# UNDERSTANDING PSYCHOPATHOLOGY

## AN INTEGRAL EXPLORATION

**R. Elliott Ingersoll**

**Andre Marquis**

Boston Columbus Indianapolis New York San Francisco Upper Saddle River
Amsterdam Cape Town Dubai London Madrid Milan Munich Paris Montréal Toronto
Delhi Mexico City São Paulo Sydney Hong Kong Seoul Singapore Taipei Tokyo

Vice President and Editorial Director: Jeffery W. Johnston
Senior Acquisitions Editor: Meredith Fossel
Editorial Assistant: Janelle Criner
Executive Field Marketing Manager: Krista Clark
Senior Product Marketing Manager: Christopher Barry
Project Manager: Kerry Rubadue
Operations Specialist: Michelle Klein
Senior Art Director: Diane Ernsberger
Text Designer: S4Carlisle Publishing Services
Cover Designer: Jayne Conte
Cover Image: Andre Marquis
Media Project Manager: Noelle Chun
Full-Service Project Management: S4Carlisle Publishing Services
Composition: S4Carlisle Publishing Services
Printer/Binder: Courier Westford
Cover Printer: Moore Langen
Text Font: 10/12 ITC Garamond Std

Credits and acknowledgments for materials borrowed from other sources and reproduced, with permission, in this textbook appear on the appropriate page within the text.

Every effort has been made to provide accurate and current Internet information in this book. However, the Internet and information posted on it are constantly changing, so it is inevitable that some of the Internet addresses listed in this textbook will change.

---



**Library of Congress Cataloging-in-Publication Data**

Ingersoll, R. Elliott, author.
Understanding psychopathology: an integral exploration/R. Elliott Ingersoll, Andre Marquis.—First edition.
pages cm
Includes bibliographical references and index.
ISBN-13: 978-0-13-159438-8
ISBN-10: 0-13-159438-9
1. Mental health counselors—Vocational guidance. 2. Psychology, Pathological. I. Marquis, Andre (Mental health counselor), author. II. Title.
RC466.I54 2015
616.89—dc23 2014003342

10 9 8 7 6 5 4 3 2 1

ISBN 10: 0-13-159438-9
ISBN 13: 978-0-13-159438-8

## Dedication

*This book project turned out to be the academic equivalent of what we in the "Cross-Fit" community call "Beast Mode." That is why my dedication for this book goes to my Cross-Fit trainers Lisa Shiu and Charlie Dunnifer and my extended family at All Heart Cross Fit in Kent, Ohio. I learned more there about getting up after being knocked down than in any area of my life. Thanks for those painful lessons in perseverance—train on!*

Elliott Ingersoll

*I dedicate this book to my wife, Erica Crane, for her support, understanding, encouragement, and love.*

Andre Marquis

# ABOUT THE AUTHORS

***Elliott Ingersoll*** is a licensed psychologist and clinical counselor in Ohio. He is a professor of counseling/counseling psychology and "Distinguished Faculty Member" at Cleveland State University. His research interests span a broad spectrum including psychopathology, mental health diagnosis, psychopharmacology, and spirituality in counseling and psychotherapy. He has authored or co-authored six books and dozens of peer-reviewed articles and book chapters on mental-health-related topics, including *Integral Psychotherapy: Inside Out/Outside In* with David Zeitler. What unites his research interests is a freethought approach to Integral theory. His latest project is educating people about the lies perpetrated by the pharmaceutical industry, especially where medicating children is concerned. His TEDxCleveland talk on this topic can be found at http://www.tedxcle.com/.

Elliott has been performing music professionally for 30 years. He has been inspired and influenced by the Free Thought movement of the late 19th century and particularly by Robert Green Ingersoll, a leading freethinker of that time. He believes the most important skill for a human being is critical thinking. As a singer/songwriter he created "FreeThought Folk Music," which he performs throughout northeastern Ohio. His CD *American Infidel* was released in 2013.

***Andre Marquis*** is a licensed mental health counselor in New York; he is also an associate professor in counseling and human development at the University of Rochester. His teaching, research, and scholarly interests include counseling theories, psychotherapy integration and unification, group therapy, relational psychodynamics, developmental constructivism, human change processes, and Integral theory as it provides a framework to coherently organize theory and practice. Other scholarly interests of his include critical analyses of dominant trends within the mental health field, from the ways that mental disorders are constructed and conceptualized to methodological issues involved in the empirically supported treatment and evidence-based practice movements. Marquis has authored *The Integral Intake: A Guide to Comprehensive Idiographic Assessment in Integral Psychotherapy*, *Theoretical Models of Counseling and Psychotherapy,* and dozens of peer-reviewed scholarly articles. Marquis serves various editorial roles for national publications, including the *Journal of Psychotherapy Integration*, the *Journal of Unified Psychotherapy and Clinical Practice*, and the *Journal of Integral Theory and Practice,* and is on the advisory board of the *Unified Psychotherapy Project*. He has taught more than 20 different courses in psychology, counseling, and human development.

Andre is an avid fisherman, outdoorsman, and music lover. He lives in the Finger Lakes region of western New York with his wife Erica, their dog Nelson, and their cat Sparkle.

# PREFACE (DON'T SKIP THIS—IT MATTERS!)

Ask yourself a few questions. Why do people get mental illness? What—exactly—causes mental disorders? When someone is suffering psychologically, how can we know the best way to treat that person? How is it that we can decode a genome but cannot figure out definitive, clear-cut answers to these questions? Questions like these—as well as our best current answers to these questions—are what this book is about.

This is a book about understanding as much as we can about the etiology and treatment of some of the most common mental disorders and psychological symptoms. Understanding etiology—the study of the causes and origins of diseases or abnormal conditions—is of extreme importance to effective treatment. If you believe a plague is caused by angry gods (as did the author of *The Iliad*), then you "treat" the plague by appeasing the gods. If, as science has demonstrated, plagues are caused by bacterial infections, then effective treatment depends upon antibiotics (and prevention depends upon proper hygiene and/or immunization); that's a big difference. In this text, we use an Integral framework to review empirical and theoretical literature related to the psychological, physiological, cultural, and social aspects of the etiology and treatment of the disorders and symptoms that prompt people to seek the help of mental health professionals. That said, it is *not* a book *solely* about the *Diagnostic and Statistical Manual of Mental Disorders,* Fifth Edition (known as the DSM-5). This book is best used as a *companion* to the DSM-5. Although we cover some disorders proper (e.g., Bipolar I Disorder), many distressing symptoms appear in multiple disorders, so you will read about them in multiple chapters. This book is timed to be released soon after the DSM-5. In our research and writing, we have scrupulously studied the DSM-5 Task Force reports and read hundreds of papers on the development of the DSM-5, as well as books put together by the American Psychiatric Association explaining the changes that occurred in the DSM-5. Finally, when the DSM-5 was released, we fact-checked our work against the new manual. Most of the references to the DSM in this book are to the DSM-5 unless otherwise noted. We also have to remember that as of this time—because the DSM-5 was just published—there is little research on DSM-5 diagnoses; most research is based in DSM-IV-TR diagnoses.

Most important, we want to repeat that we have covered cutting-edge research in each chapter on both etiology and treatment. Thus, it really doesn't matter if the DSM label for a disorder has changed. What we know about the causes and treatment of a given disorder does not change just because the DSM label or criteria change. Although we feel we have done a thorough job of following DSM-5 developments, we ask you to keep this in mind. Changes in the DSM labels or criteria do not change the extant empirical research for, or theoretical understanding of, the underlying symptoms and problems for which people seek treatment. We believe that there is no book like this currently on the market, and while we ask a lot of the reader, we also offer a lot, and hope that you find the journey as exciting and informative as we have.

# ACKNOWLEDGMENTS

First and foremost, I (Ingersoll) want to thank my friend and colleague Andre Marquis for being willing to do this project with me. I never could have done this without his exhaustive efforts, incisive critiques, penetrating questions, and moral support. I also want to thank the research assistants who have been so helpful to me in tracking down papers and researchers from across the globe. These assistants include Nadine Ndanema, Doreen George-Thomas, Laura McIntyre, and Kevin Blake. Carlene Ortiz from The Centers for Families and Children provided enormous support helping me think through ideas and write in a language students could connect with. Thanks to Paulina Alanisz for her hours of conversations about states of consciousness and cultural identification. Finally, I want to thank Cleveland State University for the release time and technical support to complete this book. CSU has been a great place to work and explore my diverse interests with supportive colleagues and the best students on the planet!

I (Marquis) want to thank Elliot Ingersoll for beginning this project (I doubt I would have initiated such an ambitious undertaking!) and for all of the excellent research he did in preparation for this book. I continue to feel at home in the Counseling and Human Development program at the University of Rochester, and deeply appreciate the support and camaraderie of my colleagues there. I am grateful for the support and friendship of my brother, Ro; my parents; my friend and fishing partner, Brian Connors; and my sister Melinda and her husband Clint. I also want to thank Erica Crane, my wife, for her thoughtful proofreading of my chapters.

We also thank Meredith Fossel and Kerry Rubadue from Pearson who believed in this project and worked hard to get us over many hurdles. Additionally, we want to thank Roxanne Klaas from S4Carlisle Publishing Services who worked so hard on the final pages and was a real trooper with helping us think through last minute changes.

We also would like to thank the reviewers of this first edition: Jenelle C. Fitch, Texas Women's University; Jeffrey Longhofer, Rutgers University; Kathryn Ecklund, Azusa Pacific University; Elizabeth C. Pomeroy, University of Texas at Austin; and Marleen S. Williams, Brigham Young University.

# BRIEF CONTENTS

# CONTENTS

# 1

# Introduction

We are embarking on a journey together—you the reader, and we the authors. We assume you are training to become a mental health practitioner, perhaps a counselor, a social worker, or a psychologist. What is it that you should know about psychopathology? Perhaps most important, we want the reader to understand that this is a book about psychopathology that describes multiple causes and treatments for the most common psychiatric/psychological symptoms that clients present with. That said, this is not a book about how to use the *Diagnostic and Statistical Manual of the American Psychiatric Association*, 5th Edition, commonly referred to as DSM (American Psychiatric Association [APA], 2013a). Rather, this book is designed as a companion to the current edition of the DSM as well as other diagnostic systems for mental and emotional disorders.

The DSM (which we'll cover in greater depth in the next chapter) is a system of categorical psychiatry that provides symptom clusters based on their relationship to one another and the category they are grouped under (e.g., Major Depressive Disorder). The DSM does not attempt to state what causes the disorders (etiology) or the best way to treat the disorders once they are identified. There was an attempt to do this in the DSM-II (APA, 1968), such as describing depression as "endogenous" (more biological in basis) or "exogenous" (triggered by external events). Because researchers failed (and still fail) to find biological markers that would conclusively demonstrate that a case of depression was "endogenous," these attempts at etiology were deleted from DSM-III (APA, 1980).

Thus, studying the DSM by itself is of little clinical value if your work is treating clients rather than matching their symptoms to the ones listed in the DSM. Our primary goal is that this book will help you understand theories and evidence regarding the causes of the symptoms and disorders clients suffer from and, secondarily, various ways to treat symptoms and disorders. Although the DSM edition changes over the years (like the recently released DSM-5), how a disorder is labeled or how many symptoms you must have to be diagnosed with a disorder does not change what *causes* the disorder or *how best to treat the disorder*. While we have just transitioned from DSM-IV-TR (APA, 2000) to DSM-5 (APA, 2013a), the transition has not affected the research on etiology and has had only minimal effect on treatment.

Diagnostic systems for children that you should be aware of include the *Diagnostic Classification of Mental Health and Developmental Disorders of Infancy and Early Childhood*, Revised Edition (DC:0-3R; Zero to Three, 2005) and the *Research Diagnostic*

*Criteria—Preschool Age* (RDC-PA; Task Force on Research Diagnostic Criteria: Infancy and Preschool, 2002). These systems were designed to serve as a complement to the DSM by providing a systematic, developmentally attuned manual to help clinicians identify and classify mental health and developmental difficulties in the first 4 years of life. In addition, there is the *Psychodynamic Diagnostic Manual* (also referred to as the PDM), which is a diagnostic framework that aims to characterize a client's full range of functioning with regard to emotional, cognitive, and social domains (PDM Task Force, 2006). The PDM is also designed to complement the DSM. Finally, there is the *International Classification of Mental and Behavioural Disorders* (ICD-10; World Health Organization, 1992). This manual is the World Health Organization's volume on mental disorders, and the DSM-5 has been designed to harmonize diagnoses in the DSM with those in the ICD. For example, next to each DSM-5 diagnostic code there is a parenthetical ICD code. The ICD-11 is due to be released in 2016. The plan is for these ICD codes to be implemented October 1st 2015, which is why the DSM-5 has both the recognizable (from earlier DSMs) five-digit numeric code (e.g., 296.32) and the parenthetical ICD alphanumeric code (e.g., F32.00). Rather than expecting students to master all these diagnostic manuals, in this book we will summarize the etiology and treatment of mental and emotional disorders including relevant information from these manuals in addition to the ICD and DSM. Finally, we should note that the National Institute of Mental Health (NIMH) announced that it will no longer rely on DSM-5 criteria in research on mental illness. Rather, it is proceeding with its ambitious Research Domain Criteria (RDoC) approach, which was drafted in 2011.[1] These criteria will focus on multiple physiological variables that may cause mental and emotional symptoms. The symptom domains the NIMH will research include symptoms that occur across DSM categories (for example, depression could emerge in Major Depressive Disorder, Persistent Depressive Disorder, or Bipolar I and Bipolar II disorder). The RDoC will include research on genetic, molecular, cellular, and behavioral variables that contribute to symptoms as well as other factors such as brain circuits.

It is important to understand the DSM-5 diagnostic system, and it is strongly recommended that instructors using this text assign the DSM-5 (or the less expensive *DSM-5 Desk Reference* [American Psychiatric Association, 2013b]) to be studied with it. Despite the many controversies surrounding the DSM-5 (Frances, 2013), it is still the most common manual that you will encounter in the field in the United States. What we think you need to understand about diagnostic systems, assessment, and treatment will drive this first chapter and lay the framework for the rest of the book. We hope that by the end of the chapter you will understand that psychiatric disorders are, first and foremost, *very different from* disorders in other branches of medicine. This must be clearly understood if any good is to result from reading this book. We also want to emphasize early on that psychiatry and psychopathology use unique jargon, and you will likely come across new words in reading this book. Keep a dictionary handy, and if you come to a word you don't know, stop, look it up, and write the definition in the margin of the page where the word appears (if you own the book). We will try to define words likely to be unfamiliar to most readers in the footnotes in each chapter.

---

[1] This decision and the links to the RDoC can be found at http://www.nimh.nih.gov/about/director/2013/transforming-diagnosis.shtml.

## FINANCIAL ISSUES SURROUNDING QUOTES FROM AMERICAN PSYCHIATRIC ASSOCIATION PUBLICATIONS

Upon completion of the DSM-5, the American Psychiatric Association set fees for reproducing any material from the DSM-5 for works like this book. We were quoted a price of $600 for every quote (properly cited) that we originally wanted to use (including criteria sets), which would have been about $30,000. This being prohibitive, we have summarized or paraphrased material from all American Psychiatric Association publications that would have been quoted had the fees not been so high.

## THE LAYOUT OF THIS BOOK

This book is designed to introduce you to theories and evidence regarding the etiology and treatment of psychopathology as well as to encourage you to think critically about these theories and data. Thinking critically includes critiques of the DSM and the process used to create it. Although some authors decry the decline of critical thinking in universities and the ascension of what they derisively term "vocational training" (Hacker & Dreifus, 2010), critical thinking is very much alive in our classrooms and the minds of our students. It is the dialogues with students (many of whom are working in mental health fields) that shaped much of our approach here.

The rest of this chapter is divided into six parts. Part I discusses the difference between psychiatry and other branches of medicine. This is important because the DSM is primarily authored by psychiatrists. Even though other mental health professionals have in recent years been part of the task force developing each section, the discipline of psychiatry dominates the process. Of the 33 members of the DSM-5 task force listed in the DSM-5, 79% have M.D. credentials.[2] Part II of the chapter deals with how we define psychopathology and answer the question "what is normal?" Our aim in this part is to encourage you to think critically and broadly about just what constitutes psychopathology and how crucial client variables like cultural identification may affect what is considered "normal." Part III provides an outline of what is sometimes called the "mind/brain problem." In this section we want you to understand that what is considered "mind," what is considered "brain," and the relationship between the two is still unclear (despite the assertions of pharmaceutical-funded researchers who want us to believe that "mind" is nothing more than electrochemical actions in the brain). Again, we include this material to encourage critical thinking. Part IV discusses the place of clinician judgment in using the DSM. Part V introduces and outlines the Integral model, and Part VI provides a case example using that model. The Integral model is subsequently presented as two illustrations in each chapter that are designed to help the reader see "at a glance" the important variables in the etiology and treatment of disorders. Finally, each chapter will have review questions at the end.

[2] A list of members of the DSM-5 task force can be found online at http://www.dsm5.org/MeetUs/Pages/TaskForceMembers.aspx and in the DSM-5.

## PART I: HOW IS PSYCHIATRY DIFFERENT FROM OTHER BRANCHES OF MEDICINE?

Before going any further, it is important for the reader (who is likely studying or working in a nonmedical mental health profession) to understand the difference between psychiatry and nonmedical mental health professions such as counseling, psychology, marriage and family therapy, chemical dependency counseling, and clinical social work. Psychiatry is a branch of medicine in the United States and other countries. The approach to medical practice in the United States is generally referred to as *allopathic* medicine. The term *allopathy* was coined in 1842 by Samuel Hahnemann, the founder of homeopathic medicine. Allopathic medicine treats disease by introducing remedies that produce effects different from those of the disease under treatment (Webster's New World, 2008). In contrast, *homeopathic* medicine was based in the assumption that drugs or other agents in smaller amounts could produce symptoms *similar to* those of an illness in healthy people and better prepare their bodies to fight disease.[3] Other approaches to medicine historically include osteopathic medicine (which traditionally emphasized the role of the musculoskeletal system in health and disease) and chiropractic medicine (a system of treating disease by manipulating the vertebral column). In the early 20th century, medical education reform was initiated by Abraham Flexner (under the aegis of the Carnegie Foundation) and his so-called "Flexner Reports." In these reports, Flexner established (under great protest from the medical community) allopathic medicine (with its then-new "germ theory") as the most progressive and thus desirable form of medical training. Since then, allopathic medicine has dominated medical training and practice in the United States to the point where osteopathic physicians are basically trained in allopathy and homeopathy has been pushed to the periphery of popular culture.

Why is this important to understand? It is important because psychiatry and the psychiatric diagnostic manual (DSM) list disorders that are radically different from non-mental health disorders in the International Classification of Diseases (ICD) of the World Health Organization in that there is not one disorder in the DSM for which we have found a physiological marker that correlates 100% with any symptom cluster (Practice Management Information Corporation, 2006). It has been pointed out by several sources that as far as biological markers go, psychiatry has failed to find even one for a single DSM disorder (Charney et al., 2002; Paris, 2013). Charney and colleagues (2002) went so far as to note that such a dearth of markers places psychiatry 50 to 100 years behind other branches of medicine. Imagine if your general practitioner was 100 years behind in the practice of medicine; he or she would not know that influenza was caused by a virus.

---

[3] Sometimes, at first glance, students may think homeopathy is similar to vaccination. Homeopathy is *very* different than the idea behind vaccinations. Homeopathy beliefs vary, but generally it is thought that by administering homeopathic agents, the agents stimulate a *vital force* to effect healing, whereas in vaccinations, the intent is to directly affect the immune system to fight a pathogen. There is no scientific evidence for homeopathy's "vital force" through studies of Reiki and acupuncture, but energy medicine and energy psychology continue to explore the possibility. Finally, homeopathy espouses the "law of dilution," which maintains that the way an agent is diluted with water or alcohol (a process called *succussion*) activates the vital force of the agent, and therefore the body will respond to that vital force with its own vital force. As you might guess from this short note, there is scant scientific support for homeopathic practices.

This is a sobering situation at a time when pharmaceutical companies have mistakenly convinced an unwitting public that conditions like depression are unilaterally caused by "chemical imbalances" in the brain.[4] There is no evidence for such a statement but the current laws governing what is called direct-to-consumer drug advertising (which is illegal in every country in the world except the United States and New Zealand) do not prohibit marketing misguided ideas like it. To say that psychiatry may be up to 100 years behind other branches of medicine is to compare psychiatry with medicine at a time when it was almost helpless in the face of the deadliest influenza epidemic in the history of the civilized world (the flu epidemic of 1917–1918). As noted, at that time doctors did not even know that influenza is caused by a virus, and there were many doctors who still contested any germ theory of disease (Barry, 2005).

The truth of our current situation is that we *do not know* precisely what (if any) disease process underlies mental and emotional disorders. In fact, assuming there *is* a physical disease process underlying all of them *may* be an error. Or, as some researchers are investigating, there may be far more variables than we can currently imagine (e.g., see Forsythe & Kunze, 2013, for a discussion of how gut microbes can affect the central nervous system). As you will see in this text, many of the disorders that we cover are what we call *overdetermined*; this means there can be multiple causes across physiological, psychological, and sociocultural aspects of one's life for the symptoms of, for example, depression or anxiety. Other disorders like Bipolar I Disorder or Schizophrenia *seem* to have a physiologic basis but we still do not know exactly what that is.

Given the lack of a definitive understanding about etiology and the fact that we have multiple diagnostic manuals for mental and emotional disorders, the framework we use in this book is the Integral model (Wilber, 1995). We will outline the model later in this chapter, but for now, we want to mention that we use the Integral model for this book because it is an integrative, unifying framework that provides multiple perspectives on symptoms clients are suffering from and thus helps clinicians look at the symptoms from different points of view. This is even more important now because DSM-5 deleted the five-axis diagnosis recording procedure that noted specific psychosocial stressors and global assessment of functioning. Being able to view symptoms from different perspectives increases the chance that a clinician will consider multiple variables related to the client's symptoms (and then treatment) that might otherwise go unnoticed. Why might they go unnoticed? It seems that human beings tend toward a type of attribution error in that if we give something a label, many of us assume that the label explains what the thing *is*, in this case a disease process. In the case of many mental and emotional disorders, the labels *actually obscure* important variables—particularly when the client is a young child.

By way of example, consider depression. It is a set of symptoms present in multiple disorders, including Major Depressive Disorder, Persistent Depressive Disorder (previously Dysthymia), Bipolar I Disorder, Bipolar II Disorder, Post-Traumatic Stress Disorder, and Schizoaffective Disorder. But even depression proper (Major Depressive Disorder) can develop from multiple etiologies. A person may become depressed for no discernable reason and not respond to antidepressant medication

---

[4] You can view the first author's "TED" talk on this at http://www.tedxcle.com/dr-elliott-ingersoll/.

or be depressed and have a lot of vegetative (physical) symptoms (appetite change, sleep disruption, decreased sexual desire) that respond fairly well to antidepressant medication. Equally, depression may follow the loss of a loved one, giving birth, or suffering a trauma. A person who grew up in a dysfunctional family may develop a negative mindset that increases the chance that he or she will become depressed (what is called a cognitive vulnerability to depression). Other people may be depressed because they have trouble forming healthy relationships, and this seems to be related to having poor relations with their parents early in their lives (what may be called interpersonally-driven depression that results from poor attachment). In each of these examples, the client "hotspots" (what we call *the positive causative factors*) differ. The Integral model, as you will see shortly, provides a framework that helps you map out the "hotspots" by considering possible contributors in several key areas. Before we introduce the Integral model, though, we want to address the concept of psychopathology and normalcy.

## PART II: PSYCHOPATHOLOGY

Psychopathology courses are sometimes labeled as "abnormal psychology." What is a "psychology," how do we define it as "normal," and what departure from that makes a psychology "abnormal"? These are the questions we want to explore with you in this section of the chapter. We'll begin with a discussion of normalcy and an idea of what is psychologically "normal." Next, we'll tackle the mind/body problem and the implications this unresolved dilemma has for understanding what is psychologically "normal" and "abnormal." Finally we'll conclude with a discussion of the way this book is structured and an introduction to the Integral model.

### What Is "Normal"?

Imagine you are sitting in a coffee shop where you and several other patrons are working on your laptops. At one point a young girl of Indian descent and dressed in a pattu pavadai[5] jumps up with a gasp, points at her computer, and says in a stifled mutter "you made me do this." Is this behavior "normal," "abnormal," or somewhere in between? Most of you are probably thinking "well, it depends." On one hand, if queried the woman may claim that she has just launched a nuclear missile to destroy North Korea because the voices in her head told her to do so. When faced with the reality of what she had done, she muttered that the voices "made her do it." On the other hand, you may find on closer examination that she spilled hot coffee in her lap (accounting for the gasp) while she was engaged in an argument with a relative via the Internet using Skype or some similar software package. In this context her actions and statements take on a new meaning that fall well within the realm of consensual reality[6] or what is "normal." So, what is normal is to a large degree based on the context, and, as developmental psychologist Jerome Kagan (2006) has noted, when we change the

---

[5] A pattu pavadai is a cone-shaped silk garment that is one of the traditional dresses of southern India for young girls.

[6] The term *consensual reality* is one way to describe agreements we make, intentionally and tacitly, as to what is "real."

context of something, the psychological meaning of that thing is also changed. Consider how even the following cases of cannibalism, potential suicide, and murder were actually publicly accepted—even celebrated—as a function of context. One man, R. C., ate the flesh of a friend of his; another man repeatedly told friends and family that he was going to drive off a cliff; and another admitted to taking the lives of several people in a series of fights.

> In the first example, R. C. was one of sixteen survivors of an airplane crash in the Andes. He and his companions remained barely alive for ten weeks in the bitter cold and barren wastes of a snow-covered mountain range. Their courageous survival [was] made possible only by their reluctant use of dead bodies for food. . . . The apparent suicide attempt was actually a well-publicized daredevil stunt performed by motorcyclist Evel Knievel. The third illustration refers to the memoirs of a crime-fighting sheriff of a small Tennessee town. (Mahoney, 1980, p. 3)

What we are calling "context" takes into account things like culture, technology, and larger dynamics such as the socioeconomic modes of production within a society and the average person's access to the latest technology. In the 1980s, I (Ingersoll) lived and worked in an inner-city area that had a centralized park. During walks around the park I would frequently encounter people muttering or talking to themselves and occasionally gesturing wildly with their hands while speaking loudly and even shouting. Most of those I encountered in the 1980s were people suffering from Schizophrenia and living on the street or in the mental health group homes that ringed the park area. Today when I walk through downtown Cleveland, it is more unusual to pass a person who is *not* talking to some unseen presence being channeled through a Bluetooth phone remote fashionably clipped onto the person's ear. In this case, the cellular phone technologies available to the average citizen have rendered outdated the notion that anyone walking along talking to herself likely suffers from some mental disorder.

The concept of what is psychologically "normal" is very hard to pin down. We can certainly set parameters that culturally similar people agree upon and say generally that anyone behaving within these parameters is "normal." But then to be culturally accommodating we may further broaden the parameters to include different cultural perspectives and call anyone functioning within these broader parameters "normal enough." But what is "enough"? It is difficult to say what is "normal" regarding physiology let alone psychology. Physiologically, one example is the idiosyncratic response many people have to prescription medications. Whereas in adults idiosyncratic responses are more often the exception, the younger a person is, the more likely the chance that he or she will have an idiosyncratic response to a medication—ask any parent who has given a child an over-the-counter antihistamine for allergies only to have the child bouncing off the walls the entire night rather than feeling sedated from the drug. Even in anatomy what is "normal" varies greatly. Some stomachs hold 12 times as much food as others. In the heart, the number of branching blood vessels differs from aorta to aorta. What is interesting is that *all of these stomachs and aortas fall within the range of what is anatomically "normal."* One criterion we may use to judge the normalcy of an organ like a stomach is whether it functions adequately: If it performs its functions adequately, we should include it in the realm of what is a normal stomach.

But can we apply this criterion of "normal" to psychological states and traits? One of the most speculative and contentious areas in psychology is personality theory. As psychologist Kenny Paris asks students in his abnormal psychology course, "what's a 'normal' person?" Answer: "someone you don't know very well." Surveying thousands of years of efforts to classify typologies of personality has turned up very little material that has predictive or explanatory power, let alone the power to describe what is psychologically "normal" (Ingersoll & Zeitler, 2010). Part of the problem here is that (hard as it is to believe) we still lack a universal definition of what "mind" is and, more important, what the relationship is between "mind" and "brain." If there is such a thing as "the mind," what is it that is functioning "normally" or "adequately" when mind is "healthy"? To even ask the question you need some background on what is called the *mind/brain problem.*

## PART III: THE MIND/BRAIN PROBLEM AND THE QUESTION OF DISTRESS OR DISABILITY

*"What is mind? No matter. What is matter? Never mind."*

George Berkeley

Are "mental" disorders mental, physical, or both? A central issue in answering this question is how we define "mind." At the outset, we are going to "cut to the chase" and tell you this issue has not been resolved. Let's start by having you reflect on your mental experience right now. You are reading. As the late author Kurt Vonnegut stated, reading is hard work. Readers of the English language must create in their minds whole worlds from horizontal lines of 26 phonetic symbols, 10 Arabic numbers, and about a dozen punctuation marks (Vonnegut & Stringer, 1999). How are you doing this right now with your mind? What is the thing you are doing it with? In addition to the work of reading, you are also likely aware of emotions, bodily sensations, and other thoughts. All of these arise in your consciousness, or your field of awareness. Do the things that arise constitute your mind, or is your mind the field of awareness within which all these things arise? Also, if either of these is your mind, does it "come from" somewhere or something like the brain, or can consciousness exist without a brain? You can begin to see what difficult questions these are! Scientists and philosophers who believe your mind comes from your brain are typically called *physicalists* or *materialists* (Churchland, 2002; Koch, 2012).

The materialist typically views the mind as something that "comes from" the activity of the brain. Exactly how this happens *no one has yet been able to explain.* Probably the best effort has been by philosopher Patricia Churchland, who clearly stated ". . . it is the *brain*, rather than some nonphysical stuff, that feels, thinks, and decides" (Churchland, 2002, p. 1). This answer, however, begs another question: How can something "mental" (i.e., nonphysical) feel, think, and decide to affect something physical? Psychologist and philosopher Daniel Robinson has noted that this question has never been adequately answered. We decide to raise our right hand and do it—how do we do that? Robinson notes that if consciousness is nothing more than electrochemical processes, why does it feel so different from electrochemical processes? He further points out that if consciousness is nothing more than physical components and their processes, we must include the matter and processes of atoms and subatomic particles that we hardly understand at all. Thus, even an exclusively materialist perspective on mind, asserting that the mind derives from the brain, leaves us with an ocean of unanswered questions (Robinson, 2008).

A second (and by no means the last) perspective is sometimes referred to as the *dual-substance approach*, which presumes that consciousness is *not* dependent on a brain for existence. There are many versions of this argument, but one sense of it can be experienced by reviewing the debate about color vision between Isaac Newton and Johann von Goethe. In 1672 Isaac Newton published a series of experiments that postulated a theory of color vision that was physiological in nature. Goethe, who was a respected writer and scientist, took issue with Newton's theory and published his own 1400-page theory of color vision in 1810. Although Goethe seems to have misinterpreted some of Newton's findings, one point he made was with regard to the *experience* of seeing in color. Goethe stated that Newton's theory explained everything about color vision *except* what it was *like* to see in color.

The differences between Newton's and Goethe's theories are sometimes credited as giving rise to a philosophical problem called the "Mary Problem," which was posed by philosopher Frank Jackson (1986). In the problem, Mary is a fictional scientist who was raised in an indoor world of black and white. She has had no access to color stimuli. She has however, through black-and-white television monitors, been able to see the outside world and has studied color vision in depth to the point where there is nothing she has not read on the topic. Being a top-rate mind, she has retained all she has read. The problem is this: In this situation, can we say that Mary "knows" everything there is to know about color vision? Jackson's initial position was that if materialism were complete knowledge, Mary should know everything about color vision. The point of course is that most people would say "no, she doesn't know everything there is to know if she hasn't had the subjective experience of actually seeing in color."

If we take Mary from her black-and-white world into a world of color that she sees for the first time, does she learn something new about color that goes beyond her encyclopedic knowledge of the topic? Many would assert that in fact she does learn something new—she learns what it *feels like* to see color. These experiences of how things seem to us—the subjective qualities of conscious experience—are called *qualia*. You are having experiences of qualia right now as you are reading—what the pages of the book feel like, how your body feels as you sit reading, perhaps (if you live near one of the Great Lakes) a feeling of sinus pressure in your head. All these are qualia and they are intimately related to your experience of mind (whatever that is). If this is the case, then mind or consciousness seems somehow irreducible to the brain, deserving of its own ontological status by virtue of its unique properties.

### Metaphysics and the Mind/Brain Problem

Before we go any further we feel it is essential that you understand what we mean by "metaphysics." Many of you may think we are referring to California-style beliefs in "higher" consciousness and yogurt enemas. We are not. We are simply referring to assumptions that underlie any assertion about what you think is real and how to explore it. Such assumptions constitute metaphysical frameworks. Two extreme positions (and there are more than two) that are instructive to the mind/brain problem reflect different metaphysical assumptions. Briefly, the physicalist or materialist asserts that mind is an epiphenomenon (or side effect) of the brain; this position assumes that all of reality (including your mental states) can be understood by understanding matter and the biochemical processes of the brain. In essence this is the ontological assumption underlying the NIMH RDoC agenda described earlier. The dual-substance argument asserts that matter and mind (or consciousness) are two distinct entities and one is not reducible to the other, although they may be intimately related to, and likely co-arise with, one another. Again, these are just two extreme positions on the mind/brain problem but we shall use them to explain metaphysical assumptions.

All arguments have metaphysical assumptions as their basis. The term *metaphysical* is derived from the editors of Aristotle's works and simply refers to the works that came "after the physics" or *ta meta ta physica* (μεταφυσικά) (or the books that came after the books on physics). As you can see, this is totally unrelated to popular phenomena like supposed psychics or beliefs about reincarnation. The topic of Aristotle's *Metaphysics* was simply what sorts of things exist, what you must *do* in order to acquire that knowledge, the limits of that knowledge, how it changes, and how we might learn about it. Two branches of metaphysics are *ontology* (the study of reality, being, and existence, as well as inquiry into what types of entities actually exist) and *epistemology* (the study of the nature of knowledge, the extent and limits regarding knowledge attainment, and *how* one attains such knowledge). So the two positions on the mind/brain problem just discussed involve different sets of metaphysical assumptions. In the materialist perspective, the ontological assumption about what is "real" is as follows: Only matter (in this case the brain) is "real"; consciousness has no "reality" in and of itself apart from the brain; given that, the best method (epistemology) to learn about consciousness is to study the brain (via empiricism). On the other hand, in the dual-substance position, the ontological assumption is that both brains and consciousness possess realities that cannot be reduced to the other; the epistemological consequences of this are that you can learn about consciousness by studying both the mind (via phenomenology) and the brain (via empiricism).

Now the important issue here is that *both* of these assumptions are leaps of faith and not science per se. Those championing the materialist position sometimes assert that its primary assumption is "scientific" (minds are "side effects" of brains). This assumption (that the mind derives from the brain) is not *in and of itself* scientific; this is the part most people fail to realize. They assume if something is claiming the mantle of science then it is—in and of itself—scientific. In all cases, though, even science rests on assumptions that are metaphysical in nature, and metaphysical frameworks are not constrained by measurement and observation in the same way that science is constrained. Metaphysical assumptions therefore can neither be proved nor disproved to be scientific. Certainly we may hypothesize that the experience of mind derives from the brain and seek to falsify this hypothesis, but that is different from claiming it is an indisputable "truth."

This may seem like philosophical hair-splitting, but it is important for students of psychopathology because even the most seemingly bias-free method—empiricism—assumes *a priori* that externally observable (empirical) data constitute the most significant form of data; because there are no empirical data that could support that assumption, it can thus be seen as an example of a leap of faith (Marquis & Douthit, 2006). If consciousness turns out to be no more than a side effect of the brain, all mental health disciplines will likely derive their treatments from what we learn from brain research and the NIMH RDoC in particular. However, presently we must find ways to accommodate information about both mind and brain. We must continue to struggle to account for consciousness, mind, and self-awareness and how all of these interact to create psychological experience. Moreover, even *if* mind and consciousness were discovered to be purely side effects of the brain, that would not negate the fact that people *experience* their minds and consciousness as central to whether they are suffering or flourishing. Thus, we cannot imagine a scenario in which only strictly scientific research on the brain will be needed to help those who are suffering psychological symptoms; the issue of values and how to find meaning amidst one's struggles will always be a central component of helping those with various psychological problems (more on this in the final chapter).

From an Integral perspective, we want to integrate what we learn in neuroscience with what we know about consciousness and the mind. We know that brain affects mind and mind affects brain, but we do not know what the exact relationship is between the two. You will have to come to your own metaphysical assumptions based on your experience. However, the biggest mistake you can make is to assume that any particular position on what the mind is carries the mantle of science is therefore *indisputable*. This is not the case, and, just like when working with a client, you must judge the evidence for yourself and come to your own conclusions.

## PART IV: DSM AND THE CONCLUSIONS OF THE THERAPIST

According to the DSM we should make a psychiatric diagnosis only if the presenting symptoms cause marked distress or disability with regard to the different domains of life (e.g., work)[7] (APA, 2013a). This of course requires that mental health practitioners use their minds to exercise discernment and judgment about what constitutes distress and impairment (not to mention the difference between "marked" and "not so marked"). How can we tell if a client's symptoms are "distressing" or "impairing" his or her life experience? Consider the experience of a client suffering from drug dependence who also meets the criteria for Borderline Personality Disorder. This client's life is practically ruled by dependence on alcohol and an inability to regulate emotional experiences. Yet, to hear the client tell it, everyone else is the problem. From the clinician's perspective, the client's life is impaired. From the client's perspective, everyone else is impaired. There are no easy approaches to such situations, and the most effective ones frequently take a great deal of time as the therapeutic relationship is built and the client learns to trust the clinician. That said, our aim is to write this book in a manner that is helpful to clinicians and people training to become clinicians. There is a vast difference between what is statistically significant in field trials of DSM symptom checklists and what the clinician experiences with a client suffering from symptoms. As psychologist Jerome Kagan (2006) has written:

> Experienced therapists have perceptual representations of their patients that are rich with details of the patients' postures, tempos of speech, timbres of voice, facial expressions and modes of dress. By contrast, the representations of patients

---

[7] It is interesting that in previous DSMs, the judgment about whether or not a person had a mental disorder rested on distress and impairment. In the DSM-5 it is distress and disability. Many clinicians that we have spoken with are still using the construct of impairment, as we are here.

> held by scientists whose knowledge of mental illness comes primarily from questionnaires, often administered over the telephone, lack the rich perceptual structures of the clinician. As a result the two groups do not always agree on which patients are depressed or anxious. . . . The two professionals "know" depression in a different way. (p. 45)

To repeat, this is why we are writing this book with an emphasis on what clinicians experience and what may help them treat clients. Clinicians must use both their knowledge of DSM criteria *as well as* their knowledge of etiology and treatment of symptoms to exercise judgment with regard to what is impairing and distressing clients. Clinicians are presented with a rich array of signals that may be clues to diagnosis and treatment. Given this, we believe that the Integral model provides an efficient way to organize and make use of all the information that clinicians are exposed to in their work as therapists.

## PART V: THE INTEGRAL MODEL

The Integral model is a trans-disciplinary theory or philosophy that exists in several forms. For the purposes of our book we use it as an integrative framework. Integrative approaches to psychotherapy allow clinicians to organize as much data about clients and treatments as possible with the aim of maximizing treatment outcomes. The Integral model began as a philosophical model (Wilber, 1995) to unite different forms of knowledge and experience. Wilber maintains that all disciplines or perspectives offer partial truths, and thus what is needed is a model that integrates the partial truths rather than settling for different schools squabbling over who has "*the* truth." The spirit of the Integral framework is that everybody is right about something, but no one is right about everything. Granted there are people who apparently are right about nothing (e.g., the late psychic Sylvia Browne) but trying to find common ground is helpful to establish dialogue. The Integral model has five primary elements: four quadrants or perspectives, lines of development, levels of development, states of consciousness, and psychological types (what is sometimes referred to as psychological styles). In this section of the chapter we will offer a brief summary of these five aspects of the model and discuss how we will use the model in the chapters to come. In addition, we will also introduce a little-used concept in the area of psychopathology: spirituality.

### The Four Quadrants or Perspectives

Right now as you read this page you have at least four aspects to your being that can be loosely called (1) your subjective psychological experience, (2) your behavior and physiological functions, (3) beliefs that you share with others (family/culture), and (4) social institutions that you are impacted by and/or participate in. These perspectives or aspects of your being are illustrated in the four quadrants or perspectives in Figure 1.1.

### The Upper-Left Quadrant: The Interior of the Individual

What is the "interior" or "inside" of the individual? This refers primarily to the phenomenological experience we all have as sentient beings. This is what we referred to

| | INTERIOR (INSIDE) | EXTERIOR (OUTSIDE) |
|---|---|---|
| INDIVIDUAL | psychological | medical |
| GROUP | cultural | social |

**FIGURE 1.1** The Four Quadrants of the Integral Model

earlier as your subjective psychological experience. For example, as you are reading this you are likely aware of thoughts and feelings as well as bodily sensations. You may have an inner monologue running that sounds like your voice. You may hear music in your mind. Put simply, the interior perspective of the individual is one's experience of awareness and the things that arise in one's field of awareness. This is where most counselors and mental health workers focus in their sessions: How are you feeling today? What's on your mind today? What are you aware of right now? All these questions are asking about a client's interior individual experience. In terms of diagnostic manuals, the *Psychodynamic Diagnostic Manual* includes an "S" axis that is intended to highlight the subjective experience of the client suffering from particular symptoms. For example, the "S" axis for depression describes "styles" of being depressed that are related to two general emotional orientations (*anaclitic* and *introjective*—both discussed in Chapter 3).

Your interior individual experience is usually expressed in first-person "I" language. We say things like "I'm feeling a little anxious today" or "I can't seem to get a certain song out of my mind." Sometimes in counseling sessions clients refer to their first-person awareness in second- or third-person language. A client may say "*you know how it is with anxiety—you have the jitters and you just can't seem to focus.*" It is as if the client is pushing away or disowning his or her first-person experience. To counter this, most counselors would direct the client to try using "I" instead of "you" in the statement about anxiety. Throughout this book, we will refer to this interior, subjective perspective as the psychological perspective.

Another way to describe the phenomenological experience pointed to by the interior individual perspective is the term *qualia*, which we described earlier in this chapter. The word *qualia* comes from the Latin language and means "what sort" or "what kind." A contemporary definition of qualia is that it refers to the quality of "what it is like" regarding mental states. In the "Mary Problem" summarized earlier, we might say that Mary knows everything there is to know about color vision except the qualia of color vision—the "what it is like" to see in color. This is critically important in counseling because clients and counselors are usually focused on what the client's psychological state or psychological life "feels like" to the client. As noted in the earlier section on the DSM, many researchers who are not clinicians miss aspects of psychological symptoms because they study them only from a third-person perspective.

They don't really capture, for example, what depression *feels like* for the client. Thus, qualia are the infinite varieties of what the things that arise in our field of awareness feel like to us. *Qualia*, by this definition, *cannot be observed from the outside*; rather, they have to be reported by the client. We can't "know" what your internal experience is unless you share it and we understand what you've shared. In this sense qualia have a hermeneutic quality about them; in other words, they require interpretation and shared understanding.

Qualia are one of the primary dimensions of the mind/brain problem because no one has ever explained how the electrochemical processes in the brain result in qualia; this is what philosopher David Chalmers (1995) terms "the hard problem" of consciousness—how and why we have the qualitative, subjective experience of consciousness at all. In contrast is what Chalmers terms "the easy problem" of consciousness; this is what most neuroscientists devote themselves to—it involves explaining how a specific mechanism in the brain is responsible for a specific function, such as the ability to focus attention, integrate information, deliberately control behavior such as walking, and so forth.

> The easy problems are easy precisely because they concern the explanation of cognitive *abilities* and *functions*. To explain a cognitive function, we need only specify a mechanism that can perform the function. The methods of cognitive science are well-suited for this sort of explanation, and so are well-suited to the easy problems of consciousness. By contrast, the hard problem is hard precisely because it is not a problem about the performance of functions. The problem persists even when the performance of all the relevant functions is explained. (Chalmers, 1995, p. 201)

In a new Foreword to his landmark book *How the Mind Works*, Harvard psychologist Steven Pinker (2009/1997) writes about some readers' misunderstanding of his work:

> Part of the misunderstanding comes from commentators' failure to distinguish two distinct problems raised by the phenomenon of consciousness. David Chalmers called them "the hard problem" and "the easy problem"; I called them "sentience" and "access," respectively. Without exception, the theories and research of the past decade that claim to attempt to illuminate the hard problem (sentience) in fact illuminate the easy problem (access). And many readers missed what I consider to be the most interesting scientific lesson of the mystery of sentience: that the feeling of mystery is itself a psychological phenomenon, which reveals something important about the workings of the human mind. (p. xi)

We know that changes in qualia may correlate with taking a pill such as an antidepressant, but they are also correlated with things like exercise, listening to music, engaging in sexual activity, playing with a child, or spending time in nature. We doubt that any reader would deny their own conscious experience at this moment while reading this page. We challenge you to seriously contemplate the idea that everything you are experiencing now is solely the result of electrochemical processes that are taking place in your nervous system. Does that feel accurate? If it is accurate, how do you account for the sense of subjectivity you are experiencing? The degree to which you agree or disagree with that assertion is the degree to which you are a believer in either the materialist or a dual-substance position on the mind/brain problem.

Obviously, the manner in which we gather information about another person's qualia can bias the responses given by that person. Many epidemiologic studies are biased simply by the types of persons who respond to such surveys. People who are more preoccupied with their symptoms or who may have experienced secondary gains from their symptoms may be more likely to fill out and return a questionnaire about symptoms. This is the type of bias that various research methodologies aim to avoid, but such avoidance is rarely possible.

## The Upper-Right Quadrant: The Exterior of the Individual

What is the "exterior" or "outside" of the individual? Simply put, it is anything that can be observed from the outside or measured and has physical properties. For example, you are engaged in a set of behaviors in reading this book. You are exercising certain muscles in the way you are sitting or holding the book. Your brain cells are firing in areas around the hippocampus, we hope moving some of the book's information from your short-term memory into your long-term memory. So, from the perspective of this quadrant, we would see physical processes and behaviors. Certainly some of these physical processes may be "inside" the individual body (like electrochemical brain processes), but in some sense we can detect their presence by measurement, even if that requires technological equipment like brain-scanning machines.

Of course, this does not necessarily mean we can always measure them accurately. No one would disagree that the neurotransmitter serotonin exists in the brain; however, we have no baseline for what is a "normal" amount of serotonin and thus we cannot speak with accuracy about serotonin balance or imbalance. The most we can say is that some but not all depressed people (about 50%), when given a serotonin-enhancing drug, report feeling less depressed after 4 to 6 weeks. This means that we can *intervene* chemically by giving the person a serotonin-enhancing drug, but that in no way implies that a chemical serotonin deficit was the *cause* of the depression.[8]

The language of the upper-right quadrant is usually third person, and, particularly, "it" language. The idea from this perspective is that one person can behold the "objective" elements of a client with a detached, scientific objectivity so that one studies behavior, blood pressure, serotonin metabolites, and so forth—whatever "it" quality is of interest. Sometimes clients will refer to aspects of themselves as "it." This can be a clue that the client is uncomfortable with some aspect of self and tries to make it "other." For example, in the famous "Gloria" films, when Gloria is with Carl Rogers she refers to her body in the third person, stating that she wants to make love to a man only when she is in love, but her body ("it") disagrees.

We will label this perspective the *medical model perspective* because, as noted, the current allopathic medical model aims to examine objective, physiological variables and understand their relation to symptoms. We will stretch this understanding to also include the behavioral perspective, which seeks to understand human psychological life through behavioral observations. Although strict behavior therapy is less common now than 50 years ago, behavioral interventions live on in our spectrum of cognitive-behavioral theories and interventions and can be very effective. Although

[8] If such an argument were true, the fact that many people feel energized after drinking coffee would mean that the fatigue they had experienced was caused by a lack of caffeine in the brain!

the DSM claims to be "a-etiological," its orientation is closest to the perspective of this quadrant (Douthit & Marquis, 2006). Many DSM symptom sets contain behavioral or physiological symptoms that nicely illustrate the perspective of this quadrant. For example, in Major Depressive Disorder, three of the nine symptoms listed under criteria for a major depressive episode include physiological symptoms such as significant weight loss or weight gain, insomnia or hypersomnia, and psychomotor retardation or agitation.

With regard to psychopathology, the medical model perspective is primarily concerned with the central nervous system and its relation to psychological experiences, including various symptoms. There is no doubt that what we call the human experience of consciousness has strong correlates with brain development and activity, and it may eventually be well demonstrated that consciousness does emerge from brain development (Churchland, 2002). For example, the neurons in the third layer of the brain's cortex undergo a burst of development early in the second year of life. These nerves develop into the corpus callosum, the network of nerves that connect the two hemispheres of the brain. At this same time in development, most children exhibit the first forms of speech, a moral sense, and what we call self-consciousness (Kagan, 1981). These psychological and physiological sets of events are clearly related, but the question that remains is whether one "causes" the other. Are mind and all the things we tie to it, like self-consciousness and morality, nothing more than the brain? What is the relationship? Some neuroscientists make a compelling case that even things like morality are, in the end, nothing more than our brains (Harris, 2010). Others, often working from a philosophical tradition, question the extent to which we can conclude that this is all there is going on (Combs, 2009).

Similarly, we know that we can image brains and show correlations between mental tasks (such as thinking about a drug one is addicted to) and activation of particular brain centers (in the case of thinking about the drug, the pleasure centers the drug activates). The "activation," though, is only a rough approximation of what is happening. In any given brain area, 20–50% of the neurons may be involved in inhibitory processes, so just because those parts of the brain "light up" on a positron emission tomography (PET) scan, we still don't know if the "lighting up" has the overall effect of an excitatory or inhibitory response (Kagan, 2006). Similarly, brain areas may be "activated" for a variety of reasons. The amygdalae (plural of amygdala) are limbic-system structures in the brain that in part mediate emotional experience, but they may be "activated" by anger, fear, or simply surprise (Kagan, 2006). As we pointed out in the discussion of the mind/brain problem, we have yet to come to a clear agreement on what the mind and brain are and whether, in fact, they constitute interacting but exclusive entities or one is merely an effect of the other. There is of course the possibility that all of these are the wrong questions.

### The Lower-Left Quadrant: The Interior of Groups

What is the interior of a group? Perhaps the clearest example is the shared beliefs that constitute a shared cultural heritage. The word *culture* comes from a Latin root meaning "to cultivate" but has a multitude of meanings across academic disciplines. In this instance we refer to the shared experiences, beliefs, values, and worldviews of those who may identify with one another based on shared ethnicity, race, sexual orientation, socioeconomic status, ability/disability, religious/spiritual path, age, or sex and gender. In counseling, psychology, and social work we have made progress in understanding the importance of cultural identification to effective therapy. For example, we know that African Americans share a history of oppression that may incline them to view Caucasians with some suspicion. In some cases this has led to institutionalized racism, as in cases where African Americans were more likely to underutilize mental health services because of well-founded mistrust based on their history of oppression (Suite, La Bril, Primm, & Harrison-Ross, 2007).

Another aspect of the interior of groups involves understanding how groups can share a common language. Shared beliefs or backgrounds lead to *shared signifieds*, as is the case when particular written or verbal signifiers (such as a written or spoken word) trigger particular mental signifieds unique to the group. For example, we would be willing to bet that when confronted with the signifiers "DSM," a majority of the readers of this book would have a thought or image related to the American Psychiatric Association's *Diagnostic and Statistical Manual of Mental and Emotional Disorders*. The letters "DSM" in that case would serve as a signifier that evokes a shared signified (a mental image of the actual manual) among most mental health professionals. We would also bet it somewhat unlikely that any 10 engineering majors sitting in a coffee shop would have the same experience when confronted with "DSM" (they may more likely think of an engineering firm—"DSM Engineering Associates"). In this example, "DSM" thus comes to share specific (and different) meanings for students and professionals in different professions. The interior of a group, when it manifests in shared beliefs or signifieds, may result in those who identify with the group forming a sense of "we," and this is frequently the pronoun used to represent this quadrant (e.g. "we believe . . . ," "we agree that . . .").

You can easily imagine the importance of knowing what cultures your client identifies with. For example, you may be seeing a client who was raised in an abusive home and currently struggles to make ends meet. In this case you would want to be aware that people raised in abusive homes and struggling with financial issues are at much higher risk for mental and emotional disorders such as depression. Currently, it is believed that combining a genetic vulnerability to depression with an impoverished environment greatly increases the risk of depression (Kaufman et al., 2004). So in this case, membership in a group that may share some signifiers also increases one's risk of developing certain symptoms.

The training models of the different mental health disciplines may come to serve as a shared signifier for a majority of individuals in those disciplines. For example, the American Psychological Association has long been associated with what is called the Boulder model of training psychologists (Frank, 1984). This model is based on an ideal known as the scientist-practitioner, in which psychologists ideally learn to both conduct research and attempt to apply research findings with clients. As several scholars have pointed out, though, most psychologists are primarily interested in research or clinical work and *rarely* engage in both (Norcross, Gallagher, & Prochaska, 1989; Snyder & Elliott, 2005), so although most psychologists know of the Boulder model, it appears that few identify with it. The debate of counselor identity continues to be a struggle to evoke a shared signified in the mind of the public when individuals hear the world *counselor*. This is one aspect of the "Counseling 20/20" campaign, and part of the problem is that most of the general public is not aware of the differences between the various mental health disciplines. Such differences are harder to make a case for when in most states the scope of practice covered by state law is the same for counseling, social work, and psychology.

Shared beliefs can also function as cultural and social currency, and not always toward positive ends. The aforementioned belief that mental and emotional disorders are "caused by" a chemical imbalance has so misinformed laypeople that they often believe that the optimal treatment for depression is antidepressant medication (Howowitz & Wakefield, 2007; Ingersoll & Rak, 2006). Similarly, many Americans turn to herbal preparations rather than allopathic medicine because they believe that "natural" remedies are safer. In believing this, they ignore the fact that many herbal preparations can prove lethal in the wrong dosage (Astin, 1998).

Other common aspects of shared beliefs that clinicians deal with are those shared by a client's current family or family of origin. Think of a family therapy session initiated because one of two children in the family suffers from depression. The depressed child is 13 years old and has an older sibling who is 19. The parents are a dual-career couple who value competition, material success, and "New Thought" spirituality that focuses on positive thinking. The older sibling is majoring in marketing at a local university and the younger sibling is barely passing his courses. In meeting with this family, the first thing you notice is that the depressed child does very little talking. The parents talk about how you have to "focus on the positive" and "pull yourself up by the bootstraps" when feeling down, and the older brother confirms this is the best approach to depression. Before long, you become aware that the older brother and parents seem to share a worldview that the younger brother doesn't buy into. When you follow up with him in individual therapy, he says "Why should I bother talking? My family already knows the meaning of life." Here is a case in which one member of the family doesn't buy into the family's shared beliefs about competition and success. This variable is likely to play at least as powerful a role in his depression as any purported chemical imbalance.

With regard to diagnostic manuals, previous editions of the DSM (previous to DSM-5) allowed clinicians to code on axis IV psychosocial stressors that may be important to a client's diagnosis, and family tensions often qualify. The Zero to Three task force in charge of authoring the DC:0-3R manual has proposed adding a family axis (axis VI) that would encourage information gathering about family history of mental illness, family structure and available supports, and family culture. Particularly when working with children, no clinician can render effective treatment without some knowledge of the family that forms the context of the child's life. The task force is piloting the family axis as of this writing. Such things can be coded in DSM-5 but there is no axis specific to those issues.

### The Lower-Right Quadrant: The Exterior of Groups

The exterior of a group is a little easier to understand. It involves all the things about groups that can be measured or observed from the outside. The group in question may be a family (as in the previous example) a social institution (such as a university), or a social dynamic (such as socioeconomic status as a function of where one lives—urban, suburban, rural, etc.). The lower-right quadrant represents the social perspective. In the family example just presented, the actual structure of the family as well as the way the individuals behave together (systems analysis) would be seen from this perspective. As you'll see in the next section on Integral diagnosing, there is a great deal of overlap between the two lower quadrants. For example, a family may be deeply involved in Roman Catholicism. In that instance the Roman Catholic Church provides both measurable structure in the institution of the church, such as codes of behavior (lower-right quadrant), as well as shared beliefs and values (lower-left quadrant) about what it means to be Catholic.

In the family example presented earlier, the parents and older brother attend religious services at a nondenominational church that emphasizes a "New Thought" version of Christianity. Needless to say, the depressed 13-year-old does not feel this is a good fit and has recently decided not to attend. Here, the structure of the family, to some extent, conforms to the shared beliefs (those shared by three out of four members). So in a sense this "outside" of the family should mirror what is happening on the "inside" or in the realm of shared beliefs. As noted, for school counselors and school psychologists, these two lower quadrants and what they tell us about the family are crucial to understanding children's mental and emotional symptoms. This is particularly true because the younger the child, the less likely the symptoms will present like those in the DSM, which has been normed on adults (House, 1999, 2002).

The social perspective is also used (in what we'll describe as Integral diagnosis) to list the potential "hotspots" in a client's life that relate to social institutions. For example, clients who are on probation are beholden to parole officers, and this can be an added stressor affecting their symptom profile; similarly, clients without sufficient financial means due to unemployment are vulnerable to a host of mental and emotional disorders that they might not be troubled by if they were enjoying better financial circumstances.

## Lines and Levels of Development

The second main element in the Integral model involves developmental dynamics. Despite the fact that school counselors (as well as many other mental health professionals) deal with children ages 5 through 18, there are few psychopathology books for counselors about mental and emotional disorders in children. In addition, the DSM is normed almost entirely on adults (with the exception of neurodevelopmental disorders), but we all know that children and adolescents may suffer from mental or emotional problems that interfere with academic achievement and cause distress or impairment (Skovagaard, Houmann, Landorph, & Christiansen, 2003). This is another reason this book is a companion to diagnostic manuals, including the DC-03. Integral theory attempts to elucidate both stages (also called levels) of development and so-called "lines" of development. In addition to the four perspectives represented by the quadrants, each individual is navigating multiple lines (or different aspects) of development. Right now you have some sense of your intellectual abilities that likely correlate with your cognitive development. In addition, you have a sense of self (sometimes called "ego") that has likely changed as you've grown. You may think of other possible lines of development, such as emotional or psychosexual as well as moral, physical, or artistic.

Although we don't currently have an accurate count of how many distinct lines of development there are, it does appear that the lines we have some empirical support for do not progress at the same rate within most individuals. This simply means that for most people, some lines of development are more developed than others. A line of development is an aspect of your being that unfolds in a predictable sequence. The various plateaus in the sequence we call *stages* or *levels*. This is a thorny issue in academic psychology because it requires enormous rigor to support the hypothesis of a stage theory. There are many so-called "pop-psychology" theories that claim to have lines of development, but most of these have little or no research to support them. That said there are some stage theories with rigorous support; these include theories of cognitive development, moral development, and ego or "self" development, all of which are clinically helpful.

Most clinicians depend, at least roughly, on their assessment of the client's cognitive development. If we think in general Piagetian terms, it is important to know whether an adult client has access to concrete operational thinking, formal operational thinking, or post-formal operational thinking. A client's level of cognitive ability is important because it guides the manner in which the clinician engages the client. For example, I (Ingersoll) was working with inmates transitioning from prison to halfway group homes. Part of the assessment included a measure of cognition using the Kaufman Brief Intelligence Test 2 (KBIT-2). Prior to reviewing one client's test score, I was discussing with him the list of things he needed to do the first day at the group home. He noted that he had accomplished two of them with one trip. I said "two birds with one stone, huh?" and his response was "*why the f*!* you goin' on 'bout birds?*" The client's cognitive abilities were more or less in a range we would describe as "concrete"; thus, metaphors, allegories, and other formal operational language were not going to be beneficial clinical tools for him.

Simply put, we can refer to a client's level of cognition as what the client is able to be aware of. Within the realm of what a client is aware of are things that he or she identifies with. These we can take as indicators of self or ego development. In this sense one's level of ego development is somewhat dependent on one's level of cognitive development. Cognition can be thought of as the "pacer" for how far a person can proceed in ego development. What we find, though, is that people can be very healthy at all conventional or postconventional ego levels, so growth is not necessary beyond a conventional sense of self. Ego (or self) development was pioneered by Jane Loevinger from the 1950s through the 1990s (e.g., Loevinger, 1998) and continues to be researched today by Susann Cook-Greuter (2000) and others. In this theory, *ego is the story you tell yourself about your life*. The construct of ego proper has three interrelated components. The operative component includes what adults see as the purpose of life, what needs they act on, and what ends they move toward. The emotional or affective component includes how the person deals with emotions and the experience of being in the world. Finally, the cognitive component addresses how a person thinks of her- or himself and the world (Cook-Greuter, 2003).

The nine levels of ego identity range from preconventional to conventional to postconventional. Similar to Kohlberg's terms in his moral development theory, preconventional ego identity means the person is really not aware of, or willing to play by, the conventions of society. As a result we see many of these people in our criminal justice system. Conventional ego identity means that individuals are aware of, and willing to play by, the conventions of whatever society they find themselves in. Finally, people with postconventional ego identities know the conventions of society but make decisions more on their own values and based on context, in contrast to rigid, universally applicable rules. We are just beginning to see research related to ego development and mental health. For example, there is some evidence that later ego identity is associated with psychosocial adjustment (Lindfors et al., 2007).

The phrase *developmental psychopathology* was coined by Thomas Achenbach in 1974. More recently, Achenbach (2009) has made the point that the categorical approach in the DSM cannot be generalized across age groups, sexes, or cultures. He is one of many who advocate for a dimensional approach to diagnosis, which we discuss in Chapter 2. In general, the past 10 years have seen a dramatic increase in the developmental literature on psychopathology. We are starting to gather evidence that the more severe disorders frequently impair progress on different lines of development. There is strong evidence that severe mental and emotional disorders impair a person's cognition and thus perspective-taking ability (Langdon, Coltheart, & Ward, 2006; Langdon, Coltheart, Ward, & Stanley, 2001; Schiffman et al., 2004). If the relationship described earlier between cognition and ego or self is accurate, then we should expect that disorders/symptoms that interfere with cognitive development will also interfere with ego or self-development.

The only real mention of developmental considerations in the DSM-5 is a half-page summary noting that the aim was to organize the chapters and the manual so that disorders and/or symptoms are presented in what is thought to be a chronological manner. That is, disorders thought to begin in infancy or childhood (e.g., neurodevelopmental disorders) are presented first and disorders thought to arise later in life (e.g., neurocognitive disorders) are presented last. This is really a general caveat, though, and appears to be intended to help guide future research rather than to illustrate the developmental implications of disorders.

## States of Consciousness

In addition to the four perspectives reflected in the four quadrants and the developmental dynamics just discussed, the Integral model also emphasizes the importance of states of consciousness. As far as understanding mental and emotional disorders, it is clear that states of consciousness may be relevant as part of the symptoms, as well as part of the "cure." Going back to our example of depression, consider the state of being depressed; for many clients, it is an overwhelming ennui—a pervasive sadness that seems to exacerbate negative thoughts and emotions. With the exception of chronic, long-term, low-grade depression (called Dysthymia), depression is a transitory state. It can be incapacitating but, like all states, it is transitory. The goal of treatment is to figure out the best way for each client to diminish the frequency and severity of the symptoms. How to do this varies from client to client but in the main, treatment may consist of medication, a form of talk therapy, exercise and dietary changes, and perhaps even meditation.

The use of mindfulness meditation as one tool for treating depression is relatively new but provides an excellent example of how a depressed state can be treated in part by teaching the client to induce a nonchemical, nonordinary state of consciousness. In this case, the non-ordinary state is focusing attention in the present and learning to view thoughts as passing mental events rather than as realities that you are immersed in. "*Mindfulness* is the awareness that emerges through paying attention on purpose, in the present moment, and nonjudgmentally to things as they are"; in mindfulness practice, you learn to watch your thoughts, feelings, and physical sensations (Williams, Teasdale,

Zindel, & Kabat-Zinn, 2007, p. 31). We have told some clients that it is like sitting on a dock by a river. The river is your awareness, and the things that float by (leaves, twigs, etc.) are akin to the things that arise in your awareness. Once you learn to watch what arises in your field of awareness, then you create a psychological space between the you who is witnessing depressing thoughts emerging and the depressing thoughts themselves. In this sense you learn that you are *not* your thoughts and feelings. In some cases this practice seems to stop negative thoughts from fueling depression; in other cases, people still have negative thoughts but they report not being so bothered or disturbed by them. By training themselves to enter states of consciousness in which they can disidentify with their thoughts ("I can watch my thoughts; therefore I am *not* my thoughts"), clients gain the capacity to change their relationship to their thoughts, emotions, and other aspects of their experience such that they are not a victim to them; rather, they develop a sense of freedom—even if the specific thoughts and feelings don't cease. Even if the shift away from depression only lasts a few minutes, it becomes evidence that clients are really not their thoughts and thus have some degree of control over the extent to which they are overwhelmed by the negative thoughts that accompany depression. Like all forms of treatment, this will be helpful for some but not all clients.

In addition to viewing the client's life experience through the four perspectives of the quadrants and understanding relevant developmental dynamics, the Integral model reminds us to note relevant states of consciousness—both those that are related to the symptoms and those related to relief. In some disorders, such as chemical dependency, clients may be using altered states to numb out emotional pain. In such cases, clinicians need to help the client replace a state that poses medical, psychological, and legal risks with one that is generally better for the client. This can be challenging, as the case of Maggie demonstrates. Maggie was dependent on heroin and frequently used it to stifle her panic attacks. Her problems multiplied when the onset of heroin withdrawal would actually seem to cause a panic attack, which would then lead to more self-medicating with heroin. In addition to the risk of putting an illicit substance in her body, she was putting herself at risk for infectious illnesses through needle sharing, and possible legal complications from trafficking illicit drugs. Clearly for people like Maggie, medical intervention (known as "detox") was necessary to help her body wean off the heroin. Following that, a structured, restrictive treatment environment was needed to help her begin to face life without drugs. However, most of Maggie's treatment focused on her states of mind and how to change them while remaining sober.

## Types or Styles

The final element in the Integral model is what we call types or styles; it is really a "shorthand" word for personality. Although Integral theorists initially used this construct to refer to psychological typologies, we prefer to view this as a client's style of being in the world because there is little evidence that personality is expressed as exclusive types (Ingersoll & Zeitler, 2010). From the Myers-Briggs Type Indicator to the Enneagram, it seems that, at best, typologies can function only as metaphors—not as valid constructs with reliable psychometric properties. From the time Theophrastus took over the Lyceum from Aristotle (Sandys, 1909), people have tried to "type" personality, and in every instance they have failed. It is this failure that has led us to the factorial approach illustrated in the Five-Factor Model. The controversy over types began, in part, with the work of psychologist Walter Mischel (1968). He published a critique of all personality assessments (including typologies) and concluded that only a small amount of the variance in a person's behavior can be accounted for by personality tests. Mischel made the commonsense point that human beings are far more complex than most of the subjects in experimental psychology (e.g., rats, mice, monkeys) and that this complexity had not been captured by psychological assessment. This critique rippled through the psychological community and called into question the legitimacy of personality theories and personality assessment.

Given this state of affairs, personality theories are not terribly useful guides in diagnosing and treating psychopathology. The idea of a personality *style*, however, can give some insights into how the person sees the world and what sorts of psychological defenses the person may use. Although we remain skeptical that there is such a thing as a "disordered personality," it is clearly true that some people have personality styles that exacerbate their suffering.[9] Consider the case of Janice, a 26-year-old engineering graduate student who has an excellent academic record but who suffers from consistently volatile personal relationships. Janice grew up in a single-parent household with her mother and was the victim of sexual abuse at the hands of two of her mother's boyfriends. Janice never experienced the safe environment that allows children to develop emotionally. As a result, she has not learned how to set healthy boundaries in relationships and struggles to manage her emotions and the emotions of others. In treatment, I (Ingersoll) talked with Janice about her style of navigating relationships in a way that allowed her to engage my efforts at a therapeutic alliance but not in a way in which she felt I was "damning" the very self she identified with. We may also see that clients manifest particular symptoms with a certain "style," as in the case of anxiety. Anxiety may be experienced primarily as physical symptoms (sweating, racing heart), cognitive symptoms (racing or catastrophic thoughts), or emotional symptoms (fear and a desire to escape anxiety-producing situations).

## Spirituality

Another element in the Integral model that rarely shows up in treatments of psychopathology is spirituality. Although popular treatments of psychology are inundated with supposed references to spirituality, mainstream counseling and psychotherapy is really just beginning to integrate this aspect of human experience into topics such as psychopathology. In fact, as recent as 25 years ago, most references to spirituality in the psychopathology literature implied that a spiritual orientation or belief was itself pathological (Wulff, 1996). This has changed to the point where legitimate problems related to one's spiritual life are treated, at least minimally, in the DSM. In the DSM-IV and DSM-IV-TR these were listed under the "V" code "Religious or Spiritual Problem" (Lukoff, Lu, & Turner, 1992). In the DSM-5 the "V" codes are listed alongside the "Z" codes of the ICD-10; thus in the DSM-5 "Religious or Spiritual Problem" is listed as both V62.89 and Z65.8.

In a scholarly approach to psychological topics we have to "operationalize" terms. Operationalizing means that we describe in observable terms what we mean

[9] Psychodynamic diagnosis (McWilliams, 1994) always attends to two interacting dimensions of a client - both the defensive style (i.e., obsessive, dependent, schizoid, paranoid) and the developmental level of personality organization (i.e., psychotic, borderline, neurotic, or "normal"). Thus, a given personality style that manifests in a "normal" or mild neurotic manner is not necessarily dysfunctional; however, any of those same styles will constitute a disorder at borderline or psychotic levels of personality organization, but that is a function of the developmental level of severity rather than the style per se.

when we use a particular construct; in psychotherapy, that usually is through references to what clients are experiencing. For example, anxiety is defined as a negative mood state that can be characterized by somatic symptoms, apprehension about the future, or a set of behaviors (e.g., fidgeting, looking worried). Many studies of anxiety look at only one of these or some combination of two out of three, and researchers admit that anxiety in humans is very hard to measure (Barlow & Durand, 2002). The same can be said of spirituality, and probably the best descriptions of it in relation to psychotherapy state that it is frankly hard to define (Miller, 1999; Wiggins-Frame, 2003).

Spirituality is operationalized in many ways in the psychological literature. In the mid to late 20th century, mental health professionals were just beginning to offer general descriptions of what spirituality meant. Here is a sampling: Spirituality has been described as the ultimate or deepest needs of the self that, when met, move the individual toward meaning and purpose (Bollinger, 1969) and as one's journey toward union with God (Magill & McGral, 1988). Counselor Mel Witmer (1989) described spirituality as a belief in a force or thing greater than oneself. Psychiatrist Gerald May (1988) noted that spirituality has an elusive nature in that it seems paradoxically indwelling yet rooted in something eternal. Counselor Howard Clinebell (1992) described spirituality as living in meanings, hopes, and beliefs about what is ultimately important.

In all of these samples, you'll note the dearth of reference to religion and religiosity. That is likely because William James (1902) set the tone of investigation into the healthy aspects of religion in his famous Gifford Lectures, and Gordon Allport (1950) followed this lead in his book *The Individual and His Religion*. Psychologists from James to Allport thus birthed the construct of religiosity, but in the late 20th century more references were made to "spirituality." Psychologist Carl Thoresen (2007) addressed the complexity of teasing apart religiosity and spirituality. He noted that

> both concepts are complex with several facets or features, some of which are latent, that is, not directly observable but are inferable. . . . Very important concepts remain difficult to articulate and lack complete agreement about how best to define them . . . given this complexity there is no clear consensus on how to best describe, define, or measure spirituality and religion. Both concepts are clearly related to each other and both contain a connection to what is perceived as sacred in life. (p. 5)

In an effort to more clearly specify what is meant by spirituality, many researchers—beginning with sociologist David Moberg (1979)—began looking more at constructs that implied spiritual health or wellness. These included spiritual well-being, spiritual wellness, and spiritual health. As I (Ingersoll, 1994) summarized these efforts, the idea was that because spirituality was described in so many different ways, perhaps focusing on measurable aspects of people who had a spiritual practice would clarify what healthy spirituality meant for clients (and clinicians). These efforts were more precise and led to the development of some scales to measure spiritual wellness but diverged sharply from the manner in which clients described their spirituality. Clients rarely come in, sit down, and say "I had a spiritual experience that is best operationalized by Ellison's [1983] subscale on existential well-being."

In the last 10 to 15 years, it seems that a second round of efforts has been made to more clearly operationalize both religiosity and spirituality. The gap between spirituality and religion continues, as psychologist David Wulff (1996) explained:

> sensing that the words *religious* and *religion* fail today to denote certain positive inward qualities and perceptions but, to the contrary, seem increasingly to be associated with prejudicial attitudes, violence, and narrow social agendas, people in various walks of life are choosing to use the terms *spiritual* and *spirituality* instead. (p. 47)

Psychologists Scott Richards and Allan Bergin (2000) noted that

> . . . by spiritual, we also mean those experiences, beliefs, and phenomena that pertain to the transcendent and existential aspects of life . . . the transcendental relationship between the person and a Higher Being, a quality that goes beyond a specific religious affiliation, that strives for reverence, awe, and inspiration, and that gives answers about the infinite. (p. 13)

These same two authors, 3 years later (Richards & Bergin, 2000), owned the Western biases in the previous description and added a full-page table of the differences between Western and Eastern worldviews. Bruce Scotton (1996) differentiated spiritual and religious when he wrote that

> *Religious* refers to the belief system of a specific group, whose members usually gather around specific contents and contexts that contain some transpersonal elements. *Spiritual* refers to the realm of the human spirit, that part of humanity that is not limited to bodily experience. *Transpersonal experience* in addressing all human experience beyond the ego level, includes spiritual experience but also includes embodied human experience of higher levels. (p. 4)

Most recently, authors have focused on the difficulty of defining words like *spirituality* and *religion*, with some authors devoting entire chapters to the problem (Aten & Leach, 2009; Sperry & Shafranske, 2005). Psychologists Brian Zinnbauer, Kenneth Pargament, and Allie Scott (1999) conducted an analysis of the panoply of definitions and asserted that spirituality and religiousness had been polarized by contemporary theorists in three ways. The first was the polarization between organized religion and personal spirituality. The second was substantive religion in contrast to functional spirituality. The third was negative religiousness in contrast to positive spirituality. The authors then integrated these constructs, concluding that the polarizations unnecessarily constricted the definitions. Their solution is twofold. First, they noted that there is a need to resolve the tension between remaining pluralistic enough to include the varieties of spiritual and religious experiences while also allowing researchers to be specific enough to carry out a coherent research program. Second, they felt there had to be a way to distinguish between spirituality and religion without polarizing them. To accomplish these aims, they endorsed Kenneth Pargament's description of spirituality as "a search for the sacred" and his definition of religion as a search for significance in ways related to the sacred. In these definitions, spirituality is central to religion and religion can be the culturally shaped vessel that ideally nurtures the search for the sacred.

To recognize the complexity of this issue, we will draw on many of the previous descriptions of spirituality throughout the book and will include them when they are relevant to certain symptom sets (for example, there are types of depression described in mystical literature called a "dark night of the senses" or "dark night of the soul"). We will include spiritual considerations when we are able to, although there is limited literature to draw upon in this arena. In some cases we will, following philosopher Robert Solomon (2002), simply describe spirituality as a thoughtful love of life.

## PART VI: CASE EXAMPLE: PULLING TOGETHER AN INTEGRAL DIAGNOSIS

At this point we have introduced all the elements of the Integral framework that we will refer to in this book. For the most part, though, we will focus on the four perspectives offered by the quadrants and how these can help us in the process of diagnosing. One approach that we recommend, and that we both use in our private practices, is to complement our DSM diagnoses (which we'll discuss more in depth in the next chapter) with what has been called an Integral assessment and diagnosis (Ingersoll, 2002; Marquis, 2008). To demonstrate one way to use this model, consider the following case.

---

Katie is a 29-year-old, African American mother of three children (ages 9 months, 3, and 4). She identifies as an Evangelical Christian (meaning a belief in the historicity and general inerrancy of scripture, the exclusive divinity of Jesus of Nazareth, and a Calvinist emphasis on personal conversion). This client was originally seen at an agency for financial counseling and was subsequently referred for personal counseling. She stated that she had been "wrestling with strong demons" and said she had been meeting with her pastor about them. The "demons" were feelings of fear about the future, her children's welfare, and her husband's drinking problem. Her husband had been drinking more alcohol (unusual for him) almost every night and becoming sullen and distant. Katie thought he was drinking because of their financial problems but also feared he was drinking because she was not as good a wife as she should be. Her husband had also snapped at her verbally several times a week—also uncharacteristic of him.

Katie discussed times when she felt "attacked" and was beset with heart palpitations, sweating, chest pain and nausea, and a frightening feeling that she was going crazy. She had four such attacks in the 3 months prior to the evaluation. She said she constantly worried about having these attacks and that they were going to cause her to go crazy. As a result of the attacks, she started seeing her pastor for counseling and had tripled her prayer time. She was dismayed that she still had the attacks despite her prayer and was growing increasingly despondent because she was starting to doubt her religious convictions because her prayer time had not resulted in any appreciable lessening of her symptoms. In her religious faith community, traditional gender roles were the norm and she felt that her husband's behavior may have been her fault.

She agreed to let the therapist speak with her pastor, and he noted that Katie's life was stressful and he hoped that their sessions gave her comfort and some ways to access the power of the Spirit to help her. The pastor noted that she didn't seem to feel any better in the 2 months that she had been seeing him, and he stated that he was glad she was seeking additional help. Katie was relieved that her pastor supported her work in counseling, as she felt that her anxiety was interfering with her ability to perform daily tasks. Because of increasingly pervasive religious doubts, she was also ambiguous about her pastor's ability to help her with her problems. Katie presented cognitively as someone who has access to formal operational thinking. Her sense of self was very conventional in that, up to this point, she felt her religious faith was a complete guide for how to live her life.

Katie had no history of mental health interventions and her physician had confirmed that she also suffered from Irritable Bowel Syndrome (IBS). She had no medical disorders that would mimic anxiety and there was no evidence of any drug use/abuse. In the third session with Katie, she revealed an experience late one night when she was up worrying about the family's problems. She said she was suddenly "overwhelmed" by a sense of peace. For about an hour she said she felt on the one hand as if she were merely watching her fears—like they were someone else's—but that she didn't feel "numb" to them. She said she wondered if this had been a state of grace. Whereas her counselor suggested she was dissociating due to stress, Katie felt there was something more to the experience because it was comforting. The experience has not recurred.

## DSM-IV-TR and DSM-5 Diagnoses of Katie

Under the DSM-IV-TR (APA, 2000), Katie's five-axis diagnosis would have been as follows:

Axis I: 300.01 Panic Disorder Without Agoraphobia
R/O V62.89 Religious or Spiritual Problem
Axis II: V71.09 No Diagnosis on Axis II
Axis III: 564.1 Irritable Bowel Syndrome
Axis IV: husband's drinking problem, financial stressors
Axis V: 58

Under the DSM-5 (American Psychiatric Association, 2013a) the five-axis diagnosis has been eliminated, leaving us with a nonaxial system. Using the DSM-5, clinicians can list what used to be on axes I, II, and III together (again mirroring the ICD-10) and then make additional comments about psychosocial factors and assessment of functioning (formerly axes IV and V) (American Psychiatric Association, 2013a).

So from the DSM-5 perspective, Katie's diagnosis would look like this:

F41.0 Panic Disorder; R/O Z65.8 Religious or Spiritual Problem. Client's husband appears to be abusing alcohol and the couple is experiencing financial stress. Some third-party payers will switch to numbered lines for diagnoses with the change to ICD codes. In that format all relevant issues (including psychosocial stressors) are listed like this:

1. F41.0 Panic Disorder
2. R/O Z65.8 Religious or Spiritual Problem
3. Relational stress due to spouse's alcohol use.

| | Quadrants/Perspectives | |
|---|---|---|
| | **INTERIOR (INSIDE)** | **EXTERIOR (OUTSIDE)** |
| **INDIVIDUAL** | Questioning her faith<br>Feels persecuted by demons<br>Fear of losing her mind<br>Questioning her worth<br>Concern about secular counselor | Physiological symptoms of anxiety<br>Panic attacks<br>Irritable bowel syndrome<br>Increased religious behaviors (prayer) |
| **GROUP** | Norms of the faith community<br>Breakdown in communication w/husband | Structure of the church<br>Creditors' interest rates and demands for payment |

**FIGURE 1.2** Integral Summary of Katie's Case

Doing away with the five-axis format will likely minimize many of the contextual elements the multi-axial system represented. It is for this reason that we feel it is more important than ever to have some integrative system that is complementary to the DSM diagnosis, as this approach will capture what used to be captured in axes III, IV, and V; the Integral quadrant approach provides this.

## Complementary Integral Diagnosis Related to the Quadrants

Using the four quadrants, Figure 1.2 illustrates how the material from the written case about Katie fits into the elements of the Integral framework.

**DEVELOPMENTAL TASKS** Katie and her husband have recently had a third child and, in addition to the added financial stress, are having to find a new family rhythm.

**STATES** Clearly Katie is suffering with states of anxiety but has also had one state that was nonordinary for her and was, by her description, comforting. Katie also experiences a great deal of distress due to her perception of the woman's role in the family. She feels stress because she believes it is the woman's job to keep up family morale.

**TYPES OR STYLES** Katie appears to have a conventional, conservative sense of self that, until recently, has been more or less embedded in her church community. While she is questioning some aspects of her faith, the community still plays an important role with regard to her sense of self. We also see that Katie has a "style" of being anxious that manifests in physical symptoms.

Now we will discuss what we placed in each quadrant. The idea of using the four-quadrant diagram is to be able to catch, "at a glance," what the "hotspots" seem to be for the client's experience. Recall that each quadrant is simply one aspect of a person's life experience.

**Exterior Individual Quadrant—The Medical Model Perspective** Katie is clearly suffering from many physiological symptoms of anxiety, given the confirmation from her physician that she is otherwise healthy. Her behavior of increasing her prayer time is a logical response given her worldview, which, however, may cause distress depending upon her expectations and subsequent results. She also has the diagnosis of IBS. The objective signs tell us that Katie's predominant "style" of anxiety is physical, and this informs the shape the intervention will take. Her IBS is likely exacerbated by the stress and anxiety she is experiencing. One important aspect of the treatment must be to decrease the frequency and intensity of the panic attacks and objectively measure these to assess the effectiveness of treatment as it progresses.

**Interior Individual Quadrant—The Psychological Perspective** Katie feels like she is being persecuted by demons—a construct that makes sense from, and generates more anxiety in, her worldview. It is important to understand that the way she talks about "demons" reflects her worldview rather than what some might think is delusional thinking. She harbors some apprehension about secular counseling. She fears that she is losing her mind and her faith all at once. She also is questioning her worth as a woman, largely because of her husband's alcohol problem. Katie must use the therapeutic dialogue to explore new understandings of herself, her values, and her sense of the resources she will need to cope with her life circumstances. The experience Katie describes as being "at peace" seems to qualify as a "peak experience" for her. Katie's reported distress is remarkable. She is experiencing self-defeating and other irrational thoughts that may be targeted with cognitive therapy. She is also experiencing doubts about her faith that are having a strong emotional impact on her (in addition to her other worries). These may in fact be adding to her anxiety response.

**Interior Group Quadrant—The Cultural Perspective** Katie has grown up with an Evangelical Christian worldview and has derived support from her faith and faith community. Her faith tradition has supported her sense of the primacy of family; however, the current problems with her family have religious as well as interpersonal significance for her. Further, developmentally Katie may have grown (or be growing) beyond aspects of her understanding of her faith tradition (e.g., the righteous are rewarded, the wicked are punished), and that may require some attention from her pastor, or possibly the counselor working with her.

**Exterior Social Quadrant—The Social Perspective** The church and the fiscal institutions of society are impinging on Katie the most right now. She is beset with phone calls from collection agencies and feels shame in response to these interactions. Although she understands there are bankruptcy laws in place that may offer one solution to her family's debt, her shared worldview from the lower-left quadrant does not affirm the use of them. She feels dissonance about her place in her church community and is not sure how she fits in that community right now. Katie must develop strategies that help her cope with the pressure of her creditors as well as make a decision about where she fits in her faith community.

## Review Questions

1. Compare and contrast the DSM, the DC:0-3R, and the PDM. What seems to be strengths and weaknesses of each manual?
2. How do you define what is psychologically normal and abnormal? How does your cultural background seem to affect your definition of these terms?
3. Given the overview of mind and brain, do you feel closer to the materialist/physicalist perspective or the dual-substance perspective? Why and what influences from your background seem to play into your answers?
4. If a DSM diagnosis can be made only if a client suffers distress or impairment from his or her symptoms, how would you handle a client dependent on alcohol who claims to be a "functional alcoholic" but who has been charged with drunk driving and given a written warning at work for coming in late?
5. How would you summarize the elements of the Integral model? Which elements are harder for you to understand?

## References

Achenbach, T. M. (1974). *Developmental psychopathology.* Oxford, UK: Oxford University Press.

Achenbach, T. M. (2009). Some needed changes in DSM-5: But what about children? *Clinical Psychology: Science and Practice, 16,* 50–53.

Allport, G. W. (1950). *The individual and his religion: A psychological interpretation.* Cambridge, MA: Harvard University Press.

American Psychiatric Association. (1968). *Diagnostic and statistical manual of mental disorders* (2nd ed.). Washington, DC: Author.

American Psychiatric Association. (1980). *Diagnostic and statistical manual of mental disorders* (3rd ed.). Washington, DC: Author.

American Psychiatric Association. (2000). *Diagnostic and statistical manual of mental disorders* (4th edition, text revision). Washington, DC: Author.

American Psychiatric Association. (2013a). *Diagnostic and statistical manual of mental disorders* (5th ed.). Washington, DC: Author.

American Psychiatric Association. (2013b). *Desk reference to the diagnostic criteria from DSM-5.* Washington, DC: Author.

Astin, J. A. (1998). Why patients use alternative medicine: Results of a national study. *Journal of the American Medical Association, 279,* 1548–1553.

Aten, J. D., & Leach, M. M. (Eds.). (2009). *Spirituality and the therapeutic process: A comprehensive resource from intake to termination.* Washington, DC: American Psychiatric Association.

Barlow, D. H., & Durand, V. M. (2002). *Abnormal psychology: An integrative approach* (3rd ed.). New York: Thomson.

Barry, J. M. (2005). *The great influenza: The story of the greatest pandemic in history.* New York: Penguin.

Bollinger, T. E. (1969). *The spiritual needs of the aging: In need for a specific ministry.* New York: Knopf.

Chalmers, D. J. (1995). Facing up to the problem of consciousness. *Journal of Consciousness Studies, 2*(3), 200–219.

Charney, D. S., et al. (2002). Neuroscience research agenda to guide development of a pathophysiologically based classification system. In D. J. Kupfer, M. B. First, & D. A. Regier (Eds.), *A research agenda for DSM-5* (pp. 31–84). Washington, DC: American Psychiatric Association.

Churchland, P. S. (2002). *Brain-wise: Studies in neurophilosophy.* Cambridge, MA: MIT.

Clinebell, H. (1992). *Well-being: A personal plan for exploring and enriching the seven dimensions of life.* San Francisco: Harper.

Combs, A. (2009). *Consciousness explained better: Towards an integral understanding of the multifaceted nature of consciousness.* St. Paul, MN: Paragon.

Cook-Greuter, S. (2000). Mature ego development: A gateway to ego transcendence? *Journal of Adult Development, 7,* 227–240.

Cook-Greuter, S. (2003). *Ego development: Nine levels of increasing embrace.* Wayland, MA: Cook-Greuter & Associates.

Douthit, K. Z., & Marquis, A. (2006). Empiricism in psychiatry's post-psychoanalytic era: Contemplating DSM's "atheoretical" nosology. *Constructivism in the Human Sciences, 11*(1), 32–59.

Ellison, C. W. (1983). Spiritual well-being: Conceptualization and measurement. *Journal of Psychology and Theology, 11,* 330–340.

Forsythe, P., & Kunze, W. A. (2013). Voices from within: Gut microbes and the CNS. *Molecular Life Science, 70,* 55–69.

Frances, A. (2013). *Saving normal: An insider's revolt against out-of-control psychiatric diagnosis, DSM-5, big pharma, and the medicalization of ordinary life.* New York: Morrow.

Frank, G. (1984). The Boulder model: History, rationale, and critique. *Psychology: Research and Practice, 15,* 417–435.

Hacker, A., & Dreifus, C. (2010). *Higher education? How colleges are wasting our money and failing our kids—and what we can do about it.* New York: Times Press.

Harris, S. (2010). *The moral landscape: How science can determine human values.* New York: Free Press.

House, A. E. (1999). *DSM-IV diagnosis in schools.* New York: Guilford.

House, A. E. (2002). *The first session with children and adolescents: Conducting a comprehensive mental health evaluation.* New York: Guilford.

Howowitz, A. V., & Wakefield, J. C. (2007). *The loss of sadness: How psychiatry transformed normal sorrow into depressive disorder.* Oxford, UK: Oxford University Press.

Ingersoll, R. E. (1994). Spirituality, religion, and counseling: Dimensions and relationships. *Counseling & Values, 38,* 98–112.

Ingersoll, R. E. (2002). An integral approach for teaching and practicing diagnosis. *The Journal of Transpersonal Psychology, 34,* 115–127.

Ingersoll, R. E., & Rak, C. F. (2006). *Psychopharmacology for helping professionals: An Integral approach.* New York. Cengage.

Ingersoll, R. E., & Zeitler, D. A. (2010). *Integral psychotherapy: Inside out/Outside in.* Albany, NY: SUNY.

Jackson, F. (1986). What Mary didn't know. *Journal of Philosophy, 83,* 291–295.

James, W. (1902). *The varieties of religious experience: A study in human nature.* New York: Holt.

Kagan, J. (1981). *The second year: The emergence of self-awareness.* Cambridge, MA: Harvard University Press.

Kagan, J. (2006). *An argument for mind.* New Haven, CT: Yale University Press.

Kaufman, J., Yang, B. Z, Douglas-Palumberi, H., Hooshyer, S., Lipschitz, D., Krystal, J. H., & Gelertner, J. (2004). Social supports and serotonin transporter gene modulate depression in maltreated children. *Proceedings of the National Academy of Sciences, 101,* 17316–17321.

Koch, C. (2012). *Consciousness: Confessions of a romantic reductionist.* Cambridge, MA: MIT Press.

Langdon, R., Coltheart, M., & Ward, P. B. (2006). Empathetic perspective-taking is impaired in schizophrenia: Evidence from a study of emotion attribution and theory of mind. *Cognitive Neuropsychiatry, 11,* 133–155.

Langdon, R., Coltheart, M., Ward, P. B., & Stanley, V. (2001). Visual and cognitive perspective-taking impairments in schizophrenia: A failure of allocentric simulation? *Cognitive Neuropsychiatry, 6,* 241–269.

Lindfors, K., Elovainio, M., Wickman, S., Vuorinen, R., Sinkkonen, J., Dunkel, L., & Raappana, A. (2007). Brief report: The role of ego development in psychosocial adjustment among boys with delayed puberty. *Journal of Research on Adolescence, 17,* 601–612.

Loevinger, J. (1998). Completing a life sentence. In P. M. Westenberg, A. Blasi, & L. Cohn (Eds.), *Personality development: Theoretical, empirical and clinical investigations of Loevinger's conception of ego development* (pp. 347–355). Mahwah, NJ: Erlbaum.

Lukoff, D., Lu, F., & Turner, R. (1992). Toward a more culturally sensitive DSM-IV: Psychoreligious and psychospiritual problems. *Journal of Nervous and Mental Disease, 180,* 673–682.

Magill, F. N., & McGral, I. P. (Eds.). (1988). *Christian spirituality: The essential guide to the most influential spiritual writings on the Christian tradition.* San Francisco: Harper.

Mahoney, M. J. (1980). *Abnormal psychology: Perspectives on human variance.* San Francisco: Harper & Row.

Marquis, A. (2008). *The integral intake: A guide to comprehensive idiographic assessment in integral psychotherapy.* New York: Routledge.

Marquis, A., & Douthit, K. Z. (2006). The hegemony of "empirically supported treatment": Validating or violating? *Constructivism in the Human Sciences, 11*(2), 108–141.

May, G. (1988). *Addiction and grace: Love and spirituality in the healing of addictions.* San Francisco: Harper.

McWilliams, N. (1994). *Psychoanalytic diagnosis: Understanding personality structure in the clinical process.* New York, NY: The Guilford Press.

Miller, W. R. (Ed.). (1999). *Integrating spirituality into treatment: Resources for practitioners.* Washington, DC: American Psychological Association.

Mischel, W. (1968). *Personality and assessment.* Mahwah, NJ: Erlbaum.

Moberg, D. O. (1979). *Spiritual well-being: Sociological perspectives.* Washington, DC: University Press of American.

Norcross, J. C., Gallagher, K. M., & Prochaska, J. O. (1989). The Boulder and/or Vail model: Training preferences of clinical psychologists. *Journal of Clinical Psychology, 45,* 822–828.

Paris, J. (2013). *The intelligent clinician's guide to the DSM-5.* New York: Oxford University Press.

PDM Task Force. (2006). *Psychodynamic diagnostic manual.* Silver Spring, MD: Alliance of Psychoanalytic Organizations.

Pinker, S. (2009/1997). *How the mind works.* New York: W. W. Norton & Company, Inc.

Practice Management Information Corporation. (2006). *International classification of diseases* (9th ed., clinical modification). Downers Grove, IL: Author.

Richards, P. S., & Bergin, A. E. (2000). Religious diversity and psychotherapy: Conclusions, recommendations, and future directions. In P. S. Richards & A. E. Bergin (Eds.), *Handbook of psychotherapy and religious diversity* (pp. 469–489). Washington, DC: American Psychological Association.

Robinson, D. (2008). *Consciousness and mental life.* New York: Columbia.

Sandys, J. E. (1909). *The characters of Theophrastus: An English translation from a revised text with introduction and notes by R.C. Jebb.* London: Macmillan.

Schiffman, J., Lam, C. W., Jiwatram, T., Ekstrom, M., Sorensen, H., & Mednick, S. (2004). Perspective-taking deficits in people with schizophrenia spectrum disorders: A prospective investigation. *Psychological Medicine, 34,* 1581–1586.

Scotton, H. W. (1996). Introduction and definition of transpersonal psychiatry. In B. W. Scotton, A. B. Chinen, & J. R. Battista (Eds.), *Textbook of transpersonal psychiatry and psychology* (pp. 4–8). New York: Basic Books.

Skovagaard, A. M., Houmann, T., Landorph, S. L., & Christiansen, E. (2003). Assessment and classification of psychopathology in epidemiological research of children 0–3 years of age: A review of the literature. *European Child and Adolescent Psychiatry, 13,* 337–346.

Snyder, C. R., & Elliott, T. R. (2005). Twenty-first century graduate education in clinical psychology: A four level matrix model. *Journal of Clinical Psychology, 61,* 1033–1054.

Soloman, R. C. (2002). *Spirituality for the skeptic: The thoughtful love of life.* Oxford, UK: Oxford University Press.

Sperry, L., & Shafranske, E. P. (Eds.). (2005). *Spiritually oriented psychotherapy.* Washington, DC: American Psychological Association.

Suite, D. H., La Bril, R., Primm, A., & Harrison-Ross, P. (2007). Beyond misdiagnosis, misunderstanding and mistrust: relevance of the historical perspective in the medical and mental health treatment of people of color. *Journal of the National Medical Association, 99,* 879–885.

Task Force on Research Diagnostic Criteria: Infancy and Preschool. (2002). Research diagnostic criteria—preschool age (RDC-PA). Retrieved from http://www.infantinstitute.org/RDC-PA.htm

Thoresen, C. E. (2007). Spirituality, religion, and health: What's the deal? In T. G. Plante & C. E. Thoresen (Eds.), *Spirit, science, and health: How the spiritual mind fuels physical wellness* (pp. 3–10). Westport, CN: Praeger.

Vonnegut, K., & Stringer, L. (1999). *Like shaking hands with God: A conversation about writing.* New York: Washington Square Press.

Webster's New World. (2008). *Webster's new world medical dictionary* (3rd ed.). New York: Author.

Wiggins-Frame, M. (2003). *Integrating religion and spirituality into counseling: A comprehensive approach.* Pacific Grove, CA: Brooks/Cole.

Wilber, K. (1995). *Sex, ecology, spirituality: The spirit of evolution.* Boston: Shambhala.

Williams, M., Teasdale, J., Zindel, S., & Kabat-Zinn, J. (2007). *The mindful way through depression: Freeing yourself from chronic unhappiness.* New York: Guilford.

Witmer, J. M. (1989). Reaching toward wholeness: An integrated approach to well-being over the life span. In T. J. Sweeney (Ed.), *Adlerian counseling: A practical approach for a new decade.* Muncie, IN: Accelerated Press.

World Health Organization. (1992). *The ICD-10 classification of mental and behavioural disorders.* Geneva: Author.

Wulff, D. M. (1996). The psychology of religion: An overview. In E. P. Shafranske (Ed.), *Religion and the clinical practice of psychology* (pp. 43–70). Washington, DC: American Psychological Association.

Zero to Three. (2005). *Diagnostic and classification of mental health and developmental disorders of infancy and early childhood: Revised edition (DC:0-3R).* Washington, DC: Zero to Three Press.

Zinnbauer, B. J., Pargament, K. I., & Scott, A. B. (1999). The emerging meanings of religiousness and spirituality: Problems and prospects. *Journal of Personality, 67,* 879–919.

# 2

# The DSM and Other Manuals: History and Overview

As we noted in Chapter 1, it is important that you have a general understanding of the *Diagnostic and Statistical Manual of the American Psychiatric Association*, 5th edition, and its history, as well as some awareness of other mental health diagnostic manuals, such as the *Psychodynamic Diagnostic Manual* (PDM; PDM Task Force, 2006) and the *Diagnostic Classification of Mental Health and Developmental Disorders of Infancy and Early Childhood* (DC:0-3R; Zero to Three, 2005). As we also emphasized, the DSM is *unlike* medical systems of diagnosis in that we have yet to find specific, reliable physiological markers for any of the disorders listed in it (Charney et al., 2002; Frances, 2013; Paris, 2013).

The DSM-5 was supposed to be different from previous editions of the DSM, and include biological markers for disorders, but not one has been found (Charney et al., 2002). Although biological variables likely play a role in many disorders, we do not yet know what the role is or exactly what the variables are. We are closer to isolating brain circuits that may play dominant roles in disorders like Obsessive-Compulsive Disorder (OCD), but there is still a "chicken–egg" paradox between mind and brain in such cases (Schwartz & Begley, 2002).[1] Many DSM disorders (like our example of depression in Chapter 1) appear to be *overdetermined*, meaning that they appear to have multiple causes (Frances, 2013). This does not stop some parties, such as pharmaceutical companies, from alluding to clear-cut physiological origins of mental disorders, but if you listen to such claims critically, the claimant always fails to produce evidence. One example is historian Jonathan Engel (2008), who in his description of mental disorders makes

[1] Schwartz and Begley performed a study demonstrating the power of the mind to change brain structures. Their subjects were people with OCD and compulsions to wash their hands. These subjects were supposed to stand in front of a sink with running water. Those who were able to do so without washing their hands had brains that had changed similarly to matched-subjects who had been given medication for their OCD. In short, "mental force" changed their brains. Of course the brain is known for its plasticity but questions still remain about how much change can be guided mentally versus with medication.

statements like "psychiatric disorders clearly had biological causes" or ". . . schizophrenia, that most physiological of psychiatric disorders . . ." (p. 226) but then fails to name or cite even one study illustrating what the biological or physiological basis is. Although many disorders like Schizophrenia and Bipolar I Disorder *seem* to have biological substrates, we do not know what they are—until we do, those premises should be stated as hypotheses. Again, critical thinking is an ethical imperative for your clients and an important tool for your ongoing development as a clinician.

In this chapter we provide a brief history of the DSM, an overview of other manuals we will draw from in subsequent chapters, and a look at important issues related to the DSM-5. Perhaps the most important thing for you to remember is that the DSM is not a "gospel" or sacred canon. As psychiatrist, renowned researcher on Schizophrenia, and DSM-IV task force leader Nancy Andreasen and her colleagues have written, the DSM ". . . is not the Ark of the Covenant, the Ten Commandments, the Talmud, or the Holy Bible" (Andreasen, Flaum, & Arndt, 1992, p. 616). Although it serves a useful purpose, it should not be accorded excessive reverence, and excessive faith should not be placed in it. At best, the DSM is a work in progress that helps in diagnosing some but not all clients.

This said, you should also be aware that the DSM is a political document. As Alfred Korzybski (1958) has stated ". . . those who rule symbols, rule us" (p. 76). One of the reasons that the release of the DSM-5 publication was delayed three times is the current battle regarding how broadly psychiatric diagnoses should be defined/construed/written. Some of the harshest criticism of the DSM-5 revision process has come from psychiatrists Robert Spitzer and Allen Frances. Spitzer headed the DSM-III task force and Frances headed the DSM-IV task force. Both have been deeply involved in DSM development, from the DSM-III in 1980 to the present (Aldhouse, 2009). Frances (2009b) contends that the initial aim of the DSM-5 was to focus on biological markers for mental and emotional disorders. He wrote that because biological markers are thus far unattainable, the shift has gone to diagnosing sub-threshold and prodromal disorders, which he claims will result in many people (especially children) being prescribed psychiatric medication when they may not even have a disorder. In an interview with journalist Jon Ronson (2012), Frances stated that the diagnosis of Bipolar I Disorder in children is one of three false epidemics in psychiatry (the other two being Attention Deficit–Hyperactivity Disorder [ADHD] and Autism). Bipolar I Disorder is a fairly rare psychiatric disorder thought to afflict at most 1.6% of the population with early onset being age 13. In one survey (Danner et al., 2009), it was estimated that in a 6-year period the number of children being medicated for Bipolar I Disorder had increased 245%. Many of these children had subthreshold symptoms, meaning they did not meet all the criteria. Can you imagine if you went to your physician and she said "well you have subthreshold symptoms of strep throat, so we're going to load you up on antibiotics just in case"? If that wouldn't raise your eyebrows, it should. One addition to the DSM-5 is Disruptive Mood Dysregulation Disorder, located under the Depressive Disorders. Because many children diagnosed (likely misdiagnosed) with Bipolar I Disorder are diagnosed this way (based on disruptive moods), the hope is that by separating out a disorder for disruptive moods, fewer children will be diagnosed with Bipolar I Disorder (Margulies, Weintraub, Basile, Grover, & Carlson, 2012). Others fear it will simply inflate the number of diagnosed children by adding the new disorder (Jairam, Prabhuswamy, & Dullur, 2012; Raven & Parry, 2012). Time will tell.

Groups such as pharmaceutical companies (which fund a great deal of research on both diagnosis and treatment) have much to gain if disorders are broadened in such a way that more people meet the criteria for any given disorder and are prescribed psychotropic medication. This is one reason Spitzer and Frances believe DSM revisions should be as public as possible. Whereas many laypeople are not trained to understand the diagnoses in the DSM, nonmedical mental health therapists are, and their critiques could prove important to the further development of the DSM.

Robert Spitzer (2009) has been outspoken in his criticism of the secrecy with which DSM-5 revisions have been undertaken. He claims that the confidentiality agreement that all DSM-5 task force members signed violates the spirit of public science in which findings and deliberations are supposed to be open to peer review. The confidentiality agreement prohibited their sharing of any information about the revision process, including:

> . . . all work product, unpublished manuscripts and drafts and other prepublication materials, group discussions, internal correspondence, information about the development process and any other written or unwritten information in any form that emanates from or relates to my work with the APA Task Force or Workgroup. (Spitzer, 2009, p. 2)

Since Spitzer's protest, some of the DSM-5 deliberations have been made public, but mental health clinicians should be mindful that this is another illustration of the political dimension of the manual. Particularly because of these political dynamics, we believe critical thinking about the manual is imperative. The lack of scientific certainty in the DSM leaves a gap that can be bridged only by a leap of faith or a critical understanding of what the manual can and cannot do. Clearly, we prefer the path of critical thinking and hope that this book gives you the tools to engage in that process. To be clear, the DSM is a work in progress. While some disorders are overdetermined (e.g., there are many ways to get depressed, and some of them are psychological), others appear to be rooted primarily in genetics and/or the nervous system (e.g., Schizophrenia and Bipolar I Disorder, which are usually lifelong). The Research Domain Criteria (RDoC) of the National Institute of Mental Health (NIMH), described in Chapter 1, is designed to root out much of the physical and behavioral underpinnings of disorders.

## NOSOLOGICAL SYSTEMS

Taxonomy is the science or technique of classification. A nosology is a type of taxonomy, and the term *nosology* is frequently used in medical literature to refer to the systematic classification and knowledge of diseases (the Greek root *noso* means "disease" and the suffix *ology* refers to "a science or branch of knowledge"). In the strict meaning of the word, nosology is probably not an accurate label for the classification of mental disorders. This again promotes the misunderstanding that mental disorders can be equated with, and understood as, physical or medical diseases. As we have said multiple times, that is not the case. In terms of classifying mental disorders, there is a paradox to referring to that classification as a nosology.

The paradox is this: In physical disorders the symptom depends on the disease—meaning that when a symptom appears, a medical doctor tries to trace it to an underlying disease process (although there are diseases that may be asymptomatic for long periods of time). Take, for example, the medical disease colloquially referred to as strep throat (streptococcal pharyngitis). In most cases, patients report soreness in the throat, difficulty swallowing, and perhaps a fever. Doctors can do several tests for the presence of the bacteria that causes the symptoms (Group A Streptococcal infection). Tests include Rapid Antigen Detection Test (RADT) or growing a culture from the patient's throat in blood on an agar plate. If the test shows that Group A Streptococcus is growing in the person's throat, the doctor prescribes antibiotics that in most cases kill the bacteria. In this case the doctor examines the symptoms of the patient and then runs tests based on the symptoms that lead to confirmation of a disease.

This is not the case with mental disorders. In mental disorders, rather than symptoms leading to tests that reveal a disease process, *the symptoms—in combinations determined by the DSM—are themselves considered the disease.* Of the hundreds of diagnoses in the DSM-5, *not one* qualifies as a specifically identifiable disease process (which has a physiological/neurological marker) underlying the set of symptoms from which the client suffers. Thus, identification of the symptom configuration is the end of the line, so to speak. So, in general medicine, the symptom derives from the disease; in mental disorders, the "disease" *is* the set of symptoms (Goncalves, Machado, Korman, & Angus, 2002).

Despite all these problems, the fact remains that the DSM categorical system is designed to parallel the coding and descriptions for mental disorders in the *International Classification of Diseases* (ICD) of the World Health Organization. In addition to the categories, the DSM-5 does have some dimensional elements, which we discuss in the next section.

## DSM HISTORY: CATEGORIES AND DIMENSIONS

One way to understand the DSM as a work in progress and to practice critical thinking is to learn about its history. In particular, the differences between a *dimensional* description of symptoms and a *categorical* description of symptoms will help you understand how the DSM has evolved, including some of the changes in the DSM-5. In addition, it should help you understand the approach we took while writing the rest of this book.

### Categorical Diagnosis

The categorical approach to diagnosis is sometimes called the "descriptive" approach because the categories are supposed to describe the diagnoses. Categories in the DSM constitute the diagnoses most readers are familiar with, such as Major Depressive Disorder (MDD) or Bipolar I Disorder (BPI). Each category or diagnosis in the DSM has a list of symptoms and *threshold instructions* like those in MDD, in which clients must meet five of the nine symptoms listed under criterion "A." Ideally, the threshold derives from well-designed and carefully analyzed research, but sometimes—more often than not—the threshold is set based upon "expert consensus." Thus, categories present each clinician with a bimodal choice: The client either meets the criteria in the category or does not. With this type of a classification/diagnostic system, a person with four of the symptoms for depression does not have MDD, whereas someone with five of the symptoms does (although one can always opt for the diagnosis of Other

Specified Depressive Disorder or Unspecified Depressive Disorder[2]). Do you see the weaknesses of such a system? Do you see the potential problems of making a diagnosis categorically (yes or no) in contrast to dimensionally (how severe is this person's depression?)? Although the categorical approach simplifies the diagnostic decision in some ways, many clinicians believe that a clinically useful diagnosis is rarely that simple.

One problem with this is that categorical approaches treat each diagnosis as a distinct entity. Thinking of DSM diagnoses as distinct is difficult, especially given the high levels of comorbidity (when a client meets criteria for two or more disorders) seen in clinical practice. This is one reason the RDoC are set up to research *across* different disorders (for example, one could experience depression in Major Depressive Disorder, Bipolar I Disorder, and Schizoaffective Disorder, among others). Moreover, the younger clients are, the more prevalent comorbidity is (House, 1999). Here again this illustrates how DSM diagnoses differ from medical diagnoses. Comorbidity in DSM diagnoses (especially in children) has been much more the rule than the exception (Kessler, 1995; Kessler et al., 1994). In some studies, clients meeting the criteria for one disorder had a 50% chance of meeting criteria for at least one additional disorder. Can you imagine going to the doctor and having her tell you that because you have strep throat, there is a 50% chance you have some other disease? With regard to diagnostic practices based upon the DSM, in many cases that is the situation, and we believe this points to the limitations of the categorical approach (Angold, Costello, & Erkanle, 1999; Aragona, 2009; Clark, Watson, & Reynolds, 1995).

## Dimensional Diagnosis

One proposed remedy to the weaknesses of the categorical approach is the dimensional approach to diagnosis. There are several ways that one can diagnose dimensionally. In the DSM-5, dimensionality is addressed in initial groupings of dimensions that envelop many diagnoses. For example, internalizing disorders would include depression, anxiety, and related cognitive symptoms, and externalizing disorders include things like substance use and impulse control problems (American Psychiatric Association [APA], 2013; Andrews et al., 2009; Krueger & South, 2009; Wittchen, Beesdo, & Gloster, 2009). Although this is currently primarily a research endeavor, it could have profound impact on future DSMs.

Dimensions may also be used to represent the degree of severity for a defined set of symptoms. In this case, dimensional diagnosis allows for diagnoses to be presented on a continuum. For example, you could look at depression on a continuum that runs from mild to moderate to severe in terms of the intensity of the symptoms the client is experiencing. In this sense, Major Depressive Disorder would be diagnosed when a client's symptoms exceed a cutoff on the continuum, similar to how hypertension (high blood pressure) is diagnosed when systolic and diastolic blood pressure levels exceed a particular threshold.

The dimensional model also allows for subthreshold levels of symptoms to be identified as the target of interventions. For example, the literature on Personality

[2] These are the options presented in the DSM-5. In previous DSMs, the option was Major Depressive Disorder, not otherwise specified (NOS).

Disorders shows that in 50% of the cases in which a Personality Disorder is comorbid with an axis I disorder (such as depression or anxiety), there are personality variables that contribute to the axis I disorder but are not diagnosable in the current DSM (Westen, Kegley-Heim, Morrison, Patterson, & Campbell, 2002). Of course, this type of model complicates certain aspects of clinical practice, some of which involve third-party payment. Also significant is who sets the threshold (and *how*—the process by which that threshold is established) beyond which the client is said to have a "disorder" and below which the client is said to simply be struggling with problems of living. This is similar to how it was decided that it's five symptoms out of nine that will lead to a diagnosis of depression, not four or six.

The DSM-5 presents the Personality Disorders in the same format as those in DSM-IV. The initial DSM-5 revision of Personality Disorders was so radical it was decided to present the revised dimensional approaches to these disorders in an appendix. Also included in that appendix is an alternative model for assessing impairment in personality traits or functions in a dimensional manner. For example, a general level of personality functioning can be measured by the Level of Personality Functioning Scale (also included in the same appendix). Other domains, such as grandiosity or deceitfulness, are proposed for similar dimensional measures. Again, time and more research will tell if this revised approach will become standard practice in future manuals.

Dimensional diagnosis can also refer to symptoms or personality dimensions that—in combination—produce a variety of psychopathologies. Much of the research on the relationship of the Five-Factor Model of personality and Personality Disorders uses this understanding of dimensional diagnosis (Nestadt et al., 2008). Dimensions can also be used to reflect genetic vulnerabilities as well as specific biological parameters. For example, we know that the heritability of mental disorders is more accurately described as *genetic vulnerability*. This means that we may have a higher risk for a mental disorder because one of our parents has suffered from one. The increased risk is because the disorder is related to the genome (genotype) we inherited from the person suffering from the disorder.

The challenge here is that the expression of genetic vulnerabilities (gene expression is referred to as phenotype) is dependent on environmental triggers, but we don't know exactly which environmental triggers trigger which genetic vulnerabilities. The relation of gene expression to environmental triggers is referred to as *epigenetics*. As we learn more specifically what sorts of environments trigger which sorts of genetic variables, then dimensional approaches for the environmental triggers can be used to complement the existing categorical structure of the DSM.

By way of example, imagine a child who has one parent suffering from Schizophrenia. In this scenario, assume we have a correlation between increased risk for the development of any mental disorder if the child suffers from poor attachment to caregivers and/or the stresses associated with lower socioeconomic status. In this case, we would add these dimensions to the child's chart and try to quantify his socioeconomic status and degree of attachment. In our view, this type of multidimensional diagnosis gets closer to ideal assessment, and also makes it more likely that we will engage in prevention by trying to increase the probability of healthy attachment and decrease the stressors related to lower socioeconomic status.

## DSM HISTORY: THE EVOLUTION OF THE DSM

The DSM began as War Department Technical Bulletin Medical 203 (hereafter referred to as Medical 203), first drafted in 1943 (War Department, 1946). Medical 203 began in a committee chaired by Brigadier General William Menninger, a psychiatrist and brother of Karl Menninger (who, with their father, founded the Menninger Clinic in Topeka, Kansas). William Menninger was serving in the Office of the Surgeon General when Medical 203 was created. Menninger was instrumental in the utilization of nonmedical mental health professionals (psychologists and social workers) to conduct mental health assessments in the U.S. Army. It is important to understand that prior to World War II, organized psychiatry did not conduct outpatient practices with "normal" individuals, and the fields of clinical psychology, social work, and counseling either didn't exist or were just getting started (Houts, 2000).

The military had known that life circumstances (particularly combat experiences) could produce or trigger mental illness, but with the droves of veterans returning from WWII, the public began to realize it too. Psychiatrist Adolf Meyer (1866–1950) introduced the concept of mental disturbances as psycho-biologic reactions. In his work in New York and later at Johns Hopkins, Meyer (like Freud before him) had hoped to trace mental disorders to something physiological (even then this was the ultimate hope). He eventually realized, however, that because no physiological causes had been discovered that had consistently underlain mental disorders, it was more accurate to understand mental disturbances as *reactions* of the person to emotional states brought on by circumstances (this came to be known as the "reaction concept"). Again, Freud (1950 [1895]) ran into the same obstacle with his Project for a Scientific Psychology: being unable to identify and correlate physiological markers with mental disorders (Meyer, 1908). Meyer was exceptional in his desire to build theories based upon data, rather than mere speculation. He approached psychiatry in a pragmatic sense and advocated nonadherence to theory in understanding mental illness. Meyer also distanced himself from what he viewed as cultish dynamics in psychoanalytic circles, in which he believed that a type of faith seemed to play a stronger role than science (Engel, 2008). Although we agree with many of the strong arguments that have been made pointing out the impossibility of a truly "atheoretical" diagnostic system (Douthit & Marquis, 2006), we also admire Meyer's goal of trying to be as unbiased by theory as possible. With psychoanalytic theory, this turned out to be very important because it has been falsified on some counts and written in a way that makes it impossible to falsify on other counts.

Psychoanalytic theory did play a role in both Medical 203 and the DSM-I. The spread of psychodynamic thinking within psychiatry ". . . coincided with the expansion of medical-school training programs funded by the newly founded National Institute of Mental Health" (Houts, 2000, p. 942). This expansion shifted the priorities of psychiatry in that prior to WWII, it is estimated that about 60% of the members in the American Psychiatric Association were employed in inpatient hospitals. In 1956 (4 years after the appearance of the DSM-I), that number had fallen to 17% (Grob, 1991). The infusion of psychodynamic thinking in medical school psychiatric rotations was given a large boost when William Menninger served as president of the American Psychoanalytic Association and then the American Psychiatric Association (hereafter referred to as APA). Medical 203 was described as the document that paved the way for psychodynamic concepts to dominate the study of psychopathology for 30 years (Barton, 1987). Thus, Medical 203 had a substantial influence on the first DSM (DSM-I; American Psychiatric Association, 1952).

Prior to the DSM-I, psychiatric taxonomies were produced by multiple organizations (such as the New York Academy of Medicine and the American Medico-Psychological Association [the precursor to the APA]), mostly for use in state mental institutions. The treatment of soldiers during and after WWII changed that focus because the increase in soldiers suffering mental problems required diagnoses to help bring order to the increasingly chaotic field (Raines, 1952). The APA Committee on Nomenclature was heavily influenced by psychiatrists who had used Medical 203 during the war to the extent that the first draft of the DSM-I was ". . . some amalgamation of Medical 203 . . ." (Houts, 2000, p. 945). The final draft of the DSM-I was approved by the APA in 1951 and released in 1952. The categories in the DSM-I were directly based on many Medical 203 categories, including organic psychoses, disorders of intelligence, psychotic disorders, psychoneurotic disorders, character and behavior disorders, and simple personality disorders. Psychoanalytic terms were particularly reflected in neurotic, psychotic, and character disorders.

In both Medical 203 and the DSM-I, the basic idea was that mental disorders were caused by ". . . some aberration in the development of the personality, most likely, but not necessarily, combined with stressful environmental circumstances" (Houts, 2000, p. 946). This was an early version of what is today called the *diathesis-stress model.* "Diathesis-stress" is an unfortunate label in that it is grammatically awkward and colloquially vague. The "diathesis" can be thought of as a "weak link" or inherent vulnerability that is then exacerbated or broken by stress, which then results in the disorder. The World Health Organization (also influenced by Medical 203) included a section on mental disorders for the first time in its sixth edition of the International Classification of Diseases (ICD) in 1948.

The bottom line is that Medical 203 and the DSM-I combined psychoanalytic concepts with Adolph Meyer's idea of psychobiologic reactions. This is ironic given Meyer's skepticism about psychoanalysis in general and the orthodoxy of its practitioners in particular. The DSM-II, which was published in 1968, retained the psychoanalytic concepts but did away with Meyer's reaction concept (American Psychiatric Association, 1968). In the foreword to the DSM-II, committee chairperson Ernest Gruenberg noted that the committee could not agree on the etiology of disorders such as Schizophrenia, so the concept of reaction was deleted. The DSM-II was designed to mirror the mental disorders listed in the 8th edition of the International Classification of Diseases (ICD-8), which was released in 1966. The ICD-8 also retained much of the psychoanalytic thinking about mental disorders. Disorders were viewed as problems rooted in personality and intrapsychic conflict. Karl Menninger captured the thinking of this era when he wrote that mental disorders were the failure of the person to adapt to his or her environment; the problem was "what was behind the symptom" (Menninger, 1963, p. 325). It has been argued that this psychodynamic system did an unsatisfactory job of separating unhealthy from healthy individuals (Grob, 1987), although similar criticisms can be made of all other DSMs. The DSM-I and the DSM-II were artifacts that reflected the esteem that psychoanalytic thinking had in the psychiatric profession at that time; however, that esteem was not to last. The DSM-III would be a radical departure from the previous two versions.

Why did the DSM-III so radically depart from its two predecessors? The simple answer is for the survival of psychiatry. Even well before 1980—when the DSM-III was released—the psychiatry, psychology, and social work professions were all becoming painfully aware of the weaknesses of psychoanalytic theory. How was it that a theory that claimed to have explanations for most human behavior failed to ameliorate the very symptoms it supposedly understood with such omniscience? One problem began at the root of psychoanalysis with Sigmund Freud's famed intolerance of colleagues who disagreed with his theory. His shunning of any dissenters quickly established a cult-like orthodoxy wherein the master's theory was to be believed, not tested. The reliance on psychodynamic terms in the DSM produced what has been called a crisis of legitimacy for psychiatry in the 1970s (Mayes & Horwitz, 2005).

As the fields of psychology and psychiatry aimed to practice more scientifically, their practitioners aimed to practice the scientific method that required theoretical assertions to be tested against empirical data. If a theory cannot be tested or cannot predict the course of treatment, is it any different from any other leap of faith, whether religious or philosophical? The need for descriptive criteria that could be tested empirically paved the way for the categorical method pioneered in the DSM-III and that is still used in the DSM-5. If we think of the DSM as a work in progress, we can appreciate that the current DSM has its weaknesses but also that it is a vast improvement over the earlier psychoanalytically-based manuals (Frances & Egger, 1999).

## The Role of the World Health Organization in Changing the DSM

Due to the lack of empirical support for the mental disorder taxonomies in the DSM I, DSM II, ICD-6, and ICD-7, the World Health Organization initiated a comprehensive review of diagnostic issues. The review was conducted by British psychiatrist Erwin Stengel. His work is credited with advancing the practice of diagnosis and operationalizing labels to increase reliability (APA, 2000). The development of the DSM-III (begun in 1974 and published in 1980) coincided with the ICD-9 (published in 1977) and introduced the categorical approach (with each category listing specific symptoms). The DSM-IV (published in 1994) introduced the five-axis approach that was supposed to give a more well-rounded picture of the client by taking an atheoretical stance with regard to the cause of the disorders. It is interesting to note that the DSM-5 (APA, 2013) did away with the five-axis diagnostic system because it was claimed that the five-axis system had never been scientifically validated (APA, 2013). However, many of the categories in the DSM-III and DSM-IV were inconsistent and in some cases the criteria were still unclear. This led to revisions, the DSM-III-R in 1987 and the DSM-IV-TR in 2000.

The DSM-III was also heavily influenced by the work of psychiatrist John Feighner and what some have called the "Feighner Criteria." In his third year of residency, Feighner began to develop criteria for specific disorders (Editorial, 1989). This led to his development of the Schedule for Affective Disorders and Schizophrenia (SADS; Endicott & Spitzer, 1972). Using the SADS, patients were to be assigned a diagnosis only if they met a certain number of the total criteria listed. Most of the criteria were based on symptoms, but in some cases history and prior mental health problems were included. This approach was used in the DSM-III and remains with us today in the DSM-5. To increase the reliability of the diagnostic system, the SADS was revised and simplified. The revised assessment is the Structured

**TABLE 2.1 Number of Diagnoses in, and Length of, All the DSMs**

| Version | Year | Total Number of Diagnoses | Total Number of Pages |
|---|---|---|---|
| I | 1952 | 106 | 130 |
| II | 1968 | 182 | 134 |
| III | 1980 | 265 | 494 |
| III-R | 1987 | 292 | 567 |
| IV | 1994 | 365 | 886 |
| IV-TR | 2000 | 365 | 943 |
| 5 | 2013 | approx. 350 | 946 |

Clinical Interview for DSM-III (SCID; Spitzer, 1983; Spitzer, Williams, Gibbon, & First, 1992). Since its inception, there have been numerous versions of the SCID, including a clinical version, a research version, and a version specifically for Personality Disorders.[3]

The DSM-III contained 265 disorders; the DSM-III-R, published in 1987, contained 292; and the DSM-IV, published in 1994, increased the total number of diagnoses to 365. Table 2.1 summarizes the increases in diagnoses and page length with each subsequent DSM version.

Reviewing the increase in diagnoses and general length raises some interesting questions about the DSM in general. Although mental disorders are not like physical, allopathic illnesses, it would seem that we "discover" new mental disorders each time the manual is revised; in fact, some authors have even suggested that the DSMs are "making us crazy" (Greenberg, 2013; Kutchins & Kirk, 1997). To be fair, we would expect that as we study criteria sets we may come up with "subdivisions" of a particular set, thus creating a new disorder, but it is hard to tell if that is what is happening in the DSMs. For the first time since its inception, the DSM (in the current version, the DSM-5) actually has fewer disorders than its predecessors (unless you include all the modifications of disorders, such as mild, moderate, or severe).

Some researchers have claimed that the proliferation of diseases in the ICD is radically different than the proliferation of disorders in the DSM. Part of this is a function of how disorders are conceptualized in the DSM. From the DSM-III onward, the concept of dysfunction is equated with disorder, and this has led to the proliferation of diagnostic categories (mental disorders) in the DSMs (Houts, 2001). Psychologist Arthur Houts has published numerous papers on this topic. His main point revolves around the remarkable increase in the number of diagnoses in the four decades separating DSM-I and DSM-IV. He also notes that, not coincidentally, at the same time, we have seen a drastic increase in the number of mental health professionals in practice (driven strongly by the licensing of master's-level therapists in counseling and social work) (Houts, 2002).

[3] Materials on the SCID can be found at http://www.scid4.org/index.html.

First and foremost, the intent of DSMs III through 5 is "to facilitate clinical practice and communication" (Clark et al., 1995). The idea of the DSM being atheoretical and a-etiological was a direct reflection of the failure of psychoanalytic theory (or any other theory of personality, for that matter) to further our knowledge of mental and emotional disorders. In plain English: we don't know the exact causes of these disorders, just as we don't have much agreement on what personality and mind are and how they may contribute to mental disorders.[4] Again, this is in sharp contrast to most of the disorders found in the ICD, and one of the many differences between the DSM and the ICD. The new approach in the DSM-III was based upon field trials of criteria that *described (not explained)* the symptoms that seemed to cluster together (for example, fatigue, appetite disturbance, and anhedonia[5] cluster together under the category "Major Depressive Disorder"). In this manner, symptoms and their categories could then be tested in different settings to see how clearly they were being described ("clear" in this sense means helping clinicians correctly diagnose clients). From this point of view, even if we don't know the specific etiology of mental disorders, if we describe them accurately, we enable subsequent research to investigate the etiology. The editors of the DSM (from III onward) have used this categorical approach (derived from the Feighner Criteria), which aims to create categories of symptoms based on an observable pattern of behaviors or experiences that is reproducible across individuals and causes significant distress or impairment of functioning. In this system, literature reviews and clinical trials are used to determine how many of the criteria in a given category must be met for the person to be diagnosed with the disorder.

## THE DISEASE MODEL IN DSM

Although the editors of the DSM claim that the manual is "atheoretical," critics have pointed out that such claims seem intended to mask that the model is in fact a medical or disease model of psychopathology that is biased toward psychiatrists and away from nonmedical mental health therapists (Douthit & Marquis, 2006; Malik & Beutler, 2002). According to the American Psychiatric Association, the five-axis diagnoses of the previous versions of DSM were supposed to facilitate "comprehensive and systematic evaluation," capture "the complexity of clinical situations," and provide a more holistic model that allows for comments on clients' current levels of functioning and psychosocial stressors (APA, 2000). The five-axis system that was eliminated in the DSM-5 was supposed to reflect physician George Engel's (1977, 1997) biopsychosocial paradigm as a holistic alternative to the medical model that focused disproportionately on the physical aspects of illness.

Engel noted that to practice from the allopathic medical model (described in Chapter 1) is to operate from what is called the "disease model." Recall that the allopathic model treats disease with agents that produce effects different from the disease process, with the hope of ameliorating it. For example, if the inattention in Attention Deficit–Hyperactivity Disorder (ADHD) is believed to be correlated with a deficiency

---

[4] This is an old problem dating back to Mischel (1968). See also the chapter on types in Ingersoll and Zeitler (2010).

[5] As we'll describe in Chapter 3, anhedonia is one of the vegetative signs of depression that manifests as a loss of pleasure or joy in things that used to give the client pleasure or joy.

in dopamine activity in the brain, one allopathic approach is to administer medications that increase dopamine activity (e.g., amphetamines) in the brain, with the hope of reducing symptoms and increasing the client's ability to attend. Engel contended that all branches of medicine (including psychiatry) should be taught such that clinicians consider biological, psychological, and social variables when dealing with patients' symptoms. Many psychiatrists lament that Engel's call was not heeded in any branch of medicine and that in psychiatry, the allopathic approach, or disease model, has won the political day; this appears particularly true given the loss of the five-axis diagnosis system (Cohen, 1993; Victor, 1996).

The disease model got a real boost when psychiatric nosology adopted the descriptive format of the DSM-III. Up to that point, psychiatric practice and the labeling of disorders had a more dimensional quality to it. The dimensions were varied and related to the severity of symptoms or the client's manifestation of diverse symptom sets that seemed to go together (such as symptoms of both anxiety and depression). However, as previously mentioned, much of the dimensional quality of the first two DSMs relied on psychoanalytic concepts, and many critics thought that reliance too heavy, especially given that psychoanalytic approaches tend to rely heavily on the client's reported subjective experience, in contrast to the more "objective" statistical procedures that characterize the DSM-III onward.

These critics turned to researchers of mental disorders who used more objective statistical techniques to conclude that certain symptoms tend to occur together and can be organized as syndromes. As psychiatrist Stephen Dilts (2001) noted, the syndromes are described by the symptoms that compose them; thus, the approach is called "descriptive," in contrast to dimensional. Dilts added that the descriptive model does not capture everything about a particular disease state or client; he also proposed a more rigorous use of the biopsychosocial approach. Once again, his recommendations have not been followed. Currently, many psychiatrists are challenging the descriptive model and urging an integration of the dimensional model in the DSM-5 (Helzer & Hudziak, 2002; Maser et al., 2009; Tackett, Balsis, Oltmanns, & Krueger, 2009). Although dimensions are included in some categories, they are really "add-ons" rather than changes to the categorical structure of the DSM-5.

## Challenges to a Psychiatric Disease Model

The disease model that underlies the DSM has been called into question on many counts. Critics like Thomas Colbert (2000) and Seymour Fisher and Roger Greenberg (1997) have written whole volumes illustrating that psychological disorders are overdetermined and, in that sense alone, very different from allopathic disorders. In their view, there is a world of difference between a streptococcus infection and depression. Whereas the former can clearly be conceptualized and treated through the allopathic approach, the latter may or may not respond to allopathic approaches and may require hermeneutic therapies (approaches that depend upon intersubjective dialogue, discussion, interpretation, and shared understanding between client and therapist, rather than the procedural administration of objective knowledge). Other critics have challenged the validity of DSM categories of disorders. For example, psychiatrist David Healy (1997) has documented how the concept of depression was "sold" by the medical community and the pharmaceutical industry through the descriptive (DSM) model.

The correlation of certain symptoms occurring together was first labeled "depression." Then the construct of depression was "sold" via the DSM. After the concept of depression was "bought" by the medical establishment, antidepressants were marketed as a treatment for the disorder because, as Healy has pointed out, people must have a disorder before they will be interested in purchasing a cure for it. Healy has also documented how, in the United States, the Food and Drug Administration (FDA) regulations reinforce the descriptive model of psychiatry because potential drugs must show efficacy for the treatment of some disorder. Without the DSM categories, there are no disorders on which drugs may be shown to have an effect. In other words, the FDA will not allow pharmaceutical companies to market a drug unless there is a clearly defined disease (mental disorder) that the drug ameliorates (Healy, 2004). It probably isn't hard for you to see why the pharmaceutical industry would be invested in maintaining and proliferating an artifact such as the DSM, without which it could not garner its huge profits. We are not trying to deny how invaluable some pharmaceuticals are to many people; we are merely trying to highlight the complex economic and political (social, lower-right quadrant) dimensions regarding what actually constitutes a mental disorder and how they have come to be defined the way they are.

Whatever the validity and reliability of particular DSM diagnoses, what used to be axis I diagnoses tend to be the primary focus of third-party payers, and this bias is reflected in psychology and other mental health training. Such dynamics have likely fueled the negative reaction many therapists have to the topic of diagnosis. As Thomas Hohenshil (1994) has noted, many clinicians question the necessity of diagnosis and feel it is an unproductive labeling process based on oversimplified categories to describe complex human dynamics. Ideal training in the use of the DSM requires an approach that acknowledges the spirit of the biopsychosocial model advocated by Engel but that goes beyond it to include the full spectrum of the human condition; unfortunately, this type of training is quite rare.

## HOW ARE DSM CATEGORIES DEVELOPED?

DSM categories and symptoms are created and explored by workgroups in a process using literature reviews, data analysis and re-analysis, and field trials. The literature reviews begin with each workgroup (organized by diagnosis) identifying issues relevant to the group's topic and then conducting a literature review. The domains to be considered should include clinical utility, descriptive validity, reliability, and psychometric properties of individual criteria. The literature reviews can potentially be biased by several factors. First and most obvious, papers with statistically significant findings are more likely to be published than papers without statistically significant findings, so many studies that found no significant difference are never publicly available. Also, pharmaceutical companies that have a vested interest in the diagnoses related to their products fund a great deal of the research reviewed. In many instances, the pharmaceutical company has a contract with the researchers that allows the company to withhold nonsignificant findings.[6] What this means is that a drug company may run

[6] For a summary of this problem, see Ingersoll and Rak (2006).

five clinical trials and not obtain any significant findings until the fourth and fifth trial. With such a contract, the company can legally (although not ethically) report that the drug has been found repeatedly effective in clinical trials, without any mention of the first three trials in which the drug was not effective.

Data analysis and re-analysis can include unpublished data sets. There were 40 data re-analyses for the DSM-IV and in several cases they produced new criteria sets tested in the field trials. The number of re-analyses for reliability in the DSM-5 is a point of contention, with critics claiming that important steps were skipped (Frances, 2013) while the American Psychiatric Association defends the rigor of the task-force approach (American Psychiatric Association, 2012a). Again, though, all of the literature review and data analysis questions are derived from the expert opinions of the work-group members. Significantly, the manner in which these work group members are chosen often has more to do with each member's theoretical approach, ideological stance, and other political factors than with "objective," value-free science. The field trials allow the workgroups to see how new criteria sets perform in the field and begin anticipating the impact that changes to the existing DSM will have on the field. The editors of the DSM had some guidelines for developing criteria that included trying to make the criteria as clear and simple as possible, striking a balance of making the DSM as compatible as possible with the ICD, and collecting as much evidence as possible to support the changes. Before moving on, it is important to explicitly examine reliability and validity with regard to the DSM.

## Reliability

Readers may recall the two constructs of reliability and validity from their research or testing courses. Reliability is the first criterion needed to document the quality of a diagnostic category. Simply phrased, reliability is the degree to which a diagnosis holds up across raters and across time. As with validity, there are multiple ways to explore reliability—including internal consistency, inter-rater, and test-retest. An example of internal consistency in diagnostic categories is when the different symptoms in the same diagnostic category are in fact quite consistently present in people diagnosed with that category, as opposed to only a few of the different symptoms manifesting together in a more occasional or random manner. Inter-rater reliability is when multiple raters using DSM criteria independently assign the same diagnosis for the same client. Some diagnoses have high inter-rater reliability (like Major Depressive Disorder) while others have practically none (most of the Personality Disorders). Finally, test-retest reliability is when the same criteria are applied across time and the same outcome results; in other words, a person who is diagnosed with specific mental disorder is diagnosed with the same disorder 6 and 12 months later. As you can imagine, this is complicated and difficult with mental health diagnoses because a client may improve (or worsen) during the time interval.

Perhaps the chief challenge to reliability is that few clinicians follow a standardized interview format when making diagnoses (Aboraya, 2008). Although the DSM mentions interviews, associated laboratory findings, and associated physical examination findings, clinicians rarely collect this type of data unless they are ruling out substance-induced disorders or perhaps something like medication-induced delirium. The DSM-5 also allows that if a patient is incoherent (e.g., unable to make psychological contact), clinicians may obtain information from family members or other informants. Despite these exceptions, making a diagnosis is usually done solely with information obtained directly from the client. To deal with this problem, semistructured and fully structured interviews have been developed (Meyer, 2002). In one review, inter-rater reliability approached .92 using the Composite International Diagnostic Interview (CIDI), which can be administered by a computer or a clinician (Wittchen, 1994). Even in these cases, the increased reliability comes at the cost of depending more on client self-report than on clinician expertise (Meyer, 2002). While diagnoses made from unstructured interviews rely heavily on client self-report too, they also involve the clinician's ability to synthesize the information.

So, although there are drawbacks and benefits to both structured and unstructured interviews, they may yield different results for different reasons. Structured interviews are vulnerable to clients' memory problems, denial, or deliberate efforts to present oneself in an inaccurate (usually more positive) manner (John & Robins, 1994). Many readers may recall the famous study by David Rosenhan wherein he secretly planted eight pseudopatients in several psychiatric units and instructed them to say during their diagnostic interviews that they heard different sounds (empty, hollow, and thud-type sounds). Aside from these few fabrications (made only at intake), the pseudopatients were told to simply give honest details from their lives (with the exception of their true identities). Immediately after their admission, all of the patients stopped displaying symptoms and interacted with staff in a normal manner. Despite their normal behaviors, seven of the eight were diagnosed with Schizophrenia (Rosenhan, 1973). Perhaps even more interesting, many of the actual inpatients surmised that they were more "normal" than the other inpatients, an important fact that the psychiatrists/mental health staff did not recognize.

In a follow-up study, Rosenhan found another psychiatric institution that agreed to having pseudopatients sent over a 3-month period. This particular institution had staff who did not believe a study like Rosenhan's could be replicated under their system. During the 3-month period that Rosenhan told them to expect the pseudopatients, 41 out of 118 screened were identified as pseudopatients—despite the fact that Rosenhan had sent no such patients during the agreed-upon time frame (Rosenhan, 1984). Both Rosenhan studies highlight the problems regarding the reliability and validity of diagnostic labels that are the result of clinical interviews with clients.

One of the controversies over the DSM-5 concerns the reliability of many diagnoses. According to Allen Frances (chair of the DSM-IV task force), there should have been two stages of reliability testing but the design of the field trials was so complicated that only one stage was completed. Frances feels the problems also lie with the fact that the criteria sets in the DSM-5 are unclear (Frances, 2009a, 2009b, 2012). Another part of the problem is that whereas the DSM-IV field trials were funded by the NIMH, the American Psychiatric Association failed to find such external funding for the DSM-5. Because of the NIMH funding the methodology for the DSM-IV had to go through the peer-review process, but the methodology for the DSM-5 was not subjected to peer review that could have improved the methodology. As a result, Frances (2013) contends that the DSM-5 researchers focused exclusively on reliability, avoiding questions of validity and practical utility. The methodology problems led to incomplete reliability testing, and the reliability of many diagnoses was far lower than in previous

DSMs. As noted, technically, there were supposed to be two stages in reliability testing for the DSM-5. Diagnoses that had reliability problems in the first round could then be changed and tested again in a second round; however, only the first round was completed (Frances, 2009b, 2009c; Jones, 2012). The APA has defended the work on its website, but only time will tell if the DSM-5 is an improvement or not.

## Validity

Validity can be thought of as the extent to which your construct (in this case a DSM category) describes what you believe it describes. There are six ways to judge validity: face validity, content validity, convergent validity, discriminant validity, predictive validity, and construct validity. We'll describe each type using a DSM category as an example. Face validity is simply the extent to which your diagnostic category "looks like" what you believe it to be. Therefore fatigue, lethargy, and sadness all support the face validity of Major Depressive Disorder (MDD). Interestingly, face validity relies on the mental, psychological, subjective aspects of a disorder. Those materialists who think psychological suffering is a direct result of the electro-chemical symphony in the brain will never achieve face validity. Content validity is the extent to which the content of a category relates to what you believe you are measuring. Again, significant numbers of clients who suffer from depression report fatigue, lethargy, and sadness. Convergent validity is the degree to which a category is similar to other categories or tests. For example, people who are diagnosed with MDD often score in the depressed range on inventories like the Beck Depression Inventory (Beck, Steer, Ball, & Ranieri, 1996) or the Hamilton Rating Scale for Depression (Williams, 1989). Discriminant validity is the degree to which a category or diagnosis is different from things presumed to be antithetical to it. For example, people with diagnoses of MDD do not meet the criteria for scores in the 90–100 range (high to very high functioning) on the DSM-IV's Global Assessment of Functioning (GAF). Predictive validity is the extent to which a diagnosis is predictive of a certain course. For example, diagnoses of Schizophrenia predict a poor prognosis for later functioning, whereas diagnoses of Brief Psychotic Episode do not. Finally, construct validity is the extent to which a diagnosis is similar to related psychological constructs; that is, a diagnosis of MDD should present similar symptoms to what is psychologically referred to as depression.

Interestingly, for all we know about what should happen in validating a diagnosis, it is very hard to actually carry out. In 1970, Eli Robins and Samuel Guze (Robins & Guze, 1970) published a paper that proposed the most rigorous validity process for psychiatric diagnoses. They recommended five dimensions that should be assessed: careful clinical description, laboratory studies, delimitation from other disorders, follow-up research, and family studies. The most important steps for Robins and Guze were the last two, which would demonstrate continuity over time and give researchers a sense of how much of the diagnosis emerged longitudinally in families. When Robins and Guze used these five dimensions, they felt only 16 diagnoses were validated. Spitzer (1991) contrasted this with the DSM-III's over 200 diagnoses that were based on clinical judgment. Spitzer concluded that, in fact, expert consensus will continue to play a large role in diagnostic validation. One consistent problem in the DSM-III, III-R, and IV is that the knowledge bases from which different criteria have been developed and validated differ drastically across diagnoses. The take-home message: not all diagnoses are equally valid (Rounsaville et al., 2002).

As you'll see throughout the book, this can be a problem in a society where pharmaceutical companies have inordinate influence in crafting the public's understanding of what a "disease" is. As of this writing, pharmaceutical companies have two lobbyists for every senate and congressional representative in the federal government (Petersen, 2008). In addition, a 1992 federal law now allows drug companies to pay "user fees" to the FDA to have their products approved more quickly. Prior to this law, the only function of the FDA was to protect consumers and police companies (Petersen, 2008). In addition, with the exception of New Zealand, the United States is the only country in the world where direct-to-consumer (DTC) advertising of medications is legal. The DTC advertising of psychotropic medication has exponentially correlated with increased sales of those drugs advertised (whether they effectively treat a disorder or not). Some of the disorders that appear in these advertisements have been shown to be concocted by drug companies (e.g., "overactive bladder"), whereas at other times the advertisements use a more saleable title, such as calling Social Phobia "Social Anxiety Disorder," which prior to the DSM-5 only appeared parenthetically. Many times, companies lose a patent on a medication (as with Prozac/fluoxetine[7]) and then go on to create a new formulation of the same drug to recapture patent status (as with converting Prozac to Sarafem) (Petersen, 2008). Sarafem is nothing more than a time-release formulation of fluoxetine that has been marketed by Eli Lilly to treat symptoms of Premenstrual Dysphoric Disorder (PDD). The problem is that PDD was first introduced in the DSM-IV as a condition warranting further study. Even before it was validated and included as a Depressive Disorder in the DSM-5, medications were being developed to treat it. To return to the main point of this section, if expert consensus is a primary mode of validating a diagnostic category, then having experts paid as consultants by pharmaceutical companies should be a conflict of interest. A recent study investigated relationships between pharmaceutical companies and workgroups writing clinical practice guidelines for the American Psychiatric Association for the treatment of Schizophrenia, Bipolar Disorder, and Major Depressive Disorder. In this study, 18 workgroup members (90%) had at least one financial tie to the pharmaceutical industry (Cosgrove, Bursztain, Krimsky, Anaya, & Walker, 2009). All of the clinical practice guideline authors who had industry relationships had financial relationships with companies whose products were considered or included in the guidelines they authored (Cosgrove et al., 2009). This should be very disturbing to you; we cannot understand how or why this is legal. The American Psychiatric Association (2012b) has challenged the Cosgrove study as not fairly assessing the steps task-force members took to divest themselves of financial affiliations. In creating DSM-5, work-group members were asked to complete financial conflict of interest (FCOI) forms, as this was not done with DSM-IV. The result was that approximately three-fourths of DSM-5 panel members had financial ties to the pharmaceutical industry and the panel groups with the most ties were studying disorders where medication is considered a first-line treatment intervention (Cosgrove & Krimsky, 2012).

---

[7] Throughout this book, when we refer to a psychotropic medication we will name the brand name (e.g., Prozac) followed by the generic name (e.g., fluoxetine).

Surprising as this is, it is important to understand these political dynamics and their potential relationship to the approval of new diagnostic categories and how the process may be influenced by those with money, power, and more to gain by the approval of new diagnoses. Equally, we must be willing to hear both sides of the story, as the appearance of undue influence can be as damaging as actual undue influence. From an Integral perspective, the lower quadrants remind us to consider how political, social, and cultural dynamics influence the way psychopathology is understood and defined. Again, this is where critical thinking on the part of clinicians is needed.

## WHAT IS "STATISTICAL" ABOUT THE DIAGNOSTIC AND STATISTICAL MANUAL?

In early versions of the DSM, the word "statistical" reflected the intended use of the manual, which was to statistically gauge the prevalence and incidence of disorders (Kraemer, Shrout, & Rubio-Stipec, 2007). Beginning with the DSM-III, there was more emphasis on statistical assessment of the reliability (see earlier discussion) of the diagnoses. In other words, in a study in which several clinicians were diagnosing the same individual by observing a diagnostic interview, what was the inter-rater reliability between them? More simply put, what was the probability that the clinicians would all reach the same diagnosis for the same client? It has been argued that since the DSM-III, many of the problems in the DSM were created by the statisticians. One particular argument (particularly pronounced in the DSM-5) was that in the process of focusing on reliability, the statisticians sacrificed validity—which is more important to clinicians (Kirk & Kutchins, 1992).

The DSM-IV, DSM-IV-TR, and DSM-5 attempted to place greater emphasis on the role of empirical evidence as a requirement to change diagnostic rules. As noted, the DSM-5 had two stages of reliability studies planned, but stage two was never completed. This resulted in far less statistical rigor than was hoped for by the DSM-5 task force (Kraemer et al., 2007). One of the most important decisions that statisticians play a role in is to clarify what we mean by "disorder." The word *disorder* is used when the etiology is unknown; when the etiology is known, the word *disease* is used (World Health Organization, 1992). Furthermore, a "diagnosis" should help clinicians decide whether a client is suffering from a particular syndrome. The quality of any diagnosis depends on how well the clinician's assessment corresponds to the client's condition and what has been documented about other clients with the same diagnosis (Kraemer et al., 2007).

Statisticians can also assess whether changes to diagnostic categories bring researchers closer to things such as risk factors, causal factors, or even progress toward effective prevention and treatment. Again, when a category is changed, the DSM task force must test the reliability and validity of the changes. Ideally, this is done across multiple sites in the field trials phase of developing the categories or changes to existing categories. Without going into too much detail, it is important to note that the proper use of statistics requires that an appropriate statistical test be performed for the proper reasons under the best possible conditions. As Anne Spence and her colleagues (Spence, Greenberg, Hodge, & Vieland, 2003) have noted, statisticians frequently will be drawn to a field because of employment opportunities or because the field is new and exciting. In these cases, rather than deeply understanding the basis of a diagnosis, they look for applications of statistical skills they already know. This can lead to the development of new statistical designs that are poorly adapted to the needs of the field in which the statistical practices are being applied (Spence et al., 2003).

## A PRACTICAL GUIDELINE FOR DSM USE

What we hope you take away from this part of the chapter is, again, an active practice of critical thinking with regard to the DSM. Now that we have provided a critical view of the DSM, we'd like to suggest an outline form of how to use it with this text. Throughout the text we'll include cases that you can practice both DSM and Integral diagnoses with. Similar to the case of Katie in Chapter 1, we'll note a client's presenting concern and then encourage you to practice narrowing down the narrative to what seem to be presenting symptoms. With cases presented in written format it is harder to do an accurate diagnosis because many aspects of the clinical interaction are missing. Toward that end, we want to start with a summary of one approach to using the DSM to diagnose, and then we'll offer a briefer version for practicing with written cases. The following summary is taken from Ekkehard and Sieglinde Othmers's (1994a, 1994b) two volumes on clinical interviewing. These are to be understood as general guidelines. Some agencies and practices may have you use a formal interview format like the Structured Clinical Interview for DSM (SCID), mentioned earlier.

### Four Components to the Clinical Interview

The four components of the clinical interview are establishing rapport, gathering information, assessing mental status, and making a diagnosis. We now describe each component in detail.

**RAPPORT** How the client and the clinician relate is one of the most important aspects of clinical assessment, and the client–clinician relationship has been shown to be a primary factor in psychotherapy outcome (Duncan, Miller, Wampold, & Hubble, 2009). Think of rapport as including your ability to put the client at ease, recognize the client's state of mind, warm the client up with a brief explanation of what you'll be doing in the session, and meet the client where she or he is psychologically. Your ability to establish rapport with the client is directly related to the client's level of comfort in talking about what are often difficult things to share. Typically, rapport has been discussed in psychodynamic and descriptive frameworks. You can use aspects of both in establishing rapport.

The psychodynamic framework typically conceptualizes rapport in terms of *transference* and *countertransference.* Transference is when the client responds toward the interviewer in a manner that resembles the way the client responds to significant others in his or her life. For example, when I (Ingersoll) was interviewing an African American inmate preparing for release from prison, he said "you just tell me what you want 'cause that's what this about anyway." As we interacted, it was pretty clear that he viewed me as one more privileged Caucasian "cog" in the machinery of a society that had no place for him. Whether or not that was an accurate description of my role in his release was not important—that he *believed* it was what was important and as Yalom and Leszcz (2005) have noted, to ignore something of such emotional import would pretty much guarantee that we wouldn't get much else done in the session.

Whether or not you accept psychodynamic theories as a whole, most of us have moments when we react to people in ways that mirror our history more than our present interaction with a given person.

The other approach to rapport is descriptive, which derives more from humanistic and, particularly, client-centered theory. In this approach to rapport, the ideal is that the client–clinician interview progresses from understanding to trust. The ideal is that you can empathize with the client's experience and accurately reflect back to the client issues that are of most concern, based upon his or her narrative. When clients experience you as someone who is listening to both content and emotion (because you are reflecting feelings as well as content), you can at times increase the trust they have in you.[9] One example of this was a client who had a laundry list of issues but, at root, she was in counseling because she found life to be overwhelming. In this instance, the clinician reflected "I hear all your concerns about your marriage and children, getting back to working at least part-time, and fear of being criticized by your friends. It seems, though, that a connecting thread is fear or perhaps anxiety that you'll never be able to address it all. Does that feel accurate?" This response not only drew the client into the interview more; it seemed to also focus the session on what the client wanted relief from.

**STRATEGIES FOR GATHERING INFORMATION ABOUT THE CLIENT** The second component of the clinical interview is sometimes called technique. This involves the methods used to establish rapport and the theories the clinician relies on to guide the methods. Othmer and Othmer (1994a) summarize three strategies focusing on client complaints, resistance, and defenses. Client complaints are perhaps the most obvious thing to listen for, but they may point you in numerous directions. For example, a client who is suffering from aural hallucinations (hearing voices) may want you to stop the voices. In this example, the symptom is ego-dystonic, meaning *it is incongruent* with how the client sees himself—he wants to get rid of the symptom. You need to meet him where he is, while at the same time, gather enough information to create a treatment plan that will help him. Another client's problem may be the way she interacts with others and her lack of emotional boundaries; clients who meet the criteria for Personality Disorders may show these sorts of signs. She may seem overly complimentary—saying she knows you'll cure her in no time, for example. In this case, we say the problem is ego-syntonic, meaning it is *congruent* with how the client sees herself, and more often than not, people with ego-syntonic problems do not recognize their problems as problems (they are unable to make their problems the object of their awareness); they see others or the world as the problem.

Sometimes, the way clients resist questions or psychological contact with the clinician can give you insight into what problems they may need to tackle in clinical work. Expressing acceptance when a client is reluctant to talk may help the client overcome what might be a fear of ridicule or judgment. In these cases, to help him overcome his resistance you can encourage him and reflect what you think the fear is (e.g., "I'm guessing that you're hesitant to talk because you don't know me and wonder if I might judge you"). Another approach is gently confronting the resistance or, in other words, making what the client is doing an object of awareness. In one session

[9] This is, of course, a paraphrase of one of Carl Rogers's (1957) six core conditions for therapeutic change.

we supervised, a client would change the subject every time the clinician brought up the topic of emotions. Finally, the counselor said "It seems to me that when I mention emotions, you shift the discussion onto another topic. I'm wondering if emotions are hard for you to talk about."

For clients who are more actively resistant (and aware that they are resisting), you can still talk about the process. One client who was in treatment for heroin dependence kept shifting the discussion away from her use and onto unrelated topics, stating that she didn't want to talk about her use anymore. In this case the therapist stated "It seems that you really have trouble facing the way you've lived your life these past 2 years." To this, the client responded that she really didn't have trouble facing it but just didn't want to stop. That opened up a more important topic: her lack of commitment to sobriety.

Another route to understanding the client's difficulties can be through addressing defenses. The DSM-5 (like its predecessors) offers a list of defenses in the glossary. They are psychodynamic in nature but may be useful in identifying what a client needs to work on. In the case of the heroin-dependent client just described, denial continued to be a problematic defense for her. Bear in mind that defenses are necessary and serve healthy psychological needs (if you doubt it, consider how many days you've gotten through without a rationalization). One client tended to use humor in ways that, over time, appeared to be hurting him more than it was helping him. In the initial interview, he offered to shake hands, then pulled his hand back before the clinician could shake it. The client said "isn't that what crazy people do doc?" His humor was usually aggressive and focused on others, and this led to identifying his anger as one of the things he sought relief from.

**MENTAL STATUS** Mental status refers to the client's state of mind during the interview. In particular, we start by assessing whether a client is oriented to person (who she is), place (where she is), time (when she is—"what time/year is it?"), and situation ("what is this interview about?"). A client who is able to respond within the boundaries of consensual reality is said to be "oriented × 4" or to possess "clear sensorium." If the client is able to make psychological contact, you can usually discern this in the interview without going through special questions to determine the client's orientation. If the client seems confused as to person, place, time, and/or situation, you can proceed in a direction that more directly assesses mental status (Faber, 2009; Davis & Zimmerman, 1994; Strub & Black, 1993).

Mental status exams can be helpful if you suspect that a client may have suffered an organic injury (e.g., stroke, head trauma), is under the influence of intoxicating substances, is suffering from a side effect of a medication, or perhaps is suffering from a psychotic disorder. It is often not easy to tell the difference between these things, and that is when the client needs to be referred for a medical evaluation. In private practice, it is helpful if the client has had a medical checkup in the past year, but frequently clients will not have had this and may not have the insurance to pay for such an exam. In these instances, you have to make your best clinical guess regarding when to refer for medical evaluation.

Although this is not a text about diagnostic interviewing, it is important to at least list other sources of information about a client (Hamstra, 1994). The client's appearance—including body type, hygiene/grooming, clothing, posture, eye contact, and poise (the way a client holds him- or herself)—can give you clues as to things that may be part of the presenting problem. One client came in to a July session wearing an overcoat, winter hat, and earmuffs. While his statement that the clothes kept the voices away gave a primary clue that he was likely suffering from a severe disorder, his attire helped the clinician more quickly confirm that. Another client who suffered from Bipolar I Disorder (formerly known as Manic-Depressive Illness) would start wearing very bright colors prior to suffering a manic episode. In this case, family members came to be able to preclude several episodes by getting him to his doctor when his attire changed to the flashier clothing.

Another important component of assessment is the client's attitude. Does the client want to be in the interview or not? Is the client suspicious, angry, apathetic, or showing great apprehension? For example, apprehension is common in people suffering from Anxiety Disorders; thus apprehension can be a sign in the initial session that points the clinician in the correct direction. Another thing to observe is the client's speech. Sometimes obvious problems with speech can point to organic disorders or head trauma. Clients who are depressed frequently speak with softer volume and in a less animated way. This leads to other things to observe: mood and affect. Mood is considered to be the client's emotional state as reported by the client, whereas affect refers to the outward expression of emotion as observed by the clinician. Affect is revealed by facial expressions, body movements, and sometimes vocal tone, and it can change quickly.

Thought process and thought content are also important to assess in the clinical interview. Thought content is basically what the client shares as the content of his or her thoughts. Content such as delusions, hallucinations, or obsessions may point to various disorders, including Psychotic Disorders and Obsessive-Compulsive Disorder.

With regard to levels of development (discussed in Chapter 1), thought process gives clues about the cognitive tools a client has access to. A client who uses metaphors appropriately, can follow a train of abstract thought, and is able to discuss the same thing in different contexts likely has the capacity for formal operational thinking. Clients who speak more concretely and seem puzzled by metaphors may be limited to concrete operational thinking.

There are particular thought problems that show up in several DSM disorders that can be clues to the presenting disorder or problem. Loose associations are when ideas that the client expresses do not seem to be related. Flight of ideas is when a client seems to jump rapidly from one idea to the next. Perseveration is when a client seems to get stuck on a particular word or phrase. In one case, the client shared "I know you doc; you're not the kind of person who is phony to be with. I know you doc; you don't think they are treating me right at work. I know you doc; you should see the way they treat me at work. I know you doc . . .," and so forth.

**DIAGNOSING** Finally, the fourth component to the interview is actually providing a diagnosis of the client—if that is within the scope of your practice. Most states allow (licensed) psychiatrists, psychologists, social workers, counselors, and psychiatric nurses to diagnose mental and emotional disorders, but you must make sure you understand the law and scope of practice for the state you are working in. The more you learn about clients—their strengths and weaknesses, their deficits and resources, and the complaints they present with—the better able you are to get into the appropriate diagnostic ballpark. As noted earlier, you may use a structured diagnostic interview (like the SCID) or a structured intake form that covers concerns related to both body and mind (and spirit, if that is part of the client's worldview) (Marquis, 2008).

One diagnostic tool that came with DSM-IV was the decision trees in Appendix A of that manual. These offer flow charts for differential diagnosis of Mental Disorders Due to General Medical Condition, Substance-Induced Disorders, Psychotic Disorders, Mood Disorders, Anxiety Disorders, and Somatoform Disorders. These can be helpful guidelines, but they are no substitute for clinical judgment. Clinical judgment develops with experience, but the intake assessment, your experience of the client, and the other areas we previously noted should provide you enough information to outline both a DSM and an Integral diagnosis (discussed in Chapter 1). Before moving on, here is another sample case that we'll flesh out first with an Integral diagnosis and then discuss how that can be used to arrive at a DSM-5 diagnosis.

## CASE OF JORGE

Jorge is a 43-year-old owner of two small sandwich shops. His family is from Peru and moved here when he was 3. He has no mental health history, no history of substance abuse, and is oriented × 4. Because of his cultural background, he was also given the Cultural Formulation Interview (CFI) that is newly included in the DSM-5. Several responses to CFI items suggested that he feels some of his shyness and awkwardness with others is due to his temperament and some the result of growing up with his Peruvian family in a primarily Caucasian, Midwest suburb. He has trouble sustaining eye contact when speaking, and speaks without much inflection. He lives alone with his dog and has few friends. He says he tried attending churches but is not religious. He hoped to meet some people there but felt he didn't really fit in. He says he spends most of his time working and says that at his job is really the only place he feels like he fits in. He can converse easily with customers because he says he knows they don't expect anything from him other than service. One of the things that makes his problems harder to cope with is his lack of a family support system. Jorge has one brother who lives on the West Coast and some contact with his mother (his father died 4 years ago).

His presenting complaint is difficulty sleeping, due to anxiety. Jorge presents as well dressed and well groomed but also unsure of himself. In the interview, he keeps correcting himself. First he says "I am not sleeping," then "No, that's not right; I'm anxious and that is why I don't sleep well." His attitude seems cautious, although sincere, and when the clinician states "You seem like you may be a little wary of counseling," Jorge responds "Wary, yeah, I've . . . you know . . . never done anything like this." After discussing what happens in counseling, Jorge shares more about his current concerns. He states that his business has "taken a hit" in the economy, although he thinks things are beginning to improve. When asked if that is a main source of stress, he says "not really." Jorge shares that he sometimes feels like he is having a heart attack. He says ". . . my heart races, I sweat, and then I start thinking like I've got to run out of the shop." He has had a full assessment by his doctor, who says he is in excellent cardiac health.

Jorge tends to rationalize when the clinician speaks about anxiety. He says ". . . oh yeah, I know it's all in my head, I guess everyone has this problem." After half an hour of discussion, it seems that the panic Jorge experiences as well as his anxiety are the primary problems. He says ". . . well they may be, but I wonder if there is some kind of pill you can take for this that doesn't make you tired." His doctor had prescribed a low dose of Xanax/alprazolam, but Jorge said it made him sleepy. The doctor tried a low dose of Lexapro/escitalopram, but Jorge didn't like the sexual dysfunction side effect. When the clinician summarizes that he didn't seem to like the medications his doctor prescribed, Jorge says ". . . well, yeah . . . I thought maybe there was something else without side effects." Jorge's thought processes seem normal enough, but he says his thoughts race when he has panic episodes. He also says he tends to dwell on negative thoughts sometimes. He read a book about positive thinking but it didn't seem to help him. He wonders if he fits in anywhere besides at work.

When asked what the negative thoughts are about, he responds "Well this will seem weird, but I worry about my heart and my business. I know they are both OK but I start wondering, what if they are not?" It appears that there are no compulsions accompanying his obsessions. He finally says "I guess it is the panic that is the biggest problem." His panic comes on only when he is at work, but not every time he is at work. It happens about six times a month and he worries about it happening again. He twice called in sick to avoid an attack. He hated to do that because, in his words, "work is my life."

| | **INTERIOR** | **EXTERIOR** |
|---|---|---|
| **INDIVIDUAL** | Feelings of panic<br>Unrealistic fears and obsessions<br>Anxiety as racing thoughts<br>Worries about fitting in | Calling in sick to avoid an attack<br>Tried medication but didn't like it<br>Trouble maintaining eye contact<br>Speaks without much inflection |
| **GROUP** | Does not feel a sense of community in his life business<br>Comes across as socially awkward | Economic stressors<br>Tried churches but didn't feel he fit in<br>Lives alone |

Integral Diagnosis for Jorge

It seems that Jorge could use some coaching on social interactions and ways to meet other people. For him, we might view that as a *developmental* task, addressing the *line* of interpersonal development. The problematic *states* for Jorge are anxiety and panic. As far as types go, Jorge appears to be very conventional in his sense of self. The idea of fitting in (belonging) is very important for him. Again, the *four quadrants* give us a sense of the "hotspots" for Jorge. He is beset with panic and anxiety symptoms, wants to fit in, is starting to engage in avoidance behavior because of the panic symptoms, and would like a sense of community but doesn't know how to find it.

With the DSM-5, we would document Jorge's diagnosis as

F41.0 Panic Disorder; client has cultural concerns about "fitting in" and is experiencing financial stress.

Between the Integral diagnosis and Jorge's DSM diagnosis, we have several important pieces of information. As we noted in Chapter 1, we view the two assessments (Integral and DSM-5 diagnoses) as complementary. The DSM diagnosis gives us codes that, if accurate, are paired in many cases with treatment manuals that offer good summaries of peer-reviewed literature on the most effective treatments for the disorder (Gabbard, 2001). The Integral diagnosis gives us more insight into the client's experiential perspective as well as cultural and social issues that used to be represented in the five axes of the DSM-IV-TR diagnosis.

## AN OVERVIEW OF THE DC:0-3R AND THE PDM

The last part of this chapter is a brief overview of the *Diagnostic Classification of Mental Health and Developmental Disorders of Infancy and Early Childhood* (DC:0-3R) and the *Psychodynamic Diagnostic Manual* (PDM). As noted in Chapter 1, both of these manuals can complement the DSM. In particular, the DC:0-3R is important because most of the disorders in the DSM (with the exception of Neurodevelopmental Disorders) are normed on adults and the criteria for adults frequently do not generalize to children. In some cases, such as for Major Depressive Disorder, the DSM will note different symptom manifestations for children, but in general, clinicians are on their own in determining the extent to which the disorders can be applied to child and adolescent clients.

This has become particularly problematic with Bipolar I Disorder. As noted earlier, there has been an explosion in the diagnosis of Bipolar I Disorder in children as young as 2 years old, and this has been a controversial topic in child psychiatry (Paris, 2009; Youngstrom, Birmaher, & Findling, 2008). It is estimated that a *40-fold increase* in the diagnosis of Bipolar I Disorder in children took place between 1994 and 2003. Many of these children had what are called "subthreshold" symptoms, meaning the symptoms did not meet the adult criteria for severity. Here again, we see that the ontological assumptions of researchers are important in understanding the type of research they do. Those who want to believe that the increase in diagnoses is legitimate try to make the case that Bipolar I Disorder is actually part of a spectrum and that we should diagnose this entire spectrum (Merikangas et al., 2007). Bear in mind that there is no conclusive evidence to support this, other than the conjecture of the researchers (one of whom was consultant to 13 pharmaceutical companies, and there is a note at the end that the preparation of the article was supported by AstraZeneca) (Merikangas et al., 2007, p. 551). Other (more critical) researchers note that many of the symptoms in the supposed Bipolar Spectrum diagnoses are comorbid with Attention Deficit–Hyperactivity Disorder (ADHD), and suggest that these may in fact be side effects of stimulant medication (Sahling, 2009).

Bipolar I Disorder is one of the disorders in which it appears that we need diagnostic criteria specific to children and adolescents. Although the DC:0-3R does not cover Bipolar Disorders, the idea is that it sets a precedent for looking at children's disorders differently than adult disorders. This is imperative because of the radically different nature of the nervous system and mind between children and adults, not to mention different developmental levels in general. In many cases, the children are "acting out" or showing what is called mood lability or aggression; whether this actually constitutes Bipolar I Disorder remains to be determined (Duffy, 2007).

### The DC:0-3R

The DC:0-3R is a slim 75-page volume that offers initial mental health and developmental diagnoses for infants and children ages 0–3. The DC:0-3R task force developed a five-axis diagnostic system that is better suited to reflect the lives of the young clients that are its focus. Axis I is considered the Primary Diagnosis and clinical disorders are coded on it; these include Posttraumatic Stress Disorder, Deprivation/Maltreatment

Disorder, Disorders of Affect, Prolonged Bereavement/Grief Reaction, Anxiety Disorders of Infancy and Early Childhood, Mixed Disorder of Emotional Expressiveness, Regulation Disorders of Sensory Processing, Sleep Behavior Disorder, Feeding Behavior Disorder, Disorders of Relating and Communicating, and Multisystem Developmental Disorders.

Axis II is different than the DSM in that it focuses on Relationship Disorders and provides a series of assessments. These include a Parent-Infant Relationship Global Assessment Scale (PIR-GAS), which ranges from "well adapted" to "documented maltreatment." Next, there is a Relationship Problems Checklist (RPCL) that covers descriptive features of a relationship's qualities—ranging from "overinvolved" to "underinvolved"—and lists a set of emotional qualities that may be observed in the relationship (e.g., angry or hostile, anxious or tense, and categories such as abusive).

Axis III is devoted to Medical and Developmental Disorders and Conditions, and particular emphasis is given to medical disorders that can cause what appear to be psychiatric symptoms. Among the common examples listed are endocrine disorders causing mood symptoms, metal toxicity causing irritability and restlessness, Pediatric Autoimmune Neuropsychiatric Disorders Associated with Streptococcus (PANDAS) causing obsessive or compulsive symptoms, and hearing or speech problems that manifest as irritability, frustration, and behavior problems.

Axis IV, similar to the DSM-IV, is devoted to psychosocial and environmental stressors. Psychosocial stressors can be acute (time-limited) or enduring. Normal events in the life of a family (like the arrival of a new baby) can be inordinately stressful for some children. What is also assessed is the extent to which the caregiving environment can shield the child from stressors. This is assessed with the Psychosocial and Environmental Stressor Checklist. The checklist helps clinicians identify multiple sources of stress as well as the duration and severity of stress.

Finally, Axis V is for Social and Emotional Functioning; it reflects the young child's affect and interaction with important caregivers in relation to expectable patterns of development. This is done by rating the child's capacities for emotional and social functioning using the Capacities for Emotional and Social Functioning Rating Scale. Capacities the child is rated on include attention and regulation (usually observable between birth and 3 months), forming relationships and mutual engagement (observable between 3 and 6 months), intentional two-way communication (observable beginning between 4 and 10 months), complex gestures and problem solving (observable between 10 and 18 months), use of symbols to express thoughts and feelings (observable between 18 and 30 months), and connecting symbols logically (observable between 30 and 48 months). Whether the DC-03R will be revised to eliminate the multiple axes (like the DSM-5) has yet to be decided.

## The Psychodynamic Diagnostic Manual (PDM)

The PDM is the result of collaboration between the American Psychoanalytic Association, the International Psychoanalytical Association, the Division of Psychoanalysis (division 39) of the American Psychological Association, the American Academy of Psychoanalysis and Dynamic Psychiatry, and the National Membership Committee on Psychoanalysis in Clinical Social Work. The manual is supposed to be a diagnostic framework that attempts to reflect a client's emotional, cognitive, and social functioning (PDM Task Force, 2006).

The PDM aims toward a multidimensional approach to describe the intricacies of a client's overall functioning and the way the client engages the therapeutic process. To do this, the PDM utilizes three dimensions labeled "P," "M," and "S." The "P" axis stands for Personality Patterns and Disorders. This axis uses a dimensional continuum for the client's personality ranging from "healthier" to "more disordered." In addition, the way the client organizes mental functioning and engages the world is described on this axis. The "M" axis stands for Mental Functioning. This offers a more descriptive profile of emotional functioning, including the capacities that contribute to a client's personality and overall level of psychological health or pathology. The third dimension, the "S" dimension, stands for Manifest Symptoms and Concerns. This dimension begins with DSM categories and proceeds to describe what we refer to as experiential states, cognitive processes, somatic experiences, and relational patterns that are typical for the client. The PDM refers to symptom clusters as useful *descriptors* but does not regard them as demarcated biopsychosocial phenomena. The editors note that their main goal is to not go beyond the knowledge base in the field (PDM Task Force, 2006).

Although far fewer clinicians use the PDM than use the DSM, from an Integral standpoint it is an important contribution to the literature because its editors have aimed to look at mental disorders from a strictly psychodynamic point of view. In this sense, the PDM can be a useful complement to our Integral diagnosis, particularly the experiential perspective (upper-left quadrant). It is interesting that although fewer clinicians use the PDM, Gordon (2009) found that psychologists in his study gave the PDM a 90% approval rating.

## Concluding Thoughts

We have covered a great deal of material in this chapter. The rest of the book will deal with particular types of psychopathology, starting in Chapter 3 with depression. We hope that these first two chapters have given you some reasons to approach the DSM with a critical mind as well as introduced you to some of the other efforts at diagnostic systems that are available. We also hope that this chapter has given you an outline for how to begin using the DSM while reading through cases in this book. With that said, we will now turn to the various manifestations of depression.

## Review Questions

1. What is the difference between the categorical and dimensional approaches to diagnosis?
2. What is the status of the search for consistent biological markers that cause specific mental disorders?
3. What seems to be the relationship between *epigenetics* and *gene expression*?
4. How did the DSM-III radically differ from its predecessors, and why were the changes made?
5. What is the general relationship between the ICD and the DSM?
6. What is "statistical" about the *Diagnostic and Statistical Manual of Mental Disorders*?
7. What are four general components of the clinical interview?
8. What aspects of the initial interview provide information about the client and the client's diagnosis?
9. What are the four components of the mental status exam orientation?
10. How do the DSM axes differ from the DC:0-3R axes?

## References


Aboraya, A. (2008). Do psychiatrists use structured interviews in real clinical settings? *Psychiatry, 5,* 26–27.

Aldhouse, P. (2009). Psychiatry's civil war. *New Scientist, 18.* Retrieved from http://www.newscientist.com/article/mg20427381.300-psychiatrys-civil-war.html?full=true&print=true

American Psychiatric Association. (1952). *Diagnostic and statistical manual of mental disorders.* Washington, DC: Author.

American Psychiatric Association. (1968). *Diagnostic and statistical manual of mental disorders* (2nd ed.). Washington, DC: Author.

American Psychiatric Association. (2000). *Diagnostic and statistical manual of mental disorders* (4th ed., text revision). Washington, DC: Author.

American Psychiatric Association. (2012a). Reliability and prevalence in the DSM field trials. Retrieved from http://www.dsm5.org/Documents/Reliability_and_Prevalence_in_DSM-5_Field_Trials_1-12-12.pdf

American Psychiatric Association. (2012b). Statement for John Oldham, M.D.: President of the American Psychiatric Association. Retrieved from http://www.dsm5.org/Documents/APA%20Refutes%20Secondary%20Analysis%20of%20DSM-5%20Disclosures.pdf

American Psychiatric Association. (2013). *Diagnostic and statistical manual of mental disorders* (5th ed.). Washington, DC: Author.

Andreasen, N. C., Flaum, M., & Arndt, S. (1992). The comprehensive assessment of symptoms and history (CASH): An instrument for assessing diagnosis and psychopathology. *Archives of General Psychiatry, 49,* 616.

Andrews, G., Goldberg, D. P., Krueger, R. F., Carpenter, W. T., Hyman, S. E., Sachdev, P., & Pine, D. S. (2009). Exploring the feasibility of a meta-structure for DSM-V and ICD-11: Could it improve utility and validity? *Psychological Medicine, 39,* 1993–2000.

Angold, A., Costello, E. J., & Erkanle, A. (1999). Comorbidity. *Journal of Child Psychiatry, 40,* 57–87.

Aragona, M. (2009). About and beyond comorbidity: Does the crisis of the DSM bring on a radical rethinking of descriptive psychopathology? *Philosophy, Psychiatry and Psychology, 16,* 29–33.

Barton, W. E. (1987). *The history and influence of the American Psychiatric Association.* Washington, DC: American Psychiatric Press.

Beck, A. T, Steer R. A., Ball R., & Ranieri, W. (1996). Comparison of Beck Depression Inventories-IA and -II in psychiatric outpatients. *Journal of Personality Assessment, 67,* 588–597.

Charney, D. S., Barlow, D. H., Botteron, K., Cohen, J. D., Goldman, D., Gur, R. E., . . . Zalcman, S. F. (2002). Neuroscience research agenda to guide development of a pathophysiologically based classification system. In D. J. Kupfer, M. B. First, & D. A. Regier (Eds.), *A research agenda for DSM-V* (pp. 31–84). Washington, DC: American Psychiatric Association.

Clark, L. A., Watson, D., & Reynolds, S. (1995). Diagnosis and classification of psychopathology: Challenges to the current system and future directions. *Annual Review of Psychology, 46,* 121–153.

Cohen, C. I. (1993). The biomedicalization of psychiatry: A critical overview. *Community Mental Health Journal, 29,* 509–521.

Colbert, T. C. (2000). *The four false pillars of biopsychiatry: One hundred years of medical nonsense.* Tustin, CA: Kevco.

Cosgrove, L, Bursztain, H. J., Krimsky, S., Anaya, M., & Walker, J. (2009). Conflicts of interest and disclosure in the American Psychiatric Association's clinical practice guidelines. *Psychotherapy and Psychosomatics, 78,* 228–232.

Cosgrove, L., & Krimsky, S. (2012). A comparison of DSM-IV and DSM-5 panel members' financial associations with industry: A pernicious problem persists. *PLoS Medicine, 9,* 1–4.

Danner, S., Fristad, M. A., Arnold, E., Youngstrom, E. A., Birmaher, B., Horwitz, S. M., Demeter, C., Findling, R. L., Kowatch, R. A., & The LAMS Group. (2009). Early-onset bipolar spectrum disorders: Diagnostic issues. *Clinical Child and Family Psychological Review, 12,* 271–293.

Davis, F. A., & Zimmerman, M. (1994). *Interview guide for evaluating the DSM-IV psychiatric disorders and the mental status examination.* East Greenwich, RI: Psych Products Press.

Dilts, S. L. (2001). *Models of the mind: A framework for biopsychosocial psychiatry.* Philadelphia, PA: Brunner/Rutledge.

Douthit, K. Z., & Marquis, A. (2006). Empiricism in psychiatry's post-psychoanalytic era: Contemplating DSM's "atheoretical" nosology. *Constructivism in the Human Sciences, 11*(1), 32–59.

Duffy, A. (2007). Does bipolar disorder exist in children? A selected review. *The Canadian Journal of Psychiatry, 52,* 409–417.

Duncan, B. L., Miller, S. D., Wampold, B. E., & Hubble, M. A. (2009). *The heart and soul of change: What works in therapy* (2nd ed.). Washington, DC: American Psychological Association.

Editorial. (1989). This week's citation classic. *Archives of General Psychiatry, 43,* 14.

Endicott, J., & Spitzer, R. L. (1972). The schedule for affective disorders and schizophrenia. *Archives of General Psychiatry, 35,* 837–844.

Engel, G. L. (1977). The need for a new medical model: A challenge for biomedicine. *Science, 196,* 129–136.

Engel, G. L. (1997). From biomedical to biopsychosocial: Being scientific in the human domain. *Psychosomatics: Journal of Consultation Liaison Psychiatry, 38,* 521–528.

Engel, J. (2008). *American therapy: The rise of psychotherapy in the United States.* New York: Gotham.

Faber, R. A. (2009). The neuropsychiatric mental status exam. *Seminars in neurology, 29,* 185–193.

Fisher, S. F., & Greenberg, R. P. (Eds.). (1997). *From placebo to panacea: Putting psychiatric drugs to the test.* New York: Wiley.

Frances, A. (2009a). A warning sign on the road to DSM-V: Beware of its unintended consequences. *Psychiatric Times, 26.* Retrieved from http://www.psychiatrictimes.com/display/article/10168/1425378

Frances, A. (2009b). Whither DSM-V? *The British Journal of Psychiatry, 195,* 391–392.

Frances, A. (2009c). Limitations of field trials. *American Journal of Psychiatry, 166,* 1322.

Frances, A. (2012). Newsflash from APA meeting: DSM-5 has flunked its reliability tests. *HuffPost Science.* Retrieved from http://www.huffingtonpost.com/allen-frances/dsm-5-reliability-tests_b_1490857.html

Frances, A. (2013). *Saving normal: An insider's revolt against out-of-control psychiatric diagnosis, DSM-5, big pharma, and the medicalization of ordinary life.* New York: Morrow.

Frances, A. J., & Egger, H. L. (1999). Whither psychiatric diagnosis? *Australian and New Zealand Journal of Psychiatry, 33,* 161–165.

Freud, S. (1950 [1895]). *The standard edition of the complete psychological works of Sigmund Freud, Volume I (1886–1899): Pre-psycho-analytic publications and unpublished drafts,* (pp. 281–391). London: Vintage.

Gabbard, G. (Ed.). (2001). *Treatments of psychiatric disorders* (vol. I & II, 3rd ed.). Washington, DC: American Psychiatric Association.

Goncalves, O. F., Machado, P. P. P., Korman, Y., & Angus, L. (2002). Assessing psychopathology: A narrative approach. In L. E. Beutler & M. L. Malik (Eds.), *Rethinking the DSM: A psychological perspective* (pp. 149–176). Washington, DC: American Psychological Association.

Gordon, R. M. (2009). Reactions to the *Psychodynamic Diagnostic Manual (PDM)* by psychodynamic, CBT and other non-psychodynamic psychologists. *Issues in Psychoanalytic Psychology, 31*(1), 55–62.

Greenberg, G. (2013). *The book of woe: The DSM and the unmaking of psychiatry.* New York: Blue Rider Press.

Grob, G. (1987). The forging of mental health policy in American: World War II to the New Frontier. *Journal of the History of Medicine & Allied Sciences, 42,* 410–446.

Grob, G. N. (1991). Origins of DSM-I: A study in appearance and reality. *American Journal of Psychiatry, 148,* 421–431.

Hamstra, B. (1994). *How therapists diagnose: Professional secrets you deserve to know and how they affect you and your family.* New York: St. Martins Griffin.

Healy, D. (1997). *The antidepressant era.* Cambridge, MA: Harvard University Press.

Healy, D. (2004). *The creation of psychopharmacology.* Cambridge, MA: Harvard.

Helzer, J. E., & Hudziak, J. J. (Eds.). (2002). *Defining psychopathology in the 21st century: DSM-V and beyond.* Washington, DC: American Psychiatric Association.

Hohenshil, T. H. (1994). DSM-IV: What's new? *Journal of Counseling and Development, 73,* 105–107.

House, A. E. (1999). *DSM-IV diagnosis in the schools.* New York: Guilford.

Houts, A. (2000). Fifty years of psychiatric nomenclature: Reflections on the 1943 War Department Technical Bulletin, Medical 203. *Journal of Clinical Psychology, 56,* 935–967.

Houts, A. C. (2001). The diagnostic and statistical manual's new white coat and circularity of plausible dysfunctions: response to Wakefield, Part 1. *Behaviour Research and Therapy, 39,* 315–345.

Houts, A. (2002). Discovery, invention, and the expansion of the modern manuals of mental disorders. In L. E. Beutler & M. L. Malik (Eds.), *Rethinking the DSM: A psychological perspective* (pp. 17–68). Washington, DC: American Psychological Association.

Ingersoll, R. E., & Rak, C. F. (2006). *Psychopharmacology for helping professionals: An integral approach.* Pacific Grove, CA: Brooks Cole.

Ingersoll, R. E., & Zeitler, D. A. (2010). *Integral psychotherapy: Inside out/outside in.* Albany, NY: SUNY.

Jairam, R., Prabhuswamy, M., & Dullur, P. (2012). Do we really know how to treat a child with Bipolar Disorder or one with severe mood dysregulation? Is there a magic bullet? *Depression Research and Treatment, 2012,* 1–9.

John, O. P., & Robins, R. W. (1994). Accuracy and bias in self-perception: Individual difference in self-enhancement and the role of narcissism. *Journal of Personality and Social Psychology, 66,* 206–219.

Jones, D. K. (2012). A critique of DSM-5 field trials. *Journal of Nervous & Mental Disease, 200,* 517–519.

Kessler, R. C. (1995). The epidemiology of psychiatric comorbidity. In G. E. P. Zahner (Ed.), *Textbook of psychiatric epidemiology* (pp. 179–197). New York: Wiley.

Kessler, R. C., McGonagle, K. A., Zhao, S., Neson, C. B., Hughes, M., Eshleman, S., . . . Kendler, K. S. (1994). Lifetime and 12-month prevalence of DSM-III-R psychiatric disorders in the United States. Results from the National Comorbidity Survey. *Archives of General Psychiatry, 51,* 8–19.

Kirk, S. A., & Kutchins, H. (1992). *The selling of the DSM: The rhetoric of science in psychiatry.* New York: Aldine De Gruyter.

Korzybski, A. (1958). *Science and sanity: An introduction to non-Aristotelian systems and general semantics* (5th ed.). Brooklyn, NY: Institute of General Semantics.

Kraemer, H. C., Shrout, P. E., & Rubio-Stipec, M. (2007). Developing the diagnostic and statistical manual V: What will "statistical" mean? *Social Psychiatry and Psychiatric Epidemiology, 42,* 259–267.

Krueger, R. F., & South, S. C. (2009). Externalizing disorders: Cluster 5 of the proposed meta-structure for DSM-V and ICD-11. *Psychological Medicine, 39,* 2061–2070.

Kutchins, H., & Kirk, S. (1997). *Making us crazy: DSM: The psychiatric bible and the creation of mental disorders.* New York: Free Press.

Malik, M. L., & Beutler, J. E. (2002). The emergence of dissatisfaction with the DSM. In L. E. Beutler & M. L. Malik (Eds.), *Rethinking the DSM: A psychological perspective.* Washington, DC: American Psychological Association.

Margulies, D. M., Weintraub, S., Basile, J., Grover, P. J., & Carlson, G. A. (2012). Will Disruptive Mood Dysregulation Disorder reduce false diagnosis of Bipolar Disorder in children? *Bipolar Disorders, 14,* 488–496.

Marquis, A. (2008). *The integral intake: A guide to comprehensive idiographic assessment in integral psychotherapy.* New York: Routledge.

Maser, J. D., Norman, S. B., Zisook, S., Everall, I. P., Stein, M. B., Schettler, P. J., & Judd, L. L. (2009). Psychiatric nosology is ready for a paradigm shift in DSM-V. *Clinical Psychology: Science and Practice, 16,* 24–40.

Mayes, R., & Horwitz, A. V. (2005). DSM-III and the revolution in the classification of mental illness. *Journal of the History of the Behavioral Sciences, 41,* 249–267.

Menninger, K. (1963). *The vital balance.* New York: Viking.

Merikangas, K. R., Akiskal, H. S., Angst, J., Greenberg, P. E., Hirschfeld, R. M. A., Petukhova, M., & Kessler, R. C. (2007). Lifetime and 12-month prevalence of bipolar spectrum disorder in the national comorbidity survey replication. *Archives of General Psychiatry, 64,* 543–552.

Meyer, A. (1908). The problems of mental reaction-type, mental causes and diseases. *Psychological Bulletin, 5,* 385–403.

Meyer, G. J. (2002). Implications of information-gathering methods for a refined taxonomy of a psychopathology. In L. E. Beutler & M. L. Malik (Eds.), *Rethinking the DSM: A psychological perspective* (pp. 69–106). Washington, DC: American Psychological Association.

Mischel, W. (1968). *Personality and assessment.* Mahwah, NJ: Erlbaum.

Nestadt, G., Costa, P. T., Hsu, F.-C., Samuels, J., Bienvenu, O. J., & Eaton, W. W. (2008). The relationship between the five-factor model and latent *Diagnostic and Statistical Manual of Mental Disorders*, Fourth Edition Personality Disorder dimensions. *Comprehensive Psychiatry, 49,* 98–105.

Othmer, E., & Othmer, S. C. (1994a). *The clinical interview using DSM-IV: Volume 1: Fundamental.* Washington, DC: American Psychiatric Association.

Othmer, E., & Othmer, S. C. (1994b). *The clinical interview using DSM-IV: Volume 2: The difficult patient.* Washington, DC: American Psychiatric Association.

Paris, J. (2009). The bipolar spectrum: A critical perspective. *Harvard Review of Psychiatry, 17,* 206–213.

Paris, J. (2013). *The intelligent clinician's guide to the DSM-5.* New York: Oxford University Press.

PDM Task Force. (2006). *Psychodynamic diagnostic manual.* Silver Springs, MD: Alliance of Psychoanalytic Organizations.

Petersen, M. (2008). *Our daily meds: How the pharmaceutical companies transformed themselves into slick marketing machines and hooked the nation on prescription drugs.* New York: Sarah Crichton. ["two for each member of congress" p. 10; the 1992 law is described on pp. 330–331]

Raines, G. N. (1952). Foreword. In American Psychiatric Association (Ed.), *Diagnostic and statistical manual of mental disorders* (pp. v–xi). Washington, DC: American Psychiatric Association.

Raven, M., & Parry, P. (2012). Psychotropic marketing practices and problems: Implications for DSM-5. *The Journal of Nervous and Mental Disease, 200,* 512–516.

Robins, E., & Guze, S. B. (1970). Establishment of diagnostic validity in psychiatric illness: Its application to schizophrenia. *The American Journal of Psychiatry, 126,* 983–986.

Rogers, C. R. (1957). The necessary and sufficient conditions for therapeutic change. *Journal of Consulting Psychology, 21,* 95–103.

Ronson, J. (2012). *The psychopath test: A journey through the madness industry.* New York: Riverhead.

Rosenhan, D. (1973). On being sane in insane places. *Science, 179,* 250–258.

Rosenhan, D. (1984). On being sane in insane places. In P. Watzlawick (Ed.), *The invented reality: How do we know what we believe we know?* (pp. 117–144). New York: Norton.

Rounsaville, B. J., Alarcon, R. D., Andrews, G., Jackson, J. S., Kendell, R. E., & Kendler, K. (2002). Basic nomenclature issues for DSM-V. In D. J. Kupfer, M. B. First, & D. A. Regier (Eds.), *A research agenda for DSM-V* (pp. 1–30). Washington, DC: American Psychiatric Association.

Sahling, D. L. (2009). Pediatric bipolar disorder: Underdiagnosed or fiction? *Ethical Human Psychology and Psychiatry, 11,* 215–227.

Schwartz, J. M., & Begley, S. (2002). *The mind and the brain: Neuroplasticity and the power of mental force.* New York: RegenBooks.

Spence, M. A., Greenberg, D. A., Hodge, S. E., & Vieland, V. J. (2003). The emperor's new methods. *American Journal of Human Genetics, 72,* 1084–1087.

Spitzer, R. (1983). Psychiatric diagnosis: Are clinicians still necessary? *Comprehensive Psychiatry, 24,* 399–411.

Spitzer, R. L. (1991). An outsider-insider's views about revising the DSMs. *Journal of Abnormal Psychology, 100,* 294–296.

Spitzer, R. L. (2009). DSM-V transparency: Fact or rhetoric? *Psychiatric Times, 26.* Retrieved from http://www.psychiatrictimes.com/display/article/10168/1385346?verify=0

Spitzer, R. L., Williams, J. B., Gibbon, M., & First, M. B. (1992). The Structured Clinical Interview for DSM-III-R (SCID). I: History, rationale, and description. *Archives of General Psychiatry, 49,* 624–629.

Strub, R. L., & Black, F. W. (1993). *The mental status exam in neurology* (3rd ed.). Philadelphia: F.A. Davis.

Tackett, J. L., Balsis, S., Oltmanns, T. F., & Krueger, R. F. (2009). A unifying perspective on personality pathology across the life span: Developmental considerations for the fifth edition of the *Diagnostic and Statistical Manual of Mental Disorders. Development and Psychopathology, 21,* 687–713.

Victor, B. S. (1996). Psychopharmacology and transpersonal psychology. In B. W. Scotton, A. B. Chinen, & J. R. Battista (Eds.), *Textbook of transpersonal psychiatry and psychology* (pp. 327–334). New York: Basic Books.

War Department. (1946). Nomenclature of psychiatric disorders and reactions: War department technical bulletin, Medical 203. *Journal of Clinical Psychology, 2,* 289–296.

Westen, D., Kegley-Heim, A., Morrison, K., Patterson, M., & Campbell, L. (2002). Simplifying diagnosis using a prototype-matching for the next edition of the DSM. In L. E. Beutler & M. L. Malik (Eds.), *Rethinking the DSM: A psychological perspective.* (pp. 221–250). Washington, DC: American Psychological Association.

Williams, J. B. W. (1989). A structured interview guide for the Hamilton Depression Rating Scale. *Archives of General Psychiatry, 45,* 742–747.

Wittchen, H.-U. (1994). Reliability and validity scales of the WHO-Composite International Diagnostic Interview (CIDI): A critical review. *Journal of Psychiatric Research, 28*, 57–84.

Wittchen, H.-U., Beesdo, K., & Gloster, A. T. (2009). A new meta-structure of mental disorders: A helpful step into the future or a harmful step back to the past? *Psychological Medicine, 39*, 2083–2089.

World Health Organization. (1992). *The ICD-10 classification of mental and behavioural disorders: Clinical descriptions and diagnostic guidelines.* Geneva: Author.

Yalom, I. D., & Leszcz, M. (2005). *Theory and practice of group psychotherapy* (5th ed.). New York: Basic Books.

Youngstrom, E. A., Birmaher, B., & Findling, R. L. (2008). Pediatric bipolar disorder: Validity, phenomenology, and the recommendations for diagnosis. *Bipolar Disorders, 10,* 194–214.

Zero to Three. (2005). *Diagnostic and classification of mental health and developmental disorders of infancy and early childhood: Revised edition (DC:0-3R).* Washington, DC: Zero to Three Press.

# 3

# Understanding Depression

The incidence of depression has increased dramatically in Western societies in the last 50 years. One reason for this is that the pace of life has become more frantic and the individual has less community support to metabolize the stress. Although we could spend a chapter simply exploring the reasons for the increased rates of depression, our primary focus in this chapter is exploring the following questions: Why do people get depressed? Is it because they lack the motivation to enjoy life? Is it because they have a "chemical imbalance"? Is it because they inherited the disease? Is it because they have recently suffered a trauma? Finally, what is the best way to treat people who are depressed? The answers are more complex than any of these questions, and the first part of the chapter will explore that complexity. In the second half, we will focus on the range of treatments available for someone who is suffering from depression.

In the *Diagnostic and Statistical Manual of Mental Disorders*, Fifth Edition (DSM-5), the new category *Depressive Disorders* includes Major Depression, Persistent Depressive Disorder (previously called Dysthymia), Premenstrual Dysphoric Disorder, depression related to medications or medical conditions, and Disruptive Mood Dysregulation Disorder (discussed in Chapter 6) (American Psychiatric Association [APA], 2013). We focus on depression in general to follow the Research Domain Criteria (RDoC) of the National Institute of Mental Health (NIMH) and because depression occurs in many disorders in addition to those listed in the Depressive Disorders section of DSM-5. In this chapter we will focus on common themes found across different theories about why people suffer depression and how best to treat it.

Depression is one of the most overdetermined symptom sets that mental health clients present with. Recall that the word *overdetermined* means that there are many variables (and combinations of variables) that can contribute to feeling depressed. So to begin, you must consider that we do not know what *causes* depression. We know this is asking a lot of the reader, particularly in the United States, where we are conditioned to look for certainty, particularly from experts in a discipline. Americans excel at a type of "word magic" in which an illusion of certainty is created with words although, in truth, no certainty has been consistently confirmed. The news that there is no one thing causing depression is actually good because we know that many variables influence whether or not a person suffers depression, and the more we know about these variables, the more help we are to clients.

It is more resourceful for clinicians and researchers to focus on risk factors than causal mechanisms. Risk factors increase the probability of a condition, whereas causal mechanisms explain the processes through which risk factors bring about a condition. In this chapter, think of depression as a large territory that is currently being mapped by several mapmakers with different skills and agendas. Each mapmaker contributes a partial truth to our understanding of why people get depressed and the best way to treat depression. When you use an integrative model to organize your maps and assess your client, you are drawing on the best of all worlds and decreasing the risk of a category error.[1]

In this chapter we will cover three terrains of depression and discuss treatments relevant to each. The three terrains are the body (physiological theories of depression), the mind (psychological theories of depression), and the spirit (existential/trans-ego understandings of depression). In addition, we'll explore social, cultural, and developmental variables in depression.

When we use the word *depression*, we are referring to any number of or combination of the symptoms listed under Major Depressive Disorder in the DSM. We realize that in operationalizing depression this way we immediately incur the wrath of those who prefer narrow, more specific descriptions of depression. Such preferences are usually aimed at diagnostic clarity, but the more they narrow and clarify the list of symptoms in the DSM, the farther they depart from the clinical reality of most clients. This said, an integral perspective is crucial for clinicians because it allows for the heterogeneous manifestation of symptoms or, in easier language, the sloppiness of being human. The symptoms for a Major Depressive Episode proper found in the DSM-5's Depressive Disorders still include self-report of depressed mood, anhedonia (a loss of pleasure in things you used to enjoy), weight changes of 5% or more of normal body weight, sleep problems, inappropriate guilt, trouble concentrating, and possibly thoughts of suicide. In the DSM, clients must have five or more of the listed symptoms in a 2-week period.

The symptoms for Persistent Depressive Disorder (previously Dysthymic Disorder), thought to be a low-grade depression, are very similar to those just listed. In fact, the symptoms just listed may manifest in many DSM disorders, including (but not limited to) Major Depressive Disorder and Persistent Depressive Disorder. Depressive symptoms are also a significant factor in Bipolar I and Bipolar II Disorders, Cyclothymia, Schizoaffective Disorder, Disruptive Mood Dysregulation Disorder, Obsessive-Compulsive Disorder, many of the so-called Personality Disorders, and are frequently comorbid with Anxiety Disorders. In addition, depressive symptoms can occur after childbirth (depression with postpartum onset), as a side effect of prescription and illicit drugs, and in relation to seasonal fluctuations (Seasonal Affective Disorder), and can be comorbid with hormonal fluctuations (Premenstrual Dysphoric Disorder). Depression is comorbid with different types of trauma, for example, in victims and perpetrators of abuse (particularly in women

[1] A category error involves the error of presenting things as if they are of the same kind, when they are actually of radically different kinds. In Integral theory, we say a category error is when someone tries to account for all quadrants (perspectives) with only one or two quadrants or perspectives.

who are victims of violent abuse) (Hegarty, 2011). More recent research suggests that environmental stressors like trauma, genetics, and sex (gender) all interact to account for the higher prevalence of reported depression in females (Vigod & Taylor, 2013). Depression can also be directly related to a medical disorder (such as multiple sclerosis, Parkinson's disease, hepatitis, diabetes, AIDS, and other infectious diseases). There are also emerging links between general medical conditions and the etiology of depression, one example being disorders involving inflammation and effects on the brain resulting in depression (Anisman, 2011). Finally, in the DSM-5 depression can be labeled "other—specified" or unspecified.

As we will illustrate, the DSM categories can be useful in planning treatment but to be truly helpful as a clinician you should consider all the partial truths in the three maps we will cover. The categories also remind us that there are differences *between* categories in the manifestation of depression. Dysphoria may be of clinical importance, but it also may differ in etiology from depression. Research has yet to offer us firm conclusions on such distinctions.

As noted, we do not know what "causes" depression because "depression" is many different things to many different people with similar symptoms. By listening to, learning about, and being in relationship with our clients, we can learn how they have come to experience a depressed state and what the most resourceful treatment for them will be.

Consider the following vignettes in which depression plays a prominent role in all of the clients described:

#1: Franklin was admitted to an inpatient psychiatric unit in an inner-city hospital. He was suffering from psychotic symptoms upon his arrival, claiming the moon and stars were talking to him and lighting his way to fame. He was also suicidal and experiencing hopelessness, meaninglessness, anhedonia, and loss of weight and appetite. He had been eliminated from tryouts for a semi-professional soccer team a week before-putting an end to his dream of professional athletics. Franklin's psychotic symptoms remitted completely in 10 days, leaving only the depressive symptoms.

#2: José has been struggling to find gainful employment for 2 years. He, his wife, and their three children have an income that puts them below the poverty level in the United States and are living in a dangerous inner-city area. José is a skilled construction worker and found a good job with a firm last month. José and his family came to the country illegally from Mexico and are considered illegal immigrants. He never knew his parents and was raised by neighbors and lived for 6 years in a church orphanage. When the state government cracked down on the hiring of illegal workers, José lost the one good job he had found. He was brought to a neighborhood clinic by his cousins because he was depressed and suicidal, although the clinic does not have a bilingual counselor and José speaks only Spanish. He says he feels worthless and that the world is against him. He doesn't think things will ever change.

#3: James was formerly a Roman Catholic priest; he left the priesthood for a position in which he provided mental health services to victims of torture in Central America. He remains a very spiritual person and is involved in daily practice of a form of contemplative prayer called Centering Prayer. He grapples with inhumanity and what he calls "the darkest aspects of the human species." James recently returned to the United States after experiencing profound depression for over 2 months. He is in treatment for his depression.

#4: Alicia began suffering depressive episodes at puberty and has had them nearly every month around the onset of her menstrual cycle. She had been in counseling on and off for 3 years but found it did little to decrease the episodes. Her family physician, after charting the episodes, determined they were strongly correlated with her menstrual cycle and prescribed an antidepressant that Alicia takes 2 weeks out of each month around the time of her period. She reports that the episodes are either less severe or nonexistent each month. She says when she is depressed, her first "take" on things is always negative. For example, she was offered a promotion at work during her last episode and she said "the first thing that popped into my mind is that I will mess this up somehow."

#5: Ingrid has suffered from bouts of depression off and on for the last 3 years and seems to have a chronic, low-grade depression as well (this is sometimes referred to as "double depression.") One look at Ingrid and people can tell she has low self-efficacy. Her posture is slouched; she frequently sighs deeply, and seems oblivious to others in the environment. She has responded quite well to an antidepressant (Paxil/paroxetine) but still speaks in a low, clipped voice. Most of her observations and comments are negative and people find her to be a "downer." In fact, Ingrid seems to identify with her symptoms as if they define her. She regularly calls herself an "ambulatory depressive."

#6: Janice began experiencing depressive episodes when she was 19. Her symptoms seem to worsen in the winter months and improve in the spring and summer. She is now 28 and has increasingly been experiencing severe joint pain and fatigue. Last year she was diagnosed with fibromyalgia. Her doctor began her treatment with a mild cocktail of medications to help her sleep. Her sleep has improved and her joint pain and mood symptoms have dramatically decreased.

When reading the latter vignettes, it is easy to see that depression is overdetermined. It would be absurd to simply try to reduce the causes of depression in all the vignettes to something like a *chemical imbalance* in the brain.[2] Clients may share some similar genetic vulnerability to depression (Kamata et al., 2011), and if we could consistently find genomic patterns that correlate with depression, we could consider that a physiological marker. To date we have found no such marker. In reality, all of the clients described in the vignettes had multiple factors impinging on them and their mood. Alicia's case is the closest that we have to any kind of "imbalance," and the map of the body is the most useful in understanding her depression. Her depressive symptoms fluctuated around the hormonal shifts that occurred as part of her menstrual cycle. As far as we could determine, there were no precipitating psychological traumas or negative associations with sexuality (and thus the onset of menses).

In José's case, his depression seems to be a psychological response to living in poverty, experiencing what does seem like a hopeless situation, and feeling that there is nothing that can be done. Although there may be biochemical events that correlate with the psychological meaning José attributes to his situation, these events are clearly not the "cause" of his depression.

[2] Recall that there is no support for the idea that mental illnesses are caused by chemical imbalances in the brain. Sometimes we can intervene chemically and help to alleviate depression, but that in no way means the chemicals affected by the intervention were unbalanced to begin with.

Franklin's psychotic and depressive symptoms seem to be directly related to the "loss of face" that accompanied failing to win a place on the semi-professional soccer team. In this sense the psychological map of depression and understanding how the ego deals with a severe "loss of face" is most resourceful to begin planning treatment. Franklin had built this up in his mind for years and talked about it a great deal with family and friends. His failure, in his eyes, was ultimate and led to the ensuing symptoms. Franklin went through an 8-month course of treatment with counseling and antidepressant medication and has been symptom-free now for 9 years.

For James, his spiritual practice seems to have moved him to a place where he is open and undefended in the face of enormous suffering. He himself would admit that the practice opened his heart but he had not yet learned to metabolize the suffering he then embraced. James's depression is what we could call existential or spiritual in nature. Using the spiritual map to understand James's symptoms, we see that he is psychologically at a point where his ego is becoming an object of awareness, but this leaves his awareness less defended in the face of suffering and renders him more vulnerable to depressive responses. It is common across many spiritual paths that spiritual practice increases one's capacity to see the existential givens in the world (including suffering), but the individual has not yet reached a point where he or she can say "yes" to those givens without being dragged down emotionally.

Ingrid certainly suffers depressive symptoms, but her mindset is also quite negative. In her case we must explore the extent to which the depressive symptoms and her negative mindset fuel each other.

In Janice's case, the depression seems to be better accounted for as a symptom of fibromyalgia. There is still debate about the extent and role of auto-immune disorders like fibromyalgia, but in Janice's case the proof seems to be in the treatment, so to speak. One theory regarding fibromyalgia is that fine tendon repair takes place during the rapid eye movement (REM) stage of sleep, so if you improve the client's REM sleep, the repair can take place and symptoms should decrease (Anderson, Maes, & Berk, 2012; Gracely, Ceko, & Bushnell, 2011).

So, why do people get depressed? As the latter vignettes illustrate, it depends, and the answer may differ depending on the person, situation, and time of life. Again, this is where the categories of the DSM, and *categorical psychiatry* in general, depart from allopathic medicine and where a DSM diagnosis should be only one part of an overall client profile (Frances, 2013). To pretend that depression is a "disease" like a bacterial infection is confusing psychiatric categories with allopathic medical diseases. As we noted in Chapter 1, the approach of categorical psychiatry used in the DSM has been estimated to be 50 to 100 years behind diagnostic practices in other branches of medicine. This is why integrative models (in this case, the Integral model we are using) are useful to map a client's depressive symptoms. In this chapter we will use the Integral model to review what we know about the etiology and treatment of depression.

First we review theories about the etiology of depression from the biological, psychological, and spiritual maps. Where data exists, we review cultural, social, and developmental factors. Finally, we discuss the recommended treatment for depression and offer some case studies to practice applying the concepts covered in both etiology and treatment.

## THE ETIOLOGY OF DEPRESSION

It helps to remember that reality is complex, and complexity is our friend. This is particularly important with an overdetermined symptom set like that for depression. Solid research and clinical wisdom can guide us in mapping some of the signposts on the journey to becoming depressed, but not everyone takes the same road and the signposts differ from client to client. Why do people get depressed? The question is simple and the answer is complex. The variables contributing to depression include biological, psychological, and environmental. As noted, we will add spiritual variables to this list,[3] recognizing that adding such variables implies a transformed psychotherapy to deal with these symptoms, whether they reflect states or stages of development. We will elaborate on these and use the Integral model as a framework to understand them as complementary rather than competing maps. We begin by viewing depression through the map of the body.

### Physiological Theories of Depression: The Map of the Body

We know that we cannot account for depression exclusively with physical variables, but we also know it would be foolish to rule them out. We have learned a great deal in the last 25 years about which physical variables are highly correlated with depression. Despite years of research, however, we know little about the pathophysiology[4] of depression or even if there is such a thing (Lipsman & Lozano, 2011). Similarly, we know little about the causative molecular mechanisms of antidepressant therapy that can lead to clinical benefit. As Sahay and Hen (2007) summarized ". . . the heterogeneity of depression indicates that its origin may lie in dysfunction of multiple brain regions" (p. 1110). As long as you remember that there is a complex interplay between physical variables, the mind, and the environment you can avoid the trap of thinking that the physical variables *cause* depression.

One of the reasons we've learned so much about depression in the past 25 years is that advances in medical technology have allowed us to peer more deeply into the central nervous system and the cells and structures of the brain. In a recent study on the most-cited works about depression, the 243 most-cited studies (400 or more citations) deal primarily with the etiology and epidemiology of the disorder (Lipsman & Lozano, 2011). As we've noted in earlier chapters, there is a strong relationship between the medical technologies available and the theories of why certain symptoms develop. Theories about why people get depressed based in physiological explanations are one of the clearest examples of this relationship. Whereas the first two versions of the DSM were based on a psychodynamic model, beginning with the DSM-III, the categorical approach described in Chapter 1 was used, and thus began the search for biological "markers" for depression. All such "marker" studies are in their infancy (e.g., Goodwin, New, Triebwasser, Collins, & Siever, 2010). Despite the fact that no

---

[3] Spirituality as we discussed it in Chapter 1.

[4] Pathophysiology is the study of the disturbance of biochemical and other physical functions either by disease or other condition. This is a basic discipline in allopathic medicine and may be inappropriate in studying mental and emotional disorders for reasons discussed in Chapter 1.

universal markers have been found, the theories and physiologically based treatments that grew from the search play an important (but partial) role in diagnosing and treating depressive symptoms.

## A Note on "Chemical Imbalances"

Before launching into the physiological theories of depression we have gleaned from examining the map of the body, it is important to clear up a phrase that has been the source of much misunderstanding in the late 20th and early 21st centuries. That phrase is "chemical imbalance." That phrase, used today, is what we refer to as *word magic*—attempting to create an illusion of certainty with words where in fact no certainty exists, or at least where no certainty has been confirmed and/or replicated in scientific models. Exploring a topic integrally requires a willingness to explore political agendas, biases, and the role context plays in the topic under study. All of these are pertinent when considering the idea of a chemical imbalance. First, a bit on how the phrase developed.

When some of the early medications for depression (monoamine oxidase [MAO] inhibitors and tricyclic antidepressants) began to show positive results for treating depression, it was quickly learned that one of the first things these drugs do is increase the levels of a neurotransmitter called norepinephrine (abbreviated as "NE"). Thus, it was only human to assume that if the drugs correlated with an increase in NE and a decrease of symptoms, perhaps the drugs corrected an "imbalance" in NE. What we find, of course, in reviewing the theories of how antidepressants work is that their mechanism of action is far more complicated than increasing the levels of a given neurotransmitter. That is only one of many mechanisms of action.

Despite that, the idea that depression was somehow caused by a chemical imbalance took hold, particularly because the idea made it easier to market antidepressant medications. In addition, the chemical imbalance metaphor has been a mainstay of psychiatric training similar to gene expression (which is an equally poor phrase that we'll address later). Kemker and Khadivi (1995) noted that "regarding chemicals as the cause of mental illness is a growing trend, despite flaws in the logic of this model" (p. 247). These authors noted that given the stresses of psychiatric training, it is far easier to describe suffering as chemical rather than undertaking the time-intensive task of understanding the client's psychological and emotional context.

**CAUSATION AND CORRELATION** Just because a drug that has chemical properties is correlated with symptom reduction in *some but not all* clients,[5] this does not mean that these clients' brain chemistries were "unbalanced" in the first place. We consulted with a client who bleakly shared that her doctor told her that her depression was caused by a chemical imbalance. We asked her what type of test her doctor used to check her brain chemistry—blood test? spinal tap? She responded that the doctor did no such test. We then told her that many doctors use the phrase "chemical imbalance" more as

[5] This phrase will be a staple phrase in this book. Most studies on interventions only show results in "some but not all" clients. In many studies, "some but not all" equals about 50%.

a metaphor because ingesting chemicals (antidepressants) can be helpful in reducing the symptoms. "In other words," we told her, "just because we intervened chemically does not mean your brain chemicals were the problem." Her mood improved a great deal after that discussion. Imagine being told by a doctor that you had a thyroid imbalance, but the doctor never tested the levels of thyroid-stimulating hormone in your blood. The fact that ingesting chemicals (antidepressants) is correlated with symptom reduction in *some but not all* clients does not mean the symptoms were *caused by* an imbalance in the same chemicals. It merely means that some alleviation of the symptoms may be accomplished through chemical intervention. This may sound like hair-splitting, but it is an important point because there is a great deal of lobbying from pharmaceutical companies and some corners of biological psychiatry to conceptualize mental and emotional disorders as basically *allopathic* brain disorders. This is not the case as noted in several places in Chapter 1. Particularly, depression is an overdetermined disorder that very likely results from a complex interplay of physical, psychological, and environmental variables. There is certainly a chance we will discover some aspect of the brain or genetic variable that "causes" depression, and when that can be consistently confirmed we will have to upgrade our understanding of the disorder. One promising field of study is viewing depression as an immune inflammatory disorder (Anderson et al., 2014). Even though this recent theory of depression focuses on physical variables (immune system functions drawing tryptophan away from serotonin and melatonin) it is still overdetermined in terms of multiple physical variables being involved.

Having said that, though, there *are* numerous physiological changes that correlate with the reduction of, or remission of, depressive symptoms. These correlations appear after several weeks of treatment with antidepressant medications. The physiological theories related to depression describe many of them quite well. The question remains, though: Are these theories about the etiology of depression or theories of antidepressant action? Because, as noted in Chapter 1, the mind impacts the brain as the brain impacts the mind, we are faced with the proverbial "chicken/egg" problem. The most resourceful way to understand these physiological theories is as partial truths. Only when we weave all the partial truths together (physiological, psychological, environmental, cultural, and spiritual) do we approach a way of thinking about depressive symptoms that honors the complexity of each client.

Finally, it is important to note that we begin this review of the physiological variables related to depression with the question "Why do people get depressed?" The answers from the physiologic theories, however, most often address the question "When a medication seems to help reduce symptoms of depression, what is that medication doing in the body, particularly in the central nervous system?" This of course is quite different from asking "Why do people get depressed?" Isolating one mechanism of action for an antidepressant is not the same as isolating a cause of depression. If taking an antidepressant raises the levels of norepinephrine (NE) in synapses, that does not mean these synapses were somehow deficient in NE prior to the medication. It simply means we have isolated a variable that correlates with taking an antidepressant.

This bears repeating because too often we hear such variables irresponsibly turned around to "explain" why people get depressed (e.g., "if taking antidepressants increases the levels of NE, then depression must be caused by an NE deficit"). This results in poor and even irresponsible explanations that quickly become entrenched in the popular culture (e.g., "Depression is caused by a neurochemical imbalance"). Imagine if someone felt better after smoking cannabis and then proposed he had a cannabinoid imbalance in his brain (although some have proposed that exogenous cannabinoids may have antidepressant properties; Ashton & Moore, 2011). It doesn't really make sense. So, fascinating as these theories are, please hold them lightly as important partial truths that take us one step closer to understanding our clients and how to treat them.

**THE MONOAMINE THEORY OF DEPRESSION** An early physiological theory of why people get depressed grew out of treatment with the first antidepressant medications in the 1950s: MAO inhibitors and tricyclic antidepressants.[6] This theory was called the monoamine hypothesis and its origins are attributed to a biochemist named Albert Zeller from Northwestern University. An amine is any compound that is derived from ammonia by replacement of one or more hydrogen atoms with organic compounds. A monoamine is an amine that has a single binding site in its structure. Monoamines include the neurotransmitters dopamine (DA), epinephrine (EP), and norepinephrine (NE). MAO inhibitors and tricyclic antidepressants both increase the levels of norepinephrine (NE) in the synaptic cleft.[7] MAO inhibitors do this by deactivating the enzyme that disables NE.[8] Tricyclics increase NE by inhibiting its reuptake by transporter molecules.[9] So essentially, because antidepressants helped some (but not all) patients with their depression and because they increased levels of NE, the hypothesis was that depressed people did not have enough NE and thus had a "chemical imbalance."

The permissive hypothesis is in a way an amendment of the amine hypothesis. It asserts that depression is caused by an imbalance between the neurotransmitters serotonin (abbreviated 5-HT for 5-hydroytryptamine) and norepinephrine.[10] This theory postulates that antidepressants that increase the availability of serotonin then allow serotonin to regulate the release and effects of norepinephrine. This theory basically allows that neurotransmitters other than amines be implicated in depression. The antidepressants related to this theory are the selective serotonin reuptake inhibitors (SSRIs) and the serotonin norepinephrine reuptake inhibitors (SNRIs).

---

[6] MAO inhibitors inhibit an enzyme (monoamine oxidase) that in turns breaks down the neurotransmitter NE after it is released from the neurons. Inhibiting the breakdown of NE leaves more NE in the synapse to bind to receptors. Tricyclic antidepressants are named for their molecular structure, which resembles three interlocking rings. These drugs work primarily by inhibiting the reuptake of NE, again resulting in more NE in the synapse. Both drugs have several other mechanisms of action. For a full description, see Ingersoll and Rak (2006).

[7] "Synaptic cleft" and "synapse" are synonymous. Both refer to the space between the end of one neuron and the beginning of another.

[8] This discovery that enzymes, including MAO, disable neurotransmitters was made by Zeller, thus laying what was to become one of the foundation blocks for amine theory.

[9] Transporter molecules are proteins that bind to neurotransmitters that have been fired from neurons and take them back into the neuron to be used/fired again. This process is akin to recycling the neurotransmitter. Julius Axelrod eventually won a Nobel Prize in 1970 for this research, which he began 20 years earlier.

[10] Norepinephrine is also referred to as noradrenalin. The former name is derived from the Greek language (*epi* means "on" and *nephron* means "kidney"), and the latter is derived from Latin (*ad* again means "upon" and *renal* means "kidney").

**THE DOWNREGULATION THEORY OF ANTIDEPRESSANT ACTION** The monoamine hypothesis was a logical but overly simplistic hypothesis. Clinicians knew that it could take between 2 and 6 weeks for antidepressants to have their full therapeutic effect, but the increases in NE occur within an hour of taking the drug. Thus, the increases of NE could not fully account for the therapeutic effects. What was later discovered was that the increases in NE (or serotonin for drugs like Prozac/fluoxetine) led to a decrease in the number and sensitivity of postsynaptic receptors, called downregulation. This decrease in the number and sensitivity of the receptors takes approximately 2 to 6 weeks to occur. Eureka! Thus was born the downregulation theory of how antidepressants work. This second theory was still a variation on the chemical imbalance theory. It stated that a depressed person takes an antidepressant and quickly increases the levels of NE available in the synaptic cleft. This increase in NE then causes the downregulation (decrease in the number and sensitivity of postsynaptic receptors) and this translates into relief from symptoms of depression. The downregulation theory still held that some sort of mythic "balance" was achieved through the medications, and this theory was then generalized to other types of antidepressants, including SSRIs and so-called third-generation antidepressants like Wellbutrin/bupropion and Cymbalta/duloxetine. Again, though, this was not the end of the story.

It is important to note a missing link in both the monoamine and downregulation hypotheses. We began with the question "Why do people get depressed?" The answers increasingly come to address the mechanism of action for antidepressants, which stops short of explaining how increasing NE and effecting downregulation actually changes mood. The answer is that, at this point, we simply don't know why people get depressed, but many writers in the field appear reluctant to admit this. With the next theory of antidepressant action, we come one step closer to actually beginning to understand why antidepressants (and other things such as exercise and psychotherapy) may improve mood.

**MOLECULAR/CELLULAR THEORY OF ANTIDEPRESSANT ACTION** The cellular/molecular theory of antidepressant action was an exciting development that clearly linked depression with the presence of ligands[11] in the central nervous system (Duman, Heninger, & Nestler, 1997; Sharp, 2013). The cellular/molecular theory builds on the amine and downregulation theories by describing what happens inside the neurons while increased NE and downregulation of receptors are happening outside. This theory is built in large part on the technologies that allow us to actually learn what is happening inside neurons. It is a pivotal theory, and will surely be one important puzzle piece in a series of findings utilizing intracellular technologies. In a nutshell, the molecular/cellular theory points out that after initially ingesting an antidepressant, when the levels of neurotransmitter targeted by the antidepressant increase (norepinephrine or serotonin or both, depending on which drug was ingested), there is also an increase inside the cell in the levels of cyclic adenosine monophosphate (cyclic AMP).

Cyclic AMP is a molecule important to many biological processes. Inside the neurons of the brain, cyclic AMP governs the production and processing of brain-derived neurotrophic factor, which is a protein that helps the survival of existing neurons as

[11] A ligand (from the Latin *ligandum*, meaning "binding") is a molecule that can bind with a biomolecule to serve a biological purpose. A biomolecule is any molecule produced by a living organism. Neurotransmitters are a class of ligand. This use of the term is distinct from its use in metalorganic and inorganic chemistry.

well as encouraging the growth and development of new neurons (referred to as neurogenesis) (Malberg & Blendy, 2005).[12] The following is the key sequence of events in the molecular/cellular theory of how antidepressants act on the body. For the sake of the example, we'll assume the antidepressant taken is an SSRI.

1. Within an hour of taking the SSRI, the level of serotonin in the synapses increases.
2. At the same time, the levels of cyclic AMP inside of the postsynaptic neuron also increase.
3. Over 2 to 6 weeks, the number and sensitivity of the postsynaptic serotonin receptors decrease. While the levels of cyclic AMP inside the postsynaptic cell decrease, they remain *higher* than they were in the pre-medication condition.
4. It is believed that the overall increase in cyclic AMP in the postsynaptic neurons results in more brain-derived neurotrophic factor (BDNF) and thus healthier existing neurons and a greater chance for the growth and development of new neurons. There are also some studies that suggest decreased plasma levels of BDNF are correlated with depression (Lee et al., 2007).

There is some promising initial research support for this theory. We have known for some time that there is a significant relationship between stress, affective disorders, and BDNF. Exposure to stress, the stress hormone *corticosterone*, and social isolation have been shown to *decrease* the expression of BDNF in rats (Dwivedi, Rizavi, & Pandey, 2006; Licinio & Wong, 2002). In addition, both stress and social isolation are correlated with depression in humans. Two research groups have recently found lower plasma levels of BDNF in depressed patients when compared to a nondepressed matched population (Scaccianoce et al., 2006). In addition, at least one study has demonstrated that antidepressants reverse BDNF decreases induced by the stress hormone corticosterone.

It is with the molecular/cellular theory that we really start looking at a chain of physiological events that correlates with the decrease of depressive symptoms, and that is much more realistic than stating that the physiological variables *cause* depression. As early as 2004, researchers had concluded that although deficits in neurogenesis (related to deficits in BDNF) may play a subtle role in depression, these deficits do not *cause* depression (Henn & Vollmayr, 2004). As we'll see in studying psychological theories of depression, the mind/brain interaction is such that certain psychological experiences in response to environmental stimuli could impact and change the way the brain is working. Recall from Chapter 1 that the brain has a degree of plasticity that is now recognized as far greater than was once believed. This is one of the most exciting directions for clinicians because there are activities such as exercise that begin in the mind as will or motivation and then can actually have an impact on the brain. In the case of exercise, studies have concluded that exercise is correlated with a decrease in depressive symptoms (Erickson, Miller, & Roecklein, 2012) and increases in BDNF (Adlard & Cotman, 2004). In some part, the correlation of exercise with reduced depressive symptoms may come about because exercise also increases levels of BDNF. It is important to qualify this, though, and note that researchers think that BDNF stimulates the action of antidepressants but antidepressants do not correct an "imbalance" of BDNF (Wolkowitz et al., 2011).

---

[12] It used to be believed that once a person was born, that person had all the neurons he or she would in life and no new ones would develop. This turned out to be incorrect, as several areas of the brain can grow new neurons throughout the lifespan.

At this point we come full circle in the sense of theory informing clinical practice. We've always known that physical activity could be a useful way to improve mood and decrease anxiety, but now we're starting to understand some of the physical mechanisms involved. When a client is told that depression is caused by a chemical imbalance, it can reinforce the very *external locus of control* that contributes to feeling helpless or hopeless (both of which are shown in cognitive research to increase one's *vulnerability to depression*). On the other hand, if a client is told that exercise can enhance levels of "chemicals" that help brain cells work optimally, the locus of control includes some internal variables. Many clients benefit greatly from a 6-month regimen of antidepressants but, during that 6 months, they also make changes in their lives that allow them to maintain gains after titrating off of antidepressants. Presenting this to clients is simply a matter of summarizing what we know clearly and free of the pharmaceutical industry bias that pushes us to define things in terms of physical diseases that can be helped *only* by taking medication.

## Other Physiological Theories of Depression

**GENETICS** If we have learned anything about the role of physiology in developing depressive symptoms, it is that science is always, by definition, incomplete—a work in progress. Many scientists understand this, but commercial marketing and the mass media frequently misunderstand it, leaving us with inaccurate phrases like "chemical imbalance." We see the same problem in trying to isolate the role of genetics in the development of mental and emotional disorders (Brown, 1998).

The role of *gene expression* is important in studying any mental or emotional symptoms that constitute a disorder. To start with, the phrase "gene expression," if not word magic, is pretty inaccurate. Genes do not intentionally "express" themselves. Genes are simply akin to blueprints or a parts list regarding how to make proteins. This is no small task because the average person makes about 50,000 proteins for a multitude of tasks. Genes are found on chromosomes, which are in the nuclei of cells. Each of your cell nuclei contains 23 pairs of chromosomes (with the exception of reproductive cells). Most chromosomes are approximately 50% deoxyribonucleic acid (DNA) and 50% proteins. DNA is shaped as the double helix discovered by Francis Crick and James Watson.[13] If you were to unwrap the double helix, you would have something akin to a ladder. The sides of the ladder are composed of sugars and phosphates. The rungs are composed of four ligands called bases (also sometimes called nucleotides or letters). These bases are adenosine, thymine, guanine, and cytosine. A gene is simply a group of these base pairs on a DNA molecule. Each group is a set of instructions for protein synthesis. We noted that the chromosome itself is about 50% protein. This protein is a sort of sheath or sleeve covering the DNA that makes up the gene. To "express," the sheath must be withdrawn so that messenger ribonucleic acid (mRNA) can "see" the "blueprint" and then initiate a series of events leading to synthesis of that protein.

[13] It should be noted that Rosalind Franklin is now historically credited with providing the data Crick and Watson used to discern the DNA shape. It has been alleged that these data were shown to Watson without her approval. Her data were essential to solving the mystery of the double helix. Maddox (2003) argues that sexism, egoism, and anti-Semitism all played a role in her being left out of history.

So what is the point here? The point is that genes don't actually "express" themselves; rather, their parts lists can be read and instructions carried out when the cell, responding to events external to it (and even the body of which it is a part), is configured in such a way that the protein sheath is temporarily withdrawn and the blueprint is available to mRNA. This paragraph is critical to making sense of the role genetics plays in mental health. The initial hope of researchers was that single genes might be correlated with disorders like Schizophrenia much in the same way as single genes have been identified as underlying disorders like muscular dystrophy or cystic fibrosis. This has not turned out to be the case. What we will consistently refer to in this book is the idea of *genetic vulnerability* to disorders. From a geneticist's point of view, vulnerability explains why for a pair of monozygotic twins with a history of Schizophrenia in their family, only one will develop it while the other does not. Although they share the same genome, their reactions to the environment can be radically different. The role of the environment and one's psychological reaction to it comprises the discipline now called epigenetics (*epi* means "near or around"). Thus epigenetics is the study of events (in the body, mind, and environment) that trigger the withdrawal of protein sheaths around genes and allow their blueprints to be carried out.

So while we'll continue using the phrase "gene expression," it is important that we understand it as the ability of a gene's instructions for protein synthesis to be carried out. This much is straightforward enough but, just as with the phrase "chemical imbalance," the phrase "gene expression" can be used inaccurately to the point where it too constitutes word magic. In that sense, the statement "depression is caused by gene expression" tells us absolutely nothing, and we might as well say depression is caused by "karma," "poor temperament," or the impending end of the Mayan calendar in 2012.[14] This is so because if "gene expression" is triggered by events in the environment or the mind perceiving the environment, those events (rather than the expression triggered) are the ones of research and clinical import. Even hypotheses stating that symptoms like depression are reactions or a vulnerability to life events and are genetically determined only account for, at most, less than half the variance between those who do and those who do not suffer from depression. More specific theories about gene expression and depression are being developed, one related to what are called "clock genes" and how they may underlie the sleep disturbances that often are part of depression (Coogan & Thome, 2012).

To make matters more complex, the manner in which gene expression occurs is currently being debated. In the 1970s, the idea that genes operate individually became a fundamental belief in the field of genetics. In limited cases (like those noted earlier) a particular disease could be tied to a particular gene. This began as the idea that each gene in any organism carries the information it needs to synthesize one (and only one) protein. In July of 2007, The United States National Human Genome Research Institute published findings suggesting that rather than genes functioning independently and

[14] At the time we were writing this book, the 2012 phenomenon was making a mark on the culture, with people predicting everything from another harmonic convergence to a magnetic pole reversal that would destroy all electronics to a supervolcanic eruption that would plunge the Northern Hemisphere of the planet into a quasi-nuclear winter. While we were open to something happening that might transcend our understanding, in 2011 we were still renewing our magazine subscriptions as well as planning our New Year's party.

linking to a single function (like a predisposition to depression), they operate in complex networks and interact as well as overlap with each other in ways we don't fully understand. More recently, scientists discovered that what was previously referred to as "junk DNA" is actually millions of switches communicating with genes about what to do and when to do it (Ritter, 2012).

This is important particularly because the popular press frequently misinterprets genetic research. For example, if scientists publish a paper showing a correlation between a genetic anomaly and alcohol dependence, the newspapers will frequently report it with a headline like "Gene for Alcoholism Found." As the most recent findings about genes working in networks suggest, gene expression is a complex aspect of nature and in its infancy as a science.

When we talk to clinicians about the role of genetics in mental health, they frequently are under the misguided impression that biology *is* destiny and that if your parents suffered from a particular disorder, then you will suffer from the same or similar disorders. Although it is true that having first-degree relatives who suffer from depression increases the probability that you *may* suffer depressive symptoms, it is not destiny for the simple reason that a genetic code is not some concrete computer program moving irreversibly toward one outcome. As noted, it is a system of millions of codes, some of which will get triggered or "played out" and others of which will not. The prevalence of depression in a given population can change quickly, whereas gene pool changes would take years to occur. Our genes (or networks of genes, as we are now learning) are expressed in intricate interplay with the environment and our psychological reactions to the environment (Charney, 2004). As Ernest Rossi (2002) noted, genetic determinism is a misconception. He wrote

> Our genes are not deeply buried in biology, remote from our daily consciousness and concerns. On the contrary, our genes express themselves every moment of our lives in response to everything that stirs our curiosity, wonder, and fascination. Our genes are expressed in continually changing dramas that flow with meaningful life events. Our genes are switched on and off in response to our conscious efforts to cope with outer stresses as well as to our inner hopes, wishes, fantasies, and dreams. (p. xvi)

The realization that "significant life events can turn on genes that lead to the synthesis of proteins that, in turn, generate new neurons and connections between them in the brain" has profound implications for the practice of counseling and psychotherapy, as we will see in the later section on treatment.

So while we all carry within our genetic codes certain predispositions, whether a particular gene (or network of genes) is expressed and the degree to which it is expressed depends on environmental conditions. Such gene expression could be implicated in health and disease. This is a very different understanding of genetics from the academically safe pronouncements that depression seems to run in families or that having female relatives who were severely depressed before age 30 increases your overall risk of becoming depressed. While the latter is helpful in generally understanding a person's risk factors, the former can be the basis for an effective treatment and prevention program. In case the reader is wondering, there has been no successful attempt to find a single gene underlying depression. As with many of the disorders covered in this book, to the extent that there are genetic variables involved, these variables include multiple genes, environmental factors, and psychological responses to the environment.

Although it is important to remember that mental disorders are likely polygenic to the extent genes are involved, one of the more promising genes studied in relation to mental illness is called the Disrupted in Schizophrenia 1 (DISC-1) gene. This gene is currently thought to play a role in depression, Bipolar Disorders, and Schizophrenia. It was discovered in 2000 and is considered a risk gene for these disorders (but is not a guarantee you will get any of the disorders if you have the gene). The theory is that this gene might impact a molecule (D-Serine) that plays a role in signaling neurotransmitter receptors for a neurotransmitter called glutamate (Glu). The DISC-1 gene seems related to levels of D-Serine, with implications for the three disorders listed (Ma et al., 2012).

**HORMONES** One of the disorders that moved from the appendix in the DSM-IV-TR (APA, 2000) to Depressive Disorders in the DSM-5 is Premenstrual Dysphoric Disorder (PMDD; previously known as Late-Luteal Phase Dysphoric Disorder). The DSM-5 describes the essential features of PMDD as symptoms such as markedly depressed mood, marked anxiety, marked affective lability, decreased interest in activities, sense of being overwhelmed, and physical symptoms like breast sensitivity. In PMDD these symptoms are noted to occur the final week before the onset of menses and are absent the week post-menses (Futterman & Rapkin, 2006). Eleven symptoms are listed, five of which are required for the diagnosis:

1. feeling sad, hopeless, or self-deprecating
2. feeling tense, anxious, or “on edge”
3. marked lability of mood interspersed with frequent tearfulness
4. persistent irritability, anger, and increased interpersonal conflicts
5. decreased interest in usual activities or withdrawal from social relationships
6. difficulty concentrating
7. feeling fatigued, lethargic, or lacking in energy
8. marked changes in appetite that may be associated with binge eating
9. hypersomnia or insomnia
10. subjective feeling of being out of control or overwhelmed
11. physical symptoms like headaches, breast tenderness, or sensations of bloating

It is important to note that part of the controversy over this diagnosis was the issue of pathologizing a natural process in women. The conclusion researchers have come to is that PMDD is in fact a severe set of symptoms that occur in only a minority of women during the last week of the luteal phase of the menstrual cycle.[15] The disorder can also be diagnosed in adolescents (Rapkin & Mikacich, 2006).

---

[15] The menstrual cycle occurs in four phases divided equally by the event of ovulation. The first is the menstrual phase, which begins the first day of menstrual bleeding and continues approximately 4 days. The second phase, which lasts days 5–13, is the follicular phase in which the lining of the uterus thickens in response to the release of estrogen; follicles are developed and one or two become dominant. Ovulation is the divide between the four phases when a dominant follicle releases an egg or ovum. The third phase is the luteal phase, which occurs oin days 15–26. In this phase the remains of the dominant follicle become the corpus luteum (Latin for yellow body), which produces large amounts of progesterone which to prepares the uterine lining for the possible implantation of an embryo. The final phase oin days 27 and 28 is the ischemic phase, where, if embryo implantation does not occur, there are sharp drops in estrogen and progesterone, leading back to the first phase of the cycle.

What is most interesting about PMDD is that the symptoms respond remarkably well to SSRI antidepressants administered only during the luteal phase. This is quite different from the use of SSRIs in the treatment of depression, which requires continuous treatment and in which therapeutic effects may take 2 to 6 weeks to occur. Intermittent dosing with SSRIs for women suffering from PMDD appears to have a positive impact on their quality of life (MacQueen & Chokka, 2004). Although the causes of PMDD remain unknown, some researchers have tied the syndrome to serotonergic dysregulation, which of course may or may not be tied to gene expression, which may or may not be tied to the environment and the person's psychological reaction to the environment. *Serotonergic dysregulation* is grammatically much more accurate than the phrase "chemical imbalance," as it simply points to the neurotransmitter system that may be implicated without speculating exactly *how* it is implicated. Jovanovic and colleagues (2006) found differences in the binding potential of certain serotonin receptors in women suffering from PMDD compared to those who were not. If these findings are replicated, it may help explain how PMDD develops and who is at risk for it.

If nothing else, the research on depression in PMDD highlights the importance of differential diagnosis. If you are treating adolescent or adult female clients who appear to be depressed, it is important that you have them chart their symptoms and their menstrual cycle to see if the depressive symptoms correlate with the last week of the luteal phase of the cycle. If so, treatments other than or in addition to counseling or psychotherapy may be particularly beneficial. These include medication treatment with SSRIs, aerobic exercise, dietary changes, and dietary supplements. It is also important to know if your female clients have met the criteria for PMDD because it is now linked to a higher risk for postpartum depression (Bloch et al., 2005).

**RESEARCH INVOLVING BRAIN STRUCTURES AND NEUROGENESIS** Some research has implicated particular brain structures in the expression of depressive symptoms. One useful line of research attempted to isolate the areas of the brain that regulate emotion and to see if those areas functioned differently in depressed subjects compared to euthymic subjects.[16] In a summary of 15 years of neuroimaging studies, researchers concluded that there are no areas of the brain that are abnormally overactive or underactive in depressed subjects (Steele, Currie, Lawrie, & Reid, 2007). This may seem like something of an anticlimax, but the finding is important. As these researchers allude to in their conclusions, oversimplified theories that try to link something as complex as depression to malfunction of a brain structure tend to be unreliable and result in inconsistent findings. As these authors stated, more sophisticated concepts of depression should likely lead to more reproducible findings. This type of meta-analysis is important particularly because writers in the popular press misunderstand simplistic hypotheses and present them as fact in the mass media. In one popular example, a journalist tried to correlate specific brain structures with specific symptoms and then went on to propose that different psychotropic medications acted directly on these brain structures. Without research like the brain-imaging studies just mentioned, such misrepresentations will persist.[17]

---

[16] Euthymia is actually a word derived from Greek that means "tranquil" or "joyous." Its original meaning has quite been lost in clinical language where its use means simply "neither manic nor depressed."

[17] In a particularly irksome example Jonathan Engel (2008) claimed chemical imbalances caused mental illness and biology was found to be the root of most disorders yet did not cite one study supporting his assertions.

Research following up on what we have learned about the role of neurotransmitter systems has also contributed to our understanding of symptoms that are comorbid with and possibly part of depression for some (but not all) people. Stahl and Briley (2004) traced particular serotonergic and noradrenergic pathways implicated in depression and proposed that based on their function, disruption in these pathways *could* contribute to somatic symptoms in depression, pain in particular. Although somatic symptoms are *not* universal in depression, it is important to explore the connection when clients present with somatic symptoms in addition to depression. This is important research, but it raises the question of differential diagnosis from pain syndromes like fibromyalgia and chronic fatigue syndrome (Michielson et al., 2006). Both the latter include symptoms of depression for many afflicted parties. This highlights the importance of a physical exam before engaging clients in counseling or psychotherapy.

More recently, McCarthy et al. (2012) postulated what they call glutamate-based depression. Glutamate (Glu) is a nonessential amino acid classed as an excitatory neurotransmitter. Several types of Glu receptors have been identified, and *N*-Methyl-D-aspartic acid (NMDA) is implicated in this theory of depression. Glu acts at NMDA receptors, and too much can cause excitotoxicity and cell death. Since the year 2000, several studies have found that injections of ketamine can decrease or eliminate depressive symptoms in one dose (Mathew et al., 2012). Although ketamine is used as an anesthetic in veterinary medicine, it is also classed as a potential drug of abuse.[18] Since Skolnick (2012) reported evidence that all antidepressants to some extent inhibit NMDA receptors, those findings, and the ketamine reports, make them a logical target for both a theory and an intervention. In particular, NMDA receptors in an area of the brain called Brodmann's area 25 in the cerebral cortex (also called the subgenual cingulate) may play a major role in the etiology of depression. Basically, McCarthy et al. (2012) hypothesize that a disruption in Glu transmission may underlie depression. Although more research is necessary, it is a promising lead, and several pharmaceutical companies are looking at ways to create oral doses of ketamine to treat depression.

## Psychological Theories of Depression: The Map of the Mind

Remember the cases of José and Franklin at the beginning of this chapter? José was living in chronic poverty and suffering from the stress of trying to support his family. Franklin was dealing with the "loss of face" that occurred when he failed to attain a long-cherished dream. Both of these men clearly met the criteria for depression, but the stressors precipitating the depression originated in the environment and the mind. Although the environment and mind may have had some impact on the body (specifically the brain), clearly we have to take into account the psychosocial stressors in both cases.

In exploring what the map of the mind has to offer us regarding the etiology of depression, we will journey into several well-known theories and fascinating research, and we will learn that in many cultures psychological theories about depression are considered before biological ones. The psychological theories about why people get depressed will take us back to psychoanalysis and through the cognitive revolution in psychology. What we will see is that, to paraphrase the poet John Milton (1969), the mind is its own place and can make a heaven of hell and a hell of heaven.

---

[18] Ketamine seems to induce what feel like out-of-body experiences. Ketamine was used extensively by John Lilly in his development of the sensory deprivation tank, and he felt it had therapeutic potential. See Lilly (1981).

**PSYCHODYNAMIC THEORIES OF DEPRESSION** In 1917 Sigmund Freud wrote a paper called "Mourning and Melancholia" in which he distinguished grief (mourning) from melancholic depression. Grief, he said, was a normal reaction to the loss of a loved person, whereas depression was a pathological reaction to the loss of a loved person.[19] Frequently this loved object is a parent or other caregiver who, early in life, abandons the child. Affective states experienced by people suffering from depression have been grouped by Sidney Blatt into two orientations: anaclitic (dependent) and introjective (self-critical). The anaclitic model of depression is similar to Freud's idea of melancholia. Anaclitic depressive patterns are frequently experienced by people whose relationship with their primary caregiver was disrupted in some way. This evolves into feelings of weakness, helplessness, inadequacy, fears of abandonment, desires to be soothed, difficulty tolerating delay of gratification, and difficulty expressing anger (for fear of driving another loved person away).

Introjective depressive patterns manifest as an experience of "harsh, punitive, unrelenting self-criticism; feelings of inferiority, worthlessness, and guilt; a sense of having failed to live up to expectations and standards; fears of the loss of approval, recognition, and love from important others; and fears of the loss of acceptance of assertive strivings" (Blatt & Zuroff, 1992, p. 539).

Being able to differentiate these two psychodynamic patterns of depression contributes to the ability to choose effective treatment. Some researchers have noted that anaclitic depression seems to affect one's interpersonal line of development[20] relating to issues of dependence and threatened (real or imagined) loss of loved ones. People suffering from anaclitic depression frequently report feeling lonely, weak, and helpless. They experience an intense desire for love and approval as well as intense fear of rejection. Aggression is repressed for fear of driving loved ones away ("If I tell you I am angry you will leave me"), and this repression is thought to be responsible for psychosomatic symptoms, which can include different types of pain.

Introjective depressive patterns focus on difficulties with ". . . self-appraisal, self-definition, self-criticism, and identity" (Meurs, Vliegen, & Cluckers, 2005, p. 207). Again, these patterns can result from disruption in the relationship with an early caregiver but in this case the resulting symptoms derive from harsh inner criticism. Such criticism also disrupts current relationships through the resultant sense that one is not worth loving. Blatt and Shahar (2005) have suggested that there are some sex-related tendencies in these depressive styles, with women more frequently presenting with anaclitic patterns and men with introjective patterns. In Western societies, traditional gender roles may reinforce these patterns.

Both anaclitic and introjective experiences of depression have been linked to attachment theory. Attachment theory proposes that consistently loving, protective, and nurturing relationships with our parents or caregivers promote our ability to form healthy relationships with others throughout life. Attachment theory suggests that we develop internal models of self and others from early relationships. If those relationships

[19] Features that distinguish the depressive reaction as pathological include—among other things—a profoundly painful dejection, a significant lowering of self-regard, an inability to love, and a loss of interest in the outside world.

[20] As noted in Chapter 2, there are dozens of hypothesized lines of development. Some of these constructs are well developed and some are simply artifacts of pop psychology. As also noted in Chapter 2, interpersonal development is intricately tied to ego development, which is a robust construct.

go reasonably well, the models we develop work reasonably well and are the basis for a healthy attachment style. If the relationships are of poor quality (e.g., neglect, abuse), then the models we develop are also of poor quality and result in an insecure attachment style. Reis and Grenyer (2002) summarized variations on unhealthy attachment styles and noted that the styles with negative views of self are linked to anaclitic and introjective depression. The person who is preoccupied with relationships, has a negative view of self, and has a positive view of others is thought to be vulnerable to anaclitic depression. The person who has a negative view of self and is dismissive of and fearful of relationships is vulnerable to the introjective style of depression.

**Other Psychodynamic Theories of Depression** Psychodynamic patterns of depression were also detailed by Melanie Klein (1957) and Karen Horney (1940), who felt it was an emotional state that was the result of a fragmented or divided self. This caused *intrapersonal* confusion where the self experienced numerous subpersonalities[21] struggling to break into awareness, be recognized, and be accepted. Horney (1940) wrote that clients must be helped to retrieve disowned parts of themselves, become aware of real feelings and wants, evolve their own values, and relate to others on the basis of these changes. In Horney's treatment, the client was aided in bringing these subpersonalities to awareness and integrating them into the self or ego. Arieti and Bemporad (1980) provided a discussion of depression in relation to the goals that a client is pursuing. In psychodynamic theory, the "over-I" (mistranslated as "superego") is a combination of one's introjected authorities as well as one's personal sense of an ideal self. The idea is that pursuit of unrealistic goals that have their origin in the "over-I" can be the cause of depression because the real self is in no way capable of achieving these. Psychiatrist John Bowlby (1977) elaborated on the theme presented in anaclitic depression, namely that disruption in early attachments and early interpersonal conflicts render one vulnerable to later depressive episodes. Finally, many of the self-psychologists focused on depression as a result of the belief that important personal needs and desires in depressed people were not being met.

**Clarifying Psychodynamic Depressive Patterns** Many clinicians unfamiliar with psychodynamic thinking may still be a bit mystified by how disruption in the relationship with one's early caregiver can result in adult depression. As Freud himself realized, we cannot state with certainty that psychological events trigger predictable neurological sequences.[22] In healthy growth, we (the subjects) take aspects of ourselves and our lives and consistently make them objects of awareness. For example, when you are angry, if you are able to be aware that you are angry and own your anger you have far more choices about what to do with it. A person with an anaclitic depressive pattern begins to become aware of her anger just as you might, but, unlike you, as soon as she begins to be aware of her anger, she becomes afraid that expressing it will upset and

[21] Subpersonalities is a construct developed by Roberto Assagioli (1975), founder of psychosynthesis, and defined as "autonomous configurations within the personality as a whole" that are similar to what Jung and Adler described as complexes.

[22] Early in his career, Freud was inspired by the ground-breaking work of Nobel Prize–winning anatomist Santiago Ramon y Cajal to attempt such a correlation in his *Project for a Scientific Psychology*. He abandoned this project, realizing that the science of his day was unable to clearly link experiences to predictable sequelae in the central nervous system. This research is still being carried out by another Nobel Prize winner, Dr. Eric Kandel (2006).

perhaps drive away someone she loves. Then, in order to protect her current relationships from the imagined threat that derives from early abandonment, she pushes the anger out of awareness or, in psychodynamic parlance, she represses the anger. In this latter example, rather than the subject consistently making her anger an object of awareness, she denies it, in essence making it "other." This has been called the "subject/other" dynamic of psychopathology.

Another way to understand these patterns is through what Blatt and Shahar (2005) referred to as a dialectical model of self-development. In this model, the authors point out that our ego or proximate-self is intimately linked to our experience and internalized representations of significant others. Drawing on Erik Erikson's (1950) model of psychosocial development, these authors saw the self evolving dialectically through three general interpersonal levels of development: basic trust, cooperation, and intimacy. The inability to negotiate these developmental levels has implications for emotional and behavioral dimensions. Failure to establish early relations of trust leads to an emotional sense of worthlessness and inhibition of behaviors of initiation. In plain English, this means that when we do not learn to trust, we feel worthless and fail to start things because of that feeling. Moving from trust to a capacity for cooperation depends on the child's ability to develop a sense that one is autonomous and capable of participating in cooperative relationships such as those found in play. Finally, this capacity to engage in cooperative relationships leads to further refinement of self and identity that then make it possible to engage in intimate relationships (much in the same way that Horney's treatment required the person to relate to others on the basis of changes made in awareness of wants, needs, and values). Thus, "the sense of self and the quality of interpersonal relatedness develop in a reciprocal, mutually facilitating, dialectic transaction" (Blatt & Shahar, 2005, p. 138).

**COGNITIVE-BEHAVIORAL THEORIES OF DEPRESSION** The earliest behavioral theories of depression were set forth in part to break from the psychodynamic theories that dominated up until the mid-20th century. The gist of early behavioral theories was that those vulnerable to depression tend to either suppress behaviors that elicit positive responses from others or enact behaviors that elicit negative feedback from others. As we will see later in the chapter, these theories gave birth to interpersonal theories of depression. A more straightforward behavioral theory of depression was Lewinsohn, Weinstein, and Shaw's (1969) model that associated depression with a lack of social skills and proposed that if the depressed people learned social skills, their depressive symptoms would lessen. The goal of these therapies was to alter behavior to increase the probability of positive reinforcement from the environment and decrease the probability of negative feedback or punishment. Although such approaches are useful in a small number of cases, the majority of people suffering from psychogenic[23] depression have far more complex causes. The social skills approach is particularly useful with people suffering severe mental and emotional disorders and whose lack of social skills causes secondary depression.

Perhaps the most enduring behavioral paradigm is Martin Seligman's (1975) paradigm of learned helplessness. This began as a behavioral paradigm and was easily

---

[23] *Psychogenic* means of psychological origin or etiology.

adapted to complement what was becoming a cognitive-behavioral approach to understanding depression. The initial work in this area involved giving dogs electric shocks in situations where escape was impossible. When the dogs were moved to a shock condition where escape *was* possible, they failed to attempt it. Seligman and Maier (1967) were able to demonstrate that this behavior was caused by the uncontrollability of the original shocks. This became the animal model of the theory that when external events are beyond a person's control, they may lead to depression. This is similar to the earlier behavioral formulations outlined previously in the chapter (that depression is due to a lack of positive reinforcement from the environment as well as perhaps punishment or negative consequences in the environment). Seligman and others always presumed that this would account for some but not all depressive symptoms, and the evidence was strong enough to support that claim. The learned helplessness theory was later critiqued and reformulated because of several weaknesses. The revisions deal with weaknesses that stem from generalizing from an animal model to human beings (Alloy et al., 2000; Alloy et al., 2006).[24]

The sentience or self-awareness of human beings is better accounted for in the revised theory. It differentiates between helplessness that is universal (affecting all people) versus helplessness that is personal (affecting one or a few people rather than all people). Personal helplessness is correlated with an internal attribution, whereas universal helplessness is correlated with an external attribution. The revised theory of learned helplessness also deals with whether or not the helplessness is specific or global. Helplessness that occurs in a broad range of situations is global and helplessness that occurs in a narrow range of situations is specific. If the person perceives the helplessness as global, he or she is more vulnerable to depression. The time course of helplessness may also vary from person to person, with some instances lasting minutes and others lasting years. Here the revised theory differentiates between transient and chronic helplessness, with chronic being the more depressogenic of the two.

The reformulated theory of helplessness in depression is as much a theory of attributions. The reformulated theory is essentially as follows:

1. Depression causes problems in motivation, cognition, emotions, and one's self-sense.
2. When individuals believe that getting what they want is unlikely (or suffering what they don't want is likely) and there is nothing they can do to change it, they will suffer depression.
3. The depression is shaped by how the depressed person makes attributions. Problems with motivation or emotions may worsen if attributed to general helplessness. The more stable the belief in one's helplessness, the more chronic the symptoms will be. If this sense of helplessness is internalized, it will damage the person's self-sense.
4. The intensity of the depression increases and one's sense of helplessness increases. The more important the outcomes the person feels he or she is lacking, the more chronic the depression is likely to be. (Abramson, Seligman, & Teasdale, 1978)

---

[24] The idea of generalizing from animal models to human beings began with Charles Darwin's idea that "human behavior evolved from the behavioral repertory of our animal ancestors. That idea gave rise to the notion that experimental animals could be used as models to study human behavior" (Kandel, 2006, p. 40).

Thus, cognition begins to become part of the theory as attributions requiring some level of sentience are integrated. As Abramson and colleagues concluded, ". . . the properties of the attribution predict in what new situations and across what span of time the attribution of helplessness will be likely to recur" (1978, p. 59).

**COGNITIVE THEORIES OF DEPRESSION** To the extent that we view attributions as types of cognitions, we have moved toward a cognitive theory of depression. As Haaga, Dyck, and Ernst (1991) noted ". . . there has been widespread agreement that cognitive *therapy* of depression is effective (but) there has been less consensus on the validity of cognitive *theory*" (p. 221). The search for an underlying cognitive theory of depression is noteworthy because it has resulted in the different schools of thought being brought together in an integrative manner.

The psychological theory of depression most studied in recent years is the cognitive vulnerability theory of depression. Simply stated, this theory proposes that negative cognitive styles confer vulnerability to depression when people confront negative life events. For our purposes, a negative cognitive style can be defined as a tendency to explain negative events in stable and global terms. The cognitive vulnerability theory of depression is really the result (and combination) of two earlier theories: Aaron Beck's theory of depression and the hopelessness theory of depression.

**Beck's (1987) Cognitive Theory of Depression** Simply stated, Aaron Beck's theory focused on specificity, the cognitive triad of depression, the cognitive distortion bias, automaticity, and schemas. Specificity refers to the idea that depressive cognitions are specific in perceiving final and definite loss. In the case of James at the beginning of this chapter, the loss was a loss of faith in humanity (and he also suffered from symptoms of Post-Traumatic Stress Disorder [PTSD]). The cognitive triad of depression refers to the idea that depressed people think more negatively about themselves, the future, and the world than people who are not depressed. José's case illustrates the cognitive triad in his sense of worthlessness, the world being against him, and nothing changing. The cognitive distortion bias is a selective memory for negative things and inability to identify or remember positive things. Consider the case of Ingrid—she sees the negative in everything and people consider her a "downer." Automaticity refers to the fact that negative thoughts are experienced as repetitive and uncontrollable. Finally, Beck's idea of schemas is very similar to psychodynamic idea of unconscious organizing principles, or internal working models.

A schema, in Beck's theory, is a cognitive map of sorts, and depression-generating schemas are beliefs (conscious and unconscious) that increase the likelihood of negative cognitions.[25] Young, Klosko, and Weishaar (2003) noted that a schema is a broad pervasive theme comprised of memories, emotions, thoughts, and bodily sensations that developed during childhood or adolescence and is elaborated throughout one's life. Beck recognized there was a need for further attention to things like the disruption of early relationships (ala John Bowlby) as well as to the environment of depressed people. Although another change noted as important was limiting

[25] This idea of cognitive maps derives from the work of Edward Tolman (1948). We have found our students do better with this concept if they think of it as a "cognitive map" rather than a "schema." You can use the terms synonymously.

cognitive theories of depression to "non-endogenous" types of depression, the dearth of success in finding pathophysiological variables associated with depression makes that change look premature.

**The Hopelessness Theory of Depression** The hopelessness theory of depression began as a subtype of depression. Abramson, Metalsky, and Alloy (1989) proposed that people with negative cognitive styles, when faced with negative life events, tend to become hopeless and develop a depression characterized by hopelessness (Spangler et al., 1993). Using the Beck Depression Inventory (Beck, Steer, & Brown, 1996), Thomas Joiner and his colleagues (2001) determined that there was a cluster of items in their analysis that related to hopelessness and supported hopelessness depression as a subtype. Similar to the work described earlier on attributions, research on the hopelessness subtype of depression seemed to indicate that the people who suffered from this subtype were predisposed to it in the way they made meaning of life (as evidenced by their cognitions). It appeared, then, that hopelessness depression and depression as Beck had earlier described it both resulted from a cognitive vulnerability. It is to this theory that we now turn.

**THE COGNITIVE VULNERABILITY THEORY OF DEPRESSION** The idea that all depression is to some extent significantly associated with increased negative thinking has consistently been supported. Although some of the research just reviewed also supported specific subtypes of depression like the hopelessness subtype, it appears that the negative cognitive style is the cognitive hallmark of people suffering from depression. Therefore, it makes sense for a theory of etiology to target negative cognitive styles directly. Do some people have a vulnerability toward developing a negative cognitive style and thus to developing depression? The answer seems to be "yes." Again, the case of Ingrid earlier in this chapter is one example.

**The Temple-Wisconsin Study** One of the most ambitious projects designed to explore this question of cognitive vulnerability was the Temple-Wisconsin Cognitive Vulnerability Project. Between September 1990 and June 1992, freshmen at Temple University and the University of Wisconsin were screened for participation in the study. A total of 419 met the screening criteria and, of these, 349 agreed to take part in the study. The students were put in high- and low-risk categories based on evidence of their cognitive styles. As one would expect, students with negative cognitive styles were thought to be more vulnerable to depression. This finding was supported in that students in the high-risk group had higher lifetime prevalence for Major Depression and hopelessness depression subtype, and marginally higher risks for minor depression.

In the Temple-Wisconsin study, we also learned about the characteristics of negative cognitive styles. For example, students in the high-risk group showed ". . . greater endorsement, faster processing, and better recall of negative depression-relevant adjectives involving themes of incompetence, worthlessness, and low motivation" (Alloy et al., 2000, p. 129). High-risk students were also less likely to recall positive adjectives like "successful" and "loving" than low-risk participants. The high-risk participants were more likely than low-risk students to develop suicidal ideation during follow-up.

**INFORMATION PROCESSING AND DEPRESSION** One information-processing theory related to cognitive vulnerability to depression is that people with negative cognitive styles cognitively process information differently than those without negative cognitive styles. In *dual-processing theory*, human beings possess two styles of cognitive processing called associative and reflective. *Associative processing* (also called quick or intuitive processing) allows us to make quick, effortless processes in relation to well-learned associations. It is thought of as parallel rather than linear and thus quicker. Associations are usually made at the preconscious level, so we are aware of the output of such processing but not the information used to produce the output. The case of Alicia presented earlier is a good example. She was offered a promotion that she wanted and her first thought was that she would somehow "mess it up." This negative thought that "popped into" her mind is the outcome of associative processing.

*Reflective processing* (also known as conscious or rational) is slow, effortful, and based on rule-based inferences. Reflective processing requires more attention and awareness than associative processing. Reflective processing is linear and takes more time than associative processing. The rules that guide reflective processing can come from logic, the media, one's culture, or oneself.

One important relationship between associative and reflective processing is that reflective processing is frequently used to correct what one feels is faulty associative thinking. Beevers (2005) demonstrated that "a cognitive vulnerability to depression is observed when negatively biased associative processing is uncorrected by reflective processing" (p. 975). This, in a nutshell, is a description of what cognitive therapy aims to do—make objects of awareness of irrational or incorrect associative conclusions (assuming one is a "loser" if one does not get a promotion one applied for) then using a system of reflective associations based on the guidelines of cognitive therapy (e.g., "what evidence do you have that failing to get a promotion means you are globally a loser?").

The cognitive vulnerability hypothesis of depression has been supported in several studies. Young, Watel, Lahmeyer, and Eastman (1991) proposed a dual-vulnerability hypothesis for Seasonal Affective Disorder (SAD).[26] In this theory, people whose moods worsen in fall and winter are believed to be physiologically and cognitively vulnerable. Enggassar and Young (2007) tested that hypothesis and found that in a sample of people suffering from seasonal variations in mood, those with more dysfunctional attitudes, ruminative response styles, and a more internal attributional style for negative events suffered more severe mood symptoms during the fall and winter.

Singer and Dobson (2007) designed a treatment study based on the information-processing model of cognitive vulnerability. Their findings supported that, prior to a negative mood induction, acceptance training based on becoming aware of one's feelings in the here and now was correlated with significantly decreased intensity of

---

[26] SAD is currently a specifier in the DSM (Seasonal Pattern Specifier) and refers to episodes of major depression that may occur in Major Depressive Disorder or Bipolar I and II Disorders. Arguments have been made that Seasonal Affective Disorder should have been its own disorder in the DSM-5 rather than a specifier (Rosenthal, 2009). The key is that the depression worsens in fall and winter and remits in spring. See Young et al. (1991).

sad moods and an alteration in their attitudes toward temporary moments of sadness. Murray, Woolgar, Cooper, and Hipwell (2001) found that cognitive vulnerability to depression was related to being exposed to a depressed mother. Finally, Gibb, Alloy, Abramson, Beevers, and Miller (2004) determined that cognitive vulnerability to depression was best represented as a dimension that is present to a greater or lesser extent in all of us and that the strength of the vulnerability is positively correlated with the severity of depressive symptoms.[27]

The construct of cognitive vulnerability and the research supporting it raises a question: What contributes to one developing the cognitive vulnerability that, in turn, makes one more vulnerable to depression and other disorders? Here, as in the physiologically based theories of depression, we have come full circle back to psychodynamic theories of how trauma and disruption in early relationships can render one more vulnerable to depression. Recall that the anaclitic and introjective theories of depression suggested that neglect or abandonment by caregivers set in motion dynamics that increase the likelihood of a person suffering from depression. Some of the reasons that people develop cognitive vulnerability to depression sound strikingly similar to the psychodynamic explanations, and it is to this topic that we now turn.

**CONTRIBUTORS TO COGNITIVE VULNERABILITY** We have come a long way from early psychodynamic theories of depression to refutation of those theories by behaviorists, to cognitive therapists' addition of attributions and schemas to learned helplessness. The hopelessness theory of depression was combined with Beck's work to lead us to the cognitive vulnerability to depression. This then led to research to learn what makes people cognitively vulnerable.

Goldberg (2001) summarized research on vulnerability as defined by openness to experience and neuroticism. These in turn were linked to early childhood adversity. This led other researchers to attempt to more comprehensively assess how parenting and abuse/neglect correlated with cognitive vulnerability. As you can guess, the findings were significant.

Rose and Abramson (1992) suggested that children who experience maltreatment seek the causes in an effort to attach meaning to the experience. The younger a child is, the more the self is a reference point to the extent that it might be said that development is a journey away from narcissism. Rose and Abramson (1992) confirmed this in the sense that because children internalize all events, they see themselves as the cause of maltreatment. This internalizing process leads to a negative attributional style that renders one more vulnerable to depression. Then, if negative events are repetitive and occur in relationships with parents or primary caregivers, the events undermine the child's positive sense of self and hope for the future. The persistence of the events and the negative attributional style increase the vulnerability to depression. Ingram and Ritter (2000) have noted that this combination becomes almost trait-like and serves as a foundation for hopelessness.

---

[27] Recall from Chapter 1 that many researchers and clinicians believe that the DSM should utilize dimensional constructs rather than categorical ones because the former more accurately represent the complexity of human beings. Here again is another example of how such a reformulation would be beneficial. See Gibb et al. (2004).

Some researchers have also demonstrated the link between particular parental characteristics and depression. Although relational patterns with those other than parents may also produce vulnerability, ". . . the data clearly suggest that various kinds of parent-child interactions are a primary source of cognitive vulnerability to depression" (Ingram & Ritter, 2000, p. 80). For example, Whisman and Kwon (1992) researched relationships between current levels of attachment in adults and depressive symptoms. They found that insecure attachment was correlated with higher levels of depressive symptoms. Earlier in this chapter we summarized introjective styles of depression as characterized by strong self-criticism. McCranie and Bass (1984) found in a sample of nursing students that higher levels of self-criticism were related to students' reports of inadequate parenting. Finally, several studies have supported the idea that disruption in parent–child bonding is associated with cognitive vulnerability to depression. One example found that cognitive patterns associated with emotional regulation are correlated with recollections of parental warmth or rejection.

Although there are always limits on retrospective studies (i.e., asking people to recollect what their parents were like), the results are consistent with the other research done on cognitive vulnerability. In an attempt to test the hypothesis that deficits in early relationships were related to cognitive vulnerability, Ingram and Ritter (2000) compared formerly depressed and never depressed people on measures designed to learn if people who had suffered depression had a tendency to attend to negative emotional stimuli when they were in a negative mood. These findings were confirmed and, furthermore, the investigators also found relationships between the formerly depressed subjects, their tendency to focus on negative stimuli when their mood was negative, and perceived deficits in bonds with their parents.

Recently, a research team attempting to summarize the relationship between vulnerability to depression and parental care concluded there is evidence for a link between depression in children and exposure to parenting characterized by low care, high psychological control, and the provision of negative feedback (Cicchetti & Rogosch, 2002). Inferential feedback is basically what the parents infer and communicate to the children about the cause of problems that arise in the children's lives. A second team of researchers supported the hypothesis that if parents had negative ideas about problems in life, children would develop similar negative inferences. These inferences are thought to be part of a negative cognitive style that renders one more vulnerable to depression. Additionally, they found that depressogenic cognitive styles were related to parents' negative cognitive styles and general negative parenting practices (such as lack of emotional warmth).

At this point it is important to understand how, similar to physiological explanations for depression, we have come full circle in our attempt to forge psychological explanations of why people get depressed. The earliest psychodynamic theories were focused on the family, and after moving through behavioral and cognitive research on the problem, we have ended up in a similar place. "Similar" (but not identical) because there are important differences. Early psychodynamic theory is inextricably linked to a prescribed treatment (long-term psychoanalysis or similar methods). In addition, although the observations of Freud and many other psychodynamic theorists were accurate, their explanations for what they observed were mostly inaccurate. The shift of focus to the role of attachment in producing cognitive vulnerability to depression frees us from some of the less utilitarian psychodynamic theory while honoring the important observations that are clearly psychodynamic in origin. It would be easier to have one set of labels for psychological phenomena that we could use across theories; however, this is antithetical to the nature of human endeavors, which are characterized by a territoriality similar to that seen in other mammals (and likely related to the pursuit of university tenure in humans). Enthusiasts for particular theories prefer to use the jargon of those theories. An Integral approach to the theories of etiology is particularly resourceful as it allows the clinicians of today to draw from all the theories mentioned in this summary to address the complexity of the clients they are treating.

**OTHER PSYCHOLOGICAL THEORIES OF DEPRESSION** Although we've covered much material on depression, there are still other understandings of how it develops. The interpersonal theory of depression has important findings of clinical relevance across the lifespan (Cole, Jacquez, & Maschman, 2001; Dow & Craighead, 1987). While biological and cognitive theories were dominating discourse, researchers were amassing data to support that interpersonal variables could be directly related to depression. Probably the most referenced interpersonal model of depression is Coyne's (1976, 1999) interactional model. Coyne (1976) posited that the interpersonal behavior of people who are depressed tends to increase rejection from others, which of course is also *depressogenic*. Recall the case summary of Ingrid at the beginning of this chapter. Even though she reported improved mood after taking the antidepressant, her "paralinguistics" and the content of her speech were decidedly negative. Several researchers have explored and found support for the interpersonal model of depression. Coyne himself has noted that his paper was only a poor attempt at theory formulation and there is much more to do in developing and researching the theory. Some of that research is summarized here.

The *paralinguistic behaviors* (vocal rate, volume, pitch, and length of pauses) of depressed people were rated as less clear than those of nondepressed people. There is also some evidence that depressed subjects in studies are harder to hear and show different patterns of eye contact than nondepressed subjects. Not surprisingly, the verbal content of depressed speakers contains more negative statements than that of nondepressed speakers. In addition, there are differences in the facial expressions of depressed and nondepressed people, with the former being less facially animated than the latter (Schwartz, Fair, Salt, Mandel, & Klerman, 1976a, 1976b).

These findings all contributed to the interpersonal theory in that they are partial aspects of interactions with others. By starting with studying these aspects, researchers were able to quantify aspects of social behavior before moving to the more qualitative aspects of interactions, such as peer acceptance. Kistner (2006) noted that low peer acceptance is clearly associated with depression, elevated depressive symptoms, and diagnosed depression. This was confirmed in research with children (Garber, 2006). Depression tends to elicit negative responses from peers, and internalization of negative feedback from peers fuels depression. Even in brief conversations, it appears that depressed people are far more likely than nondepressed people to be rejected. Clearly, the interpersonal researchers integrated what was being discovered by cognitive researchers but then took the next step by integrating cognitive findings into a context of social interactions. In Ingrid's case, although her mood lifted with antidepressants, she didn't really start enjoying her life until she began practicing social skills and making her interpersonal style an object of awareness.

Thus far we see how one set of theories clearly builds on previous ones as well as how we might isolate our client's depression to one or two primary variables. For example, a client may have been abused as a child and developed unhealthy attachment, which created a schema that made her vulnerable to depression. Whereas a psychodynamic theorist might label the depression "anaclitic" and focus on making the difficult childhood an object of awareness through transference analysis, a cognitive therapist may try to make the client's dysfunctional schema an object of awareness by teaching the client how to identify and challenge irrational thoughts. These irrational thoughts of course may manifest in interpersonal interactions, increasing the probability of rejection from peers and, consequently, exacerbating the depression. Later in the chapter we will lay this out in the four-quadrant schematic of Integral theory and explain how the therapist can use it for treatment. Before doing that, however, it is important to explore one more less-researched but important area.

**THE OUTER LIMITS OF PSYCHOLOGICAL UNDERSTANDINGS OF DEPRESSION: EXISTENTIAL AND SPIRITUAL UNDERSTANDINGS** We use the phrase "outer limits" of depression to refer to less-well-researched but clinically useful ideas about it. Particularly, existential and spiritual variables related to depression are important to consider. Although this is important material to include from an Integral perspective, the material is less well researched and requires some extrapolation from theory to clinical utility. An important caveat to remember is what we noted in Chapter 1: We must be clear about how we are operationalizing words like *spirituality*.[28] Recall James, who was introduced at the beginning of this chapter. He was practicing a spiritual discipline called Centering Prayer and was struggling psychologically with the darker aspects of human nature.

If you could meet James, you would find that it is hard to account for his depressive symptoms exclusively with the frameworks presented thus far in this chapter. By all accounts he had a healthy family life growing up, there is no significant history of any mental or emotional disorders in his family, he himself has not ever met the criteria for a disorder, and he certainly did not manifest any of the characteristics we associate with a negative cognitive style. In addition, when interacting with others, James could easily be described as attractive and charismatic—hardly evidence for James's depression being caused by a lack of social skills. So how do we account for his depression? There are two areas of philosophy and psychotherapy that were useful in treating James: existentialism[29] and spirituality.

**Existential Understandings of Depression** Key concepts in existentialism are authenticity, responsibility, and freedom to choose. In the late 19th century Friedrich Nietzsche proclaimed that modern man's soul had gone stale and all about humanity was the smell of failure. The failure was not living authentically, and this manifests as

---

[28] Integral theory (Wilber, 2006) describes five different definitions of spirituality. Briefly, they include spirituality as a line of development, as the upper levels of any line of development, as peak experience, as an attitude, and, finally, as synonymous with one's religious practice.

[29] Drawing on Yalom's (1980) definition, we define existential approaches to therapy as those that focus on concerns that are rooted in a person's existence and their perception of their existence. Individuals' perception of their existence is filtered through their proximate self or ego. Thus, ego development also plays a large part in assessing what existential givens individuals acknowledge and how their ego identity relates to their symptoms.

depression. Nietzsche was fond of paraphrasing the Greek poet Pindar by exclaiming "You should become him who you are!" This idea of "becoming" rather than "being" was central to his existential philosophy. Each person is a work in progress and the existential givens (things like suffering, illness, injustice, and death) are viewed as the very things necessary to become who we are. As Nietzsche scholar Walter Kaufmann (1974) noted, "nature must be transformed, and man must become like a work of art." It is in saying "yes" to the existential givens and the possibility of transformation that we live an authentic life.

Part of saying "yes" to life is constantly questioning our own assumptions. Refusing to think beyond our assumptions is what Nietzsche would have described as moral corruption, and this in turn will inevitably result in unnecessary suffering. In Nietzsche's (1999) own words, ". . . men of convictions are prisoners" (p. 153). For Nietzche, life could be fully lived only when one possessed the courage to face it directly without the diversions and distractions of society and those who control society. Engaging in diversions was thus a form of sleep and ended in lack of meaning. The idea, then, is that by facing life we truly become who we are. By running from life's inevitable suffering, we remain unfinished and unhappy. The problem, of course, is that in facing life, we must frequently accommodate new skills, as James did in facing the extent of human suffering.

Recall from Chapter 1 the different levels of ego identity that have been confirmed by Jane Loevinger (Loevinger & Wessler, 1978) and Susann Cook-Greuter (Cook-Greuter & Soulen, 2007).[30] Developmentally, one can use existential therapy at most if not all levels, but the issues treated by existential philosophy become far more pronounced for people once they enter the Pluralist level of ego identity. At this level, a person has worked through the ability to live life rationally and focus on his or her individual judgments. At the Pluralist level, the person is capable of holding multiple perspectives in his or her mind and realizing that there is no "one right way" of thinking or living. Rather, people very different from the individual hold different views and still succeed. This gives rise to an ability to cognitively reflect back on one's self and, in so doing, recognize that one's self is, at least partially, constructed in relation to what others and our society tell us we are or should be. To consciously engage life authentically becomes a developmental task at this point.

People can also be struck by this idea of authentic living in what is called the "midlife crisis." Have I lived my own life or a life others crafted for me? Do I feel alive and excited about living? What is it that I really want? These are all existential questions that can become pronounced at midlife even for those at earlier stages of ego development. These questions may be asked after a profound onset of depressive symptoms. Existential approaches to depression particularly focus on meaning-making, as both personal meaning and spiritual meaning have been correlated with lower rates of depression (Mascarao & Rosen, 2006, 2008).

**SPIRITUAL ISSUES AND DEPRESSION** If we hold the broad definition of spirituality[31] discussed in Chapter 1, there are several ways that depression can relate to

---

[30] These levels include Impulsive, Conformist, Expert, Achiever, Pluralist, Strategist, Magician, and Unitive.

[31] See note 16 earlier in the chapter.

spiritual experiences. Many cases of depression can grow out of what are referred to in the DSM as "Religious or Spiritual Problems" (this was a "V" code—V62.89—in the DSM-IV and is now a "Z" code in the DSM-5/ICD alphanumeric system—Z65.8). One example is what Ingersoll (2000) called the "Job Syndrome," in which a person outgrows his or her understanding of a faith tradition and, lacking support for making new meaning of the tradition, goes into a state of depression. In these cases a person's level of ego identity has frequently outgrown that of her or his community. In one case a woman who identified as a Jehovah's Witness was living in a nursing home and suffering a great deal of pain from a broken hip that could not be set properly so she would walk again. Her community members had stopped visiting her (unusual for a close-knit group) and she became depressed over a period of 3 months. In discussing this with her it was clear she believed that "the righteous are rewarded and the wicked are punished. I am suffering and feeling punished so I must not have lived the good life I thought I had." In the Job Syndrome, a person (like the protagonist of the Jewish poem[32]) wrestles with his or her concrete understanding of the Divine because his or her life experience seems to contradict it. Sometimes to resolve the dissonance, as in the case just described, individuals might find it easier to assume they had been "wicked" than that their doctrine about the wicked being punished was incorrect.

In this case the client was able to come to a more complex appreciation of God, the role of suffering, and her life. She did not need a different faith but needed to delve deeper into the tradition she had. Clearly this is not necessarily a spiritual problem per se, but a psychological problem related to spiritual life. There are many examples of depressive symptoms related to spiritual issues, and we can still use a psychological frame of reference for these. The field trials for the Religious or Spiritual Problem V-code listed other examples where depression may be a problem, including loss of faith, conversion to a new faith, intensification of practices, and involvement in cults. This V-code also includes problems that are of a more spiritual nature but that have psychological sequelae. These include near-death experiences, transpersonal experiences, and things like mystical states. Depression can be one symptom of what is called a spiritual emergency. This is when a person is experiencing spiritual growth but, for whatever reason, is not prepared to do so.

Some studies have focused on the role spirituality plays in reducing vulnerability to depression, but the results are mixed (Dein, 2006; Nolan, 2006; Westgate, 1996; Young, 2005). Part of the problem seems to be the operational definitions of spirituality. Sometimes the definition is simply one's religious practice, sometimes it is operationalized around spiritual wellness (factors thought to be associated with spiritual health), and other times it is described metaphorically because of its ineffable quality. Although studies have found relationships between religion and decreased levels of depression, there are still multiple variables that may be affecting the outcome of these studies (e.g., the role of community and social support, spiritual maturity, intrinsic versus extrinsic faith). Until we can agree on operational definitions that reflect cultural and developmental diversity, it will be hard to draw conclusions about the role of spirituality and depression. What does seem apparent (and will be discussed in the next section) is that some of the practices from spiritual traditions have been effective in helping clients who are depressed.

[32] Most readers are familiar with the "Book of Job" in the sacred writings of both Judaism and Christianity, but it is technically a poem. See Mitchell (1979).

## TREATING DEPRESSION

Although this is a book on psychopathology, it is important to provide an overview of treatment in light of the enormous number of etiological variables covered in an Integral treatment. This section will provide such an overview. Readers wanting to understand more about specific treatments can consult the sources used in this part of the chapter. In many ways, an Integral approach to understanding psychopathology makes the topic more complicated, but better that than to oversimplify our understanding of clients who, as human beings, are the most complex organisms on the planet. First we will review all the theories of etiology for depression using the Integral quadrants.[33] As we noted in Chapter 1, these quadrants reflect various aspects of the client and serve to highlight clinical "hotspots." Because we know that we can account for some but not all depressive symptoms with the theories in this chapter, we can look at them as variables that may be part of a client's given case presentation. In this sense, once we identify one or more of these variables as "hotspots" for the client in question, they will guide our treatment decisions. Figure 3.1 illustrates variables we have covered in this chapter that may influence depression.

With this figure in mind, let's review the case of José from the beginning of the chapter:

José has been struggling to find gainful employment for 2 years. He, his wife, and their three children have an income that puts them below the poverty level in the United States and are living in a dangerous inner-city area. José is a skilled construction worker and found a good job with a firm last month. José and his family came to the country illegally from Mexico and are considered illegal immigrants. He never knew his parents and was raised by neighbors and lived for 6 years in a church orphanage.

| | INSIDE | OUTSIDE |
|---|---|---|
| INDIVIDUAL | Sequelae of abandonment, neglect<br>Negative cognitive schemas<br>Vulnerability to depression<br>Existential crises<br>Associative cognition | Gene expression<br>Role of BDNF<br>Hormones<br>Learned helplessness<br>Paralinguistic behavior<br>Reflective cognition |
| GROUP | Unhealthy attachment<br>Interpersonal variables | Toxic environments<br>Social skill set<br>Use of social skills<br>Family dynamics of neglect or abuse |

**FIGURE 3.1** Variables Related to Depression by Quadrant

[33] These quadrants are described in Chapter 1. They provide four perspectives that are aspects of all of our beings. The four perspectives are individual subjective experience (upper-left quadrant), individual objective phenomena (upper-right quadrant), interpersonal or intersubjective experience (lower-left quadrant), and objective social factors (lower-right quadrant).

| | INSIDE | OUTSIDE |
|---|---|---|
| INDIVIDUAL | Sequelae of abandonment, neglect<br>Negative cognitive schemas<br>Vulnerability to depression | Gene expression? (link to triggers in lower-right and upper-left quadrants)<br>Role of BDNF? |
| GROUP | Attachment issues? | Use of social skills<br>Family dynamics of neglect or abuse<br>Toxic environments<br>Lack of economic opportunity |

**FIGURE 3.2** "Hotspots" in the Case of José

When the state government cracked down on the hiring of illegal workers, José lost the one good job he had found. He was brought to a neighborhood clinic by his cousins because he was depressed and suicidal. He says he feels worthless and that the world is against him. He doesn't think things will ever change.

Using what we know about depression, we might begin conceptualizing the "hotspots" in José's symptoms as in Figure 3.2.

According to the theories that we have reviewed in this chapter, there is a possibility that José's upbringing may have led to attachment issues that may have increased his vulnerability to depression. The extent to which genetics and BDNF play a role are hard to determine, but they may be variables. Clearly he has had negative life experiences that would lead many people to develop negative schemas and also be more vulnerable to depression. Finally, the role of economic factors and José's living conditions cannot be ignored in addressing his situation.

José was fortunate in that he was able to receive treatment at a clinic for illegal aliens. He was treated with antidepressant medication and cognitive psychotherapy. Because any thought of sexual side effects was disturbing to him, the prescribing doctor prescribed Wellbutrin/bupropion (an antidepressant not associated with sexual side effects). This also helped him feel "heard" in the session. His bilingual therapist helped him weigh the benefits and risks of staying in the country illegally as well as find resources that were accessible to him through charitable organizations and food banks. Ideally, we would also recommend things like regular exercise (with a physician's approval), but for people in José's situation, this may not be realistic. At last contact, José had found migrant labor work and was still seeking ways to support his family. He did stay on the antidepressant medication for 8 months and seemed to benefit from the medicine, the therapy, and knowing what resources were available. José's therapist confirmed that José had many negative cognitive schemas that rendered him vulnerable to depression, and was able to encourage José in his religious faith as well as help him challenge irrationally negative conclusions. Although José was likely to be moving from place to place and possibly homeless for the near future, he did learn some skills in targeting negative thoughts and negative schemas that he could take with him. Clearly, though, José had a lot to be depressed about, and his case demonstrates the challenge of helping clients who are dealing with difficult social system dynamics.

An important cultural observation about José's case is that for him, the symptoms and diagnosis were "ego dystonic," meaning he did not see them as part of who he was—they were not a part of his identity. He grew up in Mexico, where depressive symptoms were viewed more as something to be denied or something you would seek help for through your religious practices (Beltran, 2005). Contrast that with an increasingly American phenomenon of making one's symptoms an identity of sorts. Since Elizabeth Wurtzel's (1994) *Prozac Nation*, more memoirs have been published discussing this issue (also see Sharpe, 2012). Recall the case of Ingrid, in which she called herself an "ambulatory depressive." This is the client using the label of the disorder as an identity—a practice we condemn in mental health professionals (e.g., "I have two depressives and a borderline today"). Even when the client refers to herself this way, it can be therapeutic to gently challenge the idea that the symptoms are the person. Of course, there are many degrees of this, and each therapist must tailor the intervention to the client.

## General Treatment Summary

Even for Major Depressive Disorder the treatment recommendations span a spectrum, including electroconvulsive therapy (ECT), repetitive Transcranial Magnetic Stimulation (rTMS), antidepressant medication, cognitive-behavior therapy, behavior therapy, interpersonal therapy, psychodynamic therapy, and marital therapy. Typically, the more severe the depression, the more likely an intrusive intervention such as medication, rTMS, or ECT will be used. For the purposes of summarizing the spectrum of treatments available, we will group them in headings similar to those used in the etiology section: body, mind, and spirit.

## Body-Based Interventions for Depression

Body-based interventions—those focusing on the physical body—include antidepressant therapy, electroconvulsive therapy, and newer interventions such as vagus nerve stimulation (O'Reardon, Cristanch, & Peshek, 2006), as discussed in the following sections.

**ANTIDEPRESSANT THERAPY** Antidepressants have been a mainstay of treatment for depression of various kinds for approximately 50 years. Although the number and kinds of antidepressants have increased exponentially, without exception, the clinical trial efficacy for all types is reported to be around 70%. Simply put, approximately 70% of clients taking antidepressants in clinical trials were thought to experience some statistically significant reduction in depressive symptoms. However, this 70% statistic can be misleading. For example, approximately 40% of subjects in some trials experience only moderate relief and may still meet the criteria for Major Depressive Disorder. In addition, it is now clear that many trials in which the antidepressant effects are no better than those of the placebo never get published, and so the 70% figure is inflated. Meta-analyses of studies on antidepressants in the Food and Drug Administration (FDA) database demonstrated that *in over 50% of the trials, investigators found no significant difference between placebo and the antidepressant* (Berton & Nestler, 2006; Khan, Leventhal, Khan, & Brown, 2002). As early as 1995 (Antonuccio, Danton, & DeNelsky, 1995) we had evidence that for some clients medication and therapy and sometimes therapy alone were better than antidepressant medication alone.

Certainly antidepressants can be very helpful to clients, but all come with side effects and many medications stop working if a client is on them for extended lengths of time. Some antidepressants have a tolerance and withdrawal syndrome associated with them, and clients must be titrated off the medications by a physician to avoid the withdrawal (referred to as "discontinuation syndrome").[34] Antidepressants play a life-saving role for some clients in the short term, but they are best used in conjunction with counseling or psychotherapy. It is best to gauge the severity of the depression, the client's preference, and the risk of harm to self or others prior to making a referral for medication.

**ELECTROCONVULSIVE THERAPY** Although many people have unrealistic images of electroconvulsive therapy (ECT) from films and television, it is still in use and shows efficacy for severe and treatment-resistant depression (Kellner et al., 2006). Some studies suggest ECT has better efficacy than antidepressant medication (Pagnin, de Queiroz, Pini, & Cassano, 2004) while others suggest the efficacy is about the same (Guillen, Abad, Hernandez de Pablo, & Moreno, 2004). ECT has a good response rate in treatment even though laypersons still regard it negatively and we are unclear about how it works. In this treatment electrical current is introduced into the brain via electrodes placed on the temples. Whereas earlier uses of the treatment were bilateral (one electrode on either side of the head), currently unilateral is the preferred method. The electrical current induces a seizure for approximately 25 seconds, although there is no standard minimum length of time for the seizure (Rasimas, Stevens, & Rasmussen, 2007). The procedure is done anywhere from 4 to 10 times over a period that varies by client (Charlson et al., 2004). Although this type of therapy shows efficacy, the relapse rates appear to be similar to those of other types of treatment, and antidepressant medication may still be used immediately following ECT. Due to the high relapse rate in both patients treated with ECT and those treated with medication, better means of relapse prevention are still required.[35] It should be noted that the efficacy of ECT has been challenged by Ross (2006), who reviewed "sham" ECT procedures where patients were put under anesthesia but not given ECT. Those in the sham conditions (in Ross's review) did as well as those who actually got the ECT.

**NEWER BODY-BASED INTERVENTIONS** Repetitive transcranial magnetic stimulation (rTMS) and vagus nerve stimulation (VNS) are two of the newest body-based treatments for depression. In rTMS, weak electrical currents are induced in brain tissue by electromagnetic induction. Although the actual mechanisms of action remain unclear, current theory holds that rTMS works by magnetic pulses causing excitation of neurons (Fleischmann et al., 1995). This method is less invasive than ECT and in that sense could be an improvement although further research is needed. rTMS does not require that the client be sedated or under anesthesia. The magnetic pulses pass unimpeded through the skull and brain to produce depolarization[36] in the cortex. This

---

[34] Symptoms of discontinuation syndrome can include a rebound of depression and anxiety as well as flu-like symptoms and in some cases a strange sensation in the skull that some liken to an "electric" jolt (Sharpe, 2012).

[35] We recommend a short "TEDtalk" by Sherwin Nuland who shares his own experience with ECT at http://www.ted.com/talks/sherwin_nuland_on_electroshock_therapy.html.

[36] Recall from Chapter 2 that the brain uses electrical and chemical signals, and depolarization is the equivalent of increasing the probability that a neuron will fire.

depolarization appears to alter excitability in the dorsolateral prefrontal cortex in the brain. The mood-enhancing properties were discovered as a side effect of using the treatment for patients suffering from Parkinson's disease. No treatment is without side effects, though, and rTMS side effects include headache, mood and cognitive effects, scalp pain and burns, temporary auditory threshold shifts, and in some cases seizures. Initial studies show rTMS to be a promising treatment for depression (Baekan et al., 2006; Hu, Gu, Wang, & Shi, 2011; Zanardini et al., 2006).

Vagus nerve stimulation (VNS) is thought to work by enhancing the excitability of the anterior cingulate, the subgenual cingulate, and the amygdale in the brain. This is an invasive procedure that involves implanting a neurostimulator in the neck that sends impulses to the left vagus nerve.[37] Research is being done on transcutaneous devices that will not require surgical insertion and its accompanying possible risk to the vagus nerve and the surrounding tissue. The vagus nerve is the 10th of 12 paired cranial nerves and begins in the brainstem and reaches to the chest and abdomen. The mechanism of action of VNS is unclear but appears to be related to two brain structures: the median dorsal raphe nucleus and the locus coeruleus. The former is serotonergic and the latter noradrenergic, and both of these neurotransmitter systems are believed to be implicated in depression. Common side effects of VNS include voice alterations, neck pain, coughing, and labored breathing (dyspnoea). Although this is a drastic measure, it accentuates how severe untreated depression can be for the client who becomes suicidal. Both rTMS and VNS are quite new, and more research is necessary to compare their efficacy with that of antidepressant treatment and ECT.

## Psychotherapeutic Interventions for Depression

From an Integral perspective, understanding the "hotspots" for each client should guide the clinician in the choice of psychotherapy. Also, it is common for many clients to be taking antidepressant medication at least for the first 6 months of psychotherapy. This can provide a chemical window of opportunity for the client to *accommodate* new ways of *translating* life in the therapeutic process.

Many varieties of cognitive therapies have shown efficacy for depression, including cognitive therapy (Beck, 1983) dialectical behavior therapy (DBT) (Chapman, 2006) and mindfulness-based cognitive-behavior therapy (CBT) (Baer, 2003). Because CBT (including mindfulness-based CBT) is so effective in the treatment of depression, many clinicians start with one of these approaches. If the client evidences negative schemas and/or signs of vulnerability to depression, CBT can be a good starting point for therapy (Haaga et al., 1991).

In many cases, exploration of negative schemas leads to histories of abuse, neglect, or abandonment in childhood. These in turn may have resulted in an unhealthy attachment and/or anaclitic or introjective styles of depression. Although there are many approaches to psychodynamic therapy, the basis is helping clients make objects of awareness of aspects of themselves or their lives that they have pushed out of awareness because they were painful or threatening. Consistently making painful aspects of ourselves or our lives objects of awareness frees up the energy we would

[37] There are two vagus nerves in your body, and they are 2 of 12 paired cranial nerves that extend from the brain to the abdomen.

otherwise devote to repressing them. This energy can then be used in pursuit of a more satisfying life. One newer development called mindfulness-based training can help clients make painful memories objects of awareness without being debilitated by pain.

Mindfulness is a technique used in both Eastern and Western spiritual practices. As noted in Chapter 1, mindfulness is watching your thoughts and feelings arise in the field of awareness, not judging or attaching to any one of them in particular, but just noting how they come and go. Kabat-Zinn's (2003) initial work applying mindfulness with patients was in the area of chronic pain, and his latest work is in applying it to the treatment of depression. This latter work is as close to an Integral approach as can be found in the literature on depression. In it, the authors provide a summary of how mind, body, and emotions work together in depressive states and how mindfulness can be used to disrupt depressive symptoms by making them objects of awareness (Kabat-Zinn, Lipworth, & Burney, 1985). The application of mindfulness to depression and other disorders is one of the most powerful contributions of a spiritual lineage to psychological science.

## Integrally Informed Treatment of Depression

As noted in Chapter 1, using the entire Integral model[38] can be helpful in guiding treatment of all disorders. In addition to using the quadrants for checking "hotspots," the quadrants reflect four areas of the client that can be part of the treatment. Recall that the upper quadrants reflect the subjective states of the client (upper left) and the behavioral and physiological aspects of the client (upper right). The subjective states the client experiences (upper-left quadrant) reflect the client's ongoing psychological experience. We aim to help the client become more familiar with his or her mind, thoughts, and feelings to the degree that even depressive states can be tolerated and effectively worked through. In the upper-right quadrant, we focus on the client's body, including making sure the client knows how to support wellness with proper diet and exercise. After getting a physician's clearance for physical activity, it can be helpful to have a physical trainer on your treatment team who can help the client develop and benefit from an exercise program because exercise, like antidepressants, increases levels of brain-derived neurotrophic factor thought to be so critical for neurons (Russo-Neustadt, Beard, & Cotman, 1999).

The two lower quadrants reflect culture and shared values as well as social institutions the client is impacted by. The lower-left quadrant, among other things, reflects the client's interpersonal health and if the client "hotspot" is in this area, interpersonal psychotherapy may be the best treatment option. Allowing relationship issues to be part of the therapeutic work may be important for some clients. Finally the lower-right quadrant tells us how the client is situated in society. Which institutions are sources of strength for the client? Which institutions are sources of stress? What is the client's socioeconomic status? In addition to the quadrants, assessing the client's level of ego development can be helpful. Ego identity is a robust construct and can guide us in what the client values and how to language our interventions (meaning how to use

[38] The entire model is the four quadrants that reflect the four aspects of the client's being, lines and levels of development, states of consciousness, and types with regard to personality.

language in a way that resonates with the client's sense of self). Finally, teaching the client to monitor states of consciousness is part of relapse prevention (as well as mindfulness training if that is appropriate).

### Treatment at the Outer Limits: Existential and Spiritual Approaches

As noted, existential treatment can be done at most developmental levels because we all face the givens of existence. We find it particularly useful with clients who do not appear to have pervasive biological variables (e.g., mood fluctuations around the menstrual cycle or multiple vegetative symptoms) to assess (formally or informally) the client's cognitive skill set as well as his or her level of ego development. Late-stage ego development brings with it an ability to take multiple perspectives but not necessarily metabolize what those perspectives reveal about suffering and life in general. This can lead to existential crises that include depression as one of the symptoms. Existential therapy can be creatively blended with cognitive therapy to address many of the problems that arise for people at later stages of ego identity. Finally, existential therapies for depression have also been developed to bring the family into treatment as well as the identified client. This offers the advantage of situating the client in session in the context of the existential givens of family.

We have seen that mind-based therapies use techniques from spiritual traditions, but what of spiritual traditions themselves? Have they been effective in helping clients recover from depression? There are few studies to cite, and the question remains open. It does appear, however, that although spiritual practices have positive psychological benefits and psychological therapy may have spiritual benefits, the two are different realms and sometimes individuals need therapy, and sometimes they need their spiritual practice. One interesting approach discussed by Arife Hammerle (2005) is a Sufi[39] treatment of depression. The treatment aims to help align the client with a unified sense of connection to humanity. As Hammerle (2005) states, "The healing dimension in all religions is an effort to increase the capacity to see our selves as belonging to the whole existence as a form of unity . . ." (p. 259). Although there are no peer-reviewed studies on this treatment, it is a pioneering conceptual effort that may bear fruit in years to come.

## Summary

Why do people get depressed? As we hope you have seen, there is no one answer to this question. The real value of the question is what it has taught us about the large number of variables that can underlay depressive symptoms, how these variables may influence each other, and how the variables teach us to intervene in a number of ways to ease the suffering of our clients. As one of the most overdetermined symptom sets, depression reflects the complexity of human beings. Please remember: reality is complex and complexity is our friend. The more familiar we become with the complexity of depression, the more we have to offer clients in the form of effective treatment.

[39] Sufism is a mystical sect of Islam. Sufis are not recognized by many mainstream Muslims but have made powerful contributions to transformational practices.

## Review Questions

1. Assume a client comes to you saying that her doctor told her she was depressed because she had a chemical imbalance. How would you respond based on the latest research on depression?
2. Describe the relationship between the amine theory of depression, downregulation, cyclic AMP and brain-derived neurotrophic factor.
3. What is the basis for anaclitic and introjective styles of depression? How do the styles of each manifest in the experience of the client?
4. What is the cognitive vulnerability theory of depression, and how does it relate to unhealthy attachment?
5. Describe the aim of mindfulness-based cognitive therapy for the treatment of depression.
6. What do you view as the benefits and drawbacks of clinicians having a fully informed body–mind–spirit understanding of variables that may underlay depression?
7. What spiritual techniques could be useful in the treatment of depression?

## References


Abramson, L. Y., Metalsky, G. I., & Alloy, L. B. (1989). Hopelessness depression: A theory-based subtype of depression. *Psychological Review, 96,* 358–372.

Abramson, L. Y., Seligman, M. E. P., & Teasdale, J. D. (1978). Learned helplessness in humans: Critique and reformulation. *Journal of Abnormal Psychology, 87,* 49–74.

Adlard, P. A., & Cotman, C. W. (2004). Voluntary exercise protects against stress-induced decreases in brain-derived neurotrophic factor protein. *Neuroscience, 124,* 985–992.

Alloy, L. B., Abramson, L. Y., Hogan, M. E., Whitehouse, W. G., Rose, D. T., Robinson, M. S., Kim, R. S., & Lapkin, J. B. (2000). The Temple-Wisconsin cognitive vulnerability to depression project: Lifetime history of axis-I psychopathology in individuals at high and low cognitive risk for depression. *Journal of Abnormal Psychology, 109,* 403–418.

Alloy, L. B., Abramson, L. Y., Smith, J. M., Gibb, B. E., & Neeren, A. M. (2006). Role of parenting and maltreatment histories in unipolar and bipolar mood disorders: Mediation by cognitive vulnerability to depression. *Clinical Child and Family Psychology Review, 9,* 23–64.

American Psychiatric Association. (2000a). *Diagnostic and statistical manual of mental disorders* (4th ed., text revision). Washington, DC: Author.

American Psychiatric Association. (2000b). *Practice guidelines for the treatment of psychiatric disorders.* Washington, DC: Author.

American Psychiatric Association. (2013). *Diagnostic and statistical manual of mental disorders* (5th ed.). Washington, DC: Author.

Anderson, G., Maes, M., & Berk, M. (2012). Biological underpinnings of the commonalities in depression, somatization, and Chronic Fatigue Syndrome. *Medical Hypotheses, 78,* 752–756.

Anderson, G., Berk, M., Moylan, S., & Maes, M. (2014). Role of immune-inflammatory oxidative and nitrosative stress pathways in the etiology of depression: Therapeutic implications. *CNS Drugs, 28,* 1–10.

Anisman, H. (2011). Inflaming depression [Editorial]. *Journal of Psychiatry and Neuroscience, 36,* 291–295.

Antonuccio, D. O., Danton, W. G., & DeNelsky, G. Y. (1995). Psychotherapy versus medication for depression: Challenging the conventional wisdom with data. *Professional Psychology: Research and Practice, 26,* 574–585.

Arieti, S., & Bemporad, J. (1980). The psychological organization of depression. *American Journal of Psychiatry, 137,* 1360–1365.

Ashton, C. H., & Moore, P. B. (2011). Endocannabinoid system dysfunction in mood and related disorders. *Acta Psychiatrica Scandinavica, 124,* 250–261.

Assagioli, R. (1975). *Psychosynthesis: A manual of principles and techniques.* London: Turnstone.

Baekan, C., De Raedt, R., Van Hore, C., Clerinx, P., De Mey, J., & Bussuyt, A. (2006). HF-rTMS treatment in medication-resistant melancholic depression: Results from FDG-PET brain imaging. *CNS Spectrum, 14,* 439–448.

Baer, R. A. (2003). Mindfulness training as a clinical intervention: A conceptual and empirical review. *Clinical Psychology: Science and Practice, 10,* 125–143.

Beck, A. T. (1983). Cognitive therapy of depression: New perspectives. In P. J. Clayton & J. E. Barrett (Eds.), *Treatment of depression: Old controversies and new approaches* (pp. 265–284). New York: Raven.

Beck, A. T. (1987). Cognitive models of depression. *Journal of Cognitive Psychotherapy: An International Quarterly, 1,* 5–37.

Beck, A. T., Steer, R. A., & Brown, G. K. (1996). *Beck depression inventory, 2nd edition manual.* San Antonio, TX: The Psychological Corporation.

Beevers, C. G. (2005). Cognitive vulnerability to depression: A dual-process model. *Clinical Psychology Review, 25,* 975–1002.

Beltran, I. S. (2005). The relation of culture to differences in depressive symptoms and coping strategies: Mexican-American and European-American college students. Doctoral Dissertation, University of Texas at Austin.

Berton, O., & Nestler, E. J. (2006). New approaches to antidepressant drug discovery: Beyond monoamines. *Nature Reviews Neuroscience, 7,* 137–153.

Blatt, J. S., & Shahar, G. (2005). A dialectic model of personality development and psychopathology: Recent contributions to understanding and treating depression. In J. Corveleyn, P. Luyten, & S. J. Blatt (Eds.), *The theory and treatment of depression: Towards a dynamic interactionism model* (pp. 137–162). Mahwah, NJ: Erlbaum.

Blatt, S. J., & Zuroff, D. C. (1992). Interpersonal relatedness and self-definition: Two prototypes for depression. *Clinical Psychology Review, 12,* 527–562.

Bloch, M., Rotenberg, N., Koren, D., & Klein, E. (2005). Risk factors associated with the development of postpartum mood disorders. *Journal of Affective Disorders, 88,* 9–18.

Bowlby, J. (1977). The making and breaking of affectional bonds: Aetiology and psychopathology in the light of attachment theory. *British Journal of Psychiatry, 120,* 201–210.

Brown, G. W. (1998). Genetic and population perspective on life events and depression. *Social Psychiatry and Psychiatric Epidemiology, 33,* 363–372.

Chapman, A. L. (2006). Dialectical behavior therapy: Current indications and unique elements. *Psychiatry, 9,* 62–68.

Charlson, R., Siskind, D., Doi, S. A., McCallum, E., Broome, A., & Lie, D. C. (2004). ECT efficacy and treatment course: A systematic review and meta-analysis of twice vs. thrice weekly schedules. *Journal of Affective Disorders, 138,* 1–8.

Charney, D. S. (2004). Life stress, genes, and depression: multiple pathways lead to increased risk and new opportunities for intervention. *Science's STKE: Signal, Transduction Knowledge Environement, 225,* re5.

Cicchetti, D., & Rogosch, F. A. (2002). A developmental psychopathology perspective on adolescence. *Journal of Consulting and Clinical Psychology, 70,* 6–20.

Cole, D. A., Jacquez, F. M., & Maschman, T. L. (2001). Social origins of depressive cognitions: A longitudinal study of self-perceived competence in children. *Cognitive Therapy and Research, 25,* 377–395.

Coogan, A. N., & Thome, J. (2012). Special issue: Circadian rhythms, clock genes, and neuropsychiatry: Interesting times. *Journal of Neural Transmission, 119,* 1059–1060.

Cook-Greuter, S. R., & Soulen, J. (2007). The developmental perspective in integral counseling. *Counseling & Values, 51,* 180–192.

Coyne, J. C. (1976). Toward an interpersonal description of depression. *Psychiatry, 39,* 29–40.

Coyne, J. C. (1999). Thinking interactionally about depression: A radical restatement. In T. Joiner and J. C. Coyne (Eds.), *The interactional nature of depression* (pp. 365–392). Washington, DC: American Psychological Association.

Dein, S. (2006). Religion, spirituality and depression: Implications for research and treatment. *Primary Care and Community Psychiatry, 11,* 67–72.

Dow, M. G., & Craighead, W. E. (1987). Social inadequacy and depression: Overt behavioral and self-evaluation processes. *Journal of Social and Clinical Psychology, 5,* 99–113.

Duman, R. S., Heninger, G. R., & Nestler, E. J. (1997). A molecular and cellular theory of depression. *Archives of General Psychiatry, 54,* 597–608.

Dwivedi, Y., Rizavi, H. S., & Pandey, G. N. (2006). Antidepressants reverse corticosterone-mediated decrease in brain-derived neurotrophic factor expression: Differential regulation of specific exons by antidepressants and corticosterone. *Neuroscience, 139,* 1017–1029.

Engel, J. (2008). *American therapy: The rise of psychotherapy in the United States.* New York: Gotham.

Enggassar, J. L., & Young, M. A. (2007). Cognitive vulnerability to depression in seasonal affective disorder: Predicting mood and cognitive symptoms in individuals with seasonal vegetative changes. *Cognitive Therapy Research, 31,* 3–21.

Erickson, K. I., Miller, D. L., & Roecklein, K. A. (2012). The aging hippocampus: Interactions between exercise, depression and BDNF. *The Neuroscientist, 18,* 82–97.

Erikson, E. H. (1950). *Childhood and society* (2nd ed.). New York: Norton.

Fleischmann, A., Prolov, K., Abarbanel, J., & Belmaker, R. H. (1995). The effect of transcranial magnetic stimulation of rat brain on behavioral models of depression. *Brain Research, 699,* 130–132.

Frances, A. (2013). *Saving normal: An insider's revolt against out-of-control psychiatric diagnosis, DSM-5, big pharma, and the medicalization of ordinary life.* New York: Morrow.

Futterman, L. A., & Rapkin, A. J. (2006). Diagnosis of premenstrual disorders. *Journal of Reproductive Medicine, 51*(Suppl.), 349–358.

Garber, J. (2006). Depression in children and adolescents: Linking risk research and prevention. *American Journal of Preventive Medicine, 31*(Suppl. 1), s99–s103.

Gibb, B. E., Alloy, L. E., Abramson, L. Y., Beevers, C. G., & Miller, I. W. (2004). Cognitive vulnerability to depression: A taxonomic analysis. *Journal of Abnormal Psychology, 113,* 81–89.

Goldberg, D. (2001). Vulnerability factors for common mental illnesses. *British Journal of Psychiatry, 178*(Suppl.), s69–s71.

Goodwin, M., New, A. S., Triebwasser, J., Collins, K. A., & Siever, L. (2010). Phenotype, endophenotype and genotype comparisons between Borderline Personality Disorder and Major Depressive Disorder. *Journal of Personality Disorder, 21,* 38–59.

Gracely, R. H., Ceko, M., & Bushnell, M. C. (2011). Fibromyalgia and depression. *Pain Research and Treatment, 2012,* 486–490.

Guillen, J. M. B., Abad, C. S., Hernandez, de Pablo, M. E., & Moreno, S. P. (2004). Efficacy of electroconvulsive therapy: A systematic review of scientific evidence. *Actas Esp Psiquiatr, 32,* 153–165.

Haaga, D. A., Dyck, M. J., & Ernst, D. (1991). Empirical status of cognitive theory of depression. *Psychological Bulletin, 110,* 215–236.

Hammerle, A. E. (2005). Journey into the heart: Sufi ways for healing depression. In S. G. Mijares & G. S. Khalsa (Eds.), *The psychospiritual clinician's handbook: Alternative methods for understanding and treating mental disorders* (pp. 259–281). Binghamton, NY: Haworth.

Hegarty, K. L. (2011). The relationship between abuse and depression. *The Nursing Clinics of North America, 46,* 437–444.

Henn, F. A., & Vollmayr, B. (2004). Neurogenesis and depression: Etiology or epiphenomenon? *Biological Psychiatry, 56,* 146–150.

Horney, K. (1940). *Our inner conflicts: A constructive theory of neurosis.* Lund: Humphries.

Hu, M. L., Gu, Z. T., Wang, X. Y., & Shi, H. P. (2011). Treatment of depression using sleep electroencephalogram modulated repetitive transcranial magnetic stimulation. *Chinese Medical Journal, 124,* 1779–1883.

Ingersoll, R. E. (2000). Gentle like the dawn: A dying woman's healing. *Counseling and Values, 44,* 129–134.

Ingersoll, R. E., & Rak, C. F. (2006). *Psychopharmacology for helping professionals: An integral exploration.* Pacific Grove, CA: Brooks Cole.

Ingram, R. E., & Ritter, J. (2000). Vulnerability to depression: Cognitive reacitvity and parental bonding in high-risk individuals. *Journal of Abnormal Psychology, 109,* 588–596.

Joiner, T. E., Steer, R. A., Abramson, L. Y., Alloy, L. B., Metalsky, G. I., & Schmidt, M. B. (2001). Hopelessness depression as a distinct dimension of depressive symptoms among clinical and nonclinical samples. *Behaviour Research and Therapy, 39,* 523–536.

Jovanovic, H., Cerin, A., Karlsson, P., Jundberg, J., Halldin, C., & Nordstrom, A-L. (2006). A PET study of 5-HT1A receptors at different phases of the menstrual cycle in women with premenstrual dysphoria. *Psychiatry Research, 148,* 185–193.

Kabat-Zinn, J. (2003). Mindfulness based interventions in context: Past, present, and future. *Clinical Psychology Science and Practice, 10,* 144–156.

Kabat-Zinn, J., Lipworth, L., & Burney, R. (1985). The clinical use of mindfulness meditation for the self-regulation of chronic pain. *Journal of Behavioral Medicine, 8,* 163–190.

Kamata, M., Suzuki, A., Yoshida, K., Takahashi, H., Higuich, H., & Otani, K. (2011). Genetic polymorphisms in the serotonergic system and symptom clusters of major depressive disorder. *Journal of Affective Disorders, 135,* 374–376.

Kandel, E. (2006). *In search of memory: The emergence of a new science of mind.* New York: Norton.

Kaufmann, W. (1974). *Nietzsche: Philosopher, psychologist, antichrist* (4th ed., p. 156). Princeton, NJ: Princeton University Press.

Kellner, C. H., Knapp, R. G., Petrides, G., Rummans, T., A., Husain, M. M., Rasmussen, K., . . . Fink, M. (2006). Continuation electroconvulsive therapy versus pharmacotherapy for relapse prevention in major depression. *Archives of General Psychiatry, 63,* 1337–1344.

Kemker, S. S., & Khadivi, A. (1995). Psychiatric education: Learning by assumption. In C. A. Ross & A. Pam (Eds.), *Pseudoscience in biological psychiatry* (pp. 241–254). New York: Wiley.

Khan, A., Leventhal, R. M., Khan, S. R., & Brown, W. A. (2002). Severity of depression and response to antidepressants and placebo: An analysis of the Food and Drug Administration database. *Journal of Clinical Psychopharmacology, 22,* 40–45.

Kistner, J. (2006). Children's peer acceptance, perceived acceptance, and risk for depression. In T. E. Joiner, J. S. Brown, & J. Kistner (Eds.), *The interpersonal, cognitive, and social nature of depression* (pp. 1–22).

Klein, M. (1957). *Envy and gratitude and other works.* London: Hogarth.

Lee, B. H., Kim, H., Park, S. H., & Kim, Y. K. (2007). Decreased plasma BDNF level in depressive patients. *Journal of Affective Disorders, 101,* 239–244.

Lewinsohn, P. M., Weinstein, M. S., & Shaw, D. A. (1969). Depression: A clinical research approach. In R. D. Rubin & C. M. Franks (Eds.), *Advances in behavior therapy* (pp. 231–240). New York: Academic Press.

Licinio, J., & Wong, M. L. (2002). Brain-derived neurotrophic factor in stress and affective disorders. *Molecular Psychiatry, 7,* 519.

Lilly, J. (1981). *The deep self: Consciousness exploration in the isolation tank.* New York: Warner.

Lipsman, N., & Lozano, A. M. (2011). The most cited works in major depress: The "Citation classics." *Journal of Affective Disorders, 134,* 39–44.

Loevinger, J., & Wessler, R. (1978). *Measuring ego development 1: Construction and use of a sentence completion test.* San Francisco: Jossey-Bass.

Ma, T. M., Abazyan, S., Abazyan, B., Nomura, J., Yang, C., Seshadri, S., . . . Pletnikov, M. V. (2012). Pathogenic disruption of DISC1-serine racemase binding elicits schizophrenia-like behavior via D-serine depletion. *Molecular Psychiatry, 18,* 557–567.

MacQueen, G., & Chokka, P. (2004). Special issues in the management of depression in women. *The Canadian Journal of Psychiatry, 49, Suppl. 1,* 27s–40s.

Maddox, B. (2003). *The dark lady of DNA.* New York: Harper.

Malberg, J. E., & Blendy, J. A. (2005). Antidepressant action: To the nucleus and beyond. *Trends in Pharmacological Sciences, 26,* 631–638.

Mascarao, N., & Rosen, D. H. (2006). The role of existential meaning as a buffer against stress. *Journal of Humanistic Psychology, 46,* 168–190.

Mascarao, N., & Rosen, D. H. (2008). Assessment of existential meaning and its longitudinal relations with depressive symptoms. *Journal of Social and Clinical Psychology, 27,* 576–599.

Mathew, S. J., Shah, A., Lapidus, K., Clark, C., Jarun, N., Ostermeyer, B., & Murrough, J. W. (2012). Ketamine for treatment-resistant unipolar depression. *CNS Drugs, 26,* 189–204.

McCarthy, D. J., Alexander, R., Smith, M. A., Pathak, S., Kanes, S., Lee, Chi-Ming, & Sanacora, G. (2012). Glutamate-based depression GBD. *Medical Hypotheses, 78,* 675–681.

McCranie, E. W., & Bass, J. D. (1984). Childhood family antecedents of dependency and self-criticism: Implications for depression. *Journal of Abnormal Psychology, 93,* 3–8.

Meurs, P., Vliegen, N., & Cluckers, G. (2005). Closed doors and landscapes in the mist 2: Depression in psychoanalytic developmental psychopathology: From single track models to complex developmental pathways. In J. Corveleyn, P. Luyten, & S. J. Blatt (Eds.), *The theory and treatment of depression: Towards a dynamic interactionism model* (pp. 189–226). Mahwah, NJ: Erlbaum.

Michielson, H. J., Van Houdenhove, B., Leirs, I., Vandenbroeck, A., & Onghena, P. (2006). Depression, attribution style and self-esteem in chronic fatigue syndrome and fibromyalgia patients: is there a link? *Clinical Rheumatology, 25*(2), 183–188.

Milton, J. (1969). *Paradise lost* (p. 25). Garden City, NY: International Collectors Library.

Mitchell, S. (1979). *Into the whirlwind: A translation of the book of Job.* New York: Doubleday.

Murray, L., Woolgar, M., Cooper, P., & Hipwell, A. (2001). Cognitive vulnerability to depression in 5-year-old children of depressed mothers. *Journal of Child Psychology and Psychiatry, 42,* 891–899.

Nietzsche, F. (1999). *The antichrist* (p. 77). Translated by H. L. Mencken. Tucson, AZ: See Sharp Press.

Nolan, J. A. (2006). Religious participation effects on mental and physical health. Unpublished doctoral dissertation, Cornell University.

O'Reardon, J. P., Cristanch, P., & Peshek, A. D. (2006). Vagus nerve stimulation and the treatment of depression: To the brain stem to beyond. *Psychiatry, 3,* 54–62.

Pagnin, D., de Queirox, V., Pini, S., & Cassano, G. B. (2004). Efficacy of ECT in depression: A meta-analytic review. *The Journal of ECT, 20,* 13–20.

Rapkin, A. J., & Mikacich, J. A. (2006). Premenstrual syndrome in adolescents: Diagnosis and treatment. *Pediatric Endocrinology Reviews: PER, 3,* 132–137.

Rasimas, J. J., Stevens, S. R., & Rasmussen, K. G. (2007). Seizure length in electroconvulsive therapy as a function of age, sex, and treatment number. *Journal of ECT, 23,* 14–16.

Reis, S., & Grenyar, B. F. S. (2002). Pathways to anaclitic and introjective depression. *Psychology and Psychotherapy: Research and Practice, 75,* 445–459.

Rose, D. T., & Abramson, L. Y. (1992). Developmental predictors of depressive cognitive style: Research and theory. In D. Cicchetti & S. L. Toth (Eds.), *Developmental perspectives on depression* (pp. 323–350). Rochester, NY: University of Rochester Press.

Rosenthal, N. E. (2009). Issues for DSM-5: Seasonal Affective Disorder and Seasonality. *American Journal of Psychiatry, 166,* 10–11.

Ross, C. A. (2006). The Sham ECT literature. In *Ethical Human Psychology and Psychiatry* (vol. 8, 17–28).

Rossi, E. L. (2002). *The psychobiology of gene expression: Neuroscience and neurogenesis in hypnosis and the healing arts.* New York: Norton.

Russo-Neustadt, A., Beard, R. C., & Cotman, C. W. (1999). Exercise, antidepressant medications, and enhanced brain derived neurotrophic factor expression. *Neuropsychopharmacology, 21,* 679–682.

Sahay, A., & Hen, R. (2007). Adult hippocampal neurogenesis in depression. *Nature Neuroscience, 10,* 1110–1115.

Scaccianoce, S., Del Bianco, P., Paolone, G., Caprioli, D., Modafferi, A. M., Nencini, P., & Badiani, A. (2006). Social isolation selectively reduces hippocampal brain-derived neurotrophic factor without altering plasma corticosterone. *Behavior Brain Research, 168,* 323–325.

Schwartz, G. W., Fair, P. L., Salt, P., Mandel, M. R., & Klerman, G. L. (1976a, 1976b). Facial expression and imagery in depression: An electromyographic study. *Psychosomatic Medicine, 38,* 337–347.

Seligman, M. (1975). *Learned helplessness: On depression, development and death.* San Francisco: Freeman.

Seligman, M. E. P., & Maier, S. F. (1967). Failure to escape traumatic shock. *Journal of Experimental Psychology, 74,* 1–9.

Sharp, T. (2013). Cellular and molecular mechanisms of antidepressant action. *Current Topics in Behavioral Neurosciences, 14,* 309–325.

Sharpe, K. (2012). *Coming of age on Zoloft: How antidepressants cheered us up, let us down, and changed who we are.* New York: Harper.

Singer, A. R., & Dobson, K. S. (2007). An experimental investigation of cognitive vulnerability to depression. *Behaviour Research and Therapy, 45,* 563–575.

Skolnick, P. (2012). Antidepressants for the new millennium. *European Journal of Pharmacology, 375,* 31–40.

Spangler, D. L., Simons, A. D., Monroe, S. M., & Thase, M. E. (1993). Evaluating the hopelessness model of depression: Diathesis-stress and symptom components. *Journal of Abnormal Psychology, 102,* 592–600.

Stahl, S., & Briley, M. (2004). Understanding pain in depression. *Human Psychopharmacology, 19, Suppl 1,* S9–S13.

Steele, J. D., Currie, J., Lawrie, S. M., & Reid, I. (2007). Prefrontal cortical functional abnormality in major depressive disorder: a stereotactic meta-analysis. *Journal of Affective Disorders, 10,* 1–11.

Tolman, E. C. (1948). Cognitive maps in rats and men. *The Psychological Review, 55,* 189–208.

Vigod, S. N., & Taylor, V. H. (2013). The psychodynamic psychotherapist's guide to the interaction among sex, genes, and environmental adversity in the etiology of depression for women. *Psychodynamic Psychiatry, 41,* 541–552.

Westgate, C. E. (1996). Spiritual wellness and depression. *Journal of Counseling and Development, 75,* 26–35.

Whisman, M. A., & Kwon, P. (1992). Parental representations, cognitive distortions, and mild depression. *Cognitive Therapy and Research, 16,* 557–568.

Wilber, K. (2006). *Integral spirituality: A startling new role for religion in the modern and postmodern world.* Boston: Shambhala.

Wolkowitz, et al. (2011). Serum BDNF levels before treatment predict SSRI response in depression. *Progress in Neuro-Psychopharmacology & Biological Psychiatry, 35,* 1623–1630.

Wurtzel, E. (1994). *Prozac nation: Young and depressed in America; A memoir.* Boston: Houghton Mifflin.

Yalom, I. (1980). *Existential psychotherapy.* New York: Basic.

Young, J. E., Klosko, J. S., & Wieshaar, M. E. (2003). *Schema therapy: A practitioner's guide.* New York: Guilford.

Young, J. S. (2005). Reduction in depression through participation in selected spiritual discipline. Unpublished doctoral dissertation, Oral Roberts University.

Young, M. A., Watel, L. G., Lahmeyer, H. W., & Eastman, C. I. (1991). The temporal onset of individual symptoms in winter depression: Differentiating underlying mechanisms. *Journal of Affective Disorders, 22,* 191–197.

Zanardini, R., Gazoli, A., Ventriglia, M., Perez, J., Bignotti, S., Rossini, P. M., Gennarelli, M., & Bocchio-Chiavetto, L. (2006). Effect of transcranial magnetic stimulation on serum brain-derived neurotrophic factor in drug resistant depressed patients. *Journal of Affective Disorder, 91,* 83–86.

# 4

# Anxiety Disorders

*"There is no question that the problem of anxiety is a nodal point at which the most various and important questions converge, a riddle whose solution would be bound to throw a flood of light on our whole mental existence."*

FREUD, INTRODUCTORY LECTURES ON PSYCHOANALYSIS[1]

*"I would say that learning to know anxiety is an adventure which every man [sic] has to affront if he would not go to perdition either by not having known anxiety or by sinking under it. He therefore who has learned rightly to be anxious has learned the most important thing."*

KIERKEGAARD, THE CONCEPT OF DREAD[2]

## INTRODUCTION

Many people—including many prominent psychologists (Barlow, 2004; Beck & Emery, 1985; Freud, 1926/1943; Gold, 1993), philosophers (Kierkegaard, 1957; Sartre, 1943/1993), and spiritual teachers (Almaas, 1996; Walsh, 1999)—consider anxiety a universal human experience, and a significant majority of clinical psychologists acknowledge that psychological development and what it fundamentally means to be human involves and even *requires* anxiety (Mahoney, 1991). Anxiety disorders are *the* most common of all mental health problems in the United States (Danton & Antonuccio, 1997).[3] Each year, millions of people seek professional help for anxiety-related problems. Considering the variety of anxiety-related disorders—which includes Generalized Anxiety Disorder (GAD), Specific Phobia, Social Anxiety Disorder, Panic Disorder, Agoraphobia, Separation Anxiety

---

[1] Cited in May, R. (1977). *The meaning of anxiety*. New York: W. W. Norton & Company, p. xxi.

[2] Cited in May, R. (1977). *The meaning of anxiety*. New York: W. W. Norton & Company, p. xxi.

[3] To cite one large epidemiological study (that is consistent with other similar studies), Swendsen and colleagues interviewed more than 8,000, randomly sampled noninstitutionalized Americans; anxiety disorders were the most prevalent of any class of disorders (cited in Barlow, 2004).

Disorder, Obsessive-Compulsive Disorder (OCD), Post-Traumatic Stress Disorder (PTSD), Acute Stress Disorder, Selective Mutism, Anxiety Disorder Due to Another Medical Condition, Substance/Medication-Induced Anxiety Disorder, Other Specified Anxiety Disorder, and Unspecified Anxiety Disorder—25–29% of all U.S. citizens will at some point in their lifetime meet diagnostic criteria for an anxiety-related disorder[4] (Mineka & Zinbarg, 2006; Preston, O'Neal, & Talaga, 2002).

The costs of anxiety—from mental health costs to lost productivity to decreased quality of living—are truly staggering. Different studies have estimated that nearly one-third of all mental health-care costs are accounted for by anxiety disorders (approximately $46 billion per year); mood disorders and schizophrenia, by way of comparison, accounted for $22 billion and $20 billion, respectively (DuPont et al., 1996; Rice & Miller, 1993). Moreover, the continued frantic pace of contemporary America is a sociocultural dynamic that only increases the likelihood that these high incidences will continue, if not increase. This is particularly alarming in light of the fact that the costs of health-care services for those with anxiety disorders is twice as great as they are for those without anxiety disorders, even if the latter have physical illnesses (Simon, Ormel, Von Korff, & Barlow, 1995). A significant feature of anxiety disorders is that, in contrast to Major Depressive Disorder, which tends to have episodes that remit at least temporarily regardless of whether treated or not (the average duration is 9 months), anxiety disorders tend to be more chronic and often persist in less severe forms even when "successfully" treated (Barlow, 2004; Keller et al., 1992). After summarizing dozens of studies, David Barlow, in his seminal *Anxiety and Its Disorders*, concludes with ". . . one overriding fact: Anxiety disorders represent the single largest mental health problem in the country" (Barlow, 2004, p. 22).

Anxiety is costly not only in terms of direct and indirect financial costs and the diminishment of a fulfilling life; severe anxiety can also be deadly—literally. The primary causes of death that are associated with anxiety disorders are cardiovascular disease, suicide, and excessive substance use. For example, in one study, the risk of dying from coronary heart disease was three times as great for men in the highest level category of phobic anxiety than for men with lower-level anxiety (Kawachi, Sparrow, Vokonas, & Weiss, 1994). Although most people naturally associate death by suicide with depression, some researchers have found the frequency of suicide to be equal among those with anxiety disorders and matched groups of people with depression (Coryell, Noyes, & House, 1986; Noyes, 1991). Numerous other researchers have discovered that the comorbidity of anxiety and substance use disorders is very high; different studies report that between 25% and 60% of clients with severe alcoholism also have an anxiety disorder (Barlow, 2004); and some of these researchers have suggested that the etiology of anxiety and substance use disorders may be linked (Swift & Mueller, 2001). It appears that many of these individuals are self-medicating. However, even after extensive analyses, it still is not clear to what extent the anxiety comes first, then

[4] In the *Diagnostic and Statistical Manual of Mental Disorders*, 4th Edition, Text Revision (DSM-IV-TR; American Psychiatric Association [APA], 2000), OCD, PTSD, and Acute Stress Disorder were categorized as Anxiety Disorders. In the DSM-5 (APA, 2013), OCD is listed under Obsessive-Compulsive and Related Disorders; PTSD and Acute Stress Disorder are listed under Trauma- and Stressor-Related Disorders, both of which are new chapters in the DSM. These three chapters are presented sequentially in the DSM-5 because of the similarities among them.

to be medicated with a substance, or that the excessive use of substances eventually leads to an anxiety disorder. However, with regard to phobic disorders specifically, there is clear evidence that the phobia precedes the alcohol use disorder (Swendsen et al., 1998). After reviewing a tremendous amount of research, Barlow concluded that "Whether anxiety disorders precede substance use disorders or follow them, the alcohol (or drug) use seems to have a deleterious effect on mood, creating a vicious cycle. . . . anxiety and panic, when self-medicated with alcohol, result in an ever-increasing downward self-destructive spiral—not only from the effects of alcohol (or drug) addiction, but also from the exacerbating effects of the drugs on the anxiety and panic" (Barlow, 2004, pp. 16–17).

Like other mental disorders, anxiety can be viewed using the Integral framework. Clearly, the experience of worry, apprehension, fear, and dread (upper-left quadrant) that characterizes anxiety has genetic and biological components (upper-right quadrant). However, to diminish the role that our current "age of anxiety" (Auden, 1974) plays—in the form of its hyper-fast-paced and competitive culture, and the erosion of traditional family structures, values, and myths to inform one's choices without the creation of new myths and other meaning-making systems (lower-left quadrant)—and how that combines with alarming ecological crises (e.g., climate change) and political and global unrest (lower-right quadrant) would be to suffer a limited understanding of anxiety in contemporary America.

Although anxiety has played essential roles across the spectrum of psychotherapeutic theories, it has been conceptualized in considerably different ways. As is widely known, anxiety was perhaps the central etiological and experiential concern of Freud's psychoanalysis. Freud's final position regarding anxiety is in his *Inhibitions, Symptoms, and Anxiety* (1926/1959). There, Freud posited that anxiety (German word *angst*)[5] signals *anticipated* danger (technically, he wrote that anxiety of a specific object is better described with the word "fear"; German word *furcht*) and reproduces the feelings of helplessness that the person originally experienced directly in infancy and/or during birth.[6] Wolfe concurs with this point and stated that the catastrophic imagery that most anxious and phobic clients experience symbolizes "their sense of helplessness, powerlessness, and doom originally experienced much earlier in their lives" (Wolfe, 2003, p. 374).

Even if you are doubtful of, or opposed to, psychoanalysis and the notion that much of our psychological lives rests outside of our awareness, the unconscious aspects of anxiety are significant. Aaron Beck, who was originally trained as a psychoanalyst

---

[5] The German word *angst* itself derives from the Latin and Greek *angh*, from which we get the English words *anxiety, anguish*, and *anger* (Barlow, 2004). As Barlow points out, the distinctions between fear and anxiety, as well as words such as *dread, apprehensiveness*, and *fright*, have become so blurred that various descriptive—often theoretical—terms were enlisted, such as *unconscious, conscious, cognitive, somatic, signal, free-floating*, and so on. However, he believes these descriptors actually often create further confusion. Moreover, Rollo May points out that there really is no apt English equivalent to the German *angst*. Because the closest English terms are *dread* and *anguish*, he views "anxiety" as a "watered-down affect" in comparison to *angst* (May, 1958, p. 51).

[6] According to the DSM-5, fear involves an emotional reaction to a real or currently perceived danger; in contrast, anxiety involves an emotional reaction to a future, anticipated danger. The DSM-5 notes that these two emotional reactions overlap, yet are different.

yet left that tradition and became the founder of Cognitive Therapy, wrote in *Anxiety Disorders and Phobias* that

> Few of our psychological processes are conscious; most are involuntary. In no area is the operation of the nonvolitional processes more apparent than in the anxiety disorders—in which, for no apparent reason, one may suddenly become mute, find one's mind going blank, and become rooted to the spot. (Beck & Emery, 1985, p. xvi)

Beck differentiates fear and anxiety almost conversely of how many other theorists do so. According to Beck,

> Anxiety. . . . is an emotional process while fear is a cognitive one. Fear involves the intellectual appraisal of a threatening stimulus; anxiety involves the emotional response to that appraisal . . . Fear then, is the appraisal of danger; anxiety is the unpleasant feeling state evoked when fear is stimulated. (Beck & Emery, 1985, p. 9)

Many anxiety theorists, from Freud to May, would argue something of the reverse: that fear is the emotional reaction and anxiety (in addition to being affective) involves the more cognitive appraisal of potential danger. Philosopher Soren Kierkegaard wrote the only known work prior to Freud that was devoted to anxiety. Interestingly, he analyzed not only anxiety but also the despair and depression that likewise result from the individual's estrangement from himself. In that work, Kierkegaard (1954) was probably the first to differentiate fear from anxiety, the latter of which he usually termed *dread*. For him, fear is always fear of *some* thing, whereas anxiety is fear of *no* thing "—'not,' as he wryly noted, 'a nothing with which the individual has nothing to do'"(cited in Yalom, 1998, p. 193). Rollo May agreed with this conceptualization, doubting whether the phrase "fear itself" is a logical statement; he proceeded to argue that "anxiety" is what "fear itself" is (May, 1977). Whereas excessive anxiety may interfere with or prevent adaptive action,[7] fear actually prepares us to act adaptively. If anxiety (without a readily identifiable object) interferes with optimal performance and/or action, then what might be the value of anxiety? Various philosophers and psychologists, especially those with existential leanings, respond that anxiety is actually necessary to help us realize our full potentials as human beings and a deeper appreciation of existence. Thus, existentialists believe that the source of much of our anxiety is not in the external world, but within us—from our fear of death and nonbeing to our not utilizing our freedom to act in accord with our deepest values.

Anxiety is widely regarded as both adaptive and natural (Beck & Emery, 1985) as well as "the mother of all psychopathology" (Fosha, 2000, p. 47). In its most inclusive sense, most psychologists would agree that anxiety includes both affective and cognitive (appraisal) components and that it, in general, signals some form of

---

[7] The Yerkes-Dodson law states that people will perform optimally when they are moderately anxious, whereas excessive anxiety interferes with performance and too little anxiety usually does not sufficiently motivate one to adequately prepare and therefore perform at one's maximum potential (Ingersoll & Rak, 2006). See Yerkes and Dodson (1908).

danger—whether internal or external, realistic or unrealistic. For Freud, anxiety signaled some form of anticipated danger that would result if various impulses were expressed rather than defended against. Intense affect of almost any persuasion (from shame, loneliness, fear, and vulnerability to joy, pride, and exultation) can potentially lead to anxiety and the defensive exclusion (whether external avoidance or internal defending) of all experiences that are associated with them (Beck & Emery, 1985). Anxiety also changes somewhat developmentally across the lifespan, from more diffuse somatic excitation in early childhood to more psychic anxiety and finally to more of a signal function (PDM Task Force, 2006).

The professional psychotherapeutic literature includes at least three different types of anxiety: normal, neurotic, and existential. Integral psychology also recognizes a fourth type of anxiety that one encounters in the process of authentic, self-transcending spiritual practice. *Normal anxiety* adaptively draws our attention to potential dangers. In contrast to neurotic or pathological anxiety—which exaggerates the magnitude of the threat—normal anxiety is appropriate to consensus reality and serves to energize, motivate, and mobilize our responses (Freeman & Simon, 1989). According to Freud, perceiving internal danger—that is, when unconscious drives threaten to seek expression—results in *neurotic anxiety*. Also called unrealistic or pathological anxiety, neurotic anxiety involves exaggerating the magnitude or likelihood of threat, is more persistent than is reasonable to a situation, or significantly diminishes life satisfaction. Part of healthy psychological development involves learning to modify and modulate one's expression of anxiety from the more intense and disruptive forms to an imperceptible form referred to as "signal anxiety," which functions to immediately trigger or "signal" a defensive reaction. "Thus, normal anxiety is limited in intensity and duration, and is associated with adaptive defenses. Anxiety is self-defeating or pathological when it is noticeable, intense, disruptive, and paralyzing, or when it triggers self-defeating defensive processes, also called 'symptoms'" (Barlow, 2004, p. 11). *Existential anxiety* can result from confronting issues such as death, freedom (i.e., it may be a response to not living as a free, responsible agent for oneself—not living authentically or in accord with one's own values and meaning-making system), meaninglessness, and isolation. We will address all of these forms of anxiety in more detail subsequently.

Although the DSM-5 includes numerous anxiety-related disorders that can, to varying degrees, be diagnostically differentiated from one another, some researchers have argued that many of the different anxiety-related disorders actually involve the activation of similar, if not identical, brain responses. In a bit more detail, Ohman stated that "when comparing the physiological responses seen in phobics exposed to their feared objects with those seen in PTSD patients exposed to relevant traumatic scenes for the disorder, and with physiological responses during panic attacks, one is much more struck by the similarities than by the differences" (Ohman, 1992). For this reason, as well as the unfeasibility of covering all anxiety-related disorders in any detail in a single chapter, much of this chapter will address anxiety disorders in general. Later in this chapter, the specific anxiety disorders with the highest prevalence will be addressed individually. In the meantime, we would do well to remember anxiety authority David Barlow's position that "anxiety disorders, in the last analysis, are emotional disorders" (Barlow, 2004, p. xi).

## ETIOLOGY

> It is almost universally accepted that the capacity to experience fear and anxiety is adaptive, enabling, as it does, rapid and energetic response to imminent danger or preparation for more distal challenges. However, *the nature of maladaptive fear and anxiety remains controversial, and despite many hopeful leads, there is still no consensus about the etiology of any of the anxiety disorders* . . . Indeed, the current anxiety disorders . . . are characterized by enormous etiological heterogeneity. (Poulton, Pine, & Harrington, 2009, pp. 111–112, italics added)

Similar to depression, anxiety disorders are among the most overdetermined symptom-sets with which clients present (Whiteside & Ollendick, 2009). As is the case with many, if not most, mental disorders, different professional fields—from counseling, social work, and psychology to psychiatry and neuroscience—debate what the exact source and cause of anxiety disorders is. Integral psychotherapists recognize true but partial claims in all of these positions and posit that anxiety stems from complex interactions of genetic, affective, cognitive, and existential factors as well as interpersonal, cultural, and systemic factors. Thus, based on the current evidence that we have available to us, we do not believe there is adequate warrant to speak of a simple, unilateral *cause* of anxiety disorders. As you will soon see, there appear to be a plethora of contributing factors that influence the likelihood of a person developing the symptoms that would lead to being diagnosed with an anxiety disorder. Moreover, whereas the DSM-III and the DSM-IV were strictly descriptive and purportedly atheoretical, many researchers and clinicians suggested that the DSM-5 attempt to develop and communicate etiological knowledge (Andrews, Charney, Sirovatka, & Regier, 2009). However, it does not appear that the DSM-5 has provided insight into the etiological complexities involved in most mental disorders.

David Barlow has put forth a well-supported "triple vulnerability model" positing that the development of anxiety disorders usually requires the interaction of *generalized psychological vulnerabilities* (i.e., external locus of control; highly reactive temperament; behavioral inhibition; Kagan, 1997; Muris, 2006; Rotter, 1975) and *generalized biological vulnerabilities* (genetic traits such as being nervous, highly biologically reactive to environmental changes, and "high-strung") with *specific psychological vulnerabilities* (i.e., people with Panic Disorder tend to be hypervigilant to suffocation cues or other somatic sensations that make them intensely afraid, perhaps that they are dying; Barlow, 2004). Once again, the Integral model provides an excellent framework within which to organize these sundry etiological factors. An example of how the Integral model is helpful, especially in reminding us not to be reductionistic, is with regard to the following quote of cognitive therapists Freeman and Simon: "We *experience* the emotion of anxiety because of the physiological correlates" (1989, p. 347, italics in original) such as those occurring within respiratory, circulatory, gastrointestinal, dermal, or muscular systems. Integral theory posits that the dimensions of the four quadrants emerge together; in other words, no single quadrant consistently has more ontological significance or etiological influence than the others—they all influence one another. If you look back at the Freeman and Simon quote, you can see that they are privileging the upper-right quadrant—which is the domain of physiology, as well as genes, neuroscience, and other more objective perspectives—by writing that the *reason* we experience anxiety is "*because*" of physiology. However, there are many individuals whose physiologies include tachycardia, increased sweating, and gastrointestinal problems, yet these individuals do not experience anxiety problems. Thus, physiology is not a unilateral cause of anxiety so much as it is one of many influential factors. Let's go through the four quadrants and explore the numerous theories of etiology from each of those perspectives.

## Individual-Exterior Perspectives (Upper-Right Quadrant): From Genes to Behaviorism

**EVOLUTIONARY AND GENETIC VIEWS** Anxiety and fear are intimately involved in various forms of escape from, or avoidance of, potential danger. From an evolutionary perspective, possessing "anxious genes" that lead to more "false positives" or false alerts to danger—rather than "false negatives" in which actual danger is not noticed—is a biologically adaptive trait (Beck & Emery, 1985; LeDoux, 1996). Many fears/anxieties (i.e., of heights, animals, the dark) actually decrease the likelihood of suffering harm. For example, an animal that is more vigilant and responds to the slightest danger cue is more likely to escape from a dangerous situation than a less vigilant, less danger-sensitive animal. We can observe similar "avoidance-of-potentially-dangerous-situations" processes occurring in many of the anxiety disorders. For example, a heightened concern of being humiliated and negatively evaluated by others (as in Social Anxiety Disorder) could function to deter behaviors that could lead to social alienation. Likewise, an individual with an anxious attachment history may exhibit agoraphobic responses in an attempt to maintain a bond with her "secure base," a notion with clear adaptive value. In addition to helping a person or animal escape from a dangerous situation, there is also evidence that those who are more vigilant also seem to learn more quickly and easily (Liddell, 1949, as cited in Barlow, 2004).

> The vigilant animal, occupied as it is with future threat, is concerned with what is going to happen in the immediate future. In a very fundamental sense, the animal is planning for that future by taking an orientation to the future best characterized by the question "What happens next?" The planning function is apparent. In humans, this is extremely adaptive. (Barlow, 2004, p. 9)

It is now widely accepted that our genes contribute 30% to 50% of the variance in the expression of generalized anxiety traits (Barlow, 2004). However, genes do not operate in a vacuum; gene expression is largely a function of environmental factors. In fact, the virtually universal, even if not highly specific, consensus is that gene–environment interaction is involved in the development of anxiety disorders. In addition, research by Fanous and Kendler suggests that some genes operate as "modifier genes" that affect the course and clinical features of an anxiety disorder, in contrast to "susceptibility genes" that influence the likelihood of developing an anxiety disorder. Again, Poulton and colleagues conclude that "Despite promising developments in the field of psychiatric genetics, we still know little about how genes and their products (RNA, polypeptides, proteins) interact with one another, let alone how they interact with a host of environmental factors impacting people at different points across the life course" (Poulton et al., 2009, p. 117).

Of critical importance, "the strong consensus is that anxiety and related emotional disorders (such as depression) have a *common* genetic basis, and that specific differences in these disorders are best accounted for by environmental factors . . . there is no reasonable evidence to date confirming the existence of a specific 'anxious gene.' Instead, weak contributions from many genes in several different areas on chromosomes (i.e., a polygenic model) seem to contribute to a generalized biological vulnerability to become anxious" (Barlow, 2004, p. 253, italics added).[8] Despite the strong consensus just mentioned, research by Hettema and colleagues suggests that genes may be implicated in individuals' tendencies to develop one of two broad categories of anxiety disorders, the specific phobias or the panic-generalized-agoraphobic disorders (Hettema, Annas, Neale, Kendler, & Fredrikson, 2003). However, for every study that seems to suggest specificity, there are others suggesting a more common genetic vulnerability. For example, one study reviewed 23 twin studies as well as 12 family studies involving the comorbidity of anxiety and depression; their results showed that a *shared/common genetic vulnerability* for both anxiety and depression explained the comorbity found in the twin studies. Whereas some of the family studies support that conclusion, other family studies highlight that one of the two disorders is an epiphenomenon of the other—in other words, that anxiety symptoms are often secondary and derivative of the depression, or vice versa (Middledorp, Cath, Van Dyck, & Boomsma, 2005). In either case—whether anxiety and depression share a common genetic basis or are epiphenomenal of each other—from a genetic perspective, they do not appear to be as distinct as the DSMs suggest.

In short, there are evolutionary and genetic reasons for us to be anxious. At the same time, excessive anxiety not only diminishes life satisfaction; the *cumulative* consequences of pathological anxiety can actually result in death. This is one of the paradoxes of anxiety and it poses the question: how could the accumulation of adaptive genes result in such a negative state of affairs?

One response to this question is offered by the notion of *preparedness*. Martin Seligman (1971) had previously demonstrated that laboratory-conditioned fear in rats bore some striking differences from human anxiety. For one thing, animals in labs will quickly extinguish prior avoidance conditioning if their avoidance response is prevented and they don't experience punishment. In stark contrast, most phobias in humans are far more resistant to extinction. Seligman proposed that the key difference involved the *arbitrary* stimuli used in lab experiments (buzzers, flashing lights), in contrast to the very meaningful (nonarbitrary) situations or objects that humans fear (heights, snakes, spiders, bears, etc.). Summarizing Seligman's view, LeDoux stated that "perhaps we are prepared by evolution to learn about certain things more easily than others, and that these biologically driven instances of learning are especially potent and long lasting. Phobias, in this light, reflect our evolutionary preparation to learn about danger and to retain the learned information especially strongly" (1996, p. 236).

The work of Susan Mineka and colleagues (1984) strongly supports preparedness theory. Mineka demonstrated that what was believed to be monkeys' genetically inherited fear of snakes was actually *learned* by observing the fear reaction of other monkeys' fear reaction to snakes (if presented for the first time with a snake in the

---

[8] Research exploring the underlying genetic and environmental risk factors in anxiety disorder comorbidity among men and women suggests that both men and women share a similar underlying structure with regard to environmental and genetic risk factors (Hettema, Prescott, Myers, Neale, & Kendler, 2005).

absence of other monkeys, monkeys do not display a fear reaction). However, consistent with preparedness theory, monkeys learn this (prepared) fear reaction extremely quickly, yet they do not learn about nondangerous stimuli in such an efficient manner, "suggesting that there is something special about biologically relevant stimuli that makes them susceptible to rapid and potent observational learning" (LeDoux, 1996, p. 237). Albert Bandura has likewise demonstrated that observational learning—similar to that in Mineka's study with rhesus monkeys and notions of preparedness—is often involved in the development of pathological anxiety (as cited in LeDoux, 1996). Numerous researchers have stressed that this evolutionarily endowed tendency to learn avoidance of certain stimuli more rapidly and potently than others must be genetic in nature (Mineka, Davidson, Cook, & Keir, 1984; Ohman, 1986). Ohman demonstrated that humans' conditioned fear responses to dangerous stimuli that have existed for millennia (e.g., snakes) are far more resistant to extinction than responses to modern fear-relevant stimuli (e.g., guns), evidence that insufficient time has passed since guns have existed for evolution to have "prepared" us to fear them. In addition, Ohman was able to use conditioned stimuli that were not consciously perceived by participants to demonstrate prepared conditioning without participants' awareness of the conditioned stimuli (as cited in LeDoux, 1996). Thus, even from a behavioral perspective, phobias can be learned without conscious awareness of their origins; consistent with Integral theory's positing five different forms of unconscious processes (Marquis, 2008, pp. 160–164; Wilber, 1983), not everything we're unconscious of is due to repression.

**PHYSIOLOGY** The behavioral component of fear and anxiety has been described as "fight or flight" or more recently as "freeze, flight, fight." Autonomic and endocrine processes that increase blood flow to the leg and arm muscles and the brain and decrease blood flow to other organs and tissues support such "fight-or-flight" behaviors (Debiec & Ledoux, 2009).

Various physical symptoms are associated with a significantly increased likelihood that someone will meet the criteria for an anxiety disorder: chest pain (even without significant cardiovascular disease), unexplained faintness, palpitations, dizziness, and irritable bowel syndrome correlate with Panic Disorder; and chronic respiratory illness, vestibular abnormalities, and gastrointestinal symptoms correlate with other anxiety disorders (Barlow, 2004). However, psychologist Michael Mahoney stressed how important it is to note that despite there being various physiological *correlates* to what individuals with anxiety disorders experience, those experiences "cannot be reduced to mere physiological 'arousal'"(Mahoney, 1991, p. 180).[9] This caution not to reduce etiology to physiology involves notions of appraisal and choice, which will be addressed in the upper-left perspectives. Nonetheless, there are important statistics involving various physiological dimensions (e.g., panic is more likely to occur in those who are supersensitive to carbon dioxide; LeDoux, 1996). According to Barlow (2004), although the process of assessing and measuring the psychophysiological aspects of anxiety is complex and methodologically difficult, two findings have garnered consensus. First, chronically anxious individuals tend to have persistently elevated sympathetic functioning, which

[9] For more details on this point, see Dienstbier (1989) and Neiss (1988).

fosters the likelihood of interpreting potentially threatening situations as, in fact, threatening; these individuals also demonstrate a relative lack of autonomic flexibility. It also appears that individuals experiencing anxiety and panic have more asymmetrical patterns of brain activity compared to nonanxious people.

**NEUROSCIENCE** Anxiety disorders—according to neuroscientist Joseph LeDoux—involve a loss of cortical control of our evolutionarily adaptive fear system. However, that is a very general and simple description of what is a set of highly complex neurobiological processes. The past decade has witnessed an explosion of research investigating the role of various brain systems and neurocircuitry in the development of anxiety and panic (Barlow, 2004; LeDoux, 1996). Whereas neurobiological research in the 1970s through the early 1990s tended to focus on single, relatively isolated segments of brain functioning, usually on a single neurotransmitter system, current trends involve studying the *interaction* of specific neurotransmitters and neuromodulator systems with emotions such as anxiety, particularly the neurobiological processes of the HPA axis as a neuromodulator of anxiety.[10] Although the evidence is not incontrovertible (Barlow, 2004, p. 43), there is little doubt that exposure to severe and/or prolonged stress results in long-term changes in the neuroendocrine and neurotransmitter functioning that are implicated in many anxiety disorders (Barlow, 2004; Moreno, Lopez-Crespo, & Flores, 2007). Based upon research by Lang (1994), Gray and McNaughton (1996), and LeDoux (1996), Barlow stated that even after the new emphases of current research paradigms, "fine-grained neuroanatomical exploration will never offer a full explanation, even at a basic neurobiological level, of the workings of emotions" (2004, p. 43). What Barlow means by such a statement is that because neurobiology (i.e., biological stress response systems, neurotransmitters, etc.) is particularly susceptible to the effects of stressful environments during earlier developmental periods—when brain circuits are more highly plastic and synaptic connections are more rapidly being elaborated and refined—a comprehensive description of the etiology of anxiety must include not only neuroscience, but an understanding of how environmental experiences, psychology, and other such variables interact with neurobiological processes in the development of anxiety disorders. Nonetheless, an Integral perspective views neuroscience as an important, although partial, component of understanding, so we will briefly discuss some of the prevailing views.

Very briefly, when a person perceives danger, the amygdala sends a message to the hypothalamus, which signals the pituitary gland to release the stress hormone ACTH (adrenocorticotropic hormone). With its connections to the hypothalamus, the amygdala can activate the HPA axis and the sympathetic nervous system (SNS). Whereas the amygdala is signaling danger, the hippocampus is part of a control system regulating how much pituitary and adrenal stress hormones are released; more on control systems and neurotransmitters in a moment. It seems that information involving potential threat can be relayed to the amygdala via two different pathways. In the first, which LeDoux (1996) terms the "low road," signals proceed quickly from the thalamus to the

---

[10] HPA axis stands for hypothalamic-pituitary-adrenal axis, which is constituted by the interactions of the hypothalamus, the pituitary gland, and the adrenal glands. As part of the neuroendocrine system, it is responsible for regulating reactions to stress, emotions, and moods, among other things.

amygdala; by bypassing cortical processing, this brain circuitry allows for immediate action. In contrast, in what LeDoux (1996) terms the "high road," information travels from the thalamus to the cortex and then to the amygdala; although this pathway does not allow for an immediate action, it does result in more considered action, probably by recalling memories of similar potentially threatening situations.

Experimental studies with rats demonstrate that under too persistent or intense stress, the hippocampus fails to control the release of stress hormones. The effects of such excessive stress on the hippocampus is also likely responsible for different sorts of memory failures that are associated with traumatic experiences. Bruce McEwen has demonstrated that severe but transitory stress causes the dendrites in the hippocampus to shrivel. However, this shriveling is reversible—provided that the severe stress is not prolonged; if it is prolonged, hippocampal cells irreversibly degenerate and memory loss—according to McEwen—appears to be permanent (McEwen, 1992).

Severe stress can also alter the prefrontal cortex, which, like the hippocampus, is involved in controlling the amount of stress hormones released by the adrenal and pituitary glands. Morgan and LeDoux (1995) demonstrated that damage to the medial prefrontal region resulted in what they termed "emotional perseveration"—the failure to extinguish conditioned fear responses. As LeDoux (1996) points out, different individuals' brains are differentially predisposed to develop an anxiety disorder. Those who are more likely to develop a phobia appear to have an amygdala that is hypersensitive to certain prepared stimuli or have frontal lobes that lead them to develop anxiety reactions that resist extinction, even in the absence of prepared stimuli.

Another important brain circuit involved in fear and anxiety is the behavioral inhibition system (BIS; McNaughton & Gray, 2000). Triggered from the brainstem by any potentially threatening cue—from external audiovisual cues to internally felt visceral changes—this circuit connects the limbic system with the frontal cortex. When activated, the BIS prompts behavioral freezing, cognitive vigilance regarding danger, and the experience of fear and/or anxiety (Barlow & Durand, 2002).

Various neurotransmitters are involved in the control and regulation of fear and anxiety responses. Although selective serotonin reuptake inhibitors (SSRIs) are sometimes helpful in treating the symptoms of anxiety disorders (i.e., several serotonin agonists appear to reduce anxiety), research into serotonergic activity as a basis for anxiety and panic has been inconclusive (Barlow, 2004); it seems most likely that SSRIs are not targeting anxiety per se, but rather are merely temporarily inhibiting emotional arousal in general (Breggin, 1997).

Norepinephrine is also involved in anxiety. Both norepinephrine (synonymous with noradrenaline) and epinephrine (synonymous with adrenaline) are central to the flight-or-fight response that is regulated by the locus coeruleus, a small brain structure consisting of neurons that project to most other norepinephrine neurons in the brain. The locus coeruleus appears to be one of the players involved in directing attention to threat-relevant stimuli. By triggering the release of norepinephrine, the locus coeruleus can stimulate the SNS, resulting in increased heart rate, sweating, tremors, and the experience of anxiety.

In the late 1970s, researchers began exploring the role of benzodiazepine receptors in anxiety. Much of the supporting evidence for the benzodiazepine system derives from the effects of that class of anxiolytics in research involving the provoking of fear and anxiety in animal studies. One hypothesis is that there is an endogenous benzodiazepine molecule that binds with receptor molecules to reduce anxiety, and that a deficiency of this causes anxiety disorders. Even if this is the case (which has yet to be demonstrated), it will be an important but only partial explanation for the development of anxiety disorders.

GABA, perhaps the predominant inhibitory neurotransmitter in the brain, seems quite certainly involved in anxiety disorders.[11] One example of research supporting the notion that GABA binding decreases anxiety is the laboratory finding that GABA antagonists increase anxiety in animals (Gray, 1985). However, similar to what we have encountered before, other researchers point out that the diversity of functions that the GABA system plays make it more likely to be a general inhibitory transmitter, rather than specifically anxiolytic (Zillman & Spiers, 2001). Likewise, benzodiazepines may be less specifically anxiolytic and more reducing of emotion or arousal in general (Lader, 1988). It now appears that not only is the benzodiazepine–GABA system more complex than had been previously supposed, it is also more intricately involved with other systems than had been appreciated a few decades ago (Barlow, 2004). Adrenocortical functioning is not completely understood either; a series of well-designed studies found normal or even decreased adrenocortical functioning among people with anxiety disorders. As a result of these inconsistent findings, research into neuroendocrine function lost vitality during the late 1980s and early 1990s (Barlow, 2004). It has become increasingly clear that many if not all of these systems—from serotonergic and noradrenergic systems to the benzodiazepine–GABA system—function globally, rather than specifically, in alerting potential threat. Thus, neuroscientists are now studying not isolated systems but networks and interactions of systems. Finally, it is important to remember the logical error of "reasoning backward from what helps"; this logical fallacy may become clear with the following example: "When I take aspirin, my headache goes away. Thus, the reason I get headaches is because my aspirin level is too low" (Abramowitz, Storch, McKay, Taylor, & Asmundson, 2009). In other words, the finding that increasing the level of a neurotransmitter decreases anxiety does not necessarily mean that the cause of the anxiety was a deficiency of that neurotransmitter.

Interestingly, in the past decade, several neuroscientists have made statements along the lines of "Psychotherapy: Just another way to rewire the brain" (LeDoux, 1996, p. 263) or "Therapy is just another way of creating synaptic potentiation in brain pathways that control the amygdala" (LeDoux, 1996, p. 265).[12] These statements involve the concept of neuroplasticity, or the brain's capacity to form new neuronal connections in response to various changes in the environment, whether that environment is physical or social, or even in response to "mental force" (Schwartz & Begley, 2002). Thus, and consistent with an Integral perspective, it is not that either neuroscience is correct or psychological theories are correct, but rather, they are more complementary than adversarial, both offering important but incomplete explanations; more on psychological perspectives subsequently.

---

[11] GABA stands for gamma-aminobutyric acid, which is the primary inhibitory neurotransmitter in human and other mammalian nervous systems.

[12] See also Damasio (1999) and Siegel (2007).

**BEHAVIORISM** From a behavioral perspective,

> Anxiety is the primary learning problem in psychopathology. Once anxiety is established as a habitual response to specific stimuli, however, it can undermine or impair other aspects of behavior and lead to secondary symptoms. . . . These secondary symptoms [from sleep disturbances and sexual dysfunction to tension headaches and stomach upsets] themselves may elicit anxiety because of their painfulness, their association with learned fears of physical or mental disorder, or simply their embarrassing social consequences. If these secondary problems produce additional anxiety, then new learning may occur, and a "vicious circle" is created that leads to more complicated symptoms. . . . Over time, the primary complaint is no longer anxiety but the phobias and drug abuse patients have developed in order to avoid anxiety. Of course, a drug habit itself can produce anxiety and can lead to further drug abuse in order to reduce the new anxiety, and the vicious circle goes on. (Prochaska & Norcross, 2003, pp. 285–286)

In the simplest of behavioral terms, *anything that reduces a person's anxiety is highly reinforcing*. It is important to remember that what is being avoided can include both *external events* (i.e., avoiding going to a social event and thus the anxiety of possibly acting foolish and being rejected), and *internal events* (i.e., mental maneuvers or any other intrapsychic actions that distract one from anxiogenic thoughts, as well as unconscious memories that signal real or imagined danger). The (negatively) reinforcing avoidance of anxiogenic situations simultaneously diminishes felt anxiety in the moment, while perpetuating and entrenching the anxiety disorder because such patterns of negative reinforcement lead to a reduction of seeking novel experiences. Unfortunately, this diminishes the likelihood of new learning that could potentially disconfirm the anxiogenic representations and expectations that the person so vigilantly anticipates or "feeds forward."

High anxiety levels also interfere with accurate information processing and tend to cloud the clarity of thought an individual may be capable of when experiencing low to moderate anxiety, all of which tend to confirm the person's previously established anxiogenic expectations (Gold, 1993). Barlow (2004) summarized large bodies of research and concluded that the vicarious (social) learning of anxiety, and how that anxious apprehension is focused on specific objects (from somatic experiences in those with panic, to specific feared objects in those with specific phobias, to the potentially threatening aspects of social situations in those with social anxiety disorder), is clearly implicated in the development of specific psychological vulnerabilities, which interact with generalized biological and psychological vulnerabilities to produce anxiety disorders.

Despite the formidable constraints that genetics, physiology, brain chemistry, and learning histories exert upon people with anxiety disorders, not all of the etiological influences are externally observable. For example, referring to the behavioral approach he had used in his earlier work with phobic clients, Wolfe was "increasingly struck by the irony that unconscious conflicts were being elicited by a therapeutic approach that denied their existence" (2003, p. 374). Moreover, neurobiological researchers, having provoked and studied panic in laboratories for decades, have more recently confirmed that it is mediated primarily by psychological factors, of which lacking a sense of control—which derives from early developmental experiences—appears central (Barlow, 2004).

## Interior Perspectives (Upper-Left and Lower-Left Quadrants): From Cognitive and Psychodynamic to Existential

**COGNITIVE PERSPECTIVES** Aaron Beck has argued that the core of anxiety disorders is a sense (not always accurate or grounded in good evidence) of vulnerability, "defined as a person's perception of himself as subject to internal or external dangers over which his control is lacking or is insufficient to afford him a sense of safety" (Beck & Emery, 1985, p. 67). Beck views acute anxiety as particularly paradoxical in that it increases the likelihood that the feared situation will come to pass. Consistent with his approach, Beck emphasized a component of anxiety that had traditionally been neglected: cognition. Beck has also posited a specific cognitive profile for many mental disorders. For many of the anxiety disorders, Beck notes that core beliefs involve themes of excessively persistent and exaggerated concerns about impending threat/danger (whether the perceived threats are internal or external; involve one's sense of individuality, identity, and freedom; or social acceptance, bonding, and belonging) as well as an excessive devaluing of one's actual coping skills. Moreover, the distorted cognitions not only reflect but also perpetuate systematic biases in information processing (Beck & Weishaar, 2008). "This bias takes several characteristic forms, called cognitive distortions, that can be detected beneath the voluntary thought level of the client's cognitive system—in his automatic thoughts, intermediate thoughts, and core beliefs" (Fall, Holden, & Marquis, 2010, p. 274). Some of the cognitive distortions that are implicated in anxiety disorders include:

- Arbitrary inference: jumping to conclusions despite a lack of adequate supporting evidence or in the face of contradictory evidence. For example, an "A" student makes one bad grade on an exam and persistently worries that he is not cut out for college.
- Selective abstraction: thinking about a situation by focusing on one aspect of the situation and ignoring other important aspects. For example, at a social gathering, most people smile at and laugh with John; however, one person grimaces at him and John believes that no one at the party liked him because all he can think of is that one unpleasant interaction.
- Overgeneralization: taking a general rule from an isolated incident and applying it to unrelated situations. For example, one of Erin's professors gives what she thinks is an unfair exam and Erin concludes that professors can't be trusted to be fair.
- Dichotomous thinking: black-or-white thinking in which any shade of gray is labeled either white or black. For example, Bill struggles with Social Anxiety Disorder and considers any social situation either completely safe or completely dangerous, with no middle area that would be uncomfortable but unlikely to cause serious danger to him.

Another cognitive variable that appears to be implicated in the etiology of anxiety disorders is *anxiety sensitivity*: believing that sensations associated with anxiety (such as autonomic arousal) will result in negative physical, social, and/or psychological consequences (Schmidt, Zvolensky, & Maner, 2006; Taylor, Jang, Stewart, & Stein, 2008). Whereas many researchers have pointed to the role that anxiety sensitivity plays in the development of anxiety and depression, one study demonstrated that several parental behaviors that have been viewed as pathogenic (hostile, threatening, and rejecting behaviors) appear to predict children's overall level of anxiety sensitivity (Scher & Stein, 2003). Thus, while acknowledging that those parental behaviors are implicated in the development of anxiety, those behaviors are also implicated in the development of anxiety sensitivity, the latter of which may function as a mediating variable between childhood experience and anxiety.

Other cognitive factors relevant to anxiety disorders include false beliefs about worry, intolerance of ambiguity, cognitive avoidance, negative problem orientation, selective attention, judgmental bias, and sense of control (Kindt & Van Den Hout, 2001; Rheingold, Herbert, & Franklin, 2003). Whereas it is widely acknowledged that anxiety amplifies selective attention, Kindt and Van Den Hout reported research pointing to the role that selective attention plays in increasing anxiety levels as well as the fact that those with anxiety disorders struggle to inhibit selective attention. Thus, selective attention appears to play a maintenance—even if not etiological—role in anxiety disorders. Judgmental biases regarding threat-relevant stimuli have been shown to be implicated in Social Anxiety Disorder: one study found that adults with Social Anxiety Disorder exaggerated the likelihood that a negative social event would occur, as well as rating it as more distressing than did a nonanxious control group (Rheingold et al., 2003).

Numerous researchers have demonstrated the significant role that one's sense of control plays in the development of anxiety disorders. In short, the more internal one's locus of control, the more one is able to mitigate the intensity of anxious apprehension. Conversely, higher levels of external locus of control correlate with higher levels of experienced anxiety. This is readily understandable in that one's perception that one is incapable of controlling or impacting one's environment naturally leads one to feel less secure and more anxious. As will soon be suggested, although anxiety is *experienced within* a person (subjectively), it often *originates between people* (intersubjectively or interpersonally), as in the case of abuse, neglect, unresponsiveness, abandonment, and so forth—all of which are interpersonal in nature. Consistent with the multidimensional nature of the etiology of anxiety, one's sense of control (upper-left [UL] quadrant) is powerfully influenced by one's caregivers' parenting styles (lower-right [LR] quadrant) and the perceptions children have of their relationships with caregivers (lower-left [LL] quadrant), which leads us to attachment theory.

**ATTACHMENT THEORY** According to attachment theory (Bowlby, 1987, 1988; Fosha, 2000; Gold, 1993; Guidano, 1987), anxiety is the felt experience of a threatened attachment bond. From this perspective, optimal psychological development requires that children have a predictable and secure relationship—a "secure base"—with their caregivers. According to Sroufe (1990), when caregivers fail to change their behavior in response to an infant's cues of need and/or distress (i.e., if the caregivers' behavior is not *contingent*), the developing child is likely to internalize a lack of control over the environment, which is a component of a generalized psychological vulnerability. Thus, it is the caregiver's contingent responsiveness to the infant's cues—and the sense of safety and security that such responsiveness endows—that affects the "attachment representations" that children develop. Fosha stated that "If there is no feeling of safety, anxiety, the mother of all psychopathology, takes hold. Anxiety is a reaction to the nonavailability or nonresponsiveness of the caregiver and is rooted in the feeling of being alone in the face of psychic danger" (2000, p. 47).

According to attachment theory, insecure attachment histories are major etiological factors in subsequent anxiety disorders. Infants and children who lacked a "secure base"—an available, sensitive, empathically attuned and responsive caregiver—are more likely to suffer from anxiety and less likely to explore their external environments (physical or social) or capacities (external or internal; Bowlby, 1987, 1988; Fosha, 2000). Of significance, psychological aloneness amplifies any anxiety that one may experience. Thus, feeling alone (UL)—whether with others or not—and the poor attachment histories that often accompany feelings of pervasive aloneness are viewed as causally implicated in anxiety disorders.

Although not completely comprehensive from an Integral perspective, attachment theorists from Bowlby and Guidano to Gold and Fosha posit that one can usually trace a client's anxiety disorder to problematic attachment histories with early caregivers (Guidano, 1987). The idea here is not that attachment dynamics are the sole cause of anxiety disorders, but rather, are central to the psychological vulnerabilities (stress) that must interact with a genetic vulnerability (diathesis) to produce an anxiety disorder:

> Once attachments or exploration are structuralized in negative and dangerous terms, a considerable portion of the person's activity is organized around identifying threats to the tenuous ties to safety which exist in his or her own experiences, thoughts, wishes, and behavior, and in the actions of others. As even the possibility of such a threat can be the stimulus for tremendous anxiety, a hypervigilant and protective perceptual set is established, along with an overemphasized need for control or protection in those areas of life which represent, actually or symbolically, the person's subjective point of vulnerability to loss, abandonment, irrevocable separation, or to the surrender of autonomy and independence. (Gold, 1993, p. 295)

Support for attachment theory perspectives is not just theoretical. In a study examining the reciprocal influence of attachment status, child-rearing styles, and temperament with anxiety, van Brakel and colleagues found that higher levels of insecure attachment and parental control correlated with higher levels of both anxiety symptoms and disorders (Van Brakel et al., 2006). Bosquet (2001)—in a longitudinal dissertation using a developmental psychopathology perspective to examine the course of anxiety symptoms among a high-risk community sample from infancy through adolescence—found that those children who lacked confidence in their secure base and who had struggled with stage-salient developmental tasks were the most likely to develop anxiety symptoms (the risk factor of lacking a secure base was greater for females than males). Moreover, those who initially had anxiety symptoms but also perceived a secure base were more likely to have their anxiety symptoms remit. Another long-term study reported that anxious/resistant attachment at 1 year of age correlated with anxiety disorders at age 17, even after controlling for each mother's anxiety and each child's temperament (Warren, Huston, Egeland, & Sroufe, 1997).

"Exploration" is among the most important constructs in attachment theory. Those with insecure attachments, like those with anxiety disorders, tend to explore less, whether that exploration is external (trying new behaviors in the world, such as initiating conversations, public speaking, or confronting any feared situation) or internal (allowing a more fully felt visceral experience of emotion rather than defensively excluding emotions because one is afraid of being overwhelmed or being out of control). The unfortunate irony is that people with phobias or other anxiety disorders need to explore and confront what they fear in order to overcome their problem, but their lack of security makes it more difficult for them to do this.

**OTHER PSYCHODYNAMIC VIEWS** In general, psychodynamic approaches view phobias and other anxiety disorders as primarily rooted in unconscious conflicts stemming from early childhood trauma that—although sometimes is sexual or aggressive in nature—is more often a function of caregivers' unreliability, unavailability, unresponsiveness, lack of empathic attunement, neglect, or abandonment. To varying degrees, these approaches also posit that the phobogenic or anxiogenic situation is symbolically related to repressed traumas and/or other intrapsychic conflict, and that transferring one's fears or anxieties to a more concrete, often external, situation renders the fear or anxiety more manageable (Wolfe, 2005).

In reference to childhood trauma, we concur with Kohut, Bowlby, and Wolfe that the occurrence of "real traumas" is far more common than most psychotherapists acknowledge; however, what constitutes "trauma" is far less often the dramatic episodes of sexual or physical abuse than repeated experiences of having self needs left unmet, whether due to caregivers' own psychological deficits, the child's temperament, or other cultural, social, and family structures—as well as the interactions of some or all of those (Kohut, 1984). Such childhood trauma, whether more overt abuse or sustained neglect, reaps a heavy toll on one's sense of self and the ensuing sense of tenuous, if any, connection to safety, security, and reliable and attuned responsiveness from others. Although all of this may sound rather different from behavioral views of anxiety disorders, both perspectives share the notion (even if they use different terminology) that anxiety disorders derive from some sort of traumatic or otherwise aversive learning experience(s).

Essential to attachment theory and psychodynamic theories[13] of psychopathology is the fundamental role that anxiety plays in influencing behavior, thinking, and feeling. "Central to both is the tenet that contact with the attachment figure counteracts anxiety, whereas the experience of aloneness exacerbates it. The experience of aloneness in the face of what is experienced as psychically dangerous is at the core of AEDP's understanding of psychopathogenesis" (Fosha, 2000, p. 37).[14] Moreover, dynamic theorists from Sullivan and Horney to Fosha and Wachtel posit that personality is fundamentally a function of the person's experience of anxiety and the defensive maneuvers enlisted to quell it (Fosha, 2000; Horney, 1945; Sullivan, 1953; Wachtel, 2008). The internal working models—or internalized representations of self and others—that become structuralized in childhood as a result of child–caregiver interactions not only influence the person's regulation of affective experience and subsequent relating/attaching to others, they profoundly impact all exploratory behavior.

[13] Attachment theory is in many regards a form or subset of psychodynamics.

[14] AEDP stands for Accelerated Experiential Dynamic Psychotherapy.

Children will defensively exclude not only thoughts and behaviors that lead them to feel anxious, *they will also*—in order to decrease the likelihood of their caregivers' turning away in unavailability—*exclude those aspects of their experience that their caregivers cannot tolerate.* We agree with Fosha's conceptualization regarding how dependent a child's self-development is on the caregiver's capacity to establish secure attachment with the child and the concomitant feelings of safety that ensue. "In secure attachment, fear and anxiety are kept at bay as a result of reliable, responsive caregiving; in insecure attachment styles, fear and anxiety are kept at bay through reliance on defense mechanisms" (Fosha, 2000, p. 41). Similarly, Leslie Greenberg (2002)[15] views childhood and other relational experiences that were unpredictable or characterized by a sense of lacking interpersonal control as causal in many maladaptive anxieties, particularly those involving issues of intimacy, fears of abandonment, and other relational anxieties. Whereas Greenberg (2002) views fear as "a compelling survival-oriented signal to escape from danger or seek protection . . . Anxiety, on the other hand is a response to 'threats' sensed in the mind—symbolic, psychological, or social situations rather than an immediately present, physical danger. . . . Fear and anxiety operate tacitly and automatically" (p. 143).

We already mentioned that any behavior a person engages to avoid the anxiogenic situation will simply sustain the underlying pathology—for the simple reason that the reduction of anxiety is inherently highly (negatively) reinforcing. Thus, anxiety disorders are rarely a function of only intrapsychic (UL) dynamics. Although not the norm, I (Marquis) have counseled clients with Social Anxiety Disorder (previously referred to as Social Phobia) whose anxieties significantly diminished after only a few weeks of social skills training (LR), lots of role-plays, and lots of behavioral (interpersonal) homework outside of the sessions. More commonly, people with Social Anxiety Disorder simply avoid the feared situation and this avoidance is then reinforced by diminished anxiety.

Wachtel (1982) has demonstrated how internalized representations of self and others (UL) interact with real-world interactions (LR) in "vicious circles" (p. 259). For example, if Bob attempts to face his feared situation and actually asks a woman for a date, a "vicious circle" might manifest as Bob's anticipatory anxiety—experienced viscerally as shortness of breath, trembling, sweating, and tachycardia (UR) and cognitively as expectations of rejection and appraisals of oneself as unattractive, incompetent, and undesirable (UL)—influencing Bob to actually behave in an odd, uncomfortable manner that makes the woman more likely to actually avoid or reject him (LR). Thus, Bob's real-world behaviors and his interactions with others—both of which can be observed "from the outside" (UR, LR)—seem to confirm his intrapsychic representations of himself as an unappealing, unattractive, undesirable failure that no one will love (UL), as well as negatively influence the meanings he assigns to his inability to establish a romantic relationship (LL). In short, it's not all intrapsychic (UL) or neurochemical (UR). Whatever occurs culturally, socially, and interpersonally, including the person's actual social skills, profoundly influences many of the anxiety disorders. Bob also demonstrated secondary anxiety (also called meta-anxiety): the tendency

---

[15] Greenberg has developed an emotion-focused, experiential approach that is nonetheless a person-centered approach, and is also considered by many to be an expert on emotions.

to suffer anxiety or other painful emotions in response to the primary anxiety: "First, they become anxious either for some unknown reason or because of the situation in which they currently find themselves; second, they become anxious about being anxious . . . the fear of fear rapidly escalates the intensity of the original fear and may well be a specific catalytic process by which anxiety spikes into panic" (Wolfe, 2003, pp. 376–377).[16]

Interestingly, the *Psychodynamic Diagnostic Manual* conceptualizes Generalized Anxiety Disorder not as one of the other anxiety disorders but as a personality disorder, primarily because, in addition to it being chronic and pervasive, it can be the primary psychological organizing experience of the individual suffering from it (PDM Task Force, 2006, pp. 56–57, 96–97).

**EXISTENTIAL VIEWS** From the perspective of existential philosophers and existential psychotherapists, anxiety is an absolutely unavoidable aspect of human existence that stems from our awareness of and confrontation with the "ultimate concerns of existence" (also referred to as the "givens of existence"): death, freedom, meaninglessness, and isolation.[17] From this perspective, *existential anxiety is necessary for mental health* because such anxiety is often a sign that one is not realizing one's potentials as a free and responsible human being (Yalom, 1980). Therefore, avoiding one's existential anxiety results in living a life that is relatively vapid, hollow, and inauthentic.

In general, existential therapists agree with Freud's dynamic structure of anxiety (drives → anxiety → defense mechanisms), but believe that the ultimate sources of anxiety are less the threat of acting out our sexual and aggressive impulses and more a function of our confrontation with the "ultimate concerns" (awareness of ultimate concerns → anxiety → defense mechanisms). Other points of agreement with psychodynamic conceptualization are that people resort to a host of defense mechanisms in order to ward off or lessen anxiety and that each individual's configuration of defenses constitutes his or her psychopathology; even though the defenses provide a sense of protection and safety, they ultimately restrict the person's experience and development (Yalom, 1998). Importantly, existential anxiety itself is not considered pathological; rather, its absence or avoidance is (Frankl, 1985).

Critical to the existentialists is distinguishing existential anxiety from neurotic anxiety.[18] One thing that both forms of anxiety share in common is conflict. However, whereas neurotic anxiety involves conflict between what the id impulsively would like to do and the retribution that would result from society or one's superego, existential anxiety involves the conflict generated by the givens of existence: conflict between being and nonbeing; conflict between wanting to live with the comfort and security afforded by the conventions of society versus living as an authentic, self-transcending

---

[16] Barry Wolfe (2003) prefers to call this "metappraising."

[17] Kierkegaard (1954) and Tillich (1952) pointed out that although existential anxiety is inevitable, it is tempered by the activity of self-reflection and courageously assuming authorship of one's life. They further emphasized that to not even recognize one's existential anxiety is a far greater form of dread and despair.

[18] Existentialists such as Rollo May often use the word "normal anxiety" synonymously with "existential anxiety," which we consider somewhat unfortunate because anxiety regarding one's outcome on a final exam, a social performance, etc. (what most would refer to as "normal" anxiety) is a far cry from the depths of existential anxiety.

individual; and so forth. In order to become aware of existential anxiety, it is often necessary to first confront and clarify one's neurotic anxieties, or to realize that one is concerned with them as a defense against the more terrifying existential anxieties from which they stem (more on this in the treatment section).

Importantly, existential anxiety is not one emotion among others, such as anger, happiness, or sadness. Rather, *existential anxiety is an ontological characteristic of being human*. In other words, *we don't merely have existential anxiety*—it is not merely a part of the human condition—rather, *existential anxiety is an essential aspect of who we are as human beings* (May, 1958, 1977). Unlike neurotic anxieties, existential anxiety is never peripheral: "[existential] anxiety is *the experience of the threat of imminent non-being* . . . this threat of dissolution of the self is not merely something confined to psychotics but describes the neurotic and normal nature of anxiety as well" (May, 1958, p. 50, italics in original; brackets added). Whereas *fears* can be objectified (made objects of one's awareness) and thus made to not subsume a person, *anxiety*—as ontological—assaults the core of one's being: "Anxiety is ontological, fear is not. Fear can be studied as an affect among other affects, a reaction among other reactions. But anxiety can be understood only as a threat to *Dasein*. . . . It is an experience of threat which carries both anguish and dread, indeed the most painful and basic threat which any being can suffer, for it is the threat of loss of existence itself" (May, 1958, pp. 51–52).[19] This notion is captured by existential analyst Ludwig Binswanger's claim—which Heidegger previously posited—that "the source of anxiety is existence itself" (Binswanger, 1958, p. 206).

As previously mentioned, a fundamental source of anxiety stems from our awareness and fear of our mortality and other ultimate concerns such as our freedom and the need to create meaning from our experience. Although the bulk of our culture, as well as most Western psychology, operates from a denial of *death*, deep down, we know that our existence (as well as that of those we love) will end and this death anxiety pervades much of our lives, even if at largely unconscious levels (Becker, 1973).[20] Although many laypeople do not have negative connotations to the concept of freedom, it is because of *freedom* that we are responsible for ourselves, and because we often do not assume such responsibility, we live in "bad faith"—existential philosopher Jean-Paul Sartre's (1943/1993) term for the condition in which a person denies his freedom and deceives himself of the fact that he is always responsible for his choices. This condition of *inauthenticity,* in which one passively and uncritically thinks and acts like the majority (under the "tyranny" of the masses, crowd, or "herd"), rather than with authenticity—responsibly, creatively, and courageously choosing to live in accord with one's individually chosen values and commitments—is *a primary source of anxiety*. Inauthenticity is a signal that one is not living as a fully free human being. "In order to pass from inauthentic to authentic existence, a man [sic] has to suffer the ordeal of despair and 'existential anxiety,' i.e., the anxiety of a man [sic] facing the

---

[19] *Dasein* is a term used most famously by the existential phenomenologist Martin Heidegger. Although it is in many regards "untranslatable" into English, it denotes the quality of human beings' mode of existence (Ellenberger, 1958).

[20] For more on this issue, consult Yalom's (2009) most recent book: *Staring at the Sun: Overcoming the Terror of Death*. As you can glean from the title, the entire work is devoted to the issue of death anxiety and how it often masquerades under many other guises.

limits of his existence with its fullest implications: death, nothingness. This is what Kierkegaard calls the 'sickness unto death'" (Ellenberger, 1958). When existentialists refer to the ultimate concern of *meaninglessness*, they do not mean that there is no meaning to human life. Rather, they assert that we must imbue our lives with meaning; in other words, meaning is not inherent—as most traditional religious views maintain—in existence. Another primary source of our anxiety is *isolation*: "The experience of separateness arouses anxiety; it is indeed the source of all anxiety" (Fromm, 1956, p. 7).[21] From a spiritual perspective, and echoing one of the Upanishads of Hinduism, "where there is an other, there is fear." In other words, if we are exclusively identifying with a sense of self that is separate from existence, it is perfectly reasonable to be afraid; after all, something out there can hurt and kill you!

Rather than directly facing and dealing with such ultimate concerns, which we can never completely solve or resolve, people often displace the anxieties stemming from them onto more concrete and surmountable things, which is what Kierkegaard meant when he wrote "the nothing which is the object of dread becomes, as it were, more and more a something" and Rollo May meant when he wrote "anxiety seeks to become fear" (as cited in Yalom, 1998, pp. 193–194). Paraphrasing Rollo May (1958), it is not so difficult to see that neurotic forms of anxiety develop (at least in part) because one has been unable or unwilling to accept and deal with the existential dimensions of anxiety.

Sartre (1943/1993) demonstrated that, even in the most extreme circumstances, people have the freedom to choose, even if those choices are limited to how they will view their circumstances. Although a whole host of circumstances—from the genes we inherit to the political and socioeconomic conditions into which we are born—may place severe constraints upon us, they cannot force a free being to choose one option over another. The fact that we know that our choices have consequences for which we are responsible leads to anguish and dread—in other words, anxiety. Related to existential anxiety, when an individual denies or fails to fulfill her potentials, she may experience existential guilt—feeling guilty against herself for failing to realize what she has been given as a human being. To illustrate that such claims involving freedom are not mere abstractions, let us briefly consider the life and work of another existential therapist, Victor Frankl.

Frankl was a psychiatrist and a prisoner of Nazi concentration camps during World War II, in which his mother, father, brother, and wife were killed. During his time in the concentration camps, Frankl (1985) came to believe that humans' most fundamental need is for the "will-to-meaning." Consequently, Frankl's *logotherapy* is primarily concerned with the individual's creation of, and engagement with, meaning—a position highly consonant with Nietzsche's (1954) dictum that "He who has a why to live can bear almost any how." Under such terrible conditions, Frankl could have easily fallen into despair and resolved that his life was meaningless, but he didn't. Despite his body being imprisoned, he nonetheless exercised his freedom to choose how to relate to his circumstances and created meaning in his life by helping (loving) his fellow prisoners.

Although many Integral theorists differentiate existential and transpersonal stages of development, existential concerns are present throughout the lifespan. For the purposes of this chapter, we do not believe the spiritual dimensions of anxiety need to be treated completely discretely from the preceding discussion of existential anxiety,

---

[21] Eric Fromm was a social psychologist, existential-humanistic philosopher, and member of the Frankfurt School of critical theory.

although certainly there are some unique features of spiritual anxieties depending on the specific spiritual culture, beliefs, and practices a person is from and/or engaged in. Before delving into some of the spiritual dimensions of anxiety, it is important to know that from an Integral perspective, all spiritual traditions have both legitimate and authentic dimensions.

According to Wilber (1997), *legitimate spirituality* (also referred to as translative spirituality) is the more common form and function of religion, which involves fortifying one's sense of self. Through a system of beliefs and rituals, people are helped to understand and minimize the inherent suffering of the separate self; thus, legitimate spirituality fosters feelings of security, comfort, consolation, protection, and fortification (Wilber, 1997). Legitimate spirituality is so called because it provides a certain sense of legitimacy to one's beliefs about the world and one's place therein. In contrast, *authentic spirituality* (also referred to as transformative spirituality) constitutes a less common function of religion: to transcend (include and develop beyond) one's sense of self:

> Rather than consoling, fortifying, or legitimizing the self, it dismantles, transmutes, transforms, and liberates the self—ultimately from its illusion of separateness—through a series of deaths and rebirths of the self into ever more inclusive developmental waves [stages]. Authentic spirituality inquires into legitimate spirituality and concludes that the latter tends to entrench a person in one's current wave of development and, thus, prolong—even if more comfortably—the illusion of separateness that is, ironically, the actual source of suffering. (Marquis, Holden, & Warren, 2001, p. 227)

From an Integral perspective, both legitimate and authentic spirituality are important. Equally important, however, is discrimination between the two because of their different goals and processes. It is worth emphasizing that a key feature of authentic spirituality is that it facilitates developmental transformation via self-transcending practices. Thus, given the heavy emphasis on self-transcendence by many existentialists, you can probably recognize the spirituality inherent in existentialism: "*Self-transcendence*, I would say, is the essence of existence; and existence, in turn, means the specifically human mode of being" (Frankl, 1967, p. 74). As Albert Einstein put it: "What is the meaning of human life, or for that matter of the life of any creature? To find a satisfying answer to this question means to be religious" (as cited in Frankl, 1967, p. 93). And finally:

> If we are to understand a given person . . . we cannot avoid the dimension of transcendence . . . *transcendere*—literally "to climb over and beyond"—describes what every human being is engaged in doing every moment when not seriously ill or temporarily blocked by despair or anxiety. (May & Yalom, 1995, p. 267)

What does all of this have to do with spirituality and anxiety? At the heart of most, if not all, authentic spirituality is the activity of transcending one's self (that with which one identifies), which confronts one directly with the dread of nonbeing. Whether through Zen meditation, Christian centering prayer, or selfless service, one is encouraged to let go of oneself. In fact, the dynamic involved in the transformation from any developmental stage to the next involves dis-identifying with one's current self-sense (read: dying to one's current sense of self), identifying with the subsequent developmental sense of self, and then integrating the two (Wilber, 2000). What makes this process more terrifying at transpersonal or post-post-conventional stages of development is the lack of solidity of the potential future selves; not to mention that many spiritual teachings emphasize that one should let go of *all* forms of self-identification. In other words, authentic spiritual practice is often about meeting the death of one's self-sense head-on! Is it any wonder that intense, sustained, self-transcending spiritual practice can produce its own class of anxiety?[22]

With regard to legitimate spirituality, anxiety of a different nature is often involved, some of which is relatively neurotic and some of which is more existential in nature. Consider, for example, a person who is questioning her faith. This produces a whole host of anxieties, many of which share similarities to the DSM-5 *Religious or Spiritual Problem*, involving the anxiety-provoking nature of doubting spiritual values relating to one's religious upbringing or institution, questioning or losing one's faith, or converting to a new faith.

**Wolfe's Integrative Perspective: Experience and Meaning-Making as Central** In previous sections, we reviewed research suggesting that not only the different anxiety disorders, but even other categories of mental disorders (i.e., depression), share a common genetic basis. Barry Wolfe's (2005) integrative approach suggests that an important differentiating variable with regard to which of the different anxiety disorders manifest in a given individual is that of the cognitive, somatic, or affective strategies people develop in an effort to protect themselves in the face of potential threats and dangers. Although these strategies offer short-term buffering of the anxiety, they also entrench it, at the same time that the strategies themselves come to constitute part of the disorder itself (Wolfe, 2005). While not denying the contribution of genetics and other biomedical factors, Wolfe's integrative approach posits that troubled self-perceptions and experiences (UL)—what he calls "self-wounds"—are the foundational source of anxiety disorders. Moreover, both the explicit as well as implicit meanings that the anxiety has for each patient need to be addressed. Commonly, patients are aware of only the explicit meanings, which often derive from secondary reactions stemming from some perception of anxiety. Underlying such secondary reactions are the implicit meanings, which usually involve fears of catastrophic danger to the self that themselves derive from the patient's "self-wounds"—perceptions of one's self as defective, worthless, unlovable, incompetent, and so forth. Because such subjectively perceived (UL) self-wounds are as equally involved in the etiology of anxiety disorders as the more genetic, physiological and behavioral (UR) aspects, they deserve to be understood and addressed in each patient.

Thus, even though genes and stressful childhood experiences predispose one to anxiety disorders, the actual development of an anxiety disorder requires a perception of one's self as somehow "wounded"—inadequate, vulnerable, defective, incompetent, unlovable, inferior, unable to control, and so forth—suggesting a self-concept that is unable to cope with the demands of everyday life. With such a self-perception, the person enlists various coping strategies—from behavioral avoidance and emotional constriction to cognitive rituals—in an effort to defend against anxiety and other intolerable affective states, which simultaneously preclude the person's directly facing

[22] For in-depth discussions of the issue of spiritual anxieties, consult Wilber (2000), Walsh and Vaughan (1993), Walsh (1999), Steindl-Rast (1984), and Keating (1986).

those demands as well as usually producing interpersonal consequences that seem to reinforce the person's negatively-skewed self-perceptions (Wolfe, 2005). According to Wolfe, if our activity of meaning-making is given a central focus,[23] then *anxiety disorders are fundamentally disorders of (usually unconscious) anticipated dangerous, if not catastrophic, meanings.* However, many approaches fail to see this because they focus solely on the explicit, secondary aspects of the anxiety symptoms. As you probably surmise, Wolfe's treatment approach pays very close attention to clients' subjective experiences and how they make meaning of them; more on this subsequently.

### Collective-Exterior Perspectives (Lower-Right Quadrant): The Role of Family and Other Social Systems in Anxiety

> Anxiety disorders . . . result from various factors only some of which are internal to the child. Considerable evidence suggests that bioecological and ecobehavioral influences are evident. . . . Children are highly dependent on their families, schools, and communities, and, not infrequently, these contextual influences occasion and maintain anxiety in them. (Whiteside & Ollendick, 2009, p. 318)

The effects of stressful environments on brain function have been demonstrated in numerous studies. This body of research reveals the profound effects that early stressful experiences (traumatic events or environments) have upon neuroendocrine functioning, especially with regard to basal cortisol levels and hypothalamic-pituitary-adrenal (HPA) axis and corticotropin-releasing factor (CRF) activity (Barlow, 2004). As one example, correlations between childhood sexual abuse and subsequent anxiety disorders have been reported in several studies (McCauley et al., 1997).[24]

Recall that earlier in this chapter we mentioned that genes contribute 30% to 50% of the variance in the expression of generalized anxiety traits. While this is true, it is equally important to bear in mind that

> the neurobiological processes underlying anxious apprehension that may emerge from this biological (genetic) diathesis seem to be influenced substantially by early psychological processes, contributing to a generalized psychological vulnerability. In this sense, *early experiences* with controllability and predictability, *based in large part* (but not exclusively) *on interactions with caregivers*, ". . . contributes to something of a psychological template, which at some point becomes relatively fixed and diathetic. Stated another way, this psychological dimension of a sense of control is possibly a mediator between stressful experience and anxiety, and over time this sense becomes a somewhat stable moderator of the expression of anxiety" (Barlow, 2004, pp. 277–278, parentheses in original; italics added).[25]

---

[23] Wolfe is far from alone on this point; Harvard psychologist Robert Kegan (1982) emphasizes that the essence of who we are as human beings is the activity of meaning-making.

[24] It is important to note, however, that this relationship does not appear to be specific to anxiety; rather, a wide range of psychopathology correlates with childhood sexual abuse.

[25] "Diathetic" is the adjective form of diathesis, which refers to a genetic or constitutional tendency or predisposition to manifest a given pathological condition. The stress-diathesis model states that in order for many pathologies to manifest, this diathetic predisposition must combine or interact with stressful experiences (Kendler, Myers, & Prescott, 2002).

Jang and Shikishima (2009) posed the following question: "As previous research has shown, if the same genes ostensibly influence unique disorders such as GAD [generalized anxiety disorder] and major depression, what causes them to express and manifest as GAD, depression, or both?" (p. 139). They proceeded to answer that the action and interaction of the environment is responsible for such differential pathologies. For example, whereas depression seems to be largely associated with "loss events" (such as the death of a loved one or job loss), GAD appears to be predominantly associated with "danger events" (such as those that could potentially harm the person).

It appears that studies of gene–environment interactions are yielding impressive results. For example, Stein and colleagues

> . . . found a statistically significant interaction between levels of childhood emotional (or physical) maltreatment and 5-HTTLPR genotype. Specifically, people who carried two short forms of the serotonin transporter polymorphism (5-HTTLPR) allele and experienced higher levels of maltreatment had significantly higher levels of anxiety sensitivity than subjects in other groups. These results provide evidence of a specific genetic influence on anxiety sensitivity—an intermediate phenotype for anxiety (and depressive) disorders. This effect is modified by severity of childhood maltreatment, and is consistent with the notion that 5-HTTLPR operates broadly to moderate emotional responsibility to stress. (as cited in Jang & Shikishima, 2009, pp. 140–141)

Although we have already highlighted the role of the family and caregivers in the development of anxiety disorders in the discussion of attachment and psychodynamic theories, those perspectives are far from the only ones highlighting the profound role that caregivers play in children's psychological vulnerabilities that predispose them to later develop anxiety disorders, and many of these studies of family systems have been performed by observing those interactions externally, hence a lower-right quadrant view. According to Rapee and Bryant (2009), "A tremendous amount of retrospective research has pointed to an association between specific parenting styles and adult anxiety disorders" (p. 204). Moreover, Rapee and Bryant concluded that behavioral genetic research supports this view. Chorpita and Barlow (1998) reviewed much of this research and stated that parenting styles that are helpful in buffering pathological anxiety include encouraging the child's autonomy, consistently being supportive and expressing warmth and sensitivity, and responding to children contingently (based upon the child's present experience, needs, and abilities) rather than in a rigid or fixed manner. Conversely, intruding on the child's sense of autonomy, being overcontrolling and/or overprotective, having negative or critical attitudes, and being more intrusive or enmeshed and less socially engaged are associated with a lower sense of control and hence an increased psychological vulnerability for developing anxiety and other related disorders. Other implicated systemic/environmental factors include a lack of social interactions, role inversion during childhood, and vicarious learning from a relative with an anxiety disorder (Rapee & Bryant, 2009).

Parental control as a factor influencing the development of anxiety disorders appears to have almost universal consensus (Ballash, Leyfer, Buckley, & Woodruff-Borden, 2006). Again, much of this should seem similar to and consistent with attachment perspectives. However, a child's external locus of control does not necessarily result solely from separation and/or loss experiences, or even from excessively stressful experiences; a child's cognitive vulnerability for anxiety may also derive from an overinvolved, overprotective, controlling parenting style (Barlow, 2004).

Another observable family variable is that first-born children tend to have higher internal loci of control than their later-born siblings (Hoffman & Teyber, 1979). Despite the large bodies of research supporting the notion that a variety of specific family system factors contribute to the development of anxiety disorders, one review of this literature concluded that although there are clearly associations between anxiety disorders and family factors such as attachment styles, parental control and other child-rearing strategies, and family functioning dynamics (i.e., marital conflict, sibling relationships, etc.), relatively little of that research clearly indicates that those family factors are implicated specifically in anxiety disorders; rather, those family factors appear to be implicated in the development of psychopathology in general (Bogels & Brechman-Toussaint, 2006).

Another social/systemic factor involved in anxiety is social support. Experimental research on monkeys suggests that the presence of social support from one's peer group leads to significantly fewer anxiety reactions, compared to those monkeys reared in isolation (Mineka, 1985). As you can probably imagine, this finding is readily transferrable to humans, and perhaps most interesting here is that it is not only the receiving but also the giving of social support that appears to reduce anxiety. Along similar lines, and particularly interesting from a social (LR) perspective are the studies that Rachman (1979) reviewed in which children in a variety of "high-risk" environments were enlisted to help others—individuals and families in their community—with substantial adversities. The children were called upon to help others cope as well as they could amidst difficult circumstances. This focus on others' well-being, reminiscent of Adler's concept of social interest, produced a measurable "steeling" or "toughening" effect in the children who were providing the help and support (as cited in Barlow, 2004).

Although most of the details remain to be discovered, virtually all researchers in the arena of anxiety disorders acknowledge a complex interaction of biological predispositions interacting with sundry psychological and environmental dynamics in the etiology of anxiety disorders; this notion is well captured by Barlow's triple vulnerability model (described on p. 114).

A topic with much less consensus involves the relative influence of shared, in contrast to nonshared, aspects of the environment: some studies suggest that the largest influence derives from *nonshared* aspects of the environment (i.e., one of four kids in the family has a life-threatening illness or receives a nationwide award), whereas other studies highlight the profound influence of *shared* aspects of the environment (i.e., all four of the kids in the family are severely disciplined, have high expectations placed upon them, and experience intrusive control from their parents). For example, much of the research studying twins with anxiety disorders suggest that an individual's *nonshared* environment is far more influential than *shared* environmental factors (Asbury, Dunn, Pike, & Plomin, 2003). In contrast, many other studies have highlighted the significant roles that *shared* environmental dynamics play in some anxiety disorders. As one example, children with similar generalized biological vulnerabilities are more likely to develop anxiety disorders if their parents encourage avoidant behaviors in the face of anxiety, compared to similarly genetically vulnerable children who are not exposed to such parental encouragement (Hudson & Rapee, 2008). Moreover, research by Boer and colleagues (2002) suggests that shared negative life events have a more significant impact than nonshared life events on anxious children and that such negative life experiences are what most clearly differentiate clinically anxious from nonclinical populations.

A potentially significant transmission mechanism deserving further research is that of *epigenetic inheritance,* which involves the transmission of gene expression (phenotype) even after the genes themselves (genotype) have been passed on. In other words, it appears that parents can transmit their phenotypic responses to stress and other environmental challenges to children even in the absence of the children's exposure to those stressful situations (Harper, 2005). However, we currently have an incomplete understanding of exactly how this occurs, specifically with regard to:

1. the effects of parents' psychopathology on children's development across a broad range of domains, including both positive and negative outcomes;
2. the mechanisms of risk transmission;
3. the reasons for discontinuities in the transmission of risk for psychopathology across generations;
4. the role of mothers' and fathers' mental health in children's development; and
5. the bidirectional nature of parents' and children's relationships—that is, children have effects on their parents just as parents have effects on their children (Poulton et al., 2009, p.117).

So far in this discussion, much of the environmental (LR) impact on anxiety has focused on the family system. However, large social systems are also implicated in the development of anxiety disorders.[26] According to Ingersoll and Rak (2006), a few of the sociocultural forces in America that contribute to heightened anxiety include the terror of 9/11 and the potential for future terrorist attacks in our country; the continued lack of equal rights for all Americans; an increasing distrust of politicians; a declining economy; and the disintegration of traditional values.

Contemporary America is often referred to as a "consumer culture," one in which we distract ourselves from various interpersonal, occupational, familial, existential and spiritual concerns with material goods, hobbies, travel, and so forth. This culture of "having" (consuming) rather than "being" offers endless possibilities to "escape from freedom" and the painful consequences of being responsible for one's choices (Fromm, 1941, 1976). Thus, many trade their freedom and responsibility for comfort and (illusory) security. I have counseled many clients who have remained in unsatisfying corporate jobs because they felt comfortable (not challenged) and their hefty salaries provided them the opportunity to travel and buy culinary, electronic, automotive, and other "toys" that kept them distracted, even if only temporarily. Compounding the matter, the United States is so wealthy that many can afford to distract themselves in endless ways until their anxiety builds to such a point that it finally bursts through acutely. One client of mine, in particular, illustrates this point. Dan was a successful businessman with two large homes, several luxury and sports cars, a yacht, and endless other "toys." Dan was referred to me by one of his family members who, from

[26] Scholars have differing positions on this point. For example, Frances (2013) emphasized that humans have evolved in environments that were always full of stress and danger; despite the stresses that many of us experience today, he argues that environmental stress is less severe now that it has been throughout most of our evolutionary history.

prior conversations with me, thought that I might be a good "fit" for him; otherwise, he likely would not have sought counseling. Despite the fact that he had obtained "success" in the business world and had all the luxuries a person could want, Dan was quite miserable. It turns out that he was wracked with existential guilt and anxiety. According to Sartre (1943/1993), he was living in bad faith. In our work together, he realized that although he had previously thought that what was most important to him were the conventional definitions of success that he had achieved, he had become deeply unsatisfied with how he was living (inauthentically). He now saw himself as a relatively shallow fraud, not in touch with the ideals that he remembered once having in his later teens and early 20s. After he realized that his unhappiness was a function of his not leading a life he could be proud of—or that his children could truly admire—he began reorienting himself, his time and his energies, toward artistic and service activities and his existential anxiety and suffering diminished greatly.

Notions about the etiological impact of larger systems in anxiety disorders do not merely "make sense"—they also have empirical support. For example, one study examined the association between mood and anxiety disorders with participants' perceptions of work stress and the degree of imbalance between work and their personal and family lives. Multivariate analyses revealed that both imbalance between work and their personal/family lives and work stress were independently correlated with both anxiety and mood disorders. In fact, those in the most stressful work situations and most imbalanced work–personal/family circumstances were four to five times as likely to have an anxiety disorder in the last month, compared to those in the least stressful, least imbalanced circumstances (Wang, 2006).

Also relevant from a social point of view is the powerful influence that managed-care exerts regarding the most appropriate treatment (which usually means what is most cost-effective).[27] Thus, today's market forces and influential corporations of the managed-care industry push for psychopharmacological interventions that rarely result in maintained benefits or a deeper understanding of oneself and what is most meaningful in one's life (anxiolytics are among the most frequently prescribed psychotropic medications in Western societies; Ingersoll & Rak, 2006).

Because people with anxiety disorders often appraise themselves as vulnerable and inadequate to the demands of a social system that is so competitive, fast-paced, and perpetually dissatisfied (always needing more progress, growth, and development), they often end up trading a life of passionate engagement with what they—in their deeper selves—deem important and meaningful for comfort and security. Thus, such people often lead restrictively avoidant lives that diminish their sense of vitality, authenticity, and self-efficacy while increasing shame, guilt, self-condemnation, and self-alienation; all of which is compounded by an increasing lack of felt-community and with it, concomitant psychological isolation.

## Developmental Dynamics in Anxiety Disorders

According to the authors of *Stress-Induced and Fear Circuitry Disorders: Advancing the Research Agenda for DSM-5,* although a developmental research framework was essential to the task of making the DSM-5 a substantial improvement over the DSM-IV,

---

[27] Because of this, managed care is often referred to as "managed cost" or "mangled care."

they doubted whether such a framework would be successfully advanced (it was not), largely because they argued that current etiological understandings of anxiety disorders are rudimentary at best (Poulton et al., 2009). Although children, adolescents, and adults do not always, or necessarily, comprise a sequence of development (because many teenagers are more developed than some adults, based upon tests of ego, cognitive, and moral development, and so forth), what the DSM-5 has to say on this point is not without value, especially in comparison to subsequently discussed perspectives.

According to the DSM-5, children and adolescents with GAD often worry about their competence and how well they perform; this occurs not only with their grades, sports, and so forth, but also in the absence of any external evaluation. They also frequently worry excessively about things on a spectrum of importance—from issues as "small" as their punctuality; to their needs to conform, obtain approval, and be "perfect"; to catastrophes such as war, tornadoes, and hurricanes. In contrast, adults with GAD tend to be anxious about a host of things, from minor daily events to career, children, health, and the state of local and world affairs, as well as larger existential concerns of authenticity, purpose, meaning, responsibility, death, isolation, freedom, and all of the many choices that must be made on those fronts. Other research has corroborated, to some extent, the general notion that fears and anxieties are differentially expressed across the life course. For example, one study found that separation anxieties are most common from ages 6 to 9; death and bodily danger fears are most common from ages 10 to 13; and fears of failure, criticism, and other social anxieties predominate from ages 14 to 17 (Weems & Costa, 2005).

The *Psychodynamic Diagnostic Manual* (PDM) has a section devoted to classifying developmental disorders in infancy and early childhood; in it, Anxiety Disorders and Developmental Anxiety Disorders are both classified as Interactive Disorders: "challenges in which infant– or child–caregiver interaction patterns play the major role" (PDM Task Force, 2006, p. 320). Importantly with regard to these disorders, the PDM emphasizes the need to take into account how contributions from (1) functional, emotional, and developmental capacities; (2) regulatory-sensory processing capacities; (3) child–caregiver and family patterns; and (4) medical and neurological diagnoses all interact to produce these disorders. The PDM emphasizes that particularly in children, the primary source and meanings of anxiety may not be clear. In its discussion of the presenting pattern of *Anxiety Disorders* (code IEC101), the PDM states that for very young children who cannot verbally communicate, the anxiety is often of a generalized nature: excessive fearfulness, agitation, tantrums, worries, panic reactions, and avoidance are persistently evidenced, even in the absence of possible separation from its caregiver. Infants only 3 to 4 months old may appear hypervigilant, overly reactive, and frequently frightened, even in the absence of danger. In contrast, older children who can verbalize their fears and anxieties may show fight-or-flight or freezing reactions and tend not to respond to reassurances (PDM, 2006).

When discussing *Developmental Anxiety Disorders* (code IEC102), the PDM begins by stating that developmental processes themselves may produce substantial anxiety, especially in children who have difficulty dealing with the changes inherent in developmental transitions. In more severe cases, the anxiety may be intensely disruptive, as in cases of children with insecure attachment styles, who may be terrified when their caregiver must separate, and consequently avoid exploring anything new, whether play activities or interacting with other children (PDM, 2006).

Consistent with the psychodynamic conceptualization that any personality or character type (i.e., dependent, histrionic, obsessive, or in this case, anxious) can exist at any developmental level or degree of pathology (neurotic, borderline, or psychotic), the PDM discusses and gives examples of anxiety manifesting at different levels of personality organization (McWilliams, 1994). *Neurotic:* "My mind is deluged with all sorts of frightening thoughts and images. My body is all nerves. I can't sit down for any period of time. . . . At my job I can't do a thing; I just feel I can't go on." *Borderline*: "My sense of self was hollow, like I didn't have a self, like I was outside myself. . . . There are all these characters who feel separate, not part of me, and they start fighting. I can't stop them or integrate them." *Psychotic*: "They have been blowing poison gas through the keyhole. It's destroying me and obliterating my thoughts" (PDM Task Force, 2006, pp. 98–99). In the neurotic quote, the type of *neurotic anxiety* that has been much discussed thus far in this chapter is evident. In the borderline quote, *fragmentation anxiety* is present: a fear of self-disintegration that, in small amounts, can be normal and tolerable; when chronic and intense, it can be unbearable and a key feature of borderline personality organization. In the psychotic quote, *annihilation anxiety* is present: a fear of being catastrophically overwhelmed, invaded, or destroyed.

Working from a different developmental perspective—one that emerged from Jane Loevinger's work with *ego development*—Susanne Cook-Greuter has described the characteristic anxieties most frequently observed in people who scored differently on her test of ego development, the Sentence Completion Test integral (SCTi). At conventional/conformist stages of development, the chief anxiety revolves around being "not-me;" "if they lose a sense of themselves as 'me-as-accepted-by-others' they lose their sense of self" (Cook-Greuter, 2010). For those who have recently grown beyond a conformist self, anxieties often revolve around concerns that they will not be strong enough to maintain their own views and commitments—that they may be drawn back to conformity. These anxieties and vulnerabilities often manifest as having an extra-strong front. For a more post conventional ("conscientious") individual, anxieties tend to revolve around the challenges involved with integrating different aspects of oneself (i.e., rational and emotional); people at this stage often feel confused by their multiplicity of selves. As people become increasingly autonomous, anxieties revolve around not fulfilling one's potentials and/or not acting in accord with one's individually chosen commitments. As a person becomes increasingly more developmentally complex, there are necessarily fewer people who can understand their experience; thus, their anxieties often involve not feeling understood.

In contrast to other sources, such as the PDM, it is surprising how little attention is given to developmental data in the recent DSMs, especially when one considers that most adult mental disorders, including the variety of anxiety disorders, have their origins in early childhood (Kim-Cohen et al., 2003; Pine, Cohen, Gurley, Brook, & Ma, 1998; Poulton et al., 2009; Whiteside & Ollendick, 2009). Given the considerable consensus on this point, Widiger and Clark (2000) stressed that "the amount of life span information that is provided in DSM-IV is only the tip of the iceberg of what should in fact be known" (p. 956).[28] In all fairness, the DSM is not alone in its dearth of developmental data: Poulton and colleagues (2009) searched the developmental literature regarding the

---

[28] We would further add that this applies to the DSM-5 as well.

etiology of anxiety disorders and reported "no studies that explicitly tested for etiological stability across the juvenile and adult period" (p. 113).

Ideally, a developmental perspective on anxiety disorders would also examine *cumulative risk*, both in terms of total risk-factor burden as well as duration of time exposed to such risk factors. For example, a study by Koenen and colleagues found that of those members in the "Dunedin" study who had at least three childhood risk factors, 58% developed Post-Traumatic Stress Disorder (PTSD; which was categorized as an anxiety disorder prior to the DSM-5) in the aftermath of experiencing a trauma, in contrast to only 25% of those members with no childhood risk factors who experienced a trauma (as cited in Poulton et al., 2009, p. 115). An optimal developmental framework would also be flexible enough to integrate new knowledge as it emerges. "If diagnosis *is* prognosis, then it seems that too little attention has been paid to developmental aspects of anxiety disorders or to considering how the interplay of biology and environment influence course, both singularly and across disorders. The current DSM [DSM-IV] provides a multiaxial system that recognizes cross-sectional heterogeneity. DSM-5 requires a developmental equivalent" (Poulton et al., 2009, p. 118, brackets added).

It is important to recognize the large amount of heterogeneity *within* many DSM diagnostic categories, because this represents a significant problem for a categorical system. A developmental perspective, however, "explicitly posits the existence of heterogeneous subtypes *within* disorders that follow quite distinctive developmental trajectories, reflected in age of onset (early versus late) and subsequent course of symptoms over time (temporary versus persistent)" (Poulton et al., 2009, p. 116, italics and parentheses in original).

Summarizing the results of a study by Kim-Cohen and colleagues that examined the degree to which adult mental disorders are derivative of juvenile disorders, Poulton et al. (2009) wrote that "adults with anxiety disorders had also had anxiety disorders in childhood or adolescence. However, adults with anxiety were also at elevated risk of having had juvenile externalizing-spectrum diagnoses of attention-deficit/hyperactivity disorder (ADHD) and conduct disorder (CD) or oppositional defiant disorder (ODD)" (p. 108). This is yet another example that highlights the *nonspecific* dimensions regarding the etiology and continuity of mental disorders.

A fundamental and misleading problem is that a great deal of research looks for various statistical correlations between variables (in this instance, the presence of a juvenile anxiety disorder and the likelihood of having an adult anxiety disorder) and because some researchers look at so many possible correlations, they frequently find some, often by chance alone, which is why (1) the results of those studies are often not replicable and (2) other studies often report highly contradictory findings. In this particular case (the study by Kim-Cohen et al.), if we are to accept the validity of the conclusion regarding the continuity of anxiety disorders in childhood, adolescence, and adulthood, we also must accept that anxiety disorders are not necessarily discrete entities—due to their high comorbidity rates with other disorders. At the same time, other research suggests that Panic Disorder, GAD, and the phobias do have distinct biological (e.g., neurochemical or neuroendocrine)—signatures (Yehuda, 2009).

## Etiology: Summary and Conclusion

As we have seen, there are many different notions about the etiology of anxiety and anxiety disorders. An Integral perspective acknowledges that each of these perspectives contains a vital component of the overall picture while also recognizing that each is also incomplete in its explanation of the origins and causes of these disorders. Thus, we concur with Poulton and colleagues (2009) that future research should no longer focus upon a traditional risk-factor approach that examines only a single or, at best, several risk factors but rather move toward approaches that aim to assess cumulative risk from as many quadratic and developmental perspectives as possible (See Figure 4.1 for a summary of the etiology of anxiety disorders from a quadratic perspective).

**UPPER-LEFT (UL): INTERIOR-INDIVIDUAL**

- Views of self as vulnerable, weak, incompetent, unlovable, etc.
- Views of the world and others as excessively dangerous, threatening, untrustworthy
- Fear, apprehension, and other distressing concerns regarding one's capacities to meet future demands
- High anxiety sensitivity
- Uncertainties about the future and a sense of (even if markedly inaccurate) one's own vulnerability, inadequacy, and/or inferiority result in varying degrees of apprehension and vigilance
- Many anxious people experience life as a relatively continuous struggle to avoid pain and other dangers
- Not assuming responsibility for living up to one's potentials as an authentic human being
- Confronting the "ultimate concerns" of existence

**UPPER-RIGHT (UR): EXTERIOR-INDIVIDUAL**

- Biological and genetic predispositions (Barlow's generalized biological vulnerabilities)
- Physical tension and increased sympathetic nervous system activity
- Avoidance of feared situations
- Extensive efforts to meet life demands and develop self-control are common
- Neurobiological processes of the hypothalamic-pituitary-adrenal (HPA) axis and corticotropin-releasing factor (CRF) activity
- Loss of cortical control of the brain's fear system
- Direct and vicarious conditioning
- Preparedness theory

**LOWER-LEFT (LL): INTERIOR-COLLECTIVE**

- Insecure attachment histories
- Psychological aloneness amplifies any anxiety that one may experience: "The experience of aloneness in the face of what is experienced as psychically dangerous is at the core of AEDP's understanding of psychopathogenesis" (Fosha, 2000, p. 37)
- Lack of intimate relationships that function as secure bases to help one mitigate the inevitable anxieties in life
- Internalized representations of others as unavailable, unreliable, and unattuned
- Maladaptive meaning-making systems (e.g., you'll go to hell for masturbating; some forms of religious education or otherwise rigid, harsh, and intolerant codes of conduct at home or school, etc.)

**LOWER-RIGHT (LR): EXTERIOR-COLLECTIVE**

- Parenting styles that are overly controlling, overly protective, intrusive, nonattuned, nonresponsive, and noncontingent
- Childhood abuse and other traumas
- Parents with insecure attachment styles and incoherent life narratives are much more likely to have children with insecure attachment styles
- Lack of social interactions or role inversions during childhood
- Vicarious learning from a relative with an anxiety disorder
- Actual interpersonal interactions that confirm anxiogenic thoughts
- Systemic structures such as both parents working, which leads them to be more stressed and tired so they have less time to foster secure attachments
- Fast-paced, long work days/weeks; we work more than most countries; we relax less and have less vacation time
- A society that is highly competitive; many are isolated/alienated and thus lack intimacy, belongingness, and social support

**FIGURE 4.1** A Quadratic Summary of the Etiology of Anxiety Disorders

## TREATMENT

### Introduction and a Caution About Empirically Supported Treatments

Treatments for anxiety disorders run quite a gamut, from pharmacological and behavioral to psychodynamic, cognitive, and existential, just to name a few. Several dozen meta-analytic reviews of treatments for anxiety disorders have been performed. Although many of these studies summarize a rather diverse array of disorders, the general conclusions are that psychotherapies demonstrate effectiveness compared to no treatment, control, or wait list comparison groups. Although this is a generalization, psychotherapeutic interventions also tend to have fewer dropouts and larger effect sizes than pharmacological interventions (Lambert & Ogles, 2004). However, to be a bit more specific, the results of meta-analytical research evaluating high-quality studies published in the 1990s emphasized that although the average patient who received "empirically supported treatments" for common disorders such as Major Depressive Disorder (MDD), GAD, and Panic Disorder improved substantially more—at the end of the study—than did the average control patient, still only about half of such patients showed such improvement, and all of those patients had passed numerous inclusion and exclusion criteria (Westen & Morrison, 2001). Thus, not only do issues of generalizability arise from such research; the data that are available suggest that even among those who were substantially better at the end of treatment, the majority did not sustain their improvements at 1- and 2-year follow-ups, especially for disorders characterized by generalized affect states such as MDD and GAD (Westen & Morrison, 2001). For these reasons, Westen and Morrison urge using terms such as "empirically supported" and "evidence-based" in more nuanced, qualified ways, being sure to acknowledge the limitations of time frames, sample selection, and the manner of reporting outcomes that can bias the conclusions one draws.

An important point in the previous paragraph is the distinction between treating a state (a temporary state of panic or anxiety) in contrast to treating a more chronic disorder such as GAD. For example, an emergency room visit can usually effectively remedy a given panic attack (state), but that is far from an effective treatment for a general disposition to be anxious with recurrent unexpected panic attacks (GAD or Panic Disorder). As the admirable research by Westen and Morrison (2001) makes clear, we do not currently know whether, or to what degree, the same interventions that have demonstrated efficacy in treating temporary states—such as depression and panic—are also effective in treating more chronic disorders—such as recurrent MDD and GAD. Studies that include long-term follow-up data are required to answer this question, and even when such claims are common in "empirically supported treatment" (EST) literature, the actual data to support such statements are difficult, if not impossible, to find (Westen & Morrison, 2001).

Across the 17 studies involving panic and the 5 studies involving GAD that Westen and Morrison (2001) examined, exclusion rates were 64% and 65%, respectively. What this means is that in an effort to isolate variables and create homogenous groups—necessary components when trying to ascertain the cause and effect relationships that are the goal of experimental research designs—the researchers whose studies were examined by Westen and Morrison *excluded* people as participants in their studies if they were suicidal, had recently had previous psychotherapy, or had comorbid diagnoses such as major depression, substance abuse or somatic disorders. Given that some of the exclusion criteria for these studies included depression and substance abuse/use disorders, which, as we have already seen, are *very common* among individuals with panic and GAD, this should lead you to seriously question the generalizability of such EST research. In short, we need to remain somewhat tentative with regard to claims regarding precisely how effective various treatments are for the average person who seeks help with any of the sundry anxiety disorders. Those who are interested in learning more about the limitations of EST research can consult Andrews (2000), Marquis and Douthit (2006), Slife et al. (2005), Wampold (1997), Westen and Morrison (2001), and Westen, Novotny, and Thompson-Brenner (2004).

## Assessment

Careful, thorough, and ongoing assessment—of not just diagnostic criteria, but also of the person—is critical because many of the specific objects/situations that clients are concerned with may represent merely the tip of the iceberg and/or may be symbolic of more significant fears/anxieties of which the person may be largely unaware. Also important is understanding each client's capacity to tolerate a deeper exploration and experience of the anxiety and what it may represent or mean to him or her. Not only do anxiety and depression often co-occur in the same person—either at the same or different times—a review of research on this topic suggests that having an anxiety disorder is perhaps the strongest single risk factor in the likelihood of developing depression (Hranov, 2007).

Although some researchers, theorists, and therapists consider anxiety and depression to be distinct disorders, the more common view today is that they are not only more closely related than the DSM categorical classification system suggests (and the DSM-5 itself acknowledges this), they are likely overlapping syndromes with common neurobiological underpinnings and that the amount of overlap is a function of whether they are described at symptom, syndrome, or diagnostic levels (Barlow, 2004; Hranov, 2007). The bottom line is that because many of the symptoms of anxiety overlap those of depression, it is not uncommon for some people with anxiety disorders (or a clinical presentation dominated by anxiety) to be erroneously diagnosed as depressed (Hranov, 2007; Ingersoll & Rak, 2006). At the same time, according to Beck and Emery (1985), people with GAD (compared to major depression) tend to have more positive views of themselves, more optimism for the future, and more positive memories of the past. Whereas depressed people tend to attribute their problems to global, structuralized deficits, anxious people more often criticize themselves for specific deficits and failure; an exception to this is that all of the social (evaluative) anxieties share a fear of being deemed inadequate or inferior (Beck & Emery, 1985). Also, because the *symptoms* of GAD and Panic Disorder can be produced by a host of medical conditions (such as hyper- and hypothyroidism, hypoglycemia, pheochromocytoma, hypercortisolism, chronic obstructive pulmonary disease, pulmonary embolus, aspirin intolerance, vestibular dysfunctions), a careful medical assessment by a physician is a critical component of an Integral assessment (not to mention the DSM category of Anxiety Disorder Due to Another Medical Condition). Finally, it is important to bear in mind the role that caffeine, cocaine, amphetamines, and other substances can play in producing anxiety symptoms, as can withdrawal from alcohol or other central nervous system (CNS) depressants (consult the DSM-5 section on Substance/Medication-Induced Anxiety Disorder).

## General (Integrative) Treatment Goals

Just as individuals are unique, so too are the goals of those who seek therapy with anxiety disorders. We value and prize diversity, individual choice, and healthy doses of nonconformity. Nonetheless, there does appear to be some general consensus that an integrative treatment of anxiety disorders (Wolfe, 2005) involves many of the following elements:

- Reducing anxiety symptoms
- Helping clients increase their tolerance for anxiety and other painful affects
- Increasing the client's sense of self-efficacy and agency
- Helping clients reduce their defensive exclusion of painful affects
- Restructuring clients' toxic self-representations
- Increasing awareness of, and modifying, how the client defends against the pain of a wounded self
- Helping clients learn to more deeply engage authentically in their relationships such that they have more intimacy, which affords the psychological safety of a secure base[29]

Another integrative approach to treating anxiety disorders is that of Jerold Gold (1993). According to him, general goals of treatment with anxious clients involve:

- Extensive assessment
- Symptom relief, cognitive and behavioral restructuring, and psychodynamic and interpersonal exploration
- Understanding and reconstructing the client's early attachment experiences; more specifically, modifying pathogenic representations; internalizing adaptive, beneficial representations of self and others; and facilitating the client's authentic, congruent self-experience

## General Approaches and Some Specific Interventions for Anxiety Disorders

In a nutshell, treating people with anxiety disorders involves helping them discover what they are *really* afraid of or concerned with, and to face those things (Barlow, 2004; Wachtel, 1977; Wolfe, 2005). Once one is aware of what the ultimate source of anxiety is, *exposure* to that source appears to be the key to effective

---

[29] Barry Wolfe (2005) has developed one of the most integrative approaches to the treatment of anxiety. This list is from page 191 of his seminal *Understanding and Treating Anxiety Disorders: An Integrated Approach to Healing the Wounded Self*. For a more abbreviated overview of Wolfe's approach to understanding and treating anxiety disorders, consult Wolfe (2003).

treatment (Deacon & Abramowitz, 2004; Foa, Huppert, & Cahill, 2006; Richard & Lauterbach, 2006). Another essential point is that virtually anything that helps a person develop a sense of control or self-efficacy, whether learning social skills or developing a sense of mastery with other coping responses, helps buffer the intensity of anxiety.

## UPPER-RIGHT TREATMENTS

**Behavioral** Behavioral interventions that appear helpful in treating anxiety disorders include modeling, behavioral skills training, assertiveness training (especially for anxiety disorders involving interpersonal interactions), and exposure treatments, the latter of which include both flooding and systematic desensitization. In essence, exposure treatments involve helping clients face what they are afraid of without retreating from it; the "without retreating from it" is referred to as "response prevention," and it is a critical component of exposure therapies because the typical response of avoiding the feared stimulus merely reinforces the activity of avoiding because such avoidance does in fact diminish one's anxiety, which is highly reinforcing. Because a variety of exposure methods have attained the status of "empirically supported treatments" (ESTs), we think it is important to reiterate that the EST movement has been critiqued by a variety of scholars.

As previously mentioned, I (Marquis) have published a critique of the EST movement because I believe that aspects of the research protocols—such as common exclusion criteria, the diversity of dynamics that are subsumed under a single diagnostic category such as depression or anxiety, and so forth—produce results and conclusions that are often not generalizable to average "real-word" clinical settings (Marquis & Douthit, 2006). However, it is also important to point out that interventions involving exposure and the prevention of avoidant responses for some of the anxiety disorders appear to be exceptions to many of the methodological problems associated with EST lists; this is because they involve associations between specific stimuli or internalized representations of such stimuli and specific responses (whether behavioral, affective, or cognitive)—for example, panic symptoms, simple phobia, specific social phobia, PTSD following a single traumatic experience, and some obsessive-compulsive symptoms. However, disorders characterized by more generalized affect states (such as GAD and MDD) violate nearly all of the foundational assumptions underlying EST methodology. Thus, it is no coincidence that "empirically supported treatments" for the latter category of disorders rarely produce clinically significant improvement at 1- and 2-year follow-ups (Westen, Novotny, & Thompson-Brenner, 2004). It is noteworthy that all five of the disorders mentioned previously as examples of disorders that may be appropriately studied via EST protocols are anxiety disorders (or the anxiety-related disorders or symptoms of PTSD and Obsessive-Compulsive Disorder [OCD]), and many of the change processes and specific interventions that are effective with them derive from behavioral approaches.

The single most important common element of behavioral approaches in the treatment of anxiety is that of exposure. Gold stresses two critical points regarding the tailoring of exposure interventions:

> First, the level of exposure must be gradual and tolerable for the patient (Wachtel, 1977). Sudden, severe jumps in the patient's anxiety will make new learning

> impossible. . . . Exposure . . . must be graded to maximize the chance of success and to reinforce the development of tolerance of anxiety to a degree that exposure becomes reinforcing of the willingness to experience slightly greater levels of discomfort. . . . The second foundation of successful exposure is the formulation by the therapist of modes and experiences in which the meaning of the source of the anxiety can be identified and changed. . . . It is highly important therefore to help the patient to learn that his or her thoughts, feelings, desires, or behaviors did not and do not have the toxic and destructive potential with which they were associated. (Gold, 1993, p. 298)

The prototypical graded exposure treatment is *systematic desensitization,* in which the therapist and the client collaboratively develop a stimulus hierarchy: a list of anxiogenic stimuli, ranked from least anxiogenic to most anxiogenic. For example, a person with a snake phobia might list imagining snakes at a zoo, imagining encountering a snake on a nature walk, watching someone on TV handle a snake, seeing an actual snake at a distance, walking nearer to the snake, and actually holding a (nonpoisonous) snake. The therapist and client then put aside the list while the client learns to relax, usually some form of progressive relaxation. After the client has learned how to reliably and consistently achieve a state of relaxation, the client considers the least frightening stimulus from the list. The client uses a subjective units of distress (SUDs) scale from 1 (low) to 10 (high) to report her level of anxiety. If the client reports an SUD of 3 or more, the therapist guides her temporarily to relax; if she reports an SUD of 1 or 2, the therapist guides her to refocus on the anxiety-eliciting stimulus. With each repetition of this process, the client remains more and more relaxed in the real or imagined presence of the conditioned stimulus, at which point the next stimulus on the hierarchy is encountered. Ultimately, the client can focus on the previously most frightening stimulus and remain relaxed, reporting an SUD of 1 or 2. After this process is successfully applied, the person encountering the previously feared stimulus now elicits the conditioned response of relaxation rather than anxiety (Fall et al., 2010).[30]

One comment on the effectiveness of exposure-based treatments is worth noting, particularly because it comes from Barry Wolfe, who co-authored a report on the effectiveness of exposure treatments with phobias with David Barlow:

> . . . the exposure-based behavioral therapy rarely cured the phobias. I was not seeing the rapid reduction or elimination of phobic symptoms in 60% to 70% of the cases I treated as I was led to expect by the research literature (Barlow & Wolfe, 1981). In my 25 years of experience with over 300 patients with anxiety disorder, I found that exposure therapy led to the rapid reduction of symptomatology in approximately 30% of the cases. (Wolfe, 2005, p. 5)

This is an excellent example of how therapy in real-world settings is often not as "neat and clean" as in random clinical trial (RCT) research, which is what is used to ascertain ESTs. While not diminishing the often times effectiveness of exposure methods,

[30] Interestingly but not surprisingly, research has found that one of the key determinants of how successful exposure treatments are for a given person is the level of physiological arousal during the exposure interventions (Borkovec & Stiles, 1979; Mineka & Thomas, 1999).

Wolfe's point highlights the need to tailor integrative treatment approaches for each individual.

**Pharmacological** Although numerous psychotropic medications appear helpful in ameliorating the symptoms of anxiety, an Integral psychotherapeutic approach not only integrates the many forms of treatment that are effective, it also considers it important to ponder why people are so anxious in our current culture, how we might be able to make our worlds safer places, and what might be the value of living constructively with anxiety. Although pervasive, the anxiety disorders, in general, are more responsive—at least in the short-term—to psychotherapeutic interventions than many other mental disorders (Ingersoll & Rak, 2006; Westen & Morrison, 2001). Thus, while honoring each client's needs and wishes, Integral therapists are mindful to inform clients who primarily desire anxiolytics that although medications may be helpful in managing the distressing *symptoms* of anxiety, they may also mask some of the very signals that are alerting the individual to important dimensions of life (meaning, choices, etc.).

The use of psychotropic medications for anxiety is an interesting case: Not only are they perhaps the most commonly prescribed psychotropics, they are also prescribed predominantly by nonpsychiatrists (more than 80% of the time; Ingersoll & Rak, 2006). As we will soon see, several classes of psychotropics are used to treat anxiety: CNS depressants, SSRI antidepressants, benzodiazepines, and unique compounds such as buspirone (BuSpar).

All CNS depressants induce behavioral depression. Thus, their effects include not only relaxation and sleep, but relief from anxiety as well. However, if used excessively, they can also result in general anesthesia, coma, and death. The primary CNS depressants used to treat anxiety are barbiturates, which were created in the late 1800s and dominated the anti-anxiety market from the early 1900s to about 1960. However, barbiturates are not specifically anxiolytic; rather, their anxiety-reducing effects stem from their overall sedating effects, not unlike the effects of drinking a lot of alcohol. Because they have so many negative side effects—ranging from cognitive inhibition, sleepiness, behavioral depression, and ataxia (loss of muscle coordination) to physical and psychological tolerance and dependence, and overdose-related death—barbiturates are not widely used to treat anxiety these days. Quaaludes are another CNS depressant that were once used to treat anxiety but are no longer regularly used because they too induce tolerance and depression and were frequently overdosed.

Today, benzodiazepines are the prototypic anxiolytic medication and account for approximately 90% of all anxiolytic treatment (Ingersoll & Rak, 2006; Stahl, 2002). There are currently more than 40 benzodiazepines on the market, ranging from the older, more fat-soluble, longer mean half-life[31] 2-Keto compounds (Valium/diazepam, Klonopin/clonazepam, Librium/chlordiazepoxide, Centrax/prazepam, and Dalmane/flurazepam, etc.) to the newer 3-Hydroxy compounds

[31] Mean half-life refers to the time it takes for half of the dose to clear out of one's body. As a general principle, the shorter the half-life of a drug, the greater its potential for tolerance and addiction. However, tolerance and addiction are also more likely to occur with benzos that are more highly potent, taken in higher doses, or taken regularly for longer periods of time (i.e., for more than 4 weeks).

(Restoril/temazepam, Ativan/lorazepam, Serax/oxazepam, and ProSom/Estazolam) to triazolo compounds (triazolam [marketed as Apo-Triazo, Halcion, Hypam, and Trilam], Xanax/Alprazolam, and Lendormin/brotizolam). Each of these three groups varies with regard to potency, duration of effect, and half-life. As mentioned in the neuroscience section on etiology, like other psychotropics, benzodiazepines do not act upon just anxiety; they also act as muscle relaxants, sedatives, intravenous anesthetics, and anticonvulsants.

It appears that benzodiazepines facilitate the binding of GABA via natural benzodiazepine receptors, inhibit synaptic action by facilitating conductance increases in chloride, and inhibit various stress-induced increases in norepinephrine, serotonin, and dopamine. Although benzodiazepines appear to reduce anxiety-related symptoms in approximately 75% of people, they are not without their side effects. First and foremost, although their potential for death by overdose is far less than that of the barbiturates, benzodiazepines are still lethal in overdose, particularly if massive quantities are taken with alcohol (Allen, 2010). Likewise, they can lead to physical tolerance, as well as physical and psychological dependence, although this is rare, especially among benzos with longer half-lives. If they are taken over only a short period of time or p.r.n. (i.e., infrequently, from the Latin *pro re nata*, meaning "as circumstances require"), then benzodiazepines tend not to induce tolerance to their therapeutic effects. Moreover, when rebound anxiety does occur during the withdrawal of benzodiazepine use, it usually lasts only 2 to 3 days (Ingersoll & Rak, 2006).[32]

Something of an "outlier" as an anxiolytic is buspirone (BuSpar), which was the first serotonergic drug to effectively treat anxiety symptoms.[33] Unlike the majority of anxiolytics, which seem to

> exert CNS depression by acting as GABA agonists, buspirone is actually a serotonin agonist and antagonist. Because serotonin is related to certain types of disinhibition of behavior and such disinhibition is also related to relief from anxiety, researchers have hypothesized since the 1980s that serotonin agonists may alleviate anxiety. (Barlow, 2004, p. 505)

Some of the advantages that buspirone has over benzodiazepines include the following: it is less likely to induce drowsiness and fatigue; it lacks hypnotic, muscle relaxant, and anticonvulsant properties; does not impair cognitive or motor functioning; has no synergistic effects with alcohol; does not induce tolerance; and has little potential for abuse and dependence (Barlow, 2004). Nonetheless, it does have side effects, which include gastrointestinal (GI) upset, dizziness, headache, and sometimes tension, restlessness, and nervousness.

Two noradrenergic anxiolytics target the SNS symptoms of anxiety, such as increased heart rate, sweating, and trembling.[34] One of these is propranolol. By blocking

---

[32] Rebound anxiety involves the anxiety one feels as a function of withdrawal symptoms (often feeling as or more anxious than one did prior to taking the medication).

[33] Interestingly, BuSpar is chemically less like an anxiolytic and more like a butyrophenone antipsychotic; it is classified as an azapirone (Barlow, 2004).

[34] Noradrenergic refers to a compound that impacts noradrenaline, the latter of which is synonymous with norepinephrine.

beta-adrenergic receptors (thus referred to as a "beta-blocker"), it decreases SNS stimulation and thereby significantly reduces the *physical* symptoms associated with anxiety. However, propranolol does not affect the psychological symptoms of anxiety. Another noradrenergic anxiolytic that appears to reduce physical but not psychological dimensions of anxiety is clonidine.

Although it may seem confusing at first, clinicians have long known that many clients taking antidepressants also experience a reduction of anxiety. Recall from earlier in this chapter that many researchers and scholars believe that depression and anxiety may share more of a common basis than what the DSM's categorical classification system suggests. At the same time, it is important to remember how idiosyncratic and unpredictable any given person's response may be to any treatment, whether psychological or pharmacological: not only have SSRIs apparently caused panic attacks in some people (Ingersoll & Rak, 2006), even progressive muscle relaxation can elicit anxiety in some clients (Mahoney, 2003).[35] Nonetheless, SSRIs also appear helpful in reducing anxiety symptoms in some people with anxiety disorders (Barlow, 2004; Ingersoll & Rak, 2006) and far more often than not, progressive muscle relaxation is an excellent method with which to facilitate relaxation and a sense of calm.

**Other Upper-Right-Quadrant Interventions** Other upper-right interventions that appear helpful in combating many anxiety symptoms include aerobic exercise, and perhaps more specifically, exercises involving balance, range of movement, and capacities to expand (Mahoney, 2003, p. 119). In one study (Broman-Fulks & Storey, 2008), 24 participants characterized as "high anxiety sensitivity" (Anxiety Sensitivity Index-Revised scores > 28) were randomly assigned to one of two groups, a no-exercise control group or the experimental group that completed six 20-minute aerobic exercise sessions. Even though aerobic exercise exposes individuals with high anxiety sensitivity to physiological cues that are very similar to those of anxiety, the aerobic exercise group had significantly less anxiety sensitivity after the exercise, whereas the control group's scores did not significantly change.

Many clients with anxiety problems breathe rapidly and from the chest. Teaching them to breathe slowly and deeply from the abdomen often helps diminish the intensity of their anxiety (Siegel, 2007). Both deep diaphragmatic breathing as well as mindful awareness of one's breathing have been found to be powerful components of anxiety reduction. Clients should not only be taught such breathwork but also be encouraged to *regularly* practice it both when they are anxious as well as when they are not, because the more one becomes proficient in using breath to regulate anxiety, the more effective it is under conditions of anxiety and panic (Greenberg, 2008; Miller, Fletcher, & Kabat-Zinn, 1995; Wolfe, 2005).

### TREATMENTS FOCUSING ON INTERIORS (UPPER-LEFT AND LOWER-LEFT)

**Cognitive** In general, cognitive approaches posit that by ameliorating dysfunctional information processing, core beliefs, and other cognitions, disturbances in anxious feelings and avoidant behaviors will diminish. Thus, cognitive therapists seek to minimize maladaptive thought processes such as catastrophic thinking, overgeneralizing,

[35] The latter most likely occurs because they experience it as a loss of control.

and exaggerating the magnitude of potential threats. Cognitive approaches also emphasize helping clients recognize earlier symptoms of anxiety and/or panic as well as helping them learn various coping strategies (e.g., decatastrophizing, questioning the evidence, distraction, thought stopping) to diminish or eliminate the anxiety and/or panic (Schoenfield & Morris, 2008).

How do cognitive therapists do this? First, clients are educated about cognitive distortions and other dimensions of faulty thinking. Another early goal is to increase each client's self-awareness such that they recognize distorted, dysfunctional thinking *as it is occurring*; after all, it is only after a client has developed the ability to identify her maladaptive cognitions that she can restructure those cognitions. Before clients will be able to consistently correct their faulty thinking on their own, therapists must help them do this many times in-session, and they do this largely through asking questions. Typical questions that Beck and Emery (1985) explore with their clients include:

- What is the evidence for or against this idea?
- What is the logic?
- Are you confusing a habit with a fact?
- Are you thinking in all-or-none terms?
- Are you taking selected examples out of context?
- Are you confusing a low probability with a high probability?
- Are you over-focusing on irrelevant factors? (pp. 196–198)

Cognitive therapists recognize the importance of a good therapeutic relationship. Thus, questions are not asked in mechanical, scripted ways. A good cognitive therapist is able to attend with warmth and empathy to each client while also teaching cognitive principles and obtaining detailed information. Guidelines to follow when asking questions include:

- Resist the inclination to answer questions for the client.
- Ask specific, direct, and concrete questions.
- Base each question on a rationale.
- Questions should be timed to foster rapport and problem solving.
- Avoid a series of rapid-fire questions.
- Use in-depth questioning.

Beck and Emery (1985) outlined three basic approaches that cognitive therapists take. They stated that

> Nearly all of the cognitive therapist's questions can be broken down to one of these questions: (1) "What's the evidence?" [analyze faulty logic, provide information, and help them learn to treat their thoughts, worries and concerns as hypotheses to be tested] (2) "What's another way of looking at the situation?" [generate alternative interpretations of the situation; help the client 'decenter' by challenging the belief that he is the point around which all things revolve; and enlarge his perspective] and (3) "So what if it happens?" [decatastrophize and help them learn new coping skills]. Some patients respond better to one approach than to another. Each patient, however, should develop skill in using all three approaches. (p. 201, brackets added)

Other cognitive interventions include:

- Understand the *idiosyncratic meanings* that the anxiety holds for the individual.
- Question/examine the evidence. However, this technique is much less effective with anxious than depressed clients because evidence that disconfirms the depressed client's view of a hopeless future powerfully negates the validity of such a view. In contrast, an anxious client's worry and concern that he *may* lose his job is much more difficult to refute; after all, even if he retains his job, he can argue that it was merely because of the extra hours he put in, which resulted in more marital discord, about which he is now anxious he will lose his marriage.
- Reattribute clients' anxiety to a host of factors, from genes (UR) and a hectic work schedule and financial worries (LR) to idiosyncratic patterns of thinking that exaggerate the person's psychological vulnerability (UL) and living within a culture in which racial, sexist, homophobic, and other threatening attitudes are present (LL).
- Develop alternatives. Help clients see that their panicky way of relating to their situation is merely one choice among others.
- Decatastrophize.
- Examine the fantasized consequences.
- Examine advantages versus disadvantages.
- Label the distortions.
- Develop replacement imagery.
- Use thought-stopping.
- Use distraction.[36]

Beck prefers to employ behavioral strategies only *after* some cognitive groundwork is laid in which clients can integrate experiences that disconfirm their catastrophic expectations (Beck & Weishaar, 2008). Various imagery techniques can be used to help clients experience their patterns of anxiety in the therapist's presence, with the therapist asking them to share their worst- and best-imagined outcomes of the scenario. This can lead to both greater perspective on the situation as well as being a type of learning experience in itself (Beck & Weishaar, 2008). Some of the more commonly used behavioral interventions include:

- Social skills training
- Assertiveness training
- Relaxation training
- Activity scheduling
- Bibliotherapy
- Shaping/graded task assignments
- Behavioral rehearsal/role-playing
- Exposure (imaginal or in vivo)[37]

---

[36] These and more cognitive interventions, as well as further descriptions of each, are from Freeman and Simon (1989).

[37] These and more behavioral interventions, as well as further descriptions of each, are from Freeman and Simon (1989).

**Psychodynamic/Attachment Theory** The more traditional psychodynamic approaches that have not developed radically beyond Freud's formulations aim, in general, to make the client conscious of how anxiety stems from unconscious impulses to act out sexual and aggressive impulses. By analyzing dreams, transference, resistance to free association, slips of the tongue and *working through*,[38] clients learn more mature ways (usually via more mature defenses such as sublimation) of dealing with their impulses such that they are able to gratify some of them with minimal anxiety.

More contemporary dynamic approaches share a common emphasis on the interpersonal (LL)—in contrast to intrapsychic (UL)—aspects of both etiology and treatment: constructive change occurs not strictly from within a person, but primarily between people (Wachtel, 2008). More recent dynamic approaches also recognize the importance of "corrective emotional experiences," in contrast to primarily intellectual insight. What this means is that it is often not enough simply to correct faulty thinking (e.g., replacing "all social interactions will result in my being humiliated" with "some social interactions may be embarrassing but they are not the end of the world and, actually, I have enjoyed and benefited from some socializing"). Rather, it is often necessary to *experience* (physically and emotionally) social interactions that are positive (and developing social skills before embarking on this may be an important component to the success of such experiences). This may sound similar to some cognitive-behavioral therapy (CBT) approaches, and many psychodynamic theorists acknowledge this (Gold, 1993; Wachtel, 2008). However, current dynamic approaches still emphasize the centrality of unconscious, conflictual, and defensive processes in most psychopathology. Thus, although CBT approaches appear more effective than dynamic ones in cases in which what is feared is clearly identifiable (as in many phobias), when the primary concerns are not readily identifiable (as with GAD, Panic Disorder, Social Anxiety Disorders, etc.), effective treatment involves exploring the client's internal and interpersonal worlds, understanding conflicts and defenses, and interpreting those to gain an understanding of the ultimate source of the person's anxiety. These sources are often interpersonal in nature; after they have been discovered, the client is repeatedly exposed to the anxiogenic situations (in person or imaginally). Wachtel points out that although most dynamic therapists do not use terminology such as "exposure" and "learning" (which are behavioral terms), that is in fact what Freud and many dynamic therapists do (Wachtel, 1987, 2008).

A good example of how a change in theoretical understanding is connected to a change in treatment interventions—and also illuminating some of the reason for the development in dynamic approaches—involves Freud's revising his understanding of anxiety. Originally, Freud posited that repression leads to anxiety.[39] If repression is thought of as "not-knowing" (i.e., unconscious forgetting), then the "cure" is insight or "knowing." However, Freud (1926/1959) revised his theory and stated that anxiety is not the consequence of repression; rather, anxiety results in the need to repress (the anxiety). Thus, if the source of pathology is anxiety/fear, then the "cure" is to become

[38] "Working through" is a gradual process of repeatedly processing insights into the client's unconscious drives, wishes, and fantasies with a goal of helping him realize how his defenses against anxiety actually create many if not most of his symptoms (Wachtel, 2008).

[39] Prior to 1926, Freud had viewed anxiety primarily as a discharge phenomenon. It was a consequence of "repression and of the damming up of libidinal tension that repression brought about" (Wachtel, 2008, p. 197).

less afraid, which is accomplished, in large measure, by being exposed to what one fears and experientially learning (emotionally as well as intellectually) that one need not fear it (or at least not as much) (Wachtel, 1987, 2008).

**Existential** Imagine a person seeking therapy to help with recurrent panic attacks, Social Anxiety Disorder, or some other anxiety disorder. Whereas most clinicians operating from a biomedical or cognitive-behavioral perspective will have as their priority the reduction of the anxiety symptoms, existential therapists tend to have rather different goals. Although they would agree with therapists of other theoretical orientations that panic attacks, excessive social anxiety, and so forth are not the essence of optimal living, existentialists view such anxiety as potentially communicating important information regarding problems, conflicts, or potentials that the person is not effectively dealing with.

> Though the existential therapist hopes to alleviate crippling levels of anxiety, he or she does not hope to eliminate anxiety. Life cannot be lived nor can death be faced without anxiety. Anxiety is guide as well as enemy and can point the way to authentic existence. The task of the therapist is to reduce anxiety to comfortable levels and then to use this existing anxiety to increase a patient's awareness and vitality. (Yalom, 1998, p. 249)

Effective work with a client's existential anxiety should recognize the meaningful message in the anxiety and motivate the person to take the action needed to live more fully one's highest purpose, which can result in more authentic engagement with life (May, 1977). Because the primal dread of existential anxiety is usually displaced or camouflaged into secondary fears and anxieties, it is often necessary to work to discern what the underlying existential anxiety is: "Primary anxiety is always transformed into something less toxic for the individual; that is the function of the entire system of psychological defenses" (May, 1977, p. 196).[40] In the event that what is primary for a given person is neurotic and not existential anxiety, then the work of the therapist is to help the client recognize the exaggerated or unnecessary nature of his anxiety and to work through it, whether that is in a relatively analytic or cognitive-behavioral manner. Even though secondary manifestations of anxiety are not primary, they are nonetheless real and existential therapists begin treatment with what the client presents as his concerns: "Thus in the treatment of many clients the existential paradigm of psychopathology does not call for a radical departure from traditional therapeutic strategies or techniques" (Yalom, 1980, p. 112). In addition to helping clients face and constructively use their existential anxiety, they also work to eradicate neurotic fears and anxieties: "Anxiety is more basic than fear. In psychotherapy, one of our aims is to help the patient confront anxiety as fully as possible, thus reducing anxiety to fears, which are then objective and can be dealt with" (May & Yalom, 1995, p. 264).

In an effort to help clients learn how to be, after Kierkegaard, "rightly anxious," existential therapists tend to confront clients' anxieties directly, sometimes even amplifying them. As Paul Tillich (1952) wrote in *The Courage to Be*, if we are not able to face

---

[40] Integral psychotherapists view existentialism, like other perspectives, as "true but partial." Thus, although some Integral therapists place a high premium on existential formulations, we do not believe that there are existential meanings in *all* anxiety conditions.

and attend to the existential anxieties that derive from what is of ultimate concern in life to us, we will never realize what it is to be human—that which sets us apart from other animals. Thus, existential therapists may ask a client "what keeps you from killing yourself?" Although this question may seem out of the ordinary, it can elicit what is most meaningful in life to that person—the "*why* to live for" in Nietzsche's dictum, which I (Marquis) paraphrase as "If you have a 'why' to live, you will find a 'how.'" Likewise, pondering how you would live if you knew you had only 1 month left to live can also reveal what is most important to you—what it is, precisely, that is most meaningful in your life. Consonant with Nietzsche's (1954) theory of eternal recurrence, if you would not like to live your life over and over again as you are currently living it, then change the way you are living.

Referring to the sickness of a variety of neuroses, including anxiety, Frankl (1985) wrote that the "cure is self-transcendence!" (p. 152). Frankl posited that we could become authentic human beings by exercising our freedom to create meaning in our lives in three fundamental ways: by doing good deeds or creative work, by loving others in such a way as to help them actualize their potentials, and by finding meaning in unavoidable suffering. In accord with Frankl's third way to create a meaningful life, the task of therapists is to help make "suffering that feels meaningless become meaningful" (Miller, 2004, p. 249).

**Spiritual** From an Integral perspective, when attempting to intervene with a client's anxiety from a spiritual perspective, it is important to discern the relative *legitimacy* and *authenticity* of that person's relationship to his or her spirituality (recall the discussion on this earlier in this chapter). If clients' spirituality is primarily legitimate, intervening will primarily involve working within their religious/spiritual system to help them make meaning of their anxieties and lives; this involves collaboratively discussing how the individuals can use their religious and/or spiritual beliefs to increase their feelings of safety and security (e.g., with devout Christians, the therapist can remind them of their belief that God's love and forgiveness is limitless and includes them). However, not all religious beliefs and practices are healthy for people, and some even contribute to their anxiety and should thus be explored and questioned. Excellent resources for distinguishing healthy and unhealthy aspects of some clients' understanding and practice of their spiritual tradition are Battista (1996) and Griffith (2010).

To the extent that the client is open to actively practicing the cultivation of virtues within her spiritual tradition, a host of meditative and other disciplines appear helpful in diminishing anxiety, even if they do not eliminate it per se. For example, various meditative techniques that tend to be subsumed under the category of *mindfulness* have been empirically demonstrated to lessen anxiety symptoms (Linehan, 1993a; Miller et al., 1995). In essence, the practice of mindfulness involves cultivating "the awareness that emerges through paying attention on purpose, in the present moment, and nonjudgmentally to the unfolding of experience moment to moment" (Kabat-Zinn, 2003, p. 145). If future worries arise, direct one's attention back to the present with an accepting, nonjudgmental attention. This requires that clients allow themselves to open to their emotional experience, which many are afraid of. Thus, teaching clients centering, balancing, and self-regulating skills is often a necessary prerequisite. A key point here is that clients must *regularly and consistently* practice meditation in order to obtain maximum benefits. On a related note, research has demonstrated that mindfulness-based interventions are more effective when performed by therapists with their own daily meditative practice (Segal, Williams, & Teasdale, 2002).

Gratefulness is another spiritual virtue that can assist clients in reducing their anxieties. In my clinical experience, I have found that with those clients with a religious or spiritual belief system, using a gratitude-related decatastrophizing intervention within their spiritual tradition makes decatastrophizing more powerful. For example, "you really want that promotion and feel like your world will collapse if you don't get it, but God will give you all you need" (therefore, cultivate gratitude for all that you currently have); or for a Buddhist client, "the self that you are worrying about is not your true nature. All of your worries will pass just as they are currently arising. Stay aware of the present moment and recognize your Buddha-nature."

**Wolfe's Integrative Approach** Wolfe (2003, 2005) outlined an integrative four-stage basic approach to anxiety disorders. First, the therapist must establish a therapeutic relationship with the client. Second, the therapist should teach the client a variety of techniques with which to lessen and regulate the anxiety. Such techniques include but are not limited to practicing being in the present moment (paying attention to bodily sensations rather than cognitive thoughts and worries); practicing deep, diaphragmatic breathing; and contradicting catastrophic thinking (this may involve examining the available evidence, self-affirmations, etc.). Third, the therapist elicits the client's panicogenic and phobogenic conflicts. Fourth, the therapist must help the client actually resolve the conflicts; this usually involves identifying the different elements of the conflict. The two-chair technique is helpful in understanding and magnifying the experience of the contrasting elements, coaching the client through various dialogues with the contrasting elements, and ultimately integrating the contrasting elements. Once this has occurred, a plan of action is created for the client to implement what was learned.[41]

Although the various exposure therapies are highly effective in treating phobias over the short term (Westen & Morrison, 2001; Wolfe, 2003), longer-term effectiveness without relapse more often requires addressing the underlying dynamics of self-experience, one of which is a general tendency of anxiety-ridden people to have great difficulty, if they are able at all, *to fully experience painful affect*. This is part of the rationale for integrating behavioral approaches with more experiential-dynamic ones (Fosha, 2000; Greenberg, 2002, 2008; Wolfe, 2003).

As Wolfe has stressed, virtually all clients fear pain, especially emotional pain. Wolfe has repeatedly observed that when anxiety-ridden clients are finally able to allow themselves to fully experience the emotions they are afraid of, their anxiety usually diminishes: "When such patients can maintain a strict attentional focus (without worrying, because worry often functions to avoid fully experiencing underlying fears) on what they fear, whether it be a specific external object or an internal sensation, they will contact the rage, humiliation, and despair that appear to be obscured by the anxiety. Often, but not always, patients will notice that experiencing these feelings is actually less painful than the anxiety" (Wolfe, 2003, p. 376).

---

[41] Although Wolfe (2003, 2005) described steps 2 and 3 in reverse order, he subsequently found that many patients need anxiety-management "tools" before they are willing to engage in the depth of work involved in eliciting panicogenic and phobogenic conflicts (personal communication, July 27, 2011).

Due to the importance of helping anxious clients deepen their affective experience, a primary component in an Integral approach involves helping clients experience previously unbearable anxiety within the context of the secure base that the therapeutic relationship offers. This affords clients the opportunity to learn (*experientially, not just intellectually*) that allowing a fully felt exploration of the anxiety is not only tolerable but it does not, in fact, result in the danger, abandonment, loss of control, or other consequences that were catastrophically feared. A primary function of attachment and the "secure base" it provides is to reduce anxiety, which diminishes the need to defensively exclude affective life. With such defensive exclusion in abeyance, "the transforming power of affect" (Fosha, 2000, p. 108) is released and the client has an immediate, visceral experience of core, healing affect that runs directly counter to his expectations: of intense emotion decreasing rather than increasing anxiety.

**INTERVENING FROM THE LOWER-RIGHT** Given that various systemic structures—from fast-paced, competitive work environments and an increasing sense of isolation from meaning-making communities to a host of inequitable social systems (economic, medical, educational, etc.)—appear to contribute to or trigger many people's anxieties, intervening at the systemic level can contribute to reductions of anxiety. Such systemic interventions may involve discussing the advantages and disadvantages of the client re-organizing her daily patterns in order to experience fewer stressors (e.g., working fewer hours/day and/or fewer days/year; making time for relationships, hobbies, exercise, meditation, etc.). Although this might involve letting go of how much one can do or accomplish, and thus diminish one's income, it often leads to an increased quality of life. I recall counseling a woman in her late 20s whose presenting complaint was anxiety. As it turned out, she was a single mother of two children, who was not only working full-time, but also attending graduate school part-time and raising her children by herself. She reported being terribly stressed by financial concerns, worrying about being able to pay for school, and having enough quality time with her children. In this case and many others, it was most beneficial for me to act as a resource advocate for my clients—helping them access and utilize various social services that have a concrete effect on their social circumstances (e.g., grants and other forms of financial aid, public assistance services, grassroots community support groups, Head Start and other preschool programs, and encouraging people to utilize free public resources such as parks and other natural areas).

In addition to helping clients access support services that are already available, intervening from the lower-right quadrant may also involve advocating for structural changes within social systems and policies that contribute to clients' suffering. For example, I once counseled a gay man named Dave who had been monogamous with his life partner, Eric, for 30 years. Eric had recently been diagnosed with cancer when I began counseling Dave. Eric was self-employed and did not have health insurance and Dave was unable to place Eric on his insurance policy because its coverage extended only to partners in marriage. In the course of our sessions, Dave shared how this social injustice exacerbated an already anxiety-provoking situation. Thus, those who are able to change social systems and/or policies—like the one impacting Dave and Eric—such that they are more just and equitable will decrease the unnecessary suffering that so many people experience.

## Treatment Conclusion and an Illustrative Case

Given that many anxious clients are snared within vicious circles, Integral therapists posit that an optimal approach takes into account the synergistic aspects of at least the four quadrants. Thus, from an upper-right perspective, modifying overt behaviors and utilizing exposure therapies is essential; also helpful at times is the use of various psychotropic medications. From an upper-left perspective, promoting insight into deeper symbolic meanings of the feared situations and modifying maladaptive cognitions and catastrophic imagery is often critical. From a lower-right perspective, any number of various systems, from occupational and familial to economic and global politics, may be implicated in the client's anxiety; working as an advocate for change of inequitable social systems is increasingly recognized as within the purview of counselors and other mental health professionals. From a lower-left perspective, it is imperative to pay attention to the specifics of the client's significant relationships (and their capacities to function as secure bases for the client) as well as the meaning-making systems they use (from implicit family-of-origin rules and messages to central belief structures of their religious affiliations) to understand themselves and their lives. The following case illustrates many of the aforementioned dynamics.

---

Maria, a 25-year-old Mexican American, was a professional chef who had recently been invited to appear on a local TV show, but declined because she was too afraid that she would have a panic attack in front of the live audience that was part of the TV show. Being so disappointed at passing up such a big opportunity was what prompted her to seek professional help. Maria reported that she had worried about many things throughout her life, including worrying about having more panic attacks; in particular, that others would think she was crazy and that she would be humiliated to have a panic attack in public. Although she often had a drink or two with dinner, and would occasionally have three or four drinks at a party, it did not appear that substance use, or any medical condition, was responsible for her panic attacks.

Based upon her descriptions, it is likely that her father had Generalized Anxiety Disorder, although he was never diagnosed or treated for it. According to Maria, he worried "all the time" and avoided a career as a professional musician because he was too afraid to perform in front of live audiences. She further related that two of her three older siblings were excessive worriers. Thus, in addition to a likely genetic component to Maria's anxiety and panic, she may have learned from her father's and her siblings' modeling not only to worry, but to avoid those situations that caused her any anxiety.

As a child, Maria lived in a poor and crime-ridden part of town in an apartment with her parents and siblings. She reports that the apartment had exposed lead paint chipping away that she remembers was eventually repaired by the landlord during her early teen years. Her family shared their home with extended family members throughout much of her life and she would often share a room with various cousins, in addition to with her sisters. Maria frequently overheard her parents discuss their worries about finances, the safety of the neighborhood, and of their extended family struggling in Mexico; hearing her parents so concerned about these social/environmental issues may have been a factor contributing to her not feeling that the world was one that she had much control over.

Maria and her siblings were the first of her family to be born in the United States, and she reported being frequently teased at school as being the child of "wet-backs." She ended up hating school, and frequently skipped school to help out at the restaurant at which her mother was a waitress (it was there that she became interested in cooking).

Although her declining the TV show was the first time that her anxiety had resulted in her actually avoiding a major event that she really wanted to participate in, it was not the first time that she had worried about being unable to ward off future panic attacks (she did not believe that she had control over her anxiety). She thus spent most of her time either alone, with her one best friend, at the restaurant, or at home with her family. Her sense of herself was of someone who was weak, lacked emotional control, and had poor social skills. Deep down, she saw herself as incompetent, inadequate, and as something of a phony—"I don't know how I ever got to be head chef at the restaurant—I guess I'm just really lucky."

As for many Mexican Americans, Maria's family was extremely important to her, and her sense of self seemed very influenced by her family. She reported that her parents were loving and very involved in her life. She also said they had always been fairly controlling and overprotective, and were quite rigid in their rules and punishments. She realized that they did not encourage her to develop independence (she still lived at home when I counseled her). She expressed that she often felt a tension between making decisions about her life based on what was best for her family versus what she wanted to do.

A crucial aspect of helping clients with anxiety disorders involves helping them become increasingly able to deepen their affective experience, and essential to this process is facilitating their experiencing previously unbearable anxiety in the presence of the therapist, with the client using the therapeutic relationship as a "secure base." I agree with Wachtel (1977) and others (Barlow, 2004; Wolfe, 2005) that treating people with anxiety disorders is fundamentally a process of discovering what they are ultimately afraid of, and helping them face those things without the dreaded consequences occurring. I was less psychodynamic/attachment focused with Maria than was usual for me—partly because she reported feeling deeply loved by her parents and her best friend, and partly because she was insistent that she wanted her anxiety and panic symptoms to "go away as quickly as possible." Maria seemed to have a fairly secure attachment style, and related warmly and openly with me; thus, Maria and I formed a strong working alliance very quickly. To help her manage her anxiety and possible panic attacks, I referred her to a psychiatrist who prescribed her Lorazepam to be taken p.r.n. (UR). I encouraged her to use the Lorazepam only when she could not regulate her anxiety with the following strategies, which I instructed her in, and she practiced in-session and at home: deep diaphragmatic breathing (UR), which she paired with her use of her rosary (which helped her become grounded; she was Catholic [LL]); cultivating mindfulness (nonjudgmental awareness that is focused on the present moment—more about sensing than thinking [UL]); and contradicting catastrophic thinking by examining the evidence that things would likely be catastrophic (UR/UL). Thus, we engaged a three-pronged approach that (1) tried to reduce her anxiety symptoms, (2) helped her increase her tolerance for anxiety, and (3) restructured her negative self-views with more positive, realistic ones. One of the ways we addressed the second task was by having her imagine a dreaded scenario occurring (such as having a panic attack on the TV show that she declined). As she would become anxious, she would practice her deep breathing but would also allow herself to more fully experience the anxiety than simply trying to minimize or avoid it. This gave her the emotional experience—not just the intellectual idea—that she could not only tolerate her anxiety, but that the catastrophes she feared were unlikely to occur (i.e., that she would be publicly humiliated and seen as incompetent). I also helped her see that she was socially quite skilled, and provided her with evidence that she was more capable and competent than she perceived herself to be (the third task). This eventually led her to feel more confident in her capacities to deal with her anxiety when it arose. The exposure work that we did together took the form of systematic desensitization, and her imagined scenarios all involved the TV show she had declined.

Cultural and social dimensions of Maria's struggles involved helping her recognize that although the racial taunting/bullying that she had experienced in school was utterly cruel and unjust, it had not occurred since her early teen years. She eventually found it helpful to acknowledge that although our society is not free from racism, she was not currently being disadvantaged or oppressed because of her ethnicity. But that was a different matter than the economic hardships (LR) that her parents, and especially her extended family in Mexico, faced on a daily basis. Here, it was helpful to point out that although her family in Mexico truly lived in poverty, she was making a decent living as a chef, and there was no evidence that she could not continue to support herself while also sending some money to her extended family. Although such cognitive strategies are a far cry from ameliorating economic inequities among different social classes, it did seem to be one helpful component of managing her anxiety symptoms. The work I did with Maria emphasized the upper, individual quadrants, but we also addressed the lower quadrants—not only with respect to her culture (Mexican American, Catholic) and socioeconomic status, but also by using our therapeutic relationship as the foundation of our work together. When we ended our work together, Maria felt confident that if she were given another opportunity to be on a TV show, she would not hesitate to accept the offer.

## A BRIEF LOOK AT THE FIVE MOST COMMON ANXIETY DISORDERS

In this section, we will explore in more detail the etiological factors involved in the five most common anxiety and anxiety-related disorders: Panic Disorder, Specific Phobia, Social Anxiety Disorder, Generalized Anxiety Disorder, and Obsessive-Compulsive Disorder. Although OCD is no longer included in the DSM-5 section on Anxiety Disorders, it is included here because it is certainly "anxiety-related." Summarizing the results of a study by Kim-Cohen and colleagues that examined the degree to which adult mental disorders are derivative of juvenile disorders, Poulton et al. (2009) pointed out that "it was noteworthy that neither GAD or OCD 'looked out of place' compared with the other anxiety disorders; their patterns of continuity closely mirrored those of PTSD, which raises questions about the exclusion of these two disorders from the anxiety disorders section for DSM-5" (p. 110).

## Panic Disorder

According to the DSM-5, the primary diagnostic criteria of Panic Disorder involves unexpected, recurrent panic attacks, the essential feature of which is intense discomfort or fear that arises and peaks very quickly, and during which four or more symptoms from the following occur: trembling or shaking; sensations of choking, smothering, or shortness of breath; sweating; chest pain; heart palpitations; sensations of numbness, tingling, heat, or chills; nausea or abdominal distress; derealization or depersonalization; feeling lightheaded, dizzy, or faint; and fear of losing control, going crazy, or dying (APA, 2013). In general, the view that panic disorder involves intense anxiety related to a person's focusing on the bodily-felt sensations that are associated with panic attacks has received considerable empirical support (Barlow, 2004). Likewise, it is largely agreed that agoraphobia (which almost always—at least in mild forms—accompanies panic disorder) represents an avoidance coping strategy—that is, avoiding those situations in which a panic attack might occur.

There are two primary perspectives on the etiology of Panic Disorder; the first emphasizes cognitive-behavioral and psychosocial processes, and the second is a biological model (Poulton et al., 2009). The cognitive dimensions of Panic Disorder involve the person's beliefs and thoughts regarding the presumed catastrophic nature of panic attacks (Barlow, 2004). For example, it is common for such individuals to believe they are having a seizure, heart attack, or stroke; they may think they are fainting, suffocating, losing control, going crazy, or actually dying. Because Panic Attacks often occur without a clear external stimulus, people suffering from Panic Disorder develop a host of faulty beliefs revolving around their own inadequacies and vulnerabilities. As we have seen throughout this chapter, avoidance of feared situations is a key feature of anxiety disorders. Panic attacks and Panic Disorder are frequently comorbid with Agoraphobia (in the DSM-IV-TR, "Panic Disorder with Agoraphobia" was a single mental disorder), and four categories of avoidance or protective behaviors appear to maintain the Panic Disorder: agoraphobic avoidance, distraction, interoceptive (somatic) avoidance, and safety behaviors.

*Agoraphobic avoidance* involves avoiding situations in which one might be embarrassed, might not be able to escape, or in which one might not receive help were one to have a panic attack. Such situations include being outside of one's home or in a crowd (e.g., grocery stores, churches, theaters, malls, restaurants); traveling in an automobile, bus, or train; or being on a bridge. *Distraction* is another strategy that is geared toward the person avoiding the signals of a potential panic attack. Essentially, people try to distract themselves from potential panic by focusing their attention elsewhere—whether by talking to someone, watching television, listening to music, or reading, and so forth. David Barlow (2004) believes that *interoceptive avoidance* is "every bit as important as more classical agoraphobic avoidance" (p. 330) and it involves the avoidance of things or activities that produce somatic symptoms similar to those involved in panic. Some of the more commonly avoided interoceptive activities include consuming food or beverages with caffeine; engaging in sports or other aerobic activities, including dancing and sexual relations; participating in intense debates; watching horror or suspense movies; or standing up quickly from a seated position. *Safety behaviors* include any action that makes the person feel more protected or secure in case a panic attack occurs. For example, going somewhere or engaging in an activity only if a "safe person" (someone who knows the person has panic attacks and would help them in the event the person does panic) is with them or always carrying a cell phone, medication, religious symbol, or a lucky charm.

Interestingly, in a study that compared the prevalence of stressful major life experiences (i.e., severe illness or death of a co-habiting relative) in 23 clients with Panic Disorder and 23 normal controls (matched for sex, age, education, and social class), the former group had significantly higher rates of stressful life events in the 2 months prior to their first panic attack (Faravelli, 1985).

The biological perspective posits that the key etiological factor involves unusually low thresholds for suffocation symptoms or other physiological responses such as respiration, heart rate, and blood pressure. However, as we have repeatedly seen in this chapter, findings have been mixed, with different studies supporting both schools of thought (Roth, Wilhelm, & Pettit, 2005; Silberg, Rutter, Neale, & Eaves, 2001). Nonetheless, genetic contributions to Panic Disorder seem clear: first-degree biological relatives of someone with Panic Disorder are eight times as likely to develop Panic Disorder as are those without such relatives (APA, 2000, p. 437).

Cognitive-behavioral approaches appear to be the most effective treatment for Panic Disorder (Barlow, 2004). Because a core feature of people experiencing Panic Disorder involves their erroneous beliefs regarding their inadequacies and vulnerabilities, it is important to deeply explore and understand what those maladaptive beliefs are so that they can be replaced and restructured with more adaptive thought processes. Such cognitive approaches appear most helpful with regard to the panic attacks themselves, whereas various exposure therapies appear to be more effective in decreasing agoraphobic and other avoidance behaviors (Barlow, 2004).

## Specific Phobia

Specific Phobia is among the most significant of all mental disorders; not only is it one of the best understood and most successfully treatable disorders, it also affects approximately 11% of the population (Barlow, 2004). According to the DSM-5, the primary diagnostic criteria of Specific Phobia include significant fear or anxiety associated with a specific situation or object that consistently provokes fear or anxiety that is disproportionate to the actual situation or object; as a result, the person either avoids the situation or object, or suffers through the fear or anxiety, either of which leads to clinically significant impairment or distress (APA, 2013). The DSM-5 delineates five specifiers of Specific Phobias: animal (spiders, snakes, dogs, etc.), natural environment (storms, heights, water, etc.), blood-injection-injury (BII; observing blood or an injury or receiving an injection), situational (flying, enclosed places, bridges, etc.), and other (cued by stimuli not better classified as one of the four subtypes, such as a fear of vomiting, choking, or contracting an illness).

There are two primary perspectives on the etiology of phobias. In the first, the associative-conditioning perspective, phobias are seen as deriving from learning experiences in which various stimuli become conditioned (via associative processes) to fear responses. In the second, the (more innate) biological view, phobias are seen as deriving primarily from endogenous, nonassociative processes (Poulton et al., 2009). As is often the case, there are numerous studies that appear to support both perspectives (Kendler, Myers, & Prescott, 2002; Mineka & Zinbarg, 2006).

The associative-conditioning perspective posits that the etiology of Specific Phobias involves associating a situation or object that is either potentially dangerous or otherwise "prepared" with a true or false alarm.[42] Bouton, Mineka, and Barlow (2001) provide powerful evidence that the emotional learning that occurs in the etiology of specific phobias operates according to the principles of conditioning; moreover, such emotional learning and fear conditioning can occur without conscious awareness (LeDoux, 1996; Ohman, 1992).

Although the data are, as usual, mixed and somewhat contradictory (Barlow, 2004),[43] overall the consensus is that genetic contributions to Specific Phobias are important, especially with regard to how such predispositions interact with early learning experiences. More specifically, it appears that there are three distinct learning processes implicated in the etiology of Specific Phobias: direct conditioning (e.g., actually being bitten and traumatized by a dog), vicarious or observational learning (e.g., observing a friend being attacked by a dog), and information/instruction (e.g., reading about or having one's parents talk about how dangerous dogs can be; Rachman, 1977). Nonetheless, it seems that experiences of direct conditioning are the most commonly reported origin of Specific Phobias. Consistent with Barlow's triple vulnerability model (2004), it appears that the etiology of Specific Phobias involves the interaction of (1) a relatively nonspecific genetic tendency to experience anxiety, fear, and/or panic; with (2) a general psychological vulnerability for anxiety; and (3) specific learning experiences.

From the perspective of treatment, "there is very little disagreement regarding the treatment of choice for specific phobias. Almost all experts agree that exposure to feared objects and situations is both necessary and sufficient for treating the vast majority of patients with this condition" (Barlow, 2004, p. 408).[44] Unlike most psychopathologies, it is widely agreed that pharmacological treatments are of minimal help for those with Specific Phobias. Moreover, it is argued that medications actually "interfere with the effects of exposure-based treatments by preventing the individual's fear from increasing to a sufficient level" (Barlow, 2004, p. 416).

## Social Anxiety Disorder (Social Phobia)

Social Anxiety Disorder is not only the most common of the anxiety disorders; it is also the third most common of all psychopathologies (Barlow, 2004). According to the DSM-5, diagnostic criteria of Social Anxiety Disorder include significant anxiety or fear that almost always arises in social situations, especially those in which it is possible—even if unlikely—to be evaluated or scrutinized by others. As the anxiety and fear are

---

[42] A true alarm is fear or panic in the presence of a potentially dangerous stimulus; a false alarm is fear or panic in the absence of such a potentially dangerous stimulus (Barlow, 2004, p. 320).

[43] "To complicate matters further, there is no consensus about etiological pathways *within* phobia categories" (Poulton et al., 2009, p. 112).

[44] Nonetheless, it's important to remember Barry Wolfe's point (earlier in this chapter): ". . . the exposure-based behavioral therapy [in-and-of itself] rarely cured the phobias. I was not seeing the rapid reduction or elimination of phobic symptoms in 60% to 70% of the cases I treated as I was led to expect by the research literature (Barlow & Wolfe, 1981). In my 25 years of experience with over 300 patients with anxiety disorder, I found that exposure therapy led to the rapid reduction of symptomatology in approximately 30% of the cases" (Wolfe, 2005, p. 5).

disproportionate to the actual social situation, the latter are usually avoided or suffered, either of which leads to clinically significant impairment or distress (APA, 2013).

In a review of etiological perspectives on Social Anxiety Disorder—from genetic factors and temperament to cognitive distortions, skill deficits, child-rearing experiences, adverse social experiences, and other negative life events—Rapee and Spence concluded that an understanding of the etiological bases of Social Anxiety Disorder is strictly limited and remains rudimentary (Rapee & Spence, 2004). Nonetheless, certain conditions seem likely to be implicated in the development of Social Anxiety Disorder. For example, even though considerable evidence suggests that individuals experiencing Social Anxiety Disorder are not deficient in social skills, they do tend to evaluate their social performances more negatively than nonsocially phobic people do, even after actual performance differences are accounted for (Rapee & Lim, 1992). From an evolutionary perspective, it makes sense that being sensitive to critical, rejecting, or angry social stimuli has its adaptive sides, and is likely a form of biologically determined readiness (Ohman, 1986).

Like other anxiety disorders, it seems virtually certain that an interaction of biological, psychological, and environmental factors contributes to the development of Social Anxiety Disorder. In fact, David Barlow (2004) stated that his "present model of the etiology of social phobia . . . follows very closely the models presented for other anxiety disorders" (p. 461), by which he is referring to the triple vulnerability model. Although it appears that genetic contributions to Social Anxiety Disorder are nonspecific, they do seem to correlate with certain temperamental variables, such as shyness and behavioral inhibition (timidity, wariness, and fearfulness when encountering novel social situations).

In a more recent review of the literature on the etiology of Social Anxiety Disorder, Beidel and Turner concluded that in addition to genes and other biologically predisposing factors, direct conditioning, parental modeling, and other vicarious conditioning, as well as information transfer (similar to what was previously mentioned with regard to specific phobias) seem to be involved (Beidel & Turner, 2007). For example, when parents communicate to their children that the world is not a safe place, that people cannot be trusted, or that people are always evaluating you and trying to discover your weaknesses in order to exploit you, this transfer of information is one of many risk factors contributing to the likelihood of developing a Social Anxiety Disorder. Moreover, referring to a multitude of studies examining the research base to support the creation of a distinct category of "stress-induced and fear circuitry anxiety disorders" for the DSM-5 (which *would* have included not only Panic Disorder, Specific and Social Phobia, but also PTSD; this category ended up not being included in the DSM-5), Fyer and Brown stated that for each disorder they examined, they "found evidence for both the distinctness and overlap of the current diagnostic categories. We conclude that the data, consistent with findings in other areas of medicine, suggest a more complicated interrelationship between potential etiological factors (e.g., genetics, environment, developmental course) and current clinical syndromes definitions" (Fyer & Brown, 2009). Moreover, Poulton and colleagues stated that our current understanding of the etiology of Social Anxiety Disorder is still rudimentary. A review of etiological factors involved in Social Anxiety Disorder that included temperament, genetic factors, negative life events, child-rearing experiences, adverse social experiences, skills deficits, and cognitive distortions emphasized the severe limits to our knowledge of the etiology of Social Anxiety Disorder (Rapee & Spence, 2004).

With regard to treatment, research supports the efficacy of cognitive-behavioral approaches (especially in its group form; Heimberg, Salzman, Holt, & Blendell, 1993), exposure therapies, social skills training (for those who need it), and—to help one get through difficult social situations but not to overcome the Social Anxiety Disorder itself—drug treatments (including SSRIs, monoamine oxidase inhibitors [MAOIs], benzodiazepines, beta-blockers, and tricyclic and other antidepressants; Barlow, 2004).

## Generalized Anxiety Disorder

According to the DSM-5, diagnostic criteria of Generalized Anxiety Disorder include exaggerated anxiety and worry—occurring more days than not—that is associated with three or more of the following: muscle tension, restlessness or feeling on edge, difficulty concentrating, becoming fatigued easily, irritability, or some form of sleep disturbance. The anxiety and worry—which the person finds hard to control—revolve around more than one aspect of life, and result in either procrastination, avoidance, repeated assurance-seeking, or significant effort and time trying to avert negative outcomes, any of which leads to clinically significant impairment or distress (APA, 2013).

Changes in the conceptualization and criteria for GAD have been heavily debated ever since it was first included in the DSM-III. Given the difficulty of reliably differentiating GAD from other anxiety disorders (and even mood disorders), it is not surprising that the validity of the GAD diagnosis continues to be debated (Schmidt, Riccardi, Richey, & Timpano, 2009). Nonetheless, because the central feature of GAD is worry, and worry is a common feature across the anxiety disorders, some experts consider GAD to be the "basic" anxiety disorder (Barlow, 2004, p. 477). Moreover, David Barlow stated that not only would a deeper understanding of the etiology of GAD shed light upon all of the anxiety disorders, but due to its close link with major depression, a greater understanding of GAD may have significant implications pertaining to all emotional disorders (Barlow, 2004).

The empirical findings of two separate large samples, in the form of taxonometric analyses, suggest a "worry taxon"—"a form of worry that is qualitatively different from most worry that is experienced."[45] Although merely identifying a taxon reveals virtually nothing of its origins or nature, the data from these two studies suggest that pathological worry may span a much broader spectrum than previously thought, which would lead to including more (previously subclinical) people in the diagnosis of GAD. The worry of those with GAD is experienced as excessive and difficult to control or stop. Worry is fundamentally a conceptual (verbal, linguistic), as opposed to imaginal, activity that generates a multitude of potential future negative events, if not catastrophes, without active attempts to cope with or solve the feared future outcome. A number of theories have attempted to explain why such a phenomenon would occur, and we will briefly look at each of them: avoidance, information-processing biases, and meta-worry.

Borkovec and colleagues have put forth an *avoidance theory* of GAD that has garnered empirical support; briefly, it posits that worry is a cognitive process that not only

[45] A taxon refers to naturally occurring, nonarbitrary categories (Schmidt et al., 2009, pp. 366, 370).

alerts people to potential threats but also serves as an insulating avoidance of deeper emotional experience (Borkovec, Alcaine, & Behar, 2004). For two reasons, worry becomes maintained through negative reinforcement. First, worry is associated with a decrease in autonomic arousal that is reinforcing; second, the feared future catastrophes (which tend to be relatively unlikely to occur from a statistical point of view) usually do not occur and the individual then attributes the nonoccurrence of the calamity with his or her worrying, thus becoming reinforced. Regarding the first point, numerous studies have demonstrated that worry actually reduces autonomic arousal. Although that might sound like a positive aspect of worry, researchers have pointed out that reduced autonomic arousal actually impedes successful emotional processing and thus prevents the new learning that could break the cycle of worry. Borkovec and colleagues also underscore the avoidant nature of worry by emphasizing that worry is not focused upon present-moment concerns, but rather, on future-oriented *potential* calamities.

From an *information-processing* perspective, it appears clear that worry is associated with attentional and interpretive biases. For example, individuals with GAD have attentional biases toward threats, exaggerate the likelihood of negative outcomes, and tend to interpret ambiguous stimuli as dangerous or threatening (Butler & Mathews, 1983; Vasey & Borkovec, 1992). Some of the information-processing theorists agree that worry not only results in exaggerating the likelihood of danger, but that the perception results less in action to meet the threat and more in avoidance because the actual danger is not elaborated or followed through in a problem-solving manner.

Not only do people experiencing GAD worry, they also often hold negative beliefs about the worry itself (e.g., that worry is undesirable, dangerous, or a sign of their inadequacy), and these negative beliefs appear to exacerbate the worry cycle. One specific type of negative belief about worry is "*meta-worry*"—worry about worry (Wells, 1999). Once one appraises one's worrying as negative and then worries about worrying, it is common to attempt to stop or at least control the worrying. Unfortunately, such efforts usually exacerbate the worry. Wegner experimentally demonstrated that trying to avoid unwanted thoughts actually increased the likelihood of having them (Wegner, 1994). In other words, "negative appraisals of worry may motivate attempts to stop worrying, but these attempts at cognitive control may paradoxically increase the frequency of worries" (Barlow, 2004, p. 495).

Although research from twin studies have posited a genetic contribution, other studies demonstrate that what is inherited genetically is a nonspecific predisposition to develop some form of emotional disorder, not just GAD or another anxiety disorder (Kendler, 1995). As Schmidt and colleagues concluded, "The diagnosis of GAD continues to evolve. This diagnosis is perhaps the least understood of all of the anxiety disorders, and we certainly have considerable work to do in order to clarify our understanding of its nature and treatment" (Schmidt et al., 2009, p. 372).

With regard to treatment, a number of pharmacological and psychotherapeutic approaches appear to have some effectiveness. However, it is worth noting that although various treatments have demonstrated some degree of efficacy with GAD, treatments for GAD are generally less effective than the extant treatments for other anxiety disorders (Barlow, 2004, pp. 506–507). The three primary categories of drugs used with GAD are benzodiazepines, azapirones, and antidepressants. Whereas benzodiazepines appear to more effectively treat the somatic symptoms of GAD, in contrast to the psychic symptoms (such worry or irritability), azapirones—such as buspirone—seem to have more effect on the psychic rather than somatic symptoms. Another benefit of buspirone is that it does not cause sedation or deficits in cognitive or psychomotor functioning that benzondiazepines sometimes do. Moreover, it has far less risk of dependence or abuse potential (Barlow, 2004).

The psychotherapeutic approaches with the most empirical support for GAD are various cognitive-behavioral therapies. It appears that the most important component of the CBTs include psychoeducation regarding the nature of fear, anxiety, and worry; self-monitoring and early detection of somatic and psychic symptoms; learning multiple methods of relaxation (diaphragmatic breathing, pleasant imagery, meditation, progressive muscle relaxation); exposure to imaginal or in vivo stimuli; learning coping skills; and cognitive restructuring. Recently, numerous researchers and therapists have found that integrating mindfulness into CBTs has enhanced the latter's effectiveness (Miller et al., 1995; Orsillo, Roemer, & Barlow, 2003).

## Obsessive-Compulsive Disorder

When the bulk of this book was written, Obsessive-Compulsive Disorder (OCD) was classified as an anxiety disorder. In the DSM-5, OCD has been reclassified into a category of "Obsessive-Compulsive and Related Disorders" (OCRDs), which include: OCD, Hoarding Disorder, Body Dysmorphic Disorder (BDD), Trichotillomania (hair-pulling disorder), Excoriation (skin-picking), Substance/Medication-Induced Obsessive-Compulsive and Related Disorder, Obsessive-Compulsive and Related Disorder due to Another Medical Condition, Other Specified Obsessive-Compulsive and Related Disorder, and Unspecified Obsessive-Compulsive and Related Disorder (i.e., obsessional jealousy, body-focused repetitive behavior disorder). The American Psychiatric Association notes that the close relationships among anxiety disorders, OCRDs, and trauma- and stressor-related disorders (which includes Post-Traumatic Stress Disorder and Acute Stress Disorder) is reflected in their sequential ordering in the DSM-5.[46] According to the DSM-5, the reasoning behind shifting OCD into this new category separate from, but related to, anxiety disorders is that it is clinically useful and that diagnostic validators point to the relatedness of OCD with other OCRDs. This rationale was elaborated by Abramowitz and colleagues in their 2009 critical review of this—at that point—proposed change:

**a.** The symptoms of OCD and OCRDs share a core feature, namely repetitive thoughts and behaviors.
**b.** There are similarities in associated features (e.g., comorbidity, familial loading) between OCD and OCRDs.
**c.** OCD and the proposed OCRDs share common genetic factors, brain circuitry, and neurotransmitter abnormalities.
**d.** OCD and the proposed OCRDs share similar treatment response profiles (Abramowitz et al., 2009, p. 330).

However, both Abramowitz and colleagues as well as Taylor and colleagues argued strongly that data do *not* support the above four claims. As is often the case, psychologists and psychiatrists who published papers on OCD between 1996 and 2006 disagreed

[46] http://www.psychiatry.org/dsm5.

regarding how to classify OCD, with approximately 60% of that sample endorsing the proposed removal of OCD from the anxiety disorders category (Abramowitz et al., 2009; Taylor, Asmundson, Abramowitz, & McKay, 2009). One form of data suggesting that OCD should have remained in the anxiety disorders category involves the fact that those with OCD and other anxiety disorders report similar psychological experiences. For example, despite the fact that the various avoidance behaviors appear topographically diverse, Panic Disorders, Specific Phobias, Social Anxiety Disorders, and OCD all involve the experience of fear that arises in relatively disorder-specific contexts. Moreover, the distorted perceptions that tend to exaggerate the likelihood of danger maintain the fear. Put another way, OCD and other anxiety disorders share a similar internal logic that is not shared with some of the OCRDs such as Trichotillomania or Excoriation. In their scholarly review of the research suggesting that OCD be placed within the OCRDs category in the DSM-5, Abramowitz and colleagues concluded that "there is inadequate empirical support for such a marked conceptual and nosological shift" (Abramowitz et al., 2009, p. 346). Despite its now being represented in the OCRDs section of the DSM-5, we are including a brief discussion of OCD here.

According to the DSM-5, essential features of Obsessive-Compulsive Disorder include the presence of obsessions or compulsions (or both) that are time consuming or result in clinically significant impairment or distress. Those suffering from OCD, in contrast to other anxiety-related disorders, often suffer some of the most severe consequences (i.e., when a person with an anxiety-related disorder is hospitalized, it is most often due to OCD; Barlow, 2004). More often than not, such people will have other debilitating comorbid disorders (especially other anxiety disorders, depression, personality disorders, and eating disorders) that increase the magnitude and complexity of their struggles, complicate the overall clinical picture, and render successful treatment more challenging. For those struggling with OCD,

> . . . gaining control and predictability over the seemingly ubiquitous dangers in life leads them to resort to magic and rituals in vain attempts to reestablish safety or prevent a dreaded event. In OCD, danger appears in the form of a thought, image, or impulse that provokes intense discomfort. This thought or image is upsetting and is avoided, much as a person with a snake phobia avoids snakes. (Barlow, 2004, p. 516)

Given that intrusive thoughts and neutralizing compulsions are common human experiences (Barlow, 2004), how are we to understand the origins and causes of OCD? It seems likely that genetic and other biological factors predispose some people to react to stress with more intense emotional responses. In addition, some research suggests that stressful experiences can lead to both intrusive thoughts and compulsions (Jones & Menzies, 1998; Mineka, 1985). Similar to the research of Faravelli (1985) regarding the prevalence of stressful life events prior to the onset of one's first panic attack, several studies have reported similar results regarding the prevalence of stressful events prior to the onset of OCD (de Loof, Zandbergen, Lousberg, Pols, & Griez, 1989; McKeon, Roa, & Mann, 1984). Also involved are the vicarious (mis)learnings that many individuals experience from their caregivers in early life in which children are repeatedly told of the extremely dangerous, "bad," and "abnormal" nature of those who have intrusive thoughts.

Other early environmental dynamics that appear implicated in the development of OCD include caregivers' encouraging young children to assume an excessive amount of responsibility and perfectionism. Research by Salkovskis and colleagues points out that some forms of religious education or otherwise rigid, harsh, and intolerant codes of conduct at home or school may facilitate thought–action fusion (i.e., thinking about doing something bad is as bad as doing it) as well as magical thinking (i.e., believing that one's thoughts or fantasies caused an event to occur) and thus could be a factor in the development of OCD symptoms (Rachman, 1993; Salkovskis, Shafran, Rachman, & Freeston, 1999). Other research supporting this notion was captured by Barlow (2004, p. 533): "That rigid beliefs may constitute a vulnerability factor for OCD is supported by the finding that the strength (but not type) of religious belief was associated with severity of OCD pathology (Steketee, Quay, & White, 1991)." Cognitive theorists posit that, as is the case in other anxiety-related disorders, those with OCD exaggerate the likelihood and magnitude of potential threats. When such threatening or unacceptable thoughts arise and people are unable to control them, they resort to various mental or behavioral rituals in an effort to neutralize the perceived danger.

Once again, Barlow's (2004) triple vulnerability model (which is consistent with the Integral perspective) is helpful in understanding the etiology of OCD in that the interactions of biological predispositions with general and specific psychological vulnerabilities seem necessary for the etiological processes of OCD to manifest:

> Specifically, intense stress-related negative affect and neurobiological reactions are triggered by negative life events (biological vulnerability). The resulting intrusive thoughts, which are commonly experienced in the normal population (and other anxiety disorders) during periods of stress, are judged unacceptable; attempts are made to avoid or suppress these thoughts. Recurrence of these thoughts causes intensification of anxiety, with accompanying negative affect and a sense that these thoughts are proceeding in an unpredictable and uncontrollable fashion (generalized psychological vulnerability). The vicious negative feedback loop of anxiety then develops, with attention narrowed onto the content of the unacceptable thoughts themselves. The specific content of the obsessions is determined by learned dispositions that certain thoughts or images are unacceptable (specific psychological vulnerability). (Barlow, 2004, p. 535)

The three primary forms of treatment that have garnered empirical support for OCD are cognitive therapies, exposure therapies geared toward the feared circumstances while preventing their normal neutralizing rituals, and medications targeting the serotonin system (Barlow, 2004).

## Conclusion

A major theme that emerged from *Current Perspectives on the Anxiety Disorders: Implications for DSM-5 and Beyond* (McKay, Abramowitz, Taylor, & Asmundson, 2009) was that a dimensional—rather than categorical—classification would vastly improve the diagnosis and treatment of anxiety disorders. Recall that whereas categorical approaches assume that disorders arise from a relatively small number of causal factors, dimensional approaches assume that disorders result from the incremental effects of many factors. Dimensional approaches are much more consistent with current conceptualizations and research regarding the role of gene–environment interactions in psychiatric disorders (Taylor et al., 2009).

In the concluding chapter of *Current Perspectives on the Anxiety Disorders: Implications for DSM-5 and Beyond*, Taylor and colleagues referred to the various proposed regroupings of anxiety disorders for the DSM-5 and stated that "In our view, such a regrouping would have little, if any, clinical significance" (Taylor et al., 2009, p. 492). In other words, such a regrouping would not affect the effectiveness of treatment. Where the impact of such a regrouping *would* be seen is in the realm of research. For example, factor analytic research has supported the distinction between fear disorders (Panic Disorder, Agoraphobia, Specific Phobia, Social Anxiety Disorder) and distress disorders (GAD, PTSD, Major Depressive Disorder, and Dysthymia) because the two categories load on separate factors (Taylor et al., 2009). By way of contrast, the empirical evidence for the OCRDs remains much more controversial.

If you have made it this far in the chapter, you've likely realized that we know two things about the etiology of anxiety disorders. First, a multitude of factors are implicated, well captured by both Barlow's triple vulnerability model and the quadratic model of Integral theory. Second, we know that we do not know precisely *how* these myriad variables dynamically interact to produce the specific anxiety disorders. From an Integral perspective, it behooves us to try to be as aware as possible of all of the different dimensions of anxiety and its sources, while striving to understand how these complexities arise within and are experienced by each unique human being.

## Review Questions

1. Define normal, neurotic, and existential anxiety.
2. Describe David Barlow's "triple vulnerability model" of the etiology of anxiety disorders.
3. Explain why genes, physiology, and other biological processes are not the sole etiological factors involved in the development of anxiety disorders.
4. Describe how anxiety, avoidance behaviors, and negative reinforcement operate together.
5. How does attachment theory view the development of anxiety disorders?
6. Describe—theoretically—why exposure treatments are often effective with anxiety disorders, then describe how they can be implemented with clients.
7. Discuss general treatment goals of integrative approaches (particularly those of Barry Wolfe and Jerold Gold).

## References

Abramowitz, J. S., Storch, E. A., McKay, D., Taylor, S., & Asmundson, G. J. G. (2009). The obsessive-compulsive spectrum: A critical review. In D. McKay, J. S. Abramowitz, S. Taylor, & G. J. G. Asmundson (Eds.), *Current perspectives on the anxiety disorders: Implications for DSM-5 and beyond.* New York, NY: Springer Publishing Company.

Allen, D. M. (2010). *How dysfunctional families spur mental disorders: A balanced approach to resolve problems and reconcile relationships.* Santa Barbara, CA: Praeger.

Almaas, A. H. (1996). *The point of existence: Transformations of narcissism in self-realization.* Berkeley, CA: Diamond.

American Psychiatric Association. (2000). *Diagnostic and statistical manual of mental disorders* (4th ed., text revision). Washington, DC: Author.

American Psychiatric Association. (2013). *Diagnostic and statistical manual of mental disorders* (5th ed.). Washington, DC: Author.

Andrews, G. (2000). A focus on empirically supported outcomes: A commentary on search for empirically supported treatments. *Clinical Psychology: Science and Practice, 7*, 264–268.

Andrews, G., Charney, D. S., Sirovatka, P. J., & Regier, D. A. (Eds.). (2009). *Stress-induced and fear circuitry disorders: Advancing the research agenda for DSM-5*. Arlington, VA: American Psychiatric Association.

Asbury, K., Dunn. J. F., Pike, A., & Plomin, R. (2003). Nonshared environmental influences on individual differences in early behavioral development: A monozygotic twin differences study. *Child Development, 74*(3), 933–943.

Auden, W. H. (1947). *The age of anxiety: A baroque eclogue*. New York: Random House.

Ballash, N., Leyfer, O., Buckley, A. F., & Woodruff-Borden, J. (2006). Parental control in the etiology of anxiety. *Clinical Child and Family Psychology Review, 9*(2), 113–133.

Barlow, D. H. (2004). *Anxiety and its disorders: The nature and treatment of anxiety and panic* (2nd ed.). New York: Guilford.

Barlow, D. H., & Durand, V. M. (2002). *Abnormal psychology: An integrative approach*. Belmont, CA: Wadsworth.

Barlow, D. H., & Wolfe, B. E. (1981). Behavioral approaches to anxiety disorders: Reports on NIMH-SUNY, Albany Research Conference. *Journal of Consulting and Clinical Psychology, 49*, 191–215.

Battista, J. (1996). Offensive spirituality and spiritual defenses. In B. Scotton, A. Chinen, & J. Battista (Eds.), *Textbook of transpersonal psychiatry and psychology* (pp. 261–270). New York: Basic Books.

Beck, A. T., & Emery, G. (1985). *Anxiety disorders and phobias*. New York: Basic Books.

Beck, A. T., & Weishaar, M. E. (2008). Cognitive therapy. In R. J. Corsini & D. Wedding (Eds.), *Current psychotherapies* (8th ed., pp. 263–294). Belmont, CA: Thomson.

Becker, E. (1973). *The denial of death*. New York: Simon & Schuster.

Beidel, D. C., & Turner, S. M. (2007). Etiology of social anxiety disorder. In D. C. Beidel & S. M. Turner (Eds.), *Shy children, phobic adults: Nature and treatment of social anxiety disorders* (2nd ed., pp. 91–119). Washington, DC: American Psychological Association.

Binswanger, L. (1958). The existential analysis school of thought. Translated by Ernest Angel. In R. May, E. Angel, & H. F. Ellenberger (Eds.), *Existence: A new dimension in psychiatry and psychology*. New York: Basic Books.

Boer, F., Markus, M. T., Maingay, R., Lindhout, I. E., Borst, S. R., & Hoogendijk, T. H. G. (2002). Negative life events of anxiety disordered children: Bad fortune, vulnerability, or reporter bias? *Child Psychiatry and Human Development, 32*, 187–199.

Bogels, S. M., & Brechman-Toussaint, M. L. (2006). Family issues in child anxiety: Attachment, family functioning, parental rearing and beliefs. *Clinical Psychology Review, 26*(7), 834–856.

Borkovec, T. D., Alcaine, O., & Behar, E. (2004). Avoidance theory of worry and generalized anxiety disorder. In R. G. Heimberg, C. L. Turk, & D. S. Mennin (Eds.), *Generalized anxiety disorder: Advances in research and practice* (pp. 77–108). New York: Guilford.

Borkovec, T. D., & Stiles, J. (1979). The contribution of relaxation and expectance to fear reduction via graded imaginal exposure to feared stimuli. *Behavior Research and Therapy, 17*, 529–540.

Bosquet, M. A. (2001, November). *An examination of the development of anxiety symptoms from a developmental psychopathology perspective*. Dissertation Abstracts International. Section B: The Sciences and Engineering. Vol. 62 (5-B), p. 2514.

Bouton, M. E., Mineka, S., & Barlow, D. H. (2001). A modern learning-theory perspective on the etiology of panic disorder. *Psychological Review, 108*(1), 4–32.

Bowlby, J. (1987). *The making and breaking of affectional bonds*. New York: Tavistock Publications.

Bowlby, J. (1988). *A secure base: Parent-child attunement and healthy human development*. New York: Basic Books.

Breggin, P. R. (1997). *Brain disabling treatments in psychiatry: Drugs, electroshock, and the role of the FDA*. New York: Springer.

Broman-Fulks, J. J., & Storey, K. M. (2008). Evaluation of a brief aerobic exercise intervention for high anxiety sensitivity. *Anxiety, Stress, and Coping: An International Journal, 21*(2), 117–128.

Butler, G., & Mathews, A. (1983). Cognitive processes in anxiety. *Advances in Behavior Research and Therapy, 5*, 51–62.

Chorpita, B. F., & Barlow, D. H. (1998). The development of anxiety: The role of control in the early environment. *Psychological Bulletin, 124*(1), 3–21.

Cook-Greuter, S. (2010). Ego-development: Nine levels of increasing embrace. White paper. Available at http://www.cook-greuter.com

Coryell, W., Noyes, R., & House, J. D. (1986). Mortality among outpatients with anxiety disorders. *American Journal of Psychiatry, 143,* 508–510.

Damasio, A. (1999). *The feeling of what happens: Body and emotion in the making of consciousness.* New York: Harcourt, Inc.

Danton, W. G., & Antonuccio, D. O. (1997). A focused empirical analysis of treatments for panic and anxiety. In S. Fischer & R. P. Greenberg (Eds.), *From placebo to panacea: Putting psychiatric drugs to the test* (pp. 229–280). New York: Wiley.

de Loof, C., Zandbergen, J., Lousberg, H., Pols, H., & Griez, E. (1989). The role of life events in the onset of panic disorder. *Behaviour Research and Therapy, 27*(4), 461–463.

Deacon, B. J., & Abramowitz, J. S. (2004). Cognitive and behavioral treatments for anxiety disorders: A review of meta-analytic findings. *Journal of Clinical Psychology, 60,* 133–141.

Debiec, J., & Ledoux, F. E. (2009). The amygdala networks of fear: From animal models to human psychopathology. In D. McKay, J. S. Abramowitz, S. Taylor, & G. J. G. Asmundson (Eds.), *Current perspectives on the anxiety disorders: Implications for DSM-5 and beyond* (pp. 107–126). New York, NY: Springer Publishing Company.

Dienstbier, R. A. (1989). Arousal and physiological toughness: Implications for mental and physical health. *Psychological Review, 96,* 84–100.

DuPont, R. L., Rice, D. P., Miller, L. S., Shiraki, S. S., Rowland, C. R., & Harwood, H. J. (1996). Economic costs of anxiety disorders. *Anxiety, 2,* 167–172.

Ellenberger, H. F. (1958). A clinical introduction to psychiatric phenomenology and existential analysis. In R. May, E. Angel, & H. F. Ellenberger (Eds.), *Existence: A new dimension in psychiatry and psychology* (pp. 92–126). New York: Basic Books.

Fall, K., Holden, J. M., & Marquis, A. (2010). *Theoretical models of counseling and psychotherapy* (2nd ed.). New York: Routledge.

Fanous, A. H., & Kendler, K. S. (2005). Genetic heterogeneity, modifier genes and quantitative phenotypes in psychiatric illness: Searching for a framework. *Molecular Psychiatry, 10,* 6–13.

Faravelli, C. (1985). Life events preceding the onset of panic disorder. *Journal of Affective Disorders, 9*(1), 103–105.

Foa, E. B., Huppert, J. D., & Cahill, S. P. (2006). Emotional processing theory: An update. In B. O. Rothbaum (Ed.), *Pathological anxiety: Emotional processing in etiology and treatment* (pp. 3–24). New York: Guildford Press.

Fosha, D. (2000). *The transforming power of affect: A model for accelerated change.* New York: Basic Books.

Frances, A. (2013). *Saving normal: An insider's revolt against out-of-control psychiatric diagnosis, DSM-5, big pharma, and the medicalization of ordinary life.* New York: Morrow.

Frankl, V. (1967). *Psychotherapy and existentialism: Selected papers on Logotherapy.* New York: Simon and Schuster.

Frankl, V. (1985). *Man's search for meaning.* New York: Washington Square Press.

Freeman, A., & Simon, K. M. (1989). Cognitive therapy of anxiety. In A. Freeman, K. M. Simon, L. E. Beutler, & H. Arkowitz (Eds.), *Comprehensive handbook of cognitive therapy* (pp. 347–365). New York: Plenum Press.

Freud, S. (1926/1959). *Inhibitions, symptoms, and anxiety* (standard Edition, vol. 20, pp. 75–155). J. Strachey, trans. London: Hogarth Press.

Fromm, E. (1941). *Escape from freedom.* New York: Holt, Rinehart & Winston.

Fromm, E. (1956). *The art of loving.* New York: Bantam Books.

Fromm, E. (1976). *To have or to be.* New York: Harper & Row.

Fyer, A. J., & Brown, T. A. (2009). Stress-induced and fear circuitry anxiety disorders: Are they a distinct group? In G. Andrews, D. S. Charney, P. J. Sirovatka, & D. A. Regier (Eds.), *Stress-induced and fear circuitry disorders: Advancing the research agenda for DSM-5* (pp. 125–135). Arlington, VA: American Psychiatric Publishing Inc.

Gold, J. (1993). An integrated approach to the treatment of anxiety disorders and phobias. In G. Stricker & J. R. Gold (Eds.), *Comprehensive handbook of psychotherapy integration* (pp. 293–302). New York: Plenum.

Gray, J. A. (1985). Issues in the neuropsychology of anxiety. In A. H. Tuma & J. D. Maser (Eds.), *Anxiety and the anxiety disorders* (pp. 5–25). Hillsdale, NJ: Erlbaum.

Gray, J. A., & McNaughton, N. (1996). The neuropsychology of anxiety: Reprise. In D. A. Hope (Ed.), *Nebraska Symposium on Motivation: Vol. 43. Perspectives on anxiety, panic, and fear.* Lincoln, NE: University of Nebraska Press.

Greenberg, L. (2008). Emotion and cognition in psychotherapy: The transforming power of affect. *Canadian Psychology, 49,* 49–59.

Greenberg, L. S. (2002). *Emotion-focused therapy: Coaching clients to work through their feelings.* Washington, DC: American Psychological Association.

Griffith, J. L. (2010). *Religion that heals, religion that harms.* New York: Guilford.

Guidano, V. F. (1987). *Complexity of the self: A developmental approach to psychopathology and therapy.* New York: Guilford.

Harper, L. V. (2005). Epigenetic inheritance and the intergenerational transfer of experience. *Psychological Bulletin, 131*, 340–360.

Heimberg, R. G., Salzman, D. G., Holt, C. S., & Blendell, K. A. (1993). Cognitive behavioral group treatment for social phobia: Effectiveness at five-year follow-up. *Cognitive Therapy and Research, 17*, 325–339.

Hettema, J. M., Annas, P., Neale, M. C., Kendler, K. S., & Fredrikson, M. (2003). A twin study of the genetics of fear conditioning. *Archives of General Psychiatry, 60*, 702–708.

Hettema, J. M., Prescott, C. A., Myers, J. M., Neale, M. C., & Kendler, K. S. (2005). The structure of genetic and environmental risk factors for anxiety disorders in men and women. *Archives of General Psychiatry, 62*(2), 182–189.

Hoffman, J. A., & Teyber, E. C. (1979). Some relationships between sibling age, spacing, and personality. *Merrill-Palmer Quarterly, 25*, 77–80.

Horney, K. (1945). *Our inner conflicts.* New York: Norton.

Hranov, L. G. (2007). Comorbid anxiety and depression: Illumination of a controversy. *International Journal of Psychiatry in Clinical Practice, 11*(3), 171–189.

Hudson, J. L., & Rapee, R. M. (2008). Family and social environments in the etiology and maintenance of anxiety disorders. In M. M. Antony & M. B. Stein (Eds.), *Oxford handbook of anxiety and related disorders* (pp. 173–189). New York: Oxford University Press.

Ingersoll. E. R., & Rak, C. F. (2006). *Psychopharmacology for helping professionals: An integral exploration.* Belmont, CA: Thomson Brooks/Cole.

Jang, K. L., & Shikishima, C. (2009). Behavioral genetics: Strategies for understanding the anxiety disorders. In D. McKay, J. S. Abramowitz, S. Taylor, & G. J. G. Asmundson (Eds.), *Current perspectives on the anxiety disorders: Implications for DSM-5 and beyond* (pp. 127–152). New York, NY: Springer Publishing Company.

Jones, M. K., & Menzies, R. G. (1998). The relevance of associative learning pathways in the development of obsessive-compulsive washing. *Behavior Research and Therapy, 36*, 273–283.

Kabat-Zinn, J. (2003). Mindfulness-based interventions in context: Past, present, and future. *Clinical Psychology: Science and Practice, 10*(2), 144–156.

Kagan, J. (1997). Temperament and reactions to unfamiliarity. *Child Development, 68*(1), 139–143.

Kawachi, I., Sparrow, D., Vokonas, P. S., & Weiss, S. T. (1994). Symptoms of anxiety and risk of coronary heart disease: The normative aging study. *Circulation, 90*, 2225–2229.

Keating, T. (1986). *Open mind, open heart: The contemplative dimension of the gospel.* Amity: Amity House.

Kegan, R. (1982). *The evolving self: Problem and process in human development.* Cambridge, MA: Harvard University Press.

Keller, M. B., Lavori, P. W., Wunder, J., Beardslee, W. R., Schwartz, C. E., & Roth, J. (1992). Chronic course of anxiety disorders in children and adolescents. *Journal of the American Academy of Child and Adolescent Psychiatry, 31*, 595–599.

Kendler, K. S. (1995). Genetic epidemiology in psychiatry. *Archives of General Psychiatry, 52*, 895–899.

Kendler, K. S., Myers, J., & Prescott, C. A. (2002). The etiology of the phobias: An evaluation of the stress-diathesis model. *Archives of General Psychiatry, 59*, 242–248.

Kierkegaard, S. (1954). *The sickness unto death.* W. Lowrie, trans. New York: Doubleday & Co.

Kierkegaard, S. (1957). *The concept of dread.* W. Lowrie, trans. Princeton, NJ: Princeton University Press.

Kim-Cohen, J., Caspi, A., Moffitt, T. E., Harrington, H., Milne, B. J., & Poulton, R. (2003). Prior juvenile diagnoses in adults with mental disorder: Developmental follow-back of a prospective-longitudinal cohort. *Archives of General Psychiatry, 60*, 709–719.

Kindt, M., & Van Den Hout, M. (2001). Selective attention and anxiety: A perspective on developmental issues and the causal status. *Journal of Psychopathology and Behavioral Assessment, 23*(3), 193–202.

Kohut, H. (1984). *How does analysis cure?* Chicago: University of Chicago Press.

Lader, M. (1988). Beta-adrenergic antagonists in neuropsychiatry: An update. *Journal of Clinical Psychiatry, 49*, 213–223.

Lambert, M. J., & Ogles, B. M. (2004). The efficacy and effectiveness of psychotherapy. In M. J. Lambert (Ed.), *Bergin and Garfield's handbook of psychotherapy and behavior change* (5th ed., pp. 139–193). New York: John Wiley & Sons.

Lang, P. J. (1994). The varieties of emotional experience: A meditation on James-Lange theory. *Psychological Review, 101*(2), 211–221.

LeDoux, J. (1996). *The emotional brain: The mysterious underpinnings of emotional life.* New York: Touchstone.

Linehan, M. (1993a). *Cognitive-behavioral treatment of Borderline Personality Disorder.* New York: Guilford.

Mahoney, M. J. (1991). *Human change processes: The scientific foundations of psychotherapy.* New York: Basic Books.

Mahoney, M. J. (2003). *Constructive psychotherapy: A practical guide.* New York: Guilford.

Marquis A. (2008). *The integral intake: A guide to comprehensive idiographic assessment in integral psychotherapy.* New York: Routledge.

Marquis, A., & Douthit, K. Z. (2006). The hegemony of "empirically supported treatment": Validating or violating? *Constructivism in the Human Sciences, 11*(2), 108–141.

Marquis, A., Holden, J. M., & Warren, E. S. (2001). An integral psychology response to Daniel Helminiak's "Treating Spiritual Issues in Secular Psychotherapy." *Counseling and Values, 44*(3), 218–236.

May, R. (1958). Contributions of existential psychotherapy. In R. May, E. Angel, & H. F. Ellenberger (Eds.), *Existence: A new dimension in psychiatry and psychology* (pp. 37–91). New York: Basic Books.

May, R. (1977). *The meaning of anxiety.* New York: W. W. Norton & Company.

May, R., & Yalom, I. (1995). Existential psychotherapy. In R. J. Corsini & D. Wedding (Eds.), *Current psychotherapies* (5th ed., pp. 262–292). Itasca, IL: F. E. Peacock Publishers.

McCauley, J., Kern, D. E., Kolodner, K., Dill, L., Schroeder, A. F., DeChant, H. K., . . . Bass, E. B. (1997). Clinical characteristics of women with a history of childhood abuse. *Journal of the American Medical Association, 277*(17), 1362–1368.

McEwen, B. S. (1992). Paradoxical effects of adrenal steroids on the brain: Protection versus degeneration. *Biological Psychiatry, 31,* 177–199.

McKay, D., Abramowitz, J. S., Taylor, S., & Asmundson, G. J. G. (Eds.) (2009). *Current perspectives on the anxiety disorders: Implications for DSM-5 and beyond.* New York, NY: Springer Publishing Company.

McKeon, J., Roa, B., & Mann, A. (1984). Life events and personality traits in obsessive-compulsive neurosis. *British Journal of Psychiatry, 144,* 185–189.

McNaughton, N., & Gray, J. H. (2000). Anxiolytic action on the behavioral inhibition system implies multiple typos of arousal contribute to anxiety. *Journal of Affective Disorders, 61,* 161–176.

McWilliams, N. (1994). *Psychoanalytic diagnosis: Understanding personality structure in the clinical process.* New York: The Guilford Press.

Middledorp, C. M., Cath, D. C., Van Dyck, R., & Boomsma, D. I. (2005). The co-morbidity of anxiety and depression in the perspective of genetic epidemiology: A review of twin and family studies. *Psychological Medicine, 35*(5), 61–624.

Miller, J., Fletcher, K., & Kabat-Zinn, J. (1995). Three-year follow-up and clinical implications of a mindfulness-based stress reduction intervention in the treatment of anxiety disorders. *General Hospital Psychiatry, 17,* 192–200.

Miller, R. B. (2004). *Facing human suffering: Psychology and psychotherapy as moral engagement.* Washington, DC: American Psychological Association.

Mineka, S. (1985). Animal models of anxiety-based disorders: Their usefulness and limitation. In A. H. Tuma & J. D. Maser (Eds.), *Anxiety and the anxiety disorders* (pp. 199–244). Hillsdale, NJ: Erlbaum.

Mineka, S., Davidson, M., Cook, M., & Keir, R. (1984). Observational conditioning of snake fear in rhesus monkeys. *Journal of Abnormal Psychology, 93,* 355–372.

Mineka, S., & Thomas, C. (1999). Mechanisms of change in exposure therapy for anxiety disorders. In T. Dalgeish & M. Power (Eds.), *Handbook of cognition and emotion* (pp. 747–764).

Mineka, S., & Zinbarg, R. (2006). A contemporary learning theory perspective on the etiology of anxiety disorders. *American Psychologist, 61*(1), 10–26.

Moreno, M., Lopez-Crespo, G., & Flores, P. (2007). Etiology of anxiety. In B. Helmut et al. (Eds.), *Antidepressants, antipsychotics, anxiolytics from chemistry and pharmacology to clinical application* (Vol. 1 & 2, pp. 667–783). Weinheim, Germany: Wiley.

Morgan, M., & LeDoux, J. E. (1995). Differential contribution of dorsal and ventral medial prefrontal cortex to the acquisition and extinction of conditioned fear. *Behavioral Neuroscience, 109,* 681–688.

Muris, P. (2006). The pathogenesis of childhood anxiety disorders: Considerations from a developmental psychopathology perspective. *International Journal of Behavioral Development, 30*(1), 5–11.

Neiss, R. (1988). Reconceptualizing arousal: Psychobiological states in motor performance. *Psychological Bulletin, 103*, 345–366.

Nietzsche, F. (1954). *The portable Nietzsche*. W. Kaufman, trans. New York: The Viking Press.

Noyes, R. (1991). Suicide and panic disorder: A review. *Journal of Affective Disorders, 22*, 1–11.

Ohman, A. (1986). Face the beast and fear the face: Animal and social fears as prototypes for evolutionary analyses of emotion. *Psychophysiology, 23*, 123–145.

Ohman, A. (1992). Fear and anxiety as emotional phenomena: Clinical, phenomenological, evolutionary perspectives, and information-processing mechanisms. In M. Lewis & J. M. Haviland (Eds.), *Handbook of the emotions* (pp. 511–536). New York: Guilford.

Orsillo, S. M., Roemer, L., & Barlow, D. H. (2003). Integrating acceptance and mindfulness into existing cognitive-behavioral treatment for GAD: A case study. *Cognitive and Behavioral Practice, 10*(3), 222–230.

PDM Task Force. (2006). *Psychodynamic diagnostic manual (PDM)*. Silver Springs, MD: Alliance of Psychoanalytic Organizations.

Pine, D. S., Cohen, P., Gurley, D., Brook, J., & Ma, Y. (1998). The risk for early adulthood anxiety and depressive disorders in adolescents with anxiety and depressive disorders. *Archives of General Psychiatry, 55*, 56–64.

Poulton, R., Pine, D. S., & Harrington, H. (2009). Continuity and etiology of anxiety disorders: Are they stable across the life course? In G. Andrews, D. S. Charney, P. J. Sirovatka, & D. A. Regier (Eds.), *Stress-induced and fear circuitry disorders: Advancing the research agenda for DSM-5* (pp. 105–123). Arlington, VA: American Psychiatric Publishing Inc.

Preston, J. D., O'Neal, J. H., & Talaga, M. C. (2002). *Handbook of clinical psychopharmacology for therapists* (3rd ed.). Oakland, CA: New Harbinger.

Prochaska, J. O., & Norcross, J. C. (2003). *Systems of psychotherapy: A transtheoretical analysis* (5th ed.). Pacific Grove, CA: Brooks Cole.

Rachman, S. (1993). Obsessions, responsibility, and guilt. *Behavior Therapy and Research, 31*, 149–154.

Rachman, S. J. (1977). The conditioning theory of fear acquisition: A critical examination. *Behaviour Research and Therapy, 15*, 375–387.

Rachman, S. J. (1979). The concept of required helpfulness. *Behaviour Research and Therapy, 17*, 279–293.

Rapee, R. M., & Bryant, R. A. (2009). Stress and psychosocial factors in onset of fear circuitry disorders. In G. Andrews, D. S. Charney, P. J. Sirovatka, & D. A. Regier (Eds.), *Stress-induced and fear circuitry disorders: Advancing the research agenda for DSM-5* (pp. 195–214). Arlington, VA: American Psychiatric Publishing Inc.

Rapee, R. M., & Lim, L. (1992). Discrepancy between self- and observer ratings of performance in social phobics. *Journal of Abnormal Psychology, 35*, 741–756.

Rapee, R. M., & Spence, S. H. (2004). The etiology of social phobia: Empirical evidence and an initial model. *Clinical Psychology Review, 24*, 737–767.

Rheingold, A. A., Herbert, J. D., & Franklin, M. E. (2003). Cognitive bias in adolescents with social anxiety disorder. *Cognitive Therapy and Research, 27*(6), 639–655.

Rice, D. P., & Miller, L. S. (1993). The economic burden of mental disorders. *Advances in Health Economics and Health Services Research, 14*, 37–53.

Richard, D., & Lauterbach, D. (2006). *Handbook of exposure therapies*. New York: Academic Press.

Roth, W. T., Wilhelm, F. H., & Pettit, D. (2005). Are current theories of panic falsifiable? *Psychological Bulletin, 131*, 171–192.

Rotter, J. B. (1975). Some problems and misconceptions related to the construct of internal versus external control of reinforcement. *Journal of Consulting and Clinical Psychology, 43*(1), 56–67.

Salkovskis, P. M., Shafran, R., Rachman, S., & Freeston, M. H. (1999). Multiple pathways to inflated responsibility beliefs in obsessional problems: Possible origins and implications for therapy and research. *Behavior Therapy and Research, 37*, 1055–1072.

Sartre, J. P. (1943/1993). *Being and nothingness: An essay on phenomenological ontology*. H. E. Barnes, trans. New York: Washington Square Press.

Scher, C. D., & Stein, M. B. (2003). Developmental antecedents of anxiety sensitivity. *Journal of Anxiety Disorders, 17*(3), 253–269.

Schmidt, N. B., Riccardi, C. J., Richey, J. A., & Timpano, K. R. (2009). Classification of worry and associated psychopathology. In D. McKay, J. S. Abramowitz, S. Taylor, & G. J. G. Asmundson (Eds.), *Current perspectives on the anxiety disorders: Implications for DSM-5 and beyond* (pp. 353–376). New York, NY: Springer Publishing Company.

Schmidt, N. B., Zvolensky, M. J., & Maner, J. K. (2006). Anxiety sensitivity: Prospective prediction of panic attacks and Axis I pathology. *Journal of Psychiatric Research, 40*(8), 691–699.

Schoenfield, G., & Morris, R. J. (2008). Cognitive behavioral treatment for childhood anxiety disorders: Exemplary programs. In M. Mayer, J. E. Lochman, & R. Van Acker (Eds.), *Cognitive-behavioral interventions for emotional and behavioral disorders: School-based practice* (pp. 204–234). New York: Guildford.

Schwartz, J. M., & Begley, S. (2002). *The mind and the brain: Neuroplasticity and the power of mental force.* New York: Harper-Collins.

Segal, Z. V., Williams, J. M. G., & Teasdale, J. D. (2002). *Mindfulness-based cognitive therapy for depression: A new approach to preventing relapse.* New York: Guilford.

Seligman, M. E. P. (1971). Phobias and preparedness. *Behavior Therapy, 2*, 307–320.

Siegel, D. J. (2007). *The mindful brain: Reflection and attunement in the cultivation of well-being.* New York, NY: Norton.

Silberg, J., Rutter, M., Neale, M., & Eaves, L. (2001). Genetic moderation of environmental risk for depression and anxiety in adolescent girls. *British Journal of Psychiatry, 179*, 116–121.

Simon, G., Ormel, J., Von Korff, M., & Barlow, W. (1995). Health care costs associated with depressive and anxiety disorders in primary care. *American Journal of Psychiatry, 152*, 352–257.

Slife, B. D., Wiggins, B. J., & Graham, J. T. (2005). Avoiding an EST monopoly: Toward a pluralism of philosophies and methods. *Journal of Contemporary Psychotherapy, 35*, 83–97.

Sroufe, L. A. (1990). Considering the normal and abnormal together: The essence of developmental psychopathology. *Development and Psychopathology, 2*, 335–347.

Stahl, S. M. (2002). Don't ask, don't tell, but benzodiazepines are still the leading treatments for anxiety disorder. *Journal of Clinical Psychiatry, 63*, 756–757.

Steindl-Rast, D. (1984). *Gratefulness, the heart of prayer: An approach to life in fullness.* New York: Paulist Press.

Steketee, G., Quay, S., & White, K. (1991). Religion and guilt in OCD patients. *Journal of Anxiety Disorders, 5*, 359–367.

Sullivan, H. S. (1953). *The interpersonal theory of psychiatry.* New York: Norton.

Swendsen, J. D., Merikangas, K. R., Canino, G. J., Kessler, R. C., Rubio-Stipec, M., & Angst, J. (1998). The comorbidity of alcoholism with anxiety and depressive disorders in four geographic communities. *Comprehensive Psychiatry, 39*(4), 176–184.

Swift, R., & Mueller, T. (2001). Comorbidity of anxiety disorders in substance abuse. In J. R. Hubbard & P. R. Martin (Eds.), *Substance abuse in the mentally and physically disabled* (pp. 11–32). New York: Marcel Dekker.

Taylor, S., Asmundson, G. J. G., Abramowitz, J. S., & McKay, D. (2009). Classification of anxiety disorders for DSM-5 and ICD-11: Issues, proposals, and controversies. In D. McKay, J. S. Abramowitz, S. Taylor, & G. J. G. Asmundson (Eds.), *Current perspectives on the anxiety disorders: Implications for DSM-5 and beyond* (pp. 481–511). New York, NY: Springer Publishing Company.

Taylor, S., Jang, K. L., Stewart, S. H., & Stein, M. B. (2008). Etiology of the dimensions of anxiety sensitivity. A behavioral-genetic analysis. *Journal of Anxiety Disorders, 22*(5), 899–914.

Tillich, P. (1952). *The courage to be.* New Haven: Yale University Press.

Van Brakel, A. M. L., Muris, P., Bögels, S. M., & Thomassen, C. (2006). A multifactorial model for the etiology of anxiety in non-clinical adolescents: Main and interactive effects of behavioural inhibition, attachment and parental rearing. *Journal of Child and Family Studies, 15*, 569–579.

Vasey, M. W., & Borkovec, T. D. (1992). A catastrophizing assessment of worrisome model for the etiology of anxiety in non-clinical adolescents: Main and interactive effects of behavioral inhibition, attachment and parental rearing. *Journal of Child and Family Studies, 15*(5), 569–579.

Wachtel, P. L. (1977). *Psychoanalysis and behaviorism: Toward an integration.* New York: Basic Books.

Wachtel, P. L. (1982). Vicious circles: The self and the rhetoric of emerging and unfolding. *Contemporary Psychoanalysis, 18*(2), 259–273.

Wachtel, P. L. (1987). *Action and insight.* New York: Basic Books.

Wachtel, P. L. (2008). *Relational theory and the practice of psychotherapy.* New York: Guilford.

Walsh, R. (1999). *Essential spirituality: The 7 central practices to awaken heart and mind.* New York: John Wiley & Sons.

Walsh, R., & Vaughan, F. (Eds.). (1993). *Paths beyond ego: The transpersonal vision.* Los Angeles: Jeremy P. Tarcher.

Wampold, B. E. (1997). Methodological problems in identifying efficacious psychotherapies. *Psychotherapy Research, 7*, 21–43.

Wang, J. L. (2006). Perceived work stress, imbalance between work and family/personal lives and mental disorders. *Social Psychiatry and Psychiatric Epidemiology, 41*(7), 541–548.

Warren, S. L., Huston, L., Egeland, B., & Sroufe, L. A. (1997). Child and adolescent anxiety disorders and early attachment. *Journal of the American Academy of Child and Adolescent Psychiatry, 36,* 637–644.

Weems, C. F., & Costa, N. M. (2005). Developmental differences in the expression of childhood anxiety symptoms and fears. *Journal of the American Academy of Child and Adolescent Psychiatry, 44*(7), 656–663.

Wegner, D. M. (1994). Ironic processes of mental control. *Journal of Personality, 62,* 625–640.

Wells, A. (1999). A metacognitive model and therapy for generalized anxiety disorder. *Clinical Psychology and Psychotherapy, 6,* 86–95.

Westen, D., & Morrison, K. (2001). A multidimensional meta-analysis of treatments for depression, panic, and generalized anxiety disorder: An empirical examination of the status of empirically supported therapies. *Journal of Consulting and Clinical Psychology,* 69, 875–899 (downloaded from Ovid web gateway, pp. 1–36).

Westen, D., Novotny, C. M., & Thompson-Brenner, H. (2004). The empirical status of empirically supported psychotherapies: Assumptions, findings, and reporting in controlled clinical trials. *Psychological Bulletin,* 130, 631–663 (downloaded from Ovid web gateway, pp. 1–65).

Whiteside, S. P., & Ollendick, T. H. (2009). Developmental perspectives on anxiety classification. In D. McKay, J. S. Abramowitz, S. Taylor, & G. J. G. Asmundson (Eds.), *Current perspectives on the anxiety disorders: Implications for DSM-5 and beyond* (pp. 303–325). New York, NY: Springer Publishing Company.

Widiger, T. A., & Clark, L. A. (2000). Toward DSM-5 and the classification of psychopathology. *Psychological Bulletin, 126,* 946–963.

Wilber, K. (1983). *Eye to eye: The quest for the new paradigm.* Boston: Shambhala.

Wilber, K. (1997). A spirituality that transforms. *What Is Enlightenment?, 12,* 22–23.

Wilber, K. (2000). *The collected works, Volume 6. Sex, ecology, spirituality.* Boston: Shambhala.

Wolfe, B. E. (2003). Integrative psychotherapy of the anxiety disorders. In J. C. Norcross & M. R. Goldfried (Eds.), *Handbook of psychotherapy integration* (pp. 373–401). New York: Oxford University Press.

Wolfe, B. E. (2005). *Understanding and treating anxiety disorders: An integrative approach to healing the wounded self.* Washington, DC: American Psychological Association.

Yalom, I. (2009). *Staring at the sun: Overcoming the terror of death.* San Francisco: Jossey-Bass.

Yalom, I. D. (1980). *Existential psychotherapy.* New York: Basic Books.

Yalom, I. D. (1998). *The Yalom reader.* New York: Basic Books.

Yehuda, R. (2009). Role of neurochemical and neuroendocrine markers of fear in classification of anxiety disorders. In G. Andrews, D. S. Charney, P. J. Sirovatka, & D. A. Regier (Eds.), *Stress-induced and fear circuitry disorders: Advancing the research agenda for DSM-5* (pp. 255–264). Arlington, VA: American Psychiatric Publishing Inc.

Yerkes, R. M., & Dodson, J. D. (1908). The relation of strength of stimulus to rapidity of habit-formation. *Journal of Comparative Neurology and Psychology, 18,* 459–482.

Zillman, E. A., & Spiers, M. V. (2001). *Principles of neuropsychology.* Belmont, CA: Wadsworth.

# 5

# Psychological Trauma

**Tim Black, Ph.D.,** ***University of Victoria;***
**Elliott Ingersoll, Ph.D.,** ***Cleveland State University***[1]

## INTRODUCTION

Psychological trauma is a common aspect of human experience. Buddhist doctrine begins with the realization that to some extent everyone suffers in life, and much of this suffering can be attributed to events that overwhelm the ability of individuals to make sense of and integrate their experience. Psychological trauma is a construct that is only now garnering broad attention as an aspect of human experience; moreover, it is one that most, if not all, therapists will encounter at some point in their careers. The experience of psychological trauma is not new, but a fundamental understanding of human traumatic experience has only been established since the inclusion of Post-Traumatic Stress Disorder (PTSD) in the *Diagnostic and Statistical Manual of Mental Disorders*, 3rd Edition (DSM-III; American Psychiatric Association [APA], 1980) under *Anxiety Disorders*. Since then, research has begun to elucidate the construct of psychological trauma.

The DSM-5 (APA, 2013) has taken PTSD out of the Anxiety Disorders section and created an entirely new category under which it is subsumed, *Trauma and Stressor-Related Disorders*. Most of us who have worked with trauma would agree that this makes more sense than keeping it in Anxiety Disorders. For one thing the category allows a number of related disorders sharing unique symptoms to be grouped together. It also highlights the unique aspects of suffering from trauma and will hopefully encourage more specialized research and training in treating trauma victims. Although the research reviewed for this chapter focuses on PTSD, much of it relates to the symptoms of other trauma and stressor-related disorders. These include Reactive Attachment Disorder, Disinhibited Social Engagement Disorder (exemplified by children who show no developmentally normal stranger anxiety), Acute Stress Disorder, and related Adjustment Disorders.

---

[1] The authors thank Laura McIntyre for her assistance with researching veterans' issues and consulting on the case of Keisha presented in this chapter.

Epidemiological research has reported two consistent findings about the human experience of trauma. First, the majority of people exposed to traumas like terrorist attacks or natural disasters report severe stress (Friedman & Harris, 2004; Galea et al., 2002). Second, most people who suffer a traumatic event do not develop PTSD (Kessler, Sonnega, Bromet, Hughes, & Nelson, 1995). PTSD point prevalence is approximately 8% across the general population. However, among traumatized men, the lifetime prevalence is 8% and among traumatized women, 20% (Schnurr, Friedman, & Bernardy, 2002). In addition, 88% of men and 79% of women with lifetime PTSD had at least one comorbid diagnosis (Kessler et al., 1995). The PTSD Treatment Guidelines Task Force concluded, in fact, that traumatic experiences can lead to the development of other disorders, including depression, anxiety, and disorders related to substance use (Foa, Keane, & Friedman, 2000).

The situation is far worse for veterans returning from wars in Iraq and Afghanistan. Self-reported rates of PTSD and depression range from 10–44% depending on the study you consult (Hoge, Auchterlonie, & Milliken, 2006; Lapierre, Schwegler, & Labauve, 2007). For example, Hoge et al. (2006) noted that over 19% of service members returning from Iraq and 11% returning from Afghanistan reported some mental health problem. In addition, military sexual trauma was reported by over 15% of women and .7% of men in a cohort of 17,580 women and 10,814 men (Kimerling et al., 2010). More recent estimates are that between 9.5% and 33% of women serving in the military experienced an attempted rape (Wieland, Haley, & Bouder, 2011). Because of the culture of silence and secrecy, estimates are hard to come by (Baltrushes & Karnik, 2013). Some studies estimate 20–43% of female service members have been sexually assaulted (Lutwak & Dill, 2013; Yaeger et al., 2006), and studies outside the military suggest the rates may be much higher (Burgess, Slattery, & Herlihy, 2013). Military sexual trauma (MST) in men has been reported at a little over 1%, although the limitations on researching this topic (ranging from silence to taboo) have led some researchers to estimate that male victims of MST are about 12% of active service members (Hoyt, Rielage, & Williams, 2011). MST is also highly correlated with PTSD.

Whereas initially researchers wondered if the suicide rates for veterans from 2005–2008 exceeded those in the general population (Katz, McCarthy, Ignacio, & Kemp, 2012), in 2012 it appeared that suicide rates were significantly higher for veterans of the Iraq and Afghanistan wars; 2012 suicide rates among veterans increased 22% from the previous year. Leon Panetta (Secretary of Defense at that time) declared the problem an epidemic (Mulrine, 2012). Initial estimates in 2012 suggested that suicide rates for veterans and nonveterans were 26.2 versus 18.8 per 100,000 individuals, respectively (Miller et al., 2012).

This chapter will begin with PTSD as a touchstone for building an integral understanding of psychological trauma. Although this chapter will focus on PTSD proper, it is important to note the previously mentioned changes in how PTSD is listed in DSM-5. Friedman, Resick, Bryant, and Brewin (2011) summarized the arguments for the changes in the DSM-5 that resulted in the new category "Trauma and Stressor-Related Disorders," which includes Reactive Attachment Disorder, Disinhibited Social Engagement Disorder, Adjustment Disorders (AD), Acute Stress Disorder (ASD), Post-Traumatic Stress Disorder (PTSD), and Trauma or Stressor Related Disorder Not Elsewhere Classified.

## POST-TRAUMATIC STRESS DISORDER (PTSD)

Post-Traumatic Stress Disorder (APA, 2013) is conceptualized in eight clusters (A through H) and numbered specifiers. Cluster A notes that the client must have experienced threat of death, serious injury, or sexual violation in one of four ways (A1–A4):

- ***A1:*** The individual directly experienced the event considered traumatic.
- ***A2:*** The client witnessed traumatic events occurring to others.
- ***A3:*** The client learned the traumatic event occurred to a person he or she was close to (cases of actual or threatened death are here thought to be violent or accidental).
- ***A4:*** The client is experiencing repeated or extreme exposure to aversive details of the event.

Cluster B is described by intrusive symptoms, including distressing memories and dreams, dissociative reactions ("flashbacks") in which the person feels the traumatic event is recurring, intense psychological distress when exposed to internal or external cues related to the event, and marked physiological reactions to reminders of the event. Cluster C describes ways in which people can persistently avoid things associated with the event (like distressing memories or external reminders). Cluster D includes examples of negative alterations in thinking and mood associated with the event (e.g., detachment or estrangement from others and negative beliefs about oneself). Cluster E describes marked alterations in arousal and reactivity, such as aggressive behavior and hypervigilance. Criterion F defines the duration of the problems as exceeding 1 month. Criterion G is that the disturbance causes distress or impairment. Finally, criterion H notes that the disturbance cannot be the direct result of a substance or medical condition. In addition, the same eight criteria are developmentally attuned to preschool-aged children.

In the DSM-5, specifiers include dissociative symptoms like depersonalization (feeling detached, as if a witness to life) and derealization (feeling the world is dreamlike). There are also different criteria sets for children 6 years old and younger. Looking at age differences is increasingly important as evidence is accumulating that even so-called "easy trauma" (e.g., seeing violence on television) can affect children's brains (Kousha & Tehrani, 2013). Although not a focus of the DSM-5 criteria, there is also mounting evidence that whether the trauma is "intentional" (deliberately executed harm and cruelty) or nonintentional (e.g., natural disaster) can help predict prevalence and course. Intentional traumas are far more likely than unintentional traumas to lead to PTSD (Santiago et al., 2013).

The field of researching and treating PTSD is still in its infancy. The formal diagnosis was introduced into the DSM three decades ago, and the complexities involved in understanding and interpreting PTSD outcome research present a challenge to researchers and clinicians alike (Black, 2004). Even the term "trauma" has currently come under scrutiny as lacking the robustness to capture the complexity of developmental trauma and the continuum of post-traumatic responses (Briere, 2006; Koenen, 2010). Despite the fact that the International Society for Traumatic Stress Studies (ISTSS) provides guidelines for the treatment of PTSD (Foa et al., 2000), a truly Integral perspective on treating PTSD does not yet exist. Human beings are complex and have multiple dimensions, all of which simultaneously affect an individual's development. Trauma complicates "normal" human development, negatively affecting individuals' ability to live healthy psychological, emotional, behavioral, interpersonal, and spiritual lives. For clarity, trauma is thought of as the traumatic event, but the symptoms of PTSD can also be traumatic. An Integral approach to understanding and treating trauma in general and PTSD in particular must take into consideration the perspectives reflected in the four quadrants, levels and lines of development, and the states of consciousness related to symptoms for each client. As with other disorders, even once we understand the dimensions of PTSD, it is far more complicated than that. In particular, Substance Use Disorders (SUDs) are commonly comorbid with PTSD and pose substantial risks for psychiatric and functional impairment (Jason et al., 2011; Najavits, Kivlahan, & Kostin, 2011).

## Etiology

It may seem odd to discuss various etiologies for PTSD. Some would ask "isn't the trauma the etiology?" It is appropriate to think of the activating trauma as the root cause of the PTSD; however, one's psychology plays a large role in how one responds to and metabolizes traumatic events, and the symptoms of PTSD may also be re-traumatizing for some clients. Individuals going through the activating trauma often fail to understand that trauma is a normal reaction to an abnormal event. If you think back to our discussion of genetic vulnerability to disorders like Bipolar I and Schizophrenia, you can apply the same thinking here. Although most clinicians agree that the psychogenic root of PTSD is the traumatic event, current research explores whether some people may be *more vulnerable* than others to developing PTSD after a trauma. To understand the ideas that guide this research you must first understand the evolutionary legacy of the nervous system.

**THE EVOLUTIONARY LEGACY OF THE NERVOUS SYSTEM** The sympathetic nervous system (SNS) and the hypothalamic-pituitary-adrenocortical (HPA) axis are clearly implicated in PTSD, as are fear conditioning and our startle reflex (Schnurr et al., 2002). Activating the SNS and mechanisms that release norepinephrine (adrenergic mechanisms) is integral to human stress responses. In people not afflicted with PTSD, when the activating event (stressor) has been successfully dealt with and passed, adrenergic activity returns to baseline (whatever the baseline is for a particular individual). This is not the case in people suffering from PTSD. Their nervous systems' adrenergic functions remain continuously elevated. Elevated levels of adrenergic metabolites are found in their urine, and these people are unusually sensitive to drugs like yohimbine that disinhibit the adrenergic systems (Schnurr et al., 2002).

With regard to the HPA axis (more will be said in the section on genetics), this system is thought to be powerfully involved in our response to stress. Metabolites of HPA axis activity can be measured in urine and lymphocyte glucocorticoid receptor levels.[2] Although results are mixed with regard to what might be different in this

[2] Glucocorticoid receptors are receptors that cortisol and other stress hormones bind to.

system in people suffering from PTSD, Schnurr et al. (2002) suggest that elevated levels and increased activity in corticotropin-releasing factor (CRF) were more common in PTSD sufferers than control subjects.

Fear conditioning helps us learn to retain information about previous threats so we can increase our chances of survival. Laboratory studies have demonstrated exacerbated fear conditioning in clients with PTSD. These individuals are exposed to visual or auditory stimuli related to their particular traumatic event. For victims of rape it may be stimuli related to sexual assault. For veterans it will be tailored around war-related stimuli. Most subjects with PTSD will show dramatic increases of SNS activity immediately after exposure to the stimuli (Schnurr et al., 2002). Similarly, the startle response reflects activation of an alarm system when we are presented with threatening stimuli. People with PTSD have increased startle responses, more resistance to normal habituation to the stimulus, and lower inhibitory control of the startle reflex (Schnurr et al., 2002). Research in these four areas and the DSM-5 task force have led to the possibility of grouping trauma- and stress-related disorders under the category of Stress-Related Fear Circuitry (Andrews, Charney, Sirovatka, & Regier, 2008).

**PTSD and Stress-Related Fear Circuitry** Animal research has identified brain circuits that mediate the processing of threatening or fearful stimuli. These findings have been generalized to humans by brain-imaging techniques discussed in other chapters. In particular, fearful or threatening stimuli activate two parts of the limbic system called the amygdalae (plural because there is one on each side of the brain). The amygdalae have connections to the hippocampus, orbital frontal cortex, locus coeruleus, and the dorsal/ventral striata. These five structures are referred to as our fear circuit. In particular, exaggerated responses in the amygdalae and decreased activation from the middle part of the prefrontal lobe seem to elevate anxiety and underlay inadequate emotional regulation (Sartory et al., 2013). Each element in this "fear circuit" plays a role in activating the nervous system to defend against threat. The hippocampus mediates memory creation and spatial learning. The orbital frontal cortex processes memories of emotional events and related behaviors. The locus coeruleus has noradrenergic projections to activate fight, flight, or freeze responses in the sympathetic nervous system. The dorsal/ventral striata instigate avoidance behaviors (Davis & Whalen, 2001). In other studies, subjects with PTSD show greater activation of the amygdalae and less activation in the hippocampus and prefrontal cortex than non-PTSD subjects (Kaufman, Aikins, & Krystal, 2004).

One theory of PTSD is that the mediating influence of the prefrontal cortex (which includes the orbital frontal cortex) has been severely disrupted (Charney, 2004). This results in disinhibition of the amygdalae and increases the likelihood of fear conditioning (Friedman & Karam, 2008). Some of this research dovetails with research on human stress response and the role of adrenergic[3] hyperactivity and HPA axis dysregulation (Charney, 2004; Friedman & Karam, 2008). If the physiological

---

[3] Adrenergic refers to the neurotransmitter norepinephrine (NE). Strange as it is, in medicine the NE system is referred to in both Latin and Greek. In Greek *epi* means "upon" and *nephron* means "kidney." The adrenal glands (one system that involves NE and NE is a precursor to epinephrine sit on the kidneys thus in Latin *ad* means "upon" and *renal* means "kidney." So there you go.

terms are making it hard for you to conceptualize this, just imagine the fear circuit as a throttle on a motorcycle. The more you twist the throttle, the more "fear activation" occurs. When you learn to ride a motorcycle, most instructors teach you to "pre-twist" your hand before putting it on the throttle so that you don't over-twist the throttle and suddenly accelerate out of control. This hand placement could be thought of as akin to the mediating influence of the prefrontal cortex. When that is taken out of the picture, you can easily (too easily, most would agree) and severely twist the throttle—potentially losing control.

It seems that human beings (and many of our evolutionary relatives) automatically respond to sensory information with "relatively stable neuronal and hormonal activation resulting in consistent action patterns: predictable behaviors that can be elicited over and over again in response to similar input" (van der Kolk, 2006, p. 278). Again, this stable activation could be thought of as akin to proper hand placement on the motorcycle throttle. In addition to being "automatic," evidence has been mounting for almost 30 years that these responses are subconscious and are set into motion well before they are recognized in the conscious parts of the mind/brain (Harris, 2012; Libet, Gleason, Wright, & Pearl, 1983). If this is the case then people suffering from PTSD are well into a dysfunctional response before they even realize it. This is why brain researchers are trying to confirm the areas of the brain involved in these responses.

Research is being done with non-self-report diagnostic assessments that involve some type of monitoring of these brain structures, establishing baselines or "normal" ranges, then demonstrating that victims of PTSD have neural responses that exceed these "normal" ranges. This is challenging but seems possible. For example, there are stimulus-driven paradigms in which subjects are exposed to reminders of the trauma that can be auditory or visual and include brief autobiographical narratives of the trauma. In such studies, subjects with PTSD show greater activation of the cardiovascular system and more changes in skin conductance (electrodermal) and electromyographic (electrical potential generated by muscle cells) readings than non-PTSD comparison subjects (Orr et al., 2004). Such tests of psychophysiological reactivity are 60–90% successful in identifying subjects with PTSD (Friedman & Karam, 2008).

**GENETIC RESEARCH** As with the other mental disorders discussed in this book, if there is a genetic vulnerability to PTSD (and there appears to be) it is a polygenic vulnerability, which makes the identification of the specific genes involved (and their interactions or interactions with "switches" that turn them on) highly challenging. The axis or brain circuit running from the hypothalamus to the pituitary and then adrenal glands (HPA axis) appears to be implicated in the symptoms of PTSD, and this may result from differences at the genetic level (Radant, Tsuang, Peskind, McFall, & Raskind, 2001). Currently many researchers (Cornelis, Nugent, Amstadter, & Koenen, 2010) advocate what are called genome-wide studies[4] that focus on discovery rather

[4] Genome-wide association studies (GWAs) are examinations of common genetic variants in a large sample to see if variations can be linked to traits. Such studies have recently been initiated in exploring the Five-Factor Model of personality and in this sense studies on PTSD would look for "traits" related to triggering the fear circuit thought to underlay PTSD.

than hypothesis testing. Whereas candidate gene studies rely on biological hypotheses to guide the choice of candidate genes, genome-wide studies compare frequencies of hundreds of thousands of what are called single nucleotide polymorphisms (SNPs) in which one single nucleotide differs. The breadth of scope is thought to be a better approach than studies guided by a hypothesis about one single candidate gene at a time (Cornelis et al., 2010).

In general it appears that the heritability of anxiety disorders (with the exception of Obsessive-Compulsive Disorder) tends to be about 20–30% (Eley, 2008; Skelton, Ressler, Norrholm, Jovanovic, & Bradley-Davino, 2012). The majority of the remaining variance (60–70%) appears due to child-specific, nonshared environment. As noted, genetic vulnerability interacts with environment factors to trigger the disorder: ". . . differential responding to environmental pathogens is perhaps one of the most important indicators of a gene-environment interaction" (Koenen, Amstadter, & Nugent, 2009, p. 416). The responses to potentially traumatic events (PTEs) may have roots at the genetic level but a potentially traumatic event is always metabolized through gene–environment interactions.

Eley (2008) summarizes three routes by which gene–environment interactions occur. The first is passive gene–environment correlation. This is when, because biological family members share both genes and environment, parents pass on both genes and expose children to behaviors that may be modeled and learned. The second is evocative gene–environment interaction, where the behavior of a child evokes reactions from others and these then influence the experienced environment. The third is active gene–environment correlations, where as people grow, they make active choices about the world that *then act back on* whatever genome they possess. Although these patterns hold research potential, it is still difficult to apply them consistently with any anxiety disorder. Efforts are being made, though, and some promising research projects draw from the Vietnam Era Twin Registry.

The Vietnam Era Twin Registry (http://www.seattle.eric.research.va.gov/VETR/Home.asp) is comprised of 4774 male twin pairs born between 1939 and 1957 with both brothers having served in the Vietnam War. The registry ". . . was originally developed to provide the best control group for Vietnam-exposed servicemen to study the long-term health consequences of service in Vietnam" (Henderson, Eisen, Goldberg, True, & Vitek, 1990, p. 368). Research with this twin cohort has supported two important hypotheses. First, that there are heritable differences in the chances that a person will be exposed to a traumatic stressor. Second, that there are heritable differences with regard to whether a person exposed to a stressor actually develops PTSD (Friedman & Karam, 2008; Koenen et al., 2002).

As with many of the research hypotheses in this book, we still do not know what the exact mechanisms mediating the differences are. One hypothesis is that the serotonin transporter gene may play a role at least in depressive symptoms and possibly in PTSD (Kaufman et al., 2004). It may be that genetic factors contribute to risk factors that increase vulnerability to developing PTSD after a trauma. Using the Vietnam Era Twin Registry, Gilbertson and colleagues (2002) studied hippocampal size (volume) in combat veterans with and without PTSD. Smaller hippocampal volume was statistically correlated with PTSD. In other words, twins with smaller hippocampi may be at higher risk for PTSD. There is also the possibility that experiencing PTSD changes the hippocampal volume. Given that the hippocampus mediates memory creation, smaller hippocampal volume may render one more vulnerable to PTSD via a problem related to memory processes.

Other studies (Morgan et al., 2000, 2001) were done with U.S. Special Forces troops exposed to a stressful training experience during which neurohormone samples were taken from the soldiers. The neurohormone in question was Neropeptide-Y (NPY), which is a 36-amino acid peptide that has been conserved through mammalian evolution and is believed to be correlated with dissociation. The soldiers who had a greater capacity to mobilize NPY and sustain elevated levels throughout the training coped with stress and performed better than non-Special Forces troops who were not able to mobilize or sustain the peptide (Friedman & Karam, 2008).

More recently, researchers have been pursuing a link between pro-inflammatory cytokines with PTSD and then with a greater risk for cardiovascular disease. This work was based on the correlation between suffering PTSD and poor self-reported physical health and risk for comorbid medical disorders, including autoimmune disorders and pulmonary and digestive problems. Gola et al. (2013) found that peripheral blood mononuclear cells[5] were significantly higher in blood counts of people suffering from PTSD versus normal controls. The authors suggest that this physiological mechanism may be one pathway from PTSD to poorer health.

**PSYCHOLOGICAL FACTORS IN ETIOLOGY** Because we know how important psychological factors are in PTSD, it makes sense to ask if there are cognitive variables that may increase (or decrease) one's chance of developing PTSD after a traumatic event. Earlier models of psychological variables related to PTSD took the diathesis-stress approach. The model is derived from the medical field and posits that an underlying pathological mechanism (which you can think of as a "weak link") remains harmless until triggered by things like stress (Ingram, Miranda, & Segal, 1998). In terms of PTSD, the underlying "weak links" were thought to be things like cognitive vulnerability. Recall from Chapter 3 on depression that cognitive vulnerability involves biases in mental processes like interpretation, memories of events, and attention. Moreover, dysfunctional thoughts and biased cognitions lead to dysfunctional behaviors such as avoidance behavior (Elwood, Hahn, Olatunji, & Williams, 2009).

Cognitive theories of PTSD have proliferated since the 1990s. Early versions postulated that a traumatic event contradicted a person's view or "cognitive map" of the world and the discrepancy between the preexisting beliefs about the world and the world suggested by the trauma experience causes PTSD (Epstein, 1991; McCann & Pearlman, 1990). Janoff-Bulman (1992) also suggested that trauma altered three fundamental assumptions (i.e., that the world was meaningful and benevolent and that the self was worthy). The alterations in these beliefs were thought to contribute to developing PTSD.

Ehlers et al. (2005) noted that individuals with PTSD were much more likely than normal controls to experience negative views about themselves, such as believing they could not cope with life or that they were generally incompetent. They were also more likely to view the world as threatening and dangerous. Additionally, Ehring, Ehlers, and Glucksman (2006) have used experimental paradigms to show that

---

[5] These are blood cells that have a round nucleus and that are critical to immune system response.

clients suffering from PTSD are quicker to respond to threats or perceived threats—suggesting an underlying negative cognitive map.

Halligan, Michael, Clark, and Ehlers (2003) found that certain psychological variables can predict the severity of PTSD. Negative views about self ("I am incompetent"), negative views of the world ("the world is unsafe"), negative interpretations of initial symptoms ("these symptoms confirm that I am weak"), negative interpretations of other peoples' responses to symptoms ("they think I am crazy"), and the sense that things have permanently changed predict the severity of PTSD 6 months to a year after the traumatic event (Huppert, Foa, McNally, & Cahill, 2008). In addition, other researchers have identified negative attributional style (Abramson et al., 1999), rumination (Nolen-Hoeksema, 1991), anxiety sensitivity (Reiss, 1991), and looming cognitive style as psychological variables related to developing PTSD.

As noted in Chapter 3 on depression, negative attributional style in PTSD (also called negative cognitive style) increases biases toward feelings like hopelessness and helplessness. Hopelessness develops when negative events are attributed to internal, stable, and global causes—particularly with regard to why the trauma occurred ("I was abused because the world is and always has been a horrible place"), the consequences of the event ("I will always be ruined as a result of this"), and inferences about how one should have responded ("I never should have put myself in that position or should have fought off the attacker") (Abramson, Metalsky, & Alloy, 1989).

Rumination is usually defined as a tendency to think repetitively and passively about negative feelings, precipitators of traumas, distress, and the meaning of distress (Elwood et al., 2009). Measurements of rumination in people suffering from PTSD have shown mixed results, but in PTSD the rumination does seem more related to increased vigilance and the fear of similar traumas occurring (Ehlers & Clark, 2000). Anxiety sensitivity is described as a fear of anxiety-related sensations based on the belief that such sensations have harmful consequences. Anxiety sensitivity has been proposed as both a vulnerability factor and a maintenance factor in PTSD (Fedoroff, Taylor, Asmundson, & Koch, 2000). Some clients view PTSD symptoms as harbingers of insanity, rejection, or even impending death. Finally, looming cognitive style is basically a set of biases that increase one's risk of anxiety as a result of creating thoughts or mental scenarios of intensifying threat or danger (Elwood et al., 2009). Elwood and colleagues (2009) have advocated for an integrative model of cognitive vulnerability to PTSD that includes all these variables, with ways to rate clients on each one.

**CULTURAL/SOCIAL ISSUES RELATED TO PTSD** Because the physiological mechanisms thought to underlay PTSD are universal human characteristics, it seems logical that we should find PTSD across cultures. Although some would argue that someone suffering vicarious trauma after watching a loved one lose his or her job is entirely different than someone being tortured in a war zone, the Buddhist idea that all people suffer reminds us that comparing different types of suffering is rarely helpful. If clients are suffering—regardless of what the cause is—we meet them where they are and try to treat their symptoms and make the trauma underlying the symptoms an object of awareness.

The work done to date does support the idea that PTSD occurs across cultures, although with some differences. Hinton and Lewis-Fernandez (2011) conducted a literature review since 1994 looking for studies on PTSD and its relation to race, ethnicity, and culture in general. They found that PTSD had general validity across cultures, with a few caveats. The authors found that endorsement of avoidance as a symptom of PTSD varied quite a bit from culture to culture, with less endorsement in African and Middle Eastern cultures. There also seem to be variations in somatic symptoms across cultures. For example, a sense of bodily heat was far more common among Salvadoran and Senegalese refuges, bodily pain among tortured refugees, dizziness in Cambodian refugees, and shortness of breath among Rwandan genocide survivors. In addition, Jobson and O'Kearney (2008) found psychological differences in PTSD sufferers from different cultures related to whether the culture in question focused on independence or interdependence. PTSD survivors from independent cultures (such as Western European, Australian, and New Zealand) differed from survivors from interdependent cultures (such as African, Asian, and Middle Eastern cultures) on trauma-centered goals, self-defining memories, and self cognitions.

## Diagnosing PTSD: An All-Quadrant Affair

Several studies explored the consequences of "expanding" the diagnostic criteria in cluster A. In one study (Kessler et al., 1995), expanding the idea of a traumatic event to include trauma that happened to close relatives led to an increase from 68% to 89% in the incidence of traumatic events. Kessler and colleagues (1995) argued that this was far higher than any of the percentages related to the PTSD incidence rate and would decrease the usefulness of the diagnostic category. Similarly, Meltzer and colleagues (2012) suggest that PTSD is already being overdiagnosed in primary-care settings. On the other hand, some researchers say both "A" criteria could be eliminated without changing the integrity of the diagnosis. In a study of hurricane victims, the incidence of PTSD diagnoses was 11.2% with or without the "A" criteria (Demyttenaere et al., 2004). In the DSM-5 the "A" criteria were expanded to include traumas that happened to close relatives, and time will tell if this unnecessarily increases the incidence of the diagnosis.

The debate about the "A" criteria raised, again, the debate about categorical versus dimensional models. Recall from Chapter 2 that the current DSM is a system of categorical psychiatry wherein a patient either meets a threshold of symptoms (3 out of 5; 5 out of 7; etc.) or does not. Dimensional models are more a question of to what extent a client exhibits a symptom. Friedman and Karam (2008) summarized the idea of partial or subsyndromal PTSD: A dimensional model would allow such diagnoses for the cohort of people who have been exposed to a traumatic event but do not quite meet all PTSD criteria. They advocate that such criteria are necessary because many of those people do suffer distress or impairment from the level of symptoms they have.

The diagnostic criteria are meant to be scientifically measurable by a variety of assessment instruments that will provide a reliable diagnosis of PTSD (e.g., Clinician Administered PTSD Scale [CAPS]; Blake et al., 1995). Looking at both the *International Classification of Mental and Behavioural Disorders* (ICD; World Health Organization, 1992) and the DSM criteria through an Integral lens, it is apparent that PTSD is more than an objectively observable mental illness. Figure 5.1 breaks down the DSM diagnostic criteria for PTSD according to in which quadrant each criterion would be placed. The reader is reminded that the two right-hand quadrants contain externally observable or propositionally "objective" information whereas the left-hand quadrants contain the subjective experiences common to PTSD.

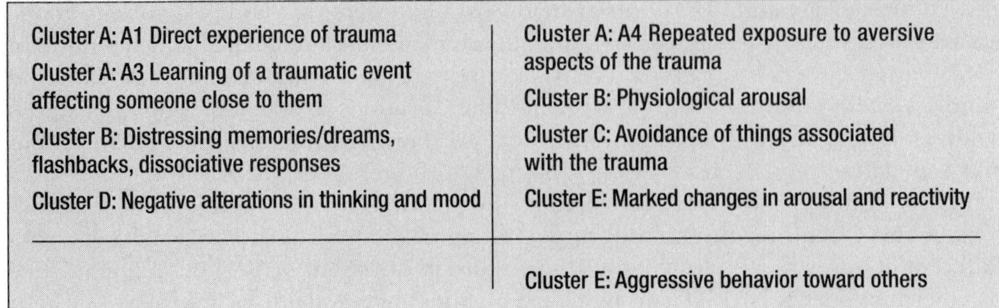


**FIGURE 5.1** PTSD Criteria Quadrant Locations—Adults Only

As Figure 5.1 illustrates, PTSD involves more than just objectively observable criteria (i.e., right-hand quadrants). The nature of symptoms such as changes in mood and the individual's distressing memories, dreams, and flashbacks are all clearly subjective, psychological phenomena. As with other disorders, these symptoms must cause clinically significant distress or impairment in social, occupational, or other important areas of functioning. Given that diagnosticians are not conducting randomly assigned experimental studies that provide definitive evidence regarding a cause-and-effect relationship between the individual's disturbance and clinically significant distress/impairment, the presence of criterion F must be established, in the best-case scenario, as a mutually agreed-upon decision (lower left [LL]) reached through a therapeutic dialogue between clinician and patient. In the worst-case scenario, the clinician can unilaterally verify or nullify the existence of criterion F because the phrasing of criterion F states that the disturbance must be "clinically significant," leaving room for interpretation, given that the DSM does not operationally define the term "clinically significant." Hence, PTSD in its current diagnostic form is not an objectively verifiable (i.e., right-hand quadrant) disorder, but, like most mental disorders, is an all-quadrant affair that is at least partially socially constructed. However, understanding how a diagnosis of PTSD relates to the four quadrants is only one part of the challenge facing therapists using the Integral approach.

## CASE EXAMPLE

Keisha is a 24-year-old African American veteran being seen at the Veterans' Administration (VA) hospital for PTSD and SUD. She was part of a mobilized National Guard unit that did two tours of duty in Iraq. Keisha joined the Guard to earn the military higher education benefits. She chose the Military Police and on deployment performed security for convoys, personnel, and prisoners of war. Keisha was initially excited about serving. Within the first 2 months she had been sexually harassed on several occasions and was sexually assaulted twice while in Iraq. She did not report the incidents for fear of reprisals from her commanding officer, who was friends with the rapist. Now, while pursuing her education, she is having significant trouble studying due to intrusive memories of the assaults, as well as severe anxiety and depressive states that are accompanied by extreme negative self-talk and some suicidal ideation. She began drinking heavily in her last year of service because it decreased her anxiety and provided a "numbing out" that was preferable to reminders of the assaults. Since transitioning home, she drinks less but still meets the criteria for PTSD and Alcohol Use Disorder. She is being treated at a local VA hospital on an outpatient basis. We will refer to Keisha's case throughout the discussion of treatment.

It is difficult to determine the accuracy of the statistics on sexual trauma in the military. The Veterans' Administration (2012) notes that 1 in 5 women and 1 in 100 men in service answered "yes" when asked if they suffered military sexual trauma. There was no attempt to collect such statistics until the Vietnam era. The statistics since 1990 reflect increasing numbers of people reporting sexual assault. Again, prevalence estimates vary; 4–9% of female service members in one study reported sexual assault (Harvin, 2004), whereas another study reported that 34% of female respondents reported a rape or attempted rape during active duty, although three-fourths of these respondents did not report it at the time for fear of reprisals, embarrassment, or being told to "suck it up" (Department of Defense Task Force on Domestic Violence, 2006). Reports in popular media (e.g., *Newsweek*) estimate that 1 in 5 females and 1 in 15 males report sexual assault by service members (Ellison, 2011). Although some have argued that the statistics are misleading because of the mean age of those serving in the military the Defense Department admits to poor handling of such assaults (Editorial, 2004).

**THE CURRENT DISCOURSE ON TREATMENT** Over the past decade, widely ranging practice guidelines for PTSD have been published worldwide and for particular groups in particular cultures. The range of guidelines for the same disorder published in different places, at different times, and for different populations can be daunting for clinicians looking for guidance in treating their clients (Forbes et al., 2010). There is a list of websites at the end of this chapter where some of the many guidelines can be found—from the United States Department of Defense to the American Psychiatric Association. In the current discourse on trauma and treatment, PTSD is considered a highly prevalent and impairing condition for which only a minority of people obtain treatment (Kessler, 2000). Certain treatments have demonstrated effectiveness in reducing the core symptoms of PTSD, including cognitive-behavioral therapies (CBTs), trauma-focused cognitive-behavioral therapy, eye movement desensitization and reprocessing (EMDR; Shapiro, 1995), and exposure techniques (Foa, 2000; Sherman, 1998; Taylor, Thordarson, Maxfield, Fedoroff, & Ogrodniczuk, 2003; Van Etten & Taylor, 1998). There are many "evidence-based" approaches that seem to have comparable efficacy (Najavits et al., 2011).

Some believe that early and aggressive outreach to treat people with PTSD could help reduce the enormous societal costs of the disorder (Kessler, 2000). This is part of the rationale for broadening the diagnostic criteria in the DSM-5. This is particularly challenging with veterans because many experience military culture as punishing any sign of weakness. Military active-duty suicides increased dramatically from 2008 to 2012, where they peaked at approximately 23 per 100,000 (up from 11 per 100,000 in 2003) (Guttierrez, Castro, Fitek, Jobes, & Holloway, 2012). In Keisha's case, she likely would not have come forward at any point. She was at a college transition program[6]

[6] College transition programs are still uncommon on American campuses. Although more are being developed, on some campuses they are protested by students. Where they do exist, many vets are hesitant to self-identify, especially if the programs are staffed with people who have never been in the military.

event for female veterans where one of the organizers (also a female vet) shared her experience of coming forward to report a sexual assault. Keisha decided that although she was not going to officially report this to the military, she was going to seek help. It is possible in the VA system to be treated for military sexual trauma (MST) and not report the incident(s).[7] She shared that she would not have likely done this without hearing a similar story from another vet.

Current treatments for PTSD fall into two broad categories: (1) psychotherapy and (2) pharmacotherapy, neither of which is comprehensive or integral in nature. Grinage (2003) states that PTSD treatment requires a multidimensional approach, including supportive patient education, cognitive behavior therapy, and psychopharmacology, echoing a call for a diversity and multiplicity of perspectives. Foa et al. (2000),[8] Bandelow et al. (2008), and Forbes et al. (2010) present practice guidelines for the effective treatment of PTSD following extensive reviews of the relevant literature in the treatment areas of: pharmacotherapy psychological debriefing, CBTs, pharmacotherapy, EMDR, group therapy, psychodynamic therapy, inpatient treatment, psychosocial rehabilitation, hypnosis, marital and family therapy, and creative therapies.

Here are key points from the literature reviews in these practice guidelines. First, it is important to recognize that there are many points of agreement across reviews and across guidelines. All guidelines support the use of trauma-focused psychological treatment in PTSD for adults and sometimes for children (Forbes et al., 2010). Second, all guidelines recognize the benefit of pharmacotherapy as a part of treatment, although the agents recommended differ depending on client response and available resources. For example, selective serotonin reuptake inhibitor (SSRI) antidepressants may be rated as a first-line or second-line intervention depending on whether trauma-focused therapy is available (Forbes et al., 2010).

Regarding pharmacotherapy, monotherapy[9] is only partly effective (Shad et al., 2011). SSRIs have generally been regarded as first-line drugs in the treatment of PTSD, perhaps because they were the first to get on-label approval of the Food and Drug Administration (FDA). Some efficacy has been demonstrated for Prozac/fluoxetine, Paxil/paroxetine, Zoloft/sertraline, as well as the serotonin norepinephrine reuptake inhibitors (SNRIs), Effexor/venlafaxine, and some tricyclic antidepressants. SSRIs and SNRIs are favored over tricyclic antidepressants because of tricyclics' overdose potential, higher incidence of side effects, and poor compliance rates (Bandelow et al., 2008). There are ongoing investigations into combining medications; for example, a norepinephrine receptor antagonist (prazosin) seems to help reduce trauma-related nightmares while propranolol (a different type of NE receptor antagonist) seems to decrease the emotional content of traumatic memories (Shad et al., 2011). Keisha was offered an SSRI as part of her therapy but refused because she did not want to suffer the potential side effects of weight gain and sexual dysfunction.

---

[7] MST is a generic label, not a diagnosis. It covers a broad range of types of traumas, many of which result in PTSD.

[8] We have relied on Foa et al. (2000) for this section, due to the legitimacy owed to it as a publication of the ISTSS and as representative of the dominant view in the current discourse, not because it represents the final or only word on the subject.

[9] Monotherapy refers to treatment with only one drug at a time.

The prescribing physician was hesitant to prescribe benzodiazepines[10] because they are cross-tolerant with alcohol.

Psychological debriefing is not considered to be effective for preventing PTSD and is in fact contraindicated as some studies show it is correlated with a worsening of symptoms (Deahl et al., 2000; Mayou, Ehlers, & Hobbs, 2000). In Keisha's case much time initially was spent in building the therapeutic relationship. Reservists like Keisha have been shown to have more difficult deployments and reintegration experiences because they did not spend extended periods of time living on a military base prior to deployment and often do not return to a base for long periods between deployment and reintegration. CBTs and trauma-focused CBT have been superior to wait-list controls (Blanchard et al., 2001). Exposure therapy initially showed positive results in some studies and negative results in others (Shalev, Bonne, & Eth, 1996) but recently the use of virtual reality computer programs is showing promising results with veterans (Rizzo et al., 2009). In addition, meditation and exposure therapy have been supported in a study of child survivors of war and tsunamis (Catani et al., 2009). Finally, one preliminary study supports the use of exposure paired with repetitive transcranial magnetic stimulation (Osuch et al., 2009).

Eye movement desensitization reprocessing (EMDR) is considered more effective than wait-list, routine-care, or active-treatment controls, but more evidence is needed to establish its effectiveness compared to other specific PTSD treatments (Taylor et al., 2003). EMDR was thoroughly reviewed by the United Kingdom National Institute for Clinical Excellence (NICE; 2005). Although the effectiveness of EMDR was generally supported, the evidence was not as strong as that for trauma-focused CBT in terms of the number of randomized, controlled trials available and the level of certainty with which clinical benefit was established (Bandelow et al., 2008). It should be noted that there is still controversy over discrepancies in meta-analytic studies on psychological treatments for PTSD. The controversy is not over whether they help but rather whether one is really better than another (Ehlers et al., 2010). In Keisha's case the therapist used a combination of mindfulness and CBT.

According to Foa et al. (2000), group therapy is recommended as potentially effective (p. 170); psychodynamic therapy did not show conclusive evidence of effectiveness due mostly to methodological issues (p. 194); and research on inpatient treatment was inconclusive but in some cases demonstrated that the use of specific inpatient treatments was warranted (p. 210). Psychosocial rehabilitation techniques are highly recommended once it is determined that clients with PTSD demonstrate a deficit in a particular domain and have identified and set goals to overcome such problems (p. 239); hypnosis is recommended as an adjunct for the treatment of PTSD (p. 270); the use of marital and family interventions to address the problems of trauma survivors has been neglected by researchers (p. 297); and, despite relatively wide use and application, the efficacy of the creative arts therapies has not been established through empirical research (p. 311).

Luxenberg et al. (2001) introduced three different treatment phases of PTSD: stabilization, processing and grieving of traumatic memories, and reconnection/reintegration with the world. Stabilization involves discussing the meaning of trauma and gaining as much knowledge as possible about the client's recurring symptoms.

[10] Benzodiazepines include drugs like Valium, Xanax, and Klonopin. They are GABA agonists.

In Keisha's case, dark, hot, enclosed spaces were triggers for memories of both assaults. One took place in a storage facility and the other in a garage. She also had many problems with males in authority, as these tended to provoke trigger situations. The VA does have an option for clients to request a therapist of the same sex, which Keisha did. Things that add to the stabilization phase include the client's physical well-being and the importance of regulating sleeping, eating, and exercise. Living in a safe environment will contribute to stabilization—for example, when a client develops a sense of trust and safety at home by creating healthy support systems.

Keisha had been living with a friend but was also looking for an apartment. In her case finding a residence where she felt safe was part of the therapy. She and her therapist narrowed down the possibilities she could afford and then, based on her triggers and need for safety, she chose a well-lit apartment that was more expensive but in a better part of town. Therapists have an active role in therapy; however, the client will be the one responsible for creating boundaries, and for building self-soothing capacities when the client is experiencing symptoms such as re-experiencing or hyperarousal. It is very important for the client to understand that trauma is not the focus of the therapy sessions; rather, healthy outcome is what the focus should be all about (Luxenberg et al., 2001). In Keisha's case, that included addressing her alcohol use and its effects on sleep and productivity. The work of apartment hunting was initially the focus of therapy for Keisha; this also helped her come to trust the therapist.

The phase of processing and grieving the traumatic memories might be the most difficult one for the client to handle during therapy. Both the client and the therapist should actively work on exploring those memories and integrating them into the client's life story. This experience should aim to normalize the emotions that the client feels when narrating her life. It is possible that the client might become overwhelmed or dissociate; thus, it is important for the therapist to be able to identify signs of those phenomena and then help the client ground herself (Luxenberg et al., 2001). This work must be carried out at the client's pace—as Keisha's therapist did, first spending time building trust. This is an example of what Lindy and Wilson (2001) call "respecting the trauma membrane" (p. 432). Keisha was dealing with powerful emotions and her therapist realized there was a danger in moving too fast. Trust is particularly important for victims of MST because the event evokes powerfully conflicting emotions. On the one hand, Keisha had built a bond of loyalty and trust with the man who raped her, while on the other hand she felt betrayal and confusion because of that. She still had to work with this man for 4 months after the second attack, which added to her confusion and fueled her alcohol use to "numb out."

For Keisha, handling the traumatic memories was the most difficult part of the therapy. She is a strong woman, which is one of the reasons she chose military police in the first place. She has always been athletic and currently does Cross-Fit workouts daily. The humiliation and shame she felt at having been threatened and overpowered were dominant feelings she used alcohol to numb. Her drinking increased at this point in the therapy because her symptoms initially worsened as she began to face the powerful emotions she had previously kept contained. After a 2-week period she was able to stop drinking again, or, as per her report, drink socially (1 or 2 drinks over the course of a 3- to 4-hour evening).

After going through the first two treatment phases, clients would then reconnect with the things that they enjoyed prior to the trauma, such as friendships, relationships, hobbies, religion, and so on. In severe cases, individuals may also require ongoing medication. Unfortunately, all medication is prescribed depending on the symptoms that the client is reporting. Zoloft/sertraline was one of the first antidepressants to get on-label approval for treatment of some PTSD symptoms and in studies is better than placebos in treating PTSD symptoms, whether from child abuse or other interpersonal traumas (Stein, van der Kolk, Austin, Fayyad, & Clary, 2006). Although nonmedical mental health professionals usually do not prescribe medications, they work with psychiatrists and other medical professionals who do. Some recommendations such professionals may make could include SSRIs (as noted earlier) for mood, anxiety, and impulsivity; benzodiazepines for anxiety, irritability, and insomnia; mood stabilizers for irritability, aggression, and hyperarousal; and antipsychotics for paranoia, thought disorder, and hallucinations (Luxenberg et al., 2001; van der Kolk, 2001). As Keisha's case illustrates, in PTSD, medication strategies are more works-in-progress than fixed treatments.

## An Integral Approach

An Integral approach to treating trauma acknowledges and attempts to incorporate, in a meaningful way, all quadrants, levels, lines, states, and types in the diagnosis, planning, treatment, follow-up, and integration of trauma work with clients. Whereas some of the chapters in this book do not integrate lines of development, personality types, and states of consciousness, we feel these are important to Integral trauma work and do include them here.[11] Despite the lack of Integral vision in the discourse on trauma treatment, an overarching treatment model has emerged and has become accepted by many in the field. The currently accepted overarching treatment model for dealing with trauma involves: (1) assessing client resources, (2) establishing safety and stabilization, (3) processing of traumatic memories, and (4) moving forward and reconnecting with life (Baranowsky, Gentry, & Schultz, 2005; Briere, 2006; Herman, 1997). Tied to the treatment literature is also a serious discussion of the risk of vicarious traumatization and secondary trauma (Pearlman, 1995; Pearlman & Saakvitne, 1995) and compassion fatigue (Figley, 2002) in the therapist. The treatment of PTSD can become more Integrally informed and therapists can bring an Integral awareness to the prevention and treatment of vicarious trauma. The following section focuses primarily on the initial stages of trauma therapy—namely, Integral approaches to establishing safety and stabilization. If we can help our clients achieve an Integrally informed sense of safety and stabilization in their lives, the processing of traumatic memories will be much less problematic and the reconnection with the world will be less intimidating.

**SAFETY AND STABILIZATION** The terms *safety* and *stabilization* have particular meaning when working with traumatized clients. Herman (1997) first alerted the therapeutic community to the necessity of establishing safety with trauma survivors. Herman's model included safety as the first of three stages of treatment in working with trauma survivors, along with remembrance/mourning and reconnection, respectively. Other

[11] These areas are also included in Dr. Sarah Hubbard's chapter on Eating Disorders. PTSD and Eating Disorders share a characteristic of being challenging to treat, and both are areas where therapists will benefit from specialized training and supervised experience.

authors (Baranowsky et al., 2005; Briere, 2006) have expanded upon Herman's (1997) ideas of safety to include *stabilization* as another key construct in trauma treatment. Baranowsky et al. (2005) refer to safety and stabilization at every stage of Herman's (1997) model, specifically focusing on the traditional therapeutic triad of cognitive, emotional, and behavioral safety and stabilization. Briere (2006) suggest psychoeducation, distress reduction and affect regulation strategies, cognitive interventions, emotional processing, and psychopharmacology. In the most recent models, the primacy of the traditional therapeutic "triad" focusing on cognitions, behaviors, and emotions is evident. Although the models represent an extremely helpful step in understanding and treating clients with PTSD, an Integral approach can complement these models with a thorough understanding of states of consciousness and taking into account as much as we know about developmental issues in trauma treatment.

**DEVELOPING INTEGRAL CLIENT RESOURCES—BASIC LEVELS OF SAFETY** The integrally informed trauma therapist assists clients as they attempt to achieve adequate[12] bodily, emotional, cognitive, and spiritual safety[13] and stabilization, understanding that the more complex levels of developmental safety (e.g., cognitive safety) can be undermined by a lack of safety in the more fundamental levels (e.g., bodily safety). In Keisha's case, the therapist recognized that it would be ill-advised to begin processing her emotionally charged trauma memories before an adequate sense of physical (biological) safety and stabilization were established. As noted, the apartment hunting that was processed in therapy was part of Keisha increasing her sense of bodily safety. Adequate safety will vary with each client and is dependent upon the clinical judgment of the therapist as well as clear communication and involvement with the client in the process. As such, some general guidelines for determining adequate safety in the basic levels of development include but are not limited to those discussed in the following subsections.

**Bodily Safety** There is minimal risk of current danger to the client's bodily self by him- or herself (e.g., suicidal ideation, high-risk behaviors), at the hands of a related other (e.g., a physically abusive or violent spouse, parent, sibling, relation, pimp, or colleague, etc.) or due to circumstances (e.g., living in or around man-made environmental disasters, war, terror, natural disasters, drive-by shootings, muggings, etc.).

**Emotional Safety** There is minimal risk of danger to the client's emotional self at the hands of a related or an unrelated other (e.g., attachment figures including parents, caregivers, family members and/or spouses are reliably present in the client's life without major disruption or toxicity involved; the client is not in contact with emotionally abusive neighbors or friends); the client is free to express his emotions without risk of suffering emotional abuse and/or manipulation in the relationship; the client understands and trusts that his emotions will not and cannot destroy him. For Keisha

---

[12] When speaking about safety and stabilization, we must be mindful to avoid treating them as dichotomous variables that one either has or is missing. We need to speak about enough "safety" to proceed in therapy without risking re-traumatization of the client.

[13] Spirituality is used here as meaning a person's ultimate concern—including her vision of material and immaterial reality, as well as an inner peace enabling the discovery of one's deepest values, meanings, and sense of being.

this required first overcoming the powerful taboos from military culture about feeling weak, defeated, and vulnerable and then talking about those feelings. Keisha noted that it was very helpful that her therapist also had a military background. Again, this is not imperative but many veterans are more able to open up if they really feel the therapist has shared life experiences.

**Cognitive Safety** There is minimal risk of danger to the client's cognitive sense of self by him- or herself or by a related or unrelated other (e.g., family, friends, spouses are at the least nonabusive and ideally supportive, offering praise and reinforcement for the client's demonstrated abilities, life choices, and self-sense; the client is not engaged in undermining negative self-talk and does not have deeply held beliefs about the lack of her value or worth as a person). Keisha's thoughts about herself as a strong person suffered a terrible blow as a result of her experiences, and this led to a downward spiral of negative self-talk.

The first three basic levels of safety are fairly straightforward. When we begin to discuss the spiritual aspects of a client's life, more complexity is required to adequately understand and appreciate how to establish safety.

**Spiritual Safety** There is minimal risk of danger to client's sense of connection to Spirit (e.g., client has a sense that God, Buddha, Jesus, Allah, etc. loves him, or the client experiences Spirit as loving kindness). Spirit can also be thought of more existentially as a connection to something greater than oneself. Such was the case with Keisha and her success with mindfulness practice. Obviously we follow the client's lead where religious or spiritual worldviews are concerned. A spiritual or religious worldview can be an asset or a problem depending on how the client relates it to the trauma. Whereas one client may feel God sustained her through her crisis, another may feel God is punishing her with the crisis.

**RELIABLE RESOURCES ACROSS THE FOUR QUADRANTS** The Integral trauma therapist will keep all these types of safety in mind as she begins dialoguing with clients about the reliable resources that clients possess in each of the four quadrants. Too often therapists over-focus on the problems in the client's life. Although understanding a client's problems is essential, establishing each client's resources (in each of the four quadrants) gives both client and therapist a good idea of areas that need to be developed prior to moving to the intense processing of traumatic material.

**Upper-Right Resources (URR)** The UR quadrant is the realm of the client's physical body and individual behaviors. Assessing the client's reliable resources includes assessing the *functioning* of the client's physical body—including aspects of physical health as well as the *behaviors* that the client engages in that can be considered resources. Examples of resources in physical *functioning* include: a healthy, disease-free body; regular, restful sleep patterns; lack of organic brain/organ dysfunction; and intact bodily senses of sight, sound, smell, touch, and taste. This is not a value judgment about people who may lack overall health in these areas but rather an acknowledgment that possessing health in these areas can be considered a reliable resource for doing trauma work. Examples of resources in *behaviors* include: adequate levels of exercise, adequate nutrition diet/eating habits, and self-soothing behaviors (e.g., taking warm baths, making favorite foods, reading inspiring literature, avoiding disturbing forms of media). Therapists and clients alike will be able to identify many such resourceful behaviors among others not included here. In Keisha's case, her Cross-Fit practice kept her in excellent physical condition and probably helped her decrease the negative effects of alcohol on her body.

**Lower-Right Resources (LRR)** The LR quadrant includes the interobjective aspects of the physical systems that impact the client's world and, hence, the client's recovery from trauma. LR resources might include: living in relatively crime-free neighborhood; having access to personal transportation or affordable public transportation; living in a community with low levels of unemployment; owning a home or renting an apartment in a building with other healthy individuals and families around; and having a job that pays the bills. This is the quadrant that the majority of therapists will not explicitly include in a discussion of client resources. In conducting this exercise clinically, one client came to realize that his home and his surrounding neighborhood were two very important resources for him that he had not recognized as such before our discussion. He realized how much he loved coming home and taking walks with his dog in the evening through his neighborhood. Even in the most dangerous neighborhoods, clients may have a physical refuge in a particular room in their apartment that feels safe and stable and can be accessed as a resource for trauma work. Keisha's apartment certainly qualifies as a resource.

**Lower-Left Resources (LLR)** The LL quadrant is the realm of interpersonal connection and relationship. Resources in this quadrant include any relationship to another person, group, or community that the client can rely upon as a resource. Therapists and clients might also explore relationships to pets and other animals as resources in this quadrant. Clients may have a multitude of reliable relationships with people and groups in their lives; they may have one good lifelong friend; or, the therapist may be their only reliable resource in this quadrant. Exploring this quadrant for resources can be very healing for clients who may not have realized how many connections they do have in their lives. What about religious and other meaning-making beliefs? This was an area where Keisha felt a void. She had two close friends in the city, one who served with her in the military. She did not accept organized religion, so that was not an option for her. She did expand her circle of friends through her Cross-Fit gym. She felt that sharing rigorous training built some of the same types of bonding she had experienced in the military.

**Upper-Left Resources (ULR)** The UL quadrant is the area in which many trauma therapists will be adept at assessing resources. This is the quadrant of the client's subjectivity and includes the client's: sense of self, beliefs, values, any spiritual connection, physical sensations, emotions, cognitions, and so forth. Again, much of therapy focuses on what is wrong in this particular quadrant, but focusing on what internal resources the client possesses can provide both therapist and client with a clear picture of how much intrapersonal work must be done before embarking upon, as well as what can be relied upon during, the "darkest moments" of the trauma work. For example, a client may firmly believe that God will never give her anything that she cannot handle. In trauma work, this belief can be drawn upon when it seems as though things will "never get any better" and the client becomes worried that she will be overwhelmed by the traumatic memories. Much of Keisha's therapy had to do with rebuilding her faith in her own abilities and trusting herself. The natural highs that come from rigorous exercise were also resources in this quadrant.

**Using the Four-Quadrant Diagram Clinically** Therapists who have an understanding of all four quadrants can use a blank quadrant diagram to write down and record with the client the client's reliable resources. This can be an illuminating process for clients that provides them with an unambiguous "map" of what work needs to be done in the safety/stabilization phase. In clinical use, one client was struck with how few resources she possessed in the UL quadrant and it became abundantly clear that prior to moving into the processing phase of the work, we needed to address her negative self-talk and change her negative automatic thoughts about her future. She had some very reliable resources in all three of the other quadrants but lacked reliable resources within herself. The diagram is a work in progress because client and therapist add resources as they become established in the client's life, providing the client with a sense of accomplishment leading up to the processing phase of treatment. Therapists will also find their own creative ways to work with the quadrant diagram in assessing client resources for doing trauma work.

Just as client and therapist can use the quadrant diagram to assess and discuss client resources, so too can they use the diagram to assess the challenges in each of the quadrants. Addressing challenges is an essential part of treatment planning and one in which most trauma therapists will be well versed. Once trauma therapists understand and begin to "see" all four quadrants in their clients' lives, they will likely begin to create new and innovative ways of using the quadrant diagram in their work.

**Resourceful Lines of Development** The Integrally informed therapist understands that clients are not merely a single and unitary self moving through time and space. Rather, they are aware that clients are complex individuals living through multiple lines of development or multiple intelligences (Gardner, 1993, 1999; Gardner & Kornhaber, 1996). The clearest example of how different lines of development can impact therapeutic work with trauma is the interplay between the cognitive line and the emotional line in adult clients. Loevinger's (1976) view is that the cognitive line of development may be differentiated from self-development in that it "leads the way" as the line that determines what a given person is, or can be, aware of. If cognition describes what a person can be aware of, self establishes what (in the realm of what the person is aware of) the person identifies with.

In practice, therapists and clients alike will be aware of how adult clients can be fully aware of the reasons *why* they are feeling the way they do and yet, despite this insight, remain unable to change the way they are feeling. A client may be fully aware that the reason she is feeling terror is due to the fact that she is being triggered by either internal or external cues and yet she still feels the terror. It could be that this occurs when the trauma happened at a developmental stage when the individual's self is identified more with emotions and cognitions. The cognitive line continues to develop new awarenesses and perspectives that the emotional line is not affected by in any substantial way, and the client remains "emotionally stuck" at an earlier developmental level. In this example, only the emotional line of development is "stuck" while the cognitive line has continued onward. The developmental lines to which the therapist attends will largely depend on each client and the nature/duration of the trauma that has brought the client to therapy in the first place.

If we hold in mind that people are not one-dimensional but possess many lines of development, we can then begin to look at resourceful lines of development that the individual can rely upon while engaged in trauma therapy. A client with severe relational trauma, such as Keisha, may develop deficits in the interpersonal line, experiencing troubles in establishing and maintaining relationships and valuing security at all costs, no matter how alone or despairing she may feel. However, despite the "damage" in the interpersonal line of development she may simultaneously possess resources in the kinesthetic/athletic line—as Keisha did in her Cross-Fit training. Integral trauma therapists will explore the multiple lines of development that the client may possess, looking at those lines of development that represent resources for doing trauma work, or that could be easily developed as resources. The following questions can be posed to explore lines of development:

***Values:*** What values do I have that will help me get through the hardest parts of my recovery process?

***Interpersonal:*** What people skills do I possess that I can rely upon to help me get to where I want to go in my therapeutic journey?

***Musical:*** What music is most inspiring to me and will help me get through the hardest parts of my recovery process?

***Cognitive:*** What is my cognitive capacity? What cognitive tools do I have at my disposal?

***Ego:*** Of the things I am aware of, what do I identify with?

***Kinesthetic:*** What exercises or physical activities give me joy or relief from the everyday stresses of life that might also give me relief during the hardest parts of my recovery process?

***Artistic:*** What artistic outlets do I have that provide me with a means of expressing myself or that provide a distraction from the everyday grind of life that I can rely upon during my therapeutic journey?

**Client and Therapist Interpersonal Lines: Trauma Counseling at the Crossroads** One of the most important lines to consider in developing trust and safety with clients is, not surprisingly, the interpersonal line. It is this line of development that some therapists (Briere, 2006) might consider to be the most important line for developing safety in clients with relational trauma. This is a very important point as issues of control and power are intimately connected to the development of safety and are issues that therapists will also struggle with when faced with their clients' "unfixable" suffering (Plomp, 1997). Therapists with high needs for interpersonal control may find working with survivors of childhood trauma overwhelming, as the demands on the therapist as a person can be intense. They may try to establish control for themselves by asserting their professional boundaries in order to prevent the client from becoming dependent on them. However, it may be that the client, in order to heal, may need to become dependent on the therapist for a short time, in order to know that another human being can be trusted not to hurt them. This subsection is really a caveat to trauma therapists and to all therapists about remaining aware of what can happen at the intersection of two different interpersonal lines of development, when one is seeking help and healing in the company of another.

**Resourceful States of Consciousness** Perhaps one of the most intriguing aspects of trauma therapy is the nature of traumatic memories and how they find expression through the client's body/mind. Particularly interesting are the experiences of flashbacks, the nondeclarative, intrusive memories of the trauma, in which clients feel as though they are reliving all or part of the event. Flashbacks are often very disturbing and are experienced as happening "in the moment" rather than as an integrated memory of a past event. In Keisha's case she was at the university on a summer night and used the elevator in the parking garage. The dark, hot, enclosed space triggered her back to her first rape, which took place in a dark storage facility.

Theories about how flashbacks occur involve discussions of the limbic system and particularly the amygdala. Flashbacks are thought to represent traumatic memories that are "stuck" in the limbic system and not processed through to become episodic memory in the cerebral cortex. The quality of the flashbacks is of the form "I am in danger" rather than "I am having a memory of when I was in danger" and can thus be considered a kind of altered state of consciousness. Another equally intriguing aspect of many traumas is the experience of dissociation, wherein clients report having left their bodies and floated up or stepped back and witnessed what was happening. The mechanisms of dissociation are not well understood by modern scientific theories. Dissociation and flashbacks constitute altered states of consciousness that many trauma clients experience and must work through during the course of their therapy. They are, however, maladaptive states of consciousness that do not generally aid the processing of traumatic memory, but rather detract from the client's ability to take advantage of therapy.

Given that PTSD often includes maladaptive states, the Integrally informed trauma therapist can also include adaptive "states training" to help clients establish safety and stabilization in their lives. A non-normal state is, by definition, a temporary shift in consciousness, away from the "usual" state in which clients find themselves. Adaptive states in trauma therapy help clients experience themselves in a nontraumatized state, and there are numerous examples from relaxation training, breath training, guided imagery (unless the person dissociates), safe-place exercise, and others that have proven to be helpful. An important factor to consider when choosing the appropriate states-training exercise is whether or not the client has a tendency to dissociate. Baranowsky et al. (2005) offer some clear guidelines in this regard. Although meditation is certainly a states-training exercise, there is some evidence that suggests Vipassana (mindfulness) types of meditation (simply noticing what arises in consciousness) may serve to lower the repression barrier, allowing a flood of unconscious material to arise, potentially overwhelming the traumatized client. We would recommend that clients start with more focused, concentrative types of meditation—such as breath awareness—in order to provide a touchstone for relief from negative self-talk, flashbacks, and other intrusive memories.

**Types and Safety—Attachment and the Interpersonal Line** The final aspect of Integral theory that the Integrally informed therapist will attend to is the notion of types. There are various instruments available to test for an individual's type, including the Enneagram, the Myers-Briggs Type Indicator, and the NEO-PI-R, to name a few, and although there is considerable interest in the notion of types in the field of counseling and psychotherapy, very little attention has been paid to how different types of people respond to treatment for trauma-related issues.[14] For example, are certain treatments better suited to more extraverted clients and others better suited to introverted

[14] This is an area where the authors recognize that types have little validity (Ingersoll & Zeitler, 2010) but can be used metaphorically with clients. Clinicians should, however, hold the concept lightly. Type systems such as the Enneagram have scant psychometric support for their validity or reliability (Ingersoll & Zeitler, 2010).

clients? One might conclude that the more extraverted client may respond better to group approaches to treating trauma and that introverted types might respond better to individual sessions. Given the attention that is now being paid to the interpersonal aspects of trauma therapy (Briere, 2006, pp. 149–164), one must begin to acknowledge that the interplay of the therapist's and the client's personality types may represent a significant factor in the healing process. One problem with personality inventories, given the finding that trauma alters an individual's personality, involves how reliable such inventories are with people who have experienced trauma (Wilson, 2006).

One typology that has received much attention in the field of developmental trauma is that of attachment styles, based on Bowlby's research and theory of attachment. Currently, there is relative agreement that the client's developmental stage at the time of traumatic exposure, as well as the specific type of trauma exposure, are essential factors in PTSD, but these factors have been deemphasized in the literature. However, studies have emerged that point to the clear relationship between adult attachment styles and post-traumatic symptomology (e.g., Dieperink, Leskela, Thuras, & Engdahl, 2001). Therefore, when we discuss *types* in the treatment of PTSD, we would do well to consider how we work with different types or styles of attachment in our adult clients.

Bakermans-Kranenburg and Ijzendoorn (1993) state that, in adults, there are three main attachment styles: (1) *autonomous or secure adults* (coded as F), (2) *dismissing adults* (coded as D), and (3) *preoccupied adults* (coded as E). Each of these classifications may receive an additional classification of *Unresolved* (U). Instruments have been developed to assist researchers and clinicians in determining an adult client's attachment style (e.g., Adult Attachment Interview [AAI], George, Kaplan, & Main, 1996), but they are not, as yet, as user-friendly as they might be, requiring in-depth analysis of interview transcripts. The biggest challenge is that many therapists do not have the means or the desire to be trained in interpreting an instrument such as the AAI. With regard to safety/stabilization in trauma treatment, understanding attachment injuries will assist clinicians in determining where to focus their efforts and what to beware of in terms of the client's interpersonal line of development. Early childhood trauma, especially early childhood relational trauma, impacts an individual's ability to attach or relate to others. If the other is a caregiver, then this impacts the client's ability to form a relational bond with a therapist. One of the most crucial aspects of trauma therapy with early childhood trauma survivors is what occurs at the intersection between the client's and the therapist's interpersonal lines of development. Identifying early childhood traumas in general, and early childhood relational traumas in particular, is essential for therapists working with traumatized clients.

The Clinician Administered PTSD Scale (CAPS; Blake et al., 1995) includes a Life Events Checklist at the back of the instrument. I (Black) have modified this particular checklist to include an indication of when the event occurred in the client's life, something that the original checklist does not include. I am calling the revised checklist the Developmental Life Events Checklist (DLEC; Blake et al., 1995). The DLEC is a user-friendly tool for practitioners to use as a possible indicator of adult attachment styles. For example, an individual who does not report any traumatic life events prior to age 15 is less likely than a person who endorses several traumatic life events having occurred in the 0–5 or 6–10 age range to have an adult attachment style that would require concerted attention on the part of the therapist in terms of treatment planning and managing of the counseling relationship dynamics. Likewise, clients who endorse more relational traumas that have occurred in the early years will be more likely to require a therapist with skill in managing, helping to create, and maintaining personal boundaries in the course of trauma therapy. Although the DLEC is not considered a reliable and valid tool for assessing adult attachment style, it can prove very useful for practitioners taking client histories and hoping to identify general issues or "red flags" in early attachment.

Personality variables other than types include Wilson's (2006) characteristics of transformation acting on the personality trying to metabolize a trauma. He explained that traumatic life experiences alter the individual's personality. Those characteristics include 12 principles that suggest knowledge of positive personal values. Principles of self-transformation in the post-traumatic self include vulnerability and illusion; pain, suffering, and transformation; acceptance; limits to ego and humility; continuity to discontinuity in life; connection and sources of meaning; balance and groundedness; empathy, compassion, and freshness of appreciation; honesty and gratitude; self-transformation and reinvention; and spiritual consciousnesses and altruism. Each of these can become the focus of treatment at any given time depending on the needs of the client. For Keisha, her mindfulness practice helped her with balance and groundedness while also allowing her to feel connected to something greater than herself. She was not a theist in the religious sense but believed there was a force that held the universe together and that mindfulness connected her with this force.

## Summary and Conclusions

Integral treatment of trauma begins with safety and stabilization in clients' lives as well as in their relationship with the therapist. Although this chapter has focused on safety and stabilization, Integral treatment of trauma also helps clients process and grieve over their traumatic memories as well as reintegrate them with the rest of their lives. If we want to help the person who has fallen victim to people or to circumstances that have overwhelmed that person's ability to cope, then we want to start by building up the whole person. Trauma therapy is an imprecise, challenging, and ultimately taxing endeavor for both therapist and client. The methods used to treat trauma have come a long way since the days when catharsis was the only goal and it was believed to be enough to achieve healing. We know more now about the treatment of psychological trauma than we ever have, and it is our hope that with an Integral map, the field will continue to grow and evolve with a consciousness that is grounded in the Buddhist doctrine of compassion and the immutable truth of suffering in human life.

## Websites with Treatment Guidelines

United States Department of Defense:
*http://www.healthquality.va.gov/ptsd/PTSD-FULL-2010a.pdf*

Agency for Health Care Research and Quality (Multiple Guidelines):
*http://www.guideline.gov/search/search.aspx?term=ptsd*

United Kingdom Institute for Health and Clinical Excellence:
*http://www.nice.org.uk/Guidance/CG26*

International Society for Traumatic Stress Studies:
*http://www.istss.org/Home.htm*

American Academy of Child and Adolescent Psychiatry:
*http://www.aacap.org/galleries/PracticeParameters/PTSDT.pdf*

## Review Questions

1. How do PTSD epidemiology statistics differ in veterans versus the civilian population?
2. What is military sexual trauma, and how does it relate to the DSM-5?
3. What is the HPA axis, and how is it implicated in PTSD symptoms?
4. What findings from genetics have informed our understanding of why certain people develop PTSD?
5. How does a negative attributional style impact the person suffering from a recent trauma?
6. What is the meaning of safety and stabilization with regard to PTSD treatment?
7. How might a client's spirituality play a role in PTSD treatment?

## References

Abramson, L. Y., Alloy, L. B., Hogan, M. E., Whitehouse, W. G., Donovan, P., Rose, D. T., et al. (1999). Cognitive vulnerability to depression: Theory and evidence. *Journal of Cognitive Psychology, 13,* 5–20.

Abramson, L. Y., Metalsky, G. I., & Alloy, L. B. (1989). Hopelessness depression: A theory-based subtype of depression. *Psychological Review, 96,* 358–372.

American Psychiatric Association. (1980). *Diagnostic and statistical manual of mental disorders* (3rd ed.). Washington, DC: Author.

American Psychiatric Association. (2013). *Diagnostic and statistical manual of mental disorders* (5th ed.). Washington, DC: Author.

Andrews, G., Charney, D. S., Sirovatka, P. J., & Regier, D. A. (Eds.). (2008). *Stress-induced and fear circuitry disorders: Refining the research agenda for DSM-5.* Washington, DC: American Psychiatric Association.

Bakermans-Kranenburg, M. J., & van Ijzendoorn, M. H. (1993). A psychometric study of the Adult Attachment Interview reliability and discriminant validity. *Developmental Psychology, 29*(5), 870–879.

Baltrushes, N., & Karnik, N. S. (2013). Victims of military sexual trauma—you see them too. *The Journal of Family Practice, 62,* 120–125.

Bandelow, B., Zohar, J., Hollander, E., Kasper, S., Moller, H.-J., & the WFSBP Task Force on Treatment Guidelines for Anxiety, Obsessive-Compulsive, Post-Traumatic Stress Disorders. (2008). World Federation of Societies of Biological Psychiatry (WFSBP) Guidelines for the pharmacological treatment of anxiety, obsessive-compulsive and post-traumatic stress disorders—first revision. *The World Journal of Biological Psychiatry, 9,* 248–312.

Baranowsky, A. B., Gentry, J. E., & Schultz, D. F. (2005). *Trauma practice: Tools for stabilization and recovery.* Toronto: Hogrefe & Huber Publishers.

Black, T. G. (2004). Psychotherapy and outcome research in PTSD: Understanding the challenges and complexities in the literature. *Canadian Journal of Counselling, 38*(4), 277–288.

Blake, D. D., Weathers, F. W., Nagy, L. M., Kaloupek, D. G., Gusman, F. D., Charney, D. S. et. al. (1995). The development of a clinician-administered PTSD scale. *Journal of Traumatic Stress, 8,* 75–90.

Blanchard, E. B., Hicking, E. J., Devineni, T., Veazy, C. H., Galovski, T. E., et al. (2001). A controlled evaluation of cognitive behavioral therapy for posttraumatic stress in motor vehicle accident survivors. *Behavior Research Therapy, 41,* 79–96.

Briere, J. (2006). Dissociative symptoms and trauma exposure: specificity, affect regulation and post traumatic stress. *The Journal of Nervous and Mental Disease, 194,* 78–82.

Burgess, A. W., Slattery, D. M., & Herlihy, P. A. (2013). Military sexual trauma: A silent syndrome. *Journal of Psychosocial Nursing and Mental Health Services, 51,* 20–26.

Catani, C., Kohiladevy, M., Ruf, M., Schauer, E., Elbert, T., & Neuner, F. (2009). Treating children traumatized by war and Tsunami: A comparison between exposure therapy and meditation-relaxation in North-East Sri Lanka. *BMC Psychiatry, 9,* 9–22.

Charney, D. S. (2004). Psychobiological mechanisms of resilience and vulnerability: Implications for the successful adaption to extreme stress. *American Journal of Psychiatry, 161,* 195–216.

Cornelis, M. C., Nugent, N. R., Amstadter, A. B., & Koenen, K. C. (2010). Genetics of post-traumatic stress disorder: Review and recommendations for genome-wide association studies. *Current Psychiatry Rep, 12,* 313–326.

Davis, M., & Whalen, P. J. (2001). The amygdala: vigilance and emotion. *Molecular Psychiatry, 1,* 13–34.

Deahl, M., Srinivasan, M., Jones, N., Thomas, J., Neblett, C., & Jolly, A. (2000). Preventing psychological trauma in soldiers: the role of operational stress training and psychological debriefing. *British Journal of Medical Psychology, 73,* 77–85.

Demyttanaere, K., Bruffaerts, R., Posada-Villa, J., Gasquet, I., Kovess, V., Lepine, J. P., et al. (2004). Prevalence, severity, and unmet need for treatment of mental disorders in the World Health Organization World Mental Health Surveys. *JAMA, 291,* 2581–2590.

Department of Defense Task Force on Domestic Violence. (2006). Retrieved from http://www.refusingtokill.net/rape/domesticviolenceinthemilitary.htm

Dieperink, M., Leskela, J., Thuras, P., & Engdahl, B. (2001). Attachment style classification and posttraumatic stress disorder in former prisoners of war. *American Journal of Orthopsychiatry, 71*(3), 374–378.

Editorial. (2004). Military report aims to combat sex assault. *Contemporary Sexuality, 38,* 9.

Ehlers, A., Bisson, J., Clark, D. M., Creamer, M., Pilling, S., Richards, D., . . . Yule, W. (2010). Do all psychological treatments really work the same in posttraumatic stress disorder? *Clinical Psychology Review, 30,* 269–276.

Ehlers, A., & Clark, D. M. (2000). A cognitive model of posttraumatic stress disorder. *Behavior Research and Therapy, 38,* 319–345.

Ehlers, A., Clark, D. M., Hackmann, A., McManus, F., & Fennell, M. (2005). Cognitive therapy for posttraumatic stress disorder: Development and evaluation. *Behavior Research and Therapy, 43,* 413–431.

Ehring, T., Ehlers, A., & Glucksman, E. (2006). Contributions of cognitive factors to the prediction of post-traumatic stress disorder, phobia and depression after motor vehicle accidents. *Behavior Research and Therapy, 44,* 1699–1716.

Eley, T. C. (2008). The genetic basis of anxiety disorders. In G. Andrews, D. S. Charney, P. J. Sirovatka, & D. A. Regier (Eds.), *Stress-induced and fear circuitry disorders: Refining the research agenda for DSM-5* (pp. 145–157). Washington, DC: American Psychiatric Association.

Ellison, J. (2011). The military's secret shame. Retrieved from http://www.newsweek.com/2011/04/03/the-military-s-secret-shame.html

Elwood, L. S., Hahn, K. S., Olatunji, B. O., & Williams, N. L. (2009). Cognitive vulnerabilities to the development of PTSD: A review of four vulnerabilities and the proposal of an integrative vulnerability model. *Clinical Psychology Review, 29,* 87–100.

Epstein, S. (1991). Impulse control and self-destructive behavior. In L. P. Lipsitt & L. L. Mitnick (Eds.), *Self-regulatory behavior and risk takings: Causes and consequences* (pp. 273–284). Norwood, NJ: Ablex.

Fedoroff, I. C., Taylor, S., Asmundson, G. J. G., & Koch, W. J. (2000). Cognitive factors in traumatic stress reactions: Predicting PTSD symptoms from anxiety sensitivity and beliefs about harmful events. *Behavioral and Cognitive Psychotherapy, 28,* 5–15.

Figley, C. R. (2002). Compassion fatigue: Psychotherapists' chronic lack of self care. *Journal of Clinical Psychology, 58,* 1433–1441.

Foa, E. B. (2000). Psychosocial treatment of posttraumatic stress disorder. *Journal of Clinical Psychiatry,* 61, 43–48.

Foa, E. B., Keane, T. M., & Friedman, M. J. (2000). *Effective treatments for PTSD: Practice guidelines from the International Society for Traumatic Stress Studies.* New York: The Guilford Press.

Forbes, D., Creamer, M., Bisson, J. I., Cohen, J. A., Crow, B. E., Friedman, M. J., . . . Ursano, R. J. (2010). A guide to guidelines for the treatment of PTSD and related conditions. *Journal of Traumatic Stress, 23,* 537–552.

Friedman, M. J., & Harris, W. W. (2004). Toward a national PTSD brain bank. *Psychiatry, 67,* 383–390.

Friedman, M. J., & Karam, E. G. (2008). Posttraumatic stress disorder. In G. Andrews, D. S. Charney, P. J. Sirovatka, & D. A. Regier (Eds.), *Stress-induced and fear circuitry disorders: Refining the research agenda for DSM-5* (pp. 3–29). Washington, DC: American Psychiatric Association.

Friedman, M. J., Resick, P. A., Bryant, R. A., & Brewin, C. R. (2011). Considering PTSD for DSM-5. *Depression and Anxiety, 28,* 750–769.

Galea, S., Ahern, J., Resnick, H. S., Kilpatrick, D. G., Bucuvalas, M. J., Gold, J., & Vlahov, D. (2002). Psychological sequelae of the September 11 terrorist attacks in New York City. *New England Journal of Medicine, 346,* 982–987.

Gardner, H. (1993). *Multiple intelligences: The theory in practice.* New York: Basic.

Gardner, H. (1999). *Intelligence reframed: Multiple intelligences for the 21st century.* New York: Basic.

Gardner, H., Kornhaber, M., & Wake, W. (1996). *Intelligence: Multiple perspectives.* Fort Worth, TX: Harcourt Brace.

George, C., Kaplan, M., & Main, N. (1996). *Adult Attachment Interview.* Boston: Routlege.

Gilbertson, M. W., Shenton, M. E., Ciszewski, A., et al. (2002). Smaller hippocampal volume predicts pathologic vulnerability to psychological trauma. *Natural Neurosciences, 5,* 1242–1247.

Gola, H., Engler, H., Sommershof, A., Adenauer, H., Kilassa, S., Schedlowski, M., . . . Kolassa, I.-T. (2013). Posttraumatic stress disorder is associated with an enhanced spontaneous production of pro-inflammatory cytokines by peripheral blood mononuclear cells. *BMC Psychiatry, 40,* 40–48.

Grinage, B. D. (2003). Diagnosis and management of Post-traumatic Stress Disorder. *American Family Physician, 68*(12), 2401–2408.

Gutierrez, P. M., Castro, C. A., Fitek, D. J., Jobes, D., & Holloway, M. (2012). Status of Department of Defense funded suicide research. Retrieved from http://www.dcoe.health.mil/Content/Navigation/Documents/SPC2012/2012SPC-Gutierrez-etal-Status_of_DoD_Funded_Suicide_Research_panel.pdf

Halligan, S. L., Michael, T., Clark, F. M., & Ehlers, A. (2003). Posttraumatic stress disorder following assault: The role of cognitive processing, trauma memory, and appraisal. *Journal of Consulting and Clinical Psychology, 71,* 419–431.

Harris, S. (2012). *Free will.* New York: Free Press.

Harvin, S. (2004). The experiences of women who survived an attack by an intimate partner relationship. *Evidence Based Nursing, 7,* 91.

Henderson, W. G., Eisen, S., Goldberg, J., True, W. R., & Vitek, M. E. (1990). The Vietnam era twin registry: A resource for medical research. *Public Health Reports, 105,* 368–373.

Herman, J. (1997). *Trauma and recovery: The aftermath of violence—from domestic abuse to political terror.* New York: Basic Books.

Hinton, D. E., & Lewis-Fernandez, R. (2011). The cross-cultural validity of posttraumatic stress disorder: Implications for DSM-5. *Depression and Anxiety, 28,* 783–801.

Hoge, C. W., Auchterlonie, J. L., & Milliken, C. S. (2006). Mental health problems, use of mental health services, and attrition from military service after returning from deployment to Iraq or Afghanistan. *JAMA, 295,* 1023–1032.

Hoyt, T., Rielage, J. K., & Williams, L. F. (2011). Military sexual trauma in men: A review of reported rates. *Journal of Trauma and Dissociation, 12,* 244–260.

Huppert, J. D., Foa, E. B., McNally, R. J., & Cahill, S. P. (2008). Role of cognition in stress-induced and fear circuitry disorders. In G. Andrews, D. S. Charney, P. J. Sirovatka, & D. A. Regier (Eds.), *Stress-induced and fear circuitry disorders: Refining the research agenda for DSM-5* (pp. 175–193). Washington, DC: American Psychiatric Association.

Ingersoll, R. E., & Zeitler, D. A. (2010). *Integral psychotherapy: Inside out/outside in.* Albany, NY: SUNY.

Ingram, R. E., Miranda, J., & Segal, Z. V. (1998). *Cognitive vulnerability to depression.* New York: Guilford.

Janoff-Bulman, R. (1992). *Shattered Assumptions: Towards a new psychology of trauma.* New York: Free Press.

Jason, L. A., Milcuiciute, I., Aase, D. M., Stevens, E., DiGangi, J., Contrera, J. R., & Ferrari, J. R. (2011). How type of treatment and presence of PTSD affect employment, self-regulation and abstinence. *North American Journal of Psychology, 13,* 175–186.

Jobson, L., & O'Kearney, R. (2008). Cultural differences in personal identity in post-traumatic stress disorder. *British Journal of Clinical Psychology, 47,* 95–109.

Katz, I. R., McCarthy, J. F., Ignacio, R. V., & Kemp, R. N. (2012). Suicide among veterans in 16 states, 2005 to 2008: Comparisons between utilizers and nonutilizers of veterans health administration (VHA) services based on data from the national death index, the national violent death reporting system and VHA administrative records. *American Journal of Public Health, 102,* S105–S117.

Kaufman, J., Aikins, D., & Krystal, J. (2004). Neuroimaging studies in PTSD. In J. P. Wilson & T. M. Keane (Eds.), *Assessing psychological trauma and PTSD* (2nd ed., pp. 389–418). New York, NY: Guilford Press.

Kessler, R. C. (2000). Posttraumatic stress disorder: The burden to the individual and to society. *Journal of Clinical Psychiatry, 61*(Suppl. 5), 4–12.

Kessler, R. C., Sonnega, A., Bromet, E., Hughes, M., & Nelson, C. B. (1995). Posttraumatic stress disorder in the National Comorbidity Survey. *Archives of General Psychiatry, 52,* 1048–1060.

Kimerling, R., Street, A. E., Pavao, J., Smith, M. W., Cronkite, R. C., Holmes, T. H., & Frayne, S. M. (2010). Military-related sexual trauma among Veterans' Health Administration patients returning from Afghanistan and Iraq. *American Journal of Public Health, 100,* 1409–1412.

Koenen, K. C. (2010). Developmental origins of posttraumatic stress disorder. *Depression and Anxiety, 27,* 413–416.

Koenen, K. C., Amstadter, A. B., & Nugent, N. R. (2009). Gene-environment interaction in posttraumatic stress disorder: An update. *Journal of Traumatic Stress, 22,* 416–426.

Koenen, K. C., Harley, R., Lyons, M. J., Wolfe, J., Simpson, J. C., Goldberg, J., Eisen, S. A., & Tsuang, M. T. (2002). A twin registry study of familial and individual risk factors for trauma exposure and posttraumatic stress disorder. *The Journal of Nervous and Mental Disease, 190,* 209–218.

Kousha, M., & Tehrani, S. M. (2013). Normative life events and PTSD in children: How easy stress can affect children's brain. *Acta Medica Irania, 51,* 47–51.

Lapierre, C. B., Schwegler, A. F., & Labauve, B. J. (2007). Posttraumatic stress and depression symptoms in soldiers returning from combat operations in Iraq and Afghanistan. *Journal of Traumatic Stress, 20,* 933–943.

Libet, B., Gleason, C. A., Wright, E. W., & Pearl, D. K. (1983). Time of conscious intention to act in relation to onset of cerebral activity (readiness-potential): The unconscious initiation of a freely voluntary act. *Brain, 106,* 623–642.

Lindy, J. D., & Wilson, J. P. (2001). Respecting the trauma membrane: Above all, do no harm. In J. P. Wilson, M. J. Friedman & J. D. Lindy (Eds.), *Treating psychological trauma and PTSD* (pp. 432–445). New York: Guilford.

Loevinger, J. (1976). *Ego Development.* San Francisco: Jossey-Bass.

Lutwak, N., & Dill, C. (2013). Military sexual trauma increases risk of post-traumatic stress disorder and depression thereby amplifying the possibility of suicidal ideation and cardiovascular disease. *Military Medicine, 178,* 359–361.

Luxenberg, T., Spinazzola, J., Hidalgo, J., Hunt, C., & van der Kolk, B. A. (2001). Complex trauma and disorders of extreme stress (DESNOS), part two: Treatment. *Directions in Psychiatry, 21,* 395–414.

Mayou, R. A., Ehlers, A., & Hobbs, M. (2000). Psychological debriefing for road traffic accident victims. Three-year follow-up of a randomized controlled trial. *British Journal of Psychiatry, 176,* 589–593.

McCann, I., & Pearlman, L. A. (1990). *Psychological trauma and the adult survivor: Theory, therapy and transformations.* New York: Brunner-Mazel.

Meltzer, E. C., Averbuch, T., Samet, J. H., Saitz, R., Jabbar, K., Lloyd-Travaglini, C., & Liebschutz, J. M. (2012). Discrepancy in diagnosis and treatment of post-traumatic stress disorder (PTSD): Treatment for the wrong reason. *The Journal of Behavioral Health Services & Research, 39,* 190–202.

Miller, M., Barber, C., Young, M., Azrael, D., Mukamai, K., & Lawler, E. (2012). Veterans and suicide: A reexamination of the national death index—linked national health interview survey. *American Journal of Public Health, 102,* S154–S159.

Morgan, C. A., Wang, S., Rasmusson, A., Hazlett, G., Anderson, G., & Charney, D. S. (2001). Relationship among plasma cortisol, catecholamines, neuropeptide Y and human performance during exposure to uncontrollable stress. *Psychosomatic Medicine, 63,* 412–422.

Morgan, C. A., Wang, S., Southwick, S. M., Rasmusson, A., Hazlett, G., Hauger, R. L., & Charney, D. S. (2000). Plasma neuropeptide-Y concentrations in humans exposed to military survival training. *Biological Psychiatry, 47,* 902–909.

Mulrine, A. (2012, August 7). Suicide "epidemic" in army: July was worst month, Pentagon says. *Christian Science Monitor.* Retrieved from http://www.csmonitor.com/USA/Military/2012/0817/Suicide-epidemic-in-Army-July-was-worst-month-Pentagon-says

Najavits, L. M., Kivlahan, D., & Kosten, T. (2011). A national survey of clinicians' views of evidence-based therapies for PTSD and substance abuse. *Addiction Research and Theory, 19,* 138–147.

National Institute for Clinical Excellence (NICE). (2005). *Post-traumatic stress disorder: The management of PTSD in adults and children in primary and secondary care.* Leicester (UK): Gaskell.

Nolen-Hoeksema, S. (1991). Responses to depression and their effects on the duration of depressive episodes. *Journal of Abnormal Psychology, 100,* 569–582.

Orr, S. P., Metzger, L. J., Miller, M. W., et al. (2004). Psychophysiological assessment of PTSD: Science and practice. In J. P. Wilson & T. M. Keane (Eds.), *Assessing psychological trauma and PTSD* (2nd ed., pp. 425–446). New York, NY: Guilford Press.

Osuch, E. A., Benson, B. E., Luckenbaugh, D. A., Geraci, M., Post, R. M., & McCann, U. (2009). Repetitive TMS combined with exposure therapy for PTSD: A preliminary study. *Journal of Anxiety Disorders, 23,* 54–59.

Pearlman, L. A. (1995). Self-care for trauma therapists: Ameliorating vicarious traumatization. In B. H. Stamm (Ed.), *Secondary traumatic stress: Self-care issues for clinicians, researchers, and educators* (pp. 51–64). Baltimore, MD: The Sidran Press.

Pearlman, L. A., & Saakvitne, K. W. (1995). Treating therapists with vicarious traumatization and secondary traumatic stress disorders. In C. R. Figley (Ed.), *Compassion fatigue: Coping with secondary traumatic stress disorder in those who treat the traumatized* (pp. 150–177). Philadelphia, PA: Brunner/Mazel.

Plomp, L. M. (1997). Confronting unfixable suffering: The lived experience of police officers. Unpublished master's thesis, University of British Columbia, Vancouver, BC.

Radant, A., Tsuang, D., Peskind, E. R., McFall, M., & Raskind, W. (2001). Biological markers and diagnostic accuracy in the genetics of posttraumatic stress disorder. *Psychiatry Research, 102,* 203–214.

Reiss, S. (1991). Expectancy model of fear, anxiety and panic. *Clinical Psychology Review, 11,* 141–153.

Rizzo, A. A., Difede, J., Rothbaum, B. O., Johnston, S., McLay, R. N., Reger, G., . . . Pair, J. (2009). VR PTSD exposure therapy results with active duty OIF-OEF combatants. *Medicine Meets Virtual Reality, 17,* 277–289.

Santiago, P. N., Ursano, R . J., Gray, C. L., Pynoos, R. S., Spiegel, D., Lewis-Fernandez, R., . . . Fullerton, C. S. (2013). A systematic review of PTSD prevalence and trajectories in DSM-5 defined trauma exposed populations: Intentional and non-intentional traumatic events. *PLOS One, 8,* 1–5.

Sartory, G., Cwik, J., Knuppertz, H., Schurholt, B., Lebens, M., Seitz, R. J., & Schulze, R. (2013). In search of the trauma memory: A meta-analysis of functional neuroimaging studies of a symptom provocation in posttraumatic stress disorder (PTSD). *Plos One, 8,* 1–11.

Schnurr, P. P., Friedman, M. J., & Bernardy, N. C. (2002). Research on posttraumatic stress disorder: Epidemiology, pathophysiology and assessment. *Psychotherapy in Practice, 58,* 877–889.

Shad, M. U., Suris, A. M., North, C. S. (2011). Novel combination strategy to optimize treatment for PTSD. *Hum Psychopharmacol, 26,* 4–11.

Shalev, A. Y., Bonne, O., & Eth, S. (1996). Treatment of posttraumatic stress disorder: A review. *Psychosomatic Medicine, 58,* 165–182.

Shapiro, F. (1995). *Eye movement desensitization and reprocessing: Basic principles, protocols, and procedures.* New York: The Guilford Press.

Sherman, J. J. (1998). Effects of psychotherapeutic treatments for PTSD: A meta-analysis of controlled clinical trials. *Journal of Traumatic Stress,* 11, 413–435.

Skelton, K., Ressler, K. J., Norrholm, S. D., Jovanovic, T., & Bradley-Davino, B. (2012). PTSD and gene variants: New pathways and new thinking. *Neuropharmacology, 62,* 628–637.

Stein, D. J., van der Kolk, B. A., Austin, C., Fayyad, R., & Clary, C. (2006). Efficacy of Sertraline in posttraumatic stress disorder secondary to interpersonal trauma or childhood abuse. *Annals of Clinical Psychiatry, 18,* 243–249.

Taylor, S., Thordarson, D. S., Maxfield, L., Fedoroff, I. C., & Ogrodniczuk, J. (2003). Comparative efficacy, speed, and adverse effects of three PTSD treatments: Exposure therapy, EMDR, and relaxation training. *Journal of Consulting and Clinical Psychology,* 71, 330–338.

van der Kolk, B. A. (2001). The psychobiology and psychopharmacology of PTSD. *Human Psychopharmacology: Clinical and Experimental, 16,* S49–S64.

van der Kolk, B. A. (2006). Clinical implications of neuroscience research in PTSD. *Annals of the New York Academy of Sciences, 1071,* 277–293.

Van Etten, M. L., & Taylor, S. (1998). Comparative efficacy of treatments for post-traumatic stress disorder: A meta-analysis. *Clinical Psychology and Psychotherapy, 5,* 126–144.

Veterans' Administration. (2012). Military sexual trauma. Retrieved from http://www.mentalhealth.va.gov/docs/mst_general_factsheet.pdf

Wieland, D. M., Haley, J. L., & Bouder, M. (2011). Military sexual trauma. *The Pennsylvania Nurse, 66,* 17–21.

Wilson, J. P. (2006). Trauma and transformation of the self: Restoring meaning and wholeness to personality. In J. P. Wilson (Ed.), *The posttraumatic self: Restoring meaning and wholeness to personality* (pp. 399–424). New York, NY: Routledge.

World Health Organization. (1992). *The ICD-10: Classification of mental and behavioral disorders: Clinical descriptions and diagnostic guidelines.* Geneva: World Health Organization.

Yaeger, D., Himmelfarb, N., Cammack, A., & Mintz, J. (2006). DSM-IV diagnosed post traumatic stress disorder women veterans with and without sexual trauma. *Journal of General Internal Medicine, 21, Suppl,* S65–S69.

# 6

# Bipolar I Disorder

**R. Elliott Ingersoll, Ph.D.,** ***Cleveland State University;***
**Jessica Haberman, M.S.** ***Cleveland State University***

Alex is a 48-year-old Caucasian female who has suffered from episodes of major depression and mania since she was 19. Alex has been on five different types of medications and currently takes a combination of Lithobid/lithium and Divalproex/valproic acid. She struggles between episodes with residual symptoms of depression. Alex currently lives in a mental health boarding home paid for by government assistance. She has never been able to function in a stable way that allows her to hold a job for more than a year. She says she hates her life, that it is not worth living, and she is frequently suicidal. Her episodes often follow psychosocial stressors. Although she takes her medication as prescribed, she suffers relapses every 12 to 16 months. She has been in and out of therapy and rarely goes more than three sessions before quitting. Her most recent relapse began last October following an argument with her sister, who said she no longer wanted Alex to visit her because she felt Alex was negatively affecting her children (ages 7 and 9). After this Alex could not sleep well. Within a week Alex began wearing increasingly brighter clothing and make-up. Over a 2-week period she began showing increasingly manic symptoms that culminated on election day when she went to the local polling place in extravagant makeup and her nightgown, stood up on the poll workers' table, and announced her candidacy for mayor. She was hospitalized at this point and stabilized after 2 weeks. One thing the doctor negotiated upon release was that Alex stay in supportive psychotherapy to try to increase the quality of her life and her life satisfaction. This included metabolizing the argument with her sister and trying to re-open communication with a willingness to change behaviors that her sister found problematic.

As Alex's case illustrates, Bipolar I Disorder appears to be a chronic disorder that is a leading cause of disability among psychiatric conditions (Andreazza et al., 2008). Hippocrates and Areteus are thought to be the first to describe symptoms of manic-depressive illness, but as David Healy (2008) points out, many translations of Hippocrates' works are disputed and in cases where the translation is agreed upon, the "mania" described is often after a long bout of fever, making it more likely that the "mania" was delirium. Manic-depressive illness was first defined by Jean Pierre Falret (1854) as having its classic swings from mania to severe depression. Later in a revision of his book on mental medicine, Emil Kraepelin included a form of Falret's manic-depressive illness. Falret and Kraepelin's disorders seem to be historically closest to what we call Bipolar I Disorder. Bipolar I Disorder (hereafter referred to as BPI) is also one of the disorders that appear to have a strong physiological basis as well as psychological and environmental factors that may act as triggers for whatever physiological variables underlay the disorder. This exemplifies how the Integral model helps us understand and integrate the potential factors in developing the disorder without giving the mistaken impression that we fully understand it. As we have written many times, it is critical that mental health professionals assume the burden of comprehending the complexity of the etiology of disorders like BPI rather than relying on inaccurate platitudes (e.g., "chemical imbalances") that tell us little and may do harm to clients and their families by promoting the idea that there are simple solutions to the problem of the disorder. Although the information coming from biological psychiatry and neuroscience is complex, we trust that graduate students can understand an introductory overview of what we know about the etiology of BPI.

In the *Diagnostic and Statistical Manual of Mental Disorder*, 5th Edition (DSM-5; American Psychiatric Association [APA], 2013), BPI is the basis of a new category, *Bipolar and Related Disorders*. BPI is the centerpiece of this section, which also includes Bipolar II Disorder, Cyclothymic Disorder, Bipolar Disorders related to substance use or medical conditions, and other specified and unspecified Bipolar and Related Disorder. While Disruptive Mood Dysregulation Disorder was ostensibly introduced to stem the misdiagnosis of children as having BPI, as noted in Chapter 3, it is in the section on Depressive Disorders. This may be in part to avoid the impression that Bipolar Disorders constitute a spectrum of sorts.

BPI has many physiological, as well as psychological, effects; and, if untreated, may even yield a greater likelihood of mortality due to general medical conditions as well as suicide. According to the DSM, suicidality is common with BPI. In fact, although it is hard to quantify exactly (Pompili et al., 2006), it is estimated that of the individuals suffering from BPI, up to 59% experience suicidal ideation, 25–56% make at least one suicide attempt, and almost 20% die from suicide (De Abreu, Lafer, Baca-Garcia, & Oquendo, 2009; Rihmer, 2009). These are clearly tragic statistics that we aim to change with accurate diagnosis and up-to-date knowledge about etiology and treatment.

There is still much confusion about the relationship between BPI, Bipolar II, and Cyclothymia disorders. In preparation for the release of the DSM-5, some advocated that all these disorders should be placed on a continuum called Bipolar Spectrum Disorder (Akiskal & Benazzi, 2006; Ghaemi, Ko, & Goodwin, 2002; Paris, 2009). Thankfully, that did not happen. Bipolar and Related Disorders were given their own category (taken out of what were Mood Disorders in the DSM-IV-TR). The concern with the spectrum idea was the possibility that clients who showed symptoms of irritation or inattention (especially children and adolescents) would get misdiagnosed under the bipolar spectrum umbrella with Bipolar I Disorder (Baroni, Lunsford, Luckenbaugh, Toubin, & Leibenluft, 2009; Paris, 2009). Although some researchers (Alloy et al., 2012; Walsh, Royal, Brown, Barrantes-Vidal, & Kwapil, 2012) have explored what they call a "soft" Bipolar Spectrum, currently BPI, BPII, and Cyclothymia should be conceived of as discrete disorders rather than thinking of Cyclothymia or Bipolar II as leading to BPI.

Because BPI is the most severe of the Bipolar and Related Disorders, this chapter will focus on BPI. To make things more complex, brain studies from the past 5 years suggest that categorically separating BPI and Schizophrenia may not be the best way to think of these disorders. Evidence is mounting that they derive from similar (in some cases, perhaps the same) underlying brain pathologies and it may be only a question of degree that separates the disorders (Craddock & Owen, 2007; Lin & Mitchell, 2008). Thus, much of the material in this chapter and the chapter on Schizophrenia will cover similar territory as we try to summarize an astonishing period of research that is leading us to new ways to think about severe mental illness.

Substance use and abuse are also common comorbid features of BPI Disorder. Unfortunately, individuals who experience symptoms of the disorder at an earlier age also have a greater likelihood of having a history of substance use problems. Other comorbid psychological conditions include Eating Disorders such as Anorexia Nervosa or Bulimia Nervosa, Attention Deficit–Hyperactivity Disorder (ADHD), and Anxiety Disorders such as Panic Disorder and Social Phobia. The essential feature of BPI is the experience of at least one manic or mixed episode. Although many individuals with BPI have also experienced major depressive or hypomanic episodes, they are not necessary for a diagnosis of the disorder. Before continuing, it would be helpful for the reader to have a working knowledge of what these different types of episodes entail.

A manic episode is characterized as such if symptoms are present for at least 1 week (less if hospitalization is required). Manic episodes, by definition, cause marked impairment. Hypomanic episodes, in contrast, are not severe enough to cause marked impairment in social or occupational functioning. A hypomanic episode shares the same symptoms of a manic episode; however, a hypomanic episode lasts at least 4 days. Regardless of the duration or type of episode (either manic or hypomanic), the individual has an unusually elevated, unrestrained, or irritable mood. For the diagnosis of BPI, the client must have suffered a manic episode. In addition to an abnormal and lasting mood, the person also presents with at least three of the following other symptoms (four if the mood is only irritable):

- inflated self-esteem;
- decreased need for sleep;
- pressured and/or talkative speech that is difficult to interrupt;
- flight of ideas or racing thoughts;
- distractibility;
- increased goal-directed activity that may include increased sexual drive, fantasies, and/or behavior; and
- excessive involvement in activities that may have negative consequences (e.g., buying sprees, reckless driving, abnormal sexual behavior) (APA, 2000a).

A major depressive episode lasts at least 2 weeks and a manic episode 1 week, and also includes the experience of either a depressed mood or the loss of interest or pleasure in nearly all activities for at least 2 weeks. Along with a depressed mood (for children and adolescents, the mood may be irritable rather than sad), a major depressive episode is diagnosed if the individual is also experiencing at least four of the following symptoms:

- changes in appetite or weight;
- changes in sleep;
- changes in psychomotor activity (either psychomotor retardation or activation nearly every day);
- decreased energy;
- feelings of worthlessness or guilt;
- difficulty thinking, concentrating, and making decisions; and
- recurrent thoughts and/or attempts of suicide.

Finally, mixed episodes present as a combination of both manic and major depressive episodes. Subthreshold symptoms from the opposite end of the pole can be present during a manic or depressive episode and that would qualify as a mixed episode. Other than the labile mood, some of the most common symptoms in a mixed episode include psychomotor agitation, sleep disturbances (especially insomnia), changes in appetite, psychotic features (e.g., hallucinations, delusions), and suicidality.

It is important to look beyond merely mood symptoms to understand BPI. In a presentation on mood-stabilizing drugs, Dr. Roy Chengappa and Dr. Paul Keck (PsychLink Video, 2001) present the four domains of symptoms in BPI shown in Figure 6.1.

## WHO GETS BIPOLAR I DISORDER?

According to the DSM, there is no particular race or ethnicity with a greater prevalence of BPI compared to any other racial or ethnic group. In some ethnic groups and in younger age groups, there may be a tendency to over diagnose Schizophrenia rather than BPI, but this seems to be a lingering effect of institutional racism rather than accurate diagnoses (Ingersoll & Rak, 2006). There is no evidence to conclude that the actual experience of bipolar symptoms is more or less prevalent in people with different racial/ethnic backgrounds.

**Manic, Mood, and Behavior Symptoms**
Euphoria
Grandiosity
Pressured speech
Impulsivity
Recklessness
Diminished sleep

**Dysphoric and Other Mood Symptoms**
Depression
Anxiety
Irritability
Hostility
Violence or suicide

**Psychotic Symptoms**
Delusions
Hallucinations
Sensory hyperacuity

**Cognitive Symptoms**
Racing thoughts
Distractibility
Poor insight
Disorganization
Inattention
Confusion

**FIGURE 6.1** Symptom Domains in BPI

In comparing the prevalence of the disorder in men and women, it is interesting to note that the number of men versus the number of women who experience symptoms of BPI is approximately equal. However, men tend to experience more manic episodes, whereas women tend to present with more symptoms of major depressive episodes. This seems congruent with the information conveyed in Chapter 3 that twice as many women than men report symptoms of Major Depressive Disorder.

Typically, an individual begins to display symptoms of, and be diagnosed with, BPI around the age of 20, with early onset thought to be no earlier than age 13. However, there is some speculation regarding the disorder in pediatric populations, although most studies exploring early onset are done with adolescents, so we do not have adequate data for pediatric populations (particularly because the symptom sets are normed on adults) (Birmaher & Axelson, 2006; Duffy, 2007). As noted, one of the controversies in the creation of the DSM-5 was blurring the boundaries between clinical and subclinical symptoms and referring to Bipolar Spectrum Disorder rather than the more specific Bipolar I Disorder. Some of the researchers who advocated the idea of Bipolar *Spectrum* Disorder (Ghaemi et al., 2002) suggested that the prevalence of bipolarity is actually much higher in the general U.S. population than noted in the DSM (Merikangas et al., 2007). The idea of the *spectrum* is that there are many individuals who live with symptoms of Bipolar Disorder, but these symptoms are below the threshold of being classified as a full-blown disorder. In fact, research on this issue estimates that 2.4% of the American population has experienced Bipolar I Disorder at subthreshold levels at some point in their lives; and these prevalence estimates are 1.4% within the last 12 months alone. As noted, this is highly controversial, particularly when one considers the agenda of the pharmaceutical companies that fund much of this research (Petersen, 2008). A temporary solution for the DSM-5 was the creation of Disruptive Mood Dysregulation Disorder under Depressive Disorders. The jury is still out on whether this will reduce the false diagnosis of BPI in children (Margulies, Weintraub, Basile, Grover, & Carlson, 2012) or, for that matter, how we should treat Disruptive Mood Dysregulation (Jairam, Prabjuswamy, & Dullur, 2012).

Genetics seem to play a substantial role in the development of BPI. According to the DSM, those individuals who have a first-degree relative with Bipolar I Disorder have anywhere between a 4% and 24% chance of displaying symptoms of the disorder themselves. For individuals who have a first-degree relative with *any* mood disorder, the likelihood that they will experience symptoms of Bipolar I Disorder at an age younger than 20 years is greater than that for a person without such a relative. We will further discuss the genetic link subsequently.

## HOW PREVALENT IS BIPOLAR I DISORDER?

As noted, BPI is commonly found among first-degree relatives. Of course, such prevalence does not guarantee that an individual will experience symptoms of the disorder simply because someone in his or her family experiences those symptoms. It does indicate, however, that a person with a familial pattern of the disorder does have a greater likelihood of presenting symptoms than someone without such a pattern. According to the DSM, anywhere from 0.4–1.6% of the general population experiences the disorder.

## ETIOLOGY

It is dismaying that despite advances in neuroscience technologies and a consensus that biological factors are implicated, we have yet to develop a clear understanding of the etiology of BPI (Young & Wang, 2007). Probably the most concise summary of the state of our knowledge is that BPI is ". . . a continuous interaction between genetic vulnerability, neurobiological dysregulation and environmental events (Miklowitz & Johnson, 2008, p. 372), or ". . . bipolar disorder requires a genetic diathesis interacting with environmental, epigenetic and stochastic[1] components" (Hasler, Drevets, Gould, Gottesman, & Manji, 2005, p. 93), and finally, BPI is ". . . likely interaction between genetic predisposition and environmental influences, including stressful life events" (Rush, 2003, p. 4). Since BPI was first introduced as a topic of research and clinical importance, studies concerning its etiology have centered on ideas of genetically based causes that express as biological factors and may be triggered by psychosocial influences. Over time, however, researchers looking for precise causes of BPI have discovered that this disorder is much like many others, in that it is the product of multiple causes; in other words, it is overdetermined. There is no single gene or set of life events that has been identified as being the direct cause of an individual's developing BPI. Likewise, there currently is no specific medical test or procedure that can effectively screen for, let alone diagnose, BPI. Efforts have been made at linking BPI to everything from specific genes (McGrath et al., 2009) to quantifying the appearance of the symptoms (the phenotype) in a way similar to genetic profiling (a process called "PhenoChipping"; Niculescu et al., 2006). All of these have contributed to our knowledge but failed to produce reproducible results that zero in on the etiology of BPI.

Many factors found to be influential in the development and maintenance of BPI are physiological in nature, some are psychological, some are environmental, and others could be described as existential. There are countless theories attempting to explain BPI, but those discussed here tend to be the most represented in the current research literature. It is time for a new way to organize the research we have, and the Integral model provides an excellent framework for this. Some of the physiological theories to be discussed link BPI to genetic factors, brain structures, and brain circuits. Some of the psychological theories link the triggering or worsening of the disorder to learned behaviors and various psychosocial factors. Environmental theories focus primarily on the importance of stressful life events and disruptions in the individual's circadian and social rhythms. The last type of theory to be addressed here is primarily concerned with existential despair and how it relates to the onset and course of the BPI.

### Physiological Theories

**UNDERSTANDING ENDOPHENOTYPE** Before reviewing the physiological pieces of the puzzle of BPI etiology, we want to clarify a concept that is driving research on this disorder and has been part of the research that went into the DSM-5. Recall that genes are stable templates containing our DNA that replicate reliably. Genes interacting with environment determine phenotype or the structure, function, and morphology (structure) of the cells in which they are expressed (Kandel, 2005). The phenotype

---

[1] Stochastic derives from the Greek, meaning "random," so a stochastic process or components include random components.

is the composite of an organism's observable characteristic. In 1903, Danish botanist Wilhelm Johanssen (1911) coined these terms. He noticed, however, that phenotype was an imperfect indicator of genotype. In other words, the same genotype may give rise to a wide range of phenotypes and the same phenotype may have arisen from different genotypes.

In even plainer English, the same genes may express differently because of environment or stressful life events. For example, many relatives of people suffering from BPI have similar or even the same genes, as well as very similar brain structures, but do not manifest the disorder (McIntosh et al., 2005). There is also a new line of research that has discovered so-called "jumping genes." These are segments of DNA that can copy themselves and paste or insert themselves into new places in the genome, altering the activity of full-length genes and including the ability to "turn-on" neighboring genes. These mobile genes may play a role in our vulnerability to mental disorders as well as help to explain things such as how identical twins can develop such different personalities (Coufal et al., 2009; Gage & Muotri, 2012). This is why we say a person is genetically vulnerable to a disorder but the actual disorder (in this case the phenotype) may not develop because of how genes express when they interact with environment (epigenetics).

We have known since the mid-20th century that classifying psychiatric disorders on the basis of the phenotype (symptoms) was not going to help us trace the same symptoms back to genetic origins (Gottesman & Gould, 2003). The concept of endophenotype was borrowed from entomology (insect biology) by Gottesman and Shields (1973). They described endophenotypes as internal phenotypes (for example, the way brain structures develop from genetic instructions) that would be discoverable only through biochemical, neuroscientific, or other tests that correlated symptoms with internal conditions that might allow us to trace those internal conditions back to genetics. The closer the factor is to the person's actual genotype, the closer we are to placing that factor in an equation of variables that, we hope, will add up to the disorder. It may be that the more variables from such an "equation" a person has, the more likely he or she is to develop the disorder (Hasler et al., 2005).

Endophenotypes are described by Gottesman and Shields (1973) as filling the gaps between genes, disease processes, and observable symptoms. This is one reason there is such a variety of research on genetic factors, brain structures, and brain circuits. Using the concept of endophenotype, the hope is that we can trace from observable symptoms to internal physiological conditions, and then account for those conditions via genetics. In a way, it is an attempt to deconstruct or reverse-engineer a diagnosis or disease process in order to understand the variables that played into its expression. In this sense, examples of endophenotypes could include changes in the size or density of neurons, brain structures such as the amygdala, the glial cells coating neurons, or even brain circuits. There may be behavioral endophenotypes as well. One that is increasingly being recognized is sustained attention. The idea is that attention is measured by a continuous performance test in people diagnosed with BPI and healthy volunteers. In some studies, the subjects with BPI perform significantly worse on this task (Santos et al., 2010).

Currently the tools being used in the service of endophenotype include neurophysiological tests, biochemical analyses, neuroanatomical studies, endocrinological research, as well as cognitive and neuropsychological measures. As we have commented several times, the technological advances of our sciences provide new tools for exploring these disorders. The concept of endophenotype makes use of as many technologies as exist, including functional magnetic resonance imaging (fMRI), single photon emission computed tomography (SPECT) scans, and positron emission tomography (PET) scans. Having introduced endophenotype, we will now summarize research related to BPI from genetics, brain structure or morphology, and brain circuitry (in particular, the role of glial cells or white matter); then we will try to tie these together using the concept of endophenotype.

Before going into specific theories of etiology, we want to note that there have been studies that link BPI to what are called perinatal insults or obstetric complications that are correlated with BPI (Rush, 2003). Schwarzkopf et al. (1989) found significantly more of these complications in clients diagnosed with BPI; these clients were also more likely to have psychotic features as part of their symptom picture.

**GENETIC FACTORS** It can be stated with a good degree of confidence that BPI is a heritable disorder (McGuffin et al., 2003) and begins as a polygenic disorder (Baum et al., 2008). Even researchers looking at a single gene (the NCAN gene[2] or the DISC-1 gene mentioned in Chapter 3) hope to tie it to only one part of the disorder. In the case of the NCAN gene researchers hope to tie it to the euphoria felt in manic episodes (Miro et al., 2012). We say BPI "begins as" because in polygenic disorders, genetics is not necessarily destiny; rather, it is vulnerability. Thus, the current state of the art for polygenic models is called a multifactorial threshold model. This model asserts that when many genetic factors contribute to a disorder, the effects of a single factor are small but risk accumulates as factors accumulate; once combined, the effects of these factors pass a critical value that is perhaps triggered by or signals other "cascade effects" in the brain and manifests the disorder (Hasler et al., 2005). Put another way, as the client possesses the susceptibility genes, it creates a gradient of liability. The more genes the client has, the more susceptible or vulnerable he or she is to the disorder (Rush, 2003). As you can see, this is a hypothesis, but it has the potential to unite many areas of research into a model that helps us understand the etiology of the disorder. As complex as this model is, it is simpler than trying to trace the symptoms of BPI (or other severe mental/emotional disorders) directly back to genetic factors.

Evidence for the heritability of Bipolar I Disorder has been supported in several studies, including those involving monozygotic and dizygotic twins; however, the estimates vary. For example, Evardsen and colleagues (2008) estimated that relatives of people with Bipolar I Disorder have a 3–8% risk of developing the disorder (see also Hajek et al., 2008; Mick, Wozniak, Eilens, Biederman, & Faraone, 2009; Pliszka, 2003), although most children with parents suffering from BPI do not develop it (Goldstein et al., 2010). At the other end of the spectrum, Belmaker (2004) estimated that 50% of people suffering from BPI have a family history of the disorder. In identical twins, when one suffers from the disorder, the other has a 40% probability of developing it, and in fraternal twins the concordance ranges between 5% and 38% (which is still quite broad) (Bertelsen, 2004). As with all other polygenic mental and emotional disorders, BPI sometimes manifests through the maternal side, and at other times through

[2] NCAN is an abbreviation for "neurocan," which is a protein (neurocan core protein) encoded by the NCAN gene.

the paternal side. However, genetics alone does not explain the onset of the disorder. Interplay between a genetic predisposition and various environmental factors seems to best explain the experience of symptoms of bipolar episodes (Shi et al., 2008).

A different theory of genetic etiology for BPI is tied to mitochondrial DNA. Mitochondrial DNA is transmitted to offspring from the ova in the mother. The DNA in most of our cells and the DNA in the mitochondria are believed to have different origins. Mitochondrial DNA is thought to be derived from bacteria that were basically "swallowed up" by the precursors to today's eukaryotic cells.[3] In a summary of research on this topic, Jun-Feng Wang (2007) suggests that people suffering from BPI may have defects in the mitochondrial electron transport chain. An electron transport chain creates an electrochemical proton gradient that in turn generates energy in the form of adenosine triphosphate (ATP). The damage in this chain may then cause oxidative damage in neurons. The damage may then manifest as the symptoms of BPI. Wang suggests that perhaps mood-stabilizing drugs work (when they work) by providing neuroprotection against oxidative stress. Thus, in this theory, the symptoms of BPI are hypothesized to derive from oxidative damage in neurons rooted in problems with mitochondrial DNA (Wang, 2007). Although we do not expect all of our readers to have a full grasp of molecular biology, we want to emphasize the complexity of theories of etiology and how far we have come from oversimplified (and incorrect) theories—such as those resorting simply to the word magic of "chemical imbalances" to attempt to explain the cause of complex mental disorders. It is far better to strain your brain to try to understand these variables than to try to oversimplify what is a very complex condition.

As with all theories of genetic vulnerability, environmental stress may play a key role for a genetic predisposition to be expressed as BPI. As early as 1992, Post (1992) hypothesized that environmental stressors played the greatest role in the early stages of the disorder, and the early episodes then affect the brain so as to increase the chance of subsequent episodes. He proposed this *kindling effect*, in which one episode acts as "kindling" (as in kindling for fires) for future episodes. Not all researchers agree with this model; however, it does fit Wang's (2007) oxidative stress theory. If mitochondrial DNA problems result in oxidative stress, and mood stabilizers provide neuroprotection, then the more BPI episodes a person suffers, the more oxidative-stress-induced damage would result. This is similar to what is called the sensitization model; in this model, clients suffering from BPI become more and more reactive to stress as the disorder progresses (Hammen & Gitlin, 1997). In clinical settings, it is best not to adhere rigidly to any such model; rather, it is better to hold them lightly as guides that may help you understand the course of a particular patient's symptoms.

**BRAIN STRUCTURE** Some professionals believe that genetic vulnerability may express as differences in the physiology of the brains of individuals susceptible to and/or diagnosed with BPI, compared to the brains of those individuals without the disorder or a genetic predisposition for it. This has led to extensive study of brain structure/morphology (called brain morphometry). Again, the idea is that if we can tie anomalies in brain structure to symptoms that clients suffer from, then using endophenotypic

---

[3] This theory is called the endosymbiotic theory.

thinking we may be able to tie the brain anomalies to specific genetic configurations. Further, if we understand—even generally—what the brain structures that are supposedly different actually do, we may better understand why the symptom picture is what it is.

There are currently many methods available with which to study neuroanatomy, and each has its strengths and limitations. The most common technique is magnetic resonance imaging (MRI), which produces three-dimensional anatomical images that show gray matter (neurons), white matter (glial cells), and cerebrospinal fluid (CSF). Diffusion tensor imaging (DTI) is a newer MRI method that can highlight microstructural changes in the white matter of the brain or glial cells (Emsell & McDonald, 2009). This is becoming more important since we discovered that, far from being only glue or insulation for neuronal axons (*glia* comes from the Greek word for *glue*), glial cells actually send neurotransmission and communicate with other cells (Fields, 2009, 2010; Sasaki, Matsuki, & Ikegaya, 2011).

There are also multiple techniques for extracting information from MRI scans. The most common quantitative techniques are "region of interest" (ROI) and computational morphometry studies. In ROI analysis, a trained rater manually traces a brain region of interest using "boundary rules" to compare sizes between different brains scanned. Computational morphometry is an automated method of comparing brain structures between different populations in a study. The most common variation is called voxel-based morphometry (VBM), which allows viewing of gray matter, white matter, and cerebrospinal fluid (Emsell & McDonald, 2009).[4] Finally, there are also deformation-based morphometry (DBM) and tensor-based morphometry (TBM). Both techniques are used to compare brain structures, but they rest upon different theoretical assumptions.

That said, we also must resist the temptation to oversimplify the results of these complex technologies. One such temptation is that of coining simplistic metaphors that suggest that brain structures are somehow more important than the networks that connect them (or even the mental processes that, in part, shape them). In some cases, structures seem to do the bulk of the work (e.g., as Broca's area in the left temporal lobe does for language) but in most cases, we are dependent upon networks that we do not fully understand, and simplifying function to structure tends to obscure the importance of the circuitry between structures (Shermer, 2008). Learning about anomalies in structure is an important piece of the puzzle, but only one piece of that puzzle.

Again, although we don't expect nonmedical mental health therapists to understand all the intricacies of this research, we are all ethically bound to have a general understanding of how this and other disabling disorders are being studied and what the general results are of such study. If you understand some of the general contours of this research, you'll understand why simplistic answers ("you have a chemical imbalance in your brain") are not only incorrect but misleading for clients and their families. Also, if you understand the range of techniques being used to study the brains of people suffering from BPI, you will understand why many studies produced conflicting data.

**Where to Start?** Two good places to start summarizing research on the size and function of brain structures and their relation to BPI is to look at meta- and mega-analyses.

---

[4] As with any approach, VBM has received criticism because of the assumptions on which it is based. See Ashburner and Friston (2001) and Bookstein (2001).

In statistics, meta-analysis is a method for combining the results of different studies that address similar research hypotheses. For example, the question of differences in brain structure has been raised in BPI, Major Depressive Disorder, and Schizophrenia; so it makes sense to combine multiple MRI studies to look for effect sizes across those three clinical populations (Lewine, Hudgins, Brown, Caudle, & Risch, 1995). Meta-analysis, like any other statistical procedure, can be done well or poorly, as evidenced by the contradictory findings in meta-analyses of, for example, psychic phenomena (Milton & Wiseman, 1999).

Mega-analysis, introduced by Carlson and Miller (1987), is newer and more controversial. In this approach, data on multiple individuals from multiple studies is pooled and analyzed. Mega-analysis has been critiqued (Cialdini & Fultz, 1990) but is being used more and more to group data from multiple neuroimaging studies. It is also important to bear in mind that there is great heterogeneity (diversity) in the presentation of BPI as well as the imaging technologies themselves. Although we are reporting research that is at an early stage of its development, further research will hopefully utilize longitudinal, multisite trials that more accurately tease out the effects of medication, comorbid drug abuse, and sex differences in the human brain (Emsell & McDonald, 2009).

***Results of Meta- and Mega-Analyses*** What have we learned from these new ways of imaging the brain? First, there do seem to be some statistically significant anomalies that show up with regularity in the brains of people suffering from severe mental disorders. We know the last sentence is a mouthful, but you must always be mindful that inferential research statistics give us probabilities, not cause-and-effect conclusions. In probability, the most significant results in a study will always be "some but not all subjects . . ." It is also interesting that this research is suggesting common factors that underlay disorders as diverse as Major Depressive Disorder, Bipolar I Disorder, and Schizophrenia. If the multifactorial threshold model described earlier is accurate, it may be that as the variables of genetic vulnerability increase, the severity of mental disturbance increases. Although we usually observe only the outcome in the symptoms, and then classify those as discrete categories (e.g., "Schizophrenia" versus "Major Depressive Disorder"), the severity may reflect the number of factors operating in a given individual; thus, a dimensional model may be more accurate than the model of discrete, categorical psychiatry.

One of the earliest studies (Lewine et al., 1995) of 325 subjects (108 suffering from Schizophrenia, 20 from Schizoaffective Disorder, 27 from Major Depressive Disorder, 20 from BPI, and 150 healthy volunteers) found that males with Schizophrenia had the most brain anomalies, followed by males and females suffering from Schizoaffactive Disorder, Major Depression, and BPI, respectively. The most obvious difference was larger brain ventricles, particularly in males with Schizophrenia. Initially, the idea was that the larger brain ventricles were related to surrounding tissue atrophy or loss, which is in turn related to the disorder (Wright et al., 2000). As such, this was a theory of "gray matter reduction," in which "gray matter" refers to neurons and reduction suggests the larger ventricles damaging the neurons. Nonspecific as this was, it did provide a starting point.

More recently, it appears that whole-brain volume is fairly well preserved in people with BPI (Konarski et al., 2008) but there are differences in the size of the lateral ventricles. People suffering from BPI are more likely to have enlargement in the lateral ventricles, and the larger these ventricles, the more severe the client's symptoms (McDonald et al., 2004). There also appear to be regional brain differences in some clients with BPI. Many studies report regional deficits in gray (neuronal) and white (glial) matter, as well as increases in spaces that hold cerebral spinal fluid (which may imply atrophy of the surrounding brain tissue) (Emsell & McDonald, 2009). What confounds these findings is that other studies find no differences between the brains of healthy volunteers and people with BPI (e.g., McDonald et al., 2005), as well as some studies in which there are *increases* in the brain region of interest in the BPI subjects (Adler et al., 2006). The regions of interest that have shown differences between healthy volunteers and people with BPI include the prefrontal cortex (which is involved with personality, decision making, and morality) and the anterior cingulate cortex (or ACC, which is linked to executive, emotional, and cognitive functions). The AAC can be divided into the anterior cingulate, which is involved with attention, memory, and processing of noxious stimuli (toxins) in the brain, and an affective division that includes the amygdala, hippocampus, nucleus accumbens, and orbitofrontal cortex. The central role of the ACC in mood and affect regulation has made it a target for imaging studies in BPI (Emsell & McDonald, 2009). One consistent finding involves asymmetries and volume differences in the ACC that may reflect neurodevelopmental vulnerability in the etiology of BPI (Fornito et al., 2007). It is also interesting that patients with BPI who respond to lithium show increased ACC volume as compared to patients who do not respond to lithium—suggesting that one way that lithium treats symptoms is by serving a neuroprotective function (Javadapour et al., 2007).

***Differences in Sub-Cortical Structures: The Amygdala*** Because of the role of the amygdala in identifying emotionally relevant stimuli, researchers have tried to discern if there are noticeable differences in the amygdalae[5] of clients suffering from BPI, compared to healthy controls. Kruger, Seminowicz, Goldapple, Kennedy, and Mayberg (2003) used PET scans and found that clients diagnosed with BPI disorder had statistically significantly more activity in their amygdalae than controls. Other studies using fMRI have found that some (but not all) people suffering from BPI have significantly larger amygdalae than controls. The theory here is that larger amygdalae would render the person more emotionally sensitive (Chang et al., 2004). Other studies have found diminished volume in the prefrontal cortex, basal ganglia, hippocampus, and anterior cingulated cortical regions in some (but not all) clients with BPI. These researchers speculate that diminished activity in these regions may interfere with the ability to regulate emotions (Phillips, Drevets, Rauch, & Brannan, 2003).

***Differences in Sub-Cortical Structures: The Hippocampus*** The hippocampus is involved with memory formation as well as recall, spatial, episodic, and semantic forms of memory. It has also been linked to the hypothalamic-pituitary-adrenal (HPA) axis. Feedback between the hypothalamus, pituitary, and adrenal glands is a major part of the neuroendocrine system, and contributes to regulation of mood, emotions, sexuality, the immune system, and energy storage and expenditure. Hippocampus volume

---

[5] You have an amygdala in the medial temporal lobes on each side of your brain; when referring to both (plural), the term is *amygdalae*.

has been found to be reduced on the left side in many patients with BPI. As with the ACC, lithium-responsive clients show volume increase in the hippocampus, suggesting the neuroprotective properties of lithium in BPI.

***Differences in White Matter*** As noted earlier, since we learned that glial cells do more than we previously thought, differences in white matter (glial cells) are increasingly being studied. Glial cells make up 85% of our brain cells and interact with neurons (the remaining 15%). Glial cells can also exert control over neurons. Glial cells in the central nervous system are made up of astrocytes, oligodendroglia, Schwann cells, and microglia. Astrocytes support cells that makeup the blood-brain barrier and provide nutrients to neurons. Oligodendroglia and Schwann cells make multiple segments of myelin that wrap around neuronal axons. Microglia respond to injury and disease in the brain—killing invading germs and initiating cell repair. Neurons are dependent on glial cells to fire electrical impulses and to send neurotransmitters across synapses. Like neurons, glial cells are also outfitted with receptors for neurotransmitters and can release neurotransmitters through channels in their membranes (Fields, 2011).

The idea that white matter may be implicated in mental illness goes back to the 1930s when Hungarian pathologist Ladislas von Meduna (while performing autopsies) noticed that glial cells were decreased in the cerebral cortex of people who had suffered from depression or Schizophrenia. He had also noted that people suffering from epilepsy seemed to have more white matter in the same areas, and thought it developed to regulate electrical activity in the brain. This was one origin of electro-shock treatment for people with severe depression and schizophrenia. It was thought that putting a mild electrical charge through the brain might stimulate the production of white matter and alleviate symptoms (Fields, 2011).

Although there is no difference in the total volume of white matter between healthy subjects and those with BPI (Scherk et al., 2008), abnormalities in the white matter of many BPI subjects have been observed some in brain-scanning studies. One theory is that abnormalities in the microstructure of the glial cells affect the brain's neuroanatomy (possibly in terms of connections between brain structures) and may be central to BPI. Glial cells in the central nervous system are made up of oligodendroglia. Each oligodendrocyte makes multiple segments of myelin that wrap around neuronal axons. The most prevalent abnormalities are called white matter hyperintensities. The name comes from the way that these areas show up on brain scans. They are essentially lesions in the white matter that may reflect differing levels of myelination or even damage to cells in the brain ventricles referred to as *ependymal loss* (Grangeon et al., 2010). The ependymal cells line the walls of the brain ventricles and form a substance that secretes spinal fluid. These cells can be injured by things such as infections and strokes. It may be that some people are genetically vulnerable to such injuries, which may then be one variable in the development of severe mental illnesses such as BPI or Schizophrenia.

Differences in white matter connectivity between and within the brain hemispheres may also play a role in BPI. Because white matter is essential to the creation of neural networks and the forming of functional circuits, deficits in white matter may contribute to disruptions in the circuits, which in turn may result in symptoms like those seen in BPI. As with all brain-imaging studies, the results of studies on white matter vary, but differences have shown up in the brains of subjects with BPI in their temporal, frontal, parietal, and occipital lobes (Kafantaris et al., 2009). Differences have also been found in white matter connectivity in the corpus callosum in pediatric and adult bipolar patients (Brambilla, Bellani, Yeh, Soares, & Tansella, 2009).

Oligodendroglia have been found to function abnormally in people suffering from BPI. In addition, many people with BPI seem to have decreased expression (downregulation) of genes related to the functioning of white matter, which may account for reduced density of the white matter in the frontal cortex of clients with BPI (Brambilla et al., 2009). It may be that the immune system will also be implicated in these problems with white matter. There appear to be associations between genetic vulnerability for BPI and immune related functions such as inflammation and interleukin genes (Papiol et al., 2004). As Brambilla et al. (2009) wrote, dysfunction in the oligodendrites (the particular glial cells) and problems in the health and repair of those cells may be caused by a problem in the immune system, and the resulting cellular abnormalities may be related to developing BPI disorder.

**Cellular Plasticity Cascades** Neuroplasticity is the ability of neurons and synapses to undergo and maintain change, and it is thought to be essential to the healthy functioning of the nervous system. Neuroplasticity involves changes in signaling cascades (how neurons trigger other neurons in a cascade effect) and gene regulation inside the neuron. Synaptic plasticity refers to changes that affect the strength of a signal that is transmitted through the synapse. Both of these affect neurotransmitter release and communication, axonal and dendritic structure, and neurogenesis (Schloesser, Huang, Klein, & Manji, 2008).

This theory postulates that BPI ". . . arises from abnormalities in cellular plasticity cascades, leading to aberrant information processing in synapses and circuits mediating affective, cognitive, motoric and neuro-vegetative functions" (Schloesser et al., 2008, p. 111). This is really a theory about how endophenotypes may give rise to disruptions in the way brain circuits work. Because endophenotypes derive from genetic vulnerability, this is still a version of the multifactorial model. In this case, however, the goal would be to target the cascades in the treatment of BPI in order to stabilize the symptoms and reduce the frequency and severity of mood episodes.

**What About Chemical Imbalances? Neurotransmitters** Throughout this chapter, we have emphasized that the old metaphor of mental and emotional disorders being caused by chemical imbalances in the brain is not accurate. Although "chemical imbalance" is a popular phrase that began being used in the 1980s, there are no studies that supported the idea of chemical imbalances as the basis of mental and emotional disorders. Using "chemical imbalance" or "chemical imbalances" as search phrases in MedLine produces not a single study supporting the idea, but only articles that dispute the idea or studies that allude to it as if it were true (see Baughman, 2006; Insell, 2009). That said, neurotransmitters are still a target of study and intervention in BPI. As noted in earlier chapters, neurotransmitters function by sending messages from cell to cell throughout the brain. Of particular interest for their roles in BPI are dopamine (DA), norepinephrine (NE), serotonin (5-HT), and gamma aminobutyric acid (GABA).

The problem remains, however, that we have yet to reach consensus on what is "normal" and "abnormal" with regard to levels of any neurotransmitter. NE activates neurons that are related to vigilance and attentiveness to the environment. In Bipolar I Disorder, abnormal levels of this neurotransmitter *might* trigger euphoria and grandiosity (Young et al., 1994). Serotonin (5-HT) functions in the regulation of mood, appetite, sleep, arousal, and pain; 5-HT is believed to inhibit the activity of some neurons and behaviors that would cause a dysregulation in these functions, particularly mood. Like serotonin, GABA is an inhibitory neurotransmitter that aids in the stability of the brain, keeping neurons from firing uncontrollably. For its role in BPI, GABA *may work* to inhibit dopamine and norepinephrine neurons, acting as a block against manic symptoms (Dean, Scarr, & MacLeod, 2005). As you can see, all of these findings are tentative, and research in molecular biology and psychiatry may make all these theories about the etiology of BPI obsolete.

Dopamine (DA) is important for its role in movement, attention, learning, and the reinforcing effects of pleasurable activities. Excess L-dopa (the amino acid synthesized into DA) *may be* responsible for triggering manic episodes in people vulnerable to them to begin with (Carlson, 2005). Berk et al. (2007) have hypothesized that alternating high and low levels of DA may trigger mania and depression, respectively, in BPI. This has not been supported thus far, although this is likely because the model is based on the response of Parkinson's patients to DA-elevating medications (O'Sullivan, Evands, & Lees, 2009). Whereas Parkinson's disease has a clear pathophysiological etiology involving the DA system, BPI does not.

Regarding their particular effects on the brain in individuals with BPI, it used to be thought that the levels of these neurotransmitters (especially the monoamines) are either too high or too low (Post, Ballenger, & Goodwin, 1980). Others have argued that there is dysregulation in the neurotransmitter systems that can be researched with so-called "challenge" procedures (Sobczak, Honig, van Duinen, & Riedel, 2002). In these challenge procedures, a neurotransmitter is stimulated by a dose of a relevant drug that leads to measureable effects, usually increases in the blood levels of modulating hormones such as prolactin or cortisol. The challenge procedure may also show clinical or psychological effects. The problem is that these challenge procedures have been criticized for being nonstandardized and not accounting for the fact that the challenge drug may induce the effects thought to be related to the disorder under study (Gijsman, Cohen, & van Gerven, 2004).

Other researchers argue that mental and emotional disorders are related to a change in the sensitivity of neurotransmitter receptors on one's nerve cells (Bernstein, Penner, Clarke-Stewart, & Roy, 2008). We now know these theories are too simplistic—in part because brain chemistry is so complex that we have virtually no idea what constitutes a "balanced" baseline, and such baselines may vary broadly from person to person. Although neurotransmitters may be implicated in BPI, their role does not appear to be the primary cause of the disorder; in fact, neurotransmitter differences may even be a product—rather than cause—of the disorder (Goodwin & Jamison, 2007; Thase, Jindal, & Howland, 2002).

## Psychological Theories

**PSYCHOLOGICAL BEHAVIORISM** In an attempt to provide an integrative developmental approach to the causes of BPI, some researchers have proposed that some psychopathology is a result of learned behaviors (Riedel, Heiby, & Kopetskie, 2001). This idea posits that there are three types of *basic behavioral repertoires* at work in the development of psychopathologies such as BPI: emotional-motivational, sensory-motor, and language-cognitive processes. According to psychological behaviorism, all three of these basic behavioral repertoires are affected by both learning and predisposed individual differences (Riedel et al., 2001).

Emotional-motivational processes are said to define for each individual the different stimuli that provoke various emotional states. Sensory-motor includes things like basic functional ability and vocational, educational, social, and recreational skills; variations in any of these may contribute to an individual's experience of psychopathology. Deficits in social skills, for example, are characteristic of many psychological disorders included in the DSM. Finally, language-cognitive processes are said to be largely influenced by classical and operant conditioning. As a result, phenomena such as maladaptive thoughts (like those associated with psychopathologies) are the likely consequence of learned language and cognitive skills.

In its conceptualization of BPI, psychological behaviorism does take into account a variety of influences on the individual's development, such as biological and psychosocial factors. Ultimately, however, from the behavioral standpoint, an individual's basic behavioral repertoires likely account for a large part of the onset and maintenance of symptoms of BPI. More specifically, it has been hypothesized that these basic behavioral repertoires may lead to the exhibition of thoughts and behaviors characteristic of the disorder. It is certainly possible that basic behavioral repertoires and the environments they are responses to could *trigger* genetic vulnerability to BPI, but more research is needed to make this endophenotypic link.

Here again, hopefully you can see the promise of how these theories could fit together to give us a clearer understanding of the etiology of BPI. One starts with a genetic vulnerability, the vulnerability leads to anomalies in brain structure, and these anomalies in interaction with the environment (and responses to it) then exacerbate the genetic vulnerability to the point where the disorder is developed. It likely doesn't bear repeating, but this is clearly a more accurate—even if more complicated—way to understand how the disorder develops than merely assuming and asserting a simple imbalance in brain chemicals.

**PSYCHOSOCIAL FACTORS** Some researchers have looked to a combination of various psychosocial factors to help explain the etiology of BPI (Holmes & Rahe, 1967; Scott & Colom, 2005). Factors such as an individual's current environment or living situation, his or her cognitive and personality styles, and even the person's developmental history have been areas of interest as potential partners in the onset and maintenance of BPI.

Some researchers suggest that age, education level, and marital and employment statuses are related to the experience of the disorder. One study surveyed over 9000 people in the general population in the United States. Results indicated that BPI is inversely related to both age and educational level. This means that the older and more educated one is, the less likely he or she will be to experience symptoms of the disorder. Now, we could also argue that if individuals have BPI onset in the late teens or early 20s, they are far less likely to attain advanced education because of their symptoms and perhaps the costs associated with the disorder. Moreover, prevalence rates of BPI (at least at subthreshold levels) are greater for those individuals who are separated or divorced than for those who are currently married. These results are similar for those individuals who are unemployed, compared to those who are employed, and could point to stressors that perhaps exacerbate genetic vulnerability or stress brain structures that have been impaired by the genetic vulnerability.

Although these results are very interesting, they should be interpreted with caution. One cannot say, for instance, that older individuals who are highly educated and who have a spouse and a job do not or cannot also experience symptoms of BPI. Similarly, one cannot conclude that a younger person who is divorced and has little education and no job will have BPI. The point, here, is that these are just relationships that have been observed in the general population. Although it is *less likely* for an older, married, well-educated, employed person to have BPI, it is nonetheless possible. Likewise, it is *more likely,* but far from a certainty, for a younger, previously married, uneducated, unemployed person to experience symptoms of the disorder.

## Environmental Theories

**LIFE EVENTS** The evidence indicating a biological link for BPI is strong—as we have emphasized throughout this chapter. This is widely recognized by researchers and clinicians alike (Rush, 2003). However, countless professionals have remained diligent in their search for other etiological variables involved in the disorder. Several studies have reviewed evidence of stressful life events acting as predictors of BPI. The psychological etiology of BPI is described in a very similar way today as it was decades ago. In 1967, the *Social Readjustment Rating Scale* was created (it later became known as the *Life Events Scale*) (Dohrenwend, Krasnoff, Askenasy, & Dohrenwend, 1978). The purpose of this instrument was to confirm the idea that psychopathology is influenced, at least partially, by significant life events. This idea acknowledged the fact that there are other factors involved in the development and maintenance of psychopathology. Although stressful life events (and behaviors like substance abuse) are not sufficient to cause a particular disorder such as BPI, they may, as noted, exacerbate genetic or other vulnerabilities to the disorder.

There are various difficulties in assessing the importance of stressful life events to an individual's experience of BPI (Goodman et al., 2001). One difficulty concerns the issue of *when* individuals and their stressors are assessed. Because a person with BPI typically is no stranger to stressful life events (Hayward, Wong, Bright, & Lam, 2002), some approaches to assessment could potentially overestimate how much these events actually trigger symptoms in the disorder. In other words, because individuals with BPI typically experience high levels of stress on a somewhat regular basis due to the nature of the disorder and things like careless behavior during manic episodes, it may be difficult to determine whether various life events are more stressful right before an episode, compared to other times in the individual's daily life.

Another difficulty associated with the assessment of these life events concerns the subjectivity with which the events are deemed stressful. This is a point made very clear simply by looking at items on the *Life Events Scale*. Some of the items listed on the scale are easily identified as what would typically be considered stressful (e.g., death of a spouse, dismissal from work, imprisonment). Other items, however, may not be as easily identified as such. In fact, some of the items on the *Life Events Scale* would typically be considered positive events (e.g., getting married, vacation, gaining a new family member). What is important to note is that even positive life events can be stressful (what we call *eustress*); the amount of stress experienced by an individual as a result of a particular event is quite subjective. So, although subjectivity may prove to be a difficulty in terms of assessing the risk for symptoms of psychopathologies such as Bipolar I Disorder, it is important for researchers and clinicians to keep in mind that life events, regardless of their positive or negative nature, can nonetheless be stressful, and may contribute to both the onset and the course of psychopathology.

**INSTABILITY HYPOTHESIS** The instability hypothesis (Jones, Hare, & Evershed, 2005) proposed that the experience of stressful life events may also have an *indirect* effect on the onset and maintenance of BPI. These stressful life events exert their effect by creating an instability or imbalance in the individual's circadian rhythms (or "biological clock"). Stressful life events have the potential to significantly affect an individual's sleep patterns, as well as other social patterns that one might typically maintain during daily life (e.g., the number of people with whom one ordinarily socializes; the time one typically gets up, eats, and goes to work; the types of activities one might do in his or her spare time). Not surprisingly, the instability hypothesis suggests that these imbalances in an individual's circadian rhythms may be at least partly responsible for the onset of the depressive and manic episodes seen in BPI. Recall the case of Alex at the beginning of this chapter. After the stressful argument with her sister, she began having sleep difficulties. Shortly after that, she began to decompensate. We would add that the instability (in our endophenotypic scheme) would exacerbate preexisting vulnerabilities in genes or brain structures.

Some researchers (Miklowitz, 2002) have noted that although stressful life events have the potential to significantly affect the functioning of any one individual, this potential seems greater for those with a vulnerability or predisposition to develop BPI. Such an individual is more vulnerable to a manic episode, for example, when he or she experiences some event that disrupts his or her usual way of living.

**AN EXISTENTIAL PERSPECTIVE** Some scholars (Havens & Ghaemi, 2005) suggest that because depression is one of (if not *the*) most common symptoms in BPI, it should be the focus of attention when trying to understand the disorder's etiology, course, and treatment. From this perspective, the depression associated with BPI may not always be caused by some physiological or psychological factor. Rather, in some cases, the depression one may experience in such a disorder might, in fact, be the result of *existential despair*. This despair (and, similarly, the resulting depression) may be exacerbated by the losses one has suffered in his or her life because of the overarching disorder. For example, some feelings of depression could be the product of some failed hope(s) brought about during a manic episode. This despair might also be explained as a loss of one's self-meaning for one's life, connection with the world, and hope for the future (Kierkegaard, 1954). Again, in Alex's case, her suicidality was exacerbated (and likely caused by) the despair that accompanies having a chronic disorder that has prevented her from attaining her dreams and living life the way she desires.

Before moving into treatment, we will use the Integral model to summarize what we know about etiology. Figure 6.2 illustrates the etiologic factors, including factors that may trigger vulnerabilities. Physiologic variables thought to underlay the disorder are followed by an (E) for etiology. Variables thought to trigger symptoms are labeled with a (T) for trigger. You can see that the primary vulnerabilities are in

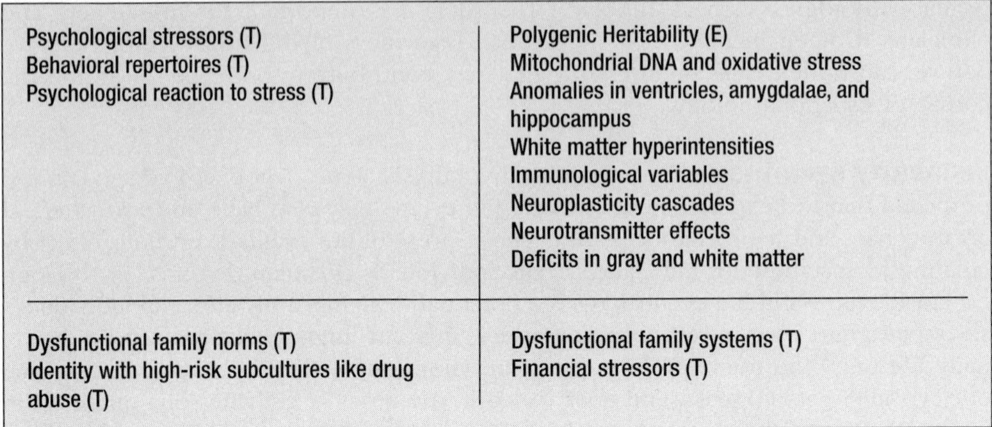


**FIGURE 6.2** Etiological and Trigger Variables in BPI Disorder

the upper-right quadrant (physiological) while the triggers populate the other three quadrants.

## HOW IS BIPOLAR I DISORDER TREATED?

BPI can be treated in a variety of ways. The most common treatment is pharmacotherapy to deal with the symptoms augmented by talk therapy—especially for developing insight into the disorder and the life-management skills that are necessary in light of the disorder (Fountoulakis & Vieta, 2008). Psychotherapy may also be used to help the individual cope with the mood-related symptoms of the disorder, as well as to refrain from engaging in the behavior-related symptoms. The most difficult aspect regarding the treatment of BPI is that, particularly in terms of medication, the treatment may vary depending on the phase of the disorder. There is a so-called prodromal[6] phase during which an at-risk person may show mood symptoms that are below the clinical threshold, an acute phase during which the symptoms are predominantly manic or depressive (except in cases of mixed state specifier), and a maintenance phase during which the symptoms are, to some extent, relieved or fully treated. The clinical implication is that clinicians should have a general sense of which phase the client is in before deciding on treatment. We will briefly summarize treatments for the acute manic, acute depressive, and maintenance phases.

There are also multiple sets of treatment guidelines (33 sets as of 2008) that do not always agree; nonetheless, they are available for clinicians, clients and client family members. Examples include the Texas Medication Algorithm Project (TMAP; Suppes et al., 2009), the World Federation of Societies of Biological Psychiatry guidelines (Grunze et al., 2009), and the Canadian Network for Mood and Anxiety Treatments (Yatham et al., 2009).

---

[6] The Latin and Greek roots for *prodromal* mean a "precursor"—in this case a precursor signaling the onset of the disorder.

## Physiological Treatment

The physiological treatments for BPI (in all its phases) are pharmacological or use electro-convulsive therapy (ECT) (American Psychiatric Association APA, 2000b; Fountoulakis & Vieta, 2008). The majority of pharmacological agents used for BPI are colloquially referred to as "mood stabilizers,"[7] although in reality, they represent radically different drug classes ranging from antipsychotics to anticonvulsants (Moller & Nasrallah, 2003). The phrase "mood stabilizer" is a bit oxymoronic because mood by its very definition is seldom "stable." Be that as it may, the best mood stabilizer should be effective in each cycle of the disorder, without exacerbating the other cycles. In other words, an ideal mood stabilizer treats symptoms of mania and depression without exacerbating either and has a prophylactic effect in decreasing relapses. This is rarely the case, which explains why more than one drug may be necessary.

**ACUTE-PHASE TREATMENT OF MANIA** ECT has been used in the acute phase of mania for over 50 years and is effective in controlling symptoms. In reviewing 50 years of such research, Mukherjee, Sackeim, and Schnur (1994) noted that ECT is associated with remission or marked improvement in 80% of manic patients. More recently, Hiremani, Thirthalli, Tharayil, and Gangadhar (2008) performed a double-blind, randomized, controlled study and noted that the placement of the electrodes also seems to be related to the speed of recovery (bifrontal electrode placement being slightly better than bi-temporal placement). Some of the risks of ECT are that it may actually provoke mania, and ECT in combination with lithium use may cause delirium. Other than caveats such these, there are no absolute contraindications to administering ECT for the treatment of acute mania (APA, 2000b).

There are many pharmacological agents that may be used to treat acute mania, and the ones with the best results encompass different types of antipsychotics (Abilify/aripiprazole, Haldol/haloperidol, Zyprexa/olanzapine, Seroquel/quetiapine, Risperdal/resperidone, and Geodon/ziprasidone), anticonvulsants (Tegretol/carbamazepine, and Divalproex/valproate), as well as lithium (Fountoulakis & Vieta, 2008; Yatham et al., 2009). Generally, after considering the type and severity of manic symptoms, doctors will choose a single agent with good demonstrated efficacy. If, after 2 weeks, the client has a good response and the medication has efficacy for maintenance, he or she is continued on it. If there is no response or a partial response, doctors may combine the first medication with a second one, or switch to another first-line drug (a drug with efficacy as a first line of treatment). If the client is still not responding to the first drug, doctors may consider a combination of two first-line drugs (Grunze et al., 2009). In Alex's case, she was stabilized on Haldol/haliperodal while her lithium was discontinued and her divalproex maintained, and to this her doctor added Lamictal/lamotrigine.

**ACUTE-PHASE TREATMENT OF DEPRESSION** It has long been noted that if people with BPI are given antidepressants, the antidepressants can trigger or exacerbate mania (Post et al., 2006). If first-line treatments that have some efficacy for depression (e.g., quetiapine, olanzapine, and lithium) are not relieving enough of the symptoms, then a second

[7] The phrase "mood stabilizer" did not exist prior to 1995 when Abbot laboratories obtained a license for using Valproate to treat manic symptoms. They used that term to market Valproate for that purpose (Healy, 2006).

drug, often an antidepressant, will be added (Yatham et al., 2009). One of the first systematic studies of multiple medications was the Texas Medication Algorithm Project (Suppes et al., 2009). In bipolar depression not related to mixed states or rapid cycling, the studies suggested starting clients on lithium and a selective serotonin reuptake inhibitor (SSRI) antidepressant (e.g., Zoloft/sertraline). If clients become unstable, the next step is to change the antidepressant. A third step would be trying a different combination. For bipolar depression with a mixed state or rapid cycling states, the first step is a combination of mood stabilizers until as many symptoms as possible are addressed. More recently, in the Systematic Treatment Enhancement Program for Bipolar Disorder (STEP-BD), researchers have recommended stabilizing the client on a mood stabilizer and then adding an antidepressant (Miklowitz et al., 2007). ECT is a third option for bipolar depression when clients fail to respond to multiple iterations of drug treatment.

**TREATMENT IN THE MAINTENANCE PHASE** The primary goals of treatment in the maintenance phase are preventing relapse and maximizing gains from treatment. A large part of preventing relapse includes developing insight into one's symptoms and learning how lifestyle changes can help prevent relapse. This feeds into the second goal of the maintenance phase—maximizing gains. Effective treatment in the acute phase is defined in the DSM as a clinically significant reduction (e.g., 50%) in symptom severity (Sachs & Rush, 2003). While in maintenance we are aiming both to prevent the return of symptoms as well as to expand the response into complete remission. Sustained remission for 6 months or longer is considered recovery. Although this sounds straightforward, in clinical practice it is more complicated, and there is no consensus regarding definitions of recovery (Sachs & Rush, 2003). We will address this further in the section on psychological treatments. As far as medication for the maintenance phase, most treatment guidelines recommend that the client remains on medications that they have been responsive to; these could include lithium, olanzapine, resperidone, divalproex, quetiapine, and lamotrigine (Fountoulakis & Vieta, 2008; Smith, Cornelius, Warnock, Bell, & Young, 2007). Here again, you can see that drugs for the maintenance phase may be primarily lithium, anticonvulsants, or antipsychotics, or some combination of drugs; it depends on which medications the client responded to in the acute phase and how well the client continues to tolerate them.

## Psychological/Psychosocial Treatment

**PSYCHOTHERAPY** Biological factors undoubtedly have a large degree of influence on the development and maintenance of BPI. Likewise, biological interventions (i.e., medications) are an important part of treatment. Despite the biological aspect of this disorder, however, it can also be significantly influenced by psychosocial factors. Moreover, pharmacological treatments, by themselves, do not consistently keep the disorder in remission (Rothbaum & Astin, 2000). Full recovery is rare, and recurrence with incomplete remission is the rule (Angst & Sellaro, 2000). Historically, psychosocial factors have been thought to contribute significantly to relapse (Scott, 1995). It follows that psychosocial interventions, such as psychotherapy, would also contribute significantly to the treatment of the disorder—especially in the maintenance phase. In Alex's case, after 6 months of dialectical behavior therapy, she did endorse an increase in her social activities and her life satisfaction. Therapy also helped her adhere to more structure concerning exercise, sleep, and diet. Although she has a long way to go, she is doing better.

Given these limitations, realistic desired outcomes could be limited to ongoing, short-term goals of acute symptom control, suicide prevention, and enhancing insight and quality of life (Sachs & Rush, 2003). We are beginning to get data on the efficacy of psychotherapy with clients suffering from BPI. Ball et al. (2006) performed a study with 52 patients diagnosed with BPI and found that the group receiving cognitive therapy had lower depression scores and better outcomes at 12 months than a control group receiving medication only. A larger randomized-controlled trial with 293 patients found that those patients receiving intensive therapy had significantly higher year-end recovery rates (approximately 64% versus 51% in the control group). Although three different types of therapy were used (family-focused, interpersonal, and social rhythm therapy), no significant differences were found between the three therapies (consistent with what we know about psychotherapy outcomes in general) (Miklowitz et al., 2007).

Psychotherapy can be used to help people deal with the symptoms of the disorder that are not addressed by medication. It can also be used to help with the prevention of repeated episodes. Just as there are different biological interventions (i.e., different medications) used in treatment, there are also several different psychotherapeutic approaches. Based on the literature, the most effective of these include psychoeducation and a variety of therapies: cognitive-behavioral, marital and family, interpersonal and social rhythm, and any adjunctive interventions that may be necessary (e.g., treatment for substance use).

Cognitive-behavioral therapy (CBT) is a therapeutic approach that helps the individual identify and change maladaptive thought and behavior patterns. Clients with BPI undergoing CBT can learn to recognize manic or depressed thoughts and emotions, and also learn how to change behaviors that contribute to these episodes (e.g., ways to refrain from excessive spending or unhealthy sexual practices during manic episodes or ways to counteract the negative mood during depressive episodes). Over 25 years of research has shown that, compared to pharmacotherapy alone, CBT combined with pharmacotherapy is more effective in helping clients improve medication adherence, leading to early detection and intervention of BPI, assisting with stress and lifestyle management, helping to treat comorbid conditions, leading to fewer manic and depressive episodes and related hospitalizations, and improving social and occupational functioning (Miklowitz & Craighead, 2007).

Insight is particularly important for people living with BPI. Being able to tell when they are decompensating, understanding things that may trigger relapse, and adjusting their lifestyle to regular rhythms are all related to insight. Part of the problem seems to be that insight is related to what is called neurocognitive functioning, and the latter is impaired in people with BPI (Dias, Brissos, & Carita, 2008). Some researchers think that such neurocognitive deficits are rooted in the brain anomalies discussed previously. For example, Varga et al. (2009) suggested that reduced insight and symptom awareness were related to atrophy in the cortex and subcortex (the volume differences in brains of people suffering BPI). As such, reduced insight contributes to high-risk behaviors, which increase the risk of relapse.

Insight can generally be divided into two types: insight into treatment and insight into the recognition of the illness. Insight into treatment is defined as understanding and accepting the need for treatment. Clients who lack insight into treatment and who have a greater number of previous hospitalizations have poorer prognoses than clients who have insight into treatment (Yen et al., 2008). Not surprisingly, insight is also correlated with medication adherence, although the degree of adverse side effects that are associated with some medications can decrease the patient's quality of life (Yen et al., 2008). This illustrates the primary dilemma confounding treatment: Even for clients with insight, if multiple medications may be needed and need to be changed depending on the stage of the disorder, this increases the chance that the client will experience adverse side effects and thus decreased quality of life and perhaps even decreased adherence to medication.

Another therapy technique—interpersonal and social rhythm therapy (IPSRT)—works from the idea that interpersonal problems, loss of sleep, changes in eating habits, and other disruptions in daily activities can trigger the onset of manic and depressive episodes in BPI. Used in conjunction with appropriate medications, IPSRT combines interpersonal psychotherapy with behavioral therapy techniques to help individuals address problems in their interpersonal styles and relationships, and establish more regular daily routines.

The interpersonal component of IPSRT addresses the fact that problems with relationships, and how one interacts with others, can contribute a significant amount of stress. This stress can then trigger the onset of a depressive or manic episode. The behavioral component of IPSRT addresses disruptions in an individual's daily routine (especially the sleep-wake cycle). By controlling the regularity of daily activities, one can also exhibit some control over the experience of Bipolar I symptoms (Frank, 2000).

## AN INTEGRAL APPROACH

Some scholars and other professionals have acknowledged the invaluable advances in the research regarding the causes and treatment of BPI. At the same time, such authors have also argued for the need for a more integrative approach to understanding this disorder, as well as the factors that influence its onset and maintenance. The push for an integrative approach is fueled by the fact that, time and time again, research has shown that there is no single cause for BPI: There is no single genetic, cognitive, emotional, developmental, or environmental factor responsible for the disorder.

Because there is no single precipitating factor, it follows that there is also no single treatment for the disorder either. From the discussion in this chapter, you may have noticed that much of the research on the treatment for BPI focuses on a combination of approaches (e.g., pharmacotherapy and psychotherapy), rather than a single treatment method.

This push for an integrated approach to understanding and treating BPI can easily be explained in the context of Integral theory. Rather than looking at various parts of an individual's life, this approach focuses on the whole person, including the culture and systems in which the person is embedded. The idea, here, is that there are multiple causes and explanations for what happens in a person's life. These multiple causes and explanations acknowledge the importance of what goes on internally, neurobiologically and behaviorally, culturally, and socially, therefore providing a whole picture. With regard to the understanding and treatment of BPI, an Integral approach looks at all of these dimensions in a person's life to provide a more comprehensive explanation for a particular individual's experiences, as well as how best to address symptoms and treat the disorder. Figure 6.3 illustrates the Integral approach to Alex's treatment.

| | |
|---|---|
| Dialectical behavior therapy<br>Exploring suicidality<br>Increasing sense of life satisfaction | Pharmacotherapy<br>Daily activity schedule for regular sleep, exercise, diet |
| Dialogue with sister with willingness to change behaviors<br>Group therapy with other people suffering from BPI | Increasing healthy social activities<br>Debt consolidation |

**FIGURE 6.3** Integral Approach to Alex's Treatment

## PEDIATRIC BIPOLAR DISORDER

In recent years, there has been controversy and debate regarding the age of onset for BPI. Beginning in 1996, psychiatrist Joseph Biederman and colleagues (1996) began publishing a series of papers suggesting that pediatric patients who were diagnosed with Attention Deficit–Hyperactivity-Disorder (ADHD) were actually exhibiting juvenile mania and should be diagnosed as having BPI. Several studies and roundtables followed, all of which were heavily funded by pharmaceutical companies. According to Healy (2008) the professionals involved seemed eager to develop guidelines for diagnosing and treating pediatric BPI in the absence of evidence. Whereas adult manic-depressive mood states persist for weeks or months, they were willing to assume children's dysfunctional moods would oscillate rapidly (several times a day), although there was no evidence that this was the case. Second, these drugs were causing severe side effects, including visible weight gain, tardive dyskinesia, and diabetes, and in some cases had proved lethal. The sales of mood-stabilizing drugs skyrocketed with the increase in pediatric diagnoses.

There is considerable controversy regarding the appropriateness of a BPI diagnosis in children. Questions regarding the appropriateness of such a diagnosis are founded on the idea that criteria for BPI may overlap with criteria for developmental issues; other disorders usually diagnosed during infancy, childhood, or adolescence (e.g., what the DSM-5 calls Neurodevelopmental Disorders); and other problems known to affect people of all ages (e.g., depressive, anxiety, substance use, and impulse-control disorders) (Chang, 2008). Further, there are currently no pediatric diagnostic guidelines for BPI in children, and it is inappropriate to use the DSM criteria for BPI because they were normed on adults (Kowatch et al., 2005; Sahling, 2009).

One of the most problematic issues is assuming that any type of irritability or acting out is somehow related to the invalid notion of a "bipolar spectrum." Differentiating between irritability (very common in children and adolescents) and symptoms of BPI is an ethical imperative for clinicians, particularly those working in foster care or with other children and adolescents who have no one to advocate for them (Banaschewski, 2009; Sahling, 2009). Although published studies using functional brain-scanning technologies to investigate early-onset BPI are few, some show brain anomalies similar to those that correlate with adult BPI (Frazier et al., 2005). Only longitudinal studies will answer the question regarding how predictive such anomalies are for the development of BPI because brain scans can only suggest endophenotypes that are related to vulnerability to a disorder (Jackson, 2006).

Between 1994 and 2003, there has been a 40-fold increase in the diagnosis of bipolar disorder in children (much of it Bipolar Disorder Not-Otherwise-Specified) (Moreno et al., 2007). Such an increase is unlikely to reflect an accurate reporting of previously "missed" diagnoses, and many have suggested that this is driven by political agendas such as pharmaceutical companies finding new markets for medications that have questionable efficacy (Ingersoll & Rak, 2006; Sahling, 2009).

Some researchers have set about developing pediatric diagnostic guidelines for BPI. This is an important start because almost all agree it is inappropriate to generalize criteria developed on adults to children and adolescents. Danner et al. (2009) suggested expanding the phenotypes (ways the disorder is thought to present): In addition to what they call the narrow phenotype (which is outlined in the DSM criteria), there should be two additional phenotypes. The first would be one that includes episodes of shorter duration (1–3 days) and the second would involve episodic irritability; the latter might be called severe mood and behavioral dysregulation (SMD) and could include hyperarousal, markedly increased reactivity to negative emotional stimuli, and abnormal mood present for at least 12 months without symptom-free periods of at least 2 months. Danner and colleagues (2009) tried to differentiate normal from abnormal behavior at different ages. For example, they considered normal a 7-year-old who is highly energetic and happy at a party or when seeing family members; they considered abnormal a 7-year-old who dances around her classroom singing about how wonderful the world is. For a sample 11-year-old, they suggest it is normal for him to zoom around the house gathering up football equipment the night before a first game; it is abnormal for the same 11-year-old to gather his football gear, organize and shine his toy car collection, and start several homework assignments without finishing any of these endeavors.

Youngstrom, Birmaher, and Findling (2008) suggested that the following symptoms have high specificity to pediatric bipolar disorder: elated, expansive, or euphoric mood; frequent and intense mood swings and lability; decreased need for sleep; and hypersexuality. Symptoms that may signal BPI in adults but not in pediatric bipolar disorder include irritable mood and distractibility (particularly because ADHD is often comorbid with BPI). Youngstrom and colleagues (2008) emphasized that Bipolar Disorder Not-Otherwise-Specified was to be thought of as on a spectrum with BPI, even though that requires the "core-positive" symptoms of abnormally elevated, expansive, or irritable mood. Here we see something of the contradictions inherent in this research area: on the one hand, Youngstrom et al. (2008) suggest irritable mood is not illustrative of BPI in children, while also listing it as a core-positive symptom.

The problems with the exponential increase in diagnosing pediatric bipolar disorder are many. In many children, rapid mood swings can be normal. The treatment guidelines (Kowatch et al., 2005) admit that "no one can say for sure what these children will look like when they grow up" (p. 214). This is a disturbing statement because BPI, properly diagnosed, is thought to be a chronic disorder. The authors of the treatment guidelines admit that the DSM symptoms for adult mania are problematic when used for children, but then they recommend continuing to use them. Overall, the treatment guidelines fail to draw distinctions between normal children and those really afflicted with BPI (Sahling, 2009).

It is also disturbing that each year, powerful mood-stabilizing and antipsychotic medications are being prescribed in greater numbers to children thought to have some variation of bipolar disorder—despite a lack of evidence for their efficacy, their high numbers of side effects, and their potential lethality. In particular, there is a problematically high comorbidity between bipolar disorder and ADHD in children, ranging from 60–98% (DelBello, 2004; Olfman, 2007). It has been suggested that what some clinicians are diagnosing as symptoms of bipolar disorder may be iatrogenically-induced side effects of stimulant medications used to treat ADHD (Masi et al., 2006; Olfman, 2007). Until methodologically sound research explores these issues more fully, clinicians would be wise to assume early-onset BPI is no earlier than age 13. Until we can untangle the rich spectrum of normal childhood behavior from what is clinically significant—using indices of distress and impairment as well as longitudinal studies to validate our observations—we should take as conservative an approach as possible to the idea that children can be diagnosed with any variation of bipolar disorder.

As for Dr. Joseph Biederman, he was under investigation as early as 2009 for failing to report over $1 million dollars paid to him by drug companies related to his work on childhood BPI disorder. According to a story from the *New York Times*, Biederman failed to tell university officials about more than a million dollars received from drug makers from 2000 to 2007. In addition, he promised Johnson & Johnson research results that would benefit the drug company apparently prior to doing the research being proposed (Harris, 2009). In 2012, Johnson & Johnson tentatively agreed to a $2.2 billion settlement to resolve a federal investigation into the company's marketing. This included a $400 million fine for illegal promotion of Risperdal/resperidone, one of the drugs Johnson & Johnson paid Dr. Biederman to investigate (Citizens Commission on Human Rights International, 2012). Biederman was disciplined by Harvard University, where he was faculty, for violating conflict-of-interest policies (Yu, 2011). No further information was available at the time of this writing.

## Summary

This chapter has provided a quick overview of BPI: what it is, who typically experiences its symptoms, what some of its causes are thought to be, and how it is usually treated. Other issues, such as the validity of Bipolar Spectrum Disorder and pediatric BPI, have also been discussed. Regardless of the age at onset or the degree of severity of symptoms, it should be noted that BPI is a significantly impairing disorder. It can have multiple causes and affect all domains of a person's life. On a more positive note, however, the disorder is treatable; and different treatment approaches are utilized to address the multiple causes of the disorder as well as the different areas of a person's life it affects. Although the disorder is unlikely to be cured, there is a significant amount of success in its treatment; and, as discussed earlier, the best treatment success is a product of an Integral approach to treatment—looking at the whole person in context.

## Review Questions

1. What is the best way to describe the etiology of Bipolar I Disorder?
2. Reviewing the different brain structures that may be involved in BPI, what seem to be differences in the brains of people suffering from BPI compared to unaffected controls?
3. What are the common medications used to treat BPI, and what do we know about how they work?
4. What psychological variables can trigger or exacerbate symptoms of BPI?
5. What is the relationship between structured schedules and BPI relapses?
6. Why is pediatric BPI such a questionable diagnosis? What are the political pressures that may be keeping it alive?
7. Assume an educated 29-year-old client correctly diagnosed with BPI Disorder asks you how she got it. What would you tell her?

## References


Adler, C. M., Adams, J., DelBello, M. P., Holland, S. K., Schmithorst, V., Levine, A., . . . Stratkowski, S. M. (2006). Evidence of white matter pathology in bipolar disorder adolescents experiencing their first episode of mania: A diffusion tensor imaging study. *American Journal of Psychiatry, 163,* 322–324.

Akiskal, H. S., & Benazzi, F. (2006). The DSM-IV and ICD-10 categories of recurrent [major] depressive and bipolar II disorders: evidence that they lie on a dimensional spectrum. *Journal of Affective Disorders, 92,* 45–54.

Alloy, L. B., Urosevic, S., Abramson, L. Y., Jager-Hyman, S., Nusslock, R., Whitehouse, W. G., & Hogan, M. (2012). Progression along the bipolar spectrum: A longitudinal study of predictors of conversion from bipolar spectrum conditions to bipolar I and bipolar II. *Journal of Abnormal Psychology, 121,* 16–27

American Psychiatric Association (APA). (2000a). *Diagnostic and statistical manual of mental disorders* (4th ed., text revision). Washington, DC: Author.

American Psychiatric Association (APA). (2000b). *Practice guidelines for the treatment of psychiatric disorders: Compendium 2000.* Washington, DC: Author.

American Psychiatric Association. (2013). *Diagnostic and statistical manual of mental disorders* (5th ed.). Washington, DC: Author.

Andreazza, A. C., Kauer-Sant'Anna, M., Frey, B. N., Stertz, L., Zanotto, C., Ribeiro, L. et al. (2008). Effects of mood stabilizers on DNA damage in an animal model of mania. *Journal of Psychiatry & Neuroscience, 33*(6), 516–524.

Angst, J., & Sellaro, R. (2000). Historical perspectives and natural history of bipolar disorder. *Biological Psychiatry, 48,* 445–457.

Ashburner, J., & Friston, K. J. (2001). Why "voxel-based morphometry" should be used with imperfectly registered images. *Neuroimage, 14,* 1238–1243.

Ball, J. R., Mitchell, P. B., Corry, J. C., Skillecorn, A., Smith, M., & Malhi, G. S. (2006). A randomized controlled trial of cognitive therapy for bipolar disorder: Focus on long-term change. *Journal of Clinical Psychiatry, 67,* 277–286.

Banaschewski, T. (2009). Editorial: Mood irritability—do we need to refine the diagnostic validity of oppositional defiant disorder and paediatric bipolar disorder? *The Journal of Child Psychology and Psychiatry, 50,* 201–202.

Baroni, A., Lunsford, J. R., Luckenbaugh, D. A., Toubin, K. E., & Leibenluft, E. (2009). Assessment review: The diagnosis of Bipolar I Disorder in children and adolescents. *Journal of Child Psychology and Psychiatry, 50,* 203–215.

Baughman, F. (2006). There is no such thing as a psychiatric disorder/disease/chemical imbalance. *PLoS Medicine, 3,* 318–319.

Baum, A. E., Akula, N., Cabanero, M., Cardona, I., Corona, W., Klemens, B., . . . McMahon, F. J. (2008). A genome-wide association study implicates diacylglycerol kinase eta (DGKH) and several other genes in the etiology of bipolar disorder. *Molecular Psychiatry, 13,* 197–207.

Belmaker, R. H. (2004). Medical progress: Bipolar Disorder. *The New England Journal of Medicine, 351,* 476–486.

Berk, M., Dodd, S., Kauer-Sant'Anna, M., Malhi, G. S., Bourin, M., Kapczinski, F., & Norman, T. (2007). Dopamine dysregulation syndrome: Implications for a dopamine hypothesis of bipolar disorder. *Acta Psychiatrica Scandinavica, 116*(Suppl. 434), 41–49.

Bernstein, D., Penner, L. A., Clarke-Stewart, A., & Roy, E. (2008). *Psychology* (8th ed.). Florence, KY: Wadsworth Publishing.

Bertelsen, A. (2004). Contributions of Danish registers to understanding psychopathology: Thirty years of collaboration with Irving I. Gottesman. In L. F. DiLalla (Ed.), *Behavior genetics principles: Perspective in development, personality and psychopathology* (pp. 123–133). Washington, DC: American Psychological Association.

Biederman, J., Faraone, S., Mick, E., Wozniak, J., Chen, L., Ouellette, C., . . . Lelon, E. (1996). Attention-deficit hyperactivity disorder and juvenile mania: An overlooked co-morbidity? *Journal of the American Academy of Child and Adolescent Psychiatry, 35,* 997–1008.

Birmaher, B., & Axelson, D. (2006). Course and outcome of bipolar spectrum disorder in children and adolescents: A review of the existing literature. *Development and Psychopathology, 18,* 1023–1035.

Bookstein, F. L. (2001). "Voxel-based morphometry" should not be used with imperfectly registered images. *Neuroimage, 14,* 1454–1462.

Brambilla, P., Bellani, M., Yeh, P. H., Soares, J. C., & Tansella, M. (2009). White matter connectivity in bipolar disorder. *International Review of Psychiatry, 21,* 380–386.

Carlson, M., & Miller, N. (1987). Explanation of the relation between negative mood and helping. *Psychological Bulletin, 102,* 91–108.

Carlson, N. R. (2005). *Foundations of physiological psychology* (6th ed.). Boston, MA: Pearson.

Chang, K., Adleman, N. E., Dienes, K., Simeonova, D. J., Menon, V., & Reiss, A. (2004). Anomalous prefrontal-subcortical activation in familial pediatric Bipolar Disorder: A functional magnetic resonance imaging investigation. *Archives of General Psychiatry, 61,* 781–792.

Chang, K. D. (2008). The bipolar spectrum in children and adolescents: Developmental issues. *Journal of Clinical Psychiatry, 69*(3), e9.

Cialdini, R. B., & Fultz, J. (1990). Interpreting the negative mood-helping literature via "mega" analysis: A contrary view. *Psychological Bulletin, 107,* 210–214.

Citizens Commission on Human Rights International. (2012). The business of ADHD. Retrieved from http://www.cchrint.org/tag/joseph-biederman/page/2/

Coufal, N. G., Garcia-Perez, J. L., Peng, G., Yeo, G. W., Mu, Y., Lovci, M. T., . . . Gage, F. H. (2009). L1 retrotransposition in human neural progenitor cells. *Nature, 460,* 1127–1133.

Craddock, N., & Owen, M. J. (2007). Rethinking psychosis: The disadvantages of a dichotomous classification now outweigh the advantages. *World Psychiatry, 6,* 84–91.

Danner, S., Fristad, M. A., Arnold, L. E., Youngstrom, E. A., Birmaher, B., Horwitz, S. M., . . . The LAMS group. (2009). Early-onset bipolar spectrum disorders: Diagnostic issues. *Clinical Child and Family Psychological Review, 12,* 271–293.

De Abreu, J. N., Lafer, B., Baca-Garcia, E., & Oquendo, M. A. (2009). Suicidal ideation and suicide attempts in bipolar disorder type I: an update for the clinician. *Revista Brasileira de Psiquiatria, 31,* 223–234.

Dean, B., Scarr, E., & MacLeod, M. (2005). Changes in hippocampal $GABA_A$ receptor subunit composition in bipolar 1 disorder. *Molecular Brain Research, 138,* 145–155.

DelBello, M. (2004). Diagnostic complexities and treatment issues in childhood bipolar disorder. *Medscape Psychiatry and Mental Health, 2.* Retrieved from http://www.medscape.com/viewartical/491489

Dias, V. V., Brissos, S., & Carita, A. I. (2008). Clinical and neurocognitive correlates of insight in patients with bipolar I disorder in remission. *Acta Psychiatry Scandinavia, 117,* 28–34.

Dohrenwend, B. S., Krasnoff, L., Askenasy, A. R., & Dohrenwend, B. P. (1978). Exemplification of a method for scaling life events: The PERI Life Events Scale. *Journal of Health and Social Behavior, 19,* 205–229.

Duffy, A. (2007). Does bipolar disorder exist in children? A selected review. *The Canadian Journal of Psychiatry, 52,* 409–417.

Emsell, L., & McDonald, C. (2009). The structural neuroimaging of bipolar disorder. *International Review of Psychiatry, 21,* 297–313.

Evardsen, J., Torgersen, S., Røysamb, E., Lygren, S., Skre, I., Onstad, S., & Øien, P. A. (2008). Heritability of bipolar spectrum disorders. Unity or heterogeneity? *Journal of Affective Disorders, 106*(3), 229–240.

Falret, J. (1854). Memoire sur la folie circulaire. *Bulletin de la Academie Imperiale de Medicin, 19,* 382–400.

Fields, R. D. (2009). *The other brain: From dementia to schizophrenia, how new discoveries about the brain are revolutionizing medicine and science.* New York: Simon & Schuster.

Fields, R. D. (2010). Change in the brain's white matter. *Science, 330,* 768–769.

Fields, R. D. (2011). The hidden brain: Flashy neurons may get the attention, but a class of cells called glia are behind most of the brain's work—and many of its diseases. *Scientific American Mind, 22,* 53–59.

Fornito, A., Malhi, G. S., Lagopoulos, J., Ivanovski, B., Wood, S. J., Velakoulis, D., . . . Yucel, M. (2007). *In vivo* evidence for early neurodevelopmental anomaly of the anterior cingulate cortex in bipolar disorder. *Acta Psychiatry Scandanavia, 116,* 467–472.

Fountoulakis, K. N., & Vieta, E. (2008). Treatment of bipolar disorder: A systematic review of available data and clinical perspectives. *International Journal of Neuropsychopharmacology, 11,* 999–1029.

Frank, E. (2000). Interpersonal and social rhythm therapy: Managing the chaos of bipolar disorder. *Biological Psychiatry, 48*(6), 593–604.

Frazier, J. A., Ahn, M. S., DeJong, S., Bent, E. K., Breeze, J. L., & Guiliano, A. J. (2005). Magnetic resonance imaging studies in early-onset bipolar disorder: A critical review. *Harvard Review of Psychiatry, 13,* 125–140.

Gage, F. H., & Muotri, A. R. (2012). What makes each brain unique? How can identical twins grow up with different personalities? "Jumping genes" move around in neurons and alter the way they work. *Scientific American, 306,* 26–31.

Ghaemi, S. N., Ko, J. Y., & Goodwin, F. K. (2002). "Cade's disease" and beyond: Misdiagnosis, antidepressant use, and a proposed definition for bipolar spectrum disorder. *Canadian Journal of Psychiatry, 47,* 125–134.

Gijsman, H. J., Cohen, A. F., & van Gerven, J. M. A. (2004). The application of the principles of clinical drug development to pharmacological challenge tests of the serotonergic system. *Journal of Psychopharmacology, 18,* 7–13.

Goldstein, B. I., Shamseddeen, W., Axelson, D. A., Kalas, C., Monk, K., Brent, D. A., . . . Birmaher, B. (2010). Clinical demographic and familial correlates of bipolar spectrum disorders among offspring of parents with bipolar disorder. *Journal of the American Academy of Child and Adolescent Psychiatry, 49,* 388–396.

Goodman, L. A., Salyers, M. P., Mueser, K. T., Rosenberg, S. D., Swartz, M., Essock, S. M., et al. (2001). Recent victimization in women and men with severe mental illness: Prevalence and correlates. *Journal of Traumatic Stress, 14,* 615–632.

Goodwin, F. K., & Jamison, K. R. (2007). *Manic-depressive illness: Bipolar disorders and recurrent depression.* New York: Oxford University Press.

Gottesman, I. I., & Gould, T. D. (2003). The endophenotype concept in psychiatry: Etymology and strategic intentions. *American Journal of Psychiatry, 160,* 636–645.

Gottesman, I. I., & Shields, J. (1973). Genetic theorizing and schizophrenia. *British Journal of Psychiatry, 122,* 15–30.

Grangeon, M. C., Seixas, C., Quarantini, L. C., Miranda-Scippa, A., Pompili, M., Steffens, D. C., . . . Reis de Oliveira, I. (2010). White matter hyperintensities and their association with suicidality in major affective disorders: A meta-analysis of magnetic resonance imaging studies. *Central Nervous System Spectrum, 15,* 375–381.

Grunze, H., Vieta, E., Goodwin, G. M., Bowden, C., Licht, R. W., Moller, H. J., Kaser, S., & WFSBP task force on treatment guidelines for bipolar disorders. (2009). The World Federation of Societies of Biological Psychiatry (WFSBP) guidelines for the biological treatment of bipolar disorders: Update 2009 on the treatment of acute mania. *The World Journal of Biological Psychiatry, 10,* 85–116.

Hajek,T.,Bernier,D.,Slaney,C.,Propper,L.,Schmidt,M., Carrery, N., . . . Alda, M. (2008). A comparison of affected and unaffected relatives of patients with bipolar disorder using proton magnetic resonance spectroscopy. *Journal of Psychiatry & Neuroscience, 33*(6), 531–540.

Hammen, C., & Gitlin, M. J. (1997). Stress reactivity in bipolar patients and its relation to prior history of the disorder. *American Journal of Psychiatry, 154,* 856–857.

Harris, G. (2009, March 20). Drug maker told studies would aid it, papers say. *New York Times,* p. A16.

Hasler, G., Drevets, W. C., Gould, T. D., Gottesman I. I., & Manji, H. K. (2005). Toward constructing an endophenotype strategy for bipolar disorders. *Biological Psychiatry, 60,* 93–105.

Havens, L. L., & Ghaemi, S. N. (2005). Existential despair and bipolar disorder: The therapeutic alliance as a mood stabilizer. *American Journal of Psychotherapy, 59*(2), 137–147.

Hayward, P., Wong, G., Bright, J. A., & Lam, D. (2002). Stigma and self-esteem in manic depression: An exploratory study. *Journal of Affective Disorders, 69*, 61–67.

Healy, D. (2006). The latest mania: Selling bipolar disorder. PloS Medicine at http://www.plosmedicine.org/article/info%3Adoi%2F10.1371%2Fjournal.pmed.0030185 retrieved March 4, 2014.

Healy, D. (2008). *Mania: A short history of Bipolar Disorder*. Baltimore, MD: Johns Hopkins Press.

Hiremani, R. M., Thirthalli, J., Tharayil, B. S., & Gangadhar, B. N. (2008). Double-blind randomized controlled study comparing short-term efficacy of bifrontal and bitemporal electroconvulsive therapy in acute mania. *Bipolar Disorders, 10,* 701–707.

Holmes, T. H., & Rahe, R. H. (1967). The social readjustment rating scale. *Journal of Psychosomatic Research, 11*(2), 213–218.

Ingersoll, R. E., & Rak, C. F. (2006). *Psychopharmacology for helping professionals: An integral exploration*. Pacific Grove, CA: Brooks Cole.

Insell, T. R. (2009). Disruptive insights into psychiatry: Transforming a clinical discipline. *The Journal of Clinical Investigation, 119,* 700–705.

Jackson, G. E. (2006). A curious consensus: "Brain scans prove disease?" *Ethical Human Psychology and Psychiatry, 8*, 55–60.

Jairam, R., Prabjuswamy, M., & Dullur, P. (2012). Do we really know how to treat a child with Bipolar Disorder or one with severe mood dysregulation? Is there a magic bullet? *Depression Research and Treatment, 2012,* 1–9.

Javadapour, A., Malhi, G. S., Ivanovski, B., Chen, X., Wen, W., & Sachdeve, P. (2007). Increased anterior cingulate cortex volume in bipolar I disorder. *The Australian and New Zealand Journal of Psychiatry, 41,* 910–916.

Johannsen, W. (1911). The genotype conception of heredity. *American Naturalist, 45,* 129–159.

Jones, S. H., Hare, D. J., & Evershed, K. (2005). Actigraphic assessment of circadian activity and sleep patterns in bipolar disorder. *Bipolar Disorders, 7,* 176–186.

Kafantaris, V., Kingsley, P., Ardekani, B., Saito, E., Lencz, T., Lim, K., & Szeszko, P. (2009). Lower orbital frontal white matter integrity in adolescents with bipolar I disorder. *Journal of the American Academy of Child and Adolescent Psychiatry, 48,* 79–86.

Kandel, E. R. (2005). *Psychiatry, psychoanalysis and the new biology of mind.* Washington, DC: American Psychiatric Association.

Kierkegaard, S. (1954). *Fear and trembling and the sickness unto death*. Garden City, NY: Doubleday.

Konarski, J. Z., McIntyre, R. S., Kennedy, S. H., Rafi-Tari, S., Soczynska, J. K., & Ketter, T. A. (2008). Volumetric neuroimaging investigations in mood disorders: Bipolar disorder versus major depressive disorder. *Bipolar Disorders, 10,* 1–37.

Kowatch, R. A., Fristad, M., Birmaher, B., Wagner, K. D., Findling, R. L., Hellander, M., & The Child Psychiatric Workgroup on Bipolar Disorder. (2005). Treatment guidelines for children and adolescents with bipolar disorder. *Journal of the American Academy of Child & Adolescent Psychiatry, 44,* 213–235.

Kruger, S., Seminowicz, S., Goldapple, K., Kennedy, S. H., & Mayberg H. S. (2003). State and trait influences on mood regulation in Bipolar Disorder: Blood flow differences with an acute mood challenge. *Biological Psychiatry, 54,* 1274–1283.

Lewine, R. R. J., Hudgins, P., Brown, F., Caudle, J., & Risch, S. C. (1995). Differences in qualitative brain morphology findings in schizophrenia, major depression, bipolar disorder and normal volunteers. *Schizophrenia Research, 15,* 253–259.

Lin, P. I., & Mitchell, B. D. (2008). Approaches for unraveling the joint genetic determinants of schizophrenia and bipolar disorder. *Schizophrenia Bulletin, 34,* 791–797.

Margulies, D. M., Weintraub, S., Basile, J., Grover, P. J., & Carlson, G. A. (2012). Will disruptive mood dysregulation disorder reduce false diagnosis of bipolar disorder in children? *Bipolar Disorder, 14,* 488–496.

Masi, G., Perugi, G., Toni, C., Millepiedi, S., Bertini, N., & Pfanner, C. (2006). Attention-deficit hyperactivity disorder–bipolar comorbidity in children and adolescents. *Bipolar Disorders, 8,* 373–381.

McDonald, C., Bullmore, E., Sham, P., Chitnis, X., Suckling, J., MacCabe, J., . . . Murray, R. M. (2005). Regional volume deviations of brain structure in schizophrenia and psychotic bipolar disorder: Computational morphometry study. *British Journal of Psychiatry, 186,* 369–377.

McDonald, C., Zanelli, J., Rabe-Hesketh, S., Ellison-Wright, I., Sham, P., Kalidindi, S., . . . Kennedy, M. (2004). Meta-analysis of magnetic resonance imaging brain morphometry studies in bipolar disorder. *Biological Psychiatry, 56,* 411–417.

McGrath, C. L., Glatt, S. J., Sklar, P., Le-Niculescu, H., Kuczenski, R., Doyle, A. E., . . . Tsuang, M. T. (2009). Evidence for genetic association of *RORB* with bipolar disorder. *BMC Psychiatry, 7,* 1–9.

McGuffin, P., Rijsdijk, F., Andrew, M., Sham, P., Katz, R., & Cardno, A. (2003). The heritability of bipolar affective disorder and the genetic relationship to unipolar depression. *Archives of General Psychiatry, 60,* 497–502.

McIntosh, A. M., Job, D. E., Moorhead, W. J., Harrison, L. K., Whalley, H. C., Johnstone, E. C., & Lawrie, S. M. (2005). Genetic liability to schizophrenia or bipolar disorder and its relationship to brain structure. *American Journal of Medical Genetics, 141B,* 76–83.

Merikangas, K. R., Akiskal, H. S., Angst, J., Greenberg, P. E., Hirschfeld, R. M. A., Petukhova, M., & Kessler, R. C. (2007). Lifetime and 12-month prevalence of bipolar spectrum disorder in the national comorbidity survey replication. *Archives of General Psychiatry, 64,* 543–552.

Mick, E., Wozniak, J., Eilens, T. E., Biederman, J., & Faraone, S. V. (2009). Family-based association study of the BDNF, COMT, and serotonin transporter genes and DSM-IV bipolar-I disorder in children. *BMC Psychiatry, 9*(2), 1–6.

Miklowitz, D. A., Otto, M. W., Frank, E., Reilly-Harrington, N. A., Wisniewski, S. R., Kogan, J. N., . . . Sachs, G. S. (2007). Psychosocial treatments for bipolar depression: A 1-year randomized trial from the Systematic Treatment Enhancement Program. *Archives of General Psychiatry, 64,* 419–426.

Miklowitz, D. J. (2002). *The Bipolar Disorder survival guide: What you and your family need to know.* New York, NY: The Guilford Press.

Miklowitz, D. J., & Craighead, W. E. (2007). Psychosocial treatments for Bipolar Disorder. In P. E. Nathan & J. M. Gorman (Eds.), *A guide to treatment that works* (3rd ed., pp. 309–322). New York: Oxford University Press.

Miklowitz, D. J., & Johnson, S. L. (2008). Bipolar Disorder. In W. E. Craighead, D. J. Miklowitz, & L. W. Craighead (Eds.), *Psychopathology: History, diagnosis, and empirical foundations* (pp. 366–402). New York: Wiley.

Milton, J., & Wiseman, R. (1999). Does psi exist? Lack of replication of an anomalous process of information transfer. *Psychological Bulletin, 125,* 387–391.

Miro, X., Meier, S., Dreisow, M. L., Frank, J., Stromaier, J., Breuer, R., . . . Zimmer, A. (2012). Studies in humans and mice implicate neurocan in the etiology of mania. *American Journal of Psychiatry, 169,* 982–990.

Moller, H. J., & Nasrallah, H. J. (2003). Treatment of bipolar disorder. *Journal of Clinical Psychiatry, 64*(Suppl. 6), 9–17.

Moreno, C., Laje, G., Blanco, C., Jiang, H., Schmidt, A., & Olfson, M. (2007). National trends in outpatient diagnosis and treatment of bipolar disorder in youth. *Archives of General Psychiatry, 64,* 1032–1039.

Mukherjee, S., Sackeim, H. A., & Schnur, D. B. (1994). Electroconvulsive therapy of acute manic episodes: A review of 50 years' experience. *The American Journal of Psychiatry, 151,* 169–176.

Niculescu, A. B., Lulow, L. L., Ogden, C. A., Le-Niculescu, H., Salomon, D. R., Schork, N. J., . . . Lohr, J. B. (2006). PhenoChipping of psychotic disorders: A novel approach for deconstructing and quantitating psychiatric phenotypes. *American Journal of Medical Genetics Part B, 141B,* 653–662.

Olfman, S. (Ed.). (2007). *Bipolar children.* Westport, CT: Praeger Publishers.

O'Sullivan, S. S., Evands, A. H., & Lees, A. J. (2009). Dopamine dysregulation syndrome: An overview of its epidemiology, mechanisms and management. *CNS Drugs, 23,* 157–166.

Papiol, S., Rosa, A., Gutierrez, B., Maring, B., Salgado, P., Catalan, R., . . . Fananas, L. (2004). Interleukin-1 cluster is associated with genetic risk for schizophrenia and bipolar disorder. *Journal of Medical Genetics, 41,* 219–223.

Paris, J. (2009). The bipolar spectrum: A critical perspective. *Harvard Review of Psychiatry, 17,* 206–213.

Petersen, M. (2008). *Our daily meds: How the pharmaceutical companies transformed themselves into slick marketing machines and hooked the nation on prescription drugs.* New York: Sarah Crichton Books.

Phillips, M. L., Drevets, M. C., Rauch, S. R., & Lane, R. (2003). Neurobiology of emotion perception I: The neural basis of normal emotional perception. *Biological Psychiatry, 54,* 504–514.

Pliszka, S. R. (2003). *Neuroscience for the mental health clinician.* New York: Guilford.

Pompili, M., Tondo, L., Grispini, A., De Pisa, E., Lester, D., Angeletti, G., . . . Tatarelli, R. (2006). Suicide attempts in bipolar disorder patients. *Clinical Neuropsychiatry: Journal of Treatment Evaluation, 3,* 327–331.

Post, R. M. (1992). Transduction of psychosocial stress into the neurobiology of recurrent affective disorder. *American Journal of Psychiatry, 149,* 999–1010.

Post, R. M., Alshuler, L. L., Leverich, G. S., Frye, M. A., Nolen, W. A., Kupka, R. W., . . . Denicoff, K. D. (2006). Mood switch in bipolar depression: Comparison of adjunctive venlafaxine, bupropion and sertraline. *British Journal of Psychiatry, 189,* 124–131.

Post, R. M., Ballenger, J. C., & Goodwin, F. K. (1980). Cerebrospinal fluid studies of neurotransmitter function in manic and depressive illness. In J. H. Wood (Ed.), *The neurobiology of cerebrospinal fluid* (Vol. 1, pp. 57–104). New York, NY: Plenum Press.

PsychLink Video. (2001). *What makes a drug a good mood stabilizer?* New York: Interactional Medical Networks.

Riedel, H. P. R., Heiby, E. M., & Kopetskie, S. (2001). Psychological behaviorism theory of bipolar disorder. *The Psychological Record, 51,* 507–532.

Rihmer, Z. (2009). Suicide and bipolar disorder. In H. K. Manji (Ed.), *Bipolar depression: Molecular neurobiology, clinical diagnosis and pharmacotherapy* (pp. 47–56). Cambridge, MA: Birkhauser.

Rothbaum, B. O., & Astin, M. C. (2000). Integration of pharmacotherapy and psychotherapy for Bipolar Disorder. *Journal of Clinical Psychiatry, 61*(Suppl. 9), 68–75.

Rush, A. J. (2003). Toward an understanding of bipolar disorder and its origin. *Journal of Clinical Psychiatry, 64*(Suppl.), 4–17.

Sachs, G. S., & Rush, A. J. (2003). Response, remission and recovery in bipolar disorder: What are realistic treatment goals? *Journal of Clinical Psychiatry, 64*(Suppl. 6), 18–22.

Sahling, D. L. (2009). Pediatric bipolar disorder: Underdiagnosed or fiction? *Ethical Human Psychology and Psychiatry, 11,* 215–228.

Santos, A. I., Teijeira, C., SanchezMorla, E. M., Bescos, M. J., Argudo, I., Torrijos, S., . . . Cabranes-Diaz, J. A. (2010). Sustained attention as a potential endophenotype for bipolar disorder. *Acta Psychiatric Scandinavia, 122,* 235–245.

Sasaki, T., Matsuki, N., & Ikegaya, Y. (2011). Action-potential modulation during axonal conduction. *Science, 331,* 599–601.

Scherk, H., Kemmer, C., Usher, J., Reith, W., Falkai, P., & Gruber, O. (2008). No change to grey and white matter volumes in bipolar I disorder patients. *European Archives of Psychiatry, 258,* 345–349.

Schloesser, R. J., Huang, J., Klein, P. S., & Manji, H. K. (2008). Cellular plasticity cascades in the pathophysiology and treatment of bipolar disorder. *Neuropsychopharmacology, 33,* 110–133.

Schwarzkopf, S. B., Nasrallah, H. A., Olson, S. C., et al. (1989). Perinatal complications and genetic loading in schizophrenia: Preliminary findings. *Psychiatric Research, 56,* 162–180.

Scott, J. (1995). Psychotherapy for Bipolar Disorder. *The British Journal of Psychiatry, 167,* 581–588.

Scott, J., & Colom, F. (2005). Psychosocial treatments for bipolar disorder. *Psychiatric Clinics of North America, 28,* 371–384.

Shermer, M. (2008). Why you should be skeptical of brain scans: Colorful scans have lulled us into an oversimplified conception of the brain as a modular machine. *Scientific American Mind, 19,* 67–71.

Shi, J., Badner, J. A., Hattori, E., Potash, J. B., Willour, V. L., McMahon, F. J., . . . Liu, C. (2008). Neurotransmission and bipolar disorder: A systematic family-based association study. *American Journal of Medical Genetics Part B (Neuropsychiatric Genetics), 147*(7), 1270–1277.

Smith, L. A., Cornelius, V., Warnock, A., Bell, A., & Young, A. H. (2007). Effectiveness of mood stabilizers and antipsychotics in the maintenance phase of bipolar disorder: a systematic review of randomized controlled trials. *Bipolar Disorders, 9,* 394–412.

Sobczak, S., Honig, A., van Duinen, M. A., & Riedel, W. J. (2002). Serotonergic dysregulation in bipolar disorders: A literature review of serotonergic challenge studies. *Bipolar Disorder, 4*(6), 347–356.

Suppes, T., Swann, A. C., Dennehy, E. B., Habermacher, E. D., Mason Crimson, M. L., Toprac, M. G., . . . Altshuler, K. Z. (2009). Texas Medication Algorithm Project: Development and feasibility testing of a treatment algorithm for patients with bipolar disorder. *Journal of Clinical Psychiatry, 62,* 439–447.

Thase, M. E., Jindal, R., & Howland, R. H. (2002). Biological aspects of depression. In C. L. Hammen & I. H. Gotlib (Eds.), *Handbook of depression* (pp. 192–218). New York: Guilford.

Varga, M., Babovic, A., Flekkoy, K., Ronneberg, U., Landro, N. I., David, A. S., & Opjordsmoen, S. (2009). Reduced insight in bipolar I disorder: Neurofunctional and neurostructural correlates. A preliminary study. *Journal of Affective Disorders, 116,* 56–63.

Walsh, M. A., Royal, A., Bronw, L. H., Barrantes-Vidal, N., & Kwapil, T. R. (2012). Looking for bipolar spectrum psychopathology: Identification and expression in daily life. *Comprehensive Psychiatry, 53*, 409–421.

Wang, J. F. (2007). Defects of mitochondrial electron transport chain in bipolar disorder: Implications for mood-stabilizing treatment. *The Canadian Journal of Psychiatry, 52,* 753–762.

Wright, I. C., Rabe-Hesketh, S., Woodruff, P. W., David, A. S., Murray, R. M., & Bullmore, E. T. (2000). Meta-analysis of regional brain volumes in schizophrenia. *American Journal of Psychiatry, 157,* 16–25.

Yatham, L. N., Kennedy, S. H., Schaffer, A., Parikh, S. V., Beaulieu, S., O'Donovan, C., . . . Kapczinski, F. (2009). Canadian Network for Mood and Anxiety Treatment (CANMAT) and International Society for Bipolar Disorders (ISBD) collaborative update of CANMAT guidelines for the management of patients with bipolar disorder: Update 2009. *Bipolar Disorders, 11*, 225–255.

Yen, C.-F, Cheng, C.-P, Huang, C.-F, Yen, J.-Y, Ko, C.-H, & Chen, C.-S. (2008). Quality of life and its association with insight, adverse effects of medication and use of atypical antipsychotics in patients with bipolar disorder and schizophrenia in remission. *Bipolar Disorders, 10,* 617–624.

Yen, C.-F, Chen, C.-S, Yen, J.-Y, & Ko, C.-H. (2008). The predictive effect of insight on adverse clinical outcomes in bipolar I disorder: A two-year prospective study. *Journal of Affective Disorders, 108,* 121–127.

Young, L. T., Li, P. P., Lish, S. J., & Warsh, J. J. (1994). Cerebral cortex beta-adrenoceptor binding in bipolar affective disorder. *Journal of Affective Disorders, 30,* 89–92.

Young, L. T., & Wang, J. F. (2007). Applying molecular approaches to understand the etiology and treatment of bipolar disorder. *The Canadian Journal of Psychiatry, 52,* 751–752.

Youngstrom, E. A., Birmaher, B., & Findling, R. L. (2008). Pediatric bipolar disorder: Validity, phenomenology and recommendations for diagnosis. *Bipolar Disorders, 10,* 194–214.

Yu, X. (2011, July 2). Three professors face sanctions following Harvard Medical School inquiry. *The Harvard Crimson.* Retrieved from http://www.thecrimson.com/article/2011/7/2/school-medical-harvard-investigation/

# 7

# The Puzzle of Schizophrenia

Schizophrenia has been said to be the centerpiece of the psychotic disorders (Andreasan, 1999). Like Bipolar I Disorder, Schizophrenia appears to have a pervasive physiological basis that begins as genetic vulnerability or perhaps an in utero insult; it then develops slowly through what is called a prodromal period to a full-blown psychotic episode, and it usually leaves residual symptoms even when treated with medication and therapy. This chapter will repeat many of the same concepts discussed in the chapter on Bipolar I Disorder because researchers are coming to find common variables that may underlay both disorders. These concepts bear repeating because they are new to most of us (particularly those of us in nonmedical mental health fields). In this chapter we will summarize what we know about etiology, focusing particularly on the physiological clues researchers are trying to trace as well as discussing important psychological, cultural, and social variables in diagnosis and treatment.

In the *Diagnostic and Statistical Manual of Mental Disorders*, Fifth Edition (DSM-5; American Psychiatric Association [APA], 2013), the section previously titled "Schizophrenia and Other Psychotic Disorders" in earlier versions of the DSM has been changed to "Schizophrenia Spectrum and Other Psychotic Disorders." The DSM-IV-TR (APA, 2000) subtypes for Schizophrenia have been eliminated because they lacked reliability and validity. The idea of the "spectrum" as indicated in the title includes Schizotypal Personality Disorder, as this is now seen as a milder form of a psychotic disorder (although is technically still classified as a Personality Disorder). Also, it has been suggested that Schizophrenia may not be a unitary disorder and may be several different disorders with different etiologies (Allardyce, Gaebel, Zielasek, & van Os, 2007). If this is the case, again the spectrum idea may have greater clinical utility rather than thinking of Schizophrenia as a solitary disorder. Further, the DSM-5 Schizophrenia Spectrum is expected to be revised to include a "0–4" dimensional assessment so that clinicians can rate severity as part of the diagnosis (Pagsberg, 2013).

Currently we know that Schizophrenia has an approximate lifetime risk of .7–1.1%, but if a parent (or sibling) suffers the disorder, the risk for offspring rises to 10–12% (Costello, 2012). Schizophrenia in children younger than age 13 is considered very early onset, and its prevalence is 1 in 10,000. Early-onset Schizophrenia is between ages 13 and 17 (Masi & Liboni, 2011). Schizophrenia is more common in males than females; has a higher prevalence in lower-socioeconomic-status classes; is highly heritable, with genetic variables thought to represent 80% of vulnerability to the illness; and has a higher incidence in urban areas. Environmental factors thought to contribute to triggering genetic vulnerability include winter/spring birth, prenatal infection, famine, bullying, substance abuse, obstetric and perinatal complications, older fathers, and social stress (Cantor-Graae, 2007). There are multiple physiological anomalies associated with Schizophrenia but none conclusively point to an underlying cause. The diagnostic boundaries between Schizophrenia and other psychotic disorders are blurred (Stober et al., 2009). Remissions are generally incomplete, with persistent cognitive impairments that correlate with increased risk for substance use and abuse and suicidality (Tandon, Keshavan, & Nasrallah, 2008b).

## HISTORY OF THE DIAGNOSIS

Despite being one of the top 10 leading causes of disease-based disability in the world (World Health Organization, 2001) and the topic of approximately 5000 publications per year (Tandon et al., 2008b), we know very little about its etiology. In addition to this (or likely because of it), pharmacological treatments for Schizophrenia are at best "only modestly effective" (Tandon et al., 2008a, p. 4). As with every other disorder we discuss in this book, Schizophrenia has (as yet) no visible neuropathic markers—despite 20 years of efforts in the fast-developing brain sciences (Andreasan, 1999; Stober et al., 2009). This is incredibly frustrating for both those who suffer from the disorder and their loved ones. How can a condition so disabling be so difficult to "see" in the brain? Again, this reflects the brain's complexity as much as the fact that we are really just getting to the point where our technologies can allow us to view what is happening at the cellular level. What is noteworthy is that in the history of psychiatry and diagnosis of mental illness, although Schizophrenia has been given different labels, the symptoms listed to describe it have been fairly consistent across hundreds of years of exploration. This suggests that different researchers from different times have been looking at the same pervasive symptoms. But the question of what causes these symptoms remains unanswered. In a rare, candid passage, Allardyce et al. (2010) noted that "If our definition of schizophrenia does not represent a 'real' construct in nature, then it will not delineate the true pathology and causal mechanisms underlying psychosis; it will obfuscate etiology" (p. 2). Our current "best guess" is that Schizophrenia may actually be the end result of several disease processes that have what is called a multifactorial etiology (caused by multiple factors) in which multiple genes interact with each other and with environmental risk factors to cause what we see as the symptoms (Allardyce et al., 2010; Tandon, Nasrallah, & Keshavan, 2010).

The presentation of Schizophrenia (the phenotype) that is currently standard throughout the world developed in the 19th century (Regier, 2010). The current descriptions of Schizophrenia lean more toward clinical utility than providing any information about the fundamental nature or structure of Schizophrenia (Allardyce et al., 2007). One of the earliest labels for the disorder was coined by Benedict Morel in 1852 and later Emil Kraeplin in 1896—*demence precoce (dementia praecox)*, meaning "youthful insanity." This label was chosen by both clinicians because of the observed early onset (especially in males) in the late teens to early 20s. This is a pattern still seen today in many clients suffering from the disorder, although the onset in females tends to be later. The label "Schizophrenia" is probably not as accurate as it could be and has led to some misunderstandings about what the disorder is. The term *Schizophrenia* was coined by Eugene Bleuler and derived from the Greek *schizein*, which means "to cleave or cut." This etymology seems to have contributed to the misunderstanding that Schizophrenia involves a "split" personality.[1] Keshavan et al. (2013) has advocated eliminating the name "Schizophrenia" because it conveys an inaccurate characterization of the symptoms, has acquired a negative connotation (like "lunacy") and belies what we are learning neurobiologically about the disorder. Keshavan has suggested an acronym "CONCORD" which stands for "youth onset conative, cognitive and reality distortion" (Keshavan et al., 2013, p. 1). As Keshevan notes, we do not take lightly renaming a disorder but the label Schizophrenia seems to be obsolete.

Part of the reason the name is obsolete is that we now think of Schizophrenia more as a group of psychoses rather than a single entity. Bleuler (1911) was one of the first to point out that Schizophrenia may be more accurately described as a group of psychoses rather than a single entity—a conceptualization that, as noted, has evolved into the Schizophrenia Spectrum in the DSM-5, which contains almost a dozen different disorders, although, of course, many or all of them may share an underlying etiology. The DSM-5 includes Schizophrenia, Schizophreniform Disorder, Schizotypal Personality Disorder, Delusional Disorder, and Brief Psychotic Disorder, which differ mainly in duration of symptoms, with Brief Psychotic Disorder lasting 1 day to 1 month, Schizophreniform Disorder lasting 1 to 6 months, and Schizophrenia more than 6 months.

Bleuler (1911) also identified what he called the "4 A's" of the disorder: loose associations, affective blunting, autistic thinking, and ambivalence. What is interesting is that these are similar to the categories now in use of positive and negative symptoms (loose associations and autistic thinking being more related to what used to be called thought disorder, and affective blunting and ambivalence being what we now call negative symptoms). This pattern was continued in 1959 by Kurt Schneider (1959), who elaborated on this list with what he called first- and second-rank symptoms. First-rank symptoms correspond to what are now called positive symptoms (things that are present and shouldn't be, such as hallucinations, illusions, and delusions). Schneider first-rank symptoms included thought broadcasting, thought insertion, thought withdrawal, delusions, and hallucinations. His second-rank symptoms correspond to what are now called negative symptoms (things that should be present but are lacking) and included perplexity and emotional blunting. The English neurologist John Hughlings Jackson was the first to use the phrases positive symptoms and negative symptoms in the early 20th century. For Jackson (Berrios, 1985), positive symptoms included delusions, hallucinations, grandiosity, excitability, suspiciousness, and hostility; negative symptoms included emotional blunting, social withdrawal, and poor grooming and hygiene.

---

[1] There is an old joke that the psychiatrist told the client: "I have good news and bad news. The good news is I've figured out what is wrong with you—you are suffering from schizophrenia." The client said "what is the bad news?" The psychiatrist said "I'm going to have to charge you double now."

Currently, positive symptoms of Schizophrenia are thought to be excesses or distortions of normal functions and include hallucinations, illusions,[2] delusions, and paranoia. Negative symptoms appear to be a diminution or loss of normal functions and include affective blunting, poor hygiene and grooming, social withdrawal, lack of expressiveness, and few peer relationships (APA, 2013). The criteria for Schizophrenia proper include five characteristic symptoms (delusions, hallucinations, disorganized speech, grossly abnormal psychomotor behavior including catatonia, and negative symptoms). Clients should experience two or more of these symptoms over a 1-month period (less if successfully treated), and at least one of the symptoms should be delusions, hallucinations, or disorganized speech. In addition, the person should experience social or occupational dysfunction and continuous signs of disturbance for 6 months. Disorganized thinking is still thought to be an important feature of the disorder but because thoughts are expressed in speech, the current DSM focuses on disorganized speech—assuming it reflects what used to be called "thought disorder." Whereas the DSM-IV proposed five subtypes of Schizophrenia, these have been deleted in the DSM-5 due to low diagnostic stability.

There has been great dissatisfaction with the DSM concept of Schizophrenia in North America and even more so in Europe (Stober et al., 2009). Psychiatrists in the developing world have been said to assert that the current diagnosis ignores the issues of three-fourths of the world's population. As with other disorders, dimensional models and hybrid models (dimensions plus categories) were developed with the hope they would be considered for the DSM-5 (Dutta et al., 2007). The only real use of the dimensional models, though, was in the case of Personality Disorders. As such, the changes in the DSM-5 have addressed some of the validity and reliability issues (e.g., eliminating the subtypes of Schizophrenia), but in some ways this has moved from a less specific and more general understanding of Schizophrenia. Chances are this situation will not be adequately resolved unless we find the pathophysiological marker we are hoping to find underlying the disorder.

In the following section on etiology and pathophysiology, we will use the four-quadrant model of the Integral perspective to guide our discussion.

## ETIOLOGY AND PATHOPHYSIOLOGY

### Individual-Exterior (Upper-Right) Perspectives

**PHYSIOLOGICAL VARIABLES** This section of the chapter (like previous chapters) summarizes what we have gleaned from studies of the genome, brain, and central nervous system and their role in Schizophrenia. In this area, genetics and epigenetics are often thought of as primary etiological factors and the development of abnormal brain structures or processes are viewed as deriving from genetic and epigenetic variables. Although this is still speculative, this section will begin with genetic variables and studies in heritability and then move on to studies of brain structures and processes. As in Bipolar I Disorder, the concept of endophenotype is also part of the search for the etiology of Schizophrenia.

---

[2] Hallucinations differ from illusions in that the former are perceived stimuli where in fact there appear to be no stimuli; the latter are distortions of existing stimuli.

**MODELS AND FACTS** Keshavan, Tandon, Boutros, and Nasrallah (2008) (echoing Popper [1959/2002]) wrote that ". . . the scientific process is not simply a random sequence of fact gathering: the facts assembled will need to generate explanatory models from which testable hypotheses may be derived" (p. 100). Current explanatory models for Schizophrenia fall into three types: pathophysiological models, theories of pathogenesis, and etiological models. Pathophysiological models ask the question "what is wrong at the biological or neurobiological level?" that is causing the illness. Theories of pathogenesis focus on the timing and nature of the pathology (e.g., "when does this occur?"); this would include a developmental perspective such as derailment of synaptic pruning in adolescence. Finally, etiological models address the root of "why did this occur?" and focus on genetics, abnormal gene expression, and epigenetics (Keshavan et al., 2008). Keshavan and colleagues (2008) assert that only integrative theories that tie the facts together across three types of theories will likely unravel the puzzle.

Such integrative theories can be built only when biological markers consistent with the disorder can be used as endophenotypes. Recall from the chapter on Bipolar I Disorder that endophenotypes are intermediate phenotypes that will hopefully help researchers get closer to understanding the origin of the disorder (Gottesman & Shields, 1973). In order to be designated an endophenotypic marker, a biological marker must meet five criteria:

1. Be correlated/associated with the disorder in the relevant population
2. Exist independent of transitory states (particularly, it must be present in both periods of health and illness)
3. Be a heritable factor
4. Co-segregate with the illness in families in which the illness is present
5. Be present in unaffected family members more often than in the general population (Keshavan et al., 2008)

As you'll see, many of the biological markers being investigated in connection with Schizophrenia have small effect sizes (meaning they occur in some but not all afflicted subjects) and overlap with other disorders. This raises the question noted in Chapter 4 of whether severe mental illnesses are all actually variations on some common underlying factors (Allardyce et al., 2007). This further raises a question asked in Chapter 2: Could the entire system of categorical psychiatry be inadequate to account for common underlying factors? Even Emil Kraeplin, who dichotomized "dementia praecox" and "manic-depressive insanity" in the 19th century, came to doubt this approach and in 1920 suggested changing to a more dimensional model that allowed for common underlying etiological factors (Dutta et al., 2007). That said, let's review what we know about the heritability of Schizophrenia.

**HERITABILITY AND GENETICS** Schizophrenia ". . . definitely involves genetic factors the precise genes and gene-environment interactions are yet to be clarified" (Keshavan, Narallah, & Tandon, 2013, p. 4). Often when laypeople hear about genetic findings, they are frequently under the misguided impression that we have located "the gene" for this or that disorder. As noted in Chapter 4, there are to date no "single-gene" mental disorders. And to complicate things, genetic vulnerability must be understood in interaction with environmental stressors and risk factors, as none of these operate in isolation (Tsuang, Bar, Stone, & Faraone, 2004). As Stober et al. (2009) concluded, "the phenotypic complexity, together with the multifarious nature of the 'group' of 'schizophrenic psychoses' limits our ability to form a simple and logical biologically based hypothesis of the disease group" (p. 129). Schizophrenia shares many heritable factors with Bipolar I disorder, suggesting there may be an underlying genetic basis for both disorders that runs on a continuum. At the more severe end of the continuum, the person is afflicted with Schizophrenia; at the less severe end (if it is fair to use that phrase in regard to any of these disorders), the person is afflicted with Bipolar I Disorder (McIntosh et al., 2006). Ultimately, though, as Owen, Craddock, and O'Donovan (2005) caution, Schizophrenia is a disorder with a heterogeneous presentation involving multiple genes that may each have relatively small effects.

Although having a family member afflicted with Schizophrenia increases your risk from 1% to between 10 and 15%, two-thirds of cases occur without the client having an identified family member equally afflicted (Tandon et al., 2008b). One way that genetic risk is assessed is by looking for the disorder in children adopted away from parents, one of whom suffered from the disorder. A second way is studying children adopted by parents, one of whom later developed Schizophrenia. In support of the genetic basis of the disorder, we have known for over 50 years that the risk of the disorder is related to the presence of the illness in biological parents but not adoptive parents (Heston, 1966; Kety, Rosenthal, Wender, & Schulsinger, 1968). These studies refuted (and in a sense falsified) psychological explanations for the disorder like the misguided "double-bind" dynamic[3] proposed by Bateson, Jackson, Haley, and Weakland (1956). This was important work because in the mid-20th century, psychological explanations tended to focus blame on mothers using psychodynamic ideas that they withheld love (which, although it happens, does not "cause" Schizophrenia).

Dizygotic twins that share 50% of their genetic material have a 10–15% risk of developing Schizophrenia if their twin suffers from the disorder. This is similar to the increase in risk for siblings who have a brother or sister diagnosed with Schizophrenia (Kendler et al., 1993). In monozygotic twins (who share 100% of their genetic material), the risk of one twin developing Schizophrenia jumps to 40–50% if the other twin has the disorder (Sullivan, Kendler, & Neale, 2003). Here again we see the importance of environmental influences on gene expression. A recent breakthrough in this area is the so-called "jumping-gene" phenomenon. These are segments of DNA that can copy themselves and paste or insert themselves into new places in the genome, altering the activity of full-length genes and even including an ability to "turn on" neighboring genes. These mobile genes may play a role in our vulnerability to mental disorders as well as explaining things like how identical twins can develop such different personalities (Coufal et al., 2009; Gage & Muotri, 2012).

A quick review of terms may help understand the next section. A chromosome is an organized structure of DNA and proteins found in our cells. A gene is a molecular unit of heredity found on chromosomes, and an allele is one of two or more forms of a gene. Current thinking is that people at risk for Schizophrenia and Bipolar I Disorder may share specific vulnerability genes and "risk alleles" (Owen,

---

[3] The double-bind dynamic is an emotionally distressing dilemma where an individual receives two conflicting messages from the same person. In Schizophrenia, it was mistakenly believed the conflicting messages were one of love and one of rejection from the mother.

Craddock, & Jablensky, 2007). Genetic linkage is the tendency of certain alleles to be inherited together, and there appear to be some linkages that make people more vulnerable to Schizophrenia. Specific chromosomal regions are identified in afflicted individuals and their family members (of course this is always "some but not all") that pass the threshold for statistical significance (Craddock, O'Donovan, & Owen, 2005). It should be added that there are several experts who suggest that ". . . our genetic conceptualization of Schizophrenia is wrong and this flawed model is the reason for our difficulties in elucidating the precise nature of the genetic basis for Schizophrenia" (Tandon et al., 2008b, p. 9). Simply put, we may be looking in the wrong place but we may not know that until we explore further and understand more about genetics.

In addition to the DISC-1 gene implicated in depression, Bipolar I Disorder, and Schizophrenia (see Chapters 3 and 6), other studies draw correlations for the presence of individual genes (although no single gene is responsible for Schizophrenia). A study in the Icelandic population implicated a gene labeled NRG1—in particular, a combination of alleles at adjacent locations (also called a "haplotype") on NRG1. The same combination was found in a large sample of afflicted patients in Scotland (Thompson et al., 2007). A second gene under investigation for its relation to Schizophrenia is labeled DTNBP1. This gene codes for a ligand[4] called dystrobrevin-binding protein 1—also known as dysbindin. Dysbindin is found in neural tissue in the brain—especially in axon bundles and terminals in the cerebellum and hippocampus. There is a strong correlation between a certain dysbindin allele and Schizophrenia (Fanous et al., 2005). These are just two examples of several candidate genes and alleles under study. Again, the challenge is understanding what combination of vulnerability genes, alleles, life/environmental stressors, and genetic "switches" (gene expression) actually results in Schizophrenia.

**BRAIN STRUCTURES** As in Bipolar I Disorder, there have been consistent anomalies in brain structure and networks found in (again, in some but not all) people suffering from Schizophrenia. There are several studies correlating brain abnormalities, neurocognitive dysfunction, and both Schizophrenia and Bipolar I Disorder (Hartberg et al., 2011; Rimol et al., 2010). Both Schizophrenia and Bipolar I Disorder have been correlated with volume reductions in brain size. In a meta-analysis, Ellison-Wright and Bullmore (2010) summarized results of several studies that identified gray matter reduction in people suffering from Schizophrenia. Generally, areas in the prefrontal cortex are reduced, the ventricles are enlarged, and some limbic structures such as the hippocampus are 5–10% smaller (Stober et al., 2009). There have also been studies that found reduction in the amygdala and the superior temporal gyri (parts of the limbic system—*gyri* is the plural form of *gyrus*, which refers to a ridge on the cerebral cortex). These volume differences are correlated with the positive symptoms of Schizophrenia, whereas reductions in the medial temporal lobes have been correlated with memory impairment (Antonova, Sharma, Morris, & Kimari, 2004). In addition, most people have an asymmetry in the hemispheres of their brains, with the larger hemisphere correlating to handedness (right hemisphere for left-handedness and left hemisphere for right-handedness). This asymmetry is decreased in many people suffering from Schizophrenia and may be specific to the disorder; it may also be related to the vulnerability genes discussed earlier (Keshavan et al., 2008).

---

[4] In biochemistry a ligand is a molecule that binds to a receptor.

**WHITE MATTER PATHOLOGY** As with Bipolar I Disorder, reductions in white matter (glial cells) show up in some but not all patients with Schizophrenia, and they appear to be related to cognitive impairments. Affected areas include the corpus callosum, the cingulum, and the arcuate fasciculus[5] (Kubicki et al., 2007). Four genes related to myelin showed statistically significant differences compared to normal controls as well as genes related to astrocytes (a type of myelin) (Barley, Dracheva, & Byne, 2009). These findings are consistent with the glutamatergic model of Schizophrenia. This model proposes that because drugs that block glutamate receptors (NMDA receptors) can cause psychotic symptoms and impair neurocognitive functioning (Javitt, 2010), these receptors may play a role in psychotic symptoms. These findings are consistent because the glutamatergic system plays a key role in glial integrity (Keshavan et al., 2008), but this is not to say that glial cell pathology may not be one primary cause of the disorder in and of itself, independent of the glutamatergic theory (Selemon & Rajkowska, 2003). Researchers have also found abnormalities in the glial cells of high-risk offspring of people suffering from Schizophrenia (Francis et al., 2013)

**NEURODEVELOPMENTAL THEORY** One set of models that researchers have posited to try to draw together all the different physiological anomalies are the neurodevelopmental models of Schizophrenia. In various ways, these all posit that the disorder begins in gene expression (Kahler et al., 2008) and then, through faulty neuronal migration and selection, the brain develops abnormally (in ways resulting in the variables discussed earlier—reduced gray matter, larger ventricles, white matter pathology, etc.). These theories also suggest that such problems in neuronal migration and selection may underlay other disorders like Bipolar I (Rapoport, Addington, Frangou, & MRC Psych, 2005). These models are also being used to research early-onset Schizophrenia (onset between childhood and adolescence) (Kinros, Reichenberg, & Frangou, 2010). As with the other models discussed in this chapter, far more research is needed to explore whether these consistently account for the changes in the brain that are noted in so many people with Schizophrenia.

**NEUROCHEMICAL VARIABLES** As has been noted elsewhere in this book, to date we do not have reliable technologies to directly measure brain chemistry per se, but there are other ways to test hypotheses about the role that neurochemicals play in Schizophrenia. Magnetic resonance spectroscopy (MRS) is one noninvasive technique to do this. MRS generates a spectrum of neurochemical "peaks" of different radio frequencies. The MRS equipment can be "tuned" much like a radio to frequencies that correspond to different chemical nuclei in the body. Not all chemicals register on this instrument. Chemicals that do register include choline-containing compounds (like acetylcholine), creatine (related to metabolism and energy), glucose, and N-acetyl aspartate (a chemical associated with myelin sheaths noted earlier). It has been suggested that although this is a new technology with unresolved error rates, it is promising in terms of understanding what is happening in the brain of a person with Schizophrenia, as well as in developing drugs to treat the disorder (Jansen, Backes, Nicolay, & Hooi, 2006; Stone & Pilowsky, 2006). N-acetyl aspartate (NAA) can be studied with MRS and appears

---

[5] Arcuate fasciculus is from the Latin, meaning curved bundle. It refers to a bundle of axons that connect parts of the temporal and parietal cortex to the frontal lobe of the brain.

reduced in several brain regions in people with Schizophrenia (Abbott & Bustillo, 2006). These NAA reductions are also seen in relatives who are genetically vulnerable to Schizophrenia (although they are seen in mood disorders as well). Perhaps more important, MRS studies point to compromised neuronal and membrane integrity in the early phases of Schizophrenia (Keshavan et al., 2008).

**Dopamine** Since the mid-20th century, dopamine (DA) has been implicated in Schizophrenia. In vivo positron emission tomography (PET) scans and single photon emission computed tomography (SPECT) scans have been used to try to understand the role of specific neurotransmitters in Schizophrenia. For decades the dopamine (DA) theory of Schizophrenia dominated the field; however, there is little direct evidence for it and indirect evidence is compromised by the presence of antipsychotic medications, DA antagonist drugs that trigger increased DA production in response to the antagonism (Davis, Kahn, Ko, & Davidson, 1991). Although the DA hypothesis partially explains the positive symptoms (indirectly, by being able to produce the symptoms with DA agonists such as amphetamines), it does not explain the cognitive deficits or negative symptoms. These have been hypothesized to be caused by a hypoactive (less active) DA functioning in the mesocortical DA system (Davis et al., 1991). Although knowing the exact role of DA in Schizophrenia requires further research, as you will see in the later section on treatment, all drugs that reduce psychotic symptoms bind to DA receptors to some extent.

**Glutamate** As noted, some researchers hypothesize that reduced glutamate may be one cause or marker of Schizophrenia. Reduced glutamate in the spinal fluid of patients with Schizophrenia is the basis for this hypothesis, but this finding has not been replicated (Keshavan et al., 2008). It has also been noted that blocking glutamate receptors, particularly NMDA receptors, can induce psychotic symptoms; however, as is the case with DA, this is indirect evidence. As noted earlier, glutamate plays a role in glial cell integrity, so that process could be implicated in Schizophrenia.

**Gamma-Amino-Butyric-Acid (GABA)** Autopsies of people who were diagnosed with Schizophrenia have consistently shown reductions in GABA in the prefrontal cortex—as measured by a ligand determining GABA synthesis (Lewis, Hashimoto, & Volk, 2005). GABA receptors can also be upregulated—indicating a compensatory response to lower GABA levels (Jarskog, Miyamoto, & Lieberman, 2007; Keshavan et al., 2008).

**Conclusions About Physiological Variables and Future Directions** To summarize current thinking about Schizophrenia, it seems to be a disorder that is rooted in physiology and that (as we'll see later in the chapter) has triggers that are psychological, cultural, and social. The core idea is that research will eventually tie together all these variables previously discussed into an equation that leads us to identify biological markers that can then be used to create endophenotypes that hopefully will lead to more effective treatment. As noted in the chapter on Bipolar Disorder, mental health clinicians are ethically bound to have a general understanding of where the researchers are looking and what they are looking at in solving the puzzle of Schizophrenia.

Two fascinating directions of current research may lead us closer to both understanding the etiology and treating the symptoms. The first is colloquially called "disease-in-a-dish," and its more technical name is cellular programming and reprogramming technology (CPART). The technology rests on the assumption that cellular deficiencies can be measured if the cells can be grown in a dish/culture. The idea is that if there is something in the genes or cells related to the disease, one would be able to observe the phenotypic expression of these differences at the cellular level (Marchetto & Gage, 2012). To accomplish this, connective tissue cells (fibroblasts) are collected from the skin cells of patients diagnosed with Schizophrenia. These cells are then turned into adult stem cells and then grown into neurons.[6] The growing culture of neurons then allows researchers to observe them for differences compared to presumed normal cells. The cells cultured from people with Schizophrenia showed significantly decreased neuronal connectivity and linked the deficit to nearly 600 genes, four times as many as previously thought implicated (but recall what we used to call "junk" DNA is actually millions of switches related to gene expression) (Brennand et al., 2011). Clearly this technology holds the potential for isolating genes responsible for cellular deficiencies related to Schizophrenia. Should we find a way to reverse these deficiencies, we may be closer to a more effective treatment for the disorder.

The second breakthrough technology is called optogenetics. Each of our cells has the same genes, but what makes the cells different from one another is the different mix of genes that get turned on or off. For example, neurons that release dopamine (DA) need certain enzymes for making and packaging the DA. The genes encoding the protein components of this operation would be turned on in a DA-producing cell but turned off in other types of cells. According to this theory, if a gene that made DA was connected to a gene that encoded for a colored dye and these were genetically engineered to function in animal cell, the animal would only produce the dye in DA cells. Thus if you could trace the dye, you could watch the DA cells in operation (Miesenbock, 2008). Biologists working 40 years ago were aware of microorganisms that produced proteins that regulated the flow of their electric charge in response to visible light. These proteins are produced by what are called "opsin" genes that extract energy and information from the microbe's environment. One of these, called bacteriorhodopsin, can be briefly activated by green light. Scientists figured out a way to splice the gene for the light-sensitive protein into the genes of a benign virus and introduce the genetic material into cells of experimental animals. Using nothing more than pulses of light, the "infected" cells could be controlled with millisecond-precision as to their pattern of firing (Deisseroth, 2011).

The result of this was that researchers were able to "infect," with a light-sensitive dye protein, the cells in the brains of flies that are responsible for an escape reflex (this reflex involves only 2 of the 150,000 cells in a fly brain). Using the flash of light to activate the dye protein, the cells for escape consistently fired, causing all the flies in the procedure to take off. Similar studies with worms and mice were equally successful. This is pointing toward a future where, if we can identify the neurons controlling circuits that are implicated in the symptoms of mental disorders, we could theoretically use a type of gene therapy to get the neurons to produce the light-sensitive dyes, figure out how to install a light source inside the skull, and then use a remote device to trigger the light source and thus affect the neurons and

---

[6] Although fascinating, this highly technical explanation has been omitted but can be reviewed in Brennand et al. (2011).

hopefully stop the symptoms as they arise. Although this seems far-fetched, we are closer to such possibilities than anyone ever dreamed of at the turn of the century (Miesenbock, 2008). Hopefully, this section of the chapter has given you a sense of that. Now we will look at psychological, cultural, and social correlates to the disorder; finally, we will discuss treatment.

## Individual-Interior (Upper Left) Perspectives: Psychological Variables

We do not currently think in terms of psychological "causes" of Schizophrenia. In the mid-20th century there were many proposed psychological etiologies for Schizophrenia. Bateson et al. (1956), for example, proposed the double-bind theory noted earlier. Again, the double-bind is when emotional distress occurs as the result of receiving two or more contradictory messages such that a successful reaction to one results in failure to the other. Although psychologically distressing, this in no way "causes" Schizophrenia. Jaspers (1959) made the case for an existential interpretation of Schizophrenia, which, again, has no support in peer-reviewed studies as an etiology for Schizophrenia (although existential issues may exacerbate existing symptoms). What we do consider are psychological variables acting as triggers, risk factors, and types of treatment (Abramson, 2010; Dickerson & Lehman, 2011; Tarrier, 2010). As with etiology, psychological risk factors are also a puzzle. We know some of the psychological variables related to relapse, but little is known about risk factors that may contribute to the development of the disorder (Klosterkotter, Schultze-Lutter, Bechdolf, & Ruhrmann, 2011). Despite this, early intervention is still a goal, and identifying the psychological risk factors involved is important (Addington, 2007). Growing numbers of variables are being identified through integrative models like the eco-epidemiology model, which, similar to the Integral model we use in this book, examines genetic, epigenetic, individual, familial, community, and social domains across the lifespan (Kirkbride & Jones, 2011).

In addition, there is the first-person, psychological experience of *having* Schizophrenia. Even here, though, the psychological experience is most frequently researched by seeking neurological correlates. For example, problems related to goal setting and motivation are correlated with impairment in the anterior cingulate and orbital function (Barch & Dowd, 2010). Deficits in emotional response are correlated with nervous system areas related to emotion (Kring & Moran, 2008). Problems in self-monitoring are thought to relate to abnormal integration of brain processes (Stephan, Friston, & Frith, 2009). Even differences in temperament (e.g., harm avoidance and cooperativeness) and personality are thought to be affected by the genetic factors or neural disease processes hypothesized to underlay Schizophrenia (Silberschmidt & Sponheim, 2007; Smith, Cloninger, Harms, & Csernansky, 2008).

People suffering from Schizophrenia have described themselves as losing their identity and having an "empty" experience of self (Lysaker, Buck, & Hammond, 2007). In a comparative study of six self-experiences grouped by theory, a general consensus suggested that many people suffering from Schizophrenia experience themselves as diminished (compared to their image of themselves prior to the illness)—feel they are less able to engage the world effectively—and this intensifies their anxiety in the face of daily life (Lysaker & Lysaker, 2008). This greatly affects the social cognition of people suffering from Schizophrenia (Green et al., 2008).

Social cognition can be thought of as the mental operations that underlay social interactions such as interpreting the intentions of others and generating responses (some of these skills are colloquially referred to as "emotional intelligence"). Researchers in this area suggest that these clients are more sensitive to negative signals from others and exaggerate the influence of such signals, decreasing their ability or willingness to trust others (Hooker et al., 2011). People with Schizophrenia are also more likely to have increased stress (compared to controls) in areas such as home environment, motivation and depression (Betensky et al., 2008). The hypothalamic-pituitary-adrenal (HPA) axis is a key mediator of stress and is being investigated for its role in exacerbating psychiatric disorders (Stahl & Wise, 2008). As will be discussed in the section on treatment, insight is critically important and is related to both medication adherence (Cheng-Fang et al., 2005) and quality of life (Cheng-Fang et al., 2008).

People suffering from Schizophrenia perform 1.5–2 standard deviations below healthy control subjects on cognitive tasks (Keefe & Fenton, 2010) and have cognitive deficits .5 standard deviations larger than those suffering from Bipolar I Disorder (Krabbendam, Arts, van Os, & Aleman, 2005). Although cognitive disturbances are referred to in the DSM description of Schizophrenia, cognitive dysfunction (formerly "thought disorder") is not listed in the criteria. People suffering from Schizophrenia have impaired cognition in the domains of working memory, psychomotor speed, executive functions, social cognition, and verbal learning (Tandon et al., 2010). Most people with this disorder show cognitive deficits, and children who eventually develop Schizophrenia start at lower cognitive baselines than healthy peers (Cannon et al., 2002). Considering how essential cognitive functioning is to one's sense of self, it is expected that disorders that induce deficits in cognitive function (such as Schizophrenia and Alzheimer's-Type Dementia) affect the self-sense as well. In addition, people with Schizophrenia suffer from deficits in what is called metacognitive capacity (the ability to think about thinking). These deficits also impair psychosocial functions and work performance (Lysaker et al., 2010).

## Lower-Quadrant Perspectives: Cultural and Social Issues Related to Etiology

**URBAN SETTINGS AND IMMIGRANT STATUS** Just as in examining the psychological variables related to Schizophrenia, with cultural and social issues we are looking primarily at things that function as triggers for the expression of the disorder, rather than things that *cause* the disorder. As noted at the beginning of this chapter, it has consistently been found (for the past 70 years) that rates of Schizophrenia are higher in urban areas (e.g., Farris & Dunham, 1939; Kelly et al., 2010; Tandon et al., 2008). It appears that the risk for Schizophrenia increases with being born and raised in urban areas, especially for males, and that this trend has actually increased in recent cohorts (Krabbendam & van Os, 2005). This connection has been found across most cultures (McGrath et al., 2004), with exceptions in Japan (Ohta, Nakane, Nishihara, & Takemoto, 1992) and Taiwan (Chien et al., 2004). Immigrant status also raises the risk for Schizophrenia and may overlap with the statistics from studies on urbanicity (meaning immigrants often settle in urban areas, so immigration status may confound the effects of living in the city).

| | |
|---|---|
| Stress from the disorder itself (t)<br>Emotional deficits (t)<br>Empty sense of self (t)<br>Low quality of life (t) | Genetic vulnerability (e)<br>candidate genes NRG1, DTNBP1<br>Volume reduction in amygdalae (e)<br>Volume differences in prefrontal cortex (e)<br>Ventricular enlargement (e)<br>Volume reduction in hippocampus (e)<br>Reduction in superior temporal gyri (e)<br>White matter pathology (e)<br>Problems in neuronal migration/selection (e)<br>Neurochemical variables (e) |
| Effects of poor social cognition<br>Social isolation | Living in an urban setting<br>Immigrant status in social system |

**FIGURE 7.1** Etiological Variables and Psychological, Cultural, and Social Triggers for Schizophrenia

One theory about this correlation is that the stressors of urban living may be more likely to exacerbate a genetic vulnerability to Schizophrenia. At the individual level, Byrne, Agerbo, Eaton, and Mortensen (2004) found that socioeconomic factors may explain this: because living in lower-socioeconomic-status conditions is more likely in urban areas, it may be less urban living itself, and more having a lower socioeconomic status, that is the factor responsible for triggering the vulnerability. At the group level, people who hold immigrant status are more likely to be diagnosed with Schizophrenia, as noted. It has been suggested that these sorts of urban variables may unduly stress the HPA axis, and this axis is also increasingly being linked with Schizophrenia (Cotter & Pariante, 2002).

The relationship between immigrant status and Schizophrenia has also persisted throughout decades of research. This has become more interesting as integrative models are increasingly appreciated. Although admitting that the etiology of Schizophrenia is likely physiological in nature, like urbanicity, immigrant status and the stressors that go with that may trigger the disorder in those vulnerable to developing it (Bourque, van der Ven, Fusar-Poli, & Malla, 2012). Growing up in disadvantaged ethnic/minority positions, with low social status, dense neighborhoods, and high degrees of discrimination, may trigger or exacerbate psychotic disorders in those vulnerable to them (Veiling & Susser, 2011). Before moving on to treatment, we want to use our quadrant model to summarize the variables related to etiology and stressors that can trigger and exacerbate symptoms. To be clear, we will label each variable with an "e" for etiology and a "t" for trigger. Again the theories of etiology are likely looking at some combination of the variables/anomalies listed in the upper-right quadrant. See Figure 7.1.

## TREATMENT OF SCHIZOPHRENIA

The treatment of Schizophrenia includes physiological/pharmacological, psychotherapeutic, and community interventions. In addition, some work is being done to see if there are ways to identify at-risk genes and preclude their expression. In other words, the best outcomes are truly integrative. Although pharmacologic interventions are currently the centerpiece of treatment, they have higher efficacy when combined with the others covered here.

## Genetic and Epigenetic Strategies

Although these treatments are still in the development stage, they are intriguing for their potential to try to get to the source of at least one important variable in developing Schizophrenia. Recall that if an identical twin suffers from Schizophrenia, the other twin's risk increases from about 1% to 50%, but that is still far from 100%. One theory is that the unaffected twin had the benefit of epigenetic silencing of certain gene patterns that were expressed in the affected twin. Some forms of Schizophrenia may be caused by inherited and environment/experience-triggered changes in gene expression for Glutamate and GABA. The theory goes that a deficiency in histone methyl and histone methylation[7] is an important part of gene expression (Connor & Akbarian, 2008). In these cases a genetic intervention would aim to correct the supposed deficit of histone methyl (Stahl, 2010).

Other interventions being researched include trying to identify and then activate "helpful" genes by inhibiting a class of enzymes called histone deacetylases. These are a class of enzymes that remove acetyl groups from an amino acid on a histone. They are important because DNA is wrapped around histones and DNA expression is regulated by acetylation and deacetylation (addition or removal of an acetyl group). Activation of genes involves acetylation (and demethylation), whereas deactivation of genes involves deacetylation (and methylation). What is being proposed here is really interfering at the level of the genes in ways that researchers hope will decrease the chances that a genetically vulnerable person will develop Schizophrenia (Nestler, 2009).

A final idea in dealing with Schizophrenia at the genetic level is identifying defective or unwanted proteins in neurons and interfering with the RNA that is related to their expression (Martinez, 2010). All cells (including neurons) have defense systems to attack viruses and other invaders by a process called RNA interference (RNAi). If scientists can "hijack" this defense system to attack RNA from unwanted genes, we could theoretically stop defective genes from being expressed. Of course, this all assumes that we will be able to more specifically narrow down the genes involved in the various endophenotypes that are associated with Schizophrenia (Stahl, 2010).

## Physiological/Pharmacological Strategies

While scientists struggle to unravel the genetic mysteries involved in Schizophrenia, clients suffering from the disorder still need treatment, and today that treatment is pharmacological and is not as different from treatment 50 years ago as we would hope. Generally, antipsychotic medications are described in two categories: typical and atypical. Typical antipsychotics work by blocking (antagonizing) dopamine-2 (D2)

---

[7] Histones are proteins found in eukaryotic cells (cells with structures enclosed in membranes) that package and order DNA into structural units. Histone methylation is the modification of amino acids in the histone itself by addition of methyl groups. A-methyl groups are chemical compounds that consist of hydrogen and carbon.

receptors. They are "dirty" drugs, meaning that they also block receptors in other neurotransmitter systems, which results in side effects that include extrapyramidal symptoms such as tardive dyskinesia (late-appearing abnormal movement), akathesia (motor restlessness), acute dystonic reactions (severe tics that may involve the head, neck, and trunk of the body), and prolactin increases that result in sexual dysfunction, among other things. There are several classes of typical antipsychotics but the most common are haloperidol/Haldol and chlorpromazine/Thorazine.[8] There are approximately 50 of these compounds and, other than trial and error, there is no way to tell which clients will respond to which medications (Tandon et al., 2010).

In the 1980s, we saw the first of 12 new compounds that were classified as "atypical" antipsychotic medications. The first of these, clozapine/Clozaril (hereafter "clozapine") was developed in the late 1960s but was kept from the market because of a potentially lethal side effect.[9] Once the side effect could be detected early with blood counts, clozapine was released. This drug worked very differently from the typical ones in that it blocked some D2 receptors but also massively blocked serotonin (5-HT) receptors. Initial tests and subsequent meta-analyses have supported the contention that clozapine is better than Haldol (the drug used in control groups as a representative of typical antipsychotics) and particularly better for treatment-resistant clients (Leucht et al., 2009). Since their release, studies have poured forth—some strongly supporting that atypical medications are more efficacious than typicals, whereas other studies question that assertion. After 20 years of studies and meta-analyses, it now appears that some atypicals are indeed better than haldol, and those include clozapine, olanzapine/Zyprexa, amisulpride/Abilify and resperidone/Risperdal (Leucht et al., 2009); however, much of their efficacy still centers on their ability to bond to D2 receptors. The massive blocking of 5-HT receptors is thought to reduce the positive symptoms in the same way 5-HT antagonists attenuate the cognitive and perceptual effects of serotonergic hallucinogens such as LSD-25 (Singh, 2005).

As noted earlier, from the mid-20th century until about 1985, it was widely believed that DA held the key to understanding Schizophrenia; however, that understanding has proven to be far more complicated than initially thought. It is true that you can decrease the positive symptoms of Schizophrenia in some but not all clients with drugs that block D2 receptors (DA antagonists), but there are also drugs that have variable actions on these receptors—based on their affinity for the receptors (like some of the newer atypical such as Zyprexa/olanzapine) and drugs whose actions on the receptors seem to vary by dosage (Abilify/amisulpride). Amisulpride tends to bind more in the limbic system than in the striatal tracts, supposedly decreasing extrapyramidal side effects. Amisulpride is a DA partial agonist (DPA), meaning the drug can act as a "silent" antagonist or an agonist, depending on dosage (Kim, Maneen, & Stahl, 2009). It is believed that in the presence of excessive DA activity, DPAs reduce signal transduction in the DA–G protein second-messenger system. Conversely, it is believed that when DA activity is deficient in some way, DPAs increase signal transduction

---

[8] For a history of the development of these drugs, see Healy, D. (2004). *The creation of psychopharmacology*. Cambridge, MA: Harvard University Press.

[9] The side effect was agranulocytosis, which is a rapid drop in the white blood cell (WBC) count, which leaves the patient vulnerable to opportunistic infections. This can be stopped if the patient's (WBC) count is monitored, and thus Clozaril was released in the 1980s.

(McKeage & Plosker, 2004). The properties of signal transduction were discovered in the 1970s. There are two steps in the process. First, a molecule outside the cell (like a drug) activates a receptor on the cell surface. Second, the second messenger (usually a G protein[10]) transmits the signal inside the cell, creating a response. In either step, the signal can be dampened or amplified due to other ligands (like DA) that are present. Thus, one molecule (or drug) may cause many responses (Reese & Campbell, 2002).

When antipsychotics work for a client, they will decrease positive symptoms in a time span beginning anywhere from a few days to several weeks. These drugs can also lessen the negative symptoms that are linked to positive symptoms but can worsen negative symptoms that are rooted in extrapyramidal side effects (Stahl & Buckley, 2007). Further, antipsychotics have no demonstrable efficacy on primary negative symptoms and can cause "neuroleptic dysphoria"[11] associated with extrapyramidal side effects. There do not appear to be any major differences between antipsychotics with regard to their effects on cognitive dysfunction. Antipsychotics are correlated with a reduction in suicide, with Clozaril/clozapine having the most robust effect (Tandon et al., 2010). Treatment with these compounds requires a good relationship with the prescribing professional because there is no way to predict which patient will respond to which compound. Further, compounds that do nothing for one patient may work well in another, contributing to the view that Schizophrenia proper is likely a heterogeneous array of disorders with different physiological variables operating as root causes.

It should be noted that electroconvulsive therapy (ECT) and repetitive transcranial magnetic stimulation (rTMS) have both been used with Schizophrenia with varying results. ECT can augment the efficacy of antipsychotic medications and in some cases speed up their onset of action; it can also be useful in treating catatonic patients, but, by and large, is not seen as a primary treatment for Schizophrenia. rTMS may be useful in treating the negative symptoms of Schizophrenia but more research is needed before conclusions can be drawn (Blumberger, Fitzgerald, Mulsant, & Daskalakis, 2010).

### Psychosocial Treatments for Schizophrenia

It is hard to imagine the distress caused by Schizophrenia—both in individuals with the disorder and their families. For this reason, many patients and family members receive different forms of psychotherapy to assist them in managing the disorder. Results of the efficacy of therapy are conflicting, and in many cases it is difficult to determine what is actually helpful in a specific case. That said, pharmacotherapy alone produces only limited improvement in negative symptoms, social functioning, cognitive deficits, and quality of life, so therapy is often important to try in addition to medication (Dickerson & Lehman, 2011; Tandon et al., 2010). Key variables in therapy include developing insight into the disorder and increasing quality of life.

Insight has been correlated with both medication adherence (Cheng-Fang et al., 2005) and quality of life (Cheng-Feng et al., 2008). Psycho-educational interventions

---

[10] G proteins are guanine nucleotide-binding proteins that help transmit signals outside a cell to the cell's interior. They function as molecular switches that can activate a cascade of further signaling events that can alter cell functions like ion channels and transporters.

[11] A depressed mood induced by the drug.

begin with providing information about the disorder to the client and relevant family members. Meta-analyses suggest that these interventions reduce strong emotion and potentially negative expressions of strong emotion in relatives as well as decrease relapses requiring hospitalization (Giron, Fernandez-Yanez, Mana-Alvarenga, Molina-Habas, & Nolasco, 2010). In this sense the interventions can certainly be thought of as decreasing stressors associated with relapse. There are also multi-family psycho-educational groups that can be offered, as it has been noted that interventions that include family members are more effective than those including only the person with Schizophrenia (Lincoln, Wilhelm, & Nestoriuc, 2007). It is important to remember that accurate information needs to be offered regarding the disorder. That is, of course, the primary aim of this book; to provide as up-to-date an analysis as possible of the disorders so that practitioners can discuss the many variables involved in a way that clients and families can understand. One cutting-edge technique in counseling for people who have a family member suffering from Schizophrenia is genetic counseling. As our understanding of the genetic variables in Schizophrenia increases, people will want to know, if they are related to someone with the disorder, what the risks are of having children. Genetic counselors are trained to work with people struggling with these issues and see genetic counseling related to mental illness as a growing field (Monaco, Conway, Valverde, & Austin, 2009). Currently a majority of clients with Schizophrenia and their family members say they feel they would benefit from genetic counseling but few individuals are being offered the service (Lyus, 2007). One group of researchers studying referrals for genetic counseling in British Columbia concluded there were only 288 referrals between 1968 and 2007 (Hunter, Hippman, Honer, & Austin, 2009). Part of the problem may be the stigma still associated with severe mental illness. Feret, Conway, and Austin (2011) found some negative attitudes toward people with Schizophrenia in genetic counselors studied. They conclude this may impede the counselor–client relationship.

All this implies that nonmedical mental health professionals are increasingly going to need a level of what Clark (2007) calls "genomic competence." Such competence would include a basis of genomic knowledge, identification of resources and relevant issues for clients and family members, referral protocols, and provision of education and support (Clark, 2007). There is research that demonstrates heritability trends for people who had one parent suffering from Schizophrenia and related disorders (risk goes from approximately 1% to 7%) versus people who had two parents suffering from it (risk goes from approximately 1% to 39%) (Gottesman, Laursen, Bertelsen, & Montenson, 2010). Although genetic counselors can help people think through choices about pregnancies and lifestyle, there is (as stated earlier) no direct genetic test for Schizophrenia. If research continues, we may identify candidate genes that can be scanned for. Currently 1–2% of people with Schizophrenia have a subtle chromosomal abnormality called 22q11 deletion syndrome (or DiGeorge syndrome) (Rideout et al., 2009). Although a test for this abnormality would not be recommended as a direct screening for Schizophrenia, if it came up in screening for related disorders (e.g., endocrine disorders) it could be viewed as one risk factor for Schizophrenia.

In general, there is a great deal of debate regarding how much clients with Schizophrenia can really benefit from psychotherapy. While on the one hand the disorder itself fragments the client's identity, agency, and personal worth (Lysaker, Buck, & Hammoud, 2007), on the other hand the cognitive deficits afflicting most clients with Schizophrenia limit the amount of benefit that can be gained from more traditional models of therapy. That said, there are still ways to construct therapy interventions that can be helpful. There are mixed reviews on the efficacy of cognitive-behavioral therapy (CBT) for clients who continue to suffer from symptoms even when on maximal doses of medication. The idea is that CBT can approach delusions and hallucinations as misinterpretations and irrational attributions caused by deficits in self-monitoring (Tandon et al., 2010). Ideally, CBT would help clients learn to challenge the conclusions they are making; however, given the level of cognitive impairment in many clients suffering from Schizophrenia, it is hard to say just how effective this will be and it likely depends on a cognitive assessment prior to therapy that is done on a case-by-case basis. Some meta-analytic evaluations have found CBT to be helpful (Pfammatter, Junghan, & Brenner, 2006), whereas (as always) others question the findings (Kingdon, 2010). Tarrier (2010) has postulated that the challenges for researchers in this area are weighing risk to the client and treating comorbidity as well as other nonpsychological conditions that could limit recovery. He felt that if researchers and clinicians address these in their CBT interventions, results would improve.

Tandon et al. (2010), in their summary of treatment, noted that data from studies of CBT for treating positive symptoms are ". . . modest at best" (p. 8). They did find that interventions aimed at the cognitive remediation of deficits in attention, working memory, motor speed, executive function, verbal learning, and social cognition seem more promising and more specific to the challenges facing people diagnosed with Schizophrenia. Again, recall that people with Schizophrenia tend to score 1.5—2 standard deviations *below* "healthy" controls on tests of cognition (Keefe & Fenton, 2010). This will limit the benefits of cognitive interventions, although the *right type of* intervention could be very useful. That is the idea behind cognitive remediation. Cognitive remediation interventions teach clients how to organize information, use reminders that can be posted in the environment (e.g., for times to take medication), and use a range of techniques to improve social functioning (Eack et al., 2010). Cognitive remediation seems to have more of an impact when paired with psychiatric treatment. Questions remain about the durability of the benefits of cognitive remediation, and more long-term study is needed (Tandon et al., 2010). Cognitive remediation interventions focused on social cognition overlap with social skills training (SST), the latter of which has been used for decades in assisting clients with Schizophrenia to enhance their social interactions and increase their quality of life. Although there are many approaches to social skills, one of the challenges has been getting the skills to transfer outside of the therapeutic setting. As with the research on CBT, the reviews of SST are mixed, with the strongest effects seen in improvements in community skills and community functioning and fewer effects with regard to symptoms and relapse (Kurtz & Mueser, 2008).

Assertive Community Treatment (ACT) is intended to offer integrated delivery of services to clients with severe mental illness. It is multidisciplinary in its approach, aiming toward high frequency of contact with patients and low patient-to-therapist ratios (Tandon et al., 2010). As you can imagine, this approach requires financial resources not available to many community mental health systems in the United States, which limits its implementation. As with all the psychosocial interventions discussed here, studies are mixed regarding the efficacy of ACT.

## Spiritual Considerations

What can we say about spirituality and Schizophrenia? First and foremost, as has been our mission throughout this book, it is important to separate romanticized images of severe mental illness from the actual experience of it. For a short period in the 20th century, some theorists attempted to make the argument that Schizophrenia in some way involves "spiritual energies" and that what the mystic is experiencing is similar to what someone suffering from Schizophrenia is experiencing. As Mendelssohn (2004) wrote, "It is my own belief that every schizophrenic is a medium, an intermediary between worlds, between spiritual and cosmic dimensions" (p. 597). Mendelssohn claims in that editorial to have "cured" someone diagnosed with Schizophrenia in one visit. We have been able to find no double-blind support for such claims. The concepts that differentiate Schizophrenia from supposed mental health have also been challenged as culturally determined (Stanghellini, 2005).

Similarly, psychiatrist John Perry (1962) and mythologist Joseph Campbell (1972) wrote of Schizophrenia as an "inward journey" where the psychotic episode is viewed as a mythic journey into the self and, similar to a shaman in societies that have such healers, the person in the psychotic state should be allowed to have the psychosis run its course and then he or she will emerge psychically whole. One has only to have acquaintance with people suffering from Schizophrenia who remain untreated (whether due to volition or access to treatment) to see that this is a false and romanticized view of the disorder. It is more forgivable to have a belief in this idea in the mid-20th century than in the 21st century.

From a cultural perspective, Dr. Julian Silverman (1967) explored supposed similarities between psychosis and shamanic initiation. He concluded that it was the cultural context that made the difference. Whereas the shaman had a culture that supported the crisis in some way and expected the individual to "get better" and return to the society in the function of a healer, Silverman noted that our society rejected the psychological significance of the episode and thus contributed to the person being unable to work through it. Again, this is a highly speculative and romanticized image of Schizophrenia that does not hold up for those who work with people suffering from the disorder. When the traditional approach tends to pathologize mystical states, there is the opposite danger of spiritualizing psychotic states (Grof & Grof, 1989). That in no way excuses romanticizing what is a terrible disorder, whatever its etiology may be. Still, there is a place for spirituality in the lives and recovery of people suffering from Schizophrenia.

We also need to acknowledge that even in the 21st century there are religious groups grappling with the belief in the existence of metaphysical evil and to what extent this relates to disorders like Schizophrenia. Although pastoral care has improved immensely even in the past 50 years, there are many gray areas where people of different faiths grapple with the extent to which metaphysically evil agents (e.g., the devil) play a role in the etiology and maintenance of psychopathology. Clinicians need to be sensitive to cultural context while at the same time try to discern the extent to which the beliefs of a particular community may exacerbate symptoms (Yarhouse, Butman, & McRay, 2005).

Since the late-20th century, psychiatry has recognized the need to at least affirm patients' religious and spiritual convictions (Dein, 2005). This is part of the Recovery

Model advocated by the landmark 1999 Surgeon General's report on mental health. She urged all mental health systems to adopt the model that specifically addresses spirituality (Lukoff, 2007). Religion and spirituality have been shown to be highly prevalent in people diagnosed with Schizophrenia. This affiliation stays stable over time and can be a resource that contributes to positive change. However, spiritual and religious beliefs can be highly labile in such populations as clients struggle with the injustice of the disorder and what it says about "God" or other spiritual beings (Mohr, Brandt, Borras, Gillieron, & Huguelet, 2006; Mohr et al., 2010).

Shah et al. (2011) found that sound spiritual, religious, or related belief systems were associated with active, adaptive coping skills in subjects diagnosed with Residual Schizophrenia.[12] Even in inpatient units, spiritual matters are addressed by many clinicians. Revheim, Greenberg, and Citrome (2010) and Revheim and Greenberg (2007) describe an inpatient study where a spirituality-based group was developed for clients suffering from Schizophrenia. For those who attended, spirituality was significantly correlated with self-efficacy with regard to symptoms and social functioning. The attendees were more hopeful than nonattendees, and hopefulness was correlated with the extent to which members identified as "spiritual." Overall self-efficacy and quality of life did not differ between those who attended and those who didn't, but for the spiritually inclined, the results seem to suggest that groups like this can be a positive variable in treatment.

Several studies just discussed allude to the need for the clinician to make a judgment about the "soundness" of the client's expressed spiritual/religious affiliation. This is where established traditions offer real strengths. If the client identifies with a mainstream practice that includes a lineage and a community of practitioners, it may be easier for clinicians to differentiate sound versus unsound religious/spiritual experiences and identification. Clearly this is to some extent in the eye of the beholder, as Scientology is (at least according to its adherents and the Internal Revenue Service) an established religion but it is not mainstream. By way of example, Franklin was a member of the African Methodist Episcopal Church. Franklin engaged in Bible study and a form of spiritual direction. He was supported in his congregation and able to achieve semi-independent living situation once his symptoms were stabilized. His minister could also detect shifts in Franklin's beliefs that signaled a return of symptoms. Whereas an atheist may say that the entire theology of the church is delusional, in the church context there was a clear lineage and degrees of spiritual experience concomitant with spiritual practice. Particularly, when Franklin reported "command voices" he thought came from God, the "commands" were very different from what the lineage of practitioners would agree was in the realm of spiritual experience. In these cases, Franklin's minister was on target and Franklin met with his doctor for a med-check. Again, one has to consider the context of the religious/spiritual community, the beliefs, and how those beliefs relate to mainstream society. This is another area where the DSM-5 Cultural Formulation Interview can be of help.

That said, it is important to emphasize that the spiritual experience of the client will not always be positive or comforting. Theologically, conditions like Schizophrenia

---

[12] This study was done using DSM-IV-TR criteria, which still retained the subtypes of Schizophrenia that have been eliminated in the DSM-5.

raise questions of what is called "theodicy," or the attempt to reconcile the existence of evil with the belief in a loving God. Because clients suffering from severe mental illness are more likely to have a religious or spiritual identity, this is an area many clinicians will encounter. Groups like the one described by Revheim and Greenberg (2007) can provide a supportive environment where these difficult issues can be explored. Both Mohr et al. (2010) and Phillips and Stein (2007) describe how clients' beliefs may change in the course of grappling with the existential dimensions of having a chronic mental illness. Phillips and Stein (2007) discussed "reappraisals" of beliefs that clients engaged in over the course of treatment outlined by Pargament, Koenig, and Perez (2000). Benevolent reappraisals represent attempts to redefine problems as having spiritual benefits. In Franklin's case, he frequently wondered aloud if he were learning about compassion by suffering from Schizophrenia. Phillips and Stein (2007) found such reappraisals to be correlated with higher levels of coping and growth, thus having positive implications.

Less commonly, clients may engage in two other reappraisals that are correlated with negative outcomes and decompensation. Reappraising Schizophrenia as punishment from God for one's sins is a common variant of this. Another variation is reappraising one's sense of God's power after a stressor fails to resolve despite fervent, sincere prayer. In Franklin's case, whenever he was decompensating he began dwelling in an almost paranoid sense on the idea that God may be punishing him. Although a legitimate concern, the way he expressed this carried "red flags" for his minister. In one example, Franklin's concern was stated illogically (in the framework of the theology of the African Methodist Episcopal Church). Whereas when doing well Franklin could live with ambiguities like the Trinity,[13] when he was decompensating, he would focus on the Father sending the Holy Ghost with symptoms specifically for Franklin. This paranoid personalizing was a sign to his minister that Franklin might be decompensating. Exploring the realities of theodicy carried personal import for Franklin, but he also needed support to avoid such ruminations when his symptoms were worsening. As you can tell, this is a delicate balancing act for the clinician and particularly so for clinicians who may identify as "nonbelievers." Before concluding, we would like to summarize treatment components using our Integral quadrants in Figure 7.2.

| | |
|---|---|
| Developing insight<br>Psycho-education for client<br>Cognitive remediation interventions<br>Appropriate spiritual support | Developmental genetic therapies hold promise<br>Psychopharmacology<br>ECT if indicated |
| Psycho-education of family | Assertive Community Treatment<br>Genetic counseling of family |

**FIGURE 7.2** Integral Summary of Treatment for Schizophrenia

[13] In many versions of Christianity, the Trinity is a doctrine that describes God as being three divine persons: Father, Son, and Holy Ghost. The doctrine states that these three persons are distinct yet coexist in unity.

## Conclusion

In sorting out the puzzle of Schizophrenia, it appears that many of the pieces are physiological in nature. Similar to Bipolar I Disorder, if progress is to be made in the diagnosis and treatment of Schizophrenia, we will have to sort out what these pieces mean in terms of gene expression and brain structure and function. Unlike Bipolar I Disorder, in which clients may still have adequate functioning between episodes, Schizophrenia is more impairing—particularly in the cognitive domain—and this requires that any psychosocial approaches to treatment be crafted to the client's abilities, aiming toward what can be the best level of inter-episode functioning possible. As with all the disorders in this book, nonmedical mental health professionals must understand what the current research tells us about the disorder and convey that honestly and compassionately to clients and their families.

## Review Questions

1. Assume that you are meeting the parents of a client who is suffering from Schizophrenia. They ask you what causes the disorder. How would you respond?
2. How would you describe the risks of living in urban areas in relation to developing Schizophrenia?
3. What are the primary differences between "typical" and "atypical" antipsychotic medications?
4. What is the role of the mental health professional with regard to the treatment of Schizophrenia?
5. In an ideal world, what would seem to be the best treatment for someone suffering from Schizophrenia?
6. Review in the DSM the differences between Schizoaffective Disorder, Schizophrenia, and Schizophreniform Disorder; summarize the distinctions.

## References


Abbott, C., & Bustillo, J. (2006). What have we learned from proton magnetic resonance spectroscopy about Schizophrenia? A critical update. *Current Opinion in Psychiatry, 19*, 135–139.

Abramson, R. (2010). Psychotherapy of psychoses: Some principles for practice in the real world. *Journal of the American Academy of Psychoanalysis and Dynamic Psychiatry, 38*, 483–502.

Addington, J. (2007). The promise of early intervention. *Early Intervention in Psychiatry, 1*, 294–307. Publisher info - "American Psychiatric Association in Washington DC".

Allardyce, J., Gaebel, W., Zielasek, J., & van Os, J. (2010). Deconstructing Psychosis Conference February 2006. In C. A. Tamminga, P. J. Sirovatka, D. A. Regier, & J. van Os (Eds.), *Deconstructing psychosis: Refining the research agenda for DSM-5* (pp. 1–10). Washington, DC: American Psychiatric Association.

American Psychiatric Association. (2000). *Diagnostic and statistical manual of mental disorders* (4th edition, text revision). Washington, DC: Author.

American Psychiatric Association. (2013). *Diagnostic and statistical manual of mental disorders* (5th ed.). Washington, DC: Author.

Andreasan, N. C. (1999). Understanding the causes of Schizophrenia. *New England Journal of Medicine, 340*, 645–647.

Antonova, E., Sharma, T., Morris, R., & Kimari, V. (2004). The relationship between brain structure and neurocognition in Schizophrenia: A selective review. *Schizophrenia Research, 70*, 117–145.

Barch, D. M., & Dowd, E. C. (2010). Goal representations and motivational drive in Schizophrenia: The role of prefrontal-striatal interactions. *Schizophrenia Bulletin, 36,* 919–934.

Berrios, G. E. (1985). Positive and negative symptoms and Jackson: A conceptual history. *Archives of General Psychiatry, 42,* 95–97.

Barley, K., Dracheva, S., & Byne, W. (2009). Subcortical oligodendrocyte- and astrocyte-associated gene expression in subjects with Schizophrenia, Major Depression and Bipolar Disorder. *Schizophrenia Research, 112,* 54–64.

Bateson, G., Jackson, D., Haley, J., & Weakland, J. H. (1956). Towards a theory of Schizophrenia. *Behavioral Science, 1,* 251–264.

Betensky, J. D., Robinson, D. G., Gunduz-Bruce, H., Sevy, S., Lencz, T., Kane, J. M., . . . Szeszko, P. R. (2008). Patterns of stress in Schizophrenia. *Psychiatry Residency, 160,* 38–46.

Bleuler, E. (1911). Dementia Praecox oder die Gruppe der Schizophreinien. In G. Aschaffenburg (Ed.), *Handbook of psychiatry* (pp. 98–145). Leipzig/Wien: Deuticke.

Blumberger, D. M., Fitzgerald, P. B., Mulsant, B. H., & Daskalakis, Z. J. (2010). Repetitive transcranial magnetic stimulation for refractory symptoms in Schizophrenia. *Current Opinion in Psychiatry, 23,* 85–90.

Bourque, F., van der Ven, E., Fusar-Poli, P., & Malla, A. (2012). Immigration, social environment and onset of psychotic disorders. *Current Pharmaceutical Design, 18,* 518–526.

Brennand, K. J., Simone, A., Jou, J., Gelboin-Burkhart, C., Tran, N., Sangar, S., . . . Gage, F. H. (2011). Modelling Schizophrenia using human induced pluripotent stem cells. *Nature, 473,* 221–229.

Byrne, M., Agerbo, E., Eaton, W. W., & Mortensen, P. B. (2004). Parental socioeconomic status and risk of first admission with Schizophrenia—a Danish national register based study. *Social Psychiatry and Epidemiology, 39,* 87–96.

Campbell, J. (1972). *Myths to live by.* New York: Viking.

Cannon, M., Caspi, A., Moffitt, T. E., Harrington, H., Taylor, A., Murray, R. M., & Poulton, R. (2002). Evidence for early-childhood, pan-developmental impairment specific to Schizophreniform Disorder: results from a longitudinal birth cohort. *Archives of General Psychiatry, 59,* 449–456.

Cantor-Graae, E. (2007). The contribution of social factors to the development of Schizophrenia: A review of recent findings. *Canadian Journal of Psychiatry, 52,* 277–286.

Cheng-Fang, Y., Cheng-Sheng, C., Chih-Hung, K., Ming-Li, Y., Shang-Ju, Y., Ju-Yu, Y., . . . Chia-Chen, W. (2005). Relationships between insight and medication adherence in outpatients with Schizophrenia and Bipolar Disorder: Prospective study. *Psychiatry and Clinical Neurosciences, 59,* 403–409.

Cheng-Fang, Y., Chung-Ping, C., Chi-Fen, H., Ju-Yu, Y., Chih-Hung, K., & Cheng-Sheng, C. (2008). Quality of life and its association with insight, adverse effects of medication and use of atypical antipsychotics in patients with Bipolar Disorder and Schizophrenia in remission. *Bipolar Disorder, 10,* 617–624.

Chien, I. C., Chou, Y. J., Lin, C. H., Bih, S. H., Chou, P., & Chang, H. J. (2004). Prevalence and incidence of Schizophrenia among national health insurance enrollees in Taiwan, 1996–2001. *Psychiatry and Clinical Neuroscience, 58,* 611–618.

Clark, W. G. (2007). Schizophrenia and genomics: Linking research to practice. *Journal of Psychosocial Nursing, 45,* 25–28.

Connor, C. M., & Akbarian, S. (2008). DNS methylation changes in Schizophrenia and Bipolar Disorder. *Epigenetics, 3,* 55–58.

Costello, V. (2012). *A lethal inheritance: A mother uncovers the science behind three generations of mental illness.* Amherst, NY: Prometheus.

Cotter, D., & Pariante, C. M. (2002). Stress and the progression of the developmental hypothesis of Schizophrenia. *British Journal of Psychiatry, 181,* 363–365.

Coufal, N. G., Garcia-Perez, J. L., Peng, G., Yeo, G. W., Mu, Y., Lovci, M. T., . . . Gage, F. H. (2009). L1 retrotransposition in human neural progenitor cells. *Nature, 460,* 1127–1133.

Craddock, N., O'Donovan, M. C., & Owen, M. J. (2005). The genetics of Schizophrenia and Bipolar Disorder: Dissecting psychosis. *Journal of Medical Genetics, 42,* 193–205.

Davis, K. L., Kahn, R. S., Ko, G., & Davidson, M. (1991). Dopamine in Schizophrenia: A review and reconceptualization. *The American Journal of Psychiatry, 148,* 1474–1486.

Dein, S. (2005). Spirituality, psychiatry, and participation: A cultural analysis. *Transcultural Psychiatry, 42,* 526–544.

Deisseroth, K. (2011, November). Controlling the brain with light. *Scientific American, 12,* 49–55.

Dickerson, F. B., & Lehman, A. F. (2011). Evidence-based psychotherapy for Schizophrenia: 2011 update. *Journal of Nervous and Mental Disorders, 199,* 520–526.

Dutta, R., Greene, D. R., Addington, T., McKenzie, K., Phillips, M., & Murray, R. M. (2007). Biological, life course, and cross-cultural studies all point toward the value of dimensional and developmental ratings in the classification of psychosis. *Schizophrenia Bulletin, 33,* 868–876.

Eack, S. M., Hogarty, G. E., Cho, R.Y., Prasad, K. M., Greenwald, D.P., Hogarty, S.S., & Keshavan, M. S. (2010). Neuroprotective effects of cognitive enhancement therapy against gray matter loss in early Schizophrenia: Results from a 2-year randomized controlled trial. *Archives of General Psychiatry, 67,* 674–682.

Ellison-Wright, I., & Bullmore, E. (2010). Anatomy of bipolar disorder and Schizophrenia: A meta-analysis. *Schizophrenia Research, 117,* 1–12.

Fanous, A. H., van den Oord, E. J., Riley, B. P., Aggen, S. H., Neale, M. C., O'Neill, F. A., . . . Kendler, K. S. (2005). Relationship between a high-risk haplotype in the DTNBP1 (dysbindin) gene and clinical features of Schizophrenia. *American Journal of Psychiatry, 162,* 1824–1832.

Farris, R. E. L., & Dunham, H. W. (1939). *Mental disorder in urban areas.* Chicago: University of Chicago Press.

Feret, H., Conway, L., & Austin, J. C. (2011). Genetic counselors' attitudes towards individuals with Schizophrenia: Desire for social distance and endorsement of stereotypes. *Patient Education and Counseling, 82,* 69–73.

Francis, A. N., Bhojraj, T. S., Prasad, K. M., Montrose, D., Eack, S. M., Rajarhathinam, R., . . . Keshavan, M. (2013). Alterations in the cerebral white matter of genetic high risk offspring of patients with Schizophrenia Spectrum Disorder. *Progress in Neuropsychopharmacology and Biological Psychiatry, 40,* 187–192.

Gage, F. H., & Muotri, A. R. (2012). What makes each brain unique? How can identical twins grow up with different personalities? "Jumping genes" move around in neurons and alter the way they work. *Scientific American, 306,* 26–31.

Giron, M., Fernandez-Yanez, A., Mana-Alvarenga, S., Molina-Habas, A., & Nolasco, A. (2010). Efficacy and effectiveness of individual family intervention on social and clinical functioning and family burden in severe Schizophrenia. *Psychological Medicine, 40,* 73–84.

Gottesman, I. I., Laursen, T. M., Bertelsen, A., & Montenson, P. B. (2010). Severe mental disorders in offspring with 2 psychiatrically ill parents. *Archives of General Psychiatry, 67,* 252–257.

Gottesman, I. I., & Shields, J. (1973). Genetic theorizing and Schizophrenia. *British Journal of Psychiatry, 122,* 15–30.

Green, M. F., Penn, D. L., Bentall, R., Carpenter, W. T., Gaebel, W., Gur, W. C., . . . Heinssen, R. (2008). Social cognition in Schizophrenia: An NIMH workshop on definitions, assessment, and research opportunities. *Schizophrenia Bulletin, 34,* 1211–1220.

Grof, S., & Grof, C. (1989). *Spiritual emergency: When personal transformation becomes a crisis.* Los Angeles, CA: Tarcher.

Hartberg, C. B., Sundet, K., Rimol, L., Haukvik, U. K., Lange, E. H., Nesvag, R., . . . Agartz, I. (2011). Subcortical brain volumes relate to neurocognition in Schizophrenia and Bipolar Disorder and healthy controls. *Progress in Neuro-Psychopharmacology & Biological Psychiatry, 35,* 1122–1130.

Heston, L. L. (1966). Psychiatric disorders in the foster home reared children of schizophrenic mothers. *British Journal of Psychiatry, 112,* 819–825.

Hooker, C. I., Tully, L. M., Verosky, S. C., Fisher, M., Holland, C., & Vinogradov, S. (2011). Can I trust you? Negative affective priming influences social judgments in Schizophrenia. *Journal of Abnormal Psychology, 120,* 98–107.

Hunter, M. J., Hippman, C., Honer, W. G., & Austin, J. C. (2009). Genetic counseling for Schizophrenia: A review of referrals to a provincial medical genetics program from 1968 to 2007. *American Journal of Genomics, 152A,* 147–152.

Jansen, J. F. A., Backes, W. H., Nicolay, K., & Hooi, M. E. (2006). H MR spectroscopy of the brain: Absolute quantification of metabolites. *Radiology, 240,* 318–332.

Jarskog, L. F., Miyamoto, S., & Lieberman, J. A. (2007). Schizophrenia: New pathological insights and therapies. *Annual Review of Medicine, 58,* 49–61.

Jaspers, K. (1959). *General psychopathology: Volume II.* Berlin: Springer-Verlag.

Javitt, D. C. (2010). Glutamatergic theories of Schizophrenia. *The Israel Journal of Psychiatry and Related Sciences, 47,* 4–16.

Kahler, A. K., Djurovic, S., Julle, B., Jonsson, E. G., Agartz, I., Hall, H., . . . Andreassen, O. A. (2008). Association analysis of Schizophrenia on 18 genes involved in neuronal migration: MDGA1 as a new susceptibility gene. *American Journal of Medical Genetics Part B: Neuropsychiatric Genetics, 147B,* 1089–1100.

Keefe, R. S. E., & Fenton, W. S. (2010). How should DSM-5 criteria for Schizophrenia include cognitive impairment? In C. A. Tamminga, P. J. Sirovatka, D. A. Reigier, & J. van Os (Eds.), *Deconstructing psychoses: Refining the research agenda for DSM-5* (pp. 83–98). Washington, DC: American Psychiatric Association.

Kelly, B. D., O'Callaghan, E., Waddington, J. L., Feeney, L., Browne, S., Scully, P. J., . . . Larkin, C. (2010). Schizophrenia and the city: A review of literature and prospective study of psychosis and urbanicity in Ireland. *Schizophrenia Research, 116,* 75–89.

Kendler, K. S., McGuire, M., Greunberg, A. M., O'Hare, A., Spellman, M., & Walsh, D. (1993). The Roscommon family study 1. Methods, diagnosis of probands, and risk of Schizophrenia in relatives. *Archives of General Psychiatry, 50,* 527–540.

Keshavan, M. S., Tandon, R., Boutros, N. N., & Nasrallah, H. A. (2008). Schizophrenia, "just the facts": What we know in 2008. Part 3: Neurobiology. *Schizophrenia Research, 106,* 89–107.

Keshavan, M. S., Tandon, R., Boutros, N. N., & Nasrallah, H. A. (2013). Renaming schizophrenia: Keeping up with the facts. *Schizophrenia Research, 148,* 1–2.

Kety, S. S., Rosenthal, D., Wender, P., & Schulsinger, F. (1968). The types and prevalence of mental illness in the biological and adoptive families of adopted schizophrenics. *Journal of Psychiatric Residency, 1,* 345–362.

Kim, D. H., Maneen, M. J., & Stahl, S. M. (2009). Building a better antipsychotic: Receptor targets for the treatment of multiple symptom dimensions of schizophrenia. *Neurotherapeutics, 6,* 78–85.

Kingdon, D. (2010). Over-simplification and exclusion of non-conforming studies can demonstrate absence of effect: A lynching party. *Psychological Medicine, 40,* 25–27.

Kinros, J., Reichenberg, A., & Frangou, S. (2010). The neurodevelopmental theory of Schizophrenia: Evidence from studies of early onset cases. *The Israel Journal of Psychiatry and Related Sciences, 47,* 20–27.

Kirkbride, J. B., & Jones, P. B. (2011). The prevention of Schizophrenia—what can we learn from eco-epidemiology? *Schizophrenia Bulletin, 37,* 262–271.

Klosterkotter, J., Schultze-Lutter, F., Bechdolf, A., & Ruhrmann, S. (2011). Prediction and prevention of Schizophrenia: What has been achieved and where to go next? *World Psychiatry, 10,* 165–174.

Krabbendam, L., Arts, B., van Os, J., & Aleman, A. (2005). Cognitive functioning in patients with Schizophrenia and Bipolar Disorder: A quantitative review. *Schizophrenia Research, 80,* 137–149.

Krabbendam, L., & van Os, J. (2005). Schizophrenia and urbanicity: A major environmental influence—conditional on genetic risk. *Schizophrenia Bulletin, 31,* 795–799.

Kring, A. M., & Moran, E. K. (2008). Emotional response deficits in Schizophrenia: Insights from affective science. *Schizophrenia Bulletin, 34,* 819–834.

Kubicki, M., McCarely, R., Westin, C. F., Park, H. J., Maier, S., Kikinis, R., . . . Shenton, M. E. (2007). A review of diffusion tensor imaging studies in Schizophrenia. *Journal of Psychiatric Research, 41,* 15–30.

Kurtz, M. M., & Mueser, K. T. (2008). A meta-analysis of controlled research on social skills training for Schizophrenia. *Journal of Consulting and Clinical Psychology, 76,* 491–504.

Leucht, S., Corves, C., Arbter, D., Engel, R. R., Chunbo, L., & Davis, J. M. (2009). Second-generation versus first-generation antipsychotic drugs for Schizophrenia: A meta-analysis. *The Lancet, 373,* 31–41.

Lewis, D. A., Hashimoto, T., & Volk, D. W. (2005). Cortical inhibitory neurons and schizophrenia. *Nature Reviews: Neuroscience, 6,* 312–324.

Lincoln, T. M., Wilhelm, K., & Nestoriuc, Y. (2007). Effectiveness of psychoeducation for relapse, symptoms, knowledge adherence and functioning in psychotic disorders: A meta-analysis. *Schizophrenia Research, 96,* 232–245.

Lukoff, D. (2007). Spirituality in the recovery from persistent mental disorders. *Southern Medical Journal, 100,* 642–646.

Lysaker, P. H., Buck, K. D., & Hammond, K. (2007). Psychotherapy of Schizophrenia: An analysis of requirements of individual psychotherapy with persons who experience manifestly barren or empty selves. *Psychology and Psychotherapy: Theory, Research, and Practice, 80,* 377–387.

Lysaker, P. H., Dimaggio, G., Carcione, A., Procacci, M., Buck, K. D., Davis, L. W., & Nicolo, G. (2010). Metacognition and Schizophrenia: The capacity for self-reflectivity as a predictor for prospective assessments of work performance over six months. *Schizophrenia Research, 122,* 124–130.

Lysaker, P. H., & Lysaker, J. T. (2008). Schizophrenia and alterations in self-experience: A comparison of 6 perspectives. *Schizophrenia Bulletin, 36,* 331–340.

Lyus, V. L. (2007). The importance of genetic counseling for individuals with Schizophrenia and their relatives. *American Journal of Medical Genetics Part B, 144b,* 1014–1021.

Marchetto, M. C., & Gage, F. H. (2012). Modeling brain disease in a dish: Really? *Cell Stem Cell, 10,* 642–645.

Martinez, M. A. (2010). *RNA interference and viruses.* New York: Caister Academic Press.

Masi, G., & Liboni, F. (2011). Management of Schizophrenia in children and adolescents. *Drugs, 71,* 179–208.

McGrath, J., Saha, S., Welham, J., El Saadi, O., MacCauley, C., & Chant, D. (2004). A systematic review of the incidence of Schizophrenia: The distribution of rates and the influence of sex, urbanicity, migrant status and methodology. *BMC Med, 2,* 13.

McIntosh, A. M., Job, D. E., Moorhead, W. J., Harrison, L. K., Whalley, H. C., Johnstone, E. C., & Lawrie, S. M. (2006). Genetic liability to Schizophrenia or Bipolar Disorder and its relationship to brain structure. *American Journal of Medicao Genetics Part B (Neuropsychiatric Genetics), 141B,* 76–83.

McKeage, K., & Plosker, G. L. (2004). Amisulpride: A review of its use in the management of Schizophrenia. *CNS Drugs, 18,* 933–956.

Mendelssohn, S. (2004). From a healer to scientists: On duality. *The Journal of Alternative and Complementary Medicine, 4,* 597–606.

Miesenbock, G. (2008, October). Lighting up the brain: A clever combination of optics and genetics is allowing neuroscientists to map—even control—brain circuits with unprecedented precision. *Scientific American,* 52–59.

Mohr, S., Borras, L., Rieben, I., Betrisey, C., Gillieron, C., Brandt, P. Y., . . . Huguelet, P. (2010). Evolution of spirituality and religiousness in chronic Schizophrenia or Schizo-Affective Disorders: A 3-years follow-up study. *Social Psychiatry Epidemiology, 45,* 1095–1103.

Mohr, S., Brandt, P., Borras, L., Gillieron, C., & Huguelet, P. (2006). Toward an integration of spirituality and religiousness into the psychosocial dimension of Schizophrenia. *American Journal of Psychiatry, 163,* 1952–1959.

Monaco, L. C., Conway, L., Valverde, K., & Austin, J. C. (2009). Exploring genetic counselors' perceptions of and attitudes towards Schizophrenia. *Public Health Genomics, 13,* 21–26.

Nestler, E. J. (2009). Epigenetic mechanisms in psychiatry. *Biological Psychiatry, 65,* 189–190.

Ohta, Y., Nakane, Y., Nishihara, H., & Takemoto, T. (1992). Ecological structure and incidence rates of Schizophrenia in Nagasaki City. *Acta Psychiatry Scandanavia, 86,* 113–120.

Owen, M. J., Craddock, N., & Jablensky, A. (2007). The genetic deconstruction of psychosis. *Schizophrenia Bulletin, 33,* 905–911.

Owen, M. J., Craddock, N., & O'Donovan, M. C. (2005). Schizophrenia and genes at last? *Trends in Genetics, 21,* 518–525.

Pagsberg, A. K. (2013). Schizophrenia Spectrum and other psychotic disorders. *European Child and Adolescent Psychiatry, 22,* S2–S9.

Pargament, K. I., Koenig, H. G., & Perez, L. M. (2000). The many methods of religious coping: Development and initial validation of RCOPE. *Journal of Clinical Psychology, 56,* 519–543.

Perry, J. W. (1962). Reconstitutive process in the psychopathology of the self. *Annals of the New York Academy of Medicine, 96,* 853–873.

Pfammatter, M., Junghan, U. M., & Brenner, H. D. (2006). Effectiveness of psychoeducation for relapse, symptoms, knowledge adherence and functioning in psychotic disorders: Conclusions from meta-analyses. *Schizophrenia Bulletin, 32,* S64–S80.

Phillips, R. E., & Stein, C. H. (2007). God's will, God's punishment or God's limitations? Religious coping strategies reported by young adults living with serious mental illness. *Journal of Clinical Psychology, 63,* 529–540.

Popper, K. (1959/2002). *The logic of scientific discovery.* New York: Routledge.

Rapoport, J. L., Addington, A. M., Frangou, S., & MRC Psych. (2005). The neurodevelopmental model of Schizophrenia: Update 2005. *Molecular Psychiatry, 10,* 434–449.

Reece, J., & Campbell, N. (2002). *Biology.* San Francisco: Benjamin Cummings.

Publisher info - "American Psychiatric Association in Washington DC"

Revheim, N., & Greenberg, W. M. (2007). Spirituality matters: Creating a time and place for hope. *Psychiatric Rehabilitation Journal, 30,* 307–310.

Revheim, N., Greenberg, W. M., & Citrome, L. (2010). Spirituality, Schizophrenia, and state hospitals: Program description and characteristics of self-selected attendees of a spirituality therapeutic group. *Psychiatric Quarterly, 81,* 285–292.

Rideout, A. L., Carroll, J. C., Blaine, S. M., Cremin, C., Dorman, H., Gibbons, C. A., . . . Allanson, J.

(2009). Genetics Schizophrenia. *Canadian Family Physician, 55,* 1207.

Rimol, L. M., Hartberg, C. B., Nesvag, R., Fennema-Notestine, C., Hagler, D. J., Pung, C. J., . . . Agartz, I. (2010). Cortical thickness and subcortical volumes in Schizophrenia and Bipolar Disorder. *Biological Psychiatry, 68,* 41–50.

Schneider, K. (1959). *Clinical psychopathology.* New York: Grune & Stratton, Inc.

Selemon, L. D., & Rajkowska, G. (2003). Cellular pathology in the dorsolateral prefrontal cortex distinguishes Schizophrenia from Bipolar Disorder. *Current Molecular Medicine, 3,* 427–436.

Shah, R., Kulhara, P., Grover, S., Kumar, S., Malhotra, R., & Tyagi, S. (2011). Relationship between spirituality/religiousness and coping in patients with residual Schizophrenia. *Quality of Life Research, 20,* 1053–1060.

Silberschmidt, A. L., & Sponheim, S. R. (2007). Personality in relation to genetic liability for Schizophrenia and Bipolar Disorder: Differential associations with the COMT. *Schizophrenia Research, 100,* 316–324.

Silverman, J. (1967). Shamans and acute Schizophrenia. *American Anthropologist, 69,* 20–32.

Singh, B. (2005). Recognition and optimal management of Schizophrenia and related psychoses. *Internal Medicine Journal, 35,* 413–418.

Smith, M. J., Cloninger, C. R., Harms, M. P., & Csernansky, J. G. (2008). Temperament and character as Schizophrenia-related endophenotypes in non-psychotic siblings. *Schizophrenia Research, 104,* 198–205.

Stahl, S. M. (2010). Fooling mother nature: Epigenetics and novel treatments for psychiatric disorders. *CNS Spectrum, 15,* 358–365.

Stahl, S. M., & Buckley, P. F. (2007). Negative symptoms of Schizophrenia: A problem that will not go away. *Acta Psychiatrica Scandinavica, 115,* 4–11.

Stahl, S. M., & Wise, D. D. (2008). The potential role of a Corticotropin-releasing factor recept-1 antagonist in psychiatric disorders. *CNS Spectrum, 13,* 467–476.

Stanghellini, G. (2005). Schizophrenic consciousness, spiritual experience, and the borders between things, images and words. *Transcultural Psychiatry, 42,* 610–629.

Stephan, K. E., Friston, K. J., & Frith, C. D. (2009). Dysconnection in Schizophrenia: From abnormal synaptic plasticity to failures of self-monitoring. *Schizophrenia Bulletin, 35,* 509–527.

Stober, G., Ben-Shachar, D., Cardon, M., Falkai, P., Fonteh, A. N., Gawlik, M., . . . Riederer, P. (2009). Schizophrenia: From the brain to peripheral markers. A consensus paper of the WFSBP task force on biological markers. *The World Journal of Biological Psychiatry, 10,* 127–155.

Stone, J. M., & Pilowsky, L. S. (2006). Antipsychotic drug action: Targets for drug discovery with neurochemical imaging. *Expert Review of Neurotherapeutics, 6,* 57–70.

Sullivan, P. F., Kendler, K. S., & Neale M. C. (2003). Schizophrenia as a complex trait. Evidence from a meta-analysis of twin studies. *Archives of General Psychiatry, 60,* 1187–1192.

Tandon, R., Keshavan, M. S., & Nasrallah, H. A. (2008a). Schizophrenia: "Just the facts": What we know in 2008. Part 1: Overview. *Schizophrenia Research, 100,* 4–19.

Tandon, R., Keshavan, M. S., & Nasrallah, H. A. (2008b). Schizophrenia: "Just the facts": What we know in 2008. Part 2: Epidemiology and etiology. *Schizophrenia Research, 100,* 1–18.

Tandon, R., Nasrallah, H. A., & Keshavan, M. S. (2010). Schizophrenia, "just the facts" 5: Treatment and prevention: Past, present and future. *Schizophrenia Research, 122,* 1–23.

Tarrier, N. (2010). Cognitive behavior therapy for Schizophrenia and psychosis: Current status and future directions. *Clinical Schizophrenia & Related Psychoses, 4,* 176–184.

Thompson, P. A., Christoforou, A., Morris, S. W., Adie, E., Pickard, B. S., Porteous, D., . . . Evans, K. L. (2007). Association of neuregulin 1 with Schizophrenia and Bipolar Disorder in a second cohort from the Scottish population. *Molecular Psychiatry, 12,* 94–104.

Tsuang, M. T., Bar, J. L., Stone, W. S., & Faraone, S. V. (2004). Gene-environment interactions in mental disorders. *World Psychiatry, 3,* 73–83.

Veiling, W., & Susser, E. (2011). Migration and psychotic disorders. *Expert Review of Neurotherapeutics, 11,* 65–76.

World Health Organization. (2001). *Mental health report 2001. Mental Health: New understanding, New Hope.* Geneva: Author.

Yarhouse, M. A., Butman, R. E., & McRay, B. W. (2005). *Modern psychopathologies: A comprehensive Christian approach.* Downers Grove, IL: Intervarsity Press.

# 8

# Substance-Related Disorders[1]

*We Americans—like most all other human cultures, ancient and modern, primitive and civilized—are a drug-using people. Indeed, homo sapiens is a drug-using species, and has been for thousands of years. . . . [Also obvious] is the relative rarity of non-drug-users in our culture. No estimate has been made of the number of American adults who have never used a mind-affecting drug . . . but the number must be very small, a few percent of the population at most. The nonuse of mind-affecting drugs, indeed, can be described as aberrant behavior, deviating from the norms of American society.*

BRECHER, 1972, PP. 480–481

## INTRODUCTION

The desire to experience various altered states of consciousness appears to be normal and innate, not to mention that people routinely take a variety of licit and illicit drugs in response to stress and other aversive experiences (Carlson, 2006; Mahoney, 1980; Weill, 2004). Some noteworthy individuals—from William James, Huston Smith, and Aldous Huxley to Roger Walsh, Ram Das, and Timothy Leary—have even gone so far as to stress that some drugs (particularly psychedelics) actually heighten our awareness of consciousness and reality:

> Some years ago I myself made some observations on this aspect of nitrous oxide intoxication, and reported them in print. One conclusion was forced upon my

[1] In the Diagnostic and Statistical Manual of Mental Disorders, 4th edition, text revision (DSM-IV-TR; American Psychiatric Association [APA], 2000), the diagnostic category was titled "Substance-Related Disorders." In the DSM-5 (APA, 2013), this category was changed to "Substance-Related and Addictive Disorders," which includes Gambling Disorder (previously listed in DSM-IV-TR under the category of Impulse-Control Disorders Not Elsewhere Classified). This chapter focuses only on Substance-Related Disorders.

> mind at that time, and my impression of its truth has ever since remained unshaken. It is our normal waking consciousness, rational consciousness as we call it, is but one special type of consciousness, whilst all about it, parted from it by the filmiest of screens, there lie potential forms of consciousness entirely different. We may go through life without suspecting their existence; but apply the requisite stimulus, and at a touch they are there in all their completeness, definite types of mentality which probably somewhere have their field of application and adaptation. No account of the universe in its totality can be final which leaves these other forms of consciousness quite discarded. How to regard them is the question . . . (William James, 1902, as cited in Walsh & Vaughan, 1993, p. 94)

At the same time, substance-related problems have been a detriment to individuals and societies throughout history, and some estimates suggest that Substance Use Disorders reflect the most significant health problem in 21st-century United States (Bevins & Bardo, 2004). The incidence of alcohol dependence[2] alone is staggering: between 12.5–15% of U.S. adults will meet the criteria at some point in their lives (APA, 2000; Hasin, Stinson, Ogburn, & Grant, 2007). The consequences of substance-related problems are enormous: from lethal overdoses and increased incidences of crime and violence to a host of associated illnesses (cirrhosis, lung cancer, hepatitis B and C, etc.), increased birth defects in the offspring of addicted mothers, and a diminished capacity to parent effectively (Bry, 1983; Johnson & Belfer, 1995). In the United States, substance-related problems are also among the most common causes of adolescent mortality, and it appears that adolescent drug use is increasing, with many youths beginning at younger ages (Allen, 2003; Sussman, Skara, & Ames, 2008; Weinberg, Rahdert, Colliver, & Glantz, 1998). This is particularly alarming because the younger the age when individuals begin using various substances, the more likely they will develop a Substance Use Disorder (SUD; Kassel et al., 2010).

Whereas historical explanations of addiction tended to blame the individual for moral/spiritual bankruptcy, demonic possession, or willful misbehavior, today's theories are becoming increasingly complex and multifaceted (Childress, 2006; Giese, 1999). Nonetheless, "although our explanations have become more sophisticated, our understanding of addiction is far from complete" (DiClemente, 2003, p. 3). The majority of researchers in this field have emphasized that SUDs are not confined to a

[2] The DSM-III and DSM-IV included separate categories for substance abuse and substance dependence, the latter being the more severe condition. DSM-5 collapsed abuse and dependence into "Substance Use Disorder," which is accompanied by a severity scale: mild, moderate, or severe. Whereas in the DSM-IV one criteria was required for substance abuse, and three criteria were required for substance dependence, two criteria are required for the DSM-5 diagnosis of Substance Use Disorder. The DSM-5 states that eliminating the diagnoses of substance abuse and substance dependence was due to the common confusion of "dependence" with "addiction" (i.e., the tolerance and withdrawal that characterize substance dependence are also normal, nonpathological responses to many prescribed medications and thus do not necessarily indicate an addiction). According to the DSM-5 Substance Use Disorders Workgroup (n.d.), the rationale for this change involved several empirical findings: "the high correlations between dependence and abuse raised questions about the utility of the two-factor solutions. . . . The large body of literature on the structure of abuse and dependence criteria in clinical and general population samples suggest that the DSM-IV abuse and dependence criteria can be considered to form a unidimensional structure, with abuse and dependence criteria interspersed across the severity spectrum." Because this book is going to press shortly after the release of DSM-5, there is no extant research on the single category of "Substance Use Disorder." Therefore, much of the research cited here refers to the DSM-IV categories of substance abuse and substance dependence.

specific class or type of individuals (there is no such thing as a "typical" alcoholic or drug abuser) and that they are related not only to the brain, but also to a host of psychological, cultural, and societal factors (Carroll & Miller, 2006; DiClemente, 2003).

In many regards, the problem of drug abuse captures the essence of many mental health problems: how and why people often repeatedly engage in self-destructive behavior; the tensions between immediate gratification and long-term well-being of self, family, and community; and the dynamic interplay of biology and choice, individual and society (Carroll & Miller, 2006). On the other hand, most other mental health problems are *not* "appetitive" or engaged due to their inherently pleasurable and reinforcing effects (i.e., depressive and psychotic episodes are not pleasurable, in contrast to the effects of most drugs and alcohol; DiClemente, 2003).

As is the case with most of the disorders in this text, the etiology of Substance Use Disorders is multidimensional and somewhat idiosyncratic to any given individual. For example, taking a specific drug in order to *induce* a specific, desired experiential state of consciousness is the principle driving force for some who later develop an addiction. In contrast, others may begin taking substances in order to *escape* from aversive emotions or in order to establish and/or maintain membership in various social networks. Moreover, the preceding factors interact with a given person's willful choice and the presence of other (non-substance-related) reinforcing activities; with one's physiology, brain circuitry, and other genetic factors; as well as one's sociocultural conditions—all of which have an impact regarding whether and to what extent a person develops a Substance Use Disorder.

One thing that you will repeatedly encounter in this chapter is the notion that "the labeling of substance use as 'deviant' is hardly a pure and unproblematic act" (Mahoney, 1980, p. 348) and that the line between substance use and a Substance Use *Disorder* is anything but universally clear-cut. One issue is that of what constitutes a drug. For example, do you consider caffeine a drug? If not, you should know that most of the literature in this arena considers a drug something that we ingest or otherwise take into our bodies that is not normally required for its nutritional properties (Mahoney, 1980). Moreover, caffeine not only affects the mind, body, and behavior with stimulating properties, but routinely drinking as few as five cups of coffee each day may produce physical dependence, and those who habitually drink coffee and quit usually experience withdrawal symptoms—from lethargy and nervousness to headaches and irritability. Why is this drug not only not prohibited, but virtually exalted by our society? Could it be because it often improves the caffeine user's productivity, which is so valued by our society? And why does the DSM-5 include a "Use Disorder" for every class of substances except caffeine—despite the fact that many caffeine users meet all of the criteria for substance dependence (which require more criteria than Substance Use Disorder)?[3] Even though many of our cultural customs involve caffeine (from coffee and chocolate to tea and soft drinks) and we regularly introduce our children to them at very early ages, excessive use of caffeine is nonetheless unhealthy.[4]

---

[3] The same was true of the DSM-IV-TR (APA, 2000, p. 192). Although the DSM-5 does include caffeine-related disorders (i.e., intoxication, withdrawal, etc.), caffeine is the only substance (of the 10 classes of substances the DSM-5 lists) for which the diagnosis of Substance Use Disorder does not apply.

[4] Not only can large doses of caffeine lead to insomnia, muscle tremors, irregular pulse, respiratory problems, and convulsions—doses of approximately 10 grams may be lethal, even though that would require consuming nearly 100 cups of coffee (Mahoney, 1980).

According to the DSM-5, a Substance Use Disorder is a problematic pattern of substance use that results in clinically significant distress or impairment, accompanied by two (or more) of the following criteria within a 12-month period: increasing amounts of the substance are used, or for longer than intended; the person craves the substance; the person repeatedly wants to decrease or cease the substance use, or has tried unsuccessfully; the person spends a lot of time acquiring, or recovering from, the substance; use of the substance interferes with the person's responsibilities at home, school, or work; the person reduces or ceases occupational, social, or recreational activities that were previously important to him; the person continues to use the substance even though it has caused or magnified problems with his relationships; the person continues to use the substance even though he knows it is causing or magnifying a psychological or physical problem; the person uses the substance in contexts that are physically dangerous; the person has developed tolerance to the substance; the personal has withdrawal symptoms to the substance.

As Tarter, Vanyukov, and Kirisci (2008) have pointed out, to comprehensively understand the etiology of SUDs, research would need to identify not only the risk factors that are common to all SUD categories (i.e., the severity level of the SUD—mild, moderate, severe), but also those that are specific to each SUD (i.e., Alcohol SUD, Tobacco SUD, Amphetamine SUD, etc.). However, in those instances in which SUD-specific variables have been found, they are confined primarily to catabolic pathways and pharmacological actions, a far cry from a comprehensive understanding. For the vast majority of cases, the biological, genetic, environmental, sociocultural, and developmental risk factors that have been identified are common to *all* SUD categories (Tarter et al., 2008); for this reason, this chapter will focus primarily on the etiological factors common to all SUDs.

## Terminology: What You Call It Makes a Difference

Although the DSM-IV-TR stated that substance abuse "should not be used as a synonym for 'use,' 'misuse,' or 'hazardous use'" (APA, 2000, p. 198), many authors in the substance field prefer to use non-DSM terms such as "troublesome use" (Carroll & Miller, 2006; DiClemente, 2006; Humphreys & Gifford, 2006), "misuse" (Carlson, 2006), "addictions" (Childress, 2006; DiClemente, 2003; Koob, 2006), and "addictive behaviors" (Miller, 2006). As Carroll and Miller (2006) stress, "What you call it matters" (p. 5). After all, consider what it implies about how one conceptualizes the dynamics of the issue, as well as the consequences for those struggling with substances, to refer to people who drink heavily or use illicit drugs as "drunkards," "alcoholics," "problem drinkers," "addicts," drug abusers," "dope fiends," "drug-dependent," or "criminals."

Two things seem clear to us. First, it seems important to recognize that, like most mental health problems, substance-related issues manifest across a spectrum, from completely nonproblematic *use* (such as occasional drinking or smoking marijuana in safe circumstances), to *heavy use* (such as more regular use of substances that does not currently interfere with one's health, relationships, or work; mild SUD), to *misuse, abuse,* or potentially *hazardous use* (chronic, heavy use of substances that is interfering to some extent with one's health, relationships, or work; moderate SUD), to outright unhealthy *dependence* (as in the case of an uncontrollable heroin addiction; severe SUD). According to Miller and Carroll (2006), "the

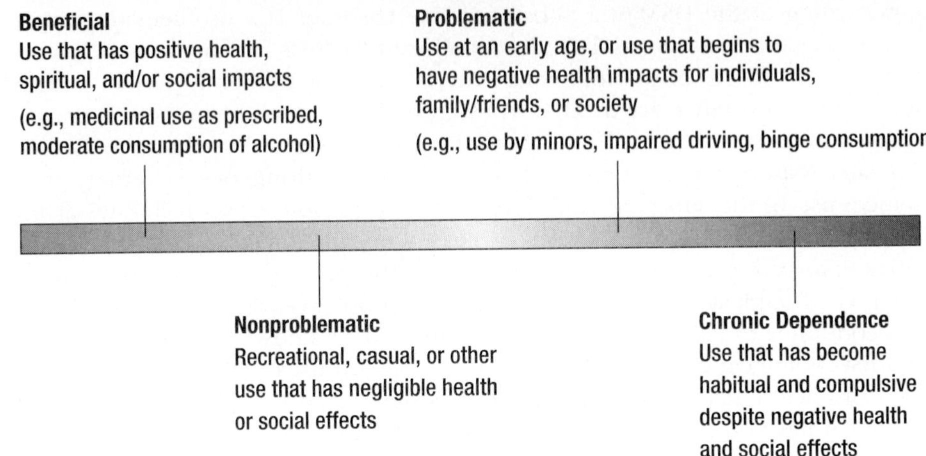


**FIGURE 8.1** The Spectrum of Psychoactive Substance Use[5]

diagnostic criteria for classifying people with 'drug abuse' and 'drug dependence' represent arbitrary cut points along a gradual continuum" (p. 296). Many, if not most, researchers in this field agree with a continuum or "spectrum" view of substance use (see Figure 8.1). In this chapter, we will primarily use the term Substance Use Disorders (SUDs), although we will also use other terms, such as "addiction," in the context of quoting others' work.

It is important to remember that according to the DSM-5, a diagnosis of a Substance Use Disorder requires not just the use of substances, but "clinically significant impairment or distress." This view is widely held among experts in the field:

> Alcoholism (now more accurately called *alcohol dependence*) is a disorder that is defined by its consequences. The amount a person consumes is an important clue, but the diagnosis itself is based on the effects drinking has on the individual and the environment. (Morrison, 2008, p. 100)

Like other disorders covered in this book, SUDs are anything but homogenous conditions:

> Not only are there significant differences in how individuals progress to substance abuse and dependence and whether they get out early in the progression of problematic use, there are also very big differences in the lifetime careers of alcohol and substance abusers. Some seem able to maintain a pattern of abuse or binge use over long periods without moving on to severe dependence. Others continue frequent or daily use for many consecutive years. Still others have a variable pattern and show periods of dependence and periods of abstinence mixed with periods of nonabusive use. (DiClemente, 2006, p. 86)

---

[5] Reproduced with permission from British Columbia Ministries of Health Services and Children and Family Development (2010, November 1). *Healthy Minds, Healthy People: A 10-Year Plan to Address Mental Health and Substance Use in British Columbia*. Victoria, British Columbia.

## Comorbidity Issues

The comorbidity of substance-related disorders and other mental health disorders is high, and increases as the latter becomes more severe: lifetime prevalence of substance-related disorders is approximately 25–30% in those with depression or anxiety disorders and approximately 50% among those with Schizophrenia or Bipolar Disorder (Muesser, Drake, Turner, & McGovern, 2006). Of great clinical significance is the all-too-well-known reality that such comorbidity increases the complexity of a person's struggles and makes treatment considerably more difficult. There have been long-standing debates regarding whether or not SUDs are the cause or consequence of other psychopathology. Whereas some (e.g., Bean-Bayog, 1988) have argued that SUDs are themselves forms of trauma that are responsible for causing other forms of psychopathology, others have argued for the converse—that is, that substance use is a response to previously existing mental health struggles. Meanwhile, others have emphasized that "the complexities of human suffering associated with substance abuse cannot be reduced to simplistic either-or conclusions about whether alcoholism and addiction are a result or cause of that suffering" (Khantzian, 1987, p. 522).

After reviewing the literature on overarching meta-models that attempt to explain these high comorbidities,[6] Muesser and colleagues concluded that none of the models sufficiently account for the high comorbidities observed between substance-related and other mental health disorders; they even went so far as stating that "the basic monolithic fact is that we understand relatively little about the etiologies of individual psychiatric and substance use disorders. Therefore accounting for comorbidity is a complex conundrum" (Muesser et al., 2006, p. 122).[7] As will be discussed subsequently in more detail, interventions that target SUDs and comorbid mental health disorders separately have demonstrated very little success (Muesser et al., 2006). Because of the high comorbidity found between SUDs and the following disorders, it is highly recommended that clinicians screen for these when working with people with SUDs: depression (McDowell & Clodfelter, 2001); anxiety (Barlow, 2004; Swift & Mueller, 2001); Schizophrenia (Buckley, 1998); Bipolar Disorders (Clodfelter & McDowell, 2001); Post-Traumatic Stress Disorder (PTSD) (Ouimette & Brown, 2002); Conduct Disorder (Weinberg et al., 1998); Antisocial and Borderline Personality Disorders (Compton,

---

[6] Some of these meta-models include secondary substance abuse models (i.e., the "self-medication" hypothesis in which people use specific substances to reduce or counter the symptoms of their mental health disorders); secondary psychopathology models (i.e., that some types of substances—such as LSD, stimulants, and cannabis—may cause not only transient psychotic episodes but also more enduring mental health disorders); common factor models (i.e., that independent factors common to both conditions—such as poverty and cognitive impairment—are responsible for the comorbidity); and bidirectional models (i.e., substance use may trigger the onset of an anxiety disorder and then substances are used to medicate the symptoms of the anxiety disorder; Muesser et al., 2006). Interestingly, Edward Khantzian—a Harvard Medical School professor of psychiatry who co-originated the self-medication hypothesis—eventually arrived at a more nuanced position on the debate regarding substance dependence being either a cause or consequence of other psychopathology: "there is much that can be seen as complementary rather than competing. The issue is not whether substance dependence is a cause or consequence of psychopathology, but how we can begin to integrate the findings of the various perspectives and clarify the complex interrelationships between psychopathology and substance dependence" (Khantzian, 1987, p. 525).

[7] Moreover, most epidemiological studies addressing such comorbidity issues focus on a "between-persons" level of analyses; because of this, we know relatively little with regard to how such comorbidity derives at the level of the individual person (Kassel & Veilleux, 2010).

Thomas, Stinson, & Grant, 2007; Linehan, 1993); Attention Deficit–Hyperactivity Disorder (ADHD; Childress, 2006); and Eating Disorders (Katz, 1990).

## ETIOLOGY

*"Addiction is not well understood."*

BICKEL & POTENZA, 2006, P. 8

In the field of Substance Use Disorder treatment, it is widely agreed that as our understanding of the etiology of SUDs improves, so will our ability to prevent and treat them (Glantz, Weinberg, Miner, & Colliver, 1999), and laypeople hold similar views. In a study by Kuppin and Carpiano (2008), laypeople's beliefs regarding whether or not substance problems are biological in nature correlate with their beliefs regarding the most appropriate form of treatment.

Like depression and anxiety, addiction appears to be highly overdetermined or, as Bickel and Potenza (2006) state, "a complex multicomponent phenomenon. . . . there is no centralized control by a singular process in addiction" (p. 9). Whereas researchers and clinicians have traditionally sought singular, simple mechanisms to explain SUDs, such as mesolimbic dopaminergic neurotransmission (UR), craving (UL), or familial, macro-environmental or other sociocultural ills (LR/LL), we suggest that Integral theory again provides an excellent framework with which to understand some of the complexities involved in SUDs. "When it comes to addictions," writes DiClemente (2003), "single-cause etiological models have been woefully inadequate" (p. 6). Not only are a host of quadratic and developmental factors involved in the etiology of SUDs; the latter is usually not a person's sole problem, but rather one part of a larger set of problems, including mood, anxiety, and other mental disorders; child abuse and neglect and other serious family disturbances; poverty, unemployment, financial problems, and homelessness; health problems, injuries, and disability; as well as violence and crime (Miller & Carroll, 2006). Thus, understanding why some people are able to use alcohol or other drugs and not develop a problem whereas others develop severe SUDs requires a complex model capable of revealing the interplay of a host of biological, experiential, cultural, and social factors (DiClemente, 2003; Donovan & Marlatt, 1988; Glantz & Pickens, 1992).

On this issue it is important to remember that "despite all of our disclaimers that alcoholism/addiction is no one thing and that it has multiple determinants, we almost invariably, if not necessarily, fall prey to considering our own formulations, concepts, and data to the exclusion of other perspectives" (Khantzian, 1987, p. 521). With this in mind, let us turn to specific etiological views of SUDs.

### Upper-Right Perspectives: From Behaviorism to Neuroscience

"Addiction is a self-organizing complex disorder that emerges from the interaction of evolutionarily old behavioral processes and their associated brain regions" (Bickel & Potenza, 2006, p. 9). Part of what this means is that multiple processes interact—some of which have co-evolved over millennia via natural selection—and become a system that orders and perpetuates itself without the intentional intervening of an external agent. Among the most powerful components of this complex set of interactions is that of operant conditioning and how its processes impact the brain (O'Brien, 2007). We will address the conditioning processes first, followed by the neuroscience of SUDs.

**BEHAVIORAL PERSPECTIVES** As we have seen in earlier chapters, much of our behavior—including those behaviors resulting in a mental disorder diagnosis—is a function of positive and negative reinforcement. The positive reinforcing effects of alcohol and other substances (making us feel good or better; or viewing ourselves, others, and the world in a more enjoyable manner) play very significant roles in the development of SUDs.[8] Noteworthy is the finding that people with less access to non-substance-related positive reinforcement, fewer stress-buffering resources, and less stimulating environments are at an increased risk for SUDs, for the simple reason that substances—in contrast to gratifying work, hobbies, relationships, and so forth—are the main or only source of enjoyment in their lives (de Wit & Phan, 2010).[9] In contrast to those who use substances primarily to enhance the pleasure of an activity they are already enjoying, those who use substances as a means of *escaping* from or *avoiding* dealing with life problems are more at risk for developing a substance problem; the latter are using substances more for their negatively reinforcing properties (the removal of aversive experience) than for their positively reinforcing properties (the addition of pleasurable experience) (McCarthy, Curtin, Piper, & Baker, 2010). To compound matters, if individuals—in addition to having avoidant coping styles—also expect or believe that alcohol, for example, will have positively reinforcing effects, this combination increases the likelihood of substance use becoming a Substance Use Disorder (Cooper, Russell, & George, 1988).

Once one has initiated drug use, withdrawal symptoms—such as depressed mood, anxiety, or irritability—are common experiences, and escaping from such unpleasant affect is highly (negatively) reinforcing. Individuals' learning that drug use diminishes withdrawal symptoms or other aversive affect is considered by many to be a central motive for continued use that may result in an SUD (McCarthy et al., 2010). However, research has demonstrated that withdrawal symptoms do not always predict drug use, and such evidence suggests that negative reinforcement is not always a primary factor in the development of SUDs.[10] To account for such data, Baker, Piper, McCarthy, Majeskie, and Fiore (2004) developed a reformulated negative reinforcement model of drug motivation that added three components to traditional negative reinforcement models. First, Baker et al. (2004) posit that escaping from or avoiding affective—in contrast to somatic—dimensions of withdrawal is the primary motivation of continued drug use. Second, they suggest that although people are normally aware that they are using drugs, they are often unaware of the motivational and decision-making processes that led them to use the drug(s). Finally, the negative reinforcing principles involved are generalized to *any* aversive affective experiences, not just

[8] It is of great importance that whereas the positive experiential effects of most drugs are relatively immediate, the negative consequences are usually quite delayed.

[9] High-quality, intimate relationships with people who do not use alcohol or substances are a major protective factor, as are other coping skills that reduce stress and provide positive reinforcement (exercise, meditation, journaling, spending time in nature, hobbies, and attending to one's life difficulties—whether with counseling/psychotherapy or informally).

[10] It seems critically important to bear in mind that negative reinforcement occurs not only with the removal or lessening of withdrawal symptoms but with the removal or lessening of *any* aversive experience.

those involved in withdrawal: "we propose that addicted individuals use drugs to escape distress, whether the distress is due to drug deprivation or environmental stress" (McCarthy et al., 2010, p. 20). In addition, positive and negative reinforcement principles work together; they are not mutually exclusive or contradictory:

> the reformulated model does not hold that distress is the sole precipitant of urges or self-administration, although it does assert that escape or avoidance of distress is the dominant motive for use . . . the reformulated model . . . acknowledges the role that positive reinforcement plays in drug use, particularly during initiation of use or after a period of abstinence in which tolerance diminishes. (McCarthy et al., 2010, p. 21)

According to Miller and Carroll (2006),

> Some drugs hijack the central reinforcement system of the brain by (1) artificially stimulating it and powerfully reinforcing drug use, (2) dysregulating and undermining natural reward systems, and (3) simultaneously evoking stress and aversive states likely to increase hunger for positive reinforcement. These drug effects in themselves can lead to a stable preference for drug use and displacement of natural sources of reinforcement. (pp. 296–297)

The conceptual framework of neurobiologist George Koob (2006) emphasizes the transition from merely using a substance to being addicted to that substance, the latter of which involves experiencing irritability, anxiety, dysphoria, and other aversive emotional states when the person is unable to use the substance. Here again we encounter an aspect of the issue regarding the nonequivalence of substance use and Substance Use Disorders: at the most dangerous end of the continuum are those people with minimal or no nondrug reinforcements who use substances primarily to escape from their pain and suffering (negative reinforcement); at the less dangerous end are people who enjoy satisfaction from many different outlets (work, relationship, hobbies, etc.) yet also use substances as an additional source of stimulation or pleasure (positive reinforcement).

Paraphrasing Bickel and Potenza (2006, pp. 17–18), brief, intense stimuli (which characterizes the action and effects of most substances) are more powerfully reinforcing than stimuli that are less intense and/or of a longer duration; as a result, some people will devote increasing amounts of their time and behavior to acquiring and experiencing such brief, intense stimuli. A significant consequence of attending more and more to such stimuli is a shortened temporal horizon that consequently tends to reduce the reinforcing effects of less intense, more protracted stimuli (such as those that derive from an activity one devotes oneself to such as meaningful work, learning to play a musical instrument, developing an athletic skill, or practicing a hobby such as painting or pottery). In other words, spending an increasing proportion of one's time engaging in drug use that is intensely reinforcing shortens one's perspective of time and makes engaging in long-term, delayed-yet-gratifying projects more difficult.[11]

---

[11] From the reformulated affective procession model of negative reinforcement, drug cues (which are usually of high incentive value—in other words, brief and intensely rewarding) not only recruit one's attention, they also recruit one's cognitive control. Thus, the perceived value of any alternative incentives or sources of positive reinforcement becomes obscured because of the hyper-salience of the drug cues (Baker et al., 2004): "When very attractive incentives are available, cognitive control resources may be recruited to ensure that the opportunity for reinforcement is not missed" (McCarthy et al., 2010, p. 26).

Thus, as people devote more of their time, attention, and energy to acquiring the brief, intense stimuli that substances often provide, they tend to devalue and discount long-term activities that yield healthy reinforcement, which increases the likelihood of developing dependence on the substance(s). In short, the more one discounts and devalues delayed rewards, the more likely one is at risk for substance-related problems; and to make this dynamic even more powerful, substance use tends to amplify the discounting process. Related to this point, some researchers have stressed that—motivational factors notwithstanding—proactively taking almost any form of *action* in the desired direction of change (i.e., away from unhealthy substance use) may be more critical than the specific actions that are taken (Miller & Carroll, 2006).

**GENETIC FACTORS** Hereditary risk factors clearly put some people at an increased or decreased risk for developing SUDs (Prescott, Piper, McCarthy, Majeskie, & Fiore, 2006). This is most clear for alcohol problems (Bohman, Sigvardsson, & Cloninger, 1981; Cloninger, Bohman, & Sigvardsson, 1981), but evidence is also accumulating that suggests that genetic predispositions play important roles in other substance problems (Miller & Carroll, 2006); for example, when their biological father has an SUD, children are four to seven times more likely to develop an SUD (Tarter & Vanyukov, 2001).

> Genetically predisposed individuals' ingestion of alcohol reduces their autonomic stress response following an aversive stimulus to a greater degree than is observed in non-genetically predisposed individuals. Genetically predisposed people may be more sensitive to the pharmacologically reinforcing qualities of drug use and therefore be more inclined to use these drugs heavily relative to non-genetically predisposed people. (Kassel et al., 2010, p. 198)

However, genes influence everything from neurotransmitters to substance-related behaviors in highly intricate ways, and a single gene will rarely explain why some people are at increased risks (Hasin, Hatzenbuehler, & Waxman, 2006); and, as is the case with other disorders, genetic and environmental factors interact in complex ways (Dick et al., 2006; Jacob et al., 2001). One example of a gene–environment interaction involves the moderating effect of religiosity on female alcohol use: among those women with low religiosity, genetic effects vastly exceeded those of the environment; in contrast, among women high in religiosity, environmental effects were large and genetic effects were virtually absent (Hesselbrock & Hesselbrock, 2006). In two adoption studies exploring genetic and environmental influences on drug abuse and dependence, the authors concluded that although one component of family influence is genetic, family environments also directly influence the behaviors of adoptees that result in their subsequently developing SUDs (Cadoret, Troughton, O'Gorman, & Heywood, 1986; Cadoret, Yates, Troughton, Woodworth, & Steward, 1996). More specifically, when adoptees' biological relatives had a history of antisocial behavior, the adoptees were likely to have an antisocial personality, which is strongly associated with SUDs; in addition, when adoptees' biological relatives had a history of alcohol problems, the adoptees were likely to have SUDs; finally, nonbiological parental disturbances—whether divorce, substance-related, or any other psychiatric problem—also significantly increased the likelihood of the adoptees' drug abuse (Cadoret et al., 1986).

In general, alcohol dependence displays a heritability of 50–60%, whereas the heritabilities for other substance disorders vary more, most likely because the conditions being observed in studies of the latter themselves vary more (i.e., some included only abuse and dependence whereas others included both moderate and heavy drug use). However, in general, studies of drug dependence suggest levels of heritability similar to those for alcohol dependence (Hasin et al., 2006). Another important factor is that whereas environmental factors appear to play a more significant role in initial use and continued use beyond experimenting, genetic influence seems to play a larger role in the transition from use to dependence (Hasin et al., 2006).

The considerable heritability of substance-related problems suggests that brain differences may play important roles in these phenomena (see the neuroscience section later in the chapter; Childress, 2006). The reinforcing properties of drugs are sometimes genetically determined. For example, the aversive effects of alcohol are increased by metabolic processes that are common in some Asian groups, thus decreasing the likelihood that members of those groups will develop alcohol problems. Conversely, some people inherit a capacity to "hold their liquor"—a relative insensitivity to the adverse effects of drinking heavily—and this increases their chance of developing an alcohol problem (Miller & Carroll, 2006).

A final point worth mentioning involves the well-known fact that alcohol and drug disorders are more common among men than women, thus raising questions regarding potential gender differences with regard to genetic determinants. However, Hasin and colleagues' (2006) review of family and twin studies concluded that gender differences among alcohol disorders are not due to genetic influences; such results for other substance use disorders are currently unavailable. Although genetic factors are clearly implicated in substance disorders, they are not deterministic; after all, the majority of children born from an alcoholic parent will *not* develop an alcohol-related problem (Hesselbrock & Hesselbrock, 2006). As we will soon see, a host of personal and social variables play equally important roles.

**NEUROSCIENCE** Many neuroscientists are increasingly viewing SUDs as brain diseases (O'Brien, 2007; Goldstein & Volkow, 2002; Volkow, Fowler, Wang, Swanson, & Telang, 2007). At the same time, most neuroscientists acknowledge that the brain does not operate in a vacuum. According to Nora Volkow and colleagues (2007), addiction is fundamentally a complex brain disease that derives from recurrent intoxication and is modulated by a host of genetic, psychological (perhaps most notably, positive and negative reinforcement), environmental, experiential, and developmental factors. Whereas most neurological studies focusing on drug addiction used to focus on limbic subcortical structures, frontal cortical structures are now receiving increased attention—in particular, the anterior cingulate gyrus and the orbitofrontal cortex, both of which are neuroanatomically connected to the limbic system (Goldstein & Volkow, 2002). These two frontal cortical areas are activated in addicted individuals during craving, bingeing, and intoxication, and are deactivated during withdrawal. Of significance is that these same areas are critical to motivational and other higher-order cognitive functions, including the capacity to appraise the salience of potential reinforcers and the ability to inhibit or otherwise control behavioral responses. The results of neuroimaging studies expand the notion that addiction involves brain structures and processes beyond the limbic system's responses to rewards and pleasure to a host of cortically regulated emotional and cognitive processes, the end product of which is the overvaluing of substances as reinforcers, the devaluing of alternative sources of reinforcement, and deficits in inhibiting responses to drug cues (Goldstein & Volkow, 2002).

Emerging brain-imaging data suggest that different brains vary greatly with regard to (1) the capacity to manage impulses toward immediate gratification, which involves weighing the potential consequences of one's choices around desired rewards, and (2) the ancient reward circuitry that underlies humans' strong motivation for, and response to, natural rewards—that is, food and sex, as well as one's experience of, and response to, alcohol and drugs. Childress (2006) refers to the former as the brain's "STOP!" system (an inhibitory "put on the brakes" system that entails critical processes involved in pursuing any long-term goals, including maintaining motivation and commitment to abstinence) and the latter as its "GO!" system (which is highly influential in what substances a given person experiences as rewarding). Differences in these two systems are likely implicated in the finding that some people are able to cease long-term substance use without professional help whereas others appear unable to remain abstinent for even a week, despite enduring terrible consequences of their substance use.

Regarding the brain's "GO!" system, when adults who are addicted to heroin, cocaine, nicotine, or alcohol are presented with drug cues, their brains' reward circuitry displays different reactions than do those of nonaddicted people. For example, cocaine-addicted adults have lower levels of $D_2$ dopamine receptors.[12] Regarding the brain's "STOP!" system, deficits in the frontal region of the brains of adults addicted to cocaine or alcohol have been observed, including lower metabolism, less blood flow, and less-dense gray matter. Such deficits in brain function may play a significant role pertinent to why some people struggle so much in response to the cues of various substances. Another important brain-imaging finding is that adolescents with frontal region defects are at an increased risk of developing an SUD. The hypothesis that even mild frontal defects add to the vulnerability of a developing "STOP!" system is corroborated by data showing that untreated mental disorders that involve frontal defects—such as conduct disorder and ADHD—increase the risk of substance use in adolescents[13] (Childress, 2006).

A central process in the development of an SUD appears to involve changes in the brain's reward system (i.e., how one responds to various reinforcers); thus the neurobiological bases for the acutely reinforcing effects of substances are key factors in understanding the etiology of SUDs. Evidence has accumulated that implicates the mesocorticolimbic dopamine system as critical in the rewarding effects of substances:

> During the development of dependence, there occurs both a change in function of neurotransmitters associated with the acute reinforcing effects of drugs of abuse (the "light side": dopamine, opioid peptides, serotonin, and GABA) and a recruitment of the brain's stress system neurotransmitters (the "dark side": corticotropin-releasing factor [CRF] and norepinephrine) and dysregulation of the neuropeptide Y [NPY] brain antistress system. (Koob, 2006, p. 38)

---

[12] Other authors have pointed out that it is unclear whether the observed changes in the $D_2$ receptors are a cause or consequence of substance abuse (Chipkin, 1994).

[13] At the same time, other research suggests that ADHD without conduct disorder does not appear to be a risk factor for SUDs, at least in males; evidence for ADHD as a SUD risk factor in females is quite limited (Lynskey & Hall, 2001).

Neurotransmitters—including dopamine, endocannabinoids, gamma-amino-butyric acid (GABA), opioid peptides, and nicotinic acetylcholine—in the "extended amygdala" (a specialized basal forebrain superstructure) are known to mediate the acutely reinforcing effects that many abused substances exert upon the person ingesting the substance (Koob, 2006). In the course of the development of substance-related problems, these "reward" neurotransmitters, as well as other brain stress systems, become dysregulated; more specifically, CRF (which is involved in the activation of the stress response) increases and NPY (which has antistress effects) decreases (Helig, Koob, Ekman, & Britton, 1994).

Although excessive drug use clearly dysregulates the reward system of the brain, sundry environmental and genetic factors can either protect or lend vulnerability to any aspect of neurotransmission function or dysregulation during the development of a drug use disorder—those affecting both brain reward systems and stress systems (Koob, 2006). The neurotransmitters involved in the acutely reinforcing effects of cocaine and amphetamines are dopamine and GABA; for opiates and THC (the active ingredient in marijuana), they are opioid peptides, dopamine, and endocannabinoids; for nicotine, they are nicotinic acetylcholine, dopamine, GABA, and opioid peptides; and for alcohol, they are dopamine, endocannabinoids, GABA, and opioid peptides (Koob, 2006).

**SUDS AS SELF-ORGANIZING SYSTEMS** Another phenomenon that has been noted by addiction researchers is that in the course of developing an SUD, the person's substance use—as well as its concomitant problems—becomes a self-organizing and self-perpetuating system (Bickel & Potenza, 2006; Miller & Carroll, 2006). What this means is that the various dimensions of the drug use—from the people the user comes into contact with while acquiring the substance and the time spent acquiring it, to adverse health and relational effects—actually take on a life of their own (which is not to suggest that choice and will are completely absent) and increase the system's organization without the person's awareness of such activities becoming self-regulating (Bickel & Potenza, 2006, p. 14). Thus, for many addicted people, their lives revolve around, and are ordered by, the many functions and processes served—even if maladaptively—by their substance use. Some of these processes are biological in nature, whereas others clearly serve psychological needs—from the need to feel good to a drive to alter one's consciousness—to which we now turn.

## Upper-Left Perspectives: From Cognitive to Affective Views

**COGNITIVE FACTORS** Despite the significant roles that positive and negative reinforcement, genes, and neurochemical/brain structures play in SUDs, cognitive processes are also clearly involved (Kassel et al., 2010).[14] Numerous cognitive variables have been found to influence the development of SUDs: general level of cognitive functioning (poor foresight, less capacity to use thought processes to regulate behavior), expectancy, attentional biases, and cognitive control.[15] However, "to date, specific

---

[14] It is critical to note that "cognitive processes are intimately influenced by, and influence, emotional response. . . [and that] cognition cannot merely be identified with conscious thought" (Kassel et al., 2010, pp. 62–63, bracketed text added).

[15] Cognitive control is the "effortful, controlled activation and allocation of attention in order to select and process goal-relevant information that facilitates behavioral adaptation in tasks involving high difficulty, novelty, decision uncertainty, or response conflict" (McCarthy et al., 2010, pp. 22–23).

cognitive deficits in persons at risk for developing substance abuse problems have not been consistently reported" (Hesselbrock & Hesselbrock, 2006, p. 102).

**Expectancy** Bandura's social learning theory (Bandura, 1977a, 1977b) posits two different types of expectancies: outcome expectancies and efficacy expectancies. The former consists of beliefs such as "If I do behavior A, I should expect outcome B"; the latter consists of one's beliefs regarding one's ability to successfully perform a given behavior (Scheier, 2010b). A person's outcome expectancies about a given drug play a significant role in one's reaction to that drug. For example, if someone believes that alcohol makes him less anxious, he will often report feeling less anxious after drinking, even when what he drank was (unbeknown to him) a nonalcoholic drink; conversely, when such a person unknowingly consumes alcohol, he often reports little or no reduction of anxiety (Wilson & Abrams, 1976). Other alcohol-related outcome expectancies include beliefs of enhanced social relating, increased personal power, enhanced sexual pleasure and performance, and increased relaxation (Hesselbrock & Hesselbrock, 2006). Many cognitive perspectives emphasize the power of an outcome expectancy that alcohol will help an individual cope with a difficult situation, particularly if that person's efficacy expectancy is poor (i.e., the person has low coping efficacy—he does not believe he will be able to use adaptive strategies to successfully cope with difficulties; Collins, Blane, & Leonard, 1999).

Expectancy perspectives do not suggest that there are not also powerful physiological effects of alcohol and other substances, but they do underscore the significance of the interaction of biology, psychology (e.g., the desire for relaxation, social relating, power, etc.), and social factors (e.g., the impact of advertising or observing others who are drinking; Hesselbrock & Hesselbrock, 2006). Reviews of the literature make it clear that alcohol expectancies not only correlate with adolescent drinking status but also "are prospectively predictive of onset of alcohol use among adolescents who had not drank previously and of the onset of problem drinking" (Collins et al., 1999, p. 158). Although most of the research on expectancies has been with alcohol, evidence is now accumulating that suggests similar findings with nicotine, cocaine, and marijuana (Collins et al., 1999). Moreover, "burgeoning evidence collectively implicates drug expectancies in all critical periods of the drug use trajectory, from initiation through relapse" (Kassel et al., 2010, p. 72).

In addition to the power of positive outcome expectancies to predict the frequency and amount of substance use, expectations regarding the diminishment or cessation of negative affect states (i.e., expectancies of negative reinforcement) have also been repeatedly shown to correlate with the development of SUDs (Cooper, 1994; Shiffman, 1984). Also of significance is that although drug outcome expectancies are in many ways stable and trait-like, they have also been shown to vary across context, from environmental (home, bar, alone vs. in a group) and physical (urges, withdrawal symptoms) to affective (emotions, mood) and cognitive (availability of drug-related information) contexts (Kassel et al., 2010). In particular, the context of negative affect (experiencing some form of aversive affect) continues to be shown to correlate with positive outcome expectancies and thus increased substance use (Hufford, 2001; McKee, Wall, Hinson, Goldstein, & Bissonnette, 2003); more on this topic will be subsequently presented.

**Attentional Biases** Those with SUDs often exhibit biases in selective attention with regard to drug cues, and such attentional biases display a bidirectional association with subjective drug craving. In other words, among those with substance problems, as their craving for a substance increases, the salience of drug-related cues increases; moreover, their attentional biases further escalate their experience of craving (Field, 2006).

**Cognitive Control** Given the potency of prior conditioning involved in drug use, cognitive control is a crucial factor in an individual's ability to overcome previous reinforcement histories and the strong stimulus–response associations that have derived from routinized patterns of drug use (McCarthy et al., 2010). Individuals vary with regard to how much cognitive control they possess; thus, it can be either a risk or protective factor. However, even among those at the higher end of the cognitive control spectrum, increased distress impairs a person's cognitive control, and as you will soon see, affective distress is a major factor motivating drug use. When a person decides to try to reduce or quit drug use, her level of cognitive control is crucial to whether or not she will be able to attend to and choose nondrug behaviors as they compete with previously learned drug behaviors (McCarthy et al., 2010).

**EARLY PSYCHOANALYTIC AND CONTEMPORARY PSYCHODYNAMIC VIEWS** Freud viewed alcoholism as a manifestation of oral fixation and self-destructive tendencies; Alfred Adler saw alcoholism as a response to feelings of inferiority. The empirical evidence for these views is scant at best, and many of today's psychoanalysts find such concepts "highly speculative and embarrassingly unuseful" (Khantzian, 1987, p. 531).

From a contemporary psychodynamic perspective, however, SUDs derive from deficits of self functions, such as the capacity to organize a coherent sense of self characterized by vitality, initiative, values, and talents; capacities to regulate self-esteem and meet a host of self needs; abilities to regulate affect; and so forth. Thus, a fundamental cause of SUDs involves chronic affective distress (although the degree to which a person consciously experiences such distress varies significantly) and disruptions in users' relationships with self and others (Kassel et al., 2010; Khantzian, 1987; PDM Task Force, 2006). At one end of the continuum, individuals experience acutely painful, intolerable emotions, whereas for those at the other end, affect is either unrecognized or less defined—more vaguely dysphoric and confusing, often including feelings of boredom and emptiness. Similarly, individuals with SUDs may display a range of underlying psychopathology, from psychotic and borderline disorders to anxiety and mood disorders. In any case, psychodynamic views stress that SUDs derive—at least in part—from patterns of aversive emotional experience and a deficit in self-care functions; thus, they represent a form of self-medication or an attempt to exert control (PDM Task Force, 2006). Whereas many people who abuse substances are unable to recognize, understand, regulate, or control their emotional lives,

> when they take drugs they counter this state of affairs or feelings because they produce a condition which over time they come to recognize, understand, and control, even if the effects and aftereffects are unpleasant and painful. That is, they often choose to substitute a dysphoria they invent and control in place of a dysphoria which is elusive and which they do not control. (Khantzian, 1987, p. 533)

In the main, psychodynamic theorists posit that addictive vulnerabilities are the result of developmental deficits in ego and self-organization related to neglectful, abusive, and chaotic family environments that often derive from the substance abuse of caregivers and other significant others. Capacities for regulating emotions, self-esteem, relationships, and self-care are deeply affected by these deficits. Substances are thus used to ameliorate, control, change, or mute affective experiences that are too intense, confusing, or otherwise aversive (PDM Task Force, 2006).

Because distressing affects often motivate the use of substances, the specific affects that are common for a given person often lead them to abuse a certain class of substances. For example, alcohol and other sedatives (benzodiazepines, barbiturates) are often used to "numb out" intense anxiety or other intensely aversive affect. In contrast, those who feel weak, low energy, or unloved often resort to stimulants; opiates reportedly make many people feel more "normal," calm, or mellow (PDM Task Force, 2006).

As noted in some of the preceding chapters, attachment theory is closely associated with psychodynamic perspectives, and some research has suggested that one's attachment style and one's concomitant experiences of emotional bonding and merging play important roles in the etiology of SUDs (Stapleton, 2004). In short, a lack of secure attachments and its associated merger experiences leaves individuals with heightened anxiety in response to life's vicissitudes, and such anxiety is strongly correlated with substance abuse (Barlow, 2004). Moreover, Stapleton (2004) argues that people with insecure attachment styles use alcohol and other substances to help them experience alternative merger experiences.

**PERSONALITY AND TEMPERAMENT TRAITS** Many studies have reported correlations between certain temperament traits and SUDs. According to Tarter, Kabene, Escaller, Laird, and Jacob (1990), individuals' behavioral activity level, attention span/persistence, sociability, emotionality, and soothability influence their capacities for behavioral and emotional regulation, and those who are more dysregulated—both affectively and behaviorally—are at increased risks for SUDs (Glantz, Conway, & Colliver, 2005; Kassel et al., 2010; Tarter, 2002). Other temperament traits that are associated with behavioral dysregulation and substance abuse in adolescence include antisociality (Sanford, 2001), delinquency[16] (Hawkins, Lishner, Catalano, & Howard, 1985), impulsivity and an inability to commit to delayed gratification (Dawe et al., 2007), psychoticism (Hesselbrock & Hesselbrock, 2006), and novelty-seeking behavior (Grande, Wolf, Schubert, Patterson, & Brocco, 1984). In general, negative affectivity—being more likely to experience depression and other aversive emotions—appears to influence the likelihood of developing SUDs (Hesselbrock & Hesselbrock, 2006).

Tarter and colleagues (1990) suggest that neurological and somatic developmental derailments, exacerbated by adverse environments, increase the likelihood of affective and behavioral dysregulation, and that such "dysregulation progresses via epigenesis [the biological process in which genes interact with the environment to produce specific structures and functions] from difficult temperament in infancy to conduct problems in childhood to substance use in early adolescence and to severe

[16] Other research concludes that the relationship between delinquency and alcohol use is more spurious than causal (Felson, Savolainen, Aaltonen, & Moustgaard, 2008).

SUD by young adulthood" (p. 657, bracketed text added). Although 40 years of both longitudinal and cross-sectional data suggest that childhood behavioral problems strongly correlate with adolescent and adult substance abuse (especially those characteristic of Conduct Disorder, Oppositional-Defiant Disorder, and ADHD),

> many of these studies often fail to take into account the effect of co-occurring conduct problems or sample children with only hyperactivity or attention deficit disorder. There is little evidence for the independent contribution of either hyperactivity or attention deficit disorder alone to the susceptibility for alcoholism. (Hesselbrock & Hesselbrock, 2006, p. 100)

**WILL AND CHOICE** The dimensions of will and choice, as they relate to substance-related problems, is often downplayed or outright denied (Miller & Carroll, 2006). Highlighting that individuals have made choices that have resulted in their SUD is not meant to suggest that they are therefore morally deficient or deserving of harsh, moralistic treatment. Even though drug use is a behavior that is certainly influenced by both neurobiology and behavioral principles such as reinforcement, that does not diminish the fact that drug use is a behavior that is chosen from a variety of behavioral options (Miller & Carroll, 2006). From this perspective, individuals with SUDs are viewed as responsible choosing agents—not so that they can be blamed for their choices, but rather so that they can be enlisted as active participants in treatment. In fact, the majority of people who recover from substance-related problems actually do so *without* formal treatment (DiClemente, 2006; Miller & Carroll, 2006). Such "do-it-yourself" recovery usually involves an important "click," decision, or commitment, reflected in the popular notion of "hitting bottom" (Miller & Carroll, 2006). Despite the fact that an individual's choices are an important dimension of subsequently developing substance-related problems, nobody consciously chooses to become addicted to substances. Rather, addictions and other related problems develop gradually, over time, and not in the absence of other variables, such as genetics, relationships, social systems, and the availability of other reinforcers in one's environment.

**MOTIVATION** It is widely acknowledged that motivational dynamics (defined broadly)[17] are key, although not the only, components in the development of SUDs (Miller, 2006). When people who have ceased troublesome substance use on their

---

[17] Even though this section on motivation is placed within the upper-left quadrant (UL; interior of the individual), neither Miller nor Integral theorists view motivation as simply an intrapersonal phenomenon. In addition to subjective, intrapersonal aspects of motivation (such as craving, temptation, compulsion, expectancies regarding the effects of a substance, perception of the substance use being a problem, decisional processes, perceived ability to change, will, and so forth), motivation is actually a product of all four quadrants. Thus, motivation is also a function of one's biology, genes, and other more "objective" dimensions of the person (UR); relational and other social variables—from the interpersonal influence of friends and family to advertising, media, economic, education, public policy, and other social systems (LR)—to the shared meanings and values of a given person's ethnicity, gender, religion, or other relational and cultural dimensions (LL). Much evidence suggests that interpersonal factors strongly influence an individual's motivation to change their alcohol or substance abuse (Miller, 2006). Similarly, the motivational work of self-determination theorists highlights not only the significance of motivation in SUDs but also that concepts such as self-determination and intrinsic motivation are not separate from needs for relatedness and autonomy-supportive relationships (Ryan, Lynch, Vansteenkiste, & Deci, 2010).

own (i.e., without professional treatment) talk about why and how they did so, they often mention a choice or turning point (Miller & Carroll, 2006). Likewise, transtheoretical research (DiClemente, 2003, 2006) highlights the stages of change through which substance users progress, beginning with an increased motivation or concern for change, decisional considerations and making the commitment to change, and ending in taking and maintaining the actions needed to change. According to Miller and Carroll (2006), many individuals do not need much assistance making the desired change once they have developed a personal commitment to change. Moreover, motivation—especially for changing substance-related problems—is quite malleable; the notion that a person must hit rock bottom before that person can be helped is simply mistaken (Miller & Carroll, 2006). The practical implication of this is that friends and family can often exert an influence to increase someone's motivation to change.

**OTHER EXPERIENTIAL FACTORS** While testing their hypothesis that low self-concept is an etiological factor in SUDs, Samuels and Samuels (1974) found that adolescent participants reported the following factors as influential in their substance use: boredom and curiosity (92%), low self-concept (76%), peer pressure (68%), and the pleasure derived (65%). Although such research is far from comprehensive, it points to experiential states (i.e., boredom, curiosity, pleasure) as important contributors in the initiation and development of SUDs.

**EMOTION AND AFFECTIVE PERSPECTIVES** Would people abuse substances if there were no emotional payoffs? In response to this question, Panskepp et al. (2004), Kassel and Veilleux (2010), and others respond with an emphatic "No." However, it does not follow that those with SUDs are merely hedonists with no impulse control. In fact, it is important to remember that any observed associations between drug use and emotion ultimately reveal relationships that reflect the intense emotional pain experienced by the vast majority of those with severe SUDs. Indeed, the personification of the "happy drunk," or the addict as a hedonist run amok, is rarely exhibited by individuals in the throes of addiction. Instead, clinicians treating people with SUDs almost always witness individuals with marked affective distress (Kassel & Evatt, 2010, p. 282).

A field of study has emerged to address the complex relationships between emotion and substance use and misuse, and consists of scholars from disciplines as diverse as affective neuroscience, developmental psychopathology, and neuropsychology to behavioral pharmacology and pharmacodynamics. Distilling data from these disparate but related fields of study, Kassel and Evatt (2010) stress that "from virtually every perspective, emotion appears to play a central role in the consumption and abuse of addictive substances" (p. 281). However, the exact nature of the role of affect is unclear. For example,

> We know that people who experience heightened levels of affective distress are more likely to use and abuse drugs. Burgeoning evidence also supports the reciprocal relationship: People who abuse drugs are more likely to experience disorders of affect. We view these findings as important for several reasons. First, they point to the obvious (but frequently overlooked) fact that substance abuse

> is almost always accompanied by emotional pain; that is—and counter to the notion entertained earlier that addiction may simply reflect uncontrolled hedonistic desire—individuals who abuse drugs are most often depressed, anxious, or manifesting any number of symptoms of affective distress. (Kassel & Veilleux, 2010, p. 7)

Related to the previous statement that substance abuse is usually accompanied by emotional pain, recall the high comorbidities of SUDs with emotionally distressing disorders such as depression, anxiety, Bipolar Disorders, and Schizophrenia.[18] Nonetheless, the relationship between affect and SUDs is likely much more complex than it seems on the surface, and we must remember that most of the data supporting this relationship is correlational; thus, we cannot draw causal conclusions at this point in time (Kassel et al., 2010). Moreover, the emotional effect of substances on individuals is also a function of the social context in which those substances are used. For example, Armeli and colleagues (2003) reported that the stress-mitigating effects of alcohol in their study occurred only when the subjects drank in the presence of others. With the importance of social contexts in mind, we now turn to a range of systemic variables and their role in the development of SUDs.

## Lower-Right Perspectives: From Family Systems to Public Policy

Many researchers and clinicians in the field of SUDs consider SUDs more of a social problem than a problem centered in the individual (Peyrot, 1984; Scheier, 2010a). Various dimensions of social contexts—from families, schools, and peer groups to work and neighborhood environments, public policies, and other large-scale systemic factors—can either increase or decrease the risk of developing substance-related problems. However, consistent with Integral theory, such social factors dynamically interact with an individual's biology and choices in reciprocal, mutually constitutive ways to result in that person's specific pattern of substance use or abstinence. As a simple example, we know that an adolescent's peer-group modeling and approval of substance use increases the likelihood of the adolescent's use, and potential misuse, of substances. However, the adolescent is not merely a passive victim and has some choice regarding who is chosen as one's peer group. Similarly, reciprocally influential processes occur between children and their parents: a lack of parental monitoring and support may facilitate an adolescent's initial substance use, which, in turn, may trigger a sense of discouragement and hopelessness in the parents and thus even less parental monitoring and support. Or, similarly, families that lack intimacy appear to increase the chance that members will resort to substance use as a coping mechanism only to have escalating substance use magnify the previous family-intimacy dysfunction, creating a vicious cycle that is often transmitted to future generations (Coleman, 1982). Thus, like genetic, behavioral, cultural, experiential, and other factors, social contexts have a powerful influence on the likelihood that one will develop a substance problem, but they are far from unidimensional causes of such problems. Individual choices, genetics, and other factors always interact in complex ways to result in any

[18] Comorbidity of SUDs and externalizing disorders such as Antisocial Personality Disorder are even higher than they are for internalizing disorders such as anxiety and mood disorders (Kassel et al., 2010).

given outcome. Unfortunately, most research is not currently able to ascertain the specifics of such complex interactions:

> Despite the multifactorial etiology of drug abuse . . . drug abuse research has focused and continues to focus largely on individual risk factors at the expense of an understanding of the interaction of broader and interrelated [social factors]. . . . the social epidemiology of drug use necessarily involves an examination of the interaction of individual factors with familial, biological, and socioenvironmental factors, and the accumulation of these interactions over time and across generations. (Thomas, 2007, p. S141; bracketed text added)

**FAMILY INFLUENCE** Research supports the significant influence that families and other close relationships play in the protection against, as well as the initiation of, development of, course of, and recovery from SUDs (Friesen, 1983; Kliewer, 2010; McCrady, 2006; Moos, 2006). Although many laypeople hold stereotypical, oversimplified ideas of what are actually a complex network of social relationships, some general findings appear quite robust. For example, a huge risk factor for youth beginning to use and misuse substances is their parents' substance use (Friesen, 1983; Hawkins et al., 1985; Kliewer, 2010; Moos, 2006). Not only are parents with SUDs more likely to abuse their children, they are also less likely to parent in a manner that buffers their children from the risks of drug problems. Moreover, parents' modeling of substance use increases youngsters' positive expectancies about such use. In contrast, parents who monitor and disapprove of substance use are more likely to delay their children's first use of substances, which lowers the risk that such use will develop into an SUD (Grant & Dawson, 1997; Hawkins, Graham, Maguin, Abbott, Hill, & Catalano, 1997):

> It is quite clear from numerous studies using a variety of samples, methods, and research designs that parents' drug use increases the odds that their children will use. . . . Notably, most of these associations were present after accounting for demographics and in many cases controlling statistically for peer influence. (Kliewer, 2010, p. 372)

Many young men report that they drink their first alcohol with their fathers—fathers who apparently did not offer many opportunities for shared activities or closeness. Other children report having been "pulled in" to a habit of using substances by a parent who abused substances. In such cases, children and young adults had few opportunities to be close to their parents unless they were drinking or using substances with them (PDM Task Force, 2006).

Summarizing an edited volume addressing the scientific research on SUDs and their etiological influences, Miller and Carroll (2006) stressed that optimal parenting styles are supportive, consistent, and authoritative (a moderately structured style that is neither authoritarian-punitive nor permissive-neglectful); involve monitoring children's activities and friends; and involve children in religious and/or other social structures that not only provide support but also model desirable behaviors. In contrast, parental styles associated with increased risks for SUDs include abusive, neglectful, or uninvolved parenting; a spousal relationship characterized by high emotional conflict; and diffuse and blurred cross-generational boundaries (Friesen, 1983). In a study "designed to establish a causal relationship between childhood victimization and young adults' substance abuse. . . . Childhood physical abuse proved a strong predictor of young adults' current substance abuse, although sexual abuse did not" (Lo & Cheng, 2007, p. 139). Prenatal behaviors also exert an influence; in particular, maternal nutrition and illness, as well as the smoking or drinking of the pregnant mother, are associated with increased risks for SUDs in the offspring. Although much of the information just presented represents considerable consensus by social scientists, such conclusions are the result of primarily correlational data and thus are not capable of discerning causal inferences.

The work of developmental psychologist Wendy Kliewer (2010) has focused on three primary components through which families and parents affect adolescent drug use behavior: modeling (the behavior of parents observed by children; which has been alluded to previously), coaching (verbal messages parents give their children), and family context (aspects of the familial environment such as emotional tone and rules that can support or buffer child behavior). Significantly, Kliewer posits that these three features affect children's coping skills, which is central to the development of SUDs. In general, adolescents who approach problems and stressors with active (approach-oriented) coping strategies fare better than those with avoidance strategies, the latter of which correlate with drug use in adolescence (Kliewer, 2010; Wills & Filer, 1996).

Parental coaching messages include both attitudes toward drug use as well as coping strategies relevant to drug use. It is clear that parents' values around drug use—usually defined in terms of explicit disapproval—are correlated with fewer drug-related problems among their adolescents (Kliewer, 2010). Moreover, the coping strategies that parents verbally encourage are correlated to their adolescents' coping styles; not only are avoidant coping strategies associated with more drug use, drug use itself appears to be a form of avoidant coping (Kliewer, 2010).

Family context has been extensively researched with regard to the etiology of drug use and SUDs. As an overarching concept, family context includes the categories of parental mental health, family structure, family management (rule and boundary setting, monitoring, and discipline strategies), quality of adolescent–parent relationships (how much warmth, support, affection, mutual attachment, etc.), and general family climate (emotional expression, cohesion, conflict); and all five of these categories correlate with drug use and/or SUDs (Kliewer, 2010). In short, the following are associated with increased adolescent substance use and/or SUDs: parents with more psychopathology; families with an absent father; less parental monitoring; lack of warm, affectionate parent–adolescent relationships, as well as lack of mutual attachment between parents and their children; and lack of familial cohesion and high levels of emotional conflict (Kliewer, 2010).

Families influence not only children and adolescents; they also play large roles regarding substance use and misuse by parents. Protective family factors include a cohesive family with few hostile arguments, intimate relationships, a partner who is direct and clear regarding his or her concerns about others' substance use, having a social network with nonsubstance users, and receiving support for abstinence. Conversely, family risk factors include marital dissatisfaction, having a partner who either tolerates or is indirect in communicating about the others' substance use, hostile arguments, and having and maintaining friends who use substances (McCrady, 2006).

**PEER GROUPS AND SCHOOLS** It seems clear that those who lack a nonsubstance-using social network will be at risk for initiating substance use as well as developing an SUD. Negative peer influence ranges from early peer groups to a host of group affiliations, including later adolescent environments such as college fraternities. Although we know that peer groups exert considerable influence on youngsters, it is also the case that some young people are more susceptible to negative influence than others, such as those who have a predominantly present-time perspective (in contrast to those who are more focused on the future and delayed gratification), are extroverted, have a largely avoidant/escapist style of coping, possess poorer social skills, and have low self-esteem (Moos, 2006). Schools that actively encourage student involvement in extracurricular activities, social monitoring, and discipline promote the delaying of students' initiation of substance use as well as the escalation from use to heavy use (Moos, 2006). Being socially isolated is another risk factor. Perhaps not as readily apparent (but previously mentioned) is that the availability of nondrug positive reinforcers—from sports, music, and other after-school extracurricular activities or hobbies to having a meaningful role in one's school, work, or society—tends to decrease the development of SUDs (Miller & Carroll, 2006).

**STRESSFUL/TRAUMATIC EXPERIENCES** It seems virtually self-evident that stress and trauma can contribute to people's use of substances, and research supports the notion that intense stress appears to increase the likelihood that a person will develop an SUD (Carroll & Miller, 2006). For example, in a study comparing the incidence of SUDs among Vietnam veterans as a function of whether or not they experienced heavy combat, such exposure more than doubled the likelihood that they reported developing an SUD after returning from the war (Fischer, 1991). Although other studies report that as stressful experiences increase, so do SUDs, other researchers have criticized a large majority of such research on methodological grounds. The most common error is that many studies do not adequately attend to how SUDs may actually be the *cause* of stressful life events and therefore mistake either the direction of causality or confuse correlation with causation (Allan & Cooke, 1985). Nonetheless, there is some consensus that stress can be a precipitant of relapse: "A recent factor analysis of Marlatt's relapse taxonomy found negative emotion, which includes many forms of stressors, to be a key factor in relapse" (Koob, 2006, p. 30). This dovetails with previously mentioned issues including not only the role of affect but also the negatively reinforcing effects of substance use to ameliorate stress and other aversive experiences.

**WORK** Although merely correlational, data suggest that adolescents who spend more time working (i.e., paid employment) during their high school years tend to have less healthy bonds with their parents as well as more exposure to peers modeling substance use; thus, they are at increased risks for substance use (Moos, 2006). By way of contrast, in adulthood, the monitoring and supervision that regular employment usually involves often serves to keep substance use from escalating to an SUD. Some studies have reported that being underemployed or unemployed is correlated with increased substance use (possibly due to social alienation and the absence of supervision). When analyzed with structural equation modeling, other research posits that "recent unemployment decreases alcohol use while longer unemployment increases it"

(Khan, Murray, & Barnes, 2002, p. 405). On the other hand, when a work environment is highly stressful and includes positive norms for substance use, it is likely to increase the risk of use and misuse, and such influence increases for individuals who use substances for more escapist reasons (negative reinforcement; Moos, 2006).[19]

**LARGER SOCIAL INFLUENCES** Substance use and substance-related problems arise within sociopolitical and economic contexts that range from local to global. Spooner and Hall (2002) refer to these as "macro-environmental" influences and argue that their influence is significant enough to warrant the expansion of our views of both etiology and treatment. In the 21st century, substance use trends can rapidly sweep across a country, from the recent rave phenomenon to increased heroin use in rural areas (Carlson, 2006). Although it may seem too obvious to need stating, drug use is amplified in environments in which drugs are readily available.[20] Moreover, the "culture of addiction" has its own infrastructure, from crack houses, night clubs, and bars to casinos, strip clubs, and zones of prostitution (du Plessis, 2010). Not only are drug dealers more aware than ever of potential markets for their commodities, the Internet is now used to illegally distribute pharmaceutical drugs. Thus, drugs are more available and "within reach" than ever before. Add to this the social-systemic factors of poverty, racism, unemployment, social isolation, and general inequity, and it is not difficult to understand why people with less access to the commodities of the "good life" that are so ubiquitously advertised (diminished access to less-destructive sources of positive reinforcement) increasingly resort to drug use as a source of pleasure and enjoyment.

**SOCIOECONOMIC STATUS** Given what we have already discussed regarding the role of the environment and the negative reinforcement of using substances to alleviate aversive experience, it should come as no surprise that many researchers have suggested that low socioeconomic status (SES) plays an etiological role in SUDs. For example, one study of 41 males between the ages of 24 and 70 with a high SES and 40 males of the same age range with a low SES found that the latter generally provided external attributions for their alcohol use, whereas the former tended to provide internal attributions (McKirnan, 1984). Although subjective attribution by no means equates to actual causation, it makes considerable sense that for people struggling with unemployment, poverty, or other low-status phenomena, such socioeconomic stressors could be a principal factor in their resorting to alcohol or other substance misuse, whereas internal/psychological factors may be more responsible for such misuse among those from less stressful socioeonomic conditions. Williams and Latkin (2007) demonstrated that neighborhood poverty is significantly related to SUDs, even after controlling for many

---

[19] Other reviews of the literature highlight that "the relation between full-time employment and substance use is not clear. Some studies have shown that full-time employment decreases alcohol use (Gotham et al., 1997), whereas other studies have found that it increases alcohol use (Temple et al., 1991). Still other studies have found no association between full-time employment and alcohol use (Bachman, O'Malley, & Johnston, 1984; Gotham et al., 2003)" (Jochman & Fromme, 2010, p. 569).

[20] And this is not simply because it is easier to obtain drugs when they are readily available. Environmental contexts (LR) actually affect the subjective craving or urges for drugs, and many earlier, simple etiological models failed to appreciate this. A study by Juliano and Brandon (1998) demonstrated that individuals with SUDs who know they do not have access to drugs (for example, if they are undergoing inpatient treatment) report fewer urges than when they are in an environmental context that affords drug use.

other factors such as employment and social support. At the extreme end of low SES, poverty not only appears to be associated with SUDs; using structural equation modeling, Khan and colleagues (2002) reported that increased poverty is actually *causally* implicated in alcohol-related problems (p. 405).

**DRUG POLICIES** Other systemic factors relevant to substance use and misuse are drug and alcohol policies; local enforcement of driving under the influence (DUI), underage drinking, and other drug-related laws; and state and federal policies. Of particular significance are federal laws criminalizing drug possession and the prevailing view of SUDs as more of a criminal justice issue rather than a public health or medical issue. Current public policies reflect contradictory messages about the nature of SUDs as well as the most appropriate way to treat them. We are all presented with conflicting messages about drug use—some speak of the "evils" of drugs and try to wage "war" on them, whereas other voices (from the alcohol and tobacco industries to songs, art, movies and other media) glorify and promote drugs.

The issue of drugs and the criminal justice system is essential not only to a comprehensive understanding of the etiology of SUDs, but especially to the treatment of such. The development of a problem such as an SUD—which, to repeat, many researchers consider more of a social problem than an individual problem (Peyrot, 1984; Scheier, 2010a)—is at least in part a function of political processes such as governmental policies and laws. Even though some clinics, treatment centers, and researchers emphasize SUDs as medical or clinical problems, the prevailing emphasis in terms of governmental funding is still, unequivocally, one of criminal justice (Bertram & Sharpe, 2011; Moyers, 1998). As sociologist Mark Peyrot (1984) has demonstrated, "the view of current drug abuse policy as 'medicalized' underplays the significance of the previously instituted criminal justice response" (p. 84).[21] Peyrot (1984) demonstrated how our current drug use policies are a result of different views that have been instituted during different historical eras, resulting in "a confused combination of two contradictory approaches—that of punishment and repression on one hand, and treatment and rehabilitation on the other" (p. 84). It may surprise readers to realize that drugs such as heroin, opium, cocaine, and marijuana were subject to virtually no legal restrictions prior to 1875 (Peyrot, 1984). As many scholars have suggested, local and federal legislation that resulted in criminalizing such drugs appears to have been motivated primarily out of a fear of minorities who used drugs—in particular, Chinese opium smokers and African American and Hispanic marijuana and cocaine users—and as a means of controlling and oppressing them (Helmer, 1975; Peyrot, 1984).

Most readers already know that Prohibition (under which alcohol was deemed an illegal substance for 14 years) not only failed to solve the problems associated with consuming alcohol, it actually *created* a host of new problems, from organized crime to civil disobedience (anyone who drank alcohol became a criminal). If you doubt the current failure of many of our government's current drug policies, just consider the interminable "war on drugs," a drug policy in which 70% of funding is spent trying to keep drugs out of the country or off the streets that has *not* significantly reduced

[21] For those interested in an overview of the historical development of drug policies as they bear upon conceptions of, and responses to, drug use, see Peyrot (1984).

substance-related problems in the last three decades (Bertram & Sharpe, 2011).[22] Even General Barry McCaffrey, former U.S. drug "czar," remarked that "We are spending 17 billion dollars a year to lock up 1.6 million Americans. . . . We have got to develop the political will to spend the money needed not only on prevention programs but on effective drug treatment" (as cited in Bertram & Sharpe, 2011, p. 13).

Current drug policies tend to view SUDs as fundamentally a criminal problem of deviant, misguided, or immoral individuals (Bertram & Sharpe, 2011). This traditional view persists despite overwhelming evidence from the fields of genetics, neuroscience, medicine, psychology, and sociology (Hasin et al., 2006; Koob, 2006; Moos, 2006; Thomas, 2007). Why and how does the criminal justice perspective continue to prevail over medical, clinical, and/or public health perspectives? Peyrot (1984) eloquently explained that the critical historical variable is the extent to which prior remedial approaches were institutionalized. Because subsequent approaches are usually superimposed upon earlier foundations—rather than completely replacing them—the more deeply ingrained the earlier approaches, the less likely new approaches will supercede them. As an example, consider that even though criminal sanctions for drinking alcohol ended long before today's clinical approach to alcohol use disorders, previous criminal and moral views regarding alcohol abuse and dependence still exert their influence. Likewise, the criminal justice approach to drug abuse continues to play a more prominent role than do clinical, public health, medical or mental health approaches in the treatment of drug use disorders. Although Peyrot (1984) was an early voice in pointing out these dynamics, his perspective has been echoed by many contemporary substance clinicians and researchers (Beatty, 2010; du Plessis, 2010; Thomas & Conway, 2010).

It is significant to note that whereas people from all strata of society *use* drugs, enforcement of drug laws and incarceration falls more heavily on African Americans, Latinos, and those living in poor neighborhoods and/or inner cities (Beatty, 2010; Moyers, 1998). Between 65–70% of people in prison are incarcerated for substance-related problems (from possession or selling of drugs to stealing or prostituting to get money to buy drugs), and ethnic minorities are vastly overrepresented (Beatty, 2010).[23]

Another socially inequitable derivative of current public policy is that treatment for SUDs is usually unavailable to those who cannot afford to pay out of pocket; at minimum, there is usually a 3- to 6-month wait for such services (during which time, the person with the SUD will often relapse). Long-term residential treatment is rarely available to those who are not wealthy. Whereas it seems there are nearly unlimited resources when it comes to prison space, there is only a fraction of such resources for prevention, treatment, and rehabilitation. An all-too-common and unfortunate reality is that for poor people who are caught using illicit substances, what they get is a stay in prison waiting for a placement in a rehabilitation center that almost never

---

[22] Whereas criminal sanctions for substance use appear to be relatively ineffective in preventing substance use, social modeling and norms regarding substance use exert considerable influence: "Cultures in which abstinence is normative and modeled, and in which drug use is stigmatized, tend to have much lower rates of drug use and drug-related problems" (Miller & Carroll, 2006, p. 301). In stark contrast are the symbolic meanings communicated by the advertisement of substances, which tend not only to normalize their use, but simultaneously associate such use with successful, wealthy, or otherwise attractive people.

[23] That drug policies are differentially enforced with regard to ethnic status is different from the stress of being discriminated against in other ways, the latter of which can increase the likelihood of one abusing substances as a way to cope (Gibbons, Pomery, & Gerrard, 2010).

materializes. In essence, our public policy allows the wealthy person with a drug problem to go to Betty Ford whereas the poor person will likely go to jail (Moyers, 1998).

Even though the toll of alcohol and cigarettes is far greater than that of all illicit drugs combined,[24] many otherwise productive and law-abiding citizens are currently in prison for smoking marijuana.[25] Another example of contradictory policies and drug laws involves the case of marijuana. Marijuana became an "illicit" drug in 1937, prior to which some physicians prescribed it for muscle relaxation, asthma, and relief of pain (Mahoney, 1980). Today, it is still one of the best anti-nausea medications and it is also used to treat the pain and other symptoms of a host of medical diseases (e.g., AIDS, glaucoma, cancer, multiple sclerosis). Nonetheless, the federal Controlled Substances Act considers marijuana a Schedule I drug (which is the most strict classification, and includes heroin, whereas Schedule II drugs include amphetamines and cocaine). In contrast, consider the claim of noted scholar and science writer Edward Brecher (1972), who was best known for his contributions to addiction research:

> The individual and social harm (including the destruction of young lives and growing disrespect for law) caused by the present use of the criminal law to attempt to suppress cannabis far outweighs any potential for harm which cannabis could conceivably possess, having regard to the long history of its use and the present lack of evidence . . . For all of these reasons, it is said, cannabis should be made available under government-controlled conditions of quality and availability. (p. 466)

Although far from being legalized at the federal level, 25 states, as well as the District of Columbia, have either legalized or decriminalized recreational marijuana, or have legalized the use of medical marijuana (Wikipedia, n.d.). Having just covered a number of societal dynamics, the role that observable, measurable social systems (such as SES, laws, and public policy) play in the etiology of SUDS is not clearly distinct from many of the intersubjective, relational, and cultural factors that we will now address.

### Lower-Left Perspectives: From Cultures of Addiction to Cultures That Fill Our Hunger for Ecstatic Connectedness

Although this is a simple and general statement, it is important to recognize and remember that substance-related problems develop in sociocultural and relational contexts (Khantzian, 1987; Kliewer, 2010; PDM Task Force, 2006), some of which were addressed in the preceding lower-right quadrant discussion. Moreover, different cultures and subcultures prescribe highly divergent roles to the use of psychoactive substances: from social lubricants, medicinal roles, and sacramental purposes that induce heightened states of consciousness, to vilified evils. However, before we address

[24] More than 400,000 people die annually from tobacco/nicotine and more than 100,000 die annually from alcohol; alcohol is also involved in 60% of murders and 38% of reported child abuse incidents (Bertram & Sharpe, 2011; Moyers, 1998).

[25] One of the key factors that has led many otherwise politically conservative people to favor the decriminalization of some drugs is just that—the fact that such laws make criminals out of otherwise law-abiding citizens. Moreover, many citizens would rather have prison space allotted to murderers, rapists, and thefts than to those with non-violent SUDs (Moyers, 1998). An alternative to viewing drug abuse as primarily a crime is to conceive of it as a public health issue, implications of which would involve sending first- and second-time offenders to treatment/rehabilitation rather than to prison.

different cultural dynamics involved in the etiology and maintenance of SUDs, we need to say a bit about states of consciousness.

**STATES OF CONSCIOUSNESS** Despite the fact that episodes of depression, mania, anxiety, panic, delirium, and even psychoses are almost always *states* of consciousness—in other words, most people are *not permanently* depressed, manic, anxious, delirious, or psychotic—few forms of psychopathology revolve so centrally around states of consciousness as do SUDs. After all, why do people use substances? To alter their state of consciousness: "It is obvious that drug use and addiction are associated with altered states of consciousness [ASC]; however, addiction has seldom been analyzed from the perspective of consciousness theory or cross-cultural patterns of the use of ASC" (du Plessis, 2010, p. 76; bracketed text added). As mentioned early in this chapter, the desire to seek ASC appears to be innate (Weill, 2004); from this perspective, drug use is not inherently abnormal, nor should moderate to heavy substance use be seen as fundamentally different from the problems experienced by those who chronically overeat (Wang et al., 2001).

Different cultures value ASC in highly discrepant ways. In fact, anthropologists such as Laughlin, McManus, and Shearer (1993) have highlighted the restrictive nature of Western culture's "monophasism": valuing and deriving a worldview from a single state of consciousness—the normal waking state. In contrast, most cultures are "polyphasic" in that their values and worldviews reflect an appreciation of multiple states of consciousness, including waking, dreaming, and numerous contemplative, mystical, or drug-induced states. Numerous researchers have highlighted that most treatment programs fail to address the fact that people desire and need to experience ASC and that this lack of attention to ASC is part of the reason for the high relapse rates of those seeking most forms of recovery treatment (du Plessis, 2010; McPeake, Kennedy, & Gordon, 1991). Winkleman likewise describes the

> widespread Western biases against ASCs, manifested in efforts to marginalize, persecute, or pathologize them . . . [in] contrast with most cultures' group rituals to enhance access to ASCs. These cultural biases inhibit recognition of the factors that contribute to drug abuse and prevention. . . . Although cultures differ in their evaluation of and support of ASCs, people in all cultures seek ASC experiences because they reflect biologically based structures of consciousness for producing holistic growth and integrative consciousness. This near-universality of institutionalization of ASC induction practices reflects human psychobiological needs. . . . Since contemporary Indo-European societies lack legitimate institutionalized procedures for accessing ASCs, they tend to be sought and utilized in deleterious and self-destructive patterns—alcoholism, tobacco abuse and illicit substance dependence. (cited in du Plessis, 2010, pp. 76–77)

One partial but highly intriguing view of how our contemporary sociocultural forces do not provide the type of ecstatic, regenerative altered states that our evolutionary ancestors participated in for millennia—and thus why some seek for such ecstatic states in potentially degenerative sources such as drugs and alcohol—is that of philosopher Bruce Wilshire, discussed next.

"**Missing is any sense that anything is missing**" (Wilshire, 1999, p. xiv). Humans evolved over the course of millions of years, during which time our prehuman and human ancestors survived by a deep engagement with "wild Nature"

(Wilshire, 1999).[26] Biological survival—including hunting, gathering, and the provision of shelter and other basic needs—likely dominated the consciousness of early humans and probably resulted in an intense and emotional life, even when the emotions were fear and terror. Wilshire posits that humans—at least on one level—still hunger for that type of *primal* engagement, connection, and excitement; however, that hunger is largely suppressed and confounded by our modern processes of socialization, the endless distraction of technology, and the relative ease and comfort of modern life. The culture of our "civilized" way of living no longer affords the connectedness and ecstasy of such deep engagement with wild Nature and her cycles:

> I think addictions stem from breaking the participatory bond our species has had with regenerative source, with wild Nature over the ages—kinship with plants and animals, with rocks, trees, and horizons. Even terror is a bond with what terrifies. In such moments we are "out of ourselves," ecstatic,[27] spontaneous, full of the swelling presences of things. Addictions try to fill the emptiness left by the loss of ecstatic kinship. They are substitute gratifications that cannot last for long—slavishly repeated attempts to keep the emptiness at bay. (Wilshire, 1999, pp. x–xi)

In other words, when our primal, biopsychospiritual needs are not met, we are not true to ourselves and we often gratify a vague urge not with what will actually meet the need in a regenerative way; rather, we provide ourselves with a substitute, degenerative source of pleasure in the form of substances, which ultimately leaves us spiraling through endless cycles of desire and momentary satisfaction. Some have even gone so far as to say that our entire culture is addicted, whether to food, money, sex, TV, virtual social networking, or other aspects of the Internet (Schaef, 1987).

Anthropologist Robert Carlson points out that in any given culture, psychoactive substances vary as a function of whether they are more symbolic mediators or commodities. In the former, various substances (such as hallucinogens)

> can be used to mediate or link the domains of everyday life and a spiritual world (the profane and the sacred) in various ways. The same can be said of the use of peyote in some Native American religions as well as the use of wine in other religions. (Carlson, 2006, pp. 205–206)

In the role of symbolic mediators, psychoactive substances can assist people in dealing with the fundamental problem of being biologically separate from one another as well as feeling separate from domains of reality that are largely culturally defined:

> In relation to psychoactive substances, symbolic mediation takes three general forms: (1) linking perceived domains of reality that are culturally defined as separate [i.e., the spiritual/sacred from the earthly/profane]; (2) marking transitions or boundaries relative to some aspect of life, whether changes in life status (e.g., birth, marriage), the Sabbath and the rest of the week, or changes in

---

[26] For 99% of the genus *Homo*'s existence, our ancestors have lived in wilderness as hunters and gatherers (Kellert & Wilson, 1993).

[27] The word *ecstasy* derives from the Greek *ek-stasis*, which means "a standing out" or "to stand outside of one's self." To be ecstatic is not merely to "feel good" but to be absorbed in and embraced by something greater than one's self: "this experience of belonging in what catches us up ecstatically is the experience of the sacred. . . . Loss of ego is a kind of sacrament that leaves room for something much greater than ego" (Wilshire, 1999, p. 13).

> prescribed behavior (e.g., the transition from work to relaxation); and (3) facilitating social bonding or connecting individuals through shared common experience. (Carlson, 2006, p. 207; bracketed text added)

Societies and cultures vary widely with regard to the extent to which substances are valued for their symbolic mediational properties. Moreover, once a substance becomes a commodity—a product with cash value—its constructive, symbolic mediational properties often become obscured and weakened. Rather than helping people creatively understand and link different domains of reality, commodified substances increasingly alienate users from the rest of society (Carlson, 2006). The "rest of society," and intimate, healthy relationships in particular, are critical in understanding SUDs.

Not only do severe SUDs often lead to the deterioration or loss of relationships; a lack of satisfying, intimate relationships is often a key factor in the development of SUDs. According to du Plessis (2010),

> Family and friends often become perplexed and outraged by the addict's behavior, as [it] transgresses cultural norms. Eventually many addicts undergo a *cultural shift* and find themselves in a new (sub)culture where their addictive behaviors are accepted and often encouraged. (p. 72, italics in original)

This notion of a "culture of addiction" is important to the maintenance of SUDs:

> The physiological, psychological, and spiritual transformations that accompany the person-drug relationship occur within and are shaped by the culture of addiction. The progression of addiction is often accompanied by concurrent disaffiliation from society at large and on enmeshment in the culture of addiction. This cultural affiliation touches and transforms every dimension of one's existence. What begins as a person-drug relationship moves toward an all-encompassing lifestyle. No part of the persona is left untouched by the culture of addiction. (White, 1996, as cited in du Plessis, 2010, p. 72)

The relational and cultural affiliations of many people struggling with SUDs are among the most difficult aspects for them to change, and are key components of successful treatment. In short, substance use is a socially mediated activity in which cultural values and norms impact the sociocultural contingencies involved in substance use. These cultural values, norms, and contingencies vary as a function of place (urban, rural), religion, social class, race, gender, and so forth (Collins et al., 1999).

**RACIAL AND GENDER DIFFERENCES** "Substance use is a universal phenomenon affecting people from all ethnic and racial backgrounds" (Marsiglia & Smith, 2010, p. 289). It is important to remember that ethnicity is a complex construct, not only because of increasing proportions of mixed-heritage individuals, but also because many cultural variables—such as *machismo* and *marianismo*[28]—appear to have both

---

[28] "Machismo refers to hypermasculine gender role norms and expectations that emphasize male dominance and privilege. . . Marianismo refers to feminine gender-role norms and expectations that emphasize self-sacrifice and dedication to family and the household" (Castro & Nieri, 2010, p. 308). Whereas positive dimensions of machismo—including loyalty to family—may operate as protective factors, negative dimensions of machismo—including aggressiveness and a sense of privilege—appear to be risk factors. Likewise, positive dimensions of marianismo—including nurturance—may operate as protective factors, whereas negative dimensions of marianismo—including submission—appear to be risk factors (Castro & Nieri, 2010).

positive and negative influences on substance use (Castro & Nieri, 2010). Moreover, despite many decades of research attempting to discern how race and ethnicity relate to the etiology of SUDs, precise relations between race, ethnicity, and SUDs remain uncertain (Marsiglia & Smith, 2010). After highlighting the often contradictory differences reported in the literature on substance-related problems as a function of race and gender, Holder (2006) was able to make some summary statements: a higher percentage of male youth drink than do female youth, and this difference becomes more pronounced in adolescence and adulthood; white and Hispanic youth are more likely to drink heavily than African American youth; from the most prevalent to least, self-reported drinking by underage youth (12 years and older) is: Caucasians, Native Americans/Native Alaskans, Hispanics, African Americans, and Asians (p. 154). In adulthood, both African American and Caucasian men seem to display similar patterns of alcohol problems; however, African American men tend to report escalated alcohol problems after marrying, whereas Caucasian men tend to report a reduction after marriage. Although women are less likely to have alcohol- or drug-related problems than men, when their drinking becomes increasingly heavy, women report a higher risk of alcohol-related problems, and this gender difference is greater among Caucasians than African Americans (Holder, 2006). African Americans report more illicit drug use than Caucasians or Hispanics.[29] Among Caucasians, marijuana use is more prevalent among those with lower family income and less prestigious occupations, whereas this correlation is absent among African Americans (Holder, 2006).

At the same time, other reviews of the literature report somewhat different conclusions and emphasize that "increasingly apparent, however, is that gender and ethnicity alone do not fully explain these observed differences" (Castro & Nieri, 2010, p. 307). Moreover, it is often less helpful to consider a given culture—such as Latino or African American—as a monolithic variable than it is to inquire how specific cultural factors—such as acculturation, ethnic pride, *familism*, *machismo*, *marianismo*, traditionalism, and so forth—influence the etiology of SUDs. For example, the strong collectivist orientation, involvement and loyalty to family, in many Latino cultures—*familism*—often emphasizes social responsibility to one's family, and in this way, serves protective functions (Castro & Nieri, 2010). *Ethnic pride* is another protective factor, but appears to serve protective functions primarily for those youth who also live in *traditional* families. One interesting finding that research has consistently demonstrated is that higher levels of acculturation to American culture—the extent to which an individual from a diverse ethnic group conforms his or her values and behaviors to mainstream American culture—correlates with higher rates of SUDs (Castro & Nieri, 2010). There are several possible reasons for this finding. First, the more acculturated one is, the less likely that person will exhibit the familism, ethnic pride, and valuing of traditionalism just mentioned. Second, adapting to the comparatively more permissive stance of American culture would likely result in a greater sense of freedom and choice, including the choice to use a variety of substances.

In his review of literature regarding evidence for differential etiologies for SUDs among Caucasians and African Americans, Roberts (2000) concluded "that Whites and

---

[29] Other research suggests that both alcohol and illicit drug use is higher for Caucasians than Hispanic and African American individuals, with the exception of crack, ice, and heroin use among Hispanic youth (Jochman & Fromme, 2010).

African-American addicts differ in their underlying reasons for abusing drugs. Drug addiction among Whites appears to be related largely to psychopathology, whereas Black drug abuse is best understood in terms of social and environmental factors" (p. 667). Although Robert's conclusion is an oversimplified and partial explanation, it is not without its merit. Consider how sociocultural dynamics such as prejudice, discrimination, and hostility toward ethnic groups not only lead to inequity and stress for such groups; such dynamics may also create community-wide "oppositional cultures" that intentionally reject many of the dominant culture's values—such as sobriety—and instead adopt "an alternative subculture that can include gang activity, drug trafficking, and sanctioning illegal drug use and other antisocial behaviors" (Castro & Nieri, 2010, pp. 312–313).

Some gender differences also appear significant. In general, men are more likely to initiate and sustain substance use—from heavy drinking as well as use of illicit substances—than women (Jochman & Fromme, 2010). With regard to etiology, a study by Lev-Wiesel and Shuval (2006) reported that women with SUDs believed that familial dynamics such as domestic violence and incest were primary causes of their SUDs, whereas men believed their SUDs were more likely caused by their curiosity and the influence of friends who used substances. Although this study was conducted in Israel, and there are limitations to such self-reported perceptions of what contributed to the participants' SUDs, it suggests that there may be etiological differences between men and women that are somewhat analogous to those between Caucasians and people of other ethnicities.

## DEVELOPMENTAL DYNAMICS

From intrauterine exposure to alcohol, nicotine, and illicit substances to the potentially protective factors involved in many life transitions, developmental dynamics clearly play a role in the etiology of SUDs. Perhaps most noteworthy is the well-established correlation that the younger one begins using substances, the more likely one is to develop an SUD[30] "the vast majority of individuals who go on to become drug dependent begin taking drugs in adolescence" (Kassel et al., 2010, p. 185). The prevalence of SUDs appears to follow a clear developmental trajectory, with the highest rates found among 18- to 29-year-olds (Kassel et al., 2010). One implication of this is that many young adults with an SUD will recover on their own as they age and mature. In fact, the 20s are a key period during which substance use may peak, persist, or cease (Jochman & Fromme, 2010). Before we address the developmental period that has received the most attention from researchers—adolescence—we should consider the influence of developmental dynamics from the womb to primary school; after all, more than a decade of biopsychosocial development has already taken place by the time individuals reach adolescence (Tarter, 2002).

[30] In one study of 27,616 current and former drinkers, the lifetime alcohol dependence rates decreased from an excess of 40% among those whose first use of alcohol was before age 15 to approximately 10% among individuals who began drinking after age 19; similarly, the lifetime alcohol abuse rates decreased from more than 11% among those whose first use of alcohol was before age 17 to approximately 4% among individuals who began drinking after age 19 (Grant & Dawson, 1997). The authors of this study concluded that, after adjusting for potential confounding variables, the chance of developing alcohol dependence or abuse decreased by 14% and 8%, respectively, with each subsequent year that an individual delayed initiating alcohol use. Other studies have reported similar results (Hawkins et al., 1997), all of which highlight the importance of delaying young people's initiation of substance use.

## From Gestation and Infancy to the Preschool and Primary School Years

Numerous pathological developmental pathways appear to originate from fetal exposure to substances such as nicotine, alcohol, and other drugs. Although less is known about the effects of some specific substances, it appears clear that fetal exposure to nicotine increases the chance of subsequent tobacco abuse (Cornelius, Leech, Goldschmidt, & Day, 2000). Given that children can be born addicted to various substances that their mothers were using while pregnant, it seems that similar dynamics would operate for other substances as they do with nicotine.

Numerous variables during infancy influence the likelihood of later developing SUDs. Various temperamental factors correlate with SUDs, and these have already been discussed. Another key dynamic—also previously discussed—involves attachment processes, with insecure child–caregiver bonds increasing the likelihood of a number of childhood problems—in particular, externalizing disorders such as Oppositional Defiant Disorder, Conduct Disorder, and ADHD, which appear to be intermediary to the development of SUDs (Tarter, 2002). Children who experience neglect, maltreatment, or abuse are also at increased risk for developing SUDs. Because behavioral-, emotional-, and self-dysregulation are clearly implicated in the etiology of SUDs, any maladjustment during infancy, toddlerhood, and the preschool and primary school periods lays a foundation for subsequent substance misuse.

## Adolescence

Why is adolescence such a vulnerable time with regard to substance use? Many dynamics contribute to this phenomenon—from physical, hormonal, and brain changes to a host of developmental tasks in the emotional, cognitive, and social realms (e.g., emotional lability, pressures to think for one's self, becoming increasingly autonomous from one's parents, beginning sexual-romantic relationships, developing one's identity). In general, later adolescence and emerging adulthood (the early 20s) involve more freedom and autonomy than the person has previously experienced, yet fewer responsibilities than characterizes adulthood (Jochman & Fromme, 2010). Particularly noteworthy is that the frontal cortex is not fully developed until age 25; this accounts for a host of underdeveloped executive cognitive functions, including affect regulation, impulse control, decision making, and the evaluation of risk-taking behaviors (Tarter, 2002).[31] In addition, other changes in brain structure likely affect much psychological and behavioral functioning during adolescence, and such neurodevelopmental transformations include:

> alterations in the mesocorticolimbic dopaminergic systems, which have been implicated in modulating the reinforcing properties of drugs and alcohol. In addition, maturation of the prefrontal cortex and the amygdala occurs in adolescence, and these brain regions are involved in goal-directed behaviors, emotional processing, and emotional reactivity. . . . Hence, during adolescence, development takes place in brain regions and systems responsible for regulating critical aspects

[31] Together, these functional capacities are referred to as neurobehavioral disinhibition, and preliminary research suggests that such neurobehavioral disinhibition is a better predictor of a person developing an SUD than the amount of the substances consumed (Tarter, 2002).

> of behavior, emotion, and cognition, as well as perceptions of risk and reward (Steinberg et al., 2004). Such neurobiological reorganization renders adolescence a unique period of vulnerability to extreme emotional lability, and as such, the propensity to use and misuse drugs is increased. (Kassel et al., 2010, p. 187)

Emotional instability and dysphoria often increase during adolescence, and these constitute significant risk factors for initiating substance use (Kassel et al., 2010; Tarter, 2002). Thus, the developmental period of adolescence is a particularly vulnerable one; in fact, most individuals' first use of alcohol and drugs occurs during this time (Compton, Thomas, Conway, & Colliver, 2005; Kassel et al., 2010).[32]

> Taken together, basic research on the emotional experiences of adolescents, along with the current understanding of neurocognitive development, suggests that an immature, or in some cases dysfunctional, cognitive control system, as well as changes in sensitivity of motivational systems, result in poor regulation of emotion and behavior. This occurs at a critical time when autonomy increases, time spent with adults declines, peer relationships become an important influence, and the adolescent has few adult responsibilities. The convergence of these developmental changes may lead some adolescents to engage in high levels of risky behavior, including substance use, either to cope with negative affect or to enhance positive affect. (Colder, Chassin, Lee, & Villalta, 2010, p. 113)

According to the *Psychodynamic Diagnostic Manual*, adolescents (and to a lesser extent, children) are often motivated to use substances by various affective states. These affects can vary from the excitement that derives from experimentation and the desire to feel that one belongs to a peer group to the anxiety that ensues from various developmental and social challenges, such as embarrassment, humiliation, emptiness, depression, and rage (PDM Task Force, 2006).

A good example of how developmental dynamics pertain to the etiology of SUDs comes from a study by Fischer (1991) mentioned earlier in the trauma section. Younger soldiers—presumed to have less developmental stability and integration—who experienced heavy combat were significantly more likely to report SUDs than older soldiers who experienced similar severities of combat. In this case, developmental dynamics and environment (trauma) interacted, with age operating as a moderating variable.

Giese (1999) investigated the role of "personal meaning"—a developmentally related ability to anticipate the consequences of risk-taking behaviors—in alcohol abuse and found that as adolescents' personal meanings developed, they were less likely to abuse alcohol, and if a given adolescent had protective factors, the impact of such was greater for those with higher levels of personal meaning. Both the Fischer (1991) and Giese (1999) studies suggest that in addition to being risk factors, some developmental dynamics can serve as buffers to the likelihood of developing SUDs.

---

[32] Kassel and colleagues (2010) report that

> 73% of 12th graders have tried alcohol. . . . More than a quarter (27%) of youth have used an illicit drug other than marijuana, with marijuana being the most popular illicit drug, with prevalence rates of 31.5% among high school students. Of even greater concern, many adolescents begin using drugs or alcohol before high school; 19.5% of eighth graders reported having been drunk sometime in their lives; and to repeat, earlier age at first use has been associated with greater drug use in adulthood. (p. 185)

## Early Adulthood

Early adulthood often presents developmental transitions that frequently encourage one to change problematic substance use. Many of these transitions involve assuming more responsibility than one previously had—as in the case of beginning a career, marriage, or parenthood—which appears to result in many people decreasing their substance use. Part of the reason for this transition is that the consequences of problematic use during such transitions take on greater significance. For example, a DUI cited to a single 19-year-old tends not to have as much impact as one delivered to a recently married, new father who has just begun a career-oriented job (DiClemente, 2006).

## Older Adulthood and Late Life

Older adults tend to display different patterns of substance use and misuse than younger adults, with problematic alcohol use and polypharmacy[33] being the most common substance-related problems among the elderly. Although the prevalence of heavy drinking declines after age 50—primarily due to premature demise, problematic diagnostic criteria,[34] and underreporting—more than a third of geriatric populations with Alcohol Use Disorders develop their disorder after age 60 (Kennedy, 2000). Moreover, according to the National Health Interview Survey, among those 60 years or older who reported drinking within a year of the survey, 39% of the women and 50% of the men were almost daily drinkers (as cited in Trevisan, 2008). Moreover, 57% of the female population takes 5 or more prescription medications, and 12% takes 10 or more (Trevisan, 2008). In a study of 196 outpatients who were taking 5 or more medications and were 65 years old or older, 65% were found to be taking inappropriate medications, and the "use of one or more inappropriate medications was documented in 128 patients (65%), including 73 (37%) taking a medication in violation of the Beers drugs-to-avoid criteria and 112 (57%) taking a medication that was ineffective, not indicated, or duplicative" (Steinman et al., 2006, p. 1516).

It is important to realize how often SUDs go undetected in geriatric populations; because of this, the Substance Abuse Among Older Adults Consensus Panel for the Treatment Improvement Protocol Series urges all clinicians to screen clients 60 years or older for alcohol and prescription drug misuse. This problem is virtually certain to escalate in the upcoming years as baby boomers—who either experimented with illicit drugs and alcohol or used them more heavily than previous generations—enter late life (Trevisan, 2008); it thus warrants more research and clinical attention.

---

[33] Polypharmacy involves taking multiple medications, particularly when the medications are not clinically warranted, the dosages are too high, or one or more of the medications adversely interacts with or supplicates the mechanisms of another medication. "The incidence of addiction to illicit substances after the age of 65 approaches 0 . . . [they] more often 'mellow out,' die, or transition to alcohol or prescription medications with abuse potential" (Kennedy, 2000, p. 209). Polysubstance dependence, which was a mental disorder in the DSM-IV-TR, has been eliminated in the DSM-5.

[34] Because the majority of this population is retired, adverse occupational and social effects of alcohol misuse may be difficult or impossible to detect: "the retired, socially isolated older male may fill the void with alcohol yet genuinely not report loss of social or occupational activities associated with drink" (Kennedy, 2000, pp. 211–212).

## ETIOLOGY: SUMMARY AND CONCLUSION

As Cambridge neuroscientist Jeff Dalley and colleagues state, even after decades of research, it is still unclear why some people are so susceptible to alcohol and drug addiction, whereas others can use such substances without such horrid consequences (Dalley et al., 2009). As we have seen, the complex interactions that genetic, biological, environmental, personality, experiential, cultural, social, and developmental dynamics exert in the etiology of SUDs is exceedingly difficult to understand in detail, and much of the current literature is overwhelming and often contradictory (Hesselbrock & Hesselbrock, 2006; Pihl, 1999; Scheier, 2010a). Nonetheless, "each perspective has an advantage in describing certain features and etiologic determinants of substance dependence. Each also has its limitation" (Khantzian, 1987, p. 534). The inconsistencies or apparent contradictions that you may have noticed from the different sections/perspectives in this chapter do not necessarily mean that one of the perspectives is right and that the others are wrong; rather, it is more likely a function of some perspectives being better at accounting for and explaining some dimensions of SUDs whereas they are more limited in accounting for other aspects of SUDs. For example, neuroscientific, genetic, behavioral, statistical, and other right-quadrant perspectives offer powerful scientific insights into the workings of brain processes, physiology, and how those interact with reinforcement dynamics; however, they often seem removed or distant from phenomenological experience and the struggles with which people with SUDs suffer. Psychodynamic, existential, and other left-quadrant perspectives are able to complement—not contradict—the right-quadrant perspectives by illuminating some of the experiential and cultural dimensions, meanings, and functions that substances serve for a given person. As Hesselbrock and Hesselbrock (2006) emphasized, "alcohol and other drug use disorders are multiply determined by a complex association of genetic, environmental, personality, and other factors" (p. 103). For example, consider three people, each representing a different position on the spectrum of etiological risk for developing an SUD.

John is an Caucasian from a family with many members who have SUDs, and thus John likely has genes and a physiology (upper-right [UR] risk factor) that predisposes him to develop an SUD. In addition, John grew up in a verbally and physically abusive family (lower-right [LR] risk factor) that was not empathically responsive to his needs and consequently he did not develop good emotion regulation skills (upper-left [UL] risk factor). Because the parental relationships that were modeled were highly dysfunctional, John has struggled to form intimate relationships (lower-left [LL] risk factor) and he often feels isolated and alienated; he does not feel that he fits in or belongs anywhere. Living in poverty in an inner city, he has little access to opportunities or activities that could provide him with less destructive forms of reinforcement, and many of the people he is in contact with use a variety of illicit substances (LR risk factor).

Alex is a recently married African-American and he and his wife hope to begin having children (potentially a developmental and/or LL protective factor). Alex was raised in a family that operated with the rule of "we don't talk about unpleasant things," and his parents and older siblings modeled an avoidant style of coping with life's problems (LR risk factor). His parents were social drinkers, not appearing to misuse alcohol. When he was in his late teens and 20s, he was a member of a touring and recording rock band (LR risk factor) and he routinely drank a bottle of vodka nightly.

His band's popularity dwindled when he was 26, and, suddenly, his life and future began appearing quite bleak and empty to him (UL risk factor). It was then that he met the woman he recently married and decided to quit drinking (UL decision point).

Lee is a Chinese student at an Ivy League university, where she not only excels in her music performance major, but is also on the tennis team, and a popular member of a sorority (LR protective factors). She grew up in an upper-middle-class family with highly attentive parents who were happily married and used no illicit substances (LR protective factor); when they did drink alcohol, they did so in moderation. Her genetics and physiology result in her experiencing drinking more than two drinks as highly aversive (UR protective factor). Moreover, despite the fact that alcohol and other drugs are common at the sorority parties she enjoys, she has many other sources of satisfaction (from violin and tennis to her friends and family; LR protective factors) and is free of any serious mental health problems; thus, she does not experience any need to resort to substances either to experience pleasure or to avoid excessively unpleasant affective states (lack of UL risk factors). None of her closest friends, with whom she frequently socializes, drink or use substances (LL protective factor).

If you consider the three people just described, it is not hard to see that they are ordered from most to least likely to develop an SUD. Of course, we can never know with certainty who will or will not develop an SUD, in part because an individual's willful choices and the positive influences from significant relationships and nonsubstance-related sources of reinforcement cannot be perfectly predicted. Nonetheless, let us consider why John is most at risk and Lee is least at risk. From a quadratic perspective, John has risk factors in all four quadrants, and research has shown a positive relationship between alcohol misuse and number of risk factors (Giese, 1999). Although it is difficult to separate the genetic/physiological components from other (environmental) family influences, the negative impact of growing up in a family in which drug use was modeled, and in which he was abused and not empathically attuned to, will only intensify any genetic predispositions that he inherited. Moreover, his lack of affect regulation skills will make the effects of many substances all the more negatively reinforcing (rather than using deep-breathing, affirming self-talk, and other self-regulation skills to counter aversive affect, he will likely resort to alcohol or other affect-numbing substances). Moreover, his peer groups in the inner city reduce the number of non-using social networks available to him and it may be that he finds a sense of belonging only among these substance users.

In contrast, Lee appears to have no SUD risk factors, but many protective factors. She gains a sense of enjoyment and purpose from playing tennis and violin, as well as from her close friends, none of whom encourage her to use substances. Even if her friends did drink heavily, her physiology would decrease the probability of her developing an alcohol-related problem. Moreover, her being female makes her statistically less likely to develop an SUD.

With regard to the likelihood of developing an SUD, Alex is in between John and Lee. Although he had risk factors from his avoidant coping style, the culture of most rock bands (you know, the "sex, drugs, and rock-n-roll" cliché), and his life seeming bleak, his recently being married and likely to assume the role of a father may make him more likely to succeed in his commitment to remain abstinent.

| UPPER-LEFT (UL): INTERIOR-INDIVIDUAL | UPPER-RIGHT (UR): EXTERIOR-INDIVIDUAL |
|---|---|
| • cravings<br>• negative affect<br>• choice and will<br>• outcome and efficacy expectancies<br>• cognitive control<br>• poor affect regulation<br>• avoidant coping style | • genetic predisposition<br>• mesolimbic dopaminergic neurotransmission<br>• the positive and negative reinforcement action of substances<br>• sensitization<br>• deficits/defects in the frontal region of the brain |
| **LOWER-LEFT (LL): INTERIOR-COLLECTIVE** | **LOWER-RIGHT (LR): EXTERIOR-COLLECTIVE** |
| • lack of satisfying relationships<br>• alienation and loneliness<br>• heavy drinking/substance use in one's culture and/or family<br>• social cohesion/sense of belonging<br>• the "culture of addiction"<br>• cultural bias against altered states of consciousness<br>• a culture that does not encourage participation in ecstatic engagement with Nature or what is regeneratively ecstatic for the person | • family influence (parental role modeling, parental monitoring, history of being abused or neglected)<br>• parenting quality<br>• significant stressors/trauma, some of which may be due to racial discrimination and other social injustices<br>• low SES<br>• lack of social supports or social network that does not misuse substances<br>• peer-group pressure<br>• local availability<br>• social policies<br>• lack of access to alternative sources of reinforcement<br>• residential stability/instability |

**FIGURE 8.2** A Quadratic View of the Etiology of Substance-Related Disorders

Given that so many variables are clearly implicated in the development of SUDs (see Figure 8.2), and compounded by the complex interaction of those variables as well as oftentimes contradictory findings from different disciplines, some authors have suggested that it is less productive to continue trying to decipher the specific etiology of SUDs than it is to understand how SUDs are maintained (Mello, 1983). With this in mind, let us briefly overview some forms of treatment for SUDs—ways to help people interrupt the processes that maintain their SUDs.

## TREATMENTS

### Introduction and Overview

The U.S. health-care system's approach to treating SUDs is in dire straits, and some researchers have stressed that, in many ways, an organized system with which to address SUDs is nonexistent:

> With drastic cuts in financial support for already starved treatment and prevention efforts, many alcohol and drug treatment programs across the United States have simply closed. Major gaps persist between what has shown to be effective

> and what is actually practiced in clinical settings. Services for drug problems continue to be stigmatized, marginalized, and isolated from the rest of the health care system. (Carroll & Miller, 2006, p. 4)

The gap between research and practice[35] alluded to in this quote appears to be prevalent not only in community clinics but in schools as well: "although considerable progress has been made in identifying effective prevention approaches, there is a large gap between what research has shown to be effective and the methods generally used in schools" (Botvin, 2000, p. 887). Having reviewed the literature on risk factors for substance-related problems from a developmental perspective, it seems clear that prevention efforts are most effective when begun at early ages and they should target not only the individual, but also peer groups, families, communities, and social policies (Hesselbrock & Hesselbrock, 2006). Thus, compared to most disorders listed in the DSMs, SUDs get more attention with regard to primary prevention (gearing intentional actions toward helping adolescents and others *prevent* predictable adverse consequences, preserving current health, and promoting desired outcomes) in comparison with treatment (focusing actions to lessen or eliminate existing problems) (Leukefeld, McDonald, Stroops, Reed, & Martin, 2005). On this point, it appears that the most effective prevention efforts are those operating from a psychosocial perspective, geared toward early adolescence (when many are beginning to experiment with substances) and emphasizing not only skills to help students resist pro-drug social influences, but also correcting inaccurate normative beliefs and teaching social and coping skills (Botvin, 2000). These programs assume that many adolescents' onset of drug use is due to their lacking the skills or confidence to resist peer influences to drink, smoke, or use illicit drugs. Although the effects of such prevention programs do decrease over time, some studies have demonstrated a reduction of drug use that persisted through the end of high school.[36]

Most researchers in the field view SUDs as diseases, not as a weakness of character. As is the case with other chronic diseases, it is more accurate to say that people with SUDs are helped or treated, not "cured"; moreover, there is no single approach that works for everyone.

Most people who seek help for SUDs do so because environmental pressures—employers, the legal system, family or friends—have encouraged or forced them to do so (Bickel & Potenza, 2006). As is well known, people with SUDs often deny their misuse of substances, but they are more likely to be honest with regard to their use of substances in the presence of a therapist who inquires about substance use in a way that is free of critical or moralizing overtones (PDM Task Force, 2006).

Because most people with an SUD have a host of other problems, including likely having another mental disorder, *interventions are more likely to be successful when they address a broad range of a person's life, rather than just the SUD.* In addition,

[35] Kassel and Evatt (2010) concur: "the field of substance abuse and dependence—arguably more so than any other field of psychopathology—has historically been plagued by deep chasms between the worlds of research and clinical delivery" (p. 283). As discussed earlier, this is largely due to the public policy view of SUDs as more of a criminal justice issue than a mental health, clinical, or public health issue.

[36] On the other hand, "some of the most widely used school-based prevention approaches are ineffective. Notable among these are approaches that rely [primarily] on providing information concerning the adverse consequences of drug abuse" (Botvin, 2000, p. 894; bracketed text added).

abstinence is often low on their priority list, and because successful treatment usually involves helping addicted people have more rewarding, satisfying lives that do not depend on substance use as their only source of pleasure, focusing solely on their substance-related problems in a treatment program makes little sense (Miller & Carroll, 2006). In order to help them increase non-drug reinforcements, clients must develop positive relationships and other healthy coping skills. Moreover, and as mentioned earlier, once someone develops an SUD—particularly if it is on the more severe end of the spectrum—it becomes a self-organizing system that is particularly difficult to destabilize unless multiple entrance points are addressed in one's (integrative) treatment (Bickel & Potenza, 2006; Miller & Carroll, 2006). In other words, addressing only one aspect of the system (such as just physiology, just behavior, just emotions, just social systems) rarely leads to significant, lasting change.

In the past, it was commonly—although mistakenly—believed that people with SUDs could not recover on their own. By way of contrast, DiClemente (2006) stresses that people with SUDs have demonstrated the capacity to recover from every abusable substance without formal, professional intervention. Of great significance, "natural recovery is not a process that differs from treatment-assisted recovery" (DiClemente, 2006, p. 94). When a person seeks professional treatment, such treatment actually interacts with self-change[37] processes and is a time-limited component of that person's entire process of self-change. DiClemente (2006) thus views all substance abuse recovery as self-change, with any formal interventions serving a facilitating role. Such a perspective places greater emphasis on the person—rather than the treatment—struggling with substance misuse, his experiences and values, his developmental status, his stage of change, and the role that substances play in his unique life.

Therapeutic intervention begins with a thorough assessment of not only the patterns and amounts of substance use and any negative life consequences, but also comorbidity issues,[38] motivation, and strengths and resources to draw upon in recovery (especially alternative sources of positive reinforcement). One of the most common obstacles in the early stages of treatment or help seeking is the substance user's ambivalence regarding having a problem—believing that his problem is not severe enough to warrant changing. In such cases, motivational interviewing (Miller & Rollnick, 2002) is recommended.[39]

In the concluding chapter of their excellent edited volume *Rethinking Substance Abuse*, Miller and Carroll (2006) provide the following 10 recommendations regarding intervening in the realm of SUDs:

1. Intervention is not a specialist problem but a broad social responsibility that should be shared by many public and private sectors.

---

[37] "Self-change" is DiClemente's (2006) term for recovery from substance problems without formal or professional treatment or assistance; a change that is fundamentally directed by the person him- or herself.

[38] Some interventions have been developed to treat such comorbidity dynamics. For example, Ouimette and Brown (2002) have combined cognitive-behavioral therapy (CBT) and exposure therapy for those with an SUD and PTSD. For those with comorbid SUD and Schizophrenia, clozapine has been shown to decrease alcohol, smoking, and cocaine use (Buckley, 1998).

[39] Motivational interviewing involves a combination of client-centered, empathic understanding with semi-directive questioning that often engages or amplifies the client's intrinsic motivation to change her substance use by highlighting and exploring the pros and cons of not changing, reflecting discrepancies or contradictions in her expressions, and resolving her ambivalence.

2. Screen for and address the full range of drug problems, and not just the most severe.
3. Understand drug use and problems in a larger life context, and provide comprehensive care.
4. Look beyond the individual for the causes and solutions to drug use and problems.
5. Enhancing motivation for and commitment to change should be an early goal and key component of intervention.
6. Changing a well-established pattern of drug use usually begins by interrupting the pattern to produce an initial period of abstinence.
7. Enhance positive reinforcement for nonuse and enrich access to alternative sources of positive reinforcement.
8. Diminish the rewarding aspects of drug use.
9. Make services easily accessible, affordable, welcoming, helpful, potent, rapid, and attractive.
10. Use evidence-based approaches.[40] (pp. 302–310)

## Upper-Left Treatments

Given the significant roles that emotions, expectancies, and motivation play in SUDs, it makes sense that treatment for those trying to recover from SUDs must attend to different dimensions of their subjective experience. With regard to emotional regulation, clients can be helped to develop distress tolerance skills, calming strategies, and other means of achieving desirable affective states (deep breathing, positive self-talk, thought stopping, attentional focusing skills, etc.; Jongsma, Peterson, & Bruce, 2006; Linehan, 1993; McCarthy et al., 2010). Mindfulness practices can be used to help the person become more attuned to her affective and cognitive experience, as well as to strengthen her cognitive control. Mindfulness and other forms of meditation are also important because they potentially offer healthy ways of accessing the altered states of consciousness (ASCs) that many people strongly desire.[41] Alcoholics Anonymous emphasizes the importance of such with its call for "a new state of consciousness and being" (cited in du Plessis, 2010, p. 77). One recent study involving an incarcerated population found that, compared to a treatment-as-usual control group, participants in a mindfulness-based course had significant reductions in marijuana, crack cocaine, and alcohol use (Bowen et al., 2006).

Because outcome expectancies clearly contribute to substance use, treatment (from preventative approaches to working to prevent relapse) should include expectancy modification (Kassel et al., 2010). In general, cognitive approaches explore how clients' schemas may impact self-perceptions, efficacy expectations, and other

[40] For all 10 of these, the interested reader is referred to Miller and Carroll (2006) for an elaboration of these recommendations. For example, under the recommendation to use evidence-based approaches, they qualify their point by stating "As a closing piece of advice, we do not recommend ossifying practice into a list of 'approved' evidence-based treatments. . . . While interventions with a strong evidence base are a good starting point, a creative service system will also encourage innovation to accomplish specified goals and to monitor outcomes to know which practices do, in fact, promote the achievement of those goals" (p. 311).

[41] Unfortunately, accessing such ASCs through meditation alone often requires years of diligent practice. As you will see in the Upper-Right Treatments section, technologically assisted, nondestructive ways of achieving ASCs can vastly accelerate this process.

beliefs that may increase their discouragement or weaken their resolve to remain abstinent. Helping clients examine the evidence for such beliefs, as well as any evidence regarding the pros and cons of continuing using, is also helpful.

## Upper-Right Treatments

A widely recognized phenomenon is that undergoing a period of abstinence from substance use is a key component of destabilizing dependence on a substance,[42] and such abstinence may be instigated by different means—from incarceration or a family's intervening to prosocial reinforcement for nonuse, antagonist medication, or the user's willful choice (Miller & Carroll, 2006). If the client does not recognize and admit that he has a problem with substances, it may be helpful to refer him for a physical exam to see if there are any negative medical/physical consequences of his substance use (i.e., liver damage in chronic, heavy drinking). Such objective data are often more persuasive than, for example, asking him to list ways that his substance use has negatively affected his life.[43] Particularly if the client has comorbid diagnoses, it may be appropriate to refer him to a psychiatrist for psychotropic medications (Jongsma et al., 2006).

Assigning clients bibliotherapy or other psycho-educational materials about chemical dependency, and then processing such with them, can be an important component of treatment. Likewise, having clients meet with an Alcoholics Anonymous (AA) or Narcotics Anonymous (NA) member who has been successful in a 12-step program is suggested; as soon as possible, clients should be encouraged to attend AA or NA meetings and then process with the therapist their experience of the meetings (Jongsma et al., 2006).

From a behavioral perspective, given that SUDs usually derive, at least in part, from the brief, intense stimuli provided by the substance, applying immediate prosocial reinforcers can be a countervailing force that is often an effective component of treatment (Bickel & Potenza, 2006). According to Miller (2006), "Substance use is highly responsive to contingent positive reinforcement. Even severely dependent substance users can and do abstain from or modify their drinking or drug use in response to positive incentives to do so" (p. 149). In addition to finding alternative sources of reinforcement, it is also important to alter the stimulus–response associations the person has with the substance(s). Classically conditioned extinction by repeated *exposure* to a range of urge-producing drug cues (from somatic, emotional, and cognitive cues to environmental, social, and relational cues) without drug use usually weakens the associations between such stimuli (cues) and the response of drug use.

---

[42] Although an *initial* period of abstinence appears very important in effective treatment, not all researchers and clinicians agree that abstinence must be the goal for all those who have experienced substance-related problems:

> In the field of alcohol, we remain without guidelines concerning who must really stop drinking in order to recover from DSM-IV alcohol dependence, and who can recover stably from dependence even while drinking moderately. While many guidelines exist on *how* to cut down or stop in terms of psychological (e.g., motivation, cognitive planning) and environmental changes (new peer groups, avoidance of cues for bingeing), these do not address the question of abstinence versus controlled drinking. (Hasin et al., 2006, pp. 75–76)

[43] From an LL/LR perspective, it is often useful to have a few of the client's close friends or family members make such a list or even write a letter describing how they have observed the person's substance use adversely affecting his and/or their lives.

In addition, rewards and other reinforcements for eschewing drug use should further decrease drug urges (McCarthy et al., 2010). These authors proceeded to stress that the key to success is the person's "extensive practice of alternative responses across diverse internal and external contexts. . . . Such repetition will be essential to compete with the overlearned, strongly mapped response of drug-seeking in various contexts" (McCarthy et al., 2010, p. 31). Shortly thereafter, they stress that even with extensive practice, repetition alone will be unlikely to successfully ameliorate most SUDs; other issues, such as selecting peers and environments that do not trigger drug-use associations, are equally important.

It is also helpful to teach clients the difference between a lapse (an initial, reversible use of a substance) and a relapse (a decision—made with varying degrees of conscious intention—to return to a pattern of substance misuse). Clients should be encouraged to regularly practice and utilize the skills they have learned in therapy (from cognitive restructuring, exposure and response prevention, engaging in alternative sources of non-substance positive reinforcement, etc.) in a variety of different situations (Jongsma et al., 2006).

**PHARMACOTHERAPY** The role and effectiveness of pharmacotherapy varies greatly as a function of the specific substances being misused. For example, pharmacotherapy is a principal treatment for nicotine dependence, and only minimal behavioral interventions are normally required as a complement. In contrast, for stimulants such as amphetamines and cocaine, there are currently no pharmacotherapies approved by the Food and Drug Administration (FDA) (O'Malley & Kosten, 2006). Opiate dependence is another case in which pharmacotherapy (methadone, suboxone) is a mainstay of treatment, and naltrexone has rapidly gained acceptance in the last 15 years as a treatment for alcohol dependence.

Using pharmacological agents in the treatment of SUDs falls into two main categories: (1) those used to manage acute withdrawal symptoms or to facilitate an initial period of abstinence and (2) those used to help prevent relapse (O'Malley & Kosten, 2006). Such pharmacological agents can act in four different ways:

> *Agonist drugs* directly stimulate the receptor—for example, methadone binds to the opiate receptors—and are often used as replacements for the abused drug. Other medications can act as *indirect agonists* by increasing the levels of the transmitter indirectly. . . . *Partial agonists* act like agonists but do not stimulate the receptor to the same degree. *Antagonists* bind to the receptor but do not stimulate it and prevent agonists from binding. (O'Malley & Kosten, 2006, p. 241)

Although their pharmacological actions are efficacious, antagonists are often clinically ineffective due to problems with clients' adherence, and pharmacotherapies that make the substance of choice aversive (i.e., disulfiram for alcohol) are even more likely to have compliance problems (O'Malley & Kosten, 2006).

In addition to practicing different forms of meditation, there are technologically assisted, non-destructive ways of achieving altered states of consciousness, and these vary from electroencephalogram (EEG) biofeedback (neurotherapy) to brainwave entrainment (BWE) technologies (du Plessis, 2010; Trudeau, 2005). BWE technologies, in particular, quickly help people enter the alpha and theta brain-wave states that advanced meditative states (and many substances) induce.

## Lower-Right Treatments

Many people with substance-related problems will not seek treatment in the absence of external, environmental forces, such as losing loved ones, losing employment, becoming incarcerated, and so forth (Bickel & Potenza, 2006). Thus, Lower-Right dynamics are critical to many substance abusers' recovery. Moreover, the very act of entering some form of treatment—from inpatient rehabilitation and 12-step programs to outpatient counseling—constitutes a social system of recovery. Not only is avoiding the "people, places, and things" associated with their substance use critical to avoiding relapse, living within some form of supportive community—even if that is only a few friends or family members—is essential for most people in this process (du Plessis, 2010).

**PUBLIC POLICY** From a public health perspective, not only the person with the SUD but also the entire community must be taken into account. Perhaps even more important to this perspective is treating SUDs as a health issue—not as a criminal justice or moral issue (Compton, 2005). Treating drug problems as a public *health* issue is actually more cost effective than responding to drug problems as a criminal justice matter (Miller & Carroll, 2006). In response to someone who has tried once or twice to quit drinking or smoking cigarettes, virtually no one would say "you've had your chance, you can't try to quit again"; but to the person misusing illicit drugs, our current policies essentially say "if you do not succeed after the first or second time, you are not going to succeed—you must not have the will to quit, so you're going to jail." It follows that we need to bring a similar attitude to illegal drug use and recovery that we have with people trying to overcome problems with alcohol and nicotine, especially when considering that from medical and physiological perspectives, distinguishing between the two makes no sense at all.

> The United States has particularly relied on judicial and correctional systems to combat drug use. Although criminal sanctions may deter initial use, incarceration is largely ineffective and sometimes counterproductive in suppressing established drug dependence. We support normal accountability and sanctions for offenses committed in relation to drug use, as well as the diversion of nonviolent offenders to evidence-based treatment rather than incarceration.
>
> Because drugs with high abuse potential gratify basic human needs, a societal solution to drug problems is unlikely to be found in deprivation and punishment. Attempts to prevent people from using such drugs are ill-fated without providing access to alternative natural sources of positive reinforcement. Prevention and treatment efforts can address modifiable protective factors, connecting people with personal and social resources that diminish the need for what Aldous Huxley called "artificial paradises." (Miller & Carroll, 2006, p. 306)

According to Bill Moyers (1998), the "war on drugs" has become the Vietnam of our time; we keep the same policies and hope for different results. Seen from this perspective, policymakers' denial (regarding the ineffectiveness of responding to drug problems primarily as a criminal justice matter) seems comparable to that of many addicts.

> Addiction to these illegal substances is seen not primarily as a health problem, but as a crime problem, to be deterred and punished largely through the criminal justice system. Since the early 1980s, approximately 70 percent of the federal drug

war budget has been devoted to law enforcement efforts to eradicate and interdict drugs, and to arrest and prosecute dealers and users. Prevention, treatment, and research on drug abuse and addiction have commanded only 30 percent of federal budgets. Unfortunately, the drug war has failed to significantly reduce levels of supply or addiction. (Bertram & Sharpe, 2011, p. 12)

Another systemic issue is that even though there is social stigma against alcoholism, it is far less than that of heroin, cocaine, or other illicit drug misuse; there are also fewer people working to create treatment centers for illicit drug users. Finally, when considering that treatment is not effective with all substance misusers, it is important to remember that treatment is not effective for all of those with any health problem, whether depression, anxiety, cancer, or diabetes.

**FAMILY SYSTEMS APPROACHES** Due to the centrality of family dynamics in the development of children and adolescents, "many scholars believe that parents are the most underused resource in preventing youth drug abuse" (Kliewer, 2010, p. 366). Family systems approaches posit that because familial dynamics are part of what is responsible for the development of substance problems, addressing such dynamics is a key component of treatment. In general, family systems approaches focus on creating clear, direct communication patterns; creating boundaries that are neither too rigid nor too diffuse; setting clear, reasonable limits; and helping members feel both autonomy and membership in the family (Friesen, 1983). "Effective interventions with families have tended to focus on two factors in particular: (1) strengthening family skills for positive communication and monitoring, and (2) building family reciprocity in exchanging and sharing positive reinforcement" (Miller & Carroll, 2006, p. 300).

In addition, effective family-involved interventions include multicomponent programs that address multiple dimensions of risk, such as: emphasizing family management (i.e., parents are encouraged to monitor their adolescents more, and set clearer rules and firm boundaries for acceptable behavior); creating an emotional tone at home that is warm, affectionate, and cohesive; intervening very early for those in the highest-risk families; using highly attractive incentives to increase treatment retention; and using case management strategies to help people who do not have functional social networks (Kliewer, 2010; McCrady, 2006). Although peer groups become an increasingly influential force during adolescence, families remain important in the prevention of adolescent drug use and misuse, and should be enlisted in service of such (Kliewer, 2010).

It is important for clinicians to assess the role that the clients' living circumstances are playing in their substance use; this could range from living with friends or family members who also use such substances to living in a neighborhood where substance use is normative. In such situations, helping the client develop a plan to change his living circumstances is suggested (Jongsma et al., 2006). When marital dynamics are involved in the client's SUD, couples counseling or marital therapy is recommended.

It should never be forgotten how powerful familial influence is. Miller (2006) repeatedly emphasizes how clearly research supports the notion that a person's motivation to change alcohol or substance abuse can be increased from the unilateral intervention of significant others such as a spouse, parent, or other close family members and friends. Different versions of such "interventions" abound, but surprisingly, approximately 80% of families report that the confrontational intervention is unacceptable to them, and thus do not go through with it; however, among those families that do intervene in such a manner, a very high percentage of substance users do enter treatment (Miller, 2006).

People who live in rural areas experience even more obstacles to treatment than most, ranging from cultural norms against seeking mental health treatment and the increased difficulty of maintaining confidentiality to that of the "urbanocentric distribution" of substance abuse treatment facilities, and thus the need to travel greater distances to receive treatment (Johnson, 2009; Simanksy, 2008). This is particularly troublesome given that the incidence of substance abuse among adolescents in rural areas is now equal to or greater than that in urban areas (Simansky, 2008).

**SOCIAL STIGMA** When giving reasons why they chose not to seek professional help, many people with substance-related problems cite social stigma. In other words, society's viewing problematic substance use as deviant and/or criminal simultaneously creates a barrier to their seeking help and promotes an overidentification with other substance users that increases the difficulty of changing. That being said, the desire to avoid being stigmatized as an "addict" may also help motivate some—who are concerned about their use but do not want to seek professional treatment for a stigmatized condition—to change on their own (DiClemente, 2006).

## Lower-Left Treatments

Given that SUDs develop in the context of relationships (often dysfunctional ones), it should not be surprising that "recovery occurs in a context of caring relationships" (Khantzian, 1987, p. 533).[44] Miller and Carroll (2006) echo this point when they underscore how differentially effective some counselors are in working with clients with SUDs; for one thing, "counselors who are higher in warmth and empathy have clients who show greater improvement in drug use and problems. . . . A confrontational style that puts clients on the defensive appears to be countertherapeutic" (p. 301). Regarding other caring relationships, couples counseling, according to McCrady (2006), is often more effective in reducing drinking and drug use than is individual counseling. Moreover, "any form of treatment that does not acknowledge and understand the principles behind the culture of addiction as well as the need for a healthy recovery culture is bound to be ineffective" (du Plessis, 2010, p. 73). A culture of affiliation that supports someone's recovery is perhaps one of the main reasons that 12-step programs are effective—they provide a recovery culture that gives each member a sense of belonging and acceptance. Healthy recovery cultures also provide healthy rites of passage: "The 'chip' or key-ring that addicts receive during their milestones in NA meetings satisfy deep 'archetypal' human needs; they function as 'symbols of initiation' and are often proudly displayed" (du Plessis, 2010, p. 73). Along similar lines, helping clients develop "sobriety buddies" and engaging in recreational and social activities that are not associated with substance use are paramount to remaining abstinent.

---

[44] Although religious involvement is one of the more powerful buffers against developing drug and alcohol problems, it does not appear very effective in treating such problems once they have developed (Carroll & Miller, 2006).

One study of a male African American clinical population found that they not only considered their cultural pain and anger as contributing to their developing substance-related problems, they also reported (in both surveys and focus group interviews) considerable distrust of substance abuse professionals who were from the dominant culture (Williams, 2008). Although meta-analytical research—regarding psychotherapy as a whole, not SUDs in particular—has *not* supported enhanced outcomes as a function of the ethnic matching of therapist and client (Norcross, 2010), the findings of Williams (2008) remind us of the importance of diversity competence and the need to be sensitive to each client's cultural identity, especially when clients are from nondominant groups. The need for cultural sensitivity when working with Hispanic Americans was also stressed by Gullickson and Ramser (1996), particularly with regard to their valuing of family and cooperation; their preferring a counseling approach that is action-oriented and directive; and the constructs of *respeto*, *personalismo*, and *simpatia*.

## An Integrated Approach

One example of an integrated approach to treating SUDs is du Plessis's (2010) Integrated Recovery (IR) Model.[45] As an Integrally-informed treatment approach, the IR Model emphasizes and implements six dimensions of recovery:

1. ***Physical:*** Physical exercises including walks on nearby beaches and mountains; surfing lessons; yoga; Tai Chi; Kung Fu; nutritional assessment and supplements . . . nutritional education; acupuncture; psychiatric assessment and pharmacological intervention by a psychiatrist, if necessary; neurological assessment and neurotherapy using EEG biofeedback and QEEG assessment
2. ***Mental:*** Psychosocial education in the form of lectures, workshops, and written work; Dialectical Behavior Therapy adapted for addicted populations; Rational Emotive Behavior Therapy workbooks; Cognitive Behavior Therapy; 12 Step education and written work; psychological assessments
3. ***Emotional:*** Individual counseling; psychotherapeutic groups, including gender groups; grief groups; eating disorder groups (incorporating mindful eating practices); sex and love addiction groups; emotional literacy and regulation skills
4. ***Spiritual:*** Daily mindfulness meditation adapted from a Mindfulness-Based Stress Reduction program and assisted by Brainwave Entrainment technology; mindfulness practice groups using *Ikebana* and *Bonsai* as focus activities; music and art groups; spirituality group focusing on spiritual education and discussion; existential group focusing on the pursuit of meaningful activities in recovery
5. ***Social:*** Regular attendance of 12 Step fellowship meetings and service activities; 12 Step sponsor; family program; family conjoints; use of ritual and initiation in phase-based treatment processes
6. ***Environmental:*** Community and environmental service; participation in recycling activities; permaculture gardening; *curriculum vitae* design; administrative life skills and financial education; guidance in finding safe accommodation. (du Plessis, 2010, pp. 74–75).

[45] Another example of an integrated treatment approach is Guajardo, Bagladi, and Kushner (2004).

It should be clear that the IR Model is implemented in a formal recovery center, in contrast to outpatient therapy.[46] Nonetheless, the IR Model can be adapted and used by therapists who are not working within a formal recovery environment. In essence, the IR Model involves "mindfully practicing one's physical, emotional, mental, spiritual, and financial dimensions as part of an Integrative Recovery Lifestyle that is geared towards continued personal growth in relation to self, others, and the transcendent" (du Plessis, 2010, p. 75).

## TREATMENT SUMMARY

Because the aforementioned treatments are, by themselves, often ineffective, this suggests that each treatment approach is addressing only one aspect of the multidimensional origins and nature of SUDs. Because so many different variables are involved in the development of SUDs, interventions that are most likely to be effective are integrative and address each—or at least most—of the components, from biological and environmental to social, cultural, and experiential (see Figure 8.3; du Plessis, 2010; Pickins & Svikis, 1991). Moreover, resources should be devoted to prevention efforts,

| UPPER-LEFT (UL): INTERIOR-INDIVIDUAL | UPPER-RIGHT (UR): EXTERIOR-INDIVIDUAL |
|---|---|
| • If needed, increase client's motivation for and commitment to change<br>• Healthy coping skills (from positive self talk to emotional regulation)<br>• Mindfulness and other spiritual practices<br>• Participating in activities that provide enjoyment (positive reinforcement)<br>• Existential-humanistic approaches | • Interrupt the pattern of substance use with a period of abstinence<br>• A physical exam to determine if the substance use has caused any negative medical/physical consequences<br>• Pharmacotherapy such as methadone, buprenorphine, and the nicotine patch<br>• Cognitive behavioral approaches<br>• EEG biofeedback and BWE |
| **LOWER-LEFT (LL): INTERIOR-COLLECTIVE** | **LOWER-RIGHT (LR): EXTERIOR-COLLECTIVE** |
| • Unilateral "interventions" from concerned significant others<br>• Healthy relationships with people who do not use substances<br>• A culture of affiliation that supports the person's recovery<br>• A culture that encourages participation in ecstatic engagement with Nature or what is regeneratively ecstatic for the person<br>• Psychodynamic and attachment theory approaches | • Increasing access to alternative sources of positive reinforcement<br>• Attending AA or NA meetings<br>• Avoiding the "people, places, and things" associated with substance use<br>• Family systems approaches<br>• Changing SUDs from primarily a criminal justice issue to a public health issue |

**FIGURE 8.3** A Quadratic View of the Treatment of Substance-Related Disorders

[46] du Plessis (2010) developed and implements the IR Model at Tabankulu Secondary Addiction Recovery Center in Cape Town, South Africa.

be geared toward early adolescence, and involve not only families and communities but larger social policies as well. Finally, the social stigma attached to having and seeking professional help for an SUD must be reduced, and rehabilitation services need to be made more affordable, accessible, welcoming, and attractive to those struggling with substance use.

## Conclusion

As you have seen, Substance Use Disorders represent a complex issue, and labeling substance use as aberrant or as a "disorder" is itself difficult and potentially problematic. The etiology of SUDs is clearly overdetermined, with complex interactions that are far from being completely understood. Even though we have addressed many of the etiological principles—from genetic predispositions, neurotransmission, reinforcement histories, experiencing aversive affect, and having poor impulse control to a host of familial and sociocultural dynamics—the development of SUDs is often idiosyncratic to specific individuals. It is worth repeating that some people are able to use substances in beneficial or nonproblematic ways, whereas others' use is clearly problematic, abusive, and destructive.

Treatment of SUDS is likewise complex and is more likely to succeed when it addresses the multidimensional nature of the person's life, not just the SUD. A warm, caring, nonjudgmental stance is essential for clinicians who treat those suffering from SUDs. Healthy relationships are critical not only between clients and clinicians; those in recovery must have such relationships, as well as a "culture of affiliation" that supports their recovery and affords prosocial means of experiencing enjoyment so that they do not need substances as substitute gratifications.

## Review Questions

1. What do you think are the most appropriate terms with which to describe the topic of this chapter (i.e., addiction, alcoholism, substance abuse, substance dependence, substance misuse, hazardous use, substance use disorder, substance-related problem) and why?
2. Reflect upon Figure 8.1, The Spectrum of Psychoactive Substance Use. What are your reactions to it? Support your reactions and thoughts with as much evidence as possible.
3. How would you respond to someone who said "my struggle with alcoholism is due completely to the genes I've inherited"?
4. Discuss why people who use substances primarily for their negatively reinforcing properties (i.e., the removal of aversive experience) are more likely to eventually develop serious problems with those substances than those who use them primarily for their positively reinforcing properties (i.e., to gain a pleasurable experience). Also include other relevant factors that contribute to the likelihood of substance use becoming a SUD (i.e., the availability of other means of achieving enjoyment and other coping skills the person has, etc.).
5. How prominent do you consider will and choice in an individual's development of an SUD?
6. The chapter emphasizes that part of the problem with regard to understanding, preventing, and treating SUDs is that American society tends to view them more as criminal justice issues than public health or medical/mental health issues. What do you think about this? Support your position with as much evidence as possible.
7. What role do families, schools, and other systems play with regard to the prevention or development of SUDs? Bear in mind the repeatedly encountered finding that the earlier a person initiates substance use, the more likely that person will eventually develop an SUD.

## References


Allan, C. A., & Cooke, D. J. (1985). Stressful life events and alcohol misuse in women: A critical review. *Journal of Studies on Alcohol, 46*(2), 147–152.

Allen, D. (2003). Treating the cause not the problem: Vulnerable young people and substance misuse. *Journal of Substance Use, 8*(1), 47–54.

American Psychiatric Association. (2000). *Diagnostic and statistical manual of mental disorders* (4th ed., text revision). Washington, DC: Author.

American Psychiatric Association. (2013). *Diagnostic and statistical manual of mental disorders* (5th ed.). Washington, DC: Author.

Armeli, S., Tennen, H., Todd, M., Carney, M. A., Mohr, C., Affleck, G., & Hromi, A. (2003). A daily process examination of the stress-response dampening effects of alcohol consumption. *Psychology of Addictive Behaviors, 17,* 260–276.

Baker, T. B., Piper, M. E., McCarthy, D. E., Majeskie, M. R., & Fiore, M. C. (2004). Addiction motivation reformulated: An affective processing model of negative reinforcement. *Psychological Review, 111,* 33–51.

Bandura, A. (1977a). Self-efficacy: Toward a unifying theory of behavior change. *Psychological Review, 84,* 191–215.

Bandura, A. (1977b). *Social learning theory.* Englewood Cliffs, NJ: Prentice-Hall.

Barlow, D. H. (2004). *Anxiety and its disorders: The nature and treatment of anxiety and panic* (2nd ed.). New York: The Guilford Press.

Bean-Bayog, M. (1988). Alcohol and drug abuse: Alcoholism as a cause of psychopathology. *Hospital and Community Psychiatry, 39*(4), 352–354.

Beatty, L. A. (2010). Drug abuse research: Addressing the needs of racial and ethnic minority populations. In L. Scheier (Ed.), *Handbook of drug use etiology: Theory, methods, and empirical findings* (pp. 325–340). Washington, DC: American Psychological Association.

Bertram, E., & Sharpe, K. (2011). The politics of addiction. Retrieved from http://www.google.com/search?q=politics+of+addiction+moyers&ie=utf-8&oe=utf-8&aq=t&rls=org.mozilla:en-US:official&client=firefox-a

Bevins, R. A., & Bardo M. T. (Eds.) (2004). *Motivational factors in the etiology of drug abuse: Volume 50 of the Nebraska symposium on motivation.* Lincoln, NE: University of Nebraska Press.

Bickel, W. K., & Potenza, M. N. (2006). The forest and the trees: Addiction as a complex self-organizing system. In W. R. Miller & K. M. Carroll (Eds.), *Rethinking substance abuse: What the science shows, and what we should do about it* (pp. 8–24). New York: The Guilford Press.

Bohman M., Sigvardsson S., & Cloninger, C. R. (1981). Maternal inheritance of alcohol abuse. *Archives of General Psychiatry, 38,* 965–969.

Botvin, G. J. (2000). Preventing drug abuse in schools: Social and competence enhancement approaches targeting individual-level etiological factors. *Addictive Behaviors, 25*(6), 887–897.

Bowen, S., Witkiewitz, K., Dillworth, T. M., Chawla, N., Simpson, T. L., Ostafin, B. D., et al. (2006). Mindfulness meditation and substance use in an incarcerated population. *Psychology of Addictive Behaviors, 20*(3), 343–347.

Brecher, E. M. (1972). *Licit and illicit drugs.* Mt. Vernon, NY: Consumers Union.

Bry, B. H. (1983). Substance abuse in women: Etiology and prevention. *Issues in Mental Health Nursing, 5,* 253–272.

Buckley, P. F. (1998). Substance abuse in schizophrenia: A review. *Journal of Clinical Psychiatry, 59*(3), 26–30.

Cadoret, R. J., Troughton, E., O'Gorman, T. W., & Heywood, E. (1986). An adoption study of genetic and environmental factors in drug abuse. *Archives of General Psychiatry, 43*(12), 1131–1136.

Cadoret, R. J., Yates, W. R., Troughton, E., Woodworth, G., & Steward, M. A. (1996). An adoption study of drug abuse/dependency in females. *Comprehensive Psychiatry, 37*(2), 88–94.

Carlson, R. G. (2006). Ethnography and applied substance misuse research: Anthropological and cross-cultural factors. In W. R. Miller & K. M. Carroll (Eds.), *Rethinking substance abuse: What the science shows, and what we should do about it* (pp. 201–222). New York: The Guilford Press.

Carroll, K. M., & Miller, W. R. (2006). Defining and addressing the problem. In W. R. Miller & K. M. Carroll (Eds.), *Rethinking substance abuse: What the science shows, and what we should do about it* (pp. 3–7). New York: The Guilford Press.

Castro, F. G., & Nieri, T. (2010). Cultural factors in drug use etiology: Concepts, methods, and recent findings. In L. Scheier (Ed.), *Handbook of drug use etiology: Theory, methods, and empirical findings* (pp. 305–324). Washington, DC: American Psychological Association.

Childress, A. R. (2006). What can human brain imaging tell us about vulnerability to addiction and to relapse? In W. R. Miller & K. M. Carroll (Eds.), *Rethinking substance abuse: What the science shows, and what we should do about it* (pp. 46–60). New York: The Guilford Press.

Chipkin, R. E. (1994). D2 receptor genes: The cause or consequence of substance abuse? *Trends in Neuroscience, 17*(2), 50.

Clodfelter, R. C., & McDowell, D. M. (2001). Bipolar disorder and substance abuse: Considerations of etiology, comorbidity, evaluation, and treatment. *Psychiatric Annals, 31*(5), 194–199.

Cloninger, C. R., Bohman, M., & Sigvardsson, S. (1981). Inheritance of alcohol abuse. *Archives of General Psychiatry, 38*, 861–868.

Colder, C. R., Chassin, L., Lee, M. R., & Villalta, I. K. (2010). Developmental perspectives: Affect and adolescent substance use. In J. D. Kassel (Ed.), *Substance abuse and emotion* (pp. 109–135). Washington, DC: American Psychological Association.

Coleman, E. (1982). Family intimacy and chemical abuse: The connection. *Journal of Psychedelic Drugs, 14*(1–2), 153–158.

Collins, R. L., Blane, H. T., & Leonard, K. E. (1999). Psychological theories of etiology. In P. J. Ott, R. E. Tarter, & R. T. Ammerman (Eds.), *Sourcebook on substance abuse: Etiology, epidemiology, assessment, and treatment* (pp. 153–165). Boston: Allyn & Bacon.

Compton, W. M. (2005). Applying a public health approach to drug abuse research. *Journal of Drug Issues, 35*(3), 461–467.

Compton, W. M., Thomas, Y. F., Conway, K. P., & Colliver, J. D. (2005). Developments in the epidemiology of drug use and drug use disorders. *American Journal of Psychiatry, 162*, 1494–1502.

Compton, W. M., Thomas, Y. F., Stinson, F. S., & Grant, B. F. (2007). Prevalence, correlates, disability, and comorbidity of DSM-IV drug abuse and dependence in the United States. *Archives of General Psychiatry, 64*, 566–578.

Cooper, M. L. (1994). Motivations for alcohol use among adolescents: Development and validation of a four-factor model. *Psychological Assessment, 6*, 117–128.

Cooper, M. L., Russell, M., & George, W. H. (1988). Coping, expectancies, and alcohol abuse: A test of social learning formulations. *Journal of Abnormal Psychology, 97*(2), 218–230.

Cornelius, M., Leech, S., Goldschmidt, L., & Day, N. (2000). Prenatal tobacco exposure: Is it a risk factor for early tobacco experimentation? *Nicotine Tobacco Research, 2*, 45–52.

Dalley, J. W., Fryer, T. D., Aigbirhio, F. I., Brichard, L., Richards, H. K., Hong, Y. T., . . . Robbins, T. W. (2009). Modeling human drug abuse and addiction with dedicated small animal positron emission tomography. *Neuropharmacology, 56*(1), 9–17.

Dawe, S., Loxton, N. J., Gullow, M. J., Staiger, P. K., Kambouropoulos, N., Perdon, L., & Wood, A. (2007). The role of impulsive personality traits in the initiation, development, and treatment of substance misuse problems. In P. M. Miller & K. Kavanagh (Eds.), *Translation of addictions science into practice* (pp. 321–339). New York, NY: Elsevier Science.

de Wit, H., & Phan, L. (2010). Positive reinforcement theories of drug use. In J. D. Kassel (Ed.), *Substance abuse and emotion* (pp. 43–60). Washington, DC: American Psychological Association.

Dick, D. M., Agrawal, A., Schuckit, M. A., Bierut, L., Hinrichs, A., Fox, L., . . . Begleiter, H. (2006). Marital status, alcohol dependence, and GABRA2: evidence for gene-correlation and interaction. *Journal of Studies on Alcohol, 67*(2), 185–194.

DiClemente, C. C. (2003). *Addiction and change: How addictions develop and addicted people recover.* New York: The Guilford Press.

DiClemente, C. C. (2006). Natural change and the troublesome use of substances: A life-course perspective. In W. R. Miller & K. M. Carroll (Eds.), *Rethinking substance abuse: What the science shows, and what we should do about it* (pp. 81–96). New York: The Guilford Press.

Donovan, D. M., & Marlatt, G. A. (Eds.). (1988). *Assessment of addictive behaviors.* New York: Guilford Press.

DSM-5 Substance Use Disorders Workgroup. (n.d.). Proposed revision. Retrieved from http://www.dsm5.org/ProposedRevision/Pages/proposedrevision.aspx?rid=452#

du Plessis, G. P. (2010). The integrated recovery model for addiction treatment and recovery. *Journal of Integral Theory and Practice, 5*(3), 68–85.

Felson, R., Savolainen, J., Aaltonen, M., & Moustgaard, H. (2008). Is the association between alcohol use and delinquency causal or spurious? *Criminology: An Interdisciplinary Journal, 46*(3), 785–808.

Field, M. (2006). Attentional biases in drug abuse and addiction: Cognitive mechanisms, causes, consequences and implications. In M. Munafo & I. P. Alperly (Eds.), *Cognition and addiction* (pp. 73–99). New York: Oxford University Press.

Fischer, V. J. (1991). Combat exposure and the etiology of postdischarge substance abuse problems among Vietnam veterans. *Journal of Traumatic Stress, 4*(2), 251–277.

Friesen, V. I. (1983). The family in the etiology and treatment of drug abuse: Toward a balanced perspective. *Advances in Alcohol and Substance Abuse, 2*(4), 77–89.

Gibbons, G. X., Pomery, E. A., & Gerrard, M. (2010). Racial discrimination and substance abuse: Risk and protective factors in African American adolescents. In L. Scheier (Ed.), *Handbook of drug use etiology: Theory, methods, and empirical findings* (pp. 341–362). Washington, DC: American Psychological Association.

Giese, J. K. (1999). The role of personal meaning and multiple risk factors in adolescent alcohol abuse. *Dissertation Abstracts International: Section B: The Sciences and Engineering, 59*(11-B), 6064.

Glantz, M. D., Conway, K. P., & Colliver, J. D. (2005). Drug abuse heterogeneity and the search for subtypes. In Z. Sloboda (Ed.), *Epidemiology of drug abuse* (pp. 15–27). New York, NY: Springer.

Glantz, M. D., & Pickens, R. (Eds.). (1992). *Vulnerability to drug use.* Washington, DC: American Psychological Association.

Glantz, M. D., Weinberg, N. Z., Miner, L. L., & Colliver, J. D. (1999). The etiology of drug abuse: Mapping the paths. In M. D. Glantz & C. R. Hartel (Eds.), *Drug abuse: Origins and interventions* (pp. 3–45). Washington, DC: American Psychological Association.

Goldstein, R. Z., & Volkow, N. D. (2002). Drug addiction and its underlying neurological basis: Neuroimaging evidence for the involvement of the frontal cortex. *American Journal of Psychiatry, 159*(10), 1642–1652.

Grande, T. P., Wolf, A. W., Schubert, D. S. P., Patterson, M. B., & Brocco, K. (1984). Associations among alcoholism, drug abuse, and antisocial personality: A review of literature. *Psychological Reports, 55*(2), 455–474.

Grant, B. F., & Dawson, D. A. (1997). Age at onset of alcohol use and its association with DSM-IV alcohol abuse and dependence: Results from the national longitudinal alcohol epidemiologic survey. *Journal of Substance Abuse, 9*, 103–110.

Guajardo, H. S., Bagladi, V. L., & Kushner, D. L. (2004). Integrative psychotherapy in addictive disorders. *Journal of Psychotherapy Integration, 14*(3), 290–306.

Gullickson, T., & Ramser, P. (1996). Review of Hispanic substance abuse. *Contemporary Psychology: APA Review of Books, 41*(1), 83–84.

Hasin, D., Hatzenbuehler, M., & Waxman, R. (2006). Genetics of substance use disorders. In W. R. Miller & K. M. Carroll (Eds.), *Rethinking substance abuse: What the science shows, and what we should do about it* (pp. 61–80). New York: The Guilford Press.

Hasin, D., Stinson, F. S., Ogburn, E., & Grant, B. F. (2007). Prevalence, correlates, disability, and comorbidity of DSM-IV alcohol abuse and dependence in the United States: Results from the National Epidemiologic Survey on Alcohol Related Conditions. *Archives of General Psychiatry, 64*(7), 830–842.

Hawkins, J. D., Graham, J. W., Maguin, E., Abbott, R., Hill, K. G., & Catalano, R. F. (1997). Exploring the effects of age alcohol use initiation and psychosocial risk factors on subsequent alcohol misuse. *Journal of Studies on Alcohol, 58*(3), 280–290.

Hawkins, J. D., Lishner, D. M., Catalano, R. F., & Howard, M. O. (1985). Childhood predictors of adolescent substance abuse: Toward an empirically grounded theory. *Journal of Children in Contemporary Society, 18*(1–2), 11–48.

Helig, M., Koob, G. F., Ekman, R., & Britton, K. T. (1994). Corticotropin-releasing factor and neuropeptide Y: Role in emotional integration. *Trends in Neurosciences, 17*, 427–440.

Helmer, J. (1975). *Drugs and minority oppression.* New York: Seabury Press.

Hesselbrock, V. M., & Hesselbrock, M. N. (2006). Developmental perspectives on the risk for developing substance abuse problems. In W. R. Miller & K. M. Carroll (Eds.), *Rethinking substance abuse: What the science shows, and what we should do about it* (pp. 97–114). New York: The Guilford Press.

Holder, H. D. (2006). Racial and gender differences in substance abuse: What should communities do about them? In W. R. Miller & K. M. Carroll (Eds.), *Rethinking substance abuse: What the science shows, and what we should do about it* (pp. 153–165). New York: The Guilford Press.

Hufford, M. R. (2001). An examination of mood effects on positive alcohol expectancies among undergraduate drinkers. *Cognition and Emotion, 15*, 593–613.

Humphreys, K., & Gifford, E. (2006). Religion, spirituality, and the troublesome use of substances. In W. R. Miller & K. M. Carroll (Eds.), *Rethinking substance abuse: What the science shows, and what we should do about it* (pp. 257–274). New York: The Guilford Press.

Jacob, T., Sher, K. J., Bucholz, K. K., True, W. T., Sirevaag, E. J., Rohrbaugh, J., . . . Heath, A. C. (2001). An integrative approach for studying the etiology of alcoholism and other addictions. *Twin Research and Human Genetics, 4*(2), 103–118.

Jochman, K. A., & Fromme, K. (2010). Maturing out of substance use: The other side of etiology. In L. Scheier (Ed.) *Handbook of drug use etiology: Theory, methods, and empirical findings* (pp. 565–578). Washington, DC: American Psychological Association.

Johnson, A. O. (2009). The geographic availability of substance abuse treatment facilities and services to rural veterans of the Unites States armed forces. *Dissertation Abstracts International: Section B: The Sciences and Engineering, 69*(7–B), 4121.

Johnson, E. M., & Belfer, M. L. (1995). Substance abuse and violence: Cause and consequence. *Journal of Health Care for the Poor and Underserved, 6*(2), 113–121.

Jongsma, A. E., Peterson, L. M., & Bruce, T. J. (Eds.). (2006). *The complete adult psychotherapy treatment planner.* Hoboken, NJ: Wiley.

Juliano, L. M., & Brandon, T. H. (1998). Reactivity to instructed smoking availability and environmental cues: Evidence with urge and reaction time. *Experimental and Clinical Psychopharmacology, 6*, 45–53.

Kassel, J. D., & Evatt, D. P. (2010). Afterword: New frontiers in substance abuse and emotion. In J. D. Kassel (Ed.), *Substance abuse and emotion* (pp. 281–286). Washington, DC: American Psychological Association.

Kassel, J. D., Hussong, A. M., Wardle, M. C., Veilleux, J. C., Heinz, A., Greenstein, J. E., & Evatt, D. P. (2010). Affective influences in drug use etiology. In L. Scheier (Ed.), *Handbook of drug use etiology: Theory, methods, and empirical findings* (pp. 183–205). Washington, DC: American Psychological Association.

Kassel, J. D., & Veilleux, J. C. (2010). Introduction: The complex interplay between substance abuse and emotion. In J. D. Kassel (Ed.), *Substance abuse and emotion* (pp. 281–286). Washington, DC: American Psychological Association.

Katz, J. L. (1990). Eating disorders: A primer for the substance abuse specialist: II. Theories of etiology, treatment approaches, and considerations during co-morbidity with substance abuse. *Journal of Substance Abuse Treatment, 7*(4), 211–217.

Kellert, S., & Wilson, E. O. (1993). *The biophilia hypothesis.* Washington, DC: Island Press.

Kennedy, G. K. (2000). *Geriatric mental health care: A treatment guide for professionals.* New York: Guilford.

Khan, S., Murray, R. P., & Barnes, G. E. (2002). A structural equation model of the effect of poverty and unemployment on alcohol abuse. *Addictive Behaviors, 27*(3), 405–423.

Khantzian, E. J. (1987). A clinical perspective of the cause-consequence controversy in alcoholic and addictive suffering. *Journal of the American Academy of Psychoanalysis, 15*(4), 521–537.

Kliewer, W. (2010). Family processes in drug use etiology. In L. Scheier (Ed.), *Handbook of drug use etiology: Theory, methods, and empirical findings* (pp. 365–381). Washington, DC: American Psychological Association.

Koob, G. F. (2006). The neurobiology of addiction: A hedonic Calvanist view. In W. R. Miller & K. M. Carroll (Eds.), *Rethinking substance abuse: What the science shows, and what we should do about it* (pp. 25–45). New York: The Guilford Press.

Kuppin, S., & Carpiano, R. M. (2008). Public conceptions of serious mental illness and substance abuse, their causes, and treatments. Findings from the 1996 General Social Survey. *American Journal of Public Health, 98*(1), S120–S125.

Laughlin, C., McManus, J., & Shearer, J. (1993). Transpersonal anthropology. In R. Walsh & F. Vaughan (Eds.), *Paths beyond ego: The transpersonal vision* (pp. 190–194). Los Angeles, CA: Jeremy P. Tarcher.

Leukefeld, C. G., McDonald, H. M. S., Stroops, W. W., Reed, L., & Martin, C. (2005). Substance misuse and abuse. In T. P. Gullotta & G. R. Adams (Eds.), *Handbook of adolescent behavioral problems: Evidence-based approaches to prevention and treatment* (pp. 439–465). New York: Springer.

Lev-Wiesel, R., & Shuval, R. (2006). Perceived causal and treatment factors related to substance abuse. *European Addiction Research, 12*(2), 109–112.

Linehan, M. (1993). Cognitive-behavioral treatment of Borderline Personality Disorder. New York: Guilford.

Lo, C. C., & Cheng, T. C. (2007). The impact of childhood maltreatment on young adults' substance abuse. *The American Journal of Drug and Alcohol Abuse, 33*(1), 139–146.

Lynskey, M. T., & Hall, W. (2001). Attention deficit hyperactivity disorder and substance use disorders: Is there a causal link? *British Journal of Addiction, 96*(6), 815–822.

Mahoney, M. J. (1980). *Abnormal psychology: Perspectives on human variance.* San Francisco, CA: Harper & Row.

Marsiglia, F. F., & Smith, S. J. (2010). An exploration of ethnicity and race in the etiology of substance abuse: A health disparities approach. In L. Scheier (Ed.), *Handbook of drug use etiology: Theory, methods, and empirical findings* (pp. 289–304). Washington, DC: American Psychological Association.

McCarthy, D. E., Curtin, J. J., Piper, M. E., & Baker, T. B. (2010). Negative reinforcement: Possible clinical implications of an integrative model. In J. D. Kassel (Ed.), *Substance abuse and emotion* (pp. 25–42). Washington, DC: American Psychological Association.

McCrady, B. S. (2006). Family and other close relationships. In W. R. Miller & K. M. Carroll (Eds.), *Rethinking substance abuse: What the science shows, and what we should do about it* (pp. 166–181). New York: The Guilford Press.

McDowell, D. M., & Clodfelter, R. C. (2001). Depression and substance abuse: Considerations of etiology, comorbidity, evaluation, and treatment. *Psychiatric Annals, 32*(4), 244–251.

McKee, S. A., Wall, A. M., Hinson, R. E., Goldstein, A., & Bissonnette, M. (2003). Effects of an implicit mood prime on the accessibility of smoking expectancies in college women. *Psychology of Addictive Behaviors, 17*, 219–225.

McKirnan, D. J. (1984). The identification of alcohol problems: Socioeconomic status differences in social norms and causal attributions. *American Journal of Community Psychology, 12*(4), 465–484.

McPeake, J. D., Kennedy, B. P., & Gordon, S. M. (1991). Altered states of consciousness therapy: A missing component in alcohol and drug rehabilitation treatment. *Journal of Substance Abuse Treatment, 8*, 75–82.

Mello, N. (1983). Etiological theories of alcoholism. *Advances in Substance Abuse, 3*, 271–312.

Miller, W. R. (2006). Motivational factors in addictive behaviors. In W. R. Miller & K. M. Carroll (Eds.), *Rethinking substance abuse: What the science shows, and what we should do about it* (pp. 134–152). New York: The Guilford Press.

Miller, W. R., & Carroll, K. M. (2006). Drawing the scene together: Ten principles, ten recommendations. In W. R. Miller & K. M. Carroll (Eds.), *Rethinking substance abuse: What the science shows, and what we should do about it* (pp. 293–312). New York: The Guilford Press.

Miller, W. R., & Rollnick, S. (2002). *Motivational interviewing: Preparing people to change.* New York: Guilford Press.

Moos, R. H. (2006). Social contexts and substance use. In W. R. Miller & K. M. Carroll (Eds.), *Rethinking substance abuse: What the science shows, and what we should do about it* (pp. 182–200). New York: The Guilford Press.

Morrison, J. R. (2008). *The first interview* (3rd ed.). New York: The Guilford Press.

Moyers, B. (1998). The politics of addiction [from the PBS series: Close to Home /DVD].

Mueser, K. T., Drake, R. E., Turner, W., & McGovern, M. (2006). Comorbid substance use disorders and psychiatric disorders. In W. R. Miller & K. M. Carroll (Eds.), *Rethinking substance abuse: What the science shows, and what we should do about it* (pp. 115–133). New York: The Guilford Press.

Norcross, J. C. (2010, May). Psychotherapy relationships that work II: Evidence-based practice and practice-based evidence. Presented at the Society for the Exploration of Psychotherapy Integration, Florence, Italy.

O'Brien, C. P. (2007). Brain development as a vulnerability factor in the etiology of substance abuse and addiction. In D. Romer & E. F. Walker (Eds.), *Adolescent psychopathology and the developing brain: Integrating brain and prevention science* (pp. 388–398). New York: Oxford University Press.

O'Malley, S. S., & Kosten, T. R. (2006). Pharmacotherapy of addictive disorders. In W. R. Miller & K. M. Carroll (Eds.), *Rethinking substance abuse: What the science shows, and what we should do about it* (pp. 240–256). New York: The Guilford Press.

Ouimette, P., & Brown, P. J. (Eds.) (2002). *Trauma and substance abuse: Causes, consequences, and treatment of comorbid disorders.* Washington, DC: American Psychological Association.

Panskepp, J., Nocjar, C., Burgdorf, J., Panskepp, J. B., & Huber, R. (2004). The role of emotional systems in addiction: A neurobiological perspective. In R. A. Bevins & M. T. Bardo (Eds.), *Nebraska Symposium on Motivation: Vol. 50. Motivational factors in the etiology of drug abuse* (pp. 85–126). Lincoln, NE: University of Nebraska Press.

PDM Task Force. (2006). *Psychodynamic diagnostic manual.* Silver Spring, MD: Alliance of Psychoanalytic Organizations.

Peyrot, M. (1984). Cycles of social problem development: The case of drug abuse. *The Sociological Quarterly, 25*, 83–96.

Pickins, R. W., & Svikis, D. S. (1991). Prevention of drug abuse: Targeting risk factors. In L. Donohew, H. E. Sypher, & W. J. Bukoski (Eds.), *Persuasive communication and drug abuse prevention* (pp. 35–49). Hillsdale, NJ: Lawrence Erlbaum Associates, Inc.

Pihl, R. O. (1999). Substance abuse: Etiological considerations. In T. Millon, P. H. Blaney, & R. D. Davis (Eds.), *Oxford textbook of psychopathology* (pp. 249–276). New York, NY: Oxford University Press.

Prescott, C. A., Piper, M. E., McCarthy, D. E., Majeskie, M. R., & Fiore, M. C. (2006). Challenges in genetic studies of the etiology of substance use and substance use disorders: Introduction to the special issue. *Behavior Genetics, 36*(4), 473–482.

Roberts, A. (2000). Psychiatric comorbidity in White and African-American illicit substance abusers: Evidence for differential etiology. *Clinical Psychology Review, 20*(5), 667–677.

Ryan, M. R., Lynch, M. F., Vansteenkiste, M., & Deci, E. L. (2010). Motivation and autonomy in counseling, psychotherapy, and behavior change: A look at theory and practice. *The Counseling Psychologist, 39*(2), 193–260.

Samuels, D. J., & Samuels, M. (1974). Low self-concept as a cause of drug abuse. *Journal of Drug Education, 4*(4), 421–438.

Sanford, M. (2001). The relationship between antisocial behaviour and substance abuse in childhood and adolescence: Implications for aetiology, prevention and treatment. *Current Opinion in Psychiatry, 14*(4), 317–323.

Schaef, A. W. (1987). *When society becomes an addict.* San Francisco: Harper and Row.

Scheier, L. (Ed.). (2010a). *Handbook of drug use etiology: Theory, methods, and empirical findings.* Washington, DC: American Psychological Association.

Scheier, L. (2010b). Social cognitive models of drug use etiology. In L. Scheier (Ed.), *Handbook of drug use etiology: Theory, methods, and empirical findings* (pp. 93–112). Washington, DC: American Psychological Association.

Shiffman, S. (1984). Cognitive antecedents and sequelae of smoking relapse crises. *Journal of Applied Social Psychology, 14*, 296–309.

Simansky, J. A. (2008). Rural adolescent perceptions of the availability and accessibility of substance abuse treatment. *Dissertation Abstracts International: Section B: The Sciences Vol. 68*(12-B), p. 8412.

Spooner, C., & Hall, W. (2002). Preventing drug misuse by young people: Why we need to do more than "just say no." *Addiction, 97*(5), 478–481.

Stapleton, M. T. (2004). Attachment theory and psychological merging: Understanding the etiology and treatment of substance abuse. *Dissertation Abstracts International: Section B: The Sciences and Engineering, 65*(1), 453.

Steinman, M. A., Landefeld, C. S., Rosenthal, G. E., Berthenthal, D., Sen, S., & Kaboli, P. J. (2006). Polypharmacy and prescribing quality in older people. *Journal of the American Geriatric Society, 54*, 1516–1523.

Sussman, S., Skara, S., & Ames, S. L. (2008). Substance use among adolescents. *International Journal of the Addictions, 43*(12–13), 1802–1828.

Swift, R., & Mueller, T. (2001). Comorbidity of anxiety disorders in substance abuse. In J. R. Hubbard & P. R. Martin (Eds.), *Substance abuse in the mentally and physically disabled* (pp. 11–32). New York: Marcel Dekker.

Tarter, R. E. (2002). Etiology of adolescent substance abuse: A developmental perspective. *The American Journal on Addictions, 11*(3), 171–191.

Tarter, R. E., Kabene, M., Escaller, E. A., Laird, S. B., & Jacob, T. (1990). Temperament deviation and risk for alcoholism. *Alcoholism: Clinical and Experimental Research, 14*, 380–392.

Tarter, R. E., & Vanyukov, M. (2001). Introduction: Theoretical and operational framework for research into the etiology of substance use disorders. *Journal of Adolescent Chemical Dependency, 10*(4), 1–12.

Tarter, R. E., Vanyukov, M., & Kirisci, L. (2008). Etiology of substance use disorder: Developmental perspective. In Y. Kaminer & O. G. Bukstein (Eds.), *Adolescent substance abuse: Psychiatric comorbidity and high-risk behaviors* (pp. 5–27). New York: Routledge.

Thomas, Y. F. (2007). The social epidemiology of drug abuse. *American Journal of Preventive Medicine, 32*(6S), S141–S146.

Thomas, Y. F., & Conway, K. (2010). The epidemiology of drug abuse: How the National Institute on Drug Abuse stimulates research. In L. Scheier (Ed.), *Handbook of drug use etiology: Theory, methods, and empirical findings* (pp. 19–28). Washington, DC: American Psychological Association.

Trevisan, L. A. (2008). Baby boomers and substance abuse. *Psychiatric Times, 25*(8), 28–36.

Trudeau, D. L. (2005). EEG biofeedback for addictive disorders—the state of the art in 2004. *Journal of Adult Development, 12*(2–3), 139–146.

Volkow, N. D., Fowler, J. S., Wang, G., Swanson, J. M., & Telang, F. (2007). Dopamine in drug abuse and addiction: Results of imaging studies and treatment implications. *Archives of Neurology, 64*(11), 1575–1579.

Walsh, R., & Vaughan, F. (Eds.) (1993). *Paths beyond ego: The transpersonal vision.* Los Angeles, CA: Jeremy P. Tarcher.

Wang, G. J., Volkow, N. D., Logan, J., Pappas, N. R., Wong, C. T., Zhu, W., et al. (2001). Brain dopamine and obesity. *The Lancet, 357*, 354–357.

Weill, A. T. (2004). *The natural mind: A revolutionary approach to the drug problem.* New York: Houghton Mifflin Company.

Weinberg, N. Z., Rahdert, E., Colliver, J. D., & Glantz, M. D. (1998). Adolescent substance abuse: A review of the last 10 years. *Journal of the American Academy of Child Psychiatry, 37*(3), 252–261.

Wikipedia (n.d.). Medical cannabis. Retrieved from http://en.wikipedia.org/wiki/Medical_cannabis#Safety_of_cannabis

Williams, C. (2008). Cultural pain and anger as causal factors to substance abuse in an African-American male clinical population. An exploration with implications for treatment. *Dissertation Abstracts International: Section B: The Sciences and Engineering, 69*(6), 3863.

Williams, C., & Latkin, C. A. (2007). Neighborhood socioeconomic status, personal network attitudes, and the use of heroin and cocaine. *American Journal of Preventive Medicine, 32*(6S), S203–S210.

Wills, T. A., & Filer, M. (1996). Stress-coping model of adolescent substance abuse. In T. H. Ollendick & R. J. Pinz (Eds.), *Advances in clinical child psychology* (Vol. 18, pp. 91–132). New York: Plenum Press.

Wilshire, B. (1999). *Wild hunger: The primal roots of modern addiction.* Lanham, MD: Rowan & Littlefield Publishers, Inc.

Wilson, G. T., & Abrams, D. (1976). Effects of alcohol on social anxiety: Cognitive versus pharmacological processes. *Cognitive Therapy and Research, 1*, 195–210.

# 9

# Attention Deficit–Hyperactivity Disorder

**Kathryn Z. Douthit, Ph.D.,** ***University of Rochester***
**Tami K. Sullivan, Ph.D.,** ***State University of New York at Oswego***

*"Is a medical model of ADHD therapeutically helpful? Quite the opposite; it offers a decontextualised and simplistic idea that leads to all of us—parents, teachers and doctors—disengaging from our social responsibility to raise well-behaved children. We thus become a symptom of the cultural disease we purport to cure. It supports the profit motive of the pharmaceutical industry, which has been accused of helping to create and propagate the notion of ADHD in order to expand its own markets. By acting as agents of social control and stifling diversity in children, we are victimizing millions of children and their families by putting children on highly addictive drugs that have no proven long-term benefit . . . and have been shown in animal studies to have brain-disabling effects. . . ."*

TIMIMI & TAYLOR, 2004, P. 8

## INTRODUCTION

Many of the psychological challenges that have earned a place in the *Diagnostic and Statistical Manual of Mental Disorders* (DSM) seem, in the public eye, to merely depict common everyday struggles in adjusting to life's demands. The blurry lines between, for example, Major Depressive Disorder and deep sadness or grief, Oppositional Defiant Disorder and lack of discipline in children, Social Anxiety Disorder and shyness, or mania and the frenetic, multitasking skills required to survive in a 21st-century world, represent a divergence of public sensibility and psychiatry's powerful push toward the medicalization of atypical behavioral patterns and normative psychological distress.

Few DSM diagnoses have received as much public criticism as that of Attention Deficit–Hyperactivity Disorder (ADHD). The behaviors associated with ADHD have been christened with diverse etiological attributions ranging from absentee fathers, failure to discipline, and distant mothers to video game excesses, food dyes and additives, and schools out of sync with the needs of children. It is precisely this wide range of attributions, all of which comport a persuasive partial truth but lack the comprehensiveness typically sought in explanation, that make ADHD a compelling focus for an Integral analysis.

This chapter begins with a description of the rich and enduring history of ADHD building to the present day, 5th edition of the DSM (DSM-5) (American Psychiatric Association [APA], 2013) conceptualization of this disorder. We then enter a four-quadrant discussion of the etiology of ADHD that includes, when applicable, the Integral model's concepts of lines, levels, and states. Any discussion of ADHD would be woefully incomplete without a consideration of the disorder's extensive comorbidity patterns. These patterns are a major determinant in predicting life-course outcomes for individuals diagnosed with ADHD, and they will therefore be presented here in some detail. Finally, we will consider the most widely used ADHD-related assessment tools, and the range of ADHD interventions currently being utilized in clinical settings. A case example will be used to illustrate how an Integral model can be applied to construct a multidimensional picture of the disorder.

## THE HISTORY OF ADHD

### Early Brain-Damage Models

The terms *ADHD* and *Attention Deficit Disorder* (ADD) were not part of the psychiatric lexicon until the release of the third edition of the DSM, DSM-III, in 1980. Prior to this time the behaviors that we associate with ADHD (i.e., hyperactivity, impulsivity, and inattention) were framed in accordance with the bio-historical and philosophical moments of the day. The first historical moment in the rise of ADHD actually occurred in 1798 when Scottish-born physician Sir Alexander Crichton introduced the term *mental restlessness* in the "attention" chapter of his book: *An Inquiry into the Nature and Origin of Mental Derangement: Comprehending a Concise System of the Physiology and Pathology of the Human Mind and a History of the Passions and Their Effects* (cited in Palmer & Finger, 2001). His description characterized those with mental restlessness as having a psychomotor agitation that prevented afflicted individuals from attending to important tasks requiring concentration and endurance.

The next historical moment came when physician George Still (1902) introduced 20 of the children in his clinical practice, exhibiting the hallmarks of current-day ADHD-like behavior, to the Royal College of Physicians (Barkley, 2006b). The children in Still's group were characterized as being impulsive, recalcitrant, difficult to discipline, highly emotional, and unable to sustain attention. Still believed that the children in his charge where plagued by a neurologically predicated inability to sustain moral control, and he characterized the disorder as typically chronic. He predicted, based on his observation and conjecture, that the more chronic cases would be prone to criminality later in life.

It was also Still's observation that his patients' behaviors differed significantly from that of their same-age peers (Barkley, 2006b). This observation introduced the practice of diagnosing childhood ADHD using the young patient's deviation from age-appropriate behaviors and thus marks a century-old practice of considering cognitive and emotional lines and levels of development, a practice that remains central to the identification of ADHD children in contemporary psychiatry.

Although Still reports observing ADHD-like behavior in children raised in both troubled and functional homes, it was his contention that if children subjected to a poor home life were excluded from his population of ADHD-like patients, a pure form of the disorder would emerge, capturing individuals who most likely had inherited their behavioral patterns or were impacted by a pre- or postnatal injury (Barkley, 2006b). It was also Still's contention that any form of neural modification that could cause retardation in an earlier, milder, undetected form could cause the disturbing behaviors typical of these children with ADHD-like symptoms (Barkley, 2006b).

The notion that mild, early, permanent brain damage is responsible for the ADHD-like behavior in children remained popular through the late 1950s and into the early 1960s. Toward the middle of the 20th century, the mild damage paradigm would be supported by a series of naturalistic observations in which physical injury or the neurotropic sequelae of infectious diseases caused the impairments that are typical of children with ADHD-like symptoms, that is, problems with attention, hyperactivity, and impulsivity (Barkley, 2006a). These naturalistic models included one population of children who had survived encephalitis infection, another group suffering from measles sequelae, and others injured by lead toxicity or trauma. The mounting evidence in psychiatric and medical circles demonstrating that damage to the central nervous system often results in impulsive, recalcitrant, and hyperkinetic behavior ultimately led professionals to coin the term *minimal brain damage*, or MBD—a term that was euphemistically changed by the 1950s and 1960s to *minimum brain dysfunction* (Barkley, 2006a).

A certain degree of hopelessness developed around MBD-diagnosed children in that the prevailing clinical wisdom assumed that this condition was impervious to medical intervention. Then, between 1937 and 1941, a series of papers was published claiming that children diagnosed with MBD and treated with amphetamines showed less of a tendency toward disruptive behavior and demonstrated improved academic performance (Bradley, 1937; Bradley & Bowen, 1941). For many contemporary scholars of ADHD, this discovery marked the dawn of a revolution in ADHD treatment, whereas for others it marked the beginning of an often disconcerting marriage between medicine and commercial interest (Conrad, 1976; Kohn, 1989; McGuinness, 1989).

## A Psychoanalytic Model

The turbulent, antiauthoritarian political climate of 1960s extended its reach into the world of psychiatry. An increasingly popular antipsychiatry movement was spawned that disparaged the biological determinism reflected in the medically based MBD model (Laing, 1967; Szasz, 1970) and favored a more interpretive, psychodynamic understanding of psychological affliction. In Integral terms, the prevailing thought began to shift away from a primarily exterior-individual orientation to one that favored interior-individual and interior-collective explications and interventions.

Russell Barkley, who is arguably among the most influential ADHD scholars of the late 20th century, derided this period of psychoanalytic ascendency as a regression in the understanding and treatment of ADHD. Barkley used terms like "excessive," "convoluted," and "pedantic" to describe the emergent anti-biomedical scholarship of the time and is highly critical of the blame placed on parents and family dynamics (Barkley, 1990, p. 10).

## The Rise of the Triumvirate: Hyperkinesis, Inattention, and Impulsivity

MBD's marriage with psychoanalysis was particularly brief and was soon replaced by a descriptive model with hyperkinetic behaviors at its core (Chess, 1960). The new hyperactive child syndrome was an example of an emerging trend in psychiatry—namely, a focus on symptoms in lieu of a search for etiology. In the language of Integral theory, the "exterior-individual" perspective re-emerged to a position of prominence in our understanding of MBD. This new iteration of MBD would be dubbed "hyperkinetic reaction of childhood" and would be indelibly codified through its inclusion in the second edition of the DSM (DSM-II) (APA, 1968).

As the research on hyperkinetic children progressed through the 1970s, attention deficits and impulsivity began to take center stage in identification of MBD. Virginia Douglas (1972) proposed that attention deficits and problems in impulse control were more likely to generate the difficulties suffered by this group than mere hyperkinesis. Barkley (1990) asserted that the new theory highlighting attention deficits and impulsivity was bolstered by the work of Gabrielle Weiss. Weiss followed a cohort of children, all of whom displayed hyperactivity, inattention, and impulsivity, into adolescence and found that as these individuals aged, their hyperactive behavior subsided while much of the inattention and impulsivity remained (Weiss & Hechtman, 1986).

What was arguably among the most influential turns in this historical moment was Douglas' (1972) assertion that children who were administered stimulant medications showed extraordinary improvement in tests of sustained attention (Barkley, 1990). The improvement in attention fixation was taken as direct evidence of a neurophysiological defect in the control of attention/impulse, and was, by all appearances, the foundation for an unprecedented surge in the use of stimulant medications for treatment of disorders of attention (Zito et al., 2000).

Another historical turn, rivaling the stimulant milestone for the reach of its influence, was the publication of the third edition of the DSM-III in 1980. The DSM-III (APA, 1980), a radical transformation from the DSM-II, took the final step toward purging psychoanalytic theory from the annals of psychiatric thought in favor of a descriptive, biomedical nosology (Douthit & Marquis, 2006). What emerged was a classification that included circumscribed boundaries for hundreds of discrete mental disorders, among them, attention deficit disorder (ADD). The ADD entry in the DSM-III introduced a new lens for understanding the disorder, which divided it into two types—namely, ADD with hyperactivity (ADD+H) and ADD without hyperactivity (ADD−H) (APA, 1980). Despite limited empirical evidence supporting this decision, the creation of the new categories was a springboard for research agendas comparing the two groups in terms of response to drug therapy, aggression, and social adaptability (Barkley, 1990). Although there were many conflicting results arising from this research, Carlson (1986) and later Lahey and Carlson (1991) were able to show that the ADD−H children were more likely to be lethargic and underachieving when compared to ADD+H children but less likely to display aggression and difficulty with peer relationships. Although the Carlson and Lahey findings were compelling, they did not emerge in time to be considered in a revised edition of the DSM-III (DSM-IIIR) (APA, 1987; Barkley, 1990). The result was the elimination of ADD−H, and a new name, ADHD.

## Current ADHD Classification

With the APA's publication of the fourth edition of DSM (DSM-IV) in 1994, the text revision edition of the DSM-IV (DSM-IV-TR) in 2000, and the publication of the fifth edition of DSM (DSM-5) in 2013, ADHD emerged in a form that reflects current-day classification of the disorder. This disorder category builds on a set of basic assumptions that the symptoms being observed: (1) are developmentally atypical in relation to age, (2) have emerged before the age of 12, (3) are observable across multiple settings, and (4) interfere with one's ability to successfully negotiate the rules and expected behaviors related to work, relationships, play, and school. In its current iteration (APA, 2013), ADHD can manifest as one of three subtypes, with each subtype reflecting contrasting symptom clusters. These subtypes, which match the subtype profile in the DSM-IV-TR, include Attention Deficit–Hyperactivity Disorder Predominantly Inattentive Type, Attention Deficit–Hyperactivity Disorder Predominantly Hyperactive-Impulsive Type, and Attention Deficit–Hyperactivity Disorder Combined Type. The first of these subtypes, Attention Deficit–Hyperactivity Disorder Predominantly Inattentive Type, manifests primarily as a problem of inattention, whereas the Predominantly Hyperactive-Impulsive Type is marked by symptoms recognized as hyperactive and impulsive, and the individual with Combined Type has a threshold of symptoms for both hyperactivity-impulsivity and inattention.

The symptoms for inattention describe an inability to focus attention. Individuals are given the designation of "inattentive" when they meet at least six of the nine criteria for inattention for a period of 6 months. These inattention criteria include being forgetful, loosing important items, having difficulty maintaining focus on prolonged activities, and being unable to follow directions. Likewise, the diagnosis for hyperactivity-impulsivity requires that an individual manifest a minimum of six symptoms of hyperactivity and/or impulsivity for at least 6 months. The criteria for hyperactivity generally involve some form of excessive physicality such as fidgeting, an inability to remain seated, extreme levels of running and climbing, excessive amounts of talking, and, particularly in adolescents and adults, feelings of restlessness. In contrast, the criteria for impulsivity focus on the inability of individuals to display measured behaviors that would allow them to conform to rules of social engagement. Some of these impulsive behaviors include not taking turns, interrupting, prematurely blurting out answers to questions that have not been fully articulated, using others' possessions without permission, and, particularly in the case of adults and adolescents, inappropriately attempting to take over a situation. When diagnosing ADHD, it is essential that the observable behaviors forming the basis of the diagnosis are not due to another mental disorder such as Schizophrenia, Substance Intoxication or Withdrawal, Mood Disorder, or Anxiety Disorder.

In its current form, the prevalence of ADHD is thought to be 5% in children and 2.5% in adults (APA, 2013), and epidemiological studies suggest that when similar methodology is utilized, the disorder has a uniform global distribution (Polanczyk, de Lima, Horta, Biederman, & Rohde, 2007). The disorder is difficult to diagnose in children before the age of 4 because behavior in younger children is more variable and many developmentally appropriate behaviors are consistent with features of ADHD (APA, 2013). Typically, diagnosis of ADHD occurs after a child has entered elementary school where the new, structured environment presents difficulty for hyperactive, impulsive, and inattentive children (APA, 2013). Although some individuals will experience a decline in ADHD symptoms over time, many will continue to have symptoms, particularly those related to impulsivity and inattention, which persist into adulthood (APA, 2013). The disorder outcomes vary considerably among subtypes, with the Combined Type being most trenchant and most commonly associated with aggression, serious conduct problems including criminality, and substance use involving tobacco, alcohol, and/or other drugs (Spencer, Biederman, & Mick, 2007).

Although increasing attention being given to the predominantly inattentive subtype of ADHD has bolstered the estimates of female ADHD prevalence, the DSM-5 still reports a male-to-female ratio of 2:1 in children and 1.6:1 in adults (APA, 2013). In addition, a study by Biederman et al. (2002) revealed distinct gender differences in the phenotypic expression of ADHD in a clinic-referred sample of ADHD-diagnosed children consisting of 140 boys and 140 girls. The results of this study indicated that females were more likely than males to manifest the predominantly inattentive subtype of ADHD, but were less likely to have learning disabilities in the areas of reading or mathematics and were also less likely to have problems in school or during leisure activities. Data also pointed to a statistically significant gender-by-ADHD interaction in the association between ADHD and alcohol or drug abuse and dependence. Specifically, females with ADHD were more likely than males with ADHD to manifest Substance Use Disorders when compared with age- and gender-matched controls.

## Noteworthy Changes to ADHD in the Transition from the DSM-IV-TR to the DSM-5

Although the ADHD entry in the DSM-5 (APA, 2013) retained the well-known DSM-IV-TR hallmarks of ADHD (i.e., inattention and/or hyperactivity/impulsivity), several noteworthy changes were included in the fifth edition. The most significant changes included an increase in age, from 7 to 12 years, marking the cut-off before which symptoms of ADHD must manifest, and criterion descriptions that have been modified to include more adolescent and adult manifestations of the disorder.

The change in age, from 7 to 12 years, before which symptoms of ADHD must appear in order to be considered as diagnostic, reflects a general trend in the DSM-5 to "cast a wider net," thus expanding the number of individuals captured by given diagnostic categories (Frances, 2010). In the case of ADHD, the change in designated age allows for individuals whose symptoms manifested after age 7 but before age 12 to now receive a diagnosis that was previously restricted to those manifesting symptoms before age 7.

The expanded number of age-inclusive criterion descriptions in the DSM-5 presentation of ADHD (i.e., descriptions including those seen in adolescents and adults) represents a departure from the more child-focused nature of the ADHD diagnosis in the DSM-III, IV, and IV-TR. For example, in the case of the inattentive criterion related to forgetfulness, the late adolescent/adult description includes references to paying bills on time, returning phone calls, and reliably keeping appointments (APA, 2013).

## ETIOLOGY

An Integral quadratic analysis that draws from extant literature on ADHD inevitably reflects the overwhelming bias in contemporary ADHD etiology and intervention research. Biomedicine, heavily weighted toward neuroscience, genetics, and pharmaceutical development, currently dominates the discourse related to ADHD. This bias is indeed palpable in the DSM-IV-TR and DSM-5 representation of ADHD. In spite of the DSM claim to theoretical neutrality in its portrayal of so-called "mental disorder" (APA, 2000, 2013), a deconstructive analysis of the ADHD entry in the DSM-IV-TR reveals a distinct bias toward medicalization in the cluster of symptoms currently known as ADHD (Douthit, 2001; Douthit & Marquis, 2006).

Historically, more professional attention was given to understanding ADHD in the context of factors such as children's psychosocial challenges, the adaptive psychological imprints of advanced technology, and the general permissiveness of the postmodern parent. Much of this alternative literature has now faded into obscurity and has been replaced by a highly productive and amply funded research agenda focusing, with laser-like sharpness, on the biological underpinnings of the disorder. Hence the apparent partiality of this present quadratic analysis unavoidably favors the exterior-individual quadrant and needs to be understood not as the bias of the authors of this chapter, but as an accurate reflection of currently available data.

In spite of the bias in favor of biological explanations of ADHD mechanisms, the idea of etiological heterogeneity has gained momentum recently, prompting further research exploring how multiple causal pathways may lead to somewhat different manifestations of the disorder. This focus on heterogeneity sheds light on the emerging concept that ADHD may have etiological "types" and causal pathways not recognized by the DSM-IV-TR, but that are emerging in the DSM-5 conceptualization (APA, 2013; Sonuga-Barke, 2003). Sonuga-Barke (2005) urged a shift in the etiological evaluation of ADHD from a single core dysfunction to multiple developmental pathways with varying degrees of deficits and symptoms overlapping and operating differently within a range of neuropsychological mechanisms. It is in the spirit of etiological heterogeneity that we begin this four-quadrant exploration of ADHD.

### Individual-Exterior (Upper-Right) Perspectives

Russell Barkley, a psychologist whose long and illustrious career has been devoted to elucidating the etiological foundations of ADHD, is a leading voice in the field. Barkley's "unequivocal" (2006a, p. 220) assertion that contextual factors, such as family discord, video games, attachment-related issues, and the fast-paced tempo of contemporary life, in and of themselves, cannot provide a sufficient explanatory framework for our understanding of ADHD etiology, is reflective of more general trends in psychopathology research where data generated in the biological sciences, including genetics, neuroscience, and psychopharmacology, has often been interpreted using a disciplinarily-constrained lens.

An understanding of the dangers inherent in constrained forms of scientific inquiry is an important prelude to a discussion of ADHD and its relationship to the upper-right quadrant. Biological evidence, which generally comes in a form that is appealingly tangible, visually compelling (e.g., various forms of neuroimaging), and based on the truth claims of positivist, empirical research, cannot always be taken merely at face value. For example, finding "a gene" for ADHD, or using a brain-imaging technique on individuals harboring the symptoms of ADHD to reveal abnormal structures or defective neurological pathways, does not equate to unveiling "the" etiology of ADHD. Genetic research provides an apt illustration of what can be called the "biogenic fallacy" that often characterizes interpretation of data in the sciences. This biogenic fallacy uncritically assumes that biological evidence, such as the statistically significant presence of a particular gene in individuals with ADHD, tells us something about the basic cause of ADHD. Such genetic determinism

> . . . assumes that an inescapable lockstep mechanism drives gene expression. If individuals have "the gene" for depression, genetic determinism tells them that they are destined to have depression. One's genes, according to genetic determinism, are an inflexible, unyielding blueprint that single-handedly determines every nuance of one's physical being. (Douthit, 2006, pp. 17–18)

Contrary to notions of determinism, a contemporary understanding of psychiatric genetics underscores that, for the most part, genes do not cause mental disorder without interacting with other variables. Rare examples of direct genetic causality include early-onset Alzheimer's dementia (Bertram & Tanzi, 2008) and dementia related to Huntington's disease (Walker, 2007). Most psychiatrically significant behaviors/symptoms represent a composite of many genes (i.e., polygenetic) whose expressions are environmentally regulated, and much of that regulation is the interplay of the physical self and extant conditions related to the three remaining quadrants, as well as developmental dynamics. In some cases, regulated, polygenetic expression may result in certain behavioral proclivities that are at odds with social norms, hence creating conditions, depending on the particular context, in which the individual may be socially ostracized, criminalized, or exalted for their exceptionality. In any case, the lesson to be taken from this short description of genetic determinism is that *biological data must be analyzed critically. Genes—in and of themselves—don't generally cause mental disorders and, likewise, abnormally appearing brain structures or brain chemistry may be the outcome of environmentally induced biological outcomes.*

Having underscored this caveat concerning the interpretation of biological data, this section on the individual-exterior quadrant will consider evidence of how this domain relates to the cluster of symptoms that we call ADHD. We begin with an overview of the genetics of ADHD and then discuss some of the neuroscientific findings that have emerged in recent years.

**AN OVERVIEW OF ADHD GENETICS** Within psychiatric circles, ADHD is reputed to be among the most heritable of mental disorders (Barkley, 2006a; Faraone & Mick, 2010). The basis for such claims is predicated on three primary lines of evidence: genetic linkage studies, gene association studies, and monozygotic (MZ)/dizygotic (DZ) twin and adoption studies. Each of these three sources of data has its own strengths and weaknesses but, in any case, provides a springboard for additional lines of inquiry. Perhaps the largest untapped data source in the Integral study of ADHD heritability is in the realm of epigenetics. Epigenetics is a burgeoning area of research that considers phenotypes or traits that arise through heritable (i.e., they can be passed from one generation to the next) and reversible regulation of gene expression achieved through an environmentally mediated molecular manipulation of genes that does not include any changes in basic DNA structure. The study of epigenetic mechanisms is particularly germane to Integrally informed inquiry because it provides an empirical platform for our understanding of how some of the most basic elements of human biological functioning (UR) can be linked, in a tangible "flesh-and-blood" way, to the UL, LR, and LL quadrants and to various lines and levels of development.

**GENETICS AND HERITABILITY** ADHD, relative to other DSM disorders, has a heritability factor that is quite high, at upwards of 76–78% (Faraone & Mick, 2010; Sklar, 2005). The high heritability calculations of ADHD, relative to other DSM mental disorder categories, has been the focus of a plethora of studies attempting to elucidate a genetic basis for the behaviors associated with this highly prevalent disorder. Because the research in this realm is so abundant, an overview of the extant findings can be extracted from numerous reviews and meta-analyses.

**GENE LINKAGE** Gene linkage studies in ADHD aim to reveal parts of chromosomes that would be expected to be shared more often by blood-relative family members who harbor the symptoms of ADHD. Studies generally involve gene comparisons of similarly afflicted first-degree relatives and often will target siblings. By revealing shared genes, geneticists are able to determine the degree to which specific genes are likely to play a part in generating the symptoms of the disorder in question. In a review of studies involving full genome scans, Faraone and Mick (2010) concluded that the results of ADHD gene linkage research suggest that "many genes of moderately large effect size are unlikely to exist" (p. 160); that is, the relative risk of having the disorder due the presence of any single known gene is small. As Sklar (2005) asserts, ADHD is genetically quite complex and no single genetic locus has emerged that has proved to be replicable across studies. This lack of replicability has several explanations, including: (1) ADHD has many phenotypes, not all of which are reflected in the DSM-5 (APA, 2013) criterion sets; (2) ADHD, which is defined in the DSM through etiologically atheoretical criteria (Douthit & Donnelly, 2010), actually represents a cluster of etiologically unrelated disorders having similar descriptive manifestations; and (3) the heritability that has been observed in twin studies is actually a reflection of heritable epigenetic, rather than genetic, transmission. All of this suggests that there might be much heterogeneity across samples thus jeopardizing the likelihood that reliable replication of findings will emerge. In any case, for ADHD, as well as other genetically complex disorders, the fact remains that to achieve replicable statistical power in the face of heterogeneity and subtle, albeit pervasive, genetic effects requires prohibitively large sample sizes (Risch & Merikangas, 1996). In such cases, a method entitled "genetic association" holds more promise for unlocking genetic contributions to disorder than linkage studies (Faraone & Mick, 2010; Risch & Merikangas, 1996).

**GENE ASSOCIATION STUDIES** Association studies, in contrast to the linkage studies just discussed, have greater ability to detect modest effects and are more methodologically suitable in the case of modest effect disorders such as ADHD (Risch & Merikangas, 1996). The general aim of association studies is to uncover disorder-related alleles (i.e., small areas on chromosomes that are related to disorder) that are either more or less common in individuals having the symptoms of a particular disorder than in the general population. As Sklar (2005) asserts, for ADHD and other complex genetic diseases, "the underlying signal will be less strong because multiple genes contribute to disease risk in an individual linkage study" (p. 1358).

In contrast to linkage studies, an abundance of association studies are available and have implicated a number of candidate genes. Several meta-analytic studies underscore the association between ADHD and the dopamine D4 receptor gene (DRD4) (see, for example Li, Sham, Owen, & He, 2006). As discussed later in the chapter, the association with this particular gene is consistent with what we know about how individuals diagnosed with ADHD respond to stimulant medications. Unfortunately, numerous gene scans have failed to capture other theoretically compelling gene associations (Faraone & Mick, 2010). In a review of gene association studies, Faraone and Mick report that the genes to date that have the strongest associations with ADHD etiology are DRD4, DRD5, SLC6A3, SNAP-25, and HTR1B, and that in spite of their small effects, the role of these genes is becoming increasingly clear as the phenotypic heterogeneity within ADHD populations comes into sharper focus:

> . . . Examination of refined phenotypes that may reduce heterogeneity, is beginning to bear fruit, but more research is needed to extend the work focused on ADHD subtypes (e.g., inattentive subtype and HTR1B); comorbid psychopathology or cognitive impairment (e.g., depression and SNAP-25, reading disability and ADRA2A), and gene-environment interactions (e.g., prenatal or psychosocial risk factors for ADHD and SLC6A3). It is also possible that ADHD genetics research will benefit from the study of endophenotypes such as neuropsychological functioning or brain imaging. (Faraone & Mick, 2010, pp. 170–171)

**USING ENDOPHENOTYPES TO CLARIFY GENETIC INFLUENCE** As the previous quotation from the work of Faraone and Mick (2010) suggests, ADHD-related genetic research aided by the use of endophenotypes could prove to be quite fruitful in the search for clinically relevant genetic influence. A brief discussion of gene-endophenotype research is particularly warranted in the context of an Integral understanding of DSM disorders because endophenotype research acknowledges the etiological heterogeneity of disorder categories and could provide a window into our understanding of how ADHD is shaped by the full ecology of the developmental influence reflected in the four quadrants of Integral theory.

The term *endophenotype* has a long history that began outside the confines of clinical research. Within the realm of psychiatric molecular genetics, endophenotype can be understood as a single characteristic or marker that is "more proximal to the biological etiology of a clinical disorder than its signs and symptoms and [is] influenced by one or more of the same susceptibility genes as the condition" (Doyle et al., 2005, p. 1324). Taking ADHD endophenotypic research as an example, more conventional ADHD genetic research begins by identifying a population of subjects, all of whom meet the DSM-5 criteria for diagnosis of the disorder. Endophenotype advocates would purport that among the many observable behaviors that constitute an ADHD diagnosis: (1) the behaviors or observable features of ADHD are most likely controlled by a complex array of genes, important gene–environment interactions, biological assaults unrelated to genetic function (e.g., lead), and environmental conditions related to the larger ecology of development; (2) the complexity surrounding the actual manifestations of ADHD DSM criteria leads to an understandable etiological heterogeneity among individuals receiving the DSM diagnosis; and (3) because of the potential variation in etiology, it may be more fruitful, in the search for specific genes with direct influence on disorder manifestation, to sort through either some of the disorder behaviors or perhaps other types of shared neurophysiological or neuroanatomical markers that are not part of the DSM diagnosis to see if any of these are more closely regulated by genes than others. In the case of ADHD, an endophenotype (i.e., a characteristic associated with the disorder that has direct genetic control) might be performance on a neuropsychological test of inhibitory control or perhaps an important component of inhibitory control such as visual-spatial memory.

Numerous potential endophenotypes for ADHD have emerged in recent years. In particular, twin, family, and adoption studies suggest that aspects of executive functioning, in addition to "processing speed, visual attention, and response to variability may be associated with the genetic liability to ADHD" (Doyle et al., 2005, p. 1328). Likewise, other twin studies have highlighted the potential endophenotypic value of electroencephalogram (EEG) and event-related potential (ERP) measures as well as certain assessments of brain volume (Doyle et al., 2005). Although findings related to ADHD endophenotypes have held some promise, in previous studies, no single endophenotype emerged that was consistently found in ADHD-diagnosed participants, "particularly one that was reliable, heritable, and cofamilial" (Doyle et al., 2005, p. 1331).

**ADHD, ENVIRONMENTAL FACTORS, AND THE EMERGING FIELD OF EPIGENETICS** Epigenetics, broadly speaking, can be defined as the study of mechanisms involved in non-DNA-sequence-related phenotypic variations in traits, that is, variations in traits that are not due to differing DNA sequences (Bonasio, Tu, & Reinberg, 2010). Epigenetic factors are considered to be key mediators in an organism's response to environmental conditions and hence an important focus in the study of mental health. Most epigenetic information is contained in self-reproducing "molecular signatures" that are, in essence, molecular imprints of a stimulus, including stimuli generated through contextual experience and the intrapsychic processes that mediate contextual experience. These molecular signatures, which act through physical contact with genes, come in a number of forms. A review of these various forms is beyond the scope of this chapter, but suffice it to say that epigenetic processes are one method by which our physical being becomes a reflection of the particular idiographic configuration of our individual developmental ecologies.

Although the science of epigenetics is still in its infancy, it is nonetheless emerging as an important dimension of our understanding of the complex etiology of mental disorder and is particularly germane to our attempts to build a model that assimilates all four quadrants of Integral theory. In the case of ADHD, epigenetics provides a platform for integrating the volumes of data that show very credible associations between ADHD symptoms and an array of intrapsychic, psychosocial, socioeconomic, cultural, and other variables. Discussions of many of these associations can be found in other sections of this chapter, but some variables that have been the focus of more intense scrutiny as candidates for epigenetic transformation of phenotype will be mentioned here. As this discussion unfolds, it is important to understand that *the power of an environmental or other force to change gene expression (i.e., epigenetic transformation) does not necessarily equate to a particular genetic predisposition for epigenetic transformation.* Although some inherited genes may, in fact, be more epigenetically malleable than others, in other cases the external force driving epigenetic process may be very powerful and may drive transformation of phenotype across a range of gene susceptibilities to epigenetic change. The kinds of epigenetic transformations that are seen in mental disorder can actually be understood as a form of environmentally driven dysregulation leading to psychological or psychiatric suffering (Mill & Petronis, 2008).

Much of the speculation concerning ADHD-related epigenetic processes points to pre- and perinatal environmental risk. The large majority of known risk factors for ADHD seem to exert their influence on either the developing fetus or in the early neonatal period (Mill & Petronis, 2008). This pattern of early influence is consistent with the emerging "developmental origins of health and disease (DOHaD) hypothesis [that] argues that a poor environment in pre- and early postnatal life manifests itself in permanent changes to various metabolic processes in the body" (p. 1021). As this discussion unfolds, however, it is important to be mindful of the notion that genetic and/or environmental forces bearing responsibility for the developmental origins of ADHD may or may not be implicated in eventual outcomes, that is, experience and disability in the developing child, adolescent, and adult (Thapar, Langley, Asherson, & Gill, 2007). It is also important to bear in mind that the precise mechanisms that occur under the rubric of DOHaD are largely under-researched, thus leaving specific gene–environment mechanisms open to conjecture.

Maternal smoking in the prenatal period, when combined with certain genes involved in the dopamine pathway, appears to significantly raise the risk of the child receiving an ADHD diagnosis, when compared to children with prenatal exposure to cigarette smoke who do not carry the dopamine pathway gene (Neuman et al., 2007). Likewise, Becker, El-Faddagh, Schmidt, Esser, and Laucht (2008) found that in males, the impact of prenatal smoke exposure was dependent on the particular dopamine-pathway-related genotype of the child and resulted in significantly higher levels of hyperactivity-impulsivity in males who carried the vulnerable genotype when compared to males without the genotype. Further suspicion is raised regarding the dopamine pathway in a study in which children with a vulnerable genotype are more likely to be diagnosed with ADHD when the vulnerable genotype interacts with the mother's marital instability (Waldman, 2007).

Other environmental variables that are promising candidates in epigenetic studies include a sizable list shown to have an association with ADHD (Mill & Petronis, 2008). These variables include prenatal exposure to maternal stress (Cottrell & Seckl, 2009; van den Bergh et al., 2006; van den Bergh, Mulder, Mennes, & Glover, 2005); prenatal organophosphate pesticide exposure as determined by the mother's pesticide blood level (Bouchard, Bellinger, Wright, & Weisskopf, 2010); low birth weight, although findings are mixed, with several studies showing very low birth weight not to have a significant association (Mick, Biederman, Prince, Fischer, & Faraone, 2002); and prenatal exposure to industrial by-products such as polychlorinated biphenyls (PCBs) (Eubig, Aguiar, & Schantz, 2010; Sagiv et al., 2010), lead (Eubig et al., 2010), glucocorticoids (Kapoor, Petropoulos, & Matthews, 2008), and cocaine (Accornero et al., 2007). Although an association has been demonstrated between ADHD symptoms and prenatal alcohol exposure (Mick, Biederman, Faraone, Sayer, & Kleinman, 2002), subsequent studies designed to differentiate between causation related to alcohol exposure and genetic causation suggest that a genetic propensity for alcohol abuse in mothers is predictive of ADHD-like symptoms in offspring and is a more powerful predictor than alcohol exposure independent of genetic influence (Knopik et al., 2006).

**STRUCTURAL AND FUNCTIONAL ABNORMALITIES REVEALED THROUGH NEUROIMAGING** Advances in neuroimaging techniques in the past several decades have spawned a vigorous line of scholarship focusing on structural abnormalities associated with ADHD symptoms. Although the majority of studies have generally included less than 20 participants and have thus been underpowered, more robust studies have confirmed many of the conclusions coming from these small-scale studies (Seidman, Valera, & Makris, 2005). Another limitation in imaging studies is the insufficient attention given to various sources of heterogeneity in the ADHD population. This heterogeneity includes a number of factors that underscore an Integral model of ADHD depicting a range of ADHD etiologies and clinical presentations, all of which need to be considered in any comprehensive study of structural and functional correlates of the disorder. Included among these factors are subtype, perinatal exposure to environmental toxins, antenatal and postnatal maternal stress, family discord, early childhood trauma, family history of ADHD, family history of substance abuse, medication history, comorbidity patterns, and birth complications (Seidman et al., 2005). It is important, when considering data from imaging studies, to remember that the presence of an anatomical abnormality does not lead directly to the conclusion that the etiology of the abnormality necessarily originates in the upper-right quadrant. Although images can be quite compelling, those that are outside the realm of what is considered to be normative structure or function can result from familial, social, and cultural forces that impact neuroanatomy and neurophysiology through epigenetic and other mechanisms.

The tools that are available in the field of neuroimaging are increasingly sophisticated and are able to provide data regarding the relative volume of brain structures as well as the level of metabolic activity (e.g., measures of oxygen consumption, and blood flow associated with various functional brain units). At the most basic level, computerized axial tomography (CAT) provides radiographic images of brain structures that can be used to assess anatomical features such as size and shape. Magnetic resonance imaging (MRI) can be used to generate clearer anatomical data and, through technological advances that include functional MRI (fMRI), positron emission tomography (PET), and single photon emission computed tomography (SPECT), researchers are able to produce images that are a window into the level of metabolic activity in areas of the brain.

Numerous reviews have been published that have identified emergent patterns in ADHD brain-imaging data. In a systematic review of over two dozen studies, Bush, Valera, and Seidman (2005) confirmed the long-held view that frontostriatal circuit abnormalities known to be related to executive functioning are central to ADHD symptomatology. In the same review, as well as others (Cherkasova & Hechtman, 2009; Dickstein, Bannon, Castellanos, & Milham, 2006), additional areas of importance came to light, such as the frontoparietal circuit and the cerebellum, the latter being known to have connections to the prefrontal cortex and to be involved in a number of functions germane to ADHD, such as planning, processing of temporal data, working memory, attention shifting, emotional regulation, and executive functioning (Cherkasova & Hechtman, 2009).

**PHYSIOLOGICAL MODELS OF ADHD** One of the important contributions of this book is its explicit articulation of the complex ecology of both healthy and injurious forms of human development. Complex ecology, aptly captured in iterations of Integral theory applied to counseling and psychotherapy (Ingersoll & Zeitler, 2010; Marquis, 2007, 2008), underscores the difficulty in attributing "psychological symptoms" to exclusively intra-individual biological causes. Perhaps the closest approximation of an uncontested biological model of ADHD comes from studies utilizing animal strains with a propensity for ADHD-like behavior, animal populations subjected to selective brain injury, or animals subjected to neurotoxin exposure that results in symptoms typically associated with ADHD. The advantages of animal models are well known: such populations are relatively genetically homogeneous; have no previous exposure to toxins such as alcohol, nicotine, lead, and so forth; are not subject to complex family dynamics or larger social dynamics, have uniform diets, and do not bring confounding comorbidities to the research arena (Davids, Zhang, Tarazi, & Baldessarini, 2003). An exemplary animal ADHD model would be expected to "resemble a clinical disorder in as many details as possible, including symptomatic expression, treatment responses, pathophysiology, and ideally, etiology" (Davids et al., 2003, p. 2). The connection between human and animal research is often direct and explicit. Findings from animal studies may also directly inform research questions in the realm of human-focused biomedical inquiry.

Rat and mouse studies have informed some of the most widely supported models of ADHD etiology. For example, selective inbreeding responsible for the Wistar-Kyoto strain of spontaneously hypertensive rats (SHR) has resulted in an animal strain that exhibits behavioral qualities characteristic of ADHD (Sagvolden, 2000). Research with SHR points to a problem of impaired dopamine release from nerve terminals located in rat brain sites analogous to those commonly identified as suspect in human imaging studies. Included among these suspect sites are the prefrontal cortex, nucleus accumbens, neostriatum, and caudate-putamen. The SHR model has also provided a medium through which some post-synaptic neurotransmission abnormalities involving protein kinase II, an important enzyme in the neurotransmission process, have been implicated. Further evidence that SHR physiology echoes human ADHD physiology is gleaned from the SHR response to stimulant medications, in which ADHD-like behaviors of SHR are diminished through what is assumed to be a correction of impaired dopaminergic neurotransmission (Davids et al., 2003; Russell, Sagvolden, & Johansen, 2005; Sagvolden, 2011). Other rodent models, including the dopamine transporter knockout mouse, the coloboma mutant mouse, and the Naples high-excitability rat, provide additional evidence for the notion that ADHD is rooted in impairment of dopaminergic neurotransmission (Davids et al., 2003).

## Interior-Collective (Lower-Left) Perspectives

ADHD, as a psychopathological construct that is over a century old (Still, 1902), has been the object of considerable scrutiny and critique. This close examination of ADHD has not been the sole purview of science and medicine; rather, a lively multidisciplinary discourse has emerged with some topics that refute the actual existence of the disorder, others that are aligned with a now conventional biomedical view, those that attempt to understand ADHD as a historically and geographically delimited cultural construction, and, finally, those that nobly attempt to conceptualize complex cross-disciplinary models of the disorder. Given that much has already been said in this chapter about the contemporary dominance of biomedical explications of ADHD, this section focuses on sociocultural representations of ADHD etiology.

In keeping with other nonbiomedical explanations of ADHD, the volume of literature focusing on cultural considerations has waned considerably since the 1980s and early 1990s. In spite of the age of this literature, however, its relevance to a robust Integral analysis of ADHD has not diminished. This section begins by introducing the work of Peter Conrad, a scholar well known among sociologists for his work on the medicalization of deviance. The work of Sami Timimi, an ADHD critic whose work also underscores the role of biomedicalization in our understanding of ADHD type symptoms, is then described. The section then turns to the work of Thom Hartmann, a progressive journalist and social critic whose compelling 1993 work on ADHD provided a cultural, historical framework for ADHD that attempted to normalize behaviors commonly seen in individuals diagnosed with the disorder.

**CONRAD'S MEDICALIZATION OF DEVIANCE** Conrad (1976, 1980, 2006, 2007) posits that among the many consequences of an increasingly powerful, pervasive medical establishment is a trend toward medicalizing socially deviant forms of behavior. From an Integral perspective, Conrad's thesis underscores the importance of understanding that scientific data are not value neutral and that the meaning attributed to upper-right influences must be considered in the context of social, cultural, and historical forces. Conrad (1976, 2007) asserts that sources of deviance ranging from alcoholism, drug abuse, obsessive sexual behavior, obesity, violence, and hyperactivity—all previously described in terms of moral turpitude—are now largely the purview of medical science and, rather than being treated punitively, are subject to surgical, pharmacological, or behavioral intervention.

Conrad challenges the construct of illness as an objective state of disease or pathology by underscoring that much of what we term "illness" is in fact a culturally relative assessment of an individual's condition. In Conrad's words, "An entity or condition is a disease or illness only if it is recognized and defined as one by the culture" (1980, p. 104). Conrad thus introduces the concept that cultures attach meaning to various states of organic reshuffling—that is, the physiological states that produce the conditions of "disease"—and in this way they construct roles, rituals, and expectations around various physiological states. Because there is cultural meaning attached to any constructed illness label, to be deemed "ill" carries the weight of nonbiological consequences. For example, individuals face different social positioning depending on whether they are labeled as being lazy and irresponsible versus victims of chronic fatigue syndrome. This cultural positioning, conceptualized as an interior-collective (LL) phenomenon, contributes to the subjective (interior-individual/UL) experience of the disease. Thus the mere creation of a diagnostic category such as ADHD is itself a cultural judgment of what is considered to be within the bounds of "normality" and dictates to a certain degree how the afflicted individual will experience his physiological state.

Although deviance is usually viewed as willful and illness as un-willful, both conditions hamper the ability of the individual to perform behaviors associated with their particular role performance (Parsons, 1951; Widiger, Livesley, & Clark, 2009). Sharper contrast between deviance and illness emerges, however, when remediation is considered. For the ill, there is a culturally legitimated but conditional sick role in which the individual is not expected to function normally. In order to maintain that legitimate status, however, the sick individual must enter a relationship with a physician who is expected to alter the physical condition that precludes that individual from performing in her particular social roles. For the deviant, remediation comes through punishment that aims to alter the motivation of the deviant individual to enter into more socially acceptable social roles (Conrad, 1980).

It is certainly not difficult to understand how this narrow, culturally relative definition of physical disorder might be reductionistic to a fault. However, Conrad's cultural relativity is less problematic when applied to phenomena involving behavioral deviancy. "In this light it is understandable that conditions defined as illness reflect the social values and general *weltanshauung* of a society"[1] (Conrad, 1980, p. 107).

Conrad (1980) posits that the shift toward the medicalization of deviance is attributable to several factors, including the ascendency of psychoanalytic practice, which generally seeks to understand the embodiment of social phenomena, and the emergence of a powerful medical profession. He proposes a set of conditions that, when linked to a behavioral phenomenon, sets the stage for the process of medicalization to take hold. These conditions include:

1. A behavior or set of behaviors must be defined as deviant and as a problem in need of remedy by some segment of society . . .
2. (P)revious or traditional forms of social control are seen as inefficient or unacceptable . . .
3. (S)ome form of medical control needs to be available . . .
4. (There must exist) some ambiguous organic data as to the source of the problem . . .
5. It is essential for the medical profession to accept the deviant behavior within their jurisdiction. (Conrad, 1980, pp. 111–114)

Conrad (1980), with his specific interest in hyperactivity, demonstrates the ways in which this particular disorder fits the conditions just listed: (1) hyperactivity has been deemed by mothers and school personnel alike as deviant and in need of remediation; (2) corporal punishment in classrooms is out-moded and the expulsion of disruptive children from school is no longer viewed as an ethically viable form of social control; (3) the discovery that stimulant medication has a paradoxical, calming effect on hyperactive children gives the medical establishment a means of treatment; (4) a number of bio-physiological theories have implicated organic mechanisms in hyperactive behavior, including genes, environmental toxins, difficulties at birth, prenatal environment, brain injury, and food additives; and (5) approximately one dozen physicians and behavioral scientists acted as medical entrepreneurs by publishing a number of papers "promoting hyperactivity and exhorting the usefulness of medical treatment, and advocating the identification and treatment of hyperactive children" (p. 116). Medicalization of hyperactivity was then symbolically approved by a "blue ribbon professional investigative committee . . . (T)his approval came in a report submitted to the Department of Health, Education and Welfare's Office of Child Development in 1971" (p. 116).

While there seems to be little question that hyperactivity, and ADHD more broadly, at least for the economically advantaged, has undergone the transition from deviance to illness, the question remains as to why the medicalization process should

[1] *Weltanshauung* refers to one's worldview—the set of ideas and beliefs with which an individual perceives herself and the world around her.

be of concern. Conrad (1980) addresses this question, bringing to light a number of issues. First, medicalization tends to exonerate the individual by diminishing the likelihood of autonomous, willful action. Second, medicine continues to expand its purview regardless of the effectiveness of its interventions and is bolstered by a highly profitable and omnipresent pharmaceutical industry. Third, although medicine is assumed to be the product of neutral science, it is actually considerably influenced by the social-moral order. Fourth, medicalization restricts dialogue and understanding of human and social problems to appointed medical experts, and along with this restrictive dialogue comes a "dominance and hegemony of medical definitions . . . (that) are often taken as the last scientific word" (p. 119). Fifth, the techniques used by medicine to treat deviant behavior can often alter the personality of the individual and in some cases are irreversible. These powerful treatment modalities are instituted in the name of adherence to social convention. Lastly, by focusing on remediation of individual pathology, the collective social dimension of human behavior is eclipsed.

Echoing Conrad's cultural critique of the ADHD construct, Timimi (2005) posits that contemporary cultural conditions drive much of the hyperactive behavior seen in children, and include realities such as the dissolution of extended family systems, waning of the moral authority of adults, competing paradigms regarding child discipline, the "hyperactive" state of family life, and "a market economy value system that emphasizes individuality, competitiveness, and independence" (Timimi & Taylor, 2004, p. 8). When this market economy value system is then overlaid with "the profit-dependent pharmaceutical industry and a high status profession looking for new roles . . . we have the ideal cultural precondition for the birth and propagation of the ADHD construct" (Timimi & Taylor, 2004, p. 8).

As pediatric psychiatry, and psychiatry more generally, attempt to secure their places in modern medicine, human behaviors are increasingly viewed through the decontextualized lens of medicalization (Timimi & Taylor, 2004). Underscoring adults' complicity in creating and sustaining the ADHD construct, Timimi and Taylor argue that this decontextualization causes adults, whether caregivers, teachers, or medical professionals, to relinquish responsibility for raising well-behaved children. They further assert: "By acting as agents of social control and stifling diversity in children, we are victimizing millions of children on highly addictive drugs that have no proven long term benefit (Timimi, 2002) and have been shown in animal studies to have brain disabling effects (Moll et al., 2001; Sproson et al., 2001; Breggin, 2002)" (Timimi & Taylor, 2004, p. 8). Whether it is a case of medicalization of deviance or the forces of a market economy, sweeping macro-level constructs are shaping the nature of institutions and interpersonal communication to create the internalized "perfect storm" that is ADHD. It is important, however, to understand that the artifacts of interior-collective action are reproduced and perpetuated by people with agency and the dynamic interchange between forces in all four quadrants. Still, the interior-collective elements in the case of ADHD provide a powerful set of "realities" that inform beliefs, behaviors, and experiences.

**HARTMANN'S SOCIOBIOLOGICAL REFRAMING OF ADHD** The claim has been made that an important contribution to the escalation of ADHD diagnoses relates to practices within American education that pathologize male attributes (Stolzer, 2009). Concurring with this notion, Hartmann (1993) is ill at ease with the reality that 10% of the general population and upwards of 20% of all males could be afflicted with a mental disorder.

In an attempt to construct a more naturalistic explanation for the high prevalence of ADHD among males, Hartman suggests that individuals manifesting the symptoms of the disorder actually represent the "hunter" end of a spectrum of behaviors that are characterized at one end by hunter-like behavior and at the other end by farmer-like behavior. It is Hartmann's contention that the behaviors that characterize ADHD are, in a hunting society, behaviors that are essential for success and ultimate survival. Unfortunately for those whose display predominantly hunter qualities in a contemporary, Western, postindustrial milieu, schooling and the world of work favor the qualities of the steady, persistent, and fastidious "farmer."

In efforts to reframe ADHD, Hartmann (1993) compiled a list of ADHD characteristics that he compellingly reinterpreted in the context of the competent hunter. He also contrasts these hunter behaviors with those of the competent farmer under similar conditions. For example, in the case of the ADHD behavior, Hartmann reframes distractibility as an essential tool for successful hunters who must relentlessly survey their environment. In contrast, he notes that the successful farmer must display a steadfast disposition in which the focus on a slow-moving and often unstimulating set of repetitive tasks is essential for survival. Likewise, ADHD behaviors associated with impulsivity and disorganization can be reframed as the flexibility and preparedness for quick changes in strategy that are the mark of an accomplished hunter and the nemesis of the farmer who needs to maintain a strategy and remain organized and focused on a plan in the face of disruptive circumstances. Other ADHD behaviors reframed by Hartmann include a short attention span punctuated with hypervigilance, a distorted sense of time, acting in ways that prevent physical danger, and being impatient and results oriented.

Although Hartmann sees ADHD characteristics as adaptive in a hunting society, it is his contention that those same characteristics can prove beneficial in modern sociocultural settings as well. Trial lawyer, salesperson, and entrepreneur are just a few of the vocations that resonate with hunter behaviors. Hartmann is also quick to assert that ADHD children, because of their relatively unbridled perspective, tend to be creative thinkers and that many American presidents and "founding fathers" have tended toward the hunter end of the hunter–farmer continuum.

**MICRO-INTERACTIONAL DIMENSIONS OF INTERIOR-COLLECTIVE INFLUENCE** Whereas the works of Conrad, Timimi, and Hartmann address the internal experience of collective influence, many scholars prior to the turn of the 21st century were concerned with how micro-interactional processes impact internal experience and possibly generate the symptoms of ADHD. Much of the research supporting micro-interactional psychosocial influences on the etiology of ADHD harkens back to work done in the 1970s and 1980s, an era still strongly imprinted with the interpretivist epistemology of psychoanalytic thought. A central aim of psychoanalysis is to understand the internalization of social experience, and hence in the world of psychopathology, psychoanalysis provides a lens that brings into sharp focus the transformation of social structure into interior, psychological process. The publication of the DSM-III in 1980 marked the beginning of biomedicine's meteoric rise to prominence in the world of psychiatry and the precipitous decline of psychoanalysis. This epistemological and philosophical turn redirected the focus of psychotherapeutic attention away from intrapsychic (UL) and intersubjective (LL) processes toward biological (UR) attributions and marked the ascendancy of quantifiable, observable criteria in our understanding and assessment of mental disorder.

Although the post-psychoanalytically driven medical model promotes the theory of the "neurologically disordered brain," alternative explanations for how social experience leads to ADHD-type behavior exists within bodies of literature that consider interpersonal attachment relationships with caregivers, family systems dynamics, and the role that the child's temperament plays in determining the quality of close relationships. Each of these arenas of possible interior-collective influence will be explored in depth in the following subsections.

**ATTACHMENT** Viewing ADHD behaviors through the lens of attachment theory provides a basis for understanding the interpersonal and emotional challenges of ADHD within a contextual framework (Erdman, 1998; Newman, 1996; Olson, 1996; Stiefel, 1997). Now an anchoring concept in relational psychology, attachment is understood as the predominant and enduring pattern that characterizes the ways in which a parent and their infant relate to one another (Ainsworth, Blehar, Waters, & Wall, 1978; Bowlby, 1982). The infant attempts to establish a secure base with the primary caregiver from whom they develop functional or dysfunctional exploratory behaviors. In this way, the developing infant depends on the caregiver's ability to provide a secure base upon which self-regulatory capacities are developed. These self-regulatory capacities are built on what will ideally be the caregiver's sensitive responses to the infant's signals (Cassidy, 1994). The "secure attachment" patterns that emerge from a healthy infant–caregiver relationship are important for how the child will relate to others in life and how he or she experiences the environment. In Integral terms, attachment can be seen as a backdrop of the inner experience of relationships captured in the collective-interior (LL) quadrant.

Attachment patterns thus have profound implications for the child's feelings of security and her capacity to form trusting relationships. If the caregiver is inconsistent or does not respond to the child's needs, the child may become "insecurely attached" and exploratory attempts become extremely stressful and often discouraging for the child. Insecure attachment, in turn, is associated with affective and behavioral regulation problems in childhood (Cassidy, 1994). The child's positive and negative experiences with the primary caregiver thus become instantiated and provide a blueprint upon which all later relationships with adults and peers are formed.

Bowlby (1988) referred to this instantiation as the child's "internal working model." These working models of attachment can be dormant in the child's day-to-day functioning until mobilized by specific experiential triggers (Bowlby, 1982). Whereas secure attachment is responsible for adaptive and healthy later functioning, an unhealthy attachment style is less adaptive and strongly influences later behavioral problems. Insecurely attached infants come to view the world as "comfortless and unpredictable; and they respond either by shrinking from it or doing battle with it" (Bowlby, 1973, p. 208). A parent–child relationship characterized by mistrust and anxiety places the child at risk for adaptational failures. Bowlby (1982), in fact, proposes that adaptational failures caused by ruptures in the attachment relationship are the main cause of psychopathology more generally.

Thus, a child's insecure attachment with the primary caregiver creates a great deal of interpersonal challenge and puts the child at risk for experiencing difficulties in social functioning. Psychologists have long known that insecurely attached children experience more problems in interpersonal relationships than those with healthy attachment patterns (Erickson, Stroufe, & Egeland, 1985). What is most germane to this chapter is that there are striking similarities between the deficits associated with ADHD and those linked to insecure attachment. The impairments of insecure attachment, which are also characteristic of the self-regulatory deficits in ADHD, affect the child's ability to regulate impulses, self-soothing behaviors, initiative, perseverance, patience, and inhibition (Clark, Ungerer, Chahoud, Johnson, & Stiefel, 2002; Olson, 1996; Stiefel, 1997). Barkley (1997) underscores the centrality of self-regulation to the impairments seen in ADHD. These self-regulatory abilities, when functioning optimally, enable the child to effectively adapt behavior across multiple contexts and integrate cognitive, affective, and motor functions in response to varying situational demands (Barkley, 1997).

A well-developed body of research supports the purported relationship of attachment-related problems to ADHD. Early micro-interactional research, developed in the 1970s, revealed a number of undesirable patterns among children with ADHD symptoms and their caregivers. When compared to child–caregiver dyad controls, caregiver–hyperactive child dyads displayed higher levels of directive behavior, more expression of disapproval or negativity, and less response from caregivers to the child's attempts to engage in social commentary about ongoing child–caregiver activities (Barkley, Karlsson, & Pollard, 1985; Campbell, 1973, 1975; Cunningham & Barkley, 1979). The same body of research showed that the hyperactive child is less conforming, more disruptive, and less likely to persist in on-task behavior than "normal" controls.

At the time these micro-interactional data were released, their interpretation raised some controversy and divided ADHD scholars into two opposing factions. Some, asserting that a caregiver deficiency model was causally involved, believed that ADHD's behavioral and relational difficulties arose because parenting deficiencies, such as those that would impact the quality of the attachment relationship, created fewer positive parent–child interactions (Campbell, 1987, 1990; Campbell & Ewing, 1990). They further contended that sustained oppositional and hyperactive behavior over time is partially related to the parent's use of directive and critical language.

Scholars refuting the caregiver deficiency model asserted that children with ADHD symptoms elicit negative caregiver responses by acting in unmanageable ways (Barkley & Cunningham, 1979; Barkley, Karlsson, Pollard, & Murphy, 1985; Cunningham & Barkley, 1979). Support for their position comes from research that assessed changes in parental behavior following administration of methylphenidate to children diagnosed with ADHD (Barkley & Cunningham, 1979). Results from these methylphenidate studies showed that pharmacological abatement of negative and noncompliant behavior in children resulted in a corresponding decrease in negative and directive maternal conduct. The conclusion was thus drawn that mothers' undesirable parenting practices are in direct response to negative child behaviors.

Moving away from this early debate, more recent studies provide evidence for the role of attachment in generating ADHD symptoms. One such study suggested that hostility between family members during the child's toddler years predicts ADHD symptoms in grade school (Jacobvitz, Hazen, Curran, & Hitchens, 2004). Likewise, the first longitudinal study assessing the developmental trajectory of attention problems in children found evidence that home environments have a moderating effect (Jester et al., 2005). It appears from this latter work that parent–child relationships may be influenced by impulsive, negative, attention-seeking, and hyperactive behavior that is part of the child's repertoire in his or her attempts to gain the attention of an emotionally unavailable caregiver. Another longitudinal study by Carlson, Jacobvitz, and Stroufe (1995) also demonstrated the predictive ability of early attachment measures in relation to the onset of ADHD symptoms. Maternal intrusiveness and insensitivity when the child was 6 months of age more powerfully predicted distractibility in early childhood and hyperactivity in middle childhood than did biological or temperamental factors.

Another ADHD association that may be related to attachment and the ability of parents to attend to the needs of young children is in the realm of parental mental disorder. Maternal depression, for example, has been found to be a risk factor for developing later conduct problems in ADHD (Chronis et al., 2007). Also, high rates of mood, conduct, substance abuse, and anxiety disorders among first-degree relatives, either accompanied or unaccompanied by ADHD (Biederman et al., 1992), may either predict attachment issues and general family dysfunction, or reflect a genetic predisposition for mental health disorder more generally.

It is difficult to talk about the relationship between attachment and ADHD symptoms without drawing on individual-exterior (UR) contributions to our understanding of this relationship. Neuroscience has provided insight into how negative parent–child interactions lead to disturbances in attachment relationships. More specifically, neuroscientists have observed that severe disruption in early development can affect psychological and neurological development by altering the dopaminergic, noradrenergic, and other neural pathways that support regulatory capabilities in the child (Nigg, 2006). The individual-exterior section of this chapter contains an extended discussion of the role of neurotransmitters and neural pathways in the production of ADHD symptoms. Individual-exterior forces also play a role in the quality of the caregiving provided by caregivers. For example, the genetic propensity of the caregiver for some degree of autism spectrum or schizoid behavior would likely impede the ability of the caregiver to empathically mirror the growing child or otherwise respond effectively to the child's needs. Likewise, a parent or caregiver suffering subclinical neurological damage due to occupational hazards, such as pesticide or heavy metal exposure, may not have the attention capacity, executive functioning, or affective stability required for effective parenting. Such compromises in caregiver capacity would likely be further challenged by a child having some degree of biological propensity for ADHD-like behavior. In any case, many of the examples in the collective-interior quadrant can easily be tied to a causal chain that involves other quadrants, thus underscoring the importance of understanding the reciprocal interplay between etiological dynamics in all four quadrants.

## Collective-Exterior (Lower-Right) Perspectives

When grappling simultaneously with the complexity of Integral theory and the range and density of ADHD research, it is often difficult to confine the outcomes of ADHD research to any one Integral quadrant. Hence, the preponderance of data presented in this section could arguably be located in another quadrant. In particular, many of the concepts presented here under the rubric of "collective-exterior" are gleaned from biological (UR) studies that underscore how social structures (LR) can be a driving force in biological outcomes. As described in the discussion on epigenetics, pre- or postnatal exposure to any one of a variety of environmental toxins is associated with development of ADHD-like behaviors. What is important to this discussion is that the presence of these toxins in the environment is the result of collective-exterior forces that most often, although not always, relate to structural inequality predicated on socioeconomic status, race, gender, age and a host of other sources of socio-structural injustice. Keeping in mind the notion that quadrants do not generally work in isolation to produce outcomes, the following examples of exterior-collective influence on ADHD generally use the medium of the exterior-individual quadrant to demonstrate their ultimate link to the symptoms of ADHD.

**LEAD EXPOSURE** Inorganic lead is a known neurotoxin and one of the most commonly cited environmental risk factors associated with ADHD and other developmental challenges. Evidence of this association has been garnered from both human and animal studies. Although the relationship between ADHD features and high blood lead levels (i.e., above 10 µg/dl) has been well documented for several decades, these findings have not attracted much attention because levels this high are relatively uncommon in countries where government regulation has restricted allowable lead levels in ubiquitous products such as paint and gasoline (Nigg, 2008). Recent work has examined the association between the lower, more commonly observed blood lead levels (i.e., 1–3 µg/dl) in countries adopting strict lead regulation laws (Fewtrell, Pruss-Ustun, Landrigan, & Ayuso-Mateos, 2004) and ADHD-related dysfunctions and behaviors (Canfield, Kreher, Cornwell, & Henderson, 2003; Nigg et al., 2008). Findings from these recent studies reveal an association between ADHD and these lower blood lead levels (i.e., those in the 1- to 3-µg/dl-range).

Numerous collective-exterior factors, including low-socioeconomic status, minority racial status, and low-quality housing, are known risk factors for exposure to lead (Tong, von Schirnding, & Prapamontol, 2000). The sources of lead related to low-income housing are particularly easy to trace. Homes built in the United States before the late 1970s, particularly those that have not been maintained, are likely sources of ingestible chipping and peeling lead-based paint and present a serious hazard to infants, toddlers, and unborn children. It is not uncommon for leaded paint chips and dust to be present on windowsills and dusty carpets and floors, and it is often present in soil surrounding homes where old chipping and peeling paint are a problem.

Another possible link between poverty and lead toxicity may be related to what has long been known about lead toxicity and children's calcium intake: young children whose diets are rich in calcium may be more resistant to the neurotoxic effects of lead (Mahaffey, 1995). Although this intersection of diet and toxicity is, at the end of the causal chain, an exterior-individual phenomenon, the question of early childhood and prenatal nutrition is one that is intimately tied to social and economic policies, racial and socioeconomic marginalization, educational opportunity, and access to quality food sources; all of which are factors situated in the exterior-collective (LR) quadrant.

**POLYCHLORINATED BIPHENYL AND ORGANOPHOSPHATE EXPOSURE** Lead does not stand alone as an ADHD-related neurotoxic substance whose etiological causal chain integrates both upper-right and lower-right influences. Two other substances of note with integrated pathways are polychlorinated biphenyls (PCBs) and organophosphate pesticides. PCBs, belonging to a group of organic substances known as organochlorides, are environmental contaminants that, until the 1970s, were used in coolants, cement and paint plasticizers, flame retardants, lubricating oils, sealants, pesticide extenders, and other substances that are ubiquitous in industrialized settings. Considerable evidence points to a relationship between prenatal PCB exposure and ADHD symptoms (Grandjean et al., 2001; Sagiv et al., 2010). In a study of children born to mothers living near a PCB-contaminated harbor in New Bedford, Massachusetts, Savig et al. (2010) found that even among children whose mothers had low umbilical cord blood PCB levels relative to several population studies showing a positive association between organochloride levels and ADHD-like symptoms, a moderate association was still found. The possible ADHD–PCB causal chain echoes the interplay of upper-right and lower-right quadrant factors characterizing the lead–ADHD causal chain. Although housing compromised by industrial waste contamination is not exclusive to low income areas, it is often the case that inexpensive housing options are located near current or former industrial production sites or near areas where disposal of industrial waste compromises water, soil, and/or air quality. Hence, the final step in the PCB cascade of etiological factors resulting in ADHD-like symptoms may be distinctly biological; but industrial regulatory policies; prevailing social attitudes that turn a blind eye to the dangers, across the lifespan, of low-income housing; and deeply entrenched systems of social reproduction involving substandard education, racial marginality, and lack of economic opportunity are equally culpable. This is not to imply that income provides a guarantee of immunity from environmental contamination. We are all living in a closed ecological system in which industrial chemicals and other neurotoxic hazards are accumulating and thus rendering increasing amounts of real estate uninhabitable.

The interplay of quadrants is also a salient feature in organophosphate-pesticide-related ADHD criteria. Organophosphate substances include a host of pesticides, among them the well-known insecticides malathion and parathion, and the more sinister weapons of chemical warfare commonly known as sirin and VX nerve agent. These agents are able to irreversibly disable the enzyme (acetylcholinesterase) that degrades excess amounts of the neurotransmitter acetylcholine in nerve synapses and are also able to attach to acetylcholine receptors in the synapse. When acetylcholine function is compromised, this in turn leads to a disrupted cellular response to dopamine, a neurotransmitter implicated in ADHD etiology (van Hienen, 2010). Exposure to organophosphates typically occurs through ingestion of residual pesticide contamination of fruits and vegetables, drinking water, and residential use of pesticides. As a reflection of lower-right quadrant involvement, organophosphate exposure can be a serious threat to individuals living near farms or farm workers, commonly immigrants, involved in maintaining and harvesting crops (Eskenazi, 2010; United States National Research Council cited in Bouchard et al., 2010). Although data are limited, studies investigating exposure to organophosphates in utero and in childhood have linked these substances to problems in attention and other neurodevelopmental abnormalities (Bouchard et al., 2010; Grandjean, Harari, Barr, & Debes, 2006; Marks et al., 2010).

**TOBACCO AND ALCOHOL EXPOSURE** The relationship between ADHD and prenatal exposure to a number of licit and illicit substances has been the focus of numerous investigations. Although results are varied, a large body of evidence coming from case-control studies points to an association between prenatal exposure to tobacco and ADHD symptoms (Linnet et al., 2003). Tobacco is particularly relevant to a discussion of exterior-collective influences on ADHD in that a clear association exists between socioeconomic status and tobacco use (Centers for Disease Control and Prevention, 2011), and tobacco advertising often targets lower-income racial and ethnic populations (Stoddard, Johnson, Boley-Cruz, & Sussman, 1997).

In one tobacco-related case-control study, children with an ADHD diagnosis were 2.1 times more likely to have mothers who smoked during pregnancy (Mick et al., 2002), while in another study, offspring of mothers who smoked during pregnancy were four times more likely to manifest characteristics of ADHD than control subjects (Milberger, Biederman, Faraone, & Jones, 1998). Likewise, a large-scale retrospective study of over 4700 children, ages 4 to 15, showed an ADHD-adjusted odds ratio of 2.5 for prenatal tobacco exposure (Braun, Kahn, Froehlich, Auinger, & Lanphear, 2006).

Recent studies investigating the link between prenatal tobacco exposure and ADHD have focused on the role of genes in children's vulnerability to ADHD. Findings to date offer convincing evidence that certain dopamine transporter alleles, particularly in males with the severe combined hyperactive-inattentive subtype ADHD, are associated with an increased risk of the developing infant suffering the ADHD-related effects of tobacco exposure (Becker et al., 2008; Neuman et al., 2007).

Alcohol consumption during pregnancy has exterior-collective influences that somewhat resemble the patterns observed in tobacco use in that two of the major risk factors for prenatal alcohol exposure are poverty and homelessness (Bhuvaneswar, Chang, Epstein, & Stern, 2007). Considerable research has been designed to uncover an association between ADHD in children and maternal alcohol consumption during pregnancy. Although the evidence supporting this association is not as well established as the evidence for prenatal tobacco use, some research does suggest that prenatal alcohol exposure is predictive of ADHD in children and that, as mentioned, genetics play a role in determining the vulnerability of the developing fetus to maternal alcohol use (Knopik et al., 2006; Mick et al., 2002). In one case-control study, children with an ADHD diagnosis were 2.5 times more likely than controls to have a mother who consumed alcohol while pregnant (Mick et al., 2002). A number of studies, several of which are included in a review by Linnet et al. (2003), failed to find an association between ADHD and maternal prenatal alcohol consumption.

## Individual-Interior (Upper-Left) Perspectives

The many social and emotional difficulties associated with ADHD behavior can have a deleterious effect on the self-development of the child and often result in descriptions of self and events that are frequently characterized by negative attribution patterns (Hoza, Waschbusch, Pelham, Molina, & Milich, 2000). Although we embrace the notion that self-identities of children are socially, biologically, and culturally constructed and can hence be traced to phenomena occurring in other quadrants, in this section we will heuristically consider the enduring view of self to be a reflection of the interior-individual (UL) quadrant.

**SELF-PERCEPTIONS** In a qualitative study exploring adolescents' experience with ADHD as it related to their sense of self-experience, individuals were more "antagonistic and negative than researchers expected" (Krueger & Kendall, 2001, p. 64). Descriptions of self were entangled within an ADHD-defined self, even prior to a diagnosis, and focused upon inadequacy in girls and upon anger and defiance in boys. The researchers identified the self-development processes of these adolescents as deeply enmeshed in the negative attitudes and stigmatizing beliefs surrounding the disorder: "I've had pretty negative thoughts about myself and ADHD since I was little, especially when people are nagging me about things when I mess up. I try to do things right, but I can't. I think it's the way I'll always be" (p. 66).

The impact that ADHD has on a child's inner experience was also explored in a qualitative study that looked at the self-perceptions of 39 children (Kendall, Hatton, Beckett, & Leo, 2003). Many of these children described ADHD in terms of how badly they felt much of the time. Feeling sad, mad, frustrated, and ashamed were common themes throughout the interviews, indicating that these responses were most often a result of the learning and behavioral problems they were experiencing. The children's identity was deeply intertwined with ADHD, what the researchers labeled an "ADHD-identity" (p. 122).

The children's narratives in the previously mentioned studies bring into awareness the impact of history, sociology and culture on the developing self, that is, the development of self as a "self-as-a-story-told" (Benson, 2001, p. xi), in which the narratives are constructed upon the "repertoires of cultural-historical options" (p. xi). Kendall et al. (2003) identified differences in identity formation between children who considered ADHD an illness and those who viewed ADHD simply as a dimension of self. Those who thought of ADHD as "just the way you are" (p. 123) considered it a relatively normal part of their identity. Children who generally viewed ADHD as a disease reported difficulties with adjustment, living with the disorder, and identifying coping strategies. The formalized diagnosis through authority figures, usually a physician or teacher, created the reality of ADHD in these children's lives. Thus ADHD became, for these children, a salient feature of their self-definition.

Racial and ethnic differences have been found in self-identify formation among African American, Hispanic, and White children diagnosed with ADHD. African American children described themselves with the word "bad," while Hispanic children used the word "trouble." In contrast, White children with ADHD referred to themselves as "weird" or "whacko" (Kendall et al., 2003).

**TEMPERAMENT** Temperament could arguably be situated in multiple quadrants because it is a medium through which we process, experience, and respond to our outer-world interface. For heuristic purposes we are situating it under the heading of individual-interior phenomena with the caveat that temperament can be located at the beginning, middle, or end of causal chains involving other quadrants.

The function of temperament is to mediate transactions with the outer world and act as a substrate for inner experience. A child's temperament consistently predicts his or her cognitive and emotional skills in negotiating the social environment. In the context of ADHD etiology, child temperament may not only interfere with the development of regulatory and attention capacities (Johnston & Mash, 2001), it may also be an important force in shaping the internal experience of children as they transact with their particular idiographic ecologies. For example, children who are highly active, irritable, difficult to soothe, and resistant to environmental change will not only have an inner experience fraught with negative emotions, they are also challenging to parent (Campbell, 1990). In this case, difficult temperament may exacerbate parents' difficulties in reading their child's needs and responding to those needs in a sensitive manner. Ultimately, the parental response will likely result in a negative internal experience for the child already experiencing some level of dysregulation. Such temperamental challenges may also make parents less likely to engage with the child out of fear of having to negotiate unpleasant and emotionally challenging interactions.

Numerous temperament-related traits have been shown to affect the neuropsychological functions that comprise emotional responses central to incentive-motivation systems. Among these traits, approach and withdrawal have been salient in ADHD research. Approach traits, elements of the behavioral activation system (Gray, 1991), have been associated with reward-response abnormalities seen in ADHD. ADHD diagnosed children with reward-response abnormalities have difficulty in tolerating delay (Sonuga-Barke, 2003), trouble learning from mistakes (Johansen, Aase, Meyer, & Sagvolden, 2002), and a tendency to favor immediate over delayed (and larger) rewards (Solanto et al., 2001).

Withdrawal traits are elements of the behavioral inhibition system (Gray, 1991) that influence effortful control. They are temperamental dimensions of self-regulation involving suppression of the dominant response. Children with intact behavioral inhibition system function are able to resist impulses in order to plan and execute more adaptive behaviors in response to stimuli. The traits associated with withdrawal affect focus, attention capacities, inhibition of impulses, and executive functions such as problem solving and managing negative emotions (Rothbart, 2003). These withdrawal traits also affect the development of self-control and punishment-related responding, rendering a child insensitive to impending punishment. Thus children with withdrawal traits develop inappropriate behaviors characterized by impulsiveness and poorly regulated and socially inappropriate behavior. The withdrawal trait has been shown to be elevated in a range of psychopathological conditions, including ADHD, in which difficulty coping with stress and high anxiety are salient features (Nigg et al., 2002).

Studies on the impact of withdrawal on the quality of the parent–child relationships have revealed problems in the realms of positive social exchanges, anticipatory guidance, monitoring of child activities, and the affective expressiveness of the parent (Greenberg, Speltz, & DeKlyen, 1993). Also, irritable, impulsive children are at risk for aggressive and antisocial acts (Sanson, Hemphill, & Smart, 2004). As the child reacts with defiance and disobedience, parents become increasingly stressed (Coplan, Bowler, & Cooper, 2003). A bidirectional relationship is thus formed between the child's difficulties and negative parenting, which promotes the child's negative, impulsive, and hyperactive style. Hence, the affective quality of the parent–child relationship may establish a developmental trajectory that leads transactionally to ADHD-type behavior. Conversely, children whose parents are responsive, sensitive, and who facilitate the development of self-regulatory capacities by providing a nurturing and responsive environment may attenuate or even terminate ADHD symptoms, even if these children have a biological predisposition for the disorder (Johnston & Mash, 2001).

## ETIOLOGY: SUMMARY AND CONCLUSION

The sizeable number of empirically and otherwise supported models of ADHD etiology, with compelling representation in all four quadrants, underscores the importance of an Integral analysis of conditions of "psychopathology." The breadth of etiological explanations for ADHD—ranging from genetic and epigenetic mechanisms; environmental toxins; and prenatal stress and tobacco exposure to attachment problems in early childhood; parental psychopathology; turbulent family life; and cultural demands, at odds with masculine drives, for measured responses and impulse suppression—while of interest in and of themselves, speak to the need for assessments that distinguish specific forms of the disorder from its many potential variants, and interventions that are tailored to the particular etiological mechanisms responsible for disorder genesis in a given individual. As much of the remainder of this chapter reveals, *ADHD assessment and intervention too often targets behaviors of the disorder rather than its root causes*. This symptom-focused approach is often of considerable value; however, in many cases, it is clear that assessment tools and intervention strategies need to be subject to the same critical quadratic analysis that is applied to etiology. Until such an analysis is implemented, root causes will remain unaddressed while assessment is largely informed by variations on DSM criteria and intervention is aimed at eradicating symptoms through pharmacological and behavioral strategies.

## ADHD COMORBIDITY

As the analysis of interior-individual phenomena illustrates, the internal world of the child with ADHD is fraught with anxiety, anger, conflict, isolation, and sadness. It is not surprising, therefore, that children diagnosed with ADHD commonly have additional psychological challenges complicating their clinical picture. The wide range of comorbid disorders that frequently accompany ADHD raises important questions whose answers hold keys to effective prevention and treatment of the various presentations that the disorder commonly displays in complex, real-world settings. See Figure 9.1.

| UPPER-LEFT (UL): INTERIOR-INDIVIDUAL | UPPER-RIGHT (UR): EXTERIOR-INDIVIDUAL |
|---|---|
| • Self-development processes enmeshed in negative attitudes and beliefs surrounding the disorder<br>• Negative self-perceptions<br>• Difficulty with adjustments<br>• Temperament traits and related compromise of emotional responses and self-regulation<br>• Heightened anxiety<br>• Low self-efficacy<br>• Susceptible to isolation and sadness | • Genetic linkages, associations, and endophenotypes<br>• Epigenetic mechanisms<br>• Frontostriatal circuit abnormalities<br>• Neurotransmission<br>• Prenatal environment<br>• Difficulties at birth |
| **LOWER-LEFT (LL): INTERIOR-COLLECTIVE** | **LOWER-RIGHT (LR): EXTERIOR-COLLECTIVE** |
| • Labels used in social positioning<br>• Culturally legitimized expectations in school, home, and community<br>• Social control of diversity-related normative behaviors<br>• Attachment patterns that create interpersonal challenges<br>• Learning challenges<br>• Experiences with family life<br>• Experiences of competing paradigms of family discipline<br>• Experience of racial and ethnic overrepresentation<br>• Waning of the moral authority of adults<br>• Challenges in social interactions and friendship-making<br>• Medicalization of ADHD behaviors seen in need of remediation | • Neurotoxin exposure<br>• Dietary intake<br>• Environmental contaminants<br>• Maternal tobacco and alcohol exposure during pregnancy<br>• Low SES<br>• Racial minority status<br>• Poor conflict resolution skills<br>• Parental mental disorders |

**FIGURE 9.1** A Quadratic View of the Etiology of ADHD

Comorbidity is a particularly important topic in any discussion of ADHD because, as Gillberg et al. (2004) suggest, depending on the characteristics of the sample, comorbidity is present in 60–100% of individuals diagnosed with ADHD. The most common ADHD comorbid disorders include the so-called "disruptive behavior" disorders—namely, Oppositional Defiant Disorder (ODD) and Conduct Disorder (CD); internalizing disorders related to depression and/or anxiety; Learning Disorders, Substance Abuse and Dependency Disorders; and Tourette's Disorder. Although a thorough discussion of underlying mechanisms in these comorbidity patterns is beyond the scope of this chapter, there has been some compelling speculation suggesting that ADHD with disruptive behavior represents a form of ADHD that is distinct from forms of the disorder accompanied by internalizing disorders and that failure to diagnostically separate them represents an error that is an expected consequence of a system of classification that does not consider etiology (Douthit & Donnelly, 2010; Jensen, Hinshaw, Kraemer et al., 2001).

## Disruptive Behaviors

Among the most notable ADHD comorbid diagnoses are so-called "externalizing" disorders characterized by disruptive behavior and known in the language of DSM as ODD and CD (APA, 2000). ODD is typically identified in young children and is characterized mainly by noncompliance, opposition, tantrums, and interpersonally provocative, aggressive behaviors. Once established in early childhood and grade school, the less serious disruptive behaviors of ODD often lead to the more grave behaviors associated with CD, a disorder characterized by socially deviant acts such as stealing, lying, fire setting, truancy from school, interpersonal violence, and property destruction (APA, 2000; Campbell, 1990; McGee, Partridge, Williams, & Silva, 1991; Richman, Stevenson, & Graham, 1982).

In young children ranging in age from 3 to 8 years, there is significant correlation between ADHD and behaviors of noncompliance, opposition, tantrums, and interpersonally provocative behaviors that increase the probability of fighting or other forms of aggression (Campbell, 1990). Aggression and parental reports of externalizing behaviors are relatively stable from toddlerhood over time, and when the symptoms reach a diagnosable level in school-age children and adolescents, these individuals become relatively resistant to treatment (Campbell, Shaw, & Gilliom, 2000). In a study of preschool-age children, Wilens et al. (2002) reported that disruptive behaviors, meeting the full diagnostic criteria for ODD, occurred in 59% of children with ADHD. Moreover, the same study found that 23% of the same children with ADHD had comorbidities that included the more extreme CD. Notably, parenting practices characterized by coercive interaction styles, inconsistent discipline, and lack of parental involvement have been correlated with ODD and CD (Pfiffner, McBurnett, Rathouz, & Judice, 2005).

Although the causes for the comorbidities of ADHD, ODD, and CD are not fully understood, the correlations among these externalizing disorders are significant, perhaps reflecting some overlap in the symptoms used to describe them (Greenberg et al., 1993). Other interpretations of the data concerning comorbidity with disruptive behavior lend themselves particularly well to an Integral analysis. For example, intersubjective communication patterns (LL) that typically arise in families of children with ADHD may foster negative attention-seeking behaviors on the part of the child. When the primary connection between parents or caregivers and their ADHD child reliably fall into a cycle of disruption and disapproval (LL), ADHD-diagnosed children may not only feed this cycle to ensure the ongoing existence of the attachment, but they may also unwittingly foster a self-identity of deviance (UL). This deviance identity may, in turn, compromise certain developmental lines, including the development of healthy self-schema and moral development as the child is increasingly wedded to deviance as a coping mechanism, and cognitive development as children are alienated from the community of engaged learners in the classroom and at home.

Snyder, Reid, and Patterson (2003) reported that the breakdown in parenting skills played a causal role in oppositional, defiant, and aggressive behaviors seen in children. A more broadly reaching risk-factor model for the etiology of disruptive behavior patterns in early childhood proposed by Greenberg et al. (1993) includes a number of salient risk factors, such as difficult temperament, child biologic vulnerability, poor parental management strategies, family adversity, and parent psychopathology. Consistent with the Greenberg et al. model, Pfiffner et al. (2005) found that impoverished attachment, operationalized as a mother's lack of warmth and interpersonal involvement with her child, was associated with an increased risk of a diagnosis of ADHD comorbid with CD when compared with healthier attachment relationships.

Children with ADHD alone are clearly distinguishable from children with combined ADHD-CD in several different ways. For example, an early study by Lahey et al. (1988) asserted that children with an ADHD-CD diagnosis are more likely to come from lower-socioeconomic backgrounds—a statistic that could have much to do with issues of privilege (LR) and cross-cultural misunderstanding (LL)—and are more likely to have a father with a history of aggression, incarceration, and persistent violation of laws (possible involvement of all or any of the quadrants) than children from control groups. The same study also linked the presence of CD symptoms to substance abuse and antisocial personality traits in the father, and antisocial personality traits, substance abuse, or somatization disorder in mothers (Lahey et al., 1988). A more recent study by Brook, Brook, Zhang, and Koppel (2010) demonstrated a clear association between CD symptoms in ADHD children and Substance Use Disorders in adulthood.

Children diagnosed with a combination of ADHD and CD, when compared with children diagnosed with ADHD alone, are more likely to have learning difficulties, including higher rates of Reading Disorder and impaired verbal, visual-spatial, and visual-motor integration skills. It is not clear, however, what the unique contribution of the combined ADHD-CD pairing is to these cognitive and sensory impairments given that CD alone is correlated with this particular cluster of learning challenges. Thus the notion that ADHD-CD diagnosed individuals represent a unique subtype is neither supported nor refuted by these patterns of phenotype expression.

## Internalizing Disorders

A well-developed body of ADHD comorbidity literature consistently asserts that ADHD is associated with both Mood and Anxiety Disorders. In a review of the literature on the co-occurrence of ADHD and Mood Disorder, Pliszka (1998) underscores the challenges inherent in documenting internalized comorbidities, which have a symptom profile that, unlike the profile of CD, is not directly observable. Child reports and parent reports, when viewed separately, often give a piecemeal profile of symptoms, leaving researchers and clinicians with the burden of having to decide whether a legitimate diagnosis can be made from multiple sources of input concerning children's overall cluster of symptoms (Pliszka, 1998).

Major Depressive Disorder (MDD) in children is characterized by both the DSM-5 criteria for MDD as well as symptoms that are unique to child and adolescent populations. In keeping with the DSM definition of MDD (APA, 2013), children may be sad or irritable and take little pleasure in things that would otherwise be pleasurable for them. They may also have appetite changes, fatigue, problems with sleep, and feelings of worthlessness, guilt, and suicidal ideation. Unlike their adult counterparts, children may show changes in their performance in school, refuse to go to school, act in aggressive and antisocial ways, and have stomachaches, headaches, and other somatic complaints. Mania also manifests in distinctive ways in children. Children with mania may be extremely irritable with moods that are explosive and extremely disruptive to family and other relationships. In less severe cases, the symptoms of mania more closely match the DSM-5 description (APA, 2013) and include an increase in goal-directed activity, thrill-seeking, poor judgment, decreased need for sleep, and heightened energy level (Spencer et al., 2007).

In a review of the literature on comorbid ADHD and MDD, Pliszka (1998) reported prevalence estimates ranging from 9–38%, and Spencer et al. (2007) reported that in prospective studies, 4-year follow-up revealed that children with an ADHD diagnosis had a baseline comorbid depression of 29% that jumped to 45% at an average age of 15. The same prospective studies revealed that children who received a baseline MDD diagnosis were more likely than children without MDD to have compromised psychosocial and interpersonal functioning, and to have higher rates of hospitalization. A similar increase in frequency was noted with mania. At baseline, mania was noted in 11% of children (at a mean age of 11), and 4 years later, 23% of children were diagnosed with mania. As with MDD, children with a mania diagnosis had severe difficulties with psychosocial functioning and were more likely to be hospitalized than children with ADHD alone.

In a review of ADHD comorbidity, Pliszka (1998) estimated that 25% of children diagnosed with ADHD meet the criteria for an Anxiety Disorder. This figure of 25% represents an increase of 10–20% over what would be expected in the general population. In a review of the literature, Schatz and Rostain (2006) found that when ADHD-diagnosed children were compared with ADHD-and-comorbid-anxiety-diagnosed children, the latter were more likely to display aggression and have lower self-esteem. Schatz and Rostain also report that data from the large Multimodal Treatment Study of ADHD suggested that ADHD-diagnosed children with comorbid anxiety tend to be more inattentive than impulsive and have less disordered conduct. Externalizing symptoms have much to do with how children with ADHD are identified and subsequently treated; hence, the lack of externalizing symptoms may increase the chances that a child's need for intervention will be overlooked.

## Substance Use

Studies exploring the link between substance use and ADHD have consisted of a spectrum of substances including tobacco, alcohol, and illicit drugs. The outcomes of these studies show a clear and enduring association between substance use and a diagnosis of ADHD. Collecting retrospective accounts from adults and observations of youth, it was determined that "juveniles with ADHD are at increased risk for cigarette smoking and substance use during adolescence . . . [and that] ADHD youth disproportionately become involved with cigarettes, alcohol, and then drugs" (Spencer et al., 2007, p. 77). It was also determined that, independent of comorbidity, individuals diagnosed with ADHD were more likely to have a prolonged substance abuse disorder when compared with non-ADHD controls (Spencer et al., 2007). It should be noted that although the association between ADHD and substance use was shown to be independent of comorbidity, certain ADHD comorbidities, most notably Conduct, Major Depressive, and Anxiety Disorders, demonstrated particularly high rates of tobacco use (Milberger, Biederman, Faraone, Chen, & Jones, 1997). It is also noteworthy that a significant correlation was found between tobacco use and drug abuse (Milberger et al., 1997).

### Learning Disorders

The prevalence of Learning Disorders among children with ADHD varies with the actual definition of Learning Disorder (LD) that is used to identify research subjects. For example, Lambert and Sandoval (1980) suggest an approach that compares outcomes on standardized tests of math and verbal achievement with the scores on standardized tests of intelligence. Another approach is to simply designate as LD all individuals falling 1.5–2.0 standard deviations below the mean for standardized tests of achievement (Barkley, 1990). Finally, Rutter, Tizard, and Whitmore (1970) calculated expected performance outcomes from a regression equation generated from general population data looking at performance, intelligence quotient, and chronological age. In a review of LD comorbidity where LD includes disabilities in math, spelling, or reading, Pliszka (1998) notes that more liberal estimates of LD generate prevalence figures of 40–60% of ADHD children, whereas more conservative figures identify 20–30%. In addition to their performance difficulties on achievement and intelligence tests, LD-diagnosed children have lower grades in school, are more likely to be required to repeat grades, and are more likely to be placed in special classes (Barkley, 2006a).

### Tourette's Disorder

Tourette's disorder is a hereditary syndrome involving both motor and vocal tics that last for more than 1 year (APA, 2000). Although only 7% of ADHD individuals are simultaneously diagnosed with Tourette's Disorder (Barkley, 2006a), Erenberg (2006), in a review dating back to 1980, found that in populations of clinic-referred children with Tourette's Disorder, the occurrence of ADHD ranged from 35–95%. There has been some speculation that the use of stimulant medications in ADHD children may actually be a causative factor in Tic Disorder. However, Erenberg (2006), based on a review of the literature, concluded that when the group data were analyzed, there was no significant association between stimulant medication and tics.

## ASSESSMENT OF ADHD IN CHILDREN

ADHD is a disorder that reflects deficits and/or delays in a child's behavioral, cognitive, and emotional abilities. Assessing ADHD in children is a comprehensive process that includes current functioning, the history of difficulties, and the degree of impairment these ADHD-related problems cause in the child's life. More specifically, the assessment of ADHD should take into account important aspects of the disorder that include: (1) the consideration that ADHD is regarded as a biopsychosocial disorder, and that assessment should therefore be broad-based; (2) assessment can vary based upon the age and developmental level of the child; (3) symptoms of ADHD may present differently in children depending on the context; and (4) the disorder manifestations impart a variety of meanings across environments and are perceived by informants through lenses that include culture, social positioning, and psychosocial history (Barkley & Edwards, 2006; Pliszka & the AACAP Work Group on Quality Issues, 2007).

As discussed earlier, ADHD often exists with other disorders. Over 40% of children diagnosed with ADHD have at least one other psychiatric disorder that significantly impairs their social, emotional, and cognitive functioning (Barkley, 2006a). Given this high rate of co-occurrence, assessment must distinguish ADHD from other disorders and determine if the criteria that are outlined in the DSM-5 confirm the diagnosis of ADHD. Although the primary characteristics of ADHD are easy to observe, it is often difficult to differentiate the diagnostic features of other disorders that may mirror the behaviors characterizing ADHD. *Not all children who are inattentive, hyperactive, distracted, or exhibit less-than-optimal decision making have ADHD.* These ADHD-like behaviors could exist for a number of reasons, for example, another psychological disorder such an anxiety or mood disorders, decreased motivation, emotional disturbances, frustration, or a reaction to family stress and dysfunction. In many instances, however, the symptoms of another disorder exist in addition to ADHD, rather than to its exclusion (Barkley, 2006a).

A broad-based assessment is often conducted by a team of professionals working in conjunction with the parents of the child with ADHD. Generally, numerous professionals are involved in the assessment process, including, but not limited to, physicians, clinical and school psychologists, counselors, clinical social workers, learning specialists, and educators. Members of the assessment team can each address unique aspects of the child's symptoms. Parents usually initiate an evaluation through their child's school or a clinical setting in the community. Assessment is usually not expeditious or clear-cut as there is no single psychological or neurological test for ADHD. A thorough assessment generally includes the collection of comprehensive behavioral data across multiple settings and multiple informants, and involves interviews, rating scales, observations, and direct assessment of the child's behavior.

## Interviews

Interviews are used to obtain information about a child's specific problems and how the child performs in real-life settings. Information needs to be obtained about the child's challenges and strengths, and his or her social, academic, developmental, and medical history. This information is ideally provided by multiple informants, including parents, caregivers, teachers, and the child. Parents, caregivers and teachers are valuable sources of information regarding the child's functioning in home and school settings. Children are not always aware of, or able to describe, their difficult behaviors, so interviews with parents and teachers can generally help to generate a more complete data set than can be gleaned from interviewing the child undergoing assessment (Smith, Barkley, & Shapiro, 2006). It is important, nonetheless, to bear in mind that children with ADHD-like behaviors often have complex profiles and that many of the problems emanating from the various Integral quadrants are mediated in one way or another through interactions with parents, caregivers, and/or teachers in troubled schools. The astute practitioner will thus critically consider all available data and will make every effort to construct a comprehensive picture of the ecology of child.

Both structured and semistructured interviews with informants, when combined, offer an ecologically valid, reliable, and efficient way to collect information about the frequency, intensity, and severity of the child's troublesome behaviors (Barkley & Edwards, 2006). The most widely used structured interview instruments, with sound psychometric properties, are the Diagnostic Interview for Children and Adolescents-IV, (DICA-IV) and the Diagnostic Interview Schedule for Children (DISC) (Barkley & Edwards, 2006). These instruments offer a reliable and efficient way to collect information regarding the 18 ADHD symptoms listed in the DSM-5 and provide information about the child's functional impairments across multiple settings. Semistructured interviews are conducted with a fairly open framework that allows for a wide scope of discussion and the potential for rich data. Direct questions about parents' perceptions of and reactions to the child are recommended because these are central to the child's behavioral patterns in relationship to the environment. In addition to serving a diagnostic purpose, semistructured interviews can help the clinician understand parent–child interactions, family relationships, how the child's behavior is managed, and the degree of distress the child's problems create for the family (Barkley & Edwards, 2006).

Interviews with teachers can be an indispensable source of information about the child's difficulties in the school environment. Although parents may understand that their child experiences difficulties in the school setting, they may underestimate the severity of the problem (Mitsis, McKay, Schultz, Newcorn, & Halperin, 2000). Teachers can further clarify how the child's problems affect academic progress, classroom behavior, and relationships with peers, and the conditions that may contribute to these problems. Furthermore, teachers can provide information that may be useful in planning interventions by identifying strategies, practices, or interventions that may have been used successfully to address the child's problems in school. Teachers also have a central role in making accommodations in the classroom environment to provide structure, support, and help with academic work.

Children with ADHD are at a higher risk of being identified as having a learning disability. The rates of learning disabilities vary greatly in children with ADHD, with an overall range of 15–40% having been reported (Rucklidge & Tannock, 2002). Children diagnosed with ADHD have the rights to special evaluation as well as educational and related services as a part of the Individuals with Disabilities Education Act (IDEA) under the categories of learning disabilities or behavior/emotional disturbance (IDEA, 2004). Even without the diagnosis of a learning disability, children with ADHD are more likely to experience difficulties with school tasks in organization, scheduling and planning, academic skill, control of their activity level, mood, and self-esteem issues that interfere with their daily academic tasks, handwriting, and the ability to sustain careful approaches to school work (Barkley & Edwards, 2006). Teachers can be tremendously beneficial in the identification of problems in school that may be attributed to inattention, distractibility, and/or hyperactivity.

## Rating Scales

Rating scales and checklists are popular tools for assessing the symptoms of ADHD and providing information about the degree to which the child's problems deviate from well-established norms. Rating scales and checklists are convenient and require little time and effort to administer and score. There are numerous rating scales for parents and teachers. Some of these are broad in scope and identify ADHD as well as other childhood disorders, whereas others are narrow-band scales that focus on the assessment of specific symptoms (e.g., disruptive behavior, social skills, peer rating, parent stress). Most of the rating scales provide standardized scores on a number of factors related to attention span, hyperactivity, self-regulation, social skills, disruptive behaviors, mood, and anxiety. Three widely employed, clinically sound, broad-range scales that have versions for both parents and teachers are the Behavioral Assessment System for Children-Second Edition (BASC-2; Reynolds & Kamphaus, 2004), the Child Behavior Checklist (CBCL/6-18; Achenbach & Rescorla, 2001), and the Conners' Rating Scales-Revised (Conners, 2001).

## Observation

It is generally useful to observe the child in multiple settings and on different days to obtain enough data to understand the situational and behavioral manifestations of ADHD. Direct observation of the child in naturalistic settings such as multiple classrooms, interacting with peers, or in the home can be extremely useful to obtain a comprehensive understanding of the child's difficulties. Behavioral observations can provide the clinician with information about the frequency, duration and intensity of problem behaviors, and the relationships the child has with others (Forehand & McMahon, 1981). These observations can also generate data essential to the practitioner's understanding of the dynamics interacting to generate the symptom profile of the child. Information about situations or consequences that exacerbate or ameliorate academic and behavioral problems can be extremely valuable for assessment and planning interventions.

One liability related to the use of direct observation is that it can be time consuming and expensive. An alternative observation-based assessment procedure, which can still be used in a naturalistic setting, is an observational coding system. Coding systems enable clinicians to conduct observations in a reliable and valid manner, and to identify patterns of interaction as well as specific child behaviors (Forehand & McMahon, 1981). A clinician can develop a coding system that quantifies parent–child interactions, the positive and negative aspects of parenting skills, and child behavior problems. Generally, an interval sampling procedure is used to record these behaviors during a specified observational period. In addition, the clinician's office may serve as a convenient observational setting to observe parent–child interactions, specific behaviors during test administration, and the child's learning strategies.

## Other Sources of Assessment Data

To refine the assessment of ADHD, psychological tests and continuous-performance tests are often used as "objective" measures that can supplement interviews, rating scales, and observations of the child (Gordon, Barkley, & Lovett, 2006). Standardized tests of intelligence and academic achievement can provide useful information in identifying cognitive factors that contribute to a child's academic difficulties. Overall cognitive ability can be assessed with standardized intelligence tests that measure the child's use of language, reasoning, memory, and perception. Achievement tests can examine the child's weaknesses in subject areas such as reading, written language, and arithmetic. Both kinds of tests are helpful in determining the child's baseline of expected performance.

Continuous-performance tests are specific tests that evaluate the child's degree of impulsivity, and sustained and selective attention. Computerized continuous-performance tests (CPTs) are widely used and require the child to respond in a specific way to stimuli presented on a computer screen (Gordon et al., 2006). The stimuli can be sounds, letters, symbols, or shapes and can vary in the speed and order of presentation. The child is instructed to respond to a certain number of patterned stimuli. The stimuli are presented repeatedly over a period of time thus requiring the child to maintain focus. Among the more commonly used CPTs are the Integrated Visual and Auditory CPT (Sandford & Turner, 2000), Test of Variables of Attention (T.O.V.A.) (Greenberg, Kindschi, Dupuy, & Hughes, 2007), Conners Continuous Performance Test-Second Edition (CPT-II) (Conners, 1995), and the Gordon Diagnostic System (GDS) (Gordon et al., 2006).

Neuropsychological tests represent a battery of instruments that have been useful in research settings but have not demonstrated reliability in ADHD assessment (Pliszka & the AACAP Work Group on Quality Issues, 2007). Neuropsychological tests measure and compare actual cognitive functioning in different domains. Tests that measure neuropsychological functions can be particularly useful in identifying deficits in executive functioning, but as Pliszka and the AACAP Work Group on Quality Issues assert, not all individuals diagnosed with ADHD have executive function impairment, and the utility of such testing is thus limited.

Finally, medical evaluations are necessary to differentiate symptoms of ADHD from other medical conditions, assess conditions that may require medical management, and determine if any medical or developmental factors exist that may influence the child's treatment plan (Barkley & Edwards, 2006).

## TREATMENTS

### Introduction

Devising a comprehensive, Integrally informed treatment plan for individuals diagnosed with ADHD is often a thorny process resulting in a treatment regimen that is an amalgamation of interventions. In many cases, these interventions reflect multiple etiologies and span multiple quadrants. Likewise, attempting to assign a given intervention to a specific Integral quadrant is often fraught with a logic that is decidedly contestable. For example, although pharmacological interventions would seem to have a clear place in the upper-right quadrant, the reader may rightly question whether a stimulant medication is actually helping to address an inherent, biological disorder or placate a teacher (LL) unable to accommodate adaptive behaviors in a disruptive child that are reflective of a challenging home environment (LR). Hence, in spite of the clarity and simplicity that might come from organizing ADHD treatments using the Integral quadrant heuristic, such an organization would not reflect the modal complexity inherent in *in vivo* practices. We will thus refrain from assigning interventions to a given quadrant within the text and refer the reader interested in speculating as to

| UPPER-LEFT (UL): INTERIOR-INDIVIDUAL | UPPER-RIGHT (UR): EXTERIOR-INDIVIDUAL |
|---|---|
| • Discovery and acceptance of differences<br>• Healthy coping skills<br>• Mindfulness/meditation | • Pharmacotherapy<br>• Cognitive-behavioral approaches<br>• Combined pharmacotherapy and behavioral therapy |
| **LOWER-LEFT (LL): INTERIOR-COLLECTIVE** | **LOWER-RIGHT (LR): EXTERIOR-COLLECTIVE** |
| • Family and peer relations<br>• Awareness of how assimilation, language barriers, and views of the disorder impact development and functioning<br>• Building healthy interpersonal relationships | • School-wide and classroom systems of supports<br>• Supports that wrap around to home and community<br>• Family systems approaches<br>• Increased awareness of how neighborhood, community, and school variables affect child development<br>• Lead and other toxic substance abatement<br>• Remediation of skill deficits<br>• Parent training<br>• Supports and services to improve school performance |

**FIGURE 9.2** A Quadratic View of ADHD Interventions

the Integral nature of ADHD interventions to Figure 9.2, where we have attempted, with some hesitation, to assign treatment modalities or aspects of treatment modalities to a specific location within the quadrant heuristic.

## Psychopharmacological Interventions

> *. . . [T]he National Institute of Mental Health (NIMH) has just started an unprecedented study on the use of medications to treat ADHD in preschoolers (three-year-olds). This is the single most important moral question the scientific community will face in the next decade. The ethics of genetically altered tomatoes, health care rationing, organ transplants, prescription drug reimbursements, and even assisted suicide are just a walk in the park compared to the ethics of exposing a developing brain to a psychotropic drug.*
>
> Leo, 2002, p. 52

Although much of the lexicon of psychopharmacology is outside the awareness of the general public, the most common, current-day pharmaceutical intervention for ADHD transcends professional and lay boundaries. The notion that the stimulant Ritalin is one of the first lines of defense in the treatment of ADHD is a well-known fact of popular culture and is often used in satirical humor relating to "out-of-control" children, adolescents, and adults (e.g., "He must have skipped his Ritalin this morning!"). After the introduction of Attention Deficit Disorder in the 1980 publication of the DSM-III, an era was spawned in which school lunch time marked a daily ritual during which many boys, and a few less girls, would form a line outside the school nurse's office to get their midday dose of Ritalin. The rapid ascent of stimulant use, beginning in the 1980s, has persisted to the present day as a centerpiece of the intervention profile for children and adults diagnosed with ADHD. Since that time, stimulants have been joined by several other classes of psychotropic drugs, including norepinephrine-reuptake inhibitors, and sympatholytic $\alpha_2$ and $\alpha_{2A}$ adrenergic agonists. Each of these categories of pharmacological intervention is described in more detail in the following subsections.

**STIMULANTS** The advent of stimulant use in the treatment of disruptive behavior actually began by happenstance many years prior to the post-1980 surge in attention deficit diagnoses. In 1937, Charles Bradley, treating a group of hyperactive children for complaints of headache, fortuitously discovered that the newly synthesized stimulant, Benzedrine, while having no analgesic value, did a remarkable job of subduing the hyperactive tendencies in these children (Whitaker, 2010). Although Bradley's discovery did not translate into immediate widespread use of stimulants to treat hyperactivity and other disruptive behaviors in children, it set the stage for its burgeoning use in the 1980s and 1990s. Presently, stimulants are the most widely used medications for the treatment of ADHD symptoms (National Resource Center on ADHD, 2011). The Centers for Disease Control reported in 2007 that approximately 1 in 23 children between the ages of 4 and 17 was receiving stimulant medication (Whitaker, 2010).

Stimulants, which have been subjected to hundreds of randomized controlled trials (RCTs), consistently demonstrate their ability to control many of the symptoms of ADHD (Pliszka, 2007). In Swanson et al.'s (1993) landmark "review of reviews," short-term stimulant-generated improvements were found in dozens of studies involving subjects ranging in age from preschoolers to adults. Pliszka (2007) reports that of the 5899 patients receiving stimulant treatment in these RCTs, 65–75% saw improvement, albeit to widely varying degrees (National Resource Center on ADHD, 2011), in their symptoms. This improvement stood in contrast to the 4–30% of patients who were assigned to placebo groups. Based on their study, Swanson et al. (1993) offered a summary of the expected outcomes for children who were administered stimulant pharmacotherapy, which included: ability to control motor behaviors involved in overactivity, better ability to sustain attention, better ability to control the symptoms of impulsivity, more compliance, more sustained effort, less physical and verbal aggression, less negative interpersonal behavior, increased academic productivity, and increased accuracy in academic work.

Although the name "stimulant" evokes distressing images of hyperactive children being further aroused, the mechanism underlying the success of stimulant medications is related to their ability to activate dopaminergic pathways that are essential to attention, self-control, and a host of executive functions that are important for meeting the demands of contemporary schooling practices. Stimulants are based on various manipulations of the basic amphetamine molecule, which has served as a foundation for many psychoactive pharmaceuticals. Some of the most popular stimulant drugs used in the treatment of childhood ADHD include the brand names Ritalin, Dexedrine, and Adderall, known generically as methylphenidate, dextroamphetamine, and amphetamine/dextroamphetamine, respectively (Ingersoll & Rak, 2006). Other brand names of stimulants include Concerta, Metadate, Focalin, Dextrostat, Cylert, and the potentially addictive methamphetamine hydrochloride, whose brand name is Desoxyn (National Resource Center on ADHD, 2011). In recent decades, research and development in the pharmaceutical industry has expanded the available formulations of stimulants to include ample selections of both long- and short-acting options

(Pliszka, 2007). The longer-acting versions allow children and adolescents to avoid the often-stigmatizing midday dosing line at the school nurse's office that characterized earlier stimulant use.

The side effects attributable to stimulants can be distressing for both the child taking the drug and their caregivers. Side effects include headache, loss of appetite, trouble sleeping, mania, and a "let-down" effect that occurs as the drug is metabolized to below therapeutic levels. Two reviews (Faraone, Biederman, Morley, & Spencer, 2008; Poulton, 2005) assert that there is reason to believe that a stimulant drug regimen, particularly in the first 1 to 3 years of drug consumption, can lead to decrease in height gain relative to what would be expected in control groups.

Another disturbing side effect of stimulants was underscored by Herbert Rie (cited in Whitaker, 2010), who in 1987 conducted a double-blind study of Ritalin on 28 so-called "hyperactive" children. The following is his own accounting of his observations during that study:

> Children who were retrospectively confirmed to have been on active drug treatment appeared, at the times of evaluation, distinctly more bland or "flat" emotionally, lacking both the age-typical variety and frequency of emotional expression. They responded less, exhibited little or no initiative or spontaneity, offered little indication of either interest or aversion, showed virtually no curiosity, surprise, or pleasure, and seemed devoid of humor. Jocular comments and humorous situations passed unnoticed. In short, while on active drug treatment, the children were relatively but unmistakably affectless, humorless, and apathetic. (Rie, 1978, quoted in Whitaker, 2010, p. 223)

As Breggin (2001) and others assert, this reduced repertoire of behaviors, while imparting a compliance that is better suited to classroom decorum than previous behaviors, does not necessarily generate outcomes that prove to be a positive experience for the ADHD child. In Integral terms, it appears that children experience a "state" change that is somewhat dissociative in its essence, in which pleasure and spontaneity are suppressed.

Sleater, Ullmann, and von Neuman (1982), in an attempt to ascertain children's experiences with stimulant medication, gathered the opinions of 52 subjects. When asked about their experiences taking stimulants, the comments of these children included: "It makes me sad and I like to eat. I don't want to participate. I wouldn't talk or smile or anything. I don't want to play. Makes me feel strange. Like I was under hypnosis. Don't like myself" (p. 477). What is even more distressing is that there is evidence from animal studies that this state change may extend into adulthood. Rats treated with methylphenidate for only a 15-day period during preadolescence, and left undisturbed until they reached an age of 90 days, suffer effects that include anxiety, depression, and decreased response to natural (i.e., sugar) and drug (i.e., morphine) rewards (Bolaños et al., 2008). Although Bolaños and his group found that these effects could be somewhat mitigated with the administration of fluoxetine (i.e., Prozac), they underscore the urgent need for research into the long-term neurodevelopmental effects of stimulant medication.

**NONSTIMULANTS** Although stimulants, and methylphenidate in particular, are the first line of defense in ADHD pharmacotherapy (Zito et al., 2000), several other classes of medication have emerged as intervention alternatives to stimulants. Atomoxetine (brand name Strattera) is a norepinephrine-reuptake inhibitor that has been shown to be effective for managing the symptoms of ADHD in children, adolescents, and adults (Michelson et al., 2001, 2002, 2003). Atomoxetine may be of particular use in ADHD with comorbid anxiety (Geller et al., 2007) and/or tics (Allen et al., 2005). The Food and Drug Administration (2005) warns that atomoxetine carries the risk of liver toxicity and suicidal ideation, although these severe side effects are relatively uncommon. Other less severe side effects include insomnia, irritability, aggression, and dizziness (Ingersoll & Rak, 2006).

Atomoxetine is not the only alternative for treatment of ADHD with tics. Another class of pharmaceuticals, the alpha-agonists, has also shown promising results (Tourette's Syndrome Study Group, 2002). This particular group of sympatholytic compounds has been used elsewhere to treat blood pressure, Panic Disorder, various Anxiety Disorders, and Tourette's disorder. Included in this group are two closely related compounds, clonidine and guanfacine.

Children with comorbid ADHD and Major Depressive Disorder present a complicated picture. The Texas Children's Medication Algorithm Project (CMAP), which has formulated guidelines for the administration of ADHD medications, recommends assessing the severity of both the ADHD and the Major Depressive Disorder, and treating the more severe of the two (Pliszka, 2007). According to Pliszka, the algorithm suggests that if the ADHD is treated first and the Major Depressive Disorder subsides, no further treatment of the major depression is needed. If the major depression persists, an antidepressant or psychosocial intervention is recommended.

### Combining Psychopharmacological and Behavioral Interventions: Multimodal Studies

In 1992, the National Institute of Mental Health engaged six well-established ADHD scholars and their respective research teams to participate in a landmark, multisite clinical ADHD intervention trial known as the Multimodal Treatment of Attention-Deficit Hyperactivity Disorder (MTA) study. These trials, described by Jensen, Hinshaw, Swanson et al. (2001), included a total of 579 first through fourth graders, 80% male and 20% female, ages 7.0 to 9.9 years, none of whom were excluded on the basis of comorbidity profiles. The children, who were followed for 14 months, were divided into four groups: (1) medication alone, in which subjects received close monitoring and adjustment of medication (the majority of which was methylphenidate); (2) behavioral intervention alone; (3) combined close medication supervision and behavioral therapy; and (4) community comparison, in which individuals secured treatment from community providers. The large majority of children in the community comparison group were receiving medication alone, which was provided by primary care physicians in the community and was less closely monitored than the medication being administered in the medication alone and combined medication-behavioral therapy groups.

The outcome of this study, which has driven both professional practices and the prevailing popular wisdom on the topic of ADHD intervention, showed that the combination therapy and the medication-only therapy options were both more likely to abate the symptoms of ADHD than the behavioral treatment alone (Jensen, Hinshaw, Swanson et al., 2001). All of the experimental conditions were superior to the outcomes in the community comparison group (Jensen, Hinshaw, Swanson et al., 2001).

Although the MTA outcomes are generally portrayed as definitive and are widely cited in the ADHD literature, the study is not without its harsh critics. Leo (2002) describes major flaws in subject recruitment and data collection. The subjects, rather than being randomly sampled, were the children of self-referred parents. These parents were already aware of the nature of the study and were comfortable with the medical model of ADHD. In addition, the majority of data comes from parent and teacher reports of children's behaviors, but neither the parents nor the teachers were blind to the child's group assignment (i.e., parents and teachers knew how their children were being treated).

The flawed method upon which this study is built bears mentioning for several reasons. The MTA is frequently cited in professional journals ranging from those in the basic medical sciences to others that are designed for use by practitioners. With such far-reaching impact, and with the potential long-term risk incurred by medicating the brains of developing children, bias could come at a very high price.

From an Integral perspective, a flaw in the MTA study is that it bolstered an intervention paradigm that favored a biomedical and behaviorist, individual-external lens. Although it is certainly possible that the behavioral interventions and medications administered in the MTA could aid, for example, collective-internal family and peer relations, such an outcome would be tangential to the main focus of the therapy—that is, symptom reduction—and would be fortuitous at best. Likewise, individual-interior issues such as the internal experience of trauma-related abuse or neglect, or collective-exterior issues such as crime in unsafe neighborhoods, parental unemployment, and parental incarceration were neglected while the focus of intervention was to eradicate behavioral symptoms apart from their root causes. Finally, potential exterior-collective issues related to assimilation, language barriers, and views of psychiatric disorder that can have profound impact on how children function in structured, culturally disparate settings were also not considered in the intervention strategies. In summary, we contend that it is essential to base ADHD intervention on a rigorous Integral assessment (Marquis, 2008) of the child's condition. Childhood depression, anxiety, anger, diet, sleep patterns, home responsibilities for siblings, and many other factors can produce symptoms that are very difficult to distinguish from ADHD, and for which stimulants, nonstimulants, and behavioral interventions are, at best, inappropriate.

## Psychosocial Interventions

Given the pervasive nature of ADHD, psychosocial interventions, unlike more invasive pharmacotherapy, carry the benefit of building healthy interpersonal relationships and functional family systems while imposing none of the risks to neurologically developing children that are associated with psychotropic medications. Even if used in combination with medication, rigorously employed psychosocial interventions can reduce the amount of stimulant medication necessary to control associated problems of ADHD such as self-regulation, focus, and task engagement (Daly, Creed, Xanthopoulos, & Brown, 2007). Due to their efficacy and safety, psychosocial interventions appear prominently in the guidelines for the treatment of ADHD in the American Academy of Pediatrics and the American Academy of Child and Adolescent Psychiatry (Diller, 2006). Compared to pharmacological approaches, behaviorally oriented interventions put more emphasis on improving functional domains such as social and family relationships and school performance.

Evidence-based psychosocial interventions described in this section include behaviorally based parent training programs designed to manage behavior and/or emotional problems at home, educational interventions aimed at remediating ADHD children's identified skill deficits, and academic interventions developed to improve on-task behavior and rates of work completion.

## Parent Training

Parent training directly addresses many of the problems with ADHD child–parent interactions that were detailed in the collective-interior quadrant analysis of ADHD. Parenting a child with ADHD can be a continuous challenge. There is considerable conflict between the parent and child, with parents' communications with their ADHD children being less rewarding, more directive, and more negative when compared with non-ADHD-diagnosed counterparts (Barkley, 2006a). Parents can become overwhelmed by the needs and demands of these children, and the behavioral and emotional problems associated with ADHD may contribute to family difficulties and high levels of parental stress.

The severity of problems manifested by children with ADHD varies greatly from family to family. There is also considerable variation in parents' reactions and discipline tactics. Difficulties experienced in families of a child with ADHD can include lowered sense of parenting competence, increased isolation from extended family and friends, increased marital conflict, increased substance abuse by the parents, and increased rates of divorce (Barkley, 2006a).

More than one hundred studies of parent and teacher interventions with children with ADHD demonstrate the effectiveness of interpersonal psychosocial intervention in reducing disruptive behaviors (Daly et al., 2007; Maughan, Christiansen, Jenson, Olympia, & Clark, 2005; Pelham, Wheeler, & Chronis, 1998; Pelham et al., 2005). Parent training (PT) provides parents with a variety of skills to assist them in managing their child's challenging and disruptive behavior in the home (Kazdin, 1997), specific ADHD-related behavior problems (Chronis, Chacko, Fabiano, Wymbs, & Pelham, 2004), and coercive and manipulative parent–child interactions (McMahon & Forehand, 2003). The degree of effectiveness of PT is influenced by the age of the child (Chronis et al., 2004); PT is best suited for parents of children with ADHD between the ages of 4 and 12 years (Anastopoulos, Rhoads, & Farley, 2006).

As children mature into adolescents, parent-directed discipline tactics become less effective. Adolescence is a time when children seek to discover their identity and depend less on family members as they strive for independence. Interventions in this developmental period focus on providing parents with the tools they need to give more freedom and opportunity to the child so that the developing adolescent can manage his own life. Behavioral interventions can be tailored to adolescents by including the adolescent in identifying his or her target behaviors, using privileges to reinforce responsible behavior, and teaching self-management skills to foster independence (Robin, 2006). Interventions such as problem-solving and positive communication skills can guide the adolescent to learn the skills necessary to become an independent, responsible young adult and are the most effective during this age period.

**THERAPEUTIC OBJECTIVES** PT programs vary somewhat in format and length, but they share the goal of teaching child management techniques. The broad reaching therapeutic objectives of PT are first to provide a foundation of knowledge about ADHD so that parents can better understand the biological basis of the disorder and, second, to teach parents how to use more rewards and nonpunitive consequences while implementing preventative interventions with their ADHD children. Evidence indicates that benefits are maintained for up to 12 months postintervention (Daly et al., 2007). Parents commonly have a frame of reference for ADHD that leads to unproductive and self-defeating parenting practices. Parents' directive, coercive, and maladaptive attempts to manage their child's problem behaviors may become counterproductive and may even perpetuate their child's problematic behavior (Daly et al., 2007). The usual discipline tactics such as explaining, reasoning, warning, and reprimanding can often be ineffective. Out of frustration, parents may attribute their child's difficulties to laziness, manipulation, or defiance, and attribute adolescent behavior to malicious and purposeful motives. Moreover, parents may also begin to view themselves as lacking basic parenting skills (Anastopoulos et al., 2006).

Parents may also harbor a burden of guilt based on the assumption that they have caused the problem in their child. Having knowledge about ADHD and the effects it can have on their child's behavior, socialization, academic performance, and home life can alleviate some of the frustration and sense of powerlessness that parents may feel. A greater understanding of their child's difficulties can increase the use of positive methods of discipline and assist the child in gaining self-control (Barkley, 2006a).

Therapeutic considerations aimed at parents ideally incorporate both emotional support and instruction in behavioral management strategies to help them manage their ADHD-diagnosed child. Behavior management skills, designed to change problematic patterns of interaction with the child, are taught to parents in controlled learning environments (McMahon & Forehand, 2003). Therapists, through didactic instruction, teach discrete parenting skills such as modeling and role-playing. "Successful" management of child behavior is viewed as bringing the child's behavior under control, facilitating the child's understanding of behavioral consequences, ameliorating the development of comorbidity, and reducing the stress on the family (Anastopoulos & Farley, 2003). Teaching parents behavioral interventions to reduce ADHD symptoms diminishes family distress and improves parenting skills and parents' sense of competence (Daly et al., 2007).

Chronis et al. (2004) outline a successful behavioral intervention program for parents that emphasizes the management of the core symptoms of ADHD and associated noncompliance and defiance. Topics include: (1) education concerning the nature of ADHD; (2) improving the parent–child relationship; (3) social learning theory and behavioral management techniques; (4) developing and enhancing parental attention to child behavior; (5) attending to appropriate behavior while ignoring minor inappropriate behavior; (6) establishing a reinforcement system that includes token reinforcements, response cost, and time-out from positive reinforcement; (7) how to enforce behavior across multiple settings; (8) problem-solving techniques; and (9) strategies for maintenance and relapse prevention. Because ADHD is recognized as a chronic condition, parents also must learn how to manage future misbehavior and are given follow-up sessions to learn how to maintain interventions over the long term (Smith, Barkley, & Shapiro, 2006). Findings from a meta-analysis of behavioral interventions supported the efficacy of treatment across study methods and designs (Chronis et al., 2004; Fabiano et al., 2009).

## Educational Interventions

Many children with ADHD experience extreme difficulty in school and have lower productivity, grades, and academic achievement than their non-ADHD counterparts (Mash & Wolfe, 2010). This pattern of academic difficulty is particularly problematic because research has shown that chronic school failure can result in grade retention, expulsion, school drop-out, and impairment in occupational functioning in adolescence and adulthood (Loe & Feldman, 2007). Fortunately, educational interventions can improve children's performance in school by implementing behavioral interventions and by modifying methods of teaching.

A majority of children with ADHD have academic skill deficits, and nearly 80% qualify for a Learning Disorder diagnosis by late childhood (Mash & Wolfe, 2010). About 25% of these children experience a significant delay in reading, arithmetic, or spelling that affects their general intellectual functioning or are identified as extremely low in achievement in a specific academic subject (Barkley, 2006a). Students with ADHD are less actively engaged in academic instruction than their classmates, display less on-task behavior during instruction, and require more instruction and practice to keep pace with their peers who do not have learning difficulties (Barkley, 2006a). Although some children with ADHD are placed in a special education class for some or part of the day, most children with ADHD are assigned to mainstream classes because they don't need the intensive assistance that smaller, special education programs offer (Mash & Wolfe, 2010). Both the National Rehabilitation Act and the IDEA are legislative efforts requiring appropriate educational services for children with ADHD. In 1991 the U.S. Department of Education stipulated that ADHD can be used as a qualifying condition under Part B of the "Other Health Impaired" category if the school determines that the child is disabled (Barkley, 2006a).

**BEHAVIORAL CLASSROOM MANAGEMENT** Research indicates that behavioral classroom management interventions are a well-supported educational treatment for children with ADHD (Pelham & Fabiano, 2008). Classroom behavior management strategies are often contingency management procedures such as teacher-implemented reward programs, point systems, and response-cost procedures that are individualized to the child (Pelham & Fabiano, 2008). Behavioral modification systems have three basic characteristics: (1) expectations about the child's behavior are clearly identified and communicated, (2) a system is in place for increasing desirable behaviors and decreasing undesirable ones, and (3) rules are clearly stipulated (Forehand & McMahon, 1981). These modifications are managed by a consultant—such as a school psychologist, school counselor, or special education teacher—who collaborates with the classroom teacher (Daly et al., 2007). Teachers are crucial in influencing the learning environment in their classroom and can be instrumental in the implementation of an effective behavioral classroom management plan.

Teachers generally appear to favor positive behavioral supports over negative contingencies for children with ADHD in the classroom (Pfiffner, Barkley, & DuPaul, 2006). The consequences of a child's behavior in the classroom can be manipulated using selective attention, giving positive reinforcement with praise for appropriate or on-task behavior, and by ignoring and redirecting inappropriate or off-task behavior. An effective method to encourage behavior change is a token economy system. A token economy system is a contract between the teacher and the child stating that if the child meets agreed upon behavioral expectations, the teacher will provide certain rewards and/or privileges. Tokens such as stickers or points can be accumulated and exchanged for back-up reinforcers that are selected by the child. Social reinforcement that involves visible records of achievement, direct verbal praise, or provides positive reinforcement to a group of students may increase the effectiveness of a token economy system (Daly et al., 2007).

Another effective positive behavioral support in the classroom is contingency contracting (Daly et al., 2007). The teacher and child sign a written contract that specifies how the child will behave and the contingencies that will accrue. Often, contracting is a process of negotiation between the child and the teacher that specifies (1) behaviors targeted for change, (2) goals for behavior, and (3) consequences for attaining goals. Communication between the classroom and the parents regarding the child's performance is essential. A daily report card sent home to parents could provide information about how the child is progressing toward meeting the desired target behaviors.

To improve the performance and the behavior of children with ADHD, an effective supplement to positive behavior supports involves a strategic application of negative consequences, such as response-cost procedures or "time-out," designed to punish disruptive or off-task classroom behaviors (Pfiffner et al., 2006). Response-cost procedures involve the loss, following inappropriate or unproductive behavior, of a reinforcer such as privileges, activities, or tokens. Pfiffner et al. (2006) advise that when negative consequences are used in a child's behavior modification program, teachers should teach and reinforce alternative appropriate behaviors that are incompatible with inappropriate behaviors. Time-out from positive reinforcement (e.g., teacher attention, peer attention, preferred activities) is a negative consequence that is effective in managing disruptive or noncompliant behavior in children with ADHD (Fabiano et al., 2009). Time-out procedures vary in types and levels of restriction. It is generally recommended that time-out procedures be implemented starting with the least restrictive condition (Mercugliano, Power, & Blum, 1999).

**ACADEMIC INTERVENTIONS** In addition to behavioral interventions that target disruptive behavior and task engagement, teacher-mediated academic interventions—that is, teaching methods that are modified to meet the unique needs and challenges of children with ADHD—are important additions to a multipronged program designed to ensure the overall academic success of children with ADHD (Pfiffner et al., 2006). Children are more likely to pay attention when they know what is expected from them and when teachers use developmentally appropriate, well-organized, and predictable instructional material. Oral directions that are supplemented with visual aids and cues for work completion may be especially helpful for children with ADHD. Ways of altering the instructional material and methods of instruction that include varying the modalities of instruction, repeating instructions, providing extra time to complete assignments, reducing the length of written assignments, using a systematic approach to note taking, pairing verbal instructions with written ones, and employing visual aids to improve organization can increase the likelihood that children with ADHD will pay attention and complete classwork (Pfiffner et al., 2006).

Children with ADHD are more likely to pay attention when they use novel, hands-on learning materials (Barkley, 2006a). Attention span can be improved and hyperactivity reduced when instructional materials are varied, materials are presented in color, and students have the opportunity to engage in tasks that require an active, motoric response (Mercugliano et al., 1999). Computer-assisted instruction (CAI) programs are helpful for engaging children in that they simplify tasks, can be targeted to the child's specific learning needs, can accurately identify skill levels, and can improve mental organization (Pfiffner et al., 2006). CAI programs provide highly stimulating instruction in a game-like format that makes dull and repetitive tasks, like practicing math computation and word recognition skills, fun and rewarding.

## Meditation

Meditation has been shown to be effective in managing problematic behaviors related to ADHD, but study designs to date have largely failed to exclude participants actively taking ADHD-related medications, thus weakening conclusions regarding the effects of meditation alone (Krisanaprakornkit, Ngamjarus, Witoonchart, & Piyavhatkul, 2010; Zylowska et al., 2008). The two types of meditation that have been shown to be effective in the reduction of ADHD symptoms are concentrative meditation and mindfulness meditation (Krisanaprakornkit et al., 2010). Whereas it may be obvious how concentrative forms of meditation can help ADHD children increase their attentiveness, the attentional practices of mindfulness meditation facilitate an opening of awareness that leads to improved cognitive, emotional, and behavioral self-regulation (Brown, Ryan, & Creswell, 2007).

Grosswald, Stixrud, Travis, and Bateh (2008) demonstrated the feasibility of using Transcendental Meditation™ (TM), a concentrative meditation that emphasizes sustained attention, with middle school students. The study showed that after 3 months of meditating twice daily for 10 minutes, 10 students with ADHD, 8 of whom were taking stimulant medication, improved executive functioning and behavior regulation. The students reported a 50% reduction in stress, anxiety, and stress-related ADHD symptoms. A second study involved 18 ADHD-diagnosed children, ages 11 to 14 years, 10 of whom were medicated. The children practiced TM for 6 months, and showed improved brain functioning and language-based skills that resulted in improved focus on schoolwork, organizational skills, and independent learning (Travis, Grosswald, & Stixrud, 2011).

Mindfulness meditation as an approach to stress reduction has also been incorporated into the treatment of ADHD. The emphasis of mindfulness meditation is on an open awareness to mental processes and nonjudgmental acceptance of one's present emotional state. In a study of 24 adults and 8 adolescents with ADHD, some of whom were also medicated for their ADHD symptoms, subjects participated in an 8-week mindfulness meditation-training program. Researchers found that 78% of the participants in this mindfulness program experienced a reduction in self-reported ADHD symptoms (Zylowka et al., 2008). Participants in the study reported that mindfulness meditation helped improve their emotional regulation, cognitive inhibition, and attention. Moreover, both anxiety and depression improved among the adult participants. From this study, Zylowska and Smalley developed the Mindful Awareness Practices for ADHD (MAPs for ADHD) (Zylowska, Smalley, & Schwartz, 2009). The MAPs program is delivered in a group format and includes psychoeducation, guided meditations, weekly practice assignments, cognitive-behavioral coaching strategies, and a loving-kindness meditation designed to address the low self-esteem problems commonly associated with ADHD.

### Considering Systemic Intervention Strategies

Although the central focus of this book is to guide mental health practitioners in their conceptualization of individual mental health challenges, the many potential ADHD etiologies situated in the lower-right quadrant warrant some consideration of the value of wider systemic intervention strategies. More specifically, assisting and encouraging clients in their attempts to prevail upon legislators, community leaders, educators, law enforcement, and commercial interests to enact policies and practices that address systemic issues—such as lead abatement, toxic waste disposal, school based wrap-around programs, and neighborhood safety—could be considered key prevention and intervention strategies. Such systemically focused action would fall under the general heading of client advocacy and empowerment, both central concepts in a transdisciplinary, Integral understanding of mental health practice.

## THE CASE OF ANTHONY JONES

Anthony Jones is a 9-year-old boy in the third grade who was referred by his school psychologist and assistant principal to an outpatient community mental health clinic. This referral follows his second out-of-school suspension for throwing school furniture at a teacher. Anthony's mother, Ms. Jones, was reluctant to bring her son to the clinic, saying that there was nothing wrong with him and that her son was provoked. As a single mother, she relied on Anthony to be the "man of the house," but stated that he "seemed to always be getting into trouble in school" and "that the teachers thought he was out of control." One of the school's recommendations for Anthony's return to school after his expulsion was that he be evaluated in the clinic. Major concerns included Anthony's temper, aggression, distractibility, difficulty completing tasks, verbal impulsivity, and restlessness. Ms. Jones and Anthony came into the clinic reluctantly so that Anthony could make arrangements to return to school.

Ms. Jones reports that Anthony is a very bright, creative child who loves to draw portraits of his extended family. He loves to read and Ms. Jones notes that he "always wants to do more, to be challenged." She comments that she doesn't understand why he doesn't do his homework, or even bring it home for that matter. When asked which subjects he likes in school, Anthony reports that the only ones he likes are those that are related to science (the class was currently studying volcanoes). Anthony's behaviors with others are troublesome. He says that he has no real friends at school and that they are "all really stupid." Ms. Jones reports that she has tried to set up play dates for Anthony in her apartment complex with neighboring boys but the children frequently fight. When Anthony returns to the house after play dates, he locks himself in his room and doesn't come out, even for meals. Anthony is verbally impulsive, frequently blurting out remarks that are harmful to his mother.

At the beginning of the year Anthony was referred by his teacher to the school counselor. The school counselor reports that he has become less manageable than he had been at the beginning of the school year 4 months ago. Initially, he had been charming and often joked around with his teacher and other adults in the school, but as he became more familiar with the classroom, his behavior became more difficult. Anthony averaged several tantrums a week, each of which consisted of verbal tirades about how useless the assignments were. He would run around pushing peers out of his way and crying that he didn't want to do "all of this dumb work." As the school year progressed, Anthony became unable to collect himself when he got upset; his behaviors were severe enough to have him sent out of the classroom to the in-school-suspension room for the remainder of the day.

His classroom teacher reports that Anthony is very easily distracted, has difficulty organizing assignments and completing tasks, and often forgets to bring the needed classroom materials from home. In addition, Anthony often has difficulty sitting still, fidgets in his seat, and gets up from his desk to walk around the classroom, humming. Anthony needs frequent reminders to stay on task when working independently or in groups and he often blurts out comments not related to the work. A discussion with the school psychologist revealed that Anthony's intelligence level was in the high-average range. In addition, his overall level of tested achievement was low average, but not more than 2 standard deviations from his intelligence test score. Anthony did not qualify for a diagnosis of a Learning Disorder.

## Case Analysis

A cursory analysis of Anthony's behavior reveals a pattern that is commonly, albeit not exclusively, seen in boys with ADHD. The fact that Anthony is "very easily distracted, has difficulty organizing assignments and completing tasks, and often forgets to bring the needed classroom materials from home" are reflective of diagnostic criteria related to inattention, while descriptions indicating that he has "difficulty sitting still, fidgets in his seat, gets up from his desk to walk around the classroom, humming . . . needs frequent reminders to stay on task when working independently or in groups, and . . . often blurts out comments not related to the work" are reflective of hyperactive-inattentive criteria. Assuming that these criteria are displayed in multiple settings, and are clearly not due to a major disruption or trauma in his life, a medical condition, or a substance problem, a diagnosis of ADHD, Hyperactive-Inattentive Type would be consistent with his presentation.

The comorbidity section of this chapter talks about the externalizing and internalizing comorbid disorders that often accompany ADHD and underscores that it is more common for boys to suffer from externalizing comorbid disorders such as ODD and CD, whereas girls are more likely to endure internalizing comorbid disorders such as depression and anxiety. Anthony's behavior in and out of the classroom, including his tantrums, verbal tirades, fighting, and explosive anger, are reflective of a child with ODD. Although some of his outbursts are bordering on the antisocial behaviors associated with CD, it is not at all clear that Anthony has consistent, premeditated intent to do harm to people, animals, or property, or engage in other antisocial acts.

It is important in Anthony's case to consider alternative diagnoses or explanations for his behavior. This case description relies heavily on individual-exterior quadrant variables and leaves many questions unanswered regarding how Anthony's behavior is being shaped by the remaining three quadrants. Additional issues to consider in a discussion of Anthony would begin with circumstances in his home life, including his relationship with his mother; the presence or absence of a father; the quality of his relationship with any another significant male presence; relationships with siblings; socioeconomic stressors, including parental unemployment, housing quality, racial or economic marginalization, and neighborhood safety; death; separation; divorce; illness; and parental substance abuse. With Anthony being the "man of the house" at 9 years of age, one can infer that either there is no male parent in the home or that the male figure who is present is impaired to an extent that precludes his acting in the capacity of a fully participative parent. In any case, Anthony may be "acting out" in response to very difficult life circumstances, and children who are depressed, anxious, or distressed will often become angry and irritable, thus giving the outward appearance of being disruptive, defiant, and distracted.

It would also be important to get more information on Anthony's classroom experience. Is he, perhaps, the only African American child in an otherwise homogeneous, White classroom? Is he the object of bullying? Is he having particular difficulty with the teacher? Is he having an ADHD-related challenging transition into the academic demands of the third grade?

Barring any particularly challenging life circumstances in Anthony's psychosocial history, and assuming that he has no medical or substance issues complicating his clinical picture, a diagnosis of Combined-Type ADHD with comorbid ODD would be consistent with his presentation. Possible interventions would include providing Anthony's mother with behavioral management techniques, psycho-educational material regarding ADHD, and a support group for parents of children with ADHD. Anthony should receive a multipronged approach that includes a complete medical evaluation, social skills training, age-appropriate psychoeducational intervention, behavioral management techniques that he can use to manage his time in the classroom, anger management, a psychotherapeutic intervention to help him cope with adjustment to both his disorder and exacerbating contextual circumstances, and mindfulness training to help him manage some of the dysregulated emotion that he experiences. Stimulant medication for his disorder could be considered if nonpharmacological interventions fail to address problematic behaviors. Finally, it would be important that Anthony's teachers be apprised of effective pedagogical and motivational classroom interventions. The fact that Anthony has the cognitive capacity for academic success can serve as the foundation of an assets-based approach in the classroom. In particular, drawing on his interest in "hands-on" science can provide the teacher with insight into Anthony's learning style and curiosity about the world around him.

## Conclusion

ADHD is a disorder that reverberates through families, schools, churches, clubs, sports teams, and virtually every other setting where predictable, ordered social engagement is an expectation. It is also a disorder that can be devastating to its victims—leaving them isolated, angry, ashamed, confused, anxious, depressed, and with diminishing feelings of self-worth. A salient feature of this disorder is that the etiology of the suffering is represented by dynamics interacting in, and among, all four quadrants. Unlike the experience of depression or anxiety, which persistently generates psychological pain even in the absence of contextual influence, ADHD victimization almost always involves complicity among family members, institutional structures, social hierarchies, and cultural expectations. Hence, healing the wounds of ADHD requires conceptualizing it as an ecological phenomenon in which the individual-in-relation is a primary focus of therapeutic intervention.

## Review Questions

1. Describe some of the salient research regarding the genetic basis of ADHD.
2. Discuss Peter Conrad's concerns about the increasing trend to medicalize aspects of human difference (deviance).
3. What do you think about Hartmann's notion that ADHD characteristics reflect natural characteristics of a spectrum that ranges from hunter-like behavior at one end to farmer-like behavior at the other?
4. How are attachment-related dynamics implicated in ADHD?
5. Describe how exposure to lead, PCBs, and organophosphates is a good example of the interplay of UR and LR dynamics, and how they are etiological factors in ADHD.
6. Describe some of the more salient temperament traits that are associated with ADHD.
7. What is your reaction to the high comorbidity found among ADHD and other DSM disorders? What are possible explanations for such high comorbidities?
8. Describe the pros and cons of both psychosocial and pharmacological intervention with ADHD.

## References


Accornero, V. H., Amado, A. J., Morrow, C. E., Xue, L., Anthony, J. C., & Bandstra, E. S. (2007). Impact of prenatal cocaine exposure on attention and response inhibition as assessed by continuous performance tests. *Journal of Developmental Behavioral Pediatrics, 28*, 195–205.

Achenbach, T. M., & Rescorla, L. A. (2001). *Manual for ASEBA school-age forms and profiles*. Burlington, VT: University of Vermont, Research Center for Children, Youth, & Families.

Ainsworth, M. D. S., Blehar, M. C., Waters, E., & Wall, S. (1978). *Patterns of attachment: A psychological study of the strange situation*. Hillsdale, NJ: Erlbaum.

Allen, A. J., Kurlan, R. M., Gilbert, D. L., Coffey, B. J., Linder, S. L., Lewis, D. W., . . . Spencer, T. J. (2005). Atomoxetine treatment in children and adolescents with ADHD and comorbid tic disorders. *Neurology, 65*, 1941–1949.

American Psychiatric Association. (1968). *Diagnostic and statistical manual of mental disorders* (2nd ed.). Washington, DC: Author.

American Psychiatric Association. (1980). *Diagnostic and statistical manual of mental disorders* (3rd ed.). Washington, DC: Author.

American Psychiatric Association. (1987). *Diagnostic and statistical manual of mental disorders* (3rd ed., rev.). Washington, DC: Author.

American Psychiatric Association. (2000). *Diagnostic and statistical manual of mental disorders* (4th ed., text rev.). Washington, DC: Author.

American Psychiatric Association. (2013). *Diagnostic and statistical manual of mental disorders* (5th ed.). Arlington, VA: American Psychiatric Publishing.

Anastopoulos, A. D., & Farley, S. E. (2003). A cognitive-behavioral training program for parents of children with attention-deficit/hyperactivity disorder. In A. E. Kazdin & J. R. Weisz (Eds.), *Evidence-based psychotherapies for children and adolescents* (pp. 187–203). New York: Guilford Press.

Anastopoulos, A. D., Rhoads, L. H., & Farley, S. E. (2006). Counseling and training parents. In R. A. Barkley (Ed.), *Attention-deficit hyperactivity disorder: A handbook for diagnosis and treatment* (3rd ed., pp. 453–479). New York: Guilford Press.

Barkley, R. A. (1990). *Attention-deficit hyperactivity disorder: A handbook for diagnosis and treatment* (1st ed.). New York: Guilford Press.

Barkley, R. A. (1997). *ADHD and the nature of self-control.* New York: Guilford Press.

Barkley, R. A. (2006a). *Attention-deficit hyperactivity disorder: A handbook for diagnosis and treatment* (3rd ed.). New York: Guilford Press.

Barkley, R. A. (2006b). The relevance of the Still Lectures to Attention Deficit Hyperactivity Disorder: A commentary. *Journal of Attention Disorders, 10,* 137.

Barkley, R. A., & Cunningham, C. E. (1979). The effects of methylphenidate on the mother-child interactions of hyperactive children. *Archives of General Psychiatry, 36,* 201–208.

Barkley, R. A., & Edwards, G. (2006). Diagnostic interview, behavior rating scales, and the medical examination. In R. A. Barkley (Ed.), *Attention-deficit hyperactivity disorder. A handbook for diagnosis and treatment* (pp. 337–368). New York: Guilford Press.

Barkley, R. A., Karlsson, J., & Pollard, S. (1985). Effects of age on the mother-child interactions of hyperactive children. *Journal of Abnormal Child Psychology, 13,* 631–638.

Barkley, R. A., Karlsson, J., Pollard, S., & Murphy, J. (1985). Developmental changes in the mother-child interactions of hyperactive boys: Effects of two doses of Ritalin. *Journal of Child Psychology and Psychiatry, 26,* 705–715.

Becker, K., El-Faddagh, M., Schmidt, M. H., Esser, G., & Laucht, M. (2008). Interaction of dopamine transporter genotype with prenatal smoke exposure on ADHD symptoms. *The Journal of Pediatrics, 152,* 263–269.

Benson, C. (2001). *The cultural psychology of self: Place, morality and art in human worlds.* New York: Routledge.

Bertram, L., & Tanzi, R. E. (2008). Thirty years of Alzheimer's disease genetics: The implications of systematic meta-analysis. *Nature Reviews Neuroscience, 9,* 768–778.

Bhuvaneswar, C. G., Chang, G., Epstein, L. A., & Stern, T. A. (2007). Alcohol use during pregnancy: Prevalence and impact. *The Primary Care Companion to the Journal of Clinical Psychiatry, 9,* 455–460.

Biederman, J., Faraone, S. V., Keenan, K., Benjamin, J., Krifcher, B., Moore, C., . . . Tsuang, M. T. (1992). Further evidence for family genetic risk factors in attention deficit hyperactivity disorder: Patterns of comorbidity in probands and relatives in psychiatrically and pediatrically referred samples. *Archives of General Psychiatry, 49,* 728–738.

Biederman, J., Mick, E., Faraone, S. V., Braaten, E., Doyle, A., Spencer, T., . . . Johnson, M. A. (2002). Influence of gender on Attention Deficit Hyperactivity Disorder in children referred to a psychiatric clinic. *American Journal of Psychiatry, 159,* 36–42.

Bolaños, C. A., Willey, M. D., Maffeo, M. L., Powers, K. D., Kinka, D. W., Grausam, K. B., & Henderson, R. P. (2008). Antidepressant treatment can normalize adult behavioral deficits induced by early-life exposure to methylphenidate. *Biological Psychiatry, 63,* 309–316.

Bonasio, R., Tu, S., & Reinberg, D. (2010). Molecular signals of epigenetic states. *Science, 330,* 612–616.

Bouchard, M. F., Bellinger, D. C., Wright, R. O., & Weisskopf, M. G. (2010). Attention-Deficit/Hyperactivity Disorder and urinary metabolites of organophosphate pesticides. *Pediatrics, 125,* e1270–e1277.

Bowlby, J. (1973). Separation: Anxiety and anger. *Attachment and loss. Vol. 2.* London: Hogarth Press.

Bowlby, J. (1982). *Attachment and loss. Vol. 1: Attachment* (2nd rev. ed.). New York: Basic Books. (Original work published 1969).

Bowlby, J. (1988). *A secure base: Parent-child attachment and healthy human development.* New York: Basic Books.

Bradley, C. (1937). The behavior of children receiving Benzedrine. *American Journal of Psychiatry, 94,* 577–585.

Bradley, C., & Bowen, M. (1941). Amphetamine (Benezedrine) therapy of children's behavior disorders. *American Journal of Orthopsychiatry, 11,* 92–103.

Braun, J. M., Kahn, R. S., Froehlich, T., Auinger, P., & Lanphear, B. P. (2006). Exposures to environmental toxicants and attention deficit hyperactivity disorder in U.S. children. *Environmental Health Perspectives, 114,* 1904–1909.

Breggin, P. R. (2001). *Talking back to Ritalin: What doctors aren't telling you about stimulants and ADHD.* Cambridge, MA: Perseus.

Brook, D. W., Brook, J. S., Zhang, C., & Koppel, J. (2010). Association between attention-deficit/hyperactivity disorder in adolescence and substance use disorder in adulthood. *Archives of Pediatrics and Adolescent Medicine, 164,* 930–934.

Brown, K. W., Ryan, R. M., & Creswell, J. D. (2007). Mindfulness: Theoretical foundations and evidence for its salutary effects. *Psychological Inquiry, 18,* 211–237.

Bush, G., Valera, E. M., & Seidman, L. J. (2005). Functional neuroimaging of attention-deficit/hyperactivity disorder: A review and suggested future directions. *Biological Psychiatry, 57,* 1273–1284.

Campbell, S. B. (1973). Mother-child interaction in reflective, impulsive, and hyperactive children. *Developmental Psychology, 8,* 341–349.

Campbell, S. B. (1975). Mother-child interactions: A comparison of hyperactive learning disabled and normal boys. *American Journal of Orthopsychiatry, 45,* 51–57.

Campbell, S. B. (1987). Parent-referred problem three-year-olds: Developmental changes in symptoms. *Journal of Child Psychology and Psychiatry, 28,* 835–846.

Campbell, S. B. (1990). *Behavior problems in preschool children: Clinical and developmental issues.* New York: Guilford Press.

Campbell, S. B., & Ewing, L. J. (1990). Follow-up of hard-to-manage preschoolers: Adjustment at age nine years and predictors of continuing symptoms. *Journal of Child Psychology and Psychiatry, 31,* 871–889.

Campbell, S. B., Shaw, D. S., & Gilliom, M. (2000). Early externalizing behavior problems: Toddler and preschoolers at risk for later maladjustment. *Development and Psychopathology, 12,* 467–488.

Canfield, R. L., Kreher, D. A., Cornwell, C., & Henderson, C. R. (2003). Low-level lead exposure, executive functioning, and learning in early childhood. *Child Neuropsychology, 9,* 35–53.

Carlson, C. (1986). Attention Deficit Disorder Without Hyperactivity: A review of preliminary experimental evidence. In B. Lahey & A. Kazdin (Eds.), *Advances in clinical child psychology* (Vol. 9, 99, pp. 153–176). New York: Plenum.

Carlson, E. A., Jacobvitz, D., & Stroufe, L. A. (1995). A developmental investigation of inattentiveness and hyperactivity. *Child Development, 66,* 37–54.

Cassidy, J. (1994). Emotion regulation: Influences of attachment relationships. *Monographs of the Society for Research in Child Development, 59*(2/3), *The development of emotion regulation: Biological and behavioral considerations,* 228–249.

Centers for Disease Control and Prevention. (2011, September 9). Vital signs: Current cigarette smoking among adults aged ≥ 18 years—United States, 2005–2010, *Morbidity and Mortality Weekly Report, 60*(35), 1207–1212. Retrieved from http://www.cdc.gov/mmwr/preview/mmwrhtml/mm6035a5.htm?s_cid=mm6035a5_w

Cherkasova, M. V., & Hechtman, L. (2009). Neuroimaging in attention-deficit hyperactivity disorder: Beyond the frontostriatal circuitry. *Canadian Journal of Psychiatry, 54,* 651–664.

Chess, S. (1960). Diagnosis and treatment of the hyperactive child. *New York State Journal of Medicine, 60,* 2379–2385.

Chronis, A. M., Chacko, A., Fabiano, G. A., Wymbs, B. T., & Pelham, W. E. (2004). Enhancements to the behavioral parent training paradigm for families of children with ADHD: Review and future directions. *Clinical Child and Family Psychology Review, 7,* 1–27.

Chronis, A. M., Fabiano, G. A., Gnagy, E. M., Onyango, A. N., Pelham W. E., Lopez-Williams, A., . . . Seymour, K. E. (2004). An evaluation of the summer treatment program for children with attention deficit/hyperactivity disorder using a treatment withdrawal design. *Behavior Therapy, 35,* 561–585.

Chronis, A. M., Lahey, B. B., Pelham, W. E., Williams, S. H., Baumann, B. L., Kipp, K., . . . Rathouz, P. J. (2007). Maternal depression and early positive parenting predict future conduct problems in young children with attention-deficit/hyperactivity disorder. *Developmental Psychology, 43,* 70–82.

Clark, L., Ungerer, J., Chahoud, K., Johnson, S., & Stiefel, I. (2002). Attention deficit hyperactivity disorder is associated with attachment insecurity. *Clinical Child Psychology and Psychiatry, 7,* 179–196.

Conners, C. K. (1995). *Conners' continuous performance test.* Toronto: Multi-Health Systems Inc.

Conners, C. K. (2001). *Conners' rating scales-revised: Technical manual.* North Tonawanda, NY: Multi-Health Systems.

Conrad, P. (1976). *Identifying hyperactive children: The medicalization of deviant behavior.* Lexington, MA: Lexington Books.

Conrad, P. (1980). On the medicalization of deviance and social control. In D. Ingleby (Ed.), *Critical psychiatry.* New York: Pantheon Books.

Conrad, P. (2006). The shifting engines of medicalization. *Journal of Health and Social Behavior, 46,* 3–15.

Conrad, P. (2007). *The medicalization of society: On the transformation of human conditions into treatable disorders.* Baltimore: Johns Hopkins University Press.

Coplan, R. J., Bowler, A., & Cooper, S. M. (2003). Parenting daily hassles, child temperament, and social adjustment in preschool. *Early Childhood Research Quarterly, 18,* 376–395.

Cottrell, E. C., & Seckl, J. R. (2009). Prenatal stress, glucocorticoids and the programming of adult disease. *Frontiers in Behavioral Neuroscience, 3,* 1–9.

Cunningham, C. E., & Barkley, R. A. (1979). The interactions of hyperactive and normal children with their mothers during free play and structured tasks. *Child Development, 50,* 217–224.

Daly, B. P., Creed, T., Xanthopoulos, M., & Brown, R. T. (2007). Psychosocial treatments for children with Attention deficit/hyperactivity disorder. *Neuropsychological Review, 17,* 73–89.

Davids, E., Zhang, K., Tarazi, F. I., & Baldessarini, R. J. (2003). Animal models of attention-deficit hyperactivity disorder. *Brain Research Reviews, 42,* 1–21.

Dickstein, S. G., Bannon, K., Castellanos, F. X., & Miham, M. P. (2006). The neural correlates of attention deficit hyperactivity disorder: An ALE meta-analysis. *The Journal of Child Psychology and Psychiatry, 47,* 1051–1062.

Diller, L. H. (2006). *The last normal child.* Westport, Connecticut: Praeger.

Douglas, V. I. (1972). Stop, look, listen: The problem of sustained attention and impulse control in hyperactive and normal children. *Canadian Journal of Behavioral Sciences, 4,* 259–282.

Douthit, K. Z. (2001). The psychiatric construction of attention deficit/hyperactivity disorder: A critical evaluation of the theoretical precepts. (Unpublished doctoral dissertation). University of Rochester, Rochester, NY.

Douthit, K. Z. (2006). The convergence of counseling and psychiatric genetics: An essential role for counselors. *Journal of Counseling and Development, 84,* 16–28.

Douthit, K. Z., & Donnelly, D. (2010). Theoretical neutrality in DSM classification: Diagnosing the manual. Unpublished manuscript, Counseling and Human Development Program, University of Rochester, Rochester, NY.

Douthit, K. Z., & Marquis, A. (2006). Empiricism in psychiatry's post-psychoanalytic era: Contemplating DSM's atheoretical nosology. *Constructivism in the Human Sciences, 11,* 32–59.

Doyle, A. E., Willcutt, E. G., Seidman, L. J., Biederman, J., Chouinard, V. A., Silva, J., & Faraone, S. V. (2005). Attention-deficit/hyperactivity disorder endophenotypes. *Biological Psychiatry, 57,* 1324–1335.

Erdman, P. (1998). Conceptualizing ADHD as a contextual response to parental attachment. *American Journal of Family Therapy, 26,* 177–185.

Erenberg, G. (2006). The relationship between Tourette syndrome, attention deficit hyperactivity disorder, and stimulant medication: A critical review. *Seminars in Pediatric Neurology, 12,* 217–221.

Erickson, M. F., Sroufe, L. A., & Egeland, B. (1985). The relationships between quality of attachment and behavior problems in preschool in a high-risk sample. *Monographs of the Society for Research in Child Development, 50*(1/2), *Growing Points of Attachment Theory and Research,* 147–166.

Eskenazi, B. (2010). Organophosphate pesticide exposure and attention in young Mexican-American children: The CHAMACOS study. *Environmental Health Perspectives, 118,* 1768–1774.

Eubig, P. A., Aguiar, A., & Schantz, S. L. (2010). Lead and PCBs as risk factors for attention deficit/hyperactivity disorder. *Environmental Health Perspectives, 118,* 1654–1667.

Fabiano, G. A., Pelham, W. E., Coles, E. K., Gnagy, E. M., Chronis-Tuscano, A., & O'Connor, B. C. (2009). A meta-analysis of behavioral treatments for attention-deficit/hyperactivity disorder. *Clinical Psychology Review, 29,* 129–140.

Faraone, S. V., Biederman, J., Morley, C. P., & Spencer, T. J. (2008). Effect of stimulants on height and weight: A review of the literature. *Journal of the American Academy of Child and Adolescent Psychiatry, 47,* 994–1009.

Faraone, S. V., & Mick, E. (2010). Molecular genetics of attention deficit (sic) hyperactivity disorder. *Psychiatry Clinics of North America, 33,* 159–180.

Fewtrell, L. J., Pruss-Ustun, A., Landrigan, P., & Ayuso-Mateos, J. L. (2004). Estimating the global burden of disease of mild mental retardation and cardiovascular diseases from environmental lead exposure. *Environmental Research, 94,* 120–133.

Food and Drug Administration. (2005). New warning for Strattera. Retrieved from http://www.fda.gov/bbs/topics/ANSWERS/2004/ANS01335.html

Forehand, R. L., & McMahon, R. J. (1981). *Helping the noncompliant child.* New York: The Guilford Press.

Frances, A. (2010). Opening Pandora's box: The 19 worst suggestions for DSM5. *Psychiatric Times.* Retrieved from http://www.psychiatrictimes.com/home/content/article/10168/1522341?pageNumber=2&verify=0

Geller, D., Donnelly, C., Lopez, F., Rubin, R., Newcorn, J., Sutton, V., . . . Sumner, C. (2007). Atomoxetine treatment for pediatric patients with Attention-Deficit/Hyperactivity Disorder and comorbid Anxiety

Disorder. *Journal of the American Academy of Child & Adolescent Psychiatry, 46,* 1119–1127.

Gillberg, C., Gillberg, I. C., Rassmussen, P., Kadesjo, B., Soderstrom, H., Rastam, M., . . . Niklasson, L. (2004). Co-existing disorders in ADHD—Implications for diagnosis and intervention. *European Child and Adolescent Psychiatry, 13* (Suppl. 1), i80–i92.

Gordon, M., Barkley, R. A., & Lovett, B. J. (2006). Tests and observational measures. In R. A. Barkley (Ed.), *Attention-deficit hyperactivity disorder: A handbook for diagnosis and treatment* (pp. 369–388). New York: The Guilford Press.

Grandjean, P., Harari, R., Barr, D. B., & Debes, F. (2006). Pesticide exposure and stunting as independent predictors of neurobehavioral deficits in Ecuadorian school children. *Pediatrics, 117,* e546–e556.

Grandjean, P., Weihe, P., Burse, V. W., Needham, L. L., Storr-Hansen, E., Heinzow, B., . . . White, R. F. (2001). Neurobehavioral deficits associated with PCB in 7-year-old children prenatally exposed to seafood neurotoxicants. *Neurotoxicology and Teratology, 23*(4), 305–317.

Gray, J. A. (1991). Neural systems, emotion, and personality. In J. Madden (Ed.), *Neurobiology of learning, emotion, and affect* (pp. 273–306). New York: Raven Press.

Greenberg, L. M., Kindschi, C. L., Dupuy, T. R., & Hughes, S. J. (2007). *T.O.V.A.® clinical manual: Test of variables of Attention Continuous Performance Test.* Los Alamitos, CA: The TOVA Company.

Greenberg, M. T., Speltz, M. L., & DeKlyen, M. (1993). The role of attachment in the early development of disruptive behavior problems. *Development and Psychopathology, 5,* 191–213.

Grosswald, S. J., Stixrud, W. R., Travis, F., & Bateh, M. A. (2008). Use of the transcendental meditation technique to reduce symptoms of Attention Deficit Hyperactivity Disorder (ADHD) by reducing stress and anxiety: An exploratory study. *Current Issues in Education, 10*(2), December 2008. Retrieved from http://cie.ed.asu.edu/volume10/number2/

Hartmann, T. (1993). *Attention-Deficit Disorder: A different perception.* Lancaster, PA: Underwood-Miller.

Hoza, B., Waschbusch, D. A., Pelham, W. E., Molina, B. S. G., & Milich, R. (2000). Attention-deficit/hyperactivity disorder and control boys' responses to social success and failure. *Child Development, 71,* 432–446.

Individuals with Disabilities Education Improvement Act of 2004, Pub. L. No. 108-446. 118 Stat. 328. (2004).

Ingersoll, E. R., & Rak, C. F. (2006). *Psychopharmacology for helping professionals: An integral exploration.* Belmont, CA: Thomson Brooks/Cole.

Ingersoll, R. E., & Zeitler, D. M. (2010). *Integral psychotherapy: Inside and out.* Albany, NY: SUNY Press.

Jacobvitz, D., Hazen, N., Curran, M., & Hitchens, K. (2004). Observations of early triadic family interactions: Boundary disturbances in the family predict symptoms of depression, anxiety, and attention-deficit/hyperactivity disorder in middle childhood. *Development and Psychopathology, 16,* 577–592.

Jensen, P. S., Hinshaw, S. P., Kraemer, H. C., Lenora, N., Newcom, J. H., & Abikoff, H. B. (2001). ADHD comorbidity findings from the MTA study: Comparing comorbid subgroups. *Journal of the American Academy of Child and Adolescent Psychiatry, 2,* 147–158.

Jensen, P. S., Hinshaw, S. P., Swanson, J. M., Greenhill, L. L., Conners, C. K., Arnold, L. E., . . . Wigal, T. (2001). Findings from the NIMH Multimodal Treatment Study of ADHD (MTA): Implications and applications for primary care providers. *Developmental and Behavioral Pediatrics, 22,* 60–72.

Jester, J. M., Nigg, J. T., Adams, K., Fitzerald, H. E., Puttler, L. I., Wong, M. M., & Zucker, R. A. (2005). Inattention/hyperactivity and aggression from early childhood to adolescence: Heterogeneity of trajectories and differential influence of family environment characteristics. *Development and Psychopathology, 17,* 99–125.

Johansen, E. B., Aase, H., Meyer, A., & Sagvolden, T. (2002). Attention deficit/hyperactivity disorder behavior explained by dysfunctional reinforcement and extinction processes. *Behavioural Brain Research, 130,* 37–45.

Johnston, C., & Mash, E. J. (2001). Families of children with attention-deficit/hyperactivity disorder; Review and recommendations for future research. *Clinical Child and Family Psychology Review, 4,* 183–207.

Kapoor, A., Petropoulos, S., & Matthews, S. G. (2008). Fetal programming of hypothalamic-pituitary-adrenal (HPA) axis function and behavior by synthetic glucocorticoids. *Brain Research Reviews, 57,* 586–595.

Kazdin, A. E. (1997). Parent management training: Evidence, outcomes and issues. *Journal of the American Academy of Child and Adolescent Psychiatry, 36,* 1349–1356.

Kendall, J., Hatton, D., Beckett, A., & Leo, M. (2003). Children's accounts of attention deficit/hyperactivity disorder. *Advances in Nursing Science, 16,* 114–130.

Knopik, V. S., Heath, A. C., Jacob, T., Slutske, W. S., Bucholz, K. K., Madden, P. A., . . . Martin, N. G. (2006). Maternal alcohol use disorder and offspring ADHD: Disentangling genetic and environmental effects using a children-of-twins design. *Psychological Medicine, 36,* 1461–1471.

Kohn, A. (1989, November). Suffer the restless children. *Atlantic Monthly,* pp. 90–100.

Krisanaprakornkit, T., Ngamjarus, C., Wittonchart, C., & Piyavhatkul, N. (2010). Meditation therapies for Attention-Deficit/Hyperactivity Disorder (ADHD). *Cochrane Database of Systematic Reviews*, Issue 6, Art. No.: CD006507.

Krueger, M., & Kendall, J. (2001). Descriptions of self: An exploratory study of adolescents with ADHD. *Journal of Child and Adolescent Psychiatric Nursing, 14,* 61–72.

Lahey, B. B., & Carlson, C. L. (1991). Validity of the diagnostic category of Attention Deficit Disorder without Hyperactivity: A review of the literature. *Journal of Learning Disabilities, 24,* 110–120.

Lahey, B. B., & Piacentini, J. C., McBurnett, K., Stone, P., Hartdagen, S., & Hynd, G. W. (1988). Psychopathology in the parents of children with conduct disorder and hyperactivity. *Journal of the American Academy of Child and Adolescent Psychiatry, 27,* 163–170.

Laing, R. D. (1967). *The politics of experience and the bird of paradise.* Harmondsworth: Penguin.

Lambert, N. M., & Sandoval, J. (1980). The prevalence of learning disabilities in a sample of children considered hyperactive. *Journal of Abnormal Child Psychology, 8,* 33–50.

Leo, J. (2002). American preschoolers on Ritalin. *Society, 39*(2), 52–60.

Li, D., Sham, P. C., Owen, M. J., & He, L. (2006). Meta-analysis shows significant association between dopamine system genes and attention deficit hyperactivity disorder (ADHD). *Human Molecular Genetics, 15*(14), 2276–2284.

Linnet, K. M., Dalsgaard, S., Obel, C., Wisborg, K., Henriksen, T. B., Rodriguez, A., . . . Jarvelin, M. (2003). Maternal lifestyle factors in pregnancy risk of Attention Deficit Hyperactivity Disorder and associated behaviors: Review of the current evidence. *American Journal of Psychiatry, 160,* 1028–1040.

Loe, I. M., & Feldman, H. M. (2007). Academic and educational outcomes of children with ADHD. *Journal of Pediatric Psychology*, 32, 643–654.

Mahaffey, K. (1995). Nutrition and lead: Strategies for public health. *Environmental Health Perspectives, 103*(Suppl. 6), 191–196.

Marks, A. R., Harley, K., Bradman, A., Kogut, K., Barr, D. B., Johnson, C., . . . Eskenazi, B. (2010). Organophosphate pesticide exposure and attention in young Mexican-American children: The CHAMACOS study. *Environmental Health Perspectives, 118*(12), 1768–1774.

Marquis, A. (2007). What is integral theory? *Counseling and Values, 51*(3), 164–179.

Marquis, A. (2008). *The integral intake: A guide to comprehensive idiographic assessment in integral psychotherapy.* New York: Routledge.

Mash, E. J., & Wolfe, D. A. (2010). *Abnormal child psychology.* Belmont, CA: Wadsworth.

Maughan, D. R., Christiansen, E., Jenson, W. R., Olympia, D., & Clark, E. (2005). Behavioral parent training as a treatment for externalizing behavior disorders: A meta-analysis. *School Psychology Review, 34,* 267–286.

McGee, R., Partridge, F., Williams, S. B., & Silva, P. A. (1991). A twelve-year follow-up of preschool hyperactive children. *Journal of the American Academy of Child and Adolescent Psychiatry, 30,* 224–232.

McGuiness, D. (1989). Attention deficit disorder: The emperor's clothes, animal "pharm," and other fiction. In S. Fisher & R. P. Greenburg (Eds.), *The limits of biological treatments for psychological distress* (pp. 151–187). Hillsdale, NJ: Lawrence Erlbaum.

McMahon, R. J., & Forehand, R. (2003). *Helping the noncompliant child: A clinician's guide to effective parent training.* New York: Guilford.

Mercugliano, M., Power, T. J., & Blum, N. J. (1999). *The clinician's practical guide to Attention Deficit Hyperactivity Disorder.* Baltimore: Paul H. Brookes.

Michelson, D., Adler, L., Spencer, T., Reimherr, F. W., West, S. A., Allen, A. J., . . . Milton, D. (2003). Atomoxetine in adults with ADHD: Two randomized, placebo-controlled studies. *Biological Psychiatry, 53,* 112–120.

Michelson, D., Allen, A. J., Busner, J., Casat, C., Dunn, D., Kratochvil, C., . . . Harder, D. (2002). Once daily atomoxetine treatment for children and adolescents with attention deficit hyperactivity disorder: A randomized, placebo-controlled study. *American Journal of Psychiatry, 159,* 1896–1901.

Michelson, D., Faries, D., Wernicke, J., Kelsey, D., Kendrick, K., Sallee, F. R., & Spencer, T. (2001). Atomoxetine in the treatment of children and adolescents with attention-deficit hyperactivity disorder: A randomized, placebo-controlled, dose-response study. *Pediatrics, 108*(5), 1–9.

Mick, E., Biederman, J., Faraone, S. V., Sayer, J., & Kleinman, S. (2002). Case-control study of attention-deficit hyperactivity disorder and maternal smoking, alcohol use and drug use during pregnancy. *Journal of the American Academy of Child and Adolescent Psychiatry, 41,* 378–385.

Mick, E., Biederman, J., Prince, J., Fischer, M. J., & Faraone, S. V. (2002). Impact of low birth weight on attention-deficit hyperactivity disorder. *Journal of Developmental & Behavioral Pediatrics, 23,* 18–22.

Milberger, S., Biederman, J., Faraone, S. V., Chen, L., & Jones, J. (1997). ADHD is associated with early initiation of cigarette smoking in children and adolescents. *Journal of the American Academy of Child and Adolescent Psychiatry, 36,* 37–44.

Milberger, S., Biederman, J., Faraone, S. V., & Jones, J. (1998). Further evidence of an association between maternal smoking during pregnancy and attention deficit hyperactivity disorder: Findings from a high-risk sample of siblings. *Journal of Clinical Child Psychology, 27,* 352–358.

Mill, J., & Petronis, A. (2008). Pre- and peri-natal environmental risks for attention-deficit hyperactivity disorder (ADHD): The potential role of epigenetic processes in mediating susceptibility. *Journal of Child Psychology and Psychiatry, 49*(10), 1020–1030.

Mitsis, E. M., McKay, K. E., Schulz, K. P., Newcorn, J. H., & Halperin, J. M. (2000). Parent-teacher concordance for DSM-IV attention-deficit/hyperactivity disorder. *Journal of the Academy of Child and Adolescent Psychiatry, 39,* 308–313.

National Resource Center on ADHD. (2011). Diagnosis & treatment: Managing medication for children and adolescents with ADHD (WWK3). Updated February 2008. Retrieved from http://www.help4adhd.org/en/treatment/medication/WWK3

Neuman, R. J., Lobos, E., Reich, W., Henderson, C. A., Sun, L., & Todd, R. D. (2007). Parental smoking exposure and dopaminergic genotypes interact to cause a severe ADHD subtype. *Biological Psychiatry, 61,* 1320–1328.

Newman, L. (1996). ADHD—Rethinking the epidemic. *Australian and New Zealand Journal of Family Therapy, 17,* 107–108.

Nigg, J. T. (2006). *What causes ADHD?: Understanding what goes wrong and why.* New York: Guilford Press.

Nigg, J. T. (2008). ADHD, lead exposure and prevention: How much lead or how much evidence is needed? *Expert Reviews in Neurotherapeutics, 8,* 519–521.

Nigg, J. T., John, O. P., Blaskey, L. G., Huang-Pollock, C. L., Willcutt, E. G., Hinshaw, S. P., & Pennington, B. (2002). Big Five dimensions and ADHD symptoms: Links between personality traits and clinical symptoms. *Journal of Personality and Social Psychology, 83*(2), 451–469.

Nigg, J. T., Knottnerus, G. M., Martel, M. M., Nikolas, M., Cavanaugh, K., Karmaus, W., & Rappley, M. D. (2008). Low blood levels associated with clinically diagnosed Attention-Deficit/Hyperactivity Disorder and mediated by weak cognitive control. *Biological Psychiatry, 63,* 325–331.

Olson, S. (1996). Developmental perspectives. In S. Sandberg (Ed.), *Hyperactivity disorders of childhood. Cambridge Monographs in Child and Adolescent Psychiatry* (pp. 149–194). Cambridge: Cambridge University Press.

Palmer, E. D., & Finger, S. (2001). An early description of ADHD (Inattentive Subtype): Dr. Alexander Crichton and the "Mental Restlessness" (1798). *Child Psychology and Psychiatry Reviews, 6,* 66–73.

Parsons, T. (1951). *The social system.* Glencoe, IL: Free Press.

Pelham, W. E., Burrows-MacLean, L., Gnagy, E. M., Fabiano, G. A., Coles, E. K., & Tresco, K. E. (2005) Transdermal methylphenidate, behavioral, and combined treatment for children with ADHD. *Experimental and Clinical Psychopharmacology, 13,* 111–126.

Pelham, W. E., Jr., & Fabiano, G. A. (2008). Evidence-based psychosocial treatments for attention-deficit/hyperactivity disorder. *Journal of Clinical Child and Adolescent Psychology, 37,* 184–214.

Pelham, W. E., Wheeler, T., & Chronis, A. (1998). Empirically supported psychosocial treatments for Attention Deficit Hyperactivity Disorder. *Journal of Clinical Child Psychology, 27,* 190–205.

Pfiffner, L. J., Barkley, R. A., & DuPaul, G. J. (2006). Treatment of ADHD in school settings. In R. A. Barkley (Ed.), *Attention-deficit hyperactivity disorder: A handbook for diagnosis and treatment* (3rd ed., pp. 547–589). New York: Guilford Press.

Pfiffner, L. J., McBurnett, K., Rathouz, P. J., & Judice, S. (2005). Family correlates of oppositional and conduct disorders in children with ADHD. *Journal of Abnormal Child Psychology, 33,* 551–563.

Pliszka, S. R. (1998). Comorbidity of attention-deficit/hyperactivity disorder: An overview. *Journal of Clinical Psychiatry, 59,* 50–58.

Pliszka, S. R. (2007). Pharmacologic treatment of attention-deficit/hyperactivity disorder: Efficacy, safety, and mechanisms of action. *Neuropsychological reviews, 17,* 61–72.

Pliszka, S. R., & the AACAP Work Group on Quality Issues. (2007). Practice parameter for the assessment and treatment of children and adolescents with attention-deficit/hyperactivity disorder. *Journal of the Academy of Child and Adolescent Psychiatry, 46,* 894–921.

Polanczyk, G., de Lima, M. S., Horta, B. L., Biederman, J., & Rohde, L. A. (2007). The worldwide prevalence of ADHD: A systematic review and meta-regression analysis. *American Journal of Psychiatry, 164,* 942–948.

Poulton, A. (2005). Growth on stimulant medication; clarifying the confusion: A review. *Archives of Diseases of Childhood, 90,* 801–806.

Reynolds, C. R., & Kamphaus, R. W. (2004). *Behavioral Assessment System for Children, Second Edition (BASC-2).* Bloomington, MN: Pearson Assessments.

Richman, M., Stevenson, J., & Graham, P. J. (1982). *Preschool to school: A behavioural study.* London: Academic Press.

Risch, N., & Merikangas, K. (1996). The future of genetic studies of complex human diseases. *Science, 273,* 1516–1517.

Robin, A. L. (2006). Training families with adolescents with ADHD. In R. A. Barkley (Ed.), *Attention-deficit hyperactivity disorder: A handbook for diagnosis and treatment* (3rd ed., pp. 499–546). New York: Guilford Press.

Rothbart, M. K. (2003). Temperament and the pursuit of an integrated developmental psychology. *Merrill-Palmer-Quarterly, 50,* 492–505.

Rucklidge, J. J., & Tannock, R. (2002). Neuropsychological profiles of adolescents with ADHD: Effects of reading difficulties and gender. *Journal of Child Psychology and Psychiatry, 43,* 988–1003.

Russell, V. A., Sagvolden, T., & Johansen, E. B. (2005). Animal models of attention-deficit hyperactivity disorder. *Behavioral and Brain Functions, 1*(9), 1–17. Retrieved from http://www.behavioralandbrainfunctions.com/content/1/1/9

Rutter, M., Tizard, J., & Whitmore, K. (Eds.). (1970). *Education, health, and behavior.* London: Longman and Green.

Sagiv, S. K., Thurston, S. W., Bellinger, D. C., Tolbert, P. E., Altshul, L. M., & Korrick, S. A. (2010). Prenatal organochlorine exposure and behaviors associated with attention deficit hyperactivity disorder in school-aged children. *American Journal of Epidemiology, 171,* 563–601.

Sagvolden, T. (2000). Behavioral validation of the spontaneously hypertensive rat (SHR) as an animal model of attention-deficit/hyperactivity disorder (ADHD). *Neuroscience and Biobehavioral Reviews, 24,* 31–39.

Sagvolden, T. (2011). Impulsiveness, overactivity, and poorer sustained attention improve by chronic treatment with low doses of l-amphetamine in an animal model of Attention-Deficit/Hyperactivity Disorder (ADHD). *Behavioral and Brain Functions,* 7(6), 1–10. Retrieved from http://www.behavioralandbrainfunctions.com/content/7/1/6

Sandford, J. A., & Turner, A. (2000). *Integrated visual and auditory continuous performance test manual.* Richmond, VA: Brain Train.

Sanson, A., Hemphill, S. A., & Smart, D. (2004). Connections between temperament and social development: A review. *Social Development, 13,* 142–170.

Seidman, L. J., Valera, E. M., & Makris, N. (2005). Structural brain imaging of attention-deficit/hyperactivity disorder. *Biological Psychiatry, 57,* 1263–1272.

Schatz, D. B., & Rostain, A. L. (2006). ADHD with comorbid anxiety: A review of the current literature. *Journal of Attention Disorders, 10,* 141–149.

Sklar, P. (2005). Principles of haplotype mapping and potential applications to attention-deficit/hyperactivity disorder. *Biological Psychiatry, 57,* 1357–1366.

Sleator, E. K., Ullmann, R. K., & von Neuman, A. (1982). How do hyperactive children feel about taking stimulants and will they tell the doctor? *Clinical Pediatrics, 21,* 474–479.

Smith, B. H., Barkley, R. A., & Shapiro, C. J. (2006). Attention deficit/hyperactivity disorder. In E. J. Mash & R. A. Barkley (Eds.), *Treatment of childhood disorders* (3rd ed., pp. 65–136). New York: Guilford.

Snyder, J., Reid, J., & Patterson, G. R. (2003). A social learning model of child and adolescent antisocial behavior. In B. B. Lahey, T. E. Moffitt, & A. Caspi (Eds.), *Causes of conduct disorder and juvenile delinquency* (pp. 27–48). New York: Guilford.

Solanto, M. V., Abikoff, H., Sonuga-Burke, E., Schachar, R., Logan, G. D., & Wigal, T. (2001). The ecological validity of delay aversion and response inhibition as measures of impulsivity in AD/HD: A supplement to the NIMH Multimodal Treatment Study of AD/HD. *Journal of Abnormal Child Psychology, 29*, 215–228.

Sonuga-Barke, E. J. S. (2003). The dual-pathway model of ADHD: an elaboration of neuro-developmental characteristics. *Neuroscience and Behavior Review, 27*, 593–604.

Sonuga-Barke, E. J. S. (2005). Causal models of attention-deficit/hyperactivity disorder: From common simple deficits to multiple developmental pathways. *Biological Psychiatry, 57*, 1231–1238.

Spencer, T. J., Biederman, J., & Mick, E. (2007). Attention-deficit/hyperactivity disorder: Diagnosis, lifespan, comorbidities, and neurobiology. *Ambulatory Pediatrics, 7*, 73–81.

Stiefel, I. (1997). Can disturbance in attachment contribute to attention deficit hyperactivity disorder? A case discussion. *Clinical Child Psychology and Psychiatry, 2*, 45–64.

Still, G. F. (1902). Some abnormal psychical conditions in children: The Goulsonian lectures. *Lancet, 1*, 1008–1012.

Stoddard, J. L., Johnson, C. A., Boley-Cruz, T., & Sussman, S. (1997). Targeted tobacco markets: Outdoor advertising in Los Angeles minority neighborhoods, *American Journal of Public Health, 87*, 1232–1233.

Stolzer, J. M. (2009). Attention deficit hyperactivity disorder: Valid medical condition or culturally constructed myth? *Ethical Human Psychology and Psychiatry, 1*, 5–15.

Swanson, J. M., McBurnett, K., Wigal, T., Pfiffner, L. J., Lerner, M. A., Williams, L., . . . Fisher, T. D. (1993). Effect of stimulant medication on Children with attention deficit disorder: A "review of reviews." *Exceptional Children, 60*, 154–162.

Szasz, T. (1970). *The manufacture of madness*. New York: Harper Colophon.

Thapar, A., Langley, K., Asherson, P., & Gill, M. (2007). Gene-environment interplay in attention-deficit hyperactivity disorder and the importance of a developmental perspective. *The British Journal of Psychiatry, 190*, 1–3.

Timimi, S. (2005). *Naughty boys: Antisocial behavior, ADHD and the role of culture*. New York: Palgrave MacMillan.

Timimi, S., & Taylor, E. (2004). ADHD is best understood as a cultural construct. *British Journal of Psychiatry, 184*, 8–9.

Tong, S., von Schirnding, Y. E., & Prapamontol, T. (2000). Environmental lead exposure: A public health problem of global dimensions. *Bulletin of the World Health Organization, 78*, 1068–1077.

Tourette's Syndrome Study Group. (2002). Treatment of ADHD in children with tics: A randomized controlled study. *Neurology, 58*, 527–536.

Travis, F., Grosswald, S., & Stixrud, W. (2011). ADHD, brain functioning, and transcendental meditation practice. *Mind & Brain, The Journal of Psychiatry, 2*(1), 73–79. Retrieved from http://content.yudu.com/Library/A1t5r8/MindampBraintheJourn/resources/index.htm?referrerUrl=http%3A%F%2Fwww.yudu.com%2Fitem%2details%2F371567%2FMind--Brain--the-Journal-of-Psychiatry-Volume-2Issue-1

van den Bergh, B. R. H., Mennes, M., Stevens, V., Van der Meere, J., Börger, N., Stiers, P., Marcoen, A., & Legae, L. (2006). ADHD deficit as measured in adolescent boys with a continuous performance task is related to antenatal maternal anxiety. *Pediatric Research, 59*, 78–82.

van den Bergh, B. R. H., Mulder, E. J. H., Mennes, M., & Glover, V. (2005). Antenatal maternal anxiety and stress and the neurobehavioral development of the fetus and child: Links and possible mechanisms. A review. *Neuroscience and Biobehavioral Reviews, 29*, 247–258.

van Hienen, F. J. W. (2010). Organophosphate based pesticides and ADHD. Unpublished doctoral dissertation. University Utrecht, Utrect, The Netherlands.

Waldman, I. D. (2007). Gene-environment interactions reexamined: Does mother's marital instability interact with the dopamine receptor D2 gene in the etiology of childhood attention-deficit/hyperactivity disorder? *Development and Psychopathology, 19*, 1117–1128.

Walker, F. O. (2007). Huntington's disease. *Lancet, 369*, 218–228.

Weiss, G., & Hechtman, L. (1986). *Hyperactive children grown up*. New York: Guilford Press.

Whitaker, R. T. (2010). *Anatomy of an epidemic: Magic bullets, psychiatric drugs, and the astonishing rise of mental illness in America*. New York: Crown.

Widiger, T. A., Livesley, W. J., & Clark, L. A. (2009). An integrative dimensional classification of personality disorder. *Psychological Assessment, 21*, 243–255.

Wilens, T. E., Biederman, J., Brown, S., Tanguay, S., Monuteaux, M., Blake, C., & Spencer, T. J. (2002).

Psychiatric comorbidity and functioning in clinically referred preschool children and school-age youths with ADHD. *Journal of American Academy Child and Adolescent Psychiatry, 41*, 262–268.

Zito, J. M., Safer, D. J., dosReis, S., Gardner, J. F., Boles, M., & Lynch, F. (2000). Trends in the prescribing of psychotropic medications to preschoolers. *Journal of the American Medical Association, 238,* 1025–1030.

Zylowska, L., Ackerman, D. L., Yang, M. H., Futrell, J. L., Horton, N. L., Hale, T. S., . . . Smalley, S. L. (2008). Mindfulness meditation training in adults and adolescents with ADHD: A feasibility study. *Journal of Attention Disorders, 11*, 737–746.

Zylowska, L., Smalley, S. L., & Schwartz, J. M. (2009). Mindful awareness and ADHD. In F. Dodonna (Ed.), *Clinical handbook of mindfulness* (pp. 319–338). New York: Springer.

# 10

# Sexual Disorders

**Deborah Hudson, Ph.D. Candidate, *University of Rochester***
**Jessica Germano-Fokin, Ed.D., *Sexual Health Discoveries***
**Andre Marquis, Ph.D., *University of Rochester***

*"Sexuality, just like other basic needs such as intimacy, contact, emotional expression and love, is an integral component of human life."*

(Crooks & Baur, 2011)

## INTRODUCTION

Sexual disorders are a conglomerate of various sexual problems that together cause a considerable amount of distress to those afflicted by them, their partners, their families, and, in some cases, communities at large (Laumann, Paik, & Rosen, 1999; Sadovsky & Nusbaum, 2006). There are a large number of sexual disorders, some of which are quite prevalent;[1] many share commonalities, whereas others have distinct differences (Crooks & Baur, 2011; Laumann et al., 1999; Sadovsky & Nusbaum, 2006). The majority of people will experience some sort of sexual concern at some point in their lives (Mezzich & Hernandez-Serrano, 2006). There is also significant controversy regarding where to draw the line between normal and abnormal sexual functioning, and some take issue with specific diagnostic categories (Althof, Dean, Derogatis, Rosen, & Sisson, 2005; Balon & Wise, 2011; Fagan, 2004; Singy, 2010).

Despite the distress these disorders cause, as well as their frequency of occurrence, there remains a tendency for sexual disorders to be neglected or understudied by researchers, and relatively ignored by clinicians and physicians

---

[1] Although there is general agreement regarding the high prevalence of Sexual Dysfunctions, an exact number is difficult to determine (Kingsberg & Althof, 2009). According to the *Diagnostic and Statistical Manual of Mental Disorders*, 4th Edition, Text Revision (DSM-IV-TR), a comprehensive survey suggested the following prevalence estimates for various sexual complaints: 3% for male dyspareunia, 15% for female dyspareunia, 10% for male orgasm problems, 25% for female orgasm problems, 33% for female hypoactive sexual desire, 27% for Premature Ejaculation, 20% for female arousal problems, and 10% for male erectile difficulties (APA, 2000, p. 538).

(Kingsberg & Althof, 2009; Maurice & Yule, 2010; Mezzich & Hernandez-Serrano, 2006; Sadofsky & Nusbaum, 2006). Moreover, there is even less research on female sexuality than male sexuality (Kingsberg & Althof, 2009). On a positive note, there has been a recent resurgence of interest in the area of sexual functioning, including the unique needs of women (Laumann et al., 1999; Sutherland, 2012). There are wide variations in how sexual dysfunctions are experienced, across disorders, individuals, and couples. In addition, cultural factors have an important bearing on how sexual experiences are perceived (American Psychiatric Association [APA], 2013; Crooks & Baur, 2011). Thus, it is critical to be empathically attuned to each client in terms of his or her unique experience (Tiefer, 1991).

The multifaceted nature of Integral theory is helpful in that it allows for both an idiosyncratic and comprehensive conceptualization of each client or client system[2] (Dallos, Wright, Stedman, & Johnstone, 2006). Specifically, the experience of self-consciousness and performance anxiety (UL) is a significant factor in sexual dysfunction; biological and physiological factors (UR) have been highly privileged in recent thought pertaining to Sexual Dysfunction Disorders; relationship factors and cultural issues (LL) are clearly implicated, as wider sociocultural views and specific circumstances pertaining to a person's sexual partner(s) are significant determinants in how an individual's sexuality will manifest; and systemic issues (LR) are also relevant, particularly in the case of some of the Paraphilic Disorders,[3] with which legal issues are apt to arise.

In the DSM-5, the sexual disorders are grouped into two categories: Sexual Dysfunction Disorders and Paraphilic Disorders.[4] Sexual Dysfunction Disorders involve clinically significant disturbance in an individual's capacity to enjoy sex or respond sexually (APA, 2013). Paraphilic Disorders involve persistent and intense sexual attraction not involving foreplay or genital stimulation with consenting, physically mature human partners (APA, 2013). Gender Dysphoria is a rare occurrence (APA, 2000); it will be covered very briefly at the end of the chapter.

Prior to turning our attention to the Sexual Dysfunction Disorders and Paraphilic Disorders, we will lay a contextual foundation to facilitate a clearer understanding of the evolution of thought pertaining to sexual health. We begin with a discussion of Sigmund Freud. Freud had a huge influence on societal views of sexuality, asserting that sexuality was innate in women as well as men (Crooks & Baur, 2011). Freud placed much emphasis on the effect of a frustrated sex drive, believing it "represented the single most conflictual experience for a young child that, consequently, exerted the most influence over personality" (Fall, Holden, & Marquis, 2004, p. 48). Freud's theory of psychosexual development framed psychological development in the context of psychosexual stages, and postulated that individuals could become stuck, or fixated, at a given stage (Fall et al., 2004). Freud's seven-volume book *Studies in Psychology of Sex* posited that any sexual activity—including homosexuality and masturbation, which were often deemed perversions—was healthy provided that no one was harmed (Crooks & Baur, 2011). Based on the view that the clitoris was a "stunted penis"

---

[2] Another multifaceted approach is the "perspectives" view, first put forth by McHugh and Slavney (1998) and applied specifically to sexual disorders by Fagan (2004).

[3] These disorders were termed Paraphilias in the DSM-IV-TR.

[4] The bulk of this chapter was written during the transition from the DSM-IV-TR to the DSM-5.

(Crooks & Baur, 2011, p. 169), and the related conclusion that clitoral orgasms were more in line with a masculine way of experiencing sexuality, Freud suggested that a female should progress from experiencing clitoral to vaginal orgasms by the end of adolescence. If she were unable to do so, she was considered to be less mature. Although much of Freud's seminal (pun intended) work has been challenged and refuted, relics of his theory are still noticeable in the sexology literature today, even as views of human sexuality continue to evolve.

Next, we turn to the groundbreaking work of Alfred C. Kinsey and colleagues (Kinsey, Pomeroy, & Martin, 1948; Kinsey, Pomeroy, Martin, & Gebhard, 1953) who, in the 1940s and 1950s, were the first to study real-life sexual practices in the general population (Crooks & Baur, 2011; Mezzich & Hernandez-Serrano, 2006). Devoted to the scientific method, Kinsey and colleagues (1948) described their research as "a fact finding survey in which an attempt is being made to discover what people do sexually, and what factors account for differences in sexual behavior among individuals, and among various segments of the population" (p. 3). Kinsey et al. (1948, 1953) used a methodology wherein sex survey interviews were conducted with a large sample of 5300 White male and 5940 female Americans from all areas of the country, which were then coded and analyzed using primarily descriptive statistics (Kinsey et al., 1948, 1953; Mezzich & Hernandez-Serrano, 2006). No attempt was made to differentiate between those who would be considered psychologically healthy or unhealthy (Kinsey et al., 1948, 1953). Despite Kinsey's (1948, 1953) staunch commitment "to ignore sexual politics and attend simply to the 'facts'" (Irvine, 1990, p. 39), his research led to an uproar in American society because the results indicated that the commonly espoused morality of the time was not congruent with actual sex practices (Crooks & Baur, 2011; Irvine, 1990; Mezzich & Hernandez-Serrano, 2006). Another useful finding of Kinsey et al. (1948, 1953) was that sexual practices differ widely across individuals, which makes the concept of normality extremely difficult to define (Edwards & Booth, 1994; Udry & Campbell, 1994).

## THE SEXUAL RESPONSE CYCLE

Following on the heels of the pioneering work by Kinsey and colleagues came William Masters and Virginia Johnson (1966, 1970), who were the first to offer sex therapy to resolve sexual problems (Green, 1994). Kinsey and colleagues (1948, 1953) paved the way for Masters and Johnson by bringing the topic of sexuality into the open for the mainstream American population, as well as through initial discussions of the physiology of male and female sexual responses, wherein the similarity between the genders was emphasized (Irvine, 1990).

Through direct laboratory observation of masturbation and coitus with a homogeneous sample of healthy, orgasmic participants, Masters and Johnson (1966) first identified the human sexual response cycle (HSRC; Crooks & Baur, 2011). Their work was revolutionary and highly influential, to the extent that the HSRC served as the framework for diagnosing Sexual Dysfunction Disorders in the DSM-IV-TR (Balon, Segraves, & Clayton, 2001; Crooks & Baur, 2011; Tiefer, 1991). Specifically, sexual dysfunctions are typically viewed as a malfunction at some point in the HSRC, which is generally held to be the model of normal sexual functioning for both men and women (APA, 2000; Balon et al., 2001; Troisi, 2008).

## Postmodern Critique of the Human Sexual Response Cycle (HSRC)

Before we delve further into the physiological aspects of sexual functioning and explain the HSRC from a biological point of view, we would be remiss not to mention that the HSRC has fallen prey to strong criticism by some, calling its validity and applicability into question, especially for women (Association of Reproductive Health Professionals [ARHP], 2008; Bancroft, 2002; Basson, 2000, 2001a, 2001b, 2005; Crooks & Baur, 2011; Hinderliter, 2010; Tiefer, 1991). Although the work of Masters and Johnson (1966) has served an important purpose in terms of "helping to orient treatment and research along clinically relevant dimensions" (Schiavi, 2000, p. 267) and has withstood "the test of time" (Crooks & Baur, 2008, p. 37), there are criticisms stemming largely from a social constructionist view, which holds "that there is no such thing as a value-free science, that the concepts we use are popular or persistent not because they are valid but because they are socially and politically useful" (Rossi, 1995, p. 5). A critique is put forth by Tiefer (1991), who states: "It is my impression that the widespread utilization of [the HSRC] model has received little scientific or intellectual analysis, and has been adopted prematurely, primarily to meet professional needs" (p. 2).

Despite Kaplan's (1974) addition of desire to Masters and Johnson's (1966) HSRC model, Tiefer (1991) nonetheless critiqued the revised model based upon research, clinical, and feminist rationales. First, she suggests that it neglects the concept of desire as an initiating mechanism for sexual behavior (Tiefer, 1991). Tiefer (1991) maintains that this omission is critical in terms of distinguishing between a sexuality that is individually constructed and determined, as opposed to one that is fixed in all human beings—a sort of "essential human quality" (Rossi, 1995, p. 5). More specifically, the HSRC model does not allow for variations in sexual responsiveness, suggesting that the normative person will move progressively and sequentially through separate and distinct phases in a linear fashion, with an emphasis on genital changes (Basson, 2000, 2001a, 2001b, 2005; Crooks & Baur, 2011).

A second criticism is that Masters and Johnson's (1966) research is not generalizable to the population at large because their using volunteer subjects likely generated biased research results (Bentler & Abramson, 1980; Crooks & Baur, 2011; Rosenthal & Rosnow, 1969; Rowland, 1999). More specifically, Tiefer (1991) notes several selection biases in Masters and Johnson's (1966) methodology. First, a requirement for subjects was that they have a "positive history of masturbatory and coital orgasmic experience" (Tiefer, 1991, p. 311). As Tiefer (1991) points out, this would call into question the applicability of the results for individuals and couples experiencing sexual difficulties. In addition, the HSRC implies that the only satisfactory sexual experience must include orgasm, reifying orgasm as a stage to be achieved and the sole purpose of sexual intercourse, rather than legitimizing sex as a means of experiencing pleasure in nonspecific ways and connecting on a personal level, with or without orgasm (Basson, 2000, 2001a, 2001b, 2008; Basson et al., 2004; Levine, 1992; Tiefer, 1991). To the extent that women place a higher value on interpersonal connection than on achieving orgasm, the HSRC is preferential in the direction of a masculine style of experiencing sexuality (Tiefer, 1991; Crooks & Baur, 2011). Similarly, the subjects chosen for Masters and Johnson's laboratory research were required to show a significant amount of interest in sex (Masters & Johnson, 1966). We speculate that this quality is also more likely to be absent among individuals experiencing sexual problems.

In addition to subject selection bias, the laboratory studies used in Masters and Johnson's (1966) research were held in an artificial setting and are replete with experimenter bias, which calls the validity of their work into question (Rosenthal, 1966; Tiefer, 1991). Specifically, Masters and Johnson (1966) emphasized performance issues, which was readily communicated to research subjects with words such as "success" and "failure" to comment on occurrences in the laboratory (Masters & Johnson, 1966; Tiefer, 1991). In summary, the HSRC model is primarily a physiological perspective, focusing heavily on bodily responses and the genitals, with a lack of emphasis on the emotional and psychological aspects of sexual experiencing (Tiefer, 1991). It has likely led to the commonly held perception that sexual responses are largely physiological in nature, rather than psychological or relational (Crooks & Baur, 2011).

## Description of the Human Sexual Response Cycle

Masters and Johnson (1966) originally proposed the HSRC in 1966 as a linear model of sexual response for both men and women (Crooks & Baur, 2011). Masters and Johnson (1966) tracked two primary physiological mechanisms: vasocongestion and myotonia (vasocongestion and myotonia pertain to increases in blood flow and muscle tension, respectively). The HSRC as originally conceptualized by Masters and Johnson (1966) is comprised of four stages: excitement, plateau, orgasm and resolution. Masters and Johnson (1966) also believed that males had an additional phase: a refractory period, also known as a recovery period, during which further genital stimulation would not produce another orgasm (Crooks & Baur, 2011).

Given the importance of the HSRC in the conceptualization of sexual dysfunction, we will now describe it in greater detail. True to the original model, the emphasis in this section will be on genitalia and physiological processes. The first stage of the HSRC is excitement. Often referred to as foreplay, it happens when an individual (either male or female) is exposed to sexual stimuli. There are wide variations in what constitutes stimuli for a particular person; visual images, thoughts/fantasies, and physical touch are all likely sources of sexual stimuli (Haber & Runyon, 1984). The primary indicator that a male is experiencing sexual excitement is that his penis will become engorged with blood and he will develop an erection (Crooks & Baur, 2011). His testicles will begin to rise, and his nipples may become hard (Sipski & Alexander, 1997a). For a female, the signs include clitoral expansion, lubrication of the vagina, swollen breasts, and erect nipples (Haber & Runyon, 1984). In both genders, respiratory rate, heart rate, and blood pressure begin to climb, myotonia increases, and a pink rash may develop that is called the sex flush (Crooks & Baur, 2011; Haber & Runyon, 1984; Satterfield & Stayton, 1980).

Following the excitement phase is the plateau phase, during which there is a powerful intensification of sexual reactions and sensations (Crooks & Baur, 2011). The penis and testes become more enlarged in males, and a drop of fluid may be secreted from the penis. Females will experience a lessening of lubrication and a retraction of the clitoris beneath its hood, while breasts become larger. In both genders, myotonia, heart rate, and blood pressure will continue to increase (Crooks & Baur, 2011).

Sexual pleasure climaxes in the orgasm phase, when people experience "a transient peak sensation of intense pleasure" (Kingsberg & Althof, 2009, p. S36). In both genders, respiratory rate, heart rate, and blood pressure peak (Levine, 1992). The male experience of orgasm consists of ejaculation and simultaneous penile contractions

(Crooks & Baur, 2011), preceded by an intense pleasure state known as "ejaculatory inevitability" (Levine, 1992, p. 33). The female experiences similar, intense contractions and throbbing in the vicinity of the vagina (Crooks & Baur, 2011; Haber & Runyon, 1984). Although orgasm is often framed as the primary goal of sexual intercourse, it is important to note that sex can be extremely rewarding and pleasurable even when orgasm does not occur (Basson, 2005; Basson et al., 2004).

Following orgasm, there is an experience of release, and the bodily changes that occurred during intercourse will return to their baseline, pre-excitement levels (Crooks & Baur, 2011). This is known as the resolution phase, which may be experienced as a time of closeness for a couple, during which they may hold and caress each other, and engage in intimate conversation (Levine, 1992). For men, there is usually an additional refractory period, during which they are unable to experience an orgasm (Levine, 1992; Sipski & Alexander, 1997a). Women do not have a refractory period and are able to experience multiple orgasms during a single sexual encounter (Crooks & Baur, 2011).[5]

Also highly influential in the arena of sex therapy is psychiatrist and psychoanalyst Helen Singer Kaplan (1974, 1979), who is known for integrating multiple approaches (psychodynamic, cognitive, interpersonal, and behavioral) to sexual difficulties (Mezzich & Hernandez-Serrano, 2006; Schiavi, 2000). In 1974, Kaplan modified Masters and Johnson's (1966) original model by adding the concept of desire, which is defined as "sensations that motivate the person to initiate or respond to sexual stimulation" (Sipski & Alexander, 1997a, p. 77), and condensing the excitement and plateau phases. Kaplan (1979) suggested that most sexual difficulties involve at least one of these three phases, and an individual may experience difficulty with one phase while functioning well in the others (Crooks & Baur, 2011). An important contribution of Kaplan's (1979) model is that it addresses aspects of the sexual response cycle other than genital changes, especially desire (Crooks & Baur, 2011; Ferreira, Narciso, & Novo, 2012). Kaplan's (1979) model, which she initially referred to as a triphasic model, has been integrated with the earlier work of Masters and Johnson (1966).

The HSRC, incorporating Kaplan's (1979) changes, is comprised of four stages: desire, excitement, orgasm, and resolution. The desire stage consists of stimulating the mind through engagement in fantasies about sensual and/or sexual activity and encounters. The excitement stage is characterized by physiological changes in preparation for orgasm. The orgasmic stage is the most heightened point of sexual pleasure, resulting in the release of tension as a result of sexual satiation. The final stage is resolution, during which the individual comes down from a sexually heightened state, generally feeling quite relaxed with an overall sense of well-being (APA, 2000; Crooks & Baur, 2008; Mezzich & Hernandez-Serrano, 2006).

## Alternative Models of Sexual Response

It has been suggested that despite the addition of the desire phase to Kaplan's (1979) model, it remains incomplete (Crooks & Baur, 2011), and it is clear that not all sexual

---

[5] There is some contradiction about multiple orgasms and refractory periods in the literature. It appears that in some cases, men can experience multiple orgasms (Chia & Abrams, 1997), and some women do experience a refractory period. For more detailed information on the HSRC, the reader is referred to *Our Sexuality* (Crooks & Baur, 2011).

expression includes spontaneous sexual desire (Basson, 2001b; Basson et al., 2004; ter Kuile, Both, & van Lankveld, 2010). Basson (2001a) suggests multiple motivations for engaging in sexual activity, especially for women. For example, a woman may be motivated to begin a given act of sex not by sexual desire itself, but rather by factors such as desiring emotional intimacy or the desire to increase her feelings of being feminine, attractive, and desired by her partner.

As alluded to previously, some have questioned the use of the HSRC model with women, taking issue with the fact that it assumes that male and female sexual response patterns are virtually the same (Basson, 2000; Kingsberg & Althof, 2009; Sutherland, 2012; Tiefer, 1991; Troisi, 2008). Whipple and Brash McGreer (1997) emphasize that there are multiple ways that women can experience sexual pleasure other than orgasm, charging health professionals "to be aware that there is no right or normal way to have a sexual experience. Each person is unique and responds differently depending on many variables" (p. 516). Research shows that, for women, a combination of factors along with biology, such as context, psychology, and interpersonal issues, are influential in a woman's sexual experiences, and women may choose to participate in sex for a wide variety of reasons (Basson, 2000; Kingsberg & Althof, 2009; Sutherland, 2012; Troisi, 2008; Whipple & Brash McGreer, 1997). In fact, being discriminating in terms of requiring positive relationship factors in order to be sexually responsive may actually serve an evolutionary purpose, preventing the conception of children in sexual partnerships that are unstable or unsatisfying (Troisi, 2008).

Hence, alternative models have been proposed that are more reflective of women's needs. David Reed's Erotic Stimulus Pathway Model focuses less on genitalia and more on the psychology and social behaviors that make up the human sexual response (Sexual Health Network, 2004). Reed postulates that there are four stages: Seduction, Sensation, Surrender, and Reflection. In the Seduction stage, we participate in those behaviors that will lead us and/or a potential partner to engage in sexual activity, such as attending to physical appearance, smelling good, and planning to spend time together. In the Sensation stage, we engage our senses, taking in and interpreting potential sexual stimuli, which leads to arousal. In the Surrender stage, we experience orgasm, which requires relinquishing control and trusting one's self and/or partner. In the Reflection stage, we look back on the sexual experience and consider whether it was positive and pleasurable. This stage is considered to be very important because whether or not a sexual experience was felt to be positive will either serve as reinforcement and set the stage for a future sexual encounter or lead to future resistance to sexual experiencing (Sexual Health Network, 2004). Whipple and Brash McGreer (1997) have extended Reed's model, suggesting that "the model is circular, with the reflection phase leading to the seduction phase of the next sexual experience" (p. 526).

Basson (2008) has also constructed a nonlinear model of female sexual response, emphasizing the interrelated effects of emotional intimacy, sexual stimuli, and relationship satisfaction. According to Basson (2001b), a woman may choose to participate sexually for reasons other than desire, such as to be responsive to her partner or experience emotional connection. She further points to the interconnectedness between physical and psychological factors (body/UR and mind/UL), stating that women frequently report phases of sexual responses that not only overlap and vary sequentially, but also meld both mental and bodily components (Basson, 2005). In Basson's (2001a) model, she begins from a place of "sexual neutrality," in which a woman is open to sexual stimuli, yet does not seek it out (ARHP, 2008). When that stimulus is encountered, psychological and biological factors lead to increased desire and arousal. If not interrupted, desire and arousal culminate in a satisfying emotional and physical experience, which will make her more likely to be desirous of, and open to, a sexual encounter the next time around (ARHP, 2008; Basson, 2000). Basson's (2001a) model clarifies that the goal of sexual activity is not necessarily to achieve an orgasm, but rather to experience personal satisfaction, which can involve physical satisfaction (orgasm) and/or emotional satisfaction (a feeling of intimacy and connection with a partner).

## THE BIOPSYCHOSOCIAL PERSPECTIVE ON SEXUAL FUNCTIONING AND AN ETIOLOGICAL PREVIEW

The works of early sexologists such as Kinsey et al. (1948, 1953), Masters and Johnson (1966), and Kaplan (1974) fit readily with the disease model that is in vogue today, and recent approaches to human sexuality have been highly medicalized (Bancroft, 2002; DeLamatar & Sill, 2005; Mezzich & Hernandez-Serrano, 2006; Rosen & Leiblum, 1995; Rossi, 1995; Sutherland, 2012; Tiefer, 2001, 2004). Previously, the emphasis had been on psychological factors, and psychoanalysis was the primary approach for treating sexual problems (Schiavi, 2000). From the perspective of Integral theory, the majority of sexual problems were first viewed as subjective, upper-left quadrant phenomena; more recently, they have tended to be viewed largely as upper-right quadrant phenomena. Currently, it is estimated that etiological influences are close to evenly split between psychological and physiological causes (Mezzich & Hernandez-Serrano, 2006). The dichotomy between mind and body approaches to sexuality is, at best, a substantial impediment for a comprehensive understanding of all that goes into an individual's experience of sexuality. At worst, it is erroneous and downright problematic in terms of arriving at an effective approach toward human sexuality and the treatment of sexual difficulties, particularly in women (Basson, 2001b; Mezzich & Hernandez-Serrano, 2006; Rossi, 1995; Sadovsky & Nusbaum, 2006; Schiavi, 2000; Sutherland, 2012; Tiefer, 2001, 2004). In addition to psychology and physiology, interpersonal and sociocultural influences (lower-left and lower-right quadrant phenomena) are important in the conceptualization and treatment of sexual issues (Basson, 2001a; DeLamater & Sill, 2005; Mezzich & Hernandez-Serrano, 2006; Rossi, 1995; Sutherland, 2012; Tiefer, 2001).

Hence, there is an evolving trend away from unidimensional approaches to human sexuality and toward a biopsychosocial perspective on sexual health that attends to the interaction of biological, psychological, social, environmental, and cultural factors (Bergeron, Meana, Binik, & Khalife, 2010; Fagan, 2004; Mezzich & Hernandez-Serrano, 2006; Rossi, 1995). Writing in 2006 on behalf of the World Psychiatric Association's Educational Program on Sexual Health, Mezzich and Hernandez-Serrano (2006) took a global perspective, and stressed the value of including cultural considerations when approaching matters of sexual health. It is also important to note that these factors are multifaceted, interrelated, and fluid, exerting mutual influences on each other that are circular and dynamic, as opposed to linear and fixed (Mezzich & Hernandez-Serrano, 2006):

> Physical aspects of sexuality such as anatomy and biochemistry cannot be treated in isolation from psychological factors such as development, personality, identity,

> thoughts and feelings or from social factors such as gender roles, interpersonal relationships, and structures of inequality. Cultural considerations are also of importance since definitions, expressions, regulations, and meanings associated with human sexuality are culturally based and informed. (p. 3)

Due to its breadth of scope and integrative nature, a biopsychosocial view is congruent with Integral theory, and is readily incorporated into an Integral approach to sexual functioning. Now, having laid a foundation, we turn our attention to the Sexual Dysfunction Disorders.

## SEXUAL DYSFUNCTION DISORDERS

As defined in the DSM-5, sexual dysfunctions refer to an impaired capacity to respond sexually and/or have a pleasant sexual experience (APA, 2013). There are 7 primary Sexual Dysfunction Disorders in the DSM-5: Delayed Ejaculation, Erectile Disorder, Female Orgasmic Disorder, Female Sexual Interest/Arousal Disorder, Genito-Pelvic Pain/Penetration Disorder, Male Hypoactive Sexual Desire Disorder, and Premature (Early) Ejaculation. In addition, there are diagnostic categories for Medication or Substance-Induced Sexual Dysfunction, and Other/Unspecified Sexual Dysfunction, for situations in which an individual is experiencing distress related to symptoms indicative of a sexual dysfunction, while not meeting the diagnostic criteria for the 7 sexual dysfunction disorders listed above.

Sexual dysfunction, as well as being a common occurrence (Heiman & Meston, 1998; Simons & Carey, 2001), is a highly complex problem, with many contributory factors and quite a bit of overlap across the Sexual Dysfunction Disorders (Balon & Wise, 2011; Crooks & Baur, 2008; Mahan, 2003). For example, a person who has difficulty achieving orgasm is likely to also have difficulties with desire and arousal. In turn, a person experiencing difficulties with desire and arousal will often struggle to achieve orgasm (APA, 2000; Crooks & Baur, 2008).[6] In addition, an individual may exhibit a sexually disordered behavior without fitting into specific DSM criteria for a sexual disorder (Fagan, 2004). It may be that this complexity and overlap is a factor that leads many clinicians to avoid the problem of sexual dysfunction altogether (Mahan, 2003). Furthermore, how a person's sexual functioning is perceived will vary from individual to individual. Despite the occurrence of what some might consider a sexual difficulty, it does not necessarily follow that the person will be dissatisfied with his or her sexual functioning or experience distress (Balon & Wise, 2011; Crooks & Baur, 2008). Other factors, such as an individual's emotional health and the quality of his sexual relationship, may impact his perception of his sexual experiences (Chao et al., 2011; Crooks & Baur, 2008).

Sexual dysfunction is also common with certain mental health diagnoses, such as Major Depressive Disorder, Obsessive-Compulsive Disorder, and Posttraumatic Stress Disorder. In the event that a sexual dysfunction is explained primarily by another mental health diagnosis, only the latter diagnosis is given (APA, 2013).

---

[6] Perhaps due to this overlap, Hypoactive Sexual Desire Disorder and Female Sexual Arousal Disorder have been subsumed under the new Sexual Interest/Arousal Disorder diagnostic category in the DSM-5 (APA, 2010, 2013).

## Sexual Desire Disorders

Sexual desire is defined "as a wish, need or drive to seek out and/or respond to sexual activities or the pleasurable anticipation of such activities" (Giargiari, Mahaffey, Craighead, & Hutchison, 2005). Levine (1992) has further divided desire into three separate components, as described by Kingsberg and Althof (2009):

> The first component is *drive*, the biological component based on neuroendocrine mechanisms and evidenced by spontaneous sexual interest. Patients recognize this as feeling "horny". . . . The second component is *cognitive*, which reflects a person's expectations, beliefs, and values related to sex. The third component of desire is the emotional or interpersonal component of desire and characterized by the willingness of a person to engage in sexual activity and is labeled as *motivation*. (p. S35)

The two DSM-IV-TR Sexual Desire Disorders—Hypoactive Sexual Desire Disorder (HSDD) and Sexual Aversion Disorder—are similar in that they are associated with a lessening of sexual desire. Hence, they both represent difficulties in the desire-phase of the sexual response cycle (Crooks & Baur, 2008). In the case of Hypoactive Sexual Desire Disorder, although the client lacks interest in sexual activity, she can usually participate once the sexual act has been initiated (APA, 2000; Morrison, 2006).[7] In the case of Sexual Aversion Disorder, the client is disgusted by the concept of contact to her genitals (APA, 2000; Morrison, 2006). In many cases, these two disorders overlap, and are often diagnosed together; hence the rationale for combining them in one diagnosis in the DSM-5. Although the decision to combine diagnostic categories met with some resistance (DeRogatis, Clayton, Rosen, Sand, & Pyke, 2011), the decision was made to do so based on the evidence "that women with low desire often present with difficulties in most or all areas of their sexual functioning" (Brotto, Graham, Binik, Segraves, & Zucker, 2011, p. 222).

## Sexual Arousal Disorders

Sexual Arousal Disorders involve individuals who are desirous of sexual activity yet nevertheless do not become sufficiently aroused to complete the sex act (APA, 2000; Crooks & Baur, 2008; Morrison, 2006). These disorders occur in the excitement phase of the sexual response cycle and were Female Sexual Arousal Disorder and Male Erectile Disorder in the DSM-IV-TR (APA, 2000; Crooks & Baur, 2008; Morrison, 2006). Whereas Erectile Disorder has remained in the DSM-5, Female Sexual Arousal Disorder has been subsumed into Female Sexual Interest/Arousal Disorder, as indicated previously. These disorders are likely to cause psychological distress to the individual and disruption to the love relationship (APA, 2000). There has been a fair amount of confusion concerning Female Sexual Arousal Disorder (FSAD), which has made it difficult to determine its frequency, and epidemiological studies have shown wide variations in its rate of occurrence (Simons & Carey, 2001; Spector & Carey, 1990). FSAD is "defined as the inability to complete sexual activity with adequate lubrication. Absent or impaired genital responsiveness to sexual stimulation is the essential DSM-IV-TR

---

[7] As Basson (2000, 2001a, 2001b, 2005) points out, this may actually be the norm for some women, and she recommends including the concept of receptivity in the conceptualization of sexual desire in women.

diagnostic criterion" (Kingsberg & Althof, 2009, p. S36). The process of sexual arousal in women is complex, and in many cases, FSAD overlaps considerably with other Sexual Dysfunction Disorders—Hypoactive Sexual Desire Disorder in particular—which contributes to the lack of understanding pertaining to this dysfunction (APA, 2000; Basson, 2008).[8] Again, this lack of clarity led to the decision to merge women's sexual desire and arousal disorders in the DSM-5 (Brotto et al., 2011).

Male Erectile Disorder (ED), which is sometimes referred to as impotence (Rosen & Leiblum, 1992), is characterized by a recurrent or persistent incapacity to achieve, or sustain until the sexual interaction is complete, an adequate erection (APA, 2013). ED may occur at varying points during sexual intercourse, including at the beginning of the sex act, while attempting to penetrate, or when thrusting (APA, 2013). Some men are able to attain an erection only under certain circumstances, such as upon waking, during masturbation, or when with a prostitute (APA, 2013; Morrison, 2006). When ED occurs only intermittently, or when there has been inadequate stimulation, a diagnosis is not warranted.

## Orgasmic Disorders

Orgasmic Disorders occur during the orgasm phase of the sexual response cycle, and are experienced by both men and women (Crooks & Baur, 2011). Problems related to orgasm include the capacity to experience an orgasm (at least as much as one would like), as well as how long it takes to climax—too fast or too slow (Crooks & Baur, 2011). Congruent with other sexual dysfunctions, Orgasmic Disorders have the potential to cause significant distress in the form of embarrassment, lowered self-esteem, social isolation, negative body image, infertility, and disrupted love relationships (APA, 2000; Mahan, 2003). The DSM-IV-TR identified three different Orgasmic Disorders: Female Orgasmic Disorder, Male Orgasmic Disorder, and Premature Ejaculation. All three of these disorders have remained in the DSM-5, albeit with slightly different nomenclature. Female Orgasmic Disorder has kept its name, whereas Male Orgasmic Disorder was renamed Delayed Ejaculation, and Premature Ejaculation was renamed Premature (Early) Ejaculation, in an effort to use terminology that is more accurate and less pejorative (APA, 2010). Female and Male Orgasmic Disorder are each defined as "a persistent or recurrent delay in, or absence of, orgasm following a normal sexual excitement phase" (APA, 2000, p. 547).[9] Premature (Early) Ejaculation is very common in men, with community prevalence rates of around 25– 40% (Levine, 1992; Rosen & Leiblum, 1995); it is defined as "the persistent or recurrent onset of orgasm and ejaculation with minimal sexual stimulation before, on, or shortly after penetration and before the person wishes it" (APA, 2000, p. 552).

---

[8] Female Sexual Arousal Disorder (FSAD) has been combined with Hypoactive Sexual Desire Disorder (HSDD) and subsumed under the diagnostic category of Sexual Interest/Arousal Disorder in Women in the DSM-5. We endorse this change, given the large amount of overlap between HDDD and FSAD.

[9] Based upon recent research pertaining to female sexual response, Basson (2005) revised the definition of Orgasmic Disorder such that even though the woman reports being highly sexually aroused, her orgasms are either considerably delayed, lacking, or significantly diminished in intensity. This definition takes into account that many women, including healthy, orgasmic women, experience orgasm situationally—with only certain types of stimulation—and do not experience orgasm through intercourse alone (Crooks & Baur, 2008; Donahey, 2010; Kingsberg & Althof, 2009). Taking issue with the DSM diagnostic criteria descriptor "interpersonal difficulty," the revised definition stresses that a woman is not to be pathologized and labeled as sexually disordered if she doesn't experience an orgasm, unless she herself is distressed by it (Basson, 2000).

### Sexual Pain Disorders

There were two sexual pain disorders in the DSM-IV-TR: Dyspareunia and Vaginismus (APA, 2000). These have been subsumed into one disorder, Genito-Pelvic Pain/ Penetration Disorder, in the DSM-5 (APA, 2010, 2013). Although both men and women may have pain during intercourse, these disorders are primarily experienced by women (Crooks & Baur, 2011; Morrison, 2006; Rosen & Leiblum, 1995). In circumstances when a male experiences pain during sex, it is frequently associated with a medical condition (Crooks & Baur, 2011; Morrison, 2006). The pain may occur at any point in the sexual response cycle, but it commonly happens during intercourse, and especially at the time of penetration (APA, 2000; Crooks & Baur, 2008; Morrison, 2006).

Sexual pain disorders are likely to have a significant negative impact on sexual satisfaction, and may be interwoven with other sexual dysfunctions, such as sexual desire and orgasmic disorders (Crooks & Baur, 2011; Morrison, 2006). In addition, they can lead to anxiety, frustration, low self-esteem, feelings of rejection, and erectile problems (Morrison, 2006). Sexual pain disorders may cause great harm to sexual relationships, and are capable of preventing the consummation of a marriage or the conception of a child (APA, 2000; Morrison, 2006).

Having provided an overview of the Sexual Dysfunction Disorders, we will now discuss their etiology. The etiology of sexual dysfunctions is highly complex—in part because of the overlap among the Sexual Dysfunction Disorders. We will begin by discussing these complexities, and then proceed to address what is known about the etiology of Sexual Dysfunction Disorders.

## ETIOLOGY OF SEXUAL DYSFUNCTION

We begin this section by emphasizing the complexity involved in determining the etiology of any particular individual's or couple's sexual dysfunction (Mezzich & Hernandez-Serrano, 2006). The etiology of sexual disorders is complicated not only because biological, psychological, and sociocultural variables are involved and interact, but also because the relative salience of those factors differs from individual to individual (Troisi, 2008). In addition to the significant overlap among the various Sexual Dysfunction Disorders, in some cases—such as female Sexual Arousal Disorder and Dyspareunia, or Premature Ejaculation and Erectile Dysfunction—one disorder can actually cause the other (Mezzich & Hernandez-Serrano, 2006). According to Fagan (2004), although we know a considerable amount about sex, we do not know much about the multidimensional, interacting causal influences—in particular, of biology and culture—of sexual behavior. Because it is virtually impossible to identify a single, unilateral cause for any of the sexual dysfunctions, we will discuss the etiology of Sexual Dysfunction Disorders together as a group, utilizing an Integral framework. This approach departs from dualistic historical trends that have pitted psychological and medical aspects of sexual functioning against each other, and is more in line with the biopsychosocial model of sexuality discussed previously (DeLamater & Sill, 2005).

### Upper-Right Perspectives: Biological and Physiological Factors

**EVOLUTIONARY AND GENETIC VIEWS** From the standpoint of evolutionary psychology, it is imperative to keep in mind the concepts of functionality and adaptability to an individual's specific environment when determining whether a particular thought or behavior is "disordered" (Hinderliter, 2010). In other words, we must know what is functional before we can know what is dysfunctional (Troisi, 2008). In the case of human sexuality, the theory of sexual selection is particularly relevant, which elucidates how differences in psychology, responses to social cues, and mating strategies have evolutionary origins (Troisi, 2008).

Considering the sexual disorders together as a whole for a moment, there is a far greater occurrence of sexual dysfunction in women than in men, whereas there is a far greater occurrence of Paraphilic Disorders in men than in women; this is likely due to the differing approaches to mating seen in males, in contrast to females (Troisi, 2008). According to evolutionary theory, males have a tendency toward casual sex and tend to discriminate less when it comes to deciding whether or not to participate sexually in a given situation. Women, on the other hand, are much more discriminating, largely due to the high level of investment that is required of them in order to rear offspring (Troisi, 2008). In this context, sexual dysfunction, which is more prevalent in women than in men, is seen as an exaggeration of the natural tendency to be sexually selective. Troisi (2008) explicated how, often, what is labeled a sexual dysfunction in a woman is actually an extreme form of what have evolutionarily been adaptive mating strategies (i.e., the ability to exercise sexual restraint, evaluating her potential mate's fitness, and exercising more deliberation with regard to whom she mates with). This is congruent with what recent research has shown regarding the importance of relational factors to the quality of women's sexual experiences. When relationship dynamics are unsatisfactory, lack of sexual desire may be construed as a normative and adaptive response for women (Troisi, 2008). Specifically, "the use of an evolutionary perspective can help clinicians to pay appropriate attention to evolved sex differences in sexual psychology and to avoid transposing to women the pattern of male sex response" (Troisi, 2008, p. 461).

**PHYSIOLOGY** Physiological factors such as age, hormones, illness, surgery, disability and medications often play a role in sexual problems (Annon, 1976; Crooks & Baur, 2011; DeLamater & Sill, 2005; Kedde, Van De Wiel, Weijmar Schultz, Vanwesenbeek, & Bender, 2010; Miller & Hunt, 2003; Satterfield & Stayton, 1980). For example, in the case of Sexual Desire Disorders, the DSM-5 states that general medical conditions may adversely affect sexual desire in nonspecific ways—from pain and weakness to survival concerns and disturbed body image (APA, 2013). It is important to note that there is often an overlap, or an interactional effect, between physiological and other factors in sexual dysfunction (Crooks & Baur, 2011; Kedde et al., 2010). In the case of genito-pelvic pain, many physical conditions can cause intercourse to be painful, including infection, herpes, abnormalities of the pelvis (scarring, adhesions, endometriosis), pelvic inflammatory disease, estrogen deprivation, vaginal changes related to menopause, gastrointestinal problems, and urinary tract irritation/infection (APA, 2000; Morrison, 2006; Saks, 1999).[10] A very common physical malady that leads to pain in approximately 10% of women is called vulvar vestibulitis syndrome[11] (Bergeron et al., 2010; Heiman, 2002).

[10] For further detail, we refer the reader to Crooks and Baur (2011).

[11] For a detailed description of vulvar vestibulitis syndrome, see Basson (2005).

When genito-pelvic pain is known to be caused by a medical condition or physical abnormality, it would not be diagnosed as a mental disorder (APA, 2013). It is also possible for genito-pelvic pain to result from substance use, in which case it would be categorized as a Substance/Medication-Induced Sexual Dysfunction (APA, 2010, 2013; Balon & Wise, 2011). In the case of genito-pelvic pain, as well as sexual disorders in general, it makes sense to coordinate care with a medical provider. Other co-occurring mental disorders must be ruled out as well, including anxiety disorders, mood disorders, psychotic disorders, and Somatization Disorder (Granot, Zisman-Ilani, Ram, Goldstick, & Yovell, 2011), for which painful intercourse is included in its diagnostic criteria (APA, 2000). Kingsberg and Althof (2009) make the excellent point that even when there are significant biological factors contributing to a sexual problem, it is still necessary to attend to psychological and behavioral aspects of the difficulty. For example, some simple, short-term remedies for genito-pelvic pain include the use of vaginal lubricants and trying different sexual positions (Crooks & Baur, 2011; Saks, 1999).

Painful intercourse in men is quite rare. When it occurs, it is often related to medical conditions (Crooks & Baur, 2011; Morrison, 2006). Some possibilities include a tight foreskin or an infection beneath the foreskin of a male who has not been circumcised, other infections occurring in the region of the genitalia, sexually transmitted diseases, and Peyronie's disease. In the case of painful intercourse in males related to such causes, medical treatment is imperative, and often leads to a resolution of the problem (Crooks & Baur, 2011).

**Overall Health and Wellness** Good physical health is the foundation for positive sexual experiences (Chao et al., 2011; Crooks & Baur, 2011). Even in the absence of a physical illness, the condition of one's body at any given time will have an impact on sexual functioning. For example, ineffective stress management can lead to a physiological state of tension, which can be a factor in sexual dysfunction; fatigue is a factor in diminished sexual desire; and the strength of the pubococcygeal (PC) muscles plays a role in achieving orgasm and ejaculatory control (Mezzich & Hernandez-Serrano, 2006).

**Age** Research shows a relationship between sexual desire and aging, although aging by no means precludes having an enjoyable sex life (Chao et al., 2011; Kontula & Haavio-Mannila, 2009; Sipski & Alexander, 1997a).[12] However, some research suggests that there may be mitigating factors influencing the relationship between age and sexual functioning, and that age alone may not have a negative impact on sexuality (Chao et al., 2011; DeLamater & Sill, 2005). One such factor is a reduction in sex hormone levels (Crooks & Baur, 2011; DeLamater & Sill, 2005). Another is medication, as a large number of prescription and over-the-counter drugs have side effects that negatively impact sexual functioning (Crooks & Baur, 2011; DeLamater & Sill, 2005). Mitigating psychological factors are a propensity for increased depression (Lourenço, Azevedo, & Gouveia, 2011), negative attitudes toward sexuality in older persons, as well as ageist biases in mainstream culture against sexual activity in elders (DeLamater & Sill, 2005). Similarly, issues of self-esteem, body image, and insecurity related to body changes, with the possibility of concomitant performance anxiety, can have a negative impact

---

[12] Excellent resources for the reader interested in aging and sexuality are DeLamater and Sill (2005) and Sipski and Alexander (1997a).

on sexual experiences (Kontula & Haavio-Mannila, 2009; Sipski & Alexander, 1997a). Hence, in the case of inhibited sex drive, it is important to consider the possibility that psychological factors may be underlying the dysfunction, rather than assuming an organic, age-related cause (Levine, 1992). As Chao and colleagues (2011) point out, ". . . sexual desire is a psychological state" (p. 400).

**Hormones** Hormones also have a significant influence on sexual functioning (DeLamater & Sill, 2005; Mezzich & Hernandez-Serrano, 2006), and illnesses and surgeries that impact sex hormone production are likely to harm sexual functioning (Satterfield & Stayton, 1980). The term "sex hormones" refers to hormones that have an impact on libido; they are androgens and estrogens. Androgens (primarily testosterone) are generally considered male sex hormones, and estrogens are generally considered female sex hormones, although both sex hormones are produced to some extent by both sexes (Crooks & Baur, 2011; Satterfield & Stayton, 1980). Androgens and estrogens are steroid hormones, and are secreted by the adrenal glands—the testes (in males) and the ovaries (in females). In addition, neuropeptide hormones produced by the brain, such as oxytocin, are important in human sexuality (Crooks & Baur, 2011).

Testosterone deficiency has been implicated in diminished sexual desire, erectile problems, and reduced sexual pleasure in males (Crooks & Baur, 2011; Mezzich & Hernandez-Serrano, 2006). In fact, a man must have normal testosterone levels in order to function sexually (Mezzich & Hernandez-Serrano, 2006). Hypogonadism—the medical term associated with decreased levels of blood testosterone—is implicated in as many as 35% of cases of Erectile Dysfunction (Mezzich & Hernandez-Serrano, 2006). Testosterone also plays an important role in female sexual functioning. When there are reduced circulating levels of testosterone, the following are likely to be negatively impacted: desire, sexual fantasy physical sensitivity to sexual stimuli, arousal, capacity for orgasm, and frequency of sexual activity (Crooks & Baur, 2011; DeLamater & Sill, 2005; Mezzich & Hernandez-Serrano, 2006).

Estrogen has a feminizing effect on a woman's body, and estrogen levels have been linked with several aspects of a woman's sexuality and sexual functioning, including vaginal lubrication, sexual desire, sexual pleasure, and capacity for orgasm (Crooks & Baur, 2011; DeLamater & Sill, 2005). Estrogen also produces some nonspecific effects that may be conducive to sexual expression, such as positive mood, self-confidence, and an overall sense of well-being (Mezzich & Hernandez-Serrano, 2006).

Other hormones that have an impact on sexuality are oxytocin and progesterone. Progesterone is known to be a factor in libido (Mezzich & Hernandez-Serrano, 2006). The release of oxytocin is triggered through touch, occurs at escalating levels during sexual intercourse, and contributes to attraction, bonding, and the expression of affection in sexual partners (Crooks & Baur, 2011).

**Medical Problems** Medical problems can harm sexual functioning through their negative impact on specific biological mechanisms and bodily functioning as a whole, as well as indirectly through generalized pain, fatigue, loss of energy, and psychological effects such as negative body image (Chao et al., 2011; DeLamater & Sill, 2005; Kedde et al., 2010; Satterfield & Stayton, 1980; Sipski & Alexander, 1997b).[13] Relevant

---

[13] An excellent resource on the impact of illness and disability on sexuality is *Sexual Function in People with Disability and Chronic Illness* (1997b), edited by Sipski and Alexander.

medical problems include disability, illness, injury, and systemic conditions, which may affect the urologic, circulatory, hormonal, myotonic, and/or neurological systems (Annon, 1976; Kedde et al., 2010; Mezzich & Hernandez-Serrano, 2006). Sipski and Alexander (1997b) make the important point that any discussion of the impact of illness and disability on sexual functioning must be individualized, incorporating factors such as: "(1) the type of disability or chronic illness by which the person is affected and (2) the individual strengths and weaknesses of the person affected by the disability or chronic illness" (p. 3). Other medical illnesses that may be implicated include cardiovascular diseases such as myocardial infarction and stroke, respiratory disease, hypertension, diabetes, arthritis, prostate disease, cancer, thyroid problems, arteriosclerosis, multiple sclerosis, cerebral palsy, vaginitis, and urinary tract infections (Kedde et al., 2010; Mahan, 2003; Mezzich & Hernandez-Serrano, 2006; Sipski & Alexander, 1997b).[14] In the case that physical illness is causing a sexual dysfunction, addressing the illness will often result in improved sexual functioning (Mahan, 2003). Hence, it is crucial to partner with a qualified medical professional when attending to matters of sexual functioning.

The impact of a physical disability on sexual functioning varies; some individuals will be able to maintain or resume a satisfactory sex life following a disability, whereas others will experience irreversible damage in the realm of their sexuality (Crooks & Baur, 2011). Physiological factors impacting the relationship between disability and a person's sexual functioning include impaired motor control, reduced physical sensation, pain, difficulty performing the physical acts of masturbation and intercourse due to physical deformity, and sensory loss (Crooks & Baur, 2011; Sipski & Alexander, 1997b). Many of the illnesses mentioned in the previous paragraph result in concomitant disability. Other disabilities that affect sexual functioning include traumatic brain injury, amputation, spinal cord injury (with paralysis), cerebral palsy, blindness, and deafness (Sipski & Alexander, 1997b). In addition, some surgeries, such as abdominal surgery, hysterectomy, and surgery to a woman's genital tract, may result in sexual dysfunction (Levine, 1992; Mezzich & Hernandez-Serrano, 2006).

**Medications and Illicit Drugs** Medications and other substances are also potential causes of sexual dysfunction, including prescription medications, over-the-counter remedies, and street drugs (Crooks & Baur, 2011; Mahan, 2003).[15] As is the case with illness, medications may negatively impact sexual functioning through indirect effects on health and well-being (DeLamater & Sill, 2005; Weiner & Rosen, 1997). Illicit substance use "may be a cover up and may also be used to enhance, extend, abbreviate, replace, or otherwise modify sexual behavior" (Mezzich & Hernandez-Serrano, 2006, p. 37). The impact of the substance will be mediated by factors such as the dose, how often it is used, how long it is used, and the situation under which the use occurs. In many cases, adjusting the medication or eliminating use of the substance will remedy the sexual dysfunction (Crooks & Baur, 2011; Mahan, 2003). Some of the substances that commonly cause sexual dysfunction include anticonvulsants, antihypertensive agents, anticholesterolemic agents, gastrointestinal medications,

---

[14] For a thorough list of physical illnesses related to sexual dysfunction, the reader is referred to Mezzich and Hernandez-Serrano (2006), p. 102.

[15] An excellent resource is Weiner and Rosen (1997).

anticancer drugs, antiarrhythmic drugs, antihistamines, antidepressants (especially selective serotonin reuptake inhibitors [SSRIs]; Lourenço et al., 2011), antipsychotics, lithium, anxiolytics, sedatives, tranquilizers, and medications for motion sickness, as well as illicit substances such as alcohol, marijuana, and other street drugs (Crooks & Baur, 2011; Mahan, 2003; Weiner & Rosen, 1997).

**BEHAVIORAL PERSPECTIVES** From a behavioral perspective, sexual responses, such as orgasm, are learned behaviors (Carlson & Wheeler, 1980). Many individuals with a sexual dysfunction lack sexual skills, which may stem from inadequate knowledge of sexual anatomy and the HSRC, insufficient sex education, and sexual inexperience (Mezzich & Hernandez-Serrano, 2006). Avoidance is a related behavior that can have an important bearing on a sexual dysfunction. In other words, when an individual has struggled significantly with sexual difficulties and experiences feelings of failure and helplessness, she may eventually develop a pattern of avoiding sexual situations (Satterfield & Stayton, 1980). A repeated pattern of masturbating to pornography has been seen in individuals with Male Orgasmic Disorder (Mezzich & Hernandez-Serrano, 2006), and we hypothesize that this may be a strategy for meeting sexual needs while avoiding relations with a partner, which is more stressful for those with limited social skills or struggles with intimacy. Other behavioral problems include inability to relax; difficulty focusing on one's physical sensations during sex; and an inability to control one's bodily reactions, which often leads to performance anxiety (Mezzich & Hernandez-Serrano, 2006).

## Upper-Left and Lower-Left Perspectives: From Attitudes to Relational Factors

There are significant psychological, relational, and cultural factors that contribute to the experience of sexual dysfunction. In fact, there is evidence that attitudes toward sexuality, many of which stem from an individual's culture, have more bearing on the quality of a person's sex life than do biological factors (Crooks & Baur, 2011; DeLamater & Sill, 2005). Social and relationship factors are also important (Mezzich & Hernandez-Serrano, 2006). In this section, we will discuss psychological, relational, and cultural factors that are likely to influence whether an individual or couple will experience sexual dysfunction.

**EMOTIONAL HEALTH AND MENTAL ILLNESS** Research suggests that many who experience a sexual disorder have a coexisting mental health concern (Mezzich & Hernandez-Serrano, 2006). Common sexual difficulties among those suffering from mental illness include decreased sexual desire, problems with erection, and problems with ejaculation (Maurice & Yule, 2010). When there is a serious or chronic disorder of the psychological system, as is the case with major mental illness, it is likely that the mental health concern may be causing the sexual dysfunction (Mezzich & Hernandez-Serrano, 2006). Examples of mental illness that have the potential to disrupt sexual functioning include Schizophrenia, Obsessive-Compulsive Disorder, depression (Lourenço et al., 2011; ter Kuile et al., 2010), Bipolar Disorder, panic and other anxiety disorders (ter Kuile et al., 2010), Post-Traumatic Stress Disorder (PTSD) (Brotto, Seal, & Rellini, 2012), personality disorders, Eating Disorders, and substance abuse (Mezzich & Hernandez-Serrano, 2006; Satterfield & Stayton, 1980). When an individual is experiencing psychological distress, even if it is more along the lines of an adjustment problem and is situational in nature, it can be a factor in sexual dysfunction, manifesting as either a cause or a result of the sexual problem (Chao et al., 2011).

**LACK OF KNOWLEDGE** Lack of knowledge and experience pertaining to sexuality is a common factor in sexual dysfunction (DeLamater & Sill, 2005). According to Deida (2005), many people are handed their "genital instruments" without any real kind of instruction or examples of what healthy sexuality is. As a result, their sexual development often falls far short of what is possible, and they end up playing the same crude songs over and over, rather than enjoying the symphonies and jazz improvisations that are possible when one has more knowledge and skills in the sexual arena.

Many individuals lack even the most basic knowledge pertaining to sexual anatomy and the HSRC (Mezzich & Hernandez-Serrano, 2006). This gives rise to a lack of sexual skill, which then contributes to sexual dysfunction. Uninformed individuals also fall prey to sexual myths and misunderstandings, which often lead to false expectations. Individuals subscribing to false expectations that fail to materialize are vulnerable to feelings of disappointment, frustration, and self-doubt. All of this leads to a sexual experience that is tense, pressured, and anxious—the opposite of the relaxed and confident sexual demeanor that is necessary for optimal sexual health (Mezzich & Hernandez-Serrano, 2006).

**ATTITUDES** Attitudes toward sexuality are also extremely important to the quality of a person's sexual experience (DeLamater & Sill, 2005). Closely related to attitude are an individual's beliefs pertaining to sexuality, many of which are learned in early childhood and are intrinsically related to one's culture. Crooks and Baur (2011) emphasized how we frequently are unaware of the influence of sociocultural factors on our own sexual attitudes. More often than not, we presume our sexual urges or behaviors are natural or biologically innate, but much of our sexuality is learned from societal messages. Sociological analyses of other societies and eras clearly demonstrate that what we regard as sexually natural is clearly relative (Crooks & Baur, 2011).

As one example, discomfort with sex—often in the form of guilt and shame—is a common factor in sexual dysfunction, particularly with female orgasmic, interest, and arousal disorders (Mezzich & Hernandez-Serrano, 2006). Fears, such as of acquiring a sexually transmitted disease, also contribute. Cultural factors of significance include religious beliefs and the sexual practices that were modeled for the individual. There are also pressures in present American society to maintain high levels of sexual desire, which can lead to a sense of expectancy or inadequacy, depending on one's particular degree of sexual interest (Mezzich & Hernandez-Serrano, 2006).

In addition to the physiological changes associated with aging, there are psychological changes as well, which may have a significant impact on sexuality (Chao et al., 2011; Mezzich & Hernandez-Serrano, 2006). Specifically, there can be an increase in fearfulness related to bodily functioning, anxiety pertaining to sexual issues, distractibility, and performance pressures that can have a harmful impact on sexual experiences. The simple belief that the quality of one's sexuality will decline as one ages makes it more likely that it will. In some cases, men will desire younger partners, and women will put more attention into their work and creative endeavors, which may lead to difficulties in long-term sexual relationships. Additionally, Mezzich and

Hernandez-Serrano (2006) have coined the term "sexual burnout," which refers to people growing tired of their typical sexual practices; when this occurs, people are more likely to seek out other sexual partners, which can have a destructive effect on their relationships.

Also important is a person's attitude toward himself as a sexual being, as well as the extent of attraction for one's partner. Feelings of low self-esteem and sexual inadequacy have a deleterious effect on a sexual relationship (Mezzich & Hernandez-Serrano, 2006). Feeling pressured to participate in sex, while at the same time feeling inadequate, can lead to performance anxiety, an unhelpful state that further impedes sexual performance.

**SPIRITUAL FACTORS** Although sexuality and spirituality are often considered separate domains in modern Western cultures, with sexuality often considered to be "earthly" or "bad" and spirituality considered to be "heavenly" or "good," this has not always been the case (Copelan, 1995). In ancient cultures, sex was a major part of religious rituals, and many Eastern religions place value on melding male and female sexual energies as a component of spiritual practice (Copelan, 1995). Today, there are some individuals for whom it becomes a priority to understand how the seemingly opposite concepts of spirituality and sexuality are related (Deida 2005; Marquis, 2008; Moore, 1980).

Spiritual views of sexuality, which encompass our capacities to be relational, self-transcending, and freely committed (Eugene, 1994), embrace the concept that it is indeed possible to "find God through sex" (Deida, 2005, p. xiv), and consider sex to be much more than the discrete steps spelled out in the HSRC. When viewing sexuality through a spiritual lens, sex is an expression of love, and as such, cannot be "dysfunctional" (Deida, 2005). At times, lovemaking is "perfect"—with heart, mind, and genitals aligned. At other times, sex can be anxious and conflicted. Nonetheless, Deida does not believe it is helpful to view such experiences as "failures"; rather, they are best viewed as an opportunity to learn, grow, and open in love. This perspective lies in stark contrast to traditional Judeo-Christian religious views of sexuality. Overly rigid and moralistic approaches to sexuality are often a factor in sexual dysfunction, to the extent traditional religious beliefs commonly discourage people from learning about sexuality, thus contributing to guilt pertaining to sexual practices (Mahan, 2003). Recall that Freud recognized that conflict underlying sexual expression was a factor in mental illness and distress (Copelan, 1995; Crooks & Baur, 2011).[16]

Nonetheless, even among those who would not be assigned a Sexual Dysfunction Disorder diagnosis per se, sexual frustration is common (Deida, 2005). While not denying that sexual problems can result from biological impairment or previous sexual experiences, spiritual perspectives often point out that sexual problems derive from a closed heart and other emotional constriction. Maintaining "a completely unprotected and vulnerable heart" (Deida, 2005, p. 52) could be the antidote, not only for a less-than-fulfilling sexual experience, but for a less-than-fulfilling life.

---

[16] This is particularly salient in the case of Vaginismus (DSM-IV-TR) or Genito-Pelvic Pain/Penetration Disorder (DSM-5; Butcher, 1999).

**RELATIONAL FACTORS** Given that sexuality is often experienced in the context of a romantic partnership—beginning with whether or not a partner is present or available—a myriad of relationship factors impact sexual functioning (DeLamater & Sill, 2005). It is important to recognize that a sexual relationship may take many forms, and the type of challenges experienced will be unique to each relationship. For example, the issues that are likely to be faced by individuals involved in long-term relationships will be different than those faced by adolescents and single young adults who are new to dating and romantic relationships. Different also will be the issues faced by older adults who are dating again after the end of a marriage or other long-term partnership (Myers, 2010), and those faced by members of the lesbian, gay, bisexual, and transgendered (LGBT) community (Scott & Levine, 2010).

Meana (2010) suggests that the way in which relationship problems and sexual distress are related for any particular couple may not be immediately apparent. Significant interpersonal factors that often have an impact on sexual experiencing include the sexual skills of each partner, but also the extent to which conflict is present and whether the couple has the skills necessary to resolve conflict (Mezzich & Hernandez-Serrano, 2006). As pointed out by Meana (2010), some couples have what she calls a "battleground mentality," wherein all of a couple's life becomes a win-lose struggle, including their sexual interactions. For example, with regard to low sexual desire, the relationship with the person's love partner may be negatively affected as the individual withdraws and avoids potential sexual opportunities (Schover & LoPiccolo, 1982). It may also happen that the person lacks sexual desire *because* of relationship factors, such as frequent conflict, abuse, or pressure from one's partner. In some cases, sex is experienced as downright aversive, and the individual may experience symptoms akin to panic, including feelings of terror, intense anxiety, breathing difficulties, nausea, faintness, dizziness, and palpitations (APA, 2013). It is also possible that the behaviors chosen to avoid sexual contact may themselves become problematic; some of these behaviors include neglecting hygiene and personal appearance, substance use, and excessive involvement in outside activities such as work and socializing (APA, 2000). On the other hand, although a large number of people with relationship difficulties also experience sexual problems (Satterfield & Stayton, 1980), relationship factors are not always at the root of sexual difficulties. As stated by Meana (2010), "bad sex can happen to happy couples" (p. 104). Similarly, factors in the environment, such as whether there is safety and privacy, and whether there are children present, are influential (Scharff, 2010).

A common source of conflict occurs when members of a couple experience differing levels of desire and disagree regarding how often to have sex (Mezzich & Hernandez-Serrano, 2006).[17] In this case, if intimacy and communication skills are lacking, or if a power imbalance is present, it is likely for the problem to become entrenched, with the member of the couple experiencing less desire shrinking in response to his or her partner's dissatisfaction (Mezzich & Hernandez-Serrano, 2006). The "demand-withdrawal pattern" involves a reciprocal interactive cycle in which as one partner withdraws, the other partner demands more, and the more that partner

[17] It is common for couples to have differences between them in terms of how often they want to engage in sexual activity (Crooks & Baur, 2011). According to the 2005 Global Sex Survey, 29% of women and 41% of men want to have sex more often than they do (Crooks & Baur, 2011).

demands, the more the other partner withdraws (Meana, 2010). In the case of this sort of reactive sexual disorder, it is necessary to elicit a spirit of cooperation between the partners if the sexual problem is to be resolved (Mezzich & Hernandez-Serrano, 2006).

Other relationship factors that frequently lead to sexual difficulties are the feelings of inadequacy people often feel when they are infertile (Scharff, 2010). Women are particularly vulnerable to the impact of infertility on sexual self-esteem as well as their overall sense of well-being (Troisi, 2008). In addition, the need to structure sex as a part of fertility treatment, along with emotional states such as anxiety and disappointment, can place a heavy strain on a sexual partnership. Infidelity also has a harmful effect on a couple's sexual relationship (Scharff, 2010), and is usually related to significant relationship problems (Levine, 2010; Meana, 2010).

An example of circular causation (reciprocal influence) regarding sexual disorders and relationship difficulties is evidenced in Premature (Early) Ejaculation, which often causes significant distress and disruption to intimate relationships (Levine, 1992; Morrison, 2006), the latter of which results in anxiety, animosity, or other confounding emotions; then those emotions lead to an increased likelihood of more sexual dysfunction, and so on. Some common emotions experienced by one or both members of the couple include frustration, resentment, embarrassment, guilt, and inadequacy (Haber & Runyon, 1984; Levine, 1992; Morrison, 2006). Similar to the other male sexual dysfunctions, shame and concerns about performance can lead to anxiety (Levine, 1992), which makes matters worse, possibly resulting in a breakdown in communication, sexually avoidant behaviors, or Erectile Disorder (Morrison, 2006).

Another interpersonal/cultural dynamic is the demeaning connotation of the term *impotence*, with far reaching implications regarding such matters as masculinity, strength, and personal empowerment (Rosen & Leiblum, 1992). Tiefer (1986) asserts:

> It is no surprise, then, that any difficulty in getting the penis to do what it 'ought' can become a source of profound humiliation and despair, both in terms of immediate self-esteem and the destruction of one's masculine reputation, which is assumed will follow. (p. 581)

The severe psychological and interpersonal consequences for not maintaining an erection can lead to anticipatory anxiety and self-consciousness, which results in further difficulties maintaining an erection (Rosen & Leiblum, 1992). Hence, there is a feedback loop that reinforces ongoing problems with sexual functioning for the man with ED (Haber & Runyon, 1984; Morrison, 2006). Some have postulated that fear-based thinking around sexual performance has increased in recent decades as a result of women becoming more invested in sexual fulfillment (Frosch, 1978). Not surprisingly, ED is the most likely sexual dysfunction to compel a man to seek sex therapy (Rosen & Leiblum, 1992, 1995).

As mentioned earlier, even well-functioning couples experience challenges to a fulfilling sexual life. A common struggle for individuals in long-term relationships is keeping the sexual excitement alive (Welwood, 1996). Meana (2010) points out that the stress of daily living, which includes the myriad responsibilities involved in raising a family and concerns related to establishing a secure future, detract from sexual desire. In addition, overfamiliarity between members of a long-term relationship, diminished romance, and viewing sex as an obligation—as opposed to something one wants to do—are detrimental to fulfilled sex lives (Meana, 2010).

**CHILDHOOD EXPERIENCES** Childhood experiences have a bearing on whether an adult will develop a problem with intimacy and/or sexuality (Deida, 1995; Scharff, 2010). When there is a lack of love and affection in the home, it is more likely that adult relationships will also lack these qualities (Maurice & Yule, 2010). In addition, if a family is highly sexualized and sexuality is flaunted, there is an increased chance that sexual problems will emerge (Scharff, 2010). Ironically, this is also true if the opposite happens—if the family is sexuality suppressed. As explained by Scharff (2010), it is common for children who are raised in families that suppress sexuality to avoid, deny, or fear sex as adults. Similarly, when individuals are deprived of the opportunity to experiment with romance and sexuality during adolescence, which often occurs when an individual experiences a mental illness or developmental challenge, sexual difficulties may arise in adulthood as a result of this dearth of earlier experience (Maurice & Yule, 2010).

**History of Abuse and Trauma** Individuals who have experienced emotional, physical, or sexual abuse in childhood are more likely to experience a sexual difficulty (Brotto et al., 2012; Mezzich & Hernandez-Serrano, 2006). This is because having positive attachment relationships early in life leads to the sense of comfort and ease with a partner that is more conducive to healthy sexual relating (Scharff, 2010). As explained by Mezzich and Hernandez-Serrano (2006), even nonsexual abuse or neglect often results in an attitude of mistrust, anger, or hurt that adversely affects the victim's sexuality in adulthood, often leading to diminished sexual desire, sexual aversion, and/or painful intercourse.

Sexual abuse has a devastating effect on all aspects of a child's development (Scharff, 2010). Even if not acted out physically, when a child is placed in a parentified role and is used to meet adult needs for love that are not being fulfilled through the parental relationship, this child is likely to act highly sexualized at a younger age (Scharff, 2010). When actual sexual abuse occurs, it is tantamount to "a sexual invasion of the mind" (Scharff, 2010, p. 76) that wreaks havoc on all aspects of the child's development. From severe mental illness such as Dissociative Identity Disorder (Levine, 1992), Borderline Personality Disorder (Linehan, 1993), and Post Traumatic Stress Disorder (Brotto et al., 2012; Grillon, 2005), to living a highly sexualized lifestyle and developing a sexual disorder, sexual abuse is extremely harmful. In the case of sexual aversion and sexual pain and penetration disorders, for example, the client is viewed as defending herself against possible re-victimization (Mezzich & Hernandez-Serrano, 2006).

### Lower-Right Perspectives: Sociocultural Factors

We each learn about our role as a sexual being through societal group norms, and often feel a related pressure to conform to them, which can be unhelpful to our sexual experiences and functioning (Mosher, 1980; Satterfield & Stayton, 1980). These socioculturally imparted attitudes dictate what the level and quality of our sexual involvement should be (Mosher, 1980). For example, a woman who has a culturally reinforced passive personality style will be reticent during sex to the detriment of her pleasure and that of her partner (Satterfield & Stayton, 1980).

Gender-related double standards have historically been a contributing factor in sexual dysfunction (Crooks & Baur, 2008; Satterfield & Stayton, 1980). Consider the following societal messages people have received regarding sexuality: "women who have vaginal orgasms are more mature than those who only have clitoral orgasms," "only dirty women really enjoy sex," "a real man will get his woman to come" (Mosher, 1980). As societal mores regarding sexuality have changed, some women have been caught between requirements to be chaste, juxtaposed with more recent requirements to be highly sexually responsive (Satterfield & Stayton, 1980). Men have also experienced sexual pressure, which can lead to performance anxiety and related sexual dysfunction, such as Erectile Disorder and Early/Premature Ejaculation (Satterfield & Stayton, 1980). In the context of a sexual partnership, each member will have different role expectations based on their unique circumstances and how their sexuality developed over time. Sexual problems often occur when the role expectations between members of a couple are incongruent (Mosher, 1980). Fortunately, cultural standards regarding male and female roles have relaxed in recent years, with women feeling more free to experience the masculine aspects of their personality, and vice versa (Deida, 1995).

Having presented etiological factors from each of the four quadrants, we now turn to a case that demonstrates how these multiple influences converge. Kira and her husband Jeffrey present for couples counseling due to the status of their sexual relationship. Kira is a 32-year-old African American female born and raised in a devout Baptist/Pentecostal church, which her father pastored. She is the youngest of three girls. Arriving late in her parents' marriage, she is 9 and 6 years younger than her two sisters, respectively. Although Kira describes an overall stable childhood, she harbors the secret that she was sexually abused by her eldest sister's boyfriend on several occasions when she was between 13 and 14 years of age. Those experiences caused profound distress and shame for her, given the high spiritual value she places on keeping sexuality sacred to marriage. To this day she has not told anyone, including Jeffrey, about what happened to her, out of fear that she would be judged and subsequently rejected. Jeffrey came from a similar family of origin; he was also born and raised in an intact, devout fundamentalist Christian family. Jeffrey's sexual history revealed that his parents slept in separate bedrooms, did not show any physical affection to each other, and taught him that masturbation and sexual contact were wrong unless the latter was for the purpose of conceiving a child.

Kira and Jeffrey met while attending Bible College, and Jeffrey is now serving as the assistant pastor in their church. Having both been born and raised in Christian homes, Kira and Jeffrey were determined to be conscientious in honoring their values, and although it was sometimes challenging for them, they managed to abstain from sexual intercourse until their wedding night. They have been married for 8 years, and very much want to begin a family before Kira's "biological clock" runs out.

Coming for couples counseling in order to address their sexual health was an extremely difficult decision for Kira and Jeffrey. They are particularly concerned that their counselor has respect for their religious values pertaining to sexuality and will protect their confidentiality, given that Jeffrey holds a leadership role in their church. They acknowledge fear of being judged, along with some underlying feelings of guilt and shame, both about sexuality in general as well as the fact that they are struggling with sexual issues in their relationship. They admit to almost skipping the appointment; however, they are highly motivated to receive help due to their wish to have a child.

Despite what is described as an overall positive relationship, including good communication and companionship, Kira and Jeff rarely have sex. They are in agreement that after having waited out their courtship to engage in intercourse, their wedding night was a dismal disappointment. For Kira, the pain was intense, to the point where they were unable to continue. The thought of hurting Kira was extremely upsetting to Jeffrey, and corroborated his previously held beliefs that sex is harmful. They tried to have sexual intercourse a few times since the wedding night, but penetration remained extremely painful for Kira. She explains: "it feels like someone is shoving a broken glass bottle up inside me." Sexual experiences did not get any better for them. In fact, they seemed to worsen after each attempt, reinforcing their belief that for them, sex just didn't work.

It is noteworthy that, overall, Kira and Jeffrey are not distressed over the dearth of sexuality in their relationship. Kira is satisfied with their pleasant companionship and the overall supportiveness of their relationship. Jeffrey reports that he very rarely has erotic thoughts or urges, and when he does, he distracts himself from them by thinking about something else until they quickly pass. They were used to being together without having intercourse during their courtship, and are content with the high level of nonsexual physical affection they share, such as holding hands and cuddling.

Kira and Jeffrey's sexual experiences show how the sexual problem of an individual or couple is impacted by multiple factors, particularly relationship dynamics. Kira and Jeffrey are fortunate in that there is congruence in their idiosyncratic presentations that leads to an overall harmony in their relationship. In fact, it is questionable whether either Kira or Jeffrey would have a diagnosable sexual disorder were it not for their wish to have intercourse in order to conceive a child, because neither one of them has been experiencing "clinically significant distress" (DSM-5 diagnostic criteria; APA, 2013) up until this point. Were either one of them dissatisfied with the status quo, they probably would have experienced distress and sought help much earlier in their relationship, or perhaps their relationship would have dissolved.

For Kira and Jeffrey, upper-left quadrant dynamics are particularly salient. They each hold negative beliefs about sexuality with concomitant guilt and shame that is longstanding, which is likely a driving factor for them. For Kira, her history of sexual abuse (LR) along with the meaning she ascribed to it and her emotional experience of intense shame is a vulnerability factor for Genito-Pelvic Pain/Penetration Disorder, her likely clinical diagnosis. They also appear to lack knowledge regarding normative sexual functioning. It is probable that Jeff's belief that sex is wrong, combined with how he feels when penetration causes pain for Kira, are strong contributing factors to his low level of desire, although a medical evaluation is warranted to rule out physiological (UR) causes. An additional behavioral (UR) dynamic for Kira and Jeff is that negative beliefs about sex are likely strengthened after each unpleasant attempt, which also serves to increase anxiety over their sexual interactions and punish their efforts, rendering it less likely that future sexual events will take place. They are also sexually inexperienced, and likely lack basic sexual skills. Kira and Jeffrey's learning has taken place in a sociocultural context (LR, LL) including explicit messages from their families and religion (that sex is wrong), what was modeled in their families (sex is taboo and parents sleep in separate beds), and actual sexual experiences within the context of the home (Kira's sexual abuse). For Kira and Jeffrey, both their religious beliefs and church organizations (LL, LR), past and present, exert powerful influences in their lives.

## Developmental Dynamics, States of Consciousness, and Personality Types

**DEVELOPMENTAL DYNAMICS** Psychodynamic theories posit that developmental dynamics play a role in sexual problems, and that sexual dysfunction may be the result of developmental issues stemming from childhood (Scharff, 2010). Given that we develop our own unique sexual identity in the context of our relationships with others over time (Mosher, 1980), and the fact that developmental factors are often neglected by those providing services in sexual health, we should remain highly skeptical when clients who seek help with sexual troubles act as if, or outright say, that their sexuality is unrelated to other dimensions of their lives (Scharff, 2010). More than likely, a host of other aspects of their lives—from self-esteem and identity to trust and intimacy issues—are also involved.

When viewing sexual difficulties through a developmental lens, sexual problems are often considered representative of vulnerabilities emanating from a person's attachment style, the foundation of which was laid in childhood (Granot et al., 2011). As explained by Scharff (2010), what occurs in the context of an individual's earliest attachments will have a bearing on how sexuality is enacted in later years. Specifically, positive and stable early relationships lay the foundation for psychological maturity and a sense of safety in adult relationships that pave the way for enriching sexual experiences (Granot et al., 2011). Thus, deep intimacy and sexual satisfaction are contingent upon developmental capacities such as a solid sense of oneself, taking responsibility for one's own needs, and relating to one's partner as a separate person whose needs may differ from one's own needs (Ferreira et al., 2012; Meana, 2010).

Sexuality—like most other aspects of life—can be engaged in a deeply open, caring, loving manner, or it can be engaged in primarily selfish, childish ways (Deida, 2005). When sexual relationships are used in the service of less mature needs, comfort and security will be emphasized (Deida, 2005), and sex is viewed primarily as bodily pleasure and as a means to relieve sexual tension (Mosher, 1980). In many cases, people use love relationships to provide the illusion of a cocoon that protects them from existential concerns such as uncertainty, isolation, and death.

Conflict frequently arises in love relationships when a partner does not act in a manner conducive to the type of safety and peace that is expected, leading to withdrawal and defending one's heart (Deida, 2005; Psaris & Lyons, 2000). In contrast, more mature lovers are able to stay open and undefended in the midst of unpleasant emotional and relational occurrences, which is a pathway to further growth (Deida, 2005). When this occurs, a lover will be able to stay fully present and maintain attention; sex will be experienced as oneness with one's partner, and will surmount sensations of superficial pleasure and emotional comfort resulting in a profound sense of ecstasy and bliss (Deida, 2005). When sexual partners are content with more conventional styles of sexual lovemaking, it is likely to feel more like a "common grunt of stimulation and release" (Deida, 2005, p. 95).

**STATES OF CONSCIOUSNESS** The act of sex itself—especially when it is entered into with focused attention and a certain depth of participation—often promotes a state of consciousness different from normal waking consciousness (Levine, 1992; Mosher, 1980). In addition to the pleasurable altered states that sex may induce, anxiety and panic are states of consciousness that have significant relevance in the context of sexuality, because they frequently occur in people experiencing sexual difficulties (Annon, 1976; Satterfield & Stayton, 1980; ter Kuile et al., 2010). A particular phenomenon, called "spectatoring" in the sexology literature, refers to when a "person steps out of the role of participant and becomes an observer" (Crooks & Baur, 2005, p. 163); this obsessive sort of self-consciousness generally interferes with the sexual process (Satterfield & Stayton, 1980). Also, clients with panic disorders tend to fear the bodily sensations that occur when one is sexually aroused, and anxiety is clearly a factor in sexual aversion and Genito-Pelvic Pain/Penetration Disorder (Mezzich & Hernandez-Serrano, 2006; ter Kuile et al., 2010). Some individuals, particularly those who have experienced sexual trauma, will dissociate and become psychologically disconnected during a sexual experience, which will have "a direct negative effect upon sexual response and satisfaction" (Brotto et al., 2012, p. 3). Performance anxiety is a common occurrence. Similarly, women who struggle to experience orgasm may feel pressured by their partner and feel anxious. In an anxious state, orgasm becomes less likely (Carlson & Wheeler, 1980).

**PERSONALITY TYPES** A comprehensive understanding of human sexuality must include the concept of personality types, the most obvious and salient of which are masculine and feminine types. Beginning from the lens of evolutionary psychology, matters of type have an impact on mating strategies, with feminine types tending to be more discriminating in their choice of a sexual partner, and masculine types having more of a propensity toward casual sex. This also plays out in terms of the prevalence of sexual disorders, with Sexual Dysfunction Disorders being more common in feminine types, and Paraphilic Disorders being more common in masculine types (Troisi, 2008).

In his book *Finding God Through Sex: Awakening the One of Spirit Through the Two of Flesh*, David Deida (2005) discusses how the experience of sexuality varies based on masculine and feminine types,[18] with each gender experiencing different sexual and relational preferences. Deida (1995) also points out how masculine individuals interacting with feminine individuals serve to ignite sexual attraction and passion. Viewing sexuality from a spiritual perspective, Deida (2005) suggests that there are both feminine and masculine sexual essences.[19] For example, people with masculine styles tend to prioritize freedom and accomplishing their mission in life, whereas people with feminine styles tend to value closeness and relationship. Deida (2005) makes a strong case that whereas the feminine is fulfilled by love, the masculine is fulfilled by freedom. Deida (2005) points out that feminine individuals find it much more difficult to separate their hearts from their genitals than masculine individuals do—a woman's vagina opens along with her heart—and for her, sex and love are inextricably connected. In contrast, masculine individuals often more readily separate the two: love involves his heart and sex involves his penis.

---

[18] Deida (2005) further explains that biological gender and the gender of one's essence are not necessarily the same. Individuals vary in terms of how feminine or masculine their essence is, regardless of whether they are biologically male or female.

[19] It is important to note that a man may be feminine and women may be masculine; most of us are a mix of both.

## SUMMARY OF ETIOLOGY

We believe the utilization of an Integral framework is extremely helpful in making sense of the varying phenomena involved in the conceptualization of sexual dysfunction. We have emphasized the multidimensional nature of sexual dysfunction, focusing on interactions between biological, psychological, social, cultural, and developmental aspects of sexual experiencing. We have shown how etiological factors overlap and that it is usually impossible to identify a single unilateral cause in any particular case.

That being said, important biological and physiological factors include evolutionary processes and genetics; physical health and illness, including medical problems and substance use; age; and hormones. We have also explored behavioral influences, such as limited sexual skills and learned sexual responses. Important emotional and psychological factors include lack of knowledge pertaining to sexuality, attitudes toward sexual experiences and responses, and mental health. In addition, relational factors are highly significant, such as childhood experiences, disparate degrees of desire, the presence of conflict in the relationship, and communication skills for addressing and resolving such conflict. Also discussed were the relevance of spiritual and sociocultural factors. In our use of an Integral framework, we addressed developmental dynamics, states of consciousness, as well as masculine and feminine personality types in the context of sexual dysfunction (see Figure 10.1).

At this point, we turn to the treatment of sexual dysfunction. Specifically, we will address general principles of sex therapy prior to launching into a discussion of the predominant treatment strategies. Biological, psychological, relational, and spiritual approaches to treatment will be described.

## TREATING SEXUAL DYSFUNCTIONS

At the outset of this section on the treatment of sexual dysfunction, we would like to assert that the ultimate goal for any client is sexual health, which is a significant factor in the overall quality of life (Chao et al., 2011; Crooks & Baur, 2011; Mezzich & Hernandez-Serrano, 2006). According to Mezzich and Hernandez-Serrano (2006), sexual health is a dynamic yet balanced state of fulfilling reproductive and erotic experiences; importantly, it is not the mere absence of a sexual disorder, and it must be recognized as arising within larger contexts of well-being—from physical and emotional to interpersonal, ethical, and spiritual. Furthermore, we agree with the notion put forth by Crooks and Baur (2011) that attending to sexual health "goes beyond identifying and treating sexual problems" (p. 402). In general, a healthy body is a pre-requisite for experiencing a satisfying sex life (Copelan, 1995; Myers, 2010). Thus, maintaining good health (physically, emotionally, and spiritually) is the first step in preventing or reversing a sexual problem or dysfunction. Effective stress management, adequate rest, maintaining a healthy weight, physical exercise, and good nutrition are all positive life habits that are likely to support optimum sexual health (Brisben, 2008; Copelan, 1995). Similarly, good hygiene and a positive body image are crucial (Myers, 2010). If a major mental illness is the main cause for the sexual dysfunction, treating the mental illness is the primary treatment priority (Mezzich & Hernandez-Serrano, 2006).

The first step in attending to a person's or couple's sexual complaint is to conduct a thorough clinical evaluation, including a medical and sexual history (Donahey, 2010;

| UPPER-LEFT (UL): INTERIOR-INDIVIDUAL | UPPER-RIGHT (UR): EXTERIOR-INDIVIDUAL |
|---|---|
| – Body image<br>– Attitudes toward sexuality and one's partner<br>– Experiences of sexual failure (e.g., discouragement and helplessness)<br>– Self-esteem<br>– Personality style<br>– Lack of sexual knowledge/misinformation<br>– Dysfunctional beliefs regarding sexuality<br>– Anxiety/stress/tension<br>– Depression<br>– PTSD (detached and less responsive)<br>– Inappropriate sexual expectations (with concomitant feelings of being let down or inadequate)<br>– Self-consciousness | – Status of overall health<br>– Nutrition<br>– Medications<br>– Substance use<br>– Illness<br>– Disability<br>– Abnormal hormonal levels<br>– Body changes related to aging<br>– Avoidance of sexual situations |
| **LOWER-LEFT (LL): INTERIOR-COLLECTIVE** | **LOWER-RIGHT (LR): EXTERIOR-COLLECTIVE** |
| – Relationship factors/problems<br>– Level of attraction to the partner<br>– Conflict with partner/lack of skills for resolving conflict<br>– Capacity for intimacy<br>– Trust in the sexual relationship<br>– Power balance/imbalance in the sexual relationship<br>– Negative emotions toward partner<br>– Cultural beliefs and practices: biases pertaining to sexuality; attitudes regarding the rights of women and children; pressure to show high levels of sexual desire | – Childhood experiences: attachment to caregivers; history of abuse and/or neglect; trauma history<br>– Environment: safety; space issues in the home/adequate privacy<br>– Availability of a partner<br>– Communication with partner<br>– Infidelity |

**FIGURE 10.1** A Quadratic Summary of the Etiology of Sexual Dysfunction

Hertlein, Weeks, & Sendak, 2009). Given the overdetermined nature of sexual difficulties, it is imperative that the evaluation is comprehensive (Mezzich & Hernandez-Serrano, 2006) and ongoing (Hertlein et al., 2009). Information must be gleaned in order to diagnose the problem, identify causative and contextual factors, and develop a treatment plan (Althof et al., 2005).[20]

In the case of a sexual concern, it is often helpful to interview the couple together, as well as each individual alone (Basson, 2005; Mezzich & Hernandez-Serrano, 2006), and to take relationship dynamics into account (Ferreira et al., 2012; Granot et al., 2011; Meana, 2010; Sutherland, 2012). It is important for the clinician to initiate

[20] For helpful discussions pertaining to assessment and diagnosis, including a list of assessment instruments, the reader is referred to the work of Althof et al. (2005), Hertlein et al. (2009), Mezzich and Hernandez-Serrano (2006), and Phillips (2000).

this dialogue because many clients are reluctant to bring up the topic of sexuality (Kingsberg & Althof, 2009). Pre-appointment intake forms containing questions pertaining to sexual health can be a helpful adjunct to the clinical interview (Phillips, 2000). Mahan (2003) suggests the following questions that may be useful in identifying possible sexual difficulties:

1. Do you have any questions or concerns about your sex life?
2. Are you currently sexually active?
3. Have you recently had less interest in sex?
4. Do you have a problem with vaginal dryness/erection?
5. Are you able to have an orgasm (or to ejaculate)? (p. 90)

It is also important to determine the client's sexual orientation because concerns related to sexual identity are often linked to sexual difficulties (Phillips, 2000).

Having adequate training in counseling/psychotherapy is important when assessing and treating sexual dysfunction, due to the frequency with which sexual symptomatology is related to a psychiatric difficulty. Additionally, sex therapists must also be well versed in the basics of marriage and family therapy, cognitive-behavior therapy, and assertiveness training (Mezzich & Hernandez-Serrano, 2006). We further recommend partnering with a qualified medical professional who can conduct a physical examination, if clinically indicated, in order to determine whether an illness or other physical anomaly is causing the dysfunction (Phillips, 2000).[21] Due to the importance of upper-right quadrant factors in sexual difficulties, and the fact that sexual concerns often masquerade as other somatic complaints, it is imperative to rule out the possibility of physical causes for your client's difficulty (Phillips, 2000). Mezzich and Hernandez-Serrano (2006) point out that if a psychological treatment for a sexual problem is provided when the cause of that problem is largely physiological, the experience will be ineffective and disheartening for the client. Completing a traditional diagnostic formulation will help to ensure that key aspects of any case conceptualization are addressed.[22]

Good basic counseling skills are important when it comes to working with individuals experiencing sexual problems. Awareness of one's own values, beliefs, and attitudes pertaining to sexuality is also important, along with maintaining respect for those of the client. Some clients may wish to decline treatment. In this case, the client's right to self-determination should be respected (Phillips, 2000). It is imperative not to impose one's personal values or opinions on the client, and in some cases, a conflict in values may necessitate referral to another provider (Mezzich & Hernandez-Serrano, 2006).

### The PLISSIT Model of Sex Therapy

The PLISSIT model was developed by Jack Annon (1976) and colleagues in the mid-1970s.[23] It is a flexible model that serves as a means for organizing sex therapy

[21] To locate a medical professional with expertise in sexuality, the reader may contact the American Association of Sexuality Educators, Counselors, and Therapists (AASECT) at http://www.AASECT.org.

[22] For a helpful form to aid in completing a comprehensive diagnostic formulation for individuals with sexual disorders, the reader is encouraged to consult Mezzich and Hernandez-Serrano, 2006, pp. 91–92.

[23] For a detailed explanation of the PLISSIT model, the reader is referred to Annon's (1976) book *Behavioral Treatments of Sexual Problems: Brief Therapy*.

in stages depending on the therapist's capabilities and comfort levels (Annon, 1976). As explained by Annon (1976), the PLISSIT model "was intended to be adaptable for use by a wide range of people in the helping professions and allow for a range of treatment choices geared to the level of competence of the individual clinician" (p. 45). There are four levels of therapy specified in the PLISSIT model: the "P" stands for permission, the "LI" stands for limited information, the "SS" stands for specific suggestions, and the "IT" stands for intensive therapy (Annon, 1976). At the first level, permission, therapists inquire about the client's sexual life, share some basic facts regarding sexual functioning, and may make referrals for further treatment if clinically indicated. They also normalize any fantasies, thoughts, feelings, desires, or behaviors of the client that increase her enjoyment without adversely affecting her partner (Crooks & Baur, 2005). At the second level, limited information, therapists provide clients with information that is specific to their sexual concerns. At the third level, specific suggestions, therapists become involved in offering suggestions to help with the specific complaint of the client, with the intention of helping the client achieve the goal that brought him into treatment. The therapist may also recommend some behavioral exercises for the couple to do at home. These exercises may include versions of masturbation techniques, sensate focus (discussed subsequently), or the stop-and-start technique. Last, the intensive therapy level, which is performed by a trained sex therapist, is an in-depth treatment that must be individualized to the need of the specific client or couple who presents for treatment (Annon, 1976).

Due to its comprehensive nature, an Integral approach allows for the consideration of all relevant factors in an individual or couple's sexual health, and also looks for patterns that connect the various factors (Marquis, 2008). This, in turn, allows for the possibility of drawing from all possible resources in the service of the client. In the following section, we discuss common treatment strategies for sexual dysfunction as they are situated within the Integral model. We begin with the upper-right quadrant, biological and behavioral treatments, because traditional sex therapy tends to begin from this perspective when treating a sexual dysfunction (counseling will not be effective if there is a biological cause underlying the sexual dysfunction that has not been addressed; Mezzich & Hernandez-Serrano, 2006). In addition, biological causes may be the most simple to ameliorate; thus, they should be addressed first.

## Upper-Right Interventions for Sexual Dysfunction

**RELAXATION TRAINING** Relaxation training is an important aspect of sex therapy because physical relaxation is a prerequisite for experiencing sexual excitement. In many cases, anxiety, especially performance anxiety, plays a role in the sexual dysfunction (Mezzich & Hernandez-Serrano, 2006). Many forms of relaxation training may be helpful, including frequent and vigorous exercise, muscle relaxation, focusing on the breath, yoga, and especially exercises that help the person to tune in to his own physical sensations (Copelan, 1995). Exercises to strengthen the Kegel/pelvic muscles are also recommended (Brisben, 2008).

**PHARMACOLOGICAL TREATMENTS** Pharmacological interventions may help some individuals gain control of their sexuality by modifying their body's physiological functions (Fagan, 2004). They are used most often with men experiencing Erectile Disorder

(Mezzich & Hernandez-Serrano, 2006). We agree with Fagan (2004) that pharmacological treatment is most effective when integrated with a comprehensive treatment plan that also addresses other factors. The use of pharmacology is most warranted when there is a clear physiological cause for the dysfunction, or there is a comorbid condition negatively impacting an individual's sexual functioning; it is usually most effective when used in conjunction with psychotherapy or a psychosexual skills training program (Fagan, 2004; Mezzich & Hernandez-Serrano, 2006).

Perhaps the most well-known pharmacological treatments in use today are the vasoactive medications for Erectile Disorder: Sildenafil (Viagra), Vardenafil (Levitra), and Tadalafil (Cialis; Crooks & Baur, 2011; Mahan, 2003). Reports have shown that "almost 40,000 prescriptions were dispensed in the first 2 weeks of being on the market, and since then, Viagra has had $1 billion in annual worldwide sales . . ." (Crooks & Baur, 2005, p. 463). These oral medications help men with Erectile Disorder to initiate and sustain an erection. Research indicates that all three of the medications have approximately the same degree of effectiveness, although they vary in terms of side effects, how quickly they take effect, and how long their effects last (Mezzich & Hernandez-Serrano, 2006). It is important to note that there are risks associated with these medications for clients with heart problems, and in combination with other drugs, such as alpha-blocker antihypertensives (used to reduce blood pressure and treat an enlarged prostate) and nitrates (used to treat angina; Mezzich & Hernandez-Serrano, 2006).

Psychotropic medications such as SSRIs, anxiolytics, or neuroleptics have also been used in the treatment of sexual problems (Donahey, 2010; Rosen & Leiblum, 1995). Although psychotropic medications often have a negative impact on sexual functioning, it is also possible for them to have a positive effect and they are particularly useful when depression or anxiety is a causative factor in the sexual dysfunction (Donahey, 2010). In particular, SSRIs, such as fluoxitane (Prozac) and clomipramine (Anafranil), have been shown to prolong the time before ejaculation in men struggling with Premature (Early) Ejaculation (Levine, 1992).

**HORMONE TREATMENT** Hormonal replacement therapies may be useful in the case of testosterone deficiency in women, the symptoms of which include reduced sexual desire, diminished sexual fantasies, reduced physical sensitivity to sexual stimuli, and difficulty becoming aroused and having an orgasm (Mezzich & Hernandez-Serrano, 2006). Testosterone medications must be used with care due to a propensity for harmful side effects in large doses, the most troubling of which are liver damage, the presence of male sexual characteristics, a reduction in levels of good cholesterol, hair loss, and weight gain (Mezzich & Hernandez-Serrano, 2006). Testosterone replacement is also a useful treatment for men experiencing a condition called hypogonadism, which results in reduced blood testosterone levels. Estrogen replacement therapy is used with women, although this is another case in which caution is warranted because exogenous estrogen may actually have a negative impact on sexual functioning (Mezzich & Hernandez-Serrano, 2006).

**LUBRICANTS AND TOPICAL CREAMS** Adding an artificial lubricant may be helpful and enhance sexual pleasure, especially in women who are postmenopausal, or experience sex hormone levels that are below normal limits (Mezzich & Hernandez-Serrano, 2006).

In fact, Patty Brisben (2008), author of the self-help book *Pure Romance Between the Sheets,* goes so far as to say "Everyone should have a good lubricant. Period" (p. 153). Lubricants relieve vaginal dryness, reduce the possibility of pain and discomfort, and make sexual activity more pleasurable (Brisben, 2008). It follows that when sexual activity is experienced as pleasurable, libido will improve, desire will increase, and arousal will occur more readily.

**HERBAL REMEDIES** Some herbal remedies show promise in the alleviation of sexual difficulties. In a double-blind placebo-controlled crossover study, 900 milligrams of Korean red ginseng, a traditional Asian remedy for sexual dysfunction, three times daily was found to significantly improve erectile functioning, with no side effects (Ito, Kawahara, Das, & Strudwick, 1998). Moreover, a nutritional supplement called ArginMax, containing ginseng, ginkgo, L-arginine, damiana, and 14 other vitamins and minerals, is available over the counter that may significantly increase women's sexual desire and overall satisfaction (Mahan, 2003). It is important to note that these are relatively new treatments, and the testing of their efficacy and safety is limited.

**SURGICAL TREATMENTS** A surgical treatment called vestibulectomy, during which painful vestibular tissue is excised, is used on occasion to treat vestibulodynia in women (ter Kuile et al., 2010). Surgery may also be helpful for some men. Vascular surgery and a surgically implanted penile prosthesis are options for men with Erectile Disorder who have not had success with pharmacological treatment or other methods (Lewis, Rosen, & Goldstein, 2005).

**MECHANICAL DEVICES** Devices that suction blood to the genitals during oral sex or intercourse have been used since the mid-1980s to treat Erectile Dysfunction (Mezzich & Hernandez-Serrano, 2006) and enhance sexual pleasure. One device for use by males is an external vacuum constriction aid, which is available by prescription, and consists of a vacuum chamber, pump, and penile constriction band that is placed over the flaccid penis (Crooks & Baur, 2011). Velcro type devices that work by restraining the testicles are sometimes used to prevent Early/Premature Ejaculation (Mezzich & Hernandez-Serrano, 2006). Also helpful for some men are penile rubber rings (the slang term for this device is cock ring, or c-ring). When placed over the flaccid penis, c-rings help to slow down the blood flow, which, in turn, prolongs the release of ejaculatory fluids. Some designs allow for the attachment of a vibrator for the purpose of stimulating a partner's anus or clitoris, thereby prolonging the erection and enhancing the partner's pleasure simultaneously (Brisben, 2008).

For females, devices such as clitoral stimulators and vibrators can enhance sexual pleasure (ter Kuile et al., 2010). Clitoral stimulating devices use suction to increase blood flow in the area of the clitoris, whereas vibrators provide intense stimulation. Although there can be some resistance on the part of both men and women to use vibrators, sometimes referred to as "sex toys" (Brisben, 2008), they can be quite effective in increasing desire, promoting arousal, and enhancing orgasm (Mezzich & Hernandez-Serrano, 2006). Vibrators come in a wide variety of styles, shapes, and sizes, and may be designed to stimulate the clitoris, Graffenberg spot ("G-spot"), or both (Brisben, 2008).

**COGNITIVE-BEHAVIORAL THERAPY** Cognitive-behavioral therapy is a preferred therapy for treating sexual dysfunction (Mezzich & Hernandez-Serrano, 2006; ter Kuile et al., 2010). Cognitive-behavioral therapy assists clients in understanding the complex interactions between cognition, behavior, biology, and interpersonal functioning, which is central to the cognitive-behavioral understanding of sexual dysfunction (Mahan, 2003). For example, clients might be educated about how anxiety and other negative thoughts associated with sexual performance can distract them from erotic cues and reduce pleasure and sexual responding (Mezzich & Hernandez-Serrano, 2006; ter Kuile et al., 2010). Focusing on changing maladaptive sexual thoughts and behaviors, the San Francisco Bay Area Center for Cognitive Therapy (2006) suggests the following interventions: (1) psychoeducation, focusing on common myths and misinformation about sex; (2) scheduling and planning intimate time; (3) exposure-based treatments in which the person or couple carries out a series of specific, home-based behavioral homework assignments designed to reduce anxiety in sexual situations and increase focus on pleasurable aspects of intimacy; (4) sexual communication training; (5) cognitive restructuring to challenge negative thoughts associated with sex; (6) discussion of expanding their sexual repertoire to minimize boredom and maximize interest; (7) lifestyle interventions such as exercise and sleep hygiene that may positively impact sexual response; (8) marital therapy to resolve interpersonal conflict and enhance intimacy; and (9) individual therapy to address contributing problems, such as depression. Another cognitive-behavioral technique used in sex therapy is cognitive pacing, which entails noticing triggers that lead to sexual arousal and rank-ordering them based on potency. The individual can then draw on this knowledge to slow down or speed up arousal during intercourse (Mezzich & Hernandez-Serrano, 2006).[24]

## Upper-Left and Lower-Left Interventions for Sexual Dysfunction

**SEX EDUCATION** Given that many people do not possess even elementary knowledge of the HSRC, providing sex education is often a necessary first step in the treatment of sexual dysfunction because adequate knowledge is a prerequisite for treatment success. Misinformation can lead to unrealistic expectations and concomitant discouragement when those expectations are not met. It is helpful to normalize common sexual problems, de-bunk sexual myths, and explain the basics of human anatomy and physiology, sexual technique, and relationship skills that are relevant to sexual partnerships (ter Kuile et al., 2010). It is also helpful to educate clients about the varying paths to sexual arousal, so that they do not misinterpret the behavior of a partner who may be pursuing a different path than they are. For example, a woman who is focused on her partner while he is focusing on his own pleasure could misperceive his behavior as rejecting. Sex education may be provided in individual, couple, or group format. A helpful adjunct is bibliotherapy (Donahey, 2010); there are many useful self-help books on the market today that address the sexual needs of clients (Mezzich & Hernandez-Serrano, 2006).

---

[24] For a comprehensive summary of cognitive behavioral treatment approaches for women experiencing sexual dysfunction, see ter Kuile et al. (2010).

**ENCOURAGE A POSITIVE ATTITUDE TOWARD SEXUALITY** Basic cognitive counseling principles support the notion that how we think about events in our lives will increase the likelihood of experiencing specific emotions, which, in turn, will lead to certain physiological sensations associated with those emotions (Fall et al., 2004). In the case that individuals hold negative views regarding their bodies and sexuality, concomitant negative emotions, such as anxiety and disgust, are likely to result (Mezzich & Hernandez-Serrano, 2006). Thus, a basic task in treating sexual dysfunction is to counteract any negative views that clients have about their sexuality and instill more positive attitudes (ter Kuile et al., 2010).

**INCREASE CLIENTS' SELF-AWARENESS** Studies have shown that crucial components of satisfying sexuality include both emotional and physical self-awareness, and people who know their sexual feelings, their needs, and how their bodies respond to sexual stimuli are better able to share that information with their partner than people who are not as self-aware (Crooks & Baur, 2011). Sensual awareness training is a component of sex therapy that helps clients to be more aware of their bodies, specifically related to their response to touch (Mezzich & Hernandez-Serrano, 2006). Although it can be helpful to explore all areas of the body, not just genital regions, research has shown that masturbation exercises are a useful way for both men and women to learn more about their sexual arousal and response (ter Kuile et al., 2010).

**PSYCHODYNAMIC THERAPY** Psychodynamic therapy was the treatment of choice for sexual problems prior to the work of Masters and Johnson and Helen Singer Kaplan in the 1960s and 1970s (Mezzich & Hernandez-Serrano, 2006). Psychodynamic therapy focuses on bringing unconscious psychological conflict into the foreground of awareness, in the hope that this will cause the sexual dysfunction to remit. Unfortunately, this does not occur in the majority of cases, most likely because more immediate and surface causes are important factors in the sexual problem; thus, psychodynamic therapy is no longer the preferred method for treating sexual dysfunction (Mezzich & Hernandez-Serrano, 2006). Nevertheless, there is a role for psychodynamic therapy—when addressing the more immediate causes is not fruitful—as well as for addressing the emotional aspects of sexual difficulty (Mezzich & Hernandez-Serrano, 2006).

**SPIRITUAL TREATMENTS** For some individuals, the goal of their sexual participation is a spiritual one, wherein they transcend their sense of being a separate self and experience an I–thou unity (Mosher, 1980) that facilitates a heart-openness in which connection to the love force present in all of life can be experienced (Marquis, 2008). When this goal is achieved in the context of sexual union, there is often a simultaneous state change in which the ordinarily perceived boundaries between the other and oneself is transcended; such sexual union is so ecstatic that it often surpasses what most people believe is possible (Mosher, 1980).

For individuals who choose to view sexuality as part of a spiritual path to greater levels of openness and depth, interventions can be chosen to facilitate such objectives. Deida (2005) provides guidance for experiencing a spiritual connection during love-making. Similar to behavioral sensate focus approaches, he recommends: (1) fully experiencing one's own sensations; (2) fully tuning in to one's partner's sensual experiencing; and (3) "feeling beyond" one's partner's sensations until a spacious quality is perceived.

Deida (2005) adds that feeling *through* experience in such a manner involves ceasing to add fear, tension, or closure to the openness of the present moment, thus facilitating the experience of oneness that self-transcending sexual love can uniquely create.

Also, preparation for lovemaking is encouraged; it is suggested that effort be made to create a sensual environment that will engage all five senses, using props such as music, candles, and perfumes (Copelan, 1995). Relaxation exercises prior to lovemaking are also recommended. Erotic massage is another useful technique for enhancing sensuality. Because it helps to be fully engaged and psychologically present for the experience, practicing mental disciplines that minimize distractions are recommended (Copelan, 1995; Mosher, 1980). Regular meditation is one means whereby an individual can practice being mindful, aware, and present to current experience on an ongoing basis. Once physical contact occurs, it should be engaged in leisurely, with a focus on sharing and connecting with one's partner, as opposed to achieving a certain outcome, such as orgasm. These steps are conducive to the blissful, ecstatic, and spiritual soul-union that spiritual lovers crave (Copelan, 1995).

Tantric yoga is an Eastern practice, originating in the Hindu-Jain-Buddhist tradition, which has been used to improve intimacy, enrich sexual satisfaction and enhance orgasmic experience by living life in meditation (Muir & Muir, 1989). "Tantra could be said to embrace holistically the *ecstatic poetics* of being human, and focuses on our deepest longing for the divine . . . a personalized spiritual training requiring that practitioners commit every aspect of their lives toward the process of their enlightening" (Barratt & Rand, 2007, p. 7). It is noted, however, that in order for tantric methodologies to be effective, "participants need to be somewhat open to the experience of subtle energies within their embodiment" (Barratt & Rand, 2007, p. 7). Similar to the spiritual approach mentioned earlier, tantra brings into awareness all five of the sensual modalities: breath, movement, sound, visualization, and touch (Barratt & Rand, 2007).

In addition, the Kama Sutra is a source of ancient Indian love practices, dating from about A.D. 400. It engages philosophies of sexuality and spirituality through the use of varied sexual techniques (Crooks & Baur, 2011). Despite its ancient origins, there has been a resurgence of interest in the Kama Sutra in modern times. Hooper (2007) notes that "According to the Kama Sutra, a man has a duty to satisfy his lover" (p. 39), recommending sensual movements that include: (1) blow of the bull, which involves rubbing the penis along one side of the vagina; (2) pressing, involving pushing forcefully against the vagina; (3) sporting of the sparrow, which involves moving rapidly and lightly in and out of the vagina; (4) moving forward (straightforward penetration); (5) piercing, involving penetrating the vagina from above and pushing against the clitoris; (6) churning, which involves holding and moving the penis in the vagina; and (7) giving a blow, involving removing the penis and striking the vagina with it.

## Lower-Right Interventions for Sexual Dysfunction

**COUPLE THERAPY** Couple therapy is an important modality for the treatment of sexual dysfunction (Mezzich & Hernandez-Serrano, 2006; Rosen & Leiblum, 1992).[25] In some

[25] Volumes have been written on couple therapy for sexual dysfunction. To be succinct, we agree with Meana's (2010) recommendation: "to work simultaneously on both the sexual and relationship problems" (p. 104) in the hope that improvement in one area will lead to improvement in the other.

cases, couple therapy will be preferred; in others, it may be an important ancillary treatment to individual therapy. Effective sex therapy for couples will situate the sexual dysfunction within the context of the couple's overall relationship, and will strive for improvement in the relationship along with amelioration of the sexual problem (Meana, 2010). Mezzich and Hernandez-Serrano (2006) point out the importance of the couple functioning as intimate partners who mutually give and receive pleasure—in contrast to a "battleground mentality." It is also important to address the sexual role expectations held by each member of the couple, helping them clarify these expectations and come to an agreement regarding how they want to enact those roles in their own relationship (Mosher, 1980). Common problems addressed in couple therapy include: conflict regarding how often sex will occur, variations in the desire for sex, resolving issues emanating from childhood abuse, problems with arousal, difficulty achieving orgasm, Premature (Early) Ejaculation, genito/pelvic pain and penetration difficulties, and sexual dysfunction related to substance use or medical issues.

There are times when sexual experiencing falters in the context of an otherwise happy relationship (Ferreira et al., 2012; Meana, 2010). In short, sex becomes boring. This is because passion often dwindles in long-term relationships, becoming "lost in the shuffle of responsibilities" (Meana, 2010, p. 106) that go along with maintaining a secure family lifestyle. When people become overly familiar with each other and lack adequate differentiation, it is easy for sexual excitement to wane (Ferreira et al., 2012). The antidote in these cases is to encourage the couple to utilize creativity in prioritizing their relationship while at the same time taking distance from each other in ways that would add interest to their lives (Meana, 2010).

**Communication Training** Helping couples to communicate directly, particularly concerning sexual matters, is a standard component of sex therapy. Communication training aims to cultivate a supportive attitude between partners, as well as to foster the relaxation required for sexual intimacy. Moreover, directly discussing sexual issues with one's partner not only decreases embarrassment, guilt, and shame regarding sex—it also helps clients become clearer about their own feelings, preferences, and so forth (Mezzich & Hernandez-Serrano, 2006). Even when couples are able to communicate well on other topics, feelings such as embarrassment and guilt can make communicating about sexual topics more challenging, and people may not know how to approach what is often perceived as a sensitive subject (Crooks & Baur, 2011). Nevertheless, having a relaxed and confident attitude regarding sexual matters lends itself to positive sexual experiences. Communication exercises are often used by therapists to help partners share their feelings and to improve their listening skills (Donahey, 2010). Important skills covered under communication training include being empathic toward one's partner, refraining from blame, paraphrasing, and reflective listening (Mezzich & Hernandez-Serrano, 2006).

**COGNITIVE-BEHAVIORAL COUPLE TRAINING** Sensate focus therapy is a classic behavioral treatment for sexual dysfunction that may be incorporated into a cognitive-behavioral treatment approach (Donahey, 2010; Fagan, 2004; ter Kuile et al., 2010). Utilizing observation, behavioral goal setting, and contingency management, the goal of sensate focus therapy is to improve the quality of the couple's interactions (Fagan, 2004). In the case that a woman wishes to improve her sexual functioning on her own, exercises designed to strengthen the pubococcygeal (PC) muscles and improve her self-stimulating ability may be helpful (Satterfield & Stayton, 1980). Shown to be one of the most useful couple-oriented activities for enhancing mutual sexual enjoyment (Crooks & Baur, 2011), sensate focus therapy consists of reducing anxiety caused by a goal-driven, frustrating event (such as desire to achieve an orgasm) and helps couples to increase communication, pleasure, and closeness, thus changing the event into one that is relaxed, non-threatening and enjoyable for both partners (Fagan, 2004; Mahan, 2003). Through the use of homework, sexual partners are gradually, over a period of several weeks, guided through "a nondemanding increase of sensual and then sexual pleasuring behaviors with each other" (Fagan, 2004, p. 87). By focusing on the pleasurable effects of touch and other sensual and sexual activities, the ability to give and receive sensual and sexual pleasure is developed (ter Kuile et al., 2010). Traditionally, sexual intercourse is prohibited in the early stages (Rosen & Leiblum, 1989), and then re-introduced gradually and incrementally. At each step of the process, anxiety reduction, skills training, and minimizing performance demands and other stresses are addressed (Mezzich & Hernandez-Serrano, 2006).

There are other activities that may be incorporated into a cognitive-behavioral treatment protocol for sexual dysfunction with couples (ter Kuile et al., 2010). One such technique is "Couple Genital Exploration Relaxation Training," which is a homework assignment instructing members of a couple to alternate in leading a sensual conversation facilitating the exploration of each other's bodies; another is called "Couple Arousal Pacing Training" (Mezzich & Hernandez-Serrano, 2006, pp. 140–141), which is used to help members of a couple take charge of their sexual arousal. "The Intercourse Acclimation Technique" (Mezzich & Hernandez-Serrano, 2006, p. 142) is particularly helpful with men who are experiencing difficulties with sexual performance, and consists of a man resting his penis inside his partner's vagina or mouth until he attains an erection, and then maintaining that state for a prolonged period of time.

The "stop-start" technique, also known as the squeeze-and-release technique, was developed by James Semans to prolong the sensation before orgasm (Crooks & Baur, 2011), and is most commonly used with men with Premature (Early) Ejaculation. The stop-start technique involves stimulating the penis to the point of impending orgasm and then stopping until the pre-ejaculatory stimulation subsides, allowing ejaculation to occur in a more controllable manner. This may involve using the squeeze technique, in which strong pressure is applied with two fingers on top of the penis glans (one finger below and one finger above the corona) and the thumb on the frenulum until the urge to ejaculate subsides (Crooks & Baur, 2005). The stop-start technique is continually practiced until the man experiences progressively better ejaculatory control. It is important to mention that there have been controversial reviews of the squeeze technique because it may cause physical pain and can potentially have a negative impact on intimacy (Schnarch, 2002).

Finally, a cognitive-behavioral approach to couple sex therapy will incorporate "Progressive Intercourse: Alternative Scenarios" into a couple's sexual repertoire. This means that other activities will be introduced to allow the couple more variety and flexibility, such as oral sex, novel sexual positions, and role-play (ter Kuile et al., 2010). There are also a vast number of holistic approaches to sex therapy that may be useful, such as hypnosis, yoga, acupuncture, biofeedback, and dance. Before concluding sex therapy treatment, it is important to support the couple in establishing a plan for maintaining their gains and normalizing occasional challenges in their quest for sexual health (Mezzich & Hernandez-Serrano, 2006).

## SUMMARY OF THE TREATMENT OF SEXUAL DYSFUNCTION

In a final consideration of the treatment of sexual dysfunction, we emphasize the importance of sexual health, encompassing physical, emotional, interpersonal, and spiritual dimensions. We have included a discussion of the basic principles of sex therapy, such as the importance of completing a comprehensive assessment, adequate training in psychotherapy, self-awareness on the part of the clinician, and the PLISSIT model of sex therapy. We then situated key treatment strategies for sexual dysfunction within the Integral model. Important biological and behavioral treatments include relaxation training, pharmaceutical treatments, hormone treatments, herbal remedies, topical lubricants and creams, surgery, and mechanical devices. Cognitive-behavioral therapy for both individuals and couples is considered to be one of the most effective interventions for sexual dysfunction. Psychological, emotional, and cultural treatments include psychosexual education, psychodynamic therapy, and spiritual treatments. Relational approaches are comprised of couple therapy and communication training. Having completed our discussion of the sexual dysfunctions, we now turn our attention to the Paraphilic Disorders, which are qualitatively very different from the sexual dysfunctions.

## PARAPHILIC DISORDERS

Paraphilias[26] (the term means literally "beyond usual love;" Clipson, 2004), are defined as recurrent, intense sexually arousing fantasies, sexual urges, or behaviors generally involving (1) nonhuman objects, (2) the suffering or humiliation of oneself or one's partner, or (3) children or other nonconsenting persons that occur over a period of at least 6 months and cause clinically significant distress or impairment of functioning (APA, 2000). Previously termed "deviations" and "perversions" (Hinderliter, 2010), the Paraphilic Disorders differ from sexual dysfunctions in that the sexual response is unaffected; rather, the sexual stimulus itself constitutes the symptom (Person, 2005). As explained by Person (2005), "the sexual response is preserved, but the symptom, a significant deviation in the erotic stimulus or in the activity itself, is the precondition for sexual excitement and orgasm" (p. 1965).

The majority of individuals with a Paraphilic Disorder are men (Troisi, 2008). Although it is not possible to accurately state the prevalence of Paraphilic Disorders (Fedoroff, 2010), it appears that they are relatively common and frequently ignored by treatment providers (Berlin, Malin, & Thomas, 1995).[27] The specific disorders may be

---

[26] In the DSM-5, a distinction is made between paraphilias, which are the unusual sexual interests that cause no harm, and Paraphilic Disorders, which are determined to cause harm, either by acting it out with a nonconsenting individual or by having an experience of emotional distress or impaired functioning (APA, 2010).

[27] Although this view prevails in the literature, Person (2005) disagrees, stating: "With the possible exception of sadism and masochism, the paraphilias are relatively rare compared to sexual dysfunctions. Yet the paraphilias have claimed just as much attention as the sexual dysfunctions" (p. 1966).

divided into categories, based on whether or not they involve coercive activity.[28] The coercive paraphilias (Crooks & Baur, 2011) include Exhibitionistic Disorder (exposing one's genitals), Frotteuristic Disorder (attaining physical contact with a nonconsenting person), Voyeuristic Disorder ("peeping" at people who are disrobing, naked, or taking part in sexual activity), and Pedophilic Disorder (using prepubescent children for sexual pleasure). The noncoercive paraphilias include Fetishistic Disorder (using objects for sexual stimulation), Transvestic Disorder (dressing in clothes typically worn by the opposite gender), Sexual Masochism Disorder (being the recipient of suffering or humiliation), and Sexual Sadism Disorder (inflicting suffering or humiliation onto another).[29] There are also categories for Other Specified Paraphilic Disorder and Unspecified Paraphilic Disorder, which include paraphilias that do not meet diagnostic criteria for the categories just mentioned (APA, 2013). Whether or not the clinician chooses to explain the nature of the paraphilia and/or why the diagnosis does not meet the full criteria for a paraphilia determines whether the paraphilia is specified or unspecified. Examples of these include Zoophilia (having a sexual preference for animals), Necrophilia (desire for sexual activity with a corpse), and Coprophilia/Urophilia (becoming sexually aroused through contact with feces and urine; Brockman & Bluglass, 1996). The number of paraphilias is very large; lists have been compiled showing nearly 550 different varieties (Fedoroff, 2010).[30]

The presence of an unusual sexual preference will not necessarily result in a diagnosis. In the case of Pedophilic, Voyeuristic, Exhibitionistic, and Frotteuristic Disorders, as well as sexual sadism, the diagnosis will be made only if the individual has acted on these sexual urges, or if he is experiencing clinically significant impairment or distress in occupational, social, or other important dimensions of functioning as a result of the urges (APA, 2010). In the cases of fetishism, sexual masochism, and Transvestic Disorder, a diagnosis will be made only in cases in which the person is experiencing distress that is clinically significant, or functioning is impaired (APA, 2010).

Paraphilias, comprised of fantasies and/or behaviors, often begin in childhood, normally around the time of puberty, and once they become habitual, can endure for a lifetime (Mezzich & Hernandez-Serrano, 2006; Saleh & Berlin, 2003). For some people, paraphilic preferences dominate, and become requisite for the experience of sexual pleasure (APA, 2000). For others, paraphilic fantasy and activity is included in sexual activity intermittently, and is not required in order to experience sexual pleasure (APA, 2000; Hinderliter, 2010). Interestingly, some individuals will prefer paraphilic sexual activity when they are under stress, returning to more normative sexual activity when the stress subsides (Person, 2005).

Overlap among paraphilias is not uncommon; in other words, the same person may experience multiple paraphilias (APA, 2000; Hinderliter, 2010; Mason, 1997). Fedoroff (2010) points out that a commonality among the paraphilias is that they

---

[28] We prefer this distinction, although the DSM is not organized in this manner. It is important to note that the non-coercive paraphilias are relatively benign. As Person (2005) points out: "It is the group of paraphilias that causes harm that stigmatizes the whole group and leads one to think of paraphilias as invariably pernicious" (p. 1966).

[29] In the case that sadistic acts are forced on a nonconsenting individual, sexual sadism would be considered a coercive paraphilia (APA, 2000, 2010).

[30] Fedoroff's (2010) chapter includes a useful table showing a comprehensive list of paraphilias derived from the *International Statistical Classification of Diseases and Related Health Problems*.

usually (although not always) occur outside of the context of a "consensual, mutually reciprocal relationship" (p. 404). In many cases, people will hide their paraphilic urges and activity, experiencing them only in isolation, sometimes even hidden from their partners (Brockman & Bluglass, 1996). When discovered, these individuals may experience considerable emotional distress and the potential to lose their primary love relationship. On the other hand, some people enjoy their paraphilic sexual activity and experience no distress related to their sexual preference (Person, 2005). It is not uncommon for a person experiencing a paraphilia to have a concomitant mental health problem, such as a mood disorder, anxiety disorder, impulse control disorder, substance use disorder, or personality disorder (Brockman & Bluglass, 1996). Given the wide variety of sexual practices across cultures, it is difficult to ascertain the division between normal and disordered sexual behavior (Mezzich & Hernandez-Serrano, 2006), and there is considerable controversy regarding whether paraphilias should be considered mental disorders (Hinderliter, 2010; Moser, 2009). Particularly in the case of noncoercive sexual activity, many consider paraphilic behavior to be harmless (Crooks & Baur, 2008; Hinderliter, 2010). Person (2005) observed that "many people have strands of perverse interest woven into their sexual makeup that fly just under the radar of consciousness but that express themselves in self-evident interest in films and books that express one or another paraphilia" (p. 1966). Although unusual sexual practices make some people very uneasy (Fedoroff, 2010; Mezzich & Hernandez-Serrano, 2006), the tendency to label unusual sexual interests as deviant and pathological is of concern to the extent that such labels can be used to marginalize innocent individuals or make it more difficult for distressed individuals to seek help for a paraphilia (Hinderliter, 2010; Moser, 2009).

Moser (2009) makes a good case for the way in which sexual behaviors that deviate from societal norms are readily labeled as pathological, yet these views, being socially constructed and culturally sanctioned, are prone to change over time. Although sexuality has almost universally been viewed as a powerful force, there has also been a historical tendency to view unusual sexual preferences as either perverted, sinful, or criminal (Person, 2005). Some sexual practices that were once considered to be criminal and/or perverse are now considered to be normal sexual acts, such as homosexuality and masturbation (Hinderliter, 2010; Levine, 1992; Moser, 2009; Sadock, 2005). The possibility that mere thoughts and fantasies could place someone at risk of being marginalized and labeled as criminal remains a significant concern today (Hinderliter, 2010; Moser, 2009). However, many (if not most) paraphilias are not criminal in nature; and even among those whose paraphilic desires would be criminal if acted upon, many never act upon them (Fedoroff, 2010). Nevertheless, there is currently a great deal of fear surrounding sexual offenses. Whereas some studies report extremely high recidivism rates (Brockman & Bluglass, 1996), recent research is suggesting lower recidivism rates and increased optimism regarding the ability to effectively treat people with Paraphilic Disorders (Fedoroff, 2010).

In some cases, concern appears warranted, because certain paraphilic urges—when acted out in a coercive manner—can cause harm to innocent, nonconsenting individuals (Crooks & Baur, 2011; Hollin, 1997). Paraphilic behavior tends to involve the objectification of others, and depending on the act inflicted upon them, these individuals may feel violated, vulnerable, and fearful of further abuse (Crooks & Baur, 2011). Some paraphilias will begin as a fantasy experienced through masturbation, and then progress to behavior that occurs in the outside world as cravings intensify (Fagan, 2004). In more severe cases, victims of unwanted sexual acts may be left traumatized, or even dead (Hollin, 1997). For this reason, laws are in place to protect unwilling recipients from harm related to sexual urges, and acting out some paraphilias constitutes criminal activity (Crooks & Baur, 2011). It is also important to note that some extremely harmful sexual behaviors, such as rape, are not considered mental disorders, and will not be discussed in this chapter, despite their obviously deleterious effect on society.

For the remainder of this chapter, we will explain each Paraphilic Disorder in detail, including some etiological factors and ideas regarding treatment specifically for each disorder. We will conclude this section with general information on the etiology and treatment of the Paraphilic Disorders as a whole.[31]

## Exhibitionistic Disorder

The legal term for exhibitionism is *indecent exposure* (Rosen, 1996) and refers to a person—who is almost always a man—exposing his genitals to an unsuspecting person, who is usually a female child or adult woman (Crooks & Baur, 2011). DSM-5 (APA, 2010, 2013) diagnostic criteria include

- The occurrence of sexual arousal related to fantasies, urges, and behaviors involving the exposure of one's genitals to an unsuspecting individual;
- Recurrent arousal occurs over a period of at least 6 months;
- The individual has either acted on these urges, or is experiencing significant distress or functional impairment as a result.

Research has shown that about one-third of identified sexual offenders are exhibitionists (Laws & O'Donohue, 1997; Rosen, 1996). It is the most common of the Paraphilic Disorders, and is seen frequently by clinicians (Rosen, 1996). It appears that most people who expose themselves are males in their 20s or 30s and are married or have previously been married (Crooks & Baur, 2011). Many exhibitionists go undetected for years, and often pride themselves on their self-control and high moral standards in other areas of their lives (Rosen, 1996).

Exhibitionists often obtain sexual gratification by masturbating shortly after performing the act, in which masturbation usually involves mental visions or fantasies about the act (especially the observer's reactions, which are often shock, disgust, and/or fear) to increase his arousal (Crooks & Baur, 2011). Some sexologists take the view that the exhibitionist does not intend to participate in sexual activity with the victim. In fact, he would probably be afraid and unable to consummate physical intercourse with his victim were he to have the opportunity (Brockman & Bluglass, 1996). Others posit that at least some exhibitionists will eventually act out in sexually violent ways (Crooks & Baur, 2005; Rosen, 1996).

[31] We have chosen this structure due to the fact that there are a large number of Paraphilic Disorders, which are similar in some ways and very different in others. Given the large number of disorders that overlap and diverge, there is an inherent challenge in doing each one justice in a single book chapter. In fact, Hudson and Ward (1997) point to the need for an organizational meta-theory to solve the conundrum. In the meantime, we believe that it is necessary to organize this material in a manner that may feel a bit awkward to the reader.

Internal factors (upper-left and lower-left quadrant phenomena) are highly significant in the etiology of exhibitionism. Despite research indicating that there is no personality profile for exhibitionists (Laws & O'Donohue, 1997), it is has been noted that most who experience exhibitionist urges struggle with intimacy, are shy, and have persistent feelings of insecurity and inadequacy (Crooks & Baur, 2011), yet have the ability to function quite effectively in their daily lives. Additional etiological factors may be: (a) powerful feelings of inadequacy; (b) looking for affirmation of their masculinity; (c) seeking attention due to feelings of isolation or lack of appreciation; (d) feelings of anger or hostility toward people who have failed to notice them, which has caused emotional pain; and/or (e) they are emotionally disturbed, mentally disturbed, or intellectually disabled (Crooks & Baur, 2011). When exhibitionism occurs among the elderly, it may be the result of dementia, an upper-right quadrant phenomenon (Brockman & Bluglass, 1996).

The primary treatment of exhibitionism is cognitive-behavioral. Treatment begins with an individualized assessment, followed by individual and/or group psychotherapy (Rosen, 1996) that may include behavioral techniques, such as electric shock, covert sensitization, minimal arousal conditioning, aversion behavior rehearsal, vicarious sensitization, social skills training, and alternative behavior conditioning (Laws & O'Donohue, 1997). Other behavior techniques that have been used include masturbation techniques, fantasy change, satiation, impulse-control training, and plethysmographic feedback. Studies have shown that some psychotropic medications such as neuroleptics and SSRIs decrease exhibitionist urges (Rosen, 1996). Another medication that may be of help is Fluphenazine, which, especially when combined with Fluoxetine, often results in a significant antiandrogenic effect[32] (Laws & O'Donohue, 1997).

## Fetishistic Disorder

Fetishism refers to becoming sexually aroused by fantasies of, or viewing, inanimate objects or nongenital body parts (APA, 2013). DSM-5 diagnostic criteria include (APA, 2013; Kafka, 2010):

- The occurrence of sexual arousal related to fantasies, urges, and behaviors involving the use of nonliving objects or focus on nongenital body parts;
- Recurrent arousal occurs over a period of at least 6 months;
- The individual experiences clinically significant distress or impaired functioning in key life domains as a result of fetishistic urges or behavior;
- Objects such as clothing used while cross-dressing or genital stimulation devices are not considered when making the diagnosis.

Similar to other paraphilias, it is difficult to determine what constitutes an atypical behavior (Crooks & Baur, 2011; Moser, 2009). For example, it is not unusual for people to become sexually aroused by undergarments or specific body parts (Crooks & Baur, 2011). Some common objects used for sexual stimulation include women's undergarments, high-heeled shoes, black boots, stockings, and objects made with leather, silk, and rubber (Brockman & Bluglass, 1996; Crooks & Baur, 2011; Kafka, 2010; Mason, 1997). In some cases, the individual will require the fetishistic object to

---

[32] Androgens are the male sex hormones, such as testosterone. An antiandrogenic effect occurs when the typical physiological effects of these hormones are prevented from occurring.

be worn by a partner in order to complete the sex act. Fetishism becomes interpersonally problematic when objects become more important than people, interfering with intimacy in the relationship (Kafka, 2010; Levine, 1992). People with fetishism may also experience extreme anger when their urge to touch a fetishistic object is blocked.

Although the etiology underlying fetishism is not completely clear (Laws & O'Donohue, 1997), classical and operant conditioning—upper-right quadrant phenomena—appear to play a significant role. In simple behavioral terms: a certain object or body part is focused on during fantasy as the individual masturbates; when orgasm occurs, the fetish is associated with the pleasurable experience and the fetishistic behavior is reinforced (Crooks & Baur, 2011; Junginger, 1997). As an example, if a person is fantasizing about women's undergarments while engaging in masturbation, becomes sexually aroused, and eventually climaxes, the thought of women's undergarments alone can lead to future sexual arousal.

Another view is that fetishistic behavior evolves from childhood associations (Crooks & Baur, 2011). A child may come to associate certain objects (such as gloves or panties) of his mother, older sister, or other emotionally significant person with sexual arousal. This can lead to a child continuing to associate the fetish object with the owner into adulthood. In extreme cases, the person will engage in fetishistic behavior exclusively, and withdraw from sex with a partner (Crooks & Baur, 2011).

Although research shows that treatment for fetishistic behavior is often ineffective (Brockman & Bluglass, 1996), typical treatments may include cognitive therapy as well as the use of counterconditioning by electric shock, covert sensitization, and masturbatory satiation (Brockman & Bluglass, 1996; Laws & O'Donohue, 1997).

## Frotteuristic Disorder

Frotteurism involves a person (usually male) obtaining sexual arousal by rubbing or pressing against an involuntary person, usually a woman in a public space (APA 2013; Crooks & Baur, 2011). DSM-5 diagnostic criteria for frotteurism include (APA, 2010, 2013; Långström, 2010):

- The occurrence of sexual arousal related to fantasies, urges, and behaviors involving touching or rubbing against a nonconsenting person;
- Recurrent arousal occurs over a period of at least 6 months;
- The person has acted on these urges with a nonconsenting person, or the sexual urges or fantasies cause marked distress or impaired functioning.

This fairly common paraphilia often goes unnoticed as the act typically occurs in crowded public places, such as an elevator, subway, underground train, bus, or at a large sporting event or outdoor concert (Crooks & Baur, 2011; Rosen, 1996). Frotteurism involves the use of the perpetrator's hands to touch a person's thigh, rubbing of his clothed genitalia against another person, or brushing up against the buttocks, legs, or breasts of the victim, who may have been pre-selected (Laws & O'Donohue, 1997; Rosen, 1996). This results in feelings of arousal or orgasm during the act or, more commonly, when incorporating the mental images (fantasies) of the behavior while masturbating at a later time (Crooks & Baur, 2011; Rosen, 1996). It is important to note that it is difficult to estimate the number of people who actually engage in this behavior, as it usually happens so discretely that it often goes unnoticed by victims.

As with other coercive paraphilias, frotteurism is most commonly exhibited by males who engage in this activity due to feelings of social and sexual inadequacy (Crooks & Baur, 2011). Research has shown that frotteurism is most closely associated with characteristics commonly manifested by those who engage in exhibitionism (Crooks & Baur, 2011). As a review, these are largely upper-left and lower-left quadrant phenomena, such as shyness, a sense of inadequacy, feeling isolated and unappreciated, and feelings of resentment toward people who have failed to notice them. Some studies have shown a mutual relationship between this disorder, voyeurism, exhibitionism, and preferential rape[33] (Laws & O'Donohue, 1997).

Researchers recommend a comprehensive intake assessment, followed by cognitive-behavioral approaches, including masturbatory satiation, covert sensitization, cognitive restructuring, sex education, social skills and assertiveness training (Laws & O' Donohue, 1997).

## Pedophilic Disorder

Pedophilia is any sexual activity with a child, generally younger than 13 years of age (APA, 2000), and is a serious problem in current society (Brockman & Bluglass, 1996; Crooks & Baur, 2011). Statistics show alarming rates of child sexual abuse, with one out of every three girls and one out of every six boys being the victim of sexual abuse before the age of 18 (Araujo, 2008). Survivors of sexual abuse amount to over 60 million in the United States, which is approximately 20% of the population (Araujo, 2008). A person 16 years of age or older may be diagnosed with Pedophilic Disorder when his predominant sexual arousal occurs from children, at least 5 years younger than him, as opposed to physically mature adults. In addition, sexual interest in children must have been present for at least 6 months, must have been acted upon, or caused significant emotional distress or problems in interpersonal relationships (APA, 2010, 2013). There are also specifiers related to what age(s) and gender(s) the individual is attracted to. It is important to note that in the case of Pedophilia, experiencing distress over the urges is not always a prerequisite for the diagnosis (APA, 2013).

Pedophile offenders are not describable by any specific profile, but typically are "heterosexual males and are known to the victim" (Crooks & Baur, 2011, p. 533). Although most identify as being heterosexual, they may desire sexual encounters with children of the same gender (Groth & Birnbaum, 1978). Pedophiles, commonly known as child molesters, tend to cover the entire spectrum in terms of social status, occupation, economic status, religion, intelligence, educational status, and so forth. However, research indicates that many pedophile offenders are often lonely, shy, feel socially inadequate, relatively uniformed about sexuality, religious, and moralistic (Crooks & Baur, 2011). There also appears to be a harmful cycle of abuse, as many Pedophile offenders were themselves victims of sexual abuse as children (Crooks & Baur, 2005; Rosen, 1996). In some cases, pedophilic behavior is not commonly performed, but is rather an anomaly deriving from painful emotional experiences of the perpetrator, such as stress, loneliness, and isolation, in which case the child is an inappropriate substitute for the adult connection the perpetrator truly needs (Brockman & Bluglass, 1996).

[33] Preferential rape is defined as "a paraphilic preference for coercive sex" (Freund & Seto, 1998, p. 433).

Research shows that attachment issues are significant in the etiology of Pedophilic Disorder (Marshall & Marshall, 2002).

There is much controversy between clinicians and researchers regarding effective treatment approaches for pedophile offenders (Laws & O' Donohue, 1997). Despite the fact that psychodynamic concepts such as attachment theory (Marshall & Marshall, 2002) and object relations (Leguizamo, 2002) seem to offer valid explanations for sexually offending behavior, traditional psychotherapeutic strategies and psychopharmacology have not been shown to be effective with this population; behavioral interventions, however—such as electrical aversion, covert sensitization, and masturbatory satiation—are recommended in the treatment of pedophile offenders (Laws & O'Donohue, 1997). Innovative models for the treatment of sexual offending have also been developed by Schwartz (2002) and Longo (2002), which utilize integrative and holistic principles. Comprehensive treatment programs are considered the most effective modality for delivering treatment to pedophile offenders (Laws & O'Donohue, 1997).

## Sexual Masochism and Sexual Sadism

Sexual masochism involves becoming sexually aroused while being psychologically humiliated or physically bound, beaten, or otherwise hurt; sexual sadism involves obtaining sexual arousal from delivering such physical or psychological pain (Crooks & Baur, 2008). In order to be diagnosed, these patterns must occur for 6 months, and must result in psychological distress or impaired functioning. In addition, in the case of sexual sadism, the disorder is diagnosable if these urges have been acted out on a nonconsenting individual (APA, 2013; Krueger, 2010a).

Together, these diagnoses are commonly known as sadomasochistic behavior because they both involve "the association of sexual expression with pain" (Crooks & Baur, 2011, p. 501). The colloquial term for sadomasochism is BDSM, referring to: bondage-domination-sadism-masochism (Crooks & Baur, 2011). Individuals who enjoy some element of sexual sadomasochism are common (Person, 2005). As with other paraphilias, some take issue with defining some of these sexual preferences as disorders (Glasser, 1996; Krueger, 2010a, 2010b). Many individuals enjoy some form of aggressive interaction during sex play, and respond erotically to sadomasochistic activity (Crooks & Baur, 2011; Person, 2005).

There is no clear line of demarcation regarding where sexual masochism ends and sexual sadism begins (Brockman & Bluglass, 1996). In fact, people who engage in sadomasochistic behaviors often do not confine themselves to either sexual sadism or masochism, but alternate between both forms of sexual activity (Brockman & Bluglass, 1996; Crooks & Baur, 2011; Krueger, 2010a, 2010b). The range of this activity, often conducted through role-playing, incorporates elements of dominance/submission and control. Bondage fantasies are often enacted, utilizing restrictive devices. Whereas uninformed individuals have the misperception that pain is usually inflicted on another unwillingly, in the majority of cases, the sexual activity is consensual and enjoyed by both parties (Crooks & Baur, 2011).

At times, sadomasochistic sexual activity does become dangerous (Krueger, 2010a, 2010b). In some cases, "people may engage in dangerous or injurious behavior during their masochistic episodes" (Baumeister & Butler, 1997, p. 227) such as "electrical stimulation, hanging, or asphyxiation, nonasphyxual sexual bondage, or taking poisons" (Baumeister & Butler, 1997, p. 227). People have died from an extremely dangerous masochistic activity called "hypoxyphilia," in which sexual arousal is obtained through being deprived of oxygen (APA, 2000; Brockman & Bluglass, 1996; Krueger, 2010a). The strategy for attaining the oxygen-deprived state, such as with the use of a noose or ligature, can go awry, leading to accidental death (APA, 2000; Brockman & Bluglass, 1996). In our own anecdotal experiences with clients, we have become concerned when they meet up with virtual strangers and immediately engage in sexual activity in which they are restrained and extremely vulnerable.

There are also people who are sexual sadists as well as "predators" (Hucker, 1997).[34] At times, the course of sexual sadism may evolve from lesser to greater severity, with the requirement for pleasure becoming a need to inflict serious physical harm onto a victim (APA, 2000). As pointed out in the DSM, when sexual sadism is combined with Antisocial Personality Disorder, the risk of someone becoming seriously hurt or killed is increased (APA, 2000; Krueger, 2010b).

People who participate in sadomasochistic sexual activity are usually motivated by the desire to experience either dominance or submission, as opposed to wanting to inflict or experience pain (Crooks & Baur, 2011; Krueger 2010a). Additional motivations include: a need for additional nonsexual stimuli to achieve arousal; sexual enhancement through the experience of resistance or tension between partners; the provision of an escape from the rigid, controlled patterns of daily living; and repeating early experiences that led to a connection between sex and pain (Crooks & Baur, 2011; Laws & O' Donohue, 1997). Sadomasochistic phenomenon may also be related to guilt, conflict, and negative views about sexuality that cause people to doubt their right to experience pleasure without first experiencing pain. Hence, sadomasochistic activity can be a form of punishing or being punished for sexual pleasure (Crooks & Baur, 2011).

Given that sadomasochistic sexual activity is common in both genders (Krueger, 2010a), Person (2005) speculates that these urges are related to "power issues growing up" (p. 1969). Many people who participate in sadomasochistic activity are otherwise stable and well adjusted, without complaints pertaining to their sexuality (Crooks & Baur, 2011; Krueger, 2010a, 2010b). In such cases, treatment is not clinically indicated. When sadomasochistic activity becomes problematic and distressing, either for those involved or for unwilling recipients or victims, treatment is warranted (Hollin, 1997; Krueger, 2010a, 2010b). The aims of treatment for a sexual sadist include: to change arousal patterns; to foster empathy for the victim; to alter cognitive distortions; and to address idiosyncratic needs of the client, such as substance use issues and social skills deficits (Hollin, 1997). When treatment is indicated for clients with sexual masochism, the goal is often to expand the sexual repertoire of the client to incorporate additional possibilities for arousal (Crooks & Baur, 2011). Some potential motivations for changing this behavior include the client's dislike of being dependent on this form of arousal, as well as concomitant disturbance of intimacy with her partner (Thornton & Mann, 1997). Motivational interviewing (Miller & Rollnick, 2002) is a useful strategy, as are a variety of behavioral approaches (Thornton & Mann, 1997).

---

[34] Hollin (1997) provides a thorough exploration of these extreme cases.

## Transvestic Disorder

Transvestic fetishism involves a person obtaining sexual arousal from cross-dressing, but it must be distinguished from other forms of cross-dressing, in which sexual arousal is not the primary motivation (Crooks & Baur, 2008). Some examples of the latter include dressing in clothes of the opposite gender for entertainment purposes, gay men dressing in women's clothing to attract a partner, and transsexuals whose sexual identities are validated through cross-dressing (Crooks & Baur, 2008). In order to be diagnosed with Transvestic Disorder, sexual arousal derived from cross-dressing must have occurred for at least 6 months, and the individual must experience significant distress or functional impairment as a result (APA, 2010, 2013; Blanchard, 2010).

It is important to note that there is much controversy regarding whether transvestic fetishism should be considered pathological (Blanchard, 2010; Laws & O' Donohue, 1997). Some, including members of the transgendered community, feel strongly that cross-dressing is an acceptable sexual outlet that should not be pathologized or viewed as abnormal (Crooks & Baur, 2011).

Men experiencing transvestic fetishism may be quite masculine in their adult hobbies and career choices, and are frequently found in male-dominant occupations (Zucker & Blanchard, 1997). In addition, men with transvestic fetishism do not tend to manifest cross-dressing behaviors in prepubescence or adolescence, nor were they markedly prone to playing with girls or engaging in feminine-type activities as children (Zucker & Blanchard, 1997). Some clinicians have suggested that transvestic fetishism may result from forced cross-dressing during childhood as a form of punishment or humiliation, which is termed "petticoat punishment" (Zucker & Blanchard, 1997). Another possibility is that cross-dressing provides a sense of comfort and safety, and "when it is accompanied by sexual excitement, masturbation, and orgasm, there is an added reinforcing property" (Zucker & Blanchard, 1997, p. 271).

Treatment approaches for transvestic fetishism tend to be "behavioral in orientation, emphasizing the reduction of the abnormal behavior and reinforcement of normal behaviors" (Adshead, 1997, p. 288). Early treatment focused on the use of punishment and noxious aversion techniques including electrical, chemical, and shaming techniques with behavior therapies including masturbatory reconditioning or covert sensitization (Adshead, 1997). Antiandrogenic agents and psychotropic medications have also been considered as possible aversion approaches in the attempt to extinguish the behavior. The efficacy of these approaches is doubtful, and the use of these aversive techniques has been called into question on ethical grounds. More recent treatment approaches have focused on the use of cognitive-behavioral and psychodynamic therapies as treatments for transvestic fetishism (Adshead, 1997).

## Voyeuristic Disorder

Voyeurism involves becoming sexually aroused when observing unsuspecting others who are naked or engaging in sexual activity (APA, 2013). It has been noted that the definition is broader than this and includes: scopophilia (watching others undress), scoptophilia (watching others have sex), and triolism (observing one's partner having sex with another person) (Laws & O' Donohue, 1997; Rosen, 1996).

Conceptualizing voyeurism as a deviant behavior is somewhat controversial, because to a certain extent it is considered socially acceptable; simply consider the popularity of R- and X-rated movies, explicit magazines, live shows, and pornography (Brockman & Bluglass, 1996; Crooks & Baur, 2011). The key distinction is that true voyeuristic behavior is characterized by the nonconsenting lack of awareness on the part of the individual(s) being watched (Brockman & Bluglass, 1996). Individuals with voyeuristic characteristics often experience arousal from the mere thought of the risk of discovery, which is why nudist camps or nude beaches do not attract them (Crooks & Baur, 2011). Voyeurism may be diagnosed when an individual 18 years of age or older becomes sexually aroused as a result of watching others who are either naked, in the process of taking their clothes off, or participating in some type of sexual behavior. In addition, arousal from voyeuristic sources must occur for at least 6 months, and the person must have either engaged in voyeuristic activity with a nonconsenting victim, or be experiencing significant emotional distress or impaired functioning (APA, 2010, 2013).

Voyeuristic behavior is more commonly exhibited by men and can include peering in bedroom windows; stationing oneself by the entrance of women's bathrooms, boring holes in the walls of public dressing rooms, and video voyeurism (Crooks & Baur, 2011). Video voyeurism has grown with the accessibility of advanced and multi-functional technology devices, mainly video cameras (Crooks & Baur, 2011). Cameras may be placed in unusual spots such as smoke detectors, ceiling fixtures, and gym bags. Individuals may also develop an obsession with a particular person whom they seek to watch, which may be combined with another paraphilia and lead to a more serious offense involving physical contact. Similar to sexual sadism, voyeurism often contains elements of aggression, power, and control (Brockman & Bluglass, 1996).

Psychodynamic, social learning, and sociobiological theories are useful in explaining the etiology of voyeurism (Kaplan & Krueger, 1997). According to psychodynamic theory, voyeurism (along with other paraphilias) is considered to derive from a more fundamental psychopathology involving unresolved psychosexual conflicts (Kaplan & Krueger, 1997).

Unusual sexual interests, including voyeurism, may be indicative that a person has regressed to a developmentally earlier psychosexual stage, and may also represent psychological defenses against hostility stemming from trauma in early childhood (Kaplan & Krueger, 1997). Specifically, voyeurism in males may be related to the need to separate psychologically from one's mother, wherein one first attains a certain amount of psychological distance from one's mother, and subsequently decreases this distance by the nonmutual act of looking upon her without her knowledge (Kaplan & Krueger, 1997).

Social learning theory posits that unique expressions of one's sexuality, including voyeuristic urges, are developed and maintained as a result of behavioral principles, such as operant conditioning, modeling, and reinforcement (Kaplan & Krueger, 1997). Not only are the kinds of circumstances and types of stimulation that can evoke sexual arousal largely learned, the person's previous experiences are major determinants of the specific ways the person behaves in order to express his sexuality (Kaplan & Krueger, 1997). In other words, when pleasure is associated with a particular stimulus, that stimulus will be reinforced, and the individual is likely to establish a learned pattern of pairing the stimulus with sexual pleasure in the future. In addition, the particular stimuli that become associated with sexual excitement are contingent on the individual's environment.

Sociobiological theory invokes an evolutionary perspective on voyeuristic behavior, suggesting that males are sexually aroused at the site of female genitalia, especially genitals that they have not seen before. In turn, they experience a strong desire to view women's genitalia because such motivational processes maximized male reproductive success in our evolutionary history (Kaplan & Krueger, 1997).

Research has shown similar characteristics among people who are inclined to voyeurism and people who expose themselves (exhibitionism), such as poorly developed sociosexual skills and strong feelings of inadequacy and inferiority (Crooks & Baur, 2011). These individuals often desire to "peep" at strangers, rather than someone they might know, which increases their level of excitement by making the risk of discovery quite high (Crooks & Baur, 2011).

Although there is very little information on the treatment of this disorder, it has been suggested that treatment should include setting limits to prevent voyeuristic activity, and identifying healthier, more appropriate alternatives to the sexual fulfillment obtained through voyeuristic acts (Laws & O'Donohue, 1997).

## ETIOLOGY OF THE PARAPHILIC DISORDERS

Although it is generally accepted that many adults will respond to unusual sexual stimuli, it is unclear why some individuals will act on those urges, whereas others will not (Brockman & Bluglass, 1996). Compared to other mental disorders, little is known regarding the etiology of the Paraphilic Disorders (Fedoroff, 2010; Person, 2005), and what is known lacks a consistent, coherent organizational theory (Hudson & Ward, 1997). As is the case with the sexual dysfunctions, there are many potential factors underlying the experience of an unusual sexual preference, and an integrative, multidimensional approach is warranted (Fedoroff, 2010; Mezzich & Hernandez-Serrano, 2006; Troisi, 2008). Brockman and Bluglass (1996) have suggested an integrated approach to the conceptualization and treatment of the Paraphilic Disorders based on the principles of cognitive analytical therapy. They propose that there are some factors that serve as motivators, making it more likely for someone to engage in paraphilic behavior, and there are other factors that serve as deterrents. It appears that whether or not someone acts on unusual sexual urges depends on which side carries more weight—the motivating side or the deterring side (Brockman & Bluglass, 1996).

### Upper-Right Perspectives: Biological and Physiological Factors

**EVOLUTIONARY PERSPECTIVES** Evolutionary factors are salient to paraphilic phenomena (Freund & Seto, 1998; Trosi, 2008). Epidemiological data show that paraphiliacs are primarily men, and the difference in number between men and women with a Paraphilic Disorder is dramatic (Troisi, 2008). Evolutionary theory posits that males and females differ in their approach to mating, with men tending to discriminate much less in their requirements for sexual activity. Women, on the other hand, are more cautious, due to the high parental requirements that are demanded of them. Paraphilic Disorders, therefore, can be interpreted as an exaggeration of the male tendency to engage in sexual behavior prolifically for the biologically adaptive purpose of reproduction. As explained by Troisi (2008), paraphilias represent extreme variants of what are—for males—evolutionarily adaptive qualities: becoming easily sexually aroused and mating promiscuously with nearly any female he can.

**PHYSICAL ABNORMALITIES** Brain abnormalities, which could be due to traumatic brain injury or organic factors, lead to an increased possibility that an individual will be prone to unusual sexual behavior (Brockman & Bluglass, 1996; Freund, Seto & Kuban, 1997). Specifically, impairment of the temporal lobe and temporal lobe epilepsy can cause abnormal patterns of arousal (Brockman & Bluglass, 1996; Person, 2005). Possible explanations are:

> that a brain abnormality diminishes the individual's control over preexisting paraphiliac impulses, that it releases impulses otherwise repressed, that it disadvantages the individual thus afflicted, that it leads to paraphiliac substitutions, or that it may be a direct result of cerebral wiring. (Person, 2005, p. 1970)

Problems with the endocrine system and subsequent hormonal imbalances as well as chromosome abnormalities such as those found in Klinefelter's syndrome[35] may also be factors in paraphilic behavior (Brockman & Bluglass, 1996). Other genetic disorders that may predispose someone to a Paraphilic Disorder include fragile X syndrome, which is "a genetic defect that affects mostly male offspring and is associated with mental retardation" (APA, 2007, p. 388), and Autism Spectrum disorder (Fedoroff & Richards, 2010).

**DEVELOPMENTAL DISABILITY** There appears to be an increased tendency for paraphilic behavior in some individuals with developmental disabilities (Brockman & Bluglass, 1996). Developmental disabilities may cause concomitant problems with social learning and interpersonal skills, leading to asocial behavior (Fedoroff & Richards, 2010), and may also lessen the likelihood of having a consenting sexual partner (Brockman & Bluglass, 1996). The lack of a partner may lead to sexual frustration that cannot be met through socially sanctioned outlets. Such people also have an increased chance of having a comorbid personality disorder and a propensity for aggressive behavior, which are additional factors that could lead to paraphilic activity (Brockman & Bluglass, 1996).

**BEHAVIORAL VIEWS** From a behavioral perspective, all sexual behavior is learned—including paraphilic behavior: "there are no separate principles for 'deviant' or 'abnormal' and 'normal' sexual behavior . . . the question is, How is any behavior learned, or how does anybody come to like or value anything?" (Annon, 1976, p. 12). The hopeful aspect of this view is that anything that has been learned can be unlearned through behavioral techniques, such as aversion (Annon, 1976). Specifically, the Paraphilic Disorders would be considered problems of "behavioral excess" because they are extreme and occur when they are unwanted or not sanctioned by society (Freund et al., 1997). Annon (1976) explains the behavioral view of how unusual sexual preferences and behavior develop when arousal is paired with stimuli in the environment:

> Thinking or fantasizing about specific sexual activities may also bring on arousal, and occasionally, orgasms. By continued association of these sexual thoughts and fantasies with "neutral" stimuli, a person can learn to respond with arousal to previously neutral persons or objects. (p. 53)

---

[35] Klinefelter's syndrome is defined as "a congenital condition characterized by a short neck, low hairline, and a reduced number of vertebrae, some of which may be fused into a single mass. The condition is often accompanied by deafness and mental retardation" (APA, 2007, p. 515).

## Upper-Left Perspectives

**SEXUAL STYLE AND IDENTITY** A person's sexual style evolves over time and is a function of biological evolution, childhood experience, sociocultural influences, and numerous other factors (Deida, 2005). As explained by Person (2005),

> Each individual, whether paraphiliac or not, develops a characteristic pattern of sexual expression—sometimes called a *sex print* or *love map*. This pattern constitutes an erotic signature, signifying that the individual's sexual potential has been progressively narrowed between infancy and adulthood. (p. 1966)

This "erotic signature" includes the type of sexual fantasies and activities a person is prone to enjoy, and these sexual preferences are deeply entrenched (Person, 2005). Sexual identity is formed as an individual internalizes and identifies with his unique patterns of sexual preference. In the case of a Paraphilic Disorder, the range of fantasies and practices that will provide sexual satisfaction becomes restrictive, and often a prerequisite for sexual arousal (Person, 2005).

**EMOTIONAL HEALTH AND MENTAL ILLNESS** An individual's cognitive style and emotional state, including the presence of cognitive distortions, the experience of inner conflict, and the presence of certain emotions, such as anger, are significant to the etiology of the Paraphilic Disorders (Brockman & Bluglass, 1996). Psychological factors, such as a co-occurring mental illness (e.g., anxiety, depression, Schizophrenia, Personality Disorder) are significant as well (Brockman & Bluglass, 2006; Geffner, Franey, & Falconer, 2003; Mezzich & Hernandez-Serrano, 2006).

**ATTITUDES** Important factors regarding whether or not someone will have a tendency toward paraphilic behavior are related to the individual's cognitions and other internal dynamics (Brockman & Bluglass, 1996). As the reader may have noted in the previous descriptions of specific Paraphilic Disorders, factors such as self-esteem, the individual's views of self and others, perceptions of relational events and beliefs about those events, and his or her fantasy life are significant to the development of Paraphilic Disorders (Brockman & Bluglass, 1996).

**SPIRITUAL PERSPECTIVES** Unusual sexual preferences have been linked to spiritual ideas (Deida, 2005; Moore, 1980). Troisi (2008), who takes to an evolutionary perspective, and Deida (2005), who takes a spiritual perspective, seem to agree that unusual sexual preferences are quite common in men. Stated plainly by Deida (2005), "most men have some pretty strange sexual desires" (p. 177) that they "would be embarrassed to admit" (p. 178). In many cases, these desires are experienced solely as fantasies, and "are frequently reflections of . . . unmet spiritual needs" (Deida, 2005, p. 179). Specifically, sexual force fantasies (which occur in both masculine and feminine types) may represent a deep need to be in touch with one's inner sense of power and strength (Deida, 2005). Masochistic fantasies, which also occur irrespective of gender, may represent the need to be in touch with the wish to experience "surrender, devotion, and trust" (Deida, 2005, p. 180). Moore (1980) elaborates on this concept, suggesting that fantasies of being raped are "the sexual manifestation of the spiritual desire to surrender to the ravishing or rapturous experience of being penetrated by the 'divine masculine'" (p. 169).

### Lower-Left and Lower-Right Perspectives

Newer approaches to paraphilic phenomena emphasize the importance of relational factors—current and past relational experiences, and the individual's interpretation of these experiences—in the development of a Paraphilic Disorder (Fedoroff, 2010). Specifically, newer views regarding the etiology of the Paraphilic Disorders see them as "disorders in which consensual sexual interests have failed to develop" (Fedoroff, 2010, p. 404). Childhood events, such as whether or not one was abused, are very important, and memories can be a trigger (Brockman & Bluglass, 1996; Deida, 2005). The state of current relationships, such as whether conflict exists and whether there has been recent loss, rejection, or abandonment, is also highly relevant (Brockman & Bluglass, 1996). One's feelings for others—that is, whether there is resentment, an opportunistic sentiment, or the capacity for empathy—are significant as well. Impairment in social learning and the inability to accurately perceive social cues, which are often present in individuals with developmental disabilities, may be contributing factors in paraphilic behavior (Brockman & Bluglass, 1996).

Deficits in social skills and difficulty dealing with interpersonal conflict are highly significant in the etiology of Paraphilic Disorders (Troisi, 2008). Recognizing inadequate relationship skills as important in the manifestation of a Paraphilic Disorder is congruent with the currently preferred view that Paraphilic Disorders represent a blocked capacity to experience intimate, consensual sexual relations (Fedoroff, 2010). As explained by Troisi (2008),

> paraphiliacs with appropriate nonparaphiliac sexual arousal lack appropriate social skills. They may experience sexual arousal to possible appropriate partners, but may lack the social skills to initiate and maintain conversations, show interest and concern, and interact without anxiety. (p. 460)

It follows that many paraphiliacs will enact sexual behavior related to their unusual sexual interests because it is easier and less anxiety provoking than attempting to relate to a peer who is a potential relationship partner (Troisi, 2008).

An individual's culture and social environment have a significant bearing on how sexual preferences and behaviors become crystallized. For example, young men entering puberty are faced with the task of managing their increased sexual and aggressive urges in a socially acceptable manner (Hudson & Ward, 1997). If they live out these challenges in an invalidating environment where they are subjected to harmful behavior on the part of others, they are much less likely to learn the skills necessary to manage their urges effectively. Particularly salient environmental factors include family dynamics and a history of sexual abuse (Miranda & Davis, 2002), as well as an antisocial peer culture (Agee, 2002). Hence, a person with particular vulnerabilities located within a stressful environment is more likely to show problematic sexual behaviors (Hudson & Ward, 1997). Some important environmental contingencies are the culture of the neighborhood, including attitudes toward violence and the likelihood of violence being reported; attitudes toward women and aggression toward women; attitudes toward casual sex; prevalence of substance use; and the presence of a potential victim (Hudson & Ward, 1997). In turn, mass media exerts a significant influence on societal attitudes and modern-day culture (Cushman, 1990; Impett, Schooler, & Tolman, 2006; Moran, 2002; Russell, 2005).

## SUMMARY OF THE ETIOLOGY OF PARAPHILIC DISORDERS AND A CASE ILLUSTRATION

As the reader has likely surmised, the etiology of Paraphilic Disorders appears complex and multidimensional. Some of the factors influencing the development of a Paraphilic Disorder are displayed in Figure 10.2.

The case of Joe demonstrates both the complexities and the suffering involved in many of the Paraphilic Disorders. Joe is a 40-year-old, middle-class Caucasian male who, up until very recently, was employed as a dental hygienist at a pediatric dentist office. He lives alone with his pet golden retriever. Joe is referred for a mental health evaluation and risk assessment by the county probation office after being arrested about a month ago. Joe had been caught for the first time placing a video recorder in the bathroom of his very close friend, Mike. Joe had been a friend of Mike's family for over 20 years, since Mike and Joe attended high school together.

Joe is an only child, raised in an intact, blue-collar family. His father was employed by the mechanic shop down the street from his family home, and consistently portrayed a "tough-guy" image, both in the home and outside of it. His demeanor was distant and gruff, especially with his mother. Joe's mother was a full-time homemaker; she

| **UPPER-LEFT (UL): INTERIOR-INDIVIDUAL** | **UPPER-RIGHT (UR): EXTERIOR-INDIVIDUAL** |
|---|---|
| – Faulty cognitions/cognitive distortions<br>– Emotional conflict<br>– Anger<br>– Attitudes toward self (e.g., low self-esteem)<br>– Attitudes toward others (e.g., resentment; empathy/lack of empathy; opportunistic)<br>– Stress and tension<br>– Sexual frustration/problems with frustration tolerance<br>– Comorbid mental illness<br>– Motivation to do the sexual act vs. internal inhibitors<br>– Sexual fantasies | – Developmental disability<br>– Traumatic brain injury<br>– Brain tumors<br>– Temporal lobe epilepsy<br>– Klinefelter's syndrome/chromosomal abnormalities<br>– Endocrine abnormalities<br>– Patterns of aggressive behavior<br>– Substance abuse |
| **LOWER-LEFT (LL): INTERIOR-COLLECTIVE** | **LOWER-RIGHT (LR): EXTERIOR-COLLECTIVE** |
| – Relational loss (abandonment; rejection/perceived rejection)<br>– Conflict in relationships<br>– Deficits in social learning<br>– Misunderstanding of social cues<br>– Cultural factors (i.e., acceptance of behaviors is culture-specific) | – Social stimuli<br>– Childhood environment (e.g., history of sexual abuse as a child)<br>– Deficits in interpersonal skills<br>– Environmental factors that support or preclude acting on the sexual urge<br>– Availability of partner/victim<br>– Presence of fetish objects in the immediate environment<br>– Legal implications |

**FIGURE 10.2** A Quadratic Summary of the Etiology of Paraphilic Disorders

maintained a submissive stance with her dominant husband. Although she was caring and nurturing by nature, she was clearly unhappy in her marriage, and experienced some episodic depression. When Joe's mother was depressed Joe felt quite alone, and longed for more contact with his aloof and somewhat harsh father. He coped by withdrawing, engaging largely in imaginary play as a small child, and solitary activities such as reading, television, and video games as he matured. At school, he had few friends, and was called a "geek" by many of his peers.

When Joe and Mike first became acquainted in school, Joe was extremely grateful for the social acceptance, particularly because Mike was relatively popular at school and played on the football team. At the beginning of their friendship, there was typical camaraderie between them, mixed with some understandable admiration on Joe's part. As time went on, though, Joe started to develop romantic and erotic feelings for Mike. Joe's feelings for Mike, coupled with his sexual desire, became obsessive; Joe had little interest in establishing a conventional couple relationship with a person of either gender. Instead, he spent considerable time at Mike's home under the guise of a close friendship. Joe's feelings became even more intense when Mike was married and began having children. Mike was unaware of how Joe's feelings had evolved over time; Joe feigned friendly affection for Mike's family, and no one suspected the thoughts and feelings he was entertaining in his mind.

Eventually, Joe began to entertain sexual fantasies about Mike while he masturbated. His feelings and urges for sexual contact grew even stronger as they were fed by the fantasies, and he began to think about ways to actually see Mike naked. Joe knew there was no possibility that Mike would participate with him sexually, yet he desperately wanted a visual image to support his fantasies and masturbation. Subsequently, he purchased a small video recorder, and when he was over at Mike's house for dinner one night, he placed the camera behind the toilet, facing upward toward the front of the toilet. "I was sure this would give me a good look at Mike, but I didn't think it was a big deal," Joe reports.

The next time he was at Mike's house, he removed the camera. He was able to view the video and got a glimpse of some of Mike's body and genitalia, but it wasn't satisfying enough for him. He wanted to see more. Becoming brazen, he tried again. He placed the camera behind the toilet, a little more to the left this time, hoping it would give him a better shot. However, this time, Mike's wife found it immediately. She was horrified, and ran screaming to her husband, camera in hand. The police were called, and Joe was arrested.

Mike and his wife were concerned for their children. They misinterpreted the circumstances, believing that Joe was trying to capture pictures of their children. The arrest made it to the news, and Joe is now branded a pedophile. He was fired from his job because it involved contact with children, and is now isolating himself in his house due to fear of what others in the community may think. In the past month, he has left the house only once to attend court. Mike and his family have not spoken to him since he was arrested. With his life in ruins, Joe is now experiencing major depression with significant hopelessness and suicidal ideation.

Joe's situation reveals the far-reaching implications that the experience of a sexual disorder may have on a person's life, and his dire condition at the present time results from the interplay of factors situated in every quadrant of the Integral model. In the upper-left quadrant, the most apparent phenomenon is Joe's private experience of sexual thoughts and fantasies. In addition, there are the feelings and cognitions associated with his current depression. It is also likely, based on Joe's psychosocial history, that he has experienced at least intermittent anxiety and depression over the course of his life. In the upper-right quadrant, Joe's behavioral choice to act on his sexual urges and place the camera in the bathroom is most prominent. Joe also shows an avoidant personality style, which would involve the interplay between inner psychological defenses (UL), behavioral choices to withdraw from social contact (UR), and social reinforcement for his behavioral choices (LR). From the perspective of the lower-left quadrant, Joe's experiences in his family of origin, the meaning he placed on those experiences, and how he felt about them are also implicated. Specifically, Joe was deprived of consistent emotional contact with his parents, especially his father, and longed for positive male attention. Being the only child in a family devoid of meaningful interaction and closeness, Joe failed to develop a full spectrum of social skills, which led to further difficulties with peers and a concomitant reluctance to engage in a conventional romantic partnership. Lower-right quadrant factors include the legal system and the sociocultural responses to Joe's voyeuristic behavior. Finally, the meaning (LL) of Joe's voyeuristic act was misunderstood and mistakenly linked with pedophilia, evoking panic, stigmatism, and ostracism on the part of those in Joe's community.

## TREATMENT OF PARAPHILIC DISORDERS

The goal of treatment for an individual experiencing a Paraphilic Disorder is achieving a satisfying yet lawful sex life as an important component of a balanced and meaningful life (Fedoroff, 2010). An important distinguishing feature in the treatment of Paraphilic Disorders—as opposed to the sexual dysfunctions—is that in many cases, others are placed at risk by the paraphilic behavior. In such cases, stopping the behavior will be an important treatment goal (Berlin et al., 1995). In fact, individuals often arrive for treatment only after having incurred a legal charge for acting out their paraphilia (Mezzich & Hernandez-Serrano, 2006).

Given that large numbers of clients in treatment for a Paraphilic Disorder are mandated to undergo such treatment, it is important to ascertain the client's motivation for receiving services, as well as to avoid getting embroiled in conflicts of interest with third-party payers. Fedoroff (2010) emphasizes the need to balance obtaining as much information as possible while, at the same time, not interrogating the client and coming off as a "police detective" (p. 410). Ethical dilemmas around matters such as the client's right to self-determination and confidentiality are particularly salient. Problems can be avoided by making sure the client knows the limits of confidentiality and when others will receive reports regarding his treatment. It is especially important to report any possible child abuse, and not to give permission for the client to continue engaging in illegal activity. Fedoroff (2010) admonishes therapists to not accept clients' excuses that they "can't help it" or that they are "out of control"; firmly tell clients that they must cease any illegal acts. In other cases, individuals come for treatment to alleviate their distress or the distress of their partners (Mezzich & Hernandez-Serrano, 2006). Although there was a time when it was believed that Paraphilic Disorders could not be treated effectively, the prognosis is now significantly better, and it is important not to dash the hope of a new client by telling him that his sexual disorder is incurable (Fedoroff, 2010).

As we discussed in the previous section on sexual dysfunctions, all clients are unique, and there are multiple factors that may be involved in each individual's sexual problem. The principles previously discussed in this chapter regarding the importance of a comprehensive assessment hold true in the case of Paraphilic Disorders as well. A thorough medical examination is warranted for a client receiving treatment for a paraphilia; in some cases a medical problem, such as a neurological condition or endocrine disorder, may be contributing (Fedoroff, 2010).

Fedoroff (2010) provides a summary of effective treatment for individuals seeking help for a Paraphilic Disorder. First, a thorough clinical assessment must be conducted, and differential diagnoses are very important to rule out, just as comorbid conditions are critical to identify. Then, review your assessment and treatment options with the client; ideally, both therapist and client agree on these. Try to tailor the treatment plan according to the individual, and avoid being punitive.

## Upper-Right Quadrant Treatments

**PHARMACOLOGICAL AGENTS** Medications may be of help to individuals with a Paraphilic Disorder (Fedoroff, 2010; Nelson, Soutullo, DelBello, & McElroy, 2002). Pharmacological agents are likely to be helpful when the paraphilic behavior is related to the person's emotional state, as is the case with depression and anxiety, when obsessive-compulsive difficulties are a factor, or when a medical condition is a component of the problem (Berlin et al., 1995). Some medication regimens used in the treatment of Paraphilic Disorders may be quite complex (Schwartz, 2002). Categories of medications that may be of use include antidepressants, anxiolytics, mood stabilizers, anticonvulsants, antipsychotics, and antiobsessional medications (Berlin et al., 1995; Nelson et al., 2002). Recently, SSRIs and Buspirone have shown some success in the treatment of Paraphilic Disorders (Fedoroff, 2010; Nelson et al., 2002).

The use of antiandrogen medications, also called "chemical castration," has been applied to the treatment of Paraphilic Disorders (Nelson et al., 2002), or when the diminishment of all sexual urges is deemed to be of clinical utility (Fedoroff, 2010). Antiandrogens block the effect of natural androgens in the body, such as testosterone, and "are alternatives to surgical castration for reducing sexual drive and sexual deviant behaviors" (Nelson et al., 2002, pp. 13–6).[36] Whether or not the use of antiandrogens is helpful may be questionable because having a lower testosterone level does not necessarily equate with diminished intensity of fantasy or sexual arousal (Mezzich & Hernandez-Serrano, 2006). In addition, antiandrogens have not been shown to change the nature of an individual's sexual preferences (Nelson et al., 2002).

**BEHAVIORAL TECHNIQUES** Behavioral approaches to therapy are important in the treatment of Paraphilic Disorders. The goal of behavioral techniques is the "extinction of paraphilic arousal (both urges and fantasies)" (Berlin et al., 1995, p. 1947). Some behavioral treatments are aversive, such as electric shock therapy and olfactory aversion: having the client smell something noxious, such as ammonia

---

[36] This is how the book is numbered—"13" stands for the chapter; "6" stands for the page number within the chapter.

(Berlin et al., 1995). Nonaversive strategies include covert and assisted covert sensitization, which "are used to lessen deviant arousal by pairing it with negative associations while positively reinforcing appropriate arousal" (Schwartz, 2002, pp. 1–21)[37] and masturbatory satiation, which "involves having a patient repeat his paraphilic fantasies over and over again for a sustained period of time (often for 1 hour) into a tape recorder, beginning immediately after masturbation to orgasm" (Berlin et al., 1995, p. 1951).

**COGNITIVE-BEHAVIOR THERAPY** As is the case with the sexual dysfunctions, cognitive-behavioral therapy is useful in the treatment of Paraphilic Disorders. As stated by Schwartz (2002), "the function of cognitive-behavioral treatment is to address the thought patterns that reinforce maladaptive behavior" (pp. 1–21). Specifically, cognitive-behavior therapy with clients experiencing a Paraphilic Disorder will focus on cognitive restructuring, problem solving, and addressing problematic thought patterns. Common cognitive distortions to address in individuals with a Paraphilic Disorder are rationalization, minimization, and denial. One useful cognitive-behavioral technique, thought-blocking, consists of having the client immediately replace his paraphilic fantasies with nonparaphilic fantasies (Berlin et al., 1995).

## Upper-Left and Lower-Left Quadrant Treatments

**PSYCHOTHERAPY** Psychotherapy may be helpful to an individual with a Paraphilic Disorder when it helps the client understand how his behavior detrimentally affects others, when it facilitates insight into the underlying emotional disturbances that motivate the paraphilic behavior, and when it increases the client's self-esteem (Mezzich & Hernandez-Serrano, 2006). From a psychodynamic perspective, Paraphilic Disorders are considered representative of developmental arrest, with the individual fixated at an early stage of psychosexual development (Berlin et al., 1995). It is important to note that while a psychodynamic approach may be of some use, the value of insight as a corrective mechanism for a Paraphilic Disorder is questionable, and psychodynamic approaches are no longer the treatment of choice (Berlin et al., 1995).

Schwartz (2002) points out that some individuals who experience paraphilic urges—particularly sex offenders—are often disconnected from their feelings, and a lack of empathy is of particular concern. Hence, treatment approaches that assist clients to reconnect with their feelings and develop empathy are recommended. Possible experiential therapies that may be useful include music, drama, and art therapy. Similarly, individuals with unusual sexual preferences frequently struggle with emotional dysregulation and concomitant impulsivity. Helping clients to manage anger and control their emotions are important components of individual therapy. In cases in which substances are used to regulate emotions, it is necessary to address and resolve issues with substance abuse or dependency. In general, mental illness and mental health problems must be treated when they co-occur with paraphilic behavior (Schwartz, 2002).

---

[37] This is how the book is numbered—"1" stands for the chapter, "21" for the page number within the chapter.

### Lower-Right Quadrant Treatments

**GROUP PSYCHOTHERAPY** Effective treatment for individuals experiencing a Paraphilic Disorder often includes couple, family, and/or group psychotherapy (Mezzich & Hernandez-Serrano, 2006). Having supportive people involved in the client's care is helpful, and being in a group with others who have similar difficulties can help reduce the shame that is often associated with paraphilic urges and behavior. Fedoroff (2010) described three different types of paraphilic treatment groups that are being used at the renowned Sexual Behaviors Clinic of the Royal Ottawa Health Care Group, of which he is the director. The first group is targeted for individuals with major mental illness such as Schizophrenia, and is largely a life skills group, helping clients with issues such as positive recreation and occupational pursuits. The second, "a sex education and social skills group" (Fedoroff, 2010, p. 417), is open to all clients, and is designed to foster positive relationships. The third group is specifically for individuals who have a sexual interest in children. In addition to group therapy, it is helpful for individuals managing paraphilic behavior to have a solid network of social supports and to help these individuals relate to others in satisfactory ways (Berlin et al., 1995; Schwartz, 2002).

**MILIEU TREATMENT** Some individuals with a Paraphilic Disorder engage in behaviors that are harmful to others, and thus the legal system will become involved (Steen, 2001). When this occurs, they are apt to be incarcerated, or placed in a residential program. Supervision—to prevent the possibility that additional harm will occur—is an important component of such programs (Schwartz, 2002).[38]

## GENDER DYSPHORIA

Gender Dysphoria, termed Gender Identity Disorder in the DSM-IV-TR (APA, 2000), refers to a subjective experience (UL quadrant) of severe discontent with one's biological sex, as well as the typical expectations for behavior and traditional gender roles that go along with it (Cohen-Kettenis & Pfäfflin, 2010). In other words, the person feels "trapped in a body of the 'wrong' sex" (Crooks & Baur, 2011, p. 128), to the point where it causes extreme distress. Gender Dysphoria first manifests in children from the ages of 2 to 4 as a strong interest in activities usually associated with the other gender, and a concomitant wish to look like members of that gender (APA, 2000, 2010, 2013; Morrison, 2006; Zucker, 2010). Additional indicators of Gender Dysphoria in children include: wanting to cross-dress or wear clothing styles of the other gender; strongly preferring playmates of the other gender, and adopting their style of play (playing the other gender in fantasy games, choosing toys and activities typically chosen by individuals of the other gender, identifying with hero figures of the other gender); and wanting different sexual anatomy (disliking one's own sexual anatomy and wishing for the sex characteristics of the other gender; APA, 2010, 2013; Zucker, 2010).

For adults with Gender Dysphoria, there is great discomfort with one's biological sex and an unrelenting preoccupation with the desire to be the other gender including

[38] The reader is referred to the volume edited by Schwartz (2002) entitled *The Sexual Offender: Current Treatment Modalities and Systems Issues* for comprehensive guidance pertaining to the treatment of sexual offenders.

rejection of one's sex characteristics and wishing for the sex characteristics of the other gender, wanting to be treated as someone of the other gender, and believing that one feels and reacts the way those of the other gender do (APA, 2010, 2013; Cohen-Kettenis & Pfäfflin, 2010). The wish to be someone of the other gender is often manifested by living out societal roles geared more toward the gender of choice (APA, 2000, 2013; Crooks & Baur, 2011). For adolescents, diagnostic criteria for both children and adults will be applied, based on the youth's level of development. In order to diagnose Gender Dysphoria, the indicators must be present for 6 months or more, and there must be a clinically significant level of distress and/or impairment in functioning (APA, 2013).

Diagnosable Gender Dysphoria is extremely rare in adults; only 1 out of every 100,000 females and 3 out of every 100,000 males will grow up to be diagnosed with the disorder (Morrison, 2006). The majority of individuals who present with Gender Dysphoria in childhood will be homosexual as adults. A few will grow up to be heterosexual, and approximately 16% will be transsexuals as adults and may continue to have diagnosable Gender Dysphoria (Hewitt et al., 2012).

Despite the inclusion of Gender Dysphoria in the DSM, there has been much controversy as to whether Gender Dysphoria is truly a mental disorder (Crooks & Baur, 2011; Wyndzen, 2008). People who identify with the other gender may not experience themselves as disordered, and ". . . not all gender variance requires clinical attention . . ." (Cohen-Kettenis & Pfäfflin, 2010, p. 505). Not every transsexual person regards their own proclivities for the other gender as disordered, and we may question what constitutes so-called normal gender-specific thoughts, feelings, and behaviors. Many labels and stereotypes are socially constructed, and lead to assumptions regarding how people are likely to behave based on gender (Wyndzen, 2008). Unfortunately, these labels may "limit the range of behaviors that people are comfortable expressing" (Crooks & Baur, 2011, p. 112), and in the worst case, lead to the pathologizing of those who behave in a manner other than what would be expected based on gender.

The distress experienced by some individuals with gender identity conflict can be severe; anxiety, depression, suicidal ideation/attempts and substance abuse are all commonly associated with Gender Dysphoria (APA, 2010). As if this were not bad enough, the emotional pain of individuals experiencing Gender Dysphoria is often exacerbated by others' responses to them (LL/LR quadrants). Specifically, social isolation is common in individuals experiencing Gender Dysphoria, which is likely due to an inner sense of not fitting in, as well as actually being stigmatized and ostracized for the ways in which they are different (APA, 2000, 2013). Social isolation, in turn, can lead to other unhealthy thinking patterns and behaviors and the mental health concerns mentioned previously.

Although theories of the etiology of transsexualism abound, no conclusive evidence clearly supports one theory over another (Crooks & Baur, 2011). Viewing the phenomenon of transsexualism from an Integral lens, it is likely that the etiology is multidimensional, and varies for each individual. Psychodynamic theories (UL/LL quadrants) pertain to issues of attachment within the family of origin. For example, it is postulated that male-to-female transsexual individuals experienced "excessive mother-son symbiosis in the early years" (Green, 2005, p. 1983), with concomitant difficulty separating and individuating from the mother over time. Biological (UR quadrant) explanations include genetic and hormonal influences (Crooks & Baur, 2011; Green, 2005). A social-learning view (LR quadrant) suggests that behaviors are reinforced in transsexual children that would generally be identified with the other sex (Crooks & Baur, 2011).

The primary treatment goal for Gender Dysphoria is to bring the biological (physical) body into harmony with the client's inner identity (Wyndzen, 2008)[39]. Secondary goals are to provide support, psychoeducation, and treatment for any emotional distress the client is experiencing and to help reduce the psychological conflict the client is experiencing pertaining to gender identity issues. Family therapy may also be indicated to assist with issues that arise involving the client's partner, family of origin, or children (Green, 2005). In many cases, the client will benefit from physical treatments to change the body in order to be more congruent with the individual's gender identity. These changes may be relatively superficial, such as binding one's breasts closer to the chest wall or removing facial hair; or they may be more substantial, such as through the use of hormone therapy or sex-reassignment surgery (Crooks & Baur, 2011; Green, 2005). An important role of counseling is to assist transsexual clients in determining what treatment options will best meet their needs (Crooks & Baur, 2011).

## Summary

This chapter has been written with the intent of providing comprehensive information pertaining to the etiology and treatment of sexual disorders—Sexual Dysfunction Disorders, Paraphilic Disorders, and Gender Dysphoria—within the context of an Integral framework. In closing, we would like to emphasize the importance of viewing each individual, couple, or client system as unique in terms of how the sexual disorder is being experienced and manifested. We are firmly convinced that, given the vast differences across disorders and individuals/couples, Integral theory will be useful in integrating pertinent material in a manner that is useful for each client that presents for treatment, providing a unifying theoretical framework that will help the reader develop clinically effective case conceptualizations and treatment interventions for those who present for treatment due to a sexual disorder.

## Review Questions

1. Describe the human sexual response cycle, including Kaplan's (1979) changes.
2. Explain why—from an evolutionary perspective—sexual dysfunctions are more common in women whereas paraphilias are far more common among men.
3. Describe how an individual's attitudes toward sex (including the influence on those attitudes from society and religion) may contribute to various sexual dysfunctions.
4. Discuss how relational problems and sexual dysfunctions are often interrelated.
5. Describe the PLISSIT model of sex therapy.
6. What is your reaction to the DSM-5 classifying as pathological a paraphilia such as fetishism, in which no one is harmed by the person's need for various objects (whether lingerie or sex toys) to become sexually aroused?

---

[39] Transsexualism differs from homosexuality in that although transsexual individuals generally want to have sexual relations with an individual of their biological sex, they typically want to do so from the perspective of the other gender. Hence, they imagine themselves as someone of the opposite gender having a heterosexual experience.

## References


Adshead, G. (1997). Transvestic fetishism: Assessment and treatment. In D. R. Laws & W. O'Donohue (Eds.), *Sexual deviance: Theory, assessment, and treatment* (pp. 280–296). New York: The Guilford Press.

Agee, V. M. (2002). Creating a positive milieu in residential treatment for adolescent sexual abusers. In B. K. Schwartz (Ed.), *The sex offender: Current treatment modalities and systems issues* (Vol. IV, pp. 23-1–23-20). Kingston, NJ: Civic Research Institute.

Althof, S. E., Dean, J., Derogatis, L. R., Rosen, R. C., & Sisson, M. (2005). Current perspectives on the clinical assessment and diagnosis of female sexual dysfunction and clinical studies of potential therapies: A statement of concern. *Journal of Sexual Medicine, 2*(Suppl. 3), 146–153.

American Psychiatric Association. (2000). *Diagnostic and statistical manual of mental disorders* (4th ed., text revision). Washington, DC: Author.

American Psychiatric Association. (2007). *APA dictionary of psychology*. Washington, DC: Author.

American Psychiatric Association. (2010). DSM-5 development. Retrieved http://www.dsm5.org/Pages/Default.aspx

American Psychiatric Association. (2013). *Diagnostic and statistical manual of mental disorders* (5th ed.). Washington, DC: Author.

Annon, J. S. (1976). *Behavioral treatment of sexual problems*. New York: Harper & Row.

Araujo, A. V. (2008). An integral solution to healing sexual abuse trauma. *Journal of Integral Theory and Practice, 3*(4), 125–153.

Association of Reproductive Health Professionals. (2008). What you need to know: female sexual response. Retrieved from http://www.arhp.org/factsheets

Balon, R., Segraves, R. T., & Clayton, A. (2001). Issues for DSM-5: Sexual dysfunction, disorder, or variation along normal distribution: Toward rethinking DSM criteria of sexual dysfunctions. *American Journal of Psychiatry, 164*(2), 198–200.

Balon, R., & Wise, T. N. (2011). Update on diagnoses of sexual dysfunctions: Controversies surrounding the proposed revisions of existing diagnostic entities and proposed new diagnoses. *Advances in Psychosomatic Medicine 31*, 1–15.

Bancroft, J. (2002). The medicalization of female sexual dysfunction: The need for caution. *Archives of Sexual Behavior, 31*(5), 451–455.

Barratt, B. B., & Rand, M. A. (2007). On the relevance of tantric practices for clinical and educational sexology. *Contemporary Sexuality, 41*(2), 7–12.

Basson, R. (2000). The female sexual response: A different model. *Journal of Sex & Marital Therapy, 26*, 51–65.

Basson, R. (2001a). Female sexual response: The role of drugs in the management of sexual dysfunction. *Obstetrics & Gynecology. 98*(2), 350–353.

Basson, R. (2001b). Human sex-response cycles. *Journal of Sex & Marital Therapy, 37*, 33–43.

Basson, R. (2005). Women's sexual dysfunction: revised and expanded definitions. *Canadian Medical Association Journal, 172*(10), 1327–1333.

Basson, R. (2008). Women's sexual function and dysfunction: current uncertainties, future directions. *International Journal of Impotence Research, 20*, 466–478.

Basson, R., Leiblum, S., Brotto, L., Derogatis, L., Fourcroy, J., Fugl-Meyer, K. et al. (2004). Revised definitions of women's sexual dysfunction. *Journal of Sexual Medicine, 1*(1), 40–48.

Baumeister, R. F., & Butler, J. L. (1997). Sexual masochism: Deviance without pathology. In D. R. Laws & W. O'Donohue (Eds.), *Sexual deviance: Theory, assessment and treatment* (pp. 225–239). New York: The Guilford Press.

Bentler, P. M., & Abramson, P. R. (1980). Methodological issues in sex research: An overview. In R. Green & J. Wiener (Eds.), *Methodology in sex research: Proceedings of the conference held in Chevy Chase, Maryland November 18 & 19, 1977* (pp. 308–332). Rockville, MD: National Institute of Mental Health.

Bergeron, S., Meana, M., Binik, Y., & Khalife, S. (2010). Painful sex. In S. B. Levine, C. B. Risen, & S. E. Althof (Eds.), *Handbook of clinical sexuality for mental health professionals* (2nd ed., pp. 193–214). New York: Routledge.

Berlin, F. S., Malin, H. M., & Thomas, K. (1995). Nonpedophiliac and nontransvestic paraphilias. In G. O. Gabbard (Ed.), *Treatment of psychiatric disorders* (2nd ed., pp. 1941–1958). Washington, DC: American Psychiatric Press.

Blanchard, R. (2010). The DSM diagnostic criteria for Transvestic Fetishism. *Archives of Sexual Behavior, 39*, 363–372.

Brisben, P. (2008). *Pure romance between the sheets: Find your best sexual self and enhance your intimate relationship.* New York: Atria Books.

Brockman, B., & Bluglass, R. (1996). A general psychiatric approach to sexual deviation. In I. Rosen (Ed.), *Sexual deviation* (3rd ed., pp. 1–42). New York: Oxford University Press.

Brotto, L. A., Graham, C. A., Binik, Y. M., Segraves, R. T., & Zucker, K. J. (2011). Should sexual desire and arousal disorders in women be merged? A response to DeRogatis, Clayton, Rosen, Sand, and Pyke (2010). *Archives of Sexual Behavior 40*, 221–225.

Brotto, L. A., Seal, B. N., & Rellini, A. (2012). Pilot study of a brief cognitive behavioral versus mindfulness-based intervention for women with sexual distress and a history of childhood sexual abuse. *Journal of Sex and Marital Therapy, 38*, 1–27.

Butcher, J. (1999). Female sexual problems II: Sexual pain and sexual fears. *British Medical Journal, 318*, 110–112.

Carlson, B., & Wheeler, K. A. (1980). Group counseling for pre-orgasmic women. *Topics in Clinical Nursing, 1*(4), 9–19.

Chao, J.-K., Lin, Y.-C., Ma, M.-C., Lai, C.-J, Ku, Y.-C., Kuo, W.-H., et al. (2011). Relationship among sexual desire, sexual satisfaction, and quality of life in middle-aged and older adults. *Journal of Sex and Marital Therapy, 37*, 386–403.

Chia, M., & Abrams, D. (1997). The multi-orgasmic man: Sexual secrets every man should know. New York, NY: Harper Collins Publishers.

Clipson, C. R. (2004). Practical considerations in the interview and evaluation of sexual offenders. *Journal of Child Sexual Abuse, 12*(3/4), 257–278.

Cohen-Kettenis, P. T., & Pfäfflin, F. (2010). The DSM diagnostic criteria for Gender Identity Disorder in adolescents and adults. *Archives of Sexual Behavior, 39*, 499–513.

Copelan, R. (1995). *100 ways to make sex sensational and 100% safe.* Hollywood, FL: Lifetime Books.

Crooks, R., & Baur, K. (2005). *Our sexuality* (9th ed.). Belmont, CA: Wadsworth.

Crooks, R., & Baur, K. (2008). *Our sexuality* (10th ed.). Belmont, CA: Wadsworth.

Crooks, R., & Baur, K. (2011). *Our sexuality* (11th ed.). Belmont, CA: Wadsworth.

Cushman, P. (1990). Why the self is empty. *American Psychologist, 45*, 599–611.

Dallos, R., Wright, J., Stedman, J., & Johnstone, L. (2006). Integrative formulation. In L. Johnstone & R. Dallos (Eds.), *Formulation in psychology and psychotherapy: Making sense of people's problems.* New York: Routledge.

Deida, D. (1995). *Intimate communion: Awakening your sexual essence.* Deerfield Beach, FL: Health Communications, Inc.

Deida, D. (2005). *Finding god through sex: Awakening the one of spirit through the two of flesh.* Boulder, CO: Sounds True.

DeLamater, J. D., & Sill, M. (2005). Sexual desire in later life. *The Journal of Sex Research, 42*(2), 138–149.

DeRogatis, L. R., Clayton, A. H., Rosen, R. C., Sand, M., & Pyke, R. E. (2011). Should sexual desire and arousal disorders in women be merged? *Archives of Sexual Behavior, 40*(2), 217–219.

Donahey, K. M. (2010). Female orgasmic disorder. In S. B. Levine, C. B. Risen, & S. E. Althof (Eds.), *Handbook of clinical sexuality for mental health professionals* (2nd ed., pp. 181–192). New York: Routledge.

Edwards, J. N., & Booth, A. (1994). Sexuality, marriage, and well-being: The middle years. In A. Rossi (Ed.), *Sexuality across the life course* (pp. 233–260). Chicago: The University of Chicago Press.

Eugene, T. M. (1994). While love is unfashionable: Ethical implications of black spirituality and sexuality. In J. B. Nelson & S. P. Longfellow (Eds.), *Sexuality and the sacred: Sources for theological reflection* (pp. 105–112). Louisville, KY: Westminster/John Knox Press.

Fagan, P. J. (2004). *Sexual disorders: Perspectives on diagnosis and treatment.* Baltimore, MD: Johns Hopkins University Press.

Fall, K. A., Holden, J. M., & Marquis, A. (2004). *Theoretical models of counseling and psychotherapy.* New York: Brunner-Routledge.

Fedoroff, J. P. (2010). Paraphilic worlds. *Handbook of clinical sexuality for mental health professionals* (2nd ed., pp. 401–424). New York: Routledge.

Fedoroff, J. P., & Richards, D. A. (2010). Sexual disorders and intellectual disabilities. *Handbook of clinical sexuality for mental health professionals* (2nd ed., pp. 461–468). New York: Routledge.

Ferreira, L. C., Narciso, I., & Novo, R. F. (2012). Intimacy, sexual desire and differentiation in couplehood: A theoretical and methodological review. *Journal of Sex & Marital Therapy, 38*(3), 263–280.

Freund, S., & Seto, M. C. (1998). Preferential rape in the theory of courtship disorder. *Archives of Sexual Behavior, 27*(5), 433–443.

Freund, S., Seto., M. C., & Kuban, M. (1997). Frotteurism and the theory of courtship disorder. In D. R. Laws & W. O'Donohue (Eds.), *Sexual deviance: Theory, assessment and treatment* (pp. 111–139). New York: The Guilford Press.

Frosch, W. A. (1978, June). Psychogenic causes of impotence. *Medical Aspects of Human Sexuality,* 57–58.

Geffner, R., Franey, K. C., & Falconer, R. (2003). Adult sexual offenders: Current issues and future directions. In R. Geffner, K. C. Franey, T. G. Arnold, & R. Falconer (Eds.), *Identifying and treating sex offenders: Current approaches, research, and techniques* (pp. 1–16). New York: The Haworth Press, Inc.

Giargiari, T. D., Mahaffey, A. L., Craighead, W. E., & Hutchison, K. E. (2005). Appetitive responses to sexual stimuli are attenuated in individuals with low levels of sexual desire. *Archives of Sexual Behavior, 34*(5), 547–556.

Glasser, M. (1996). Aggression and sadism in the perversions. In I. Rosen (Ed.), *Sexual deviation* (3rd ed., pp. 279–299). New York: Oxford University Press.

Granot, M., Zisman-Ilani, Y., Ram, E., Goldstick, O., & Yovell, Y. (2011). Characteristics of attachment style in women with Dyspareunia. *Journal of Sex & Marital Therapy, 37,* 1–16.

Green, R. (1994). Sexual problems and therapies: A quarter century of developments and changes. In A. Rossi (Ed.), *Sexuality across the life course* (pp. 341–362). Chicago: The University of Chicago Press.

Green, R. (2005). Gender identity disorders. In B. J. Sadock & V. A. Sadock (Eds.), *Kaplan and Sadock's comprehensive textbook of psychiatry: Volume I* (8th ed., pp. 1979–1991. New York: Lippincott Williams & Wilkins.

Grillon, D. (2005). Anxiety disorders: Psychophysiological aspects. In B. J. Sadock & V. A. Sadock (Eds.), *Kaplan & Sadock's comprehensive textbook of psychiatry Vol. I,* (8th ed., pp. 1728–1739). New York: Lippincott Williams & Wilkins.

Groth, A. N., & Birnbaum, H. J. (1978). Adult sexual orientation and attraction to underage persons. *Archives of Sexual Behavior 7*(3), 175–181.

Haber, A., & Runyon, R. P. (1984). *Psychology of adjustment.* Homewood, IL: The Dorsey Press.

Heiman, J. (2002). Psychologic treatments for female sexual dysfunction: Are they effective and do we need them? *Archives of Sexual Behavior, 31*(5), 445–450.

Heiman, J. R., & Meston, C. M. (1998). Empirically validated treatments for sexual dysfunction. In K. S. Dobson & K. D. Craig (Eds.), *Empirically supported therapies: Best practices in professional psychology* (pp. 259–303). New York: Sage Publications.

Hertlein, K. M., Weeks, G. R., & Sendak, S. K. (2009). *A clinician's guide to systemic sex therapy.* New York: Routledge.

Hewitt, J. K., Paul, C., Kasiannan, P., Grover, S. R., Newman, L. K., & Warne, G. L. (2012). Hormone treatment of Gender Identity Disorder in a cohort of children and adolescents. *The Medical Journal of Australia, 196*(9), 578–581. Retrieved from https://www.mja.com.au/journal/2012/196/9/hormone-treatment-gender-identity-disorder-cohort-children-and-adolescents/

Hinderliter, A. C. (2010). Defining paraphilia: Excluding exclusion. *Open Access Journal of Forensic Psychology, 2,* 241–272. Retrieved from http://www.forensicpsychologyunbound.ws/

Hollin, C. R. (1997). Sexual sadism: Assessment and treatment. In D. R. Laws & W. O'Donohue (Eds.), *Sexual deviance: Theory, assessment, and treatment* (pp. 210–224). New York: The Guilford Press.

Hooper, A. (2007). *Kama Sutra for 21st-century lovers.* New York: DK Publishing, Inc.

Hucker, S. J. (1997). Sexual sadism: Psychopathology and theory. In D. R. Laws & W. O'Donohue (Eds.), *Sexual deviance: Theory, assessment, and treatment* (pp. 194–209). New York: The Guilford Press.

Hudson, S. M., & Ward, T. (1997). Future directions. In D. R. Laws & W. O'Donohue (Eds.), *Sexual deviance: Theory, assessment, and treatment* (pp. 481–500).

Impett, E. A., Schooler, D., & Tolman, D. L. (2006). To be seen and not heard: femininity ideology and adolescent girls' sexual health. *Archives of Sexual Behavior, 35*(2), 131–144.

Irvine, J. M. (1990). *Disorders of desire: Sex and gender in modern American sexology*. Philadelphia: Temple University Press.

Ito, T., Kawahara, K., Das, A., & Strudwick, W. (1998). The effects of ArginMax, a natural dietary supplement for enhancement of male sexual function. *Hawaiian Medical Journal, 57*, 741–744.

Junginger, J. (1997). Fetishism: Assessment and treatment. In D. R. Laws & W. O'Donohue (Eds.), *Sexual deviance: Theory, assessment and treatment* (pp. 92–110). New York: The Guilford Press.

Kafka, M. P. (2010). The DSM diagnostic criteria for Fetishism. *Archives of Sexual Behavior, 39*, 357–361.

Kaplan, H. S. (1974). *The new sex therapy: Active treatment of sexual dysfunctions*. New York: Brunner/Mazel.

Kaplan, H. S. (1979). *Disorders of sexual desire*. New York: Brunner/Mazel.

Kaplan, M. S., & Krueger, R. B. (1997). Voyeurism: Psychopathology and theory. In D. R. Laws & W. O'Donohue (Eds.), *Sexual deviance: Theory, assessment and treatment* (pp. 297–310). New York: The Guilford Press.

Kedde, H., Van De Wiel, H. B. M., Weijmar Schultz, W. C. M., Vanwesenbeek, W. M. A., & Bender, J. L. (2010). Efficacy of sexological healthcare for people with chronic diseases and physical disabilities. *Journal of Sex and Marital Therapy, 36*(3), 282–294.

Kingsberg, S., & Althof, S. E. (2009). Evaluation and treatment of female sexual disorders. *International Urogynecology Journal and Pelvic Floor Dysfunction, 20*(Supp. 1), S33–S43.

Kinsey, A. C., Pomeroy, W. B., & Martin, C. E. (1948). *Sexual behavior in the human male*. Indianapolis, IN: Indiana University Press.

Kinsey, A. C., Pomeroy, W. B., Martin, C. E., Gebhard, P. H. (1953). *Sexual behavior in the human female*. Philadelphia: W.B. Saunders Company.

Kontula, O., & Haavio-Mannila, E. (2009). The impact of aging on human sexual activity and sexual desire. *Journal of Sex Research, 46*(1), 46–56.

Krueger, R. B. (2010a). The DSM diagnostic criteria for sexual masochism. *Archives of Sexual Behavior, 39*, 346–356.

Krueger, R. B. (2010b). The DSM diagnostic criteria for sexual sadism. *Archives of Sexual Behavior, 39*, 325–345.

Långström, N. (2010). The DSM diagnostic criteria for exhibitionism, voyeurism, and frotteurism. *Archives of Sexual Behavior, 39*, 317–324.

Laumann, E. O., Paik, A., & Rosen, R. C. (1999). Sexual dysfunction in the United States: Prevalence and predictors. *Journal of the American Medical Association, 281*(6), 537–544.

Laws, D. R., & O'Donohue, W. (1997). Fundamental issues in sexual deviance. In D. R. Laws & W. O'Donohue (Eds.), *Sexual deviance: Theory, assessment and treatment* (pp. 1–21). New York: The Guilford Press.

Leguizamo, A. (2002). The object relations and victimization histories of juvenile sex offenders. In B. K. Schwartz (Ed.), *The sex offender: Current treatment modalities and systems issues* (Vol. IV, pp. 4-2–4-39). Kingston, NJ: Civic Research Institute.

Levine, S. (1992). *Sexual life: A clinician's guide*. New York: Plenum Press.

Levine, S. B. (2010). Infidelity. In S. B. Levine, C. B. Risen, & S. E. Althof (Eds.), *Handbook of clinical sexuality for mental health professionals* (2nd ed., pp. 87–102). New York: Routledge.

Lewis, J. H., Rosen, R., & Goldstein, I. (2005). Patient education series. Erectile dysfunction. *Nursing 35*(2), 64.

Linehan, M. M. (1993). *Cognitive-behavioral treatment of borderline personality disorder*. New York: The Guilford Press.

Longo, R. E. (2002). A holistic/integrated approach to treating sexual offenders. In B. K. Schwartz (Ed.), *The sex offender: Current treatment modalities and systems issues* (Vol. IV, pp. 3-1–3-19). Kingston, NJ: Civic Research Institute.

Lourenço, M., Azevedo, L. P., & Gouveia, J. L. (2011). Depression and sexual desire: An exploratory study in psychiatric patients. *Journal of Sex and Marital Therapy, 37*, 32–44.

Mahan, V. (2003). Assessing and treating sexual dysfunction. *Journal of the American Psychiatric Nurses Association, 9*(3), 90–95.

Marquis, A. (2008). *The Integral intake: A guide to comprehensive idiographic assessment in Integral psychotherapy*. New York: Routledge.

Marshall, L. E., & Marshall, W. L. (2002). The role of attachment in sexual offending—An examination of preoccupied-attachment-style offending behavior. In B. K. Schwartz (Ed.), *The sex offender: Current treatment modalities and systems issues* (Vol. IV, pp. 3-1–3-8). Kingston, NJ: Civic Research Institute.

Mason, F. L. (1997). Fetishism: Psychopathology and theory. In D. R. Laws & W. O'Donohue (Eds.), *Sexual deviance: Theory, assessment and treatment* (pp. 75–91). New York: The Guilford Press.

Masters, W. H., & Johnson, V. E. (1966). *Human sexual response.* Boston: Little, Brown and Company.

Masters, W. H., & Johnson, V. E. (1970). *Human sexual inadequacy.* Boston: Little, Brown and Company.

Maurice, W. L., & Yule, M. (2010). Sex and chronic and severe mental illness. In S. B. Levine, C. B. Risen, & S. E. Althof (Eds.), *Handbook of clinical sexuality for mental health professionals* (2nd ed., pp. 469–482). New York: Routledge.

McHugh, P. R., & Slavney P. R. (1998). *The perspectives in psychiatry* (2nd ed.). Baltimore: Johns Hopkins University Press.

Meana, M. (2010). When Love and sex go wrong: helping couples in distress. In S. B. Levine, C. B. Risen, & S. E. Althof (Eds.), *Handbook of clinical sexuality for mental health professionals* (2nd ed., pp. 103–120). New York: Routledge.

Mezzich, J. E., & Hernandez-Serrano, R. (2006). *Psychiatry and sexual health.* New York: Jason Aronson.

Miller, H. B., & Hunt, J. S. (2003). Female sexual dysfunction: Review of the disorder and evidence for available treatment alternatives. *Journal of Pharmacy Practice, 16*(3), 200–208.

Miller, W. R., & Rollnick, S. (2002). *Motivational interviewing: Preparing people for Change.* New York: Guilford Press.

Miranda, A. O., & Davis, K. (2002). Sexually abusive children—etiological and treatment considerations. In B. K. Schwartz (Ed.), *The sex offender: Current treatment modalities and systems issues* (Vol. IV). Kingston, NJ: Civic Research Institute.

Moore, J. (1980). *Sexuality and spirituality: The interplay of masculine and feminine in human development.* San Francisco, CA: Harper & Row.

Moran, J. (2002). *Teaching sex: The shaping of adolescence in the 20th century.* Cambridge, MA: Harvard University Press.

Morrison, J. (2006). *DSM-IV made easy: The clinician's guide to diagnosis.* New York: The Guilford Press.

Moser, C. (2009). When is an unusual sexual interest a mental disorder? *Archives of Sexual Behavior, 38,* 323–325.

Mosher, D. L. (1980). Three dimensions of depth of involvement in human sexual response. *The Journal of Sex Research, 16*(1), 1–42.

Muir, C., & Muir, C. (1989). *Tantra: The art of conscious loving.* San Francisco: Mercury House, Inc.

Myers, L. S. (2010). Single again. In S. B. Levine, C. B. Risen, & S. E. Althof (Eds.), *Handbook of clinical sexuality for mental health professionals* (2nd ed., pp. 121–137). New York: Routledge.

Nelson, E. B., Soutullo, C. A., DelBello, M. P., & McElroy, S. L. (2002). The psychopharmacological treatment of sex offenders. In B. K. Schwartz (Ed.), *The sex offender: Current treatment modalities and systems issues* (Vol. IV, pp. 13-1–13-30). Kingston, NJ: Civic Research Institute.

Person, E. S. (2005). Paraphilias. In B. J. Sadock & V. A. Sadock (Eds.), *Kaplan & Sadock's comprehensive textbook of psychiatry* (Vol. I, 8th ed., pp. 1965–1979). New York: Lippincott Williams & Wilkins.

Phillips, N. A. (2000). Female sexual dysfunction: Evaluation and treatment. *American Family Physician, 62,* 127–136, 141–142. Retrieved from http://www.aafp.org

Psaris, J., & Lyons, M. (2000). *Undefended love.* Oakland, CA: New Harbinger Publications.

Rosen, I. (1996). Exhibitionism, scopophilia, and voyeurism. In I. Rosen (Ed.), *Sexual deviation* (3rd ed., pp. 174–215). New York: Oxford University Press.

Rosen, R. C., & Leiblum, S. R. (1989). Assessment and treatment of desire disorders. In S. R. Leiblum & S. C. Rosen (Eds.), *Principles and practice of sex therapy: Update for the 1990s* (pp. 19–45). New York: Guilford.

Rosen, R. C., & Leiblum, S. R. (1992). Erectile disorders: An overview of historical trends and clinical perspectives. In R. C. Rosen & S. R. Leiblum (Eds.), *Erectile disorders: Assessment & treatment* (pp. 3–26). New York: The Guilford Press.

Rosen, R. C., & Leiblum, S. R. (1995). Treatment of sexual disorders in the 1990s: An integrated approach. *Journal of Consulting and Clinical Psychology, 63*(6), 877–890.

Rosenthal, R. (1966). *Experimenter effects in behavioral research.* New York: Appleton-Century-Crofts.

Rosenthal, R., & Rosnow, R. L. (1969). The volunteer subject. In R. Rosenthal & R. L. Rosnow (Eds.), *Artifact in behavioral research* (pp. 59–118). New York: Academic Press.

Rossi, A. S. (1995). *Eros and caritas*: A biopsychosocial approach to human sexuality and reproduction. In A. S. Rossi (Ed.), *Sexuality across the life course* (pp. 3–36). Chicago: The University of Chicago Press.

Rowland, D. L. (1999). Issues in the laboratory study of human sexual response: A synthesis for the nontechnical sexologist. *Journal of Sex Research, 36*(1). Retrieved from http://galenet.galegroup.com

Russell, S. T. (2005). Conceptualizing positive adolescent sexuality development. *Sexuality Research & Social Policy, 2*(3), 4–12.

Sadock, V. A. (2005). Normal human sexuality and sexual dysfunction. In B. J. Sadock & V. A. Sadock (Eds.), *Kaplan & Sadock's comprehensive textbook of psychiatry* (8th ed., pp. 1902–1935). Philadelphia, PA: Lippincott Williams & Wilkins.

Sadovsky, R., & Nusbaum, M. (2006). Sexual health inquiry and support is a primary care priority. *Journal of Sexual Medicine, 3*, 3–11.

Saks, B. R. (1999). Identifying and discussing sexual dysfunction. *Journal of Clinical Psychiatry Monograph, 17*(1), 4–8.

Saleh, F. M., & Berlin, F. S. (2003). Sexual deviancy: Diagnostic and neurobiological considerations. In R. Geffner, K. C. Franey, T. G. Arnold, & R. Falconer (Eds.), *Identifying and treating sex offenders: Current approaches, research, and techniques* (pp. 53–76). New York: The Haworth Press, Inc.

San Francisco Bay Area Center for Cognitive Therapy. (2006). Sexual dysfunction. Retrieved from http://www.sfbacct.com

Satterfield, S. B., & Stayton, W. R. (1980). Understanding sexual function and dysfunction. *Topics in Clinical Nursing, 1*(4), 21–32.

Scharff, D. E. (2010). How development structures relationships. In S. B. Levine, C. B. Risen, & S. E. Althof (Eds.), *Handbook of clinical sexuality for mental health professionals* (2nd ed., pp. 73–86). New York: Routledge.

Schiavi, R. C. (2000). Psychiatrists' role in the management of sexual disorders. *Current Opinion in Psychiatry, 12*, 267–269.

Schnarch, D. (2002). *Resurrecting sex: Resolving sexual problems and rejuvenating your relationship.* New York: Harper Collins.

Schover, L. R., & LoPiccolo, J. (1982). Treatment effectiveness for dysfunctions of sexual desire. *Journal of Sex & Marital Therapy, 8*(3), 179–197.

Schwartz, B. K. (2002). The JRI model for treating varied populations with inappropriate sexual behavior. In B. K. Schwartz (Ed.), *The sex offender: Current treatment modalities and systems issues* (Vol. IV, pp. 1-2–1-30). Kingston, NJ: Civic Research Institute.

Scott, D. L., & Levine, S. B. (2010). Understanding gay and lesbian life. In S. B. Levine, A. B. Risen, & S. E. Althof (Eds.), *Handbook of clinical sexuality for mental health professionals* (2nd ed., pp. 351–368). New York: Routledge.

Sexual Health Network. (2004). Human sexual response cycles. Retrieved from http://www.sexualhealth.com/article_print.php?Action=read&article_id=243

Simons, J. S., & Carey, M. P. (2001). Prevalence of sexual dysfunctions: Results from a decade of research. *Archives of Sexual Behavior, 30*(2), 177–219.

Singy, P. (2010). What's wrong with sex? *Archives of Sexual Behavior, 39*, 1231–1233.

Sipski, M. L., & Alexander, C. J. (1997a). Basic sexual function over time. In M. L. Sipski & C. J. Alexander (Eds.), *Sexual function in people with disability and chronic illness* (pp. 75–83). Gaithersburg, MD: Aspen Publishers.

Sipski, M. L., & Alexander, C. J. (1997b). Impact of disability or chronic illness on sexual function. In M. L. Sipski & C. J. Alexander (Eds.), *Sexual function in people with disability and chronic illness* (pp. 3–12). Gaithersburg, MD: Aspen Publishers.

Spector, I. P., & Carey M. P. (1990). Incidence and prevalence of the sexual dysfunctions: A critical review of the empirical literature. *Archives of Sexual Behavior, 19*(4), 389–408.

Steen, S. (2001). Contested portrayals: Medical and legal social control of juvenile sex offenders. *Sociological Quarterly 42*(3), 325–350.

Sutherland, O. (2012). Qualitative analysis of heterosexual women's experience of sexual pain and discomfort. *Journal of Sex and Marital Therapy, 38*(3), 223–244.

ter Kuile, M. M., Both, S., & van Lankveld, J. J. D. M. (2010). Cognitive behavioral therapy for sexual dysfunctions in women. *Psychiatric Clinics of North America 33*, 595–610.

Thornton, D., & Mann, R. (1997). Sexual masochism: Assessment and treatment. In D. R. Laws & W. O'Donohue (Eds.), *Sexual deviance: Theory, assessment, and treatment* (pp. 240–252). New York: The Guilford Press.

Tiefer, L. (1986). In pursuit of the perfect penis. *The American Behavioral Scientist, 29*(5), 579–599.

Tiefer, L. (1991). Historical, scientific, clinical and feminist criticisms of "the human sexual response cycle" model. *Annual Review of Sex Research, 2*(2), 1–24.

Tiefer, L. (2001). A new view of women's sexual problems: Why new? Why now? *The Journal of Sex Research, 38*(2), 89–93.

Tiefer, L. (2004). *Sex is not a natural act & other essays.* Boulder, CO: Westview Press.

Troisi, A. (2008). Psychopathology and mental illness. In C. Crawford & D. Krebs (Eds.), *Foundations of evolutionary psychology* (pp. 453–474). New York: Lawrence Erlbaum Associates.

Udry, J. R., & Campbell, B. C. (1994). Getting started on sexual behavior. In A. Rossi (Ed.), *Sexuality across the life course* (pp. 187–208). Chicago: The University of Chicago Press.

Weiner, D. N., & Rosen, R. C. (1997). Medications and their impact. In M. L. Sipski & C. J. Alexander (Eds.), *Sexual function in people with disability and chronic illness: A health professional's guide* (pp. 85–118). Gaithersburg, MD: Aspen Publishers.

Welwood, J. (1996). *Love and awakening: Discovering the sacred path of intimate relationship*. New York: HarperCollins.

Whipple, B., & Brash McGreer, K. (1997). Management of female sexual dysfunction. In M. Sipski & C. Alexander (Eds.), *Sexual function in people with disability and chronic illness: A health professional's guide* (pp. 511–536). Gaithersburg, MD: Aspen Publishers.

Wyndzen, M. (2008). All mixed up: Perspectives on transgenderism and Gender Identity Disorder. Retrieved from http://www.genderpsychology.org

Zucker, K. J. (2010). The DSM diagnostic criteria for Gender Identity Disorder in children. *Archives of Sexual Behavior, 39*, 477–498.

Zucker, K. J., & Blanchard, R. (1997). Transvestic fetishism: Psychopathology and theory. In D. R. Laws & W. O'Donohue (Eds.), *Sexual deviance: Theory, assessment, and treatment* (pp. 253–279). New York: The Guilford Press.

# 11

# Sleep–Wake Disorders[1]

**Ari J. Elliot, Ph.D. Candidate, *University of Rochester***

*"Sleep that knits up the ravelled sleave of care, The death of each day's life, sore labour's bath, Balm of hurt minds, great Nature's second course, Chief nourisher in life's feast."*

SHAKESPEARE, MACBETH

As Shakespeare poetically attested, sleep is a central and inevitable fixture of our daily lives, one indispensable to our well-being. However, W. C. Fields's wry comment that getting a lot of sleep is the best cure for insomnia highlights that availing ourselves nightly of this most natural source of nourishment may be far from a simple matter. Many of us have heard that we spend roughly a third of our lives sleeping; perhaps more intriguing than the statistic itself, however, is the variety of reactions it might elicit, thereby reflecting the diverse ways in which sleep is viewed, enacted, and experienced. For example, sleep may be perceived as time poorly or well spent, treated casually or with much care and consideration, and felt to be a source of consternation or rejuvenation (and anywhere in between). Despite being one of the most basic biological imperatives, sleep is a highly complex and multidimensional phenomenon, aspects of which still elude the scientific gaze. Furthermore, in keeping with the subject of this text, sleep disturbance is a common clinical problem in the physical and mental health domains (Chokroverty, 2009; Reite, Weissberg, & Ruddy, 2009), one that "has profound effects on the lives of millions" (Walsh & Lindblom, 1997, p. 104).

The objective of this chapter is to provide an overview of what is known about sleep disorders, broaching their nosology (the classification of various types),

[1] At the time of this writing, the extant research has addressed the *Diagnostic and Statistical Manual of Mental Disorder*, 4th Edition, Text Revision (DSM-IV-TR; American Psychiatric Association [APA], 2000) disorders, including the DSM-IV-TR distinction between Primary Insomnia (PI) and Insomnia comorbid with other mental and/or medical disorders. In the DSM-5, these two previously distinct diagnoses were collapsed into the single diagnosis of *Insomnia Disorder*. Where applicable, we will use the new diagnostic category of Insomnia Disorder; however, when the research we cite refers specifically to Primary Insomnia, we will use that term. In subsequent editions of this text, we will include research on the newer DSM-5 disorders.

epidemiology, and treatment, although focusing primarily on their etiology. Given the extensive volume of theoretical models, research findings, and clinical knowledge pertaining to sleep disorders, such a review will inevitably be an abridged one; however, the Integral framework will be utilized to provide an integrative and multidimensional, if still foundational, understanding of sleep and its pathologies. The chapter will begin by discussing the various states and processes, both experiential and biological, involved in the regulation of sleeping and waking, as well as the consequences of sleep disturbance; it will then proceed to review the various pathologies of sleep, discuss etiology from the four quadratic perspectives, and finally, provide an overview of treatment approaches. In the course of the ensuing discussion, the reader is urged to bear in mind a few cautionary points. First, in the case of certain syndromes—particularly insomnia—sleep measurements and diagnostic symptoms exhibit continuous variation across individuals (rather than being categorically present or absent), with no precisely identifiable boundary between the normal and the pathological. Second, the causes, correlates, and consequences of sleep disturbance are often difficult to distinguish from one another.

## STATES OF CONSCIOUSNESS

### Waking, NREM, and REM States

Drawing upon Advaita Vedanta (an Eastern philosophical tradition), Integral theory considers sleep to be a state of consciousness fundamentally different from wakefulness, one that is further divided into dreaming and deep sleep states (Sharma, 2004; Wilber, 2000). These distinctions also appear to be evident from a modern scientific perspective, as sleep is not a singular or uniform physiological process or state. Most broadly, rather, it is divided into rapid eye movement (REM) and non-REM (NREM) phases, which in several respects appear to be qualitatively different from the waking state and from each other (Chokroverty, 2009). In light of such findings, "it has been suggested that REM sleep constitutes a third major physiological state, with neuronal generating and control systems that are essentially independent of those associated with wakefulness and non-REM (slow-wave) sleep" (Reite et al., 2009, p. 31). The subjective experiential features of each sleep state also differentiate them: Dreaming frequently and predominantly occurs during REM sleep (Chokroverty, 2009), whereas the usual absence of recallable mental experience is one salient characteristic of deep (slow-wave NREM) sleep. In spite of these critical differences, the boundaries between states of consciousness are not absolute. For example, slow-wave sleep is but one of multiple NREM substages that span a broader continuum of brain waves. Furthermore, as noted by Reite et al. (2009), "[waking, NREM, and REM] states are not mutually exclusive, and admixtures or rapid oscillations may occur" (p. 31), although such phenomena are generally the exception rather than the norm.

### Dreaming, Consciousness, and the Transpersonal

The nature and function of dreaming remain a subject of controversy. Sigmund Freud's *The Interpretation of Dreams* (1900/1911) bestowed a conception of dreams (which he famously declared the "Royal Road to the Unconscious") as revelations of unconscious wishes. With the decline of classical psychoanalysis, the interpretation of dreams has lost much of its prominence in the field of counseling and psychotherapy; nevertheless, it continues to capture the interest of laypersons and to hold significance to many clinicians (Yalom, 2002), particularly those of existential-humanistic, psychodynamic, and Jungian orientations. Neuropsychological accounts of dreaming range from the hypothesis that dream content is entirely an epiphenomenon of random neural information processing (Hobson & McCarley, 1977) to the more recent proposition that it reflects processes of memory consolidation (Payne & Nadel, 2004). Clearly, dreams may be subjectively experienced as quite meaningful or quite random. Nevertheless, common descriptions of dreams as emotion-laden narratives that are often logically disorganized are consistent with the neurobiological finding that "There is selective activation of the amygdala and other emotion-generating limbic regions during REM sleep, along with deactivation of the dorsolateral prefrontal cortex, a region central to rational thought" (Reite et al., 2009, p. 33). Thus, to psychoanalysts and neuroscientists alike, dreams would appear to lie outside the domain of the conscious, rational awareness typical of the waking state. However, an apparent contradiction is presented by lucid dreaming, in which a person "knows that the dream is a dream—and may even to some extent be able to control the dream experience" (Reite et al., 2009, p. 33).

Another phenomenon related to sleep and consciousness is that of transpersonal experience. The waking state of consciousness tends to be dominated by the ego's sense of identity as a separate individual self. According to various spiritual traditions, in the dreaming and deep sleep states, the psyche is relatively liberated from these egoic perceptual and conceptual constraints, thereby allowing greater access to transpersonal experience (Wilber, 2000). Kuiken, Lee, Eng, and Singh (2006) provide an account of "transcendent dreams," which involve spiritually oriented aesthetic experiences and narrative themes and are associated with subsequent reports of spiritual transformation such as an increased sense of awe and renewal.

## SLEEP BIOLOGY AND PHYSIOLOGY

### Sleep Architecture

The most salient physiological correlates of sleep are brain waves, eye movements, and muscular activity (also known as muscle tone), the measurement of which are called electroencephalography (EEG), electrooculography (EOG), and electromyography (EMG), respectively. EEG activity is measured by the frequency—in cycles per second (cps)—and amplitude of brain waves, and is generally categorized as one of four rhythms based on the frequency range. From slowest to fastest, they are delta (0.5–3 cps), theta (4–7 cps), alpha (8–13), and beta (14–25 cps; Hirshkowitz, Moore, & Minhoto, 1997). Compared to the waking state, sleep is characterized by diminished alpha and beta activity and, conversely, the elevated presence of other EEG rhythms (Chokroverty, 2009). For example, slow-wave sleep (SWS) is a phase marked by a significant increase or preponderance of delta waves. In NREM sleep, eye movements are generally slow and minimal, if present at all; in contrast, rapid eye movement is one of the defining characteristics of the REM stage. During NREM sleep, muscle tone is decreased, whereas REM sleep corresponds with a near or complete loss of voluntary muscle activity such that normally, "for all intents and purposes, the individual is paralyzed during REM sleep" (Hirshkowitz et al., 1997, p. 19).

Due to considerable variation across individuals, the parameters of sleep considered "normal" are difficult to define (Lichstein, Durrence, Riedel, Taylor, & Bush, 2004). Nevertheless, various prototypic patterns have been observed, particularly in the macrostructure—the stage composition—of sleep (Chokroverty, 2009). Sleep typically consists of a cycle of alternating NREM and REM episodes, each typically lasting around 90 to 120 minutes and occurring between four and six times (Hirshkowitz et al., 1997). NREM sleep is further divided into three stages—N1, N2, and N3—in the most recent classification system (American Academy of Sleep Medicine [AASM], 2007). Following onset, sleep generally proceeds quickly (10–12 minutes) through the N1 stage, with the N2 stage lasting longer (30–60 minutes). The N3 stage (containing SWS) completes the NREM phase, with the initial REM period usually beginning 60 to 90 minutes after sleep onset (Chokroverty, 2009). NREM sleep generally comprises 75–80% of total sleep duration, with REM sleep occupying the remaining 20–25%. Most SWS occurs in the first few sleep cycles; conversely, the most prolonged REM episodes usually occur in later cycles, such that the bulk of REM sleep falls in the last third of the sleep period (Chokroverty, 2009). Table 11.1 displays the characteristic EEG activity and average percentage of total sleep time spent in each stage among adults.

Changes in the duration and structure of sleep occur with age. Total sleep time decreases from infancy through childhood and into adulthood (Reite et al., 2009). Infants spend a significantly higher proportion of sleep time (> 50%) in REM sleep, which then "declines until adolescence and stabilizes at adult levels" (Hirshkowitz et al., 1997, pp. 24–25), an observation that suggests an important role for REM sleep in neurological development (Reite et al., 2009). In addition, the amount of N3 stage and slow-wave sleep typically declines from adolescence to late adulthood (Hirshkowitz et al., 1997; Reite et al., 2009).

**TABLE 11.1 Basic Sleep Architecture**

| State | % Total Sleep Time | EEG (brain waves) | EOG (eye movements) | EMG (muscle tone) |
|---|---|---|---|---|
| Waking | – | Alpha | Normal | Normal |
| NREM | | | | |
| N1 | 2–8% | < 50% alpha, Intermixed beta and theta | Slow rolling | Decreased |
| N2 | 45–55% | Intermixed with sleep spindles, K complexes | Absent | Decreased |
| N3 | 15–20 % | Slow-wave sleep | Absent | Decreased |
| REM | 20–25% | Mostly beta range, some theta activity | Rapid | Atonia (absent) |

*Source:* Chokroverty, 2009; Hirshkowitz et al., 1997

## Polysomnography and Sleep Measurement

Polysomnography (PSG) is the recording of sleep physiology, and is used in clinical assessment as well as sleep research. Typically conducted in a laboratory,[2] it includes EEG, EOG, and EMG measurement, as well as charting of heart rate and patterns, respiration and airflow, body position, and limb movements (Reite et al., 2009). Several sleep assessment concepts are instrumental to the understanding of sleep pathology, as disturbance may occur in several dimensions of sleep. Sleep-onset latency (SOL or SL) is the amount of time it takes to fall asleep. Sleep continuity (SC) is a measure of the amount of uninterrupted sleep time, and sleep efficiency (SE) is the percentage of total time in bed (between retiring and arising) actually spent sleeping. Other variables include total sleep time (TST), number of awakenings in the course of the sleep period (NWAK), and wake time after sleep onset (WASO). These variables can be measured by laboratory or in-home PSG study, or by self-report.

## Sleep Regulation

In perhaps "the greatest biological mystery of all time," the organismic purpose of sleep has not been precisely or conclusively determined (Chokroverty, 2009, p. 19). Leading hypotheses include the "restorative theory," which proposes that sleep provides for cellular and tissue growth and restoration; the "energy conservation theory," which contends that a decrease in metabolic activity occurring during sleep reduces biological stress; the "adaptive theory," which maintains that the inactivity and energy conservation pursuant to sleep is an evolutionary adaptation shaped by selection pressures; and, finally, the "memory consolidation and reinforcement theory," which posits that sleep facilitates the processing and retention of various types of memory (Chokroverty, 2009, pp. 19–21). Human beings possess various regulatory mechanisms that govern sleep, beginning with an organismic drive to satisfy the need for sleep (Hirshkowitz et al., 1997). All else equal, the longer a person has been awake, the more sleepiness (defined as the tendency to fall asleep) he or she will experience. Slow-wave and REM sleep also exhibit a homeostatic drive: An elevated tendency to enter these stages (known as "pressure") and an increase in their respective percentage of total sleep time (known as "rebound") are observed during recovery sleep following selective deprivation of these stages (Hirshkowitz et al., 1997). Another primary regulatory mechanism is the circadian rhythm (*circa* meaning "around" and *dian* meaning "day")—a physiological pattern of sleepiness and wakefulness that generally coincides with the 24-hour day/night cycle.[3] Cyclical exposure to light and darkness acts as a "cue" that helps ensure such synchronicity (a process known as "entrainment"). However, the circadian sleep rhythm persists even in the absence of environmental stimuli, reflecting the existence of a master biological clock that has been located in the suprachiasmatic nucleus (SCN) of the hypothalamus (Zee & Manthena, 2007). Cyclical patterns of sleepiness and alertness are also evident in the face of sleep deprivation: Despite an overall increase in baseline sleepiness in the course of a 24-hour

---

[2] In-home PSG studies are also conducted, although they are typically less comprehensive.

[3] Other circadian biological rhythms coincide and may act in concert with the circadian sleep rhythm, including cycles of body temperature and hormone secretion (Chokroverty, 2009).

period without sleep, a temporary increase in energy the following morning is often observed. Thus, homeostatic ("process S") and circadian mechanisms (process "C") interact to regulate sleep (Hirschkowitz et al., 1997; Reite et al., 2009).

## CONSEQUENCES OF SLEEP PROBLEMS

Sleep is undeniably necessary for survival, and, it seems, for optimal physical and mental health: Experimental and epidemiological research have linked inadequate sleep to adverse psychological, physiological, psychosocial, and societal outcomes. We would do well to give serious consideration to the personal and public health costs of what appears to be a pervasive problem. The National Center on Sleep Disorders Research (NCSDR; 2003) has estimated that between 50 and 70 million Americans suffer from a sleep disorder, and in a recent nationally representative survey of Americans between the ages of 13 and 64, more than half (60%) of respondents reported experiencing a sleep problem every night or almost every night, including insomnia symptoms (e.g., waking in the night, waking up too early, or feeling un-refreshed in the morning) or snoring (National Sleep Foundation [NSF], 2011).

The most consistent effect of sleep deprivation is increased sleepiness (i.e., the objectively measured tendency to fall asleep; Walsh & Lindblom, 1997), and individuals whose sleep is chronically disturbed or insufficient may experience excessive daytime sleepiness (EDS), which can interfere with functioning in many areas of life (Chokroverty, 2009). Both total and partial sleep deprivation commonly result in decreased mood, particularly on indices of tension, confusion, and fatigue (i.e., the subjective report of feeling tired; Ikegami et al., 2009). Furthermore, sleep deprivation has been found to negatively impact cognitive functioning, including alertness, attention, concentration, memory, and other higher-order functions (Belenky et al., 2003; Chokroverty, 2009; Ikegami et al., 2009). The effects of partial sleep deprivation[4] (PSD) have consistently been found to be temporary and moderate (Walsh & Lindblom, 1997). However, research increasingly suggests that chronic PSD results in an accumulating "sleep debt" associated with escalating and persistent performance decrements and mood disturbance (Belenky et al., 2003; Van Dongen, Maislin, Mullington, & Dinges, 2003).

A sizeable body of research suggests that poor sleep adversely affects physical health. Persons with insomnia report substantially more medical problems (Lichstein et al., 2004). In longitudinal studies, short sleep duration has been associated with increased body mass index (BMI) and obesity (Gangswich, Malaspina, Boden-Albala, & Heymsfield, 2005), perhaps as a result of sleep-induced metabolic and endocrine changes (Taheri, Lin, Austin, Young, & Mignot, 2004). Although direct evidence of causality is still limited and the relevant physiological mechanisms largely unknown, epidemiological research has linked both excessively short and long sleep duration to an elevated risk of type 2 diabetes (Gangswich et al., 2007), cardiovascular disease in women (Ayas et al., 2003), and overall mortality[5] (Kripke, Garfinkel, Wingard, Klauber, Marler, 2002; Patel et al., 2004).

[4] In experimental sleep research, partial sleep deprivation entails restriction of sleep to between 4 to 6 hours, for varying periods of time.

[5] In both studies, the lowest mortality was observed at an average sleep duration of 7 hours per night.

Sleep disturbance may have negative psychosocial consequences, perhaps by way of lower mood, cognitive disruption, and/or excessive sleepiness. Although research on the subject is limited, the results of a few studies are suggestive. For example, parental insomnia was related to a decline in marital relationship satisfaction among first-time parent couples in the year after childbirth (Meijer & van den Wittenboer, 2007), and children's sleep problems predicted decreased parent–child closeness in subsequent years (Bell & Belsky, 2008). Societal costs of sleep disturbance include associated mortality, direct health-care costs, and lost occupational productivity. Sleepiness is a major factor contributing to vehicular and trucking accidents (Lyznicki, Doege, Davis, & Williams, 1998) and has been implicated in the Chernobyl and Three Mile Island nuclear meltdowns among other environmental disasters (Colten & Altevogt, 2006). Furthermore, sleep disturbance has been associated with workplace absenteeism, diminished productivity, and nonvehicular accidents (Leger, Massuel, & Arnaud, 2006). In the educational domain, short sleep duration (< 6 hours) is associated with poor academic performance in adolescents (Roberts, Roberts, & Duong, 2009).

In summary, the physical, psychological, and societal burden of diagnosable sleep disorders, whether occurring alone or in combination with other medical and/or mental health conditions, is extensive (Colten & Altevogt, 2006; NCSDR, 2003). When considering subclinical symptoms as well, inadequate sleep is perhaps one of the most salient examples of the "psychopathology of the average" (Maslow, 1968, p. 71) in contemporary Western society, and constitutes a major public health concern.

## DIAGNOSTIC CLASSIFICATION OF SLEEP DISORDERS

There are several diagnostic systems that classify sleep disorders; the two most commonly used are the *International Classification of Sleep Disorders* (ICSD-II; AASM, 2005) and the *Diagnostic and Statistical Manual of Mental Disorders,* Fifth Edition (DSM-5; American Psychiatric Association [APA], 2013). This review is organized primarily around the DSM-5 taxonomy, which is geared toward general mental health and medical practice as opposed to the specialty practice of sleep medicine (APA, 2013). The term *Sleep–Wake Disorders*, as codified in the current edition of the DSM, serves to emphasize that these disorders entail disruptions or abnormalities of what are coordinated neurophysiologic processes regulating the timing and transitions between sleeping and waking states. Although such disturbances and related disorders may occur independently, they commonly accompany other mental disorders, such as mood and anxiety disorders, and may influence their severity and course (APA, 2013). Furthermore, rather than inevitably remitting with the treatment of co-occurring disorders, a sleep disorder such as insomnia may warrant independent clinical attention even in a context of comorbidity. Therefore, it behooves the mental health practitioner to be familiar with various sleep disorders and their symptoms. The following section providers a brief overview of most Sleep–Wake Disorders listed in the DSM.

### Insomnia Disorder

Periodic symptoms of insomnia are quite common in the general population, affecting between 30–40% of the population, and the prevalence of the diagnosable disorder with resulting impairment is commonly estimated at between 5–10% (NCSDR, 2003;

Ohayon, 2002). As a clinical condition, the criteria used to define and assess insomnia have varied widely in sleep research, with different requirements as to frequency and severity (e.g., number of nights per week, minimum average sleep latency), daytime consequences, and self-perception of having insomnia (Lichstein et al., 2004; Ohayon, 2002). Furthermore, insomnia has both objective and subjective aspects; the importance of the latter is highlighted by the observation that not all persons with insomnia symptoms or poor sleep—as objectively measured—are dissatisfied with their sleep, whereas other persons are, despite objectively measured sleep that appears to fall within normal bounds (Lichstein et al., 2004). In the DSM-5 (APA, 2013), the central criterion for Insomnia Disorder is dissatisfaction with either the quantity or quality of sleep, as a result of difficulty falling asleep, difficulty remaining asleep (either due to repeated awakenings or difficulty resuming sleep), or excessively early waking. These symptomatic forms are often known as sleep-onset insomnia, sleep-maintenance insomnia, and terminal/late insomnia, respectively. Thus, although the stereotypical picture of insomnia is one of trouble falling asleep, this is by no means the sole manifestation of the disorder. The DSM diagnostic criteria also require that the given sleep disturbance occurs at least 3 nights per week and has been experienced for at least 3 months. As is a requirement for the diagnosis of nearly all Sleep–Wake Disorders, symptoms must cause clinically significant distress or impairment. Furthermore, the insomnia symptoms must not be exclusively attributable to nor fully explained by a different sleep–wake disorder, the effects of a substance, or a co-occurring mental disorder or medical condition. Insomnia is considered to be persistent or chronic when it has lasted more than 3 to 6 months (AASM, 2005).

## Hypersomnolence Disorder

The central criterion for Hypersomnolence Disorder is excessive sleepiness despite an ample primary sleep period (at least 7 hours), which must be accompanied by at least one of the following symptoms: recurrent episodes of sleep over the course of a single day (e.g., unintended daytime naps), a long (more than 9 hours) yet nonrestorative primary sleep period, and a lack of normal alertness after abrupt awakening. Unlike in the case of insomnia, individuals with hypersomnia typically fall asleep easily and maintain continuous sleep, although they have difficulty awakening in the morning and may display sleep drunkenness, a state of impaired mental alertness or disorientation upon awakening (APA, 2013; Reite et al., 2009). Also, whereas the course of insomnia is often discrete and episodic in response to stressors, the course of hypersomnia tends to be continuous and unremitting (APA, 2013).

## Narcolepsy

The principal diagnostic feature of Narcolepsy is the presence of repeated episodes of intense sleepiness, napping, or briefly falling asleep, occurring within the same day (APA, 2013). Another prototypic, although not universal, diagnostic feature is cataplexy: a sudden loss of muscular control usually lasting a few seconds. Cataplectic episodes may result in subtle or gross body movements, and are typically preceded or triggered by strong emotional stimulation, usually laughing or joking (APA, 2013). Other common features of Narcolepsy include hypnagogic (pre-sleep) or hypnopompic (post-wake) hallucinations, usually of a visual nature, and sleep paralysis (temporary verbal and motor incapacitation just before falling asleep or upon awakening; APA, 2013; Reite et al., 2009). Narcolepsy generally exhibits a chronic course (APA, 2013). The DSM-5 (APA, 2013) distinguishes subtypes of Narcolepsy based on the presence or absence of cataplexy and a deficiency in hypocretin (low cerebrospinal fluid levels of a specific type of neurotransmitter, an abnormality that may be involved in the pathophysiology of Narcolepsy).

### Breathing-Related Sleep Disorders

Breathing-Related Sleep Disorders involve disruptions or abnormalities in breathing that tend to result in interrupted or nonrestorative sleep. The DSM-5 classifies three specific disorders within this category. The most prevalent is Obstructive Sleep Apnea Hypopnea (more commonly called sleep apnea) in which the repeated occurrence of blockage in the upper airways results in complete cessation of airflow (apnea) or a reduction in airflow (hypopnea). Apneas or hypopneas, which are observed through polysomnography, commonly produce snoring or other disruptions in nocturnal breathing that result in repeated arousals or awakenings (APA, 2013; Reite et al., 2009). It is important to note that although Obstructive Sleep Apnea Hypopnea is most common in overweight individuals, it can affect individuals of varying age, body shape, and physical condition (Reite et al., 2009). In contrast to Obstructive Sleep Apnea Hypopnea, Central Sleep Apnea is characterized by apneas or hypopneas that result from disturbances in the underlying physiologic regulation of breathing (such as respiratory effort), rather than from airway obstruction. Finally, Sleep-Related Hypoventilation involves abnormal ventilation that results in low oxygen levels. Despite substantive differences in the pathophysiology of these disorders, all of them may result in insomnia-like symptoms, including frequent awakenings, nonrestorative sleep, and daytime sleepiness (APA, 2013). Furthermore, if left untreated, they tend to persist or even worsen over time (Reite et al., 2009).

### Circadian Rhythm Sleep Disorder

Circadian Rhythm Sleep Disorder is characterized by sleep disruption resulting from either disturbance in the circadian system or from a mismatch between the timing of the circadian system and the sleep–wake schedule that is desired or required as a result of social or professional demands (APA, 2013). It is usually the product of a misalignment between the biological sleep rhythm and environmental sleep schedule requirements, rather than an underlying dysfunction in sleep physiology. Although there are several types listed in the DSM-5 and ICSD-II, the most common are delayed sleep phase type and shift work type. In delayed sleep phase type, the individual's circadian sleep rhythm is delayed relative to the desired or required chronological sleep schedule (meaning that he or she is biologically driven to both stay up and sleep in later than the attempted bedtime and waketime), resulting in difficulty falling asleep and awakening at these hours and, often, daytime sleepiness (APA, 2013). In shift work type, the circadian sleep rhythm is disrupted by the schedule demands of night or rotating shift work, typically resulting in diminished sleep duration and quality, and often, sleepiness at work (Reite et al., 2009). Other types include advanced sleep phase type, the converse of delayed sleep phase type, and an irregular sleep–wake type that involves a disorganized and highly variable sleep–wake schedule.

## Parasomnias

Parasomnias are defined as abnormal or undesirable physical, behavioral, or experiential events that occur during the sleep period or during sleep–wake transitions (APA, 2013; Bornemann, Mahowald, & Schenck, 2006). They may involve neurological, motor, or cognitive abnormalities and may occur during REM sleep or NREM sleep (particularly slow-wave sleep). Although benign sleepwalking may be the most common parasomnia, these disorders have gained notoriety for occasionally taking the form of violent behavior or inappropriate sexual activity ("sexsomnia"), apparently outside of the individual's conscious control and without subsequent recall. "Sane automatism" (an individual acting involuntarily despite general sanity) resulting from a parasomnia has been presented successfully as a defense in several cases involving nocturnal criminal acts (Bornemann et al., 2006). Although such extreme cases are a rarity, population-based surveys suggest that parasomnias, including violent behavior and sexual activity during sleep, are not uncommon in Western societies (Bjorvatn, Grønli, & Pallesen, 2010; Ohayon, Caulet, & Priest, 1997).

**NIGHTMARE DISORDER** Nightmare Disorder is characterized by the repeated occurrence of intensely frightening or dysphoric dreams, often involving threats to safety or survival. Upon awakening from these dreams, the individual quickly regains full alertness and is able to recall details of the dream (APA, 2013). Nightmares and associated awakenings may result in difficulty attaining sufficiently restorative sleep as well as anticipatory anxiety about sleeping. Traumatic nightmares, which are common features of Post-Traumatic Stress Disorder (PTSD), typically involve highly repetitive dream sequences that reenact aspects of the traumatic experience; these nightmares may arise from NREM sleep, whereas idiopathic nightmares overwhelmingly occur during REM sleep (Hartmann, 1984; Spoormaker, Schredl, & van den Bout, 2006). In any case, it is critical to recognize that nightmares and other sleep disturbances arising from exposure to trauma may develop into a chronic and functionally autonomous disorder that is often not adequately addressed with general PTSD treatment, and requires more direct sleep-focused intervention.

**REM SLEEP BEHAVIOR DISORDER** REM Sleep Behavior Disorder is another parasomnia that, despite being rare, has garnered significant research attention in recent years, and following the ICSD-II, was recently added to the DSM. This disorder involves abnormal arousal occurring during REM sleep, including vocalizations or complex motor behaviors such as flailing of limbs or jumping from bed (APA, 2013; Reite et al., 2009). Such behaviors may result in injury to self or a bed partner. As noted, temporary muscular paralysis (atonia) is a normative feature of REM sleep; however, among persons with REM Sleep Behavior Disorder, this physiological safeguard is disabled, enabling these individuals to literally act out their dreams.

**NREM SLEEP AROUSAL DISORDERS** Parasomnias arising during the slow-wave NREM stage (typically during the first third of the major sleep episode) are often called "disorders of arousal" (AASM, 2005); they involve atypical motoric and emotional activation while "most of the brain, including the cortex, [remains] in non-REM sleep" (Reite et al., 2009, p. 151), thus leaving the individual without conscious awareness and control. As such, disorders of arousal are intriguing and seemingly paradoxical admixtures of the states of wakefulness and deep sleep. It has been theorized that these disorders involve dysfunction in the regulation of sleep–wake state partitions and transitions, although the underlying pathophysiology remains largely unknown (Reite et al., 2009). The various subtypes classified in the DSM-5 and ICSD-II differ in their symptomatic and behavioral features. Nevertheless, they are believed to be manifestations of the same underlying neurophysiologic abnormality (Bornemann et al., 2006). Although the disorders of arousal are more common in adults than previously thought (Bornemann et al., 2006), their onset is most often in childhood, and their prevalence decreases substantially with age (Laberge, Tremblay, Vitaro, & Montplaisir, 2000).

**Sleep Terror Type** Sleep terrors involve repeated episodes of sudden arousal from sleep during which an individual displays intense fear and elevated autonomic arousal (e.g., rapid heartbeat or breathing, sweating); the individual is typically unresponsive to others' attempts to awaken and reorient them, and unlike in Nightmare Disorder, is generally unable to recall dream content upon awakening (APA, 2013). During a sleep terror episode, a person may be highly vocal, screaming or crying, and may exhibit violent and complex movements (Reite et al., 2009). "Confusional arousals" are a similar but less extreme form of NREM parasomnia, in which a person displays marked agitation and disorientation, although typically without the same degree of emotional distress or physiological arousal (Reite et al., 2009).

**Sleepwalking Type** Sleepwalking (somnambulism) involves complex motor behavior arising during sleep. It usually consists of leaving bed and walking around, although, less commonly, more elaborate behaviors such as driving may take place. The individual is largely unresponsive to others during the episode and exhibits minimal recall upon awakening, but soon regains normal functioning.

**RESTLESS LEGS SYNDROME (RLS)** Recently elevated to the status of a full disorder in the current edition of the DSM, Restless Legs Syndrome (RLS) is considered to be a neurological and sensorimotor condition that is characterized by "an urge to move the legs, usually accompanied or caused by uncomfortable and unpleasant sensations in the legs" (The International Restless Legs Syndrome Group, as cited in Allen et al., 2003, p. 102). The urge to move the legs is worse when legs are at rest and during the evening/night, and is at least partly relieved by moving the legs (Allen et al., 2003; APA, 2013). The severity of symptoms varies, as does the course, which is often chronic and progressive, although in milder cases it may be intermittent. RLS often interferes with the initiation or maintenance of sleep.

## ETIOLOGY OF SLEEP-WAKE DISORDERS

As with the many other forms of psychopathology discussed in this text, sleep disorders are overdetermined: Their etiology frequently involves an interplay of biological, psychological (including cognitive, affective, and behavioral), and social factors, which are implicated to different degrees in different sleep disorders. For example, whereas various behaviors can influence the severity of Breathing-Related Sleep Disorders, physiology is the principal cause (Guilleminault & Zupancic, 2009). In contrast, psychological processes typically play a central role in chronic insomnia

(Espie, 2002; Harvey, 2002; Morin, 1993). Finally, the causes of certain sleep disorders (such as idiopathic hypersomnia) are still unknown (Reite et al., 2009).

The ensuing discussion reviews a range of phenomena—spanning the four quadrants—that have been implicated in the etiology of various sleep disorders; however, given that insomnia is the most prevalent and widely investigated form of sleep disturbance,[6] it focuses primarily on the theoretical models and empirical evidence relevant to the causes of insomnia. Accordingly, it is useful to keep in mind an overarching conceptual scheme, known as the "3-P" model (Spielman, 1986), that views insomnia as developing through an interaction of predisposing, precipitating, and perpetuating factors:

> Predisposing conditions often precede the onset of the sleep disturbance and set the stage for its occurrence by, for example, lowering the threshold for triggering the insomnia. While the intensity of a predisposing condition is, by definition, not sufficient by itself to produce an insomnia, it establishes a propensity or serves as a contributing factor in the genesis of the insomnia. Precipitating circumstances are temporally contiguous with the onset and render the insomnia manifest. Perpetuating factors are those features that sustain or support the insomnia. (Spielman, 1986, p. 14)

## Upper-Right Perspectives

**GENETICS** Twin studies have revealed significant genetic contributions to the duration, timing, and quality of sleep (Heath, Kendler, Eaves, & Martin, 1990). One study examining the self-reports of a large sample of monozygotic (MZ) and dizygotic (DZ) twins concluded that "Genetic differences accounted for at least 33% of the variance in sleep quality and sleep disturbance" (Heath et al., 1990, p. 318). Heredity also appears to underlie individual differences in basal sleep need, which ranges from 6 to 8 or more hours (Hor & Tafti, 2009) and may affect the degree of sleep debt and daytime impairment resulting from disrupted or insufficient sleep.

Genetic factors appear to play a role in the pathogenesis of many sleep disorders, although the precise mechanisms of expression and the extent of their influence largely remain to be determined (Dauvilliers, Maret, & Tafti, 2005a). With most sleep disorders, genotype is considered a predisposing factor, as it is insufficient in and of itself to explain the condition. This is because "sleep and sleep disorders are complex phenotypes, regulated by many genes, gene interactions, environment [factors], and gene–environment interactions" (Dauvilliers et al., 2005a, p. 91). As such, the hereditary contribution to the etiology of sleep disorders is typically *polygenic* (involving multiple genes), although in a few uncommon and more severe disorders it is monogenic—traceable to the presence of a specific gene or a mutation (polymorphism) on a certain chromosome (Hamet & Tremblay, 2006). For example, fatal familial insomnia (FFI—an

[6] Estimates of prevalence have varied considerably depending on definitional criteria and study methodology. Epidemiological research suggests that between 30–40% of the population has one or more periodic insomnia symptoms, that 10–20% also experience daytime consequences and dissatisfaction with sleep, and that anywhere from 1–10% meet criteria for Insomnia Disorder (APA, 2013; Lichstein et al., 2004; Ohayon, 2002).

extremely rare disorder characterized by severe insomnia and rapid, fatal degeneration of the autonomic nervous system) is caused by a mutation in the prion protein gene on chromosome 20. In Narcolepsy, researchers have identified specific alleles (principally, DQBl*0602) in the HLA complex—a set of genes related to specialized immune functioning—that are present in the vast majority (85–95%) of individuals suffering from Narcolepsy with cataplexy (Dauvilliers et al., 2005a; Hamet & Tremblay, 2006). An autoimmune dysfunction associated with the HLA system might be responsible for the abnormally low levels of neurotransmitters called hypocretins in cerebrospinal fluid and brain tissue that have been implicated in the pathophysiology of human Narcolepsy (Dauvilliers, Billiard, & Montplaisir, 2003). Nevertheless, no specific gene has been found to be either "necessary or sufficient for developing narcolepsy" (Hamet & Tremblay, 2006, p. S9). The risk of developing Narcolepsy among first-degree relatives of afflicted individuals is anywhere from 10 to 100 times greater than in the general population; nonetheless, fewer than 2% of first-degree relatives are affected, and it appears that only 25–30% of monozygotic twin pairs are concordant for Narcolepsy with cataplexy (Mignot, 1998). The data thus imply that Narcolepsy "is not a simple genetic disease," but rather, involves a genetic predisposition interacting with environmental factors (Mignot, 1998, p. S16).

Certain Circadian Rhythm Sleep Disorders are strongly influenced by genetics. Research has identified specific "clock genes" involved in circadian sleep regulation (Hamet & Tremblay, 2006) and twin studies have indicated a strong hereditary basis for the sleep schedules toward which persons will naturally gravitate, a typological dimension known as morningness/eveningness or "chronotype" (Hur, Bouchard, & Lykken, 1998). Some individuals tend to wake early and easily and are particularly energetic in the morning (a "lark"), in contrast to persons who have difficulty waking and/or feel sluggish in the morning, yet are more alert at night and tend to stay awake later (an "owl"; Chokroverty, 2009). In an especially illustrative case of gene–environment interaction, the interplay of circadian dispositions and exogenous demands on sleep timing determines the likelihood of a chronological mismatch that, if severe enough, may manifest in a circadian rhythm sleep disorder. Delayed sleep phase syndrome has been linked to a number of specific genes, and a family history is commonly reported (Dauvilliers et al., 2005a; Reite et al., 2009), but social and behavioral factors also play a contributing role (Crowley, Acebo, & Carksadon, 2007). In a more monogenic pathway, a subset of cases of advanced sleep phase syndrome (a rare condition marked by an excessively early sleep–wake cycle) has been associated with a mutation in the clock gene *Per2* (Dauvilliers et al., 2005a).

Genetics also appear to play a role in insomnia, with recent studies reporting moderate to strong heritability (Drake, Friedman, Wright, & Roth, 2011; Hublin, Partinen, Koskenvuo, & Kaprio, 2011; Watson, Goldberg, Arguelles, & Buchwald, 2006). There is some data to suggest that genetic influences may be stronger in Primary Insomnia than in insomnia that is comborbid with anxiety or depression, as well as in cases of insomnia with an earlier age of onset (Bastien & Morin, 2000; Dauvilliers et al., 2005b).

Sleep apnea is another condition influenced by genetics, to the extent that:

> most of the risk factors involved in the pathophysiology of this condition [are] largely genetically determined. This is true for instance for body fat distribution and metabolism (especially upper-body obesity), ventilatory control

abnormalities, and craniofacial dysmorphism, which predispose to the obstruction of the upper airways. (Dauvilliers et al., 2005a, p. 94)

Finally, research has suggested that a genetic predisposition is involved in the parasomnias. One twin study estimated that genetics accounted for around 45% and 37% of the variance in childhood and adult nightmares, respectively (Hublin, Kaprio, Partinen, & Koskenvuo, 1999), and there may be some common genetic underpinnings to the abnormalities in motor inhibition shared by NREM parasomnias (sleepwalking, sleep terrors) and REM Sleep Behavior Disorder (Lecendreux et al., 2003). Again, genetic and environmental factors interact to determine whether the given parasomnia will be expressed, as "in some patients, specific stressors or traumas may be necessary to elicit the symptoms, whereas in other patients with a very strong genetic loading," such psychological influences may be largely absent from the clinical picture (Reite et al., 2009, p. 50).

**EFFECTS OF SUBSTANCES** Psychoactive substances (including psychopharmacological agents and both licit and illicit drugs) are known to influence sleep and its architecture. Substances may have either pathogenic or palliative effects that are often highly specific to the given drug and individual. Antidepressants, for example, can either enhance sleep or contribute to disturbances including insomnia, hypersomnia, or EDS (Reite et al., 2009). Some of the more commonly observed effects of substances on sleep are summarized in Table 11.2.

The effects of alcohol and caffeine on sleep are particularly noteworthy given the sheer volume of consumption in Western society. Heavy consumption of caffeine produces disruptive effects on sleep (Bonnet & Arand, 1992), and even moderate amounts may inhibit sleep when consumed too late in the day. Alcohol initially facilitates sleep onset and generally suppresses REM sleep; however, after 4 hours or so it typically results in poorer sleep continuity and, often, a resurgence of REM sleep (known as "REM rebound") that may cause early waking (Partinen, 2009; Reite et al., 2009). These effects are more pronounced at higher doses, and, accordingly, heavy use of alcohol is associated with insomnia (Partinen, 2009).

Diet can affect the severity of sleep disorder symptoms. For example, heavy and carbohydrate-rich meals—especially those with rapidly absorbed (high-GI) carbohydrates—may exacerbate daytime sleepiness by increasing tryptophan levels (Partinen, 2009). By the same token, proportionally high-carbohydrate, low-protein dinners as well as a late-night snacks high in tryptophan (such as a glass of milk) may reduce sleep-onset latency (Reite et al., 2009). Certain vitamins and minerals may also affect sleep; most notably, Restless Legs Syndrome is associated with iron deficiency (more precisely, a below-average serum ferritin level), and in these cases is treated with iron supplementation (Partinen, 2009).

**MEDICAL ILLNESSES AND SLEEP** Sleep disturbance may be caused or aggravated by various medical conditions. Symptoms interfering with sleep include pain, disrupted respiration, and atypical movements, which may result from a range of illnesses. Reite et al. (2009) note that "Cardiac dysrhythmias, angina pectoris, and breathing disorders related to cardiac conditions all can cause awakenings and sleep fragmentation" (p. 173). Other medical conditions commonly associated with sleep problems include

**TABLE 11.2 Prominent Effects of Substances on Sleep**

| Drug | General Effects | Effects on Sleep Architecture | Notes |
|---|---|---|---|
| **Hypnotics and Sedatives** | | | |
| Benzodiazepines | < SL, > TST | < REM, < SWS > N2 | Risk of tolerance, rebound insomnia, withdrawal |
| Nonbenzodiazepine hypnotics (e.g., Zolpidem) | < SL, > TST | No consistent effects observed | Better risk profile than benzodiazepines |
| **Antidepressants** | | | |
| Tricyclics and monoamine oxidase inhibitors (MAOIs) | Vary with specific drug | < REM | May aid sleep or contribute to insomnia |
| Selective serotonin reuptake inhibitors (SSRIs) | > SL, < SC in some cases | < REM | May aid sleep or contribute to insomnia, hypersomnia, EDS at higher doses |
| ***Other Psychoactive Substances*** | | | |
| Antipsychotics | < SL, > SE | < REM | Effects vary depending on specific drug |
| Lithium | No consistent effects | < REM, > SWS | Implicated in NREM parasomnias |
| Alcohol | < SL, > SC early in night, then < SC Chronic/heavy use: < TST | < REM REM rebound | Worsens Breathing-Related Sleep Disorders; heavy use related to poor sleep; withdrawal effects |
| Caffeine | > SL, < SC | < SWS | Effects fairly individual and dosage/time-dependent |
| Nicotine | > SL, < SC | < REM | Effects dosage-dependent |
| Antihistamines (over-the-counter [OTC] sleep meds) | < SL, > SC | < REM | Hangover effect, quick development of tolerance |

*Source:* Reite et al., 2009; Franzen and Buysse, 2009

muscoskeletal (e.g., rheumatoid arthritis, fibromyalgia), neurological (e.g., Parkinson's disease), endocrine (e.g., hyperthyroidism), or pulmonary (e.g., emphysema) disease (APA, 2000). Persons with insomnia often link the onset of the condition to a medical stressor (Healey et al., 1981), although "it is unclear whether health problems per se or worries about health trigger insomnia" (Bastien, Vallières, & Morin, 2004, p. 57).

**NEUROBIOLOGICAL AND OTHER PHYSIOLOGICAL FACTORS IN INSOMNIA** The human nervous system is comprised of the central nervous system (consisting of the brain and spinal cord) and the peripheral nervous system, which in turn is made up of the somatic system (responsible for voluntary muscular control) and autonomic system.

The autonomic nervous system regulates many involuntary organ functions that serve to maintain internal homeostasis and respond to the environment; it consists of the sympathetic system, which governs respiration and cardiac function, and the parasympathetic system, which governs salivation, digestion, and excretion. Autonomic arousal refers to the stimulation of the sympathetic system, which may result from endogenous causes (e.g., fear, pain, and muscle tension) or exogenous sources (e.g., heat or noise; Hirshkowitz et al., 1997). As sleep coincides with proportionally reduced sympathetic activity (e.g., decreased heart rate and blood pressure) and increased parasympathetic activity (Hirshkowitz et al., 1997), it is not surprising that autonomic arousal inhibits sleep (Waters, Adams, Binks, & Varnado, 1993).

Transient, situational arousal can interfere with sleep on any given night regardless of general sleep patterns. However, a seminal study by Monroe (1967) found significant physiological differences between groups of poor and good sleepers, leading to the hypothesis that more persistently elevated levels of arousal contribute to insomnia (Bonnet & Arand, 1995). Over the past four decades, the physiological hyperarousal model of insomnia has accumulated support from additional findings that persons with insomnia (PWI) and normal sleepers (NS) differ on somatic, neurological, and endocrine measures. PWI have been shown to exhibit higher arousal than NS on a number of somatic measures, including heart rate, body temperature, and metabolic rate, both in sleeping and waking states (Adam, Tomeny, & Oswald, 1986; Bonnet & Arand, 1995; Monroe, 1967; Stepanski, Glinn, Zorick, Roehrs, & Roth, 1994). One might expect that on account of sleep loss, persons with insomnia would tend to be sleepier during the day than those without the condition. In actuality, PWI tend to exhibit equivalent if not *less* daytime sleepiness as measured by the mean sleep latency test[7] (MSLT; Stepanski, Zorick, Roehrs, Young, & Roth, 1988), implying that hyperarousal may be consistently inhibiting sleep in spite of an accumulating sleep debt.

Additional support for the physiological hyperarousal model derives from comparative neurological and endocrine data. Regarding the former, PWI generally exhibit greater high frequency EEG (particularly beta) activity and reduced low frequency EEG (particularly delta) activity in comparison with NS, implying a state of elevated cortical arousal (Cortoos, Verstraeten, & Cluydts, 2006; Krystal, Edinger, Wohlgemuth, & Marsh, 2002; Perlis et al., 2001). To the extent that it reflects greater cognitive activity (its UL quadratic correlate), higher cortical arousal may explain why PWI at times have the subjective experience of being awake when objective measures indicate that they are sleeping[8] (Cortoos, Verstraeten, & Cluydts, 2006). Furthermore, in neuroimaging research, PWI show higher cerebral glucose metabolism and a smaller reduction in metabolic activity from waking to sleep states, again suggesting a state of neurological hyperarousal (Nofzinger et al., 2004). Finally, there is some evidence for higher stress system activation (particularly hypothalamo-pituitary-adrenal [HPA] axis activity) in insomnia, as indicated by elevated plasma levels of the stress hormones cortisol and adrenocorticotropic hormone (ACTH; Vgontzas et al., 2001).

---

[7] The MSLT is a specific polysomnographic test that measures the average time to sleep onset across multiple daytime sleep opportunities.

[8] Persons with insomnia tend to overestimate sleep-onset latency, underestimate total sleep time, and even to report having been awake when aroused shortly after sleep onset (Borkovec, 1981; Carskadon et al., 1976). This phenomenon has been termed "sleep state misperception."

Of course, the correlational data contained in most studies do not preclude the possibility that higher arousal may be partly a by-product of sleep dysregulation or related stress. However, Bonnet and Arand (1995) presented experimental data implying that higher arousal is more a cause than a consequence of insomnia. In addition, normal sleepers (NS) vary in their baseline daytime sleepiness level, which is partially independent of state effects such as sleep deprivation and is associated with cardiac measures of sympathetic–parasympathetic balance; this finding is suggestive of a trait basis for sleep tendency related to level of physiological arousal (Bonnet & Arand, 2005). Finally, multiple studies have identified a subset of individuals without insomnia whose sleep is nevertheless more easily disturbed in response to laboratory stressors, effects found to be largely attributable to greater physiological reactivity (including sympathetic nervous system activation; Bonnet & Arand, 2003; Drake, Jefferson, Roehrs, & Roth, 2006; Drake, Richardson, Roehrs, Scofield, & Roth, 2004). Drake and colleagues (2006) have called this individual difference "vulnerability to stress-related sleep disturbance,"[9] and hypothesized that persons who exhibit high scores on a measure of such vulnerability are those at greatest risk for developing Primary Insomnia.

In summary, empirical findings have converged in linking insomnia to a persistent and multifaceted state of physiological hyperarousal, which may represent a trait-like tendency and constitute a key predisposition to the disorder. However, the fact that objectively poor sleep is not always accompanied by subjective complaints of insomnia suggests that "physiological arousal alone is an insufficient explanation" (Espie, 2002, p. 223). Indeed, in the case of insomnia, as with most of the mental disorders reviewed in this book, genetic or other predisposing factors do not lead to disorder in any sort of unilateral, deterministic fashion, but rather represent an underlying susceptibility that must act in concert with environmental conditions or specific experiences in order to eventuate in disorder.

**STRESSORS AND STRESS: PRECIPITATING FACTORS** The onset of insomnia usually coincides with the presence of identifiable stressors (APA, 2000; Healey et al., 1981; Morin, 1993). In an early study, PWI reported a higher occurrence of undesirable and stressful life events in the year of insomnia onset compared to other years and to NS (Healey et al., 1981). More recently, Bastien, Vallières, and Morin (2004) reported that almost 8 in 10 individuals seeking treatment for insomnia identified specific precipitating events associated with its onset, including family, health, and work or school events (the large majority of which had a negative emotional valence). In a large cohort study, Vahtera and colleagues (2007) reported that negative life events were strongly associated with subsequent reports of poor sleep. Whereas stressors can be considered environmentally based events or situations (e.g., the loss of a relationship or a job), stress is a broader, multidimensional phenomenon that encompasses an event itself, the subjective appraisal and experience of the event, and a physiological response; this response involves stimulation of the two major components of the human "stress system"—the hypothalamo-pituitary-adrenal (HPA) axis and the sympathetic nervous system (Vgontzas et al., 1998). Although the data are strictly correlational, physiological and self-report measures of stress have been associated with the degree

[9] A recent study showed a sizeable genetic as well as environmental contribution to such sleep-related reactivity (Drake et al., 2011).

of objective sleep disturbance and subjective sleep complaints, respectively (Hall et al., 2000; Vgontzas et al., 1998). Stress has also been linked to an increased frequency of nightmares (Schredl, 2003) as well as NREM episodes including night terrors and sleep-walking (Ohayon, Guilleminault, & Priest, 1999). In addition, exposure to a traumatic event,[10] an extreme form of psychological stress, is commonly followed by acute and in some cases long-term sleep problems, including insomnia symptoms and nightmares (Hefez, Metz, & Lavie, 1987; Noll, Trickett, Susman, & Putnam, 2006).

With regard to potential causal pathways, elevated levels of stress hormones associated with stimulation of the HPA axis appear to be disruptive of sleep (Van Reeth et al., 2000), and multiple studies have linked perceived stress to higher neurological arousal during sleep (i.e., decreased delta EEG and increased beta EEG activity; Hall et al., 2000, 2007). Stress might also disturb sleep by inciting intrusive mental activity (e.g., rumination, worrying, problem solving) and/or emotional arousal (e.g., anger, anxiety, dysphoria). In any case, the extent of stress-related sleep disruption would, theoretically, be contingent upon the frequency and magnitude of the stressor/s as well as the individual's reactivity to stress stimuli. Vahtera et al. (2007) observed partial support for this interaction, finding that while exposure to a severe life event within six months resulted in a higher risk of poor sleep in general, the odds were considerably higher for individuals exhibiting high liability to anxious arousal. Although further investigation is necessary to elucidate the precise mechanisms by which stress may influence sleep as well as the nature of related individual differences, a picture of elevated stress reactivity in combination with exposure to stressors goes a long way in explaining how an episode of acute insomnia can emerge. Nevertheless, one piece of Spielman's 3-P model is still missing. For transient or acute sleep disturbance to progress to chronic insomnia, it is widely agreed that perpetuating factors—those that sustain or even reinforce the disturbance—must enter the clinical picture, and most of those implicated are behavioral or cognitive in nature.

**BEHAVIORAL FACTORS** Behavior plays a significant role in various forms of sleep disturbance, particularly in chronic primary insomnia (Morin, 1993); it does so primarily by influencing the physiology of sleep, including conditioned autonomic responses and circadian regulation. With respect to the former, the physiological processes involved in sleep initiation, including the change in sympathetic/parasympathetic balance, are subject to classical conditioning; in other words, "Just as Pavlov's dog salivated to a bell after the sound was paired with food, humans can react autonomically to stimuli present in the bedroom environment" (Hirshkowitz et al., 1997, p. 26). The role of conditioning in sleep disturbance was first elaborated in the stimulus control theory introduced by Bootzin (1972). According to this model, sleep-related stimuli (which can include physical objects or settings such as the bed or bedroom, as well as the time) have normally "acquired discriminative control, in that they are potent cues associated with drowsiness and sleep onset" (Morin, 1993, p. 56). Conversely, however, when such stimuli are repeatedly paired with wakefulness[11] they are likely to become

[10] In the DSM-5 (APA, 2013), a traumatic event is defined as one in which an individual experiences perceived threat and helplessness, terror, or horror.

[11] Wakefulness in the sleep environment can range from lying awake in bed for an extended period of time to more deliberate activities such as watching television in bed.

associated with, and thus further cue, arousal rather than sleep (Bootzin, 1972). Retiring when not adequately sleepy is a common cause of excessive wakefulness in the sleep environment, which may also result from a variety of behaviors, including engaging in alerting activities (such as work or exercise) too close to bedtime, frequent or extended napping, and late or excessive caffeine intake (Reite et al., 2009).

Although the sleep-inhibiting conditioning process may occur whenever stimuli are consistently paired with wakefulness rather than sleep, it appears to be the most damaging when learned associations are made with marked emotional arousal, including frustration and anxiety, often connected to failed attempts at sleep[12] (Hirshkowitz et al., 1997). When unsuccessful, focused and effortful attempts to induce sleep, such as "trying to force sleep to come, tossing and turning to find a sleep position, lying particularly still as if asleep, and being unwilling to 'give in' and get up when not sleeping," tend to incite negative emotional arousal (Espie, Broomfield, MacMahon, Macphee, & Taylor, 2006, p. 235). Empirical evidence directly supporting the stimulus control theory is limited (Espie, 2002), although consistent with the notion of disrupted sleep-promoting associations, Robertson, Broomfield, and Espie (2002) reported that in addition to being less sleepy overall, PWI experienced a slower rate of increase in sleepiness over the hour prior to bedtime compared to NS. Furthermore, the theory is supported by clinical experience, as intervention based on the stimulus control model is an effective and widely utilized treatment for insomnia (Espie, 2002; Morin et al., 2006).

Although potentially contributing to the onset of sleep disturbance, maladaptive sleep-related behaviors may do their greatest damage in a perpetuating role. This is because acute sleep disruption that was temporally and causally linked to stressors may be aggravated and extended as a result of conditioned arousal and other disruptive effects on circadian and homeostatic processes (APA, 2000; Morin, 1993; Reite et al., 2009). As a common example, persons who have had difficulty sleeping may engage in counterproductive compensatory (or "safety") behaviors, such as deliberately prolonging time in bed (i.e., going to bed earlier or remaining in bed after awakening) in an attempt to compensate for the perceived sleep deficit. However, this tends over time to decrease sleep efficiency (Espie et al., 2006) and may actually intensify the conditioning process (Harvey, 2002).

Behavior is also implicated in the etiology of other sleep disorders. Given that obesity often contributes to the development or aggravation of obstructive sleep apnea, lifestyle behaviors that affect body weight (such as eating and exercise habits) can have a significant impact on the course and severity of the disorder (Guilleminault & Zupancic, 2009). Maintaining an irregular sleep–wake schedule can disrupt the circadian rhythm, in some cases (particularly among "owls" and other predisposed individuals) leading to the development of delayed sleep phase syndrome or another circadian rhythm sleep disorder (Reite et al., 2009). In addition, the DSM-IV (APA, 2000) reports that changes in sleep schedule may increase the likelihood of sleep terror episodes. Last, behavioral insomnia of childhood, a sleep disturbance listed in the ICSD-II, is considered to result primarily from behavioral conditioning that occurs as a consequence of parental actions (AASM, 2005). In one form, young children (typically 6 months to 3 years of age) have difficulty falling asleep or returning to sleep without

[12] In this manner, conditioned arousal can apply to behavior in combination with environmental stimuli.

an object (such as a bottle) or person to which they have become accustomed at the time of sleep onset (Reite et al., 2009). In another form, children older than 2 years of age display extreme opposition and resistance to going to bed, which is considered to result from a "lack of firm bedtime guidelines that are routinely followed" (Reite et al., 2009, p. 254).

## Upper-Left Perspectives

**COGNITIVE MODELS OF INSOMNIA** Cognitive theories of insomnia etiology emphasize the pathogenic role of cognitive arousal in insomnia, as described by Morin (1993):

> Cognitive arousal can be a negative, a neutral, or even a positive experience. It may be expressed in terms of worry, racing mind, rumination, intrusive thoughts, planning, analyzing, or difficulty in controlling exciting thoughts. According to this model, excessive cognitive activity, whether pleasant or not, interferes with the sleep process. (p. 51)

Cognitive arousal is higher among PWI than NS (Nicassio, Mendlowitz, Fussell, & Petras, 1985; Robertson et al., 2007) and in one study, was the factor most commonly blamed for sleep difficulty (exceeding somatic tension by a wide margin; Lichstein & Rosenthal, 1980). Indeed, multiple studies have suggested that cognitive arousal plays an even larger role in insomnia than does physiological arousal (Nicassio et al., 1985; Robertson et al., 2007), although they are not mutually exclusive and, in actuality, are likely to co-occur (deValck, Cluydts, & Pirrera, 2004). Perhaps all of us have had the experience, at one time or another, of lying awake thinking in bed, and most likely found that it took longer to fall asleep than usual. Although it is possible that cognitive arousal may be, to some extent, a by-product of being awake longer (Espie, 2002), experimental research has demonstrated that cognitive arousal results in greater difficulty falling asleep among normal sleepers (de Valck et al., 2004; Haynes, Adams, & Franzen, 1981).

Cognitive models of insomnia maintain that persons with insomnia do not differ from normal sleepers simply in the amount of pre-sleep mental activity, but more broadly and importantly, in the focus and content of their cognitions (Harvey, 2002; Morin, 1993). In this respect, cognition encompasses such processes as attention, perceptions, attributions, expectations, thoughts, and beliefs. Rather than forming a linear sequence, these processes are links in a chain of circular causality, and thus any particular starting point is somewhat arbitrary. Nevertheless, it is instructive to begin with the role of attention. Espie et al. (2006) draw from Abraham Maslow's (1943) hierarchy of needs theory, noting that the need for sleep, as with hunger, thirst, and other physiological needs, is one of our most pressing organismic drives. Among persons with Primary Insomnia, perceived sleep loss has likely increased the motivation to sleep as well as the danger attributed to the possibility of further sleep loss (Espie et al., 2006). As a result, sleep becomes a focus of awareness and source of concern, such that "the individual will monitor internally (i.e., body sensations) and externally (i.e., the environment) for sleep-related threats such as indicators of not getting enough sleep and of not coping or functioning well during the day" (Harvey, 2002, p. 571). This selective attention (also known as attentional bias) to sleep-related stimuli and threats, which is apt to be anxiety-laden rather than affect-neutral, may be likened to a state of hypervigilance.

On account of the heightened awareness of minor stimuli that would not likely be detected among NS, along with an interpretive bias toward threat, the individual with PI is likely to acquire a "distorted perception of deficit": an overestimation of the extent of sleep loss and resulting daytime impairment, in turn causing further preoccupation and concern (Harvey, 2002, pp. 873–874).

Although aspects of these attentional and perceptual processes may operate outside of conscious awareness, they are paralleled by certain patterns of conscious thinking that appear to be characteristic of insomnia—what Harvey (2002) has called "excessive negatively toned cognitive activity" (p. 871). According to this theory, the pre-sleep thoughts of persons with insomnia tend to be more intrusive and are more likely to be focused on sleep itself—for example, worrying about not getting enough sleep and the impact on health and daytime functioning (Harvey, 2002; Morin, 1993). Consistent with this premise, more worry—both in general and specifically about falling asleep—was reported by PWI than NS (Nicassio et al., 1985). Furthermore, negative or worrisome thinking about sleep itself is a type of thought content that appears to be more strongly linked to sleep inhibition (particularly longer sleep-onset latency) than other types of thought content (Wicklow & Espie, 2000). Haynes et al. (1981) found that experimentally induced cognitive stress actually *decreased* sleep-onset latency among PWI while increasing it among NS. Interpreting this seemingly paradoxical result, the authors suggested that for PWI, the cognitive stress may have actually served a de-arousal function by replacing the more habitual "ruminative cognitive activity, sleep-related thoughts, or attributions of internal causality for sleeping difficulties" (p. 604). Subsequent studies have also found that engagement in an alternative cognitive task (e.g., imagery) is associated with less intrusive mental activity and shorter sleep-onset latency, perhaps by occupying the "cognitive space" otherwise filled by worry and other distressing thought content (Harvey & Payne, 2002, p. 273). Finally, intrusive pre-sleep thoughts may be more or less persistent and thus disruptive depending on the manner in which the person responds to them. Consistent with Wegner's (1989) observations that thought suppression, a form of mental control that involves forcefully trying to stop thoughts, actually increases the frequency of unwanted thoughts, Harvey (2003) found that thought suppression resulted in higher estimated sleep-onset latency and lower reported sleep quality among both PWI and NS. In another study, aggressive suppression, a particularly self-recriminative form of suppression, was more common among PWI and predicted higher insomnia severity (Ree, Harvey, Blake, Tang, & Shawe-Taylor, 2005).

Contemporary cognitive theories of psychopathology rest in large part on the foundation of Aaron Beck's seminal theory (1976) explicating the causal role of core beliefs: deep-seated, implicit schemas about self and the world that underlie more explicit, habitual thinking. In addition to recurrent thought patterns like worrying about sleep, beliefs have also been implicated in the etiology of insomnia, particularly in its chronic form. Morin (1993) contends that PWI "hold more unrealistic expectations about their sleep requirements [and] stronger beliefs about the negative consequences of insomnia" (p. 127), and that their "causal attributions tend to be more external (i.e., insomnia is believed to be the result of a biochemical imbalance) and unstable (i.e., sleep is perceived as uncontrollable and unpredictable)" (p. 53). According to this theory, individuals with insomnia are more likely to believe that sleep must be near optimal in order for daytime functioning to be adequate, interpret flare-ups of sleep difficulty as reflecting a lack or loss of control over sleep, and attribute fluctuations in energy, mood, and performance strictly to sleep disturbance (Harvey, 2002; Morin, 1993). Furthermore, poor sleep may be perceived as a performance failure as well as an unsatisfied need, thereby eroding self-efficacy and contributing to negative expectations of future outcomes (Espie et al., 2006). In addition to unrealistic or negative expectations and causal misattributions, cognitive distortions are thought to operate in insomnia much as they do in other forms of psychopathology. These include magnification and catastrophizing ("if I don't get some sleep I could have a nervous breakdown"), overgeneralization ("I'll never sleep well again"), and dichotomous thinking ("my sleep was horrible"). These "dysfunctional cognitions" are considered to be problematic in leading to performance anxiety, learned helplessness, and further worry (Morin, 1993). Empirically, a measure of such dysfunctional beliefs and attitudes regarding sleep has been associated with insomnia severity (Morin, Vallières, & Ivers, 2007).

Rather than operating in a fragmented manner, the cognitive processes we have just outlined comprise a coordinated pathogenic cycle, one that Wells (2000) has called a cognitive-attentional syndrome. In a "top-down" chain of events, selective attention to threat and distorted perceptions of deficit foster negative, worrisome thinking about sleep, all of which may give rise to or reinforce dysfunctional sleep-related beliefs (Harvey, 2002). Occurring simultaneously is a "bottom-up" sequence, in which such beliefs and consequent worrying jointly promote hypervigilance and confirmatory interpretations of sleep-related events. In most cases of chronic insomnia, these cognitive processes act in tandem with the physiological mechanisms discussed previously to produce a state of elevated anxiety and arousal present in the daytime as well as the pre-sleep period (Harvey, 2002). The entire sequence thus forms a self-reinforcing feedback loop that can progressively worsen, and ultimately, then, the sleep-related worries and dysfunctional beliefs often observed in people with chronic insomnia may act as a self-fulfilling prophecy.

In addition to the cognitive-attentional syndrome, intentional states are also involved in insomnia. The role of intention is emphasized in Espie et al.'s (2006) model, which posits the operation of an attention-intention-effort (A-I-E) pathway. According to the model, a key purpose of attention is to gather the most relevant information in preparation for subsequent goal-directed action; in other words "we attend so that we can intend" (p. 229). Although this process is usually adaptive, in the case of normally automatic physiological functions like sleep, explicit intention appears to be counterproductive: A large body of clinical and experimental evidence has shown that closely monitoring and strongly intending to avoid or produce a physiologically based outcome (e.g., stuttering, blushing, sexual response) generally reduces the very likelihood of the desired outcome (Espie et al., 2006). Extrapolating from this data, Espie et al. (2006) propose that explicit and elevated intention "inhibit[s] the automaticity of normal sleep" (p. 229).

Closely associated with sleep intention is the last component of the A-I-E pathway sleep effort. If intention is "planning mode" then effort is "performance mode" (Espie et al., 2006, p. 235), both of which fall under the umbrella of "trying" to sleep (something normal sleepers do not do). The authors speculate that although attentional and intentional factors are critical, "the lasting damage, resulting in persistent insomnia, may be done when a compelling need to take control and fix the problem develops" (p. 235). Sleep effort encompasses the decidedly maladaptive "safety" behaviors described previously, although they may also include other seemingly benign sleep strategies such as thought management and relaxation techniques. Although some of these strategies might be useful in certain cases, the counterproductive expression of effort involved in these activities may supersede any beneficial effects.

Outside of counterproductive sleep behaviors, the precise mechanisms by which intention and effort interfere with sleep remain to be determined (Espie et al., 2006). Such uncertainty notwithstanding, the absence or removal of explicit intention indeed appears to promote sleep. The ICSD-II (AASM, 2005) reports that individuals with Primary Insomnia often have little difficulty falling asleep in situations in which they do not specifically intend to sleep. Empirical support derives from research on sleep interventions involving paradoxical intention—a therapeutic technique developed by Victor Frankl (1963); in sleep applications, the individual is instructed not to attempt to sleep, but rather, to try to remain passively awake. Paradoxical interventions have demonstrated some effectiveness as an insomnia treatment, and appear to operate by reducing sleep effort as well as performance anxiety (Broomfield & Espie, 2003; Morin et al., 2006).

The A, I, and E processes appear to be mutually reinforcing, such that the entire cycle can become increasingly more entrenched and impactful, thus contributing to escalating sleep impairment and the maintenance of insomnia (Espie et al., 2006). To the extent that sleep intention and effort inhibit sleep, poorer outcomes may result in even further attentional preoccupation and striving to sleep, and thus further sleep dysregulation. Although cognitive factors such as thought patterns and beliefs are often prominent in the clinical picture of insomnia, the A-I-E pathway may constitute the set of pathological processes most uniformly present across cases of primary insomnia, and whether or not it takes hold may strongly influence the course of insomnia following the resolution of a stressor. In other words, whether or not sleep becomes a focus of concerned attention and explicit intention/effort may largely determine whether the acute insomnia remits or becomes chronic (Espie et al., 2006).

## PSYCHODYNAMIC, PERSONALITY, AND AFFECTIVE FACTORS

**Insomnia** Exploration of potential psychodynamic and affective underpinnings of insomnia began with the collection of personality assessment data from persons suffering from insomnia. In a seminal study, Kales, Caldwell, Soldatos, Bixler, and Kales (1983) observed Minnesota Multiphasic Personality Inventory (MMPI) scale elevations among PWI indicative of depression, inhibition of anger, anxiety and rumination, and a preoccupation with health. The authors noted that the resulting personality profiles were relatively homogenous and consistent across a large sample, and suggested a "strong overall pattern of handling conflicts and stresses through an internalization of emotions rather than externalizing behaviors such as projection, acting out, and aggression" (p. 350). In a similar vein, having found that PWI reported being less satisfied and experienced more eating and sleeping problems as children, Healey et al. (1981) posited that this discontent was internalized in health problems rather than expressed in behavioral difficulties. Thus, from such correlational personality and psychosocial data emerged the "internalization hypothesis" (van de Laar, Verbeek, Pevernagie, Aldenkamp, & Overeem, 2010). According to this hypothesis, during waking hours, negative emotions—particularly anger—are suppressed rather than expressed and thus discharged, only to surface later during the pre-sleep period; the result is chronically elevated emotional arousal and concomitant physiological arousal, thus contributing to insomnia (Kales et al., 1983). These dynamics have been described in additional depth:

> During the day, the insomniac typically inhibits, denies, and represses conflicts. At night, however, when there is less external stimulation and distraction, defenses relax and attention is focused internally. Resentments, aggressive thoughts, and sadness begin to break through into consciousness, and as the insomniac actively struggles against the emergence of such negative feelings, sleeplessness worsens. (Kales et al., 1983, p. 28)

The personality patterns observed in the Kales et al. (1983) study have since been replicated (Kalogjera-Sackellares & Cartwright, 1997), and consistent with the model, level of "negative" affect (e.g., anxiety, dysphoria, and anger) has been associated with pre-sleep somatic tension and sleep disturbance (Waters et al., 1993). However, there is little data to directly substantiate the internalization hypothesis (van de Laar et al., 2010).

Other personality traits that have been consistently related to insomnia include perfectionism, neuroticism,[13] and anxiety (van de Laar et al., 2010). Although the nature and extent of such associations remain a matter of debate, these traits might play various mediating roles. One possibility, for example, is that persons with perfectionist tendencies are more likely to be self-critical over a perceived "failure" to sleep, and thus to engage in counterproductive sleep effort (Espie et al., 2006; van de Laar et al., 2010; Vincent & Walker, 2000). In a more generalized pathway, perfectionism, neuroticism, and anxiety may all contribute to a state of heightened physiological, cognitive, and/or emotional arousal. Thus, regardless of the specific causal pathway, certain personality traits may predispose individuals to insomnia (van de Laar et al., 2010). However, differences between PWI and NS on personality measures may also reflect more state-dependent consequences of having insomnia, and other psychopathology comorbid with insomnia (e.g., depression) is a potential confound in the interpretation of this data (van de Laar et al., 2010; Vincent & Walker, 2000).

In a study by Waters et al. (1993), negative affect was associated with pre-sleep mental activity as well as somatic tension, and to this effect, it is possible that emotional arousal may be a cause or consequence (or both) of cognitive arousal. In any case, it is clear that affective and cognitive factors interact in the etiology of insomnia, as implied by the term "excessive *negative* cognitive activity" (Harvey, 2002, p. 871, italics added). Morin (1993) submits that in addition to content, the "affective valence of cognitions . . . is an important mediating factor of insomnia" (p. 53). In other words, the emotional tone and amount of distress associated with certain thoughts may strongly influence the degree to which they are disruptive of sleep. Expectedly, the affective tone of pre-sleep cognitive activity appears to be more negative among PWI than NS (Kuisk, Bertelson, & Walsh, 1989). Although perhaps acting in concert with cognitive arousal as a predisposing factor, emotional arousal is also an important link in the chain of events and psychological responses that perpetuates Primary Insomnia: As noted previously, not falling asleep or waking repeatedly often produces frustration as well as further anxiety about

[13] On the MMPI, neuroticism refers to an enduring tendency to experience negative emotional states.

sleeping, which may incite further counterproductive effort aimed at producing sleep (APA, 2000; Espie et al., 2006; Hirshkowitz et al., 1997).

**Nightmares** As one might expect, psychodynamic theories regarding the etiology of nightmares have been developed. Consistent with his wish-fulfillment theory of dreams, Freud (1920/1961) first suggested that nightmares reflect superego wishes for punishment; however, he later moved away from this view and never provided a comprehensive or influential explanation (Hartmann, 1984). Nevertheless, subsequent accounts of nightmares rest upon the foundational Freudian premise that dreams may contain a recapitulation of the anxieties and emotional conflicts of waking life, "only in a different language—a language of visual imagery" (Yalom, 2002, p. 226). Despite different psychoanalytic theories of nightmares emphasizing different affective and interpersonal dynamics—including guilt and fear of punishment for aggressive impulses—they share the core premise that "the nightmare involves some of the earliest, most profound anxieties" (Hartmann, 1984, p. 47). In this sense, fears often present in childhood and children's nightmares (e.g., fear of abandonment or of physical harm or destruction) seem to re-occur in adult nightmares, even if they appear in different guises (e.g., threat from an army instead of a monster; Hartmann, 1984). Thus, rather than being regressive remnants of a bygone developmental age, such dream content may be more a reflection of universal human anxieties related to the ultimate concerns described by existential thinkers (e.g., fear of death, aloneness, or emptiness; Yalom, 1980). Death anxiety in particular appears to frequently take center stage in nightmares (Yalom, 1980).

Nightmares are not unusual or inherently pathological, although a subset of persons experience them regularly and may suffer extensive consequent distress (APA, 2000; Spoormaker et al., 2006). As with insomnia, researchers have attempted to discern characteristic personality patterns associated with chronic nightmares. Hartmann (1984) found that as a group, persons reporting a lifelong history and frequent occurrence of nightmares exhibited elevations on the "psychotic" scales of the MMPI (including paranoia, psychasthenia,[14] and Schizophrenia), although in contrast to persons with chronic insomnia, they did not display significant elevations on the "neurotic" scales (hysteria, depression, and hypochondriasis). Hartmann (1984) also described other observations from psychometric test results and clinical interviews suggesting that personality features common to persons with chronic nightmares included openness and lack of defensiveness, emotional sensitivity and vulnerability, and artistic tendencies. In conjunction with observed associations between nightmares and Schizophrenia,[15] these findings led him to posit that persons with chronic nightmares have "thin or permeable boundaries": most notably, dreaming/waking, ego, and interpersonal boundaries (p. 104). In other words, according to Hartmann, these persons describe dreams as extremely vivid and real; they tend to freely allow "id" material into consciousness (in contrast to persons suffering from neurotic anxiety, which typically involves overly rigid ego boundaries); and they tend to be extremely

---

[14] The MMPI psychasthenia scale measures the inability to resist certain actions or thoughts, effectively tapping obsessive-compulsive tendencies as well as excessive fears and doubts.

[15] Hartmann (1984) cites evidence that nightmares are more common among persons with Schizophrenia, and are frequently observed in the onset of a psychotic episode.

trusting and unguarded with others. As a result, although these individuals do not appear to be any more likely to have experienced childhood trauma or to be angry, hostile, or anxious, it may be that "normal fears and angers 'get through' more and become more vivid and frightening for them than for most of us" (Hartmann, 1984, p. 105). Hartmann further hypothesized that these diffuse boundaries develop in early childhood as a result of a biological predisposition in combination with environmental influences that are largely unknown, although in keeping with psychoanalytic theory, they are thought to involve aspects of early parental nurturance.

Empirical findings pertaining to nightmares and personality have been somewhat inconclusive. Nevertheless, the preponderance of data has suggested that the frequency of nightmares correlates with general psychopathology, including anxiety and depression, and in contrast to the data cited by Hartmann (1984), with the closely related personality trait of neuroticism (for a review see Spoormaker et al., 2006). Nightmare distress, a measure of the impact of nightmares on daytime functioning, is also associated with neuroticism and may be even more relevant to pathology than nightmare frequency (Kothe & Pietrowsky, 2001). In a study that included multiple trait variables, Schredl (2003) found that although nightmare frequency was indeed related to boundary thinness, the correlation with neuroticism was substantially larger. Furthermore, replicating earlier findings, Schredl (2003) observed that the level of current stress was a robust predictor of nightmare frequency, and that in the aggregate, measures of stress accounted for considerably more variance than did trait variables. The author noted that his findings:

> support the hypothesis that the effects of trait factors are mediated by state factors, i.e., persons with high neuroticism scores experience stress more often and their nightmare frequency is therefore elevated. On the other hand, the strong influence of current stressors supports the general continuity hypothesis of dreaming; nightmares reflect negative waking-life experiences. (p. 246)

## Lower-Right Perspectives

### KEY EPIDEMIOLOGICAL VARIABLES RELATED TO SLEEP DISTURBANCE

**Age and Gender** Reviews of the epidemiological research note that insomnia symptoms (particularly problems with sleep initiation) are consistently found to be more prevalent among women, as are daytime consequences and subjective dissatisfaction with sleep (Ohayon, 2002; Lichstein et al., 2004). Factors that may account for this gender disparity in risk include the higher rate of depression and anxiety among women, sleep disruption consequent to hormonal processes including menstruation and menopause, and various psychosocial events and transitions (e.g., "empty nest," elder caregiving) that have traditionally been more prominent in women's lives (Soares, 2005).

Insomnia (particularly the sleep maintenance type) is also more common in the elderly (Ohayon, 2002). In one recent large-scale and methodologically advanced epidemiological survey (Lichstein et al., 2004), insomnia was both more frequent and more severe in older than younger adults. The same study found that in a "normal" sample (excluding persons with insomnia), increasing age corresponded to a negative change on measures of number of awakenings (NWAK) and wake time (WASO), although also improvement in subjective quality rating (SQR). Furthermore, total sleep time (TST) was lowest in middle age, and steadily increased in later decades

(60s, 70s, and 80s). These results do not support the commonly held belief that a progressive worsening of sleep with aging (at least as subjectively experienced) is normative. Rather, the elevated risk of sleep difficulty and disorder may be largely a by-product of the higher rate of physiological sleep impediments (e.g., apnea) and medical illnesses among elderly adults rather than a result of age-related deterioration in sleep per se (Ohayon, 2002). As a clinical corollary, sleep complaints should be treated with equal concern among younger and older persons (Reite et al., 2009).

**Race/Ethnicity** Research examining racial and ethnic differences in sleep disturbance has primarily compared the sleep of Black or African Americans and Caucasians. In the Lichstein et al. (2004) study, the rate of insomnia was nearly identical, although its severity was higher in the former group. In the 2010 Sleep in America Poll (NSF, 2010), a similar percentage (around 20%) of Caucasians and Black Americans reported being given a sleep-related diagnosis by a doctor.

On the other hand, in the same poll, Black Americans reported significantly shorter average sleep durations than Caucasians and were significantly more likely to report having obtained less than 6 hours of sleep (which, as discussed, is associated with increased mortality), a finding echoed in another large survey (Hale & Do, 2007). Although results have not been entirely consistent, multiple self-report and home-based PSG studies have observed higher sleep-onset latency as well as lower sleep duration, continuity/efficiency, and amount of slow-wave sleep among African Americans (Hall et al., 2009; Lichstein et al., 2004; Mezick et al., 2008). Data pertaining to the sleep of other racial/ethnic groups is currently insufficient to draw reliable inferences, although in the 2010 NSF poll, Asian Americans reported better sleep than any other racial/ethnic group and half the rate of sleep-disorder diagnosis.[16] Hispanic Americans reported poorer sleep than did Caucasians, although they had about the same prevalence of diagnosis.

**SES and Implications for Racial/Ethnic Sleep Differences** Epidemiological research has supported an association between sleep—in terms of insomnia symptoms and sleep quality—and socioeconomic status (SES)—as measured by education and income—after accounting for age, gender, and ethnicity (Gellis et al., 2005; Mezick et al., 2008). It should be noted, however, that observed correlations between SES and sleep variables have generally been modest and results somewhat inconsistent, attesting to the complexity of these constructs and their interaction (Ohayon, 2002). Nevertheless, several factors have been proposed to account for a possible causal influence of SES on sleep; there is some preliminary support for the role of financial strain, negative affect, and environmental conditions (e.g., noise and room temperature) in mediating the association between SES and sleep quality (Hall et al., 2009; Mezick et al., 2008). The increased financial strain and perhaps other stressors concomitant to low-SES may act through cognitive (e.g., worry), affective (e.g., anxiety, depression), and/or physiological (e.g., somatic tension) pathways to disturb sleep (Hall et al., 2009). Adverse environmental conditions such as noise and heat would disturb sleep primarily by inciting autonomic arousal (Espie, 2002).

---

[16] This lower rate of diagnosis among Asian Americans may be partly attributable to their lower reported frequency of being asked about or discussing sleep problems with a doctor (NSF, 2010).

It has been hypothesized that systemic disparities in SES associated with race/ethnicity may explain the observed differences in sleep between African Americans and Caucasians (Mezick et al., 2008). One study found that SES and residing in an inner city attenuated the association between race/ethnicity and high-risk sleep duration (Hale & Do, 2007). Furthermore, consistent with SES and related health disparities, in a recent NSF poll (2010) Black and Hispanic Americans were nearly twice as likely as Caucasian and Asian Americans to report that personal financial concerns, employment concerns, and health-related concerns disturbed their sleep, although they were no more likely to report that relationship concerns did so. On the other hand, studies have reported race/ethnicity effects on multiple sleep measures that were independent of SES (Hall et al., 2009; Mezick et al., 2008). Considering the limited and inconsistent findings, at this point "the degree to which race and SES uniquely contribute to dimensions of sleep remains uncertain" (Mezick et al., 2008, p. 410).

**Other Institutional and Societal Influences on Sleep** Average sleep time in the United States, recently estimated at 6.7 hours,[17] has dwindled in recent years, while the prevalence of sleep problems seems to have increased (NSF, 2009, p. 45). Although there are undoubtedly myriad reasons for this trend, several institutional and societal factors may be implicated. In particular, the decline in employment and financial security associated with national and global economic instability may be contributing to sleep disruption through psychological stress (which, as discussed, may precipitate insomnia): In the 2009 Sleep in America poll, more than a quarter of respondents reported losing sleep due to financial, employment, or other economically related concerns (NSF, 2009, p. 17). Furthermore, general work-related demands on time have significant implications for insufficient sleep syndrome[18] and excessive daytime sleepiness. In recent years, the number of people reporting a sleep duration of less than 6 hours per night on weekdays has increased substantially (from 13–20%; NSF, 2009, p. 8), with around 25% now stating that their work schedule does not allow for sufficient sleep (NSF, 2010, p. 23). Specific occupational stressors associated with insomnia onset and maintenance include conflicts with supervisors or other persons, perceived demandingness and workload, and low influence over decisions (Bastien et al., 2004; Jansson & Linton, 2006). Shochat (2012) notes that flexible, compressed, and irregular work schedules appear to be increasingly common in the global economy, although they may be detrimental to sleep quality and other indices of workers' health (Martens, Nijhuis, Van Boxtel, & Knottnerus, 1999).

Finally, sleep disruption may be partly endemic to a high-tech, "24-7" society in which information and communications technology (ICT) and entertainment media are ever more prominent and accessible. Use of these devices may be siphoning hours that might be otherwise devoted to sleep. In addition, such devices tend to be mentally alerting, particularly when their use is interactive in nature, and pre-sleep exposure to

---

[17] Sufficient sleep duration is estimated by experts to be between 7 and 9 hours a night, depending on the individual.

[18] Insufficient sleep syndrome, although not a formal diagnosis, is a clinical term referring to cases in which an individual is excessively restricting his or her sleep time, usually on account of social and occupational obligations, resulting in daytime sleepiness (Reite et al., 2009). A diagnosis of insomnia requires that the disturbance occur despite adequate opportunity to sleep.

the artificial light they emit has the potential to delay the circadian rhythm and inhibit secretion of the hormone melatonin, thereby interfering with sleep (Shochat, 2012). Finally, sedentariness associated with excessive use of technology might contribute to the development of obesity and thus to risk of sleep apnea or a related disorder in children or adults (Shochat, 2012). In recognition of these trends and concerns, the sleep-related effects of technology use have attracted increased research attention in recent years. In a recent Sleep in America poll (NSF, 2011), majorities of respondents reported using various technological devices in the hour before sleep, including watching television, playing video games, or using cell phones, computers, or laptops. Research has consistently demonstrated that among children and adolescents, greater exposure to electronic media (e.g., television, video games) is associated with later bedtime and shorter sleep duration (Shochat, 2012). Findings as to similar connections with adults are more preliminary, but studies conducted in various countries have reported associations between heavy ICT/media use and poor sleep habits (Brunborg et al., 2011), self-reported insufficient sleep and shorter sleep duration (Suganuma et al., 2007), and certain symptoms of sleep disturbance (Thomée, Eklöf, Gustafsson, Nilsson, & Hagberg, 2007). Many other associations examined in these studies were statistically insignificant, and the clinical significance of the findings remains to be seen. Nevertheless, ICT/media use is increasingly being recognized as a public health concern related to sleep.

## Lower-Left Perspectives

**PSYCHOSOCIAL FACTORS AND SLEEP** As noted previously, the onset of insomnia is associated with psychosocial stressors, particularly interpersonal losses and conflicts (Bastien et al., 2004; Healey et al., 1981). Although potentially including any factors related to social functioning, the relational influence on sleep begins with the family. Consistent with a family systems model, parental variables (e.g., maternal depression, father absence) and parent–child interaction variables (e.g., general closeness/conflict and behavioral practices) have been implicated in children's sleep problems (Bell & Belsky, 2008; Reite et al., 2009). Furthermore, the influence of the family of origin appears to extend into adolescence and young adulthood: In one study, the combination of family-related and academic stress predicted higher rates of insomnia in a college population, whereas this effect was not observed for peer-related social stress (Bernert, Merrill, Braithwaite, Van Orden, & Joiner, 2007). In addition, family conflict in childhood was found to predict insomnia at age 18 after controlling for several variables; it was hypothesized that family conflict may create an enduring predisposition to sleep disturbance by inducing a greater tendency toward vigilance and worry or by leading to poor sleep hygiene (Gregory, Caspi, Moffitt, & Poulton, 2006). In a more direct precipitating capacity, familial events commonly cited by patients as being related to the onset of their insomnia include separation/divorce, marital problems, the illness or death of a family member, and the birth of a child (Bastien et al., 2004). Presumably, their disruptive effects on sleep would be mediated by the degree of subjective stress and corresponding physiological, cognitive, and emotional arousal. Importantly, social influence on sleep is by no means strictly pathogenic. For example, social support may protect against or mitigate the impact of sleep disorders such as Insomnia Disorder and Narcolepsy (Alaia, 1992; Jansson & Linton, 2006).

**CULTURAL FACTORS AND SLEEP** Intersubjective attitudes and beliefs may also serve as either pathogenic or protective influences on sleep. In a sociocultural context of ever busier lives—in which time seems to be an increasingly rare commodity, and productivity an ever more important value—sleep in excess of the bare necessity may be perceived as unaffordable or relatively expendable (the "I can sleep when I'm dead" mentality). In a similar vein, inadequate or disturbed sleep may be viewed as inevitable or trivial, and as a corollary, undeserving of professional help. For example, in the 2009 NSF poll, "accept it and keep going" was the most commonly reported coping response to daytime sleepiness (p. 23). In some social circles, functioning on little sleep may even be viewed positively—as an indication of industriousness and fortitude (Turek, 2005). A combination of such values and attitudes likely undergirds a "prevailing culture of sleepiness" that, although prominent in the Western societal milieu, seems to be particularly pronounced in the military, in certain business fields, and in medical training (Turek, 2005, p. 798). On a contrasting note, Sleep in America poll data (NSF, 2010) attest to a widespread belief that inadequate sleep has significant social, occupational, and health consequences, which would seem to be an important motivator of good sleep hygiene as well as help seeking for sleep problems. Although generalizations are useful in certain respects, it is important to note that attitudes pertaining to sleep as well as meanings ascribed to sleep disturbance likely vary across cultures (APA, 2000; NSF, 2010). At this point, however, relevant data are extremely limited.

## Summary of the Etiology of Insomnia

We have reviewed several predisposing factors involved in the etiology of insomnia, including what appear to be trait-like tendencies toward greater physiological, cognitive, and emotional arousal, particularly in response to stress. A related but somewhat divergent account has been proposed by Waters et al. (1993), who found that although PWI and NS did not differ on measures of self-reported affect, stress response, or attentional arousal, these factors were more strongly correlated with sleep variables in the former group; this observation lead the authors to posit that persons with insomnia "may have a sleep-wake system that is less robust against disruptions from emotion, stress, or novel stimuli" (p. 134). Whatever their exact nature, the phenotypic factors corresponding to a greater susceptibility to insomnia have likely resulted from an interplay of genetic and biological constitution in conjunction with formative personal experiences and environmental influences. In addition, there appears to be some differential risk of insomnia associated with demographic characteristics including age, gender, race/ethnicity, and social class. Although perhaps attributable in part to certain biological differences, elevated risk may be more a matter of disproportionate exposure to health, financial, psychosocial, and environmental stressors. As discussed, the actual onset of acute insomnia[19] is typically precipitated by such stressors, although "the severity and impact of events may need to be greater . . . in the absence of predisposing factors" (Espie, 2002, p. 219).

---

[19] Short-term, transient insomnia occurring in response to identifiable stressors is known in the ICSD-II as adjustment insomnia (AASM, 2005).

Finally, in some cases insomnia persists and becomes chronic despite the disappearance of the original precipitating conditions;[20] put differently, "insomnia may become independent of or functionally autonomous from its origins" (Morin, 1993, p. 47). To this effect, consensus holds that perpetuating factors are almost always involved in the development and maintenance of chronic insomnia (Espie, 2002; Morin, 1993). This may be the case even when stress is contributing to sleep disturbance on an ongoing basis, as one study found that dysfunctional sleep-related cognitions mediated much of the relationship between stress and insomnia (Brand, Gerber, Puhse, & Holsboer-Trachsler, 2010). Perpetuating factors implicated in the etiology of insomnia include elevated intention ("hyperintention"), various cognitive content and processes (e.g., selective attention and implicit vigilance, sleep-related worries and other intrusive thoughts, and dysfunctional beliefs), associational learning (conditioning), and counterproductive behaviors. Individually and in combination, these factors incite further physiological, cognitive, and emotional arousal and disrupt what is normally an automatic sleep process (involving a conditioned sleep response, pre-sleep de-arousal process, and relatively effortless behavioral enactment; Espie, 2002). Although integrative models of insomnia (Espie, 2002; Harvey, 2002; Morin, 1993) differ in the degree of emphasis they place on various contributing intentional, cognitive, and behavioral factors, all of them stress that these processes tend to be mutually reinforcing, thereby increasing in their intensity and impact (see Figure 11.1). Clinically speaking, therefore, a vicious cycle often develops in which hyperintention and related

| UPPER-LEFT (UL): INTERIOR-INDIVIDUAL | UPPER-RIGHT (UR): EXTERIOR-INDIVIDUAL |
|---|---|
| • Selective attention to threat-related stimuli<br>• Cognitive arousal (i.e., worry)<br>• Dysfunctional sleep-related beliefs<br>• Hyperintention<br>• Emotional arousal<br>• Anticipatory/performance anxiety | • Genetic predisposition<br>• Elevated physiological arousal and stress system reactivity (somatic, neurological, endocrine)<br>• Conditioned arousal<br>• Compensatory behaviors<br>• Medical and other psychological disorders |
| **LOWER-LEFT (LL): INTERIOR-COLLECTIVE** | **LOWER-RIGHT (LR): EXTERIOR-COLLECTIVE** |
| • Psychosocial stressors including losses and conflicts<br>• Cultural attitudes and perceptions (e.g., sleep deprivation as unavoidable or even praiseworthy; ample sleep as a luxury)<br>• Popular cultural practice of medicating sleepiness with large quantities of caffeine | • Precipitating and aggravating role of stressors/stressful events<br>• Disproportionate exposure to stressors (e.g., financial) and sleep-inhibiting environmental conditions (e.g., heat, noise) associated with certain low-SES contexts<br>• Occupational demands on time, nontraditional work hours<br>• Widespread nighttime use of ICT/media |

**FIGURE 11.1** A Quadratic Summary of the Etiology of Insomnia

[20] In this case the condition is known in the ICSD-II as psychophysiologic insomnia (AASM, 2005).

counterproductive behavior leads to adverse sleep outcomes, in turn causing hyperarousal and additional intention/effort, which further inhibits sleep (APA, 2000). The perception and experience of sleep loss feeds into the cognitive-attentional syndrome by reinforcing dysfunctional beliefs about sleep and inciting further vigilance and worry (Harvey, 2002). Thus, it becomes clear how insomnia may take a progressive course, escalating in severity and chronicity. Finally, although psychobiological and psychosocial processes comprise the principal and immediate causes of insomnia, we have also outlined several sociocultural and institutional norms and trends that may bear upon collective vulnerability to insomnia and inadequate sleep. Further research is needed to substantiate the role of these contextual factors.

It is crucial to note that the cumulative operation of these processes may, over time, produce a very real and disruptive sleep deficit. For the most part, however, the serious consequences of sleep loss for health and functioning outlined previously are cumulative effects resulting from chronic disturbance and disorder; homeostatic mechanisms normally compensate for more acute and transient sleep disruption. Thus although they are not entirely baseless or irrational, the sleep-related concerns of PWI tend to be somewhat distorted and ultimately maladaptive: Exaggerated perceptions of the day-to-day consequences of sleep disruption as well as internal causal attributions (e.g., performance failure, a serious underlying medical disorder) amplify associated distress and further intensify sleep-inhibiting arousal (Harvey, 2002).

## Insomnia and Comorbid Conditions

Comorbidity between sleep disturbance and other psychopathological symptoms and disorders has been extensively documented (Ford & Kamerow, 1989; Lichstein et al. 2004; NSF, 2009; van Mill, Hoogendijk, Vogelzangs, van Dyck, & Penninx, 2010). The DSM-5 (APA, 2013) reports that another mental disorder is present in 40–50% of cases of insomnia. Research evidence and clinical observation suggests a bidirectional relationship: Having insomnia substantially increases the risk of developing major depression and anxiety disorders (Ford & Kamerow, 1989), and conversely, disturbed sleep is a common feature of these conditions (Ohayon & Roth, 2003; Reite et al., 2009). Furthermore, sleep disturbance is increasingly considered to be a central feature (rather than secondary symptom) of PTSD (Spoormaker & Montgomery, 2008). In the case of depression, different sleep problems have been associated with different subtypes: Early morning awakening is considered to be a symptomatic feature of the melancholic depression subtype, and hypersomnia, of the atypical type (APA, 2013). Although insomnia and mood and anxiety symptoms frequently arise contemporaneously, insomnia is more likely to precede the onset of mood disorders and to follow the onset of anxiety disorders (Ohayon & Roth, 2003).

Regarding etiology, certain causal processes appear to be common to insomnia both with and without comorbid depression or anxiety, and these common processes may account for much of the relationship between insomnia and other mental health conditions. For example, one study found that after controlling for levels of stress and dysfunctional sleep-related cognitions, depression and insomnia were only weakly associated (Brand et al., 2010). Furthermore, stress system hyperactivity may be a predisposing and perpetuating factor common to both insomnia and depression (Stepanski & Rybarczyk, 2006). It is also possible that insomnia both with and without comorbid depression or anxiety result from the operation of similar processes, but to different degrees. For example, to the extent it is present in cases of Primary Insomnia, anxiety is more likely to occur in the form of anticipatory anxiety about sleep (i.e., anxiety about "failing" to sleep and the consequences thereof), whereas in insomnia comorbid with anxiety, it is likely to be more generalized and may be even more impactful. Consistent with this premise, in one study "Individuals with insomnia comorbid with [generalized anxiety disorder] reported greater presleep cognitive arousal than individuals with insomnia alone, who in turn reported greater cognitive arousal than good sleepers" (Belanger, Morin, Gendron, & Blais, 2005, p. 19). There may also be some trenchant differences in the etiology of primary versus comorbid insomnia; for example, preliminary data pertaining to family history suggest the possibility that genetics are more influential in the former than the latter (Dauvilliers et al., 2005b).

## INSOMNIA: A CASE STUDY

Luis is a 19-year old Dominican American college student who is 2 months in to his first semester at a highly selective private university in the Northeast. Luis reports that over the past few months he has experienced difficulty sleeping, which has gotten worse over the past few weeks. He says that he sometimes lies awake for about 45 minutes before falling asleep. Luis also states that although he rarely wakes up in the middle of the night, his sleep feels "restless" with lots of "tossing and turning," and he often wakes up in the morning still feeling fatigued. Luis reports experiencing trouble falling asleep or poor quality sleep about 4 to 5 nights per week. He states that he often feels sleepy during the day, and sometimes has trouble completing his schoolwork as a result. He adds that recently he's been finding himself worrying, sometimes while lying in bed, about not having enough energy for his daily activities, stating "I'm tired like all the time, and without being at 100% I don't know how I'm gonna be able to get everything done." Luis mentions that because of this concern, he often goes to bed early to "catch up" on his sleep and also tries to sleep in on weekends. Luis reports that he had no difficulty sleeping in high school, but recalls occasional difficulty sleeping as a younger child.

Luis' family resides in a lower-income urban community in the New York metropolitan area, his parents having immigrated to the United States a few years before he was born. In the Dominican Republic his mother was a schoolteacher and his father was training to become an engineer. After moving to the United States his father eventually found work in construction, and his mother works in the local middle school as an educational aide. Luis has an older brother and two younger sisters. He is the first in his family to go to college, which he says he's been motivated to do since his first year of high school. Luis reports that his parents have been very encouraging and supportive of this goal, but he mentions that his older brother, who also works in construction, often teases him, saying, "why do you want to be a poor college kid? Stay here and I'll get you a job so you can make some bucks." Although Luis received a partial merit-based scholarship, his parents have taken out sizeable loans to fund the remainder of the cost. Despite his expressions of concern about the expense, his parents have insisted that he go to college, saying, "that's why we came here." Luis reports that 2 weeks ago, his mother was laid off from her job as a result of public education cuts. His parents have repeatedly reassured him that they can still pay for his college, mentioning that his brother has been making good money lately and has been able to help out a bit with the family bills.

Luis says that although he's used to working hard and received straight A's in high school, college classes are much more difficult, "like getting up to the big leagues." He mentions that he started strong, but his grades have dipped a bit to the low B range following midterms. He says that he studied for his exams but that he "should have worked harder," although fatigue did make it difficult to study as much as he wanted to. Luis reports that he is undecided about his major, and lately has been seeing the career services office to "try to figure that out." He says he's made some friends, but also mentions feeling that in many of his classes he sticks out as "the Hispanic kid." He says he's attended a few meetings of the Latino student organization and has "met some cool people there," although "some of them are way more into the Latino thing than I am." He says that he hasn't had the time to attend many meetings or other social events, as he works part-time as part of his financial package. At one point Luis states "I've got a lot on my mind."

## TREATMENT OF SLEEP DISORDERS: AN OVERVIEW

The treatment of sleep disorders encompasses a range of modalities, both physiological and psychological in nature. Treatment indication and selection depends on a variety of factors, including the nature of the sleep complaint or diagnosis, the presumed etiology, the client's preferences, and the nature of the treatment setting (Reite et al., 2009).

### Treatment of Insomnia

**PSYCHOLOGICAL AND BEHAVIORAL TREATMENTS** Cognitive-behavioral therapy for insomnia (CBTI) has accumulated extensive empirical support (Morin et al., 2006; Morin et al., 2009) and is steadily gaining recognition as the optimal first-line treatment for chronic insomnia.[21] CBTI, which is typically delivered over four to seven sessions in individual or group formats, has been shown to provide acute symptom relief comparable to that observed with pharmacotherapy; however, its benefits are far more likely to be sustained following discontinuation of active treatment (Morin et al., 2009; National Institutes of Health, 2005). The preponderance of evidence suggests that CBTI is effective for older as well as younger and middle-aged adults (Sivertsen et al., 2006; Irwin, Cole, & Nicassio, 2006), and for both primary and comorbid insomnia (Edinger et al., 2009).

Cognitive work in CBTI attempts to correct misconceptions and facilitate more adaptive beliefs about sleep, in order to normalize periodic sleep disruption, generate more realistic perceptions of its consequences, and increase perceived control (Morin, 1993; Morin et al., 2009). The major objective of this cognitive restructuring is to break the vicious cycle described previously by reducing sleep-related anxiety and associated arousal (Morin, 1993). CBTI also incorporates several behavioral

[21] For a description of a structured treatment procedure see Morin (1993).

techniques: Stimulus control and sleep restriction, both of which have been shown to be efficacious (Morin et al., 2006), are procedures that target conditioning processes and sleep habits (also known as "sleep hygiene"). The goal of the former is to "re-establish or strengthen the associations between sleep and the stimulus conditions under which it typically occurs" (Morin, 1993, p. 115). Accordingly, individuals are encouraged to maintain a more regular sleep schedule (especially waking at a consistent time), generally avoid napping during the day, use the bed/bedroom only for sleep and sex, and avoid retiring when not sleepy or lying awake in bed (rather, to leave bed after 10–20 minutes and return only when sleepy; Morin, 1993; Morin et al., 2009; Reite et al., 2009). Sleep restriction is a common intervention that decreases total time in bed (for example, to an initial duration of 5 hours) in order to improve sleep efficiency and quality within that time; the increased homeostatic sleep pressure accompanying restriction typically results in decreased sleep fragmentation, and as sleep efficiency increases, duration is gradually expanded (Spielman, Saskin, & Thorpy, 1987). Although the technique is helpful for most people, increased daytime sleepiness in the early stages of the intervention poses a challenge to treatment adherence and success (Morin, 1993; Spielman et al., 1987). CBTI also commonly includes psycho-education aimed at promoting sleep hygiene. Patients learn how to create an optimal sleep environment (reducing light, heat, and noise, for example) and make lifestyle adjustments such as reducing caffeine and nicotine consumption, engaging in regular exercise, and avoiding work or other alerting activities too close to bedtime (Morin & Benca, 2009; Reite et al., 2009).

Despite its demonstrated effectiveness, the availability of CBTI as a treatment option is often limited. Accordingly, the aforementioned cognitive, behavioral, and psycho-educational interventions are often utilized outside of a formal CBTI program and can be incorporated into a variety of treatment settings including primary care (Edinger & Sampson, 2003). Relaxation-based interventions are also utilized for the treatment of insomnia. Morin and Benca (2009) note that "some methods (e.g., progressive muscle relaxation) focus primarily on reducing somatic arousal (e.g., muscle tension), whereas attention-focusing procedures (e.g., imagery training, meditation) target mental arousal in the form of worries, intrusive thoughts, or a racing mind" (p. 366). Mindfulness-based stress reduction (MBSR) has also been applied to the treatment of chronic insomnia, and although the extant findings have been somewhat inconsistent (Winbush, Gross, & Kreitzer, 2007), a recent randomized clinical trial (RCT) observed robust effects of MBSR on insomnia symptoms and overall sleep quality (Gross et al., 2011). For acute insomnia linked to identifiable stressors, clinical attention will likely be focused on facilitating coping and the resolution of associated concerns, although it may also be useful to directly address sleep-related symptoms by promoting sleep hygiene, teaching de-arousal strategies, or employing more formal behavioral strategies like sleep restriction (Reite et al., 2009).

### PHARMACOLOGICAL TREATMENTS

**Nonbenzodiazepine and Benzodiazepine Hypnotics** In most cases, pharmacotherapy for insomnia will entail treatment with nonbenzodiazepine hypnotics (often called "Z-drugs;" Wilson et al., 2010). Examples include Zaleplon (Sonata), Zolpidem (Ambien), and Eszopiclone (Lunesta). The short-term efficacy of nonbenzodiazepine hypnotics is well established, although unlike with CBTI, the effects are not typically sustained following discontinuation (Jacobs, Pace-Schott, Stickgold, & Otto, 2004). Evidence for the effectiveness of long-term use is still limited, although several controlled trials have provided support for the safety and potency of treatment with certain hypnotics for periods of 6 to 12 months (Krystal, Erman, Zammit, Soubrane, & Roth, 2008; Roth, Walsh, Krystal, Wessel, & Roehrs, 2005). Research has generally found minimal rebound effects or withdrawal symptoms with these hypnotics (Krystal et al., 2008; Roehrs, Randall, Harris, Mann, & Roth, 2012), and therefore they are typically considered preferable to benzodiazepine hypnotics, at least as first-line treatments (Reite et al., 2009). Benzodiazepines have sedative, hypnotic, anxiolytic, and anticonvulsant properties (Reite et al., 2009). Newer-generation benzodiazepines approved for the treatment of insomnia include triazolam (Halcion), Temazepam (Restoril), and Estazolam (ProSom). They are generally effective in inducing and maintaining sleep on an acute basis; however, there are serious drawbacks to the use of these drugs, including changes in sleep architecture (e.g., decreased SWS), a high potential for dependence, tolerance and associated rebound insomnia, and adverse withdrawal effects (Morin & Benca, 2009). Consequently, benzodiazepines are most appropriate to cases of acute insomnia comorbid with anxiety disorders (Reite et al., 2009).

Common side effects of both classes of hypnotics include "hangover" (lingering sedation and accompanying cognitive and psychomotor impairment) as well as "anterograde amnesia, a loss of memory for events that occur after taking a hypnotic" (Morin & Benca, 2009, p. 372). Various hypnotic drugs differ in their pharmacologic properties, including rate of absorption and half-life, and are thus more or less suitable depending on the insomnia complaint (sleep onset or sleep maintenance) and the degree of residual next-day sedation that is tolerable (Reite et al., 2009). Consideration of this side effect takes on added importance in the hypnotic treatment of insomnia among older adults, as resulting psychomotor impairment may increase the risk of falls, and thus hypnotics with a shorter half-life are generally preferable for this population. In general, the risk of adverse effects associated with hypnotics increases with the duration of treatment; thus, "as-needed," intermittent (non-nightly) dosing, already a common patient practice, may provide the necessary treatment effects while reducing risk (Krystal et al., 2008). Nevertheless, on account of the risks associated with hypnotics, CBTI or other non-pharmacological interventions should be strongly considered, and although medication should not be withheld in appropriate cases, an effort should be made to determine the lowest effective dose and duration of use (Reite et al., 2009).

In recognition of the long-term benefits of cognitive-behavioral intervention and the practicality and short-term utility of medication, the relative effectiveness and optimal delivery of combined pharmacotherapy and CBT for insomnia has been the focus of much recent investigation. As summarized by Morin et al. (2009), "combined CBT and medication appears to have a slight advantage over a single-treatment modality during the initial course of treatment, but their long-term effects are more variable across patients" (p. 2006). In a recent large-scale RCT (Morin et al., 2009), the addition of medication to CBTI resulted in improved outcomes relative to CBTI alone, but the best long-term outcomes occurred when medication was discontinued prior to an extended treatment phase that included maintenance CBT. In another study of individuals with both insomnia and major depression, CBTI plus medication resulted in a higher rate of both depression and insomnia remission relative to antidepressant medication alone (Manber et al., 2008).

**Other Pharmacological Agents** Antidepressants with sedating properties are frequently prescribed ("off label") for insomnia. Trazodone in particular is one of the most widely prescribed drugs for insomnia (Morin & Benca, 2009), despite a relative lack of efficacy data (Reite et al., 2009). Reasons for their use include concerns about the side effects and long-term effects of hypnotics, as well as a desire to simultaneously address comorbid symptoms such as depressed mood (Morin & Benca, 2009). Exogenous administration of melatonin, a natural hormone secreted by the pineal gland that plays a role in the regulation of the circadian rhythm, is indicated for the treatment of insomnia in certain populations. Specifically, there is considerable evidence to suggest the safety and effectiveness of melatonin in the treatment of chronic and idiopathic sleep-onset insomnia in children with Attention-Deficit Hyperactivity Disorder (ADHD; Bendz & Scates, 2010) and Autism Spectrum Disorders (Guénolé et al., 2011). In addition, prolonged-release melatonin has been shown to reduce sleep-onset latency and improve sleep quality and morning alertness among insomnia patients over age 55 (Luthringer, Muzet, Zisapel, & Staner, 2009; Wade et al., 2007). Although melatonin may not have the same potency as hypnotics, the lack of residual psychomotor impairment makes it a promising addition to the pharmacological treatment repertoire in this population (Wilson et al., 2010).

Self-medication of insomnia with alcohol and with over-the-counter (OTC) sleep aids is common (NSF, 2010; Ohayon, 2002). OTC agents almost invariably contain antihistamines such as diphenhydramine (Benadryl) or doxylamine succinate (Unisom). Although antihistamines are sedating, tolerance to their effects appears to develop rapidly, and therefore these drugs are likely to be useful only for brief periods of time (Morin & Benca, 2009). Herbal remedies such as valerian root may promote sleep for some people, and particularly in more transient and mild cases, although most have not been systematically investigated (Reite et al., 2009).

## Treatment of Other Sleep Disorders

**CIRCADIAN RHYTHM SLEEP DISORDERS** Circadian Rhythm Sleep Disorders are commonly treated with melatonin supplementation and timed exposure to bright light, as well as behavioral strategies for regulation of the sleep–wake cycle (Reite et al., 2009). Although findings have been somewhat inconsistent and the optimal dosage and timing have not been firmly established, the preponderance of evidence suggests that melatonin is effective in altering the circadian sleep rhythm (Zee & Manthena, 2007). For the treatment of delayed sleep phase disorder (thus, to advance the sleep phase), melatonin is administered in the evening, several hours before the desired bedtime. Light, in the form of sunlight or artificial bright light generated by a light box, is ideally administered in the morning following the point of lowest body temperature and should be reduced in the evening (Reite et al., 2009). The opposite approach would be taken for persons with an excessively advanced sleep phase and for sleep problems related to night shift work.

**NARCOLEPSY AND HYPERSOMNIA** Pharmacological agents commonly used in the treatment of Narcolepsy include modafinil, methylphenidate, and other stimulants to combat daytime sleepiness as well as antidepressants for cataplexy and REM sleep symptoms. Sodium oxybate (Xyrem), a central nervous system depressant taken at night, may be an effective across-the-board treatment, but its administration is complicated and it has a high potential for abuse (Reite et al., 2009). Stimulants may also be used to treat daytime sleepiness associated with idiopathic hypersomnia, although their effectiveness is not well established (Reite et al., 2009).

**PARASOMNIAS** There are few controlled clinical trials evaluating the efficacy of treatment interventions for the parasomnias (Harris & Grunstein, 2009). With respect to disorders of arousal, first-line intervention involves ensuring that the sleep environment is as safe as possible should an episode occur, as well as psycho-education and behavioral coaching to help the patient minimize exposure to known triggers (e.g., alcohol and other drugs, stress) and maintain a consistent sleep–wake schedule that affords adequate total sleep time (Wilson et al., 2010). More serious cases may call for pharmacotherapy, typically consisting of treatment with benzodiazepines such as clonazepam, and antidepressants such as imipramine or paroxetine (Harris & Grunstein, 2009). Clonazepam, melatonin, and other pharmacological agents may be attempted in the treatment of Nightmare Disorder and REM Sleep Behavior Disorder; conversely, nightmares and other symptoms may be aggravated by many common medications, including SSRIs, cholinesterase inhibitors, and beta-blockers (Reite et al., 2009; Wilson et al., 2010).

Psychological treatments that have been applied to the treatment of parasomnias include hypnotherapy and various cognitive-behavioral interventions. As a treatment for nightmares and sleep terrors, hypnotherapy has garnered considerable empirical support, and for a subset of afflicted individuals may provide long-term symptom reduction following just one or two sessions (Hauri, Silber, & Boeve, 2007). Nightmares, including those associated with trauma, have also been treated successfully with imagery rehearsal therapy (IRT), a cognitive-behavioral intervention in which the individual composes a new, nondistressing version of the dream (also known as "rescripting") and rehearses the associated imagery (Germain & Nielsen, 2003; Krakow & Zadra, 2006). Various forms of exposure and desensitization techniques as well as relaxation training have long been utilized in the treatment of nightmares (Miller & DiPilato, 1983), and a multi-component CBT intervention incorporating several of these techniques has been shown to be efficacious in the treatment of chronic nightmares among trauma-exposed adults (Davis et al., 2011).

**BREATHING-RELATED SLEEP DISORDERS** The treatment repertoire for Obstructive Sleep Apnea and other Breathing-Related Sleep Disorders includes behavioral interventions, medical devices, and surgery. Behavioral strategies include, where indicated, weight loss (which often has a considerable impact in reducing the frequency and severity of apneic events; Guilleminault & Zupancic, 2009), changing sleep position (e.g., from back to side), and avoiding smoking as well as the consumption of respiratory depressants (e.g., alcohol and sedatives), all of which can aggravate the condition (Reite et al., 2009). Medical treatment typically involves the use of a continuous positive airway pressure (CPAP) device, a small bedside machine that delivers airflow by way of a facemask and keeps airways open. Once titrated, standard CPAP devices maintain a uniform pressure. However, newer bilevel devices (BIPAP) maintain different inspiration and expiration pressures and adjust airflow depending on the individual's breathing, which can lower resistance to exhalation, increase comfort, and allow for the minimum effective breathing rate (Guilleminault & Zupancic, 2009). CPAP treatment is usually effective in improving sleep quality, continuity, and daytime wakefulness. Common side effects include nasal congestion, irritation, or dryness; runny nose; and skin discomfort, although they typically abate after a few months (Guilleminault & Zupancic, 2009). Nevertheless, "many patients have difficulty tolerating CPAP, and published compliance rates are approximately 50%–80%" (Reite et al., 2009, p. 234). As such, follow-up and support are critical.

Surgical approaches include the original technique, tracheostomy, which opens an airway in the trachea; the more common uvulopalatopharyngoplasty (UPPP), which excises tissue from the throat; and the most comprehensive, maxillomandibular advancement (MMA), which repositions the jaw. Surgery is most often utilized in more severe cases, as it is more risky and costly, and is not guaranteed to be effective. Success rates vary, from around 50% in UPPP to upwards of 90% with MMA (Guilleminault & Zupancic, 2009; Reite et al., 2009). Tonsillectomy is often indicated in cases of pediatric Obstructive Sleep Apnea (Guilleminault & Zupancic, 2009).

## Conclusion

Our understanding of sleep continues to expand into uncharted territory, and yet multiple mysteries remain. For example, what accounts for the sometimes-considerable disparity between objective and subjective reports of insomnia? What are the precise causes of Narcolepsy, hypersomnia, and the parasomnias? Furthermore, despite advancing scientific and clinical knowledge, the majority of sleep disorders still go undiagnosed and untreated (Colten & Altevogt, 2006). Another challenge is that different sleep disorders often exhibit considerable symptomatic overlap, making the assessment and differential diagnosis of sleep problems a complicated affair. Nevertheless, as sleep disturbance may be intimately involved in the onset, maintenance, and impact of depression and other psychopathologies, sleep complaints should always be investigated to determine whether direct intervention is warranted (Reite et al., 2009).

As we hope to have illustrated, sleep disorders—and particularly insomnia—commonly result from the interaction of a multiplicity of factors, including genetic, physiological, cognitive, behavioral, affective, psychosocial, and cultural influences. As such, an adequate understanding of their etiology calls for an integrative view, a task for which the quadratic framework of Integral theory is well suited. Given that sleep appears to lie at the very nexus of body and mind, comprehensive explanatory models are, at a minimum, psychobiological in nature (Espie, 2002). However, sleep is also affected by sociocultural attitudes and practices and is increasingly recognized as a critical dimension of collective as well as individual health and well-being (Walsh, 2006), thereby suggesting the value of sleep education as a public health intervention. Likewise, the necessity of quadratic holism is also evident in the context of individual treatment. As a case in point, although medical (UR) devices for the treatment of Obstructive Sleep Apnea have become quite advanced and effective, researchers have discovered that treatment adherence and overall success depends on a host of factors, including, among others, self-efficacy and motivation (UL) as well as social support (LL; Olsen, Smith, & Oei, 2008).

## Review Questions

1. What are the leading theories regarding the organismic purpose(s) of sleep?
2. Discuss the role of physiological hyperarousal as it pertains to insomnia.
3. Discuss the role of stressors and stress as they pertain to insomnia.
4. How is behavioral conditioning involved with chronic primary insomnia?
5. Describe the attention-intention-effort (A-I-E) pathway model and the ways it explains cognitive dimensions of insomnia.
6. Describe the role of SES and other social-systemic factors pertaining to insomnia.
7. How might contemporary American culture contribute to insomnia and other sleep disorders?

## References


Adam, K., Tomeny, M., & Oswald, I. (1986). Physiological and psychological differences between good and poor sleepers. *Journal of Psychiatric Research, 20*(4), 301–316.

Alaia, S. L. (1992). Life effects of Narcolepsy: Measures of negative impact, social support, and psychological well-being. *Loss, Grief & Care, 5*(3–4), 1–22.

Allen, R. P., Picchietti, D., Hening, W. A., Trenkwalder, C., Walters, A. S., & Montplaisir, J. (2003). Restless legs syndrome: diagnostic criteria, special considerations, and epidemiology: A report from the restless legs syndrome diagnosis and epidemiology workshop at the National Institutes of Health. *Sleep Medicine, 4*, 101–119.

American Academy of Sleep Medicine. (2005). *International classification of sleep disorders: diagnostic & coding manual* (2nd ed.). Westchester, IL: Author.

American Academy of Sleep Medicine. (2007). *The AASM manual for the scoring of sleep and associated events: Rules, terminology and technical specifications.* Westchester, IL: Author.

American Psychiatric Association. (2000). *Diagnostic and statistical manual of mental disorders* (4h ed., text revision). Washington, DC: Author.

American Psychiatric Association. (2013). *Diagnostic and statistical manual of mental disorders* (5th ed.). Arlington, VA: Author.

Ayas, N. T., White, D. P., Manson, J. E., Stampfer, M. J., Speizer, F. E., Malhotra, A., & Hu, F. B. (2003). A prospective study of sleep duration and coronary heart disease in women. *Archives of Internal Medicine, 163*, 205–209.

Bastien, C. H., & Morin, C. M. (2000). Familial incidence of insomnia. *Journal of Sleep Research, 9*, 49–54.

Bastien, C. H., Vallières, A., & Morin, C. M. (2004). Precipitating factors of insomnia. *Behavioral Sleep Medicine, 2*(1), 50–62.

Beck, A. T. (1976). *Cognitive therapy and the emotional disorders.* New York: International Universities Press.

Belanger, L., Morin, C. M., Gendron, L., & Blais, F. C. (2005). Presleep cognitive activity and thought control strategies in insomnia. *Journal of Cognitive Psychotherapy, 19*(1), 19–28.

Belenky, G., Wesensten, N. J., Thorne, D. R., Thomas, M. L., Sing, H. C., Redmond, D. P., & Russo, M. B. (2003). Patterns of performance degradation and restoration during sleep restriction and subsequent recovery: A sleep dose-response study. *Journal of Sleep Research, 12*, 1–12.

Bell, B. G., & Belsky, J. (2008). Parents, parenting, and children's sleep problems: Exploring reciprocal effects. *British Journal of Developmental Psychology, 26*, 579–593.

Bendz, L. M., & Scates, A. C. (2010). Melatonin treatment for insomnia in pediatric patients with Attention-Deficit/Hyperactivity Disorder. *The Annals of Pharmacotherapy, 44*(1), 185–191.

Bernert, R. A., Merrill, K. A., Braithwaite, S. R., Van Orden, K. A., & Joiner Jr., T. E. (2007). Family life stress and insomnia symptoms in a prospective evaluation of young adults. *Journal of Family Psychology, 21*(1), 58–66.

Bjorvatn, B., Grønli, J., & Pallesen, S. (2010). Prevalence of different parasomnias in the general population. *Sleep Medicine, 11*(10), 1031–1034.

Bonnet, M. H., & Arand, D. L. (1992). Caffeine use as a model of acute and chronic insomnia. *Sleep, 15*(6), 526–536.

Bonnet, M. H., & Arand, D. L. (1995). 24-hour metabolic rate in insomniacs and matched normal sleepers. *Sleep, 18*(7), 581–588.

Bonnet, M. H., & Arand, D. L. (2003). Situational insomnia: Consistency, predictors, and outcomes. *Sleep, 26*(8), 1029–1037.

Bonnet, M. H., & Arand, D. L. (2005). Performance and cardiovascular measures among normal adults with extreme MSLT scores and subjective sleepiness. *Sleep, 28*(6), 685–693.

Bootzin, R. (1972). A stimulus control treatment for insomnia. *Proceedings of the American Psychological Association*, 395–396.

Borkovec, T. D. (1981). Insomnia. *Journal of Consulting & Clinical Psychology, 50*(6), 880–895.

Bornemann, M. A. C., Mahowald, M. W., & Schenck, C. H. (2006). Parasomnias: Clinical features and forensic implications. *Chest, 130*(2), 605–610.

Brand, S., Gerber, M., Puhse, U., & Holsboer-Trachsler, E. (2010). Depression, hypomania, and dysfunctional sleep-related cognitions as mediators between stress and insomnia: The best advice is not always found on the pillow! *International Journal of Stress Management, 17*(2), 114–134.

Broomfield, N. M., & Espie, C. A. (2003). Initial insomnia and paradoxical intention: An experimental investigation of putative mechanisms using subjective and actigraphic measurement of sleep. *Behavioural and Cognitive Psychotherapy, 31*(3), 313–324.

Brunborg, G. S., Mentzoni, R. A., Molde, H., Myrseth, H., Skouverøe, K. J. M., Bjorvatn, B., & Pallesen, S. (2011). The relationship between media use in the bedroom, sleep habits and symptoms of insomnia. *Journal of Sleep Research, 20*(4), 569–575.

Carskadon, M. A., Dement, W. C., Mitler, M. M., Guilleminault, C., Zarcone, V. P., & Spiegel, R. (1976). Self-reports versus sleep laboratory findings in 122 drug-free subjects with complaints of chronic insomnia. *American Journal of Psychiatry, 133*, 1382–1388.

Chokroverty, S. (2009). An overview of normal sleep. In S. Chokroverty (Ed.), *Sleep disorders medicine: Basic science, technical considerations, and clinical aspects* (3rd ed., pp. 5–21). Philadelphia, PA: Saunders Elsevier.

Colten, H. R., & Altevogt, B. M. (Eds.). (2006). *Sleep disorders and sleep deprivation: An unmet public health problem*. Washington, DC: The National Academies Press.

Cortoos, A., Verstraeten, E., & Cluydts, R. (2006). Neurophysiological aspects of primary insomnia: Implications for its treatment. *Sleep Medicine Reviews, 10*, 255–266.

Crowley, S. J., Acebo, C., & Carskadon, M. A. (2007). Sleep, circadian rhythms, and delayed phase in adolescence. *Sleep Medicine, 8*, 602–612.

Dauvilliers, Y., Billiard, M., & Montplaisir, J. (2003). Clinical aspects and pathophysiology of narcolepsy. *Clinical Neurophysiology, 113*, 2000–2017.

Dauvilliers, Y., Maret, S., & Tafti, M. (2005a). Genetics of normal and pathological sleep in humans. *Sleep Medicine Reviews, 9*, 91–100.

Dauvilliers, Y., Morin, C., Cervena, K., Carlander, B., Touchon, J., Besset, A., & Billiard, M. (2005b). Family studies in insomnia. *Journal of Psychosomatic Research, 58*, 271–278.

Davis, J. L., Rhudy, J. L., Pruiksma, K. E., Byrd, P., Williams, A. E., McCabe, K. M., & Bartley, E. J. (2011). Physiological predictors of response to exposure, relaxation, and rescripting therapy for chronic nightmares in a randomized clinical trial. *Journal of Clinical Sleep Medicine, 7*(6), 622–631.

de Valck, E., Cluydts, R., & Pirrera, S. (2004). Effect of cognitive arousal on sleep latency, somatic and cortical arousal following partial sleep deprivation. *Journal of Sleep Research, 13*, 295–304.

Drake, C. L., Friedman, N. P., Wright Jr., K. P., & Roth, T. (2011). Sleep reactivity and insomnia: Genetic and environmental influences. *Sleep, 34*(9), 1179.

Drake, C. L., Jefferson, C., Roehrs, T., & Roth, T. (2006). Stress-related sleep disturbance and polysomnographic response to caffeine. *Sleep Medicine, 7*(7), 567–572.

Drake, C., Richardson, G., Roehrs, T., Scofield, H., & Roth, T. (2004). Vulnerability to stress-related sleep disturbance and hyperarousal. *Sleep, 27*(2), 285–292.

Edinger, J. D., Olsen, M. K., Stechuchak, K. M., Means, M. K., Lineberger, M. D., Kirby, A., & Carney, C. E. (2009). Cognitive behavioral therapy for patients with primary insomnia or insomnia associated predominantly with mixed psychiatric disorders: A randomized clinical trial. *Sleep, 32*(4), 499–510.

Edinger, J. D., & Sampson, W. S. (2003). A primary care "friendly" cognitive behavioral insomnia therapy. *Sleep, 26*(2), 177–182.

Espie, C. A. (2002). Insomnia: Conceptual issues in the development, persistence, and treatment of sleep disorder ini adults. *Annual Review of Psychology, 53*, 215–243.

Espie, C. A., Broomfield, N. M., MacMahon, K. M., Macphee, L. M., & Taylor, C. M. (2006). The attention-intention-effort pathway in the development of psychophysiologic insomnia: A theoretical review. *Sleep Medicine Reviews, 10*, 215–245.

Ford, D. E., & Kamerow, D. B. (1989). Epidemiologic study of sleep disturbances and psychiatric disorders: An opportunity for prevention? *JAMA, 262*, 1479–1484.

Frankl, V. E. (1963). *Man's search for meaning: An introduction to Logotherapy.* (I. Lasch, Trans.). London: Hodder & Stoughton.

Franzen, P. L., & Buysse, D. J. (2009). Sleep in psychiatric disorders. In S. Chokroverty (Ed.), *Sleep disorders medicine: basic science, technical considerations, and clinical aspects* (3rd ed., pp. 538–549). Philadelphia, PA: Saunders Elsevier.

Freud, S. (1911). *The interpretation of dreams* (3rd ed.). (A. A. Brill, Trans.). Retrieved from http://www.psychwww.com/books/interp/toc.htm [Original work published 1900]

Freud, S. (1961). *Beyond the pleasure principle* (rev. ed.). (J. Strachey, Trans.). London: Hogarth Press and the Institute of Psychoanalysis. [Original work published 1920]

Gangswich, J. E., Heymsfield, S. B., Boden-Albala, B., Buijs, R. M., Kreier, F., Pickering, T. G., . . . Malaspina, D. (2007). Sleep duration as a risk factor for diabetes incidence in a large US sample. *Sleep, 30*(12), 1667–1673.

Gangswich, J. E., Malaspina, D., Boden-Albala, B., & Heymsfield, S. B. (2005). Inadequate sleep as a risk factor for obesity: Analyses of the NHANES I. *Sleep, 28*(10), 1289–1296.

Gellis, L. A., Lichstein, K. L., Scarinci, I. C., Durrence, H. H., Taylor, D. J., Bush, A. J., & Riedel, B. W. (2005). Socioeconomic status and insomnia. *Journal of Abnormal Psychology, 114*(1), 111–118.

Germain, A., & Nielsen, T. (2003). Impact of imagery rehearsal treatment on distressing dreams, psychological distress, and sleep parameters in nightmare patients. *Behavioral Sleep Medicine, 1*(3), 140–154.

Gregory, A. M., Caspi, A., Moffitt, J. E., & Poulton, R. (2006). Family conflict in childhood: A predictor of later insomnia. *Sleep, 29*(8), 1063–1067.

Gross, C. R., Kreitzer, M. J., Reilly-Spong, M., Wall, M., Winbush, N. Y., Patterson, R., . . . Cramer-Bornemann, M. (2011). Mindfulness-based stress reduction versus pharmacotherapy for chronic primary insomnia: A randomized controlled clinical trial. *Explore (NY), 7*(2), 76–87.

Guénolé, F., Godbout, R., Nicolas, A., Franco, P., Claustrat, B., & Baleyte, J. M. (2011). Melatonin for disordered sleep in individuals with Autism Spectrum Disorders: Systematic review and discussion. *Sleep Medicine Reviews, 15*(6), 379–387.

Guilleminault, C., & Zupancic, M. (2009). Obstructive sleep apnea syndrome. In S. Chokroverty (Ed.), *Sleep disorders medicine: Basic science, technical considerations, and clinical aspects* (3rd ed., pp. 319–339). Philadelphia, PA: Saunders Elsevier.

Hale, L., & Do, D. P. (2007). Racial differences in self-reports of sleep duration in a population-based study. *Sleep, 30*(9), 1096–1103.

Hall, M., Buysse, D. J., Nowell, P. D., Nofzinger, E. A., Houck, P., Reynolds III, C. F., & Kupfer, D. J. (2000). Symptoms of stress and depression as correlates of sleep in primary insomnia. *Psychosomatic Medicine, 62*(2), 227–230.

Hall, M., Thayer, J. F., Germain, A., Moul, D., Vasko, R., Puhl, M., . . . Buysse, D. J. (2007). Psychological stress is associated with heightened physiological arousal during NREM sleep in primary insomnia. *Behavioral Sleep Medicine, 5*(3), 178–193.

Hall, M. H., Matthews, K. A., Kravitz, H. M., Gold, E. B., Buysse, D. J., Bromberger, J. T., . . . Sowers, M. (2009). Race and financial strain are independent correlates of sleep in midlife women: The SWAN sleep study. *Sleep, 32*(1), 73–82.

Hamet, P., & Tremblay, J. (2006). Genetics of the sleep-wake cycle and its disorders. *Metabolism Clinical and Experimental, 55*(S2), S7–S12.

Harris, M., & Grunstein, R. R. (2009). Treatments for somnambulism in adults: Assessing the evidence. *Sleep Medicine Reviews, 13*(4), 295-297.

Hartmann, E. (1984). *The nightmare: The psychology and biology of terrifying dreams.* New York: Basic Books.

Harvey, A. G. (2002). A cognitive model of insomnia. *Behaviour Research and Therapy, 40*, 869–893.

Harvey, A. G. (2003). The attempted suppression of presleep cognitive activity in insomnia. *Cognitive Therapy and Research, 27*(6), 593–602.

Harvey, A. G., & Payne, S. (2002). The management of unwanted pre-sleep thoughts in insomnia: Distraction with imagery versus general distraction. *Behaviour Research and Therapy, 40*(3), 267–277.

Hauri, P. J., Silber, M. H., & Boeve, B. F. (2007). The treatment of parasomnias with hypnosis: A 5-year follow-up study. *Journal of Clinical Sleep Medicine, 3*(4), 369–373.

Haynes, S. N., Adams, A., & Franzen, M. (1981). The effects of pre-sleep stress on sleep onset insomnia. *Journal of Abnormal Psychology, 90*(6), 601–606.

Healey, E. S., Kales, A., Monroe, L. J., Bixler, E. O., Chamberlin, K., & Soldatos, C. R. (1981). Onset of insomnia: Role of life-stress events. *Psychosomatic Medicine, 43*(5), 439–451.

Heath, A. C., Kendler, K. S., Eaves, L. J., & Martin, N. G. (1990). Evidence for genetic influences on sleep disturbance and sleep pattern in twins. *Sleep, 13*(4), 318–335.

Hefez, A., Metz, L., & Lavie, P. (1987). Long-term effects of extreme situational stress on sleep and dreaming. *American Journal of Psychiatry, 144*(3), 344–347.

Hirshkowitz, M., Moore, C. A., & Minhoto, G. (1997). The basics of sleep. In M. R. Pressman & W. C. Orr (Eds.), *Understanding sleep: The evaluation and treatment of sleep disorders* (pp. 11–34). Washington, DC: American Psychological Association.

Hobson, J. A., & McCarley, R. W. (1977). The brain as a dream state generator: An activation-synthesis hypothesis of the dream process. *American Journal of Psychiatry, 134*, 1335–1348.

Hor, H., & Tafti, M. (2009). How much sleep do we need? *Science, 325*(5942), 825–826.

Hublin, C., Kaprio, J., Partinen, M., & Koskenvuo, M. (1999). Nightmares: familial aggregation and association with psychiatric disorders in a nationwide twin cohort. *American Journal of Medical Genetics, 88*(4), 329–336.

Hublin, C., Partinen, M., Koskenvuo, M., & Kaprio, J. (2011). Heritability and mortality risk of insomnia-related symptoms: A genetic epidemiologic study in a population-based twin cohort. *Sleep, 34*(7), 957–964.

Hur, Y., Bouchard, T. J., & Lykken, D. T. (1998). Genetic and environmental influence on morningness-eveningness. *Personality and Individual Differences, 25*, 917–925.

Ikegami, K., Ogyu, S., Arakomo, Y., Suzuki, K., Mafune, K., Hiro, H., & Nagata, S. (2009). Recovery of cognitive performance and fatigue after one night of sleep deprivation. *Journal of Occupational Health, 52*, 412–422.

Irwin, M. R., Cole, J. C., & Nicassio, P. M. (2006). Comparative meta-analysis of behavioral interventions for insomnia and their efficacy in middle-aged adults and in older adults 55 years of age. *Health Psychology, 25*(1), 3–14.

Jacobs, G. D., Pace-Schott, E. F., Stickgold, R., & Otto, M. W. (2004). Cognitive behavior therapy and pharmacotherapy for insomnia: A randomized controlled trial and direct comparison. *Archives of Internal Medicine, 164*(17), 1888–1896.

Jansson, M., & Linton, S. J. (2006). Psychosocial work stressors in the development and maintenance of insomnia: A prospective study. *Journal of Occupational Health Psychology, 11*(3), 241–248.

Kales, A., Caldwell, A. B., Soldatos, C. R., Bixler, E. O., & Kales, J. D. (1983). Biopsychobehavioral correlates of insomnia. II. Pattern specificity and consistency with the Minnesota Multiphasic Personality Inventory. *Psychosomatic Medicine, 45*(4), 341–356.

Kalogjera-Sackellares, D., & Cartwright, R. D. (1997). Comparison of MMPI profiles in medically and psychologically based insomnias. *Psychiatry Research, 70*(1), 49–56.

Kothe, M., & Pietrowsky, R. (2001). Behavioral effects of nightmares and their correlations to personality patterns. *Dreaming, 11*(1), 43–52.

Krakow, B., & Zadra, A. (2006). Clinical management of chronic nightmares: Imagery rehearsal therapy. *Behavioral Sleep Medicine, 4*(1), 45–70.

Kripke, D. F., Garfinkel, L., Wingard, D. L., Klauber, M. R., & Marler, M. R. (2002). Mortality associated with sleep duration and insomnia. *Archives of General Psychiatry, 59*, 131–136.

Krystal, A. D., Edinger, J. D., Wohlgemuth, W. K., & Marsh, G. K. (2002). NREM sleep EEG frequency spectral correlates of sleep complaints in primary insomnia subtypes. *Sleep, 25*(6), 626–636.

Krystal, A. D., Erman, M., Zammit, G. K., Soubrane, C., & Roth, T. (2008). Long-term efficacy and safety of zolpidem extended-release 12.5 mg, administered 3 to 7 nights per week for 24 weeks, in patients with chronic primary insomnia: A 6-month, randomized, double-blind, placebo-controlled, parallel-group, multicenter study. *Sleep, 31*(1), 79–90.

Kuiken, D., Lee, M., Eng, T., & Singh, T. (2006). The influence of impactful dreams on self-perceptual depth and spiritual transformation. *Dreaming, 16*(4), 258–279.

Kuisk, L. A., Bertelson, A. D., & Walsh, J. K. (1989). Presleep cognitive hyperarousal and affect as factors in objective and subjective insomnia. *Perceptual and Motor Skills, 69*(3, Pt.2), 1219–1225.

Laberge, L., Tremblay, R. E., Vitaro, F., & Montplaisir, J. (2000). Development of parasomnias from childhood to early adolescence. *Pediatrics, 106*(1), 67–74.

Lecendreux, M., Bassetti, C., Dauvilliers, Y., Mayer, G., Neidhart, E., & Tafti, M. (2003). HLA and genetic susceptibility to sleepwalking. *Molecular Psychiatry, 8*(1), 114–117.

Leger, D., Massuel, M., & Arnaud, M. (2006). Professional correlates of insomnia. *Sleep, 29*(2), 171–178.

Lichstein, K. L., Durrence, H. H., Riedel, B. W., Taylor, D. J., & Bush, A. J. (2004). *Epidemiology of sleep: Age, gender, and ethnicity.* Mahwah, NJ: Lawrence Erlbaum Associates.

Lichstein, K. L., & Rosenthal, T. L. (1980). Insomniacs' perceptions of cognitive versus somatic determinants of sleep disturbance. *Journal of Abnormal Psychology, 89*(1), 105–107.

Luthringer, R., Muzet, M., Zisapel, N., & Staner, L. (2009). The effect of prolonged-release melatonin on sleep measures and psychomotor performance in elderly patients with insomnia. *International Clinical Psychopharmacology, 24*(5), 239–249.

Lyznicki, J. M., Doege, T. C., Davis, M., & Williams, M. A. (1998). Sleepiness, driving, and motor vehicle crashes. *JAMA, 279*(23), 1908–1913.

Manber, R., Edinger, J. D., Gress, J. L., San Pedro-Salcedo, M. G., Kuo, T. F., & Kalista, T. (2008). Cognitive behavioral therapy for insomnia enhances depression outcome in patients with comorbid Major Depressive Disorder and insomnia. *Sleep, 31*(4), 489–495.

Martens, M., Nijhuis, F., Van Boxtel, M., & Knottnerus, J. (1999). Flexible work schedules and mental and physical health. A study of a working population with non-traditional working hours. *Journal of Organizational Behavior, 20*(1), 35–46.

Maslow, A. H. (1943). A theory of human motivation. *Psychological Review, 50*, 370–396.

Maslow, A. H. (1968). *Toward a psychology of being.* Princeton, NJ: Van Nostrand.

Meijer, A. M., & van den Wittenboer, G. L. (2007). Contribution of infants' sleep and crying to marital relationship of first-time parent couples in the 1st year after childbirth. *Journal of Family Psychology, 21*(1), 49–57.

Mezick, E. J., Matthews, K. A., Hall, M., Strollo Jr., P. J., Buysse, D. J., Kamarck, T. W., . . . Reis, S. E. (2008). Influence of race and socioeconomic status on sleep: The Pittsburgh SleepSCORE study. *Psychosomatic Medicine, 70*, 410–416.

Mignot, E. (1998). Genetic and familial aspects of narcolepsy. *Neurology, 50*(S1), S16–S22.

Miller, W. R., & DiPilato, M. (1983). Treatment of nightmares via relaxation and desensitization: A controlled evaluation. *Journal of Consulting and Clinical Psychology, 51*(6), 870–877.

Monroe, L. J. (1967). Psychological and physiological differences between good and poor sleepers. *Journal of Abnormal Psychology, 72*(3), 255–264.

Morin, C. M. (1993). *Insomnia: Psychological assessment and management.* New York: The Guildford Press.

Morin, C. M., & Benca, R. M. (2009). Nature and treatment of insomnia. In S. Chokroverty (Ed.), *Sleep disorders medicine: Basic science, technical considerations, and clinical aspects* (pp. 361–376). Philadelphia, PA: Saunders Elsevier.

Morin, C. M., Bootzin, R. R., Buysse, D. J., Edinger, J. D., Espie, C. A., & Lichstein, K. L. (2006). Psychological and behavioral treatment of insomnia: Update of the recent evidence (1998–2004). *Sleep, 29*(11), 1398–1414.

Morin, C. M., Vallières, A., Guay, B., Ivers, H., Savard, J., Mérette, C., . . . Baillargeon, L. (2009). Cognitive behavioral therapy, singly and combined with medication, for persistent insomnia. *JAMA, 301*(19), 2005–2015.

Morin, C. M., Vallières, A., & Ivers, H. (2007). Dysfunctional beliefs and attitudes about sleep (DBAS): Validation of a brief version (DBAS-16). *Sleep, 30*(11), 1547–1554.

National Center on Sleep Disorders Research. (2003). *2003 national sleep disorders research plan* (NIH Publication No. 03-5209). Bethesda, MD: Author. Retrieved from http://www.nhlbi.nih.gov/health/prof/sleep/res_plan/index.html

National Institutes of Health. (2005). National Institutes of Health State of the Science conference statement on manifestations and management of chronic insomnia in adults. *Sleep, 28*(9), 1049–1057.

National Sleep Foundation. (2009). *2009 Sleep in America poll: Summary of findings.* Washington, DC: Author. Retrieved from http://www.sleepfoundation.org/category/article-type/sleep-america-polls

National Sleep Foundation. (2010). *2010 Sleep in America poll: Summary of findings*. Washington, DC: Author. Retrieved from http://www.sleepfoundation.org/category/article-type/sleep-america-polls

National Sleep Foundation. (2011). *2011 Sleep in America poll: Summary of findings*. Washington, DC: Author. Retrieved from http://www.sleepfoundation.org/category/article-type/sleep-america-polls

Nicassio, P. M., Mendlowitz, D. R., Fussell, J. J., & Petras, L. (1985). The phenomenology of the pre-sleep state: The development of the pre-sleep arousal scale. *Behaviour Research and Therapy, 23*(3), 263–271.

Nofzinger, E. A., Buysse, D. J., Germain, A., Price, J. C., Miewald, J. M., & Kupfer, D. J. (2004). Functional neuroimaging evidence for hyperarousal in insomnia. *American Journal of Psychiatry, 161*, 2126–2129.

Noll, J. G., Trickett, P. K., Susman, E. J., & Putnam, F. W. (2006). Sleep disturbances and childhood sexual abuse. *Journal of Pediatric Psychology, 31*(5), 469–480.

Ohayon, M. M. (2002). Epidemiology of insomnia: What we know and what we still need to learn. *Sleep Medicine Reviews, 6*(2), 97–111.

Ohayon, M. M., Caulet, M., & Priest, R. G. (1997). Violent behavior during sleep. *The Journal of Clinical Psychiatry, 58*(8), 369–376.

Ohayon, M. M., Guilleminault, C., & Priest, R. G. (1999). Night terrors, sleepwalking, and confusional arousals in the general population: Their frequency and relationship to other sleep and mental disorders. *The Journal of Clinical Psychiatry, 60*(4), 268–276.

Ohayon, M. M., & Roth, T. (2003). Place of chronic insomnia in the course of depressive and anxiety disorders. *Journal of Psychiatric Research, 37*, 9–15.

Olsen, S., Smith, S., & Oei, T. P. S. (2008). Adherence to continuous positive airway pressure therapy in obstructive sleep apnea sufferers: A theoretical approach to treatment adherence and intervention. *Clinical Psychology Review, 28*(8), 1355–1371.

Partinen, M. (2009). Sleep and nutrition. In S. Chokroverty (Ed.), *Sleep disorders medicine: Basic science, technical considerations, and clinical aspects* (3rd ed., pp. 307–318). Philadelphia, PA: Saunders Elsevier.

Patel, S. R., Ayas, N. T., Malhotra, M. R., White, D. P., Schernhammer, E. S., Speizer, F. E., . . . Hu, F. B. (2004). A prospective study of sleep duration and mortality risk in women. *Sleep, 27*(3), 440–444.

Payne, J. D., & Nadel, L. (2004). Sleep, dreams, and memory consolidation: The role of the stress hormone cortisol. *Learning & Memory, 11*(6), 671–678.

Perlis, M. L., Kehr, E. L., Smith, M. T., Andrews, P. J., Orff, H., & Giles, D. E. (2001). Temporal and stagewise distribution of high frequency EEG activity in patients with primary and secondary insomnia and in good sleeper controls. *Journal of Sleep Research, 10*, 93–104.

Ree, M. J., Harvey, A. G., Blake, R., Tang, N. K., & Shawe-Taylor, M. (2005). Attempts to control unwanted thoughts in the night: Development of the thought control questionnaire-insomnia revised (TCQI-R). *Behaviour Research and Therapy, 43*, 985–998.

Reite, M., Weissberg, M., & Ruddy, J. (2009). *Clinical manual for evaluation and treatment of sleep disorders*. Washington, DC: American Psychiatric Publishing.

Roberts, R. E., Roberts, C. R., & Duong, H. T. (2009). Sleepless in adolescence: Prospective data on sleep deprivation, health and functioning. *Journal of Adolescence, 32*(5), 1045–1057.

Robertson, J. A., Broomfield, N. M., & Espie, C. A. (2007). Prospective comparison of subjective arousal during the pre-sleep period in primary sleep-onset insomnia and normal sleepers. *Journal of Sleep Research, 16*, 230–238.

Roehrs, T. A., Randall, S., Harris, E., Maan, R., & Roth, T. (2012). Twelve months of nightly zolpidem does not lead to rebound insomnia or withdrawal symptoms: A prospective placebo-controlled study. *Journal of Psychopharmacology, 26*(8), 1088–1095.

Roth, T., Walsh, J. K., Krystal, A., Wessel, T., & Roehrs, T. A. (2005). An evaluation of the efficacy and safety of eszopiclone over 12 months in patients with chronic primary insomnia. *Sleep Medicine, 6*(6), 487–495.

Schredl, M. (2003). Effects of state and trait factors on nightmare frequency. *European Archives of Psychiatry and Clinical Neuroscience, 253*, 241–247.

Sharma, A. (2004). *Sleep as a state of consciousness in Advaita Vedanta*. Albany, NY: State University of New York Press.

Shochat, T. (2012). Impact of lifestyle and technology developments on sleep. *Nature, 4*, 19–31.

Sivertsen, B., Omvik, S., Pallesen, S., Bjorvatn, B., Havik, O. E., Kvale, G., . . . Nordhus, I. H. (2006). Cognitive behavioral therapy vs. zopiclone for treatment of chronic primary insomnia in older adults. *JAMA, 295*(24), 2851–2858.

Soares, C. N. (2005). Insomnia in women: An overlooked epidemic? *Archives of Women's Mental Health, 8*, 205–213.

Spielman, A. J. (1986). Assessment of insomnia. *Clinical Psychology Review, 6*, 11–25.

Spielman, A. J., Saskin, P., & Thorpy, M. J. (1987). Treatment of chronic insomnia by restriction of time in bed. *Sleep, 10*(1), 45–56.

Spoormaker, V. I., & Montgomery, P. (2008). Disturbed sleep in Post-Traumatic Stress Disorder: Secondary symptom or core feature? *Sleep Medicine Reviews, 12*, 169–184.

Spoormaker, V. I., Schredl, M., & van den Bout, J. (2006). Nightmares: From anxiety symptom to sleep disorder. *Sleep Medicine Reviews, 10*, 19–31.

Stepanski, E., Glinn, M., Zorick, F., Roehrs, T., & Roth, T. (1994). Heart rate changes in chronic insomnia. *Stress Medicine, 10* (4), 261–266.

Stepanski, E. J., & Rybarczyk, B. (2006). Emerging research on the treatment and etiology of secondary or comorbid insomnia. *Sleep Medicine Reviews, 10*, 7–18.

Stepanski, E., Zorick, F., Roehrs, T., Young, D., & Roth, T. (1988). Daytime alertness in patients with chronic insomnia compared with asymptomatic control subjects. *Sleep, 11*(1), 54–60.

Suganuma, N., Kikuchi, T., Yanagi, K., Yamamura, S., Morishima, H., Adachi, H., . . . Takeda, M. (2007). Using electronic media before sleep can curtail sleep time and result in self-perceived insufficient sleep. *Sleep and Biological Rhythms, 5*(3), 204–214.

Taheri, S., Lin, L., Austin, D., Young, T., & Mignot, E. (2004). Short sleep duration is associated with reduced leptin, elevated ghrelin, and increased body mass index. *PLoS Medicine, 1*(3), e62: 210–217.

Thomée, S., Eklöf, M., Gustafsson, E., Nilsson, R., & Hagberg, M. (2007). Prevalence of perceived stress, symptoms of depression and sleep disturbances in relation to information and communication technology (ICT) use among young adults–an explorative prospective study. *Computers in Human Behavior, 23*(3), 1300–1321.

Turek, F. (2005). The prevailing culture of sleepiness. *Sleep, 28*(7), 798–799.

Vahtera, J., Kivimäki, M., Hublin, C., Korkeila, K., Suominen, S., Paunio, T., & Koskenvuo, M. (2007). Liability to anxiety and severe life events as predictors of new onset sleep disturbances. *Sleep, 30*(11), 1537–1546.

van de Laar, M., Verbeek, I., Pevernagie, D., Aldenkamp, A., & Overeem, S. (2010). The role of personality traits in insomnia. *Sleep Medicine Reviews, 14*, 61–68.

Van Dongen, H. P., Maislin, G., Mullington, J. M., & Dinges, D. F. (2003). The cumulative cost of additional wakefulness: Dose-response effects on neurobehavioral functions and sleep physiology from chronic sleep restriction and total sleep deprivation. *Sleep, 26*(2), 117–126.

van Mill, J. G., Hoogendijk, W. J., Vogelzangs, N., van Dyck, R., & Penninx, B. W. (2010). Insomnia and sleep duration in a large cohort of patients with Major Depressive Disorders and anxiety disorders. *Journal of Clinical Psychiatry, 71*(3), 239–246.

Van Reeth, O., Weibel, L., Spiegel, K., Leproult, R., Dugovic, C., & Maccari, S. (2000). Interactions between stress and sleep: From basic research to clinical situations. *Sleep Medicine Reviews, 4*(2), 201–219.

Vgontzas, A. N., Bixler, E. O., Lin, H., Prolo, P., Mastorakos, G., Vela-Bueno, A., . . . Chrousos, G. P. (2001). Chronic insomnia is associated with nyctohemeral activation of the hypothalamic-pituitary-adrenal axis: Clinical implications. *Journal of Clinical Endocrinology & Metabolism, 86*(8), 3787–3794.

Vgontzas, A. N., Tsigos, C., Bixler, E. O., Stratakis, C. A., Zachman, K., Kales, A., . . . Chrousos, G. P. (1998). Chronic insomnia and activity of the stress system: A preliminary study. *Journal of Psychosomatic Research, 45*(1), 21–31.

Vincent, N. K., & Walker, J. R. (2000). Perfectionism and chronic insomnia. *Journal of Psychosomatic Research, 49*, 349–354.

Wade, A. G., Ford, I., Crawford, G., McMahon, A. D., Nir, T., Laudon, M., & Zisapel, N. (2007). Efficacy of prolonged release melatonin in insomnia patients aged 55–80 years: Quality of sleep and next-day alertness outcomes. *Current Medical Research and Opinion, 23*(10), 2597–2605.

Walsh, J. K. (2006). Insights into the public health burden of insomnia. *Sleep, 29*(2), 142–143.

Walsh, J. K., & Lindblom, S. S. (1997). Psychophysiology of sleep deprivation and disruption.

In M. R. Pressman & W. C. Orr (Eds.), *Understanding sleep: The evaluation and treatment of sleep disorders* (pp. 73–110). Washington, DC: American Psychological Association.

Waters, W. F., Adams Jr., S. G., Binks, P., & Varnado, P. (1993). Attention, stress and negative emotion in persistent sleep onset and sleep maintenance insomnia. *Sleep, 16*(2), 128–136.

Watson, N. F., Goldberg, J., Arguelles, L., & Buchwald, D. (2006). Genetic and environmental influences on insomnia, daytime sleepiness, and obesity in twins. *Sleep, 29*(5), 645–649.

Wegner, D. M. (1989). *White bears and other unwanted thoughts*. New York: Viking.

Wells, A. (2000). *Emotional disorders and metacognition*. New York: John Wiley & Sons.

Wicklow, A., & Espie, C. A. (2000). Intrusive thoughts and their relationship to actigraphic measurement of sleep: Towards a cognitive model of insomnia. *Behaviour Research and Therapy, 38*, 679–693.

Wilber, K. (2000). *Integral psychology: consciousness, spirit, psychology, therapy*. Boston, MA: Shambhala Publications.

Wilson, S. J., Nutt, D., Alford, C., Argyropoulos, S., Baldwin, D., Bateson, A., . . . Espie, C. (2010). British association for psychopharmacology consensus statement on evidence-based treatment of insomnia, parasomnias and Circadian Rhythm Disorders. *Journal of Psychopharmacology, 24*(11), 1577–1601.

Winbush, N. Y., Gross, C. R., & Kreitzer, M. J. (2007). The effects of mindfulness-based stress reduction on sleep disturbance: A systematic review. *Explore (NY), 3*(6), 585–591.

Yalom, I. D. (1980). Existential psychotherapy. New York: Basic Books.

Yalom, I. D. (2002). *The gift of therapy: An open letter to a new generation of therapists and their patients*. New York: HarperCollins.

Zee, P. C., & Manthena, P. (2007). The brain's master circadian clock: Implications and opportunities for therapy of sleep disorders. *Sleep Medicine Reviews, 11*, 59–70.

# 12

# Emptiness and Fullness: An Integral Approach to the Understanding and Treatment of Eating Disorders

**Sarah T. Hubbard, Ph.D.,** ***Center for Change***[1]

The *Diagnostic and Statistical Manual of Mental Disorders*, 5th Edition (DSM-5) changed what had previously been called Eating Disorders (ED) to Feeding and Eating Disorders (American Psychiatric Association [APA], 2013). The current manual includes Pica, Rumination Disorder and Avoidant/Restrictive Food Intake Disorder. Pica and Rumination Disorder, which used to be classified under Disorders First Diagnosed in Infancy, Childhood and Adolescence. DSM-5 includes Binge Eating Disorder (BID), which was only in the appendix of the DSM-IV-TR (for conditions warranting further study; APA, 2000), and this change is still being debated (Birgegard, Clinton, & Norring, 2013). In addition, the DSM-5 addresses one long-standing criticism of DSM Eating Disorders—that Eating Disorder Not Otherwise Specified (EDNOS) is the most common of the EDs and has been largely ignored by researchers (Grave, 2011). The DSM-5 now offers Other Specified Feeding or Eating Disorder as well as Unspecified Feeding or Eating Disorder. As the label denotes, the former refines the NOS

[1] This chapter was written while I worked at the Center for Eating Disorders at Sheppard Pratt Health System, and I would like to thank Harry Brandt, MD, and Steven Crawford, MD, for their gracious support.

category by offering guidance via specifiers such as Purging Disorder and Night Eating Syndrome. Initial studies support that these provide more clarity than the previous NOS category (Machado, Goncalves, & Hoek, 2013). Although the DSM-5 is still using a categorical approach, researchers are still advocating the addition of dimensional tools to gauge the severity of Eating Disorders (Pike, 2013). This chapter will focus on Eating Disorders (EDs), particularly Anorexia Nervosa (AN) and Bulimia Nervosa (BN). EDs are uncommon psychiatric illnesses. Lifetime prevalence rates of AN among women range from .6% to 4.0%. With regard to BN, lifetime prevalence rates among women range from 1.2% to 5.9% (Striegel-Moore, Franko, & Ach, 2006). EDs are more common among females than males; lifetime prevalence rates of AN and BN in males are unknown but are likely less than 1 percent (Collins, 2013). Prevalence of EDs is higher in urban areas than suburban areas, and age of onset for AN and BN continues to decrease (Grave, 2011). The incidence of EDs appears to be rising. Hoek and van Hoeken (2003), for instance, report a significant increase in the incidence of AN from 1935 to 1989, especially among women between 15 to 24 years of age. There are no data on prevalence rates of partial syndrome or subthreshold EDs, but clinical experience would suggest these rates are higher (Grave, 2011; Striegel-Moore et al., 2006).

Psychotherapists face unique challenges when treating clients with EDs. The clinical presentation of clients is diverse; individuals with EDs suffer from a wide range of symptoms of varying severity, and comorbid psychiatric conditions are the norm rather than the exception (Harrop & Marlatt, 2010). In addition, these individuals have earned a reputation among therapists for being difficult to treat. This reputation is not unfounded, as a hallmark sign of AN is denial of symptoms. An individual in the throes of a serious ED is, at best, profoundly ambivalent about treatment and recovery.

Given these challenges, how does one go about understanding and treating clients with EDs? Theoretical approaches including psychodynamic, cognitive-behavioral, interpersonal, and feminist are among those used to conceptualize and treat EDs. Pharmacotherapy, nutritional rehabilitation, individual therapy, group therapy, family therapy, and support groups are modalities that also play a role in treatment. Can these myriad approaches and modalities be integrated in a meaningful way? Integral theory offers a way to make informed theoretical sense of how, when, and why to apply particular treatments to clients suffering from EDs. This same model helps therapists maintain themselves as "attuned instruments" in the therapeutic process.

This chapter assumes a working knowledge of the Integral model (the quadrants, levels, lines, types, and states outlined in Chapter 1). The primary aim of this chapter is to explore the territory of EDs using the Integral map as a guide. The Integral map helps therapists know "where they are" and "what they need to pay attention to" in this vast territory. The second aim is to outline ways that the Integral map assists in the therapeutic process, as well as attunement of the "self as instrument." Because EDs are challenging, we feel that therapists will need to stretch themselves and even go beyond what research can tell us about etiology and treatment. This is not to condone reckless therapy, but to acknowledge that EDs will bring therapists to the edge of their knowledge and skill and at times they will need to grow beyond this edge. In this spirit, we have included material here (particularly on spiritual issues) that is difficult to research but may be of therapeutic value. Therapists who have adopted

Integral theory often have a spiritual orientation because the Integral model addresses the role of spiritual presence. A taste of this presence is provided in the discussion of levels and lines and therapeutic attunement. However, there is no need to embrace a particular spiritual worldview to work with this model.

## EATING DISORDERS: THE TERRITORY

We begin this journey by exploring the territory of EDs using the all-quadrants, all-levels (AQAL) framework. Our aim is to cover enough of the territory so that readers acquire a basic understanding of EDs through the Integral lens. Treatment approaches and modalities are touched upon as we traverse the territory and will be discussed more fully in a subsequent section. A comprehensive description of any phenomenon requires multiple perspectives. Integral theory suggests there are four interrelated yet irreducible perspectives on any phenomenon.

### The Four Quadrants

Because so little is understood about the etiology of EDs, we will look at common elements in both etiology and the manifestation of the disorders via the four quadrants of Integral theory. It is difficult to tease out etiology from symptoms in EDs, as many of the symptoms (and thoughts/behaviors associated with them) can exacerbate the condition or trigger further symptoms. One example is an early study that suggested caloric restriction triggers or exacerbates obsessions focused on food (Keys, Brozek, Henschel, Mickelsen, & Taylor, 1950).

**UPPER-RIGHT QUADRANT: THE EXTERIOR OF THE INDIVIDUAL** One way to understand the territory of EDs is to *look at* the characteristics of individuals who present for treatment. Using our eyes, what do we see? How does an individual with an ED behave? What can be said, *objectively*, about an individual with an ED?

The typical client with an ED is female. Estimates of the male-female prevalence ratio range from 1:6 to 1:10 (Hoek & van Hoeken, 2003). The onset of an ED is often associated with a developmental transition or stressful event, such as puberty, moving away from home, entering the workforce, the end of a significant relationship, or physical or sexual abuse (Akkermann et al., 2012; Campbell, Mill, Uher, & Schmidt, 2011; Dubose et al., 2012; Jahng, 2012; Sassaroli et al., 2011). Most individuals are adolescents or young adults at the onset of their ED. However, girls as young as 8 to 9 years and women in their 40s are also presenting for treatment with a recent onset of symptoms. In the United States, EDs appear equally common in Caucasian, Hispanic, and Native American women, and less common among African American and Asian women (Crago, Shisslak, & Estes, 1996; Striegel-Moore et al., 2003). Upon entering treatment, an individual is assigned one of the DSM-5 ED diagnoses.

An individual's percentage of ideal body weight and the presence or absence of bingeing and purging behaviors are among the criteria that depict and categorize the territory of EDs in a meaningful way. These diagnoses are descriptively helpful, but, as in most symptom sets described in this book, are only a starting point. There are two caveats with regard to the DSM-5 diagnoses that must be noted. First, there are key similarities *across* the diagnostic categories. Regardless of the specific diagnosis, the majority of individuals with EDs are extremely preoccupied with weight and shape. Most engage in periods of severe caloric restriction or compensatory behaviors in order to lose weight or prevent weight gain. These features tend to remain stable even though an individual's diagnostic classification may vary over time. For example, 50–64% of clients with AN will later develop symptoms of BN, and some clients who are initially bulimic will later develop anorexic symptoms (APA, 2006).

Up until the DSM-5, over 50% of individuals who presented for outpatient treatment were given an Eating Disorder Not Otherwise Specified (EDNOS) diagnosis (APA, 2006), which seemed to illustrate the fact that eating-disordered symptoms occur along a continuum. Currently Other Specified Feeding or Eating Disorder (or Unspecified Feeding or Eating Disorder) can be used for subsyndromal AN and BN (e.g., clients who are at a low weight but haven't lost their menstrual periods; clients who binge and purge at a frequency of less than two times a week) as well as for clients who binge without purging or who purge without bingeing.

Given that the continuum of eating disorder behaviors is broad, a second caveat pertains to the variability seen *within* the diagnostic categories. Individuals who meet the criteria for the same diagnosis may vary greatly in terms of symptom severity and type. This is why some therapists are advocating adding dimensional tools to the diagnostic categories (Pike, 2013). Indeed, therapists often assess the frequency and intensity of restricting (i.e., dieting), bingeing, and purging behaviors in clients as a guide to illness severity. Adding a dimensional quality to the exploration of these behaviors (as opposed to relying solely on the categories of the DSM) is helpful. We explore these behaviors in a rudimentary way to try to capture the "typical" ends of a dimension, knowing full well that the endpoints we have drawn are somewhat arbitrary (for examples of clinical interviews measuring the presence and severity of EDs, see the Eating Disorder Examination; Fairburn & Cooper, 1993; the Yale-Brown-Cornell Eating Disorder Scale; Sunday, Halmi, & Einhorn, 1995; and the Structured Inventory of Anorexic and Bulimic Syndromes; Fichter, Herpetz, Quadflieg, & Herpetz-Dahlmann, 1998).

Most individuals with EDs have high dietary ideals and engage in food restriction to some degree. These individuals restrict by reducing the quantity of food as well as the types of food they eat. Mild restriction may be characterized as eating 1200 calories a day of "healthy" foods. High-fat and high-sugar foods (e.g., desserts, chips) may be avoided, but no categories of food from the nutritional pyramid are routinely skipped. Severe restriction may be characterized as eating 500 calories a day of certain "safe" foods, typically fruits and vegetables. Whole categories of food such as meat and dairy may be avoided. Restriction, particularly as it becomes more severe, is often accompanied by rigid, compulsive rules around when and how to eat. Clients may need to eat at only certain times of day and may need to eat alone. They may cut their food up into tiny bites, chew each mouthful of food a certain number of times, manipulate their food, and hoard food. Eating may become a highly ritualized act that looks bizarre to the outsider.

Individuals who binge consume large quantities of food in a short period of time and experience a loss of control over their behavior. DSM criteria explicitly avoid assigning a caloric limit to "large" quantities of food and therapists must use clinical judgment in this matter. That said, clients describe binges that range anywhere from 1000 calories to greater than 5000 calories. A 5000-calorie binge, for example, may consist of one piece of cake, ½ gallon of ice cream, 2 bowls of cereal, 4 pieces of toast, 10 cookies, a bag of chips, and 32 oz. of diet coke. Clients usually binge on foods they feel are "forbidden," such as high-carbohydrate and high-fat foods, but they may also eat whatever is available. Some are so out of control that they eat all of the food in their kitchen or eat food out of garbage cans. The food eaten during a binge is often consumed quickly and until an individual is uncomfortably full. Clinically, clients present with binge eating symptoms that range in frequency from rare to multiple times a day.

Individuals with EDs usually engage in compensatory behaviors to prevent weight gain. Compensatory behaviors of the purging type include self-induced vomiting and/or the misuse of laxatives, diuretics, enemas, suppositories, diet pills, and syrup of ipecac. Clients may consume large quantities of these weight-loss aids (e.g., double or triple the standard dosage of laxatives), and purging behaviors are the source of many medical complications in EDs. Clinically, clients present with purging symptoms that range in frequency from rare to multiple times a day. Compensatory behaviors of the nonpurging type include fasting and excessive exercise. Clients may engage in a variety of exercise routines such as running, cardio machines, weights, exercise videos, and team sport practices. Some exercise for an hour a day whereas others exercise for more than 5 hours a day. Many exercise in spite of injuries (e.g., stress fractures) or illness. Even when they are not exercising, these clients are often compelled to move and fidget (e.g., leg shaking, pacing) for the benefit of burning calories.

A common feature in EDs is to observe swings back and forth between the poles of restricting and bingeing and/or binge eating and purging. It is the frequency and intensity of these behaviors that land a client in the different DSM diagnostic categories. In the case of restricting AN, the restriction pole dominates and the binge-eating pole is mild. (A client with restricting AN does not binge in the strict DSM sense of the term, but she is likely to *feel* she has binged. For her, one cookie may be experienced as a binge. This phenomenon is referred to as "subjective bingeing" by therapists.) In the case of BED, the binge-eating pole dominates and the restriction pole is mild and/or only experienced intra-psychically. In the case of BN, there is an alternating shift between the binge-eating and restricting poles and/or the binge-eating and purging poles.

Cognitive-behavioral theories suggest that strict dieting leads to physiological as well as psychological hunger, which sets individuals up for bingeing. Thus, cycles of restricting and binge-eating, and binge-eating and purging become entrenched in self-perpetuating feedback loops of deprivation and overcompensation (Wilson, Fairburn, & Agras, 1997). By normalizing eating patterns, these cycles may be broken. Nutritional education and rehabilitation have a role in this normalization.

Obsession with weight and shape is apparent in other behaviors as well. Individuals with EDs often engage in ritualistic, compulsive behaviors that are meant to monitor weight and appearance. For example, they may weigh themselves multiple times a day. They may engage in "body checking," which involves routinely measuring, pinching, touching, or otherwise investigating parts of their body. They may keep detailed lists of their calorie intake or weight. They may also engage in a number of avoidance behaviors. Some individuals never look in the mirror and wear only loose-fitting clothing in an attempt to hide their bodies. They may refuse to swim, go to the beach, or participate in other activities that could draw attention to their bodies.

There are common physical symptoms that result from EDs (APA, 2006). Clients may complain of weakness, dizziness, cold intolerance, fatigue, heart palpitations, chest pain, constipation, swollen cheeks and neck, dry and brittle hair, and menstrual dysfunction. Associated acute complications include dehydration, hypothermia, various cardiac arrhythmias, and gastrointestinal motility disturbances. With purging behaviors, complications include electrolyte disturbances, enlarged salivary glands and dental decay, as well as edema (swelling). Amenorrhea (absence of menstrual cycle) may be associated with osteopenia (low bone mineral density), which can progress to irreversible osteoporosis (weakened, fragile bones) and an associated increased risk for fractures. The seriousness of these medical complications cannot be underestimated. AN has the highest mortality rate of any psychiatric disorder (Sullivan, 1995). Death related to AN and BN is often the result of cardiac arrest, as starvation and electrolyte imbalances can seriously compromise cardiac functioning.

Research suggests that some of the clinical features associated with EDs may result from malnutrition or semi-starvation. In a classic study by Keys and colleagues, psychologically healthy volunteers were restricted to approximately half of their normal food intake for 6 months. These volunteers experienced a variety of physical, psychological, and social disturbances, including extreme food preoccupation, food hoarding, abnormal taste preferences, binge-eating, impaired concentration, depression, obsessionality, irritability, and social withdrawal (Keys et al., 1950). Some of these starvation-related phenomena may abate in clients with AN as they gain weight. However, traits such as obsessive-compulsiveness may reflect both a preexisting and enduring trait, which is exacerbated by semi-starvation, and may be only partially reversed with nutritional rehabilitation (APA, 2006). Although clients with BN are by definition not at an "anorexic" weight, they also may experience symptoms related to malnutrition if they are below their personally optimum weight range.

It is the norm, rather than the exception, for individuals with EDs to have comorbid psychiatric conditions (the following statistics are cited in APA, 2006). Lifetime comorbid Major Depressive Disorder or Persistent Depressive Disorder have been reported in 50–75% of clients with AN and BN. Comorbid anxiety disorders, particularly Social Anxiety Disorder and Obsessive Compulsive Disorder (OCD), are also common in clients with EDs. Among AN clients in particular, the lifetime prevalence of OCD has been reported as high as 25%, with OCD symptoms frequently predating the onset of AN. Substance abuse is more common among clients with BN than AN, with comorbidity estimates ranging from 23–40%. Sexual abuse has been reported in 20–50% of clients with AN and BN, and these women are more likely to present with comorbid psychiatric conditions than women who have not experienced sexual abuse. Clients with EDs may also meet the criteria for comorbid Personality Disorders, with estimates ranging from 42–75%. BN has been associated with Borderline Personality Disorder and Narcissistic Personality Disorder, and AN has been associated with Obsessive-Compulsive Personality Disorder and Avoidant Personality Disorder.

Research suggests that there is a genetic component in the development of EDs. For example, first-degree relatives of someone with AN and BN are more likely to have an ED than relatives of control subjects (Lilenfeld et al., 1998; Strober, Freeman, Lampert, Diamond, & Kaye; 2000), and monozygotic twins have a higher concordance rate of EDs than dizygotic twins. The heritability estimates for both AN and BN range from .54 to .80 (Devlin et al., 2002) and "these heritability estimates are in line with those found in studies of schizophrenia and bipolar disorder, suggesting that EDs may be as 'genetically influenced' as disorders traditionally viewed as biological in nature" (Kaye, Wagner, Frank, & Bailer, 2006, p. 124). In linkage analysis, a methodology used in molecular genetic studies, variation in the contribution of genes from mother and father to offspring is used to find disease genes or genes that influence a trait. This approach requires a large sample of families with at least two relatives (usually siblings) who have the disease or trait of interest (Mazzeo, Landt, van Furth, & Bulik, 2006). Linkage analyses from genetic studies have identified regions of genes that may be implicated in AN on a chromosome labeled 1p (Grice et al., 2002) and in BN on a chromosome labeled 10p (Bulik et al., 2003). The specifics, however, of what vulnerabilities are transferred from parent to child and the mechanisms by which these vulnerabilities contribute to the development of EDs still remain to be determined. Also, epigenetics has become increasingly part of ED research. It seems we are more likely to find connections looking at gene–environment interactions, in contrast to genetics alone (Campbell et al., 2011). There are also conflicting studies on the role of ghrelin in EDs and whether it is a causal factor or a variable related to maintenance of the disorder. Ghrelin is an amino acid peptide and hormone produced in the pancreas and cells lining the stomach. Ghrelin levels increase before meals and decrease after meals, so it has been proposed that ghrelin dysregulation plays a role in EDs (Atalayer, Gibson, Konopaka, & Geliebter, 2013). As noted, studies in this area are so far conflicting, with some supporting the hypothesis and others not.

In the last few years, a growing body of research suggests that neurobiological alterations in clients with AN and BN may contribute to the appetite dysregulation, mood problems, obsessionality, and body image distortions observed in these disorders (Jimerson & Wolfe, 2006; Kaye et al., 2006). For instance, results from physiological studies (that examined the concentration of serotonin metabolites in cerebrospinal fluid), brain-imaging studies (that identified serotonin transporter availability and receptor binding in various regions of the brain), and genetic studies are converging to suggest that abnormal serotonin functioning may play a role in AN and BN, and that persisting, possibly trait-related, alterations may reflect a biological vulnerability factor for the development of these disorders. Selective-serotonin reuptake inhibitors (SSRIs) are commonly used to treat EDs, and the U.S. Food and Drug Administration approves of fluoxetine for treatment of BN (APA, 2006).

**UPPER-LEFT QUADRANT: THE INTERIOR OF THE INDIVIDUAL** Our Integral journey continues through the territory of EDs by exploring the *subjective, experiential* component of the disorders. What thoughts, feelings, and perceptions do these individuals have of themselves, others, and the world? What is the phenomenological experience of having an ED? Typically these have included (but are not limited to) perfectionism, low self-esteem, difficulty coping with mood states, and interpersonal difficulties (Hoiles, Egan, & Kane, 2012).

The common denominator of most individuals with EDs is preoccupation with weight and excessive self-evaluation based on weight and shape (Garner, Vitousek, & Pike, 1997; Wilson et al., 1997). Such clients obsessively think about food, calories, weight, shape, and appearance throughout most of their waking hours. Their thoughts are often experienced as anxiety-producing and distressing. When entrenched in an ED, these individuals base their entire sense of self-worth upon their weight and shape. It is the magnitude of these concerns that differentiates these individuals from those merely dissatisfied with weight/shape.

Thoughts related to food and weight concerns are distorted and unrealistic in clients with EDs. Dichotomous thinking is exemplified in their categorization of foods as good or bad, the self as fat or thin, the self as "in control" and "good" when restricting or "out of control" and "bad" when eating. Their thinking may become superstitious; for example, in the belief that eating certain foods will lead instantly to fat deposited on the thighs. These individuals magnify the importance of events related to eating. For instance, eating one cookie is seen as a "disaster." This disaster may result in social isolation because the individual is now "fat;" it may result in binge-eating because the "diet is blown so I'll throw in the towel and eat whatever I want." Clients assume that how they "feel" is reality and they are unable to observe their thoughts related to weight/shape from a more objective stance. Typical assumptions include "I feel fat; therefore I am fat" and "I feel ugly; therefore I am ugly."

An internal dialogue often accompanies the swing between binge eating and restricting or binge eating and purging; it goes something like this: "I suck. My body is so fat, so gross. I'm only allowing myself one bite. Just a little bite. I can't believe I ate that! I'm such a pig. I'm going to gain 50 pounds! My body is out of control. I feel so horrible; I've got to throw up. I'm not eating anything tomorrow. I hate myself!" This dialogue may present whether the binge is 5000 calories or 20 calories. Volatile mood swings may be associated with desiring to eat, dreading to eat, and self-loathing for eating.

Individuals with EDs often experience the body as alien, as "not-me." Not only is the body not-me, it is the enemy and must be controlled. Those with AN, in particular, often wish to negate the body. They experience bodily sensations such as hunger as foreign and are terrified that the body will betray them. For example, taking even a bite of food is scary because they may not be able to stop: They fear an insatiable appetite. Some clients feel trapped in their bodies. The body is experienced as a confinement and limitation, and they just want to "crawl out of" their skin. They feel pride in seeing how far they can push their bodies through running and other sports. It is important to understand that this is not an experience of healthy embodiment; this is an experience of the body as an object to be perfected, sculpted, and punished (Bordo, 1993).

Individuals with EDs assume that "being thin" will confer desirable feelings, attributes, and outcomes. For example, being thin will lead to happiness. Being thin equates with "I'm disciplined, I'm successful, I'm worthy, and I'm loveable." "Being fat" leads to unhappiness. Being fat equates with "I'm lazy, I'm a failure, I'm unworthy, and I'm unlovable." When pressed, individuals with EDs are often unable to define being thin or being fat. At the beginning of their disorder, thinness and fatness usually equate with particular numbers on the scale. Being fat, for example, often equates to the highest weight these individuals obtained in their personal history. Being thin is often defined in an arbitrary way. It may be equated with losing 10 pounds, it may be equated with weighing a whole number (e.g., 100, 110, 120 pounds), or it may be equated with two-digit weights (i.e., less than 100 pounds). As they lose weight and achieve the number originally equated with thinness, they often do not feel happy or successful or worthy. Instead of realizing that weight loss is unconnected to these desirable outcomes, they often decide that a new and lower number on the scale must define thinness. Over time, it becomes apparent that no weight is thin enough; being thin enough is actually an unattainable goal. As well, every weight that is "not thin" becomes "fat"—there is no such thing as a neutral weight. It is this line of dichotomous reasoning that leads a clearly underweight individual with AN to proclaim with all sincerity "I'm too fat." Cognitive therapies help clients challenge these types of distorted thoughts and weight assumptions (Garner et al., 1997; Wilson et al., 1997).

It is difficult for most individuals with EDs to make an object of awareness of this ultimate paradox—the pursuit of a thinness ideal that can never be obtained. Thus, they relish their victories with weight loss and elevate the significance of each pound lost. Individuals with AN feel a sense of triumph, mastery, self-control, and superiority with weight loss. Over time, the ED informs their sense of self. These clients proclaim, "Being thin is what makes me special, it makes me different from others" and "I'm more powerful, capable, and in control when I don't eat." It is the ego syntonic nature of AN that accounts for their denial of illness and their often passionate refusal to change in treatment. Individuals suffering from BN usually feel a great deal of shame about their bingeing behavior, as they view it as a sign of weakness and failure at self-control, and thus enter treatment motivated to give up this behavior. However, these individuals are as unwilling to give up the pursuit of thinness as individuals with AN. Despite their shame, they often characterize the ED as their "best friend." Hence, they also usually lack motivation to change in treatment. Thus, motivation-to-change strategies are frequently used to help clients engage in recovery (Villapiano & Goodman, 2001).

Individuals with the diagnosis of BED report levels of eating, shape, and weight concerns comparable to individuals with BN (Marcus, Smith, Santelli, & Kaye, 1992). They too have unrealistically high dieting standards and maintain distorted beliefs about food and weight. Typically, they do not hold the same overvalued ideas about the importance of thinness. Most clients with BED feel comfortable with the notion of an average size body. As obesity is common in individuals with BED, their shame and intense dissatisfaction often comes from having an objectively larger body size. Bingeing may also be their "best friend," but they are motivated for treatment because they hope that control of their bingeing will lead to weight loss.

Although many intrapsychic similarities exist between women and men with EDs, differences have been reported (Anderson, Cohn, & Holbrook, 2000). Women are usually dissatisfied with their body shape from the waist down whereas men tend to be dissatisfied from the waist up. Women are more focused on thinness whereas men are more focused on achieving a lean and muscular physique. Some men want to increase weight to "bulk up" and believe that they cannot get big enough. This condition is known as reverse AN or body dysmorphia and it afflicts men almost exclusively (Anderson et al., 2000). Just as anorexics feel they cannot be thin enough, these men feel they cannot be big enough. Often, these men use anabolic steroids to achieve larger muscle mass.

Another paradox is that EDs serve an adaptive coping function. Some individuals are able to identify the function of their ED whereas others, especially those with AN, may be alexithymic (the inability to talk about feelings due to a lack of awareness). These clients push feelings out of awareness using both suppression and repression. The degree to which clients are able to relate to and describe their inner experiences appears to be a function of their self-organization—that is, the degree to which their bodily, cognitive, and emotional experiences are organized and integrated into a cohesive, integrated self (Goodsitt, 1997). One task of therapy is to help clients understand the function of their ED and how it serves them.

For many clients, the ED regulates overwhelming emotional states such as sadness, loneliness, anxiety, tension, boredom, anger, rejection, and stress. For example, some feel hopeless; they believe they will never be able to solve their problems. Others feel profoundly sad and alone and have a sense that no one understands them. Some experience pronounced feelings of self-loathing and guilt for taking up space in the world. Some experience an anxious perfectionism; they feel constantly on edge and tense and want to do everything perfectly. Under the cloud of a sense of impending doom, they worry about every decision, every word spoken, and every action. Sometimes this manifests as feeling very self-conscious or exposed, or as worry about how they are being judged by others. These various emotions may be part of a specific mood disorder or they may be triggered by external life events. Regardless of the origin of the feelings, there is a sense that the feelings cannot be handled or tolerated and that restricting, bingeing and/or purging help to cope with the feelings. The ED seems to distract clients from their mood state, blunt the feelings, or in some way release tension from the feelings. The end result is the re-establishment of a sense of equilibrium, albeit the sense is rooted in unhealthy coping.

The ED establishes more than emotional equilibrium for some individuals. Using the language of self-psychology, the ED facilitates a sense of cohesion and self-organization (Goodsitt, 1997). Many clients experience themselves as empty or flawed; they do not feel whole or real—there is a sense that what others see on the outside does not match up with what is felt on the inside. Some feel ineffective and incompetent at getting what they want and need. Some describe not knowing what they want or need. Some feel inferior to others; that they are somehow irreparably defective and unlovable. The ED drowns out these painful experiences of the self. The obsessive preoccupations and compulsive rituals provide these individuals with feelings of safety, predictability, and control. The process is one of projection, in which overwhelming internal states are pushed out of awareness and onto the body, and controlling the body gives the illusion of restoring control. The ED symptoms narrow down their lives to something that feels manageable (controlling the body) and become the basis for a felt sense of self. Again, in Integral terms, parts of the self are disowned and shadow is created.

For some individuals, the ED protects a fragile sense of self from failure. The disorder becomes the ultimate refuge and excuse for failing to meet expectations of self and others. If the individual is "well" and fails, the failure would be experienced as intolerable; so it is better to remain "sick."

Many suggest that EDs are a way to negotiate the developmental task of separation and individuation (Johnson, 1991a). For example, some adolescent clients feel drawn to care for and meet the needs of their parents. Parents may impose this need upon them (e.g., as in the parent who overtly places her child in a parentified, confidante role) or it may be inferred. These adolescents take it upon themselves to never be a burden, and to care for the parent. They are compliant, accommodating, and focused on serving others. At the extreme, these adolescents feel guilty for simply being. They want to negate the self, as having their own needs is "selfish" and they should live only to take care of others. Growing up and pursuing their lives poses a problem that the ED "solves." Individuals who cannot fully function in the world due to their ED often live at home or stay close to home, making them available to care for the parent. Additionally, these adolescents are scared to grow up and assume adult responsibilities. Having not had their own developmental needs for autonomy adequately met, they sense they are not prepared to, nor know how to, function in an independent manner.

At the same time, it is difficult for these adolescents to completely abandon their developmental needs, and the ED also solves this problem. It communicates, especially in individuals with AN, "Pay attention to me. Look at me. I have needs. I need to be taken care of." The disorder communicates that something has gone wrong in the maturation process and that the adolescent has unfulfilled caretaking needs. At the same time, these adolescents exert a measure of separation and independence from their parents by controlling their bodies. Parents soon learn that they cannot force their adolescent to stop the symptoms of the ED. So, the disorder serves the paradoxical function of keeping adolescents dependent, while at the same time allowing them to feel a measure of independence.

Binge eating can meet any number of needs. For example, bingeing is a way to indirectly meet needs for self-soothing, self-confirmation, and connection. Bingeing is a statement that implies, "I have legitimate needs. Some part of me is wanting and I will respond to that want. I will allow myself (psychological) sustenance. I want to be soothed, I want to be recognized, and I want to feel connected." Individuals with EDs often experience conflict around these needs. For a variety of reasons, clients feel they do not deserve to have needs. There may be a sense that they are too needy, and purging is a way to "undo" the binge. Purging punishes the individual for acting on her needs. Thus, the bingeing behavior is an assertion of the self and the purging behavior is a punishment for it (Reindl, 2001).

EDs can also be the solution to the "problem" of puberty (Crisp, 1997; Strober, 1991). The body shape of an individual with AN is prepubescent. As long as the body remains childlike, the individual may be able to avoid adult developmental challenges related to matters such as sexuality. For those who have been sexually abused or raped, the prepubescent form can be protective. It is meant to ward off unwanted sexual attention from others as well as protect the individual from having to face her own sexual urges. Similarly, weight gain associated with binge eating can be protective. These individuals attempt to avoid sexual attention by being physically undesirable (according to cultural norms) and they use fat as psychological protection. Fat "cushions" them from abuse by others as well as becoming a "wall" to distance them from abuse by others. Purging behavior can be a symbolic way to "expel" specific acts related to sexual trauma (Schwartz & Cohn, 1996).

ED symptoms may be used to communicate with others. In a deliberate manner, individuals will act on their symptoms to communicate anger, frustration, or displeasure with another. For instance, more than one adolescent has thrown up in front of her parents as a way to say, "I'm mad at you, I hope you feel bad, I want to punish you." The disorder becomes a weapon and a way to try and manipulate or guilt others into behaving as one desires.

These are some of the common intrapsychic (as well as a few interpersonal) functions an ED may serve. We want to return the reader's attention to the notion of swinging between poles on a continuum. Themes that have emerged in the discussion thus far include swinging between full and empty, indulgence and restraint, desire and deprivation, out-of-control and in-control, self-hatred and pride, anxious and calm, nurturance and self-abnegation, connected and disconnected, dependent and independent, vulnerable and protected, selfish and selfless. These are the subjective experiences that parallel the objective behaviors of bingeing and restricting. It has become apparent that EDs are about much more than food and weight; food has become loaded with alternative meanings.

**LOWER-LEFT QUADRANT: THE INTERIOR OF GROUPS** At this point in our Integral journey, we explore the *intersubjective* experience of individuals with EDs. What is their experience of being in relation with significant others? What is their experience of being in a "we space" of mutual resonance and understanding? Some of the answers to these questions have been touched upon in the previous section. This perspective examines the *cultural contexts* that individuals identify with, the "collective we," and how these contexts inform their sense of self, values, customs, and worldviews.

A natural place to begin this exploration is with the family, as the first relationships people form are with members of their immediate family. In the psychodynamic literature, much has been said about disturbances in the early mother-daughter relationship that predispose girls to develop an ED during adolescence. In cases of restricting AN, the relationship between mothers and daughters has been characterized as enmeshed (Johnson, 1991b). The mother is often described as domineering and overprotective. The mother seems unable, for a variety of reasons, to encourage developmentally appropriate growth and independence in her daughter. The mother fails to provide an adequate holding environment (Winnicott, 1965) and instead "uses" (unconsciously or consciously) the daughter to meet her own needs. For example, the mother may wish to keep the daughter close for emotional support, to be needed, or to alleviate her own fears of growing older. This over-involvement of the mother can feel intrusive, too close, and overwhelming. Some clients are conscious of this dynamic and complain of their mother's overprotectiveness and the sense that there is "no space" that is their own. Others are unaware of this dynamic and instead describe their mother as "my best friend, she knows everything about me." For the adolescent with AN, "the self-starvation is a desperate attempt to assert some autonomy, defend the fragile self against further maternal intrusiveness, and protect the fragile ego from the psychobiological demands of adulthood" (Johnson, 1991b, p. 170). Food restriction, symbolically, is an attempt to keep others out.

In cases of BN, the relationship between mothers and daughters has been characterized as one of underinvolvement (Johnson, 1991b). The mother is often described as passive, rejecting, and disengaged. These clients often feel emotionally neglected, that their mothers are unavailable in some way. These mothers may have been unable to provide an adequate holding environment for a variety of reasons such as depression, preoccupation with their own lives, an illness, or divorce. The result is a bulimic client who feels that her mother is unable to meet her needs, particularly needs for connection and self-soothing. The client is painfully aware of wanting more and of feeling that she has missed out on the right kind of parenting. Food becomes a substitute for mothering. It has the power to soothe and is readily available. Bingeing behavior, symbolically, is an attempt to take others in.

Feminist therapists add that issues related to gender identity and relational bonding are also important in understanding the mother–daughter relationship and EDs (Chernin, 1985; Rabinor, 1994). Gender roles have been in flux for the last 40 years, and girls who are coming of age today are faced with a different world than confronted their mothers. Chernin (1985) suggests that every generation measures itself against the one before, and that a daughter's experience of being female will be shaped to some extent by that of her mother: her mother's choices, her frustrations, her limits and constraints. It is this comparison between self and mother that is considered both risky and at risk, as girls today have the social and psychological opportunity to surpass the life choices of their mothers. Identification is risky because daughters can feel a great deal of rage (and underneath the rage, profound sadness and longing) at a mother who has not prepared them for this new world. As Knapp (2003) noted this is rage at a mother you did not relate to and who caused you confusion and pain. This could come from the mother trying too hard, negating her own pleasure and who can't see who you want to be in that moment.

From the perspective of the lower-left quadrant, this becomes the crux of the matter because now, the relationship with the mother is at risk. Some writers (Kaplan & Surrey, 1984) suggest that the task of identity development in women culminates in relationship-differentiation, as opposed to separation-individuation as seen in men. A woman's basic sense of self-worth is thought to be tied to her ability to find mutuality and understanding in relationships. Chernin (1985) argues that daughters experience an intolerable conflict; they are torn between remaining loyal and in connection with the mother versus forging a new role in this shifting world and becoming disconnected. This dilemma is central to EDs. The ED is a way to stay aligned with the mother, as if to say, "I'm just as self-depriving and unfulfilled as you are; we are the same." Yet, the ED is also a rejection of that alignment. Equating food with mothering, starving and purging are ways, symbolically, to reject the mother. The betrayal of leaving the mother behind also produces guilt. "How can I allow myself to have what she didn't have?" The ED is a way to atone for this betrayal—to make restitution. Essentially, it communicates "I'm leaving you, but I won't get too far." Feminist therapists work to heal and transform the mother–daughter relationship by helping girls move beyond their rage and blame (Rabinor, 1994).

The father's role in EDs has received attention in the psychodynamic literature as well. According to some authors, fathers represent the world outside of the family (Maine, 2004; Zerbe, 1993). Fathers "benevolently disrupt" the early mother-daughter bond, draw their daughters into the external world of new people and new challenges, and give their daughters permission to develop their own talents and interests (Zerbe, 1993). Fathers also play a role in accepting and encouraging their daughter's sexuality while at the same time respecting familial boundaries. Maine argues that fathers in Western culture are emotionally unavailable for their daughters, largely due to limiting myths and social patterns that keep the father outside of the family. "Father hunger" is the emptiness experienced by women whose fathers were emotionally absent. This void can lead to concerns with body image, yo-yo dieting, and disordered eating.

Humphrey (1991) suggests that deficits in nurturance, soothing, and individuation reflect a trans-generational, developmental arrest in families with EDs. The parents were never nurtured, or soothed, or had their developmental needs met appropriately, and consequently the parents try to master these deficits through re-enactments with their own children. The adaptation to these deficits differs. As Humphrey wrote, nurturing in anorexic families may be given to a daughter only if she remains dependent or childlike. In bulimic families there seems to be a lack of love or a general hunger for affection.

The result of failures in the holding environment, passed down from generation to generation, is that parent and child remain fundamentally dependent on each other for their psychological integrity and stability. Family members are unable to maintain separate identities, and the ED becomes one way for the family as a whole to establish a sense of security.

These are just a few of the theories about the "we" culture in families that contribute to EDs. The same two poles discussed in the upper-left quadrant have appeared and been expanded upon in the discussion: swings between dependence and independence, connection and disconnection, chaos and control. These theories are difficult to validate empirically, and the notion that there are *consistent* patterns in family relationships has fallen out of favor in the more recent literature on families (Dare & Eisler, 2002). The move has been toward focusing on the family as a system, and we will pick up on this discussion in the lower-right quadrant. We include these theories in the discussion here as they have conceptual utility for understanding relationship dynamics in *some* families, and research does support that family factors contribute importantly to the development and maintenance of EDs (Vandereycken, 2002).

Whereas family is the first "culture" for all individuals, culture also refers to one's affiliation with, for example, specific peer groups, sport teams, and sexual orientation. Childhood obesity and weight-related teasing by peers has been implicated in disordered eating (Becker & Fay, 2006). More than one client has said, "I will never again be rejected for being fat." The risk of EDs is higher in competitive athletes involved in appearance and weight conscious sports such as ballet, gymnastics, long distance running, and wrestling as compared to athletes in less-weight-conscious sports (APA, 2006). Focus on the individual (as opposed to a team) and the belief that lower weight will lead to increased performance are factors that may contribute to body dissatisfaction and EDs in these sports. With respect to sexual orientation, there are no differences between lesbian and heterosexual women concerning body dissatisfaction, but gay men report more appearance dissatisfaction than heterosexual men (Myers, Taub, Morris, & Rothblum, 1999). Some homosexual men develop AN in an attempt to be more attractive and to improve their relationships (Anderson et al., 2000).

Individuals with EDs usually have problems in relationships outside of the family. Interpersonal theories suggest that EDs are caused, in part, by the distress of interpersonal role disputes (i.e., discrepancies in expectations for the relationship), role transitions (i.e., change in life status), interpersonal deficits (i.e., feeling socially isolated or unfulfilled), and grief (i.e., loss of an important person or relationship; Fairburn, 1997). Clients typically assume the caretaker role in relationships and the ED may be a way to relieve them from the stress associated with this role (Tantleff-Dunn, Gokee-LaRose, & Peterson, 2004). Many clients believe the "real" self must be hidden in order to relate to others. Women with AN may fear relationships because they confuse engagement with enmeshment (Steiner-Adair, 1991). These individuals will say, "I can't need you, because if I need you I will lose myself." To compensate, they may become pseudo-independent and proclaim they do not need others. Many women with BN struggle with separation/differentiation in relationships because they fear abandonment and fragmentation (Steiner-Adair, 1991). These clients may feel, "I do need you, but I can't let you know how much I need you because my neediness is too much and you'll leave me." They are often very sensitive to the perception of others and may direct their attention to pleasing and accommodating others. Thus, for many people with EDs, relationships seem to lack genuine connection and feel false.

This difficulty with connection and intimacy may extend to an individual's spirituality (in this case, her relationship with God). Theistic views of human nature suggest that the core of identity and personality is spiritual (Richards, Hardman, & Berrett, 2006). Richards et al. (2006) suggest that EDs are a spiritual problem. The deep feelings of unworthiness and lack of identity experienced by most individuals contribute to alienation from God and significant others. For example, some women feel they are unforgivable, unacceptable, or unworthy of a relationship with God. Some blame God for their struggles, or view God as an angry, judgmental, and punishing figure. These clients place their faith in the ED instead of God, and lose touch with their spiritual identity and worth. Lelwica (1999) argues that EDs point to a spiritual hunger and a need for a sense of meaning and wholeness. She suggests that religion has failed to meet women's needs through its male chauvinism and Cartesian dualism. As a result, women have turned to the pursuit of thinness in an attempt to meet their spiritual needs for meaning and salvation. She noted that images of women on the Internet or in print media are not just images but function more as icons of being a woman. This feminine ideal is alluded to almost as some sort of transcendent truth. In that sense for many women looking at them, they almost function religiously in the sense that they promise a sense of meaning and purpose in a world of ambiguity and pain.

We will return to the role of the media in EDs in the lower-right quadrant. Relatively little research has explored the connection between EDs and spirituality, although case studies and testimonials from clients suggest that their spirituality has played an important role in recovery (Garrett, 1998; Richards et al., 2006).

In contemporary America, efforts to enhance and preserve one's beauty are considered central features of femininity. This cultural emphasis on attractiveness for girls and women is reinforced in various contexts. As Striegel-Moore (1995) summarizes, products made for young girls (e.g., clothing and toys) emphasize the importance of being pretty. Research has found that girls in school receive more attention for their physical appearance and receive less academic guidance and feedback than boys. Beauty is linked with female competence, achievement, and interpersonal success; physically attractive women are judged as more feminine than less attractive women; and women eating small meals are perceived as more feminine than women eating large meals.

This cultural backdrop, this collective "we space," has a huge impact on dieting behavior and appearance attitudes. A few statistics compiled by the National Eating Disorders Association (2005) serve to illustrate. A whopping 80% of American women are dissatisfied with their appearance. Eighty-one percent of 10-year-old girls are afraid of being fat. Forty-six percent of 9- to 11-year-olds are "sometimes" or "very often" on diets, and 82% of their families are "sometimes" or "very often" on diets. Ninety-one percent of women in college attempt to control their weight through dieting, and 22% diet "often" or "always." Twenty-five percent of American men and 45% of American women are on a diet on any given day (National Eating Disorders Association [NEDA], 2005). As well, studies suggest that weight and body image do not correlate.

The results of a *Glamour* magazine survey of 33,000 women found that 75% of women thought they were fat even though only 25% were medically overweight, and 45% of the underweight women thought they were too fat (Wolf, 1991). Many individuals who seek treatment for an ED describe the onset of their symptoms as following a period of dieting and/or weight loss. Dieting, weight and shape concerns, and negative body image have long been considered an important precursor, if not cause, of EDs (Jacobi, 2005). There is a close resonance between the drive for thinness observed in EDs and the culture's drive for thinness.

Some would call American culture's obsession with thinness a new religion (Seid, 1994). Eating habits and body weight have been elevated into a reflection of one's moral character. To be fat is shameful and dirty, and a sign of laziness. To be thin is honorable and clean, and a sign of willpower and discipline. "Weightism" (i.e., discrimination against people who are obese) is a form of prejudice that can have a major impact on the quality of one's life. As Steiner-Adair (1994) summarizes:

> Significant relationships have been identified between weight and (1) teachers' evaluations of students; (2) mental health professionals' assessments of clients (more emotional problems are attributed to large people); (3) physicians' assessments of clients (doctors judge obese people to be weak-willed, as if their weight gain were strictly a matter of insufficient willpower); (4) admissions committees' assessments of candidates for higher education; (5) personnel decisions in hiring and promotion; and (6) landlords' decisions about rental candidates. (p. 385)

Therapists who work with obese clients hear the personal stories behind these facts. Weightism tells people that dieting is the primary tool for success in this society. Weightism is why the most desired goal of 33,000 women is to lose 10 to 15 pounds; a goal that is prioritized above success in work or in love (Wolf, 1991). In short, American culture is obsessed with thinness. Narrow definitions of female beauty are promoted that include weights and body shapes that are unattainable by most. Physical appearance has become a measure of one's moral worth. This is the culture in which EDs are embedded and develop.

It is sometimes speculated that women from racial and ethnic minority groups are "immune" to developing EDs, because their cultural identity protects them against body image dissatisfaction. African American women, for instance, are thought to be less prone to EDs because their culture traditionally embraces larger body types than does the dominant culture. It is hypothesized that the process of acculturation, and the assimilation of dominant ideals, increases a woman of color's susceptibility to EDs. Research suggests that acculturation does matter, but that level of acculturation does not always predict vulnerability to EDs (Kempa & Thomas, 2000; Lake, Staiger, & Glowinski, 2000). Rather, the stage of one's ethnic identity may affect susceptibility. Ethnic identity development is generally viewed as moving from an absence of awareness about the importance of race/ethnicity, to conformity with dominant cultural stereotypes, to dissonance about those stereotypes, to rejection of dominant culture, and finally to an individuated integration (Myers, 1988). For example, individuals in the conformity stage may internalize dominant values of beauty that could lead to EDs, and that those in the dissonance stage may develop EDs as a way to cope with felt oppressive circumstances.

Contemporary American culture is also obsessed with excessive consumption, particularly in the realm of material goods. Americans seem to have channeled the pursuit of happiness into the pursuit of stuff, and women make 83% of consumer purchases in this country (Knapp, 2003). Consumer culture says, "Buy this product, it will fix what ails you." There is a collective belief that says, "If only I had those shoes, that outfit, that car, that house, then I would be OK." There is the problem of "keeping up with the Joneses." There is a resonance between the *sense of wanting and bingeing* in EDs and our collective *sense of wanting and buying material goods*. There is a collective desire to fill up; yet, no matter how much one consumes, it is never enough. Notice the broad cultural poles; swings between deny and buy, restraint and gluttony. These poles parallel the individual poles of restricting and bingeing, in-control and out-of-control.

As a culture, what do women really hunger for? What cultural longings have been converted into obsession with thinness and the possession of things? Knapp (2003) persuasively argues that women are hungry to partake in the world, to feel a sense of abundance and possibility about life, for freedom and power. Forty years after the women's movement, women have more personal freedom than ever before, but this has not translated into a *collective visceral sense* of power and competence. Societal statistics point to the reason why: Congress is 90% male, 98% of America's top corporate officers are male, only 4.4% of CEO jobs in Fortune 500 companies are held by women, and women continue to make 84 cents for every dollar a man makes. There is a gap between personal freedom and political power. Knapp (2003) has raised the questions with clients of what would satisfy them. Are there true passions underlying a goal of thinness? She notes that many women are never encouraged to explore these.

**LOWER-RIGHT QUADRANT: THE EXTERIOR OF GROUPS** We conclude our four-quadrant Integral exploration by focusing on the *interobjective* perspective of EDs. What conclusions can be drawn about the externally observable, societal aspects of EDs? We began this discussion in the previous quadrant, and we will draw parallels between the two. In particular, we look at EDs through the lens of historical, familial, social, political, and economic forces that operate in contemporary American culture.

Historical and anthropological studies suggest that women have used control of appetite and food as a form of expression dating back to the 13th century (Brumberg, 2000). For example, there are reports of women in the church ("fasting saints") who refused to eat in devotion to the Eucharist. Historians are quick to assert, however, that just because a behavior occurs across cultures or time does not necessarily mean that it has the same cause or meaning. EDs, as we know them today, are considered modern disorders.

AN was first named and identified in the 1870s, and was recognized almost simultaneously in the United States, England, and France. It emerged during the Industrial Revolution and was a distinct psychopathology of middle-class family life. It seems that the refusal to eat was a way for young girls of the bourgeois class to reject expectations to become a "proper" kind of woman and to find an appropriate, if not advantageous, marriage (Brumberg, 2000). The appearance of binge eating was first associated with AN in the 20th century, and it wasn't until 1979 that BN became recognized as a distinct disorder.

A review of the literature supports the contention that relationship dynamics among family members are important in the development and/or maintenance of EDs (le Grange, 2005). Whereas clients with BN perceive their families as conflicted, disjointed, badly organized, and lacking in nurturance or caring, observers see these clients as angrily submissive to hostile and neglectful parents. Whereas clients with AN perceive their families as stable, harmonious, and cohesive, observers see these families as rigid, overprotective, and avoidant of conflict (Vandereycken, 2002). Parents of clients with EDs report higher rates of psychopathology than controls (le Grange, 2005). An important limitation to note is that much of the research on families is cross-sectional in design. Thus, it is difficult to establish whether family issues contribute to EDs or whether EDs contribute to family dysfunction.

Some family therapists do not regard the ED as "belonging" to an individual and/or a dysfunctional family system (Dare & Eisler, 1997, 2002); rather, it is seen as a syndrome "outside" of the individual and family. Drawing on a combination of postmodern and feminist ideas, these therapists view the ED "as arising from socially constructed views as to the nature of feminity [sic], of body shape, and of the adolescent developmental process" (Dare & Eisler, 1997, p. 315). The Maudsley model (Lock, le Grange, Agras, & Dare, 2001), in particular, suggests that individual and family functioning are influenced by complex interactions between the symptom, genetic, sociocultural, and developmental/life-cycle processes. The Maudsley approach assumes that the family is a resource and source of strength in the treatment of adolescent AN; treatment consists of uniting the family to face these external forces.

Why do EDs predominantly affect women? Why are EDs apparently on the rise? What are the societal forces that align with the cultural attitudes expressed in the drive for thinness and excessive consumerism? A number of feminist writers have discussed the social and political forces operating in contemporary society and conclude, in one form or another, that patriarchy is to blame:

> *Patriarchy* . . . means the manifestation and institutionalization of male dominance over women. . . . It implies that men hold power in all the important institutions of society and that women are deprived of access to such power. It does *not* imply that women are either totally powerless or totally deprived of rights, influence, and resources. (Lerner, 1986, p. 239)

Nor does the use of the term patriarchy imply that women do not sometimes advance and extend power inequalities themselves (Bordo, 1993).

Exactly how patriarchy exerts its influence is open to debate. Most writers associate contemporary culture's obsession with thinness with the women's movement. As Steiner-Adair (1994) highlights, American society overvalues traditionally masculine traits (e.g., muscular, independent, invulnerable, in control, highly competitive) and undervalues traditionally feminine traits (e.g., round, interdependent, cooperative, nurturing). She sees idealizing thin female bodies as a symbol of American society's preoccupation with autonomy and agency as opposed to the communion and interconnectivity suggested symbolically by a more rounded body. As women have entered the workforce, they have been encouraged to adopt and project masculine ideals to succeed economically and professionally. A thin female body is the antithesis to an ample feminine body and connotes such masculine ideals as self-control and independence.

Thus, the obsession with thinness has arisen during the women's movement, in part, to advance women's position within society.

Wooley (1994) suggests that hatred of women's bodies is "structural," meaning it is built into our societal system and based upon gender politics. Since the rise of patriarchal culture, men have controlled the means of representing women's bodies. The thinning of women's bodies in modern magazines, she proposes, began with the rise of pornography in the 1950s and the women's movement in the 1960s. Pornography intensified women's self-consciousness as an object to be viewed, interpreted, and judged. As women entered the workforce, they needed representations or ideal images of women that could counter those of pornography. Seemingly sympathetic to women, women's magazines offered (and continue to offer) thin and masculine images. But these images are just as unfavorable. Wooley's conclusion is that a "fat" pornographic image represents a woman's body but no mind. The models in popular magazines seem to aim for the image of a woman with a mind but little (literally) body. The culture is still overly influenced by patriarchal views that fail to present the whole woman.

Many writers suggest that we are in the midst of a violent backlash against advances made by the women's movement (Faludi, 1991; Wolf, 1994). American culture's obsession with thinness is not meant to encourage women's power and position within society, but to undermine it. Wolf (1994) passionately argued that women with sexual and financial freedom are direct challenges to patriarchal views. Women's ability to advance in the society allows them to be themselves while dieting and obsession with thinness drains them of themselves.

Thus, thinness is really a symbol of fragility and self-effacement. The "beauty myth" is a means to control and contain women's social ambitions by directing their attention toward a thinness ideal that is unattainable by most (Wolf, 1991). Moreover, because the thin ideal is projected to women as an easily attainable goal (you just need willpower), failure to achieve the ideal further undermines their sense of self-empowerment. EDs are embedded in this sociopolitical context; feminist writers argue that this context plays a primary role in the etiology of EDs.

There is also substantial economic interest in maintaining women's concerns about shape and appearance, as appearance-related industries have grown over the last few decades. Americans spend more than $40 billion per year in the diet industry and approximately $1 million *every hour* on cosmetics (Knapp, 2003). The number of women who had breast-augmentation surgery in 1999 rose 413% from the number in 1992. In the same period, breast lifts increased by 381% and liposuction by 389%. It is vital to the interest of these industries that women continue to think they can enhance their attractiveness by dieting, purchasing products, and altering their bodies.

Advertising is a major force that both influences and reinforces cultural standards. Although advertising does not cause EDs, it helps create definitions of beauty and attractiveness, as well as emphasize the importance of body shape and size. A study of network television commercials reveals that 1 out of every 3.8 commercials send an "attractiveness message," telling viewers what is or is not attractive. It is estimated that the average adolescent sees over 5260 "attractiveness messages" per year (NEDA, 2005). Most fashion models today are thinner than 98% of American women (NEDA, 2005). In a careful and thorough review of print advertisements, Kilbourne highlights how the emphasis for girls and women is always on *being desirable*. Research suggests that advertising is having an impact, as women, more then men, appear to objectify their bodies (Kilbourne, 1999). That is, women have a tendency to view their body from the outside in—regarding physical attractiveness, sex appeal, and weight, for instance, as more central to their physical identity than health, strength, or fitness. Research has found that exposure to advertisements that show highly attractive models results in decreased satisfaction with one's own appearance (Heinberg & Thompson, 1995; Thompson, Heinberg, Altabe, & Tantleff-Dunn, 1999). The more recent objectification of men in advertising may be impacting men's sense of body dissatisfaction and predisposing them to EDs (Anderson et al., 2000).

Advertisers do more than sell Americans an image or ideal of attractiveness. Advertisers encourage Americans to develop a relationship with *things* (Kilbourne, 1999), which influences and reinforces excess material consumption. Every human emotion and every human desire has been used to sell something. The cumulative effect of all these ads is to leave people romantic about objects and cynical about humans:

> Whether it is the ice cream that will comfort us when our blind date goes wrong, the nail polish that will make us feel wild, the car that carries us away from a boring spouse, or the wristwatch that is our true pride and joy—the product promises us that it can be trusted when people let us down. (Kilbourne, 1999, cover)

The impact of these messages on the economy is notable. Americans consume more than $5 trillion worth of goods and services a year (more than double the consumption rate in the 1960s) and carry a credit card debt 60% greater than 10 years ago (Knapp, 2003). Some sociopolitical doors may be closed to women, but women are allowed, even encouraged, to want in the realms of appearance and material things. Women are encouraged to binge on consumer goods. Yet, the associated feeling is one of discord. As Knapp (2003) notes that in theory people and especially women have the freedom to feed their own appetites as they so choose they have less freedom in determining what the appetites should be and what the resulting satisfaction would feel like. Social and economic forces that are grounded in patriarchy have dictated women's wants. Women are pulled between the poles of possibility and constraint, power and powerlessness; the "dis-ease" of this context is expressed in EDs.

**FOUR-QUADRANT SUMMARY** We've covered quite a bit of the ED territory at this point in our journey. The Integrally-informed therapist is certainly not likely, nor expected, to be an expert in each theory presented in these four quadrants. The goal of the four-quadrant review is to be Integrally informed. When therapists are aware that the behavioral, experiential, cultural, and social perspectives on EDs *cannot be reduced* to one another, they are more able to dwell in the complexity of their clients' symptoms. Perhaps you were already convinced of this point, or perhaps this point has become clearer in the discussion—but do not be fooled; this Integral embrace has been hard-won. Battles over the "rightness" of one perspective over another have been fought at treatment centers, academic conferences, training universities, and in theoretical writings, and perspectives have come into and gone out of vogue over time. Integral theory highlights how each perspective contains a partial truth. These partial truths are integrated in the four quadrants, and the perspectives are seen to be mutually interdependent and interacting. Figure 12.1 summarizes some of the key variables in the etiology and *experience* of EDs. As stated, it is difficult to tease out etiology with

| | |
|---|---|
| Preoccupation with weight/body shape<br>Low self-esteem<br>Obsessive thoughts about food<br>Dichotomous thinking<br>Self-critical internal dialogue<br>Self experienced as empty, negative | Disordered eating behaviors<br>  Malnutrition/bingeing/purging<br>Possible genetic variables<br>Gene–environment interactions<br>Cycle between dieting and hunger<br>Neurobiological alterations |
| Disrupted mother/daughter relationships<br>"Father Hunger"<br>Deficits in nurturance, soothing<br>Deficits in individuation dynamics in family | Appetite control in context of need for<br>  self-expression/control<br>Patriarchal social dominance<br>  Male control of images of female body |

**FIGURE 12.1** Integral Summary of Variables Associated with Etiology and Experience of EDs

EDs so this figure contains both hypotheses about etiology (e.g. gene expression) and aspects of the ED experience that may exacerbate the ED.

## Levels and Lines

In this section we continue our Integral exploration of the territory of EDs, aided by the developmental dimension of the Integral map. We make some brief orienting comments about levels and lines, discuss "hunger" as it pertains to development, and review developmental dynamics that are particularly pertinent in understanding EDs. Although the construct of levels of consciousness is not without some speculation and disagreement, we feel it lends a dimension to understanding EDs that is helpful, particularly given the challenging nature of these disorders. This is one area where I (Hubbard) am continually growing beyond my edge as a clinician—balancing clients' needs with therapeutic possibilities (and as always, quality supervision). Instead of a case proper, I will generally describe a client's developmental journey and how stages of development may relate to EDs.

The Integral model summarizes many *levels/stages* or structures of consciousness development (Wilber, 1986, 2000). Much of this is drawn from developmental psychologists such as Jane Loevinger (1976) and Lawrence Kohlberg (1984). Although there is still debate in psychology over the nature of stages and what exactly constitutes a line of development, the concepts are useful in working with EDs and, if held lightly, can be applied ethically. I will use a general outline here to illustrate how I work with them. Psychological structures can be thought of as a sequential progression of psychological worldviews. Each worldview transcends and includes its predecessors, and as a person psychologically progresses from one to the next, their psychological experience becomes broader and deeper (Wilber, 2006).

The first set of structures comprises the *prepersonal* realm, the next three structures comprise the *personal* realm, and the final four structures comprise the *postpersonal* or transpersonal realm. A prepersonal identity simply means the sense of self has not yet been stabilized. A person with a prepersonal worldview would focus on the short-term, act impulsively, and may not understand or may disregard the conventions of society. Personal stages of identity are ones in which a person understands, supports, and to some extent identifies with the conventions of society. A *postpersonal* or transpersonal (I will use transpersonal from here on out) is a worldview where one acknowledges the conventions of society but chooses one's actions based on a combination of one's own sense of right/wrong and the context of the situation.

In addition to structures of consciousness development, there are a number of developmental *lines,* or aspects of self, that develop through these consciousness structures (e.g., lines like cognitive, affective, interpersonal, moral, spiritual, values, needs, talents, and so on). The "self-related" lines in Integral theory comprise one's identity or sense of self.

In healthy development, individuals proceed from one stage to the next by dis-identifying with the subject of the current stage and identifying with the subject of the subsequent stage. Perspectives from the current stage are transcended and then integrated at the next higher stage. The "subject of awareness" at the current stage becomes an "object of awareness" for the subject of the next later stage. The meaning-making activity of clients will differ depending upon their level of development. For instance, how clients make sense of their experiences, deal with affect, and interact with others and the world changes from one stage to the next. Integrally-informed therapists will consider how their clients' developmental levels[2] are implicated in their struggles.

Overall growth through the developmental levels can be conceptualized as a hunger to self-actualize. Hunger in the prepersonal realm is a *hunger to become*—to forge an identity. Moving through these stages of development, an individual becomes aware of her physical self, emotional self, and mental self as separate from others. She arrives at the personal realm ready to understand and explore her newly emerged sense of self as a unique individual. Hunger in the personal realm is a *hunger to be*—to refine and craft one's identity as much as possible. Moving through these stages of development, she becomes aware of things like her roles and the existential givens of her life. She elaborates upon and stabilizes her view of herself as a coherent, autonomous being unlike any who has gone before and unlike any who shall follow.

Paradoxically, she arrives at the transpersonal realm with awareness that her *hunger to be* has still left her hungry. What once seemed so glorious—her uniqueness and specialness—feels more like constriction. She has begun to awaken to a deeper hunger, a *hunger to transcend.* Moving through the transpersonal stages of growth, she expands her identity beyond the personal self, which may include a worldcentric identification with all people and perhaps an overarching spiritual reality. Sustained, contemplative practice is one way people move into transpersonal development, and such development involves the process of making more and more of one's identity and experience an object of one's awareness.

As an individual develops through the various levels, her self-boundary expands; she takes *more* into herself and the line between what is self and what is not-self recedes toward the horizon of what we may refer to as the spiritual. At first, she is only a physical self. Identification with her physical self is on one side of the line and everything else is on the other side of the line. Then she is a physical self and an emotional self. The line demarcating the self-boundary has moved. The self-side of the boundary now contains both the physical self and emotional self, whereas everything else is

---

[2] The reader is directed to the works of Cook-Greuter (2005), Cook-Greuter and Soulen (2007), and Robert Kegan (1982, 1994) for examples of comprehensive models of self-development.

not-self. And then she is a physical self, emotional self, and a mental self. If all goes well, at each level, she *identifies with more.* What is identified as self grows bigger, and "not-self" gets smaller. As noted, she could experience herself as so big that there is nothing left that is not-her. In other words, a person's sense of self could potentially be equated with all arising phenomena; in some spiritual traditions, this is described as infinite fullness and that may translate into the client being no longer hungry.

Paradoxically, as our hypothetical client navigates the levels of becoming, she not only grows but shrinks. At first, she is completely undifferentiated. Then she identifies with her physical self, and everything in her physical environment is observed as "object" outside of herself. At the next stage, she identifies with her emotional self, and her physical self and her physical environment are now objects of her awareness (e.g., she *has* a body, but no longer *is* her body). At the next stage, she identifies herself with her mental self, and the emotional self, physical self, and physical environment are objects of her awareness. In this sense, at each subsequent level, she disidentifies with more and thus *identifies with less.* As the self-boundary line moves, more and more is disidentified with until there is nothing left that is experienced as self; this results in a liberating sense of identifying with the field of awareness itself and not with the contents or objects that arise within the field of awareness. In some spiritual traditions this is described as infinite emptiness or oneness.

Considering self-related lines, the following questions can be raised as metaphors or allegories: What are individuals with EDs really hungry for? What do they need? Can hunger be a psychological or spiritual metaphor? We suggest that different levels of development have an associated "hunger," and that failures to adequately fulfill these hungers may manifest in eating disordered behavior. Listening for these hungers assists therapists in pinpointing a client's stage of development (Cook-Greuter, 2005; Kegan, 1982, 1994; Wilber, 1986, 2000). These hungers have been alluded to in the previous section and are structured more formally here.

**BASIC NEED—HUNGER FOR FOOD** For some clients, the primary hunger is for food. Their physical and cognitive functioning is impaired as a result of inadequate food intake, and real psychological work cannot be done until they are more physically stable. These clients may need the structure of an inpatient hospital to block eating disordered symptoms, as well as for nutritional rehabilitation. After stabilization is achieved, the level of hunger associated with the self's development will become more apparent.

**HUNGER FOR A PHYSICAL SELF** A newborn infant is in a symbiotic relationship with its physical environment until it learns it has a distinct physical body that is separate from others. The hunger of the prepersonal stages is *to become,* and the first "hunger" is for a bodily self. Psychoanalytic conceptions of psychosis are thought to result from failures at this stage, as the self cannot tell where its body stops and the environment begins. EDs do not usually manifest at this level of development, but we include this stage for the sake of completeness.

**HUNGER FOR A PSYCHOLOGICAL SENSE OF SELF** Emergence of the next stage occurs when the infant learns that it has a distinct emotional self and it differentiates its emotional life from others. Also known as the rapprochement phase in psychoanalytic theories of separation-individuation (Mahler, Pine, & Bergman, 1975), the infant's proximate self identifies with the impulses of the emotional-feeling body. Emotional boundaries are fluid and permeable during the emergence of this stage.

Psychoanalytic conceptions of narcissistic and borderline personality disorders are thought to result from failures at this stage. Individuals with these character pathologies do not have a clear sense of the psychological boundaries between self and other. They are driven by their impulses and are often unable to hold ambivalence in their minds; everything is seen as all good or all bad. They are easily overwhelmed and may describe a sense of falling apart. These clients feel empty. They are hungry for a psychological sense of self.

Developmental failures at this stage are observed in EDs. The ED symptoms are a way to achieve a sense of self-cohesion, a felt-sense of self. The lack of strong boundaries creates chaos for these individuals. There is a tension between feeling the loss of attunement with a perfect other and feeling angry with the self for being unable to control one's impulses (Kegan, 1982). These individuals project their inner turmoil onto the body in an attempt to manage the self. Constant preoccupation with food and the body becomes a way to control the self and to hold the self together. These clients do not *mentally identify* with their ED (they won't have that capacity until the next stage); rather, they emotionally/behaviorally *are* their ED. A goal in therapy will be to establish more solid self-other boundaries and create an individuated, psychological sense of self.

**HUNGER TO BE "SEEN"** The child's mind and body are fused until the emergence of the mental self at this next stage of development. Aided in large part by language development, the child reflects on its feelings and behaviors and develops a conceptual view of the self as distinct. The child's proximate self[3] identifies with its immediate needs, wants, and wishes and looks to the environment to acknowledge these needs and to meet these needs. Children at this stage (roughly the "latency" years) are incapable of insight into themselves and others, and they cannot take the role of other. They are "displaying" themselves at this stage; looking to others to affirm the "enduring disposition of self" that they are becoming (Kegan, 1982). As others meet their needs, the implication is acceptance of the mental/distinct self.

Individuals with EDs have not been adequately "seen" by others at this stage. There is a tension between feeling compromised because their needs have not been met and they feel angry with themselves for being too needy (Kegan, 1982). They feel that others have thwarted or curtailed the self, and the ED becomes a form of self-assertion over which others have no control. "I control my body"; "Nobody else can make me eat"; and "I have no needs" (as symbolically represented by food restriction). Underneath this facade of "I'm in control," however, is a fragile self that feels ineffective. Clients who are more in touch with their feelings of ineffectiveness will make statements such as "I don't deserve to exist"; "I don't want to take up space"; and "I don't want to be seen" (yet, not so paradoxically, these clients *are* "seen"—few sights can provoke such bewilderment and horror as the skeletal frame of an individual with AN).

[3] In integral terms, the proximate (near) self is the self, *subject*, or "I" that one feels oneself to be; this is in contrast to the distal (distant) self, which includes all of those aspects of oneself that are *objects* of one's awareness (i.e., a daughter, a teacher, brown hair, likes to play flute, etc.).

Others express more ambivalence about their hunger for a mental self. Bingeing is a way to symbolically legitimize their wants and needs, which is "undone" by purging. At this developmental level, the ED is a form of self-protection for the fragile self. Over time, clients often *identify the self with the ED* and may lose sight of why it was adopted in the first place. A goal in therapy will be to help these clients identify and "own" their real needs and wants in order to develop and strengthen a distinct, mental self.

**HUNGER FOR CONNECTION** At the next stage of development, the role-self emerges. The adolescent no longer identifies exclusively with its needs and wants, and is able to take the perspective of others. There is a hunger for belonging and connection; a desire to fit in with others, to be accepted, to be part of a group. This group may be one's family, peers, team, nation, and so on. The proximate self identifies with and conforms to the rules and norms of the group. At this stage of development, however, the self is unable to know itself separate from the group. The self is embedded within the interpersonal context. This self starts to emerge in adolescence and this is the highest level of development achieved by some adults.

Difficulties negotiating this stage are apparent in individuals with EDs. Expectations from family members, in particular, can cause significant disruptions in connection. There is a tension between feeling a "loss of myself as my own person" on the one hand and "selfish and uncaring for putting myself first" on the other hand (Kegan, 1982). As reviewed in a previous section of this chapter, the ED "solves" this conflict. In all ways except for actions related to the ED, the individual is compliant, loyal, and self-sacrificing for the sake of the relationship. For some, the norms of the family or another group come at too high a cost to the role-self. They will deny their need for others and avoid connection. They appear socially isolated; yet they deny feeling isolated. These individuals meet their hunger for connection through the ED. The ED, literally, becomes their "best friend." Others are desperate for connection, but lack adequate interpersonal skills to acquire satisfactory relationships. Individuals with frustrated needs may turn to bingeing as a way to symbolically take others in. A goal in therapy will be to establish satisfying connections with others.

Thus far, we have traversed prepersonal stages of development and entered the realm of the personal. EDs reflect pathology primarily at the emotional self, mental self, and role-self levels of development, and most individuals who present for treatment will struggle with the developmental challenges characterized by these three stages. This observation is based upon developmental assessments (e.g., the age when most EDs develop) and clinical observation and is open to empirical testing. The eating-disordered behavior is primarily a form of "self-contraction"—a kind of resistance, defense, or a "tightening" and "holding on" to the self. The behaviors can be thought of as failures of the self to negotiate stages of development because of arrest or regression.

However, the behaviors, *at times*, also reflect a desire for "self-expansion" and a "letting go"—a desire for growth to the next developmental level. Movement along the developmental continuum is fluid and dynamic. All levels of development are available as potentials and there is a constant pull for growth to the next level. Bingeing and restricting, if listened to with an ear toward growth, may express a desire to get out of oneself, to move beyond one's current meaning-making experience, to achieve a different way of being-in-the-world. Whispers of a hunger for transcendence may be heard—an existential yearning for Spirit. The emergent self[4] is speaking. Bingeing may express the desire to "let go" of one's tight self-control in order to move into a "freer" sense of self. Restriction may also express the desire for freedom, freedom from the "weight" of one's current existence to allow "expanse" into something greater. Thus, the behaviors are indicative not only of developmental arrest and regression, but may also be indicative of a desire for developmental growth—a paradoxical expression of both pathology/regression and a move towards transcendence.

## States and Types

We conclude our exploration of the Integral territory of EDs by touching briefly on states and types. States of consciousness that are of particular concern include altered states that are induced by ED symptoms. For example, some individuals with AN experience a euphoric mood state that is accompanied by increased liveliness and hyperactivity. Research with animals demonstrates that serotonergic activity is part of a reward system that encourages enhanced movement in response to starvation—presumably to increase the likelihood of finding food. This adaptation appears to "misfire" in AN, as the euphoric state that is induced by exercising during starvation may ironically reward further undernourishment and promote further exercising, contributing to the perpetuation of AN (Casper, 1998; Fessler, 2002). Current research continues to explore the link between serotonin and EDs (Akkermann et al., 2012).

Personality typologies are another dimension of the Integral model, which describe different ways individuals can "be" in the world (e.g., the Factor-Five model, the Myers-Briggs Type Indicator, the Enneagram gender). Again, many typologies are disputed as lacking reliability or validity (Ingersoll & Zeitler, 2010) but the personality styles they point to can be used in understanding the client's relationship to the ED. The observed heterogeneities within and across the AN, BN, and EDNOS diagnoses have led some to suggest that subtyping EDs on the basis of personality traits may be a more useful organizing construct than the DSM categories. Westen and Harnden-Fischer's (2001) study is representative of the research findings in this area. Employing a cluster analytic technique, they identified three groups of ED clients. Clients identified as "high functioning and perfectionistic" (overrepresented by clients with BN) function well occupationally and interpersonally, although they exhibit a blend of obsessional and depressive features and feel self-critical, competitive, and guilty. Clients identified as "constricted and overcontrolled" (overrepresented by clients with restricting AN) are restricted in all areas of their lives, chronically depressed, and feel inadequate, empty, anxious, and ashamed. Clients identified as "emotionally dysregulated and undercontrolled" (overrepresented by "bingers," but about equally often by clients at "anorexic" or "normal" weight) exhibit multiple impulsive behaviors that serve to escape or minimize distress, intense and labile emotions, and interpersonal desperation. These categorizations predicted ED symptoms, adaptive functioning (i.e., global assessment functioning scores and number of psychiatric hospitalizations), and etiological variables (i.e., sexual abuse) better than DSM-based, ED diagnoses. Although this study was conducted on clients currently ill with an ED, evidence suggests these clusters may be present in the recovered state as well, and thus may reflect enduring personality styles (Wagner et al., 2006).

---

[4] The emergent self is a developmentally later self that has yet to be realized.

The adaptive meaning of ED behaviors, Westen and Harnden-Fischer (2001) suggest, will be more dependent upon an individual's personality "style" than a DSM diagnosis. For example, the function of bingeing and purging in emotionally dysregulated clients with BN may be equivalent to substance abuse and self-mutilation, representing impulsive efforts to escape intense emotions and seek gratification. In contrast, the function of bingeing and purging in high functioning and perfectionistic clients with BN may represent efforts to manage anxiety and guilt.

## EATING DISORDERS: INTEGRALLY-INFORMED TREATMENT

Having concluded our exploration of the territory of EDs with the Integral map, we now review four ways the Integral model informs and directs treatment. Our intent is not to be exhaustive but rather to provide basic examples of application. First, the Integral map can be helpful in treatment selection. The myriad approaches and modalities in the treatment of EDs tend to align with one or two of the four quadrants. By assessing the overall "health" in these quadrants, therapists are able to make an Integrally-informed choice as to which global treatment approaches are most relevant for their clients. Second, the Integral map promotes a sensitive selection of specific interventions based upon the client's level of self-development. Third, the map is a lens through which to track the therapeutic process. Fourth, the map assists in therapist self-care and attunement of the "self as instrument."

### Treatment

An Integrally-informed treatment of EDs begins with a standard psychiatric assessment interview, supplemented with an explicit focus on a client's eating-disordered symptoms and overall functioning from the Integral perspective. The reader is directed to the Eating Disorder Examination (Fairburn & Cooper, 1993) and the Integral Intake (Marquis, 2008).

Regarding treatment, there is wide agreement in the field that an interdisciplinary team of specialists is often necessary to provide nutritional and medical stabilization, pharmacological treatment, and psychological interventions (APA, 2006). Clients usually benefit from more than one treatment approach at a time. This fact highlights the useful role that an Integrally-informed perspective brings to bear on treatment selection. The type of treatment approaches used and the intensity and duration of these treatment approaches will differ. Some clients will be able to recover in short-term outpatient individual treatment with a cognitive-behavioral approach, whereas others will need multiple inpatient hospitalizations combining multiple treatment modalities.[5]

---

[5] The course and outcome for EDs has proven to be highly variable and it is difficult to predict positive outcome. For instance, some individuals with AN, particularly adolescents who receive prompt attention, will recover after a single episode. Others will exhibit a fluctuating pattern of weight gain followed by relapse, whereas others will experience a chronic course of illness over many years (APA, 2006). The outcome in BN is also variable. A number of clients who receive treatment will recover, but some may experience a more chronic or intermittent course of illness (APA, 2006). Sullivan's (2002) review of the literature on long-term outcome (i.e., follow-up $\leq$ 10 years after clinical referral) found that 70% of clients with BN and 50% of clients with AN did not have an ED. The remaining clients had full-blown or subthreshold EDs, and 10% of the clients with AN had died. These findings highlight several points: (1) the intermittent course of illness experienced by most suggests it can take many years for clients with EDs to recover, and (2) clearly effective treatment methods for AN in particular have yet to be established.

We review the most common treatment approaches next, highlighting how perspectives from each approach align with the four quadrants.

The goals of nutritional rehabilitation, an upper-right (UR) approach, are to help clients achieve a healthy weight, normalize their eating patterns, eliminate bingeing and purging, correct the biological and psychological consequences of malnutrition, and achieve normal perceptions of hunger and satiety (APA, 2006). Education regarding healthy eating patterns and nutrition may be particularly helpful as there is much misinformation in the culture (due to fad diets and so forth).

Medications are commonly used in the treatment of EDs, based upon the client's clinical presentation. The usual goals of medication use are to treat mood disturbances, minimize preoccupations with weight and shape, and reduce the frequency of bingeing and purging. No medications have been demonstrated effective in achieving weight gain in AN, although limited research suggests that selective-serotonin reuptake inhibitors (SSRIs) may be helpful with weight maintenance. SSRIs have been empirically shown to reduce binge eating and vomiting in the treatment of BN. SSRIs are also commonly used to treat the depressive, anxious, obsessive, or compulsive symptoms that co-occur with EDs (APA, 2006).

Cognitive-behavioral therapy (CBT) aims to modify dysfunctional or irrational thoughts and maladaptive behaviors that maintain an ED and thus is an upper-left (UL) and UR approach. CBT is considered the treatment of choice in BN, and is widely used in treating clients suffering from AN and EDNOS (now Eating Disorder Unspecified in the DSM-5). Clients monitor their food intake and look for common triggers (e.g., external and internal stimuli) that are associated with their eating disordered behaviors. Alternative strategies are adopted to cope with these triggers. Food intake is normalized. Negative thoughts and assumptions about eating, weight, and shape are elicited; distortions in thinking are highlighted; evidence examining the veracity of one's thoughts is explored; and more realistic ways of thinking are introduced. Fairburn, Cooper, and Shafran have proposed a "transdiagnostic" cognitive-behavioral therapy that addresses four additional processes thought to interact with and maintain symptoms in some clients: clinical perfectionism, core low self-esteem, mood intolerance, and interpersonal difficulties (Fairburn, Cooper, & Shafran, 2003; Hoiles et al., 2012). This updated CBT model expands the territory addressed in the UL as well as adds territory in the lower-left quadrant (LL; i.e., interpersonal difficulties). Dialectical Behavioral Therapy (Linehan, 1993) incorporates many elements of traditional CBT and is sometimes used adjunctively, especially with clients who meet the criteria for comorbid Personality Disorders, to address interpersonal difficulties, affect regulation, and distress tolerance. DBT teaches mindfulness, a skill directly aimed at enhancing one's ability to witness experience by making it an object of awareness.

Psychodynamic therapies focus on intrapsychic and interpersonal conflicts and deficits (UL and LL). The therapist–client relationship plays a central role in treatment, as the actions and reactions between the therapist and client are thought to exemplify the client's interpersonal difficulties (LL). Transference reactions tend to result from attempts to defend against control by others (e.g., parents). As transference reactions are analyzed and worked through, clients gain insight into their dysfunctional efforts (e.g., the ED) to adapt. This insight, combined with the positive relational experience with the therapist, allows for change and remittance of the ED (Herzog, 1995; Johnson, 1995). Goodsitt (1997) emphasizes a developmental and self-psychological perspective, and suggests that the therapist provides a holding environment that meets previously unmet self-object needs. Therapists who specialize in the treatment of EDs and work from a psychodynamic perspective tend to integrate specific symptom management strategies as well.

Interpersonal psychotherapy is a short-term treatment approach that focuses on one or two problem areas (e.g., grief, interpersonal role disputes, interpersonal deficits, role transitions) that are thought to relate to the ED (predominantly an LL approach). The therapist helps clients develop more accurate perceptions of others, create realistic relationship expectations, and modify faulty communications. As well, the therapist helps clients assess old and new roles, address problems that arise in the acquisition of new roles, and develop strategies for coping with the new role (Wilfley, Stein, & Welch, 2003). A common theme for clients with EDs is a need to please others, and interpersonal psychotherapy helps them focus on their own needs and underlying relationship issues (Tantleff-Dunn et al., 2004).

A variety of family therapy approaches have been used with EDs (e.g., structural family therapy, strategic family therapy, Milan systems therapy). The general goal of these treatments is to establish healthy family interactions and patterns of relating (a lower-right [LR] quadrant approach). Families are encouraged to allow the child with an ED to have and to share feelings, and to reduce this child's dependency on the family (Dare & Eisler, 1997). Family therapy has been found to be superior to individual therapy in adolescents who have had AN for less than 3 years (APA, 2006). The Maudsley model suggests that the family is the most important resource in the recovery process of adolescent with AN. The parents are exonerated from blame for the ED. They are encouraged to take control of re-feeding their child, and only after their child has achieved a stable weight are other developmental tasks (e.g., increased autonomy, appropriate family boundaries) considered (Lock et al., 2001).

Feminist perspectives suggest that EDs develop when individuals internalize messages that objectify females or as a response to sociocultural messages that suggest thinness is a means to power (Gilbert, Keery, & Thompson, 2005). As well, EDs are viewed as a coping strategy for unfulfilling and unreasonable gender role expectations. Thus, LL and LR perspectives are emphasized. Treatment focuses on themes of power and role expectations in the family and in society. The therapeutic setting is a place to give voice to the pain and struggle associated with these themes (Piran, Jasper, & Pinhas, 2004). Women are encouraged to fight against weightism and reclaim round female bodies as a source of real and symbolic power.

Recently, a theistic approach toward the treatment of EDs has been investigated (Richards et al., 2006). Although not considered a standard of care, we include this perspective because a growing body of literature on spiritual and psychological interventions has accumulated during the past two decades that challenges psychology's commitment to naturalistic assumptions, and it seems likely that interest in and evidence for spiritual approaches will continue to grow in the future. Spiritual approaches to healthy functioning suggest that individuals who believe in an eternal spiritual identity, seek the influence of God's spirit, and live in harmony with universal moral principles are more likely to develop in a socially and psychologically healthy manner. At core, all healing and change—whether facilitated through medical, family, or cognitive interventions—are conceptualized as spiritual processes.

The goals of Richards and colleagues (2006) theistic approach to the treatment of EDs are to help clients discover or regain their sense of spiritual worth and identity as creation of God, and to help clients turn to God and others as their source of support and control—rather than their ED. Their model focuses predominantly on the UL and LL, as well as conventional senses of ego identity. Preliminary research findings support their theistic approach as an effective intervention (Richards et al., 2006). Women being treated inpatient for an ED were assigned to a spiritual group, a CBT group, and an emotional support control group. All women received some spiritual and cognitive exercises as a part of treatment as usual, but additional discussion and homework was provided in these treatment groups. The spiritual group completed a workbook that included topics on faith in God, adversity, spiritual identity, life purpose and meaning, responsibility, forgiveness, congruence, balance, love, belonging, gratitude, and spiritual harmony. At discharge, women in the spiritual group reported greater improvement on measures of eating, depression, and anxiety symptoms, and less interpersonal relationship distress and social role conflict than the CBT and emotional support groups.

Group therapies are often utilized in treatment. Some groups are short-term and topically focused on issues such as symptom management (UR and UL focus) and interpersonal difficulties (LL focus), whereas others are long-term and insight-oriented groups (UL and LL focus). Group therapies provide consensual validation, interpersonal feedback, models of coping, and information to members. Self-esteem and feelings of control may be enhanced through participation in helping oneself and others (Polivy & Federoff, 1997). For a sizeable number of clients with AN, group therapy is counterproductive. These clients are in competition to be the thinnest and the sickest, and the group will not be beneficial until they are further along in their recovery (Harris, Wiseman, Wagner, & Halmi, 2001).

## Developmentally Attuned Interventions

The Integral map reminds therapists to attend to each client's level of self-development. Regardless of a therapist's particular approach (e.g., psychodynamic, CBT, family systems, etc.), attention to such developmental dynamics promotes a sensitive application of therapeutic technique. As a provider of outpatient individual therapy to clients who present primarily with severe AN and BN, I (Hubbard) most frequently employ CBT techniques, which are considered by many to be the treatment approach of choice in EDs. However, common CBT interventions are more or less effective depending upon the client's level of self-development. Focusing on the emotional self, mental self, and role-self levels of self-development, I share examples that highlight how the demands of therapy can be "over the heads" (Kegan, 1994) of clients.

The "self-esteem pie" is an exercise frequently used in CBT (McCabe, McFarlane, & Olmsted, 2003). A client is asked to draw a circle, which represents her entire self-esteem, and divide the circle up into wedges—with each wedge representing a different aspect of herself that she considers important to her self-worth (the larger the wedge, the greater the importance). She "learns" that her self-esteem is exclusively tied up in shape/appearance. This situation is analogous to having all of your eggs in one basket. She is asked to consider the "usefulness" of this strategy for deriving her self-esteem. Most can see that it is not very useful. She is then asked to consider what else about herself she values, such as her talents and abilities, and the roles she assumes as a friend, student, daughter, and so on. She is encouraged to focus on and develop these talents and roles, in an effort to diminish the inappropriate emphasis on appearance. The goal is to establish a healthier sense of self by focusing on what she values, what gives her a true felt sense of meaning. For clients at the emotional self and mental self stages of development, this task is over their heads. Cognitively, they may be able to complete the assignment, but it does not truly resonate with them; they do not really understand it "deep down." Clients at the emotional self stage of development do not yet have a psychological sense of self to parcel up into a self-esteem pie. Their boundaries are fluid and permeable and the self is still largely bound up in others. Clients at the mental self stage are still learning how to identify enduring qualities of the self. Only clients at the role-self stage and beyond have the capacity to identify with various roles.

As a general rule, clients at the emotional self stage are in need of a different set of techniques to help them build and construct a sense of self. Sticking closely to the expression of their impulses and affects, the goal of this stage is to make the emotional self an object of awareness. Numerous approaches are available, such as DBT (Linehan, 1993) and schema therapy. Jeffrey Young and his colleagues (Young, Klosko, & Weishaar, 2003) have identified and labeled clusters of schemas and coping response styles that resonate for most clients. For example, clients identify and label emotions, thoughts, and behaviors that arise from the angry and impulsive child, the helpless child, the punitive parent, and so on. One moment, the client may be feeling sad, fragile, and frightened (helpless child); the next moment, she shifts into the punitive parent mode to punish the helpless child; she may then retreat into a detached protector mode to block her emotions and detach from people to protect herself. Over time, clients begin to internalize a psychological sense of a self with many aspects.

CBT techniques are frequently used to help clients identify and change maladaptive core beliefs. One common core belief is, "I'm flawed and unworthy." Clients are asked to examine the evidence for and against this belief. They learn how they have assimilated information that confirms this belief, and some can admit that they have ignored or discounted evidence that disconfirms this belief. They trace the origins of this belief to childhood. They can describe why and how the belief came into existence, which usually involved severe criticism from parents. Some will endorse that others have unconditional, unearned worth—that, for others, worthiness is inherent to being a human being. Yet, despite all of this cognitive work, the maladaptive beliefs persist for many. The bottom line sentiment is, "I'm different from others. I know it doesn't make sense, it's just the way I am." One conclusion that can be drawn is that not enough cognitive work has been accomplished—that more evidence needs to be accumulated to counter the negative core belief. Another conclusion that can be drawn is that the therapist is not skilled enough in her application of the technique. We propose another conclusion. Perhaps the intervention is "over the head" of this client. Cognitively, the client is able to complete the assignment, but perhaps this is not where her level of self development predominates. Clients at the role-self level of development cannot distinguish themselves from their relationships. They are unable to see themselves as the author (rather than merely the theater) of their inner psychological life (Kegan, 1994). To come to the conclusion that "I'm a worthy, whole being" is not possible within their interpersonal context.

Individuals at the role-self stage of development are embedded in the interpersonal context. Let's look at another example. Many clients with EDs hope that others will like them, and they try to be selfless and giving in relationships. How they feel about themselves is excessively tied up in how others perceive them. They tend to have difficulty with anger, as they fear the expression of their anger might risk their relationships. These clients seem to be too influenced by the negative opinions of others. Interpersonal and cognitive-behavioral strategies aim to teach these clients to stand up for themselves, that conflict is inevitable in relationships, that their views are as valid others', and that they can judge the "correctness" of others' opinions and chose to accept or not accept these opinions. These expectations are over their heads. Such capacities derive from the next stage of development (mature ego, conscientious self), in which an individual is able to see that she *has* relationships—as opposed to being *defined by* relationships. Clients who do not have such developmental capacities are able to parrot back what they've learned; for example, "If he doesn't like me because he thinks I'm fat then his opinion doesn't count and he doesn't matter," and "I'm learning that people don't think as badly of me as I think." However, such statements are made from the role-self stage. Notice, in the first example, how the relationship is discounted and there is no ability to maintain the relationship and discount the opinion. In the second example, coping has nothing to do with the client's ability to validate her own definition of approvability.

Strategies that address the individual more directly at the role-self stage are likely to be more beneficial. For example, one technique may be to help clients consider how close others (e.g., parents, peers, etc.) have come to be shaped as people and why they behave as they do. Relying on a client's ability for empathic identification, she may be helped to see how circumstances in another's life have contributed to the way the other acts in the relationship. As a hypothetical example, she might learn that the anger and criticism she received from her mother was really displaced anger that was generated from marital tensions. Understanding this, she may feel less harshly judged or criticized by the mother. She may be able to see how the mother truly loves her and might really want to support her independent thinking and self-assertion as a worthy person. This client is not being asked to give up her loyalty to or embeddedness in the relationship; rather, she is being encouraged to broaden her perspective within the relationship. This broader perspective may help the client learn that it's acceptable to view herself as worthy and that self-assertion is tolerable, that these actions would not necessarily mean that she is abandoning the relationship. The result would be healthier functioning at the role-self stage. The relationship with the therapist may also be helpful at this stage, as the client internalizes a more benign relationship experience in which expressions of her worth and assertion are encouraged and validated.

Treatment that emphasizes the role of culture in EDs will be more or less successful depending on an individual's level of development. The worldview of clients in the prepersonal stages is egocentric. These clients will discuss the impact of culture on their self-identity or ED in a rudimentary way, but many are turned off by this discussion as it may dismiss their experience of the ED as a unique and creative expression of their own pain. Clients in the personal and transpersonal stages have sociocentric and worldcentric views and thus are more receptive to this kind of discussion, and more likely to find it beneficial.

Although we've provided just a few examples, we hope the reader appreciates how an intervention may have different impacts depending on a client's level of development.

## Therapeutic Process

The Integral map can help therapists track the moment-to-moment therapeutic process. The map is a signpost of "where you are" in the territory of EDs. How therapists respond to the territory differs, of course, depending on their approach toward treatment. What follows are some examples of how I (Hubbard) make use of the Integral map in the therapy room. These examples are just that—examples—and should not be construed as the "best" or "right" way to conduct therapy.

The Integral map promotes balance in the therapy room. The map functions as a cue to remember each aspect of the AQAL model. For instance, I touch base with the quadrants regularly, to assess and then focus on the functioning in each. There can be a tendency to privilege one quadrant over another, a tendency that some clients collude with. Some clients, for example, prefer to focus on why they have the ED (UL) without making any behavioral changes (UR). This is a trap that therapists must avoid. As discussed previously, I listen for my client's level of self development and for material that is spoken from the "shadow self."[6] Shadow material is spoken about in the second or third person, as opposed to the first person (for example, referring to a perception of excess weight as "the weight"). This material needs to be made an object of awareness via the therapeutic relationship. The most obvious shadow for ED clients is their bodies. They often speak about their bodies in the third person, and a central task of therapy is to help them recognize and own all of their thoughts and feelings that have been projected onto the body.

The Integral map also functions as a cue to touch base with the therapeutic process from the I, We, and It perspectives: from my client's subjective point of view (UL), from my own subjective point of view (UL; particularly to access countertransference reactions), from the intersubjective "we" point of view (LL), and from more objective points of view (UR/LR).

To touch briefly on the client's subjective point of view, it is important that clients feel heard and supported. As in all psychotherapy, it is necessary to build the therapeutic alliance. Establishing an alliance with the eating disordered client can be difficult, as many are ambivalent about change. The therapist is often viewed, at least initially, as a threat—the therapist is going to make her gain weight or stop dieting and purging. One way to facilitate this alliance is to join the client at her developmental level, to speak in ways that empathically resonate with her perspective. Another alliance building technique is to assess and acknowledge a client's readiness-to-change status (McFarland, 1995; Villapiano & Goodman, 2001). Many clients move in and out of the contemplative stage of change throughout recovery. To address this stage in particular, and in a nonthreatening manner, I listen for times when a client expresses distress over something in her life—how she feels about

[6] For our purposes, "shadow self" can be thought of as the things we lie to ourselves about because they threaten our sense of self—things we thus repress, deny, project, etc.

herself, about her relationships, and so on. We talk about how the ED helps her with this distress (supporting her view), but how it also leaves her dissatisfied (challenging her entrenchment in the ED); there is a quality of just noticing these things. I'm using the motivation-to-change strategy of identifying pros and cons to change, which I use extensively and repeatedly. It's built into the dialogue and over time, it decreases the ego-syntonic nature of the ED. At a later stage in therapy, the discussion tends to evolve into perspectives from "the eating-disordered side of me" and the "noneating-disordered side of me." Most clients readily grasp this notion of two parts to the self, and elaboration and integration of these two sides is often an ongoing theme in therapy. The reader is referred to Reindl (2001), who makes use of this technique via a "beauty and the beast" metaphor.

## Self as Instrument

"Self as instrument" is the primary tool a therapist brings into the therapy room (Ingersoll & Zeitler, 2010). For those therapists who are interested, the Integral map may be used to cultivate one's own development and growth, to enhance one's capacity for presence with a client. Such a therapist can use the map for herself the same way she uses it for her clients: she assesses her own health in the four quadrants and her own level of self development, she seeks to integrate her shadow aspects of self, and she attends to other developmental aspects of herself—such as her bodily, cognitive, emotional, interpersonal, and spiritual lines. One goal of this practice is to be as pure a vessel for healing as possible—to be available and present for another human being. If she has a spiritual worldview, she may think of her practice as helping her open up so that "spirit" shines through her in her work with clients: "Not my will but Thy will be done." How one does this, of course, is unique to each individual.

I humbly provide a portion of my practice as an example. What follows is not the "correct" path or outlook, only one example of how one person is attempting to navigate the Integral waters. The backbone of my spiritual practice is mindfulness meditation—watching the arising of thoughts, feelings, and sensations in sitting mediation as well as throughout the day, the Witness of experience, no right and wrong, no judgment. Just ripples and waves on the Integral stream of levels and lines. This more awakened relationship to life brings, in the words of Prendergast (2007), an emergent sense of "spacious intimacy." When I am at home in my Being, listening from and as presence, I experience a sense of spaciousness in which I am aware of experience but not lost in the experience. This spaciousness is able to receive experience (my own and my client's) just as it is, without the need to change it, fix it, push it away, or pull it near. Additionally, I experience an increasing intimacy with my clients because at the deepest level of Being, there is the recognition that I am one with all that is. There is a way in which there is no difference between myself and my client, and that her experiences are my own. This is not a blurring of boundaries but a recognition of the Spirit we are. This spacious intimacy increases my felt sense of receptivity and attunement with my clients. Meditation is a way for me to open up my mind/heart, and to prepare to hold my clients with as much wisdom and compassion as I am able. Figure 12.2 provides an Integral snapshot of treatment options and goals for ED.

| | |
|---|---|
| CBT<br>Transdiagnostic CBT<br>DBT<br>Feminist Therapy<br>Sense of Spiritual Worth<br>Achieve normal perceptions of hunger and satiety | Achieve Healthy Weight<br>Normalize Eating<br>Eliminate Bingeing<br>Correct consequences of malnutrition<br>Use of SSRIs (with therapy) |
| Psychodynamic therapy for interpersonal conflict<br>Interpersonal Psychotherapy<br>Group therapy<br>Family therapy | Family Systems Therapy |

**FIGURE 12.2** Summary of Treatment Options for EDs

## Conclusion

The Integral map is fundamentally a map of our existence—a meta-theoretical framework in which the various ways of knowing our existence have been organized into a holistic, integrated model. Exploring phenomena through the Integral lens ensures that nothing important is overlooked or left out, that multiple perspectives are taken into account. It is well known within the academic field of EDs that etiological models explaining how multiple perspectives causally interact are needed in order to better conceptualize EDs, as well as to improve treatment. The Integral model is relevant to such a task. In addition to expanding our conceptualization of EDs, the Integral model is a powerful frame for enriching clinical treatment practice. The model can inform treatment decisions and the therapeutic process: the therapist's ability for sensitive presence, perception, and response. Nuanced application of the Integral model to etiology and treatment awaits the interested explorer and holds the promise of improving client care.

## Review Questions

1. Why is separating etiological factors from symptoms so challenging with Eating Disorders?
2. What are some of the criteria for a healthy diet in terms of calories and eating habits?
3. What is the relationship between sexual abuse and Eating Disorders?
4. What do feminist critiques of American society have to contribute to understanding Eating Disorders?
5. What sorts of family problems are common in families where one member suffers from an Eating Disorder?
6. What therapies can be used in treating clients suffering from Eating Disorders?
7. Why is therapist self-care particularly important when working with clients suffering from Eating Disorders?

## References


Akkermann, K., Kaasik, K., Kiive, E., Nordquist, N., Oreland, L., & Harro, J. (2012). The impact of adverse life events and the serotonin transporter gene promoter polymorphism on the development of Eating Disorder symptoms. *Journal of Psychiatric Research, 46,* 38–43.

American Psychiatric Association. (2000). *Diagnostic and statistical manual of mental disorders* (4th ed., text rev.). Washington, DC: Author.

American Psychiatric Association. (2006). *Practice guidelines for the treatment of patients with eating disorders* (3rd ed.) Retrieved from http://www.psychiatryonline.com

American Psychiatric Association. (2013). *Diagnostic and statistical manual of mental disorders* (5th ed.). Washington, DC: Author.

Anderson, A., Cohn, L., & Holbrook, T. (2000). *Making weight: Men's conflicts with food, weight, shape & appearance.* Carlsbad, CA: Gürze Books.

Atalayer, D., Gibson, C., Konopaka, A., & Geliebter, A. (2013). Ghrelin and Eating Disorders. *Progress in Neuropsychopharmacology and Biological Psychiatry, 40,* 70–82.

Becker, A. E., & Fay, K. (2006). Sociocultural issues and Eating Disorders. In S. Wonderlich, J. E. Mitchell, M. de Zwann, & H. Steiger (Eds.), *Annual review of Eating Disorders: Part 2—2006* (pp. 35–63). Oxford, United Kingdom: Radcliffe Publishing.

Birgegard, A., Clinton, D., & Norring, C. (2013). Diagnostic issues of binge eating in Eating Disorders. *European Eating Disorders Review, 21,* 175–183.

Bordo, S. (1993). *Unbearable weight: Feminism, western culture, and the body.* Berkeley, CA: University of California Press.

Brumberg, J. J. (2000). *Fasting girls: The history of Anorexia Nervosa.* New York: Random House Vintage Books.

Bulik, C. M., Devlin, B., Bacanu, S. A., Thornton, L., Klump, K. L., Fichter, M. M., . . . Kaye, W. H. (2003). Significant linkage on chromosome 10p in families with Bulimia Nervosa. *American Journal of Human Genetics, 72,* 200–207.

Campbell, I. C., Mill, J., Uher, R., & Schmidt, U. (2011). Eating Disorders, gene-environment interactions and epigenetics. *Neuroscience and Biobehavioral Reviews, 35,* 784–793.

Casper, R. C. (1998). Behavioral activation and lack of concern, core symptoms of Anorexia Nervosa? *International Journal of Eating Disorders, 24,* 381–393.

Chernin, K. (1985). *The hungry self: Women, eating and identity.* New York: Perennial Library.

Collins, R. (2013). Treatment challenges for men with Eating Disorders. *Canadian Medical Association Journal, 185,* 137–138.

Cook-Greuter, S. R. (2005). Ego development: Nine levels of increasing embrace. Unpublished manuscript.

Cook-Greuter, S. R., & Soulen, J. (2007). The developmental perspective in integral counseling. *Counseling & Values, 51,* 180–192.

Crago, M., Shisslak, C. M., & Estes, L. S. (1996). Eating disturbances among American minority groups: A review. *International Journal of Eating Disorders, 19,* 239–248.

Crisp, A. H. (1997). Anorexia Nervosa as flight from growth: Assessment and treatment based on the model. In D. M. Garner & P. E. Garfinkel (Eds.), *Handbook of treatment for Eating Disorders* (2nd ed., pp. 248–277). New York: Guilford Press.

Dare, C., & Eisler, I. (1997). Family therapy for Anorexia Nervosa. In D. M. Garner & P. E. Garfinkel (Eds.), *Handbook of treatment for Eating Disorders* (2nd ed., pp. 307–324). New York: Guilford Press.

Dare, C., & Eisler, I. (2002). Family therapy and Eating Disorders. In C. G. Fairburn & K. D. Brownell (Eds.), *Eating Disorders and obesity: A comprehensive handbook* (2nd ed., pp. 314–319). New York: Guilford Press.

Devlin, B., Bacanu, S., Klump, K. L., Bulik, C. M., Fichter, M. M., Halmi, K. A., . . . Kaye, W. H. (2002). Linkage analysis of Anorexia Nervosa incorporating behavioral covariates. *Human Molecular Genetics, 11,* 689–696.

Dubosc, A., Capitaine, M., Franko, D. L., Bui, E., Brunet, A., Chabrol, H., & Rodgers, R. F. (2012). Early adult sexual assault and disordered eating: The mediating role of posttraumatic stress symptoms. *Journal of Traumatic Stress, 25,* 50–56.

Fairburn, C. G. (1997). Interpersonal psychotherapy for Bulimia Nervosa. In D. M. Garner & P. E. Garfinkel (Eds.), *Handbook of treatment for Eating*

*Disorders* (2nd ed., pp. 278–294). New York: Guilford Press.

Fairburn, C. G., & Cooper, Z. (1993). The Eating Disorder Examination (12th edition). In C. G. Fairburn & G. T. Wilson (Eds.), *Binge eating: Nature, assessment, and treatment* (pp. 317–360). New York: Guilford Press.

Fairburn. C. G., Cooper, Z., & Shafran, R. (2003). Cognitive behaviour therapy for Eating Disorders: A "transdiagnostic" theory and treatment. *Behaviour Research and Therapy, 41,* 509–528.

Faludi, S. (1991). *Backlash: The undeclared war against American women.* New York: Crown Books.

Fessler, D. M. (2002). Pseudoparadoxical impulsivity in restrictive Anorexia Nervosa: A consequence of the logic of scarcity. *International Journal of Eating Disorders, 31,* 376–388.

Fichter, M., Herpetz, S., Quadflieg, N., & Herpetz-Dahlmann, B. (1998). Structured Interview for Anorexic and Bulimic disorders for DSM-IV and ICD-10: Updated (third) edition. *International Journal of Eating Disorders, 24,* 227–257.

Garner, D. M., Vitousek, K. M., & Pike, K. M. (1997). Cognitive-behavioral therapy for Anorexia Nervosa. In D. M. Garner & P. E. Garfinkel (Eds.), *Handbook of treatment for Eating Disorders* (2nd ed., pp. 94–144). New York: Guilford Press.

Garrett, C. (1998). *Beyond anorexia: Narrative, spirituality and recovery.* Cambridge, United Kingdom: Cambridge University Press.

Gilbert, S. C., Keery, H., & Thompson, J. K. (2005). The media's role in body image and Eating Disorders. In E. Cole & J. H. Daniel (Eds.), *Featuring females: Feminist analysis of media* (pp. 41–57). Washington, DC: American Psychological Association.

Goodsitt, A. (1997). Eating Disorders: A self-psychological perspective. In D. M. Garner & P. E. Garfinkel (Eds.), *Handbook of treatment for Eating Disorders* (2nd ed., pp. 205–228). New York: Guilford Press.

Grave, R. D. (2011). Eating Disorders: Progress and challenges. *European Journal of Internal Medicine, 22,* 153–160.

Grice, D. E., Halmi, K. A., Fichter, M. M., Strober, M., Woodside, D. B., Treasure, J. T., . . . Berrettini, W. H. (2002). Evidence for a susceptibility gene for Anorexia Nervosa on chromosome 1. *American Journal of Human Genetics, 70,* 787–792.

Harris, W. A., Wiseman, C. V., Wagner, S., & Halmi, K. A. (2001). The difficult-to-treat patient with Eating Disorder. In M. J. Dewan & R. W. Pies (Eds.), *The difficult-to-treat psychiatric patient* (pp. 243–271). Washington, DC: American Psychiatric Publishing.

Harrop, E. N., & Marlatt, G. A. (2010). The comorbidity of substance use disorders and Eating Disorders in women: Prevalence, etiology and treatment. *Addictive Behaviors, 35,* 392–398.

Heinberg, L. J., & Thompson, J. K. (1995). Body image and televised images of thinness and attractiveness: A controlled laboratory investigation. *Journal of Social and Clinical Psychology, 14,* 325–338.

Herzog, D. B. (1995). Psychodynamic psychotherapy for Anorexia Nervosa. In K. D. Brownell & C. G. Fairburn (Eds.), *Eating Disorders and obesity: A comprehensive handbook* (pp. 330–335). New York: Guilford Press.

Hoek, H. W., & van Hoeken, D. (2003). Review of the prevalence and incidence of Eating Disorders. *International Journal of Eating Disorders, 34,* 383–396.

Hoiles, K. L., Egan, S. J., & Kane, R. T. (2012). The validity of the transdiagnostic cognitive behavioural model of Eating Disorders in predicting dietary restraint. *Eating Behaviors, 13,*123–126.

Humphrey, L. L. (1991). Object relations and the family system: An integrative approach to understanding and treating Eating Disorders. In C. Johnson (Ed.), *Psychodynamic treatment of Anorexia Nervosa and Bulimia* (pp. 321–353). New York: Guilford Press.

Ingersoll, R. E., & Zeitler, D. M. (2010). *Integral psychotherapy: Inside out/outside in.* Albany, NY: State University of New York Press.

Jacobi, C. (2005). Psychosocial risk factors for Eating Disorders. In S. Wonderlich, J. E. Mitchell, M. de Zwaan, & H. Steiger (Eds.), *Eating Disorders review: Part 1* (pp. 59–85). Oxford, United Kingdom: Radcliffe Publishing.

Jahng, J. W. (2012). An animal model of Eating Disorders associated with stressful experience in early life. *Hormones and Behavior, 59,* 213–220.

Jimerson, D. C., & Wolfe, B. E. (2006). Psychobiology of Eating Disorders. In S. Wonderlich, J. E. Mitchell, M. de Zwann, & H. Steiger (Eds.), *Annual review of Eating Disorders: Part 2—2006* (pp. 1–15). Oxford, United Kingdom: Radcliffe Publishing.

Johnson, C. (Ed.). (1991a). *Psychodynamic treatment of Anorexia Nervosa and Bulimia.* New York, Guilford Press.

Johnson, C. (1991b). Treatment of eating-disordered patients with borderline and false-self/narcissistic disorders. In C. Johnson (Ed.), *Psychodynamic treatment of Anorexia Nervosa and Bulimia* (pp. 165–193). New York: Guilford Press.

Johnson, C. (1995). Psychodynamic treatment of Bulimia Nervosa. In K. D. Brownell & C. G. Fairburn (Eds.), *Eating Disorders and obesity: A comprehensive handbook* (pp. 349–353). New York: Guilford Press.

Kaplan, A. G., & Surrey, J. L. (1984). The relational self in women: Developmental theory and public policy. In L. Walker (Ed.), *Women and mental health policy* (pp. 79–94). Beverly Hills, CA: Sage.

Kaye, W. H., Wagner, A., Frank, G., & Bailer, U. (2006). Review of brain imaging in Anorexia and Bulimia Nervosa. In S. Wonderlich, J. E. Mitchell, M. de Zwann, & H. Steiger (Eds.), *Annual review of Eating Disorders: Part 2—2006* (pp. 113–129). Oxford, United Kingdom: Radcliffe Publishing.

Kegan, R. (1982). *The evolving self: Problem and process in human development.* Cambridge, MA: Harvard University Press.

Kegan, R. (1994). *In over our heads: The mental demands of modern life.* Cambridge, MA: Harvard University Press.

Kempa, M. L., & Thomas, A. J. (2000). Culturally sensitive assessment and treatment of Eating Disorders. *Eating Disorders, 8,* 17–30.

Keys, A., Brozek, J., Henschel, A., Mickelsen, O., & Taylor, H. L. (1950). *The biology of human starvation.* Minneapolis, MN: University of Minnesota Press.

Kilbourne, J. (1999). *Deadly persuasion: Why women and girls must fight the addictive power of advertising.* New York: Simon & Schuster Adult Publishing Group.

Knapp, C. (2003). *Appetites: Why women want.* New York: Counterpoint.

Kohlberg, L. (1984). *The psychology of moral development: Volume Two: Essays on moral development.* New York: Harper & Row.

Lake, A. J., Staiger, P. K., & Glowinski, H. (2000). Effect of Western culture on women's attitudes to eating and perceptions of body shape. *International Journal of Eating Disorders, 27,* 83–89.

le Grange, D. (2005). Family issues and Eating Disorders. In S. Wonderlich, J. E. Mitchell, M. de Zwaan, & H. Steiger (Eds.), *Eating Disorders review: Part 1* (pp. 15–25). Oxford: Radcliffe Publishing.

Lelwica, M. M. (1999). *Starving for salvation: The spiritual dimensions of eating problems among American girls and women.* New York: Oxford University Press.

Lerner, G. (1986). *The creation of patriarchy.* New York: Oxford University Press.

Lilenfeld, L. R., Kaye, W. H., Greeno, C. G., Merikangas, K. R., Plotnicov, K., Pollice, C., . . . Nagy, L. (1998). A controlled family study of Anorexia Nervosa and Bulimia Nervosa: Psychiatric disorders in first-degree relatives and effects of proband comorbidity. *Archives of General Psychiatry, 55,* 603–610.

Linehan, M. M. (1993). *Cognitive-behavioral treatment of Borderline Personality Disorder.* New York: Guilford Press.

Lock, J., le Grange, D., Agras, W. S., & Dare, C. (2001). *Treatment manual for Anorexia Nervosa: A family-based approach.* New York: Guilford Press.

Loevinger, J. (1976). *Ego development.* San Francisco: Jossey Bass.

Machado, P. P. P., Goncalves, S., & Hoek, H. W. (2013). DSM-5 reduces the proportion of EDNOS cases: Evidence from community samples. *International Journal of Eating Disorders, 46,* 60–65.

Mahler, M., Pine, F., & Bergman, A. (1975). *The psychological birth of the human infant.* New York: Basic Books.

Maine, M. (2004). *Father hunger: Fathers, daughters, and the pursuit of thinness* (2nd ed.). Carlsbad, CA: Gürze Books.

Marcus, M. D., Smith, D., Santelli, R., & Kaye, W. (1992). Characterization of eating disordered behavior in obese binge eaters. *International Journal of Eating Disorders, 12,* 249–255.

Marquis, A. (2008). *The integral intake: A guide to comprehensive idiographic assessment in Integral psychotherapy.* New York: Routledge.

Mazzeo, S. E., Landt, M., van Furth, E. F., & Bulik, C. M. (2006). Genetics of eating disorders. In S. Wonderlich, J. E. Mitchell, M. de Zwann, & H. Steiger (Eds.), *Annual review of Eating Disorders: Part 2—2006* (pp. 17–33). Oxford, United Kingdom: Radcliffe Publishing.

McCabe, R. E., McFarlane, T. L., & Olmsted, M. P. (2003). *The overcoming Bulimia workbook: Your comprehensive, step-by-step guide to recovery.* Oakland, CA: New Harbinger Publications.

McFarland, B. (1995). *Brief therapy and Eating Disorders: A practical guide to solution focused work with clients.* San Francisco, CA: Jossey-Bass.

Myers, L. (1988). *Optimal psychology: An Afrocentric perspective.* New York: Kendall/Hunt.

Myers, A., Taub, J., Morris, J., & Rothblum, E. (1999). Beauty mandates and the appearance obsession: Are lesbian and bisexual women better off? *Journal of Lesbian Studies, 3,* 15–26.

National Eating Disorders Association. (2005). *Statistics: Eating Disorders and their precursors.* Retrieved from http://www.nationaleatingdisorders.org/p.asp?WebPage_ID=286&Profile_ID=41138

Pike, K. (2013). Classification, culture and complexity: A global look at the diagnosis of Eating Disorders: Commentary on Wildes and Marcus: Incorporating dimensions into the classification of Eating Disorders. *International Journal of Eating Disorders, 46,* 408–411.

Piran, N., Jasper, K., & Pinhas, L. (2004). Feminist therapy of Eating Disorders. In J. K. Thompson (Ed.), *Handbook of Eating Disorders and obesity* (pp. 263–278). Hoboken, NJ: Wiley.

Polivy, J., & Federoff, I. (1997). Group psychotherapy. In D. M. Garner & P. E. Garfinkel (Eds.), *Handbook of treatment for Eating Disorders* (2nd ed., pp. 462–475). New York: Guilford Press.

Prendergast, J. J. (2007). Spacious intimacy: Reflections on essential relationship, empathic resonance, projective identification, and witnessing. In J. J. Prendergast & K. Bradford (Eds.), *Listening from the heart of silence: Nondual wisdom and psychotherapy* (vol. 2, pp. 35–53). St. Paul, MN: Paragon House.

Rabinor, J. R. (1994). Mothers, daughters, and Eating Disorders: Honoring the mother daughter relationship. In P. Fallon, M. A. Katzman, & S. C. Wooley (Eds.), *Feminist perspectives on Eating Disorders* (pp. 272–286). New York: Guilford Press.

Reindl, S. M. (2001). *Sensing the self: Women's recovery from Bulimia.* Cambridge, MA: Harvard University Press.

Richards, P. S., Hardman, R. K., & Berrett, M. E. (2006). *Spiritual approaches in the treatment of women with Eating Disorders.* Washington, DC: American Psychological Association.

Sassaroli, S., Apparigliato, M., Bertelli, S., Boccalari, L., Fiore, F., Lamela, C., Scarone, S., & Ruggiero, G. M. (2011). Perfectionism as a mediator between perceived criticism and Eating Disorders. *Eating and Weight Disorders, 16,* e37–44.

Schwartz, M. F., & Cohn, L. (Eds.). (1996). *Sexual abuse and Eating Disorders.* New York: Brunner-Routledge.

Seid, R. P. (1994). Too "close to the bone": The historical context for women's obsession with slenderness. In P. Fallon, M. A. Katzman, & S. C. Wooley (Eds.), *Feminist perspectives on Eating Disorders* (pp. 3–16). New York: Guilford Press.

Steiner-Adair, C. (1991). New maps of development, new models of therapy: The psychology of women and the treatment of Eating Disorders. In C. Johnson (Ed.), *Psychodynamic treatment of Anorexia Nervosa and Bulimia* (pp. 225–244). New York: Guilford Press.

Steiner-Adair, C. (1994). The politics of prevention. In P. Fallon, M. A. Katzman, & S. C. Wooley (Eds.), *Feminist perspectives on Eating Disorders* (pp. 381–394). New York: Guilford Press.

Striegel-Moore, R. H. (1995). A feminist perspective on the etiology of Eating Disorders. In K. D. Brownell & C. G. Fairburn (Eds.), *Eating Disorders and obesity: A comprehensive handbook* (pp. 224–229). New York: Guilford Press.

Striegel-Moore, R. H., Dohm, F. A., Kraemer, H. C., Taylor, C. B., Daniels, S., Crawford, P. B., & Schreiber, G. B. (2003). Eating Disorders in White and Black women. *American Journal of Psychiatry, 160,* 1326–1331.

Striegel-Moore, R. H., Franko, D. L., & Ach, E. L. (2006). Epidemiology of eating disorders: An update. In S. Wonderlich, J. E. Mitchell, M. de Zwaan, & H. Steiger (Eds.), *Annual review of Eating Disorders: Part 2—2006* (pp. 65–80). Oxford, United Kingdom: Radcliffe Publishing.

Strober, M. (1991). Disorders of the self in Anorexia Nervosa: An organismic developmental paradigm. In C. Johnson (Ed.), *Psychodynamic treatment of Anorexia Nervosa and Bulimia* (pp. 354–373). New York: Guilford Press.

Strober, M., Freeman, R., Lampert, C., Diamond, J., & Kaye, W. (2000). Controlled family study of Anorexia Nervosa and Bulimia Nervosa: Evidence of shared liability and transmission of partial syndromes. *American Journal of Psychiatry, 157,* 393–401.

Sullivan, P. F. (1995). Mortality in Anorexia Nervosa. *American Journal of Psychiatry, 152,* 1073–1074.

Sullivan, P. F. (2002). Course and outcome of Anorexia Nervosa and Bulimia Nervosa. In

C. G. Fairburn & K. D. Brownell (Eds.), *Eating Disorders and obesity: A comprehensive handbook* (2nd ed., pp. 226–232). New York: The Guilford Press.

Sunday, S. R., Halmi, K. A., & Einhorn, A. (1995). The Yale-Brown-Cornell Eating Disorder Scale: A new scale to assess Eating Disorder symptomatology. *International Journal of Eating Disorders, 18,* 237–245.

Tantleff-Dunn, S., Gokee-LaRose, J., & Peterson, R. D. (2004). Interpersonal psychotherapy for the treatment of Anorexia Nervosa, Bulimia Nervosa, and binge eating disorders. In J. K. Thompson (Ed.), *Handbook of Eating Disorders and obesity* (pp. 163–185). Hoboken, NJ: Wiley.

Thompson, J. K., Heinberg, L. J., Altabe, M., & Tantleff-Dunn, S. (1999). *Exacting beauty: Theory, assessment, and treatment of body image disturbance.* Washington, DC: American Psychological Association.

Vandereycken, W. (2002). Families of patients with Eating Disorders. In C. G. Fairburn & K. D. Brownell (Eds.), *Eating Disorders and obesity: A comprehensive handbook* (2nd ed., pp. 215–220). New York: Guilford Press.

Villapiano, M., & Goodman, L. J. (2001). *Eating Disorders: Time for change.* Philadelphia, PA: Brunner-Routledge.

Wagner, A., Barbarich-Marsteller, N. C., Frank, G. K., Bailer, U. F., Wonderlich, S. A., Crosby, R. D., . . . Kaye, W. H. (2006). Personality traits after recovery from Eating Disorders: Do subtypes differ? *International Journal of Eating Disorders, 39,* 276–284.

Westen, D., & Harnden-Fischer, J. (2001). Personality profiles in Eating Disorders: Rethinking the distinction between Axis I and Axis II. *American Journal of Psychiatry, 158,* 547–562.

Wilber, K. (1986). *Transformations of consciousness: Conventional and contemplative perspectives on development.* Boston, MA: Shambhala.

Wilber, K. (2000). *Integral psychology: Consciousness, spirit, psychology, therapy.* Boston, MA: Shambhala.

Wilber, K. (2006). *Integral spirituality: A startling new role for religion in the modern and postmodern world.* Boston, MA: Shambhala.

Wilfley, D., Stein, R., & Welch, R. (2003). Interpersonal psychotherapy. In J. Treasure, U. Schmidt, & E. Van Furth (Eds.), *Handbook of Eating Disorders* (2nd ed., pp. 253–270). West Sussex, United Kingdom: Wiley.

Wilson, G. T., Fairburn, C. G., Agras, W. S. (1997). Cognitive-behavioral therapy for Bulimia Nervosa. In D. M. Garner & P. E. Garfinkel (Eds.), *Handbook of treatment for Eating Disorders* (2nd ed., pp. 67–93). New York: Guilford Press.

Winnicott, D. W. (1965). *The maturational process and the facilitating environment: Studies in the theory of emotional development.* New York: International Universities Press.

Wolf, N. (1991). *The beauty myth: How images of beauty are used against women.* New York: William Morrow and Company.

Wolf, N. (1994). Hunger. In P. Fallon, M. A. Katzman, & S. C. Wooley (Eds.), *Feminist perspectives on Eating Disorders* (pp. 94–111). New York: Guilford Press.

Wooley, O. W. (1994). . . . And man created "woman": Representations of women's bodies in Western culture. In P. Fallon, M. A. Katzman, & S. C. Wooley (Eds.), *Feminist perspectives on Eating Disorders* (pp. 17–52). New York: Guilford Press.

Young, J. E., Klosko, J. S., & Weishaar, M. E. (2003). *Schema therapy: A practitioner's guide.* New York: Guilford Press.

Zerbe, K. J. (1993). *The body betrayed: A deeper understanding of women, Eating Disorders, and treatment.* Carlsbad, CA: Gürze Books.

# 13

# Psychopathology, Suffering, and the Moral Domain

*"No matter what mental health practitioners do or say, they have entered the moral sphere."*

(Miller, 2004, p. 19)

## INTRODUCTION

This is not a book about diagnosing, although issues related to diagnosis have been addressed from time to time. Although we have regularly referred to the description of, or criteria for, specific mental disorders in the *Diagnostic and Statistical Manual of Mental Disorders* (DSM) of the American Psychiatric Association (APA), we now return to some of the numerous problems inherent in the way that the DSM has constructed the many diagnostic categories contained within it. Our goal in this book has not been to provide everything you need to know about psychopathology in detail (that would be difficult for any book to do unless it were thousands of pages in length). Rather, our primary goal has been to help you to understand the complex dynamics involved in the etiology of commonly encountered forms of psychopathology and to teach you enough so that you don't perpetuate oversimplified misunderstandings about mental disorders (i.e., mental disorders are nothing but disorders of the brain). *It's now appropriate to discuss some of the problems involved in even using terms such as* psychopathology *and* mental disorder, *the many values involved in the construction of such categories, and how they relate to—and are potentially confounded with—the suffering that is inherent in human life.* As part of this discussion, issues central to moral philosophy and science will be examined for their role, use, and misuse in the construction and classification of psychopathology and suffering.

A central question that we will explore in this final chapter is "What *is* psychopathology?" Related to that question is what it means to have "entered the moral sphere"—as our opening quote posited. Although the modern definition of *psychopathology* is "the study of mental diseases" (dictionary.cambridge.org) or "the scientific study of mental disorders" (Oxforddictionaries.com), it is instructive to look at the components of this word that is the focus of our book, as well as its etymological roots. *Pathos* derives from the Greek for *suffering* (Partridge, 1958); *logos* means to give an account of (as in the study of something); and here, *psycho* refers to the psychological dimension. Thus, "psychopathology" is actually *the study of psychological suffering (to give an account of psychological suffering)*. What is significant about the difference between *the study of psychological suffering* and the modern, "scientific" definition is that human suffering (a multidimensional, yet immediately an experiential [UL] phenomenon) is translated into a merely objective (UR), primarily unidimensional, construct. Given the current state of political dynamics in the fields of mental health, this isn't surprising. After all, Nancy Andreasen—neuroscientist, neuropsychiatrist, and former editor of *The American Journal of Psychiatry*—wrote that "We live in a world that places a high premium on standardization and objectivity; subtlety and complexity are imperiled in that world" (Andreasen, 1995, p. 965). We urge you to remember that psychopathology and suffering are complex, multidimensional, "all-quadrants, all-levels" (AQAL) constructs with many shades of subtlety. Suffering often involves biomedical processes (UR), but it is experienced in the first and second person (UL, LL), is shaped by cultural dynamics (LL), and often derives from or is exacerbated by social forces (LR).

## SUFFERING, THE MORAL DOMAIN, AND MORAL PHILOSOPHY[1]

As you will soon see, the goal of moral philosophy has always been, and still is, the reduction of human suffering.[2] Moreover, psychology emerged as a discipline not from other branches of science, but from philosophy (Hergenhahn, 2001; Robinson, 1995). As psychology grew, it stressed the centrality of *applying* its knowledge *to ameliorate human problems* while simultaneously—given that it insisted on its scientific status—denying any overt moral claims (Miller, 2004). This section aims to show that this is a contradictory and untenable stance, and one that has resulted in the relative absence of suffering as a construct in psychology and related mental health professions. This chapter draws heavily from Ronald Miller's seminal *Facing Human Suffering: Psychology and Psychotherapy as Moral Engagement,* and we highly recommend it to interested readers. As Miller (2005) states:

> The first and most obvious observation about the concept of suffering and its role in psychology is that there is none. Suffering no longer exists as a construct

---

[1] Here, as is common in philosophy, moral and ethical are used interchangeably—fundamentally attending to the issue of how one should live one's life.

[2] Many would add the suffering not just of humans, but of all sentient beings. For example, the factory farming of livestock that is practiced by agribusiness—in which cattle, pigs, chickens, and so forth are confined in unnaturally high densities—poses serious ethical issues that are currently being debated in the United States and around the world. Having abnormally high densities of animals, in the midst of their own feces and livestock that are sick or dead, often leads the animals to discomfort, fear, distress, injury, disease, and an inability to express the normal behavior of that species (not to mention practices such as de-beaking chickens so that they don't fight and kill one another). However, it appears that those who use factory farming methods with livestock regard animals only as commodities, rather than taking their welfare as sentient beings into account; this attitude clearly results in much animal cruelty, and thus is a moral issue.

in clinical or abnormal psychology. . . . This is particularly striking considering that if one were to ask most clinical psychologists and students of clinical or abnormal psychology what the point is of studying psychology, they would probably say something about wanting to be able to help others who are suffering to lead a happier life. Yet if one looks in the mainstream textbooks of abnormal and clinical psychology (or psychiatry, for that matter) of the last 25 years, terms such as *suffering, anguish, sorrow, misery,* and even *emotional pain* hardly ever appear. In their place has arisen the vocabulary of illnesses and disorders enshrined in the *Diagnostic and Statistical Manual of Mental Disorders.* (p. 305, italics in original)

Suffering is an unavoidable part of life, and the Buddha was not the only one to realize this. Human suffering and how to reduce it has been a focus of moral philosophy for millennia. The moral dimension, moral domain, or moral concern we are discussing here is not about moralizing, moral judgmentalism, or even having moral philosophical tutorials with patients.[3] Before we can get into how psychotherapy involves the moral domain, we first need to understand what moral philosophy is.

## Moral Philosophy

Moral philosophy is that branch of philosophy that addresses questions and issues such as *how are we to live our lives?* and *how should we navigate our existence as individuals and as social creatures?* In other words, *how should we reconcile our own individual needs, desires, and feelings with those of others in ways that are fair, just, or right?* (Anchin, 2005). Moral philosophy also focuses on the issue of suffering, how to respond to it, and how to achieve "the good life." Although there are debates in every domain in philosophy, a minimum conception of behaving in a moral manner involves "at the very least, [guiding] one's conduct by reason—that is, to do what there are the best reasons for doing—while giving equal weight to the interests of each individual who will be affected by one's conduct" (Rachels, 1993, p. 13). Many scholars have demonstrated that different psychotherapeutic systems are differentially sensitive to moral issues in therapy, and some fail to recognize—or even outright deny!—that moral issues are involved (Anchin, 2005; Mahoney, 2005; Miller, 2004; Sadler, 2005).

The very act of judging[4] someone as mentally healthy or as having a mental disorder is laden with moral values—although they are usually implicit and concealed

---

[3] Even though many nonmedical mental health professionals (counselors, counseling psychologists, social workers, etc.) have been taught not to use the term "patient" because it is associated with the medical model, the word *patient* is etymologically derived from the Latin *patiens*, which means *one who suffers*; in contrast, the etymology of the word *client* refers to *one who is dependent on another*, as with a peer-contractor or consumer of expert services (Partridge, 1958). In keeping with the general thrust of this chapter, we would like mental health professionals to consider using the word *patient*, rather than *client*, while also being clear that this does not imply that patients are necessarily "sick" or "disordered." Paraphrasing Sadler, being a patient implies a certain woundedness, and words such as *client* or *consumer* are poor fits for this: "*client* and *consumer* aren't simply inappropriate terms; they are dehumanizing; they make a human existential need more closely akin to a desire for a business transaction, placing health care in the ethos of conspicuous consumption" (2005, p. 144). For more on the patient–client distinction, see Sadler (2005, pp. 142–144).

[4] Although mental health professionals—whether psychiatrists, counselors, psychologists, marriage and family therapists, or social workers—are told during their training that it is not in their purview to make "judgments" about their patients, that is exactly what they do. Although they may use terms such as "assess," "evaluate," or "diagnose," those practices are nonetheless forms of judgment; we will subsequently address moral and non-moral forms of judgment.

rather than explicit—after all, mental health is *better* because it will help us achieve the "good life." The DSMs may use terms such as "adaptive," "functional," or "healthy," but because no objective, non-morally evaluative criteria have been successfully put forth to describe those terms, they are actually just pseudonyms for *good*, a demonstrably moral construct (Miller, 2004).

If it still is not clear to you how much the moral domain is involved in providing mental health services, simply consider how often patients discuss their social and interpersonal problems—from abuse, conflict, betrayal, and abandonment to exploitation, manipulation, oppression, and other forms of injustice; these forms of struggles and the suffering they produce are the domain of moral philosophy, not biomedical disease. Patients commonly speak to their therapists with "the language of moral injury" (Miller, 2005, p. 301): despairing in the face of others' or their own sickness or death; riddled with guilt; tormented by desires they are unable to satisfy; agonizing over existential decisions they are terrified to make; struggling to find someone to love and often hating others; envious of others who appear to be "better off" and humiliated with their own lot in life; conflicted about how to meet their own needs without compromising the needs of others around them; and confused as to how to resolve all of the above. Many students, when they realize just what kind of issues they will be facing when they begin counseling patients, encounter serious doubts about their ability to help. They ask themselves—and rightly so—questions such as

> Do I really *know how* to be of help to these people? Do I *want* to help *these* people and be exposed to this side of human existence? . . . How much can I do for their suffering before I begin to suffer beyond my own tolerance. . . . Mainstream academic and clinical psychology's response to this crisis of confidence is always the same: Learn scientific psychology, practice scientifically, and do scientific (research) to build more scientific knowledge for the future. (Miller, 2004, p. 16, italics and parentheses in original)

Importantly, when a patient who has been wrongly emotionally injured (i.e., abused, betrayed, exploited) by another comes to a clinician, part of what is helpful and restorative for the patient is moral restitution. In the event that the perpetrators have not acknowledged their wrong action, it is not only helpful but critical that the therapist—a respected member of society and someone the patient looks up to—responds to what has happened to them with something along the lines of "You did *not* deserve this; X was *wrong* to have done this to you; you are *not* to blame for what happened to you." Of course, therapists should say such things only if they believe them to be true, but doing so addresses the moral domain of the patient's lived world and is a step toward making that world "right" again.

When therapists talk of the need to instill hope in patients (Mahoney, 2003), a large part of what is hoped for is a world worth living in and for (Miller, 2005; Sadler, 2005). Significantly, much of the emotional distress that patients present with involves moral evaluations, and therapists need to be able to help patients distinguish whether they or others in their life should be the recipients of guilt, shame, anxiety, and so forth. If, for example, a patient has harmed someone and that patient feels guilty, that may be perfectly appropriate and it may help the patient to *not* act that way in the future. On the other hand, some patients feel guilt or shame when others have wronged them, and appropriate responses of therapists in such cases include pointing out or validating that they have been unjustly treated, helping them prevent being treated that way in the future, and possibly pursuing restitution from the perpetrator. This type of work requires both an emotional and moral sensitivity:

> Psychotherapists need to be not only sensitive to their clients' moral dilemmas but also prepared to recognize that the psychological resolution to the clients' anxiety or conflict depends as much on finding a good moral solution as it does on managing the symptoms of anxiety or depression. (Miller, 2005, p. 329)

Even though patients' suffering is often inextricably linked to a host of biological, psychological, and sociocultural variables that are at the heart of what patients discuss with their therapists, because clinicians work to help their patients suffer less and get closer to their vision of the good life, the practice of psychotherapy is inevitably a moral practice[5] (Miller, 2005). An extremely important issue for counselors and psychotherapists to understand is that all theories of psychotherapy contain *concealed moral content* (see Appendix A at the end of this chapter). Thus, therapists of differing theoretical orientations debate about what mental health is, or what it means to flourish and achieve the "good life," but *they have the debate without being aware that the debate they are having is largely moral in nature.* It is commonplace for such debates to be conducted as though issues of personality, diagnosis, definitions of psychopathology, and the goals of therapy were merely empirical issues, when they are just as much, if not more so, moral issues (Miller, 2005; Sadler, 2005). According to Slife (2004), all approaches to psychotherapy "have implicit and often unexamined points of view that merit explication and examination" (p. 44) and "unrecognized assumptions are the worst sort of mental constraints because they exert their influence without our awareness (p. 73).

It is a detriment that "currently, we are, as a profession, at the equivalent of what Piaget called the *sensorimotor* phase with regard to our moral awareness. We are acting on moral issues with only the dimmest understanding and ability to verbalize our strategies or positions" (Miller, 2005, p. 332). Moreover,

> philosophy was created not as a sterile, abstract, intellectual exercise but as an active, forceful attempt to cope with the suffering of life [as such, it is a struggle with questions such as] Is there relief from the pain and suffering of life? What must a person do to find peace and happiness? Is there a spiritual realm that offers us a requiem from the demands of the material existence of our bodies? (Miller, 2005, p. 302)

---

[5] This does not mean that there are not also important scientific dimensions to psychotherapy. In fact, it is commonplace for seasoned psychotherapists to refer to their work as part science, part art. It is striking, however, that one rarely hears therapists refer to their work as ethical or moral. Although we believe that the work of psychotherapy is inherently a moral endeavor, that does *not* imply that we think that moral issues or "problems of living" are always the primary reason that people seek psychotherapeutic help. As we have stressed throughout this book, the etiological factors in most mental health problems are complex and involve dynamics from all four quadrants (from neurobiology, behavioral reinforcement patterns, and the influence of social systems to the impact of early childhood, trauma, one's cultural worldview, and the choices one makes). At the same time, we also believe that there are some diagnoses in the DSM that *are* primarily brain disorders (UR)—for example, Schizophrenia, Bipolar I, Autism, *severe* Clinical Depression, and Neurocognitive Disorders.

We are not arguing for a replacement of therapy with a discussion of moral philosophy with patients; rather, we are suggesting that *as clinicians, we should be able to elucidate the moral principles that guide our work, as well as justify those moral positions.* Part of what this entails is transforming nonconscious, implicit moral values into consciously examined, clear, and explicit moral values; after all, "the hallmark of science is investigation . . . including . . . its own assumptions and values" (Slife, 2004, p. 73).

Ultimately, the most important question to all of us is how to live our lives such that we minimize suffering and maximize happiness and well-being. However,

> As emotional pain, suffering, and the agonizing moral choices, personal betrayals, and injuries that occasion them are redefined as disorders of the individual produced by the brain, psyche, or environment, the meaning of human suffering is fundamentally altered, and the act of altering it is almost magically concealed. This medicalization of such a universal and fundamental aspect of human experience, and the creation of a mental health industry as the new, culturally authorized steward of these illnesses, might well be one of the most profound changes in human consciousness wrought by the 20th century. (Miller, 2005, pp. 305–306)

According to Mahoney (2005),

> Pain and suffering are the primary motivators for seeking psychotherapy . . . [yet] psychotherapy has become a profession that specializes in pain and suffering without getting too close to them . . . the profession of psychotherapy has invested itself in emotional distance, diagnostic fetishes, and illusions of simplicity. (p. 347)

To compound matters, when patients' struggles derive from social dynamics (poverty, oppression, and other social injustices), therapists may represent—not merely symbolically, but actually—the same social forces that have been primary to the patient's suffering.

You may be wondering, "Why would someone who entered a mental health field ignore the suffering of those they are trying to help?" In addition to our significant tendencies to use defense mechanisms, thus avoiding or otherwise forgetting our own and others' suffering whenever possible,

> Providers may be blind to the suffering of their patients because they have come to discount that sort of suffering by virtue of their own socioeconomic position, a position that may predate their own professional training or adoption of a theoretical model. They could not continue to exercise the privileges, authority, and power that they do in the culture and be aware of the kind of pain and suffering that result from the socioeconomic arrangements from which they benefit. . . . Indeed, if one considers what has come to be called "structural violence" . . . then the power structure of the society that the professions seek to serve would be very threatened by a full accounting of the contextualized pain and suffering of the populace. Unfortunately, rather than helping the client in this situation, the institution or practitioner "redoubles" the patient's suffering by denying its existence. (Miller, 2005, pp. 310–311)

Another reason is that most practitioners uncritically accept the paradigm in which they are educated and trained, and today, the mental health professions are all operating within a biomedical paradigm—as evidenced by the required use of the DSM, increased demand for empirically supported treatments, and escalating use of pharmacological interventions. Although we do not think that evidence-based practice or the use of psychotropics are necessarily inappropriate (see Marquis, Douthit, & Elliot, 2011; Ingersoll & Rak, 2006), the virtual wholesale adoption of the biomedical model has systematically excluded serious attention to patients' suffering. After all, the DSM catalogues "mental disorders":

> It talks of distress, disturbance, disorder, suicidal and homicidal ideas, and a whole catalogue of symptoms that indicate that a person is indeed suffering, but not of the suffering itself. *Do we suffer from mental disorders as the DSM-IV defines, or has our suffering come to be defined as mental disorders colonized by the mental health professionals as their special province of expertise?* (Miller, 2004, p. 27, italics added)

Aristotle's views of ethics are still canonical in moral philosophy, and his views of *phronesis*—practical wisdom, in contrast to theoretical or scientific knowledge—are relevant to psychotherapy. Practical wisdom depends not simply on knowing what one *should* do, but upon *actually doing that good in a specific context*; thus, it is anything but abstract. Referring to many of the ancient philosophical schools—particularly the Epicureans, Skeptics, and Stoics who, incidentally, foreshadowed many principles of cognitive therapy (Sorabji, 2000)—Nussbaum (1994) wrote that they

> all conceived of philosophy as a way of addressing the most painful problems of human life. They saw the philosopher as a compassionate physician whose arts could heal many pervasive types of human suffering. They practiced philosophy not as a detached intellectual technique dedicated to the display of cleverness but as an immersed and worldly art of grappling with human misery. (p. 3)

Unfortunately, because practical wisdom is always situated in sundry contexts—rather than resting in universal absolutes—it is not capable of certainty in the way that theoretical abstractions or mechanical productions are (Polkinghorne, 1999): "It must always be provisional and revisable because of the uniqueness and individuality of the problems" (Miller, 2004, p. 23). Practical wisdom is often discounted by psychologists such as Stanovich (1998) whose goal is to help students "think straight" about psychology and disabuse them of the notion that philosophy or folk wisdom have a place in the psychological realm.

An Integral approach to counseling and psychotherapy draws heavily from the best available scientific evidence but foundationally rests upon *phronesis*. As I have elsewhere written—and consistent with Aristotle's *Nicomachean Ethics*—the notion of therapeutic practice based *solely* upon scientific technique is misguided, erroneous, and "seriously harmful" (Mahoney & Marquis, 2002). Not only does the "tyranny of technique" potentially do violence to the individuality of the patient by encouraging in the therapist an attitude of knowing what to expect in advance, it also is teleologically associated with the product, as opposed to a teleonomic, phenomenological trust in the patient's individual process. And here enter the particulars that obscure the patterns, rendering more uncertainty to our endeavors than most would like to acknowledge. As Hoffman noted, our work

> requires an underlying tolerance of uncertainty and with it a radical, yet critical kind of openness that is conveyed over time in various ways including a readiness to soul-search, to negotiate, and to change . . . some things are always left in the dark. One might say that one of the contexts of our actions is always *the context of ignorance of contexts*. And yet, act we must. (cited in Moore, 1999, p. 122)

Thus, many of the decisions that counselors make with their patients are not made with certainty on the basis of scientific data alone, and this is a large part of the reason that the personal and moral development of clinicians is as imperative as it is. However, such practical wisdom is not as esoteric as it might sound at first; it is actually an extension of the everyday knowledge we all use in interacting with people—whether at home, work, or play. Moreover, practical wisdom is not mutually exclusive with the best scientific evidence; rather, when research conclusions have been appropriately reached that answer clinically relevant questions, such scientific data should constitute a crucial component of one's knowledge base, from which one draws to make one's clinical judgments. We would do well to remember that empiricism originally meant *derived from experience*—in contrast to derived from logic or scripture (Mahoney, 2005). We should also never forget that although there are powerful biological and psychosocial forces influencing our experience and behavior, human beings have capacities to choose and exercise freedom and creativity—even if those capacities are significantly constrained. Without the assumption that people have the potential for rational decision making—and thus to choose behaviors and how to respond to circumstances—it seems rather odd to us that anyone would become a psychotherapist.

### Science Cannot Answer Specific Moral Questions

Although it has been convincingly argued that rationality—using reason and evidence to inform one's decisions—can be helpful in discerning the relative value of differing moral stances (Harris, 2010), it has long been consensually agreed that science itself cannot provide specific answers to moral questions. This insight was first stated by the Scottish philosopher David Hume (1739/2010), and it is usually framed as the *is-ought problem*, although a similar argument is termed the "naturalistic fallacy" (Moore, 1903). Simply stated, one cannot derive a moral "ought" (a prescriptive or normative "should") from a scientific "is" (a description of the natural world). In other words, descriptive (scientific) statements refer to what *is*, and prescriptive (moral) statements refer to how things *ought* to be; although people shift from the former to the latter all the time, such inferences are not defendable on either empirical or logical grounds. The distinction between *is* and *ought*

> is of central importance to understanding the dissociation in American psychology between scientific and practical knowledge. To the extent that a proposition in psychology is truly an empirical one, it is devoid of moral content and cannot by itself dictate anything about practice. To the extent that supposedly scientific propositions claim to, in themselves, speak to practical issues, such propositions

> are pseudoscientific and already have had evaluative moral content implicitly embedded in their concepts and premises. Scientific claims about clinical practice are therefore either logically incomplete (lacking an explicit moral principle) or are pseudoscientific moral claims masquerading as objective scientific fact. (Miller, 2004, p. 25)[6]

Consider the following behavioral injunctions that are common in contemporary American culture: married people *should not* have sex outside their marriage; and children *should* stay seated and pay attention in school. In these statements, the terms *have sex, stay seated*, and *pay attention* consist of both descriptive as well as moral evaluative components, but the moral evaluations are not derived from nature or descriptive observation alone. By our assigning value to those statements, they become moral evaluations. Implicitly, we consider people who follow such injunctions as *better* than those who do not, and such implicit moral judgments are so taken for granted that we rarely deem it necessary to explicitly defend them. However, "the fact that we have a moral position that is so rarely questioned as to become invisible to those who participate in it does not obviate the fact that it is a moral position and not a factual one" (Miller, 2004, p. 88). The point of the preceding quotation is particularly relevant to ego syntonic[7] personality disorders.

> This is a rare kind of disease that the patient seeks not help with, and perhaps even enjoys, yet the physician is required to treat. Would it not be a whole lot more conceptually simple, and honest, to admit that psychiatry and psychology have taken on the responsibility of social control and the enforcement of moral standards of behavior in areas of intimate relationships and personal taste that are not amenable to criminal enforcement by the courts? We do not want to throw someone in jail for being self-absorbed, self-serving, and self-important (i.e., narcissistic personality disorder), but we do not want that person acting that way any longer, and we want someone (the therapist) to do something about it. Because the mental health professions do not diagnose people for a lack of moral rectitude, and because psychotherapy is not viewed as a moral undertaking but a technical application of scientific principles of human behavior, the project is quite doomed from the start. How can one change someone's moral character without ever discussing moral issues with him or her? One cannot, and so either the mental health professions really are not doing just technical interventions, or they are not truly addressing the narcissist's problem. Indeed, all of the DSM-IV diagnoses contain implicit moral evaluations concerning actions that are considered acceptable or unacceptable by the predominant moral values of the culture. With the personality disorders the mask is off, and the implicit moral judgment is barely disguised. (Miller, 2004, pp. 88–89)

---

[6] It is psychology's dissociation from the moral sphere that led Miller to a play on words for the title of chapter one of his 2004 work: "American Psychological *Dissociation*"

[7] Ego syntonic refers to personality traits, behaviors, feelings, or values that are acceptable to the person; in other words, the person with an ego syntonic personality disorder does not consider it a problem—in fact, he may consider those qualities to be admirable.

### A Few Clarifications

How does the preceding section jibe with what you have surely been taught—that making moral judgments has no place in counseling and that we should strive to embody a neutral, objective stance in our work with patients? Miller convincingly argues that claims to moral neutrality are grounded in misunderstandings of moral principles. In a deeply fundamental way, what therapists do *always* involves the moral domain: simply to use whatever intelligence, care, and reason one has to serve another is moral, because concern for others is a central feature of morality (Miller, 2004). To have entered the moral sphere does not imply that therapists should impose their own personal values or those of any authoritarian institutions—whether churches, synagogues, mosques, and so forth—upon patients. Unfortunately, much of contemporary America mistakenly believes that to have moral concern is primarily a function of fundamentalist religious prohibitions against sex (especially homosexuality, abortion, and contraception), other sensual pleasures, and the need to keep one's in-group free from the "contaminating immorality" of differing cultures. Such moral positions—which are often accompanied by sexism, racism, xenophobia, and other prejudices—are developmentally retarded, and it should not be difficult to acknowledge this if you rationally compare their moral discourse to the actual suffering of this world—from the degradation of the environment and climate change to poverty, war, disease, and an almost endless host of oppression and human-caused misery—and what could be done to alleviate such suffering.

## THE CONSTRUCTION OF PSYCHOPATHOLOGY AND MENTAL DISORDERS

We need to appreciate that the way we conceptualize psychopathology/mental disorder leads to convictions that powerfully influence the way we practice psychotherapy (Khantzian, 1987). Central to this appreciation is the recognition that social artifacts such as the DSM are as much constructions as they are mirrors of "reality as it actually is." In contrast to a constructivist perspective,[8] all of the versions of the

---

[8] I (Marquis) consider myself—as did Michael Mahoney—a developmental or critical constructivist, in contrast to a radical constructivist or social constructionist. Although I believe that the latter—in their weak (moderate) forms—have some important insights that are relevant to counseling and psychotherapy, I concur with Gross and Levitt (1998) that in their strong (extreme) forms, cultural constructivism and social constructionism go too far in their declarations of science as just another discourse with no epistemological or ontological superiority to other knowledge claims. This is not to say that science cannot and does not at times devolve into scientism and fall prey to a host of errors. Those who are familiar with my work know that I have published critiques of some of the most influential aspects of psychotherapy that are generally considered "scientific" (i.e., the DSM, the Empirically Supported Treatment [EST] movement, Best Practices [BPs]); this is largely due to the fact that traditional methods of scientific practice (i.e., direct observation, experimental study designs) are not always appropriately suited to the most important psychotherapeutic questions. I stand behind my previously published critiques of the DSM, ESTs, and BPs but do *not* agree with social constructionists or cultural constructivists who suggest that science is nothing more than "a highly elaborated set of conventions brought forth by one particular culture (our own) in the circumstances of one particular period; thus it is not, as the standard view would have it, a body of knowledge and testable conjecture concerning the 'real' world" (Gross & Levitt, 1998, p. 45). This position states that the claims of science have no more validity about the nature of the external world than do the claims of other traditions (whether pre-modern religion or postmodern literary theory); science is merely one discourse among many, with no privileged knowledge claims—never mind that it gave us understandings of gravity, thermodynamics, general relativity, the orbit of planets, atoms, the periodic table of elements, electricity, cells, microorganisms, germ theory, the laws of heredity, the structure of DNA, and evolution by natural selection.

DSM since 1980 view the mental disorders classified therein as objective entities that are disclosed by empirical investigation (Raskin & Lewandowski, 2000). However, many scholars—approaching this issue from radically divergent perspectives—have compellingly argued that the mental disorders in the DSMs are often not supported by objective, scientific data (Gergen & McNamee, 2000; Kirk & Kutchins, 1992; Kutchins & Kirk, 1997; Raskin & Lewandowski, 2000; Sadler, 2005; Szasz, 1974). Central among these critiques are the values (rather than merely empirical data) and political processes—often reached with votes—by which many of the decisions to include a specific disorder, as well as the criteria with which it would be diagnosed, have been made.

The DSM-IV-TR explicitly stated that its nosology was atheoretical and "neutral with respect to etiology" (APA, 2000, p. xxvi). Elsewhere, we have critiqued the atheoretical claims of the recent DSMs (Douthit & Marquis, 2006) and others have demonstrated that by "using behavioral diagnostic criteria to diagnose problems . . . [DSM] advantages approaches that attend to symptom reduction rather than psychological meaning" (Raskin & Lewandowski, 2000, p. 20). To be atheoretical with regard to mental psychopathology is not only to be without a point of view (practicing with a "view from nowhere"); it would also entail having no preconceptions about "the good life," suffering, or what it is to be healthy and flourish as a human being. We do not believe that either of these is actually possible, and thus we do not believe it is possible to be atheoretical about psychopathology.[9] Finally, it is potentially harmful to be "neutral with respect to etiology." After all, just because someone has the same or similar symptoms does not mean they have the same underlying problem, and thus may need radically different treatments. To take an example from medicine, consider a patient suffering from recurrent headaches. Like the symptoms needed to diagnose depression, the headache itself is a symptom that can result from a multitude of causes, from viral or bacterial infections, dehydration, hunger, lack of sleep, or menstruation to withdrawal from addictive substances, head injury, or the development of a brain tumor. Needless to say, depending on the etiology of the headaches, drastically different treatments are called for; likewise with most mental disorders. To take one example, depression may have a number of different etiologies, from an "anaclitic" form that involves interpersonal fears of abandonment or an "introjective" form that involves intrapsychic guilt and self-criticism (Blatt & Zuroff, 1992) to depression precipitated by the abnormal levels of hypothalamic-pituitary-adrenal axis activation associated with chronic stress (Marquis & Douthit, 2006).

Just like the moral issues previously discussed, "values are rarely addressed directly in the development of the classification of mental disorders. Frequently . . . they lurk behind the debate: silent, private, influential . . . " (Sadler, 2005, p. 4). The lack of overt dialogue about such value-laden issues contributes to many of the troubles that plague not only the construction and diagnosis of psychopathology, but the mental

[9] For a thorough unpacking of the DSM's biomedical (theoretical) perspective, see Douthit and Marquis (2006). Interestingly, the DSM-5 states—in its introduction section—that its classification is "medical," which is what Douthit and Marquis (2006) suggested. Although a medical classification is a theoretical perspective (one that differs from psychological or sociocultural theories), it nonetheless glosses over value-laden issues and the very real likelihood that there are important etiological factors that are not solely biomedical.

health fields in general: "Psychiatry [as well as psychology, counseling, and social work] has continued to avoid, deny, or minimize its intrinsic and unavoidable commitments to ideas about the Good—namely, how to live well and how to get on with living well" (Sadler, 2005, p. 5).

### DSM Categories: Science or Politics and Moral Decision Making?

According to Caplan (1995), the claim that the DSM's categories are scientifically derived is unjustifiable, and Valenstein (1998) echoed this point when he wrote that scientific considerations played far less significant roles in the development of the DSMs than did sociopolitical forces within the psychiatric profession. Although the history of psychiatric diagnosis is full of examples of conditions that are no longer considered mental disorders—from masturbation and witchcraft to draepetomania (the "compulsion" slaves had to leave their owners; Sadler, 2005)—here we will briefly consider the case of homosexuality and the DSM. Whereas the inclusion of homosexuality through the DSM-III has been viewed by some as a result of heterosexist biases (Caplan, 1995), the removal of it in the DSM-IIIR (which was accomplished by vote)[10] has been viewed by many as a prime example of political—rather than scientific—processes at work (Coleman, 1984; Raskin & Lewandowski, 2000). Democratic, political processes are often resolved by vote, but scientific principles are not; rather, the latter are derived from empirical evidence. According to Kutchins and Kirk (1997), "political considerations, personal interests, and economic pressures are major factors. Throughout the entire struggle over the inclusion or exclusion of homosexuality from DSM, the minor role played by scientific research has been striking" (p. 99). Although science and morality are not necessarily incompatible or oppositional, becoming more aware of moral dimensions—including questions of what constitutes "the good life," flourishing, and whether someone is actually ill/disordered ("mad") or morally bankrupt ("bad")—is crucial to an informed understanding of psychopathology and the DSM.

From a constructivist perspective, the concepts of normality, abnormality, health, and mental disorder are more inventions than discoveries: "we reject the very contention that the *DSM-IV* can ever be objective *at all* if objectivity means ignoring the centrality of subjective human involvement in constructing definitions of psychological disorder" (Raskin & Lewandowski, 2000, p. 16; italics in original). Thus, the problem with the DSM's nosology "isn't that value judgments are involved or that causes and purposes are presupposed. The problem is that they are disguised as objective assessments that then cannot be debated as philosophical choices" (Efran, Lukens, & Lukens, 1990, p. 110).

## VALUES IN DIAGNOSIS AND PSYCHOPATHOLOGY

It's not just that values are involved in nosology and diagnosis—in contrast to the "received view" that science and the DSMs are value neutral—there are actually many

[10] According to Coleman (1984), 5854 voted for homosexuality to be excluded, 3180 wanted it to remain included, and 367 abstained from the vote.

different types of values involved. Values are involved in *eval*uations,[11] and diagnosing psychopathology involves both moral and non-moral (purely descriptive) evaluations (Sadler, 2005). For example, if you consider some of the diagnostic criteria for Schizoid Personality Disorder in the DSM-5, we can see both types of evaluations. For the sake of our discussion, some of these criteria include the person's almost always choosing solitary activities; having no, or virtually no, interest in sexual intercourse; lacking intimate friendships outside of their family; and appearing indifferent to others' praise or criticism. Each of these four criteria is both moral and descriptive in nature. They are descriptive because it can be fairly objectively assessed that a given person engages in primarily solitary activities or has never, or rarely, had sex with another person; they are moral because the DSM-5 characterizes these qualities as "mental disorders" (and thus implicitly "bad" or otherwise undesirable) that should be remediated—even though the schizoid person is not hurting or interfering with anyone else and, oftentimes, as with the ego-syntonic personality disorders previously discussed, the person him- or herself does not consider it a problem. The issue of what is considered a "disorder" or a form of psychopathology is important because it pertains to the issue of whether someone is actually ill/disordered ("mad"), morally bankrupt ("bad"), a criminal, or simply suffering from "problems of living."[12]

On a related point, such evaluative appraisals are also central to patients' processes of understanding and deciding whether they have a problem (as well as what that problem actually is) that warrants their seeking professional help; this value-laden process may also importantly influence the type of help they will search for (mental health counselor, clergy, marriage and family therapist, psychiatrist, etc.). After all, people are rarely open to help that starkly contradicts their own worldview or frame of reference. In addition, patients' worldviews (and all of the values contained therein) are frequently implicated in the problems for which they are seeking help. The clinical difficulty is that a therapist will rarely be helpful to a client without questioning some of that client's core assumptions and perceptions; however, the client may come to view the therapist as incomprehensible or unable to understand the client if she questions such assumptions and perceptions too much or with insufficient empathic attunement or clinical tact (Miller, 2004).

---

[11] You do not have *val*ues or make *eval*uations without assigning a *val*ence (positive or negative) to that which you are evaluating. We all choose facts at hand from the chaos of experience innumerable times every day—picking those that seem important, relevant, helpful, beautiful, sacred, and so forth over the opposites of the preceding—and in this encompassing and concrete sense, "every fact issues from a valuation" (Sadler, 2005, p. 3). Although many believe that science and its favorite methodological child—empiricism—are "neutral" or value-free, numerous philosophers of science argue that this is blatantly untenable (Bartley, 1962; Polanyi, 1958; Polkinghorne, 1983). Although detailed and sophisticated explications of this matter abound (Bryceland, & Stam, 2005; Slife, 2004; Slife & Gantt, 1999; Slife et al., 2005; Wampold, 2001):

> A simple version states that a "value" signifies what matters—what we should attend to and what we can safely ignore—and empiricism does just that; it tells us to pay attention to quantifiable observables and to relegate unobservables such as meanings, emotions, motivations, dreams, lived experience, and spiritual experiences to the poets and philosophers. (Marquis & Douthit, 2006, p. 115)

[12] The term "problems of living" refers to both the normal-although-difficult wear and tear of life's vicissitudes, as well as to the sundry idiosyncrasies, foibles, limitations, and mistakes common to all of us—albeit in varying degrees.

## Science Is Only One of the Types of Knowledge Needed to Counsel Effectively

It has been our experience that many therapists-in-training are disturbed by the extent to which the practice of counseling and psychotherapy depends upon principles that are not strictly scientifically derived. In other words, scientific knowledge—especially that derived from experimental designs—is only one of many types of knowledge needed to counsel effectively. For example, a large part of one's effectiveness as a psychotherapist is a function of one's self-awareness; one's ability to build rapport and develop trusting relationships in which patients feel understood and cared for despite also being confronted with interpretations of their defenses; knowledge of the patient's culture, the local community in which they live, and the socio-historical forces that have influenced their station in life; knowledge of moral principles; and a host of other clinical concepts and theories—from listening skills and group dynamics to attachment theory and mindfulness techniques—that have been non-experimentally derived. What makes matters so grave in this regard is the extent to which many training programs suggest that all students need is to understand the "scientific" basis for clinical work;[13] moreover, many of these programs do not require that students study and become familiar with the vast (non-experimentally-derived) psychological, philosophical, and sociological literatures that more deeply address the full range of human development and other potentials.

> Worse yet, they are told no such literature exists in psychology, and they are instilled with a disdain for anything unscientific while learning a science that is largely devoid of useful information, though feigning that it is. By promoting a scientific approach to problems that are practical, contextual, highly complex, and multidimensional (social, psychological, moral, political, historical, spiritual, biological, cultural, economic, etc.) psychology has done incalculable harm by promoting pseudoscientific solutions to complex human problems. (Miller, 2004, p. 13)

It is our fervent hope that you have, or had, professors who are/were aware of the many other forms of rigorous intellectual investigation of human experience, the "farther reaches of human nature," and responses to suffering; these philosophers and psychologists did not necessarily slip into irrationality or new-age dogmatism (although some certainly have!). As Miller (2004) pointed out, those who have not accepted a purely experimental scientific approach to psychology have all but been marginalized in texts of psychology whereas it is readily demonstrable that "blind faith in the scientific method as the primary means of investigating the *practical personal problems of living* is itself a form of dogmatic belief bordering on the irrational" (p. 15; italics in original).

Perhaps it is confusing to you to read this from the same authors who supported our perspectives in the previous chapters with so much scientific research. Like William James (1907), we value experimental and other forms of scientific research when those forms of inquiry—including the study design—are appropriately matched to the research question at hand. At other times—when quantitative and stringently

---

[13] Recall the earlier quote admonishing therapists-in-training to "learn scientific psychology and practice scientifically" (Miller, 2004, p. 16).

controlled methods are not ethical or appropriate to the research question, including many questions of human suffering, meaning, and so forth—we recognize the need to use qualitative research methods or even draw upon other intellectual domains (i.e., philosophy, art and literature, etc.) to address our patients' needs (Marquis, 2013). The APA's contribution to the development of the Boulder *scientist-practitioner model of training* titled "Recommended Graduate Training Program in Clinical Psychology" listed 15 personal qualities that were deemed essential for psychology trainees; significantly, 8 of those 15 are clearly moral criteria:

> (a) regard for the integrity of others, (b) tolerance, (c) ability to develop warm relationships, (d) responsibility, (e) cooperativeness and tactfulness, (f) personal integrity and self-control, (g) discriminating sense of values, and (h) breadth of cultural background. (cited in Miller, 2004, p. 18)

In one of his last publications, Michael Mahoney (2005)[14] emphasized that

> What we want to emerge from our graduate programs are healthy beings who exemplify self-awareness; an appreciation for and celebration of human diversity; a capacity to feel deeply, to imagine what others might be feeling, and to use those capacities in the service of others. We want to nurture the development of graduates who exhibit an enduring fascination with and inquiries into the mystery of being. We want to train professionals with capacities to explore, pretend, and experiment; capacities to teach and learn in the same process; abilities to sense and honor the pervasive social embeddedness of modern existence, to feel the presence of values in all human activity, and to appreciate the complex dynamics of life span psychological development. Such abilities are more rare than they should be, and those professionals who exhibit them often do so in spite of, rather than because of, their graduate training. (p. 346)

## THE NEED FOR MULTIDIMENSIONALITY

Harvard psychiatrist and medical anthropologist Arthur Kleinman (1988), in his cross-cultural work on suffering, healing, and the human condition, distinguished three concepts that Miller (2005) believes "every graduate student in the mental health professions should be required to learn as a mantra" (p. 306): *illness, disease,* and *sickness.* Because of the importance of these three constructs, we will quote Kleinman at some length. When Kleinman (1988) speaks of *illness,* he refers to

> the innately human *experience* of symptoms and suffering. Illness refers to how the sick person and the members of the family or wider social network perceive, live with, and respond to symptoms and disability. . . . when we speak of illness, we must include the patient's judgments about how best to cope with the distress and with the practical problems in daily living it creates. . . . Illness problems are the principal difficulties that symptoms and disability create. . . . Local cultural

[14] According to Jack Anchin, the recipient of APA's 2011 Distinguished Psychologist Award, "Mahoney's work reflects comprehensive and acute knowledge of philosophical systems and their operation as fundamental underpinnings of psychological theory, research, and practice" (Anchin, 2005, p. 292).

> orientations (the patterned ways that we have learned to think about and act in our life worlds and that replicate the social structure of those worlds) organize our conventional common sense about how to understand and treat illness; thus we can say of illness experience that it is always culturally shaped . . . Illness complaints are what patients and their families bring to the practitioner. (pp. 3–5; italics added)

In contrast, *disease*

> is what the practitioner *creates* in the recasting of illness in terms of theories of disorder. *Disease is what practitioners have been trained to see through the theoretical lenses of their particular form of practice.* That is to say, the practitioner reconfigures the patient's and family's illness problems as narrow technical issues, disease problems. . . . The healer—whether a neurosurgeon or a family doctor, a chiropractor or the latest breed of psychotherapist—interprets the health problem within a particular nomenclature and taxonomy, a disease nosology, that creates a new diagnostic entity, *an "it"*—the disease.
>
> Disease is the problem from the practitioner's perspective. In the narrow biological terms of the biomedical model, this means that disease is configured *only* as an alteration in biological structure or functioning. . . . In the practitioner's act of recasting illness as disease, something essential to the experience of chronic illness is lost. . . . (Kleinman, 1988, pp. 5–6, fourth italics in original)

And to be comprehensive, Kleinman (1988) defines the third construct, *sickness*, as

> The understanding of a disorder in its generic sense across a population in relation to *macrosocial* (economic, political, institutional) *forces*. Thus, when we talk of the relationship of tuberculosis to poverty and malnutrition that places certain populations at higher risk for the disorder, we are invoking tuberculosis as sickness; similarly, when we discuss the contribution of the tobacco industry and their political supporters to the epidemiological burden of lung cancer in North America, we are describing the sickness cancer. Not just researchers, but patients, families, and healers, too, may extrapolate from illness to sickness, adding another wrinkle to the experience of disorder, seeing it as a reflection of political oppression, economic deprivation, and other social forces of human misery. (p. 6, italics added)

Kleinman's analysis fits nicely with Integral theory's quadratic model (see Figure 13.1).

Kleinman (1988) proceeded to demonstrate through a series of case studies how technically correct treatment of specific diseases can actually lead to more suffering, pain, and misery—which is not to say we should abandon evidence-based practice, but rather, that we need to supplement attention to experimental research and "empirically supported treatments" with empathic attunement to patients' suffering and mutual understanding with regard to what the illness and treatment does or can mean to them. Whereas it is understandable why a medical doctor who is confronted with a patient with a critical physical condition may view the patient's suffering and emotional pain as secondary to the task of solving the biophysical crisis at hand, in the mental health professions, the majority of what patients present to the therapist is emotional pain and suffering. Thus, for psychotherapists "to offer treatments based on

| **UPPER-LEFT (UL): INTERIOR-INDIVIDUAL**<br>**Illness**—the "*experience* of symptoms and suffering" | **UPPER-RIGHT (UR): EXTERIOR-INDIVIDUAL**<br>**Disease**—an "it"—"configured *only* as an alteration in biological structure or functioning" |
|---|---|
| **LOWER-LEFT (LL): INTERIOR-COLLECTIVE**<br>**Illness** —"Illness refers to how the sick person and the members of the family or wider social network perceive, live with, and respond to symptoms and disability" | **LOWER-RIGHT (LR): EXTERIOR-COLLECTIVE**<br>**Sickness**—"The understanding of a disorder in its generic sense across a population in relation to *macrosocial* (economic, political, institutional) *forces*" |

**FIGURE 13.1** A Quadratic View of Kleinman's Illness, Disease, and Sickness

theoretical models that exclude the consideration of the patient's suffering as the critical outcome criterion seems the height of absurdity, perhaps even dishonesty" (Miller, 2005, p. 307).

If the humanistic and constructivist emphasis on the idiographic meaning-making of each person—rather than on the DSM diagnosis that the person "has"—is taken seriously, then a radically different view of psychopathology emerges, as Italian psychiatrists Giampiero Arciero and Vittorio Guidano (2000) explain:

> If experience is considered in terms of its meanings to the individual, the explanation of clinical disorders inevitably changes. Rather than arising from an impersonal etiology (perhaps having neurocortical or biochemical origins), the genesis of disorder must be sought in the client's history of transforming his or her narrative identity throughout the life cycle. Such an approach contrasts fundamentally with an "objective" diagnosis of psychopathology in terms of signs and symptoms associated with traditional psychiatric nosology. (p. 100)

## THE PURPOSE OF DIAGNOSIS

The Preface to the DSM-5 clearly states that its primary purpose is to be useful to clinical practice (APA, 2013). We hope you never forget that the alpha and omega of diagnosing, as well as that of understanding the etiology of different forms of psychopathology, is to aid our serving of those who seek our help. Thus, if your diagnosing does not result in your being of more help to your patient, there has been no real point to the diagnosis—even if it was required for insurance purposes. That being said, it is not simple to answer questions such as "What does it mean to 'aid' the ill?", "What role does diagnosis and mental disorder classification have in aiding the ill?", and "Aid according to whom?" (Sadler, 2005, p. 450).

A related point is whether, or to what extent, diagnosing someone with a DSM disorder actually assists the clinician in helping that person. Although it makes intuitive sense that we are most likely to be helpful to patients if we correctly diagnose them first, this assumption is grounded in what is known as the *specificity hypothesis* (Hansen, 2006; Marquis, Douthit, & Elliot, 2011), which posits that—like in medicine—specific treatments are most helpful for specific diagnoses. The specificity hypothesis also rests upon the assumption that the treatment methods themselves are the principal determinant of outcome, in that the component techniques, strategies, or "ingredients" characterizing the given approach (such as cognitive restructuring in CBT) differentially target and alleviate the pathology associated with particular disorders. However, empirical research has failed to support the notion that such distinctive elements are the operative factors in producing patient change (Wampold, 2001). To the contrary, a landmark quantitative review has suggested that "common factors" shared across different theoretical approaches account for the bulk of patient change (Lambert, 2003).[15]

Another purpose of diagnosis is to render complex clinical phenomena into more simplified, manageable, and apprehensible forms. This is not an inherent liability, until the simplification becomes so grossly oversimplified as to distort the patient and his circumstances into clinical caricatures that fail to understand "what is going on" with this person who is suffering. Whereas oversimplifying is obviously not desired, keeping things simple is, and we suggest balancing such simplicity with ongoing reinterpretation (which will be subsequently addressed in the "Ongoing Reinterpretation: Resisting Diagnostic Foreclosure" section). There are other necessary functions that diagnosing from a standardized nosology provides: it allows for efficient communication between different members of treatment teams; it also facilitates some forms of research and comparison among patients, treatments, and clinicians—thus, it potentially promotes accountability of effective helping.

## PROBLEMS WITH DSM DIAGNOSIS

One of the more commonly addressed problems with DSM diagnosis is that it results in labels that both stigmatize and dehumanize the person. We do not want to suggest that the current stigma associated with psychiatric diagnoses is solely the product of the DSMs; those with mental illness have been stigmatized for millennia (Sadler, 2005). Nonetheless, if we are to engage in rendering diagnoses, we must never forget that our patients may suffer doubly—both from their psychiatric condition and from the associated stigmas. Being licensed to declare someone "mentally ill" or "mentally disordered" is an extremely powerful social sanction, and this power puts many patients' lifestyles—and lives—at stake (Sadler, 2005). In short, the conventional psychiatric diagnosis that clinicians perform via the DSM is not a neutral description or classification; it usually, if not almost always, renders a moral judgment that oftentimes adds to the struggles of the patient (Gergen & McNamee, 2000; Miller, 2004; Sadler, 2005).

Part of the difficulty with diagnosis involves integrating diagnoses that are purportedly objective into patients' subjective experience and the intersubjective therapeutic relationship. According to Searle (1992)—and consistent with Wilber (2000)—standardized diagnoses are a form of third-person knowledge. Thus, more

---

[15] This is a broad generalization; at times, accurate diagnoses are extremely important in determining general treatment decisions. For example, diagnoses of conditions such as Bipolar I or the developmental level of organization of a patient—i.e., psychotic, borderline, or neurotic (McWilliams, 1994)—should significantly alter the form of treatment provided.

often than not, the potential for an ideal Buberian I-thou relationship devolves into a dehumanized I-it relationship.

> This kind of objectification is, I would claim, an unavoidable condition of having a practice of diagnosis . . . permeate the treatment relationship. . . . It is knowledge of the outer world, it is knowledge based on the subject looking out to the world and not to the self. The sense of Buber's I-thou . . . is quite the opposite. Here the subject is looking inside, it is the subject's self-understanding, it is the encounter of the self (both selves) through encountering the Other. (Sadler, 2005, pp. 145–146)

Rather than understanding the person as a unique being in a specific set of contexts, diagnosis tends[16] to overgeneralize and thus make the patient "an example of" whatever diagnostic category is assigned.

Many of the problems associated with diagnosis involve either the confusion of, or subversion of priorities regarding, *diagnosis as noun and verb*. Diagnosis as a noun refers to the DSM category assigned to a patient; in contrast, diagnosis as a verb refers to the clinical process of understanding "what is going on" with this individual in the context of all of her life circumstances, and how all this relates to the treatment with the greatest likelihood of being of service to her. According to Sadler,

> diagnosis is answerable most of all to clinical helping, and all other practical and metaphysical priorities are derivative upon clinical helping. This means that, in the value-frame of diagnosis as noun and as verb (the verb tends to trump!), diagnostic procedure is more important than this or that diagnostic category which ultimately subserves the diagnostic process. (Sadler, 2005, p. 429)

Many believe that the introductory material is the most important part of the DSMs (Sadler, 2005; Widiger & Mullins-Sweatt, 2007). The Introduction to the DSM-5 states that the diagnostic criteria therein should not be mechanically "checked off"; rather, determining whether or not specific diagnostic criteria apply to a given patient requires clinical judgment that is informed by the psychological and social factors that have contributed to the patient's struggles (APA, 2013). Thus, good clinical judgment is absolutely imperative to the practice of diagnosis, and this involves not only a broad range of conceptual tools and clinical skills, but also how to implement those at the right time and in the right way for each individual patient.

> The DSM, and perhaps the ICDs outside the USA, are used as textbooks of psychopathology in clinical-educational settings. The DSMs encourage 'educational' uses, and the lay press loves to call the DSM the psychiatric 'bible.' But the DSM and ICDs are wretched examples of either a textbook of psychopathology or, even worse, a metaphorical 'bible' for psychiatrists and psychiatry. . . . The DSM's strength is in its comprehensive catalogue of mental ills (respecting the value

[16] We want to emphasize the "tends," because we do not think diagnosis is inherently dehumanizing or that it always objectifies the patient; nonetheless, we do think that such unfortunate tendencies are far more common than the more difficult practice of diagnosing in such a way that is empathic, contextual, and respectful of the patient's experience and meanings and thus maintains the patient's dignity and humanity.

> of 'comprehensive coverage' valiantly), but its weak spot *as a textbook of psychopathology* is its feeble handling of good, skillful, conscientious *diagnostic practice* . . . it provides only a piece of the puzzle in figuring out 'what's going on here,' and even less about *how* to figure out 'what's going on here.' (Sadler, 2005, pp. 417–418; italics in original)

Finding out "what's going on here" refers to understanding the entirety of the clinical situation as a whole—from the patient's sociocultural contexts and the individual meanings he gleans from his problems and life circumstances to the strengths and resources he also brings to the table; it also has to do with questions such as "is this person able to see meaning in what he is going through?" and "can this person think rationally and clearly about what she is experiencing?" As Allen Frances emphasized, "knowing the diagnosis is not the same as knowing the patient" (cited in Sadler, 2005, p. 267). Finally, psychiatrist Irvin Yalom (2002) stresses that "A diagnosis limits vision" (p. 4) and that "it diminishes [one's] ability to relate to the other as a person" (p. 5). More will be said about these points subsequently.

## CRITIQUES OF THE DSM'S PERSPECTIVE

Social constructionists Ken Gergen and Sheila McNamee (2000) commented that "If the goal is to cure the patient, then a diagnostic vocabulary seems reasonable enough. However, the discourse of 'disease' and 'cure' is itself optional. . . . we propose that in both therapy and diagnosis we may profitably move from disciplinary determination to dialogues of difference" (p. 336). Similarly, we do not think it is possible to offer counsel to someone without assessing or diagnosing them in some way or other (Hohenshil, 1996; Marquis, 2008); however, there are many ways of doing so and they often arise from different critical perspectives. Here, we will focus on two critiques, those from multicultural and feminist perspectives.

### Multicultural Critique

Given the substantial percentage of culturally diverse people in the United States, it behooves clinicians to understand the problems that traditional diagnostic practices—including the nosology of the DSM—have for these populations. In short, culture is increasingly considered central to a current, informed understanding of psychopathology (Dana, 2002). Multicultural advocates argue that the underlying biomedical theory of the recent DSMs (with their intrapsychic and deficit-oriented approach)[17] and their culturally biased diagnostic criteria

> help to perpetuate various forms of social injustice and cultural oppression . . . This is so because both fail to (a) properly address the environmental sources

---

[17] As alluded to earlier in this book, despite the disclaimers in the DSM, its nosology implies that mental disorders are rooted in the individual (intrapsychic). In contrast, integrative models—such as Ivey & Ivey's (2008) developmental model—view the stressor as located at times within the individual, at other times within broader social/systemic factors, or in both. Like Integral perspectives, integrative, multidimensional models acknowledge that a disorder such as depression may, at times, originate from primarily within an individual. However, for many women and ethnic minorities, their depression may originate more from the discrimination, harassment, or oppression that they experience from their social environments.

> of stress that underlie many of the psychological difficulties persons from diverse and marginalized groups encounter in their lives, (b) place the primary responsibility for one's mental health within the individual, and (c) directly or indirectly blame clients for their problems. (Zalaquett, Fuerth, Stein, Ivey, & Ivey, 2008, p. 366)[18]

Related to some of the earlier critiques mentioned—regarding the modern DSMs' purported theoretical neutrality—Douthit and Donnely (in press) write that "Rather than attempting to achieve universality through theory that reflected comprehensive cultural representation, DSM aimed to garner universality through atheoretical cultural neutrality." In response to this "cultural neutrality," a 45-member multidisciplinary Group on Culture, Diagnosis and Care (GCDC) formed early in the DSM-IV's construction. Convened under the National Institute of Mental Health (NIMH), the GCDC was charged to provide recommendations to increase the cultural relevance and cultural sensitivity of DSM-IV (Mezzich et al., 1999). In response to the work of the GCDC, the DSM-IV, DSM-IV-TR, and DSM-5 all include important cultural information pertinent to diagnosing mental disorders. The DSM-5 even acknowledges that "all" distress—including that deriving from DSM-5 disorders—is influenced by culture and is locally shaped. Thus, therapists who are not aware of patients' cultural worldviews may (mis) diagnose them with mental disorders when, in fact, their behaviors, experiences, and beliefs are normal in their culture.

Although the efforts of the authors of the DSM-IV and the DSM-5 are laudable improvements over the DSM-III, it is also clear that the DSM-IV Task Force was quite resistant to the incorporation of cultural sensitivity. First, of the nearly 400 diagnostic categories in the DSM-IV, only 76 included a section addressing "Culture, Age, and Gender Considerations" (Douthit & Donnelly, in press). Furthermore, Mezzich and colleagues (1999)—who were members of the GCDC—wrote that "proposals that challenged universalistic nosological assumptions and argued for contextualization of illness, diagnosis, and care were minimally incorporated and marginally placed. Although a step forward has been taken to introduce cultural elements in DSM-IV, much remains to be done" (p. 457). Also members of the GCDC, Manson and Kleinman (1998) wrote that "social context was systematically de-emphasized or eliminated" and that "cultural variation was minimized or off-set by reference to 'significant' or 'enormous' individual variation" (p. 383). Mezzich and colleagues (1999) accepted some responsibility for the relative failure to incorporate culture more fully into the DSM-IV, specifically pointing out that—given that social-class status is a better predictor of health status than cultural factors—not enough attention was given to social factors in the overall cultural consideration. In other words, when clinicians are unaware of how macrosystemic dynamics impact the experiences and worldviews of people of differing ethnic and socioeconomic status, they are far less likely to be very effective in helping patients from differing cultures (Herlihy & Watson, 2003).

[18] Although this quote is typed as it was printed, the authors surely meant the following: "help to perpetuate various forms of social injustice and cultural oppression. . . . This is so because both (a) fail to properly address the environmental sources of stress that underlie many of the psychological difficulties persons from diverse and marginalized groups encounter in their lives, (b) place the primary responsibility for one's mental health within the individual, and (c) directly or indirectly blame clients for their problems."

Li, Jenkins, and Sundsmo (2007) presented an overview of common problems involved in diagnosing ethnic and racial minorities:

1. Flawed assessment strategies and procedures (often because the assessment instruments were not properly standardized on minority populations and thus there are problems with the validity and reliability of those assessments with people not from the mainstream culture).
2. Symptoms are experienced and expressed differently in different cultures.
3. Lack of knowledge of different cultural norms, behaviors, values, worldviews, and so forth.
4. Clinician bias.
5. Not everyone from a given ethnic or cultural group is homogenous (within-group differences are usually greater than between-group differences).
6. Inadequate training of professionals in multicultural assessment practices. (pp. 114–117)

We need to be clear that there are major problems with cross-cultural diagnosis, and this is especially true of diagnosis done outside of Western, industrialized countries (Sadler, 2005, pp. 277–285). However, we would do well to remember that diagnosing out of the DSM is not an inherently decontextualized practice (Gergen, Hoffman, & Anderson, 1996; Sadler, 2005). At the same time, the overarching cultural critique of diagnosing psychopathology is too complex to be reduced merely to issues of particular categories and thereby remedying the problem by providing a host of exceptions, stipulations, and cross-cultural examples. To the contrary, "valid cross-cultural diagnosis is less a matter of more carefully stipulated categories and cross-validation exercises, and more a matter of skilled, anthropologically aware clinicians" (Sadler, 2005, p. 432).

Fortunately, the DSM-5 includes a "Cultural Formulation Interview" that is designed to help clinicians gather information regarding how a given patient's culture may impact key aspects of their treatment and care. This appears to be a step in the right direction.

Contrary to much of what is written with regard to multicultural critiques of diagnosis,[19] the empirical research in this area suggests that perhaps the misdiagnosis and/or overpathologizing of culturally different patients is not as drastic as is often written about, or that it is due less to ethnic bias and more to a lack of knowledge regarding the symptom presentation among different cultural groups. Ramirez (2008) hypothesized that those mental health clinicians in his study (who were mostly White) with more racial bias would be more likely to assign pathological diagnoses to Black clients, whereas those clinicians with more multicultural competence would be less likely to do so. In fact, his data did not support any of his hypotheses. Another study (Horowitz, 2006) inquired into how therapists' multicultural competencies impacted the diagnoses given to women (presented via vignettes) from different ethnic groups who presented with anxiety symptoms uniquely characteristic of their culture. When the vignette involved the most common symptom presentations of anxiety as delineated

[19] An example of this is "the token incorporation of cultural considerations in the current DSM has not appreciably diminished the over- and under-pathologizing of racial/ethnic minorities by diagnosticians" (Dana, 2008, p. 79).

in the DSM-IV-TR, study participants' diagnoses were usually correct. In the vignettes of ethnic minorities, they were more often misdiagnosed or overpathologized. However, "the frequency of misdiagnosis that occurred in this study appeared due to the unique symptom presentation and not the ethnicity of the client" (Horowitz, 2006, p. 3949). In other words, the misdiagnoses were due less to racism or ethnic bias and more to participants' not knowing the unique ways that various disorders manifest in culturally different groups (i.e., isolated sleep paralysis as a symptom of anxiety among African Americans); this appears consistent with Sadler's point noted earlier. A dissertation by Scholefield (1999)—involving 252 licensed, active psychologists presented with a vignette of either a White or Black patient with Bipolar Disorder—hypothesized that the White psychologists would more often misdiagnose the Black patient and that those psychologists with more multicultural training, clinical experience, and competence would be more accurate in their diagnoses of the Black patient than those with less multicultural competence (as measured by the Multicultural Counseling Inventory). However, "there were no significant findings" (Scholefield, 1999, p. 2366) with regard to either hypothesis. Thus, until we have more research, we need to be careful about stating what the cause of the apparent mis- and over-diagnosis of ethnic minorities actually is.

## Culturally Sensitive Diagnosis

In order to practice "culturally sensitive and culturally relative diagnosis" (Li et al., 2007, p. 102), clinicians must be knowledgeable, sensitive, and responsive to the following multicultural factors: ethnic identity; degree of acculturation; beliefs about illness as a function of the patient's culture; manifestation of symptoms as a function of the patient's culture; values/norms/worldview of the patient's culture; resiliency and other protective factors; need for systemic involvement; the patient's perceptions of mental health services as a function of her culture; and the nature of reporting common to the patient's culture (i.e., use of stories or proscriptions against disclosure). A multiculturally sensitive approach to psychopathology would also recognize racism and other forms of ethnic oppression as etiologically significant in many of the DSM disorders as well as myriad other cultural factors that play roles in distress and problems of living (Dana, 2008).

It is critical to remember that not all individuals suffering from the same problem experience the distress in the same manner, and one's culture often plays a large role in how it is experienced. To take just one example, the experience and expression of depression is clearly culturally influenced. Depressed people from many cultures are likely to communicate somatic (rather than psychological) complaints as their primary distress (APA, 2013). More specifically, those from Asian cultures often speak of tiredness, weakness, or "imbalance," whereas those from Latin and Mediterranean cultures often report headaches or "nerves" as their presenting complaint (APA, 2000). According to some, even paranoid ideation and hallucinations may be a function of sociocultural dynamics, and thus are not necessarily pathological, especially when they occur in individuals from nondominant groups:

> paranoia among African Americans may be less often part of a psychotic, pathological spectrum and more often a part of a normal experience of an oppressed individual. . . .

> many aspects of hallucinations are culturally determined . . . one must assess what was going on before and after the experience, along with the setting in which the hallucinations were experienced, to determine whether or not the hallucinations are indeed a symptom of pathology or if they are part of a culturally concordant experience. (Li et al., 2007, p. 110)

Despite the importance of being knowledgeable with regard to cross-cultural differences in how people—as a function of their culture—present or express the same disorder with different symptom sets (Abusah, 1993), some have argued that because it is not easy or feasible to infuse adequate multicultural knowledge into the current DSMs, clinicians should consult a supplemental "minority casebook" that illustrates various diagnostic dilemmas that are common when counseling multicultural patients (Good, 1996).

Similar to the Cultural Formulation Interview in the DSM-5, the DSM-IV-TR included an "Outline for Cultural Formulation" and a "Glossary of Culture-Bound Syndromes" in Appendix I (pp. 897–903). In the former, it stated that clinicians need to systematically describe: the patient's cultural identity; cultural explanations of the patient's illness; social stressors and culturally relevant interpretations of those stressors, and available social supports; how cultural factors could impact the therapist-patient relationship; and how an overall assessment of the aforementioned cultural considerations will influence the course of treatment. The DSM-IV-TR defined culture-bound syndromes as locality-specific, recurrent patterns of disturbing experiences and abnormal behavior that are not necessarily associated with a particular DSM-IV diagnosis (APA, 2000).[20] Despite the inclusion of such, many authors adamantly maintain that cultural issues still occupy only peripheral roles in DSM-IV (Paniagua, 1998). Although the DSM-5 has incorporated three cultural concepts of distress—cultural syndromes, cultural idioms of distress, and cultural explanations or perceived causes—it remains to be seen what experts in the field will say of the role that cultural issues plays in the DSM-5.

## Feminist Critique

Although feminist psychology is not unified (i.e., there are diverse viewpoints among feminist scholars), there is consensus among feminist clinicians that the actual pathologies with which therapists should be concerned are not in individuals, but in patriarchal cultures' oppressive forces—such as sexism, racism, classism, and heterosexism—thus "the feminist call to diagnose cultures, rather than people, as pathological" (Brown, 2000, p. 301).

At the same time, feminist clinicians also recognize the need to attend to individuals who are distressed and seeking professional help. Consequently, they tend to view "most psychological distress not as forms of disorder but as understandable, possibly inevitable, and therefore not per se disordered responses to a dangerous

---

[20] Although the DSM-IV-TR described 25 culture-bound syndromes, it did not include Anorexia Nervosa, the incidence of which continues to increase in Western cultures in ways that are not paralleled in other parts of the world. Thus, Abusah (1993) states that it "may be regarded as a culture-bound syndrome" (p. 68).

and painful social context" (Brown, 2000, p. 288). Feminists are particularly critical of essentialist (i.e., biological) theories of distress:

> Even a behavior that is grounded in a biological reality has meaning and value ascribed to it by the social and political milieu. Thus, any diagnosis of psychopathology reflects not only the subjective experience of distress but also the construction of the meaning of that distress within the culture. To create a "norm," whether moral or statistical, and then to construct the cultural vision of goodness as being equivalent to normalcy is a political dynamic with which mental health diagnosis is saturated. The designation of behaviors as "abnormal" is highly culturally determined; psychological diagnosis does not represent a description of that which is clearly present but a mutual decision by professionals to classify certain ways of being as outside the dominant norms. (Brown 2000, p. 290)

In short, feminist therapists honor patients' experience of distress (UL, which they maintain is primarily a function of sociocultural contexts [LR/LL]) while questioning and critiquing the hegemonic construction of psychopathology in the DSM. Although they convey important partial truths, from an Integral perspective, we cannot help but view many feminist approaches as extreme and unbalanced, as evidenced by the following examples. In response to the question "Are there feminist constructions of disorder?" Brown (2000) responded with "The answer in one word is maybe. But they are not disorders of the person. A closely applied feminist model could *never* assign disorder or pathology to a distressed individual" (p. 304; italics added). Moreover, "the feminist construction of disorder *strains* to keep away from the notion of disorder in the individual" (Brown, 2000, p. 300; italics added). We certainly agree that many of the factors that lead to real distress and suffering are rooted in unfair, inequitable, oppressive sociocultural forces (including patriarchy), but we cannot ignore that there are also dynamics rooted in individuals and early childhood experiences (from their genetic propensities and attachment histories to their object-relations and other ways they construe themselves, others, and the world) that are also constitutive of psychopathology.

## DISORDERS AS CATEGORICALLY DISCRETE VERSUS DIMENSIONAL

Stop for a moment and really think about all the people you know well. Some of them probably seem more mentally unhealthy than others, right? Of all the people you know, do they seem to fit into one of two *categories*—having a mental disorder or not? As we discussed several times in earlier chapters, it makes more sense that all of us fall somewhere along a *continuum* of mental health and unhealth. According to James Griffith (2010), a professor of psychiatry, although clearly demarcating symptoms into the discrete categories of psychiatric illness or normal human suffering makes the diagnostic process easier, it does not reflect the real world. The DSM-IV-TR stated that a categorical classification system is appropriate when there are (1) clear boundaries between the diagnostic categories, (2) when everyone who meets the diagnostic criteria for a given disorder is homogenous, and (3) when the different disorders are mutually exclusive (i.e., not characterized by high levels of comorbidity with other mental disorders). Immediately after acknowledging the limitations of a system of categorical classification, it clearly states that the DSM-IV-TR does *not* assume that (1) each mental disorder has absolute boundaries between itself and other mental disorders, (2) people with the same diagnosis are usually homogenous, or (3) a specific mental disorder is completely discrete from other mental disorders.

Anyone paying close attention to that should be rather perplexed. As scholars have pointed out, the disclaimers just mentioned, although carefully worded, are rather hollow (Widiger & Mullins-Sweatt, 2007); after all, it also stated on the same page that the DSM-IV *does* represent a categorical classification that divides mental disorders into discrete types on the basis of criterion sets with defining features (APA, 2000). As we will discuss, the categorical approach to classification—which strongly suggests that mental disorders are discrete entities, despite the disclaimers discussed earlier—has been intensely questioned and harshly criticized by many scholars (Clark, Watson, & Reynolds, 1995; First, 2003; Krueger & Markon, 2006; Widiger & Clark, 2000; Widiger & Mullins-Sweatt, 2007). In contrast to the categorical approach is the notion that there are *not* natural, demonstrably clear-cut boundaries dividing mental health and psychopathology; these are *dimensional* models of psychopathology,[21] suggesting that psychopathology is best represented as a continuum or spectrum, shading gradually from relative mental health to severe forms of psychopathology. According to the DSM-IV, a dimensional system is most appropriate when the phenomena it describes do not have clear boundaries and are distributed continuously (APA, 2000).

In its Introduction section, the DSM-5 addresses this issue and is very clear about the problems and concerns that derive from a categorical system of classification. Referring to the DSM-IV, the DSM-5 comments how it—because of its classifying each disorder as categorically separate from other disorders—was unable to reflect, capture, or understand the common overlap of symptoms across different disorders that are very clear from comorbidity studies and other diverse sources of evidence, such as genetic studies. According to the DSM-5, the scientific evidence that has accumulated in the two decades following the DSM-IV has made it clear that many (if not the majority of) mental disorders are not discrete; rather, it is more accurate to recognize not only a "spectrum" of disorder, but also that many symptoms of distress do not fit neatly within only one category of disorder (APA, 2013). The DSM-5 continues to comment how the DSM-IV failed to recognize the fluidity with which different "categories" of mental disorder flow into each other and that, now, the DSM-5 acknowledges the scientific evidence that rather than being clearly demarcated, the boundaries dividing different disorders are "porous" (APA, 2013). Despite all of this explicit critique of categorical classification, the authors did not change the foundational, categorical nature of the DSM-5, even though the proposed revisions for the DSM-5 had included substantial discussion of changing at least some of the disorders to a dimensional model.

Let us review some significant facts noted in Chapters 1 and 2: (1) no researcher has found a single laboratory marker that can identify any of the DSM disorders independently of a clinical diagnosis (Steffens & Krishnan, 2003); (2) comorbidity rates among the sundry disorders are extremely high, casting doubt upon the distinctness of the disorders; and (3) treatments that work for one disorder tend to be helpful with most of the disorders, further undermining the idea that the various disorders are radically different (Kupfer, First, & Regier, 2002).

---

[21] Interested readers are encouraged to consult Widiger and Mullins-Sweatt (2007) and Henriques (2002) for excellent discussions of this issue.

Widiger and Mullins-Sweatt make a strong case that the concept of mental disorder is undergirded by notions of *dyscontrol, impairment*, and *pathology. Dyscontrol*—or lack of voluntary self-control—is implicit in virtually all notions of mental disorder, yet there is

> no qualitative distinction between the presence and absence of self-control. . . . A continuum (or ambiguity) of self-control is particularly evident in those disorders that provide immediate benefits or pleasures to the person, such as pedophilia, intermittent explosive disorder . . . antisocial personality disorder, bulimia nervosa . . . and substance-related disorders. . . . In sum, determination of adequate versus inadequate self-control is fundamental to many social and clinical decisions, but the boundary is at best grossly ill-defined and poorly understood. (Widiger & Mullins-Sweatt, 2007, p. 5)

Many scholars and researchers—none more famously than psychiatrist Thomas Szasz (1974)—have argued that what the modern DSMs classify are less mental disorders and more varying degrees of the "problems in living" that all of us face from time to time. The requirement of *impairment*[22] that runs throughout the recent DSMs is supposed to distinguish between a normal problem in living and a bona fide mental disorder. In other words, where does genuine psychopathology end and a host of human differences—eccentricities, peculiarities, and harmless annoyances—begin? To make matters worse, not even in the "Criteria for Clinical Significance" section does the DSM-5 define what "clinically significant impairment or distress" is (APA, 2013, p. 21). To the contrary, the DSM-5 states that—due to the lack of clinically useful measures regarding the severity of most mental disorders, as well as the lack of biological markers for mental disorders—it is currently impossible to clearly demarcate pathological from normal expression of the symptoms described in the diagnostic criteria (APA, 2013). On this point, Widiger and Mullins-Sweatt (2007) write that

> New additions to the diagnostic manual rarely concern newly discovered forms of psychopathology; instead, they are typically efforts to plug holes in between existing diagnosis and normal functioning. . . . A fundamental difficulty shared by all of these diagnoses is the lack of a clear distinction with normal functioning. (p. 7)

Also central to most conceptions of mental disorder is some form of *pathology* (Wakefield, 1997; Widiger & Mullins-Sweatt, 2007). "Missing from the diagnostic criterion sets in DSM-IV, however, are references to underlying pathologies. . . . The diagnostic criterion sets emphasize instead the distress or impairment that is presumably the manifestation of an underlying pathology" (Widiger & Mullins-Sweatt, 2007, p. 8). As mentioned earlier, part of the reason for not including pathologies within criterion sets is due to a lack of definitive neurophysiological markers or other empirical support for their existence. Rather, to diagnose a person with a mental disorder from the DSM, you must evaluate the person's behavior and experience within an environmental and sociocultural context.

Another key dynamic with regard to the categorical, in contrast to the dimensional, approach is that of the high rates of comorbidity among many of the DSM's

---

[22] In the DSM-5, this is usually worded ". . . causes clinically significant distress or impairment in social, occupational, or other important areas of functioning" (APA, 2013, p. 21).

mental disorders. Are there really all of these distinct mental disorders that so frequently occur with other distinct mental disorders, or are there fewer, yet more fundamental (or dimensional), disorders that are currently classified as distinct[23] (based upon the extant diagnostic criterion sets)?

> Despite the best efforts of the leading clinicians and researchers who have been the primary authors of each revision of the diagnostic manual, diagnostic comorbidity rather than specificity is the norm. . . . "The greatest challenge that the extensive comorbidity data pose to the current nosological system concerns the validity of the diagnostic categories themselves—do these disorders constitute distinct clinical realities?" (Mineka, Watson, & Clark, 1998, cited in Widiger & Mullins-Sweatt, 2007, pp. 10–11)

The current political reality is that if a psychotherapist wants to be reimbursed for services, she must diagnose from either the DSM or the *International Classification of Mental and Behavioural Disorders* (ICD; World Health Organization, 1992), either of which results in a distinct category of mental disorder. This often perplexes and frustrates clinicians because such a practice suggests a homogeneity of presentation that is rarely the case. In contrast, dimensional classifications offer the promise of more accurate and precise descriptions of what is actually "going on" with a specific person (Widiger, Costa, & McCrae, 2002). Moreover, "a classification system that abandons the fruitless effort to make illusory distinctions among overlapping diagnostic categories in favor of a more straightforward description of each individual's unique profile will likely be much easier to use" (Widiger & Mullins-Sweatt, 2007, p. 14).

According to Widiger and Mullins-Sweatt (2007), the assumption that DSM diagnostic categories are qualitatively distinct conditions is simply false:

> An adequate understanding of the diagnosis, etiology, pathology, comorbidity, and treatment of all mental disorders may require an acknowledgment that they are not conditions qualitatively distinct from one another nor from the anxiety, depression, sexual functioning, sleep, cognitive aberrations, drug and alcohol usage, and personality traits evident within all persons. (p. 23)

It is critical to recognize that there are not absolute, clear-cut divisions between "normal" and "disordered" people[24] and that such judgments can be made only when what you know about a person is considered with the context of that person's multiple circumstances, his or her worldview and values, and the diagnostic situation itself (Johnson, Pfenninger, & Klion, 2000). Moreover, with few exceptions, both pharmacological and psychotherapeutic interventions target and ameliorate broad domains of psychopathology and other forms of psychological suffering, rather than targeting symptoms and problems unique to specific diagnostic categories (Widiger & Mullins-Sweatt, 2007).

---

[23] Regardless of the disclaimers in the Introductions to recent DSMs, a categorical approach to classification strongly implies that mental disorders are discrete, distinct entities.

[24] This is not to deny that some people are so severely disturbed (as in the case with the disorganized thinking that characterizes some people with Schizophrenia) that it is easy to ascertain that they have a serious form of psychopathology. What we mean here is that there will always be "border cases" with which it will be difficult to determine whether or not they are struggling with a "problem of living" or a true mental disorder.

## "DISORDER" IS NOT NECESSARILY THE ENEMY

According to the DSM-5, although it clearly provides a classification of mental disorders, it also admits that no definition of a mental disorder adequately demarcates the boundaries of what constitutes a mental disorder versus a normal variation of human experience and behavior (APA, 2013). From a constructivist perspective, order is a central feature of life, but periods of disorder, disorganization, and incoherence are not always a sign that something is wrong; in fact, human development *requires* episodes of novelty, disorganization, and disorder (Mahoney, 1991). Much of what psychotherapists do is distinguish between ordered, "normal" people and disordered, "abnormal" people and then classify the latter according to the DSM's elaborately ordered categories of disorder (Mahoney, 2000). In the spirit of constructivism, we urge you to resist the temptation, and contemporary pressures, to pathologize all that appears disorderly or different. In fact, episodes of disorganization, incoherence, and disorder—such as when patients feel that they are "coming unglued" or "falling apart"—may represent the very phases or subphases of human development that are required before people can reorganize and reorder themselves in a more integrated manner that allows them to flourish (Mahoney, 2000; Mahoney, 2003).

## SOME INTEGRAL-CONSTRUCTIVE ALTERNATIVES

It is important for clinicians to be mindful of how they think and communicate about diagnoses and psychopathology, because both constructs strongly evoke our tendencies to blame or stigmatize patients, which may not only blame, stigmatize, and disempower them, but may also lead to a deterioration of their relationships (from family and friends to spiritual advisors and community members), a desecration of various traditions (such as spiritual and folk traditions), or to the person's not being hired or even losing his or her job (Gergen & McNamee, 2000). Thus, if we are going to diagnose in terms of psychopathology, we must keep forefront the purpose of doing so, and most will agree that its ultimate purpose is to serve the individual's (as well as his or her relationships' and community's) well-being (Gergen & McNamee, 2000; Miller, 2004; Sadler, 2005). Critiquing standard diagnostic practices, as well as the DSM, does not mean that we think we should completely abandon such practices or such artifacts; we do not. We do, however, think that alternative ways of conceptualizing and discussing patients should be encouraged. Rather than believing that there is only one way to think about diagnosis and psychopathology, many scholars, both from within the psychiatric community and without, think that what is most helpful and healthy is the dialogue that occurs between multiple vital traditions that conceptualize psychopathology in different ways (Gergen & McNamee, 2000; Raskin & Lewandowski, 2000; Sadler, 2005).

Gergen and McNamee (2000) suggest that there are untapped potentials in discussions about such issues from multiple perspectives, which they term "transformative dialogue":

> The point of such a dialogue is not to battle over the "correct" interpretation . . . Rather, the hope would be to emerge with an expanded array of possibilities, an array that would sensitize professionals, clients, and the surrounding community to myriad factors possibly at play and a range of possible strategies, relational forms, or institutional arrangements that can serve as resources. (p. 343)

Even the authors of the DSM stated that arriving at a DSM-IV diagnosis is merely the first component of a comprehensive evaluation; in order to create an adequate treatment plan, therapists must learn much more about the whole person and his circumstances than what is sufficient to make a DSM-IV diagnosis (APA, 2000). Ideally, clinicians assess and diagnose from many different perspectives, and use their diagnostic systems flexibly—both conceptually and procedurally. One example of a way to ensure that you are assessing patients comprehensively—or at least with regard to the individual's unique characteristics and circumstances—is to use or be informed by an instrument such as the Integral Intake, which gathers information from all four quadratic perspectives, as well as developmental dynamics, various states of consciousness, and personality types that are often relevant to both the person's presenting problems and treatment considerations (Marquis, 2008).

George Kelly's (1991/1955) view was that diagnosis should always involve practical implications regarding how the client can change, thus his choice of the term *transitive diagnosis,* with "transitive" referring to helping the person *transition* from their problematic current situation to a future situation that is less distressing to them. Thus, the most important question in a transitive diagnosis is not "What is wrong with this client?" but rather "How is this client going to get well?" (Johnson et al., 2000, p. 156). Kelly and other constructivists also tend to conceptualize and practice from a non-pathologizing perspective, usually avoiding standard DSM nosology. Nonetheless, they still recognize the need to answer questions such as "How can we conceptualize this client's struggles in a way that is therapeutically useful and still communicate intelligibly with colleagues and case managers?" (Neimeyer & Raskin, 2000, p. 4).

Constructivists also tend to reject the tendency to reify mental disorders (Kelly, 1991/1955; Johnson et al., 2000; Mahoney, 2003); in other words, they are careful not to think or communicate in ways that suggest that patients have within them disease entities or a mental disorder that is a noun, rather than a verb (processes and patterns of feeling, behaving, and thinking that are distressing and/or constitute suffering).[25] In contrast to having a mental disorder (noun) within themselves, patients do live and view (verbs) the world and their experience through construct systems, and those can be anywhere along a spectrum of being very helpful or very unhelpful to the person's anticipation of events and how to function within various contexts. From Kelly's (1991/1955) perspective, a psychological disorder is constituted by the continued use of constructs that do not help the person function adaptively, as defined by the individual and her contexts. Thus, transitive diagnosis is a process of exploring and understanding the client's construct system and identifying what is keeping the person "stuck."[26]

Carl Rogers and others (Gergen & MacNamee, 2000; Seikkula et al., 1995) have stressed that diagnosis should always involve a process of *mutual understanding* between patient and therapist. Following Gergen and MacNamee, we think that ideal

---

[25] Although we are sympathetic to this point of view, we also recognize that there are many instances in which neurobiological (UR) processes are fundamentally implicated in people's suffering.

[26] A full exposition of transitive diagnosis requires a familiarity with Kelly's theory of how personal construct systems operate, and space constraints will not permit that here. For an excellent introduction to this topic, the reader is referred to Johnson et al. (2000).

diagnostic practice involves genuine dialogue. Rather than diagnosing a person primarily by gathering data from the person in order to support one's ideas about "what is wrong with this patient"—often without involving and truly consulting the individual, his family members, and so forth—a true dialogue invites the perspectives of not only the patient, but also the views of the family and any other involved members. If family members and others are not feasibly included, the clinician can—at the very least—inquire along the lines of "What would your wife say are the main problems?", "Do you agree with my thoughts about this?", and "Do you think your partner would agree with this diagnosis/interpretation?" Research has demonstrated that such "open dialogue" approaches to diagnosis and treatment planning actually reduce the number of psychotic diagnoses, psychopharmacological prescriptions, and in-patient services (Seikkula et al., 1995).

It is important to understand and perhaps discuss what being diagnosed means to patients, as well as the specific diagnosis you deem them to have. Thus, when you arrive at a diagnosis, both therapist and patient should dialogue to reach a mutual understanding of what that diagnosis does and does not imply. To do this in a manner that is helpful might involve discussing one's view that diagnostic constructs are needed for insurance purposes; that the current ways of construing mental disorder categories are—and will likely always be—incomplete; and that even though we lack certainty, some idea of what is most distressing to the patient is needed in order to begin working toward his desired goals (Johnson et al., 2000). In short, we agree with Raskin and Lewandowski (2000) when they wrote that

> constructivism encourages people to take responsibility for their personal constructions of disorder. Sharing these constructions with clients in a nondogmatic and open-minded way allows for the therapist and client to reach consensus about which life issues the client needs to address. (p. 35)

## Ongoing Reinterpretation: Resisting Diagnostic Foreclosure

Clinicians should strive to avoid certitude in their labeling of patients as this-or-that type, category, or disorder; otherwise, clinicians fall prey to what George Kelly referred to as the "attempt to cram a whole living struggling client into a nosological category" (cited in Johnson et al., 2000, p. 156). Rather than deluding themselves that they are certain that a given patient is such-and-such DSM category, Integral therapists hold their diagnoses lightly—as temporary hypotheses needed to guide their current clinical decisions—always being open to revising them as new information from the patient is brought to bear upon the situation, never forgetting that the primary imperative is to assist the person's well-being. Yalom (2002) includes a brief chapter titled "Avoid Diagnosis (*Except for Insurance Companies*)" in which he posits that "Once we make a diagnosis, we tend to selectively inattend to aspects of the patient that do not fit into that particular diagnosis, and correspondingly overattend to subtle features that appear to confirm an initial diagnosis" (p. 5).

Part of what diagnosis entails is a revealing or disclosing of that which was not previously evident (even to the patient). Such revealing of material that is potentially pathologizing, dehumanizing, stigmatizing, or otherwise threatening to the patient must be accompanied not only by a deep respect of the patient,[27] but also by a measured and respectful skepticism of one's acceptance of, or investment in, a particular theoretical view or diagnostic category. In other words, we must hold in abeyance our formulations, conceptualizations, and diagnostic hunches as the diagnostic and therapeutic processes unfold through dialogue, technical procedures, and other exchanges with the patient (Sadler, 2005). Thus, diagnostic interpretations and reinterpretations are ongoing; they should not occur only in the first few sessions (Marquis, 2008). After all,

> what therapist has not been struck by how much easier it is to make a DSM-IV diagnosis following the first interview than much later, let us say, after the tenth session, when we know a great deal more about the individual? Is this not a strange kind of science?" (Yalom, 2002, p. 5)

Such reinterpretations and re-visitings are key components of assessing the patient's progress in therapy and, if necessary, renegotiating the focus of the therapeutic work. Such ongoing diagnostic reinterpretation offers protection against the preemptive foreclosure that is so dangerous. However,

> The danger in overvaluing diagnostic reinterpretation is that, practiced in isolation from the other aesthetics of diagnosis, it may lead to interminable reflection, ruminative inaction—in other words, diagnostic indecisiveness. Considering diagnostic simplicity and diagnostic reinterpretation together is a tall order. The diagnostician should keep things simple, yet situate the patient's ordeal in a rich, revealing context. She should characterize the patient's problem(s) as simply as possible, but do so in a way that respects the complicated circumstances in which they arise. She should reduce complexity without being reductionistic, be holistic without losing focus. She should be open to the range of human experience, but disciplined in casting her interpretations. (Sadler, 2005, p. 425)

## Meaning-Making and the Patient's Experience as Central

Understanding or "diagnosing" a person's meaning-making is a key component of Kelly's transitive diagnosis, as well as the type of assessment we propose; and this process necessarily elucidates the individual's *experience* of distress, rather than merely cataloguing a cluster of behavioral symptoms (Douthit & Marquis, 2006; Marquis, 2008). According to Leitner, Faidley, and Celentan (2000),

> All experiences, rather than being symptoms to eradicate, can be better understood as communication from the self to the self about the self. In other words, all experiences should be attended to and honored to learn more about aspects of the meaning-making process. (p. 188)

---

[27] This respect is essential for at least two reasons. First, given the *ethical* requirements to respect a patient's dignity, inquiring into painful memories, religious beliefs, interpersonal liabilities, disturbing thoughts, distressing emotions, and other vulnerabilities must all be explored with an empathic sensitivity to what such disclosure means to the patient. Second, if a patient feels disrespected—psychologically invaded, probed, or offended—he will likely cease the therapy and thus we will not be able to be of help.

Stated another way, when one empathically enters the experiential world of patients, their symptoms inform you of their key struggles in life, which are necessary to know in order to help them recover, suffer less, or increasingly thrive.

While acknowledging that medicine, practiced in an ideal manner, would not only remediate disease processes but also empathically attend to patients' experience of illness, Kleinman (1988)[28] highlights the "moral core" that he believes is the primary purpose of medicine:

> When viewed from the human situations of chronic illness, neither the interpretation of illness meanings nor the handling of deeply felt emotions within intimate personal relationships can be dismissed as peripheral tasks. They constitute, rather, the point of medicine. These are the activities with which the practitioner should be engaged. The failure to address these issues is a fundamental flaw in the work of doctoring. It is in this very particular sense, then, that we can say of contemporary biomedicine: in spite of remarkable progress in the control of disease, it has turned its back on the purpose of medicine. This distortion, which results from external forces as much as from internal professional dynamics, places a great burden on the chronically ill, their families, and the practitioners who treat them. (pp. 253–254)

As Integral psychotherapists, we do not wish to be rid of the DSM; however, we do believe that both clinicians and their patients would be better served by a deeper appreciation of multiple constructions of human suffering and disorder.

> We encourage clinicians to view the inevitable judgments that they are bound to make as simply judgments, not as ultimate truth claims indicative of the defective nature of those judged. . . . Clinicians are still free to believe in their constructions of the good life but not as universals that apply across all people and contexts. In this way, the phrase *constructions of disorder* emphasizes the notion of constructions and diminishes the idea that there really are disorders of human interaction independent of those creating such disorders. (Raskin & Lewandowski, 2000, p. 34)

In contrast to such constructivist attitudes are those clinicians who adopt a "received" view in which DSM categories are taken to be accurate mirrors of disorders that exist independently of our constructions. Such clinicians are more likely to refer to their patients as their "borderline patient" or "bipolar client." What is most harmful about such an attitude is that it forecloses deeper understandings of the patient's unique individuality and often complex circumstances, and thus the "disorder" becomes the all-encompassing—even though it is circular—explanation for the person's behavior and experience (Raskin & Lewandowski, 2000). Even when our assessments—including traditional diagnoses—reassure patients that their experiences "make sense," such de-mystifying processes are ideally accompanied by a perspective that is usually difficult for patients (as well as many therapists-in-training) to accept: that a final, complete, and unequivocal diagnostic understanding is not possible (Mahoney, 2000).

---

[28] Recall that Kleinman is a physician, not a psychotherapist; his admonitions are all the more true for the practice of counseling.

## Conclusion

*"The work of therapy is largely about making suffering that feels meaningless become meaningful"* (Miller, 2004, p. 249).

The concepts and vocabulary of suffering, compassion, care, choice, and meaning are central to the work of psychotherapy as a morally engaged practice. When we invisibly objectify such experiential/subjective and intersubjective concepts into the language of psychopathology, diagnosis, and treatment plans, we contribute to the de-moralization of our profession and the de-humanizing of the people we have devoted ourselves to helping. We urge you to consider some study of moral philosophy so that you can make your clinical decisions in a more informed and deliberate fashion (a close reading of Miller's *Facing Human Suffering* is a good place to start). Regardless of how disturbing the thoughts and behavior of the person you are counseling may be, we hope that you can nonetheless view him as a moral agent—one who has the potential to be responsible for himself and his behavior—rather than merely a passive product of biological and external forces. We also think that it is vital to supplement your reading of traditional, clinical trial research with case study research, for the latter tends to illuminate the actual process of psychotherapy, including the uncertain, difficult clinical decisions that have to be made throughout the work. We also suggest that you enter your own personal therapy, and do everything you can to ensure that your own therapist is a very good one (you do not want to learn from a bad therapist!).

Finally, given that the practical wisdom needed in psychotherapy is always contingent upon contexts and is provisional, a very high tolerance for ambiguity and uncertainty is needed to be a good clinician. As Miller (2004) emphasized, "Those who have to have certain answers to life's mysteries would do best to look elsewhere for a career" (p. 254). Human beings who are suffering need more than merely technical, standardized responses; they need, in addition to whatever good science you can use to inform your clinical work, a moral response—one that is compassionate and caring. Following Miller, we recognize that the decision between cloaking yourself in a mantel of emotionally distanced objectivity, in contrast to vicariously suffering your patients' pain and misery—as well as your own existential struggles with the uncertainties of the profession you are entering—is an exceedingly difficult one; but what better way to begin your career as a mental health professional than with a difficult moral decision?

# APPENDIX A

## A Few Moral Values Associated with Different Psychotherapy Approaches

1. Behavioral and cognitive-behavioral models: Transforming unproductive, maladaptive, dysfunctional, and irrational thoughts, feelings, and behaviors into *productive, adaptive, functional, and rational thoughts, feelings, and behaviors*
2. Existential-humanistic models: Transforming inauthentic, restricted, and conformist ways of being into *more authentic, agentic, open, and genuine ways of being* (including joy, freedom, and creativity as well as heightened awareness of anxiety, responsibility, and mortality)
3. Object-relations, self-psychology, and other relational psychodynamic models: In addition to the goal of the "examined life" and accepting oneself with such self-knowledge, reducing internalized images of self and others that lead to conflict and transforming them into a *balance of autonomy and relatedness that involves love, compassion, and responsibility to both self and others*
4. Family systems models: Reducing indirect communication and rigid or diffuse familial boundaries and transforming them into *direct communication and strong yet permeable boundaries*
5. Social justice models: Transforming unjust social systems such that those who are struggling against oppressive and marginalizing social, economic, educational, and political circumstances are supported by their local communities and larger social systems so that *social arrangements become more equitable*

## References

Abusah, P. (1993). Multicultural influences in case management: Transcultural psychiatry. *Mental Health in Australia, 5*(2), 67–75.

American Psychiatric Association. (2000). *Diagnostic and statistical manual of mental disorders* (4th ed., Text revised). Washington, DC: Author.

American Psychiatric Association. (2013). *Diagnostic and statistical manual of mental disorders* (5th ed.). Washington, DC: Author

Anchin, J. C. (2005). Introduction to the special section on philosophy and psychotherapy integration and to the inaugural focus on moral philosophy. *Journal of Psychotherapy Integration, 15*(3), 284–298.

Andreasen, N. C. (1995). Posttraumatic stress disorder: Psychology, biology, and the Manichaean warfare between false dichotomies. *American Journal of Psychiatry, 152*(7), 963–965.

Arciero, G., & Guidano, V. F. (2000). Experience, explanation, and the quest for coherence. In R. A. Neimeyer & J. D. Raskin (Eds.), *Constructions of disorder* (pp. 91–118). Washington, DC: American Psychological Association.

Bartley, W. W. (1962). *The retreat to commitment.* New York: Alfred A. Knopf.

Blatt, S., & Zuroff, D. (1992). Interpersonal relatedness and self-definition: Two prototypes for depression. *Clinical Psychology Review, 12,* 527–562.

Brown, L. (2000). Discomforts of the powerless: Feminist constructions of distress. In R. A. Neimeyer & J. D. Raskin (Eds.), *Constructions of disorder* (pp. 287–308). Washington, DC: American Psychological Association.

Bryceland, C., & Stam, H. J. (2005). Empirical validation and professional codes of ethics: Description or prescription? *Journal of Constructivist Psychology, 18*, 131–155.

Caplan, P. J. (1995). *They say you're crazy: How the world's most powerful psychiatrists decide who's normal*. Reading, MA: Addison-Wesley.

Clark, L. A., Watson, D., & Reynolds, S. (1995). Diagnosis and classification of psychopathology: Challenges to the current system and future directions. *Annual Review of Psychology, 46*, 121–153.

Coleman, L. (1984). *The reign of error: Psychiatry, authority, and law*. Boston: Beacon Press.

Dana, R. H. (2002). Multicultural assessment: Teaching methods and competence evaluations. *Journal of Personality Assessment, 79*(2), 195–199.

Dana, R. H. (2008). Transitions in psychotherapy, clinical diagnosis, and assessment. In R. H. Dana & J. Allen (Eds.), *Cultural competency training in a global society* (pp. 79–94). New York: Springer.

Douthit, K. Z., & Donnely, D. (in press). Theoretical neutrality in DSM classification: Diagnosing the manual. *Journal of Mind and Behavior*.

Douthit, K. Z., & Marquis, A. (2006). Empiricism in psychiatry's post-psychoanalytic era: Contemplating DSM's "atheoretical" nosology. *Constructivism in the Human Sciences, 11*(1), 32–59.

Efrans, J. S., Lukens, M. D., & Lukens, R. J. (1990). *Language, structure, and change: Frameworks of meaning in psychotherapy*. New York: Norton.

First, M. B. (2003). Psychiatric classification. In A. Tasman, J. Kay, & J. Lieberman (Eds.), *Psychiatry* (Vol. 1, 2nd ed., pp. 659–676). New York: Wiley.

Gergen, K. J., Hoffman, L., & Anderson, H. (1996). Is diagnosis a disaster? A constructionist trialogue. In F. W. Kaslow (Ed.), *Handbook of relational diagnosis and dysfunctional family patterns* (pp. 102–118). New York: John Wiley.

Gergen, K. J., & McNamee, S. (2000). From disordering discourse to transformative dialogue. In R. A. Neimeyer & J. D. Raskin (Eds.), *Constructions of disorder* (pp. 333–350). Washington, DC: American Psychological Association.

Good, B. J. (1996). Culture and DSM-IV: Diagnosis, knowledge and power. *Culture, Medicine and Psychiatry, 20*(2), 127–132.

Griffith, J. L. (2010). *Religion that heals, religion that harms: A guide for clinical practice*. New York, NY: Guilford Press.

Gross, P. R., & Levitt, N. (1998). *Higher superstition: The academic left and its quarrels with science*. Baltimore, MD: Johns Hopkins University Press.

Hansen, J. T. (2006). Is the best practices movement consistent with the values of the counseling profession? A critical analysis of best practices ideology. *Journal of Counseling & Values, 50*(2), 154–160.

Harris, S. (2010). *The moral landscape: How science can determine human values*. New York: Free Press.

Henriques, G. (2002). The harmful dysfunction analysis and the differentiation between mental disorder and disease. *The Scientific Review of Mental Health Practice, 1*(2), 157–173.

Hergenhahn, B. R. (2001). *An introduction to the history of psychology* (4th ed.). Belmont, CA: Wadsworth/Thomson Learning.

Herlihy, B., & Watson, Z. E. (2003). Ethical issues and multicultural competence in counseling. In F. D. Harper & J. McFadden (Eds.), *Culture and counseling: New approaches* (pp. 363–378). Needham Heights, MA: Allyn & Bacon.

Hohenshil, T. H. (1996). Editorial: Role of assessment and diagnosis in counseling. *Journal of Counseling and Development, 75*(1), 64-67.

Horowitz, J. L. (2006). Culture-bound syndromes of anxiety disorders and multicultural competence. *Dissertation Abstracts International: Section B: The Sciences and Engineering*, Vol. 66 (7-B), p. 3949.

Hume, D. (1739/2010). *A treatise of human nature*. Charleston, SC: Nabu Press.

Ingersoll, R. E., & Rak, C. F. (2006). *Psychopharmacology for helping professionals: An Integral exploration*. Belmont, CA: Thomson Brooks/Cole.

Ivey, A. E., & Ivey, M. B. (2008). Reframing DSM-IV-TR: Positive strategies from developmental counseling and therapy. *Journal of Counseling and Development, 76*(3), 334–351.

James, W. (1907). *Pragmatism*. New York: Longman.

Johnson, T. J., Pfenninger, D. T., & Klion, R. E. (2000). Constructing and deconstructing transitive diagnosis. In R. A. Neimeyer & J. D. Raskin (Eds.), *Constructions of disorder* (pp. 145–174). Washington, DC: American Psychological Association.

Kelly, G. A. (1991/1955). *The psychology of personal constructs. Vol. 1: A theory of personality*. London: Routledge.

Khantzian, E. J. (1987). A clinical perspective of the cause-consequence controversy in alcoholic and addictive suffering. *Journal of the American Academy of Psychoanalysis, 15*(4), 521–537.

Kirk, S. A., & Kutchins, H. (1992). *The selling of DSM: The rhetoric of science in psychiatry*. New York: de Gruyter.

Kleinman, A. (1988). *The illness narratives: Suffering, healing, and the human condition.* New York: Basic Books.

Krueger, R. F., & Markon, K. E. (2006). Reinterpreting comorbidity: A model-based approach to understanding and classifying psychopathology. *Annual Review of Clinical Psychology, 2,* 111–133.

Kupfer, D. J., First, M. B., & Regier, D. E. (2002). Introduction. In D. J. Kupfer, M. B. First, & D. E. Regier (Eds.), *A research agenda for DSM-5* (pp. xv–xxiii). Washington, DC: American Psychiatric Association.

Kutchins, H., & Kirk, S. A. (1997). *Making us crazy: DSM: The psychiatric bible and the creation of mental disorders.* New York: Free Press.

Lambert, M. J. (2003). Psychotherapy outcome research: Implications of outcome research for psychotherapy integration. In J. C. Norcross & M. R. Goldstein (Eds.), *Handbook of psychotherapy integration* (pp. 94–129). New York: Basic Books.

Leitner, L. M., Faidley, A. J., & Celentan, M. A. (2000). Diagnosing human meaning making: An experiential constructivist approach. In R. A. Neimeyer & J. D. Raskin (Eds.), *Constructions of disorder* (pp. 175–204). Washington, DC: American Psychological Association.

Li, S. T., Jenkins, S., & Sundsmo, A. (2007). Impact of race and ethnicity. In M. Hersen, S. M. Turner, & D. C. Beidel (Eds.), *Adult psychopathology and diagnosis* (5th ed., pp. 101–121). Hoboken, NJ: John Wiley & Sons.

Mahoney, M. J. (1991). *Human change processes: The scientific foundations of psychotherapy.* New York: Basic Books.

Mahoney, M. J. (2000). Core ordering and disordering processes: A constructive view of psychological development. In R. A. Neimeyer & J. D. Raskin (Eds.), *Constructions of disorder* (pp. 43–62). Washington, DC: American Psychological Association.

Mahoney, M. J. (2003). *Constructive psychotherapy: A practical guide.* New York: Guilford.

Mahoney, M. J. (2005). Suffering, philosophy, and psychotherapy. *Journal of Psychotherapy Integration, 15*(3), 337–352.

Mahoney, M. J., & Marquis, A. (2002). Integral constructivism and dynamic systems in psychotherapy processes. *Psychoanalytic Inquiry, 22*(5), 794–813.

Manson, S. M., & Kleinman, A. (1998). DSM-IV, culture, and mood disorders: A critical reflection on recent progress. *Transcultural Psychiatry, 35,* 377–386.

Marquis, A. (2008). *The Integral intake: A guide to comprehensive idiographic assessment in Integral psychotherapy.* New York: Routledge.

Marquis, A. (2013). Methodological considerations of studying a unified approach to psychotherapy: Integral methodological pluralism. *Journal of Unified Psychotherapy and Clinical Science. 2*(1), 45–73.

Marquis, A., & Douthit, K. Z. (2006). The hegemony of "empirically supported treatment": Validating or violating? *Constructivism in the Human Sciences, 11*(2), 108–141.

Marquis, A., Douthit, K. Z., & Elliot, A. (2011). Best Practices: A critical yet inclusive vision for the counseling profession. *Journal of Counseling and Development, 89*(4), 397–405.

McWilliams, N. (1994). *Psychoanalytic diagnosis: Understanding personality structure in the clinical process.* New York: The Guilford Press.

Mezzich, J. E., Kirmayer, L. J., Kleinman, A., Fabrega, H., Parron, D. L., Good, B. J., et al. (1999). The place of culture in DSM-IV. *Journal of Nervous and Mental Diseases, 187,* 457–464.

Miller, R. B. (2004). *Facing human suffering: Psychology and psychotherapy as moral engagement.* Washington, DC: American Psychological Association.

Miller, R. B. (2005). Suffering in psychology: The demoralization of psychotherapeutic practice. *Journal of Psychotherapy Integration, 15*(3), 299–336.

Moore, G. E. (1903). *Principia ethica.* Cambridge, England: Cambridge University Press.

Moore, R. (1999). *The creation of reality in psychoanalysis: A view of the contributions of Donald Spence, Roy Schafer, Robert Stolorow, Irwin Z. Hoffman, and beyond.* Hillsdale, NJ: The Analytic Press.

Neimeyer, R. A., & Raskin, J. D. (2000). On practicing postmodern therapy in modern times. In R. A. Neimeyer & J. D. Raskin (Eds.), *Constructions of disorder* (pp. 3–14). Washington, DC: American Psychological Association.

Nussbaum, M. (1994). *The therapy of desire: Theory and practice in Hellenistic ethics.* Princeton, NJ: Princeton University Press.

Paniagua, F. (1998). *Assessing and treating culturally diverse clients: A practical guide* (2nd ed.). Newbury Park, CA: Sage.

Partridge, E. (1958). *Origins: A short etymological dictionary of modern English.* New York: The Macmillan Company.

Polanyi, M. (1958). *Personal knowledge: Towards a post-critical philosophy*. New York: Harper & Row.

Polkinghorne, D. E. (1983). *Methodology for the human sciences: Systems of inquiry*. Albany, NY: SUNY Press.

Polkinghorne, D. E. (1999). Traditional research and psychotherapy practice. *Journal of Clinical Psychology, 55*(12), 1429–1440.

Rachels, J. (1993). *The elements of moral philosophy* (2nd ed.). New York: McGraw–Hill.

Ramirez, A. M. (2008). Race bias, multicultural counseling competencies, and clinical judgment. *Dissertation Abstracts International: Section B: The Sciences and Engineering,* Vol. 69 (4-B), p. 2639.

Raskin, J. D., & Lewandowski, A. M. (2000). The construction of disorder as a human enterprise. In R. A. Neimeyer & J. D. Raskin (Eds.), *Constructions of disorder* (pp. 15–40). Washington, DC: American Psychological Association.

Robinson, D. N. (1995). *An intellectual history of psychology* (3rd ed.). Madison, WI: University of Wisconsin Press.

Sadler, J. Z. (2005). *Values and psychiatric diagnosis.* New York: Oxford University Press.

Scholefield, R. M. (1999). The impact of multicultural clinical experience, training, and self-reported competence on diagnostic bias. *Dissertation Abstracts International: Section B: The Sciences and Engineering,* Vol. 60 (5-B), p. 2366.

Searle, J. (1992). *The rediscovery of the mind.* Cambridge, MA: The MIT Press.

Seikkula, J., Aaltonen, J., Alakara, B., Haarakanga, K., Keranen, J., & Sutela, M. (1995). Treating psychosis by means of open dialogue. In S. Friedman (Ed.), *The reflecting team in action* (pp. 62–80). New York: Guilford Press.

Slife, B. (2004). Theoretical challenges to therapy practice and research: The constraints of naturalism. In M. J. Lambert (Ed.), *Bergin and Garfield's handbook of psychotherapy and behavior change* (5th ed., pp. 44–83). New York: Wiley.

Slife, B. D., & Gantt, E. E. (1999). Methodological pluralism: A framework for psychotherapy research. *Journal of Clinical Psychology, 55*, 1453–1465.

Slife, B. D., Wiggins, B. J., & Graham, J. T. (2005). Avoiding an EST monopoly: Toward a pluralism of philosophies and methods. *Journal of Contemporary Psychotherapy, 35*, 83–97.

Sorabji, R. (2000). *Emotion and peace of mind: From Stoic agitation to Christian temptation.* Oxford: Oxford University Press.

Stanovich, K. E. (1998). *How to think straight about psychology* (5th ed.). New York: Addison Wesley Longman.

Steffens, D. C., & Krishnan, K. R. R. (2003). Laboratory testing and neuroimaging: Implications for psychiatric diagnosis and practice. In K. A. Phillips, M. B. First, & H. A. Pincus (Eds.), *Advancing DSM-5: Dilemmas in psychiatric diagnosis* (pp. 85–103). Washington, DC: American Psychiatric Association.

Szasz, T. (1974). *The myth of mental illness: Foundations of a theory of personal conduct.* New York: Harper & Row.

Valenstein, E. S. (1998). *Blaming the brain: The truth about drugs and mental health.* New York: Simon & Schuster.

Wakefield, J. C. (1997). Diagnosing DSM-IV—Part 1: DSM-IV and the concept of disorder. *Behavioral Research and Therapy, 35*, 633–649.

Wampold, B. E. (2001). *The great psychotherapy debate: Models, methods, and findings.* Mahwah, NJ: Erlbaum.

Widiger, T. A., & Clark, L. A. (2000). Toward DSM-5 and the classification of psychopathology. *Psychological Bulletin, 126*, 946–963.

Widiger, T. A., Costa, P. T., & McCrae, R. R. (2002). FFM personality disorder research. In P. T. Costa & T. A. Widiger (Eds.), *Personality disorders and the Five Factor Model of personality* (2nd ed., pp. 59–87). Washington, DC: American Psychiatric Association.

Widiger, T. A., & Mullins-Sweatt, S. (2007). Mental disorders as discrete clinical conditions: Dimensional versus categorical classification. In M. Hersen, S. M. Turner, & D. C. Beidel (Eds.), *Adult psychopathology and diagnosis* (5th ed.). New York: Wiley.

Wilber, K. (2000). *The collected works of Ken Wilber (Vol. 6): Sex, ecology, spirituality: The spirit of evolution.* Boston: Shambhala.

World Health Organization. (1992). *The ICD-10 classification of mental and behavioural disorders.* Geneva: Author.

Yalom, I. D. (2002). *The gift of therapy: An open letter to a new generation of therapists and their patients.* New York: HarperCollins Publishers.

Zalaquett, C. P., Fuerth, K. M., Stein, C., Ivey, A. E., & Ivey, M. B. (2008). Reframing the DSM-IV-TR from a multicultural/social justice perspective. *Journal of Counseling and Development, 86*(3), 364–371.

# INDEX

# C

## D

## F

## G

## J



## K

# L

## Q



## R

## U

## X



## Y



## Z